FIFTH EDITION

A Second Course in Statistics: Regression Analysis

FIFTH EDITION

A Second Course in Statistics: Regression Analysis

WILLIAM MENDENHALL

University of Florida

TERRY SINCICH

University of South Florida

PRENTICE HALL

Upper Saddle River, New Jersey 07458

Library of Congress Cataloging-in-Publication Data
Mendenhall, William.
A second course in statistics: regression analysis /
William Mendenhall, Terry Sincich.—5th ed.
p. cm.
Rev. ed. of: A second course in business statistics. 4th ed. 1993.
Includes index.
ISBN 0-13-396821-9 (casebound)
1. Commercial statistics 2. Statistics. 3. Regression analysis.
I. Sincich, Terry. II. Mendenhall, William. Second course in business statistics. III. Title.
HF1017.M46 1996
519.5—dc20 95-46258
CIP

Director of Production and Manufacturing: *David W. Riccardi*
Acquisitions Editor: *Ann Heath*
Development Editor: *Millicent Treloar*
Manufacturing Buyer: *Alan Fischer*
Marketing Manager: *Evan Hanby*
Creative Director: *Paula Maylahn*
Cover/Art Director: *Jayne Conte*
Editorial Assistant: *Mindy Ince*

Simon & Schuster / A Viacom Company
Upper Saddle River, New Jersey 07458

Printed in the United States of America

10 9 8 7 6 5 4 3 2

ISBN 0-13-396821-9

Prentice-Hall International (UK) Limited, *London*
Prentice-Hall of Australia Pty. Limited, *Sydney*
Prentice-Hall Canada, Inc., *Toronto*
Prentice-Hall Hispanoamericana, S.A., *Mexico*
Prentice-Hall of India Private Limited, *New Delhi*
Prentice-Hall of Japan, Inc., *Tokyo*
Simon & Schuster Asia Pte. Ltd., *Singapore*
Editora Prentice-Hall do Brasil, Ltda., *Rio de Janeiro*

Contents

Preface

Overview

This text is designed for two types of statistics courses. The early chapters, combined with a selection of the case study chapters, are designed for use in the second half of a two-semester (or two-quarter) introductory statistics sequence for undergraduates with statistics or non-statistics majors. Alternatively, the text can be used for a course in applied regression analysis for masters' or Ph.D. students in other fields.

At first glance, these two uses for the text may seem inconsistent. How could a text be appropriate for both undergraduate and graduate students? The answer lies in the content. In contrast to a course in statistical theory, an applied regression analysis course requires only a minimal level of mathematical knowledge. Consequently, the difficulty encountered in learning the mechanics is much the same for both undergraduate and graduate students. The challenge is in the application—diagnosing practical problems, deciding on the appropriate linear model for a given situation, and knowing which inferential technique will answer a manager's practical question. This takes *experience*, and it explains why a student with a non-statistics major can take an undergraduate course in applied regression analysis and still benefit from covering the same ground in a graduate course.

Introductory Statistics Course

It is difficult to identify the amount of material that should be included in the second semester of a two-semester sequence in introductory statistics. Optionally, a few lectures should be devoted to Chapter 1 (A Review of Basic Concepts) to make certain that all students possess a common background knowledge of the basic concepts covered in a first-semester (first-quarter) course. Chapter 2 (Introduction to Regression Analysis), Chapter 3 (Simple Linear Regression), Chapter 4 (Multiple Regression), Chapter 5 (Model Building), Chapter 6 (Some Regression Pitfalls), and Chapter 7 (Residual Analysis) provide the core for an applied regression analysis course. These chapters could be supplemented with Chapter 9 (Time Series Modeling and Forecasting), Chapter 10 (Principles of Experimental Design), or Chapter 11 (The Analysis of Variance for Designed Experiments).

Applied Regression for Graduates

In our opinion, the quality of an applied graduate course is not measured by the number of topics covered or the amount of material memorized by the students. The measure is how well they can apply the techniques covered in the course to the solution of real problems encountered in their field of study. Consequently, we advocate moving on to new topics only after the students have demonstrated ability (through testing) to apply the techniques under discussion. In-class consulting sessions, where a case study is presented and the students have the opportunity to diagnose the problem and recommend an appropriate method of analysis, are very helpful in teaching applied regression analysis. This approach is particularly useful in helping students master the difficult topic of model selection and model building (Chapters 4–7) and relating questions about the model to real-world questions. The case study chapters (Chapters 12–16) illustrate the type of material that might be useful for this purpose.

A course in applied regression analysis for graduate students would start in the same manner as the undergraduate course, but would move more rapidly over the review material and would more than likely be supplemented by Appendix A (The Mechanics of a Multiple Regression Analysis), one of the computer software tutorials in Appendix D, E, F, or G (SAS, SPSS, MINITAB, or ASP), Chapter 8 (Special Topics in Regression), and other chapters selected by the instructor. As in the undergraduate course, we recommend the use of case studies and in-class consulting sessions to help students develop an ability to formulate appropriate statistical models and to interpret the results of their analyses.

Features

Readability

We have purposely tried to make this a teaching (rather than a reference) text. Concepts are explained in a logical intuitive manner using worked examples.

Emphasis on Model Building

The formulation of an appropriate statistical model is fundamental to any regression analysis. This topic is treated in Chapters 4–7 and is emphasized throughout the text.

Emphasis on Developing Regression Skills

In addition to teaching the basic concepts and methodology of regression analysis, this text stresses its use, as a tool, in solving applied problems. Consequently, a major objective of the text is to develop a skill in applying regression analysis to appropriate real-life situations.

Numerous Real Data-Based Examples and Exercises

The text contains many worked examples that illustrate important aspects of model construction, data analysis, and the interpretation of results. Numerous exercises based on data and problems extracted from news articles, magazines, and journals are located at the ends of key sections and at the ends of chapters.

Case Study Chapters

The text contains five case study chapters, each of which addresses a real-life research problem. The student can see how regression analysis was used to answer the practical questions posed by the problem, proceeding from the formulation of appropriate statistical models to the analysis and interpretation of sample data.

Data Sets

The text contains four complete data sets that are associated with the case studies (Chapter 12–16). These can be used by instructors and students to practice model building and data analyses.

Extensive Use of Statistical Software

Instructions on how to use four popular statistical software packages, SAS, SPSS, MINITAB, and ASP, are provided in Appendices D, E, F, and G, respectively. The printouts of the respective software packages are presented and discussed throughout the text.

New to the Fifth Edition

Although the scope and coverage remain the same, the fifth edition contains several substantial changes, additions, and enhancements.

Expanded Range of Applications

In response to market demand, the range of applications presented in the text has been expanded to cover numerous fields of study. Consequently, the word "Business" has been deleted from the title. In addition to business-related examples and exercises, the text now contains applications drawn from a wide variety of fields, including psychology, sociology, engineering, journalism, nursing, information systems, biology, mathematics, health sciences, chemistry, physics, and geography.

More Computer Printouts

Throughout the text, an increased number of SAS, SPSS, MINITAB, and ASP printouts appear. A printout now accompanies every statistical technique presented, allowing the instructor to emphasize interpretations of the statistical results rather than the calculations required to obtain the results.

Case Study 12: Residential Property Sale Price Data Updated

The data set for the case study on predicting sale prices of residential properties has been updated to reflect current economic trends.

Case Study 13: An Analysis of Rain Levels in California

This is a new case study that demonstrates how to detect an important omitted variable in regression with a creative analysis of residuals. The case is extracted from an article in the journal *Geography*.

Statistical Software Instructions Updated

The SAS, SPSS, MINITAB, and ASP commands for conducting a regression analysis have been updated to reflect the most recently available versions of the software.

Numerous less obvious changes in details have been made throughout the text in response to suggestions by users of the earlier editions.

Supplements for the Instructor

Instructor's Solutions Manual (by Mark Dummeldinger)

The instructor's solutions manual presents full solutions to the even-numbered exercises in the text. Solutions to the odd-numbered exercises are found in the Student's Solutions Manual.

Appendix Data Sets Available on Diskette

The three data sets in Appendices H, I, and J are available on a $3\frac{1}{2}''$ diskette (ASCII format), complimentary from the publisher.

Exercise Data Sets on Diskette

The data for all exercises containing 15 or more observations are available on a $3\frac{1}{2}''$ diskette (ASCII format). A list of these exercises follows this preface.

Supplements Available for Purchase by Students

Student's Solutions Manual (by Nancy S. Boudreau)

Fully worked solutions to all of the odd-numbered exercises are provided in this manual. Careful attention has been paid to ensure that all methods of solution and notation are consistent with those used in the core text.

Student Versions of SPSS

Student versions of SPSS's award-winning and market-leading commercial data analysis package, designed specifically for hands-on classroom teaching and learning of data analysis, statistics, and research methods, are available for student purchase. Windows and PowerMac versions of the software allow the user to take full advantage of easy-to-use graphical interface combined with the traditional power of SPSS. Details on all current products are available from the publisher.

ASP Software, Tutorial and Student Guide (by George Blackford)

A Statistical Package for Business, Economics, and the Social Sciences (ASP) is a menu-driven, user-friendly program available for use on an IBM-compatible PC with at least 512K of memory. Most students have little trouble learning to use ASP without documentation. Some, however, may want to purchase the *ASP Tutorial and Student Guide*. Bookstores or individuals may order it directly from DMC Software, Inc., 6169 Pebbleshire Drive, Grand Blanc, MI 48439. Telephone number (810) 695-6131.

Acknowledgments

We want to thank the many people who contributed time, advice, and other assistance to this project. We owe particular thanks to the many reviewers who provided suggestions and advice at the onset of the project and for the succeeding editions:

Mohammed Askalani, Mankato State University (Minnesota)

Ken Boehm, Pacific Telesis (California)

Andrew C. Brod, University of North Carolina at Greensboro

James Daly, California State Polytechnic Institute at San Luis Obispo

Assane Djeto, University of Nevada–Las Vegas

Robert Elrod, Georgia State University

James Ford, University of Delaware

Carol Ghomi, University of Houston

James Holstein, University of Missouri at Columbia

Steve Hora, Texas Technological University

K. G. Janardan, Eastern Michigan University

Thomas Johnson, North Carolina State University

Ann Kittler, Ryerson College (Toronto)

James T. McClave, University of Florida

John Monahan, North Carolina State University

Kris Moore, Baylor University

Farrokh Nasri, Hofstra University

Robert Pavur, University of North Texas

William A. Powell, University of Mississippi

P. V. Rao, University of Florida

Tom Rothrock, Info Tech, Inc.

Ray Twery, University of North Carolina at Charlotte

Joseph Van Matre, University of Alabama at Birmingham

William Weida, United States Air Force Academy

Dean Wichern, Texas A&M University

James Willis, Louisiana State University

We are particularly grateful to Charles Bond, Evan Anderson, Jim McClave, Herman Kelting, Ron Alderman, P. J. Taylor, and Mike Jacob, who provided data sets and/or background information used in the case studies (Chapters 12–16). And, finally, we give special thanks to Faith Sincich for a superb job of proofreading and transforming our notes into typed copy.

Exercise Data Sets Available on Disk

EXERCISE	PAGE	
3.70	167	Foreign revenue and assets for multinational firms (n = 20)
3.71	168	P/E ratios and R&D expenditures for companies (n = 20)
4.17	207	Man-hours, boiler capacity, design pressure, boiler type, and drum type for manufactured boiler drums (n = 35)
4.20	209	Two-year PCB levels in water samples of bays (n = 37)
4.28	227	Price, microprocessor speed, and chip type for PCs (n = 60)
4.48	250	Daily output levels for various activities at a department store (n = 52)
5.32	340	Cash compensations of CEOs in four industries (n = 32)
5.42	345	Temperature, pressure, and quality data for chemically produced products (n = 27)
6.11	370	Tar, nicotine, weight, and carbon monoxide levels of cigarette brands (n = 25)
6.12	371	Annual demand for motor fuel, weekly earnings, and average gas prices, 1965–1980 (n = 16)
6.13	371	Weekly labor hours, weight shipped, percent shipped, and average weight (n = 20)
6.17	373	Maximal oxygen uptake, age, height, weight, and chest depth of preadolescent boys (n = 10)
6.19	374	Appraisals and sale prices for residential properties (n = 15)
6.20	375	Strike activity and related variables in manufacturing (n = 50)
7.7	393	Weight percentile and number of cigarettes smoked per day in homes of children with cystic fibrosis (n = 25)
7.10	404	Dicarboxylic acid and oxidant concentration in air specimens (n = 19)
7.14	408	Leased fee values and sizes of Hawaiian properties (n = 20)
7.24	428	Employee work-hours missed and annual wages (n = 15)
7.29	438	Purchasing value of the dollar, 1970–1993 (n = 24)
7.30	439	Monthly factory sales of passenger cars (n = 24)
7.37	445	Monthly demand for used bikes and related variables (n = 15)
7.38	447	Quarterly data for absentee rate of employees (n = 20)

EXERCISE	PAGE	
7.39	447	Annual OPEC oil imports into the United States, 1974–1993 (n = 20)
8.4	456	Annual corn production, 1950–1986 (n = 37)
8.5	457	Unit cost and lot size for shipments (n = 15)
8.8	464	Residential fires: Damage and distance from station (n = 15)
8.11	470	Machine speed and number of defectives produced (n = 15)
8.12	471	Executive salary and years of experience (n = 50)
8.14	474	PC ownership status and annual income for households (n = 20)
8.15	475	Hiring status, education, experience, and sex of applicants (n = 28)
9.1	510	Quarterly housing starts, 1989–1993 (n = 20)
9.4	511	Annual crude oil imports, 1974–1993 (n = 20)
9.6	512	Quarterly S&P 500 Average, 1985–1992 (n = 32)
9.7	513	Annual price of gold, 1971–1990 (n = 20)
9.9	519	Weekly sales of single-family homes (n = 15)
9.12	520	Annual price of galvanized steel, 1971–1989 (n = 19)
9.14	521	Monthly occupancy rates for Atlanta and Phoenix hotels/motels (n = 24)
9.25	539	Quarterly Gross Domestic Product, 1990–1993 (n = 16)
9.27	540	Annual Dow Jones Industrial Average, 1971–1990 (n = 20)
9.37	553	Monthly mortgage applications for new homes, 1991–1993 (n = 36)
9.41	555	Annual U.S. beer production, 1973–1993 (n = 21)
11.10	598	Vanadium levels in oyster tissue, citrus leaves, bovine liver, and human serum (n = 14)
11.11	599	Numbers of trials until accurate decoding in each of four different training groups (n = 20)
11.21	615	Preference scores of subjects rating video display combinations (n = 70)
11.22	616	Drift ratios estimated by three programs at different building levels (n = 15)
11.23	617	Finger temperatures of students in three different sessions: live plant, no plant, and plant photo (n = 30)

FIFTH EDITION

A Second Course in Statistics: Regression Analysis

CHAPTER 1

A Review of Basic Concepts (Optional)

CONTENTS

OBJECTIVE

To review the basic concepts of statistics that are essential prerequisites to the study of regression analysis

Although we assume students have had a prerequisite introductory course in statistics, courses vary somewhat in content and in the manner in which they present statistical concepts. To be certain that we are starting with a common background, we will use this chapter to review some basic definitions and concepts. Coverage is optional.

1.1 Statistics and Data

According to *The Random House College Dictionary* (1995 ed.), statistics is "the science that deals with the collection, classification, analysis, and interpretation of numerical facts or data." In short, statistics is the **science of data**—a science that will enable you to be proficient data producers and efficient data users.

> Definition 1.1
>
> **Statistics** is the science of data. This involves collecting, classifying, summarizing, organizing, analyzing, and interpreting data.

Data are obtained by measuring some characteristic or property of the objects (usually people or things) of interest to us. These objects upon which the measurements (or observations) are made are called **experimental units**, and the properties being measured are called **variables** (since, in virtually all studies of interest, the property varies from one observation to another).

> Definition 1.2
>
> An **experimental unit** is an object (person or thing) upon which we collect data.

> Definition 1.3
>
> A **variable** is a characteristic (property) that differs or varies from one observation to the next.

All data (and consequently, the variables we measure) are either **quantitative** or **qualitative** in nature. Quantitative data are data that can be measured on a numerical scale. In general, qualitative data take values that are nonnumerical; they can only be classified. The statistical tools that we use to analyze data depend on whether the data are quantitative or qualitative. Thus, it is important to be able to distinguish between the two types of data.

> **Definition 1.4**
>
> **Quantitative data** are observations measured on a numerical scale.

> **Definition 1.5**
>
> Nonnumerical data that can only be classified into one of a group of categories are said to be **qualitative data**.

EXAMPLE 1.1

The data in Table 1.1, obtained from *Business Week*'s 1994 Executive Compensation Scoreboard, contains information on the annual salaries of 10 of the highest-paid corporate executives in the United States. For each executive, five variables are recorded: (1) company, (2) industry group, (3) total pay (in thousands of dollars), (4) return to shareholders (in dollars) on a $100 investment made 3 years earlier, and (5) pay-for-performance rating measured on a scale of 1 (excellent) to 5 (poor).

a. Identify the experimental units.
b. Classify the variables measured as quantitative or qualitative.

TABLE 1.1 **Data on 10 of the Highest-Paid Executives in 1994**

CEO	COMPANY (1)	INDUSTRY (2)	TOTAL PAY (3)	RETURN (4)	RATING (5)
M. Eisner	Walt Disney	Consumer Products	$203,011	170	5
S. Weill	Travelers	Financial Services	52,810	349	5
J. Hyde	Autozone	Service	32,220	na	na
C. Mathewson	Intl. Game Tech.	Industrial: Low Tech	22,231	1,413	3
A. Greenberg	Bear Stearns	Financial Services	15,915	296	5
H. Huizenga	Blockbuster	Consumer Products	15,557	238	3
N. Brinker	Brinker Intl.	Service	14,925	448	4
R. Goizueta	Coca-Cola	Consumer Products	14,513	199	5
C. Kidder	Duracell	Industrial: Low Tech	14,172	na	na
T. Hahn	Georgia-Pacific	Resources	13,680	197	5

na: Not available
Source: "That eye-popping executive pay." *Business Week*, Apr. 25, 1994, p. 53.

Solution

a. Because the data are recorded for each corporate executive, the 10 executives in Table 1.1 are the experimental units.
b. The first two variables (company and industry group) are qualitative because the data they produce are nonnumerical values; they can only be classified into categories or groups. The next two variables (total pay and shareholder return) are quantitative because they are measured on a numerical scale. The fifth variable (performance rating), although coded as a number (1–5), is really qualitative in nature. The performance categories are excellent, above

average, average, below average, and poor. For convenience, *Business Week* has chosen to assign numbers (i.e., 1 for "excellent," 2 for "above average," etc.) to the categories to obtain a performance rating.* This does result in a meaningful variable, however, since the higher the rating, the poorer the executive's performance. In contrast, assigning numbers to industry group (e.g., 1 for "automotive," 2 for "apparel," etc.) would not result in a meaningful quantitative variable.

EXERCISES

1.1 The data in the accompanying table were obtained from the Environmental Protection Agency (EPA) *1993 Gas Mileage Guide* for new automobiles.

MODEL NAME	MANUFACTURER	TRANSMISSION	ENGINE SIZE liters	NUMBER OF CYLINDERS	ESTIMATED CITY MILEAGE miles/gallon	ESTIMATED HIGHWAY MILEAGE miles/gallon
NSX	Acura	Automatic	3.0	6	18	23
Colt	Dodge	Manual	1.5	4	32	40
318i	BMW	Automatic	1.8	4	22	30
Aerostar	Ford	Automatic	4.0	6	16	22
Camry	Toyota	Manual	2.2	4	22	30

Source: *1993 Gas Mileage Guide,* EPA Fuel Economy Estimates, Oct. 1992.

a. Identify the experimental units.
b. State whether each of the variables measured is quantitative or qualitative.

1.2 White-collar criminal offenders (e.g., those convicted of tax evasion, fraud, or embezzlement) often receive preferential treatment in the criminal justice system. A researcher studied the social and economic damage incurred by convicted white-collar criminals (*Criminology,* Nov. 1984). From the case histories of approximately 70 offenders, the researcher collected data on several variables, listed here. Classify each of the variables as quantitative or qualitative.
a. Age in years
b. Length of sentence in years
c. Type of victim (business victim, government victim, individual victim, combination of victims)
d. Type of occupation (public/professional or private business)
e. Type of sentence (probation, work release, or incarceration)
f. Race
g. Recovery time in months (i.e., time from conviction to review of the file)

*To obtain the performance rating, *Business Week* compared an executive's return-to-pay ratio with those of other executives within the same industry group and assigned a rating of 1 to those executives with the highest ratios (relative to the others in the group), a rating of 2 to those with the next highest ratios, etc.

1.3 The *Journal of Performance of Constructed Facilities* (Feb. 1990) reported on the performance dimensions of water-distribution networks in the Philadelphia area. For one part of the study, the following data were collected for a sample of water pipe sections:

1. Pipe diameter (inches)
2. Pipe material
3. Age (year of installation)
4. Location
5. Pipe length (feet)
6. Stability of surrounding soil (unstable, moderately stable, or stable)
7. Corrosiveness of surrounding soil (corrosive or noncorrosive)
8. Internal pressure (pounds per square inch)
9. Percentage of pipe under land cover
10. Breakage rate (number of times pipe had to be repaired because of breakage)

Identify the data as quantitative or qualitative.

1.4 List five or more variables that your family physician considers while giving you a complete physical examination. State whether each is qualitative or quantitative.

1.5 "Deep hole" drilling is a family of drilling processes used when the ratio of hole depth to hole diameter exceeds 10. Successful deep hole drilling depends on the satisfactory discharge of the drill chip. An experiment was conducted to investigate the performance of deep hole drilling when chip congestion exists (*Journal of Engineering for Industry,* May 1993). Some important variables in the drilling process are described here. Identify the data type for each variable.

a. Chip discharge rate (number of chips discarded per minute)
b. Drilling depth (millimeters)
c. Oil velocity (millimeters per second)
d. Type of drilling (single-edge, BTA, or ejector)
e. Quality of hole surface

1.6 Marketers are keenly interested in the factors that motivate coupon usage by consumers. A study reported in the *Journal of Consumer Marketing* (Spring 1988) asked a sample of 290 shoppers to respond to the following questions:

a. Do you collect and redeem coupons?
b. Are you price-conscious while shopping?
c. On average, how much time per week do you spend clipping and collecting coupons?

Classify the responses to the questions as quantitative or qualitative data.

1.7 *U.S. News & World Report*'s "1994 Home Guide" provides information on prices of existing homes in 100 U.S. cities. Several of the variables recorded for each home in the *U.S. News* survey include the following:

a. City
b. Region or county
c. Home type (starter, trade-up, or deluxe)
d. Number of days on market
e. Sale price

Identify the type of data (quantitative or qualitative) produced by each variable.

1.2 Populations, Samples, and Random Sampling

When you examine a data set in the course of your study, you will be doing so because the data characterize some phenomenon of interest to you. In statistics, the data set that is the target of your interest is called a **population**. Notice that a statistical population does not refer to a group of people; it refers to a set of measurements. This data set, which is typically large, either exists in fact or is part of an ongoing operation and hence is conceptual. Some examples of phenomena and their corresponding populations are shown in Table 1.2.

TABLE 1.2 **Some Typical Populations**

PHENOMENON	EXPERIMENTAL UNITS	POPULATION	TYPE
a. Starting salary of a graduating Ph.D. biologist this year	Ph.D. biologists graduating this year	Set of starting salaries of all Ph.D. biologists who graduated this year	Existing
b. Current strength of water-distribution network in Philadelphia area	Water pipe sections	Set of breakage rates for all water pipe sections in Philadelphia	Existing
c. Quality of items produced on an assembly line	Manufactured items	Set of quality measurements for all items manufactured over the recent past and in the future	Part existing, part conceptual
d. Sanitation level on a cruise ship	Inspections	Set of sanitation levels for all inspections in the recent past and in the future	Part existing, part conceptual

Definition 1.6

A **population** is a collection (or set) of data that describe some phenomenon of interest to you.

Many populations are too large to measure (because of time and cost); others cannot be measured because they are partly conceptual, such as the set of quality measurements (population **d** in Table 1.2). Thus, we are often required to select a subset of values from a population and to make inferences about the population based on information contained in a **sample**. This is one of the major objectives of modern statistics.

Definition 1.7

A **sample** is a subset of data selected from a population.

Probability theory is used to infer the nature of a population from information contained in a sample. We observe the sample data and then consider the likelihood of observing these particular measurements for populations possessing various characteristics. Generally speaking, we infer that the sample was selected from the population most likely to have produced the observed sample. For example, if you toss a coin 10 times and observe 10 heads, you should infer either that the coin that generated the sample was biased in favor of heads or that something went wrong with your sampling (coin-tossing) procedure. Since the probability of observing a particular sample depends on how the sample was selected, the sampling procedure plays an important role in statistical inference.

The most common type of sampling procedure is one that gives every different sample of fixed size in the population an equal probability (chance) of selection. Such a sample is called a **random sample**.

Definition 1.8

A **random sample** of n experimental units is one selected from the population in such a way that every different sample of size n has an equal probability (chance) of selection.

How can a random sample be generated? If the population is not too large, each observation may be recorded on a piece of paper and placed in a suitable container. After the collection of papers is thoroughly mixed, the researcher can remove n pieces of paper from the container; the elements named on these n pieces of paper are the ones to be included in the sample. Lottery officials utilize such a technique in generating the winning numbers for Florida's weekly 6/49 Lotto game. Forty-nine white Ping-Pong balls (the population), each identified from 1 to 49 in black numerals, are placed into a clear plastic drum and mixed by blowing air into the container. The Ping-Pong balls bounce at random until a total of six balls "pop" into a tube attached to the drum. The numbers on the six balls (the random sample) are the winning Lotto numbers.

This method of random sampling is fairly easy to implement if the population is relatively small. It is not feasible, however, when the population consists of a large number of observations. Since it is also very difficult to achieve a thorough mixing, the procedure only approximates random sampling. Most scientific studies, however, rely on computers (with built-in random-number generators) to automatically generate the random sample. Almost all of the commercial statistical software packages available today (e.g., SAS, SPSS, MINITAB) have procedures for generating random samples.

EXERCISES

1.8 A panel of tobacco experts convened by the National Cancer Institute recommends that cigarette manufacturers put more descriptive labels on their cigarette packages, including a disclaimer that "light" brands are not really more healthful than "regular" (nonlight) brands (*Tampa Tribune,* Dec. 7, 1994). The panel's recommendations are based, in part, on data collected by the Federal Trade Commission (FTC). Each year, the FTC tests all domestic cigarette brands for carcinogens such as tar and nicotine. Suppose our goal is to compare the average nicotine content of all domestic light cigarette brands to the average nicotine content of all domestic regular cigarette brands. To do this, we record the nicotine contents (in milligrams) of 25 light cigarette brands and 25 regular cigarette brands.

a. Describe the target populations. (Give the precise statistical definitions.)
b. Describe the samples.
c. What are the parameters of interest?

1.9 Pesticides applied to an extensively grown crop can result in inadvertent ambient air contamination. *Environmental Science & Technology* (Oct. 1993) reported on thion residues of the insecticide chlorpyrifos used on dormant orchards in the San Joaquin Valley in California. Ambient air specimens were collected daily at an orchard site during an intensive period of spraying—a total of 13 days—and the thion level (nanograms per cubic meter) measured each day.

a. Identify the population of interest to the researchers.
b. Identify the sample.

1.10 When Nissan introduced its new Infiniti luxury cars in 1989, its television ad campaign was renowned for a novel gimmick: The automobiles were nowhere in sight. The Infiniti ads, which depicted lushly photographed trees, boulders, lightning bolts, and ocean waves (but no cars), were found by a nationwide Gallup poll of 1,000 consumers to be the best-recalled commercial on television (*Time*, Jan. 22, 1990).

a. Describe the population of interest to the pollsters.
b. What is the experimental unit?
c. Identify the sample.
d. What is the inference made by the Gallup poll?

1.11 Reporting in the *New England Journal of Medicine* (Mar. 18, 1991), the Centers for Disease Control (CDC) confirmed what many former cigarette smokers have learned from experience: People who quit smoking tend to gain weight. The CDC's research team reviewed data on 1,885 smokers and 768 former smokers who were studied over a 13-year period. Weight gain over the study period was classified as slight (3 kilograms or less), moderate (3–8 kilograms), significant (8–13 kilograms), or major (more than 13 kilograms). The smokers/quitters were also classified according to gender to compare weight gain in males versus females. The percentages of men and women in the four weight-gain categories are provided in the table.

a. What data are the experimental units for the *New England Journal of Medicine* study?
b. How many variables are measured in the study? Are they quantitative or qualitative?
c. Do the data represent populations or samples? Explain.

WEIGHT GAIN	QUITTERS		SMOKERS	
	Men	Women	Men	Women
Slight	55	50	66	63
Moderate	22	26	24	23
Significant	14	10	8	9
Major	9	14	2	5
Totals	100	100	100	100

Source: *Time*, Mar. 25, 1991, p. 55.

1.12 *Postpartum depression* is the term used to describe the usually short-lived period of emotional sensitivity that many women suffer following childbirth. Studies have indicated that nearly 90% of all mothers experience some symptoms of postpartum blues. However, new evidence shows that men, too, can suffer from postpartum depression. Suppose a developmental psychologist wants to estimate the proportion of fathers who suffer from postpartum blues. Fifty men who have recently become parents are interviewed and observed in the home, and the number experiencing some form of postpartum depression is recorded.

a. What is the population of interest to the developmental psychologist?
b. Describe the sample in this problem.
c. Suppose that 31 of the 50 men are diagnosed as having postpartum blues. The psychologist then estimates that 62% of all fathers experience postpartum depression. Do you believe that this estimate is equal to the proportion for the entire population? Explain.

1.13 Do most state lottery winners who win big payoffs quit their jobs within 1 year of winning? Not according to a study conducted by sociologist and professor H. Roy Kaplan (*Journal of the Institute for Socioeconomic Studies*, Sept. 1985). Kaplan mailed questionnaires to over 2,000 lottery winners who won at least $50,000 in the past 10 years. Of the 576 who responded, only 11% had quit their jobs during the first year after striking it rich. In this study, identify

a. the population
b. the sample
c. the inference made about the population

1.14 *Newsweek* (Nov. 16, 1987) reported on "a prescription drug that may help nervous test takers improve their Scholastic Aptitude Test (SAT) score." A researcher experimented with giving propranolol, one of the class of heart drugs called beta blockers, to nervous high school students prior to taking their SATs. The theory was that the same calming effect beta blockers provide heart patients could also be used to reduce anxiety in test takers. To test this theory, the researcher selected 22 high school juniors who had not performed as well on the SAT as they should have, based on IQs and other academic evaluations. One hour before the students repeated the test in their senior year, each student received a dose of a beta blocker. Typically, students who retake the test without special preparations will increase their scores by an average of 38 points. These 22 students, however, improved their scores by an average of 120 points.

a. Describe the population of interest to the researcher. (Give the precise statistical definition.)
b. Describe the sample.
c. Based on the sample results, what inference would you make about the use of beta blockers to increase SAT scores?

1.15 *Euthanasia,* the act of painlessly ending the life of a person suffering from an incurable and painful disease or condition, has long been a dilemma of medical ethics. Dr. Jack Kevorkian, a retired physician, strongly supports euthanasia and has himself assisted in the suicide of at least 10 suffering patients. Suppose you work for a major opinion pollster and you have been assigned the task of conducting a survey for the Concern for Dying (formerly the Euthanasia Society). The purpose of the survey is to estimate the proportion of American adults who support Dr. Kevorkian's euthanasia movement.

a. Clearly define the population of interest to the Concern for Dying.
b. Do you think it is possible to obtain the entire population? Explain.
c. Why should the sample you select for the survey be representative of the population?

1.3 Describing Data Sets Graphically

The word *inference* implies description. For example, to infer the nature of a company, we would describe its product, annual sales volume, annual profit, number of employees, and so forth. Similarly, to infer the nature of a data set, such as a population or a sample, we need to be able to describe the set.

A useful graphical method for describing quantitative data is provided by a **relative frequency distribution**. This type of graph shows the proportions of the total set of measurements that fall in various intervals on the scale of measurement. For example, Figure 1.1 shows the intelligence quotients (IQs) of identical twins. The area over a particular interval under a relative frequency distribution curve is proportional to the fraction of the total number of measurements that fall in that interval. In Figure 1.1, the fraction of the total number of identical twins with IQs that fall between 100 and 105 is proportional to the shaded area. **If we take the total area under the distribution curve as equal to 1, then the shaded area is equal to the fraction of IQs that fall between 100 and 105.**

FIGURE 1.1
Relative frequency distribution: IQs of identical twins

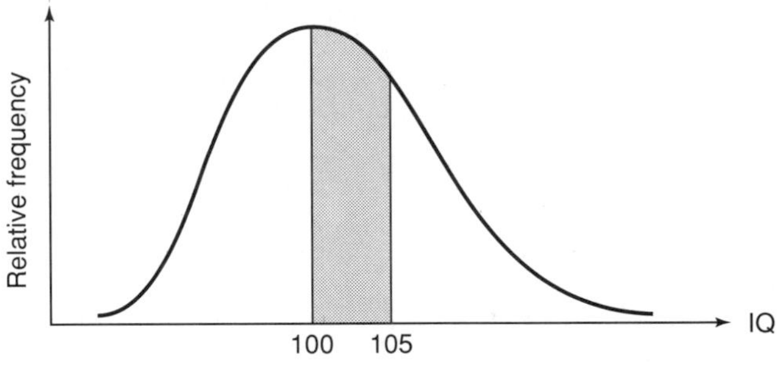

The variable measured in generating a population, denoted by the symbol y, is called a **random variable**. Observing a single value of y is equivalent to selecting a single measurement from the population. The probability that it will assume a value in an interval, say, a to b, is given by its relative frequency or **probability distribution**. The total area under a probability distribution curve is always assumed to equal 1. Hence, the probability that a measurement on y will fall in the interval between a and b is equal to the shaded area shown in Figure 1.2.

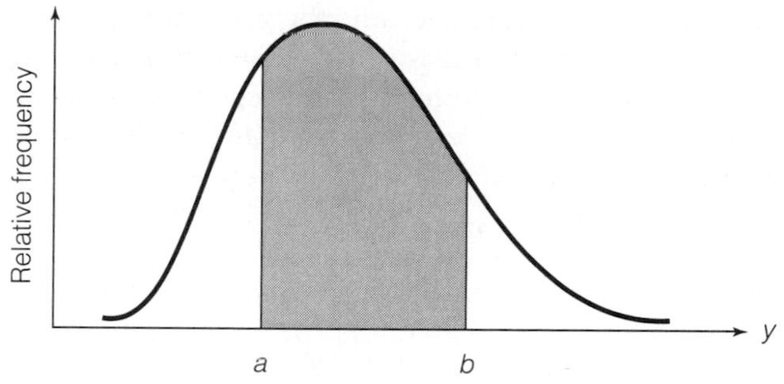

FIGURE 1.2
Probability distribution for a random variable

Since the theoretical probability distribution for a population is usually unknown, we resort to obtaining a sample from the population: Our objective is to describe the sample and use this information to make inferences about the probability distribution of the population. **Stem-and-leaf plots** and **histograms** are two of the most popular graphical methods for describing samples. Both display the frequency (or relative frequency) of observations that fall into specified intervals (or classes) of the variable's values.

For small data sets (say, 30 or fewer observations) with measurements with only a few digits, stem-and-leaf plots can be constructed easily by hand. Histograms, on the other hand, are better suited to the description of larger data sets, and they permit greater flexibility in the choice of classes. Both, however, can be generated using the computer, as illustrated in the following examples.

EXAMPLE 1.2

The data in Table 1.3 represent sale prices (in thousands of dollars) for a random sample of 25 residential properties sold in Tampa, Florida, in 1993. (These data were extracted from Appendix I. We analyze the data in Appendix I more thoroughly in Case Study 12.) A MINITAB printout of a stem-and-leaf plot for the 25 sale prices is shown in Figure 1.3. Interpret the figure.

TABLE 1.3 **Sale Prices for a Sample of Properties from Appendix I**

SALE PRICE, hundreds of dollars				
66	59	106	50	63
89	129	74	82	84
71	95	72	57	76
109	77	68	101	65
42	36	148	94	112

FIGURE 1.3 MINITAB stem-and-leaf display for sale prices in Table 1.3

```
Stem-and-leaf of salepric   N  = 25
Leaf Unit = 1.0

   1     3 6
   2     4 2
   5     5 079
   9     6 3568
  (5)    7 12467
  11     8 249
   8     9 45
   6    10 169
   3    11 2
   2    12 9
   1    13
   1    14 8
```

[*Note:* The first column gives the cumulative number of measurements in the nearest tail of the distribution, beginning with the stem row.]

Solution

In a stem-and-leaf plot, each measurement is partitioned into a stem and a leaf. MINITAB has selected the last digit in the sale price to represent the leaf and the preceding digits to represent the stem. For example, the value 148 (representing a sale price of $148,000) is partitioned into a stem of 14 and a leaf of 8, as illustrated here:

STEM	LEAF
14	8

The stems are listed in order in the second column of the plot, Figure 1.3, starting with the smallest stem of 3 and ending with the largest stem of 14. The respective leaves are then placed to the right in the appropriate stem row in increasing order. For example, the stem row of 9 in Figure 1.3 has two leaves, 4 and 5, representing the sale prices $94,000 and $95,000. Notice that the stem row of 7 (representing sale prices in the $70,000s) has the most leaves (5). Thus, 5 of the 25 sale prices (or 20%) have values in the $70,000s. Notice also that 20 of the 25 sale prices (80%) fall between $50,000 and $110,000. (That is, 20 of the sale prices have stems ranging from 5 to 10.)

EXAMPLE 1.3

Figure 1.4 is an SAS printout of a relative frequency histogram describing the sale prices (in $ thousands) of over 700 residential properties sold in Tampa, Florida, in 1993. (The data in Appendix I were extracted from this larger data set.)

FIGURE 1.4
SAS histogram for the sale prices (in $ thousands)

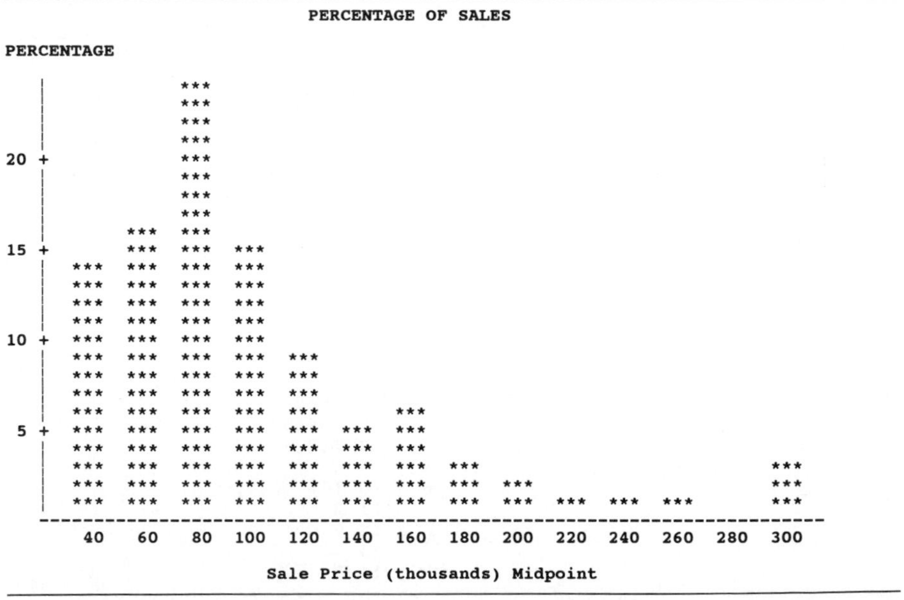

a. Interpret the graph.
b. Visually estimate the proportion of sale prices in the data set between \$70,000 and \$110,000.

Solution

a. In constructing a histogram, the values of the sale prices are divided into intervals of equal length, called **classes**. The midpoints of these classes, 40, 60, 80, etc., are shown on the horizontal axis of Figure 1.4. Thus, the classes are 30–50, 50–70, etc. The relative frequency (or percentage) of sale prices falling in each class interval is represented by the vertical bars over the class.

You can see from Figure 1.4 that the sale prices tend to pile up near \$80,000; the class interval from \$70,000 to \$90,000 has the greatest relative frequency.

Figure 1.4 also shows a tendency for the data to tail out to the high side because of a few extremely large sale prices. Distributions of data with this feature are said to be skewed to the right, or **positively skewed**. (Similarly, distributions of data are skewed left, or **negatively skewed**, if they tend to tail out to the low side because of a few unusually small measurements.)

b. The interval \$70,000 to \$110,000 spans two sale price classes: 70–90 and 90–110. The proportion of sale prices between \$70,000 and \$110,000 is equal to the sum of the relative frequencies associated with these two classes. These two class relative frequencies are (approximately) .24 and .15, respectively. Consequently, the approximate proportion of sale prices between \$70,000 and \$110,000 is

$$(.24 + .15) = .39$$
$$= 39\%$$

The steps required to construct stem-and-leaf plots and histograms by hand are summarized here. The computer commands for generating these graphs are provided in Appendices D–G.

Constructing a Stem-and-Leaf Plot

STEP 1 Decide how the stems and leaves will be defined.

STEP 2 List the stems in order in a column, starting with the smallest stem and ending with the largest.

STEP 3 Proceed through the data set, placing the leaf for each observation in the appropriate stem row. (You may want to place the leaves of each stem in increasing order.)

Constructing a Histogram

STEP 1 Examine the data to determine the smallest and largest measurements.

STEP 2 Divide the interval between the smallest and largest measurements into between 5 and 20 equal subintervals called **classes**, so that each measurement falls in one and only one subinterval. (Although the choice of the number of classes is arbitrary, you will obtain a better description of the data if you use a small number of subintervals for small data sets and a large number of subintervals for large data sets.)

STEP 3 Compute the class frequencies or the class relative frequencies.

STEP 4 Using a vertical axis of about three-fourths of the length of the horizontal axis, plot each relative frequency (or frequency) on the vertical axis as a rectangle or bar over the corresponding subinterval on the horizontal axis.

EXERCISES

1.16 Consider the following sample data:

5.9	5.3	1.6	7.4	8.6	1.2	2.1
4.0	7.3	8.4	8.9	6.7	4.5	6.3
7.6	9.7	3.5	1.1	4.3	3.3	8.4
1.6	8.2	6.5	1.1	5.0	9.4	6.4

a. Using the first digit as a stem, construct a stem-and-leaf display.
b. Construct a relative frequency histogram for the sample data.

1.17 Over half of the nearly 60,000 members of the U.S. Chess Federation (USCF) have official chess ratings. A player with a rating of 1,100 or less is a "beginner"; "average" players' ratings range between 1,100 and 1,900; "experts" range between 2,000 and 2,200; "masters" range between 2,200 and 2,400; and "grand masters" have ratings higher than 2,400. (Gary Kasparov, the reigning world champion from Russia, has a chess rating of 2,900.) The following graph from *Scientific American* (Oct. 1990), illustrates the distribution of the ratings of the 35,000 rated members of the USCF.
a. What type of graph is portrayed?
b. Visually estimate the number of USCF grand masters.
c. Are the data skewed? Explain.

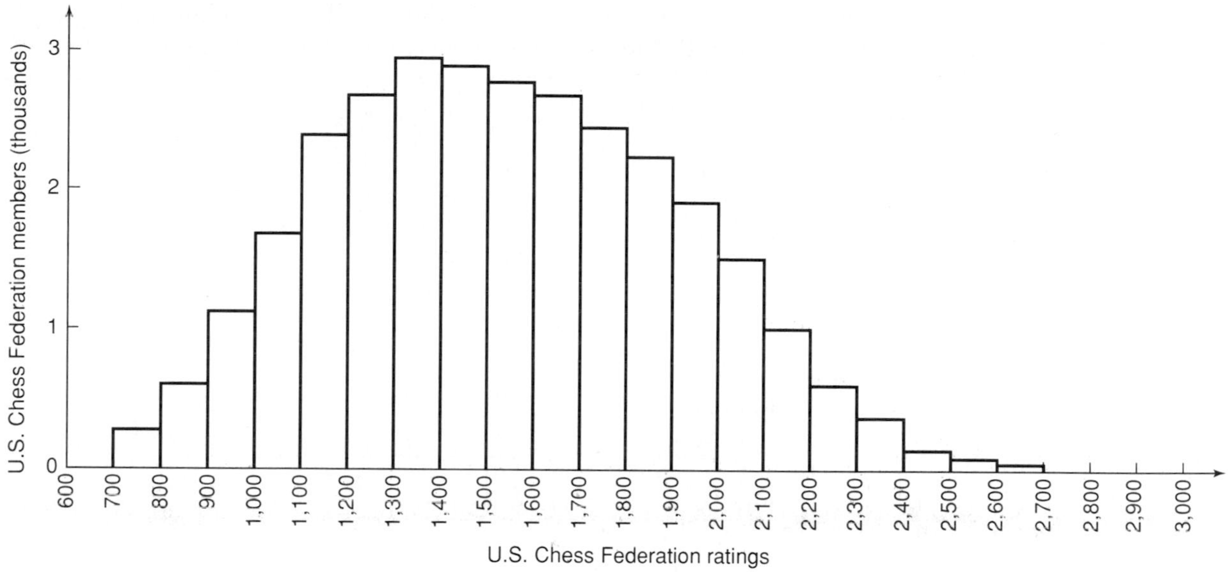

1.18 A Harris Corporation/University of Florida study was undertaken to determine whether a manufacturing process performed at a remote location could be established locally. Test devices (pilots) were set up at both the old and new locations, and voltage readings on the process were obtained. A "good" process was considered to be one with voltage readings of at least 9.2 volts (with larger readings better than smaller readings). The table contains voltage readings for 30 production runs at each location.

OLD LOCATION			NEW LOCATION		
9.98	10.12	9.84	9.19	10.01	8.82
10.26	10.05	10.15	9.63	8.82	8.65
10.05	9.80	10.02	10.10	9.43	8.51
10.29	10.15	9.80	9.70	10.03	9.14
10.03	10.00	9.73	10.09	9.85	9.75
8.05	9.87	10.01	9.60	9.27	8.78
10.55	9.55	9.98	10.05	8.83	9.35
10.26	9.95	8.72	10.12	9.39	9.54
9.97	9.70	8.80	9.49	9.48	9.36
9.87	8.72	9.84	9.37	9.64	8.68

Source: Harris Corporation, Melbourne, Fla.

a. Construct a relative frequency histogram for the voltage readings of the old process.
b. Construct a stem-and-leaf display for the voltage readings of the old process. Which of the two graphs in parts **a** and **b** is more informative?
c. Construct a frequency histogram for the voltage readings of the new process.
d. Compare the two graphs in parts **a** and **c**. (You may want to draw the two histograms on the same graph.) Does it appear that the manufacturing process can be established locally (i.e., is the new process as good as or better than the old)?

1.19 Refer to the *Journal of Engineering for Industry* (May 1993) study of deep hole drilling described in Exercise 1.5. An analysis of drill chip congestion was performed using data generated via computer simulation. The simulated distribution of the length (in millimeters) of 50 drill chips is displayed here in a frequency histogram.

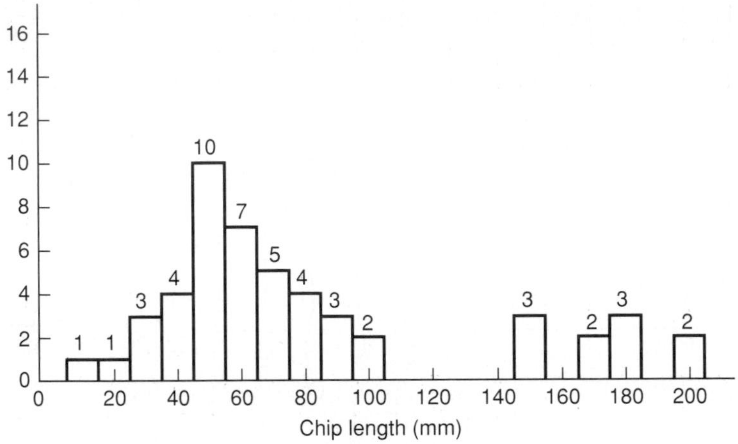

Source: Chin, Jih-Hua et al. "The computer simulation and experimental analysis of chip monitoring for deep hole drilling." *Journal of Engineering for Industry, Transactions of the ASME*, Vol. 115, May 1993, p. 187 (Figure 12).

a. Convert the frequency histogram into a relative frequency histogram.

b. Based on the graph, part a, would you expect to observe a drill chip with a length of at least 190 mm? Explain.

1.20 Researchers at Miami University (Ohio) studied the incidence of humor in advertisements placed in American, British, and German trade magazines *(Industrial Marketing Management,* 1993). A total of 665 ads were evaluated. The accompanying table gives the breakdown of the number of ads evaluated by the various industries.

INDUSTRY	NUMBER OF ADS	INDUSTRY	NUMBER OF ADS
Accountancy	21	Hotels	13
Aeronautics	20	Insurance	29
Agriculture	31	Laundry	13
Baking	35	Marketing/advertising	37
Business	26	Medical	33
Chemistry	25	Mining	27
Computers	25	Music	19
Dairy	17	Packaging	31
Dental	29	Paper/pulp	25
Electronics	16	Plastics	31
Environment	17	Safety	26
Fishing	20	Security	20
Fur	7	Toys	15
Graphics	16	Travel	19
Grocery	22		

Source: McCullough, L. S. and Taylor, R. K. "Humor in American, British, and German ads." *Industrial Marketing Management,* Vol. 22, 1993, p. 21 (Table 1).

a. Construct a stem-and-leaf display for the data, using a single-digit stem.
b. Repeat part a, using a two-digit stem.
c. Which of the two figures constructed in parts **a** and **b** provides more information about the ad data? Explain.

1.21 Are major colleges and universities lax in hiring minorities to fill top positions in their athletic programs? A *USA Today* survey of 62 Division I schools found that only 12.5% of the jobs in the athletic department are held by minorities (African Americans, Hispanics, Native Americans, and Asians). In contrast, the 1990 Census shows minorities represent 19.7% of the U.S. population (*USA Today,* Mar. 19, 1991). The results of the survey are reproduced in the table. The 62 schools were selected based on the Top 25 polls for men's and women's basketball during the 1989–1990 season and the final 1990 Top 25 football poll. (Northwestern declined to respond, and Seton Hall did not supply figures.)

SCHOOL	TOTAL POSITIONS	POSITIONS HELD BY MINORITY	PERCENT MINORITY	SCHOOL	TOTAL POSITIONS	POSITIONS HELD BY MINORITY	PERCENT MINORITY
Georgetown	30	8	26.7	Louisiana Tech	26	3	11.5
Houston	43	11	25.6	Syracuse	52	6	11.5
Miami	55	14	25.5	Arkansas	44	5	11.4
Arizona	67	15	22.4	Northern Illinois	53	6	11.3
Long Beach State	53	11	20.8	Alabama	54	6	11.1
USC	65	13	20.0	Western Kentucky	18	2	11.1
Pittsburgh	54	10	18.5	UNLV	55	6	10.9
Oklahoma State	34	6	17.6	Connecticut	37	4	10.8
Oklahoma	63	11	17.5	South Carolina	49	5	10.2
Washington	63	11	17.5	East Tennessee State	30	3	10.0
Southern Mississippi	35	6	17.1	Texas–El Paso	30	3	10.0
Stanford	71	12	16.9	Rutgers	42	4	9.5
Iowa	72	12	16.7	North Carolina State	44	4	9.1
Georgia Tech	52	8	15.4	Texas[a]	67	6	9.0
Michigan State	60	9	15.0	Michigan	58	5	8.6
Illinois	54	8	14.8	Penn State	82	7	8.5
Kentucky	54	8	14.8	St. John's	60	5	8.3
Ohio State	64	9	14.1	Nebraska	64	5	7.8
Colorado	43	6	14.0	Mississippi State	52	4	7.7
LSU	59	8	13.6	Providence	13	1	7.7
Purdue	53	7	13.2	Mississippi	40	3	7.5
New Mexico State	38	5	13.2	Florida State	53	4	7.5
UCLA	84	11	13.1	Indiana	57	4	7.0
Clemson	48	6	12.5	Tennessee[a]	73	5	6.8
North Carolina	57	7	12.3	Duke	45	3	6.7
Kansas	49	6	12.2	Virginia	60	4	6.7
Utah	33	4	12.1	BYU	51	3	5.9
Louisville	34	4	11.8	Princeton	44	2	4.5
Georgia	60	7	11.7	Notre Dame	47	2	4.3
Florida	61	7	11.5	Stephen F. Austin	27	1	3.7

[a]Numbers combined from separate men's and women's athletic programs.
Source: *USA Today*, Mar. 19, 1991.

a. Do the data represent a sample or a population? Explain.
b. Use a graphical technique to describe the data on percentage of minority positions in the athletic department of the 60 colleges and universities. Interpret the graph.

1.22 Under a voluntary cooperative inspection program, all passenger cruise ships arriving at U.S. ports are subject to unannounced inspections. The purpose of these inspections is to achieve levels of sanitation that will minimize the potential for gastrointestinal disease outbreaks on these ships. Ships are rated on a scale of 0 to 100 points, depending on how well they meet the Centers for Disease Control sanitation standards. In general, the lower the score, the lower the level of sanitation. The table lists the sanitation inspection scores for 91 international cruise ships during 1992.

SHIP	SCORE	SHIP	SCORE	SHIP	SCORE
Americana	89	Hanseatic Renaissance	82	Sea Princess	88
Amerikanis	97	Holiday	91	Seabourn Spirit	92
Azure Seas	83	Horizon	94	Seabourn Pride	99
Britanis	93	Island Princess	87	Seabreeze I	96
Caribbean Prince	84	Jubilee	89	Seaward	89
Caribe I	90	Mardi Gras	92	Sky Princess	97
Carla C	90	Meridian	95	Society Explorer	66
Carnivale	92	Nantucket Clipper	89	Song of America	95
Celebration	95	New Shoreham II	95	Song of Flower	99
Club Med 1	94	Nieuw Amsterdam	97	Song of Norway	92
Costa Classica	91	Noordam	92	Southward	89
Costa Marina	91	Nordic Empress	93	Sovereign of the Seas	93
Costa Riviera	91	Nordic Prince	92	Star Princess	94
Crown Monarch	94	Norway	84	Starship Atlantic	87
Crown Odyssey	88	Pacific Princess	88	Starship Majestic	94
Crown Princess	88	Pacific Star	70	Starship Oceanic	97
Crystal Harmony	99	Queen Elizabeth 2	98	Starward	96
Cunard Countess	96	Regent Sea	87	Stella Solaris	94
Cunard Princess	89	Regent Star	74	Sun Viking	90
Daphne	86	Regent Sun	95	Sunward	95
Dawn Princess	86	Rotterdam	92	Triton	86
Discovery I	93	Royal Princess	93	Tropicale	93
Dolphin IV	96	Royal Viking Sun	86	Universe	92
Ecstasy	94	Sagafjord	89	Victoria	96
Emerald Seas	95	Scandinavian Dawn	87	Viking Princess	90
Enchanted Isle	86	Scandinavian Song	90	Viking Serenade	96
Enchanted Seas	96	Scandinavian Sun	89	Vistafjord	94
Fair Princess	87	Sea Bird	86	Westerdam	91
Fantasy	97	Sea Goddess I	97	Wind Spirit	96
Festivale	94	Sea Lion	91	Yorktown Clipper	92
Golden Odyssey	89				

Source: Center of Environmental Health and Injury Control, Miami, Fla. (reported in *Tampa Tribune*, May 17, 1992).

a. A MINITAB stem-and-leaf display of the data is shown on page 19. Identify the stems and leaves of the graph.
b. A score of 86 or higher at the time of inspection indicates the ship is providing an accepted standard of sanitation. Use the MINITAB graph to estimate the proportion of ships that have an accepted sanitation standard.
c. Locate the inspection score of 70 (Pacific Star) on the stem-and-leaf display.

```
Stem-and-leaf of SanLevel   N  = 91
Leaf Unit = 1.0

    1     6 6
    1     6
    2     7 0
    2     7
    3     7 4
    3     7
    3     7
    3     8
    5     8 23
    7     8 44
   18     8 66666677777
   31     8 8888999999999
   42     9 00000111111
  (15)    9 222222222333333
   34     9 4444444445555555
   18     9 66666666777777
    4     9 8999
```

1.4 Describing Data Sets Numerically

Numerical descriptive measures provide a second (and often more powerful) method for describing a set of data. These measures, which locate the center of the data set and its spread, actually enable you to construct an approximate mental image of the distribution of the data set.

Note: Most of the formulas used to compute numerical descriptive measures require the summation of numbers. For instance, we may want to sum the observations in a data set, or we may want to square each observation and then sum the squared values. The symbol Σ (sigma) is used to denote a summation operation.

For example, suppose we denote the n sample measurements on a random variable y by the symbols $y_1, y_2, y_3, \ldots, y_n$. Then the sum of all n measurements in the sample is represented by the symbol

$$\sum_{i=1}^{n} y_i$$

This is read "summation y, y_1 to y_n" and is equal to the value

$$y_1 + y_2 + y_3 + \cdots + y_n$$

One of the most common measures of central tendency is the **mean**, or arithmetic average, of a data set. Thus, if we denote the sample measurements by the symbols $y_1, y_2, y_3, \ldots,$ the sample mean is defined as follows:

Definition 1.9

The **mean** of a sample of n measurements $y_1, y_2, \ldots, y_n$ is

$$\bar{y} = \frac{\sum_{i=1}^{n} y_i}{n}$$

The mean of a population, or equivalently, the expected value of y, $E(y)$, is usually unknown in a practical situation (we will want to infer its value based on the sample data). Most texts use the symbol μ to denote the mean of a population. Thus, we will use the following notation:

Notation

Sample mean: $\bar{y}$
Population mean: $E(y) = \mu$

The spread or variation of a data set is measured by its **range**, its **variance**, or its **standard deviation**.

Definition 1.10

The **range** of a sample of n measurements $y_1, y_2, \ldots, y_n$ is the difference between the largest and smallest measurements in the sample.

EXAMPLE 1.4

If a sample consists of measurements 3, 1, 0, 4, 7, find the sample mean and the sample range.

Solution

The sample mean and range are

$$\bar{y} = \frac{\sum_{i=1}^{n} y_i}{n} = \frac{15}{5} = 3$$

$$\text{Range} = 7 - 0 = 7$$

The variance of a set of measurements is defined to be the average of the *squares of the deviations* of the measurements about their mean. Thus, the population variance, which is usually unknown in a practical situation, would be the mean or expected value of $(y - \mu)^2$, or $E[(y - \mu)^2]$. We use the symbol σ^2 to represent the variance of a population:

$$E[(y - \mu)^2] = \sigma^2$$

The quantity usually termed the **sample variance** is defined in the box.

Definition 1.11

The **variance** of a sample of n measurements $y_1, y_2, \ldots, y_n$ is defined to be

$$s^2 = \frac{\sum_{i=1}^{n} (y_i - \bar{y})^2}{n - 1} = \frac{\sum_{i=1}^{n} y_i^2 - n\bar{y}^2}{n - 1}$$

Note that the sum of squares of deviations in the sample variance is divided by $(n - 1)$, rather than n. Division by n produces estimates that tend to underestimate σ^2. Division by $(n - 1)$ corrects this problem.

EXAMPLE 1.5

Refer to Example 1.4. Calculate the sample variance for the sample 3, 1, 0, 4, 7.

Solution

We first calculate

$$\sum_{i=1}^{n} (y_i - \bar{y})^2 = \sum_{i=1}^{n} y_i^2 - n\bar{y}^2 = 75 - 5(3)^2 = 30$$

where $\bar{y} = 3$ from Example 1.4. Then

$$s^2 = \frac{\sum_{i=1}^{n} (y_i - \bar{y})^2}{n - 1} = \frac{30}{4} = 7.5$$

The concept of a variance is important in theoretical statistics, but its square root, called a **standard deviation**, is the quantity most often used to describe data variation.

Definition 1.12

The **standard deviation** of a set of measurements is equal to the square root of their variance. Thus, the standard deviations of a sample and a population are

Sample standard deviation: s

Population standard deviation: σ

The standard deviation of a set of data takes on meaning in light of a theorem (Tchebysheff's theorem) and a rule of thumb.* Basically, they give us the following guidelines:

Guidelines for Interpreting a Standard Deviation

1. For *any* data set (population or sample), at least three-fourths of the measurements will lie within 2 standard deviations of their mean.
2. For *most* data sets of moderate size (say, 25 or more measurements) with a mound-shaped distribution, approximately 95% of the measurements will lie within 2 standard deviations of their mean.

EXAMPLE 1.6

Often, travelers who have no intention of showing up fail to cancel their hotel reservations in a timely manner. These travelers are known, in the parlance of the hospitality trade, as "no-shows." To protect against no-shows and late cancellations, hotels invariably overbook rooms. A recent study reported in the *Journal of Travel Research* examined the problems of overbooking rooms in the hotel industry. The data in Table 1.4, extracted from the study, represent daily numbers of late cancellations and no-shows for a random sample of 30 days at a large (500-room) hotel. Based on this sample, how many rooms, at minimum, should the hotel overbook each day?

TABLE 1.4 **Hotel No-Shows for a Sample of 30 Days**

18	16	16	16	14	18	16	18	14	19
15	19	9	20	10	10	12	14	18	12
14	14	17	12	18	13	15	13	15	19

Source: Toh, R. S. "An inventory depletion overbooking model for the hotel industry." *Journal of Travel Research*, Vol. 23, No. 4, Spring 1985, p. 27. The *Journal of Travel Research* is published by the Travel and Tourism Research Association (TTRA) and the Business Research Division, University of Colorado at Boulder.

Solution

To answer this question, we need to know the range of values where most of the daily numbers of no-shows fall. We must compute $\bar{y}$ and s, and examine the shape of the relative frequency distribution for the data.

Figure 1.5 is a MINITAB printout that shows a stem-and-leaf display and descriptive statistics of the sample data. Notice from the stem-and-leaf display that the distribution of daily no-shows is mound-shaped, and only slightly skewed

*For a more complete discussion and a statement of Tchebysheff's theorem, see the references listed at the end of this chapter.

on the low (top) side of Figure 1.5. Thus, guideline 2 in the previous box should give a good estimate of the percentage of days that fall within 2 standard deviations of the mean.

FIGURE 1.5
MINITAB printout: Describing the no-show data, Example 1.6

```
Stem-and-leaf of noshows    N  = 30
Leaf Unit = 0.10

    1     9 0
    3    10 00
    3    11
    6    12 000
    8    13 00
   13    14 00000
  (3)    15 000
   14    16 0000
   10    17 0
    9    18 00000
    4    19 000
    1    20 0

                   N      MEAN    MEDIAN    TRMEAN     STDEV    SEMEAN
noshows           30    15.133    15.000    15.231     2.945     0.538

                 MIN       MAX        Q1        Q3
noshows        9.000    20.000    13.000    18.000
```

The mean and standard deviation of the sample data, shaded on the MINITAB printout, are $\bar{y} = 15.133$ and $s = 2.945$. From guideline 2 in the box, we know that about 95% of the daily number of no-shows fall within 2 standard deviations of the mean, i.e., within the interval

$$\bar{y} \pm 2s = 15.133 \pm 2(2.945)$$
$$= 15.133 \pm 5.890$$

or between 9.243 no-shows and 21.023 no-shows. (If we count the number of measurements in this data set, we find that actually 29 out of 30, or 96.7%, fall in this interval.)

From this result, the large hotel can infer that there will be at least 9.243 (or, rounding up, 10) no-shows per day. Consequently, the hotel can overbook at least 10 rooms per day and still be highly confident that all reservations can be honored.

Numerical descriptive measures calculated from sample data are called **statistics**. Numerical descriptive measures of the population are called **parameters**. In a practical situation, we will not know the population relative frequency distribution (or equivalently, the population distribution for y). We will usually assume that it has unknown numerical descriptive measures, such as its mean μ and standard deviation σ, and by inferring (using **sample statistics**) the values of these parameters, we infer the nature of the population relative frequency distribution. Sometimes we will assume that we know the shape of the population relative frequency distribution and use this information to help us make our inferences. When we do this, we are postulating a model for the population relative frequency distribution, and we must keep in mind that the validity of the inference may depend on how well our model fits reality.

Definition 1.13

Numerical descriptive measures of a population are called **parameters**.

Definition 1.14

A **sample statistic** is a quantity calculated from the observations in a sample.

EXERCISES

1.23 Compute $\bar{y}$, s^2, and s for each of the following data sets:

a. 1, 5, 0, 2, 5, 7, 1
b. 1, 2, 0, 0, 5, 4
c. 10, 8, 12, 2
d. 3, 4, 10, 2
e. 1, 1, 20, 20, 8
f. 2, 100, 104, 2
g. $-1, -3, -2, 0, -3, -3$
h. $\frac{1}{5}, \frac{1}{5}, \frac{1}{5}, \frac{2}{5}, 2, \frac{4}{5}$

1.24 Periodically, the Federal Trade Commission (FTC) ranks domestic cigarette brands according to tar, nicotine, and carbon monoxide content. The test results are obtained by using a sequential smoking machine to "smoke" cigarettes to a 23-millimeter butt length. The tar, nicotine, and carbon monoxide concentrations (rounded to the nearest milligram) in the residual "dry" particulate matter of the smoke are then measured. The accompanying SAS printout describes the nicotine contents of the 500 cigarette brands tested in 1994 by the FTC.

a. Examine the relative frequency histogram for nicotine content. Use the rule of thumb to describe the data set.
b. Locate $\bar{y}$ and s on the printout, then compute the interval $\bar{y} \pm 2s$.
c. Based on your answer to part **a**, estimate the percentage of cigarettes with nicotine contents in the interval formed in part **b**.

```
                         UNIVARIATE PROCEDURE

                        Variable=NICOTINE

                              Moments

           N                500  Sum Wgts        500
           Mean          0.8425  Sum          421.25
           Std Dev     0.345525  Variance   0.119388
           Skewness    -0.17036  Kurtosis   0.162504
           USS         414.4775  CSS        59.57437
           CV          41.01187  Std Mean   0.015452
           T:Mean=0    54.52246  Prob>|T|     0.0001
           Sgn Rank       62625  Prob>|S|     0.0001
           Num ^= 0         500

                         Quantiles(Def=5)

            100% Max        1.9       99%        1.7
             75% Q3         1.1       95%        1.4
             50% Med        0.9       90%        1.2
             25% Q1         0.7       10%        0.4
              0% Min       0.05        5%        0.1
                                       1%        0.1

            Range          1.85
            Q3-Q1           0.4
            Mode            0.8

                             Extremes

              Lowest    Obs     Highest    Obs
                0.05(   336)       1.7(    344)
                0.05(   335)       1.8(    330)
                0.05(    93)       1.8(    333)
                 0.1(   327)       1.8(    349)
                 0.1(   325)       1.9(    152)

              Histogram                      #              Boxplot
 1.95+*                                      1                 0
     .**                                     3                 0
     .**                                     3                 |
     .**                                     3                 |
     .**                                     4                 |
     .*******                               13                 |
     .*********                             17                 |
     .*************************             49                 |
     .*********************                 42              +-----+
     .****************************          56              |     |
     .********************************      64              *-----*
     .***********************************   70              |  +  |
     .***************************           54              +-----+
     .*********                             18                 |
     .*********************                 41                 |
     .***********                           22                 |
     .**                                     3                 |
     .****                                   8                 |
     .*************                         26                 |
 0.05+**                                     3                 0
      ----+----+----+----+----+----+----+
      * may represent up to 2 counts
```

d. Use the information on the SAS histogram to determine the actual percentage of nicotine contents that fall within the interval formed in part **b**. Does your answer agree with your estimate of part **c**?

1.25 Refer to the *Journal of Performance of Constructed Facilities* (Feb. 1990) study of water-distribution networks, Exercise 1.3. The internal pressure readings (measured in pounds per square inch, psi) for a sample of pipe sections had a mean of 7.99 psi and a standard deviation of 2.02 psi.

a. Use this information to construct an interval that captures about 95% of the pressure readings sampled.

b. Would you expect to observe an internal pressure reading of 20 psi? Explain.

1.26 Refer to the Centers for Disease Control study of sanitation levels for 72 international cruise ships, Exercise 1.22. A MINITAB printout of the descriptive statistics for the data is shown here. (Recall that sanitation scores range from 0 to 100.) Interpret the numerical descriptive measures of central tendency displayed on the printout.

```
                 N      MEAN    MEDIAN    TRMEAN     STDEV    SEMEAN
sanlevel        91    91.044    92.000    91.580     5.566     0.583

               MIN       MAX        Q1        Q3
sanlevel    66.000    99.000    89.000    95.000
```

1.27 Given a data set whose largest value is 900 and whose smallest value is 50, what would you estimate the standard deviation to be? Explain the logic behind the procedure you used to estimate the standard deviation.

1.28 Based on an analysis of automobile insurance claims, the Highway Loss Data Institute (HLDI) compiles injury and collision-loss data for popular cars, station wagons, and vans. The data in the table, reported in *Consumer's Research* (Nov. 1993), are the HLDI collision-damage ratings of large station wagons and minivans. The collision-damage rating is a comparative measure of what insurance companies pay out to the model's owners for collision-damage repairs. Thus the higher the rating, the more likely the model will be involved in a collision.

VEHICLE MODEL	COLLISION-DAMAGE RATING
Chevrolet Astro 4-wheel drive	50
Plymouth Voyager	59
Chevrolet Caprice	77
Oldsmobile Silhouette	72
Dodge Caravan	60
GMC Safari	60
Mazda MPV 4-wheel drive	121
Toyota Previa	77
Chevrolet Lumina APV	71
Ford Aerostar	74
Chevrolet Astro	59
Mazda MPV	114
Pontiac Trans Sport	72

a. Compute the mean collision-damage ratings of the cars listed in the table.
b. Compute the standard deviation of the collision-damage ratings.
c. Suppose you have recently purchased a new minivan. Give an interval that is highly likely to contain the collision-damage rating of your new car.

1.29 Recently, organizational behaviorists and social psychologists have begun to study the process by which decision makers escalate their commitment to an ineffective course of action. This phenomenon has been labeled many things, including the "sunk cost" effect, the "knee-deep-in-the-big-muddy" effect, and the "too-much-invested-to-quit" effect, but is most commonly known as "entrapment."

Fifty-two introductory psychology students took part in a laboratory experiment designed to explore whether entrapment would be heightened owing to individuals' tendencies to view prior outcomes as revealing of their self-identity (*Administrative Science Quarterly*, Mar. 1986). The experiment consisted of 30 trials in which points were "awarded" based on the accuracy of students' judgments of geometric patterns of various shapes. The total points awarded on each trial are listed in the table.

5	5	4	7	24	6
10	12	11	15	11	10
3	23	4	20	5	4
7	5	6	6	15	5
15	10	13	9	4	6

Source: Brockner, J., et al. "Escalation of commitment to an ineffective course of action: The effect of feedback having negative implications for self-identity." *Administrative Science Quarterly*, Vol. 31, No. 1, Mar. 1986, p. 115. Reprinted by permission of *Administrative Science Quarterly*. Copyright 1986.

a. Compute $\bar{y}$, s^2, and s for the data.
b. Form an interval that captures most of the trial scores for the laboratory experiment.

1.30 The Trail Making Test (TMT) is frequently used in neuropsychological assessment to provide a quick estimate of brain damage in humans. Subjects taking the TMT are asked to perform a certain task as quickly as possible. The test is sensitive to the effects of age—an older person normally takes longer to complete the task. To investigate the neuropsychological deficits in alcoholics, 50 problem drinkers (25 drinkers under the age of 50 and 25 drinkers 40 years or older) were given the TMT and their performance scores observed (the higher the score, the more extensive the brain damage). The results are reported in the accompanying table.

	ALCOHOLICS UNDER AGE 40	ALCOHOLICS 40 OR OLDER
Mean performance score	39.6	49.7
Standard deviation	19.7	19.1

a. Use the information in the table to sketch your mental images of the relative frequency histograms of TMT performance scores for the two groups of alcoholics.
b. Estimate the fraction of alcoholics under age 40 who score between 19.9 and 59.3 on the TMT.
c. Approximately what percentage of alcoholics aged 40 or older score between 11.5 and 87.9 on the TMT?

1.31 Beginning in 1991, the U.S. Department of Education began taking corrective and punitive actions against colleges and universities with high student-loan default rates. Those schools with default rates above 60% face suspension from the government's massive student-loan program, whereas schools with default rates between 40% and 60% are mandated to reduce their default rates by 5% a year or face a similar penalty (*Tampa Tribune*, June 21, 1989). A list of 66 colleges and universities in Florida with their student-loan default rate is provided in the table. An SPSS printout giving descriptive statistics for the data set is shown.

COLLEGE/UNIVERSITY	DEFAULT RATE	COLLEGE/UNIVERSITY	DEFAULT RATE
Florida College of Business	76.2	Brevard CC	9.4
Ft. Lauderdale College	48.5	College of Boca Raton	9.1
Florida Career College	48.3	Florida International Univ.	8.7
United College	46.8	Santa Fe CC	8.6
Florida Memorial College	46.2	Edison CC	8.5
Bethune Cookman College	43.0	Palm Beach Junior College	8.0
Edward Waters College	38.3	Eckerd College	7.9
Florida College of Medical and Dental Careers	32.6	University of Tampa	7.6
International Fine Arts College	26.5	Lakeland College of Business	7.2
Tampa College	23.9	Pensacola Junior College	6.8
Miami Technical College	23.3	University of Miami	6.7
Tallahassee CC	20.6	Florida Institute of Technology	6.7
Charron Williams College	20.2	University of West Florida	6.3
Florida CC	19.1	Palm Beach Atlantic College	6.0
Miami–Dade CC	19.0	University of Central Florida	5.7
Broward CC	18.4	Seminole CC	5.6
Daytona Beach CC	16.9	Polk CC	5.6
Lake Sumter CC	16.7	Phillips Junior College	5.6
Florida Technical College	16.6	Nova University	5.5
Florida A&M University	15.8	Rollins College	5.5
Prospect Hall College	15.1	St. Leo College	5.5
Hillsborough CC	14.4	Gulf Coast CC	5.4
Pasco–Hernando CC	13.5	Southern College	5.3
Orlando College	13.5	Flagler College	4.7
Jones College	13.1	Florida Atlantic University	4.4
Webber College	11.8	University of South Florida	4.2
Warner Southern College	11.8	Manatee Junior College	4.1
Central Florida CC	11.8	Florida State University	4.0
Indian River CC	11.8	University of North Florida	3.9
St. Petersburg CC	11.3	Barry University	3.1
Valencia CC	10.8	University of Florida	3.1
Florida Southern College	10.3	Stetson University	2.9
Lake City CC	9.8	Jacksonville University	1.5

```
Number of Valid Observations (Listwise) =        66.00

Variable  DEFRATE

Mean            14.682               S.E. Mean         1.741
Std Dev         14.141               Variance        199.974
Kurtosis         5.427               S.E. Kurt          .582
Skewness         2.204               S.E. Skew          .295
Range           74.700               Minimum            1.50
Maximum          76.20               Sum             969.000

Valid Observations -         66      Missing Observations -        0
```

a. Locate the mean default rate on the printout.
b. Locate the variance and standard deviation of the default rates on the printout.
c. What proportion of measurements would you expect to find within 2 standard deviations of the mean?
d. Determine the proportion of measurements (default rates) that actually fall within the interval of part **c**. Compare this result with your answer to part **c**.
e. Suppose the college with the highest default rate (Florida College of Business—76.2%) was omitted from the analysis. Would you expect the mean to increase or decrease? Would you expect the standard deviation to increase or decrease?
f. Calculate the mean and standard deviation for the data set with Florida College of Business excluded. Compare these results with your answer to part **e**.
g. Answer parts **c** and **d** using the recalculated mean and standard deviation. This problem illustrates the dramatic effect a single observation can have on an analysis.

1.5 The Normal Probability Distribution

One of the most commonly used models for a theoretical population relative frequency distribution is the **normal probability distribution**, as shown in Figure 1.6. The normal distribution is symmetric about its mean μ, and its spread is determined by the value of its standard deviation σ. Three normal curves with different means and standard deviations are shown in Figure 1.7.

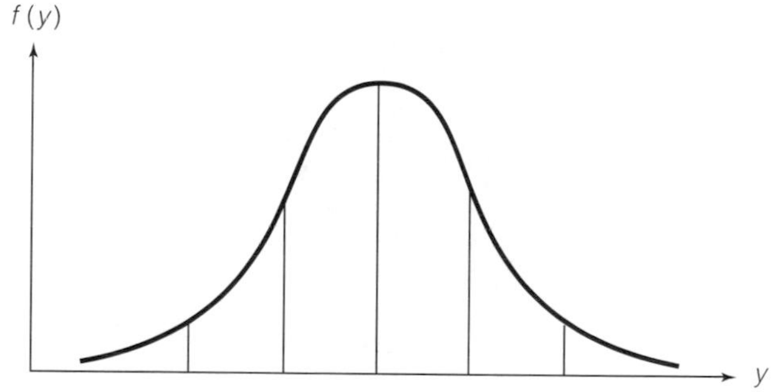

FIGURE 1.6
A normal probability distribution

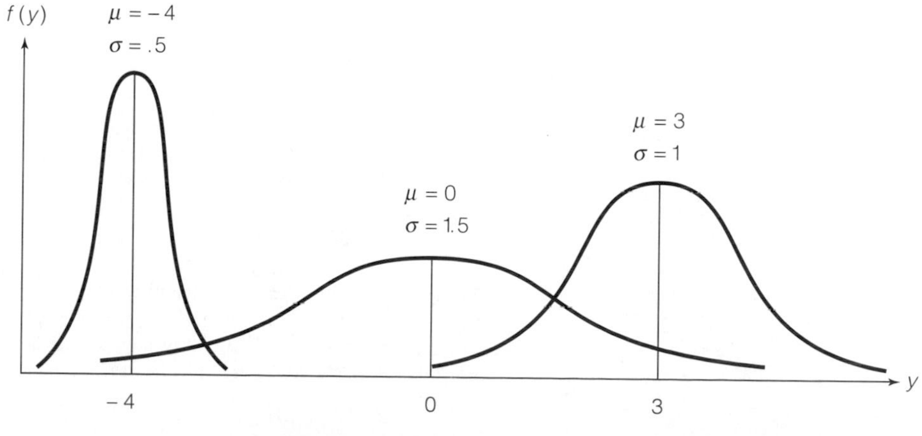

FIGURE 1.7
Several normal distributions with different means and standard deviations

Computing the area over an interval under the normal probability distribution can be a difficult task.* Consequently, we will use the computed areas listed in Table 1 of Appendix C. A partial reproduction of this table is shown in Table 1.5. As you can see from the normal curve above the table, the entries give areas under the normal curve between the mean of the distribution and a standardized distance

$$z = \frac{y - \mu}{\sigma}$$

to the right of the mean. Note that z is the number of standard deviations σ between μ and y. The distribution of z, which has mean $\mu = 0$ and standard deviation $\sigma = 1$, is called a **standard normal distribution**.

TABLE 1.5 **Reproduction of Part of Table 1 of Appendix C**

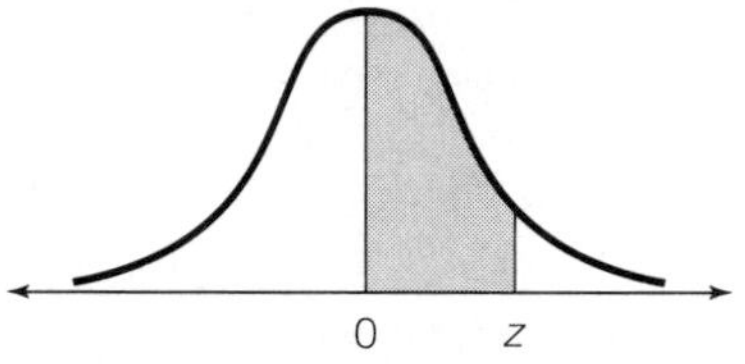

z	.00	.01	.02	.03	.04	.05	.06	.07	.08	.09
.0	.0000	.0040	.0080	.0120	.0160	.0199	.0239	.0279	.0319	.0359
.1	.0398	.0438	.0478	.0517	.0557	.0596	.0636	.0675	.0714	.0753
.2	.0793	.0832	.0871	.0910	.0948	.0987	.1026	.1064	.1103	.1141
.3	.1179	.1217	.1255	.1293	.1331	.1368	.1406	.1443	.1480	.1517
.4	.1554	.1591	.1628	.1664	.1700	.1736	.1772	.1808	.1844	.1879
.5	.1915	.1950	.1985	.2019	.2054	.2088	.2123	.2157	.2190	.2224
.6	.2257	.2291	.2324	.2357	.2389	.2422	.2454	.2486	.2517	.2549
.7	.2580	.2611	.2642	.2673	.2704	.2734	.2764	.2794	.2823	.2852
.8	.2881	.2910	.2939	.2967	.2995	.3023	.3051	.3078	.3106	.3133
.9	.3159	.3186	.3212	.3238	.3264	.3289	.3315	.3340	.3365	.3389
1.0	.3413	.3438	.3461	.3485	.3508	.3531	.3554	.3577	.3599	.3621
1.1	.3643	.3665	.3686	.3708	.3729	.3749	.3770	.3790	.3810	.3830
1.2	.3849	.3869	.3888	.3907	.3925	.3944	.3962	.3980	.3997	.4015
1.3	.4032	.4049	.4066	.4082	.4099	.4115	.4131	.4147	.4162	.4177
1.4	.4192	.4207	.4222	.4236	.4251	.4265	.4279	.4292	.4306	.4319
1.5	.4332	.4345	.4357	.4370	.4382	.4394	.4406	.4418	.4429	.4441

*Students with knowledge of calculus should note that the probability that y assumes a value in the interval $a < y < b$ is $P(a < y < b) = \int_a^b f(y)dy$, assuming the integral exists. The value of this definite integral can be obtained to any desired degree of accuracy by approximation procedures. For this reason, it is tabulated for the user.

EXAMPLE 1.7

Suppose y is a normal random variable with $\mu = 50$ and $\sigma = 15$. Find $P(30 < y < 70)$, the probability that y will fall within the interval $30 < y < 70$.

Solution

Refer to Figure 1.8. Note that $y = 30$ and $y = 70$ lie the same distance from the mean $\mu = 50$, with $y = 30$ below the mean and $y = 70$ above it. Then, because the normal curve is symmetric about the mean, the probability A_1 that y falls between $y = 30$ and $\mu = 50$ is equal to the probability A_2 that y falls between $\mu = 50$ and $y = 70$. The z score corresponding to $y = 70$ is

$$z = \frac{y - \mu}{\sigma} = \frac{70 - 50}{15} = 1.33$$

Therefore, the area between the mean $\mu = 50$ and the point $y = 70$ is given in Table 1 of Appendix C (and Table 1.5) at the intersection of the row corresponding to $z = 1.3$ and the column corresponding to .03. This area (probability) is $A_2 = .4082$. Since $A_1 = A_2$, A_1 also equals .4082, and it follows that the probability that y falls in the interval $30 < y < 70$ is $P(30 < y < 70) = 2(.4082) = .8164$. The z scores corresponding to $y = 30$ $(z = -1.33)$ and $y = 70$ $(z = 1.33)$ are shown in Figure 1.9.

FIGURE 1.8
Normal probability distribution: $\mu = 50$, $\sigma = 15$

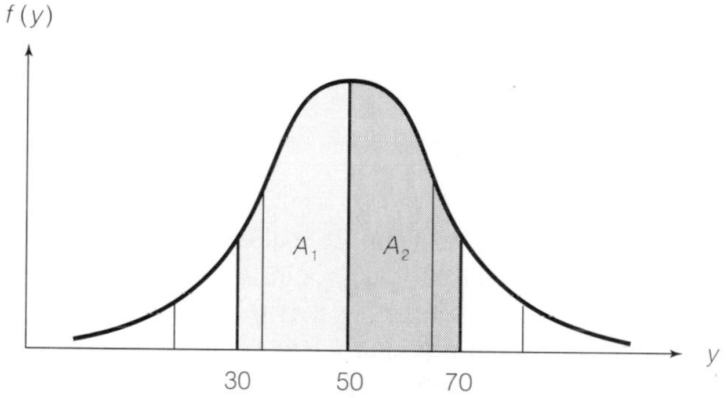

FIGURE 1.9
A distribution of z scores (a standard normal distribution)

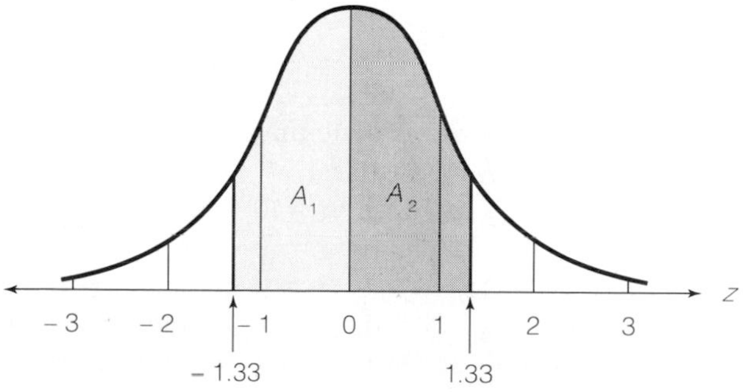

EXAMPLE 1.8

Use Table 1 of Appendix C to determine the area to the right of the z score 1.64 for the standard normal distribution. That is, find $P(z \geq 1.64)$.

Solution

The probability that a normal random variable will fall more than 1.64 standard deviations to the right of its mean is indicated in Figure 1.10. Because the normal distribution is symmetric, half of the total probability (.5) lies to the right of the mean and half to the left. Therefore, the desired probability is

$$P(z \geq 1.64) = .5 - A$$

where A is the area between $\mu = 0$ and $z = 1.64$, as shown in the figure. Referring to Table 1, we find that the area A corresponding to $z = 1.64$ is .4495. So

$$P(z \geq 1.64) = .5 - A = .5 - .4495 = .0505$$

FIGURE 1.10
Standard normal distribution: $\mu = 0$, $\sigma = 1$

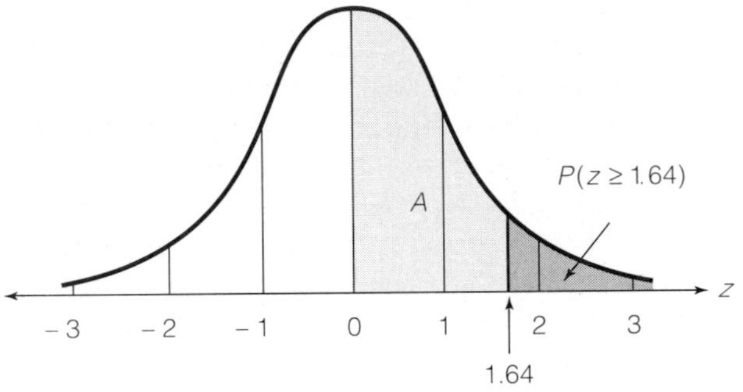

We will not be making extensive use of the table of areas under the normal curve, but you should know some of the common tabulated areas. In particular, you should note that the area between $z = -2.0$ and $z = 2.0$, which gives the probability that y falls in the interval $\mu - 2\sigma < y < \mu + 2\sigma$, is .9544 and agrees with guideline 2 of Section 1.4.

EXERCISES

1.32 Use Table 1 of Appendix C to calculate the area under the standard normal probability distribution between the following pairs of z values:

a. $z = 0$ and $z = 2$
b. $z = 0$ and $z = 1.5$
c. $z = 0$ and $z = 3$
d. $z = 0$ and $z = .5$
e. $z = -1.5$ and $z = 1$
f. $z = -.5$ and $z = .75$
g. $z = -2$ and $z = -1$
h. $z = -3$ and $z = 1.5$
i. $z = .5$ and $z = 3.5$
j. $z = -.5$ and $z = 2$

1.33 Use Table 1 of Appendix C to find each of the following:

a. $P(-1 \leq z \leq 1)$
b. $P(-1.96 \leq z \leq 1.96)$
c. $P(-1.645 \leq z \leq 1.645)$
d. $P(-3 \leq z \leq 3)$

1.34 Find a value of z, call it z_0, such that

a. $P(z \geq z_0) = .05$ b. $P(z \geq z_0) = .025$

c. $P(z \leq z_0) = .025$ d. $P(z \geq z_0) = .0228$

1.35 Find a value of z, call it z_0, such that

a. $P(z \leq z_0) = .0013$ b. $P(-z_0 \leq z \leq z_0) = .95$

c. $P(-z_0 \leq z \leq z_0) = .90$ d. $P(-z_0 \leq z \leq z_0) = .6826$

e. $P(-z_0 \leq z \leq 0) = .0596$

1.36 Given that the random variable y has a normal probability distribution with mean 100 and variance 64, draw a sketch (i.e., graph) of the frequency function of y. Locate μ and the interval $\mu \pm 2\sigma$ on the graph. Find the following probabilities:

a. $P(\mu - 2\sigma \leq y \leq \mu + 2\sigma)$ b. $P(y \geq 108)$

c. $P(y \leq 92)$ d. $P(92 \leq y \leq 116)$

e. $P(92 \leq y \leq 96)$ f. $P(76 \leq y \leq 124)$

1.37 In a laboratory experiment, researchers at Barry University (Miami Shores, Florida) studied the rate at which sea urchins ingested turtle grass (*Florida Scientist*, Summer/Autumn 1991). The urchins, starved for 48 hours, were fed 5-cm blades of green turtle grass. The mean ingestion time was found to be 2.83 hours and the standard deviation was .79 hour. Assume that green turtle grass ingestion time for the sea urchins has an approximate normal distribution.

a. Find the probability that a sea urchin will require 4 or more hours to ingest a 5-cm blade of green turtle grass.

b. Find the probability that a sea urchin will require between 2 and 3 hours to ingest a 5-cm blade of green turtle grass.

1.38 Paleomagnetic studies of Canadian volcanic rock strata known as the Carmacks Group have revealed that the northward displacement of the rock layers has an approximately normal distribution with standard deviation of 500 km (*Canadian Journal of Earth Sciences*, Vol. 27, 1990). One group of researchers estimated the mean displacement at 1,500 km, whereas a second group estimated the mean at 1,200 km.

a. Assuming the mean is 1,500 km, what is the probability of a northward displacement of less than 500 km?

b. Assuming the mean is 1,200 km, what is the probability of a northward displacement of less than 500 km?

c. If, in fact, the northward displacement is less than 500 km, which is the more plausible mean, 1,200 or 1,500 km?

1.39 Pacemakers are vital for controlling the heartbeat of cardiac patients, and over 120,000 of the devices are implanted each year. A pacemaker is made up of several biomedical components that must be of a high quality for the pacemaker to work. For manufacturers of pacemakers, it is critically important to use parts that meet the manufacturer's specifications. One particular plastic part, called a connector module, mounts on the top of the pacemaker. Connector modules are required to have a length between .304 inch and .322 inch to work properly. Any module whose length is outside these limits is "out-of-spec." *Quality* (Aug. 1989) reported on one supplier of connector modules that had been shipping out-of-spec parts to the manufacturer for 12 months.

a. The lengths of the connector modules produced by the supplier were found to follow an approximate normal distribution with mean $\mu = .3015$ inch and standard deviation $\sigma = .0016$ inch. Use this information to find the probability that the supplier produces an out-of-spec part.

b. Once the problem was detected, the supplier's inspection crew began to employ an automated data-collection system designed to improve product quality. After 2 months, the process was producing connector modules with mean $\mu = .3146$ inch and standard deviation $\sigma = .0030$ inch. Find the probability that an out-of-spec part will be produced. Compare your answer to part a.

1.40 The U.S. Department of Agriculture (USDA) has patented a process that uses a species of bacterium for removing bitterness from citrus juices (*Chemical Engineering*, Feb. 3, 1986). In theory, almost all the bitterness could be removed by the process, but for practical purposes the USDA aims at 50% overall removal. Suppose a USDA spokesperson claims that the percentage of bitterness removed from an 8-ounce glass of freshly squeezed citrus juice is normally distributed with mean 50.1% and standard deviation 10.4%. To test this claim, the bitterness removal process is applied to a randomly selected 8-ounce glass of citrus juice. Find the probability that the process removes less than 33.7%. Based on this probability, what can you infer about the spokesperson's claim?

1.41 Birdwatchers, or "birders" as the more committed prefer to be called, visiting a National Wildlife Refuge located near Atlantic City, New Jersey, report a high degree of satisfaction with their visits (*Leisure Sciences*, Vol. 9, 1987). On a standard satisfaction scale that ranged from 1 to 6 (where 1 = poor rating and 6 = perfect rating), the birders have a mean score of 5.05 and a standard deviation of .98. Assume the population of satisfaction scores of birders visiting the National Wildlife Refuge is approximately normal.

a. Find the probability that a randomly selected birder visiting the refuge will have a satisfaction score of at least 5.

b. One-fourth of the birders have satisfaction scores below what value?

1.42 The inherent risk involved with marketing a new product is a key consideration for market researchers. Various statistical models have been developed to aid speculators and businesses in making such decisions. One area of marketing research that uses decision models is called *break-even analysis*. The underlying assumption of break-even analysis is that the demand for a product is normally distributed, with known mean and standard deviation. Of interest is the relationship between actual demand D and the break-even point BE, where BE is defined as the number of units of the product the company must sell to "break even" on the investment. W. Shih* developed two practical decision criteria using break-even analysis.

Decision Rule A: Market the new product if the chance is better than 50% that demand D will exceed the break-even point BE, i.e., if $P(D \geq BE) > .5$.

Decision Rule B: For a specified level of risk p, where $0 \leq p \leq 1$, market the new product if $P(D \geq BE) > p$.

Note that decision rule A is a special case of decision rule B, with specified level of risk $p = .5$. Suppose a company utilizes break-even analysis to decide whether to market a new type of ceiling fan. From past experience, the company knows that the number of ceiling fans of this type sold per year follows a normal distribution with $\mu = 4{,}000$ and $\sigma = 500$. Marketing researchers have also determined that the company needs to sell 3,500 units to break even for the year.

a. According to decision rule A, should the company market the new ceiling fans?

b. Use your knowledge of the normal distribution to show that if $P(D \geq BE) > .5$, then it must be true that $\mu \geq BE$.

*Shih, W. "A general decision model for cost-volume-profit analysis under uncertainty: A reply." *The Accounting Review*, Vol. 56, No. 2, 1981, pp. 404–408.

c. Suppose that the minimum level of risk the company is willing to tolerate is $p = .8$. Use decision rule B to arrive at a decision.

d. Refer to part c. Find the value of BE such that the probability of at least breaking even is equal to the specified level of risk, $p = .8$.

1.6 Sampling Distributions and the Central Limit Theorem

Since we will use sample statistics to make inferences about population parameters, it is natural that we would want to know something about the reliability of the resulting inferences. For example, if we use a statistic to estimate the value of a population mean μ, we will want to know how close to μ our estimate is likely to fall. To answer this question, we need to know the probability distribution of the statistic.

The probability distribution for a statistic based on a random sample of n measurements could be generated in the following way. For purposes of illustration, we will suppose we are sampling from a population with $\mu = 10$ and $\sigma = 5$, the sample statistic is $\bar{y}$, and the sample size is $n = 25$. Draw a single random sample of 25 measurements from the population and suppose that $\bar{y} = 9.8$. Return the measurements to the population and try again. That is, draw another random sample of $n = 25$ measurements and see what you obtain for an outcome. Now, perhaps, $\bar{y} = 11.4$. Replace these measurements, draw another sample of $n = 25$ measurements, calculate $\bar{y}$, and so on. If this sampling process were repeated over and over again an infinitely large number of times, you would generate an infinitely large number of values of $\bar{y}$ that could be arranged in a relative frequency distribution. This distribution, which would appear as shown in Figure 1.11, is the probability distribution (or **sampling distribution**, as it is commonly called) of the statistic $\bar{y}$.

FIGURE 1.11
Sampling distribution for $\bar{y}$ based on a sample of $n = 25$ measurements

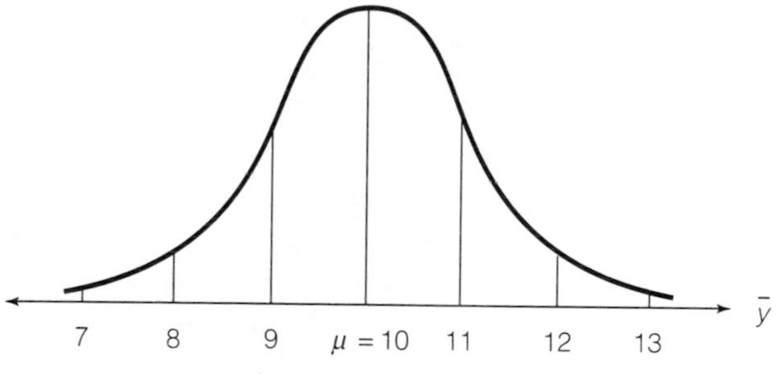

> **Definition 1.15**
>
> The **sampling distribution** of a sample statistic calculated from a sample of n measurements is the probability distribution of the statistic.

In actual practice, the sampling distribution of a statistic is obtained mathematically or by simulating the sampling on a computer using the procedure described previously.

If $\bar{y}$ has been calculated from a sample of $n = 25$ measurements selected from a population with mean $\mu = 10$ and standard deviation $\sigma = 5$, the sampling distribution shown in Figure 1.11 provides all the information you may wish to know about its behavior. For example, the probability that you will draw a sample of 25 measurements and obtain a value of $\bar{y}$ in the interval $9 \leq \bar{y} \leq 10$ will be the area under the sampling distribution over that interval.

Generally speaking, if we use a statistic to make an inference about a population parameter, we want its sampling distribution to center about the parameter (as is the case in Figure 1.11) and the standard deviation of the sampling distribution, called the **standard error of estimate**, to be as small as possible.

Two theorems provide information on the sampling distribution of a sample mean.

Theorem 1.1

If $y_1, y_2, \ldots, y_n$ represent a random sample of n measurements from a large (or infinite) population with mean μ and standard deviation σ, then, regardless of the form of the population relative frequency distribution, the mean and standard error of estimate of the sampling distribution of $\bar{y}$ will be

Mean: $E(\bar{y}) = \mu$

Standard error of estimate: $\sigma_{\bar{y}} = \dfrac{\sigma}{\sqrt{n}}$

Theorem 1.2 The Central Limit Theorem

For large sample sizes, the mean $\bar{y}$ of a sample from a population with mean μ and standard deviation σ has a sampling distribution that is approximately normal, **regardless of the probability distribution of the sampled population**. The larger the sample size, the better will be the normal approximation to the sampling distribution of $\bar{y}$.

Theorems 1.1 and 1.2 together imply that for sufficiently large samples, the sampling distribution for the sample mean $\bar{y}$ will be approximately normal with mean μ and standard error $\sigma_{\bar{y}} = \sigma/\sqrt{n}$. The parameters μ and σ are the mean and standard deviation of the sampled population.

To illustrate Theorems 1.1 and 1.2, we select 1,000 random samples of $n = 5$ measurements from a population with an **exponential relative frequency distribution** with $\mu = 1$ and $\sigma = 1$, as shown in Figure 1.12.

FIGURE 1.12
Exponential distribution with $\mu = 1$ and $\sigma = 1$

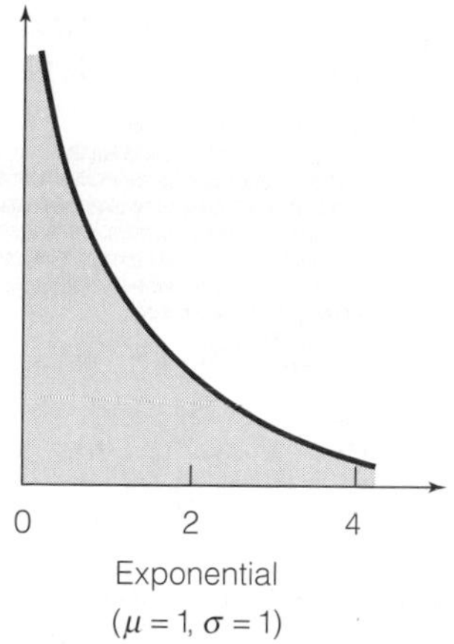

The sample mean $\bar{y}$ was calculated for each of the 1,000 samples. The resulting relative frequency histogram (generated using SPSS) is shown in Figure 1.13a. You can see that the relative frequency distribution of 1,000 sample means (which approximates the sampling distribution of $\bar{y}$) is approximately normal, and that, in fact, the mean of the approximating normal distribution is

$$\mu = 1$$

The standard error is

$$\sigma_{\bar{y}} = \frac{\sigma}{\sqrt{n}} = \frac{1}{\sqrt{5}} = .45$$

Similarly, Figures 1.13b, c, and d show SPSS histograms for the sampling distribution of $\bar{y}$ based on samples of size $n = 15$, 25, and 50, respectively. Note that the normal approximation improves when the sample size increases from $n = 5$ to $n = 50$. Also, although the mean of the four sampling distributions

FIGURE 1.13
Sampling distributions of $\bar{y}$: Exponential population

a. $n = 5$

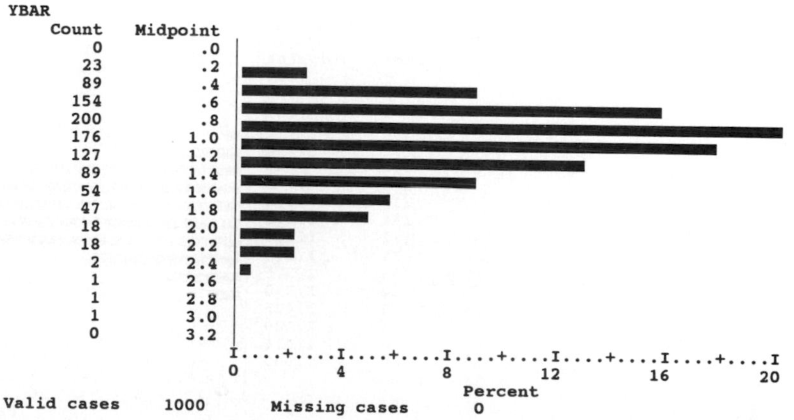

(*continued*)

FIGURE 1.13
Continued

b. $n = 15$

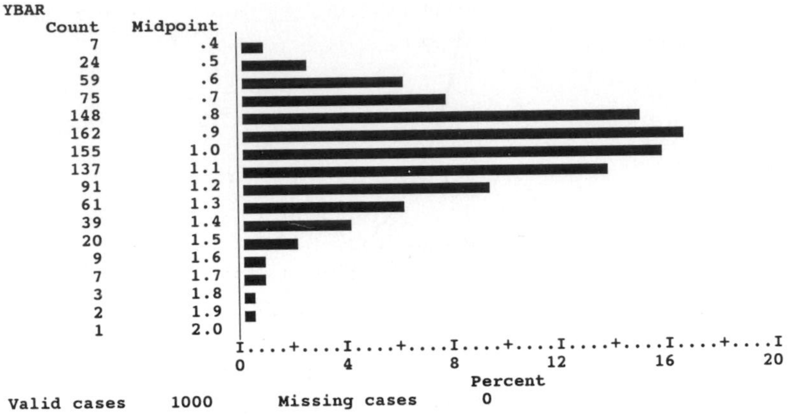

c. $n = 25$

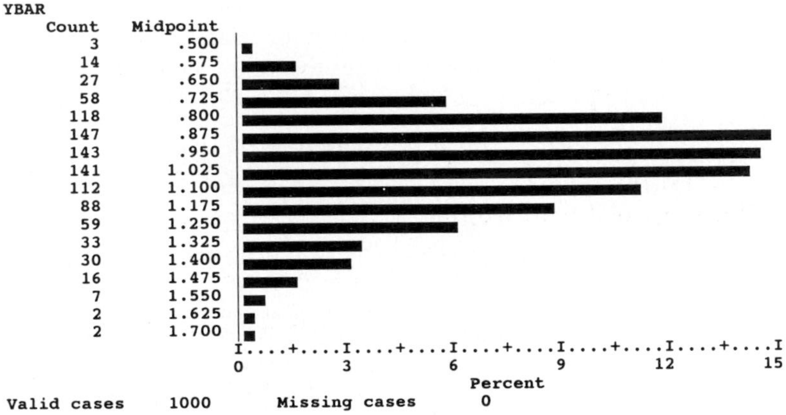

d. $n = 50$

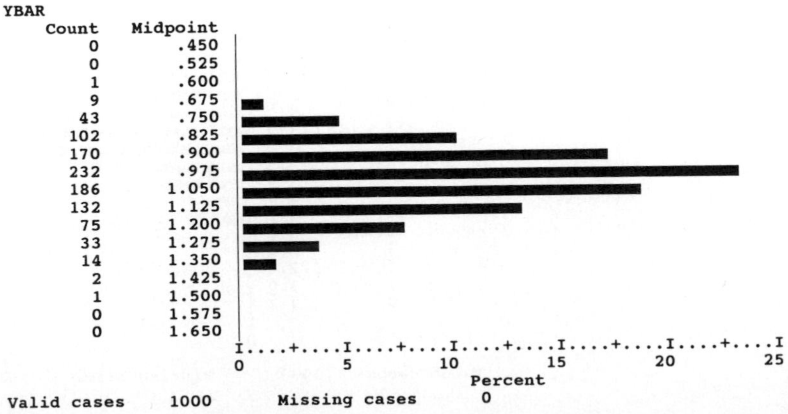

shown in Figure 1.13 is $\mu = 1$, the standard deviation $\sigma_{\bar{y}}$ decreases as n increases. For example, for $n = 50$,

$$\sigma_{\bar{y}} = \frac{\sigma}{\sqrt{n}} = \frac{1}{\sqrt{50}} = .14$$

compared to $\sigma_{\bar{y}} = .45$ for $n = 5$.

The central limit theorem can also be used to justify the fact that the *sum* of the sample measurements possesses a sampling distribution that is approximately normal for large sample sizes. In fact, since many statistics are obtained by summing or averaging random quantities, the central limit theorem helps to explain why many statistics have mound-shaped (or approximately normal) sampling distributions.

As we proceed, we will encounter many different sample statistics, and we will need to know their sampling distributions to evaluate the reliability of each one for making inferences. These sampling distributions will be described as the need arises.

1.7 Estimating a Population Mean

We can make an inference about a population parameter in two ways:

1. Estimate its value.
2. Make a decision about its value (i.e., test a hypothesis about its value).

In this section, we will illustrate the concepts involved in estimation, using the estimation of a population mean as an example. Tests of hypotheses will be discussed in Section 1.8.

To estimate a population parameter, we choose a sample statistic that has two desirable properties: (1) a sampling distribution that centers about the parameter and (2) a small standard error. If the mean of the sampling distribution of a statistic equals the parameter we are estimating, we say that the statistic is an **unbiased estimator** of the parameter. If not, we say that it is **biased**.

In Section 1.6, we noted that the sampling distribution of the sample mean is approximately normally distributed for moderate to large sample sizes and that it possesses a mean μ and standard error $\sigma/\sqrt{n}$. Therefore, as shown in Figure 1.14 (page 40), $\bar{y}$ is an unbiased estimator of the population mean μ, and the probability that $\bar{y}$ will fall within $1.96\sigma_{\bar{y}} = 1.96\sigma/\sqrt{n}$ of the true value of μ is approximately .95.*

Since $\bar{y}$ will fall within $1.96\sigma_{\bar{y}}$ of μ approximately 95% of the time, it follows that the interval

$$\bar{y} - 1.96\sigma_{\bar{y}} \quad \text{to} \quad \bar{y} + 1.96\sigma_{\bar{y}}$$

will enclose μ approximately 95% of the time in repeated sampling. This interval is called a 95% **confidence interval**, and .95 is called the **confidence coefficient**.

---

*Additionally, $\bar{y}$ has the smallest standard error among all unbiased estimators of μ. Consequently, we say that $\bar{y}$ is the **minimum variance unbiased estimator** (MVUE) for μ.

FIGURE 1.14
Sampling distribution of $\bar{y}$

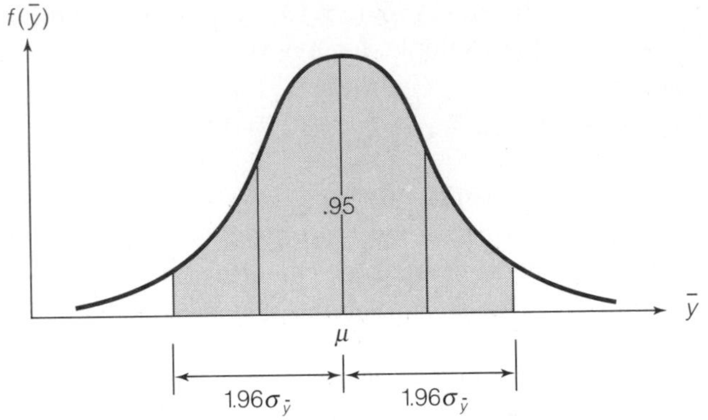

Notice that μ is fixed and that the confidence interval changes from sample to sample. The probability that a confidence interval calculated using the formula

$$\bar{y} \pm 1.96\sigma_{\bar{y}}$$

will enclose μ is approximately .95. Thus, the confidence coefficient measures the confidence that we can place in a particular confidence interval.

Confidence intervals can be constructed using any desired confidence coefficient. For example, if we define $z_{\alpha/2}$ to be the value of a standard normal variable that places the area $\alpha/2$ in the right tail of the z distribution (see Figure 1.15), then a $100(1-\alpha)\%$ confidence interval for μ is given in the box.

Large-Sample $100(1-\alpha)\%$ Confidence Interval for μ

$$\bar{y} \pm z_{\alpha/2}\sigma_{\bar{y}}$$

where $z_{\alpha/2}$ is the z value with an area $\alpha/2$ to its right (see Figure 1.15) and $\sigma_{\bar{y}} = \sigma/\sqrt{n}$. The parameter σ is the standard deviation of the sampled population and n is the sample size. If σ is unknown, its value may be approximated by the sample standard deviation s. The approximation is valid for large samples (e.g., $n \geq 30$) only.

FIGURE 1.15
Locating $z_{\alpha/2}$ on the standard normal curve

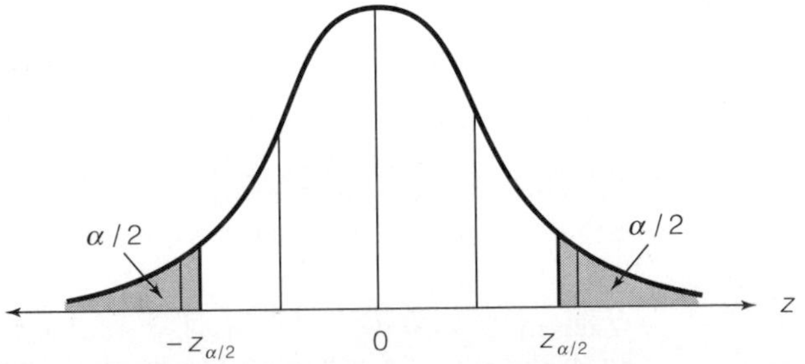

TABLE 1.6 Commonly Used Values of $z_{\alpha/2}$

CONFIDENCE COEFFICIENT $(1-\alpha)$	α	$\alpha/2$	$z_{\alpha/2}$
.90	.10	.05	1.645
.95	.05	.025	1.96
.99	.01	.005	2.576

The confidence interval shown in the box is called a large-sample confidence interval because the sample size must be large enough to ensure approximate normality for the sampling distribution of $\bar{y}$. Also, and even more important, you will rarely, if ever, know the value of σ, so its value must be estimated using the sample standard deviation s. This approximation for σ will be adequate only when $n \geq 30$.

Typical confidence coefficients and corresponding values of $z_{\alpha/2}$ are shown in Table 1.6.

EXAMPLE 1.9

A fact long known but little understood is that twins, in their early years, tend to have lower intelligence quotients and pick up language more slowly than nontwins. Recently, psychologists have speculated that the slower intellectual growth of twins may be caused by benign parental neglect. Suppose we want to investigate this phenomenon. A random sample of $n = 50$ sets of 2½-year-old twin boys is selected, and the total parental attention time given to each pair during 1 week is recorded. The data (in hours) are listed in Table 1.7. Estimate μ, the mean attention time given to all 2½-year-old twin boys by their parents, using a 99% confidence interval. Interpret the interval in terms of the problem.

TABLE 1.7 Attention Time for a Random Sample of $n = 50$ Sets of Twins

20.7	14.0	16.7	20.7	22.5	48.2	12.1	7.7	2.9	22.2
23.5	20.3	6.4	34.0	1.3	44.5	39.6	23.8	35.6	20.0
10.9	43.1	7.1	14.3	46.0	21.9	23.4	17.5	29.4	9.6
44.1	36.4	13.8	0.8	24.3	1.1	9.3	19.3	3.4	14.6
15.7	32.5	46.6	19.1	10.6	36.9	6.7	27.9	5.4	14.0

Solution

The general form of the 99% confidence interval for a population mean is

$$\bar{y} \pm z_{\alpha/2}\sigma_{\bar{y}} = \bar{y} \pm z_{.01}\sigma_{\bar{y}}$$
$$= \bar{y} \pm 2.575\left(\frac{\sigma}{\sqrt{n}}\right)$$

A SAS printout showing descriptive statistics for the sample of $n = 50$ attention times is displayed in Figure 1.16 (page 42). The values of $\bar{y}$ and s, shaded on the printout, are $\bar{y} = 20.85$ and $s = 13.41$. Thus, for the 50 twins sampled, the 99% confidence interval is

$$20.85 \pm 2.575\left(\frac{\sigma}{\sqrt{50}}\right)$$

FIGURE 1.16
SAS descriptive statistics for $n = 50$ sample attention times

Analysis Variable : ATIME

N Obs	N	Minimum	Maximum	Mean	Std Dev
50	50	0.8000000	48.2000000	20.8480000	13.4138253

We do not know the value of σ (the standard deviation of the weekly attention time given to 2½-year-old twin boys by their parents), so we use our best approximation, the sample standard deviation s. (Since the sample size, $n = 50$, is large, the approximation is valid.) Then the 99% confidence interval is

$$20.85 \pm 2.575\left(\frac{13.41}{\sqrt{50}}\right) = 20.85 \pm 4.88$$

or, from 15.97 to 25.73. That is, we can be 99% confident that the true mean weekly attention given to 2½-year-old twin boys by their parents falls between 15.97 and 25.73 hours.

The large-sample method for making inferences about a population mean μ assumes that either σ is known or the sample size is large enough ($n \geq 30$) for the sample standard deviation s to be used as a good approximation to σ. The technique for finding a $100(1 - \alpha)\%$ confidence interval for a population mean μ for small sample sizes requires that the sampled population have a normal probability distribution. The formula, which is similar to the one for a large-sample confidence interval for μ, is

$$\bar{y} \pm t_{\alpha/2}s_{\bar{y}}$$

where $s_{\bar{y}} = s/\sqrt{n}$ is the estimated standard error of $\bar{y}$. The quantity $t_{\alpha/2}$ is directly analogous to the standard normal value $z_{\alpha/2}$ used in finding a large-sample confidence interval for μ except that it is an upper-tail t value obtained from a Student's t distribution. Thus, $t_{\alpha/2}$ is an upper-tail t value such that an area $\alpha/2$ lies to its right.

Like the standardized normal (z) distribution, a Student's t distribution is symmetric about the value $t = 0$, but it is more variable than a z distribution. The variability depends on the number of **degrees of freedom, df**, which in turn depends on the number of measurements available for estimating σ^2. The smaller the number of degrees of freedom, the greater will be the spread of the t distribution. For this application of a Student's t distribution, $\text{df} = n - 1$.* As the sample size increases (and df increases), the Student's t distribution looks more and more like a z distribution, and for $n \geq 30$, the two distributions will be nearly identical. A Student's t distribution based on $\text{df} = 4$ and a standard normal distribution are shown in Figure 1.17. Note the corresponding values of $z_{.025}$ and $t_{.025}$.

*Think of df as the amount of information in the sample size n for estimating μ. We lose 1 df for estimating σ^2; hence $\text{df} = n - 1$.

FIGURE 1.17
The $t_{.025}$ value in a t distribution with 4 df and the corresponding $z_{.025}$ value

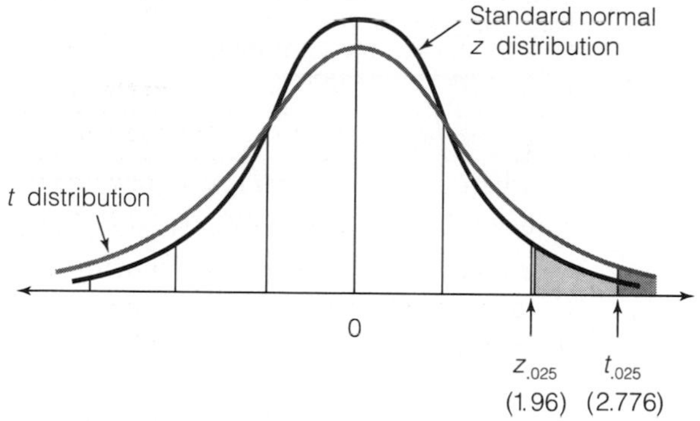

The upper-tail values of the Student's t distribution are given in Table 2 of Appendix C. An abbreviated version of the t table is presented in Table 1.8. To find the upper-tail t value based on 4 df that places .025 in the upper tail of the t distribution, we look in the row of the table corresponding to df = 4 and the column corresponding to $t_{.025}$. The t value is 2.776 and is shown in Figure 1.17.

TABLE 1.8 **Reproduction of a Portion of Table 2 of Appendix C**

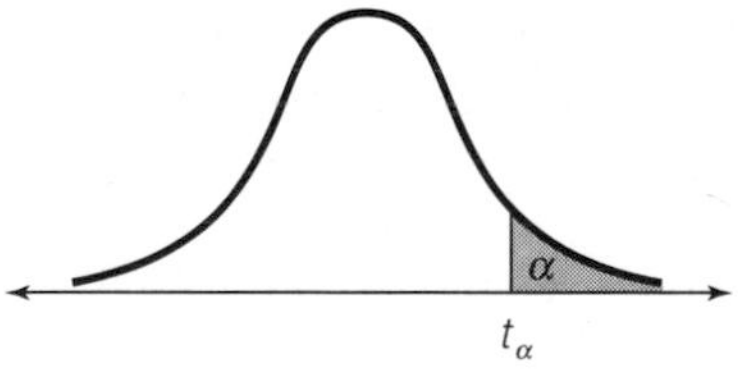

DEGREES OF FREEDOM	$t_{.100}$	$t_{.050}$	$t_{.025}$	$t_{.010}$	$t_{.005}$
1	3.078	6.314	12.706	31.821	63.657
2	1.886	2.920	4.303	6.965	9.925
3	1.638	2.353	3.182	4.541	5.841
4	1.533	2.132	2.776	3.747	4.604
5	1.476	2.015	2.571	3.365	4.032
6	1.440	1.943	2.447	3.143	3.707
7	1.415	1.895	2.365	2.998	3.499
8	1.397	1.860	2.306	2.896	3.355
9	1.383	1.833	2.262	2.821	3.250
10	1.372	1.812	2.228	2.764	3.169
11	1.363	1.796	2.201	2.718	3.106
12	1.356	1.782	2.179	2.681	3.055
13	1.350	1.771	2.160	2.650	3.012
14	1.345	1.761	2.145	2.624	2.977
15	1.341	1.753	2.131	2.602	2.947

The process of finding a small-sample confidence interval for μ is given in the next box.

Small-Sample Confidence Interval for μ

$$\bar{y} \pm t_{\alpha/2} s_{\bar{y}}$$

where $s_{\bar{y}} = s/\sqrt{n}$ and $t_{\alpha/2}$ is a t value based on $(n - 1)$ degrees of freedom, such that the probability that $t > t_{\alpha/2}$ is $\alpha/2$.

Assumption: The relative frequency distribution of the sampled population is approximately normal.

EXAMPLE 1.10

The Geothermal Loop Experimental Facility, located in the Salton Sea in southern California, is a U.S. Department of Energy operation for studying the feasibility of generating electricity from the hot, highly saline water of the Salton Sea. Operating experience has shown that these brines leave silica scale deposits on metallic plant piping, causing excessive plant outages. Jacobsen et al. (*Journal of Testing and Evaluation*, Vol. 9, No. 2, Mar. 1981, pp. 82–92) have found that scaling can be reduced somewhat by adding chemical solutions to the brine. In one screening experiment, each of five antiscalants was added to an aliquot of brine, and the solutions were filtered. A silica determination (parts per million of silicon dioxide) was made on each filtered sample after a holding time of 24 hours, with the following results:

229 255 280 203 229

Estimate the mean amount of silicon dioxide present in the five antiscalant solutions. Use a 95% confidence interval.

Solution

The first step in constructing the confidence interval is to compute the mean, $\bar{y}$, and standard deviation, s, of the sample of five silicon dioxide amounts. These values, $\bar{y} = 239.2$ and $s = 29.3$, are provided in the MINITAB printout, Figure 1.18.

FIGURE 1.18
MINITAB descriptive statistics for Example 1.10

	N	MEAN	MEDIAN	TRMEAN	STDEV	SEMEAN
ppm	5	239.2	229.0	239.2	29.3	13.1

	MIN	MAX	Q1	Q3
ppm	203.0	280.0	216.0	267.5

For a confidence coefficient of $1 - \alpha = .95$, we have $\alpha = .05$ and $\alpha/2 = .025$. Since the sample size is small ($n = 5$), our estimation technique requires the assumption that the amount of silicon dioxide present in an antiscalant solution has an approximately normal distribution (i.e., the sample of five silicon amounts is selected from a normal population).

Substituting the values for $\bar{y}$, s, and n into the formula for a small-sample confidence interval for μ, we obtain

$$\bar{y} \pm t_{\alpha/2}(s_{\bar{y}}) = \bar{y} \pm t_{.025}\left(\frac{s}{\sqrt{n}}\right)$$
$$= 239.2 \pm t_{.025}\left(\frac{29.3}{\sqrt{5}}\right)$$

where $t_{.025}$ is the value corresponding to an upper-tail area of .025 in the Student's t distribution based on $(n - 1) = 4$ degrees of freedom. From Table 2 of Appendix C, the required t value is $t_{.025} = 2.776$. Substituting this value yields

$$239.2 \pm t_{.025}\left(\frac{29.3}{\sqrt{5}}\right) = 239.2 \pm (2.776)\left(\frac{29.3}{\sqrt{5}}\right)$$
$$= 239.2 \pm 36.4$$

or 202.8 to 275.6 ppm.

Thus, if the distribution of silicon dioxide amounts is approximately normal, then we can be 95% confident that the interval (202.8, 275.6) encloses μ, the true mean amount of silicon dioxide present in an antiscalant solution. Remember, the 95% confidence level implies that if we were to employ our interval estimator on repeated occasions, 95% of the intervals constructed would capture μ.

The 95% confidence interval can also be obtained with a statistical software package. Figure 1.19 shows a MINITAB printout of the analysis. You can see that the computer-generated interval (shaded in Figure 1.19) is identical to our calculated one.

FIGURE 1.19
MINITAB confidence interval for Example 1.10

	N	MEAN	STDEV	SE MEAN	95.0 PERCENT C.I.
ppm	5	239.2	29.3	13.1	(202.8, 275.6)

EXAMPLE 1.11

Suppose you want to reduce the width of the confidence interval obtained in Example 1.10. Specifically, you want to estimate the mean silicon dioxide content of an aliquot of brine correct to within 10 ppm with confidence coefficient approximately equal to .95. How many aliquots of brine would you have to include in your sample?

Solution

We will interpret the phrase, "correct to within 10 ppm . . . equal to .95" to mean that we want half the width of a 95% confidence interval for μ to equal 10 ppm. That is, we want

$$t_{.025}\left(\frac{s}{\sqrt{n}}\right) = 10$$

To solve this equation for n, we need approximate values for $t_{.025}$ and s. Since we know from Example 1.10 that the confidence interval was wider than desired for $n = 5$, it is clear that our sample size must be larger than 5. Consequently, $t_{.025}$ will be very close to 2, and this value will provide a good approximation to $t_{.025}$. A good measure of the data variation is given by the standard deviation computed in Example 1.10. We substitute $t_{.025} \approx 2$ and $s \approx 29.3$ into the equation and solve for n:

$$t_{.025}\left(\frac{s}{\sqrt{n}}\right) = 10$$

$$2\left(\frac{29.3}{\sqrt{n}}\right) = 10$$

$$\sqrt{n} = 5.86$$

$$n = 34.3 \quad \text{or approximately} \quad n = 34$$

Remember that this sample size is an approximate solution because we approximated the value of $t_{.025}$ and the value of s that might be computed from the prospective data. Nevertheless, $n = 34$ will be reasonably close to the sample size needed to estimate the mean silicon dioxide content correct to within 10 ppm.

EXERCISES

1.43 The table contains 50 random samples of random digits, $y = 0, 1, 2, 3, \ldots, 9$, where the probabilities corresponding to the values of y are given by the formula $p(y) = \frac{1}{10}$. Each sample contains $n = 6$ measurements.

SAMPLE	SAMPLE	SAMPLE	SAMPLE
8, 1, 8, 0, 6, 6	7, 6, 7, 0, 4, 3	4, 4, 5, 2, 6, 6	0, 8, 4, 7, 6, 9
7, 2, 1, 7, 2, 9	1, 0, 5, 9, 9, 6	2, 9, 3, 7, 1, 3	5, 6, 9, 4, 4, 2
7, 4, 5, 7, 7, 1	2, 4, 4, 7, 5, 6	5, 1, 9, 6, 9, 2	4, 2, 3, 7, 6, 3
8, 3, 6, 1, 8, 1	4, 6, 6, 5, 5, 6	8, 5, 1, 2, 3, 4	1, 2, 0, 6, 3, 3
0, 9, 8, 6, 2, 9	1, 5, 0, 6, 6, 5	2, 4, 5, 3, 4, 8	1, 1, 9, 0, 3, 2
0, 6, 8, 8, 3, 5	3, 3, 0, 4, 9, 6	1, 5, 6, 7, 8, 2	7, 8, 9, 2, 7, 0
7, 9, 5, 7, 7, 9	9, 3, 0, 7, 4, 1	3, 3, 8, 6, 0, 1	1, 1, 5, 0, 5, 1
7, 7, 6, 4, 4, 7	5, 3, 6, 4, 2, 0	3, 1, 4, 4, 9, 0	7, 7, 8, 7, 7, 6
1, 6, 5, 6, 4, 2	7, 1, 5, 0, 5, 8	9, 7, 7, 9, 8, 1	4, 9, 3, 7, 3, 9
9, 8, 6, 8, 6, 0	4, 4, 6, 2, 6, 2	6, 9, 2, 9, 8, 7	5, 5, 1, 1, 4, 0
3, 1, 6, 0, 0, 9	3, 1, 8, 8, 2, 1	6, 6, 8, 9, 6, 0	4, 2, 5, 7, 7, 9
0, 6, 8, 5, 2, 8	8, 9, 0, 6, 1, 7	3, 3, 4, 6, 7, 0	8, 3, 0, 6, 9, 7
8, 2, 4, 9, 4, 6	1, 3, 7, 3, 4, 3		

a. Use the 300 random digits to construct a relative frequency distribution for the data. This relative frequency distribution should approximate $p(y)$.
b. Calculate the mean of the 300 digits. This will give an accurate estimate of μ (the mean of the population) and should be very near to $E(y)$, which is 4.5.
c. Calculate s^2 for the 300 digits. This should be close to the variance of y, $\sigma^2 = 8.25$.
d. Calculate $\bar{y}$ for each of the 50 samples. Construct a relative frequency distribution for the sample means to see how close they lie to the mean of $\mu = 4.5$. Calculate the mean and standard deviation of the 50 means.

1.44 Refer to Exercise 1.43. To see the effect of sample size on the standard deviation of the sampling distribution of a statistic, combine pairs of samples (moving down the columns of the table) to obtain 25 samples of $n = 12$ measurements. Calculate the mean for each sample.
a. Construct a relative frequency distribution for the 25 means. Compare this with the distribution prepared for Exercise 1.43 that is based on samples of $n = 6$ digits.
b. Calculate the mean and standard deviation of the 25 means. Compare the standard deviation of this sampling distribution with the standard deviation of the sampling distribution in Exercise 1.43. What relationship would you expect to exist between the two standard deviations?

1.45 Studies by neuroscientists at the Massachusetts Institute of Technology (MIT) reveal that melatonin, which is secreted by the pineal gland in the brain, functions naturally as a sleep-inducing hormone (*Tampa Tribune*, Mar. 1, 1994). Male volunteers were given various doses of melatonin or placebo; then they were placed in a dark room at midday and told to close their eyes and fall asleep on demand. Of interest to the MIT researchers is the time y (in minutes) required for each volunteer to fall asleep. With the placebo (i.e., no hormone), the researchers found that the mean time to fall asleep was 15 minutes. Assume that with the placebo treatment, $\mu = 15$ and $\sigma = 5$.
a. Consider a random sample of $n = 20$ men who are given the sleep-inducing hormone, melatonin. Let $\bar{y}$ represent the mean time to fall asleep for this sample. If the hormone is *not* effective in inducing sleep, describe the sampling distribution of $\bar{y}$.
b. Refer to part **a**. Find $P(\bar{y} \leq 6)$.
c. In the actual study, the mean time to fall asleep for the 20 volunteers was $\bar{y} = 5$. Use this result to make an inference about the true value of the μ for those taking the melatonin.

1.46 Tropical swarm-founding wasps, like ants and bees, rely on workers to raise their offspring. Interestingly, the workers of this species of wasp are mostly female, capable of producing offspring of their own. Instead, they rear the young of others in the brood. One possible explanation for this strange behavior is inbreeding, which increases relatedness among the wasps and makes it easier for the workers to pick out and aid their closest relatives. To test this theory, 197 swarm-founding wasps were captured in Venezuela, frozen at $-70°$C, and then subjected to a series of genetic tests (*Science*, Nov. 1988). The data were used to generate an inbreeding coefficient x for each wasp specimen, with the following results: $\bar{x} = .044$ and $s = .884$.
a. Construct a 90% confidence interval for the mean inbreeding coefficient of this species of wasp.
b. A coefficient of 0 implies that the wasp has no tendency to inbreed. Use the confidence interval, part **a**, to make an inference about the tendency for this species of wasp to inbreed.

1.47 When a university professor attempts to publish a research article in a professional journal, the manuscript goes through a rigorous review process. Usually, between three and five reviewers read and critique the article, then pass judgment on whether the article should be published. Recently, a study was undertaken to seek information on how reviewers for research journals pursue their activities (*Academy of Management Journal*, Mar. 1989). A sample of 73 reviewers for the Academy of Management's *Journal* (*AMJ*) and *Review* (*AMR*) were asked how many hours they spent per paper for a typical complete review process. The sample mean and standard deviation were computed to be $\bar{y} = 5.4$ hours and $s = 3.6$ hours.

a. Find a point estimate for μ, the true mean number of hours spent by a reviewer in conducting a complete review of a paper submitted to *AMJ* and *AMR*.
b. Compute a 99% confidence interval for μ.
c. Interpret the interval, part **b**.

1.48 By definition, an *entrepreneur* is "one who undertakes to start and conduct an enterprise or business, assuming full control and risks" (Funk and Wagnall's *Standard Dictionary*). Thus, a distinguishing characteristic of entrepreneurs is their propensity for taking risks. A study reported in the *Academy of Management Journal* (Sept. 1980) used a choice dilemma questionnaire (CDQ) to measure the risk-taking propensities of successful entrepreneurs. The researcher found that entrepreneurs had a mean CDQ score of 71 and a standard deviation of 12. (Lower scores are associated with a greater propensity for taking risks.) In a random sample of $n = 50$ entrepreneurs, let $\bar{y}$ be the sample mean CDQ score.

a. Describe the sampling distribution of $\bar{y}$.
b. Find $P(69 \leq \bar{y} \leq 72)$.
c. Find $P(\bar{y} \leq 67)$.
d. Would you expect to observe a sample mean CDQ score of 67 or lower? Explain.

1.49 The *Consumer's Research* (Nov. 1993) data on the collision-damage ratings of station wagons and minivans, Exercise 1.28, are reproduced here. Recall that a higher rating implies a higher likelihood that a vehicle is in a collision.

VEHICLE MODEL	COLLISION-DAMAGE RATING
Chevrolet Astro 4-wheel drive	50
Plymouth Voyager	59
Chevrolet Caprice	77
Oldsmobile Silhouette	72
Dodge Caravan	60
GMC Safari	60
Mazda MPV 4-wheel drive	121
Toyota Previa	77
Chevrolet Lumina APV	71
Ford Aerostar	74
Chevrolet Astro	59
Mazda MPV	114
Pontiac Trans Sport	72

a. In Exercise 1.28, you computed $\bar{y} = 74.31$ and $s = 20.94$ for the sample data. Use this information to construct a 98% confidence interval for μ, the true average collision-damage rating of all station wagons and minivans.
b. Is there evidence to indicate that μ is less than 100? Explain.

1.50 Let t_0 be a particular value of t. Use Table 2 of Appendix C to find t_0 values such that the following statements are true:

a. $P(t \geq t_0) = .025$ where $n = 10$
b. $P(t \geq t_0) = .01$ where $n = 5$
c. $P(t \leq t_0) = .005$ where $n = 20$
d. $P(t \leq t_0) = .05$ where $n = 12$

1.51 Many Vietnam veterans have dangerously high levels of the dioxin TCDD (2,3,7,8-tetrachlorodibenzo-*p*-dioxin) in blood and fat tissue as a result of their exposure to the defoliant Agent Orange. A study published in *Chemosphere* (Vol. 20, 1990) reported on the TCDD levels of 20 Massachusetts Vietnam veterans who were possibly exposed to Agent Orange. The amounts of TCDD (measured in parts per trillion) in blood plasma drawn from each veteran are shown in the table.

VETERAN	TCDD LEVELS IN PLASMA	VETERAN	TCDD LEVELS IN PLASMA
1	2.5	11	6.9
2	3.1	12	3.3
3	2.1	13	4.6
4	3.5	14	1.6
5	3.1	15	7.2
6	1.8	16	1.8
7	6.0	17	20.0
8	3.0	18	2.0
9	36.0	19	2.5
10	4.7	20	4.1

Source: Schecter, A., et al. "Partitioning of 2,3,7,8-chlorinated dibenzo-*p*-dioxins and dibenzofurans between adipose tissue and plasma lipid of 20 Massachusetts Vietnam veterans." *Chemosphere*, Vol. 20, Nos. 7–9, 1990, pp. 954–955 (Table I).

a. Construct a 90% confidence interval for the true mean TCDD level in the plasma of all Vietnam veterans exposed to Agent Orange.
b. Interpret the interval, part a.
c. What assumption is required for the interval estimation procedure to be valid?

1.52 According to one study, "The majority of people who die from fire and smoke in compartmented fire-resistive buildings—the type used for hotels, motels, apartments, and health care facilities—die in the attempt to evacuate" (*Risk Management*, Feb. 1986). The accompanying data represent the numbers of victims who attempted to evacuate compartmented fire-resistive buildings for a sample of 14 fires reported in the study.

FIRE	DIED IN ATTEMPT TO EVACUATE
Las Vegas Hilton (Las Vegas)	5
Inn on the Park (Toronto)	5
Westchase Hilton (Houston)	8
Holiday Inn (Cambridge, Ohio)	10
Conrad Hilton (Chicago)	4
Providence College (Providence)	8
Baptist Towers (Atlanta)	7
Howard Johnson (New Orleans)	5
Cornell University (Ithaca, New York)	9
Wesport Central Apartments (Kansas City, Missouri)	4
Orrington Hotel (Evanston, Illinois)	0
Hartford Hospital (Hartford, Connecticut)	16
Milford Plaza (New York)	0
MGM Grand (Las Vegas)	36

Source: Macdonald, J. N. "Is evacuation a fatal flaw in fire fighting philosophy?" *Risk Management*, Vol. 33, No. 2, Feb. 1986, p. 37.

a. State the assumption, in terms of the problem, that is required for a small-sample confidence interval technique to be valid.
b. Use the information in the accompanying MINITAB printout to construct a 98% confidence interval for the true mean number of victims per fire who die in their attempting to evacuate compartmented fire-resistive buildings.

```
             N        MEAN      STDEV   SE MEAN     98.0 PERCENT C.I.
numdied     14        8.36       8.94      2.39   (      2.02,     14.69)
```

c. Interpret the interval constructed in part **b**.

1.53 Chemical engineers at the University of Murcia (Spain) conducted a series of experiments to determine the most effective membrane to use in a passive sampler (*Environmental Science & Technology*, Vol. 27, 1993). The effectiveness of a passive sampler was measured by the sampling rate, recorded in cubic centimeters per minute. In one experiment, six passive samplers were positioned with their faces parallel to the air flow and with an air velocity of 90 centimeters per second. After 6 hours, the sampling rate of each was determined. Based on the results, a 95% confidence interval for the mean sampling rate was calculated to be (49.66, 51.48).
a. What is the confidence coefficient for the interval?
b. Give a theoretical interpretation of the confidence coefficient, part **a**.
c. Give a practical interpretation of the confidence interval.
d. What assumptions, if any, are required for the interval to yield valid inferences?

1.54 The *Journal of the American Medical Association* (Apr. 21, 1993) reported on the results of a National Health Interview Survey designed to determine the prevalence of smoking among U.S. adults. Over 40,000 adults responded to questions such as "Have you smoked at least 100 cigarettes in your lifetime?" and "Do you smoke cigarettes now?" Current smokers (over 11,000 adults in the survey) were also asked: "On the average, how many cigarettes do you now smoke a day?" The results yielded a mean of 20.0 cigarettes per day with an associated 95% confidence interval of (19.7, 20.3).
a. Interpret the 95% confidence interval.
b. State any assumptions about the target population of current cigarette smokers that must be satisfied for inferences derived from the interval to be valid.
c. A tobacco industry researcher claims that the mean number of cigarettes smoked per day by regular cigarette smokers is less than 15. Comment on this claim.

1.55 In the 1980s, adult students began to enroll in colleges and universities in increasing numbers, and many majored in marketing. In 1986, a study was conducted to determine the attitudes of marketing faculty toward the adult students in their classes (*Journal of Marketing Education*, Summer 1987). A sample of 290 faculty, drawn at random from the American Marketing Association's membership directory, responded to a series of attitudinal statements, the first of which was, "Adult students (i.e., undergraduates 24 years or older) participate more actively in classroom discussions than do younger students." Attitudes were measured using a 5-point Likert scale (1 = strongly agree, 2 = agree, 3 = no opinion, 4 = disagree, and 5 = strongly disagree). For the participation statement, the mean attitudinal score for the sample was 1.94 and the standard deviation was .92.
a. Estimate the true mean attitudinal score of marketing faculty with regard to classroom participation of adult students using a 98% confidence interval. Interpret the result.
b. How could you reduce the width of the confidence interval in part **a**?

1.8 Testing a Hypothesis About a Population Mean

The procedure involved in testing a hypothesis about a population parameter can be illustrated with the procedure for a test concerning a population mean μ.

A statistical test of a hypothesis is composed of the following four parts:

1. A **null hypothesis**, denoted by the symbol H_0, which is the hypothesis that we postulate is true
2. An **alternative** (or **research**) **hypothesis**, denoted by the symbol H_a, which is counter to the null hypothesis and is what we want to support
3. A **test statistic**, calculated from the sample data, that functions as a decision maker
4. A **rejection region**, values of a test statistic for which we reject the null hypothesis and accept the alternative hypothesis

The test statistic for testing the null hypothesis that a population mean μ equals some specific value, say, μ_0, is the sample mean $\bar{y}$ or the standardized normal variable

$$z = \frac{\bar{y} - \mu_0}{\sigma_{\bar{y}}} \qquad \text{where} \quad \sigma_{\bar{y}} = \frac{\sigma}{\sqrt{n}}$$

The logic used to decide whether sample data *disagree* with this hypothesis can be seen in the sampling distribution of $\bar{y}$ shown in Figure 1.20. If the population mean μ is equal to μ_0 (i.e., if the null hypothesis is true), then the mean $\bar{y}$ calculated from a sample should fall, with high probability, within $2\sigma_{\bar{y}}$ of μ_0. If $\bar{y}$ falls too far away from μ_0, or if the standardized distance

$$z = \frac{\bar{y} - \mu_0}{\sigma_{\bar{y}}}$$

is too large, we conclude that the data disagree with our hypothesis, and we reject the null hypothesis.

FIGURE 1.20
The sampling distribution of $\bar{y}$ for $\mu = \mu_0$

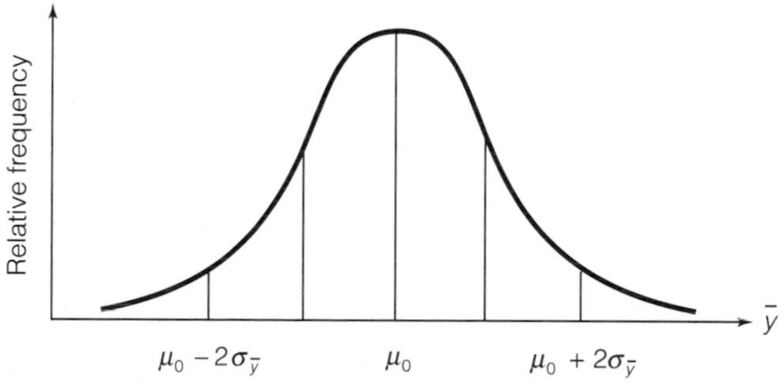

If we want to detect the alternative hypothesis that $\mu > \mu_0$, we locate the boundary of the rejection region in the upper tail of the z distribution, as shown in Figure 1.21a (page 52), at the point z_α. Similarly, to detect $\mu < \mu_0$, we place the rejection region in the lower tail of the z distribution, as shown in Figure

1.21b. These are called **one-tailed statistical tests**. To detect either $\mu > \mu_0$ or $\mu < \mu_0$—that is, $\mu \neq \mu_0$—we split α equally between the two tails of the z distribution and reject the null hypothesis if $z > z_{\alpha/2}$ or $z < -z_{\alpha/2}$, as shown in Figure 1.21c. This is called a **two-tailed statistical test**.

FIGURE 1.21 Location of the rejection region for various alternative hypotheses

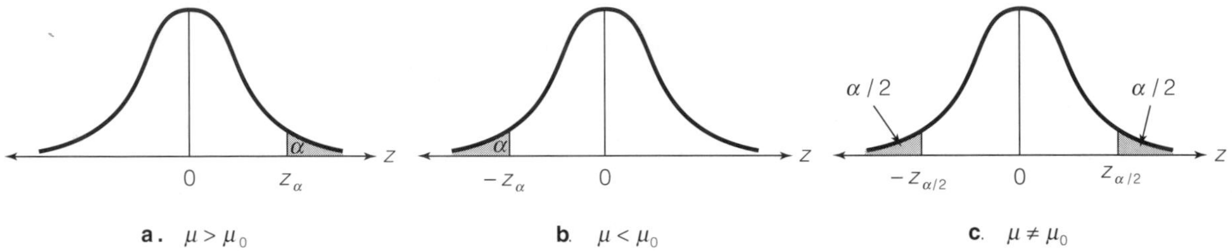

The z test, summarized in the next box, is called a *large-sample test* because we will rarely know σ and hence will need a sample size that is large enough so that the sample standard deviation s will provide a good approximation to σ. Normally, we recommend that the sample size be $n \geq 30$.

Large-Sample ($n \geq 30$) Test of Hypothesis About μ

ONE-TAILED TEST	TWO-TAILED TEST
H_0: $\mu = \mu_0$	H_0: $\mu = \mu_0$
H_a: $\mu < \mu_0$ (or H_a: $\mu > \mu_0$)	H_a: $\mu \neq \mu_0$

Test statistic: $z = \dfrac{\bar{y} - \mu_0}{\sigma_{\bar{y}}}$

Rejection region: $z < -z_\alpha$ (or $z > z_\alpha$)	*Rejection region:* $\lvert z \rvert > z_{\alpha/2}$
where z_α is chosen so that $P(z > z_\alpha) = \alpha$	where $z_{\alpha/2}$ is chosen so that $P(z > z_{\alpha/2}) = \alpha/2$

We illustrate with an example.

EXAMPLE 1.12

Humerus bones from the same species of animal tend to have approximately the same length-to-width ratios. When fossils of humerus bones are discovered, archeologists can often determine the species of animal by examining the length-to-width ratios of the bones. It is known that species A has a mean ratio of 8.5. Suppose 41 fossils of humerus bones were unearthed at an archeological site in East Africa, where species A is believed to have flourished. (Assume that the unearthed bones were all from the same unknown species.) The length-to-width ratios of the bones were measured and are listed in Table 1.9. Do these data present sufficient evidence to indicate that the mean ratio of all bones of this species differs from 8.5? Use $\alpha = .05$.

TABLE 1.9 **Length-to-Width Ratios of a Sample of Humerus Bones**

10.73	9.57	6.66	9.89
8.89	9.29	9.35	8.17
9.07	9.94	8.86	8.93
9.20	8.07	9.93	8.80
10.33	8.37	8.91	10.02
9.98	6.85	11.77	8.38
9.84	8.52	10.48	11.67
9.59	8.87	10.39	8.30
8.48	6.23	9.39	9.17
8.71	9.41	9.17	12.00
			9.38

Solution

Since we wish to determine whether $\mu \neq 8.5$, the elements of the test are

H_0: $\mu = 8.5$

H_a: $\mu \neq 8.5$

Test statistic: $z = \dfrac{\bar{y} - 8.5}{\sigma_{\bar{y}}} = \dfrac{\bar{y} - 8.5}{\sigma/\sqrt{n}} \approx \dfrac{\bar{y} - 8.5}{s/\sqrt{n}}$

Rejection region: $|z| > 1.96$ for $\alpha = .05$

The data in Table 1.9 were entered into a computer, and a SAS analysis was performed. The SAS printout is displayed in Figure 1.22.

FIGURE 1.22
SAS printout for Example 1.12

```
Analysis Variable : LWRATIO

N Obs        Minimum        Maximum          Mean        Std Dev
-----------------------------------------------------------------
   41      6.2300000     12.0000000     9.2575610      1.2035651
-----------------------------------------------------------------
```

Substituting the sample statistics shown on the SAS printout into the test statistic, we have

$$z \approx \frac{\bar{y} - 8.5}{s/\sqrt{n}} = \frac{9.26 - 8.5}{1.20/\sqrt{41}} = 4.03$$

Since the test statistic exceeds the critical value of 1.96, we can reject H_0 at $\alpha = .05$. The sample data provide sufficient evidence to conclude that the true mean length-to-width ratio of all humerus bones of this species differs from 8.5.

The *practical* implications of the result obtained in Example 1.12 remain to be seen. Perhaps the animal discovered at the archeological site is of some species other than A. Alternatively, the unearthed humeri may have larger than normal length-to-width ratios because they are the bones of specimens having unusual feeding habits for species A. **It is not always the case that a statistically significant result implies a practically significant result.** The researcher must retain his or her objectivity and judge the practical significance using, among other criteria, knowledge of the subject matter and the phenomenon under investigation.

The reliability of a statistical test is measured by the probability of making an incorrect decision. For example, the probability of rejecting the null hypothesis and accepting the alternative hypothesis when the null hypothesis is true (called a **Type I error**) is α, the tail probability used in locating the rejection region. A second type of error could be made if we accepted the null hypothesis when, in fact, the alternative hypothesis is true (a **Type II error**). Thus, you never "accept" the null hypothesis unless you know the probability of making a Type II error. Since this probability (denoted by the symbol β) is often unknown, it is a common practice to defer judgment if a test statistic falls in the nonrejection region.

A small-sample test of the null hypothesis $\mu = \mu_0$ using a Student's t statistic is based on the assumption that the sample was randomly selected from a population with a normal relative frequency distribution. The test is conducted in exactly the same manner as the large-sample z test except that we use

$$t = \frac{\bar{y} - \mu_0}{s_{\bar{y}}} = \frac{\bar{y} - \mu_0}{s/\sqrt{n}}$$

as the test statistic and we locate the rejection region in the tail(s) of a Student's t distribution with df $= n - 1$. We summarize the technique for conducting a small-sample test of hypothesis about a population mean in the box.

Small-Sample Test of Hypothesis About μ

ONE-TAILED TEST	TWO-TAILED TEST
H_0: $\mu = \mu_0$	H_0: $\mu = \mu_0$
H_a: $\mu < \mu_0$ (or H_a: $\mu > \mu_0$)	H_a: $\mu \neq \mu_0$

Test statistic: $t = \dfrac{\bar{y} - \mu_0}{s/\sqrt{n}}$

Rejection region: $t < -t_\alpha$ (or $t > t_\alpha$) where t_α is based on $(n - 1)$ df	*Rejection region:* $\lvert t\rvert > t_{\alpha/2}$ where $t_{\alpha/2}$ is based on $(n - 1)$ df

Assumption: The population from which the sample is drawn is approximately normal.

EXAMPLE 1.13

Scientists have labeled benzene, a chemical solvent commonly used to synthesize plastics, as a possible cancer-causing agent. Studies have shown that people who work with benzene more than 5 years have 20 times the incidence of leukemia than the general population. As a result, the federal government lowered the maximum allowable level of benzene in the workplace from 10 parts per million (ppm) to 1 ppm (reported in *Florida Times-Union*, Apr. 2, 1984). Suppose a steel manufacturing plant, which exposes its workers to benzene daily, is under investigation by the Occupational Safety and Health Administration (OSHA). Twenty air samples, collected over a period of 1 month and examined for benzene content, yielded the following summary statistics:

$$\bar{y} = 2.1 \text{ ppm} \qquad s = 1.7 \text{ ppm}$$

Is the steel manufacturing plant in violation of the changed government standards? Test the hypothesis that the mean level of benzene at the steel manufacturing plant is greater than 1 ppm, using $\alpha = .05$.

Solution

OSHA wants to establish the research hypothesis that the mean level of benzene, μ, at the steel manufacturing plant exceeds 1 ppm. The elements of this small-sample one-tailed test are

$$H_0: \quad \mu = 1$$
$$H_a: \quad \mu > 1$$

Test statistic: $t = \dfrac{\bar{y} - \mu_0}{s/\sqrt{n}}$

Assumption: The relative frequency distribution of the population of benzene levels for all air samples at the steel manufacturing plant is approximately normal.

Rejection region: For $\alpha = .05$ and df $= n - 1 = 19$, reject H_0 if

$$t > t_{.05} = 1.729 \quad \text{(see Figure 1.23)}$$

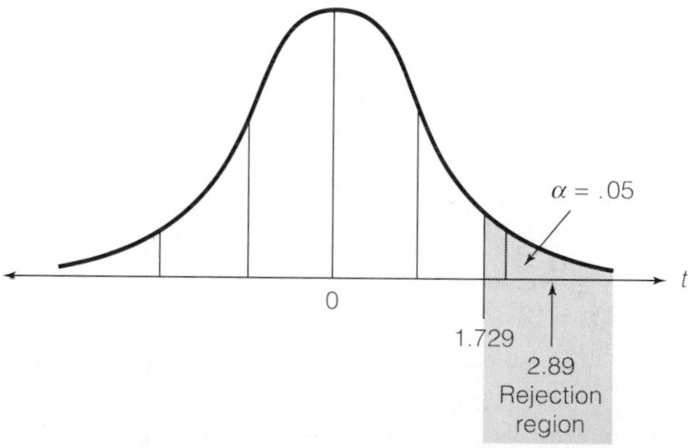

FIGURE 1.23
Rejection region for Example 1.13

We now calculate the test statistic:

$$t = \frac{\bar{y} - 1}{s/\sqrt{n}} = \frac{2.1 - 1}{1.7/\sqrt{20}} = 2.89$$

Since the calculated t falls in the rejection region, OSHA concludes that $\mu > 1$ ppm and the plant is in violation of the revised government standards. The reliability associated with this inference is $\alpha = .05$. This implies that if the testing procedure were applied repeatedly to random samples of data collected at the plant, OSHA would falsely reject H_0 for only 5% of the tests. Consequently, OSHA is highly confident (95% confident) that the plant is violating the new standards.

To conclude, we mention a second method that is useful in reporting the results of a statistical test. Some data analyzers indicate the degree to which the test statistic contradicts the null hypothesis (and hence supports the alternative hypothesis). This quantity, called the **observed significance level**, or ***p*-value**, of the test, is the probability of observing a value of the test statistic at least as contradictory to the null hypothesis as the observed value of the test statistic, *assuming the null hypothesis is true*. For example, suppose you conducted a large-sample z test to detect the alternative hypothesis $\mu > 100$, and the computed value of the test statistic was 2.12. The level of significance for this one-tailed test is the probability of observing a z value larger than 2.12 if $\mu = 100$, or

$$P(z > 2.12) = .0170$$

If the test were two-tailed (i.e., the alternative hypothesis were $\mu \neq 100$), then values more contradictory to the null hypothesis $\mu = 100$ would be z values greater than 2.12 or less than -2.12. The level of significance for this test would be $2(.0170) = .0340$.

Decisions about H_0 and H_a can be made by comparing the p-value of the test to your desired value of α, as shown in the box.

Reporting Test Results as p-Values: How to Decide Whether to Reject H_0

1. Choose the maximum value of α that you are willing to tolerate.
2. If the observed significance level (p-value) of the test is less than the maximum value of α, then reject the null hypothesis.

Most statistical software packages automatically compute the exact p-value of a test. For example, the SAS printout for the t test of Example 1.13 is shown in

Figure 1.24. The p-value for a two-tailed test is shaded under the heading **Prob> |T|** in Figure 1.24. The p-value for a one-tailed test is equal to the reported value divided by 2. Thus, the p-value for the desired test, H_0: $\mu = 1$ vs. H_a: $\mu > 1$, is

$$p = \frac{.0088}{2} = .0044$$

This implies that we will reject H_0 for any α level that exceeds p-value $= .0044$.

FIGURE 1.24
SAS printout for t test of Example 1.13

Analysis Variable : BENZLEV

N Obs	T	Prob>|T|
20	2.8937350	0.0088

EXERCISES

1.56 Define each of the following:
a. H_0 b. H_a c. Type I error d. Type II error e. α f. β

1.57 In hypothesis testing,
a. who or what determines the size of the rejection region?
b. does rejecting H_0 prove that the research hypothesis is correct?

1.58 For each of the following rejection regions, sketch the sampling distribution for z, indicate the location of the rejection region, and give the value of α:
a. $z > 1.96$ b. $z > 1.645$ c. $z > 2.576$ d. $z < -1.29$
e. $z < -1.645$ or $z > 1.645$ f. $z < -2.576$ or $z > 2.576$

1.59 According to *Chance* (Fall 1994), the average number of faxes transmitted in the United States each minute is 88,000.
a. Set up the null and alternative hypotheses for testing this claim.
b. Describe how to collect the data necessary to carry out the test, part a.

1.60 Successful deep hole drilling depends on the satisfactory discharge of the drill chip. An experiment was conducted to investigate the performance of deep hole drilling when chip congestion exists (*Journal of Engineering for Industry*, May 1993). The length (in millimeters) of 50 drill chips resulted in the following summary statistics: $\bar{y} = 81.2$ mm, $s = 50.2$ mm. Conduct a test to determine whether the true mean drill chip length, μ, differs from 75 mm. Use a significance level of $\alpha = .01$.

1.61 Farm and power equipment dealers are typically dependent on a primary supplier organization for many of their business needs. These suppliers often demand control over many of the dealers' decisions. To determine the degree to which dealers are dependent on suppliers, a national survey of 226 farm and power equipment dealers was conducted (*Academy of Management Journal*, Mar. 1989). The study revealed the following summary statistics on the total number of suppliers engaged by the dealers:

$$\bar{y} = 3.12 \qquad s = 191$$

Use this information to test the hypothesis that the true mean number of suppliers engaged by farm and power equipment dealers exceeds 2. Compute the *p*-value of the test and interpret the result.

1.62 How does lack of sleep affect one's creative ability? A recent British study, believed to be the first to measure systematically the effect of sleep loss on divergent thinking, found that loss of sleep sabotages creative faculties and the ability to deal with unfamiliar situations (*Sleep*, Jan. 1989). In the study, 12 healthy college students, deprived of one night's sleep, received an array of tests intended to measure thinking time, fluency, flexibility, and originality of thought. The overall test scores of the sleep-deprived students were compared to the average score one would expect from students who received their accustomed sleep. Suppose the overall scores of the 12 sleep-deprived students had a mean of $\bar{x} = 63$ and a standard deviation of 17. (Lower scores are associated with a decreased ability to think creatively.)

a. Test the hypothesis that the true mean score of sleep-deprived subjects is less than 80, the mean score of subjects who received sleep prior to taking the test. Use $\alpha = .05$.

b. What assumption is required for the hypothesis test of part **a** to be valid?

1.63 Radium-226 is a naturally occurring radioactive gas. Elevated levels of radium-226 in metropolitan Dade County (Florida) have been investigated (*Florida Scientist*, Summer/Autumn 1991). The data in the table are radium-226 levels (measured in picocuries per liter) for 26 soil specimens collected in southern Dade County. The Environmental Protection Agency (EPA) has set maximum exposure levels of radium-226 at 4.0 pCi/L. Use the information in the accompanying MINITAB printout to determine whether the mean radium-226 level of soil specimens collected in southern Dade County is less than the EPA limit of 4.0 pCi/L. Use $\alpha = .10$.

1.46	.58	4.31	1.02	.17	2.92	.91	.43	.91
1.30	8.24	3.51	6.87	1.43	1.44	4.49	4.21	1.84
5.92	1.86	1.41	1.70	2.02	1.65	1.40	.75	

Source: Moore, H. E., and Gussow, D. G. "Radium and radon in Dade County groundwater and soil samples." *Florida Scientist*, Vol. 54, No. 3/4, Summer/Autumn, 1991, p. 155 (portion of Table 3).

```
              N      MEAN    MEDIAN    TRMEAN     STDEV    SEMEAN
RadLevel     26     2.413     1.555     2.264     2.081     0.408

            MIN       MAX        Q1        Q3
RadLevel  0.170     8.240     0.993     3.685
```

1.64 Refer to the *Science* (Nov. 1988) study of inbreeding in tropical swarm-founding wasps, Exercise 1.46. A sample of 197 wasps, captured, frozen, and subjected to a series of genetic tests, yielded a sample mean inbreeding coefficient of $\bar{y} = .044$ with a standard deviation of $s = .884$. Recall that if the wasp has no tendency to inbreed, the true mean inbreeding coefficient μ for the species will equal 0.

a. Test the hypothesis that the true mean inbreeding coefficient μ for this species of wasp exceeds 0. Use $\alpha = .05$.

b. Compare the inference, part **a**, to the inference obtained in Exercise 1.46 using a confidence interval. Do the inferences agree? Explain.

1.65 The effect of machine breakdowns on the performance of a manufacturing system was investigated using computer simulation (*Industrial Engineering*, Aug. 1990). The simulation study focused on a single machine tool system with several characteristics, including a mean interarrival time of 1.25 minutes, a constant processing time of 1 minute, and a machine that breaks down 10% of the time. After $n = 5$ independent simulation runs of length 160 hours, the mean throughput per 40-hour week was $\bar{y} = 1{,}908.8$ parts. For a system with no breakdowns, the mean throughput for a 40-hour week will be equal to 1,920 parts. Assuming the standard deviation of the five sample runs was $s =$ 18 parts per 40-hour week, test the hypothesis that the true mean throughput per 40-hour week for the system is less than 1,920 parts. Test using $\alpha = .05$.

1.66 One of the most feared predators in the ocean is the great white shark. Although it is known that the great white shark grows to a mean length of 21 feet, a marine biologist believes that great white sharks off the Bermuda coast grow much longer because of unusual feeding habits. To test this claim, researchers plan to capture a number of full-grown great white sharks off the Bermuda coast, measure them, then set them free. However, because capturing sharks is difficult, costly, and very dangerous, only three are sampled. Their lengths are 24, 20, and 22 feet.

a. Do the data provide sufficient evidence to support the marine biologist's claim? Test at significance level $\alpha = .05$.

b. What assumptions are required for the hypothesis test of part a to be valid? Do you think these assumptions are likely to be satisfied in this particular sampling situation?

1.67 An experiment was conducted in England to compare methods of estimating the metabolizable energy content of commercial cat foods (*Feline Practice*, Feb. 1986). Method A assumes a digestibility coefficient for crude protein of .91 (called the Atwater factor for crude protein). To determine the validity of this method, the researchers monitored the diets of 28 adult domestic shorthair cats. The cats were fed a diet of commercial canned cat food over a 3-week period. At the end of the trial, the apparent digestibility coefficient was determined for each cat, with these results:

$$\bar{y} = .81 \qquad s = .042$$

Test the hypothesis that the mean digestibility coefficient for crude protein in cats is less than .91, the value assumed by method A. Use $\alpha = .01$.

1.9 Inferences About the Difference Between Two Population Means

The reasoning employed in constructing a confidence interval and performing a statistical test for comparing two population means is identical to that discussed in Sections 1.7 and 1.8. The procedures are based on the assumption that we have selected *independent* random samples from the two populations. The parameters and sample sizes for the two populations, the sample means, and the sample variances are shown in Table 1.10. The objective of the sampling is to make an inference about the difference $(\mu_1 - \mu_2)$ between the two population means.

TABLE 1.10

	POPULATION 1	POPULATION 2
Sample size	n_1	n_2
Population mean	μ_1	μ_2
Population variance	σ_1^2	σ_2^2
Sample mean	$\bar{y}_1$	$\bar{y}_2$
Sample variance	s_1^2	s_2^2

Because the sampling distribution of the difference between the sample means $(\bar{y}_1 - \bar{y}_2)$ is approximately normal for large samples, the large-sample techniques are based on the standardized normal z statistic. Since the variances of the populations, σ_1^2 and σ_2^2, will rarely be known, we will estimate their values using s_1^2 and s_2^2.

To employ these large-sample techniques, we recommend that both samples sizes be large (i.e., each at least 30). The large-sample confidence interval and test are summarized in the boxes.

Large-Sample Confidence Interval for $(\mu_1 - \mu_2)$

$$(\bar{y}_1 - \bar{y}_2) \pm z_{\alpha/2}\sigma_{(\bar{y}_1-\bar{y}_2)}{}^{*} = (\bar{y}_1 - \bar{y}_2) \pm z_{\alpha/2}\sqrt{\frac{\sigma_1^2}{n_1} + \frac{\sigma_2^2}{n_2}}$$

Assumptions: The two samples are randomly and independently selected from the two populations. The sample sizes, n_1 and n_2, are large enough so that $\bar{y}_1$ and $\bar{y}_2$ each have approximately normal sampling distributions and so that s_1^2 and s_2^2 provide good approximations to σ_1^2 and σ_2^2. This will be true if $n_1 \geq 30$ and $n_2 \geq 30$.

Large-Sample Test of Hypothesis About $(\mu_1 - \mu_2)$

ONE-TAILED TEST	TWO-TAILED TEST
H_0: $(\mu_1 - \mu_2) = D_0$	H_0: $(\mu_1 - \mu_2) = D_0$
H_a: $(\mu_1 - \mu_2) < D_0$ [or H_a: $(\mu_1 - \mu_2) > D_0$]	H_a: $(\mu_1 - \mu_2) \neq D_0$

where D_0 = Hypothesized difference between the means (this is often 0)

Test statistic: $$z = \frac{(\bar{y}_1 - \bar{y}_2) - D_0}{\sigma_{(\bar{y}_1-\bar{y}_2)}}$$

where $$\sigma_{(\bar{y}_1-\bar{y}_2)} = \sqrt{\frac{\sigma_1^2}{n_1} + \frac{\sigma_2^2}{n_2}}$$

Rejection region: $z < -z_\alpha$ (or $z > z_\alpha$)	*Rejection region:* $|z| > z_{\alpha/2}$

Assumptions: Same as for the previous large-sample confidence interval.

*The symbol $\sigma_{(\bar{y}_1-\bar{y}_2)}$ is used to denote the standard error of the distribution of $(\bar{y}_1 - \bar{y}_2)$.

EXAMPLE 1.14

Studies have shown that in a nonbusiness (e.g., academic) setting, those who tend to have job mobility are predominantly better performers. To examine the performance–turnover relationship in a business setting, a researcher examined the personnel records of a large national oil company (*Academy of Management Journal*, Mar. 1982). The sample consisted of 174 employees who were classified as "stayers" (those who stayed with the company from 1964 through 1979) and 355 former employees who were classified as "leavers" (those who left the company at varying points during the 15-year period). The company's annual performance appraisals corresponding to the initial years of service were used to form an initial performance rating for each employee. Summary statistics on initial performance for the two groups of employees are provided in Table 1.11. (The ratings were assigned using a 5-point scale, where 1 = low performance and 5 = high performance.)

a. Is there evidence of a difference between the mean initial performance ratings of stayers and leavers? Test using $\alpha = .01$.

b. If the means do, in fact, differ, how large is the difference?

TABLE 1.11 **Summary of Performance Ratings, Example 1.14**

PERFORMANCE RATINGS	
STAYERS	LEAVERS
$n_1 = 174$	$n_2 = 355$
$\bar{y}_1 = 3.51$	$\bar{y}_2 = 3.24$
$s_1 = .51$	$s_2 = .52$

Solution

a. For this problem, let μ_1 represent the mean initial performance rating of stayers and μ_2 represent the mean initial performance rating of leavers. Then the researcher wants to test the hypotheses

H_0: $(\mu_1 - \mu_2) = 0$ (i.e., no difference between mean initial performance ratings of stayers and leavers)

H_a: $(\mu_1 - \mu_2) \neq 0$ (i.e., mean initial performance ratings of stayers and leavers differ)

This two-tailed, large-sample (since both n_1 and n_2 exceed 30) test is based on a z statistic. Thus, we will reject H_0 if $|z| > z_{\alpha/2} = z_{.005}$. Since $z_{.005} = 2.575$, the rejection region is given by

$$z > 2.575 \quad \text{or} \quad z < -2.575 \quad \text{(see Figure 1.25, page 62)}$$

We compute the test statistic as follows:

$$z \approx \frac{(\bar{y}_1 - \bar{y}_2) - D_0}{\sqrt{\frac{s_1^2}{n_1} + \frac{s_2^2}{n_2}}} = \frac{(3.51 - 3.24) - 0}{\sqrt{\frac{(.51)^2}{174} + \frac{(.52)^2}{355}}} = 5.68$$

Since this computed value of $z = 5.68$ lies in the rejection region, there is sufficient evidence (at $\alpha = .01$) to conclude that the mean initial performance rating of stayers is significantly different from the mean initial performance rating of leavers. The probability of our having committed a Type I error is $\alpha = .01$.

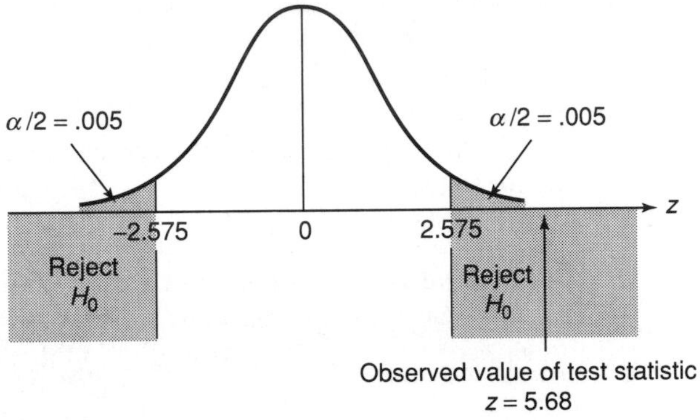

FIGURE 1.25
Rejection region for Example 1.14

b. As we discovered in Section 1.8, the information provided by a two-tailed test of hypothesis is limited. In part a, we determined that the mean initial performance ratings of the two groups of employees differ; but we have only a point estimate of the magnitude of the difference, namely, $(\bar{y}_1 - \bar{y}_2) = (3.51 - 3.24) = .27$. To find an interval estimate of the difference, we construct a 99% confidence interval for $(\mu_1 - \mu_2)$:

$$(\bar{y}_1 - \bar{y}_2) \pm z_{.005}\sqrt{\frac{\sigma_1^2}{n_1} + \frac{\sigma_2^2}{n_2}} \approx (3.51 - 3.24) \pm 2.575\sqrt{\frac{(.51)^2}{174} + \frac{(.52)^2}{355}}$$

$$= .27 \pm .12$$

or (.15, .39). Note that the interval includes only positive numbers. This implies that the difference $(\mu_1 - \mu_2)$ is positive. That is, the mean initial performance rating of stayers (μ_1) exceeds the mean initial performance rating of leavers (μ_2). This difference, although statistically significant, may be too small for the researcher to attach any practical significance to the result.

The small-sample statistical techniques are based on the assumptions that both populations have normal probability distributions and that the variation within the two populations is of the same magnitude, i.e., $\sigma_1^2 = \sigma_2^2$. When these assumptions are approximately satisfied, we can employ a Student's t statistic to find a confidence interval and test a hypothesis concerning $(\mu_1 - \mu_2)$. The techniques are summarized in the following boxes.

Small-Sample Confidence Interval for $(\mu_1 - \mu_2)$: Independent Samples

$$(\bar{y}_1 - \bar{y}_2) \pm t_{\alpha/2}\sqrt{s_p^2\left(\frac{1}{n_1} + \frac{1}{n_2}\right)}$$

where

$$s_p^2 = \frac{(n_1 - 1)s_1^2 + (n_2 - 1)s_2^2}{n_1 + n_2 - 2}$$

is a "pooled" estimate of the common population variance and $t_{\alpha/2}$ is based on $(n_1 + n_2 - 2)$ df.

Assumptions:
1. Both sampled populations have relative frequency distributions that are approximately normal.
2. The population variances are equal.
3. The samples are randomly and independently selected from the populations.

Small-Sample Test of Hypothesis About $(\mu_1 - \mu_2)$: Independent Samples

ONE-TAILED TEST

H_0: $(\mu_1 - \mu_2) = D_0$
H_a: $(\mu_1 - \mu_2) < D_0$
[or H_a: $(\mu_1 - \mu_2) > D_0$]

TWO-TAILED TEST

H_0: $(\mu_1 - \mu_2) = D_0$
H_a: $(\mu_1 - \mu_2) \neq D_0$

Test statistic: $$t = \frac{(\bar{y}_1 - \bar{y}_2) - D_0}{\sqrt{s_p^2\left(\frac{1}{n_1} + \frac{1}{n_2}\right)}}$$

Rejection region: $t < -t_\alpha$ (or $t > t_\alpha$)

Rejection region: $|t| > t_{\alpha/2}$

where t_α is based on $(n_1 + n_2 - 2)$ df

Assumptions: Same as for the small-sample confidence interval for $(\mu_1 - \mu_2)$ in the previous box

EXAMPLE 1.15

A key aspect of organizational buying is negotiation. S. W. Clopton investigated several issues pertaining to buyer–seller negotiations. One aspect of the analysis involved a comparison of two types of bargaining strategies—competitive bargaining and coordinative bargaining. A *competitive strategy* is characterized by inflexible behavior aimed at forcing concessions, whereas a *coordinative strategy* uses problem-solving in negotiations with a high degree of trust and cooperation. A sample of organizational buyers were recruited to participate in a particular negotiation experiment. In one negotiation setting where the maximum profit was fixed, eight buyers used the competitive bargaining strategy and eight buyers used the coordinative bargaining strategy. The individual savings for the two groups of buyers are provided in Table 1.12. In theory, the mean buyer savings for the competitive strategy will be less than the corresponding mean for the coordinative strategy. Test the theory using $\alpha = .025$.

TABLE 1.12 **Data for Example 1.15**

COMPETITIVE BARGAINING	COORDINATIVE BARGAINING
$1,857	$1,544
1,700	2,640
1,829	1,645
2,644	2,275
1,566	2,137
663	2,327
1,712	2,152
1,679	2,130

Source: Clopton, S. W. "Seller and buying firm factors affecting industrial buyers' negotiation behavior and outcomes." *Journal of Marketing Research*, Feb. 1984, pp. 39–53, published by the American Marketing Association.

Solution

We want to test the following hypothesis:

$$H_0: \ (\mu_1 - \mu_2) = 0 \quad \text{(i.e., no difference in mean buyer savings)}$$

$$H_a: \ (\mu_1 - \mu_2) < 0 \quad \text{(i.e., the mean buyer savings for competitive strategy is less than the mean for coordinative strategy)}$$

where μ_1 and μ_2 are the true mean savings of buyers using the competitive and coordinative bargaining strategies, respectively. Since the samples selected for the study are small ($n_1 = n_2 = 8$), the following assumptions are required:

1. The populations of buyer savings under the competitive and coordinative strategies both have approximately normal distributions.
2. The variances of the populations of buyer savings for the two bargaining strategies are equal.
3. The samples were independently and randomly selected.

If these three assumptions are valid, the test statistic will have a t distribution with $(n_1 + n_2 - 2) = (8 + 8 - 2) = 14$ degrees of freedom. With a significance level of $\alpha = .025$, the rejection region is given by

$$t < -t_{.025} = -2.145 \quad \text{(see Figure 1.26)}$$

FIGURE 1.26
Rejection region for Example 1.15

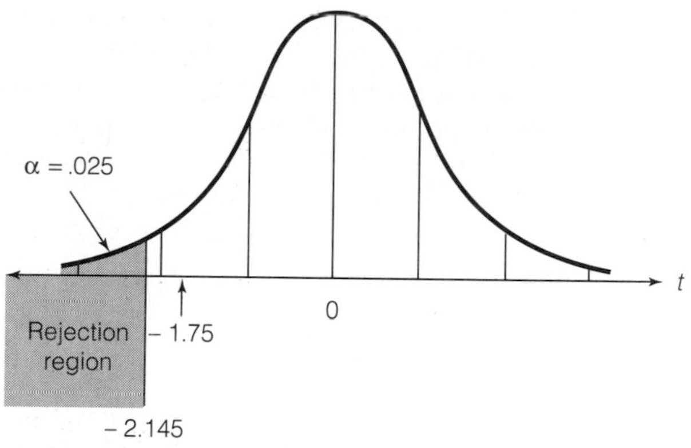

To compute the test statistic, we need to find $\bar{y}_1, \bar{y}_2, s_1$, and s_2. These summary statistics are given in the MINITAB printout, Figure 1.27, as $\bar{y}_1 = 1{,}706$, $\bar{y}_2 = 2{,}106$, $s_1 = 538$, and $s_2 = 357$.

FIGURE 1.27
MINITAB printout for Example 1.15

```
TWOSAMPLE T FOR Compete VS Coordin

           N      MEAN      STDEV    SE MEAN
Compete    8      1706        538        190
Coordin    8      2106        357        126

95 PCT CI FOR MU Compete - MU Coordin: (-890, 90)

TTEST MU Compete = MU Coordin (VS NE): T= -1.75  P=0.10  DF=  14

POOLED STDEV =           457
```

Since we have assumed that the two populations have equal variances (i.e., that $\sigma_1^2 = \sigma_2^2 = \sigma^2$), we first compute an estimate of this common variance. Our pooled estimate is given by

$$s_p^2 = \frac{(n_1 - 1)s_1^2 + (n_2 - 1)s_2^2}{n_1 + n_2 - 2} = \frac{(8 - 1)(538)^2 + (8 - 1)(357)^2}{8 + 8 - 2}$$
$$= 208{,}446.5$$

Using this pooled sample variance in the computation of the test statistic, we obtain

$$t = \frac{(\bar{y}_1 - \bar{y}_2) - D_0}{\sqrt{s_p^2\left(\frac{1}{n_1} + \frac{1}{n_2}\right)}} = \frac{(1{,}706 - 2{,}106) - 0}{\sqrt{208{,}446.5\left(\frac{1}{8} + \frac{1}{8}\right)}}$$
$$= -1.75$$

Since the computed value of t does not fall within the rejection region, we do not reject the null hypothesis (at $\alpha = .025$). There is insufficient evidence that the mean savings of bargainers using the competitive strategy is less than the corresponding mean for bargainers using the coordinative strategy.

The analysis of the data in Table 1.12 could be performed using the t test procedure available in a statistical software package. The MINITAB analysis is shown at the bottom of Figure 1.27. The p-value of the two-tailed test, shaded on the printout, is .10; hence, the p-value of the one-tailed test is

$$p = \frac{.10}{2} = .05$$

Since this one-tailed p-value exceeds $\alpha = .025$, we cannot reject H_0.

EXAMPLE 1.16

Refer to Example 1.15. Suppose you wanted to estimate the difference in mean buyer savings $(\mu_1 - \mu_2)$ correct to within \$200 with 90% confidence. How many buyers of each strategy must be sampled to obtain this estimate?

Solution

This problem is similar to Example 1.11. We want to estimate $(\mu_1 - \mu_2)$ with a confidence interval that has a half-width less than or equal to \$200. That is, we want

$$t_{.05}\sqrt{s_p^2\left(\frac{1}{n_1} + \frac{1}{n_2}\right)} = 200$$

We will use equal numbers for each strategy; i.e., we will let $n_1 = n_2$. Since the number of degrees of freedom for $t_{.05}$ depends on n (and hence is unknown) and since the value of s_p^2 depends on the data we collect, we will approximate both these values. You can see from the tabulated values of $t_{.05}$ (Table 2 of Appendix C) that $t_{.05}$ approaches $z_{.05} = 1.645$ as n gets close to 30. Consequently, $t_{.05} \approx 1.64$. The best approximation to s_p^2 would be the value computed from the samples in Example 1.15, $s_p^2 = 208{,}446.5$. Substituting these values into the equation and solving for $n_1 = n_2 = n$, we obtain

$$t_{.05}\sqrt{s_p^2\left(\frac{1}{n_1} + \frac{1}{n_2}\right)} = 200$$

$$1.64\sqrt{208{,}446.5\left(\frac{1}{n} + \frac{1}{n}\right)} = 200$$

$$\sqrt{n} = 5.29$$

$$n = 28.03$$

Therefore, we will need to sample approximately 28 buyers of each strategy to estimate the difference in mean buyer savings correct to within \$200 with confidence coefficient .90. This is an approximate solution for n_1 and n_2, but it will be fairly close to the exact solution.

The two-sample t statistic is a powerful tool for comparing population means when the necessary assumptions are satisfied. It has also been shown to be useful when the sampled populations are only approximately normally distributed. And, when the sample sizes are equal, the assumption of equal population variances can be relaxed. That is, when $n_1 = n_2$, σ_1^2 and σ_2^2 can be quite different and the test statistic will still have (approximately) a Student's t distribution.

EXERCISES

1.68 Describe the sampling distribution of $(\bar{y}_1 - \bar{y}_2)$.

1.69 To use the t statistic to test for differences between the means of two populations, what assumptions must be made about the two sampled populations? What assumptions must be made about the two samples?

1.70 Marine biochemists at the University of Tokyo studied the properties of crustacean striated muscles (*The Journal of Experimental Zoology*, Sept. 1993). It is well known that certain muscles contract faster than others. The main purpose of the experiment was to compare the biochemical properties of fast and slow muscles of crayfish. Using crayfish obtained from a local supplier, 12 fast-muscle fiber bundles were extracted and each fiber bundle tested for uptake of the cation Ca^{2+}. Twelve slow-muscle fiber bundles were extracted from a second sample of crayfish, and Ca^{2+} uptake measured. The results of the experiment are summarized here. (All Ca^{2+} measurements are in moles per milligram.) Analyze the data using a 95% confidence interval. Make an inference about the difference between the Ca^{2+} uptake means of fast and slow muscles.

FAST MUSCLE	SLOW MUSCLE
$n_1 = 12$	$n_2 = 12$
$\bar{y}_1 = .57$	$\bar{y}_2 = .37$
$s_1 = .104$	$s_2 = .035$

Source: Ushio, H., and Watabe, S. "Ultrastructural and biochemical analysis of the sarcoplasmic reticulum from crayfish fast and slow striated muscles." *The Journal of Experimental Zoology*, Vol. 267, Sept. 1993, p. 16 (Table 1).

1.71 Refer to the Harris Corporation/University of Florida study to determine whether a manufacturing process performed at a remote location could be established locally, Exercise 1.18. Test devices (pilots) were set up at both the old and new locations, and voltage readings on 30 production runs at each location were obtained. The data are reproduced in the table at the top of page 68. Descriptive statistics are displayed in the accompanying SAS printout. [*Note:* Larger voltage readings are better than smaller voltage readings.]

OLD LOCATION			NEW LOCATION		
9.98	10.12	9.84	9.19	10.01	8.82
10.26	10.05	10.15	9.63	8.82	8.65
10.05	9.80	10.02	10.10	9.43	8.51
10.29	10.15	9.80	9.70	10.03	9.14
10.03	10.00	9.73	10.09	9.85	9.75
8.05	9.87	10.01	9.60	9.27	8.78
10.55	9.55	9.98	10.05	8.83	9.35
10.26	9.95	8.72	10.12	9.39	9.54
9.97	9.70	8.80	9.49	9.48	9.36
9.87	8.72	9.84	9.37	9.64	8.68

Source: Harris Corporation, Melbourne, Fla.

```
Analysis Variable : VOLTAGE

---------------------------------- LOCATION=OLD ----------------------------

N Obs   N        Minimum        Maximum            Mean         Std Dev
-----------------------------------------------------------------------
   30  30      8.0500000     10.5500000       9.8036667       0.5409155
-----------------------------------------------------------------------

---------------------------------- LOCATION=NEW ----------------------------

N Obs   N        Minimum        Maximum            Mean         Std Dev
-----------------------------------------------------------------------
   30  30      8.5100000     10.1200000       9.4223333       0.4788757
-----------------------------------------------------------------------
```

a. Compare the mean voltage readings at the two locations using a 90% confidence interval.

b. Based on the interval, part **a**, does it appear that the manufacturing process can be established locally?

1.72 Many computer software packages utilize menu-driven user interfaces to increase "user-friendliness." One feature that can be incorporated into the interface is a stacked menu display. Each time a menu item is selected, a submenu is displayed partially over the parent menu, thus creating a series of "stacked" menus. The *Special Interest Group on Computer Human Interaction Bulletin* (July 1993) reported on a study to determine the effects of the presence/absence of a stacked menu structure on search time. Twenty-two subjects were randomly placed into one of two groups, and each was asked to search a menu-driven software package for a particular item. In the experimental group ($n_1 = 11$), the stacked menu format was used; in the control group ($n_2 = 11$), only the current menu was displayed.

a. The researcher's initial hypothesis is that the mean time required to find a target item does not differ for stacked and nonstacked menu displays. Describe the statistical method appropriate for testing this hypothesis.

b. What assumptions are required for inferences derived from the analysis to be valid?

c. The mean search times for the two groups were 11.02 seconds and 11.07 seconds, respectively. Is this enough information to conduct the test? Explain.

d. The observed significance level for the test, part **a**, exceeds .10. Interpret this result.

1.73 Some research in nursing education has been focused on teaching strategies that link scientific theory and practice. One study compared a traditional approach to teaching basic nursing skills with an innovative approach (*Journal of Nursing Education*, Jan. 1992). The innovative approach utilizes two strategies (Vee heuristics and concept maps) that consciously link theory with practice. Forty two students enrolled in an upper-division nursing course participated in the study. Half (21) were randomly assigned to labs that utilized the innovative approach. After completing the course, all students were given short-answer questions about scientific principles underlying each of 10 nursing skills. The objective of the research is to compare the mean scores of the two groups of students.

a. What is the appropriate test to use to compare the two groups?
b. Are any assumptions required for the test?
c. One question dealt with the use of clean/sterile gloves. The mean scores for this question were 3.28 (traditional) and 3.40 (innovative). Is there sufficient information to perform the test?
d. Refer to part c. The p-value for the test was reported as $p = .79$. Interpret this result.
e. Another question concerned the choice of a stethoscope. The mean scores of the two groups were 2.55 (traditional) and 3.60 (innovative) with an associated p-value of .02. Interpret these results.

1.74 Numerous studies have shown that developmentally challenged children benefit greatly when placed in preschool classes with normal developing children, but the effect upon the nonchallenged children in these classes has received less attention. To investigate this phenomenon, a study was conducted to compare the performances of two groups of nonchallenged children, those in mainstream preschools (designed primarily for nonchallenged children) and those in integrated special education preschools (designed primarily for developmentally challenged children). The Stanford–Binet Intelligence Scale, a test of child skill development, was administered to 16 children in each group. The results are summarized in the table. [*Note:* Standard deviations are estimates based on the value of the test statistic given in the article.] Is there sufficient evidence to indicate that the mean Stanford–Binet scores differ for the two groups of nonchallenged children? Test using $\alpha = .10$.

	INTEGRATED PRESCHOOL	MAINSTREAM PRESCHOOL
Sample size	16	16
Mean score	122.69	124.85
Standard deviation	10.50	10.50

Source: Odom, S. L., DeKlyen, M., and Jenkins, J. R. "Integrating handicapped preschoolers: Developmental impact on nonhandicapped children." *Exceptional Children*, Vol. 51, No. 1, Sept. 1984, pp. 41–48. Copyright 1984 by The Council for Exceptional Children. Reprinted with permission.

1.75 In the fall of 1989, the U.S. government mandated that every bottle or can of alcoholic beverages include a warning label that lists the six risks of alcohol consumption. A study was conducted to determine the awareness of these risks by adolescents both before and after the labeling law was enacted (*American Journal of Public Health*, Apr. 1993). Awareness was measured in a sample of 1,211 12th-grade students immediately before the label was required to appear (1989) and in a sample of 2,006 12th-graders 1 year after the enactment of the law (1990). (*Awareness* was measured as the number of the six risks correctly identified by the adolescent.) According to the researchers, "in 1990 the average awareness score was 4.3 (standard deviation = 1.24), which was a statistically significant (p-value $< .01$) increase over the average of 3.6 (standard deviation = 1.26) in 1989." Comment on the validity of the researchers' statement.

1.76 *End-user computing* (EUC) describes the use of computer resources by managers, professionals, and operators usually not formally educated in the computer field. Researchers at the University of Arkansas–Little Rock conducted a study of EUC systems at two types of firms: those with a formal policy controlling the EUC environment and those with no formal policy (*Journal of Computer*

Information Systems, Spring 1993). Independent random samples of 36 data processing/information systems (DP/IS) managers at firms with a formal EUC policy in place and 46 DP/IS managers at firms without a formal policy participated in the study. The managers were asked to rate (on a 5-point scale) each of 18 specific EUC policies at their firm (where 1 = no value and 5 = necessity). The mean ratings for the two groups of managers in each category are given in the table. Those means that are "significantly different" at $\alpha = .05$ are indicated by an asterisk. Interpret the results.

POLICY	MEAN RATINGS OF EUC POLICIES Formal Policy ($n = 36$)	No Formal Policy ($n = 46$)
1. Firm value	2.72	2.22
2. Goals	3.06	2.70
*3. Relationship with MIS	3.61	3.04
4. Justifiable applications	3.28	2.96
5. Hardware standards	4.39	4.22
*6. Software standards: purchases	4.50	4.17
7. Software standards: in-house	3.89	3.83
8. Compatibility	4.11	3.91
9. Role of networking	4.17	3.96
10. Justifiable types of data	3.72	3.43
11. Data security/integrity	4.06	4.35
12. Data confidentiality	4.06	4.09
13. Documentation of files	3.89	4.09
14. Ownership of files	3.67	3.83
15. Copyright infringements	3.94	3.83
*16. Movement of hardware	3.00	3.65
17. Training	2.61	2.74
*18. Accountability	3.72	3.13

Source: Mitchell, R. B., and Neal, R. "Status of planning and control systems in the end-user computing environment." *Journal of Computer Information Systems*, Vol. 33, No. 3, Spring 1993, p. 28 (Table 2).

1.77 The *Florida Scientist* (Summer/Autumn 1991) reported on a study of the feeding habits of sea urchins. A sample of 20 urchins were captured from Biscayne Bay (Miami), placed in marine aquaria, then starved for 48 hours. Each sea urchin was then fed a 5-cm blade of turtle grass. Ten of the urchins received only green blades, whereas the other half received only decayed blades. (Assume that the two samples of sea urchins—10 urchins per sample—were randomly and independently selected.) The ingestion time, measured from the time the blade first made contact with the urchin's teeth to the time the urchin had finished eating the blade, was recorded. A summary of the results is provided in the table.

	GREEN BLADES	DECAYED BLADES
Number of sea urchins	10	10
Mean ingestion time (hours)	3.35	2.36
Standard deviation (hours)	.79	.47

Source: Montague, J. R., et al. "Laboratory measurement of ingestion rate for the sea urchin *Lytechinus variegatus*." *Florida Scientist*, Vol. 54, Nos. 3/4, Summer/Autumn 1991 (Table 1).

a. Construct a 90% confidence interval for the difference between the mean ingestion times of sea urchins feeding on green and decayed turtle grass.
b. According to the researchers, "the difference in rates at which the urchins ingested the blades suggests that green, unblemished turtle grass may not be a particularly palatable food compared with decayed turtle grass. If so, urchins in the field may find it more profitable to selectively graze on decayed portions of the leaves." Does the result, part a, support this conclusion?

1.78 Due to modern advances in educational telecommunications, many colleges and universities are utilizing instruction by interactive television for "distance" education. For example, each semester Ball State University televises six graduate business courses to students at remote off-campus sites (*Journal of Education for Business*, Jan./Feb. 1991). To compare the performance of the off-campus MBA students at Ball State (who take the televised classes) to the on-campus MBA students (who have a "live" professor), a test devised by the American Assembly of Collegiate Schools of Business (AACSB) was administered to a sample of both groups of students. (The test included seven exams covering accounting, business strategy, finance, human resources, marketing, management information systems, and production and operations management.) The AACSB test scores (50 points maximum) are summarized in the table. Based on these results, the researchers report that "there was no significant difference between the two groups of students."

	MEAN	STANDARD DEVIATION
On-campus students	41.93	2.86
Off-campus TV students	44.56	1.42

Source: Arndt, T. L., and LaFollette, W. R. "Interactive television and the nontraditional student." *Journal of Education for Business*, Jan./Feb. 1991, p. 184.

a. Note that the sample sizes were not given in the journal article. Assuming 50 students are sampled from each group, perform the desired analysis. Do you agree with the researchers' findings?
b. Repeat part a, but assume 15 students are sampled from each group.

1.79 Executives of an industrial plant want to determine which of two types of power—gas or electric—will produce more useful energy at the lower cost. One measure of economical energy production, called the plant investment per delivered quad, is calculated by taking the amount of money (in dollars) invested in the particular utility by the plant, and dividing by the delivered amount of energy (in quadrillion British thermal units). The smaller this ratio, the less an industrial plant pays for its delivered energy. Random samples of 11 plants using electric utilities and 16 plants using gas utilities were taken, and the plant investment/quad was calculated for each. The data are listed in the table, followed by a MINITAB printout of the analysis of the data. Do these data provide sufficient evidence at the $\alpha = .05$ level of significance to indicate a difference in the average investment/quad between the plants using gas and those using electric utilities? What assumptions are required for the procedure you used to be valid?

ELECTRIC				GAS			
204.15	.57	62.76	89.72	.78	16.66	74.94	.01
.35	85.46	.78	.65	.54	23.59	88.79	.64
44.38	9.28	78.60		.82	91.84	7.20	66.64
				.74	64.67	165.60	.36

```
TWOSAMPLE T FOR electric VS gas

            N       MEAN      STDEV   SE MEAN
electric   11       52.4       62.4        19
gas        16       37.7       49.0        12

95 PCT CI FOR MU electric - MU gas: (-30, 59)

TTEST MU electric = MU gas (VS NE): T= 0.68  P=0.50  DF=  25

POOLED STDEV =        54.8
```

1.10 Comparing Two Population Variances

Suppose you want to use the two-sample t statistic to compare the mean productivity of two paper mills. However, you are concerned that the assumption of equal variances of the productivity for the two plants may be unrealistic. It would be helpful to have a statistical procedure to check the validity of this assumption.

The common statistical procedure for comparing population variances σ_1^2 and σ_2^2 is to make an inference about the ratio, σ_1^2/σ_2^2, using the ratio of the sample variances, s_1^2/s_2^2. Thus, we will attempt to support the research hypothesis that the ratio σ_1^2/σ_2^2 differs from 1 (i.e., the variances are unequal) by testing the null hypothesis that the ratio equals 1 (i.e., the variances are equal).

$$H_0\text{: } \frac{\sigma_1^2}{\sigma_2^2} = 1 \quad (\sigma_1^2 = \sigma_2^2)$$

$$H_a\text{: } \frac{\sigma_1^2}{\sigma_2^2} \neq 1 \quad (\sigma_1^2 \neq \sigma_2^2)$$

We will use the test statistic

$$F = \frac{s_1^2}{s_2^2}$$

To establish a rejection region for the test statistic, we need to know how s_1^2/s_2^2 is distributed in repeated sampling. That is, we need to know the sampling distribution of s_1^2/s_2^2. As you will subsequently see, the sampling distribution of s_1^2/s_2^2 depends on two of the assumptions already required for the t test, as follows:

1. The two sampled populations are normally distributed.
2. The samples are randomly and independently selected from their respective populations.

When these assumptions are satisfied and when the null hypothesis is true (i.e., $\sigma_1^2 = \sigma_2^2$), the sampling distribution of s_1^2/s_2^2 is an F **distribution** with $(n_1 - 1)$ df and $(n_2 - 1)$ df, respectively. The shape of the F distribution depends on the degrees of freedom associated with s_1^2 and s_2^2, i.e., $(n_1 - 1)$ and $(n_2 - 1)$. An F distribution with 7 and 9 df is shown in Figure 1.28. As you can see, the distribution is skewed to the right.

FIGURE 1.28
An F distribution with 7 and 9 df

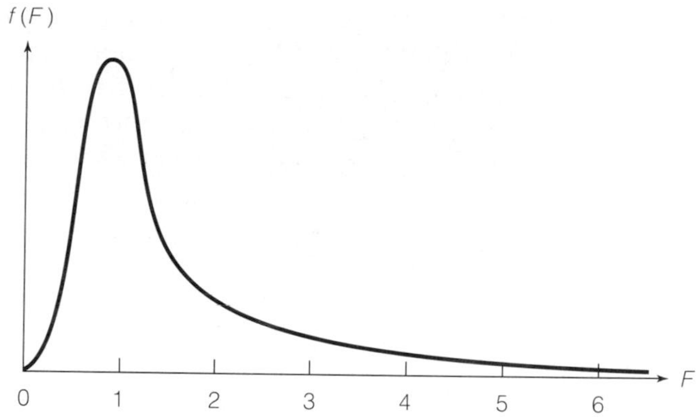

When the population variances are unequal, we expect the ratio of the sample variances, $F = s_1^2/s_2^2$, to be either very large or very small. Therefore, we will need to find F values corresponding to the tail areas of the F distribution to establish the rejection region for our test of hypothesis. The upper-tail F values can be found in Tables 3, 4, 5, and 6 of Appendix C. Table 4 is partially reproduced in Table 1.13. It gives F values that correspond to $\alpha = .05$ upper-tail areas for different degrees of freedom. The columns of the tables correspond to various degrees of freedom for the numerator sample variance s_1^2, whereas the rows correspond to the degrees of freedom for the denominator sample variance s_2^2.

TABLE 1.13 **Reproduction of Part of Table 4 of Appendix C: $\alpha = .05$**

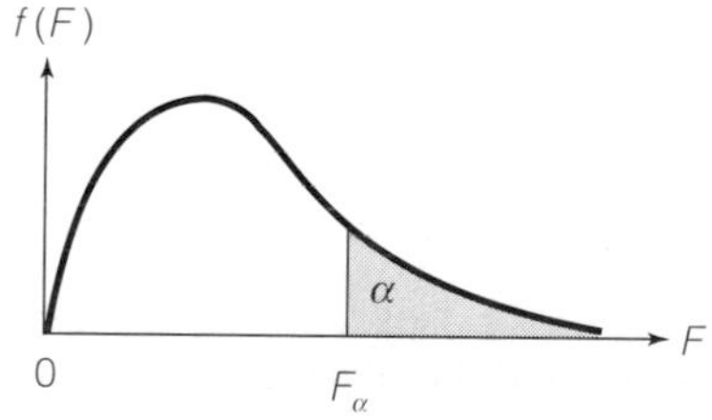

	ν_1	NUMERATOR DEGREES OF FREEDOM								
	ν_2	1	2	3	4	5	6	7	8	9
DENOMINATOR DEGREES OF FREEDOM	1	161.4	199.5	215.7	224.6	230.2	234.0	236.8	238.9	240.5
	2	18.51	19.00	19.16	19.25	19.30	19.33	19.35	19.37	19.38
	3	10.13	9.55	9.28	9.12	9.01	8.94	8.89	8.85	8.81
	4	7.71	6.94	6.59	6.39	6.26	6.16	6.09	6.04	6.00
	5	6.61	5.79	5.41	5.19	5.05	4.95	4.88	4.82	4.77
	6	5.99	5.14	4.76	4.53	4.39	4.28	4.21	4.15	4.10
	7	5.59	4.74	4.35	4.12	3.97	3.87	3.79	3.73	3.68
	8	5.32	4.46	4.07	3.84	3.69	3.58	3.50	3.44	3.39
	9	5.12	4.26	3.86	3.63	3.48	3.37	3.29	3.23	3.18
	10	4.96	4.10	3.71	3.48	3.33	3.22	3.14	3.07	3.02
	11	4.84	3.98	3.59	3.36	3.20	3.09	3.01	2.95	2.90
	12	4.75	3.89	3.49	3.25	3.11	3.00	2.91	2.85	2.80
	13	4.67	3.81	3.41	3.18	3.03	2.92	2.83	2.77	2.71
	14	4.60	3.74	3.34	3.11	2.96	2.85	2.76	2.70	2.65

Thus, if the numerator degrees of freedom is 7 and the denominator degrees of freedom is 9, we look in the seventh column and ninth row to find $F_{.05} = 3.29$. As shown in Figure 1.29, $\alpha = .05$ is the tail area to the right of 3.29 in the F distribution with 7 and 9 df. That is, if $\sigma_1^2 = \sigma_2^2$, the probability that the F statistic will exceed 3.29 is $\alpha = .05$.

FIGURE 1.29
An F distribution for 7 and 9 df: $\alpha = .05$

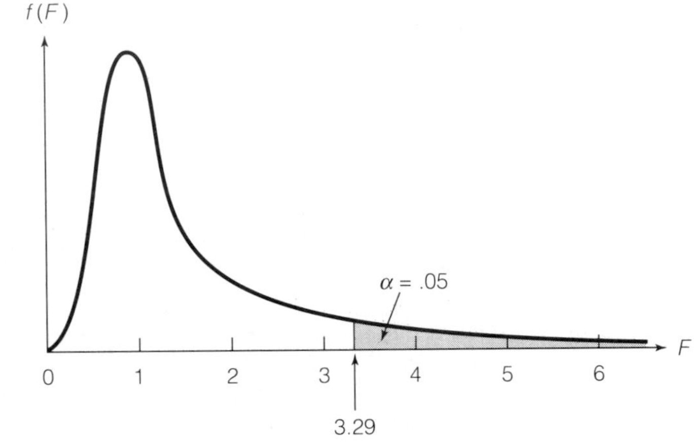

Suppose we want to compare the variability in production for two paper mills and we have obtained the following results:

SAMPLE 1	SAMPLE 2
$n_1 = 13$ days	$n_2 = 18$ days
$\bar{y}_1 = 26.3$ production units	$\bar{y}_2 = 19.7$ production units
$s_1 = 8.2$ production units	$s_2 = 4.7$ production units

To form the rejection region for a two-tailed F test, we want to make certain that the upper tail is used, because only the upper-tail values of F are shown in Tables 3, 4, 5, and 6. To accomplish this, **we will always place the larger sample variance in the numerator of the F test.** This doubles the tabulated value for α, since we double the probability that the F ratio will fall in the upper tail by always placing the larger sample variance in the numerator. In effect, we make the test two-tailed by putting the larger variance in the numerator rather than establishing rejection regions in both tails.

Thus, for our production example, we have a numerator s_1^2 with df $= n_1 - 1 = 12$ and a denominator s_2^2 with df $= n_2 - 1 = 17$. Therefore, the test statistic will be

$$F = \frac{\text{Larger sample variance}}{\text{Smaller sample variance}} = \frac{s_1^2}{s_2^2}$$

and we will reject H_0: $\sigma_1^2 = \sigma_2^2$ for $\alpha = .10$ if the calculated value of F exceeds the tabulated value:

$F_{.05} = 2.38$ (see Figure 1.30)

FIGURE 1.30
Rejection region for production example F distribution

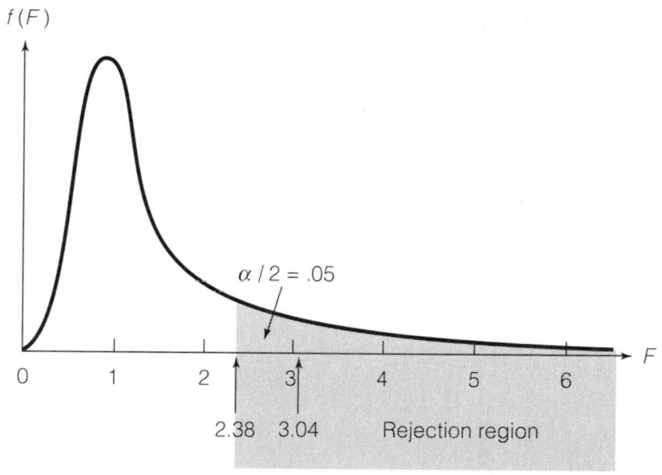

Now, what do the data tell us? We calculate

$$F = \frac{s_1^2}{s_2^2} = \frac{(8.2)^2}{(4.7)^2} = 3.04$$

and compare it to the rejection region shown in Figure 1.30. Since the calculated F value, 3.04, falls in the rejection region, the data provide sufficient evidence to indicate that the population variances differ. Consequently, we would be reluctant to use the two-sample t statistic to compare the population means, since the assumption of equal population variances is apparently untrue.

What would you have concluded if the value of F calculated from the samples had not fallen in the rejection region? Would you conclude that the null hypothesis of equal variances is true? No, because then you risk the possibility of a Type II error (accepting H_0 when H_a is true) without knowing the probability of this error (the probability of accepting H_0: $\sigma_1^2 = \sigma_2^2$ when it is false). Since we will not consider the calculation of β for specific alternatives in this text, when the F statistic does not fall in the rejection region, we simply conclude that **insufficient sample evidence exists to refute the null hypothesis that $\sigma_1^2 = \sigma_2^2$.**

The F test for equal population variances is summarized in the box at the top of page 76.

EXAMPLE 1.17

Refer to the *Journal of Marketing Research* study described in Example 1.15. The researcher's objective is to compare the mean buyer savings for two bargaining strategies, competitive and coordinative. Since both samples of buyers are small ($n_1 = 8$ and $n_2 = 8$), the t test for $(\mu_1 - \mu_2)$ requires that both sampled populations of buyer savings be normal with equal variances. To check the latter assumption, the researcher wants to determine (at $\alpha = .10$) whether the variation in the savings of buyers using the competitive strategy differs from the variation in the savings of buyers using the coordinative strategy.

F Test for Equal Population Variances

ONE-TAILED TEST	TWO-TAILED TEST
H_0: $\frac{\sigma_1^2}{\sigma_2^2} = 1$ (or $\sigma_1^2 = \sigma_2^2$)	H_0: $\frac{\sigma_1^2}{\sigma_2^2} = 1$ (or $\sigma_1^2 = \sigma_2^2$)
H_a: $\frac{\sigma_1^2}{\sigma_2^2} > 1$ (or $\sigma_1^2 > \sigma_2^2$)	H_a: $\frac{\sigma_1^2}{\sigma_2^2} \neq 1$ (or $\sigma_1^2 \neq \sigma_2^2$)
Test statistic: $F = \frac{s_1^2}{s_2^2}$	*Test statistic:* $F = \frac{\text{Larger sample variance}}{\text{Smaller sample variance}} = \frac{s_1^2}{s_2^2}$ where the samples are numbered so that $s_1^2 > s_2^2$
Rejection region: $F > F_\alpha$ where the degrees of freedom for F are: $n_1 - 1$ = df numerator sample variance; $n_2 - 1$ = df denominator sample variance	*Rejection region:* $F > F_{\alpha/2}$ where the degrees of freedom for F are: $n_1 - 1$ = df larger (numerator) sample variance; $n_2 - 1$ = df smaller (denominator) sample variance

Assumptions: 1. Both sampled populations are normally distributed.
2. The samples are random and independent.

Solution

The elements of the test are as follows:

$$H_0: \frac{\sigma_1^2}{\sigma_2^2} = 1 \quad (\text{i.e., } \sigma_1^2 = \sigma_2^2)$$

$$H_a: \frac{\sigma_1^2}{\sigma_2^2} \neq 1 \quad (\text{i.e., } \sigma_1^2 \neq \sigma_2^2)$$

$$\textit{Test statistic:} \quad F = \frac{\text{Larger sample variance}}{\text{Smaller sample variance}} = \frac{s_1^2}{s_2^2}$$

To find the rejection region, we proceed as follows: The numerator degrees of freedom are df $= n_2 - 1 = 8 - 1 = 7$ and the denominator degrees of freedom are $n_1 - 1 = 8 - 1 = 7$. From Table 4 of Appendix C, we find

$$F_{\alpha/2} = F_{.05} \approx 3.79$$

Summary statistics for the data are shown in the MINITAB printout, Figure 1.31. We now calculate

$$F = \frac{s_1^2}{s_2^2} = \frac{(538)^2}{(357)^2} = 2.27$$

This F value is not in the rejection region. Therefore, there is insufficient evidence at the $\alpha = .10$ level to refute the assumption of equal population variances.

FIGURE 1.31
MINITAB printout for Example 1.17

	N	MEAN	MEDIAN	TRMEAN	STDEV	SEMEAN
Compete	8	1706	1706	1706	538	190
Coordin	8	2106	2145	2106	357	126

	MIN	MAX	Q1	Q3
Compete	663	2644	1594	1850
Coordin	1544	2640	1766	2314

The following example shows that the F statistic is sometimes used to compare population variances in their own right, rather than just to check the validity of an assumption.

EXAMPLE 1.18

Heavy doses of ethylene oxide (ETO) in rabbits have been shown to alter significantly the DNA structure of cells. Although it is a known mutagen and suspected carcinogen, ETO is used quite frequently in sterilizing hospital supplies. A study was conducted to investigate the effect of ETO on hospital personnel involved with the sterilization process. Thirty subjects were randomly selected and randomly assigned to one of two tasks: 19 subjects were assigned the task of opening the sterilization package that contains ETO (task 1); the remaining 11 subjects were assigned the task of opening and unloading the sterilizer gun filled with ETO (task 2). After the tasks were performed, researchers measured the amount of ETO (in milligrams) present in the bloodstream of each subject. A summary of the results appears in Table 1.14. Do the data in the table provide sufficient evidence to indicate a difference in the variability of the ETO levels in subjects assigned to the two tasks? Test using $\alpha = .10$.

TABLE 1.14 **Data on ETO Levels, Example 1.18**

	TASK 1	TASK 2
Sample size	19	11
Mean	5.90	5.60
Standard deviation	1.93	4.10

Solution

Let

σ_1^2 = Population variance of ETO levels in subjects assigned task 1

σ_2^2 = Population variance of ETO levels in subjects assigned task 2

For this test to yield valid results, we must assume that both samples of ETO levels come from normal populations and that the samples are independent.

Now, following the guidelines in the box, we describe the elements of this two-tailed hypothesis test as follows:

$$H_0: \frac{\sigma_1^2}{\sigma_2^2} = 1 \quad (\text{or } \sigma_1^2 = \sigma_2^2)$$

$$H_a: \frac{\sigma_1^2}{\sigma_2^2} \neq 1 \quad (\text{or } \sigma_1^2 \neq \sigma_2^2)$$

Test statistic: $F = \dfrac{\text{Larger } s^2}{\text{Smaller } s^2} = \dfrac{s_2^2}{s_1^2} = \dfrac{(4.10)^2}{(1.93)^2} = 4.51$

Rejection region: For this two-tailed test, $\alpha = .10$ and $\alpha/2 = .05$. Thus, the rejection region is $F > F_{.05} = 1.98$ (from Table 8, Appendix C) where the distribution of F is based on $\nu_1 = (n_2 - 1) = 10$ and $\nu_2 = (n_1 - 1) = 18$ degrees of freedom.

Conclusion: Since the test statistic, $F = 4.51$, falls in the rejection region, we reject H_0. Therefore, the data provide sufficient evidence to indicate that the population variances differ. It appears that hospital personnel involved with opening the sterilization package (task 1) have less variable ETO levels than those involved with opening and unloading the sterilizer gun (task 2).

The previous examples demonstrate how to conduct a two-tailed F test when the alternative hypothesis is H_a: $\sigma_1^2 \neq \sigma_2^2$. One-tailed tests for determining whether one population variance is larger than another population variance (i.e., H_a: $\sigma_1^2 > \sigma_2^2$) are conducted similarly. However, the α value no longer needs to be doubled since the area of rejection lies only in the upper (or lower) tail area of the F distribution. The procedure for conducting an upper-tailed F test is outlined in the previous box. Whenever you conduct a one-tailed F test, be sure to write H_a in the form of an upper-tailed test. This can be accomplished by numbering the populations so that the variance hypothesized to be larger in H_a is associated with population 1 and the hypothesized smaller variance is associated with population 2.

EXERCISES

1.80 Use Tables 3, 4, 5, and 6 of Appendix C to find F_α for α, numerator df, and denominator df equal to:

a. .05, 8, 7 b. .01, 15, 20 c. .025, 12, 5
d. .01, 5, 25 e. .10, 5, 10 f. .05, 20, 9

1.81 Refer to the English study on estimating the metabolizable energy (ME) content of commercial cat foods in Exercise 1.67. In addition to the sample of 28 cats that were fed canned food, a second (independent) sample of 29 cats were fed a commercial brand of dry cat food. The ME content for each cat was measured (in kilocalories per gram) using method A, with the results shown in the table.

	CANNED FOOD	DRY FOOD
Sample size	28	29
Mean ME content	.96	3.70
Standard deviation	.26	.48

Source: Kendall, P. T., Burger, I. N., and Smith, P. M. "Methods of estimation of the metabolizable energy content of cat foods." *Feline Practice*, Vol. 15, No. 2, Feb. 1986, pp. 38–44.

Conduct a test to determine whether the variation in ME content of cats fed canned food differs from the variation in ME content of cats fed dry food. Use $\alpha = .10$.

1.82 For the perception of speech, profoundly deaf persons rely mainly on speechreading; i.e., they perceive spoken language by observing the articulatory movements, facial expressions, and gestures of the speaker. An experiment was conducted to compare the variability in the sentence perception of normal-hearing individuals with no prior experience in speechreading to those with experience in speechreading (*Journal of the Acoustical Society of America*, Feb. 1986). The sample consisted of 24 inexperienced and 12 experienced subjects. All subjects were asked to verbally reproduce sentences under several conditions, one of which was speechreading supplemented with sound-pressure information. A summary of the results (percentage of correct syllables) for the two groups is given in the table. Conduct a test to determine whether the variance in the percentage of correctly reproduced syllables differs between the two groups of speechreaders. Test using $\alpha = .10$.

INEXPERIENCED SPEECHREADERS	EXPERIENCED SPEECHREADERS
$n_1 = 24$	$n_2 = 12$
$\bar{x}_1 = 87.1$	$\bar{x}_2 = 86.1$
$s_1 = 8.7$	$s_2 = 12.4$

Source: Breeuwer, M., and Plomp, R. "Speechreading supplemented with auditorily presented speech parameters." *Journal of the Acoustical Society of America*, Vol. 79, No. 2, Feb. 1986, p. 487.

1.83 A study was conducted to compare the variation in the price of wholesale residual petroleum sold in rural (low-density) and urban (high-density) counties. In particular, the variable of interest was the natural logarithm of the ratio of the county price to state price, i.e., log (county price/state price). Based on independent random samples of 10 rural counties and 23 urban counties, the following descriptive statistics (shown in the table) were obtained. Is there evidence of a difference between the variance in the log-price ratios of rural and urban counties?

	n	$\bar{y}$	s
Rural	10	.239	.310
Urban	23	.117	.199

Source: Saavedra, P., et al. "Geographical stratification of petroleum retailers and resellers." Paper presented at Joint Statistical Meetings, Anaheim, Calif., Aug. 1990.

1.84 The quality control department of a paper company measures the brightness (a measure of reflectance) of finished paper on a periodic basis throughout the day. Two instruments that are available to measure the paper specimens are subject to error, but they can be adjusted so that the mean readings for a control paper specimen are the same for both instruments. Suppose you are concerned about the precision of the two instruments, namely, that the variation in readings from instrument 2 exceeds that for instrument 1. To check this theory, five measurements of a single paper sample are made on both instruments. The data are shown in the table. Do the data provide sufficient evidence to indicate that instrument 2 is less precise than instrument 1? Test using $\alpha = .05$.

INSTRUMENT 1	INSTRUMENT 2
29	26
28	34
30	30
28	32
30	28

1.85 Wet samplers are standard devices used to measure the chemical composition of precipitation. The accuracy of the wet deposition readings, however, may depend on the number of samplers stationed in the field. Experimenters in The Netherlands collected wet deposition measurements using anywhere from one to eight identical wet samplers (*Atmospheric Environment*, Vol. 24A, 1990). For each sampler (or sampler combination), data were collected every 24 hours for an entire year; thus, 365 readings were collected per sampler (or sampler combination). When one wet sampler was used, the standard deviation of the hydrogen readings (measured as percentage relative to the average reading from all eight samplers) was 6.3%. When three wet samplers were used, the standard deviation of the hydrogen readings (measured as percentage relative to the average reading from all eight samplers) was 2.6%. Conduct a test to compare the variation in hydrogen readings for the two sampling schemes (i.e., one wet sampler versus three wet samplers). Test using $\alpha = .05$.

Summary

The preceding sections summarize many of the basic concepts and methods presented in an introductory statistics course. We presented the concepts of a **population**, **random sampling**, and the ultimate objective of most statistical investigations, **making an inference about a population based on information contained in a sample**. Because inference implies description, we first considered methods for describing a set of data—two graphical methods (**relative frequency histogram** and **stem-and-leaf plot**) and **numerical descriptive methods** that provide measures of centrality and variability for a data set.

We noted that quantities computed from sample data—**statistics**—are used to estimate population numerical descriptive measures—**parameters**—and to make decisions about their values. To evaluate the properties of these statistics, we need to know the probabilities that they will assume specific sets of values in repeated sampling; that is, we need to know their **probability sampling distributions**. If we know the sampling distribution for a statistic, we can make probabilistic statements that measure the **reliability** of the statistic when it is used as an estimator or as the basis of a decision.

Finally, we summarized the basic concepts involved in **interval estimation** and **tests of hypotheses**. In particular, we presented **large- and small-sample confidence intervals** and **statistical tests for making inferences about a single population mean** and for **comparing two population means or variances based on independent random sampling**.

To aid in the formulation of confidence intervals and test statistics, we present two summary tables. Table 1.15 contains a list of parameters and their corresponding estimators and standard errors. Once you have identified the parameter of interest in Table 1.15, use Table 1.16 to formulate confidence intervals and test statistics.

TABLE 1.15 **Some Population Parameters and Corresponding Estimators and Standard Errors**

PARAMETER (θ)	ESTIMATOR ($\hat{\theta}$)	STANDARD ERROR ($\sigma_{\hat{\theta}}$)	ESTIMATE OF STANDARD ERROR ($s_{\hat{\theta}}$)
μ Mean (average)	$\bar{y}$	$\frac{\sigma}{\sqrt{n}}$	$\frac{s}{\sqrt{n}}$
$\mu_1 - \mu_2$ Difference between means (averages)	$\bar{y}_1 - \bar{y}_2$	$\sqrt{\frac{\sigma_1^2}{n_1} + \frac{\sigma_2^2}{n_2}}$	$\sqrt{\frac{s_1^2}{n_1} + \frac{s_2^2}{n_2}}$, $n_1 \geq 30$, $n_2 \geq 30$ $\sqrt{s_p^2\left(\frac{1}{n_1} + \frac{1}{n_2}\right)}$, either $n_1 < 30$ or $n_2 < 30$ where $s_p^2 = \frac{(n_1 - 1)s_1^2 + (n_2 - 1)s_2^2}{n_1 + n_2 - 2}$
$\frac{\sigma_1^2}{\sigma_2^2}$ Ratio of variances	$\frac{s_1^2}{s_2^2}$	(not necessary)	(not necessary)

TABLE 1.16 **Formulation of Confidence Intervals for a Population Parameter θ and Test Statistics for H_0: $\theta = \theta_0$, where $\theta = \mu$ or $(\mu_1 - \mu_2)$**

SAMPLE SIZE	CONFIDENCE INTERVAL	TEST STATISTIC
Large	$\hat{\theta} \pm z_{\alpha/2} s_{\hat{\theta}}$	$z = \frac{\hat{\theta} - \theta_0}{s_{\hat{\theta}}}$
Small	$\hat{\theta} \pm t_{\alpha/2} s_{\hat{\theta}}$	$t = \frac{\hat{\theta} - \theta_0}{s_{\hat{\theta}}}$

Note: The test statistic for testing H_0: $\sigma_1^2/\sigma_2^2 = 1$ is $F = s_1^2/s_2^2$ (see the box on page 76).

SUPPLEMENTARY EXERCISES

1.86 Tchebysheff's theorem states that at least $1 - (1/K^2)$ of a set of measurements will lie within K standard deviations of the mean of the data set. Use Tchebysheff's theorem to find the fraction of a set of measurements that will lie within:

a. 2 standard deviations of the mean ($K = 2$)

b. 3 standard deviations of the mean

c. 1.5 standard deviations of the mean

1.87 For each of the following data sets, compute $\bar{y}$, s, and s^2.

a. 11, 2, 2, 1, 9　　b. 22, 9, 21, 15

c. 1, 0, 1, 10, 11, 11, 0　　d. 4, 4, 4, 4

1.88 Use Table 1 of Appendix C to find each of the following:

a. $P(z \geq 2)$　　b. $P(z \leq -2)$　　c. $P(z \geq -1.96)$

d. $P(z \geq 0)$　　e. $P(z \leq -.5)$　　f. $P(z \leq -1.96)$

1.89 Suppose the random variable y has mean $\mu = 30$ and standard deviation $\sigma = 5$. How many standard deviations away from the mean of y is each of the following y values?

a. $y = 10$　　b. $y = 32.5$　　c. $y = 30$　　d. $y = 60$

1.90 Refer to the data on process voltage readings at two locations, Exercise 1.18. Descriptive statistics for both sample data sets are provided in the accompanying SAS printout. Use the rule of thumb to compare the voltage reading distributions for the two locations.

```
Analysis Variable : VOLTAGE

--------------------------------- LOCATION=NEW ------------------------------

N Obs   N        Minimum        Maximum          Mean        Std Dev
--------------------------------------------------------------------
   30  30      8.5100000     10.1200000     9.4223333      0.4788757
--------------------------------------------------------------------

--------------------------------- LOCATION=OLD ------------------------------

N Obs   N        Minimum        Maximum          Mean        Std Dev
--------------------------------------------------------------------
   30  30      8.0500000     10.5500000     9.8036667      0.5409155
--------------------------------------------------------------------

-------------------------------- LOCATION=NEW -------------------------------

                        UNIVARIATE PROCEDURE

Variable=VOLTAGE

                              Moments

                N                30  Sum Wgts          30
                Mean       9.422333  Sum           282.67
                Std Dev    0.478876  Variance    0.229322
                Skewness   -0.26699  Kurtosis    -0.89134
                USS        2670.061  CSS         6.650337
                CV         5.082347  Std Mean     0.08743
                T:Mean=0   107.7696  Prob>|T|      0.0001
                Sgn Rank      232.5  Prob>|S|      0.0001
                Num ^= 0         30
```

```
                        Quantiles(Def=5)

        100% Max        10.12          99%        10.12
         75% Q3          9.75          95%         10.1
         50% Med        9.455          90%        10.07
         25% Q1          9.14          10%         8.73
          0% Min         8.51           5%         8.65
                                        1%         8.51
        Range            1.61
        Q3-Q1            0.61
        Mode             8.82

                            Extremes

          Lowest      Obs     Highest     Obs
            8.51(      23)     10.03(      14)
            8.65(      22)     10.05(       7)
            8.68(      30)     10.09(       5)
            8.78(      26)      10.1(       3)
            8.82(      21)     10.12(       8)

------------------------------- LOCATION=OLD -------------------------------

                      UNIVARIATE PROCEDURE

Variable=VOLTAGE

                            Moments

        N                30   Sum Wgts          30
        Mean       9.803667   Sum           294.11
        Std Dev    0.540915   Variance     0.29259
        Skewness   -1.87787   Kurtosis    3.473528
        USS        2891.841   CSS         8.485097
        CV         5.517481   Std Mean    0.098757
        T:Mean=0    99.2704   Prob>|T|      0.0001
        Sgn Rank      232.5   Prob>|S|      0.0001
        Num ^= 0         30

                        Quantiles(Def=5)

        100% Max        10.55          99%        10.55
         75% Q3         10.05          95%        10.29
         50% Med        9.975          90%        10.26
         25% Q1           9.8          10%         8.76
          0% Min         8.05           5%         8.72
                                        1%         8.05
        Range             2.5
        Q3-Q1            0.25
        Mode             8.72

                            Extremes

          Lowest      Obs     Highest     Obs
            8.05(       6)     10.15(      22)
            8.72(      28)     10.26(       2)
            8.72(      20)     10.26(       8)
             8.8(      29)     10.29(       4)
            9.55(      17)     10.55(       7)
```

1.91 How strong is the effect of characteristics such as brand name or store name on a buyer's perception of the quality of a product? Numerous studies have been conducted to investigate this phenomenon, but the results seem to vary depending on the method used to analyze the data, type of product, price, etc. An article in the *Journal of Marketing Research* (Aug. 1989) summarized the results of 15 studies that investigated the effect of brand name on product quality and 17 studies that examined the effect of store name on quality. In all studies (the experimental units), an effect-size index was computed. The index ranges from 0 to 1; values closer to 0 indicate weaker effects, and values near 1 indicate stronger effects. Stem-and-leaf displays of effect-size index for the two groups of studies are illustrated here. Compare and contrast the two figures. Which variable, brand name or store name, seems to have the stronger effect on perceived quality? Explain.

BRAND NAME (15 STUDIES)		STORE NAME (17 STUDIES)	
STEM	LEAF	STEM	LEAF
.6	0	.6	
.5	7	.5	
.4		.4	3 4
.3	4	.3	
.2	5 5	.2	
.1	0 1 1 2 4	.1	2
.0	3 3 5 5 7	.0	0 0 0 1 1 2 2 3 3 4 6 7 8 8

Source: Rao, A. R., and Monroe, K. B. "The effect of price, brand name, and store name on buyers' perceptions of product quality: An integrative review." *Journal of Marketing Research*, Vol. 26, Aug. 1989, p. 354 (Table 2).

1.92 Do you want to avoid an Internal Revenue Service audit of your personal income tax return? If so, then try living in Newark, New Jersey, or in Boston. The Research Institute of America (RIA) found that only .55% of returns in those two cities were audited in 1987, in contrast to 1.45% in Anchorage, Alaska, 1.44% in San Francisco, and 1.36% in Manhattan (*The Wall Street Journal*, Mar. 22, 1989). For this RIA study, identify or describe the following:

a. Population
b. Sample
c. Experimental unit
d. Inference

1.93 Find a value of z, call it z_0, such that

a. $P(z \geq z_0) = .5$
b. $P(z \leq z_0) = .5199$
c. $P(z \geq z_0) = .3300$
d. $P(z_0 \leq z \leq .59) = .5845$

1.94 The random variable y has a normal distribution with $\mu = 80$ and $\sigma = 10$. Find the following probabilities:

a. $P(y \leq 75)$
b. $P(y \geq 90)$
c. $P(60 \leq y \leq 70)$
d. $P(y \geq 75)$
e. $P(y = 75)$
f. $P(y \leq 105)$

1.95 With the implantation of artificial hearts in humans, there is a chance of internal infection, a problem that has occurred with implants in animals. Experiments show that calves implanted with artificial hearts can live an average of 80 days. Suppose the distribution of the number of days that a calf implanted with an artificial heart can live is approximately normally distributed with a standard deviation of 25 days.

a. What is the probability that a randomly selected calf implanted with an artificial heart will live longer than 120 days?
b. Twenty-five percent of all calves implanted with an artificial heart live longer than d days. Find the value of d.

Show the pertinent quantities on a sketch of the normal curve for each part of the exercise.

1.96 Laws to protect infants and children as occupants of motor vehicles, i.e., *child restraint laws*, have been in effect in all 50 states since 1985. However, there is little uniformity among the laws, and in each state some children are excluded from coverage because of age, vehicle type, seating position, unregistered vehicles, etc. As part of a study to show the limiting effects of exemptions to the coverage of child restraint laws, the number of children (0–5 years) killed in motor vehicles in each state over a 5-year period was recorded, and the percentage of deaths not covered due to exemptions was calculated. The state percentages are given in the table.

STATE	PERCENTAGE	STATE	PERCENTAGE	STATE	PERCENTAGE	STATE	PERCENTAGE
AL	41	IN	27	NE	45	SC	37
AK	14	IA	10	NV	11	SD	37
AZ	49	KS	70	NH	9	TN	41
AR	44	KY	38	NJ	5	TX	30
CA	27	LA	37	NM	40	UT	50
CO	47	ME	55	NY	27	VT	50
CT	29	MD	42	NC	76	VA	47
DE	29	MA	8	ND	53	WA	18
FL	15	MI	32	OH	26	WV	26
GA	50	MN	36	OK	17	WI	46
HI	8	MS	68	OR	20	WY	60
ID	46	MO	50	PA	36		
IL	17	MT	57	RI	0		

Source: Teret, S. P., Jones, A. S., Williams, A. F., and Wells, J. K. "Child restraint laws: An analysis of gaps in coverage." *American Journal of Public Health*, Vol. 76, No. 1, Jan. 1986, p. 33 (Table 3).

a. Calculate the mean and standard deviation for the data.

b. Calculate the proportion of states with percentages falling within 1 standard deviation of the mean.

c. Calculate the proportion of states with percentages falling within 2 standard deviations of the mean.

d. Calculate the proportion of states with percentages falling within 3 standard deviations of the mean.

e. Use the rule of thumb to describe the distribution of state percentages of child motor-vehicle deaths.

1.97 Foresters "cruising" British Columbia's boreal forest have determined that the diameter at breast height of white spruce trees in a particular community is approximately normal, with mean 17 centimeters and standard deviation 6 centimeters.*

a. Find the probability that the breast height diameter of a randomly selected white spruce in the forest community is less than 12 centimeters.

b. Suppose you observe a white spruce with a breast height diameter of 12 centimeters. Is this an unusual event? Explain.

c. Find the probability that the breast height diameter of a randomly selected white spruce in the forest community will exceed 37 centimeters.

d. Suppose you observe a tree in the forest community with a breast height diameter of 38 centimeters. Is this tree likely to be a white spruce? Explain.

*Scholz, H. "Fish Creek Community Forest: Exploratory statistical analysis of selected data." Working Paper, Northern Lights College, British Columbia, Canada.

1.98 A psychologist is studying the effects of lack of sleep on the performance of various perceptual-motor tasks. After a given period of sleep deprivation, a measurement of reaction time to an auditory stimulus was taken for each of six adult male subjects. The reaction times (in seconds) are summarized as follows:

$$\bar{x} = 1.82 \qquad s = .22$$

Previous psychological studies show that the true mean reaction time for non–sleep-deprived male subjects is 1.70 seconds. Does the sample evidence indicate (at significance level $\alpha = .10$) that the mean reaction time for sleep-deprived male subjects is longer than 1.70 seconds? State any assumptions that are necessary for the hypothesis test to be valid.

1.99 Multinational corporations are firms with both domestic and foreign assets/investments. The foreign revenue (as a percentage of total revenue) generated by each of the top 20 U.S.-based multinational firms is listed in the table.

Exxon	73.2	Procter & Gamble	39.9
IBM	58.9	Philip Morris	19.6
GM	26.6	Eastman Kodak	40.9
Mobil	64.7	Digital	54.1
Ford	33.2	GE	12.4
Citicorp	52.3	United Technologies	32.9
EI duPont	39.8	Amoco	26.1
Texaco	42.3	Hewlett-Packard	53.3
ITT	43.3	Xerox	34.6
Dow Chemical	54.1	Chevron	20.5

Source: *Forbes*, July 23, 1990, pp. 362–363.

a. Construct a 90% confidence interval for the mean foreign revenue percentage of all U.S.-based multinational firms.

b. Interpret the interval, part a.

c. What assumption is required for the interval estimation procedure to be valid?

1.100 The Occupational Safety and Health Administration (OSHA) conducted a study to evaluate the level of exposure of workers to the dioxin TCDD. The distribution of TCDD levels in parts per trillion (ppt) of production workers at a Newark, New Jersey, chemical plant had a mean of 293 ppt and a standard deviation 847 ppt (*Chemosphere*, Vol. 20, 1990). A graph of the distribution is shown here. In a random sample of $n = 50$ workers selected at the New Jersey plant, let $\bar{y}$ represent the sample mean TCDD level.

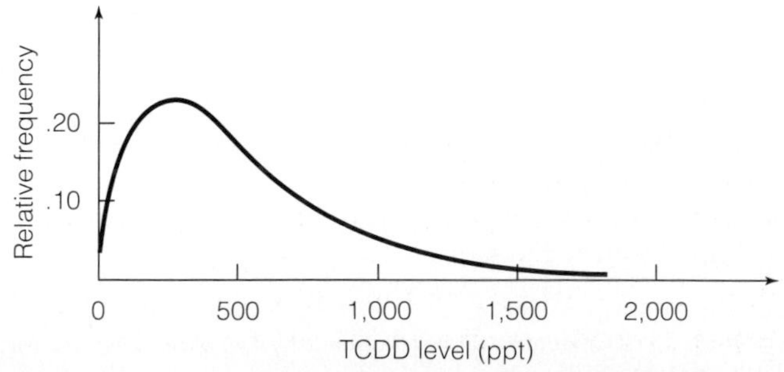

a. Find the mean and standard deviation of the sampling distribution of $\bar{y}$.
b. Draw a sketch of the sampling distribution of $\bar{y}$. Locate the mean on the graph.
c. Find the probability that $\bar{y}$ exceeds 550 ppt.

1.101 According to researchers, "One of the primary reasons relationships sour is that people stop listening to one another" (*USA Today*, Aug. 14, 1985). In a 10-year study of the listening habits of 150 couples, the researchers discovered that couples in conflict listen to each other for a maximum of 14 seconds. Assume that the relative frequency distribution for the length of time couples in conflict listen to each other has a mean of $\mu = 8$ seconds and a standard deviation of $\sigma = 5$ seconds.
a. In a sample of $n = 37$ couples in conflict, let $\bar{y}$ represent the mean length of time the couples listen to each other. Describe the sampling distribution of $\bar{y}$.
b. Find the probability that $\bar{y}$ exceeds 10 seconds.
c. Within what limits would you expect $\bar{y}$ to fall?

1.102 Let t_0 be a particular value of t. Use Table 2 of Appendix C to find the values such that the following statements are true:
a. $P(t \leq t_0) = .10$ when $n = 23$
b. $P(t \geq t_0) = .005$ when $n = 3$
c. $P(t \leq -t_0 \text{ or } t \geq t_0) = .05$ when $n = 7$
d. $P(t \leq -t_0 \text{ or } t \geq t_0) = .01$ when $n = 24$
If rejection of the null hypothesis for a particular test would cause your firm to go out of business, would you want α to be small or large? Explain.

1.103 Refer to the *Journal of Education for Business* study of interactive televised college classes, Exercise 1.78. The data, reproduced here, were used to test for a difference between the mean AACSB test scores of on-campus and off-campus students. To conduct the hypothesis test, you had to assume that $\sigma_1^2 = \sigma_2^2$. Perform an F test with $\alpha = .10$ to check that assumption. Explain the significance of your result.

	MEAN	STANDARD DEVIATION
On-campus students	41.93	2.86
Off-campus TV students	44.56	1.42

Source: Arndt, T. L., and LaFollette, W. R. "Interactive television and the nontraditional student." *Journal of Education for Business*, Jan./Feb. 1991, p. 184.

1.104 According to a popular model of managerial behavior, the current state of automation in a manufacturing firm influences managers' perceptions of problems of automation. To investigate this proposition, researchers at Concordia University (Montreal) surveyed managers at firms with a high level of automation and at firms with a low level of automation (*IEEE Transactions on Engineering Management*, Aug. 1990). Each manager was asked to give his or her perception of the problems of automation at the firm. Responses were measured on a 5-point scale (1 = no problem, . . . , 5 =

major problem). Summary statistics for the two groups of managers, provided in the table, were used to test the hypothesis of no difference in the mean perceptions of automation problems between managers of highly automated and less automated manufacturing firms.

	SAMPLE SIZE	MEAN	STANDARD DEVIATION
Low level	17	3.274	.762
High level	8	3.280	.721

Source: Farhoomand, A. F., Kira, D., and Williams, J. "Managers' perceptions towards automation in manufacturing." *IEEE Transactions on Engineering Management*, Vol. 37, No. 3, Aug. 1990, p. 230.

a. Conduct the test for the researchers, assuming that the perception variances for the two groups of managers are equal. Use $\alpha = .01$.
b. Test the assumption of part **a**. Use $\alpha = .01$.

1.105 The *American Journal of Small Businesses* (Winter 1988) reported on a survey designed to compare female managers at large firms with those at small firms (fewer than 100 employees). Previous studies tend to indicate that female managers in large and small companies are quite similar. In this study, independent random samples of 86 female managers at small firms and 91 female managers at large firms were compared on several job-related variables. The following question was asked: "How many times have you been promoted in the last three years?" The responses for the two groups of female managers are summarized in the table.

SMALL FIRMS	LARGE FIRMS
$n_1 = 86$	$n_2 = 91$
$\bar{y}_1 = 1.0$	$\bar{y}_2 = .9$
$s_1 = 1.1$	$s_2 = 1.1$

Source: Anderson, R. L., and Anderson, K. P. "A comparison of women in small and large companies." *American Journal of Small Businesses*, Vol. 12, No. 3, Winter 1988, p. 28 (Table 2).

a. Compute a point estimate for the difference between the mean number of promotions awarded to female managers at small firms and at large firms.
b. Compare the mean number of promotions awarded to the two groups of female managers with a 90% confidence interval.
c. Interpret the interval, part **b**.
d. How could the researchers reduce the width of the interval, part **b**?

1.106 *Scram* is the term used by nuclear engineers to describe a rapid emergency shutdown of a nuclear reactor. The nuclear industry has made a concerted effort to significantly reduce the number of unplanned scrams. The accompanying table gives the number of scrams at each of 56 U.S. nuclear reactor units in a recent year. A MINITAB printout showing both a graphical and numerical description of the data is also provided.

NUMBER OF SCRAMS													
1	0	3	1	4	2	10	6	5	2	0	3	1	5
4	2	7	12	0	3	8	2	0	9	3	3	4	7
2	4	5	3	2	7	13	4	2	3	3	7	0	9
4	3	5	2	7	8	5	2	4	3	4	0	1	7

MINITAB printout for Exercise 1.106

```
Stem-and-leaf of SCRAMS      N  = 56
Leaf Unit = 0.10


    6      0 000000
   10      1 0000
   19      2 000000000
  (10)     3 0000000000
   27      4 00000000
   19      5 00000
   14      6 0
   13      7 000000
    7      8 00
    5      9 00
    3     10 0
    2     11
    2     12 0
    1     13 0


                   ---------------
      --------I   +        I------------------        *   *
                   ---------------
    +---------+---------+---------+---------+---------+------SCRAMS
   0.0       2.5       5.0       7.5      10.0      12.5


                    N      MEAN    MEDIAN    TRMEAN     STDEV    SEMEAN
SCRAMS             56     4.036     3.000     3.820     3.027     0.404

                  MIN       MAX        Q1        Q3
SCRAMS          0.000    13.000     2.000     5.750
```

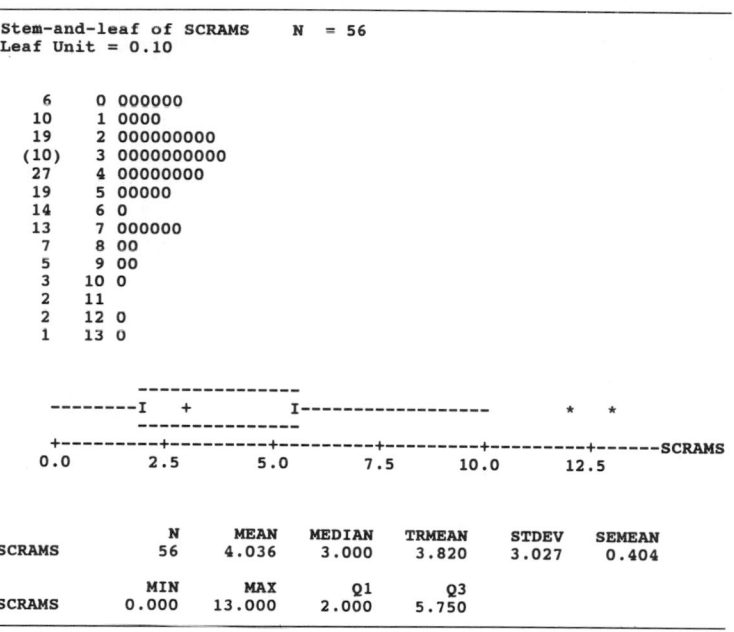

a. Fully interpret the results.
b. Would you expect to observe a nuclear reactor in the future with 11 unplanned scrams? Explain.
c. Suppose the data for nuclear reactors with 12 and 13 scrams were omitted from the analysis. Would you expect $\bar{y}$ to increase or decrease? Would you expect s to increase or decrease?
d. Recalculate $\bar{y}$ and s, excluding the observations 12 and 13. Compare these results with your answer to part **c**.

References

Freedman, D., Pisani, R., and Purves, R. *Statistics.* New York: W. W. Norton and Co., 1978.

McClave, J. T., and Sincich, T. *A First Course in Statistics,* 6th ed. Englewood Cliffs, N.J.: Prentice Hall, 1995.

Mendenhall, W. *Introduction to Probability and Statistics*, 8th ed. Boston: Duxbury, 1989.

Tanur, J. M., Mosteller, F., Kruskal, W. H., Link, R. F., Pieters, R. S., and Rising, G. R. (eds.). *Statistics: A Guide to the Unknown*, 3rd ed. San Francisco: Holden-Day, 1989.

Tukey, J. *Exploratory Data Analysis*. Reading, Mass.: Addison-Wesley, 1977.

CHAPTER 2

Introduction to Regression Analysis

CONTENTS

OBJECTIVE

To explain the concept of a statistical model; to describe applications of regression

Many applications of inferential statistics are much more complex than the methods presented in Chapter 1. Often, you will want to use sample data to investigate the relationships among a group of variables, ultimately to create a model for some variable (e.g., IQ, grade point average, etc.) that can be used to predict its value in the future. The process of finding a mathematical **model** (an equation) that best fits the data is part of a statistical technique known as **regression analysis**.

2.1 Modeling a Response

Suppose the dean of students at a university wants to predict the grade point average (GPA) of all students at the end of their freshman year. One way to do this is to select a random sample of freshmen during the past year, note the GPA y of each, and then use these GPAs to estimate the true mean GPA of all freshmen. The dean could then predict the GPA of each freshman using this estimated GPA.

Predicting the GPA of every freshman by the mean GPA is tantamount to using the mean GPA as a **model** for the true GPA of each freshman enrolled at the university.

In regression, the variable y to be modeled is called the **dependent** (or **response**) **variable** and its true mean (or **expected value**) is denoted $E(y)$. In this example,

$$y = \text{GPA of a student at the end of his or her freshman year}$$
$$E(y) = \text{Mean GPA of all freshmen}$$

> **Definition 2.1**
>
> The variable to be predicted (or modeled), y, is called the **dependent** (or **response**) **variable**.

The dean knows that the actual value of y for a particular student will depend on IQ, SAT score, major, and many other factors. Consequently, the real GPAs for all freshmen may have the distribution shown in Figure 2.1 (page 92). Thus, the dean is modeling the first-year GPA y for a particular student by stating that y is equal to the mean GPA $E(y)$ of all freshmen plus or minus some random amount, which is unknown to the dean; that is,

$$y = E(y) + \text{Random error}$$

Since the dean does not know the value of the random error for a particular student, one strategy would be to predict the freshman's GPA with the estimate of the mean GPA $E(y)$.

This model is called a **probabilistic model** for y. The adjective *probabilistic* comes from the fact that, when certain assumptions about the model are satisfied, we can make a probability statement about the magnitude of the deviation between y and $E(y)$. For example, if y is normally distributed with mean 2.5

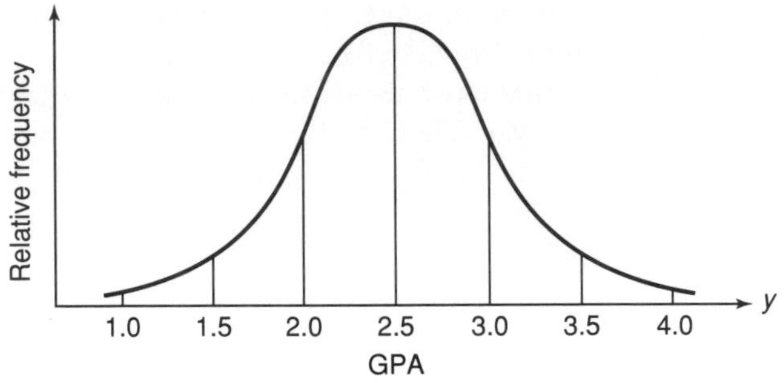

FIGURE 2.1
Distribution of freshman GPAs

grade points and standard deviation .5 grade point (as shown in Figure 2.1), then the probability that y will fall within 2 standard deviations (i.e., 1 grade point) of its mean is .95. The probabilistic model shown in the box is the foundation of all models considered in this text.

General Form of Probabilistic Model in Regression

$$y = E(y) + \varepsilon$$

where

y = Dependent variable
$E(y)$ = Mean (or expected) value of y
ε = Unexplainable, or random, error

In practice, we will need to use sample data to estimate the parameters of the probabilistic model—namely, the mean $E(y)$ and the random error ε. In Chapter 3, we will learn a standard assumption in regression: the mean error is 0. Based on this assumption, our best estimate of ε is 0. Thus, we need only estimate $E(y)$.

The simplest method of estimating $E(y)$ is to use the technique of Section 1.7. For example, the dean could select a random sample of freshmen students during the past year and record the GPA y of each. The sample mean $\bar{y}$ could be used as an estimate of the true mean GPA $E(y)$. If we denote the predicted value of y as $\hat{y}$, the prediction equation for the simple model is

$$\hat{y} = \bar{y}$$

Therefore, with this simple model, the sample mean GPA $\bar{y}$ is used to predict the true GPA y of any student at the end of his or her freshman year.

Unfortunately, this simple model does not take into consideration a number of variables, called **independent variables**,* that are highly related to a freshman's GPA. Logically, a more accurate model can be obtained by using the independent

*The word *independent* should not be interpreted in a probabilistic sense. The phrase *independent variable* is used in regression analysis to refer to a predictor variable for the response y.

variables (e.g., IQ, SAT score, major, etc.) to estimate $E(y)$. The process of finding the mathematical model that relates y to a set of independent variables and best fits the data is part of the process known as **regression analysis**.

Definition 2.2

The variables used to predict (or model) y are called **independent variables** and are denoted by the symbols x_1, x_2, x_3, etc.

For example, suppose the dean decided to relate freshman GPA y to a single independent variable x, defined as the student's SAT score. The dean might select a random sample of freshmen, record y and x for each, and then plot them on a graph as shown in Figure 2.2. Finding the equation of the smooth curve that best fits the data points is part of a regression analysis. Once obtained, this equation (a graph of which is superimposed on the data points in Figure 2.2) provides a model for estimating the mean GPA for freshmen with any specific SAT score. The dean can use the model to predict the GPA of any freshman as long as the SAT score for that freshman is known. As you can see from Figure 2.2, the model would also predict with some error (most of the points do not lie exactly on the curve), but the error of prediction will be much less than the error obtained using the model represented in Figure 2.1. As shown in Figure 2.1, a good estimate of GPA for a freshman student would be a value near the center of the distribution, say, the mean. Since this prediction does not take SAT score into account, the error of prediction will be larger than the error of prediction for the model of Figure 2.2. Consequently, we would state that the model utilizing information provided by the independent variable, SAT score, is superior to the model represented in Figure 2.1.

FIGURE 2.2
Relating GPA of a freshman to SAT score

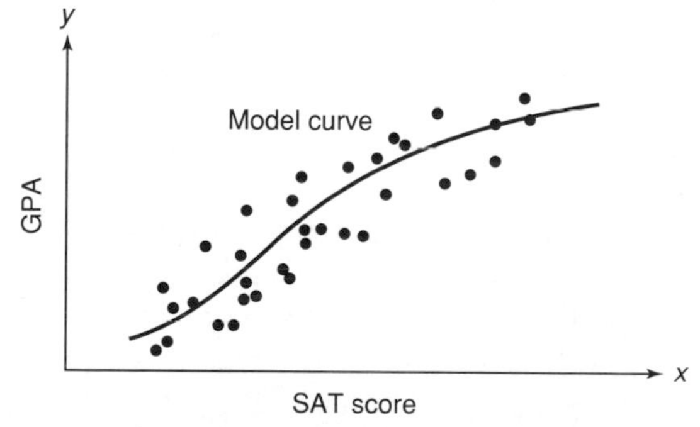

2.2 Overview of Regression Analysis

Regression analysis is a branch of statistical methodology concerned with relating a response y to a set of independent, or predictor, variables $x_1, x_2, \ldots, x_k$. The goal is to build a good model—a prediction equation relating y to the independent variables—that will enable us to predict y for given values of $x_1, x_2, \ldots, x_k$, and to do so with a small error of prediction. When using the model to predict

y for a particular set of values of $x_1, x_2, \ldots, x_k$, we will want a measure of the reliability of our prediction. That is, we will want to know how large the error of prediction might be. All these elements are parts of a regression analysis, and the resulting prediction equation is often called a **regression model**.

For example, a property appraiser might like to relate percentage price increase y of residential properties to the two quantitative independent variables x_1, square footage of heated space, and x_2, lot size. This model could be represented by a **response surface** (see Figure 2.3) that traces the mean percentage price increase $E(y)$ for various combinations of x_1 and x_2. To predict the percentage price increase y for a given residential property with $x_1 = 2{,}000$ square feet of heated space and lot size $x_2 = .7$ acre, you would locate the point $x_1 = 2{,}000$, $x_2 = .7$ on the x_1,x_2-plane (see Figure 2.3). The height of the surface above that point gives the mean percentage increase in price $E(y)$, and this is a reasonable value to use to predict the percentage price increase for a property with $x_1 = 2{,}000$ and $x_2 = .7$.

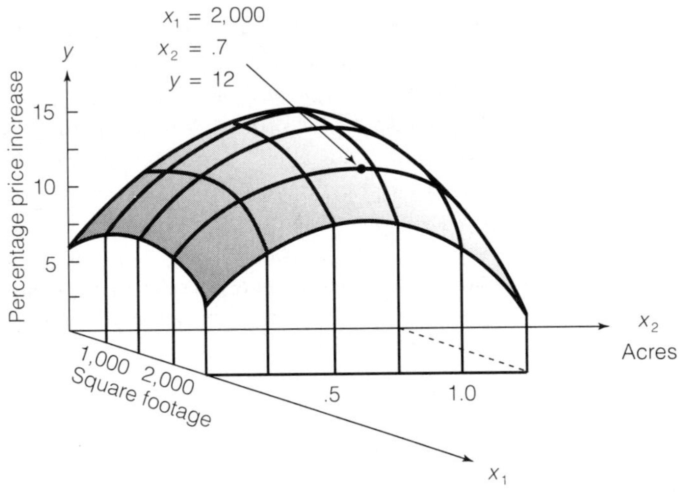

FIGURE 2.3
Mean percentage price increase as a function of heated square footage, x_1, and lot size, x_2

The response surface is a convenient method for modeling a response y that is a function of two quantitative independent variables, x_1 and x_2. The mathematical equivalent of the response surface shown in Figure 2.3 might be given by the **deterministic model**

$$E(y) = \beta_0 + \beta_1 x_1 + \beta_2 x_2 + \beta_3 x_1 x_2 + \beta_4 x_1^2 + \beta_5 x_2^2$$

where $E(y)$ is the mean percentage price increase for a set of values x_1 and x_2, and $\beta_0, \beta_1, \ldots, \beta_5$ are constants (or weights) with values that would have to be estimated from the sample data. Note that the model for $E(y)$ is deterministic because, if the constants $\beta_0, \beta_1, \ldots, \beta_5$ are known, the values of x_1 and x_2 determine exactly the value of $E(y)$.

Replacing $E(y)$ with $\beta_0 + \beta_1 x_1 + \beta_2 x_2 + \beta_3 x_1 x_2 + \beta_4 x_1^2 + \beta_5 x_2^2$ in the probabilistic model for y, we obtain the full equation for y:

$$y = \beta_0 + \beta_1 x_1 + \beta_2 x_2 + \beta_3 x_1 x_2 + \beta_4 x_1^2 + \beta_5 x_2^2 + \varepsilon$$

Now the property appraiser would obtain a sample of residential properties and record square footage, x_1, and lot size, x_2, in addition to percentage increase y in assessed value (see Section 2.4). Subjecting the sample data to a regression analysis will yield estimates of the model parameters and enable the appraiser to predict percentage increase y for a particular property. The prediction equation takes the form

$$\hat{y} = \hat{\beta}_0 + \hat{\beta}_1 x_1 + \hat{\beta}_2 x_2 + \hat{\beta}_3 x_1 x_2 + \hat{\beta}_4 x_1^2 + \hat{\beta}_5 x_2^2$$

where $\hat{y}$ is the predicted value of y, and $\hat{\beta}_0, \hat{\beta}_1, \ldots, \hat{\beta}_5$ are estimates of the model parameters.

In practice, the appraiser would construct a deterministic model for $E(y)$ that takes into account other quantitative variables, as well as qualitative independent variables, such as location and type of construction. In the following chapters, we will show how to construct a model relating a response to both quantitative and qualitative independent variables, and we will fit the model to a set of sample data using a regression analysis.

The preceding description of regression analysis is oversimplified, but it provides a preliminary view of the methodology that is the subject of this text. In addition to predicting y for specific values of $x_1, x_2, \ldots, x_k$, a regression model can be used to estimate the mean value of y for given values of $x_1, x_2, \ldots, x_k$ and to answer other questions concerning the relationship between y and one or more of the independent variables. The practical values attached to these inferences will be illustrated by examples in the following chapters.

We conclude this section with a summary of the major steps involved in a regression analysis.

Regression Modeling: Six-Step Procedure

1. Hypothesize the form of the model for $E(y)$.
2. Collect the sample data.
3. Use the sample data to estimate unknown parameters in the model.
4. Specify the probability distribution of the random error term, and estimate any unknown parameters of this distribution.
5. Statistically check the usefulness of the model.
6. When satisfied that the model is useful, use it for prediction, estimation, and so on.

2.3 Regression Applications

Regression analysis of data is a very powerful statistical tool. It provides a technique for building a statistical predictor of a response and enables you to place a bound (an approximate upper limit) on your error of prediction. For example, suppose you manage a construction company and you would like to predict the profit y per construction job as a function of a set of independent variables $x_1, x_2, \ldots, x_k$. If you could find the right combination of independent variables and could postulate a reasonable mathematical equation to relate y to these variables, you could possibly deduce which of the independent variables were causally related to profit per job and then control these variables to achieve a higher company profit. In addition, you could use the forecasts in corporate planning. The following examples illustrate a few of the many successful applications of regression analysis to real-world problems.

EXAMPLE 2.1

Psychology Perfectionists are persons who set themselves standards and goals that cannot be reasonably met or accomplished. One theory suggests that those individuals who are depressed have a tendency toward perfectionism. To study this phenomenon, 76 members of an introductory psychology class completed questionnaires using the following four scales: (1) the ASO scale, designed to measure self-acceptance; (2) the Burns scale, designed to measure perfectionism; (3) the Zung scale, designed to measure depression; and (4) the Rotter scale, designed to measure perceptions between actions and reinforcement (*The Journal of Adlerian Theory, Research, and Practice*, Mar. 1986). The researchers used the questionnaire data to build a regression model relating depression y, measured on the Zung scale, to the three independent variables: self-acceptance (ASO scale), perfectionism (Burns scale), and reinforcement (Rotter scale).

EXAMPLE 2.2

Management To reward their executives appropriately, many large corporations receive advice from consulting firms regarding the amount of compensation that each executive should receive. To provide this advice, the consulting firm collects information on the compensation y received by a large number of corporate executives. For each of these executives, the firm records the values of many independent variables, some of which are the following:

1. Experience (years)
2. College education (years)
3. Number of employees supervised
4. Corporate assets (dollars)
5. Age of the executive
6. Whether the executive is on the company's board of directors (1 if yes; 0 if no)
7. Whether the executive has international responsibility (1 if yes; 0 if no)

The consulting firm then uses a regression analysis to build a good prediction equation for y, an executive's annual compensation, as a function of the independent variables listed here. If it is successful, the company can sell its services to both participating and nonparticipating corporations, providing them with reasonable compensation projections for their executives.

EXAMPLE 2.3

Engineering The liquefaction of coal is a process used in the manufacture of synthetic fuels. An experiment was conducted to evaluate the performances of a diesel engine run on coal-derived (synthetic) and petroleum-derived fuel oil (*Journal of Energy Resources Technology*, Mar. 1990). The petroleum-derived fuel used was a number 2 diesel fuel (DF-2) obtained from Phillips Chemical Company. Two synthetic fuels were used: a blended fuel (50% coal-derived and 50% DF-2) and a blended fuel with advanced timing. The brake power (kW) and fuel type were varied in test runs, and engine performance was measured. The researchers used the experimental data to successfully build a model for predicting mass burning rate per degree of crank angle, y, a measure of engine performance. The independent variables included the quantitative variable, brake power, and the qualitative variable, type of fuel (DF-2, blended, and blended with advanced timing).

2.4 Collecting the Data for Regression

Recall from Section 2.2 that the initial step in regression analysis is to hypothesize a deterministic model for the mean response, $E(y)$, as a function of one or more independent variables. Once a model for $E(y)$ has been hypothesized, the next step is to collect the sample data that will be used to estimate the unknown model parameters (β's). This entails collecting observations on both the response y and the independent variables, $x_1, x_2, \ldots, x_k$, for each experimental unit in the sample. Thus, a sample to be analyzed by regression includes observations on several variables $(y, x_1, x_2, \ldots, x_k)$, not just a single variable.

The data for regression can be of two types: **observational** or **experimental**. Observational data are obtained if no attempt is made to control the values of the independent variables (x's). For example, suppose you want to relate an executive's compensation y to the set of predictors listed in Example 2.2. One way to obtain the data for regression is to select a random sample of $n = 100$ executives and record the value of y and the values of each of the predictor variables. The data for the first five executives in the sample are displayed in Table 2.1 (page 98). Note that in this example, the x values, such as experience, college education, number of employees supervised, etc., for each executive are not specified in advance of observing salary y; that is, the x values were uncontrolled. Therefore, the sample data are observational.

Definition 2.3

If the values of the independent variables (x's) in regression are uncontrolled (i.e., not set in advance before the value of y is observed) but are measured without error, the data are **observational**.

TABLE 2.1 **Observational Data**

	EXECUTIVE				
	1	2	3	4	5
Annual compensation, y (\$)	85,420	61,333	107,500	59,225	98,400
Experience, x_1 (years)	8	2	7	3	11
College education, x_2 (years)	4	8	6	7	2
No. of employees supervised, x_3	13	6	24	9	4
Corporate assets, x_4 (millions)	1.60	.25	3.14	.10	2.22
Age, x_5 (years)	42	30	53	36	51
Board of directors, x_6	0	0	1	0	1
International responsibility, x_7	1	0	1	0	0

How large a sample should be selected when regression is applied to observational data? In Section 1.7, we learned that when estimating a population mean, the sample size n will depend on (1) the (estimated) population standard deviation, (2) the confidence level, and (3) the desired half-width of the confidence interval used to estimate the mean. Because regression involves estimation of the mean response, $E(y)$, the sample size will depend on these three factors. The problem, however, is not as straightforward as that in Section 1.7, since $E(y)$ is modeled as a function of a set of independent variables, and the additional parameters in the model (i.e., the β's) must also be estimated. In regression, the sample size should be large enough so that the β's are both estimable and testable. This will not occur unless n is at least as large as the number of β parameters included in the model for $E(y)$. To ensure a sufficiently large sample, a good rule of thumb is to select n greater than or equal to 10 times the number of β parameters in the model.

For example, suppose the consulting firm wants to use the following model for annual compensation, y, of a corporate executive:

$$E(y) = \beta_0 + \beta_1 x_1 + \beta_2 x_2 + \cdots + \beta_7 x_7$$

where $x_1, x_2, \ldots, x_7$ are defined in Example 2.2. Excluding β_0, there are seven β parameters in the model; thus, the firm should include at least $10 \times 7 = 70$ corporate executives in its sample.

The second type of data in regression, experimental data, are generated by designed experiments where the values of the independent variables are set in advance (i.e., controlled) before the value of y is observed. For example, if a production supervisor wants to investigate the effect of two quantitative independent variables, say, temperature x_1 and pressure x_2, on the purity of batches of a chemical, the supervisor might decide to employ three values of temperature (100°C, 125°C, and 150°C) and three values of pressure (50, 60, and 70 pounds per square inch) and to produce and measure the impurity y in one batch of chemical for each of the $3 \times 3 = 9$ temperature–pressure combinations (see Table 2.2). For this experiment, the settings of the independent variables are controlled, in contrast to the uncontrolled nature of observational data in the real estate sales example.

Definition 2.4

If the values of the independent variables (x's) in regression are controlled using a designed experiment (i.e., set in advance before the value of y is observed), the data are **experimental**.

TABLE 2.2 **Experimental Data**

TEMPERATURE, x_1	PRESSURE, x_2	IMPURITY, y
100	50	2.7
	60	2.4
	70	2.9
125	50	2.6
	60	3.1
	70	3.0
150	50	1.5
	60	1.9
	70	2.2

In many studies, it is usually not possible to control the values of the x's; consequently, most data collected for regression applications are observational. (Consider the regression analysis in Example 2.2. Clearly, it is impossible or impractical to control the values of the independent variables.) Therefore, you may want to know why we distinguish between the two types of data. We will learn (Chapter 6) that inferences made from regression studies based on observational data have more limitations than those based on experimental data. In particular, we will learn that establishing a cause-and-effect relationship between variables is much more difficult with observational data than with experimental data.

The majority of the examples and exercises in Chapters 3–9 are based on observational data. In Chapters 10–11, we describe regression analyses based on data collected from a designed experiment.

Summary

Psychologists, sociologists, engineers, managers, medical researchers, physicists, chemists, and others strive for a better understanding of the phenomena that affect the variables of interest in their field of study. To achieve this understanding, they seek the assistance of mathematical models that relate the mean value of a **response** (e.g., profit) to various **independent variables** (e.g., advertising budget, size of inventory, etc.). Since even a perfect mathematical description of this relationship will still predict the response with error, a random component is included in the model to account for the many other variables that have been purposely or inadvertently excluded.

The mathematical relationship that we have described forms a model for the relative frequency distribution of the population of response measurements that would be generated when the process is in a specific state. For example, a model might represent a relative frequency distribution of the population of monthly profits that a business might generate, now and in the immediate future, when the business is operating with a \$1,000,000 inventory and a \$500,000 annual advertising budget. Estimating the unknown parameters for this population, i.e., the unknown parameters in the model, and using the model to make predictions with known reliability, is the objective of a **regression analysis**.

The sample data for regression can be either **observational** (in which the values of the x's are uncontrolled) or **experimental** (in which the x's are set in advance of observing y). For practical reasons, most regression applications in business are based on observational data.

CHAPTER 3

Simple Linear Regression

CONTENTS

OBJECTIVE

To present the basic concepts of regression analysis based on a simple linear relation between a response y and a single predictor variable x

3.1 Introduction

As noted in Chapter 2, much research is devoted to the topic of **modeling**, i.e., trying to describe how variables are related. For example, a physician might be interested in modeling the relationship between the level of carboxyhemoglobin and the oxygen pressure in the blood of smokers. An advertising agency might want to know the relationship between a firm's sales revenue and the amount spent on advertising. And a psychologist may be interested in relating a child's age to the child's performance on a vocabulary test.

The simplest graphical model for relating a response variable y to a single independent variable x is a straight line. In this chapter, we will discuss **simple linear (straight-line) models**, and we will show how to fit them to a set of data points using the **method of least squares**. We will then show how to judge whether a relationship exists between y and x, and how to use the model either to estimate $E(y)$, the mean value of y, or to predict a future value of y for a given value of x. The totality of these methods is called a **simple linear regression analysis**.

Most models for response variables are much more complicated than implied by a straight-line relationship. Nevertheless, the methods of this chapter are very useful, and they set the stage for the formulation and fitting of more complex models in succeeding chapters. Thus, this chapter will provide an intuitive justification for the techniques employed in a regression analysis, and it will identify most of the types of inferences that we will want to make using a **multiple regression analysis** later in this book.

3.2 The Straight-Line Probabilistic Model

An important consideration in merchandising a product is the amount of money spent on advertising. Suppose you want to model the monthly sales revenue y of an appliance store as a function of the monthly advertising expenditure x. The first question to be answered is this: Do you think an exact (deterministic) relationship exists between these two variables? That is, can the exact value of sales revenue be predicted if the advertising expenditure is specified? We think you will agree that this is not possible for several reasons. Sales depend on many variables other than advertising expenditure—for example, time of year, state of the general economy, inventory, and price structure. However, even if many variables are included in the model (the topic of Chapter 4), it is still unlikely that we can predict the monthly sales *exactly*. There will almost certainly be some variation in sales due strictly to **random phenomena** that cannot be modeled or explained.

Consequently, we need to propose a probabilistic model for sales revenue that accounts for this random variation:

$$y = E(y) + \varepsilon$$

The random error component, ε, represents all unexplained variations in sales caused by important but omitted variables or by unexplainable random phenomena.

As you will subsequently see, the random error ε will play an important role in testing hypotheses or finding confidence intervals for the deterministic portion of the model; it will also enable us to estimate the magnitude of the error of prediction when the model is used to predict some value of y to be observed in the future.

We begin with the simplest of probabilistic models—a **first-order linear model*** that graphs as a straight line. The elements of the straight-line model are summarized in the box.

A First-Order (Straight-Line) Model

$$y = \beta_0 + \beta_1 x + \varepsilon$$

where

y = **Dependent** variable (variable to be modeled—sometimes called the **response** variable)

x = **Independent** variable (variable used as a **predictor** of y)

$E(y) = \beta_0 + \beta_1 x$ = Deterministic component

ε = (epsilon) = Random error component

β_0 = (beta zero) = y-intercept of the line, i.e., point at which the line intercepts or cuts through the y-axis (see Figure 3.1)

β_1 = (beta one) = Slope of the line, i.e., amount of increase (or decrease) in the mean of y for every 1-unit increase in x (see Figure 3.1)

FIGURE 3.1
The straight-line model

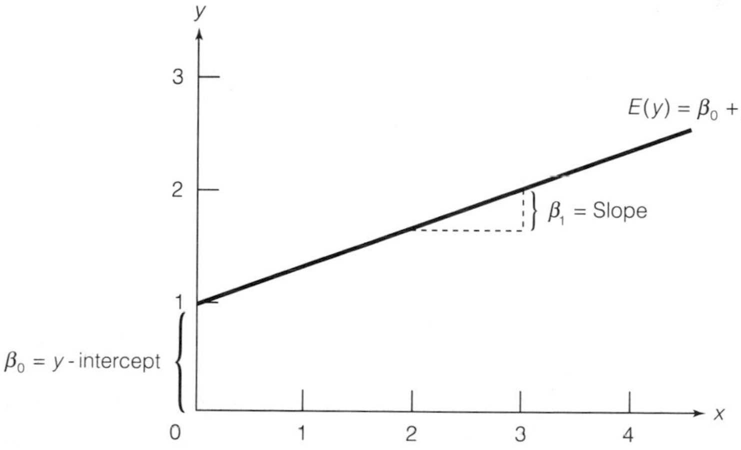

*A general definition of the expression *first-order* is given in Section 5.3.

In Section 3.4, we make the standard assumption that the average of the random errors is zero, i.e., $E(\varepsilon) = 0$. Then the deterministic component of the straight-line probabilistic model represents the line of means $E(y) = \beta_0 + \beta_1 x$. Note that we use Greek symbols β_0 and β_1 to represent the y-intercept and slope of the line. They are population parameters with numerical values that will be known only if we have access to the entire population of (x, y) measurements.

Recall from Section 2.2 that it is helpful to think of regression modeling as a six-step procedure:

STEP 1 Hypothesize the form of the model for $E(y)$.

STEP 2 Collect the sample data.

STEP 3 Use the sample data to estimate unknown parameters in the model.

STEP 4 Specify the probability distribution of the random error term, and estimate any unknown parameters of this distribution.

STEP 5 Statistically check the usefulness of the model.

STEP 6 When satisfied that the model is useful, use it for prediction, estimation, and so on.

In this chapter, we will skip step 1 and deal only with the straight-line model. In Chapters 4 and 7, we will discuss how to build more complex models.

EXERCISES

3.1 In each case, graph the line that passes through the points.
a. (0, 2) and (2, 6) b. (0, 4) and (2, 6)
c. (0, −2) and (−1, −6) d. (0, −4) and (3, −7)

3.2 The equation for a straight line (deterministic) is

$$y = \beta_0 + \beta_1 x$$

If the line passes through the point (0, 1), then $x = 0$, $y = 1$ must satisfy the equation. That is,

$$1 = \beta_0 + \beta_1(0)$$

Similarly, if the line passes through the point (2, 3), then $x = 2$, $y = 3$ must satisfy the equation:

$$3 = \beta_0 + \beta_1(2)$$

Use these two equations to solve for β_0 and β_1, and find the equation of the line that passes through the points (0, 1) and (2, 3).

3.3 Find the equations of the lines passing through the four sets of points given in Exercise 3.1.

3.4 Plot the following lines:
a. $y = 3 + 2x$ b. $y = 1 + x$ c. $y = -2 + 3x$
d. $y = 5x$ e. $y = 4 - 2x$

3.5 Give the slope and y-intercept for each of the lines defined in Exercise 3.4.

3.3 Fitting the Model: The Method of Least Squares

Suppose an appliance store conducts a 5-month experiment to determine the effect of advertising on sales revenue. The results are shown in Table 3.1. (The number of measurements is small, and the measurements themselves are unrealistically simple to avoid arithmetic confusion in this initial example.) The straight-line model is hypothesized to relate sales revenue y to advertising expenditure x. That is,

$$y = \beta_0 + \beta_1 x + \varepsilon$$

TABLE 3.1

MONTH	ADVERTISING EXPENDITURE x, hundreds of dollars	SALES REVENUE y, thousands of dollars
1	1	1
2	2	1
3	3	2
4	4	2
5	5	4

The question is this: How can we best use the information in the sample of five observations in Table 3.1 to estimate the unknown y-intercept β_0 and slope β_1?

To gain some information on the approximate values of these parameters, it is helpful to plot the sample data. Such a plot, called a **scattergram**, locates each of the five data points on a graph, as in Figure 3.2. Note that the scattergram suggests a general tendency for y to increase as x increases. If you place a ruler on the scattergram, you will see that a line may be drawn through three of the

FIGURE 3.2
Scattergram for data in Table 3.1

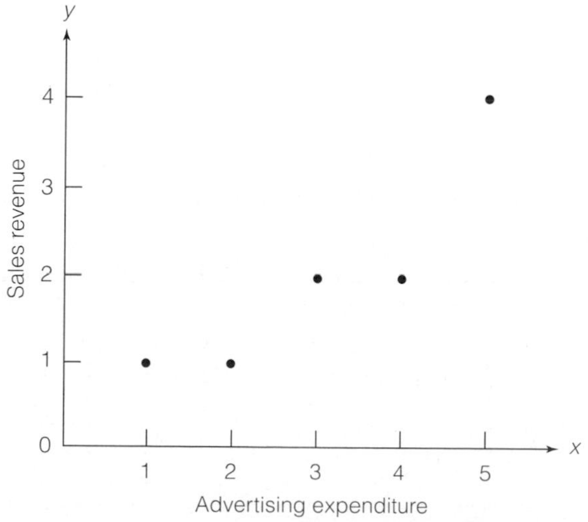

FIGURE 3.3
Visual straight-line fit to data in Table 3.1

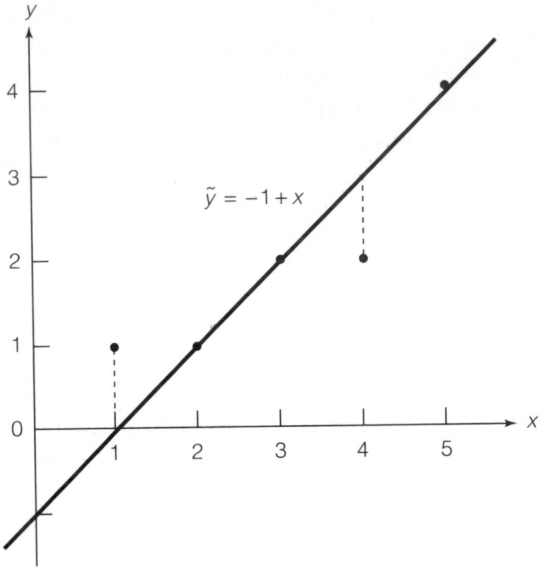

five points, as shown in Figure 3.3. To obtain the equation of this visually fitted line, notice that the line intersects the y-axis at $y = -1$, so the y-intercept is -1. Also, y increases exactly 1 unit for every 1-unit increase in x, indicating that the slope is $+1$. Therefore, the equation is

$$\tilde{y} = -1 + 1(x) = -1 + x$$

where $\tilde{y}$ is used to denote the predictor of y based on the visually fitted model.

One way to decide quantitatively how well a straight line fits a set of data is to determine the extent to which the data points deviate from the line. For example, to evaluate the visually fitted model in Figure 3.3, we calculate the magnitude of the **deviations**, i.e., the differences between the observed and the predicted values of y. These deviations, or **errors**, are the vertical distances between observed and predicted values of y (see Figure 3.3). The observed and predicted values of y, their differences, and their squared differences are shown in Table 3.2. Note that the **sum of the errors (SE)** equals 0 and the **sum of squares of the errors (SSE)**, which gives greater emphasis to large deviations of the points from the line, is equal to 2.

TABLE 3.2 **Comparing Observed and Predicted Values for the Visual Model**

x	y	$\tilde{y} = -1 + x$	$(y - \tilde{y})$	$(y - \tilde{y})^2$
1	1	0	$(1 - 0) = 1$	1
2	1	1	$(1 - 1) = 0$	0
3	2	2	$(2 - 2) = 0$	0
4	2	3	$(2 - 3) = -1$	1
5	4	4	$(4 - 4) = 0$	0
			Sum of errors (SE) $= 0$	Sum of squared errors (SSE) $= 2$

By shifting the ruler around the graph, we can find many lines for which the sum of the errors is equal to 0, but it can be shown that there is one (and only one) line for which the *SSE is a minimum*. This line is called the **least squares line**, **regression line**, or **least squares prediction equation**.

To find the least squares line for a set of data, assume that we have a sample of n data points that can be identified by corresponding values of x and y, say, $(x_1, y_1), (x_2, y_2), \ldots, (x_n, y_n)$. For example, the $n = 5$ data points shown in Table 3.2 are (1, 1), (2, 1), (3, 2), (4, 2), and (5, 4). The straight-line model for the response y in terms of x is

$$y = \beta_0 + \beta_1 x + \varepsilon$$

The line of means is

$$E(y) = \beta_0 + \beta_1 x$$

and the fitted line, which we hope to find, is represented as

$$\hat{y} = \hat{\beta}_0 + \hat{\beta}_1 x$$

The "hats" can be read as "estimator of." Thus, $\hat{y}$ is an estimator of the mean value of y, $E(y)$, and a predictor of some future value of y; and $\hat{\beta}_0$ and $\hat{\beta}_1$ are estimators of β_0 and β_1, respectively.

For a given data point, say, (x_i, y_i), the observed value of y is y_i and the predicted value of y is obtained by substituting x_i into the prediction equation:

$$\hat{y}_i = \hat{\beta}_0 + \hat{\beta}_1 x_i$$

The deviation of the ith value of y from its predicted value, called the **ith residual**, is

$$(y_i - \hat{y}_i) = [y_i - (\hat{\beta}_0 + \hat{\beta}_1 x_i)]$$

Then the sum of squares of the deviations of the y values about their predicted values (i.e., the **sum of squares of residuals**) for all of the n data points is

$$\text{SSE} = \sum_{i=1}^{n} [y_i - (\hat{\beta}_0 + \hat{\beta}_1 x_i)]^2$$

The quantities $\hat{\beta}_0$ and $\hat{\beta}_1$ that make the SSE a minimum are called the **least squares estimates** of the population parameters β_0 and β_1, and the prediction equation $\hat{y} = \hat{\beta}_0 + \hat{\beta}_1 x$ is called the **least squares line**.

Definition 3.1

The **least squares line** is one that satisfies the following two properties:

1. $\text{SE} = \Sigma (y_i - \hat{y}_i) = 0$; i.e., the sum of the residuals is 0.
2. $\text{SSE} = \Sigma (y_i - \hat{y}_i)^2$ is smaller than for any other straight-line model with $\text{SE} = 0$.

The values of $\hat{\beta}_0$ and $\hat{\beta}_1$ that minimize the SSE are given by the formulas in the box.*

Formulas for the Least Squares Estimates

Slope: $\hat{\beta}_1 = \frac{SS_{xy}}{SS_{xx}}$

y-intercept: $\hat{\beta}_0 = \bar{y} - \hat{\beta}_1\bar{x}$

where

$$SS_{xy} = \sum_{i=1}^{n} (x_i - \bar{x})(y_i - \bar{y}) = \sum_{i=1}^{n} x_i y_i - n\bar{x}\bar{y}$$

$$SS_{xx} = \sum_{i=1}^{n} (x_i - \bar{x})^2 = \sum_{i=1}^{n} x_i^2 - n(\bar{x})^2$$

n = Sample size

Preliminary computations for finding the least squares line for the advertising–sales example are given in Table 3.3. We can now calculate†

$$SS_{xy} = \sum x_i y_i - n\bar{x}\bar{y} = 37 - 5(3)(2) = 37 - 30 = 7$$

$$SS_{xx} = \sum x_i^2 - n(\bar{x})^2 = 55 - 5(3)^2 = 55 - 45 = 10$$

TABLE 3.3 **Preliminary Computations for the Advertising–Sales Example**

	x_i	y_i	x_i^2	$x_i y_i$
	1	1	1	1
	2	1	4	2
	3	2	9	6
	4	2	16	8
	5	4	25	20
Totals:	$\sum x_i = 15$	$\sum y_i = 10$	$\sum x_i^2 = 55$	$\sum x_i y_i = 37$
Means:	$\bar{x} = 3$	$\bar{y} = 2$		

*Students who are familiar with calculus should note that the values of β_0 and β_1 that minimize SSE $= \sum (y_i - \hat{y}_i)^2$ are obtained by setting the two partial derivatives $\partial SSE/\partial\beta_0$ and $\partial SSE/\partial\beta_1$ equal to 0. The solutions to these two equations yield the formulas shown in the box. (The complete derivation is provided in Appendix A.) Furthermore, we denote the *sample* solutions to the equations by $\hat{\beta}_0$ and $\hat{\beta}_1$, whereas the "^" (hat) denotes that these are sample estimates of the true population intercept β_0 and slope β_1.

†Since summations will be used extensively from this point on, we will omit the limits on Σ when the summation includes all the measurements in the sample; i.e., when the summation is $\Sigma_{i=1}^{n}$, we will write Σ.

Then, the slope of the least squares line is

$$\hat{\beta}_1 = \frac{SS_{xy}}{SS_{xx}} = \frac{7}{10} = .7$$

and the y-intercept is

$$\hat{\beta}_0 = \bar{y} - \hat{\beta}_1\bar{x}$$
$$= 2 - (.7)(3) = 2 - 2.1 = -.1$$

The least squares line is then

$$\hat{y} = \hat{\beta}_0 + \hat{\beta}_1 x = -.1 + .7x$$

The graph of this line is shown in Figure 3.4.

FIGURE 3.4
The line $\hat{y} = -.1 + .7x$ fitted to the data

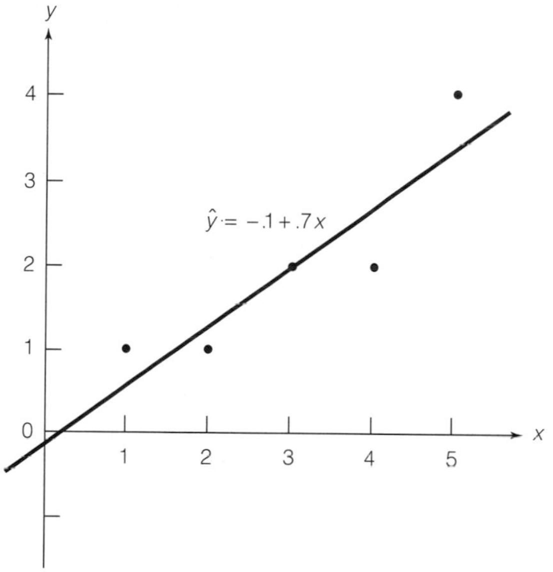

Our interpretation of the least squares slope, $\hat{\beta}_1 = .7$, is that the mean of sales revenue y will increase .7 unit for every 1-unit increase in advertising expenditure x. Since y is measured in units of \$1,000 and x in units of \$100, our interpretation is that mean monthly sales revenue increases \$700 for every \$100 increase in monthly advertising expenditure. (We will attach a measure of reliability to this inference in Section 3.6.)

The least squares intercept, $\hat{\beta}_0 = -.1$, is our estimate of mean sales revenue y when advertising expenditure is set at $x = \$0$. Since sales revenue can never be negative, why does such a nonsensical result occur? The reason is that we are attempting to use the least squares model to predict y for a value of x ($x = 0$) that is outside the range of the sample data and therefore impractical. (We have more to say about predicting outside the range of the sample data—called **extrapolation**—in Section 3.9.) Consequently, $\hat{\beta}_0$ will not always have a practical interpretation. Only when $x = 0$ is within the range of the x values in the sample and is a practical value will $\hat{\beta}_0$ have a meaningful interpretation.

The observed and predicted values of y, the deviations of the y values about their predicted values, and the squares of these deviations are shown in Table 3.4. Note that the sum of squares of the deviations, SSE, is 1.10, and (as we would expect) this is less than the SSE = 2.0 obtained in Table 3.2 for the visually fitted line.

TABLE 3.4 **Comparing Observed and Predicted Values for the Least Squares Model**

x	y	$\hat{y} = -.1 + .7x$	$(y - \hat{y})$	$(y - \hat{y})^2$
1	1	.6	$(1 - .6) = .4$	.16
2	1	1.3	$(1 - 1.3) = -.3$	.09
3	2	2.0	$(2 - 2.0) = 0$	.00
4	2	2.7	$(2 - 2.7) = -.7$	.49
5	4	3.4	$(4 - 3.4) = .6$	.36
			Sum of errors (SE) = 0	SSE = 1.10

To summarize, we have defined the best-fitting straight line to be the one that satisfies the least squares criterion; that is, the sum of the squared errors will be smaller than for any other straight-line model. This line is called the **least squares line**, and its equation is called the **least squares prediction equation**.

EXERCISES

3.6 Use the method of least squares to fit a straight line to these six data points:

x	1	2	3	4	5	6
y	1	2	2	3	5	5

a. What are the least squares estimates of β_0 and β_1?
b. Plot the data points and graph the least squares line on the scattergram.

3.7 Use the method of least squares to fit a straight line to these five data points:

x	−2	−1	0	1	2
y	4	3	3	1	−1

a. What are the least squares estimates of β_0 and β_1?
b. Plot the data points and graph the least squares line on the scattergram.

3.8 Public welfare expenditures by state governments have increased, on average, by $2 billion per year for the past 40 years. What determines the amount states spend each year on public welfare? This was the question studied in an article published in the *Journal of Socio-Economics* (Vol. 22, 1993).

The dependent variable of interest, y, was total annual public welfare expenditures aggregated over the 50 states from 1946 to 1987. To determine the best predictor of welfare expenditure, y was plotted against each of six independent variables for the 42 years: unemployment rate (x_1), total amount given to charity (x_2), Gross National Product (x_3), total amount allocated for grants-in-aid (x_4), percentage of states with Democratic governors (x_5), and percentage of states with Democratic legislatures (x_6). The six MINITAB scattergrams are shown here.* Examine the scattergrams and determine which of the six independent variables are likely to be linearly related to welfare expenditures y.

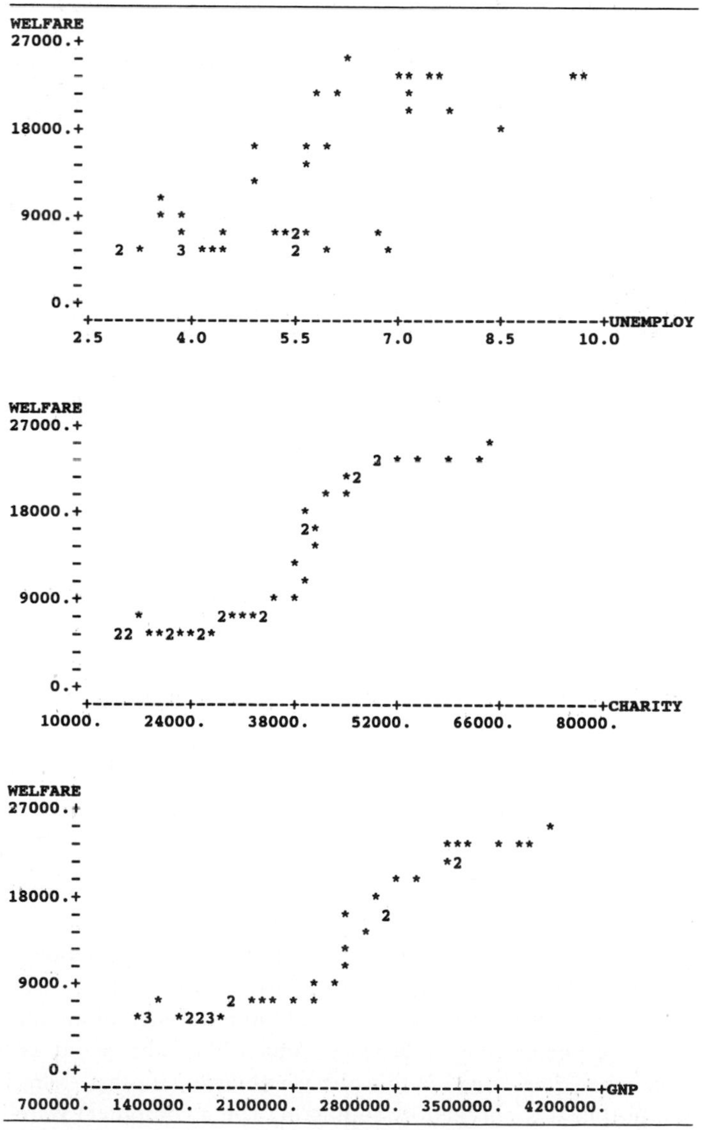

*Source: Mogull, R. G. "Determinants of states' welfare expenditures." *The Journal of Socio-Economics*, Vol. 22, No. 3, 1993, pp. 259–270 (Figures 2–5, 8–9).

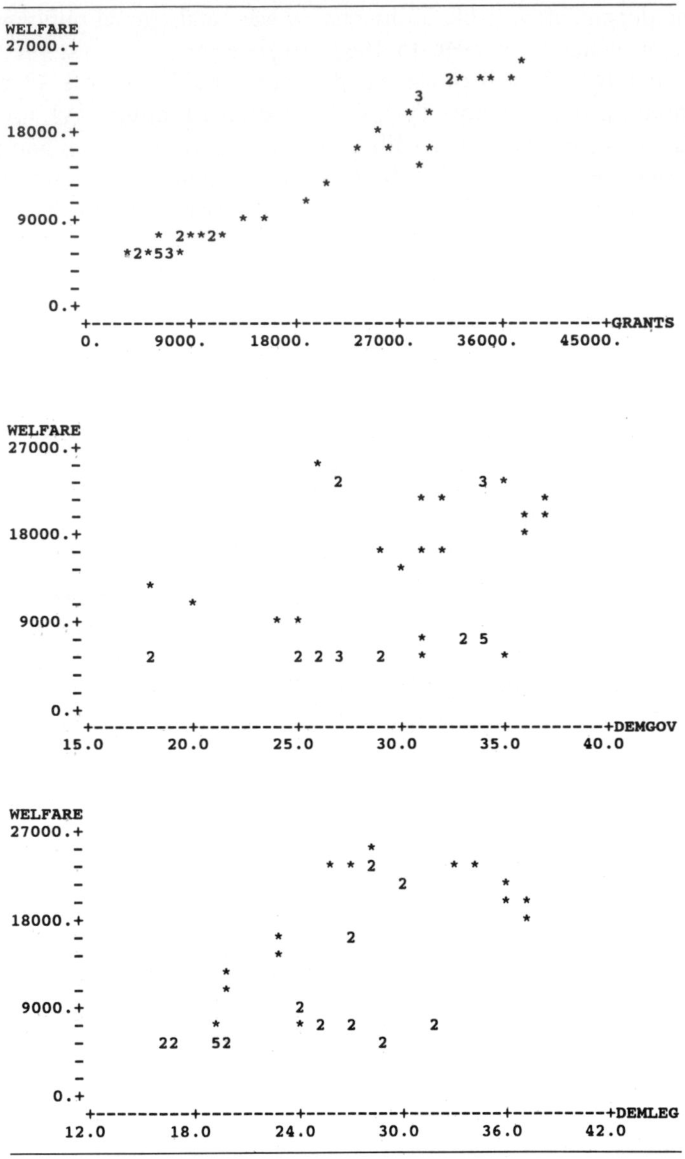

3.9 Modern warehouses use computerized and automated guided vehicles for materials handling. Consequently, the physical layout of the warehouse must be carefully designed to prevent vehicle congestion and optimize response time. Optimal design of an automated warehouse was studied in the *Journal of Engineering for Industry* (Aug. 1993). The layout assumes that vehicles do not block each other when they travel within the warehouse, i.e., that there is no congestion. The validity of this assumption was checked by simulating (on a computer) warehouse operations. In each simulation, the number of vehicles was varied and the congestion time (total time one vehicle blocked another) was recorded. The data are shown in the accompanying table. Of interest to the researchers is the relationship between congestion time (y) and number of vehicles (x).

NUMBER OF VEHICLES	CONGESTION TIME, minutes	NUMBER OF VEHICLES	CONGESTION TIME, minutes
1	0	9	.02
2	0	10	.04
3	.02	11	.04
4	.01	12	.04
5	.01	13	.03
6	.01	14	.04
7	.03	15	.05
8	.03		

Source: Pandit, R., and U. S. Palekar. "Response time considerations for optimal warehouse layout design." *Journal of Engineering for Industry*, Transactions of the ASME, Vol. 115, Aug. 1993, p. 326 (Table 2).

a. Construct a scattergram for the data.
b. Find the least squares line relating number of vehicles (x) to congestion time (y).
c. Plot the least squares line on the graph, part **a**.
d. Interpret the values of $\hat{\beta}_0$ and $\hat{\beta}_1$.

3.10 Each year, *Fortune* ranks the top U.S. cities according to their ability to provide high-quality, low-cost labor for companies that are relocating. One important measure used to form the rankings is the labor market stress index (y), which indicates the availability of workers in the city. (The higher the index, the tighter the labor market.) A second important variable is the unemployment rate (x). The values of these two variables for each of the top 10 cities in 1990 are listed in the table.

RANK	CITY	LABOR MARKET STRESS INDEX, y	UNEMPLOYMENT RATE, x
1	Salt Lake City	107	4.5%
2	Minneapolis–St. Paul	107	3.8%
3	Atlanta	100	5.1%
4	Sacramento	100	4.9%
5	Austin (Texas)	80	5.4%
6	Columbus (Ohio)	100	4.8%
7	Dallas/Fort Worth	100	5.5%
8	Phoenix	93	4.3%
9	Jacksonville (Florida)	87	5.7%
10	Oklahoma City	80	4.6%

Source: *Fortune*, Oct. 22, 1990, pp. 58–63.

a. Construct a scattergram for the data.
b. Find the least squares prediction equation.
c. Graph the least squares line on the scattergram.
d. Interpret the values of $\hat{\beta}_0$ and $\hat{\beta}_1$.

3.11 Two processes for hydraulic drilling of rock are dry drilling and wet drilling. In a dry hole, compressed air is forced down the drill rods to flush the cuttings and drive the hammer; in a wet hole, water is forced down. An experiment was conducted to determine whether the time y it takes to dry drill a distance of 5 feet in rock increases with depth x. The results (extracted from *The American Statistician*, Feb. 1991) for one portion of the experiment are shown in the table at the top of page 114.

DEPTH AT WHICH DRILLING BEGINS x, feet	TIME TO DRILL 5 FEET y, minutes
0	4.90
25	7.41
50	6.19
75	5.57
100	5.17
125	6.89
150	7.05
175	7.11
200	6.19
225	8.28
250	4.84
275	8.29
300	8.91
325	8.54
350	11.79
375	12.12
395	11.02

Source: Penner, R., and Watts, D. G. "Mining information." *The American Statistician*, Vol. 45, No. 1, Feb. 1991, p. 6 (Table 1).

a. Construct a scattergram for the data.
b. Find the least squares prediction equation.
c. Graph the least squares line on the scattergram.
d. Interpret the values of $\hat{\beta}_0$ and $\hat{\beta}_1$.

3.12 An electroencephalogram (EEG) is a tracing of brain waves recorded by an electroencephalograph. Neurologists have found that the peak EEG frequency in normal children increases with age. In one study (reported in *Science*, 1982), 287 normal children ranging from 2 to 16 years old were instructed to hold a 65-gram weight in the palm of their outstretched hand for a brief but unspecified time. The peak EEG frequency (measured in hertz) was then recorded for each child. The children were grouped according to age, and the average peak frequency for each age group was recorded. The data appear in the accompanying table.

AGE x, years	AVERAGE PEAK EEG FREQUENCY y, hertz	AGE x, years	AVERAGE PEAK EEG FREQUENCY y, hertz
2	5.33	10	7.28
3	5.75	11	7.06
4	5.80	12	7.60
5	5.60	13	7.45
6	6.00	14	8.23
7	5.78	15	8.50
8	5.90	16	9.38
9	6.23		

Source: Tryon, W. W. "Development equation for postural tremor." *Science*, Vol. 215, No. 2, 1982, pp. 300–301. Copyright 1982 by the AAAS.

a. Construct a scattergram for the data.
b. Find the least squares prediction equation.
c. Graph the least squares line on the scattergram.
d. Use the least squares prediction equation to predict the average peak EEG frequency y of $x =$ 7-year-old normal children. [*Note:* We will find a measure of the reliability of this prediction in Section 3.9.]

3.13 Civil engineers often use the straight-line equation $E(y) = \hat{\beta}_0 + \hat{\beta}_1 x$ to model the relationship between the mean shear strength $E(y)$ of masonry joints and precompression stress x. To test this theory, a series of stress tests was performed on solid bricks arranged in triplets and joined with mortar (*Proceedings of the Institute of Civil Engineers*, Mar. 1990). The precompression stress was varied for each triplet, and the ultimate shear load just before failure (called the shear strength) was recorded. The stress results for seven triplets (measured in newtons per square millimeter) is shown in the table.

TRIPLET TEST	1	2	3	4	5	6	7
Shear strength, y	1.00	2.18	2.24	2.41	2.59	2.82	3.06
Precompression stress, x	0	.60	1.20	1.33	1.43	1.75	1.75

Source: Riddington, J. R., and Ghazali, M. Z. "Hypothesis for shear failure in masonry joints." *Proceedings of the Institute of Civil Engineers, Part 2*, Mar. 1990, Vol. 89, p. 96 (Fig. 7).

a. Plot the seven data points in a scattergram. Does the relationship between shear strength and precompression stress appear to be linear?
b. Use the method of least squares to estimate the parameters of the linear model.
c. Interpret the values of $\hat{\beta}_0$ and $\hat{\beta}_1$.

3.4 Model Assumptions

In the advertising–sales example presented in Section 3.3, we assumed that the probabilistic model relating the firm's sales revenue y to advertising dollars x is

$$y = \beta_0 + \beta_1 x + \varepsilon$$

Recall that the least squares estimate of the deterministic component of the model $\beta_0 + \beta_1 x$ is

$$\hat{y} = \hat{\beta}_0 + \hat{\beta}_1 x = -.1 + .7x$$

Now we turn our attention to the random component ε of the probabilistic model and its relation to the errors of estimating β_0 and β_1. In particular, we will see how the probability distribution of ε determines how well the model describes the true relationship between the dependent variable y and the independent variable x.

We will make four basic assumptions about the general form of the probability distribution of ε:

ASSUMPTION 1 The mean of the probability distribution of ε is 0. That is, the average of the errors over an infinitely long series of experiments is 0 for each setting of the independent variable x. This assumption implies that the mean value of y, $E(y)$, for a given value of x is $E(y) = \beta_0 + \beta_1 x$.

ASSUMPTION 2 The variance of the probability distribution of ε is constant for all settings of the independent variable x. For our straight-line model, this assumption means that the variance of ε is equal to a constant, say, σ^2, for all values of x.

ASSUMPTION 3 The probability distribution of ε is normal.

ASSUMPTION 4 The errors associated with any two different observations are independent. That is, the error associated with one value of y has no effect on the errors associated with other y values.

The implications of the first three assumptions can be seen in Figure 3.5, which shows distributions of errors for three particular values of x, namely, x_1, x_2, and x_3. Note that the relative frequency distributions of the errors are normal, with a mean of 0, and a constant variance σ^2 (all the distributions shown have the same amount of spread or variability). A point that lies on the straight line shown in Figure 3.5 represents the mean value of y for a given value of x. We will denote this mean value as $E(y)$. Then, the line of means is given by the equation

$$E(y) = \beta_0 + \beta_1 x$$

FIGURE 3.5
The probability distribution of ε

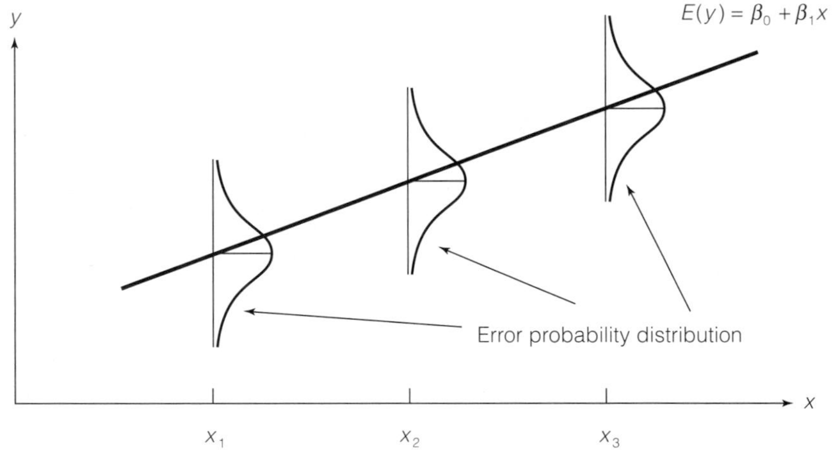

Various techniques exist for checking the validity of these assumptions, and there are remedies to be applied when the assumptions appear to be invalid. We discuss these techniques in detail in Chapter 6. In actual practice, the assumptions need not hold exactly for least squares estimators and test statistics (to be described subsequently) to possess the measures of reliability that we would expect from a regression analysis. The assumptions will be satisfied adequately for many applications encountered in business.

3.5 An Estimator of σ^2

It seems reasonable to assume that the greater the variability of the random error ε (which is measured by its variance σ^2), the greater will be the errors in the estimation of the model parameters β_0 and β_1, and in the error of prediction when $\hat{y}$ is used to predict y for some value of x. Consequently, you should not be surprised, as we proceed through this chapter, to find that σ^2 appears in the formulas for all confidence intervals and test statistics that we use.

In most practical situations, σ^2 will be unknown, and we must use the data to estimate its value. The best (proof omitted) estimate of σ^2 is s^2, which is obtained by dividing the sum of squares of residuals

$$\text{SSE} = \sum (y_i - \hat{y}_i)^2$$

by the number of degrees of freedom (df) associated with this quantity. We use 2 df to estimate the y-intercept and slope in the straight-line model, leaving $(n - 2)$ df for the error variance estimation (see the formulas in the box).

Estimation of σ^2

$$s^2 = \frac{\text{SSE}}{\text{Degrees of freedom for error}} = \frac{\text{SSE}}{n-2}$$

where

$$\text{SSE} = \sum (y_i - \hat{y}_i)^2$$

$$= \text{SS}_{yy} - \hat{\beta}_1 \text{SS}_{xy} \quad \text{(calculation formula)}$$

$$\text{SS}_{yy} = \sum (y_i - \bar{y})^2 = \sum y_i^2 - n(\bar{y})^2$$

Warning: When performing these calculations, you may be tempted to round the calculated values of SS_{yy}, $\hat{\beta}_1$, and SS_{xy}. Be certain to carry at least six significant figures for each of these quantities to avoid substantial errors in the calculation of the SSE.

In the advertising–sales example, we previously calculated SSE = 1.10 for the least squares line $\hat{y} = -.1 + .7x$. Recalling that there were $n = 5$ data points, we have $n - 2 = 5 - 2 = 3$ df for estimating σ^2. Thus,

$$s^2 = \frac{\text{SSE}}{n-2} = \frac{1.10}{3} = .367$$

is the estimated variance, and

$$s = \sqrt{.367} = .61$$

is the estimated standard deviation of ε.

You may be able to obtain an intuitive feeling for s by recalling the interpretation given to a standard deviation in Chapter 1 and remembering that the least squares line estimates the mean value of y for a given value of x. Since s measures the spread of the distribution of y values about the least squares line, we should not be surprised to find that most of the observations lie within $2s$ or $2(.61) = 1.22$ of the least squares line.* For this simple example (only five data points), all five data points fall within $2s$ of the least squares line. In Section 3.9, we will use s to evaluate the error of prediction when the least squares line is used to predict a value of y to be observed for a given value of x.

Interpretation of s, the Estimated Standard Deviation of ε

We expect most of the observed y values to lie within $2s$ of their respective least squares predicted values, $\hat{y}$.

EXERCISES

3.14 Suppose you fit a least squares line to nine data points and calculate SSE = .219.

a. Find s^2, the estimator of the variance σ^2 of the random error term ε.

b. Calculate s and interpret the result.

3.15 Calculate SSE, s^2, and s for the least squares line plotted in the following exercises. Interpret the value of s.

a. Exercise 3.7 b. Exercise 3.9 c. Exercise 3.11 d. Exercise 3.13

3.16 Calculate SSE, s^2, and s for the least squares line plotted in the following exercises. Interpret the value of s.

a. Exercise 3.6 b. Exercise 3.8 c. Exercise 3.10 d. Exercise 3.12

3.17 The Consumer Attitude Survey, performed by the Bureau of Economic and Business Research, University of Florida, is conducted using random-digit telephone dialings to Florida households. The reliability of such a telephone survey depends on the refusal rate—that is, the percentage of dialed households that refuse to take part in the study. One factor thought to be related to refusal rate is personal income. The accompanying table gives the refusal rate y and personal income per capita x for 12 randomly selected Florida counties from a recent survey.

a. Construct a scattergram for the data.

b. Find the least squares prediction equation.

c. Graph the least squares line on the scattergram.

d. Use the least squares prediction equation to predict the refusal rate for a Florida county with a per capita income of $8,000. [*Note:* We will find a measure of the reliability of this prediction in Section 3.9.]

e. Calculate SSE and s^2.

f. Calculate s and interpret its value.

---

*Another aid to interpreting s is the coefficient of variation (CV), where CV = $(s/\bar{y})(100)$. CV gives a unit-free measure of the size of s relative to the magnitude of the sample mean, $\bar{y}$.

COUNTY	REFUSAL RATE y	PER CAPITA INCOME x
1	.296	\$ 7,737
2	.498	12,330
3	.386	12,058
4	.327	9,927
5	.500	6,904
6	.333	9,463
7	.429	11,466
8	.422	10,000
9	.441	10,052
10	.191	8,636
11	.526	7,445
12	.405	9,059

Source: Bureau of Economic and Business Research, University of Florida.

3.18 A study was conducted to model the thermal performance of integral-fin tubes used in the refrigeration and process industries (*Journal of Heat Transfer*, Aug. 1990). Twenty-four specially manufactured integral-fin tubes with rectangular fins made of copper were used in the experiment. Vapor was released downward into each tube and the vapor-side heat transfer coefficient (based upon the outside surface area of the tube) was measured. The dependent variable for the study is the heat transfer enhancement ratio, y, defined as the ratio of the vapor-side coefficient of the fin tube to the vapor-side coefficient of a smooth tube evaluated at the same temperature. Theoretically, heat transfer will be related to the area at the top of the tube that is "unflooded" by condensation of the vapor. The data in the table are the unflooded area ratio (x) and heat transfer enhancement (y) values recorded for the 24 integral-fin tubes.

UNFLOODED AREA RATIO, x	HEAT TRANSFER ENHANCEMENT, y	UNFLOODED AREA RATIO, x	HEAT TRANSFER ENHANCEMENT, y
1.93	4.4	2.00	5.2
1.95	5.3	1.77	4.7
1.78	4.5	1.62	4.2
1.64	4.5	2.77	6.0
1.54	3.7	2.47	5.8
1.32	2.8	2.24	5.2
2.12	6.1	1.32	3.5
1.88	4.9	1.26	3.2
1.70	4.9	1.21	2.9
1.58	4.1	2.26	5.3
2.47	7.0	2.04	5.1
2.37	6.7	1.88	4.6

Source: Marto, P. J., et al. "An experimental study of R-113 film condensation on horizontal integral-fin tubes." *Journal of Heat Transfer*, Vol. 112, Aug. 1990, p. 763 (Table 2).

a. Fit a least squares line to the data.
b. Plot the data and graph the least squares line as a check on your calculations.
c. Calculate SSE and s^2.
d. Calculate s and interpret its value.

3.19 Amorphous alloys have been found to have superior corrosion resistance. *Corrosion Science* (Sept. 1993) reported on the resistivity of an amorphous iron–boron–silicon alloy after crystallization. Five alloy specimens were annealed at 700°C, each for a different length of time. The passivation potential—a measure of resistivity of the crystallized alloy—was then measured for each specimen. The experimental data are shown here.

ANNEALING TIME x, minutes	PASSIVATION POTENTIAL y, millivolts
10	−408
20	−400
45	−392
90	−379
120	−385

Source: Chattoraj, I., et al. "Polarization and resistivity measurements of post-crystallization changes in amorphous Fe-B-Si alloys." *Corrosion Science*, Vol. 49, No. 9, Sept. 1993, p. 712 (Table 1).

a. Fit a least squares line to the data.
b. Plot the data and graph the least squares line.
c. Calculate SSE and s^2.
d. Calculate s and interpret its value.

3.6 Assessing the Utility of the Model: Making Inferences About the Slope β_1

Refer to the advertising–sales data of Table 3.1 and suppose that the appliance store's sales revenue is *completely unrelated* to the advertising expenditure. What could be said about the values of β_0 and β_1 in the hypothesized probabilistic model

$$y = \beta_0 + \beta_1 x + \varepsilon$$

if x contributes no information for the prediction of y? The implication is that the mean of y, i.e., the deterministic part of the model $E(y) = \beta_0 + \beta_1 x$, does not change as x changes. Regardless of the value of x, you always predict the same value of y. In the straight-line model, this means that the true slope, β_1, is equal to 0. Therefore, to test the null hypothesis that x contributes no information for the prediction of y against the alternative hypothesis that these variables are linearly related with a slope differing from 0, we test

$$H_0\text{:}\quad \beta_1 = 0$$
$$H_a\text{:}\quad \beta_1 \neq 0$$

If the data support the alternative hypothesis, we will conclude that x does contribute information for the prediction of y using the straight-line model [although the true relationship between $E(y)$ and x could be more complex than a straight line]. Thus, to some extent, this is a test of the utility of the hypothesized model.

The appropriate test statistic is found by considering the sampling distribution of $\hat{\beta}_1$, the least squares estimator of the slope β_1.

Sampling Distribution of $\hat{\beta}_1$

If we make the four assumptions about ε (see Section 3.4), then the sampling distribution of $\hat{\beta}_1$, the least squares estimator of the slope, will be a normal distribution with mean β_1 (the true slope) and standard deviation

$$\sigma_{\hat{\beta}_1} = \frac{\sigma}{\sqrt{\mathrm{SS}_{xx}}} \quad \text{(See Figure 3.6.)}$$

FIGURE 3.6
Sampling distribution of $\hat{\beta}_1$

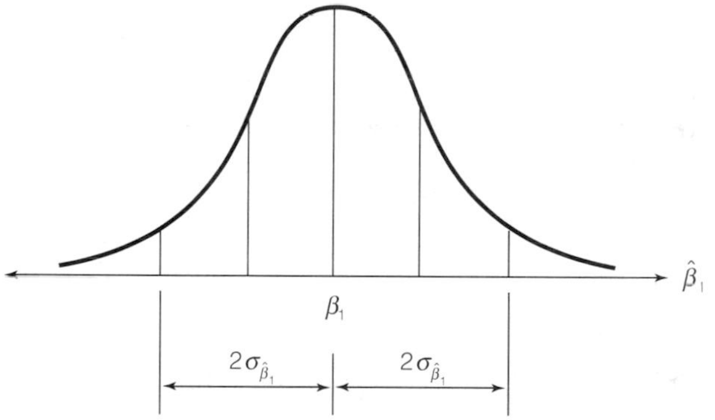

Since σ will usually be unknown, the appropriate test statistic will generally be a Student's t statistic formed as follows:

$$t = \frac{\hat{\beta}_1 - \text{Hypothesized value of } \beta_1}{s_{\hat{\beta}_1}}$$

$$= \frac{\hat{\beta}_1 - 0}{s/\sqrt{\mathrm{SS}_{xx}}}$$

where $s_{\hat{\beta}_1} = \dfrac{s}{\sqrt{\mathrm{SS}_{xx}}}$

Note that we have substituted the estimator s for σ, and then formed $s_{\hat{\beta}_1}$ by dividing s by $\sqrt{\mathrm{SS}_{xx}}$. The number of degrees of freedom associated with this t statistic is the same as the number of degrees of freedom associated with s. Recall that this will be $(n - 2)$ df when the hypothesized model is a straight line (see Section 3.5).

The test of the utility of the model is summarized in the box on page 122.

A Test of Model Utility: Simple Linear Regression

ONE-TAILED TEST	TWO-TAILED TEST
H_0: $\beta_1 = 0$	H_0: $\beta_1 = 0$
H_a: $\beta_1 < 0$ (or H_a: $\beta_1 > 0$)	H_a: $\beta_1 \neq 0$

Test statistic: $t = \dfrac{\hat{\beta}_1}{s_{\hat{\beta}_1}} = \dfrac{\hat{\beta}_1}{s/\sqrt{SS_{xx}}}$

Rejection region: $t < -t_\alpha$ (or $t > t_\alpha$)	*Rejection region:* $\lvert t \rvert > t_{\alpha/2}$
where t_α is based on $(n-2)$ df	where $t_{\alpha/2}$ is based on $(n-2)$ df

Assumptions: The four assumptions about ε listed in Section 3.4.

For the advertising–sales example, we will choose $\alpha = .05$ and, since $n = 5$, df $= (n - 2) = 5 - 2 = 3$. Then the rejection region for the two-tailed test is

$$t < -t_{.025} = -3.182 \quad \text{or} \quad t > t_{.025} = 3.182$$

We previously calculated $\hat{\beta}_1 = .7$, $s = .61$, and $SS_{xx} = 10$. Thus,

$$t = \frac{\hat{\beta}_1}{s/\sqrt{SS_{xx}}} = \frac{.7}{.61/\sqrt{10}} = \frac{.7}{.19} = 3.7$$

Since this calculated t value falls in the upper-tail rejection region (see Figure 3.7), we reject the null hypothesis and conclude that the slope β_1 is not 0. The sample evidence indicates that x contributes information for the prediction of y using a linear model for the relationship between sales revenue and advertising.

FIGURE 3.7
Rejection region and calculated t value for testing whether the slope $\beta_1 = 0$

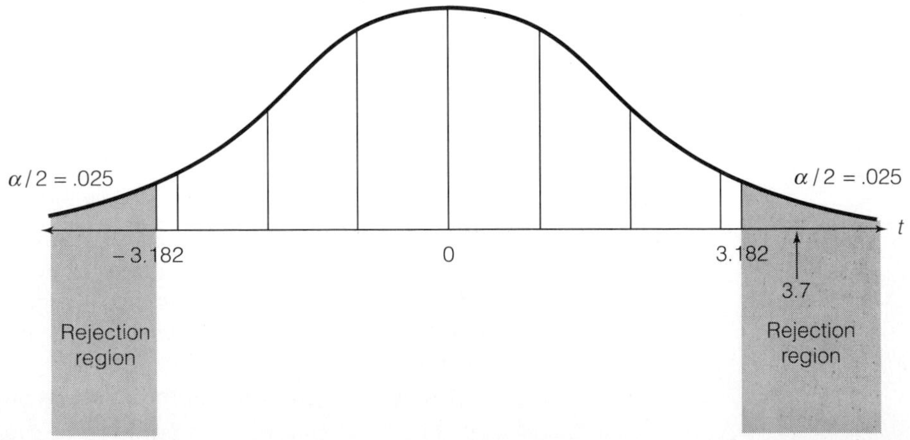

What conclusion can be drawn if the calculated t value does not fall in the rejection region? We know from previous discussions of the philosophy of hypothesis testing that such a t value does *not* lead us to accept the null hypothesis. That is, we do not conclude that $\beta_1 = 0$. Additional data might indicate that β_1 differs from 0, or a more complex relationship may exist between x and y, requiring the fitting of a model other than the straight-line model. We will discuss several such models in Chapter 4.

Another way to make inferences about the slope β_1 is to estimate it using a confidence interval. This interval is formed as shown in the next box.

A 100(1 − α)% Confidence Interval for the Simple Linear Regression Slope β_1

$$\hat{\beta}_1 \pm t_{\alpha/2} s_{\hat{\beta}_1} \quad \text{where} \quad s_{\hat{\beta}_1} = \frac{s}{\sqrt{SS_{xx}}}$$

and $t_{\alpha/2}$ is based on $(n-2)$ df

For the advertising–sales example, a 95% confidence interval for the slope β_1 is

$$\hat{\beta}_1 \pm t_{.025} s_{\hat{\beta}_1} = .7 \pm 3.182\left(\frac{s}{\sqrt{SS_{xx}}}\right)$$

$$= .7 \pm 3.182\left(\frac{.61}{\sqrt{10}}\right) = .7 \pm .61$$

Thus, we estimate that the interval from .09 to 1.31 includes the slope parameter β_1.

Remembering that y is recorded in units of \$1,000 and x in units of \$100, we can say, with 95% confidence, that the mean monthly sales revenue will increase between \$90 and \$1,310 for every \$100 increase in monthly advertising expenditure.

Since all the values in this interval are positive, it appears that β_1 is positive and that the mean of y, $E(y)$, increases as x increases. However, the rather large width of the confidence interval reflects the small number of data points (and, consequently, a lack of information) in the experiment. We would expect a narrower interval if the sample size were increased.

EXERCISES

3.20 Do the data provide sufficient evidence to indicate that β_1 differs from 0 for the least squares analyses in the following exercises? Use $\alpha = .05$.

a. Exercise 3.6 b. Exercise 3.7

3.21 Refer to *The American Statistician* investigation of dry drilling in rock, Exercise 3.11. Is there evidence to indicate that dry drill time y increases with depth x? Test using $\alpha = .10$.

3.22 Refer to the *Science* (Vol. 215, 1982) study discussed previously in Exercise 3.12. Do the data provide sufficient evidence to indicate that age, x, contributes information for the prediction of average peak frequency, y? Test using $\alpha = .05$.

3.23 Do the data in Exercise 3.17 provide sufficient evidence to indicate that refusal rate y is linearly related to per capita income x? Test using $\alpha = .01$.

3.24 Refer to the *Journal of Heat Transfer* study of the straight-line relationship between heat transfer enhancement (y) and unflooded area ratio (x), Exercise 3.18. Construct a 95% confidence interval for β_1, the slope of the line. Interpret the result.

3.25 Theophylline is a drug used to control asthma in children. To be effective, the blood concentration level of the drug must remain between 4 and 20 picograms per milliliter. Thus, frequent monitoring of theophylline concentrations is necessary for successful therapy. A study was conducted to compare the Ames Seralyzer assay system and the enzyme-multiplied immunoassay technique (EMIT), two methods of determining theophylline concentration (*American Journal of Hospital Pharmacy*, July 1986). A total of 102 blood serum samples were obtained from pediatric intensive-care unit patients who were receiving theophylline intravenously. Each sample was analyzed for theophylline concentration using both methods. The data (recorded in picograms per milliliter) were used to fit the model $y = \beta_0 + \beta_1 x + \varepsilon$, where

y = Theophylline concentration as determined by Ames Seralyzer

x = Theophylline concentration as determined by EMIT

A summary of the results follows:

$$\hat{y} = 1.737 + .953x \qquad s_{\hat{\beta}_1} = .025 \qquad s = 1.9$$

a. Construct a 95% confidence interval for β_1.

b. Interpret the interval, part **a**, and explain what it tells you about the relationship between the theophylline measurements of the two methods.

3.26 Refer to the *Chemosphere* (Vol. 20, 1990) study of Vietnam veterans exposed to Agent Orange (and the dioxin 2,3,7,8-TCDD), Exercise 1.51. The accompanying table gives the amounts of 2,3,7,8-TCDD (measured in parts per trillion) in both blood plasma and fat tissue drawn from each of the 20 veterans studied. One goal of the researchers is to determine the degree of linear association between the level of dioxin found in blood plasma and fat tissue. If a linear association between the two variables can be established, the researchers want to build models to predict (1) the blood plasma level of 2,3,7,8-TCDD from the observed level of 2,3,7,8-TCDD in fat tissue and (2) the fat tissue level from the observed blood plasma level.

a. Find the prediction equations for the researchers. Interpret the results.

b. Test the hypothesis that fat tissue level (x) is a useful linear predictor of blood plasma level (y). Use $\alpha = .05$.

c. Test the hypothesis that blood plasma level (x) is a useful linear predictor of fat tissue level (y). Use $\alpha = .05$.

d. Intuitively, why must the results of the tests, parts **b** and **c**, agree?

VETERAN	TCDD LEVELS IN PLASMA	TCDD LEVELS IN FAT TISSUE
1	2.5	4.9
2	3.1	5.9
3	2.1	4.4
4	3.5	6.9
5	3.1	7.0
6	1.8	4.2
7	6.0	10.0
8	3.0	5.5
9	36.0	41.0
10	4.7	4.4
11	6.9	7.0
12	3.3	2.9
13	4.6	4.6
14	1.6	1.4
15	7.2	7.7
16	1.8	1.1
17	20.0	11.0
18	2.0	2.5
19	2.5	2.3
20	4.1	2.5

Source: Schecter, A., et al. "Partitioning of 2,3,7,8-chlorinated dibenzo-*p*-dioxins and dibenzofurans between adipose tissue and plasma lipid of 20 Massachusetts Vietnam veterans." *Chemosphere*, Vol. 20, Nos. 7–9, 1990, pp. 954–955 (Tables I and II).

3.27 Refer to Exercise 3.26. The blood plasma and fat tissue levels of several other types of dioxin (called congeners) were also measured for each of the 20 Vietnam veterans. For each congener, a simple linear regression analysis was conducted to predict (1) fat tissue level from blood plasma level and (2) blood plasma level from fat tissue level. The results for three of these congeners are shown in the table.

CONGENER	y = FAT TISSUE LEVEL x = BLOOD PLASMA LEVEL	y = BLOOD PLASMA LEVEL x = FAT TISSUE LEVEL	t VALUE FOR TESTING β_1
2,3,4,7,8-P_n CDF	$\hat{y} = .8109 + .9713x$	$\hat{y} = .9855 + .7605x$	7.13
H_x CDD	$\hat{y} = 18.1565 + .7377x$	$\hat{y} = 5.2009 + .9018x$	5.98
OCDD	$\hat{y} = 118.6057 + .3679x$	$\hat{y} = 167.723 + 1.5752x$	4.98

Source: Schecter, A., et al. "Partitioning of 2,3,7,8-chlorinated dibenzo-*p*-dioxins and dibenzofurans between adipose tissue and plasma lipid of 20 Massachusetts Vietnam veterans." *Chemosphere*, Vol. 20, Nos. 7–9, 1990, pp. 954–955 (Table III).

a. For the congener 2,3,4,7,8,-P_n CDF, are the two regression models statistically adequate for predicting y? Test both using $\alpha = .05$.
b. Repeat part **a** for the congener H_x CDD.
c. Repeat part **a** for the congener OCDD.
d. Use the regression results to predict the level of 2,3,4,7,8,-P_n CDF in the blood plasma for a veteran with a fat tissue level of 8.0 ppt.

e. Use the regression results to predict the level of H_x CDD in fat tissue for a veteran with a blood plasma level of 24.0 ppt.
f. Use the regression results to predict the level of OCDD in blood plasma for a veteran with a fat tissue level of 776 ppt.

3.28 The data in the accompanying table consist of the average life expectancy and the population–physician ratio (i.e., the population divided by the number of physicians) for a random sample of 10 developing African countries.

COUNTRY	AVERAGE LIFE EXPECTANCY y, years	POPULATION–PHYSICIAN RATIO x
1	63.00	1,907
2	32.00	47,889
3	48.30	26,447
4	52.70	815
5	53.50	6,411
6	49.05	10,136
7	38.30	7,306
8	50.00	22,291
9	47.35	18,657
10	52.50	7,378

Source: *United Nations Statistical Yearbook.*

a. Find the least squares prediction equation $\hat{y} = \hat{\beta}_0 + \hat{\beta}_1 x$.
b. Find SSE and s^2.
c. Is there sufficient evidence to indicate that average life expectancy y in developing African countries is linearly related to population–physician ratio x? Test using $\alpha = .10$.

3.29 Researchers at the University of North Carolina–Greensboro investigated a model for the rate of seed germination (*Journal of Experimental Botany*, Jan. 1993). In one experiment, alfalfa seeds were placed in a specially constructed germination chamber. Eleven hours later, the seeds were examined and the change in free energy (a measure of germination rate) recorded. The results for seeds germinated at seven different temperatures are given in the table. The data were used to fit a simple linear regression model, with y = change in free energy and x = temperature.

CHANGE IN FREE ENERGY, kJ/mol	TEMPERATURE, °K
7	295
6.2	297.5
9	291
9.5	289
8.5	301
7.8	293
11.2	286.5

Source: Hageseth, G. T., and Cody, A. L. "Energy-level model for isothermal seed germination." *Journal of Experimental Botany*, Vol. 44, No. 258, Jan. 1993, p. 123 (Figure 9).

a. Plot the points in a scattergram.
b. Find the least squares prediction equation.
c. Plot the least squares line, part **b**, on the scattergram of part **a**.
d. Conduct a test of model adequacy. Use $\alpha = .01$.
e. Use the plot, part **c**, to locate any unusual data points (outliers).
f. Eliminate the outlier, part **e**, from the data set, and repeat parts **a–d**.

3.7 The Coefficient of Correlation

The claim is often made that the crime rate and the unemployment rate are "highly correlated." Another popular belief is that IQ and academic performance are "correlated." Some people even believe that the Dow Jones Industrial Average and the lengths of fashionable skirts are "correlated." Thus, the term *correlation* implies a relationship or "association" between two variables.

The **Pearson product moment correlation coefficient** r, defined in the next box, provides a quantitative measure of the strength of the linear relationship between x and y, just as does the least squares slope $\hat{\beta}_1$. However, unlike the slope, the correlation coefficient r is *scaleless*. The value of r is always between -1 and $+1$, regardless of the units of measurement used for the variables x and y.

Definition 3.2

The **Pearson product moment coefficient of correlation** r is a measure of the strength of the *linear* relationship between two variables x and y. It is computed (for a sample of n measurements on x and y) as follows:

$$r = \frac{SS_{xy}}{\sqrt{SS_{xx}SS_{yy}}}$$

Note that r is computed using the same quantities used in fitting the least squares line. Since both r and $\hat{\beta}_1$ provide information about the utility of the model, it is not surprising that there is a similarity in their computational formulas. In particular, note that SS_{xy} appears in the numerators of both expressions and, since both denominators are always positive, r and $\hat{\beta}_1$ will always be of the same sign (either both positive or both negative). A value of r near or equal to 0 implies little or no linear relationship between y and x. In contrast, the closer r is to 1 or -1, the stronger the linear relationship between y and x. And, if $r = 1$ or $r = -1$, all the points fall exactly on the least squares line. Positive values of r imply that y increases as x increases; negative values imply that y decreases as x increases. Each of these situations is portrayed in Figure 3.8 on page 128.

FIGURE 3.8
Values of r and their implications

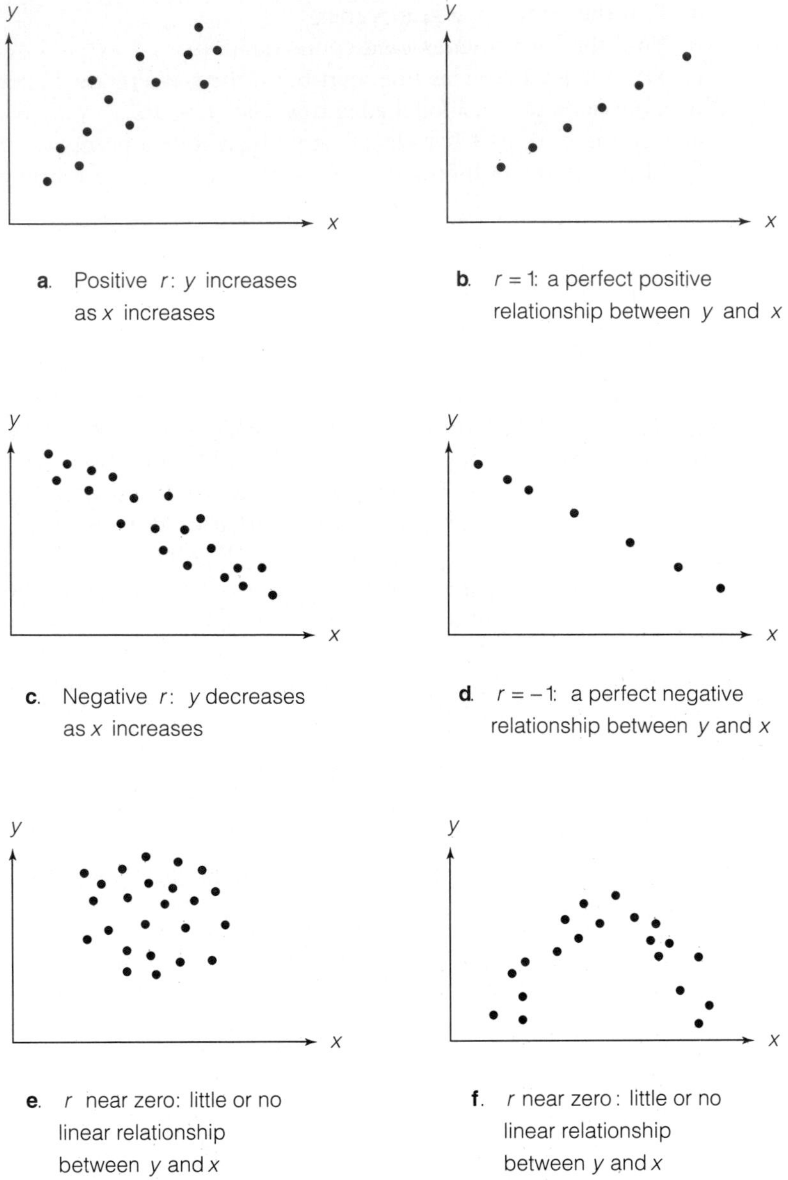

y
x
a. Positive r: y increases as x increases
b. r = 1: a perfect positive relationship between y and x
c. Negative r: y decreases as x increases
d. r = −1: a perfect negative relationship between y and x
e. r near zero: little or no linear relationship between y and x
f. r near zero: little or no linear relationship between y and x

EXAMPLE 3.1

Legalized gambling is available on several riverboat casinos operated by a city in Mississippi. The mayor of the city wants to know the correlation between the number of casino employees and the yearly crime rate. The records for the past 10 years are examined, and the results listed in Table 3.5 are obtained. Calculate the coefficient of correlation r for the data.

TABLE 3.5 **Data and Preliminary Calculations, Example 3.1**

YEAR	NUMBER OF CASINO EMPLOYEES x, thousands	CRIME RATE y, number of crimes per 1,000 population
1986	15	1.35
1987	18	1.63
1988	24	2.33
1989	22	2.41
1990	25	2.63
1991	29	2.93
1992	30	3.41
1993	32	3.26
1994	35	3.63
1995	38	4.15
	$\Sigma x = 268$	$\Sigma y = 27.73$
	$\bar{x} = 26.8$	$\bar{y} = 2.773$
	$\Sigma x^2 = 7{,}668$	$\Sigma y^2 = 83.8733$
	$\Sigma xy = 800.62$	

Solution

We need to calculate SS_{xy}, SS_{xx}, and SS_{yy} as follows:

$$SS_{xy} = \sum x_i y_i - n\bar{x}\bar{y} = 800.62 - 10(26.8)(2.773) = 57.456$$

$$SS_{xx} = \sum x_i^2 - n\bar{x}^2 = 7{,}668 - 10(26.8)^2 = 485.6$$

$$SS_{yy} = \sum y_i^2 - n\bar{y}^2 = 83.8733 - 10(2.773)^2 = 6.97801$$

Then, the coefficient of correlation is

$$r = \frac{SS_{xy}}{\sqrt{SS_{xx}SS_{yy}}} = \frac{57.456}{\sqrt{(485.6)(6.97801)}} = \frac{57.456}{58.211} = .99$$

Thus, the size of the casino work force and crime rate in this city are very highly correlated—at least over the past 10 years. The implication is that a strong positive linear relationship exists between these variables (see Figure 3.9).

FIGURE 3.9
Scattergram for Example 3.1

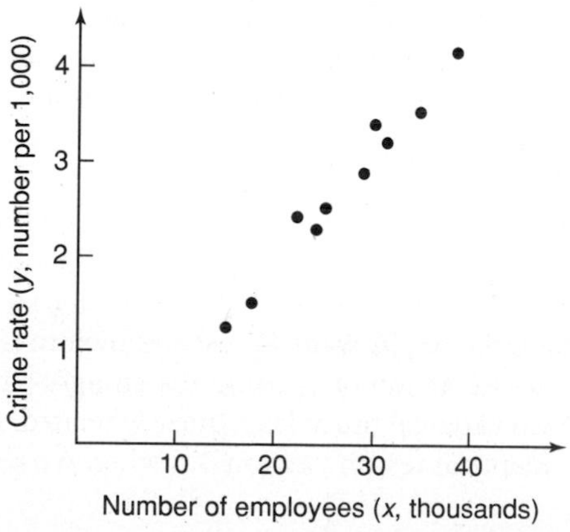

We must be careful, however, not to jump to any unwarranted conclusions. For instance, the mayor may be tempted to conclude that hiring more casino workers next year will lead to a higher crime rate. The implication of such a conclusion is that there is a *causal* relationship between the two variables. However, **high correlation does not imply causality**. The fact is, many things have probably contributed both to the increase in the casino work force and to the increase in crime rate. The city's tourist trade has undoubtedly grown since legalizing riverboat casinos, and it is likely that the casinos have expanded both in terms of services offered and in number. We must be careful not to infer a causal relationship on the basis of high sample correlation alone. The only safe conclusion when a high correlation is observed in the sample data is that a linear trend may exist between x and y. Another variable, such as the increase in tourism, may be the underlying cause of the high correlation between x and y.

Warning

High correlation does *not* imply causality. If a large positive or negative value of the sample correlation coefficient r is observed, it is incorrect to conclude that a change in x causes a change in y. The only valid conclusion is that *a linear trend may exist* between x and y.

Keep in mind that the correlation coefficient r measures the correlation between x values and y values in the sample, and that a similar linear coefficient of correlation exists for the population from which the data points were selected. The **population correlation coefficient** is denoted by the symbol ρ (rho). As you might expect, ρ is estimated by the corresponding sample statistic, r. Or, rather than estimating ρ, we might want to test

$$H_0: \quad \rho = 0$$

against

$$H_a: \quad \rho \neq 0$$

That is, we might want to test the hypothesis that x contributes no information for the prediction of y, using the straight-line model against the alternative that the two variables are at least linearly related. However, we have already performed this identical test in Section 3.6 when we tested H_0: $\beta_1 = 0$ against H_a: $\beta_1 \neq 0$.

It can be shown (proof omitted) that $r = \hat{\beta}_1\sqrt{\text{SS}_{xx}/\text{SS}_{yy}}$. Thus, $\hat{\beta}_1 = 0$ implies $r = 0$, and vice versa. Consequently, the null hypothesis H_0: $\rho = 0$ is equivalent to the hypothesis H_0: $\beta_1 = 0$. When we tested the null hypothesis H_0: $\beta_1 = 0$ in connection with the previous example, the data led to a rejection of the null hypothesis for $\alpha = .05$. This implies that the null hypothesis of a zero linear correlation between the two variables, crime rate and number of employees, can also be rejected at $\alpha = .05$. The only real difference between the least squares slope $\hat{\beta}_1$ and the coefficient of correlation r is the measurement scale. Therefore, the information they provide about the utility of the least squares model is to some extent redundant. Furthermore, the slope $\hat{\beta}_1$ gives us additional information on the amount of increase (or decrease) in y for every 1-unit increase in x. For this reason, we recommend using the slope to make inferences about the existence of a positive or negative linear relationship between two variables.

For those who prefer to test for a linear relationship between two variables using the coefficient of correlation r, we outline the procedure in the following box.

Test of Hypothesis for Linear Correlation

ONE-TAILED TEST	TWO-TAILED TEST
H_0: $\rho = 0$	H_0: $\rho = 0$
H_a: $\rho > 0$ (or H_a: $\rho < 0$)	H_a: $\rho \neq 0$

Test statistic: $t = \dfrac{r\sqrt{n-2}}{\sqrt{1-r^2}}$

Rejection region: $t > t_\alpha$ (or $t < -t_\alpha$)	*Rejection region:* $\lvert t \rvert > t_{\alpha/2}$

where the distribution of t depends on $(n - 2)$ df.

Assumption: The sample of (x, y) values is randomly selected from a normal population.

The next example illustrates how the correlation coefficient r may be a misleading measure of the strength of the association between x and y in situations where the true relationship is nonlinear.

EXAMPLE 3.2

Underinflated or overinflated tires can increase tire wear and decrease gas mileage. A manufacturer of a new tire tested the tire for wear at different pressures with the results shown in Table 3.6. Calculate the coefficient of correlation r for the data. Interpret the result.

TABLE 3.6 **Data for Example 3.2**

PRESSURE x, pounds per sq. inch	MILEAGE y, thousands
30	29.5
30	30.2
31	32.1
31	34.5
32	36.3
32	35.0
33	38.2
33	37.6
34	37.7
34	36.1
35	33.6
35	34.2
36	26.8
36	27.4

Solution

Rather than perform the calculations by hand, we use a computer to find the value of r. A SAS printout of the correlation analysis is shown in Figure 3.10. The value of r, shaded on the printout, is $r = -.11371$. This relatively small value for r describes a weak linear relationship between pressure (x) and mileage (y). The manufacturer, however, would be remiss in concluding that tire pressure has little or no impact on wear of the tire. On the contrary, the relationship between pressure and wear is fairly strong, as the scattergram in Figure 3.11 illustrates. Note that the relationship is not linear, but curvilinear; the underinflated tires (low pressure values) and overinflated tires (high pressure values) *both* lead to low mileage.

FIGURE 3.10
SAS printout of correlation analysis of data in Table 3.6

```
Pearson Correlation Coefficients / Prob > |R| under Ho: Rho=0 / N = 14

                    X               Y

   X          1.00000        -0.11371
                  0.0          0.6987

   Y         -0.11371         1.00000
               0.6987             0.0
```

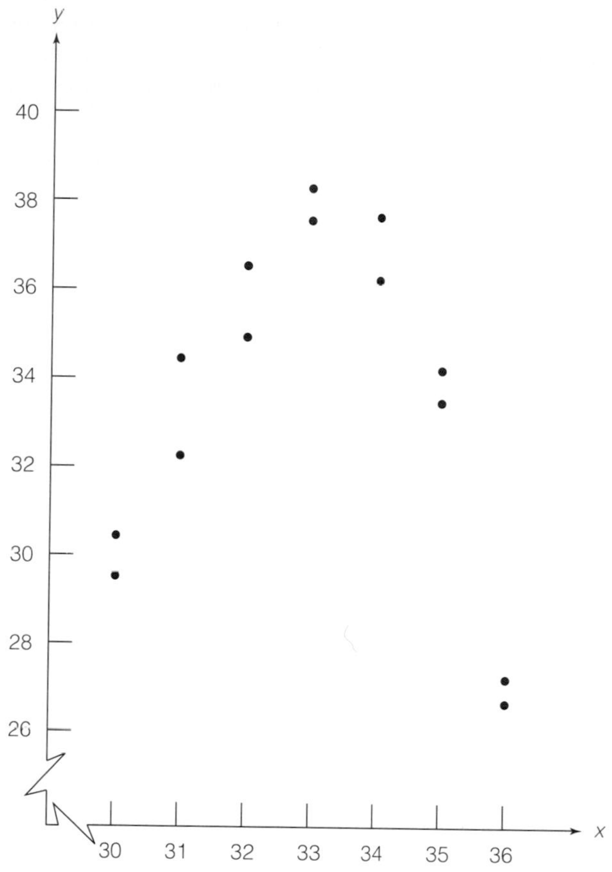

FIGURE 3.11
Scattergram of data in Table 3.6

A statistic related to the coefficient of correlation is defined and discussed in the next section.

3.8 The Coefficient of Determination

Another way to measure the contribution of x in predicting y is to consider how much the errors of prediction of y were reduced by using the information provided by x.

To illustrate, suppose a sample of data produces the scattergram shown in Figure 3.12a (page 134). If we assume that x contributes no information for the prediction of y, the best prediction for a value of y is the sample mean $\bar{y}$, which graphs as the horizontal line shown in Figure 3.12b. The vertical line segments in Figure 3.12b are the deviations of the points about the mean $\bar{y}$. Note that the sum of squares of deviations for the model $\hat{y} = \bar{y}$ is

$$SS_{yy} = \sum (y_i - \bar{y})^2$$

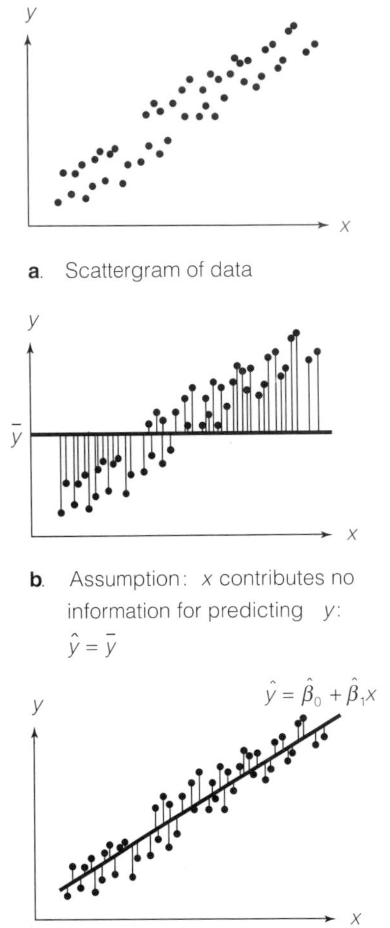

a. Scattergram of data

b. Assumption: x contributes no information for predicting y: $\hat{y} = \bar{y}$

c. Assumption: x contributes information for predicting y; $\hat{y} = \hat{\beta}_0 + \hat{\beta}_1 x$

FIGURE 3.12
A comparison of the sum of squares of deviations for two models

Now suppose you fit a least squares line to the same set of data and locate the deviations of the points about the line as shown in Figure 3.12c. Compare the deviations about the prediction lines in Figures 3.12b and 3.12c. You can see that:

1. If x contributes little or no information for the prediction of y, the sums of squares of deviations for the two lines

$$SS_{yy} = \sum (y_i - \bar{y})^2 \quad \text{and} \quad SSE = \sum (y_i - \hat{y}_i)^2$$

will be nearly equal.

2. If x does contribute information for the prediction of y, then SSE will be smaller than SS_{yy}. In fact, if all the points fall on the least squares line, then $SSE = 0$.

A convenient way of measuring how well the least squares equation $\hat{y} = \hat{\beta}_0 + \hat{\beta}_1 x$ performs as a predictor of y is to compute the reduction in the sum of squares of deviations that can be attributed to x, expressed as a proportion of SS_{yy}. This quantity, called the **coefficient of determination**, is

$$\frac{SS_{yy} - SSE}{SS_{yy}}$$

In simple linear regression, it can be shown that this quantity is equal to the square of the simple linear coefficient of correlation r.

Definition 3.3

The **coefficient of determination** is

$$r^2 = \frac{SS_{yy} - SSE}{SS_{yy}} = 1 - \frac{SSE}{SS_{yy}}$$

It represents the proportion of the sum of squares of deviations of the y values about their mean that can be attributed to a linear relationship between y and x. (In simple linear regression, it may also be computed as the square of the coefficient of correlation r.)

Note that r^2 is always between 0 and 1, because r is between -1 and $+1$. Thus, an r^2 of .60 means that the sum of squares of deviations of the y values about their predicted values has been reduced 60% by the use of $\hat{y}$, instead of $\bar{y}$, to predict y.

EXAMPLE 3.3

Calculate the coefficient of determination for the advertising–sales example. The data are repeated in Table 3.7.

TABLE 3.7

ADVERTISING EXPENDITURE x, hundreds of dollars	SALES REVENUE y, thousands of dollars
1	1
2	1
3	2
4	2
5	4

Solution

We first calculate

$$SS_{yy} = \sum y_i^2 - n\bar{y}^2 = 26 - 5(2)^2$$
$$= 26 - 20 = 6$$

From previous calculations,

$$SSE = \sum (y_i - \hat{y}_i)^2 = 1.10$$

Then, the coefficient of determination is given by

$$r^2 = \frac{SS_{yy} - SSE}{SS_{yy}} = \frac{6.0 - 1.1}{6.0} = \frac{4.9}{6.0}$$
$$= .82$$

By using the advertising expenditure x to predict y with the least squares line

$$\hat{y} = -.1 + .7x$$

the total sum of squares of deviations of the five sample y values about their predicted values has been reduced 82%. That is, 82% of the sample variation in monthly sales revenue can be "explained" by the least squares line.

Practical Interpretation of the Coefficient of Determination, r^2

About $100(r^2)$% of the sample variation in y (measured by the total sum of squares of deviations of the sample y values about their mean $\bar{y}$) can be explained by (or attributed to) using x to predict y in the straight-line model.

In situations where a straight-line regression model is found to be a statistically adequate predictor of y, the value of r^2 can help guide the regression analyst in the search for better, more useful models. For example, design engineers used a simple linear model to relate cost of mechanical work in construction (heating, ventilating, and plumbing) to floor area. Based on the data associated with 26 factory and warehouse buildings, the least squares prediction equation given in Figure 3.13 was found. It was concluded that floor area and mechanical cost are linearly related, since the t statistic (for testing H_0: $\beta_1 = 0$) was found to equal 3.61, which is significant with an α as small as .002.* Thus, floor area should be useful when predicting the mechanical cost of a factory or warehouse. However, the value of the coefficient of determination r^2 was found to be .35. This tells us that only 35% of the variation among mechanical costs is accounted for by the differences in floor areas. This relatively small r^2 value led the engineers to include other independent variables (e.g., volume, amount of glass) in the model to account for a significant portion of the remaining 65% of the variation in mechanical cost not explained by floor area. In the next chapter, we discuss this important aspect of relating a response to more than one independent variable.

FIGURE 3.13
Simple linear model relating cost to floor area

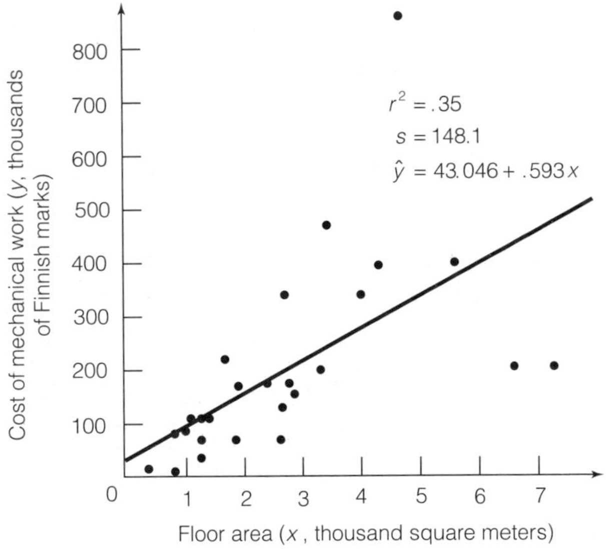

EXERCISES

3.30 Find the correlation coefficient and the coefficient of determination for the sample data of each of the following exercises. Interpret your results.
a. Exercise 3.8 b. Exercise 3.9

3.31 Do you believe that the grade point average of a college student is correlated with the student's intelligence quotient (IQ)? If so, will the correlation be positive or negative? Explain.

3.32 Research by law enforcement agencies has shown that the crime rate is correlated with the U.S. population. Would you expect the correlation to be positive or negative? Explain.

*Crandall, J. S., and Cedercreutz, M. "Preliminary cost estimates for mechanical work." *Building Systems Design*, Oct.–Nov. 1976, Vol. 73, pp. 35–51.

3.33 Give an example of two variables in your field of study that are

a. positively correlated

b. negatively correlated

3.34 Passive exposure to environmental tobacco smoke has been associated with growth suppression and an increased frequency of respiratory tract infections in normal children. Is this association more pronounced in children with cystic fibrosis? To answer this question, 43 children (18 girls and 25 boys) attending a 2-week summer camp for cystic fibrosis patients were studied (*New England Journal of Medicine*, Sept. 20, 1990). Among several variables measured were the child's weight percentile (y) and the number of cigarettes smoked per day in the child's home (x).

a. For the 18 girls, the coefficient of correlation between y and x was reported as $r = -.50$. Interpret this result.

b. Refer to part a. The p-value for testing H_0: $\rho = 0$ against H_a: $\rho \neq 0$ was reported as $p = .03$. Interpret this result.

c. For the 25 boys, the coefficient of correlation between y and x was reported as $r = -.12$. Interpret this result.

d. Refer to part c. The p-value for testing H_0: $\rho = 0$ against H_a: $\rho \neq 0$ was reported as $p = .57$. Interpret this result.

3.35 Fitts' Law is a robust and highly adopted model of human movement. According to Fitts' Law, the time T required to move and select a target of width W that lies at a distance (or amplitude) A is

$$T = a + b \log_2(2A/W)$$

where a and b are constants estimated using simple linear regression. The quantity $\log_2(2A/W)$ is termed the Index of Difficulty (ID) and represents the independent variable (measured in "bits") in the model. Research reported in the *Special Interest Group on Computer-Human Interaction Bulletin* (July 1993) used Fitts' Law to model the time (in milliseconds) required to perform a certain task on a computer. Based on data collected for $n = 160$ trials (using different values of A and W), the following least squares prediction equation was obtained:

$$\hat{T} = 175.4 + 133.2(\text{ID})$$

a. Interpret the estimates, 175.4 and 133.2.

b. The coefficient of correlation for the analysis is $r = .951$. Interpret this value.

c. Conduct a test to determine whether the model using Fitts' Law is statistically adequate for predicting performance time. Use $\alpha = .05$.

d. Calculate the coefficient of determination, r^2. Interpret the result.

3.36 The *Journal of Organizational Behavior* (1992) published a study of workload and psychological strain in the dental profession. One measure of psychological strain in dentists was job satisfaction, measured on a 20-point scale. Job satisfaction (y) was regressed against a quantitative independent variable that measured the congruence (x) between a dentist's preferred work hours and typical work hours. The simple linear regression analysis on data collected for $n = 318$ self-employed dentists resulted in a coefficient of correlation of $r = .01$. Make a statement about a possible linear relationship between job satisfaction and workload congruence for self-employed dentists.

3.37 The Environmental Protection Agency (EPA) evaluates state pollution control policies through the use of an emissions-to-job (E/J) ratio. The E/J ratio is obtained by dividing the amount (in pounds) of annual toxic emissions of an industry in a state by the number of jobs the state provides in that industry. *Environmental Technology* (Oct. 1993) investigated the relationship between the E/J ratio and spending on pollution control in the chemical industry. Data collected for $n = 19$ large chemical-producing states were used to conduct a simple linear regression analysis, where x = a state's pollution abatement capital expenditures (PACE), in millions of dollars, and y = a state's chemical industry E/J ratio, in pounds per job. [*Note:* Positive x represents overspending on pollution control, whereas negative x represents underspending.] The analysis yielded a least squares line with a negative slope and $r^2 = .587$.

a. Interpret the value of r^2.
b. Calculate the correlation coefficient r and interpret the result.
c. In theory, underspending on pollution control will result in higher emissions and fewer jobs (i.e., a higher E/J ratio). Test the theory (at $\alpha = .01$) using the results of the straight-line regression.

3.38 One controversial explanation for the consistently high homicide rates in the South is that the South constitutes a "regional culture of violence" and that as a result, people socialized in the South become inculcated with this violent tradition. If the theory is true, then Southerners can be expected to carry this "culture of violence" with them when they migrate so that the area in which they settle may exhibit a relatively higher homicide rate. An attempt to provide empirical support for the theory was reported in *Criminology* (Vol. 24, 1986). For each of the 67 Florida counties, the homicide rate y (number of homicides per 10,000 population) and percentage x of Southern-born residents were recorded. The correlation coefficient between the two variables was calculated as $r = .07$. Use this information to test the "culture of violence" theory. Test using $\alpha = .05$.

3.39 An investigation sought to determine whether there are certain collective behaviors, affective reactions, or performance outcomes associated with the maturity level of small groups (*Small Group Behavior*, May 1988). Fifty-eight undergraduate students enrolled in management information systems or communications courses at a medium-size university participated in the experiment. A 10-item questionnaire was used to measure the maturity level, y, of the students on a scale of 0–100, with more mature students receiving higher scores. One of several other variables measured was the number, x, of meetings held with their groups outside of regular class sessions. The correlation coefficient relating y to x was found to be $r = .46$. Is this sufficient evidence to indicate a positive correlation between group maturity and outside-of-class meetings? Test using $\alpha = .01$.

3.40 To examine potential gender differences in the industrial sales force, a sample of 244 males and a sample of 153 females were administered a questionnaire (*Journal of Personal Selling & Sales Management*, Summer 1990). All respondents were either sales managers or sales people at one of 16 industrial firms located in the southeastern United States. Two variables of interest to the researchers were level of organizational commitment (y) and total months experience in sales (x). For the 244 males in the study, the coefficient of correlation between x and y was $r_{\text{males}} = -.35$. For the 153 females in the study, the correlation coefficient was $r_{\text{females}} = -.06$.

a. Interpret the value of r_{males}.
b. Interpret the value of r_{females}.
c. For each gender, test the hypothesis of no linear correlation between organizational commitment (y) and experience in years (x).

3.41 The Mixed Arithmetic–Perceptual (MA-P) model is a componential model of graphic interaction that was developed based on analyses of humans interacting with graphical displays on the computer. The assumptions of the MA-P model were tested in a research article reported in the *SIG CHI Bulletin* (July 1993). Using simple linear regression, the researcher modeled response time y (in milliseconds) in a standard graph problem as a function of the number x of processing steps required to solve the problem. A summary of the regression results follows:

$$\hat{y} = 1{,}346 + 450x \qquad r^2 = .91$$

a. Interpret the value of $\hat{\beta}_1$.
b. Interpret the value of r^2.
c. Conduct a test of model adequacy at $\alpha = .01$. [*Hint:* Base the test on the value of r, the correlation coefficient.]

3.9 Using the Model for Estimation and Prediction

If we are satisfied that a useful model has been found to describe the relationship between sales revenue and advertising, we are ready to accomplish the original objectives for building the model: using it to estimate or to predict sales on the basis of advertising dollars spent.

The most common uses of a probabilistic model can be divided into two categories. The first is the use of the model for **estimating the mean value of y, $E(y)$, for a specific value of x.** For our example, we may want to estimate the mean sales revenue for *all* months during which \$400 ($x = 4$) is spent on advertising. The second use of the model entails **predicting a particular y value for a given x.** That is, if we decide to spend \$400 next month, we want to predict the firm's sales revenue for that month.

In the case of estimating a mean value of y, we are attempting to estimate the mean result of a very large number of experiments at the given x value. In the second case, we are trying to predict the outcome of a single experiment at the given x value. In which of these model uses do you expect to have more success; i.e., which value—the mean or individual value of y—can we estimate (or predict) with more accuracy?

Before answering this question, we first consider the problem of choosing an estimator (or predictor) of the mean (or individual) y value. We will use the least squares model

$$\hat{y} = \hat{\beta}_0 + \hat{\beta}_1 x$$

both to estimate the mean value of y and to predict a particular value of y for a given value of x. For our example, we found

$$\hat{y} = -.1 + .7x$$

so that the estimated mean value of sales revenue for all months when $x = 4$ (advertising = \$400) is

$$\hat{y} = -.1 + .7(4) = 2.7$$

or \$2,700 (the units of y are thousands of dollars). The identical value is used to predict the y value when $x = 4$. That is, both the estimated mean value and the predicted value of y equal $\hat{y} = 2.7$ when $x = 4$, as shown in Figure 3.14 on page 140.

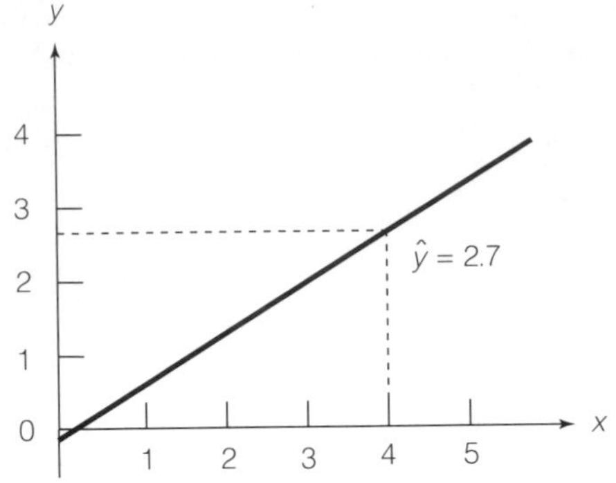

FIGURE 3.14
Estimated mean value and predicted individual value of sales revenue y for $x = 4$

The difference in these two model uses lies in the relative accuracy of the estimate and the prediction. These accuracies are best measured by the repeated sampling errors of the least squares line when it is used as an estimator and as a predictor, respectively. These errors are given in the box.

Sampling Errors for the Estimator of the Mean of y and the Predictor of an Individual y for $x = x_p$

1. The standard deviation of the sampling distribution of the estimator $\hat{y}$ of the mean value of y at a particular value of x, say, x_p, is

$$\sigma_{\hat{y}} = \sigma\sqrt{\frac{1}{n} + \frac{(x_p - \bar{x})^2}{SS_{xx}}}$$

where σ is the standard deviation of the random error ε.

2. The standard deviation of the prediction error for the predictor $\hat{y}$ of an individual y value for $x = x_p$ is

$$\sigma_{(y-\hat{y})} = \sigma\sqrt{1 + \frac{1}{n} + \frac{(x_p - \bar{x})^2}{SS_{xx}}}$$

where σ is the standard deviation of the random error ε.

The true value of σ will rarely be known. Thus, we estimate σ by s and calculate the estimation and prediction intervals as shown in the next two boxes. The procedure is demonstrated in Example 3.4.

EXAMPLE 3.4

Find a 95% confidence interval for mean monthly sales when the appliance store spends $400 on advertising.

A $100(1-\alpha)\%$ Confidence Interval for the Mean Value of y for $x = x_p$

$$\hat{y} \pm t_{\alpha/2}(\text{Estimated standard deviation of } \hat{y})$$

or

$$\hat{y} \pm t_{\alpha/2} s \sqrt{\frac{1}{n} + \frac{(x_p - \bar{x})^2}{SS_{xx}}}$$

where $t_{\alpha/2}$ is based on $(n-2)$ df

A $100(1-\alpha)\%$ Prediction Interval for an Individual y for $x = x_p$

$$\hat{y} \pm t_{\alpha/2}[\text{Estimated standard deviation of } (y - \hat{y})]$$

or

$$\hat{y} \pm t_{\alpha/2} s \sqrt{1 + \frac{1}{n} + \frac{(x_p - \bar{x})^2}{SS_{xx}}}$$

where $t_{\alpha/2}$ is based on $(n-2)$ df

Solution

For a \$400 advertising expenditure, $x_p = 4$ and, since $n = 5$, df $= n - 2 = 3$. Then the confidence interval for the mean value of y is

$$\hat{y} \pm t_{\alpha/2} s \sqrt{\frac{1}{n} + \frac{(x_p - \bar{x})^2}{SS_{xx}}}$$

or

$$\hat{y} \pm t_{.025} s \sqrt{\frac{1}{5} + \frac{(4 - \bar{x})^2}{SS_{xx}}}$$

Recall that $\hat{y} = 2.7$, $s = .61$, $\bar{x} = 3$, and $SS_{xx} = 10$. From Table 2 of Appendix C, $t_{.025} = 3.182$. Thus, we have

$$2.7 \pm (3.182)(.61)\sqrt{\frac{1}{5} + \frac{(4-3)^2}{10}} = 2.7 \pm (3.182)(.61)(.55)$$
$$= 2.7 \pm 1.1$$

We estimate that the interval from \$1,600 to \$3,800 encloses the mean sales revenue when the store spends \$400 a month on advertising. Note that we used a small amount of data for purposes of illustration in fitting the least squares line and that the width of the interval could be decreased by using a larger number of data points.

EXAMPLE 3.5

Predict the monthly sales for next month if a \$400 expenditure is to be made on advertising. Use a 95% prediction interval.

Solution

To predict the sales for a particular month for which $x_p = 4$, we calculate the 95% prediction interval as

$$\hat{y} \pm t_{\alpha/2} s \sqrt{1 + \frac{1}{n} + \frac{(x_p - \bar{x})^2}{SS_{xx}}} = 2.7 \pm (3.182)(.61)\sqrt{1 + \frac{1}{5} + \frac{(4-3)^2}{10}}$$
$$= 2.7 \pm (3.182)(.61)(1.14) = 2.7 \pm 2.2$$

Therefore, we predict that the sales next month will fall in the interval from \$500 to \$4,900. As in the case of the confidence interval for the mean value of y, the prediction interval for y is quite large. This is because we have chosen a simple example (only five data points) to fit the least squares line. The width of the prediction interval could be reduced by using a larger number of data points.

A comparison of the confidence limits for the mean value of y and the prediction interval for some future value of y for various advertising expenditure (x) values is illustrated in Figure 3.15. It is important to note that the prediction interval for an individual value of y will always be wider than the confidence interval for a mean value of y. You can see this by examining the formulas for the two intervals, and you can see it in Figure 3.15.

FIGURE 3.15
Comparison of widths of 95% confidence and prediction intervals

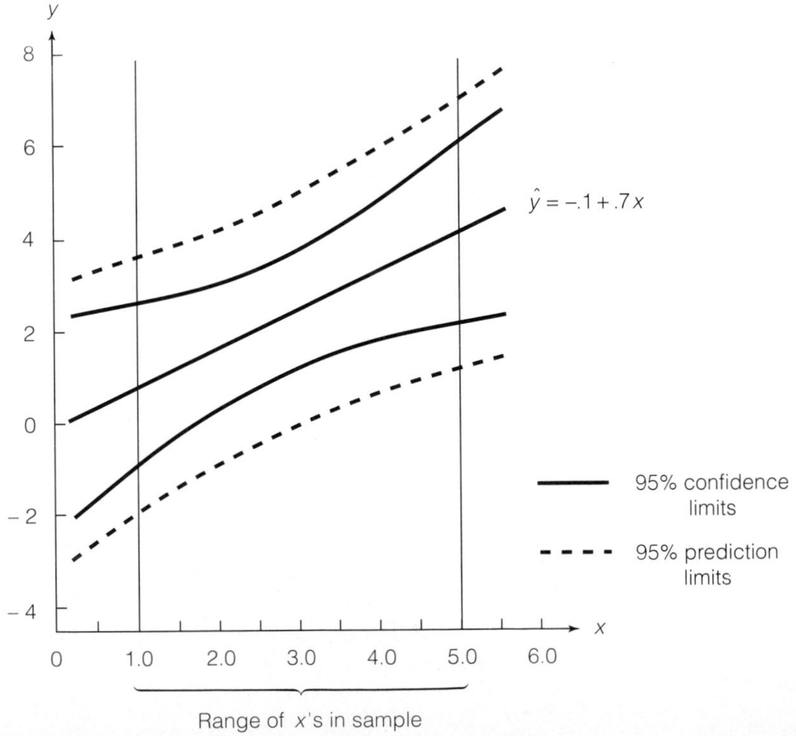

The error in estimating the mean value of y, $E(y)$, for a given value of x, say, x_p, is the distance between the least squares line and the true line of means, $E(y) = \beta_0 + \beta_1 x$. This error, $[\hat{y} - E(y)]$, is shown in Figure 3.16. In contrast, the error $(y_p - \hat{y})$ in predicting some future value of y is the sum of two errors—the error of estimating the mean of y, $E(y)$, shown in Figure 3.16, plus the random error that is a component of the value of y to be predicted (see Figure 3.17). Consequently, the error of predicting a particular value of y will always be larger than the error of estimating the mean value of y for a particular value of x. Note from their formulas that both the error of estimation and the error of prediction take their smallest values when $x_p = \bar{x}$. The farther x lies from $\bar{x}$, the larger will be the errors of estimation and prediction (see Figure 3.15). You can see why this is true by noting the deviations for different values of x between the line of means $E(y) = \beta_0 + \beta_1 x$ and the predicted line $\hat{y} = \hat{\beta}_0 + \hat{\beta}_1 x$ shown in Figure 3.17. The deviation is larger at the extremities of the interval where the largest and smallest values of x in the data set occur. In fact, when x is selected far enough away from $\bar{x}$ so that it falls outside the range of the sample data, it is dangerous to make any inferences about $E(y)$, or y, as the warning box on page 144 explains.

FIGURE 3.16
Error of estimating the mean value of y for a given value of x

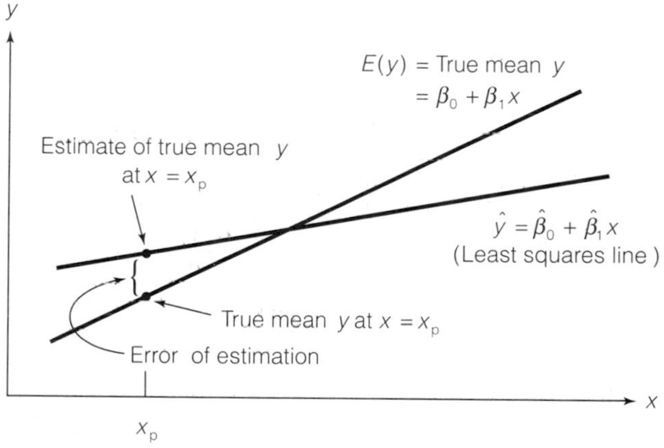

FIGURE 3.17
Error of predicting a future value of y for a given value of x

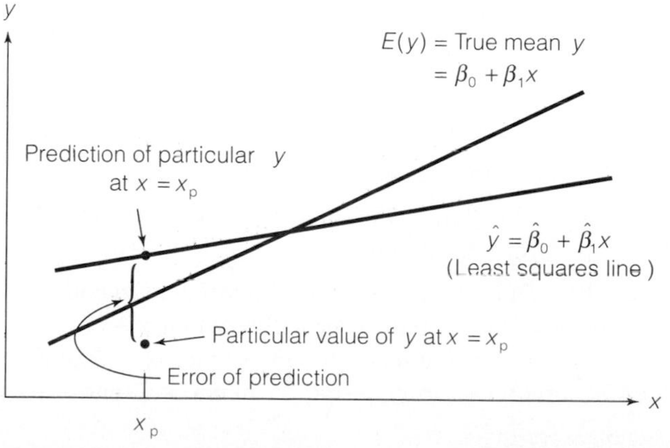

> **Warning**
>
> Using the least squares prediction equation to estimate the mean value of y or to predict a particular value of y for values of x that fall *outside the range* of the values of x contained in your sample data may lead to errors of estimation or prediction that are much larger than expected. Although the least squares model may provide a very good fit to the data over the range of x values contained in the sample, it could give a poor representation of the true model for values of x outside this region.

EXERCISES

3.42 A simple linear regression analysis for $n = 20$ data points produced the following results:

$$\hat{y} = 2.1 + 3.4x \qquad SS_{xx} = 4.77$$

$$\bar{x} = 2.5 \qquad SS_{yy} = 59.21$$

$$\bar{y} = 10.6 \qquad SS_{xy} = 16.22$$

a. Find SSE and s^2.
b. Find a 95% confidence interval for $E(y)$ when $x = 2.5$. Interpret this interval.
c. Find a 95% confidence interval for $E(y)$ when $x = 2.0$. Interpret this interval.
d. Find a 95% confidence interval for $E(y)$ when $x = 3.0$. Interpret this interval.
e. Examine the widths of the confidence intervals obtained in parts **b**, **c**, and **d**. What happens to the width of the confidence interval for $E(y)$ as the value of x moves away from the value of $\bar{x}$?
f. Find a 95% prediction interval for a value of y to be observed in the future when $x = 3.0$. Interpret its value.

3.43 Refer to Exercise 3.9. Consider an automated warehouse that operates $x = 10$ vehicles.
a. Find a 90% prediction interval for the congestion time y at this warehouse. Interpret the result.
b. Find a 90% confidence interval for the mean congestion time, $E(y)$, at all warehouses with $x = 10$ vehicles. Interpret the result.
c. Compare and comment on the sizes of the intervals in parts **a** and **b**.
d. Could you reduce the size of either or both intervals by increasing your sample size? Explain.

3.44 Refer to Exercise 3.11. Find a 95% prediction interval for drill time y when drilling begins at a depth of 300 feet. Interpret your result.

3.45 In Exercise 3.12, you found the least squares prediction equation relating average peak EEG frequency y to age x, and used it to predict peak EEG when $x = 7$.
a. Find a 95% confidence interval for $E(y)$ when $x = 7$ and interpret it.
b. Find a 95% prediction interval for y when $x = 7$ and interpret it.

3.46 a. Explain why for a particular x value, the prediction interval for an individual y value will always be wider than the confidence interval for a mean value of y.

b. Explain why the confidence interval for the mean value of y for a particular x value, say, x_p, gets wider the farther x_p is from $\bar{x}$. What are the implications of this phenomenon for estimation and prediction?

3.47 Refer to Exercise 3.17. Find a 95% prediction interval for the refusal rate of a Florida county with a per capita income of $8,000. Why is the interval so wide?

3.48 In forestry, the diameter of a tree at breast height (which is fairly easy to measure) is used to predict the height of the tree (a difficult measurement to obtain). Silviculturists working in British Columbia's boreal forest conducted a series of spacing trials to predict the heights of several species of trees. The data in the accompanying table are the breast height diameters (in centimeters) and heights (in meters) for a sample of 36 white spruce trees.

BREAST HEIGHT DIAMETER x, cm	HEIGHT y, m	BREAST HEIGHT DIAMETER x, cm	HEIGHT y, m
18.9	20.0	16.6	18.8
15.5	16.8	15.5	16.9
19.4	20.2	13.7	16.3
20.0	20.0	27.5	21.4
29.8	20.2	20.3	19.2
19.8	18.0	22.9	19.8
20.3	17.8	14.1	18.5
20.0	19.2	10.1	12.1
22.0	22.3	5.8	8.0
23.6	18.9	20.7	17.4
14.8	13.3	17.8	18.4
22.7	20.6	11.4	17.3
18.5	19.0	14.4	16.6
21.5	19.2	13.4	12.9
14.8	16.1	17.8	17.5
17.7	19.9	20.7	19.4
21.0	20.4	13.3	15.5
15.9	17.6	22.9	19.2

Source: Scholz, H., Northern Lights College, British Columbia.

a. Construct a scattergram for the data.

b. Assuming the relationship between the variables is best described by a straight line, use the method of least squares to estimate the y-intercept and slope of the line.

c. Plot the least squares line on your scattergram.

d. Do the data provide sufficient evidence to indicate that the breast height diameter x contributes information for the prediction of tree height y? Test using $\alpha = .05$.

e. Use your least squares line to find a 90% confidence interval for the average height of white spruce trees with a breast height diameter of 20 cm. Interpret the interval.

3.49 Refer to Exercise 3.19. Find a 95% confidence interval for the mean passivation potential of crystallized alloy when annealing time is 30 minutes.

3.50 Refer to Exercise 3.29. Find a 90% confidence interval for the mean change in free energy for seeds germinated at a temperature of 290°K.

3.10 Simple Linear Regression: An Example Using the Computer

In the previous sections, we have presented the basic elements necessary to fit and use a straight-line regression model. In this section, we will assemble these elements by applying them in an example where we use the computer to perform the calculations.

Suppose a fire safety inspector wants to relate the amount of fire damage in major residential fires to the distance between the residence and the nearest fire station. The study is to be conducted in a large suburb of a major city; a sample of 15 recent fires in this suburb is selected.

STEP 1 First, we hypothesize a model to relate fire damage y to the distance x from the nearest fire station. We will hypothesize a straight-line probabilistic model:

$$y = \beta_0 + \beta_1 x + \varepsilon$$

STEP 2 Second, we collect the (x, y) values for each of the $n = 15$ experimental units (residential fires) in the sample. The amount of damage y and the distance x between the fire and the nearest fire station are recorded for each fire, as listed in Table 3.8.

TABLE 3.8 **Fire Damage Data**

DISTANCE FROM FIRE STATION x, miles	FIRE DAMAGE y, thousands of dollars
3.4	26.2
1.8	17.8
4.6	31.3
2.3	23.1
3.1	27.5
5.5	36.0
.7	14.1
3.0	22.3
2.6	19.6
4.3	31.3
2.1	24.0
1.1	17.3
6.1	43.2
4.8	36.4
3.8	26.1

STEP 3 Next, we enter the data into a computer and use a statistical software package to estimate the unknown parameters in the deterministic component of the hypothesized model. The SAS printout for the simple linear regression analysis is shown in Figure 3.18.

The least squares estimates of β_0 and β_1 are found (shaded) under the column labeled **Parameter Estimate** (in the middle portion of the printout) in the rows labeled **INTERCEP** and **X**, respectively. Note that the estimate of the slope is

$$\hat{\beta}_1 = 4.919331$$

FIGURE 3.18
SAS printout for the fire damage linear regression

Dependent Variable: Y

Analysis of Variance

Source	DF	Sum of Squares	Mean Square	F Value	Prob>F
Model	1	841.76636	841.76636	156.886	0.0001
Error	13	69.75098	5.36546		
C Total	14	911.51733			

Root MSE	2.31635	R-square	0.9235
Dep Mean	26.41333	Adj R-sq	0.9176
C.V.	8.76961		

Parameter Estimates

Variable	DF	Parameter Estimate	Standard Error	T for H0: Parameter=0	Prob > |T|
INTERCEP	1	10.277929	1.42027781	7.237	0.0001
X	1	4.919331	0.39274775	12.525	0.0001

Obs	X	Dep Var Y	Predict Value	Std Err Predict	Lower95% Predict	Upper95% Predict	Residual
1	3.4	26.2000	27.0037	0.600	21.8344	32.1729	-0.8037
2	1.8	17.8000	19.1327	0.834	13.8141	24.4514	-1.3327
3	4.6	31.3000	32.9068	0.791	27.6186	38.1951	-1.6068
4	2.3	23.1000	21.5924	0.711	16.3577	26.8271	1.5076
5	3.1	27.5000	25.5279	0.602	20.3573	30.6984	1.9721
6	5.5	36.0000	37.3342	1.057	31.8334	42.8351	-1.3342
7	0.7	14.1000	13.7215	1.177	8.1087	19.3342	0.3785
8	3	22.3000	25.0359	0.608	19.8622	30.2097	-2.7359
9	2.6	19.6000	23.0682	0.655	17.8678	28.2686	-3.4682
10	4.3	31.3000	31.4311	0.720	26.1908	36.6713	-0.1311
11	2.1	24.0000	20.6085	0.757	15.3442	25.8729	3.3915
12	1.1	17.3000	15.6892	1.044	10.1999	21.1785	1.6108
13	6.1	43.2000	40.2858	1.259	34.5906	45.9811	2.9142
14	4.8	36.4000	33.8907	0.845	28.5640	39.2175	2.5093
15	3.8	26.1000	28.9714	0.632	23.7843	34.1585	-2.8714
16	3.5	.	27.4956	0.604	22.3239	32.6672	.

Sum of Residuals	-4.44089E-14
Sum of Squared Residuals	69.7510
Predicted Resid SS (Press)	93.2117

and the estimate of the y-intercept is

$$\hat{\beta}_0 = 10.277929$$

Thus, the least squares equation is

$$\hat{y} = 10.278 + 4.919x$$

This prediction equation is graphed in Figure 3.19 (page 148), along with a plot of the data points.

STEP 4 Now, we specify the probability distribution of the random error component ε. The assumptions about the distribution will be identical to those listed in Section 3.4. Although we know that these assumptions are not completely satisfied (they rarely are for any practical problem), we are willing to assume they are approximately satisfied for this example. The estimate of the variance σ^2 of ε is given (shaded) in the top portion of the printout in the column labeled **Mean Square** and the row labeled **Error**. This value is

$$s^2 = \text{MSE} = 5.36546$$

The estimated standard deviation of ε, given next to the heading **Root MSE**, is

$$s = \sqrt{5.36546} = 2.31635$$

The value of s implies that most of the observed fire damage (y) values will fall within approximately $2s = 4.64$ thousand dollars of their respective predicted values.

FIGURE 3.19
Least squares model for the fire damage data

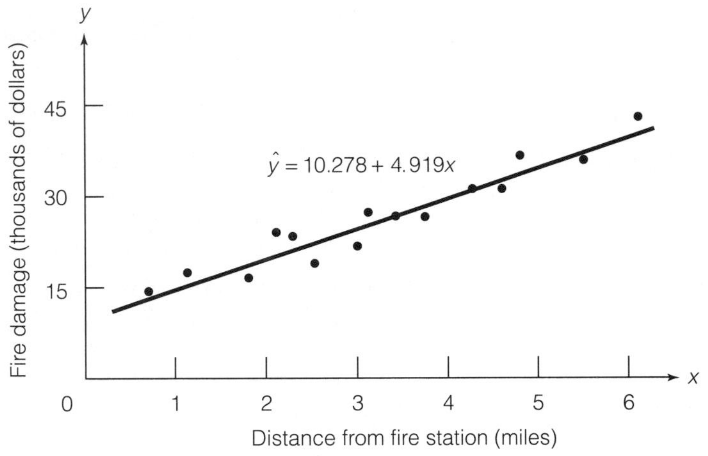

STEP 5

a. *Test of model utility* We can now check the utility of the hypothesized model, that is, whether x really contributes information for the prediction of y using the straight-line model. First, test the null hypothesis that the slope β_1 is 0, i.e., that there is no linear relationship between fire damage and the distance from the nearest fire station, against the alternative that x and y are positively linearly related. We test

$$H_0: \quad \beta_1 = 0$$

$$H_a: \quad \beta_1 > 0$$

The value of the test statistic is shaded in the middle portion of the printout under the column labeled **T for H0: Parameter=0** and the row corresponding to **X**. The value, a t statistic, is

$$t = 12.525$$

The p-value of the test is reported on the printout under the column heading **Prob >** | **T** | in the **X** row. This value (shaded) is a two-tailed p-value. The

p-value for a one-tailed test of H_0: $\beta_1 = 0$ is found by dividing the value reported in the SAS printout in half. Thus, the p-value for our test is

$$p = \frac{.0001}{2} = .00005$$

This small p-value leaves little doubt that distance between the fire and the fire station contributes information for the prediction of fire damage and that fire damage increases as the distance increases.

b. *Confidence interval for slope* We gain additional information about the relationship by forming a confidence interval for the slope β_1. A 95% confidence interval is $\hat{\beta}_1 \pm (t_{.025})s_{\hat{\beta}_1}$, where the value of $\hat{\beta}_1$ and its standard error, $s_{\hat{\beta}_1}$, are shown (shaded) on the printout. The value of $t_{.025}$, based on $n - 2 = 13$ df, is 2.160. Therefore, the 95% confidence interval is

$$\hat{\beta}_1 \pm (t_{.025})s_{\hat{\beta}_1} = 4.919 \pm (2.160)(.3927)$$
$$= 4.919 \pm .849 = (4.070, 5.768)$$

We estimate that the interval from \$4,070 to \$5,768 encloses the mean increase (β_1) in fire damage per additional mile distance from the fire station.

c. *Numerical descriptive measures of model adequacy* The coefficient of determination is found next to the heading **R-square** in the middle portion of the printout. This value (shaded) is

$$r^2 = .9235$$

which implies that about 92% of the sample variation in fire damage (y) is explained by the distance x between the fire and the fire station.

The coefficient of correlation r, which measures the strength of the linear relationship between y and x, is not shown on the SAS printout and must be calculated. Using the facts that $r = \sqrt{r^2}$ in simple linear regression and that r and $\hat{\beta}_1$ have the same sign, we find

$$r = +\sqrt{r^2} = \sqrt{.9235} = .96$$

The high correlation confirms our conclusion that β_1 differs from 0; it appears that fire damage and distance from the fire station are linearly correlated. All signs point to a strong linear relationship between x and y.

STEP 6 We are now prepared to use the least squares model. Suppose the insurance company wants to predict the fire damage if a major residential fire were to occur 3.5 miles from the nearest fire station, i.e., $x_p = 3.5$. The predicted value is shown (shaded) at the bottom of the SAS printout in the row corresponding to **X** = 3.5 and the column headed **Predict Value**. This value is

$$\hat{y} = 27.4956$$

Lower and upper prediction limits for this value are given under the columns labeled **Lower 95% Predict** and **Upper 95% Predict**, respectively. These values (shaded) are 22.3239 and 32.6672. Thus, the model yields a 95% prediction interval of \$22,324 to \$32,667 for fire damage in a major residential fire 3.5 miles from the nearest fire station.

Caution: We would not use this prediction model to make predictions for homes less than .7 mile or more than 6.1 miles from the nearest fire station. A look at the data in Table 3.8 reveals that all the x values fall between .7 and 6.1. Recall from Section 3.9 that it is dangerous to use the model to make predictions outside the region in which the sample data fall. A straight line might not provide a good model for the relationship between the mean value of y and the value of x when stretched over a wider range of x values.

In Chapter 4, we will discuss the interpretation of those portions of the SAS printout that were not mentioned here. However, the important elements of a simple linear regression analysis have been located, and you should be able to use this discussion as a guide to interpreting simple linear regression computer printouts. Details on how to perform a simple linear regression analysis on the computer using each of the four statistical software packages, SAS, SPSS, MINITAB, or ASP, are provided in Appendices D–G.

EXERCISES

3.51 The *Journal of Information Systems* (Spring 1992) published a study of a computerized intrusion-detection system. The input–output (I/O) units and the central processing unit (CPU) time (in seconds) utilized by a sample of 44 system users were recorded. The data for both variables are listed here. A simple linear regression analysis relating CPU times (y) to I/O units (x) was conducted on the data. The results are shown in the accompanying SAS printout. Locate the key elements on the printout and interpret the results.

CPU TIME	I/O UNITS	CPU TIME	I/O UNITS	CPU TIME	I/O UNITS
54	15	55	5	15	2
41	17	54	4	27	3
28	1	37	1	28	0
32	0	18	0	19	0
17	0	53	0	21	0
23	20	42	9	20	0
19	0	40	0	13	1
20	6	28	1	27	3
30	1	52	0	102	6
14	0	19	0	54	0
26	0	35	1	62	14
19	0	46	7	59	0
23	2	38	9	23	4
16	0	15	0	16	0
13	9	15	10		

Source: O'Leary, D. E. "Intrusion-detection systems." *Journal of Information Systems*, Spring 1992, p. 68 (Table 2).

```
Dependent Variable: CPU

                       Analysis of Variance

                             Sum of          Mean
Source            DF        Squares        Square       F Value       Prob>F

Model              1      937.54390     937.54390         2.975       0.0919
Error             42    13236.45610     315.15372
C Total           43    14174.00000

      Root MSE        17.75257      R-square          0.0661
      Dep Mean        32.00000      Adj R-sq          0.0439
      C.V.            55.47678

                       Parameter Estimates

                    Parameter       Standard     T for H0:
Variable   DF        Estimate          Error   Parameter=0     Prob > |T|

INTERCEP    1       28.894324     3.22564861         8.958         0.0001
IO_UNITS    1        0.904965     0.52468333         1.725         0.0919
```

3.52 Refer to the simple linear regression relating drill time y to drilling depth x, Exercise 3.11. A MINITAB printout of the results follows.

```
The regression equation is
DRILTIME = 4.79 + 0.0144 DEPTH

Predictor         Coef         Stdev      t-ratio         p
Constant        4.7896        0.6663         7.19     0.000
DEPTH         0.014388      0.002847         5.05     0.000

s = 1.432         R-sq = 63.0%       R-sq(adj) = 60.5%

Analysis of Variance

SOURCE         DF          SS           MS          F          p
Regression      1      52.378       52.378      25.54      0.000
Error          15      30.768        2.051
Total          16      83.146

Unusual Observations
Obs.    DEPTH   DRILTIME        Fit  Stdev.Fit   Residual    St.Resid
 11       250      4.840      8.387      0.376     -3.547      -2.57R

R denotes an obs. with a large st. resid.
```

a. Give the least squares prediction equation.
b. Locate the values of SSE, s^2, s, and r^2 on the printout.
c. What is the value of the test statistic for testing model adequacy?
d. Locate and interpret the p-value of the test for model adequacy.

3.53 The Federal Trade Commission (FTC) annually ranks American cigarette brands according to carbon monoxide and nicotine content (measured in milligrams). To determine the relationship between carbon monoxide content (y) and nicotine content (x), the FTC fit the straight-line model $y = \beta_0 + \beta_1 x + \varepsilon$ to data collected for a sample of 10 brands of cigarettes. The SAS printout is reproduced at the top of page 152. Locate the key elements on the printout and interpret the results.

Analysis of Variance

Source	DF	Sum of Squares	Mean Square	F Value	Prob>F
Model	1	283.93484	283.93484	325.699	0.0001
Error	8	6.97416	0.87177		
C Total	9	290.90900			

Root MSE	0.93369	R-square	0.9760
Dep Mean	9.79000	Adj R-sq	0.9730
C.V.	9.53714		

Parameter Estimates

Variable	DF	Parameter Estimate	Standard Error	T for H0: Parameter=0	Prob > |T|
INTERCEP	1	-0.534903	0.64380408	-0.831	0.4302
X	1	15.526171	0.86031171	18.047	0.0001

Obs	X	Dep Var Y	Predict Value	Std Err Predict	Lower95% Predict	Upper95% Predict	Residual
1	0.86	13.600	12.8176	0.3396	10.5265	15.1087	0.7824
2	0.17	1.200	2.1045	0.5182	-0.3579	4.5670	-0.9045
3	0.72	9.800	10.6439	0.2990	8.3831	12.9048	-0.8439
4	0.10	1.200	1.0177	0.5687	-1.5034	3.5388	0.1823
5	0.40	5.400	5.6756	0.3730	3.3570	7.9942	-0.2756
6	0.93	12.700	13.9044	0.3730	11.5858	16.2230	-1.2044
7	0.67	10.500	9.8676	0.2953	7.6094	12.1258	0.6324
8	1.02	15.400	15.3018	0.4248	12.9363	17.6675	0.0982
9	0.57	10.000	8.3018	0.3064	6.0490	10.5811	1.6850
10	1.21	18.100	18.2518	0.5541	15.7481	20.7555	-0.1518

Sum of Residuals	-6.66134E-16
Sum of Squared Residuals	6.974156
Predicted Resid SS (Press)	9.781261

3.54 In retailing ready-to-wear fashion, price concession—in the form of a markdown—is the traditional vehicle for selling slow-moving merchandise. To investigate the effect of a markdown on the rate of sale of slow-moving items, P. G. Carlson (Emory University) studied the markdown policy at Rich's department store in Atlanta. Nine styles of budget junior dresses were selected for analysis. For each style, the initial rate of sale, x, and the postmarkdown rate of sale, y, were recorded. (The initial rate of sale is the average rate of sale from the day the style was put on the floor to the time of the first markdown, whereas the postmarkdown rate of sale is the average rate of sale from the day of the first markdown to the time of either the second markdown or the end of the fashion life.) The nine data points were subjected to a simple linear regression analysis. The SPSS printout appears here.

```
* * * *   M U L T I P L E   R E G R E S S I O N   * * * *

Equation Number 1    Dependent Variable..   Y

Variable(s) Entered on Step Number
   1..     X

Multiple R              .8229
R Square                .6772
Adjusted R Square       .6311
Standard Error          .1044
```

```
Analysis of Variance
                     DF        Sum of Squares         Mean Square
Regression            1                 .1603               .1603
Residual              7                 .0764               .0109

F =      14.7064          Signif F =  .0100

------------------ Variables in the Equation ------------------

Variable              B          SE B         Beta          T   Sig T

X                2.2985         .5999        .8229      3.831   .0200
(Constant)      -0.0292         .0902                  -0.324   .5000

End Block Number   1   All requested variables entered.
```

Source: Carlson, P. G. "Fashion retailing: The sensitivity of rate of sale to markdown." *Journal of Retailing*, Spring 1983, Vol. 59, No. 1, pp. 67–76.

a. Write the least squares prediction equation.
b. Locate SSE on the printout and interpret its value.
c. Locate s on the printout and interpret its value.
d. Locate r^2 on the printout and interpret its value.
e. Is there sufficient evidence to indicate that postmarkdown rate of sale y and initial rate of sale x are linearly related? Test at $\alpha = .05$.

3.55 Refer to the simple linear regression relating heat transfer enhancement y to unflooded area ratio x, Exercise 3.18. An ASP printout of the analysis is shown here.

```
               SIMPLE LINEAR REGRESSION: HEAT(y) vrs. RATIO(x)

MODEL:   HEAT(y) = 2.42639RATIO(x) + 0.213389CNST

             COEF.    SD. ER.     t(22)      P-VALUE PT. R SQ.
           -------- -------- --------- ----------- ---------
RATIO(x) 2.42639  0.228252 10.6303   3.92489E-10 0.837041
    CNST 0.213389 0.439     0.486081 0.631717    0.0106256

R SQ. = 0.837041,   ADJ. R SQ. = 0.829634,   D. W. = 1.49972
SD. ER. EST. = 0.453826,  F(1/22) = 113.003 (P-VALUE = 3.92489E-10)
```

a. Give the least squares prediction equation.
b. Locate the values of r^2 on the printout.
c. What is the value of the test statistic for testing model adequacy?
d. Locate and interpret the p-value of the test for model adequacy.
e. The value of s for the regression is given as **SD. ER. EST.** on the ASP printout. Find and interpret this value.

3.11 Regression Through the Origin (Optional)

In practice, we occasionally know in advance that the true line of means $E(y)$ passes through the point $(x = 0, y = 0)$, called the **origin**. For example, a chain of convenience stores may be interested in modeling sales y of a new diet soft drink as a linear function of amount x of the new product in stock for a sample of stores. Or, a medical researcher may be interested in the linear relationship between dosage x of a drug for cancer patients and increase y in pulse rate of the patient 1 minute after taking the drug. In both cases, it is known that the regression line must pass through the origin. The convenience store chain knows that if one of its stores chooses not to stock the new diet soft drink, it will have zero sales of the new product. Likewise, if the cancer patient takes no dosage of the drug, the theoretical increase in pulse rate 1 minute later will be 0.

For situations in which we know that the regression line passes through the origin, the y-intercept is $\beta_0 = 0$ and the probabilistic straight-line model takes the form

$$y = \beta_1 x + \varepsilon$$

When the regression line passes through the origin, the formula for the least squares estimate of the slope β_1 differs from the formula given in Section 3.3. Several other formulas required to perform the regression analysis are also different. These new computing formulas are provided in the following box.

Formulas for Regression Through the Origin

$$y = \beta_1 x + \varepsilon$$

Least squares slope:

$$\hat{\beta}_1 = \frac{\sum x_i y_i}{\sum x_i^2}$$

Estimate of σ^2:

$$s^2 = \frac{\text{SSE}}{n-1}, \quad \text{where SSE} = \sum y_i^2 - \hat{\beta}_1 \sum x_i y_i$$

Estimate of $\sigma_{\hat{\beta}_1}$:

$$s_{\hat{\beta}_1} = \frac{s}{\sqrt{\sum x_i^2}}$$

Estimate of $\sigma_{\hat{y}}$ for estimating $E(y)$ when $x = x_p$:

$$s_{\hat{y}} = s\left(\frac{x_p}{\sqrt{\sum x_i^2}}\right)$$

Estimate of $\sigma_{(y-\hat{y})}$ for predicting y when $x = x_p$:

$$s_{(y-\hat{y})} = s\sqrt{1 + \frac{x_p^2}{\sum x_i^2}}$$

Note that the denominator of s^2 is $n - 1$, not $n - 2$ as in the previous sections. This is because we need to estimate only a single parameter β_1 rather than both β_0 and β_1. Consequently, we have one additional degree of freedom for estimating σ^2, the variance of ε. Tests and confidence intervals for β_1 are carried out exactly as outlined in the previous sections, except that the t distribution is based on $(n - 1)$ df. The test statistic and confidence intervals are given in the next box.

Tests and Confidence Intervals for Regression Through the Origin

Test statistic for H_0: $\beta_1 = 0$:

$$t = \frac{\hat{\beta}_1 - 0}{s_{\hat{\beta}_1}} = \frac{\hat{\beta}_1}{s/\sqrt{\sum x_i^2}}$$

$100(1 - \alpha)\%$ *confidence interval for* β_1:

$$\hat{\beta}_1 \pm t_{\alpha/2}s_{\hat{\beta}_1} = \hat{\beta}_1 \pm t_{\alpha/2}\left(\frac{s}{\sqrt{\sum x_i^2}}\right)$$

$100(1 - \alpha)\%$ *confidence interval for* $E(y)$:

$$\hat{y} \pm t_{\alpha/2}s_{\hat{y}} = \hat{y} \pm t_{\alpha/2}s\left(\frac{x_p}{\sqrt{\sum x_i^2}}\right)$$

$100(1 - \alpha)\%$ *prediction interval for* y:

$$\hat{y} \pm t_{\alpha/2}s_{(y-\hat{y})} = \hat{y} \pm t_{\alpha/2}s\sqrt{1 + \frac{x_p^2}{\sum x_i^2}}$$

where the distribution of t is based on $(n - 1)$ df

EXAMPLE 3.6

As part of a computer system performance evaluation, a systems manager is interested in predicting the response time for computer terminals. *Terminal response time* is defined as the length of time (in seconds) it takes the computer to respond to a command sent from a computer terminal by pressing one of the terminal's program function keys. Although many variables influence terminal response time, the systems manager will model the response time y as a function of the number x of simultaneous users (i.e., the number of users who are accessing the computer's central processing unit at the same time the command was sent). For this computer system, response time will be 0 when the number of simultaneous users is 0. Table 3.9 (page 156) gives the response times and number of simultaneous users for a sample of $n = 7$ terminal requests. Use the data to fit a straight-line regression model through the origin and calculate SSE.

TABLE 3.9 **Sample Data for Example 3.6**

NUMBER OF SIMULTANEOUS USERS x	TERMINAL RESPONSE TIME y, seconds
10	1.0
15	1.2
20	2.0
20	2.1
25	2.2
30	2.0
30	1.9

Solution

The model we want to fit is $y = \beta_1 x + \varepsilon$. Preliminary calculations for estimating β_1 and calculating SSE are given in Table 3.10. The estimate of the slope is

$$\hat{\beta}_1 = \frac{\sum x_i y_i}{\sum x_i^2} = \frac{282}{3{,}550}$$

$$= .0794366$$

and the least squares line is

$$\hat{y} = .0794x$$

The value of SSE for the line is

$$\text{SSE} = \sum y_i^2 - \hat{\beta}_1 \sum x_i y_i$$

$$= 23.3 - (.0794366)(2.82)$$

$$= .898873$$

The graph of the least squares line with the observations is shown in Figure 3.20.

TABLE 3.10 **Preliminary Calculations for Example 3.6**

x_i	y_i	x_i^2	$x_i y_i$	y_i^2
10	1.0	100	10	1.00
15	1.2	225	18	1.44
20	2.0	400	40	4.00
20	2.1	400	42	4.41
25	2.2	625	55	4.84
30	2.0	900	60	4.00
30	1.9	900	57	3.61
Totals		$\Sigma x_i^2 = 3{,}550$	$\Sigma x_i y_i = 282$	$\Sigma y_i^2 = 23.3$

FIGURE 3.20
The line $\hat{y} = .0794x$ fitted to the data in Table 3.9

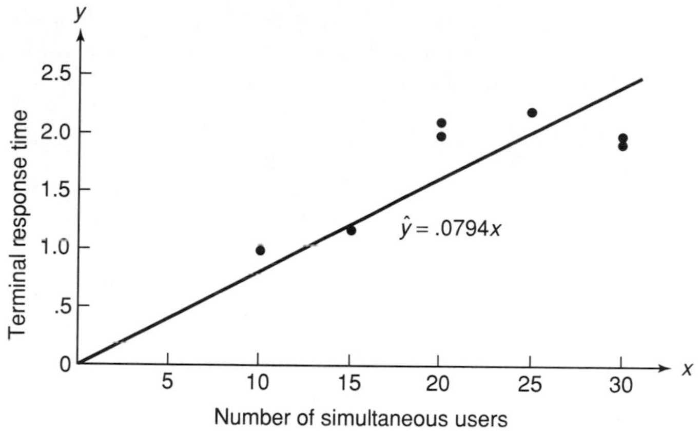

EXAMPLE 3.7

Refer to Example 3.6. Conduct the appropriate test for model adequacy. If the model is deemed adequate, predict the response time y with a 95% prediction interval, for a terminal request when $x = 23$ users are signed on to the system.

Solution

The appropriate test for model adequacy is

$$H_0: \ \beta_1 = 0$$
$$H_a: \ \beta_1 > 0$$

(We choose to do an upper-tailed test since it is reasonable to assume that if a linear relationship exists between number of users x and response time y, it is a positive one.)

To calculate the test statistic, we first compute s, where

$$s = \sqrt{\frac{\text{SSE}}{n-1}} = \sqrt{\frac{.898873}{6}} = .387056$$

Then the test statistic is

$$t = \frac{\hat{\beta}_1}{s\Big/\sqrt{\sum x_i^2}} = \frac{.0794366}{.387056/\sqrt{3{,}550}} = 12.23$$

For $\alpha = .05$, we will reject the null hypothesis if $t > t_{.05}$, where the distribution of t is based on $(n - 1) = 6$ df. From Table 2 of Appendix C, $t_{.05} = 1.943$. Thus, we will reject H_0 if

$$t > 1.943$$

Since the calculated value of t, 12.23, exceeds the critical value, there is sufficient evidence (at $\alpha = .05$) to conclude that the model is adequate for predicting terminal response time y.

To calculate a 95% prediction interval for the response time y when 23 users are signed on to the system, we first substitute $x = 23$ into the least squares prediction equation $\hat{y} = .0794x$:

$$\hat{y} = .0794(23) = 1.826$$

From Table 2 of Appendix C, $t_{.025} = 2.447$ (based on 6 df). Then, our 95% prediction interval is

$$\begin{aligned}\hat{y} &\pm t_{.025}s\sqrt{1 + \frac{x_p^2}{\sum x_i^2}} \\ &= 18.26 \pm 2.447(.387056)\sqrt{1 + \frac{(23)^2}{3{,}550}} \\ &= 18.26 \pm 2.447(.387056)(1.07192) \\ &= 18.26 \pm 1.015 \quad \text{or} \quad (.811, 2.841)\end{aligned}$$

We predict with 95% confidence that the terminal response time will range between .811 second and 2.841 seconds when 23 users are signed on to the system.

Warning: There are several situations where it is dangerous to fit the model $E(y) = \beta_1 x$. If you are not certain that the regression line passes through the origin, it is a safe practice to fit the more general model $E(y) = \beta_0 + \beta_1 x$. If the line of means does, in fact, pass through the origin, the estimate of β_0 will differ from the true value $\beta_0 = 0$ by only a small amount. For all practical purposes, the least squares prediction equations will be the same.

On the other hand, you may know that the regression passes through the origin (see Example 3.6), but are uncertain about whether the true relationship between y and x is linear or curvilinear. In fact, most theoretical relationships are *curvilinear*. Yet, we often fit a linear model to the data in such situations because we believe that a straight line will make a good approximation to the mean response $E(y)$ over the region of interest. The problem is that this straight line is not likely to pass through the origin (see Figure 3.21). By forcing the

FIGURE 3.21
Using a straight line to approximate a curvilinear relationship when the true relationship passes through the origin

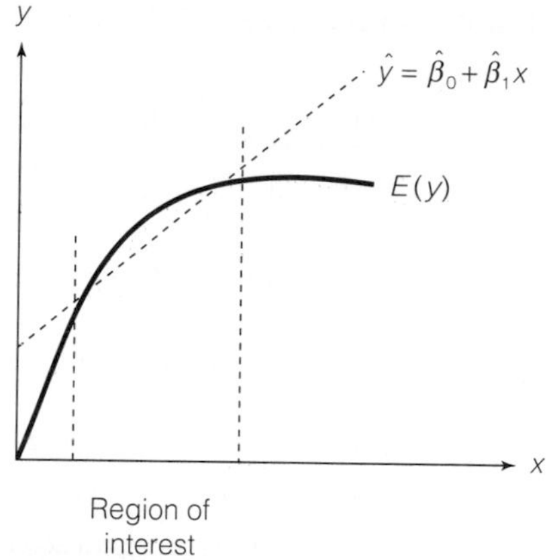

regression line through the origin, we may not obtain a very good approximation to $E(y)$. For these reasons, regression through the origin should be used with extreme caution.

EXERCISES

3.56 Consider the eight data points shown in the table.

x	−4	−2	0	2	4	6	8	10
y	−12	−7	0	6	14	21	24	31

a. Fit a straight-line model through the origin; i.e., fit $E(y) = \beta_1 x$.
b. Calculate SSE, s^2, and s.
c. Do the data provide sufficient evidence to indicate that x and y are positively linearly related?
d. Construct a 95% confidence interval for β_1.
e. Construct a 95% confidence interval for $E(y)$ when $x = 7$.
f. Construct a 95% prediction interval for y when $x = 7$.

3.57 Consider the five data points shown in the table.

x	0	1	2	3	4
y	0	−8	−20	−30	−35

a. Fit a straight-line model through the origin; i.e., fit $E(y) = \beta_1 x$.
b. Calculate SSE, s^2, and s.
c. Do the data provide sufficient evidence to indicate that x and y are negatively linearly related?
d. Construct a 95% confidence interval for β_1.
e. Construct a 95% confidence interval for $E(y)$ when $x = 1$.
f. Construct a 95% prediction interval for y when $x = 1$.

3.58 Consider the 10 data points shown in the table.

x	30	50	70	90	100	120	140	160	180	200
y	4	10	15	21	21	22	29	34	39	41

a. Fit a straight-line model through the origin; i.e., fit $E(y) = \beta_1 x$.
b. Calculate SSE, s^2, and s.
c. Do the data provide sufficient evidence to indicate that x and y are positively linearly related?
d. Construct a 95% confidence interval for β_1.
e. Construct a 95% confidence interval for $E(y)$ when $x = 125$.
f. Construct a 95% prediction interval for y when $x = 125$.

3.59 A pharmaceutical company has developed a new drug designed to reduce a smoker's reliance on tobacco. Since certain dosages of the drug may reduce one's pulse rate to dangerously low levels, the product-testing division of the pharmaceutical company wants to model the relationship between decrease in pulse rate, y (beats/minute), and dosage, x (cubic centimeters). Different dosages of the drug were administered to eight randomly selected patients, and 30 minutes later the decrease in each patient's pulse rate was recorded. The results are given in the accompanying table. Initially, the company considered the model $y = \beta_1 x + \varepsilon$ since, in theory, a patient who receives a dosage of $x = 0$ should show no decrease in pulse rate ($y = 0$).

PATIENT	DOSAGE x, cubic centimeters	DECREASE IN PULSE RATE y, beats/minute
1	2.0	12
2	4.0	20
3	1.5	6
4	1.0	3
5	3.0	16
6	3.5	20
7	2.5	13
8	3.0	18

a. Fit a straight-line model that passes through the origin.
b. Is there evidence of a linear relationship between drug dosage and decrease in pulse rate? Test at $\alpha = .10$.
c. Find a 99% prediction interval for the decrease in pulse rate corresponding to a dosage of 3.5 cubic centimeters.

3.60 Consider the relationship between the total weight of a shipment of 50-pound bags of flour, y, and the number of bags in the shipment, x. Since a shipment containing $x = 0$ bags (i.e., no shipment at all) has a total weight of $y = 0$, a straight-line model of the relationship between x and y should pass through the point $x = 0$, $y = 0$. Hence, the appropriate model might be

$$y = \beta_1 x + \varepsilon$$

From the records of past flour shipments, 15 shipments were randomly chosen and the data in the following table recorded.

WEIGHT OF SHIPMENT	NUMBER OF 50-POUND BAGS IN SHIPMENT	WEIGHT OF SHIPMENT	NUMBER OF 50-POUND BAGS IN SHIPMENT
5,050	100	7,162	150
10,249	205	24,000	500
20,000	450	4,900	100
7,420	150	14,501	300
24,685	500	28,000	600
10,206	200	17,002	400
7,325	150	16,100	400
4,958	100		

a. Find the least squares line for the given data under the assumption that $\beta_0 = 0$. Plot the least squares line on a scattergram of the data.

b. Find the least squares line for the given data using the model

$$y = \beta_0 + \beta_1 x + \varepsilon$$

(i.e., do not restrict β_0 to equal 0). Plot this line on the scatterplot you constructed in part **a**.

c. Refer to part **b**. Why might $\hat{\beta}_0$ be different from 0 even though the true value of β_0 is known to be 0?

d. The estimated standard error of $\hat{\beta}_0$ is equal to

$$s\sqrt{\frac{1}{n} + \frac{\bar{x}^2}{\text{SS}_{xx}}}$$

Use the t statistic,

$$t = \frac{\hat{\beta}_0 - 0}{s\sqrt{\frac{1}{n} + \frac{\bar{x}^2}{\text{SS}_{xx}}}}$$

to test the null hypothesis $H_0\colon \beta_0 = 0$ against the alternative $H_a\colon \beta_0 \neq 0$. Use $\alpha = .10$. Should you include β_0 in your model?

3.61 To satisfy the Public Service Commission's energy conservation requirements, an electric utility company must develop a reliable model for projecting the number of residential electricity customers in its service area. The first step is to study the effect of changing population on the number of electricity customers. The information shown in the table on page 162 was obtained for the service area from 1986 to 1995.

Since a service area with 0 population obviously would have 0 residential electricity customers, one could argue that regression through the origin is appropriate.

a. Fit the model $y = \beta_1 x + \varepsilon$ to the data.

b. Is there evidence that x contributes information for the prediction of y? Test using $\alpha = .01$.

c. Now fit the more general model $y = \beta_0 + \beta_1 x + \varepsilon$ to the data. Is there evidence (at $\alpha = .01$) that x contributes information for the prediction of y?

d. Which model would you recommend?

YEAR	POPULATION IN SERVICE AREA x, hundreds	RESIDENTIAL ELECTRICITY CUSTOMERS IN SERVICE AREA y
1986	262	14,041
1987	319	16,953
1988	361	18,984
1989	381	19,870
1990	405	20,953
1991	439	22,538
1992	472	23,985
1993	508	25,641
1994	547	27,365
1995	592	29,967

3.12 A Summary of the Steps to Follow in a Simple Linear Regression Analysis

We have introduced an extremely useful tool in this chapter—**the method of least squares** for fitting a prediction equation to a set of data. This procedure, along with associated statistical tests and estimations, is called a **regression analysis**. In six steps, we showed how to use sample data to build a model relating a dependent variable y to a single independent variable x.

Steps to Follow in a Simple Linear Regression Analysis

1. The first step is to hypothesize a **probabilistic model**. In this chapter, we confined our attention to the **first-order (straight-line) model**

$$y = \beta_0 + \beta_1 x + \varepsilon$$

2. The second step is to collect the (x, y) pairs for each experimental unit in the sample.
3. The third step is to use the method of least squares to estimate the unknown parameters in the **deterministic component**, $\beta_0 + \beta_1 x$. The least squares estimates yield a model $\hat{y} = \hat{\beta}_0 + \hat{\beta}_1 x$ with a **sum of squared errors (SSE)** that is smaller than the SSE for any other straight-line model.
4. The fourth step is to specify the probability distribution of the **random error component ε**.
5. The fifth step is to assess the utility of the hypothesized model. Included here are making inferences about the **slope β_1**, calculating the **coefficient of correlation** r, and calculating the **coefficient of determination** r^2.
6. Finally, if we are satisfied with the model, we are prepared to use it. We can use the model to **estimate the mean y value**, $E(y)$, for a given x value and to **predict an individual y value** for a specific value of x.

The concepts introduced in this chapter will be developed more fully in Chapter 4.

SUPPLEMENTARY EXERCISES

3.62 Any medical item used in the care of hospital patients is called a *factor*. For example, factors can be intravenous tubing, intravenous fluid, needles, shave kits, bedpans, diapers, dressings, medications, and even code carts. The coronary care unit at Bayonet Point Hospital (St. Petersburg, Florida) investigated the relationship between the number of factors per patient, x, and the patient's length of stay (in days), y. The data for a random sample of 50 coronary care patients are given in the following table, while a SAS printout of the simple linear regression analysis is shown at the top of page 164.

NUMBER OF FACTORS x	LENGTH OF STAY y, days	NUMBER OF FACTORS x	LENGTH OF STAY y, days
231	9	354	11
323	7	142	7
113	8	286	9
208	5	341	10
162	4	201	5
117	4	158	11
159	6	243	6
169	9	156	6
55	6	184	7
77	3	115	4
103	4	202	6
147	6	206	5
230	6	360	6
78	3	84	3
525	9	331	9
121	7	302	7
248	5	60	2
233	8	110	2
260	4	131	5
224	7	364	4
472	12	180	7
220	8	134	6
383	6	401	15
301	9	155	4
262	7	338	8

Source: Bayonet Point Hospital, Coronary Care Unit.

a. Construct a scattergram of the data.
b. Find the least squares line for the data and plot it on your scattergram.
c. Define β_1 in the context of this problem.
d. Test the hypothesis that the number of factors per patient (x) contributes no information for the prediction of the patient's length of stay (y) when a linear model is used (use $\alpha = .05$). Draw the appropriate conclusions.
e. Find a 90% confidence interval for β_1. Interpret your results.

```
Dependent Variable: Y

                         Analysis of Variance

                               Sum of          Mean
   Source           DF        Squares        Square      F Value       Prob>F

   Model             1      126.58393     126.58393       28.683       0.0001
   Error            48      211.83607       4.41325
   C Total          49      338.42000

      Root MSE        2.10077     R-square        0.3740
      Dep Mean        6.54000     Adj R-sq        0.3610
      C.V.           32.12193

                         Parameter Estimates

                       Parameter        Standard    T for H0:
  Variable   DF        Estimate           Error   Parameter=0   Prob > |T|

  INTERCEP    1        3.306032      0.67297426         4.913       0.0001
  X           1        0.014755      0.00275502         5.356       0.0001

                   Dep Var   Predict   Std Err  Lower95%  Upper95%
 Obs       X           Y     Value   Predict   Predict   Predict  Residual

   1      200          .     6.2570     0.302    1.9898   10.5242         .

Sum of Residuals               9.769963E-15
Sum of Squared Residuals           211.8361
Predicted Resid SS (Press)         234.7934
```

f. Find the coefficient of correlation for the data. Interpret your results.

g. Find the coefficient of determination for the linear model you constructed in part **b**. Interpret your result.

h. Find a 95% prediction interval for the length of stay of a coronary care patient who is administered a total of $x = 200$ factors.

i. Explain why the prediction interval obtained in part **h** is so wide. How could you reduce the width of the interval?

3.63 The relationships of five different work time dimensions with on-the-job performance were investigated in the *Journal of Business & Psychology* (Fall 1993). The researchers theorized that each work time dimension is positively related to performance. These five work time dimensions are (1) scheduling, (2) synchronization, (3) allocation of time, (4) autonomy of time use, and (5) future orientation. Based on data gathered from 122 managers at clothing manufacturing firms, the correlations shown in the following table were obtained. Use this information to test the researchers' theories at a significance level of $\alpha = .05$.

WORK TIME DIMENSION	CORRELATION (r) WITH WORK PERFORMANCE
1. Scheduling	.22
2. Synchronization	.07
3. Allocation of time	−.25
4. Autonomy of time use	−.41
5. Future orientation	.44

Source: Lim, Y. M., and Seers, A. "Time dimensions of work: Relationships with perceived organizational performance." *Journal of Business & Psychology*, Vol. 8, No. 1, Fall 1993, p. 97 (Table 1).

3.64 One common symptom of persons who suffer from hepatitis or other diseases of the biliary system (e.g., pancreas or gall bladder) is enlargement of the extrahepatic bile duct. To aid physicians in diagnosing problems of this type, an experiment was conducted to determine the effects of aging on the normal size of the bile duct (*Journal of Clinical Ultrasound*, Vol. 12, 1984). A sample of 256 healthy subjects were examined by ultrasound to locate the widest point in the extrahepatic bile duct. The inner diameter of the bile duct at the widest point was then measured (in millimeters) on the sonogram. A simple linear regression analysis relating maximal inner diameter y to age x (in years) was conducted with the following results:

$$\hat{y} = 2.72 + .06x \qquad r = .60 \qquad n = 256$$

a. Is there sufficient evidence of positive correlation between maximal inner diameter of the bile duct and age? Test using $\alpha = .01$.
b. Predict the maximal inner diameter of a 50-year-old healthy person. Would you expect all normal 50-year-olds to have maximal inner diameters equal to this value? Explain.

3.65 Refer to the experiment on estimating the metabolizable energy (ME) content of commercial cat foods in Exercise 1.67. In one phase of the study, simple linear regression analysis was used to relate the estimated ME content, x (in kilocalories per gram), to the actual ME content y for cats fed a diet of canned and dry foods (*Feline Practice*, Feb. 1986). The results for the two groups of cats are reported in the table.

DIET	$\hat{\beta}_0$	$\hat{\beta}_1$	$s_{\hat{\beta}_0}$	$s_{\hat{\beta}_1}$	r	s
Canned foods ($n = 28$)	.02	.96	.04	.04	.97	.05
Dry foods ($n = 29$)	.47	.84	.26	.09	.88	.15

a. Is there sufficient evidence to indicate that estimated ME content x is a useful predictor of actual ME content y for cats fed a diet of canned foods? Test using $\alpha = .05$.
b. Is there sufficient evidence to indicate that estimated ME content x is a useful predictor of actual ME content y for cats fed a diet of dry foods? Test using $\alpha = .05$.
c. Calculate the coefficient of determination r^2 for both regressions. Interpret these values.
d. Interpret the values of s for both regressions. What is the practical implication of this result?

3.66 Investors in real estate investment trust (REIT) stock generally prefer REITs that are internally managed and that reward management both for share performance and for performance relative to industry competitors. To better understand management compensation patterns in the REIT industry, the *Real Estate Review* (Summer 1993) studied a sample of 16 internally managed REITs. The main purpose was to establish a relationship between CEO compensation and REIT performance. Data collected on the 16 REITs from the National Association of Real Estate Investment Trusts revealed a correlation coefficient of $r = .328$ between CEO cash compensation and the 1-year annualized total return for the REIT. Is there sufficient evidence to establish a positive linear relationship between CEO cash compensation and REIT performance? Test using $\alpha = .05$.

3.67 In the business world, *Machiavellian* is a term often used to describe one who employs aggressive, manipulative, exploiting, and devious moves to achieve personal and corporate objectives. Hunt and Chonko (*Journal of Marketing*)* investigated Machiavellian tactics in marketing. One question con-

*Hunt, S. D., and Chonko, L. B. "Marketing and Machiavellianism." *Journal of Marketing*, Summer 1984, Vol. 48, No. 3, pp. 30–42.

cerned the relationship between age and Machiavellianism. Do young marketers tend to be more Machiavellian than older marketers? A sample of 1,076 members of the American Marketing Association were administered a questionnaire that measured tendency toward Machiavellianism. (The higher the score, the greater the tendency toward Machiavellianism.) The correlation coefficient between age and Machiavellian score was found to be $r = -.20$.

a. Is there evidence of a negative linear relationship between age of marketers and Machiavellian score? Test using $\alpha = .01$.

b. Calculate the coefficient of determination r^2 for the linear relationship between age of marketers and Machiavellian score. Interpret this value.

3.68 The importance of islands as sampling units for flora and fauna population studies have been widely recognized by biogeographers and evolutionists; the theory of equilibrium island biology states that larger islands should have more species than smaller islands. *The American Naturalist* (Jan. 1981) investigated whether such a relationship exists among the species of flora found in the vernal pools (pools of water formed in low-lying areas) of the Central Valley of California. At each of six sites, 10 to 20 pools were surveyed for species richness (i.e., the number of different flora species inhabiting the pool) and pool surface area. A linear model relating species richness y and surface area x (in square feet) of the pools was fitted to the data using the method of least squares with the following result:

$$\hat{y} = 18.4 + .04x$$

a. Give the null and alternative hypotheses for a test to determine whether surface area x is useful for predicting species richness y in a linear model.

b. The reported p-value for the test of part **a** is greater than .05. Interpret this result in terms of the problem.

c. The coefficient of determination for the simple linear regression is $r^2 = .06$. Interpret this value.

3.69 At major colleges and universities, administrators (e.g., deans, chairpersons, provosts, vice presidents, and presidents) are among the highest-paid state employees. Is there a relationship between the raises administrators receive and their performance on the job? This was the question of interest to a group of faculty union members at the University of South Florida called the United Faculty of Florida (UFF). The UFF compared the April 1990 ratings of 15 University of South Florida administrators (as determined by faculty in a survey) to their subsequent raises in August 1990. The data for the analysis is listed in the accompanying table. [*Note:* Ratings are measured on a 5-point scale, where 1 = very poor and 5 = very good.] According to the UFF, the "relationship is inverse; i.e., the lower the rating by the faculty, the greater the raise. Apparently, bad administrators are more valuable than good administrators."* (With tongue in cheek, the UFF refers to this phenomenon as "the SOB effect.") The UFF based its conclusions on a simple linear regression analysis of the data in the table, where y = administrator's raise and x = average rating of administrator.

a. Initially, the UFF conducted the analysis using all 15 data points in the table. Fit a straight-line model to the data. Is there evidence to support the UFF's claim of an inverse relationship between raise and rating?

b. A second simple linear regression was performed using only 14 of the data points in the table. The data for administrator #3 was eliminated because he was promoted to dean in the middle of the 1989–1990 academic year. (No other reason was given for removing this data point from

---

**UFF Faculty Forum*, University of South Florida Chapter, Vol. 3, No. 5, May 1991.

the analysis.) Perform the simple linear regression analysis using the remaining 14 data points in the table. Is there evidence to support the UFF's claim of an inverse relationship between raise and rating?

ADMINISTRATOR	RAISE[a]	AVERAGE RATING (5-PT SCALE)[b]
1	$18,000	2.76
2	16,700	1.52
3	15,787	4.40
4	10,608	3.10
5	10,268	3.83
6	9,795	2.84
7	9,513	2.10
8	8,459	2.38
9	6,099	3.59
10	4,557	4.11
11	3,751	3.14
12	3,718	3.64
13	3,652	3.36
14	3,227	2.92
15	2,808	3.00

Sources: [a]Faculty and A&P Salary Report, University of South Florida, Resource Analysis and Planning, 1990.
[b]Administrative Compensation Survey, *Chronicle of Higher Education*, Jan. 1991.

c. Based on the results of the regression, part **b**, the UFF computed estimated raises for selected faculty ratings of administrators. These are shown in the following table. What problems do you perceive with using this table to estimate administrators' raises at the University of South Florida?

RATINGS		RAISE
Very Poor	1.00	$15,939
	1.50	13,960
Poor	2.00	11,980
	2.50	10,001
Average	3.00	8,021
	3.50	6,042
Good	4.00	4,062
	4.50	2,083
Very Good	5.00	103

d. The ratings of administrators listed in this table were determined by surveying the faculty at the University of South Florida. All faculty are mailed the survey each year, but the response rate is typically low (approximately 10–20%). The danger with such a survey is that only disgruntled faculty, who are more apt to give a low rating to an administrator, will respond. Many of these faculty also believe that they are underpaid and that the administrators are overpaid. Comment on how such a survey could bias the results shown here.

e. Based on your answers to the previous questions, would you support the UFF's claim?

3.70 Is there a positive linear relationship between the foreign revenue (measured as a percentage of total revenue) and the foreign assets (measured as a percentage of total assets) of multinational firms?

Use the data in the table and the accompanying SPSS printout to conduct the analysis. Test using $\alpha = .10$.

FIRM	FOREIGN REVENUE, %	FOREIGN ASSETS, %	FIRM	FOREIGN REVENUE, %	FOREIGN ASSETS, %
Exxon	73.2	55.8	Procter & Gamble	39.9	32.2
IBM	58.9	48.6	Philip Morris	19.6	14.8
GM	26.6	25.2	Eastman Kodak	40.9	28.0
Mobil	64.7	51.1	Digital	54.1	44.2
Ford	33.2	26.9	GE	12.4	8.8
Citicorp	52.3	39.4	United Technologies	32.9	26.7
EI DuPont	39.8	29.5	Amoco	26.1	32.7
Texaco	42.3	26.6	Hewlitt-Packard	53.3	38.7
ITT	43.3	23.6	Xerox	34.6	25.4
Dow Chemical	54.1	44.9	Chevron	2.05	22.6

Source: *Forbes*, July 23, 1990, pp. 362–363. Used by permission. © Forbes Inc., 1990.

```
        * * * *   M U L T I P L E    R E G R E S S I O N    * * * *

Equation Number 1     Dependent Variable..    FOREV

Multiple R              .92825
R Square                .86166
Adjusted R Square       .85397
Standard Error         6.10121

Analysis of Variance
                        DF        Sum of Squares          Mean Square
Regression               1            4173.32066           4173.32066
Residual                18             670.04484             37.22471

F =      112.11156          Signif F =   .0000

------------------ Variables in the Equation ------------------

Variable                B           SE B          Beta          T   Sig T

FORASS            1.218908        .115119      .928255     10.588   .0000
(Constant)        1.782570       3.959089                    .450   .6579
```

3.71 For a company to maintain a competitive edge in the marketplace, spending on research and development (R&D) is essential. To determine the optimum level for R&D spending and its effect on a company's value, a simple linear regression analysis was performed. Data collected for the largest R&D spenders (based on 1981–1982 averages) were used to fit the straight-line model

$$y = \beta_0 + \beta_1 x + \varepsilon$$

where

y = Price/earnings (P/E) ratio

x = R&D expenditures/sales (R/S) ratio

The data for 20 of the companies used in the study are provided in the following table.

a. Construct a scattergram for the data.
b. Find the least squares prediction equation.
c. Plot the least squares line on your scattergram.
d. Use the least squares line to predict the P/E ratio for a company with an R/S ratio of .070.
e. Find a 90% prediction interval for the company's price/earnings (P/E) ratio.

COMPANY	P/E RATIO y	R/S RATIO x	COMPANY	P/E RATIO y	R/S RATIO x
1	5.6	.003	11	8.4	.058
2	7.2	.004	12	11.1	.058
3	8.1	.009	13	11.1	.067
4	9.9	.021	14	13.2	.080
5	6.0	.023	15	13.4	.080
6	8.2	.030	16	11.5	.083
7	6.3	.035	17	9.8	.091
8	10.0	.037	18	16.1	.092
9	8.5	.044	19	7.0	.064
10	13.2	.051	20	5.9	.028

Source: Wallin, C. C., and Gilman, J. J. "Determining the optimum level for R&D spending." *Research Management*, Vol. 14, No. 5, Sept./Oct. 1986, pp. 19–24 (adapted from Figure 1, p. 20).

f. Find a 90% confidence interval for the average (mean) (P/E) ratio of all firms with an R/S ratio of .070.

g. Compare and comment on the sizes of the intervals in parts **e** and **f**.

h. Could you reduce the size of either or both intervals by increasing your sample size? Explain.

3.72 Paper-and-pencil honesty tests of employees are common among retail stores, financial institutions, and warehouse operations where employees have access to cash and merchandise. These tests are less costly than polygraphs and can be used in states where preemployment polygraph examinations are illegal. P. R. Sackett and M. M. Harris (University of Illinois) reviewed a number of studies that examined the validity of paper-and-pencil honesty tests (*Personnel Psychology*, Summer 1984).* In one study, $n = 80$ applicants for retail management positions were given both an honesty test and a polygraph examination. The correlation coefficient between the scores of the two tests was $r = .48$. Another, independent study of $n = 17$ warehouse employees showed a correlation coefficient of $r = -.41$ between honesty test scores and dollar amount of money and merchandise stolen.

a. Is there sufficient evidence to indicate that paper-and-pencil honesty test scores and polygraph examination scores of retail management applicants are positively correlated? Test using $\alpha = .05$.

b. Calculate and interpret the coefficient of determination r^2 for the linear relationship between honesty test scores and polygraph examination scores.

c. Is there sufficient evidence to indicate that paper-and-pencil honesty test scores of warehouse employees are correlated with dollar amount of theft? Test using $\alpha = .05$.

d. Calculate and interpret the coefficient of determination r^2 for the linear relationship between honesty test scores and dollar amount of theft.

3.73 "In the analysis of urban transportation systems it is important to be able to estimate expected travel time between locations." T. M. Cook and R. A. Russell collected data in the city of Tulsa on the urban travel times and distances between locations for two types of vehicles, large hoist compactor trucks and passenger cars. A simple linear regression analysis was conducted for both sets of data (y = urban travel time in minutes, x = distance between locations in miles) with the results given in the table at the top of page 170.

*Sackett, P. R., and Harris, M. M. "Honesty testing for personnel selection: A review and critique." *Personnel Psychology*, Summer 1984, Vol. 37, No. 2, pp. 221–243.

PASSENGER CARS	TRUCKS
$\hat{y} = 2.50 + 1.93x$	$\hat{y} = 1.85 + 3.86x$
$r^2 = .676$; p-value $< .05$	$r^2 = .758$; p-value $< .01$

Source: Cook, T. M., and Russell, R. A. "Estimating urban travel times: A comparative study." *Transportation Research*, June 1980, 14A, pp. 173–175.

a. Is there sufficient evidence to indicate that distance between locations is linearly related to urban travel time for passenger cars? Test at $\alpha = .05$.
b. Is there sufficient evidence to indicate that distance between locations is linearly related to urban travel time for trucks? Test at $\alpha = .01$.
c. Interpret the values of r^2 for the two prediction equations.
d. Estimate the mean urban travel time for all passenger cars traveling a distance of 3 miles on Tulsa's highways.
e. Predict the urban travel time for a particular truck traveling a distance of 5 miles on Tulsa's highways.
f. Explain how we could attach a measure of reliability to the inferences derived in parts **d** and **e**.

3.74 Is there a link between the loneliness of parents and their offspring? Psychologists J. Lobdell and D. Perlman examined this question in an article published in the *Journal of Marriage and the Family* (Aug. 1986). The participants in the study were 130 female college undergraduates and their parents. Each triad of daughter, mother, and father completed the UCLA Loneliness Scale, a 20-item questionnaire designed to assess loneliness and several variables theoretically related to loneliness, such as social accessibility to others, difficulty in making friends, and depression. Pearson product moment correlations relating a daughter's loneliness score to her parents' loneliness scores as well as the other variables were calculated. The results are summarized here.

VARIABLE	CORRELATION (r) BETWEEN DAUGHTER'S LONELINESS AND PARENTAL VARIABLES	
	Mother	Father
Loneliness	.26	.19
Depression	.11	.06
Self-esteem	−.14	−.06
Assertiveness	−.05	.01
Number of friends	−.21	−.10
Quality of friendships	−.17	.01

Source: Lobdell, J., and Perlman, D. "The intergenerational transmission of loneliness: A study of college females and their parents." *Journal of Marriage and the Family*, Vol. 48, No. 8, Aug. 1986, p. 592. Copyright 1986 by the National Council on Family Relations, 3989 Central Ave., N.E., Suite #550, Minneapolis, MN 55421.

a. Lobdell and Perlman conclude that "mother and daughter loneliness scores were (positively) significantly correlated at $\alpha = .01$." Do you agree?
b. Determine which, if any, of the other sample correlations are large enough to indicate (at $\alpha = .01$) that linear correlation exists between the daughter's loneliness score and the variable measured.

c. Explain why it would be dangerous to conclude that a causal relationship exists between a mother's loneliness and her daughter's loneliness.

d. Explain why it would be dangerous to conclude that the variables with nonsignificant correlations in the table are unrelated.

3.75 A major portion of the effort expended in developing commercial computer software is associated with program testing. A study was undertaken to assess the potential usefulness of various product- and process-related variables in identifying error-prone software (*IEEE Transactions on Software Engineering*, Apr. 1985). A straight-line model relating the number y of module defects to the number x of unique operands in the module was fit to the data collected for a sample of software modules. The coefficient of determination for this analysis was $r^2 = .74$.

a. Interpret the value of r^2.

b. Based on this value, would you infer that the straight-line model is a useful predictor of number y of module defects? Explain.

References

Draper, N., and Smith, H. *Applied Regression Analysis*, 3rd ed. New York: Wiley, 1987.

Montgomery, D. C., and Peck, E. A. *Introduction to Linear Regression Analysis*. New York: Wiley, 1982.

Neter, J., Wasserman, W., and Kutner, K. *Applied Linear Statistical Models*, 3rd ed. Homewood, Ill.: Richard D. Irwin, 1990.

CHAPTER 4 Multiple Regression

CONTENTS

OBJECTIVE

To extend the methods of Chapter 3; to develop a procedure for predicting a response y based on the values of two or more independent variables; to illustrate the types of practical inferences that can be drawn from this type of analysis

4.1 The General Linear Model

Most practical applications of regression analysis utilize models that are more complex than the first-order (straight-line) model. For example, a realistic probabilistic model for monthly sales revenue would include more than just the advertising expenditure discussed in Chapter 3 to provide a good predictive model for sales. Factors such as season, inventory on hand, sales force, and productivity are a few of the many variables that might influence sales. Thus, we would want to incorporate these and other potentially important independent variables into the model if we need to make accurate predictions.

Probabilistic models that include terms involving x^2, x^3 (or higher-order terms), or more than one independent variable are called **multiple regression models**, or **linear statistical models**. The general form of these models is shown in the box.

> **The General Linear Model**
>
> $$y = \beta_0 + \beta_1 x_1 + \beta_2 x_2 + \cdots + \beta_k x_k + \varepsilon$$
>
> where
>
> y is the dependent variable
>
> $x_1, x_2, \ldots, x_k$ are the independent variables
>
> $E(y) = \beta_0 + \beta_1 x_1 + \beta_2 x_2 + \cdots + \beta_k x_k$ is the deterministic portion of the model
>
> β_i determines the contribution of the independent variable x_i
>
> *Note:* Remember that the symbols $x_1, x_2, \ldots, x_k$ may represent higher-order terms. For example, x_1 might represent the current interest rate, x_2 might represent x_1^2, and so forth.

The dependent variable y is now written as a function of k independent variables, $x_1, x_2, \ldots, x_k$. The random error term is added to make the model probabilistic rather than deterministic. The value of the coefficient β_i determines the contribution of the independent variable x_i, given that the other $(k - 1)$ independent variables are held constant, and β_0 is the y-intercept. The coefficients $\beta_0, \beta_1, \ldots, \beta_k$ will usually be unknown, since they represent population parameters.

At first glance it might appear that the regression model shown here would not allow for anything other than straight-line relationships between y and the independent variables, but this is not true. Actually, $x_1, x_2, \ldots, x_k$ can be functions of variables as long as the functions do not contain unknown parameters. For example, the carbon monoxide content y of smoke emitted from a cigarette could be a function of the independent variables

x_1 = Tar content

x_2 = (Tar content)$^2 = x_1^2$

x_3 = Nicotine content

and so on. In applications where the data are collected over time, you could insert a cyclical term (if it would be useful) of the form $x_4 = \sin t$, where t is a time variable. The multiple regression model is quite versatile and can be made to model many different types of response variables.

The steps we followed in developing a straight-line model are applicable to the multiple regression model.

STEP 1 Collect the sample data, i.e., the values of $y, x_1, x_2, \ldots, x_k$, for each experimental unit in the sample.

STEP 2 Hypothesize the form of the model. Choose which independent variables to include in the model.

STEP 3 Estimate the unknown parameters $\beta_0, \beta_1, \ldots, \beta_k$.

STEP 4 Specify the probability distribution of the random error component ε and estimate its variance σ^2.

STEP 5 Check the utility of the model.

STEP 6 Finally, if the model is deemed adequate, use the fitted model to estimate the mean value of y or to predict a particular value of y for given values of the independent variables.

Hypothesizing the form of the model (step 2) is the subject of Chapter 5. In this chapter, we will assume that the form of the model is known, and we will discuss steps 3–6 for a given model.

4.2 Model Assumptions

We noted in Section 4.1 that the multiple regression model is of the form

$$y = \beta_0 + \beta_1 x_1 + \beta_2 x_2 + \cdots + \beta_k x_k + \varepsilon$$

where y is the response variable that you want to predict; $\beta_0, \beta_1, \ldots, \beta_k$ are parameters with unknown values; $x_1, x_2, \ldots, x_k$ are independent information-contributing variables that are measured without error; and ε is a random error component. Since $\beta_0, \beta_1, \ldots, \beta_k$ and $x_1, x_2, \ldots, x_k$ are nonrandom, the quantity

$$\beta_0 + \beta_1 x_1 + \beta_2 x_2 + \cdots + \beta_k x_k$$

represents the deterministic portion of the model. Therefore, y is made up of two components—one fixed and one random—and, consequently, y is a random variable.

$$y = \overbrace{\beta_0 + \beta_1 x_1 + \beta_2 x_2 + \cdots + \beta_k x_k}^{\text{Deterministic portion of model}} + \overbrace{\varepsilon}^{\text{Random error}}$$

We will assume (as in Chapter 3) that the random error can be positive or negative and that for any setting of the x values, $x_1, x_2, \ldots, x_k$, ε has a normal probability distribution with mean equal to 0 and variance equal to σ^2. Further, we assume that the random errors associated with any (and every) pair of y

values are probabilistically independent. That is, the error ε associated with any one y value is independent of the error associated with any other y value. These asssumptions are summarized in the accompanying box.

Assumptions About the Random Error ε

1. For any given set of values of $x_1, x_2, \ldots, x_k$, ε has a normal probability distribution with mean equal to 0 [i.e., $E(\varepsilon) = 0$] and variance equal to σ^2 [i.e., $\text{Var}(\varepsilon) = \sigma^2$].
2. The random errors are independent (in a probabilistic sense).

The assumptions that we have described for a multiple regression model imply that the mean value $E(y)$ for a given set of values of $x_1, x_2, \ldots, x_k$ is equal to

$$E(y) = \beta_0 + \beta_1 x_1 + \beta_2 x_2 + \cdots + \beta_k x_k$$

Models of this type are called **linear statistical models** because $E(y)$ is a *linear function* of the unknown parameters $\beta_0, \beta_1, \ldots, \beta_k$.

All the estimation and statistical test procedures described in this chapter depend on the data satisfying the assumptions described in this section. Since we will rarely, if ever, know for certain whether the assumptions are actually satisfied in practice, we will want to know how well a regression analysis works, and how much faith we can place in our inferences when certain assumptions are not satisfied. We will have more to say on this topic in Chapters 6 and 7. First, we need to discuss the methods of a regression analysis more thoroughly and show how they are used in a practical situation.

4.3 Fitting the Model: The Method of Least Squares

The method of fitting multiple regression models is identical to that of fitting the first-order (straight-line) model—namely, the method of least squares. That is, we choose the estimated model

$$\hat{y} = \hat{\beta}_0 + \hat{\beta}_1 x_1 + \cdots + \hat{\beta}_k x_k$$

that minimizes

$$\text{SSE} = \sum (y_i - \hat{y}_i)^2$$

As in the case of the straight-line model, the sample estimates $\hat{\beta}_0, \hat{\beta}_1, \ldots, \hat{\beta}_k$ will be obtained as solutions to a set of simultaneous linear equations.*

The primary difference between fitting the simple and multiple regression models is computational difficulty. The $(k + 1)$ simultaneous linear equations

*Students who are familiar with calculus should note that $\hat{\beta}_0, \hat{\beta}_1, \ldots, \hat{\beta}_k$ are the solutions to the set of equations $\partial\text{SSE}/\partial\beta_0 = 0$, $\partial\text{SSE}/\partial\beta_1 = 0, \ldots, \partial\text{SSE}/\partial\beta_k = 0$. The solution, given in matrix notation, is presented in Appendix A.

that must be solved to find the $(k+1)$ estimated coefficients $\hat{\beta}_0, \hat{\beta}_1, \ldots, \hat{\beta}_k$ are often difficult (sometimes physically impossible) to solve with a pocket or desk calculator. Consequently, we resort to the use of computers. As with the straight-line model, many statistical software packages have been developed to fit a multiple regression model by the method of least squares. We will present output from several popular computer packages (ASP, SAS, SPSS, and MINITAB) in examples and exercises. Since these printouts are similar to most other statistical software packages, you should have little trouble interpreting regression output from other packages as you encounter them in the future.

To illustrate, suppose a physiologist wants to investigate the impact of exercise on the human immune system. The physiologist theorizes that the amount of immunoglobulin y in blood (called IgG, an indicator of long-term immunity) is related to the maximal oxygen uptake x (a measure of aerobic fitness level) of a person by the model

$$y = \beta_0 + \beta_1 x + \beta_2 x^2 + \varepsilon$$

To estimate the unknown parameters β_0, β_1, and β_2, values of y and x were measured for each of 30 human subjects. The data are shown in Table 4.1.

TABLE 4.1 **Data on Immunity and Fitness Level of 30 Subjects**

SUBJECT	IgG y, milligrams	MAXIMAL OXYGEN UPTAKE x, milliliters per kilogram	SUBJECT	IgG y, milligrams	MAXIMAL OXYGEN UPTAKE x, milliliters per kilogram
1	881	34.6	16	1,660	52.5
2	1,290	45.0	17	2,121	69.9
3	2,147	62.3	18	1,382	38.8
4	1,909	58.9	19	1,714	50.6
5	1,282	42.5	20	1,959	69.4
6	1,530	44.3	21	1,158	37.4
7	2,067	67.9	22	965	35.1
8	1,982	58.5	23	1,456	43.0
9	1,019	35.6	24	1,273	44.1
10	1,651	49.6	25	1,418	49.8
11	752	33.0	26	1,743	54.4
12	1,687	52.0	27	1,997	68.5
13	1,782	61.4	28	2,177	69.5
14	1,529	50.2	29	1,965	63.0
15	969	34.1	30	1,264	43.2

Notice that we include a term involving x^2 in the model because we expect curvature in the graph of the response model relating x to y. The term involving x^2 is called a **second-order**, or **quadratic**, term. Figure 4.1 illustrates that IgG appears to increase in a curvilinear manner with maximal oxygen uptake. This provides some support for the inclusion of the second-order term x^2 in the model.

Part of the SAS printout for the analysis of the data in Table 4.1 is reproduced in Figure 4.2. The least squares estimates of the β parameters (shaded on the

FIGURE 4.1
Scattergram of the data in Table 4.1

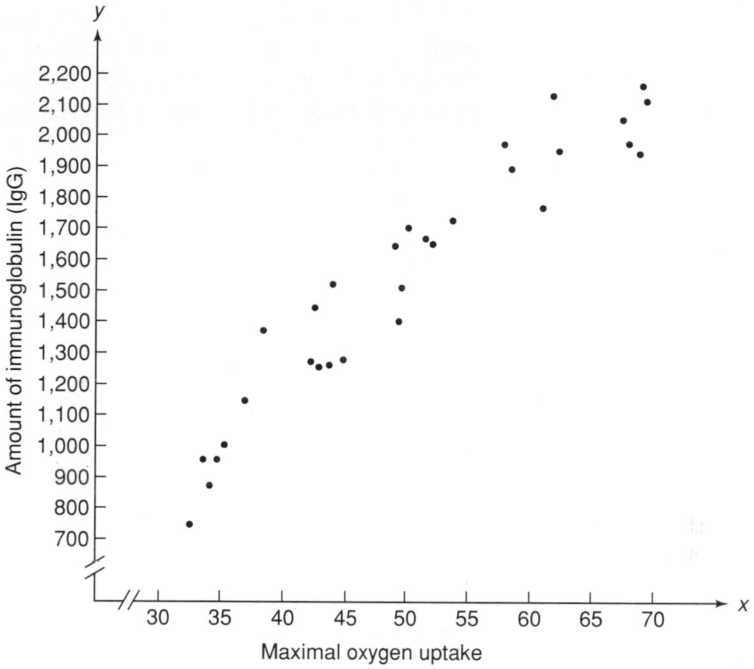

FIGURE 4.2
Portion of the SAS printout for the quadratic model

```
Dependent Variable: Y

                         Analysis of Variance

                              Sum of          Mean
      Source          DF     Squares        Square       F Value       Prob>F

      Model            2 4602145.2169 2301072.6085       203.113       0.0001
      Error           27  305883.74976  11329.02777
      C Total         29 4908028.9667

          Root MSE      106.43791     R-square        0.9377
          Dep Mean     1557.63333     Adj R-sq        0.9331
          C.V.            6.83331

                         Parameter Estimates

                     Parameter       Standard     T for H0:
    Variable  DF      Estimate          Error   Parameter=0     Prob > |T|

    INTERCEP   1  -1462.141458   411.48209286        -3.553         0.0014
    X          1     88.214044    16.47736086         5.354         0.0001
    XX         1     -0.535378     0.15822840        -3.384         0.0022
```

printout) are $\hat{\beta}_0 = -1{,}462.1$, $\hat{\beta}_1 = 88.214$, and $\hat{\beta}_2 = -.5354$. Therefore, the equation that minimizes the SSE for the data is

$$\hat{y} = -1{,}462.1 + 88.214x - .5354x^2$$

The minimum value of SSE, 305,883.7, is also shaded on the printout. [*Note:* Much of the detail on the printout has not yet been discussed. In this chapter we will shade the aspects of the printout that are under discussion.]

Note that the graph of the multiple regression model (Figure 4.3, a response curve) provides a good fit to the data of Table 4.1. Furthermore, the relatively small value of $\hat{\beta}_2$ does *not* imply that the curvature is insignificant, since the numerical value of $\hat{\beta}_2$ is dependent on the scale of the measurements.

FIGURE 4.3
Least squares fit of the quadratic model

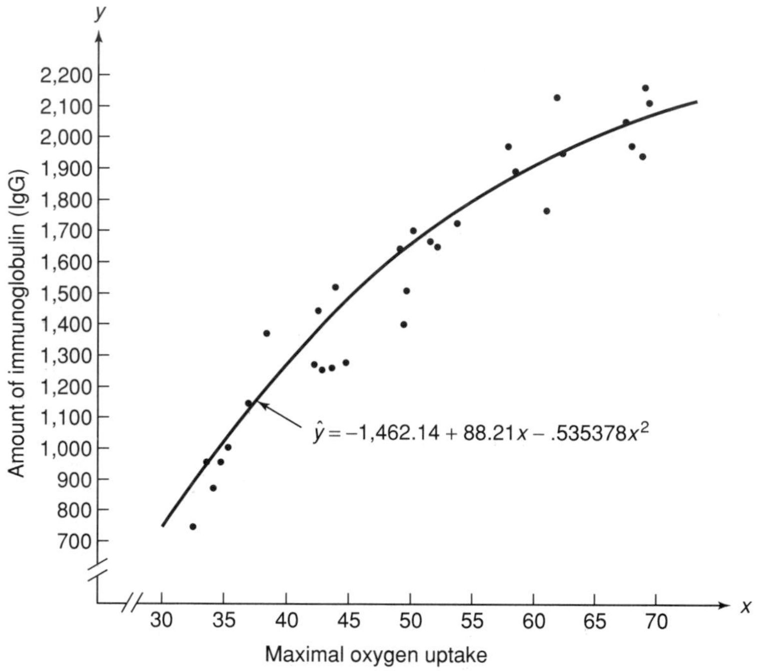

The ultimate goal of this multiple regression analysis is to use the fitted model to predict IgG y for a person with a specific maximal oxygen uptake level x. And, of course, we will want to give a prediction interval for y so that we will know how much faith we can place in the prediction. That is, if the model is used to predict IgG y for a given value x, what will be the error of prediction? To answer this question, we need to estimate σ^2, the variance of ε.

4.4 Estimation of σ^2, the Variance of ε

Recall that σ^2 is the variance of the random error ε. If $\sigma^2 = 0$, all the random errors will equal 0 and the prediction equation $\hat{y}$ will be identical to $E(y)$; i.e., $E(y)$ will be estimated without error. In contrast, a large value of σ^2 implies large (absolute) values of ε and larger deviations between the prediction equation $\hat{y}$ and the mean value $E(y)$. Consequently, the larger the value of σ^2, the greater will be the error in estimating the model parameters $\beta_0, \beta_1, \ldots, \beta_k$ and the error in predicting a value of y for a specific set of values of $x_1, x_2, \ldots, x_k$. Thus, σ^2 plays a major role in making inferences about $\beta_0, \beta_1, \ldots, \beta_k$, in estimating $E(y)$, and in predicting y for specific values of $x_1, x_2, \ldots, x_k$.

Since the variance σ^2 of the random error ε will rarely be known, we must use the results of the regression analysis to estimate its value. You will recall that σ^2 is the variance of the probability distribution of the random error ε for a given set of values for $x_1, x_2, \ldots, x_k$, and hence that it is the mean value of the squares of the deviations of the y values (for given values of $x_1, x_2, \ldots, x_k$) about the mean value $E(y)$.* Since the predicted value $\hat{y}$ estimates $E(y)$ for each of the data points, it seems natural to use

$$\text{SSE} = \sum (y_i - \hat{y}_i)^2$$

to construct an estimator of σ^2.

For example, in the second-order model describing IgG as a function of maximal oxygen uptake, we found that SSE = 305,883.7. We now want to use this quantity to estimate the variance of ε. Recall that the estimator for the straight-line model was $s^2 = \text{SSE}/(n-2)$. Note that the denominator is (n − Number of estimated β parameters), which is $(n-2)$ in the first-order (straight-line) model. Since we must estimate one more parameter, β_2, for the second-order model $y = \beta_0 + \beta_1 x + \beta_2 x^2 + \varepsilon$, the estimator of σ^2 is

$$s^2 = \frac{\text{SSE}}{n-3}$$

That is, the denominator becomes $(n-3)$ because there are now three β parameters in the model. The numerical estimate for this example is

$$s^2 = \frac{\text{SSE}}{30-3} = \frac{305{,}883.7}{27} = 11{,}329.03$$

In many computer printouts and textbooks, s^2 is called the **mean square for error (MSE)**. This estimate of σ^2 is shown in the column titled **Mean Square** in the SAS printout in Figure 4.2.

For the general multiple regression model

$$y = \beta_0 + \beta_1 x_1 + \beta_2 x_2 + \cdots + \beta_k x_k + \varepsilon$$

we must estimate the $(k+1)$ parameters $\beta_0, \beta_1, \beta_2, \ldots, \beta_k$. Thus, the estimator of σ^2 is SSE divided by the quantity (n − Number of estimated β parameters).

> **Estimator of σ^2 for Multiple Regression Model with k Independent Variables**
>
> $$s^2 = \text{MSE} = \frac{\text{SSE}}{n - \text{Number of estimated } \beta \text{ parameters}} = \frac{\text{SSE}}{n-(k+1)}$$

*Remember, we stated in Section 4.2 that $y = E(y) + \varepsilon$. Therefore, ε is equal to the deviation $y - E(y)$. Also, by definition, the variance of a random variable is the expected value of the square of the deviation of the random variable from its mean. According to our model, $E(\varepsilon) = 0$. Therefore, $\sigma^2 = E(\varepsilon^2)$.

We will use MSE, the estimator of σ^2, both to check the utility of the model (Sections 4.5 and 4.7) and to provide a measure of the reliability of predictions and estimates when the model is used for those purposes (Section 4.8). Thus, you can see that the estimation of σ^2 plays an important part in the development of a regression model.

Finally, the interpretation of $s = \sqrt{\text{MSE}}$ in multiple regression is essentially the same as that for simple linear regression. Since s estimates σ, the standard deviation of the errors of prediction, we expect most of the y values to lie within $2s$ of their least squares predicted value $\hat{y}$. On the SAS printout, Figure 4.2, $s = \sqrt{\text{MSE}} = 106.4$ is shaded next to **Root MSE**. Consequently, we expect the second-order model to predict IgG (y) to within $2s = 2(106.4) = 212.8$ milligrams of its true value.

4.5 Inferences About the β Parameters

Sometimes the individual β parameters in a model have particular practical significance, and we want to estimate their values or test hypotheses about them. For example, if IgG y is related to maximal oxygen uptake x by the straight-line relationship

$$y = \beta_0 + \beta_1 x + \varepsilon$$

then β_1 has a very practical interpretation. That is, you saw in Chapter 3 that β_1 is the mean increase in immunoglobulin y for a 1-milliliter-per-kilogram increase in maximal oxygen uptake.

As proposed in the preceding sections, suppose IgG y is related to maximal oxygen uptake x by the quadratic model

$$y = \beta_0 + \beta_1 x + \beta_2 x^2 + \varepsilon$$

Then the mean value of y for a given value of x is

$$E(y) = \beta_0 + \beta_1 x + \beta_2 x^2$$

What is the practical interpretation of β_2? As noted previously, β_2 measures the curvature of the response curve shown in Figure 4.3. If $\beta_2 > 0$, the slope of the curve will increase as x increases [see Figure 4.4a]. If $\beta_2 < 0$, the slope of the curve will decrease as x increases, as shown in Figure 4.4b.

FIGURE 4.4

The interpretation of β_2 for a second-order model

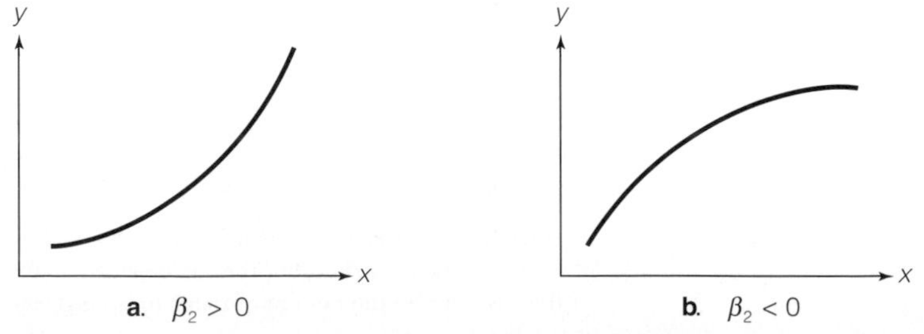

A physiologist would expect the immunoglobulin in blood y to rise almost proportionally to maximal oxygen uptake x. Then, eventually, as the aerobic fitness increases, the increase in IgG for a 1-unit increase in maximal oxygen uptake might begin to decrease. Thus, the physiologist would want to determine whether this type of curvature actually was present in the response curve, or, equivalently, the physiologist would want to test the null hypothesis

H_0: $\beta_2 = 0$ (No curvature in the response curve)

against the alternative hypothesis

H_a: $\beta_2 < 0$ (Downward curvature in the response curve)

A test of this hypothesis can be performed using a Student's t test.

The t test utilizes a test statistic that is analogous to that used to make inferences about the slope of the straight-line model (Section 3.6). The t statistic is formed by dividing the sample estimate $\hat{\beta}_2$ of the population coefficient β_2 by the estimated standard deviation of the sampling distribution of $\hat{\beta}_2$:

Test statistic: $t = \dfrac{\hat{\beta}_2}{s_{\hat{\beta}_2}}$

We use the symbol $s_{\hat{\beta}_2}$ to represent the estimated standard deviation of $\hat{\beta}_2$. The formula for computing $s_{\hat{\beta}_2}$ (presented in Appendix A) is very complex, but its computation is performed automatically as part of most standard multiple regression computer analyses. Thus, most computer packages list the estimated standard deviation $s_{\hat{\beta}_i}$ for each estimated model coefficient $\hat{\beta}_i$. In addition, they usually give the calculated t values for testing H_0: $\beta_i = 0$ for each coefficient in the model.

The rejection region for the test is found in exactly the same way as the rejection regions for the t tests in Chapters 1 and 3. That is, we consult Table 2 of Appendix C to obtain an upper-tail value of t. This is a value t_α such that $P(t > t_\alpha) = \alpha$. We can then use this value to construct rejection regions for either one- or two-tailed tests. To illustrate, in the immunoglobulin example, the error degrees of freedom is $(n - 3) = 27$, the denominator of the estimate of σ^2. Then the rejection region (shown in Figure 4.5 on page 182) for a one-tailed test with $\alpha = .05$ is

Rejection region: $t < -t_\alpha$; $\alpha = .05$, $\text{df} = 27$
$t < -1.703$

In Figure 4.6 (page 182), we again show a portion of the SAS printout for the immunoglobulin example. The estimated standard deviations for the model coefficients appear under the column labeled **Standard Error**. The t statistics for testing the null hypotheses that the coefficients β_0, β_1, and β_2 individually equal 0 appear under the column headed **T for H0: Parameter=0**. The t value corresponding to the test of the null hypothesis H_0: $\beta_2 = 0$, shaded on the printout,

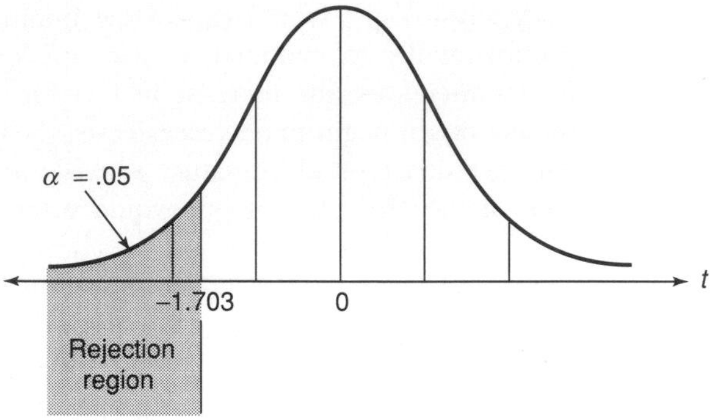

FIGURE 4.5
Rejection region for test of H_0: $\beta_2 = 0$

FIGURE 4.6
SAS printout for the quadratic model

```
Dependent Variable: Y

                         Analysis of Variance

                          Sum of          Mean
Source          DF       Squares        Square       F Value        Prob>F

Model            2  4602145.2169  2301072.6085       203.113        0.0001
Error           27  305883.74976   11329.02777
C Total         29  4908028.9667

     Root MSE     106.43791      R-square       0.9377
     Dep Mean    1557.63333      Adj R-sq       0.9331
     C.V.           6.83331

                         Parameter Estimates

                    Parameter       Standard      T for H0:
Variable   DF        Estimate          Error    Parameter=0     Prob > |T|

INTERCEP    1    -1462.141458   411.48209286         -3.553         0.0014
X           1       88.214044    16.47736086          5.354         0.0001
XX          1       -0.535378     0.15822840         -3.384         0.0022
```

is the last one in the column, i.e., $t = -3.384$. Since this value falls in the rejection region, i.e., it is less than -1.703, we conclude that the second-order term $\beta_2 x^2$ makes an important contribution to the prediction model of IgG, y.

The SAS printout shown in Figure 4.6 also lists the two-tailed observed significance levels (i.e., p-values) for each t value. These values appear under the column headed **Prob > | T |** . The observed significance level corresponding to the quadratic term is .0022 (shaded); this implies that we would reject H_0: $\beta_2 = 0$ in favor of H_a: $\beta_2 \neq 0$ at any α level larger than .0022. Since our alternative was one-sided, H_a: $\beta_2 < 0$, the observed significance level is half that given in the printout, i.e., p-value $= \frac{1}{2}(.0022) = .0011$.* Thus, there is very strong evidence of downward curvature in the relation between IgG (y) and maximal oxygen uptake (x).

*The one-tailed p-value for a t test in regression will be one-half the two-tailed p-value as long as the sign (positive or negative) of the test statistic agrees with the direction ($<$ or $>$) of the alternative hypothesis. If the signs do not agree, the one-tailed p-value equals $1 -$ (two-tailed p-value).

We can also form a 95% confidence interval for the parameter β_2 as follows:

$$\hat{\beta}_2 \pm t_{\alpha/2} s_{\hat{\beta}_2} = -.5354 \pm (2.052)(.1582)$$

or $(-.8600, -.2108)$. Note that the t value 2.052 corresponds to $\alpha/2 = .025$ and $(n - 3) = 27$ df. This interval constitutes a 95% confidence interval for β_2, the rate of change in curvature in mean IgG as aerobic fitness is increased. Note that all values in the interval are negative, reconfirming the conclusion of our test.

Testing a hypothesis about a single β parameter that appears in any multiple regression model is accomplished in exactly the same manner as described for the second-order model. The form of the t test is shown in the box.

Test of an Individual Parameter Coefficient in the Multiple Regression Model

$$y = \beta_0 + \beta_1 x_1 + \beta_2 x_2 + \cdots + \beta_k x_k + \varepsilon$$

ONE-TAILED TEST	TWO-TAILED TEST
H_0: $\beta_i = 0$	H_0: $\beta_i = 0$
H_a: $\beta_i > 0$ (or $\beta_i < 0$)	H_a: $\beta_i \neq 0$

*Test statistic:** $t = \dfrac{\hat{\beta}_i}{s_{\hat{\beta}_i}}$

Rejection region: $t > t_\alpha$ (or $t < -t_\alpha$)	*Rejection region:* $|t| > t_{\alpha/2}$

where

n = Number of observations

k = Number of independent variables in the model

and $t_{\alpha/2}$ is based on $[n - (k + 1)]$ df

Assumptions: See Section 4.2 for the assumptions about the probability distribution of the random error component ε.

EXAMPLE 4.1

A collector of antique grandfather clocks believes that the price received for the clocks at an antique auction increases with the age of the clocks and with the number of bidders. Thus, the following model is hypothesized:

$$y = \beta_0 + \beta_1 x_1 + \beta_2 x_2 + \varepsilon$$

*To test the null hypothesis that a parameter β_i equals some value other than 0, say, H_0: $\beta_i = \beta_{i0}$, use the test statistic $t = (\hat{\beta}_i - \beta_{i0})/s_{\hat{\beta}_i}$. All other aspects of the test are described in the box.

where

y = Auction price

x_1 = Age of clock (years)

x_2 = Number of bidders

A sample of 32 auction prices of grandfather clocks, along with their age and the number of bidders, is given in Table 4.2. The model is fitted to the data, and a portion of the MINITAB printout is shown in Figure 4.7. Test the hypothesis that the auction price increases as the number of bidders increases (and age is held constant), i.e., $\beta_2 > 0$. Use $\alpha = .05$.

TABLE 4.2 **Auction Price Data**

AGE x_1	NUMBER OF BIDDERS x_2	AUCTION PRICE y	AGE x_1	NUMBER OF BIDDERS x_2	AUCTION PRICE y
127	13	1,235	170	14	2,131
115	12	1,080	182	8	1,550
127	7	845	162	11	1,884
150	9	1,522	184	10	2,041
156	6	1,047	143	6	854
182	11	1,979	159	9	1,483
156	12	1,822	108	14	1,055
132	10	1,253	175	8	1,545
137	9	1,297	108	6	729
113	9	946	179	9	1,792
137	15	1,713	111	15	1,175
117	11	1,024	187	8	1,593
137	8	1,147	111	7	785
153	6	1,092	115	7	744
117	13	1,152	194	5	1,356
126	10	1,336	168	7	1,262

FIGURE 4.7
Portion of the MINITAB printout for Example 4.1

```
The regression equation is
Y = - 1339 + 12.7 X1 + 86.0 X2

Predictor        Coef       Stdev    t-ratio        p
Constant      -1339.0       173.8      -7.70    0.000
X1            12.7406      0.9047      14.08    0.000
X2             85.953       8.729       9.85    0.000

s = 133.5         R-sq = 89.2%       R-sq(adj) = 88.5%

Analysis of Variance

SOURCE         DF           SS          MS          F         p
Regression      2      4283063     2141532     120.19     0.000
Error          29       516727       17818
Total          31      4799789
```

Solution

The hypothesis of interest concerns the parameter β_2. Specifically,

H_0: $\beta_2 = 0$
H_a: $\beta_2 > 0$

Test statistic: $t = \dfrac{\hat{\beta}_2}{s_{\hat{\beta}_2}}$

Rejection region: For $\alpha = .05$, $t > t_{.05}$
where $df = n - (k + 1) = 32 - 3 = 29$
or $t > 1.699$ (see Figure 4.8)

FIGURE 4.8
Rejection region for H_0: $\beta_2 = 0$

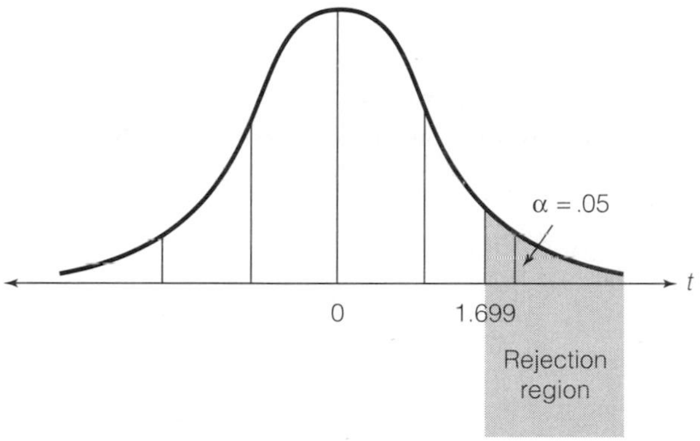

The calculated t value, $t = 9.85$, is indicated in Figure 4.7. This value exceeds 1.699 and, therefore, falls in the rejection region. Thus, the collector can conclude that the mean auction price of the clocks increases as the number of bidders increases, when age is held constant. Note that the observed significance level for the test (shaded on Figure 4.7) is p-value ≈ 0. Therefore, any reasonable value of α will lead us to reject H_0.

Note that the values $\hat{\beta}_1 = 12.7406$ and $\hat{\beta}_2 = 85.953$ (shaded in Figure 4.7) are easily interpreted. We estimate that the mean auction price increases \$12.74 per year of age of the clock when the number of bidders is held constant, and the mean price increases by \$85.95 per additional bidder, for clocks of a fixed age.

Be careful not to try to interpret the estimated intercept $\hat{\beta}_0 = -1{,}339.0$ in the same way as we interpreted $\hat{\beta}_1$ and $\hat{\beta}_2$. You might think that this implies a negative price for clocks 0 years of age with 0 bidders. However, these zeros are meaningless numbers in this example, since the ages range from 108 to 194 and the number of bidders ranges from 5 to 15. Keep in mind that we are modeling y within the range of values observed for the predictor variables and that interpretations of the models for values of the independent variables outside their sampled ranges can be very misleading.

Some statistical software packages use an F test to test hypotheses concerning the individual β parameters. If you conduct a two-tailed t test and reject the hypothesis if $t > t_{\alpha/2}$ or $t < -t_{\alpha/2}$, the corresponding F test will imply rejection if the computed value of F (which is equal to the square of the computed t statistic) is larger than F_α, because the square of the Student's t with ν (Greek nu) degrees of freedom is equal to an F statistic with 1 df in the numerator and ν df in the denominator. Thus, $t^2_{\alpha/2} = F_\alpha$, where t is based on ν df and F possesses 1 numerator and ν denominator degrees of freedom, respectively. As an example, when we tested the curvature parameter β_2 in the second-order model relating immunoglobulin in blood to maximal oxygen uptake, the computed t value was -3.384 (see Figure 4.6). The equivalent F statistic yields

$$F = t^2 = (-3.384)^2 = 11.425$$

Suppose we wanted to conduct a two-tailed statistical test, i.e., H_0: $\beta_2 = 0$ and H_a: $\beta_2 \neq 0$. The upper-tail rejection region for a two-tailed test with $\alpha = .05$ is

$$F > F_{.05}$$

where

$$F_{.05} \text{ is based on } \nu_1 = 1 \text{ df and } \nu_2 = 27 \text{ df}$$

or

$$F > 4.21$$

Note that the F value, 4.21, is equal to the square of 2.052, the value of t that corresponds to $t_{.025}$ with 27 df. In other words, you can conduct a two-tailed test of the null hypothesis H_0: $\beta_i = 0$, using either a two-tailed t test or a one-tailed F test. If you want to conduct a one-tailed test to detect H_a: $\beta_i > 0$ (or H_a: $\beta_i < 0$), the F test will not suffice. You will have to conduct the test using a t statistic.

EXERCISES

4.1 How is the number of degrees of freedom available for estimating σ^2, the variance of ε, related to the number of independent variables in a regression model?

4.2 Engineers at the University of Massachusetts studied the feasibility of using semiconductor lasers for solar lighting in spaceborne applications (*Journal of Applied Physics*, Sept. 1993). A series of $n = 8$ experiments with quantum-well lasers yielded the following observations on solar pumping threshold current (y) and waveguide A1 mole fraction (x).

a. The researchers theorize that the relationship between threshold current (y) and waveguide A1 composition (x) will be represented by a U-shaped curve. Hypothesize a model that corresponds to this theory.

b. Plot the data points in a scattergram. Comment on the researchers' theory, part **a**.

c. Use the accompanying MINITAB printout to test the theory, part **a**.

THRESHOLD CURRENT y, A/cm^2	WAVEGUIDE Al MOLE FRACTION x
273	.15
175	.20
146	.25
166	.30
162	.35
165	.40
245	.50
314	.60

Source: Unnikrishnan, S., and Anderson, N. G. "Quantum-well lasers for direct solar photopumping." *Journal of Applied Physics*, Vol. 74, No. 6, Sept. 15, 1993, p. 4226 (adapted from Figure 2).

```
The regression equation is
Y = 438 - 1684 X + 2502 X*X

Predictor       Coef        Stdev     t-ratio        p
Constant      438.31        60.54        7.24    0.001
X            -1684.3        357.3       -4.71    0.005
X*X           2502.3        470.6        5.32    0.003

s = 25.65        R-sq = 88.0%      R-sq(adj) = 83.2%

Analysis of Variance

SOURCE       DF          SS          MS          F         p
Regression    2       24163       12081      18.37     0.005
Error         5        3289         658
Total         7       27451
```

4.3 Perfectionists are persons who set themselves standards and goals that cannot be reasonably met or accomplished. One theory suggests that those individuals who are depressed have a tendency toward perfectionism. To study this phenomenon, 76 members of an introductory psychology class completed questionnaires that measure four different scales: (1) the ASO scale, designed to measure self-acceptance, (2) the Burns scale, designed to measure perfectionism, (3) the Zung scale, designed to measure depression, and (4) the Rotter scale, designed to measure perceptions between actions and reinforcement (*The Journal of Adlerian Theory, Research, and Practice*, Mar. 1986).

a. Write a first-order model relating depression (Zung scale) to self-acceptance (ASO scale), perfectionism (Burns scale), and reinforcement (Rotter scale).

b. A t test for the perfectionism (Burns scale) variable resulted in a (two-tailed) p-value of .87. Interpret this value.

4.4 Residential property appraisers make extensive use of multiple regression in their evaluation of property. Typically, the sale price (y) of a property is modeled as a function of several home-related conditions (e.g., gross living area, location, number of bedrooms). However, appraisers are not interested in the predicted price, $\hat{y}$. Rather, they use the regression model as a tool for making value adjustments to the property. These adjustments are derived from the parameter estimates of the model. The *Real Estate Appraiser* (April 1992) reported the results of a multiple regression on the price (y) of $n = 157$ residential properties recently sold in a northern Virginia subdivision. The SAS printout of the analysis is reproduced here. Note that there are 27 independent variables in the model.

Dep Variable: Sale Price

Analysis of Variance

Source	DF	Sum of Squares	Mean Square	F Value	Prob>F
Model	27	24184211898	895711551.79	20.914	0.0001
Error	129	5524834283	42828172.73		
C Total	156	29709046181			

Root MSE	6544.324	R-Square	0.8140
Dep Mean	173157.5	Adj R-Sq	0.7751
C.V.	3.779404		

Parameter Estimates

Variable	Parameter Estimate	Standard Error	95% Confidence Interval (@129df=1.98)	T for H0: Parameter=0	Prob > |T|
Intercept	96603	12530	(71794 to 121412)	7.710	.0001
Time	150	123	(-94 to 394)	1.220	.2248
Lot Size	.60	.30	(0.01 to 1.19)	2.022	.0452
Age	381	502	(-613 to 1375)	.758	.4501
GLA	22.40	3.67	(15.13 to 29.67)	6.099	.0001
Bedrooms	2263	1609	(-923 to 5499)	1.407	.1619
Half Baths	5962	2934	(153 to 11771)	2.032	.0442
Corner Lot	-1481	1692	(-4831 to 1869)	-.876	.3829
Cul-de-Sac	-56	2557	(-5119 to 5007)	-.022	.9825
Back to Woods	4086	2044	(39 to 8133)	1.999	.0477
Deck	2408	2167	(-1883 to 6699)	1.111	.2686
Fence	2896	1271	(379 to 5413)	2.279	.0243
Shed	70	1343	(-2589 to 2729)	.052	.9588
Patio	2377	1671	(-932 to 5686)	1.423	.1572
Portico	-906	2963	(-6773 to 4961)	-.306	.7603
Screen Porch	5021	2038	(986 to 9056)	2.463	.0151
In-grnd Pool	7570	3028	(1575 to 13565)	2.500	.0137
Garage	2989	1446	(126 to 5852)	2.068	.0407
Driveway	-1844	3222	(-8224 to 4536)	-.572	.5681
Fireplace	1290	1277	(-1238 to 3818)	1.010	.3144
Brick Facade	-2140	2369	(-6381 to 2551)	-.903	.3680
Updated Kit.	4171	1470	(1260 to 7082)	2.837	.0053
Remodel Kit.	6091	2367	(1404 to 10778)	2.574	.0112
Intercom	1933	2146	(-2316 to 6182)	.901	.3693
Cen. Vacuum	-4636	2166	(-8925 to -347)	-2.140	.0342
Skylights	7744	2622	(2552 to 12936)	-2.954	.0037
Air Filter	874	2506	(-4088 to 5836)	-.349	.7280
Bay Window	-3174	2086	(-7304 to 956)	-1.522	.1305

Source: Gilson, S. J. "A case study—Comparing the results: Multiple regression analysis vs. matched pairs in residential subdivision." *The Real Estate Appraiser*, Apr. 1992, p. 37 (Table 4).

a. One of the independent variables in the model is gross living area (GLA), measured in square feet. A 95% confidence interval for the β coefficient associated with GLA is shown on the printout. Interpret this interval.

b. Interpret the t test for testing the variable lot size.

c. Interpret the t test for testing the variable bay window.

4.5 *Artificial Intelligence (AI) Applications* (Jan. 1993) discussed the use of computer-based technologies in building explanation systems for regression models. As an example, the authors presented a model for predicting the scenic beauty (y) of southeastern pine stands (measured on a numeric scale) as a function of age (x_1) of the dominant stand, stems per acre (x_2) in trees, and basal area (x_3) per acre in hardwoods. A user of the AI system simply inputs the values of x_1, x_2, and x_3, and the system uses the least squares equation to predict the scenic beauty (y) value. The AI system generates information on how each independent variable can be manipulated to effect changes in the dependent variable. For example, "if all else were held constant in the stand, allowing the age (x_1) of the dominant trees in the stand to mature by 1 year will *increase* scenic beauty (y)." From what portion of the regression analysis would the AI system extract this type of information?

4.6 Refer to the *Feline Practice* (Feb. 1986) study on estimating the metabolizable energy (ME) content of commercial cat foods in Exercises 1.67 and 3.65. Three factors thought to influence ME content (y) of dry cat food are the crude protein (x_1), acid ether abstract (x_2), and nitrogen-free extract (x_3) content of the food. Data collected for 28 cats fed a diet of dry food were used to fit the multiple regression model

$$y = \beta_0 + \beta_1 x_1 + \beta_2 x_2 + \beta_3 x_3 + \varepsilon$$

with the following results:

$$\hat{y} = 2.44 + .45x_1 + 3.43x_2 + .10x_3$$

$$s_{\hat{\beta}_1} = .38$$

$$s_{\hat{\beta}_2} = .73$$

$$s_{\hat{\beta}_3} = .36$$

a. Is there sufficient evidence to indicate that crude protein x_1 is positively related to ME content y? Test using $\alpha = .05$.
b. Find a 95% confidence interval for β_3. Interpret your result.
c. The F statistic for testing H_0: $\beta_2 = 0$ was found to be $F = 22.08$. Is there sufficient evidence to indicate that ME content y is linearly related to acid ether abstract x_2? Test using $\alpha = .05$.
d. Refer to part **c**. Calculate the t statistic for testing H_0: $\beta_2 = 0$ and show that $F = t^2$.

4.7 Research on the relationship between job performance and job turnover has yielded conflicting results. Some early studies found a negative relationship (i.e., the lower the performance, the greater the likelihood of turnover) among all types of workers, whereas others detected a positive relationship (i.e., the higher the performance, the greater the likelihood of turnover) among those employed in white-collar positions. These early studies, however, focused on the linear (first-order) relationship between these variables. The possibility of a curvilinear (second-order) relationship between job performance and turnover was subsequently investigated both for white-collar workers (accountants) and for blue-collar workers (truck drivers). For each sample of workers the quadratic model $E(y) = \beta_0 + \beta_1 x + \beta_2 x^2$ was fitted, where

x = Performance rating (1 = poor, . . . , 4 = outstanding)

y_1 = Probability of turnover (i.e., likelihood of worker leaving his or her job within 1 year)

The results are shown in the table at the top of page 190.

ACCOUNTANTS (n = 169)		TRUCK DRIVERS (n = 107)	
$\hat{\beta}_1 = -1.40$	($t = -3.88$)	$\hat{\beta}_1 = 1.50$	($t = -3.83$)
$\hat{\beta}_2 = 1.13$	($t = 3.23$)	$\hat{\beta}_2 = 1.22$	($t = 4.70$)
$R^2 = .114$		$R^2 = .298$	

Source: Jackofsky, E. F., Ferris, K. R., and Breckenridge, B. G. "Evidence for a curvilinear relationship between job performance and turnover." *Journal of Management*, Vol. 12, No. 1, 1986, pp. 105–111.

a. Conduct a test of model adequacy for each of the two groups of workers. Use $\alpha = .05$.
b. Interpret the β estimates for each of the two groups of workers. Which of the $\hat{\beta}$'s have practical interpretations?
c. Is there evidence of upward curvature in the relationship between turnover and performance for accountants? Use $\alpha = .05$. What is the practical implication of this result?
d. Repeat part c for truck drivers.

4.8 Newpaper cartoons, although designed to be funny, often evoke hostility, pain, and/or aggression in readers, especially those cartoons that are violent. A study was undertaken to determine how violence in cartoons is related to aggression or pain (*Motivation and Emotion*, Vol. 10, 1986). A group of volunteers (psychology students) rated each of 32 violent newspaper cartoons (16 "Herman" and 16 "Far Side" cartoons) on three dimensions:

y = Funniness (0 = not funny, . . . , 9 = very funny)
x_1 = Pain (0 = none, . . . , 9 = a very great deal)
x_2 = Aggression/hostility (0 = none, . . . , 9 = a very great deal)

The ratings of the students on each dimension were averaged and the resulting $n = 32$ observations were subjected to a multiple regression analysis. Based on the underlying theory (called the *inverted-U theory*) that the funniness of a joke will increase at low levels of aggression or pain, level off, and then decrease at high levels of aggressiveness or pain, the following quadratic models were proposed:

Model 1: $E(y) = \beta_0 + \beta_1 x_1 + \beta_2 x_1^2$, $R^2 = .099$, $F = 1.60$

Model 2: $E(y) = \beta_0 + \beta_1 x_2 + \beta_2 x_2^2$, $R^2 = .100$, $F = 1.61$

a. According to the theory, what is the expected sign of β_2 in either model?
b. Is there sufficient evidence to indicate that the quadratic model relating pain to funniness rating is useful? Test at $\alpha = .05$.
c. Is there sufficient evidence to indicate that the quadratic model relating aggression/hostility to funniness rating is useful? Test at $\alpha = .05$.

4.9 Unions in the United States officially opposed a free trade agreement with Mexico, fearing a decrease in wages. However, in an article in the *Journal of Labor Research* (Spring 1993), one researcher used regression analysis to predict that a Mexican free trade agreement should have little influence on union wages and should increase nonunion wages. The model for union wages (y) included the independent variable years of completed education (x_1) among others.

a. The researcher hypothesized a curvilinear relationship between union wages (y) and education (x_1). Write a model for $E(y)$ as a function of x_1 that incorporates this hypothesis.
b. Refer to the model, part **a**. The researcher also hypothesized that education (x_1) will have a positive net impact on union wages (y). Specifically, wages (y) will increase with education (x_1), but at a decreasing rate. Explain how to test this hypothesis.

4.6 The Multiple Coefficient of Determination, R^2

Recall from Chapter 3 that the coefficient of determination, r^2, is a measure of how well a straight-line model fits a data set. To measure how well a general linear model (for example, a second-order model) fits a set of data, we compute the multiple regression equivalent of r^2, called the **multiple coefficient of determination** and denoted by the symbol R^2.

> **Definition 4.1**
>
> The **multiple coefficient of determination, R^2**, is defined as
>
> $$R^2 = 1 - \frac{\text{SSE}}{\text{SS}_{yy}} \qquad 0 \le R^2 \le 1$$
>
> where $\text{SSE} = \Sigma\,(y_i - \hat{y}_i)^2$, $\text{SS}_{yy} = \Sigma\,(y_i - \bar{y})^2$, and $\hat{y}_i$ is the predicted value of y_i for the multiple regression model.

Just as for the simple linear model, R^2 is a sample statistic that represents the fraction of the sample variation of the y values (measured by SS_{yy}) that is attributable to the regression model. Thus, $R^2 = 0$ implies a complete lack of fit of the model to the data, and $R^2 = 1$ implies a perfect fit, with the model passing through every data point. In general, the closer the value of R^2 is to 1, the better the model fits the data.

To illustrate, the value $R^2 = .9377$ for the immunoglobulin example is shaded in the SAS printout, Figure 4.9 (page 192). This very high value of R^2 implies that 93.8% of the sample variation in IgG (y) is attributable to, or explained by, the independent variable maximal oxygen uptake (x). Thus, R^2 is a sample statistic that tells how well the model fits the data, and thereby represents a measure of the utility of the entire model.

A large value of R^2 computed from the *sample* data does not necessarily mean that the model provides a good fit to all of the data points in the *population*. For example, a first-order linear model that contains three parameters will provide a perfect fit to a sample of three data points and R^2 will equal 1. Likewise, you will always obtain a perfect fit ($R^2 = 1$) to a set of n data points if the model

FIGURE 4.9
Portion of the SAS printout for the quadratic model

```
Dependent Variable: Y

                              Analysis of Variance

                                     Sum of          Mean
        Source             DF       Squares        Square       F Value        Prob>F

        Model               2  4602145.2169  2301072.6085       203.113        0.0001
        Error              27  305883.74976   11329.02777
        C Total            29  4908028.9667

            Root MSE        106.43791       R-square       0.9377
            Dep Mean       1557.63333       Adj R-sq       0.9331
            C.V.              6.83331

                              Parameter Estimates

                          Parameter        Standard      T for H0:
      Variable  DF         Estimate           Error     Parameter=0     Prob > |T|

      INTERCEP   1     -1462.141458    411.48209286          -3.553         0.0014
      X          1        88.214044     16.47736086           5.354         0.0001
      XX         1        -0.535378      0.15822840          -3.384         0.0022
```

contains exactly n parameters. Consequently, if you want to use the value of R^2 as a measure of how useful the model will be for predicting y, it should be based on a sample that contains substantially more data points than the number of parameters in the model.

> **Warning**
>
> In a multiple regression analysis, use the value of R^2 as a measure of how useful a linear model will be for predicting y only if the sample contains substantially more data points than the number of β parameters in the model.

As an alternative to using R^2 as a measure of model adequacy, the **adjusted multiple coefficient of determination**, denoted R_a^2, is often reported. The formula for R_a^2 is shown in the box.

> **The Adjusted Multiple Coefficient of Determination**
>
> The **adjusted multiple coefficient of determination** is given by
>
> $$R_a^2 = 1 - \frac{n-1}{n-(k+1)}\left(\frac{\text{SSE}}{\text{SS}_{yy}}\right)$$
>
> $$= 1 - \frac{n-1}{n-(k+1)}(1 - R^2)$$

Unlike R^2, R_a^2 takes into account ("adjusts" for) both the sample size n and the number of β parameters in the model. R_a^2 will always be smaller than R^2, and more importantly, cannot be "forced" to 1 by simply adding more and more independent variables to the model. Consequently, analysts prefer the more conservative R_a^2 when choosing a measure of model adequacy.

To illustrate, the value of R_a^2 is shown on the SAS printout (Figure 4.9) directly underneath the value of R^2. Note that $R_a^2 = .9331$, a value only slightly smaller than R^2. Our interpretation is that after adjusting for sample size and the number of parameters in the model, approximately 93% of the sample variation in IgG can be "explained" by the second-order model.

Despite their utility, R^2 and R_a^2 are only sample statistics. Consequently, it is dangerous to judge the usefulness of the model based solely on these values. We discuss a more formal method of checking the predictive ability of a general linear model—a statistical test of hypothesis—in the following section.

4.7 Testing the Utility of a Model: The Analysis of Variance *F* Test

The objective of step 5 in a multiple regression analysis is to conduct a test of the utility of a general linear model—that is, a test to determine whether the model is adequate for predicting y. Conducting t tests on each β parameter in a model (Section 4.5) is generally not a good way to determine whether a model is contributing information for the prediction of y. If we were to conduct a series of t tests to determine whether the independent variables are contributing to the predictive relationship, we would be very likely to make one or more errors in deciding which terms to retain in the model and which to exclude.

Suppose you fit a model with 10 independent variables, $x_1, x_2, \ldots, x_{10}$, and decide to conduct t tests on all 10 individual β's in the model, each at $\alpha = .05$. Even if all the β parameters (except β_0) in the model are equal to 0, you will incorrectly reject the null hypothesis at least once and conclude that some β parameter is nonzero approximately 40% of the time.* In other words, the overall Type I error is about .40, not .05!

Thus, in multiple regression models for which a large number of independent variables are being considered, conducting a series of t tests may cause the experimenter to include a large number of insignificant variables and exclude some useful ones. If we want to test the utility of a multiple regression model, we will need a global test (one that encompasses all the β parameters).

In particular, for the second-order model $E(y) = \beta_0 + \beta_1 x + \beta_2 x^2$ fitted to the immunoglobulin data, the test

H_0: $\beta_1 = \beta_2 = 0$

H_a: At least one of the parameters β_1 and β_2 is nonzero.

---

*The proof of this result proceeds as follows:

$$\begin{aligned} & P(\text{Reject } H_0 \text{ at least once} \mid \beta_1 = \beta_2 = \cdots = \beta_{10} = 0) \\ &= 1 - P(\text{Reject } H_0 \text{ no times} \mid \beta_1 = \beta_2 = \cdots = \beta_{10} = 0) \\ &\leq 1 - [P(\text{Accept } H_0\text{: } \beta_1 = 0 \mid \beta_1 = 0) \cdot P(\text{Accept } H_0\text{: } \beta_2 = 0 \mid \beta_2 = 0) \cdots \\ &\quad \times P(\text{Accept } H_0\text{: } \beta_{10} = 0 \mid \beta_{10} = 0)] \\ &= 1 - [(1 - \alpha)^{10}] = 1 - (.95)^{10} = .401 \end{aligned}$$

would formally test the global utility of the model. The test statistic used to test this null hypothesis is

$$\textit{Test statistic:} \quad F = \frac{\text{Mean square for model}}{\text{Mean square for error}} = \frac{\text{SS(model)}/k}{\text{SSE}/[n - (k + 1)]}$$

where n is the number of data points, k is the number of parameters in the model (not including β_0), and SS(Model) = SS(Total) − SSE. When H_0 is true, this F test statistic will have an F probability distribution with k df in the numerator and $[n - (k + 1)]$ df in the denominator. The upper-tail values of the F distribution are given in Tables 3, 4, 5, and 6 of Appendix C.

It can be shown (proof omitted) that an equivalent form of this test statistic is

$$F = \frac{R^2/k}{(1 - R^2)/[n - (k + 1)]}$$

Therefore, the F test statistic becomes large as the coefficient of determination R^2 becomes large. To determine how large F must be before we can conclude at a given value of α that the model is useful for predicting y, we set up the rejection region as follows:

$$\textit{Rejection region:} \quad F > F_\alpha \quad \text{where} \quad \nu_1 = k \text{ df and } \nu_2 = n - (k + 1) \text{ df}$$

For the immunoglobulin example, $n = 30$, $k = 2$, $n - (k + 1) = 27$, and $\alpha = .05$. Consequently, we will reject $H_0\colon \beta_1 = \beta_2 = 0$ if

$$F > F_{.05} \quad \text{where } \nu_1 = 2 \text{ and } \nu_2 = 27$$

or

$$F > 3.35 \quad \text{(see Figure 4.10)}$$

FIGURE 4.10

Rejection region for the F statistic with $\nu_1 = 2$, $\nu_2 = 27$, and $\alpha = .05$

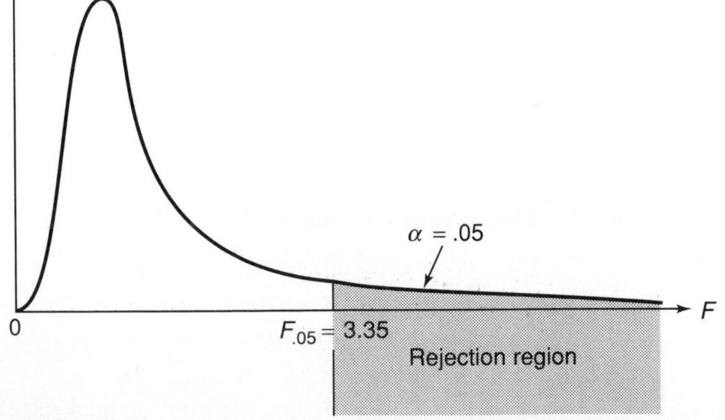

From the SAS printout shown in Figure 4.11, we find that the computed F (shaded in the upper right corner of the printout) is 203.113. Since this value greatly exceeds the tabulated value of 3.35, we conclude that at least one of the model coefficients β_1 and β_2 is nonzero. Therefore, this global F test indicates that the second-order model $y = \beta_0 + \beta_1 x + \beta_2 x^2 + \varepsilon$ is useful for predicting amount of immunoglobulin, IgG.

FIGURE 4.11
Portion of the SAS printout for the quadratic model

Dependent Variable: Y

Analysis of Variance

Source	DF	Sum of Squares	Mean Square	F Value	Prob>F
Model	2	4602145.2169	2301072.6085	203.113	0.0001
Error	27	305883.74976	11329.02777		
C Total	29	4908028.9667			

Root MSE	106.43791	R-square	0.9377
Dep Mean	1557.63333	Adj R-sq	0.9331
C.V.	6.83331		

Parameter Estimates

Variable	DF	Parameter Estimate	Standard Error	T for H0: Parameter=0	Prob > |T|
INTERCEP	1	-1462.141458	411.48209286	-3.553	0.0014
X	1	88.214044	16.47736086	5.354	0.0001
XX	1	-0.535378	0.15822840	-3.384	0.0022

Test of the Overall Utility of a Multiple Regression Model: The Analysis of Variance F Test

H_0: $\beta_1 = \beta_2 = \cdots = \beta_k = 0$

H_a: At least one of the parameters, $\beta_1, \beta_2, \ldots, \beta_k$, differs from 0.

Rejection region: $F > F_\alpha$

where the distribution of F depends on k numerator df and $n - (k + 1)$ denominator df

Test statistic:

$$F = \frac{\text{Mean square for model}}{\text{Mean square for error}} = \frac{\text{SS(Model)}/k}{\text{SSE}/[n - (k + 1)]}$$

$$= \frac{R^2/k}{(1 - R^2)/[n - (k + 1)]}$$

where

n = Number of observations

k = Number of parameters in the model (excluding β_0)

R^2 = Multiple coefficient of determination

Values of F_α for $\alpha = .10, .05, .025$, and .01 are given in Tables 3, 4, 5, and 6 of Appendix C.

We could arrive at the same decision by checking the observed significance level (p-value) of the F test, given as **Prob > F** in the SAS printout. This value (shaded in Figure 4.11) indicates that we will reject H_0 for any α greater than $p = .0001$.

EXAMPLE 4.2

Refer to Example 4.1, in which an antique collector modeled the auction price y of grandfather clocks as a function of the age of the clock, x_1, and the number of bidders, x_2. The hypothesized model was

$$y = \beta_0 + \beta_1 x_1 + \beta_2 x_2 + \varepsilon$$

A sample of 32 observations was obtained, with the results summarized in the MINITAB printout repeated in Figure 4.12. Discuss the coefficient of determination R^2 for this example and then conduct the global F test of model utility using $\alpha = .05$.

FIGURE 4.12
Portion of the MINITAB printout for Example 4.2

```
The regression equation is
Y = - 1339 + 12.7 X1 + 86.0 X2

Predictor       Coef       Stdev     t-ratio        p
Constant     -1339.0       173.8       -7.70    0.000
X1           12.7406      0.9047       14.08    0.000
X2            85.953       8.729        9.85    0.000

s = 133.5       R-sq = 89.2%      R-sq(adj) = 88.5%

Analysis of Variance

SOURCE       DF          SS         MS          F        p
Regression    2     4283063    2141532     120.19    0.000
Error        29      516727      17818
Total        31     4799789
```

Solution

The R^2 value (shaded in Figure 4.12) is .892. This implies that 89% of the variation of the y values (the auction prices) about their mean can be explained by the least squares model. We now test

H_0: $\beta_1 = \beta_2 = 0$ [*Note:* $k = 2$]

H_a: At least one of the two model coefficients is nonzero.

Test statistic: $F = \dfrac{\text{Mean square for model}}{\text{Mean square for error}} = \dfrac{\text{SS(Model)}/k}{\text{SSE}/[n - (k + 1)]}$

Rejection region: $F > F_\alpha$ where $\nu_1 = k$ and $\nu_2 = n - (k + 1)$

For this example, $n = 32$, $k = 2$, and $n - (k + 1) = 32 - 3 = 29$. Then, for $\alpha = .05$, we will reject H_0: $\beta_1 = \beta_2 = 0$ if $F > F_{.05}$, i.e., if $F > 3.33$ (obtained from Table 4 of Appendix C). The computed value of the F test statistic is 120.19 (see Figure 4.12). Since this value of F falls in the rejection region ($F = 120.19$ greatly exceeds $F_{.05} = 3.33$ and $\alpha = .05$ greatly exceeds $p = .0001$), the data provide strong evidence that at least one of the model coefficients is nonzero. The model appears to be useful for predicting auction prices.

Can we be sure that the best prediction model has been found if the global F test indicates that a model is useful? Unfortunately, we cannot. There is no way of knowing whether the addition of other independent variables will further improve the utility of the model, as the following example indicates.

EXAMPLE 4.3

Refer to Examples 4.1 and 4.2. Suppose the collector, having observed many auctions, believes that the *rate of increase* of the auction price with age will be driven upward by a large number of bidders. Thus, instead of a relationship like that shown in Figure 4.13a, in which the rate of increase in price with age is the same for any number of bidders, the collector believes the relationship is like that shown in Figure 4.13b. Note that as the number of bidders increases from 5 to 15, the slope of the price versus age line increases. When the slope of the relationship between y and one independent variable (x_1) depends on the value of a second independent variable (x_2), as is the case here, we say that x_1 and x_2 **interact.*** A model that accounts for this type of interaction is written

$$y = \beta_0 + \beta_1 x_1 + \beta_2 x_2 + \beta_3 x_1 x_2 + \varepsilon$$

Note that the increase in the mean price $E(y)$ for each 1-year increase in age x_1 is no longer given by the constant β_1, but is now $\beta_1 + \beta_3 x_2$. That is, the amount $E(y)$ increases for each 1-unit increase in x_1 is *dependent on the number of bidders* x_2. Thus, the two variables x_1 and x_2 interact to affect y.

FIGURE 4.13
Examples of no interaction and interaction models

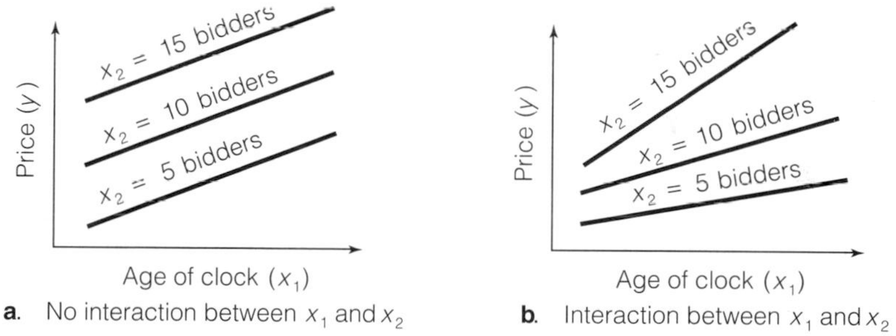

The 32 data points listed in Table 4.2 were used to fit the first-order model with interaction. A portion of the MINITAB printout is shown in Figure 4.14 on page 198. Test the hypothesis that the price–age slope increases as the number of bidders increases, i.e., that age and number of bidders, x_2, interact positively.

Solution

The model is

$$y = \beta_0 + \beta_1 x_1 + \beta_2 x_2 + \beta_3 x_1 x_2 + \varepsilon$$

and the hypothesis of interest to the collector concerns the parameter β_3. Specifically,

$$H_0: \ \beta_3 = 0$$
$$H_a: \ \beta_3 > 0$$

*A more complete discussion of interaction is given in Section 4.9 and Chapter 5.

FIGURE 4.14
Portion of the MINITAB printout for the model with interaction, Example 4.3

```
The regression equation is
Y = 320 + 0.88 X1 - 93.3 X2 + 1.30 X1X2

Predictor        Coef        Stdev     t-ratio        p
Constant        320.5        295.1        1.09    0.287
X1              0.878        2.032        0.43    0.669
X2             -93.26        29.89       -3.12    0.004
X1X2           1.2978       0.2123        6.11    0.000

s = 88.91        R-sq = 95.4%        R-sq(adj) = 94.9%

Analysis of Variance

SOURCE        DF          SS         MS          F        p
Regression     3     4578428    1526142     193.04    0.000
Error         28      221362       7906
Total         31     4799789
```

Test statistic: $t = \dfrac{\hat{\beta}_3}{s_{\hat{\beta}_3}}$

Rejection region: For $\alpha = .05$, $t > t_{.05}$
where df $= n - (k + 1)$

In this example, $n = 32$, $k = 3$, df $= n - (k + 1) = 32 - 4 = 28$, and thus, $t_{.05} = 1.701$.

The t value corresponding to $\hat{\beta}_3$ is shaded in Figure 4.14. The value, $t = 6.11$, exceeds 1.701 and, therefore, falls in the rejection region. Thus, the collector can conclude that the rate of change of the mean price of the clocks with age increases as the number of bidders increases, i.e., x_1 and x_2 interact positively. (The same conclusion can be reached by noting that the p-value of the test is approximately 0.) Thus, it appears that the interaction term should be included in the model.

One note of caution: Although the coefficient of x_2 is negative ($\hat{\beta}_2 = -93.26$) in Example 4.3, this does not imply that auction price decreases as the number of bidders increases. Since interaction is present, the rate of change (slope) of mean auction price with the number of bidders *depends on* x_1, the age of the clock. Thus, for example, the estimated rate of change of y with x_2 for a 150-year-old clock is

$$\textit{Estimated } x_2 \textit{ slope: } \quad \hat{\beta}_2 + \hat{\beta}_3 x_1 = -93.26 + 1.30(150) = 101.74$$

In other words, we estimate that the auction price of a 150-year-old clock will increase by \$101.74 for every additional bidder. Although this rate of increase will vary as x_1 is changed, it will remain positive for the range of values of x_1 included in the sample. Use extreme care in interpreting the signs and sizes of coefficients in a multiple regression model.

After we have determined that the overall model is useful for predicting y using the F test, we may elect to conduct one or more t tests on the individual

β parameters (see Section 4.5). However, the test (or tests) to be conducted should be decided a priori, i.e., prior to fitting the model. Also, we should limit the number of t tests conducted to avoid the potential problem of making too many Type I errors. Generally, the regression analyst will conduct t tests on only the "most important" β's. These are usually the β's associated with higher-order terms (x_1^2, x_1x_2, etc.). We provide insight in identifying the most important β's in a linear model in Chapter 5.

Recommendation for Checking the Utility of a Multiple Regression Model

1. First, conduct a test of overall model adequacy using the F test, i.e., test

$$H_0: \beta_1 = \beta_2 = \cdots = \beta_k = 0$$

   If the model is deemed adequate (i.e., if you reject H_0), then proceed to step 2. Otherwise, you should hypothesize and fit another model. The new model may include more independent variables or higher-order terms (see Chapter 5).
2. Conduct t tests on those β parameters in which you are particularly interested (i.e., the "most important" β's). These usually involve only the β's associated with higher-order terms (x_1^2, x_1x_2, etc.). However, it is a safe practice to limit the number of β's that are tested. Conducting a series of t tests leads to a high overall Type I error rate α.

Warning

Rejecting H_0: $\beta_1 = \beta_2 = \cdots = \beta_k = 0$ in a test of overall model adequacy does not necessarily imply that the model is best for predicting y. Another model may prove even more useful in terms of providing more reliable estimates and predictions.

EXERCISES

4.10 Refer to the *Journal of Adlerian Theory, Research, and Practice* study of depression, Exercise 4.3. Recall that the researchers fitted the model

$$E(y) = \beta_0 + \beta_1x_1 + \beta_2x_2 + \beta_3x_3$$

where

y = Zung scale of depression

x_1 = ASO scale of self-acceptance

x_2 = Burns scale of perfectionism

x_3 = Rotter scale of reinforcement

a. The model was fitted to the $n = 76$ points and resulted in a coefficient of determination of $R^2 = .70$. Interpret this value.
b. Is there sufficient evidence to indicate that the model is useful for predicting depression (Zung scale) score? Test using $\alpha = .05$.

4.11 Because the coefficient of determination R^2 always increases when a new independent variable is added to the model, it is tempting to include many variables in a model to force R^2 to be near 1. However, doing so reduces the degrees of freedom available for estimating σ^2, which adversely affects our ability to make reliable inferences. As an example, suppose you want to use the responses to a survey consisting of 18 demographic, social, and economic questions to model a college student's intelligence quotient (IQ). You fit the model

$$y = \beta_0 + \beta_1 x_1 + \beta_2 x_2 + \cdots + \beta_{17} x_{17} + \beta_{18} x_{18} + \varepsilon$$

where y = IQ and $x_1, x_2, \ldots, x_{18}$ are the 18 independent variables. Data for only 20 students ($n = 20$) are used to fit the model, and you obtain $R^2 = .95$.
a. Test to see whether this impressive-looking R^2 is large enough for you to infer that this model is useful, i.e., that at least one term in the model is important for predicting IQ. Use $\alpha = .05$.
b. Calculate R_a^2 and interpret its value.

4.12 Refer to *The Real Estate Appraiser* multiple regression model of sale price of a property, Exercise 4.4. Information from the SAS printout for the analysis is reproduced here.

DEPENDENT VARIABLE: SALE PRICE

ANALYSIS OF VARIANCE

Source	DF	Sum of Squares	Mean Square	F Value	Prob>F
Model	27	24,184,211,898	895,711,551.79	20.914	.0001
Error	129	5,524,834,283	42,828,172.73		
C Total	156	29,709,046,181			
	Root MSE	6544.324	R-Square	.8140	
	Dep Mean	173157.5	Adj R-Sq	.7751	
	C.V.	3.779404			

PARAMETER ESTIMATES

Variable	Parameter Estimate	Std Error	95% Confidence Interval (@129df=1.98)	T for H_0: Parameter=0	Prob>|T|
Intercept	96,603	12,530	(71,794 to 121,412)	7.710	.0001
Time	150	123	(−94 to 394)	1.220	.2248
Lot size	**.60**	**.30**	**(0.01 to 119)**	2.022	**.0452***
Age	381	502	(−613 to 1,375)	.758	.4501
GLA	**22.40**	**3.67**	**(15.13 to 29.67)**	6.099	**.0001***
Bedrooms	2,263	1,609	(−923 to 5,499)	1.407	.1619
Half Baths	**5,962**	**2,934**	**(153 to 11,771)**	2.032	**.0442***
Corner Lot	−1,481	1,692	(−4,831 to 1,869)	−.876	.3829

(continued)

PARAMETER ESTIMATES

Variable	Parameter Estimate	Std Error	95% Confidence Interval (@129df=1.98)	T for H_0: Parameter=0	Prob>|T|
Cul-de-sac	−56	2,557	(−5,119 to 5,007)	−.022	.9825
Back to Woods	**4,086**	**2,044**	**(39 to 8,133)**	1.999	**.0477***
Deck	2,408	2,167	(−1,883 to 6,699)	1.111	.2686
Fence	**2,896**	**1,271**	**(379 to 5,413)**	2.279	**.0243***
Shed	70	1,343	(−2,589 to 2,729)	.052	.9588
Patio	2,377	1,671	(−932 to 5,686)	1.423	.1572
Portico	−906	2,963	(−6,773 to 4,961)	−.306	.7603
Screen Porch	**5,021**	**2,038**	**(986 to 9,056)**	2.463	**.0151***
In-grnd Pool	**7,570**	**3,028**	**(1,575 to 13,565)**	2.500	**.0137***
Garage	**2,989**	**1,446**	**(126 to 5,852)**	2.068	**.0407***
Driveway	−1,844	3,222	(−8,224 to 4,536)	−.572	.5681
Fireplace	1,290	1,277	(−1,238 to 3,818)	1.010	.3144
Brick Facade	−2,140	2,369	(−6,381 to 2,551)	−.903	.3680
Updated Kit.	**4,171**	**1,470**	**(1,260 to 7,082)**	2.837	**.0053***
Remodel Kit.	**6,091**	**2,367**	**(1,404 to 10,778)**	2.574	**.0112***
Intercom	1,933	2,146	(−2,316 to 6,182)	.901	.3693
Cen. Vacuum	**−4,636**	**2,166**	**(−8,925 to −347)**	−2.140	**.0342***
Skylights	**7,744**	**2,622**	**(2,552 to 12,936)**	−2.954	**.0037***
Air Filter	874	2,506	(−4,088 to 5,836)	−.349	.7280
Bay Window	−3,174	2,086	(−7,304 to 956)	−1.522	.1305

*Indicates significance at the 5% significance level.
Source: Gilson, S. J. "A case study—Comparing the results: Multiple regression analysis vs. matched pairs in residential subdivision." *The Real Estate Appraiser*, Apr. 1992, p. 37 (Table 4).

a. Interpret the values of **F Value**, **Root MSE**, **R-Square**, and **Adj R-Sq** shown on the printout.

b. The independent variables with β coefficients significantly different from 0 (at $\alpha = .05$) are highlighted in bold on the printout. The nonsignificant variables are not highlighted. Would you advise the property appraiser to ignore any value adjustments based on nonsignificant independent variables? Explain.

4.13 According to the 1990 census, the number of homeless people in the United States is more than a quarter of a million. Yet little is known about what causes homelessness. Economists at the City University of New York used multiple regression to assist in determining the factors that cause homelessness in American intercities (*American Economic Review*, Mar. 1993). Data on the number y of homeless per 100,000 population in $n = 50$ metropolitan areas were obtained from the Department of Housing and Urban Development. In addition, the 16 independent variables listed in the table at the top of page 202 were measured for each city and a multiple regression analysis performed by fitting the first-order model: $E(y) = \beta_0 + \beta_1 x_1 + \beta_2 x_2 + \cdots + \beta_{16} x_{16}$

a. Interpret the β estimate for the independent variable, rental price.

b. Test the hypothesis that the incidence of homelessness decreases as employment growth increases. Use $\alpha = .05$.

c. Test (at $\alpha = .05$) each of the 16 independent variables to determine which are significantly related to homelessness.

d. What is the danger in performing the t tests, part **c**?

e. For this model, $R_a^2 = .83$. Interpret this result.

INDEPENDENT VARIABLE	β ESTIMATE	t VALUE
Intercept	307.54	—
Rental price (10% percentile)	2.87	3.93
Vacancy rate (10% percentile)	−872.90	−1.58
Rent-control law (yes or no)	−15.50	−.23
Employment growth	−859.09	−2.71
Share of employment in service industries	−347.69	−1.33
Size of low-skill labor market	−1,003.87	−.38
Households (per 100,000) below poverty level	.013	1.22
Public welfare expenditures	.11	.59
AFDC benefits	−.95	−2.58
SSI benefits	1.07	2.14
Percent reduction in AFDC (nonpoor percents)	146.62	1.49
AFDC accuracy rate	98.15	.13
Mental health in-patients (per 100,000)	−.83	−1.50
Fraction of births to teenage mothers	−1,173.00	−1.39
Blacks (per 100,000)	.004	1.78
1984 population (100,000's)	1.22	1.44

Source: Honig, M., and Filer, R. K. "Causes of intercity variation in homelessness." *American Economic Review*, Vol. 83, No. 1, Mar. 1993, p. 251 (Table 2).

4.14 Most academic theorists advocate group decision making as a way to resolve conflicts among a manager's subordinates. Many managers reject this proposition in practice, however, believing that airing conflict in groups is counterproductive. A study was conducted to examine this contradiction between accepted normative theory and current practice in Australia (*Organizational Behavior & Human Decision Processes*, Vol. 39, 1987). For one part of the study, multiple regression analysis was used to test "the proposition that the effective use of group discussion methods to resolve conflict depends on the manager's ability and willingness to encourage subordinates to confront conflict." A sample of 89 upper-level managers were asked to complete a questionnaire that measured the following (on a 7-point Likert scale):

y = Average performance of manager's subordinates (i.e., subordinate performance)

x_1 = Manager's preferred level of subordinate participation in decision making when conflict is present (i.e., group decision method)

x_2 = Average of subordinates' perceptions of manager's inclination to legitimize conflict (i.e., conflict legitimization)

The interaction model $E(y) = \beta_0 + \beta_1 x_1 + \beta_2 x_2 + \beta_3 x_1 x_2$ was fitted to the 89 data points, with the following results (t values in parentheses):

$$\hat{y} = 7.09 - \underset{(-1.86)}{.44x_1} - \underset{(-.01)}{.01x_2} + \underset{(1.85)}{.06x_1x_2} \qquad R^2 = .22$$

a. Conduct a test to determine whether the model is adequate for predicting subordinate performance y. Use $\alpha = .10$.

b. Use the least squares prediction equation to graph the estimated relationships between subordinate performance (y) and group decision method (x_1) for low conflict legitimization ($x_2 = 1$) and high conflict legitimization ($x_2 = 7$). Interpret the graphs.

c. Conduct a test to determine whether the relationship between subordinate performance (y) and a manager's use of a group decision method (x_1) depends on the manager's legitimization of conflict (x_2). Use $\alpha = .10$.

d. Based on the result of part **c**, would you recommend that the researchers conduct t tests on β_1 and β_2? Explain.

4.15 Marketers are keenly interested in the factors that motivate coupon usage by consumers. Three dominant motivational factors are thought to be (1) price reduction, (2) time and effort required to collect coupons, and (3) satisfaction with self (pride). Using questionnaire data collected for a sample of $n = 290$ shoppers, a trio of marketing researchers examined the relationship between coupon usage and these factors (*The Journal of Consumer Marketing*, Spring 1988). The multiple regression model took the form

$$E(y) = \beta_0 + \beta_1 x_1 + \beta_2 x_2 + \beta_3 x_3$$

where

$$y = \text{Coupon redemption rate}$$
$$x_1 = \text{Price-consciousness score}$$
$$x_2 = \text{Time-value score}$$
$$x_3 = \text{Satisfaction/pride score}$$

The results are summarized as follows (t values for testing β's in parentheses):

$\hat{\beta}_1 = .09784\ (1.444)$ $\qquad R^2 = .09226$
$\hat{\beta}_2 = -.13134\ (-1.695)$ $\qquad F = 9.6893$
$\hat{\beta}_3 = .20019\ (2.571)$

a. Conduct an overall test of model accuracy. Use $\alpha = .10$.
b. In theory, coupon users are more price-conscious than nonusers. Test the theory using $\alpha = .10$.
c. Interpret the negative β estimate for time-value score (x_2).

4.16 To what degree do the attitudes of your peers influence your behavior? There is general agreement among sociologists and psychologists that your behavior is dependent on the attitudes of and social support from your friends, neighbors, etc. However, it is unclear whether the effects of attitude and social support are additive or interactive. An attempt to resolve this attitude–behavior issue was presented in *Social Psychology Quarterly* (Vol. 50, 1987). The study included a sample of $n = 143$ adult drinkers in an urban setting characterized by high physical availability of alcoholic beverages. The goal of the study was to build a model relating frequency of drinking alcoholic beverages, y, to attitude toward drinking (x_1) and social support (x_2). Consider the interaction model

$$E(y) = \beta_0 + \beta_1 x_1 + \beta_2 x_2 + \beta_3 x_1 x_2$$

a. Interpret the phrase "x_1 and x_2 interact" in terms of the problem.
b. Write the null and alternative hypotheses for determining whether attitude (x_1) and social support (x_2) interact.
c. The reported p-value for the test, part **b**, was $p < .001$. Interpret this result.

4.8 Using the Model for Estimation and Prediction

In Section 3.9, we discussed the use of the least squares line for estimating the mean value of y, $E(y)$, for some value of x, say, $x = x_p$. We also showed how to use the same fitted model to predict, when $x = x_p$, some value of y to be observed in the future. Recall that the least squares line yielded the same value for both the estimate of $E(y)$ and the prediction of some future value of y. That is, both are the result obtained by substituting x_p into the prediction equation $\hat{y} = \hat{\beta}_0 + \hat{\beta}_1 x$ and calculating $\hat{y}$. There the equivalence ends. The confidence interval for the mean $E(y)$ was narrower than the prediction interval for y, because of the additional uncertainty attributable to the random error ε when predicting some future value of y.

These same concepts carry over to the multiple regression model. For example, suppose we want to estimate the mean IgG in blood for a given value of maximal oxygen uptake, say, $x_p = 40$ milliliters per kilogram. Assuming the quadratic model represents the true relationship between IgG and maximal oxygen uptake, we want to estimate

$$E(y) = \beta_0 + \beta_1 x_p + \beta_2 x_p^2 = \beta_0 + \beta_1(40) + \beta_2(40)^2$$

Substituting into the least squares prediction equation yields the estimate of $E(y)$:

$$\begin{aligned}\hat{y} &= \hat{\beta}_0 + \hat{\beta}_1(40) + \hat{\beta}_2(40)^2 \\ &= -1{,}462.14 - 88.21(40) - .5354(40)^2 = 1{,}209.62\end{aligned}$$

To form a confidence interval for the mean, we must know the standard deviation of the sampling distribution for the estimator $\hat{y}$. For multiple regression models, the form of this standard deviation is rather complex. However, some regression packages allow us to obtain the confidence intervals for mean values of y at any given setting of the independent variables. A portion of the SAS output for the IgG example is shown in Figure 4.15. The mean values and corresponding 95% confidence intervals are shown in the columns labeled **Predict Value**, **Lower95% Mean**, and **Upper95% Mean**. In the last row (shaded) in Figure 4.15, we observe that $\hat{y} = 1{,}209.8$ when $x_p = 40$, which agrees (with rounding) with our previous calculation. The corresponding 95% confidence interval for the true mean of y is shown to be 1,156.1 to 1,263.5 (see Figure 4.16).

If we were interested in predicting IgG in the blood of a person with a maximal oxygen uptake of 40 milliliters per kilogram, $\hat{y} = 1{,}209.8$ would be used as the predicted value. However, the prediction interval for a particular value of y will be wider than the confidence interval for the mean value. This is reflected by the printout shown in Figure 4.17 (page 206), which gives the predicted values of y and the corresponding 95% prediction intervals. Note that the predicted value for $x_p = 40$ is 1,209.8 (shaded in the last row), and the prediction interval extends from 984.9 to 1,434.7. This interval is shown graphically in Figure 4.18.

Unfortunately, not all statistical software packages have the capability to produce confidence intervals for means and prediction intervals for particular y values. This is a significant oversight, since the estimation of mean values and the prediction of particular values represent the culmination of our model-building efforts: using the model to make inferences about the dependent variable y.

FIGURE 4.15

SAS printout for estimated mean values and corresponding intervals

Obs	X	Dep Var Y	Predict Value	Std Err Predict	Lower95% Mean	Upper95% Mean	Residual
1	34.6	881.0	949.1	41.023	865.0	1033.3	-68.1312
2	45	1290.0	1423.3	26.185	1369.6	1477.1	-133.3
3	62.3	2147.0	1955.6	27.746	1898.7	2012.6	191.4
4	58.9	1909.0	1876.3	27.681	1819.5	1933.1	32.6734
5	42.5	1282.0	1319.9	25.101	1268.4	1371.4	-37.9287
6	44.3	1530.0	1395.1	25.763	1342.2	1447.9	134.9
7	67.9	2067.0	2059.3	39.222	1978.8	2139.8	7.7205
8	58.5	1982.0	1866.2	27.828	1809.1	1923.3	115.8
9	35.6	1019.0	999.8	36.959	923.9	1075.6	19.2383
10	49.6	1651.0	1596.2	28.994	1536.7	1655.6	54.8407
11	33	752.0	865.9	48.595	766.2	965.6	-113.9
12	52	1687.0	1677.3	29.600	1616.6	1738.1	9.6736
13	61.4	1782.0	1935.8	27.399	1879.6	1992.1	-153.8
14	50.2	1529.0	1617.0	29.222	1557.1	1677.0	-88.0293
15	34.1	969.0	923.4	43.253	834.7	1012.2	45.5856
16	52.5	1660.0	1693.5	29.621	1632.7	1754.2	-33.4599
17	69.9	2121.0	2088.2	47.535	1990.6	2185.7	32.8426
18	38.8	1382.0	1154.6	27.911	1097.3	1211.9	227.4
19	50.6	1714.0	1630.7	29.346	1570.5	1690.9	83.2716
20	69.4	1959.0	2081.3	45.265	1988.5	2174.2	-122.3
21	37.4	1158.0	1088.2	31.088	1024.4	1152.0	69.8017
22	35.1	965.0	974.6	38.923	894.7	1054.4	-9.5803
23	43	1456.0	1341.1	25.201	1289.4	1392.9	114.9
24	44.1	1273.0	1386.9	25.655	1334.3	1439.5	-113.9
25	49.8	1418.0	1603.2	29.075	1543.5	1662.8	-185.2
26	54.5	1743.0	1755.3	29.363	1695.1	1815.6	-12.3171
27	68.5	1997.0	2068.4	41.498	1983.2	2153.5	-71.3926
28	69.5	2177.0	2082.7	45.709	1988.9	2176.5	94.2756
29	63	1965.0	1970.4	28.253	1912.5	2028.4	-5.4276
30	43.2	1264.0	1349.6	25.262	1297.7	1401.4	-85.5612
31	40	.	1209.8	26.174	1156.1	1263.5	.

FIGURE 4.16

Confidence interval for mean IgG when $x_p = 40$

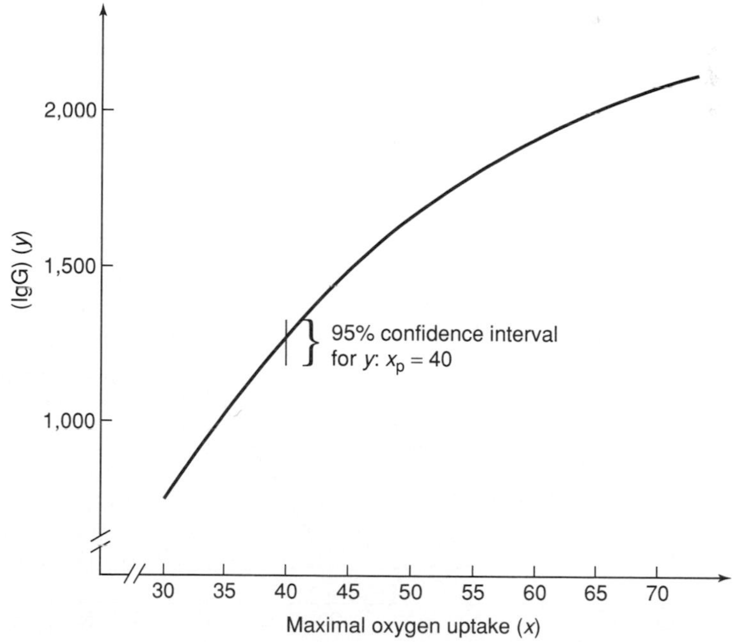

FIGURE 4.17
SAS printout for predicted values and corresponding prediction intervals

Obs	X	Dep Var Y	Predict Value	Std Err Predict	Lower95% Predict	Upper95% Predict	Residual
1	34.6	881.0	949.1	41.023	715.1	1183.2	-68.1312
2	45	1290.0	1423.3	26.185	1198.4	1648.3	-133.3
3	62.3	2147.0	1955.6	27.746	1729.9	2181.3	191.4
4	58.9	1909.0	1876.3	27.681	1650.7	2102.0	32.6734
5	42.5	1282.0	1319.9	25.101	1095.5	1544.3	-37.9287
6	44.3	1530.0	1395.1	25.763	1170.4	1619.8	134.9
7	67.9	2067.0	2059.3	39.222	1826.5	2292.0	7.7205
8	58.5	1982.0	1866.2	27.828	1640.5	2091.9	115.8
9	35.6	1019.0	999.8	36.959	768.6	1230.9	19.2383
10	49.6	1651.0	1596.2	28.994	1369.8	1822.5	54.8407
11	33	752.0	865.9	48.595	625.8	1106.0	-113.9
12	52	1687.0	1677.3	29.600	1450.6	1904.0	9.6736
13	61.4	1782.0	1935.8	27.399	1710.3	2161.4	-153.8
14	50.2	1529.0	1617.0	29.222	1390.6	1843.5	-88.0293
15	34.1	969.0	923.4	43.253	687.7	1159.1	45.5856
16	52.5	1660.0	1693.5	29.621	1466.8	1920.2	-33.4599
17	69.9	2121.0	2088.2	47.535	1849.0	2327.3	32.8426
18	38.8	1382.0	1154.6	27.911	928.8	1380.4	227.4
19	50.6	1714.0	1630.7	29.346	1404.2	1857.3	83.2716
20	69.4	1959.0	2081.3	45.265	1844.0	2318.7	-122.3
21	37.4	1158.0	1088.2	31.088	860.7	1315.7	69.8017
22	35.1	965.0	974.6	38.923	742.0	1207.1	-9.5803
23	43	1456.0	1341.1	25.201	1116.7	1565.6	114.9
24	44.1	1273.0	1386.9	25.655	1162.2	1611.5	-113.9
25	49.8	1418.0	1603.2	29.075	1376.8	1829.6	-185.2
26	54.5	1743.0	1755.3	29.363	1528.8	1981.9	-12.3171
27	68.5	1997.0	2068.4	41.498	1834.0	2302.8	-71.3926
28	69.5	2177.0	2082.7	45.709	1845.0	2320.4	94.2756
29	63	1965.0	1970.4	28.253	1744.5	2196.4	-5.4276
30	43.2	1264.0	1349.6	25.262	1125.1	1574.0	-85.5612
31	40	.	1209.8	26.174	984.9	1434.7	.

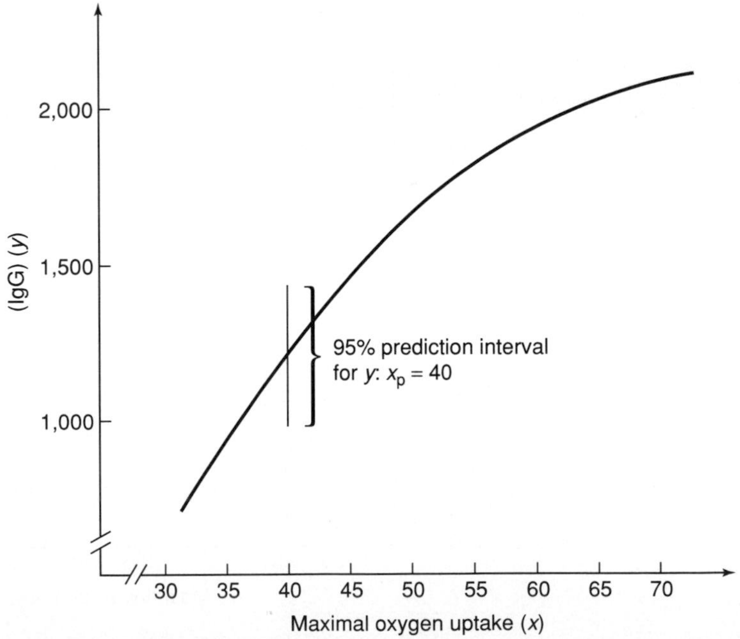

FIGURE 4.18
Prediction interval for IgG when $x_p = 40$

EXERCISES

4.17 In a production facility, an accurate estimate of man-hours needed to complete a task is crucial to management in making such decisions as the proper number of workers to hire, an accurate deadline to quote a client, or cost-analysis decisions regarding budgets. A manufacturer of boiler drums wants to use regression to predict the number of man-hours needed to erect the drums in future projects. To accomplish this, data for 35 boilers were collected. In addition to man-hours (y), the variables measured were boiler capacity (x_1 = pounds per hour or lb/hr), boiler design pressure (x_2 = pounds per square inch or psi), boiler type (x_3 = 1 if industry field erected, 0 if utility field erected), and drum type (x_4 = 1 if steam, 0 if mud). The data are provided in the table. A MINITAB printout for the model $E(y) = \beta_0 + \beta_1 x_1 + \beta_2 x_2 + \beta_3 x_3 + \beta_4 x_4$ is shown on page 208.

MAN-HOURS y	BOILER CAPACITY x_1	DESIGN PRESSURE x_2	BOILER TYPE x_3	DRUM TYPE x_4
3,137	120,000	375	Industrial	Steam
3,590	65,000	750	Industrial	Steam
4,526	150,000	500	Industrial	Steam
10,825	1,073,877	2,170	Utility	Steam
4,023	150,000	325	Industrial	Steam
7,606	610,000	1,500	Utility	Steam
3,748	88,200	399	Industrial	Steam
2,972	88,200	399	Industrial	Steam
3,163	88,200	399	Industrial	Steam
4,065	90,000	1,140	Industrial	Steam
2,048	30,000	325	Industrial	Steam
6,500	441,000	410	Industrial	Steam
5,651	441,000	410	Industrial	Steam
6,565	441,000	410	Industrial	Steam
6,387	441,000	410	Industrial	Steam
6,454	627,000	1,525	Utility	Steam
6,928	610,000	1,500	Utility	Steam
4,268	150,000	500	Industrial	Steam
14,791	1,089,490	2,170	Utility	Steam
2,680	125,000	750	Industrial	Steam
2,974	120,000	375	Industrial	Mud
1,965	65,000	750	Industrial	Mud
2,566	150,000	500	Industrial	Mud
1,515	150,000	250	Industrial	Mud
2,000	150,000	500	Industrial	Mud
2,735	150,000	325	Industrial	Mud
3,698	610,000	1,500	Utility	Mud
2,635	90,000	1,140	Industrial	Mud
1,206	30,000	325	Industrial	Mud
3,775	441,000	410	Industrial	Mud
3,120	441,000	410	Industrial	Mud
4,206	441,000	410	Industrial	Mud
4,006	441,000	410	Industrial	Mud
3,728	627,000	1,525	Utility	Mud
3,211	610,000	1,500	Utility	Mud
1,200	30,000	325	Industrial	Mud

Source: Kelly Uscategui, former graduate student, University of South Florida.

MINITAB printout for Exercise 4.17

```
The regression equation is
Y = - 3783 + 0.00875 X1 + 1.93 X2 + 3444 X3 + 2093 X4

Predictor        Coef        Stdev    t-ratio        p
Constant        -3783         1205      -3.14    0.004
X1          0.0087490    0.0009035       9.68    0.000
X2             1.9265       0.6489       2.97    0.006
X3             3444.3        911.7       3.78    0.001
X4             2093.4        305.6       6.85    0.000

s = 894.6         R-sq = 90.3%      R-sq(adj) = 89.0%

Analysis of Variance

SOURCE        DF          SS          MS          F        p
Regression     4   230854848    57713712      72.11    0.000
Error         31    24809760      800315
Total         35   255664608

SOURCE        DF      SEQ SS
X1             1   175007136
X2             1      490357
X3             1    17813090
X4             1    37544264

Unusual Observations
Obs.       X1          Y        Fit  Stdev.Fit   Residual    St.Resid
 19   1089490      14791      12022        523       2769       3.81R

R denotes an obs. with a large st. resid.

     Fit  Stdev.Fit          95% C.I.              95% P.I.
    1936        239   (    1449,     2424)   (      47,     3825)
```

a. Conduct a test of overall model adequacy.

b. A 95% prediction interval for man-hours (y) required to erect an industrial field ($x_3 = 1$) boiler with capacity $x_1 = 150{,}000$ lb/hr, design pressure $x_2 = 500$ psi, and steam drum type ($x_4 = 0$) is shown at the bottom of the MINITAB printout. Interpret the interval.

4.18 Refer to the *Artificial Intelligence (AI) Applications* study, Exercise 4.5. Recall that the authors use AI to build a regression model relating scenic beauty (y) of southwestern pine stands to age (x_1) of the dominant stand, stems per acre (x_2) in trees, and basal area (x_3) per acre in hardwoods. The AI system is designed to check the values of the input variables (x_1, x_2, and x_3) with the sample data ranges. If the input data value is "out-of-range," a warning is issued about the potential inaccuracy of the predicted y value. Explain the reasoning behind this warning.

4.19 The Florida Department of Transportation (DOT) wants to develop a model relating bid price for a road construction project to length of the road to be built or repaired and number of bidders. Since the DOT believes that the bid price increases linearly with road length and number of bidders, the following model is hypothesized:

$$y = \beta_0 + \beta_1 x_1 + \beta_2 x_2 + \varepsilon$$

where

y = Bid price (thousands of dollars)
x_1 = Length of road (miles)
x_2 = Number of bidders

Data collected on bid price, road length, and number of bidders for 32 randomly selected construction projects were used to fit the model. A portion of the SAS printout is shown here.

Dependent Variable: Y

Analysis of Variance

Source	DF	Sum of Squares	Mean Square	F Value	Prob>F
Model	2	4277159.7074	2138579.8517	120.651	0.0001
Error	29	514034.5153	17725.3281		
C Total	31	4791194.2187			

Root MSE	133.13650	R-square	0.8927
Dep Mean	665.00000	Adj R-sq	0.8853
C.V.	20.02053		

Parameter Estimates

Variable	DF	Parameter Estimate	Standard Error	T for H0: Parameter=0	Prob > |T|
INTERCEP	1	-1336.7220	173.35612607	-7.711	0.0001
X1	1	12.7362	0.90238048	14.114	0.0001
X2	1	85.8151	8.70575681	9.857	0.0001

Obs	X1	X2	Dep Var Y	Predict Value	Std Err Predict	Lower95% Mean	Upper95% Mean	Residual
32	100	7	601.5	537.6	138.771	253.81	821.39	63.9

a. Is the model useful for estimating mean bid price? Use $\alpha = .01$.
b. Test the hypothesis that the mean bid price increases as the number of bidders increases for road construction projects of the same length. Use $\alpha = .01$.
c. Interpret the 95% confidence interval given at the bottom of the printout.

4.20 Polychlorinated biphenyls (PCBs) are a family of hazardous chemicals that are often dumped, illegally, by industrial plants into the surrounding streams, rivers, or bays. The table on page 210 reports the 1984 and 1985 concentrations of PCBs (measured in parts per billion) in water samples collected from 37 U.S. bays and estuaries. An official from the Environmental Protection Agency wants to model the 1985 PCB concentration (y) of a bay as a function of the 1984 PCB concentration (x). Consider the second-order model $E(y) = \beta_0 + \beta_1 x + \beta_2 x^2$. A SAS printout of the analysis is also shown on page 210.
a. Conduct a test of overall model adequacy.
b. Interpret the prediction intervals shown at the bottom of the printout.

BAY	STATE	PCB CONCENTRATION 1984	1985
Casco Bay	ME	95.28	77.55
Merrimack River	MA	52.97	29.23
Salem Habor	MA	533.58	403.1
Boston Harbor	MA	17,104.86	736
Buzzards Bay	MA	308.46	192.15
Narragansett Bay	RI	159.96	220.6
East Long Island Sound	NY	10	8.62
West Long Island Sound	NY	234.43	174.31
Raritan Bay	NJ	443.89	529.28
Delaware Bay	DE	2.5	130.67
Lower Chesapeake Bay	VA	51	39.74
Pamlico Sound	NC	0	0
Charleston Harbor	SC	9.1	8.43
Sapelo Sound	GA	0	0
St. Johns River	FL	140	120.04
Tampa Bay	FL	0	0
Apalachicola Bay	FL	12	11.93
Mobile Bay	AL	0	0
Round Island	MS	0	0
Mississippi River Delta	LA	34	30.14
Barataria Bay	LA	0	0
San Antonio Bay	TX	0	0
Corpus Christi Bay	TX	0	0
San Diego Harbor	CA	422.1	531.67
San Diego Bay	CA	6.74	9.3
Dana Point	CA	7.06	5.74
Seal Beach	CA	46.71	46.47
San Pedro Canyon	CA	159.56	176.9
Santa Monica Bay	CA	14	13.69
Bodega Bay	CA	4.18	4.89
Coos Bay	OR	3.19	6.6
Columbia River Mouth	OR	8.77	6.73
Nisqually Beach	WA	4.23	4.28
Commencement Bay	WA	20.6	20.5
Elliott Bay	WA	329.97	414.5
Lutak Inlet	AK	5.5	5.8
Nahku Bay	AK	6.6	5.08

Source: *Environmental Quality*, 1987–1988.

SAS printout for Exercise 4.20

```
Dependent Variable: PCB85

                         Analysis of Variance

                           Sum of          Mean
Source           DF       Squares        Square       F Value       Prob>F

Model             2  1123880.6458  561940.32288       233.788       0.0001
Error            34   81723.39229    2403.62918
C Total          36  1205604.0380

      Root MSE      49.02682     R-square        0.9322
      Dep Mean     107.13351     Adj R-sq        0.9282
      C.V.          45.76236
```

SAS printout for Exercise 4.20 (*continued*)

Parameter Estimates

Variable	DF	Parameter Estimate	Standard Error	T for H0: Parameter=0	Prob > |T|
INTERCEP	1	3.460057	9.57458170	0.361	0.7201
PCB84	1	1.010904	0.05856947	17.260	0.0001
PCB84SQ	1	-0.000056597	0.00000341	-16.590	0.0001

Obs	PCB84	Dep Var PCB85	Predict Value	Std Err Predict	Lower95% Predict	Upper95% Predict	Residual
1	95.28	77.5500	99.3	8.191	-1.7496	200.3	-21.7152
2	52.97	29.2300	56.8489	8.389	-44.2331	157.9	-27.6189
3	533.58	403.1	526.7	26.577	413.4	640.1	-123.6
4	17104.86	736.0	736.0	49.027	595.1	876.9	0.00853
5	308.46	192.2	309.9	15.145	205.6	414.2	-117.7
6	159.96	220.6	163.7	9.230	62.3320	265.1	56.8839
7	10	8.6200	13.5634	9.283	-87.8407	115.0	-4.9434
8	234.43	174.3	237.3	11.829	134.8	339.8	-63.0259
9	443.89	529.3	441.0	21.916	331.9	550.2	88.2414
10	2.5	130.7	5.9870	9.499	-95.5	107.5	124.7
11	51	39.7400	54.8690	8.416	-46.2221	156.0	-15.1290
12	0	0	3.4601	9.575	-98.1	105.0	-3.4601
13	9.1	8.4300	12.6546	9.308	-88.7591	114.1	-4.2246
14	0	0	3.4601	9.575	-98.1	105.0	-3.4601
15	140	120.0	143.9	8.755	42.6672	245.1	-23.8374
16	0	0	3.4601	9.575	-98.1	105.0	-3.4601
17	12	11.9300	15.5828	9.228	-85.8007	117.0	-3.6528
18	0	0	3.4601	9.575	-98.1	105.0	-3.4601
19	0	0	3.4601	9.575	-98.1	105.0	-3.4601
20	34	30.1400	37.7654	8.706	-63.4271	139.0	-7.6254
21	0	0	3.4601	9.575	-98.1	105.0	-3.4601
22	0	0	3.4601	9.575	-98.1	105.0	-3.4601
23	0	0	3.4601	9.575	-98.1	105.0	-3.4601
24	422.1	531.7	420.1	20.797	311.9	528.3	111.6
25	6.74	9.3000	10.2710	9.375	-91.1681	111.7	-0.9710
26	7.06	5.7400	10.5942	9.366	-90.8414	112.0	-4.8542
27	46.71	46.4700	50.5559	8.479	-50.5570	151.7	-4.0859
28	159.56	176.9	163.3	9.219	61.9388	264.7	13.5810
29	14	13.6900	17.6016	9.174	-83.7617	119.0	-3.9116
30	4.18	4.8900	7.6846	9.449	-93.7830	109.2	-2.7946
31	3.19	6.6000	6.6843	9.479	-94.8	108.2	-0.0843
32	8.77	6.7300	12.3213	9.317	-89.0958	113.7	-5.5913
33	4.23	4.2800	7.7352	9.448	-93.7319	109.2	-3.4552
34	20.6	20.5000	24.2607	9.006	-77.0401	125.6	-3.7607
35	329.97	414.5	330.9	16.180	225.9	435.8	83.6341
36	5.5	5.8000	9.0183	9.411	-92.4345	110.5	-3.2183
37	6.6	5.0800	10.1296	9.379	-91.3111	111.6	-5.0496

4.9 Other Linear Models

In the preceding sections, we have demonstrated the methods of multiple regression analysis by fitting several different models, including a quadratic model and an interaction model. In this section we formally introduce other types of general linear models that are useful for relating a response variable y to a set of data.*

Models with Quantitative x's

We begin with a discussion of models using **quantitative** (numerical) independent variables. Suppose that the mean value $E(y)$ of a response y is related to two quantitative variables, x_1 and x_2, by the model

$$E(y) = 1 + 2x_1 - x_2$$

*A more complete discussion of general linear models and their role in model building is provided in Chapter 5.

Note that when $x_2 = 0$, the relationship between $E(y)$ and x_1 is given by

$$E(y) = 1 + 2x_1 - (0) = 1 + 2x_1$$

A graph of this relationship (a straight line) is shown in Figure 4.19. Similar graphs of the relationship between $E(y)$ and x_1 for $x_2 = 1$,

$$E(y) = 1 + 2x_1 - (1) = 2x_1$$

and for $x_2 = 2$,

$$E(y) = 1 + 2x_1 - (2) = -1 + 2x_1$$

are also shown in Figure 4.19.

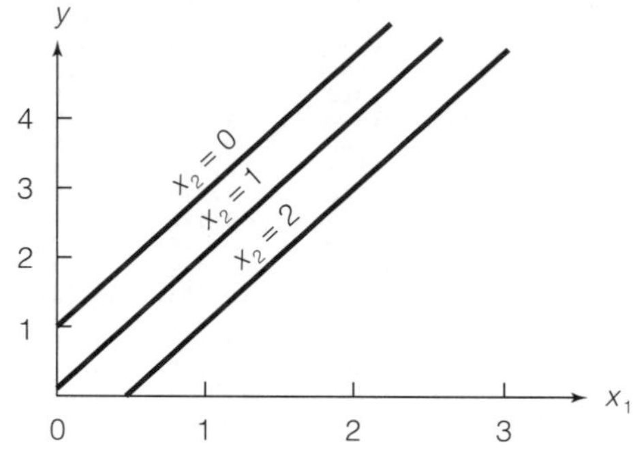

FIGURE 4.19
Graphs of $E(y) = 1 + 2x_1 - x_2$ for $x_2 = 0, 1, 2$

The model $E(y) = 1 + 2x_1 - x_2$ is an example of a **first-order linear model** in two quantitative independent variables, x_1 and x_2. A first-order linear model in five quantitative independent variables is shown in the box.

A First-Order Linear Model Relating $E(y)$ to $x_1, x_2, \ldots, x_5$

$$E(y) = \beta_0 + \beta_1 x_1 + \beta_2 x_2 + \cdots + \beta_5 x_5$$

Figure 4.19 exhibits a characteristic of all first-order models: If you graph $E(y)$ versus any one variable—say, x_1—for fixed values of the other variables, the response curve will always be a *straight line*. If you repeat the process for other values of the fixed independent variables, you will obtain a set of *parallel* straight lines. This indicates that the effect on $E(y)$ of a change in x_1 is independent of the other variables in the model. When this situation occurs (as it always does for a first-order model), we say that the independent variables in the model **do not interact**.

Now, suppose that the mean value $E(y)$ of a response y is related to two quantitative variables, x_1 and x_2, by the model

$$E(y) = 1 + 2x_1 - x_2 + x_1x_2$$

This model contains the second-order cross-product term, x_1x_2, in addition to all the terms of the first-order model. Figure 4.20 shows the graphs of the relationship between $E(y)$ and x_1 for $x_2 = 0$, 1, and 2. The straight-line equations relating $E(y)$ to x_1 are

For $x_2 = 0$: $E(y) = 1 + 2x_1 - (0) + x_1(0) = 1 + 2x_1$

For $x_2 = 1$: $E(y) = 1 + 2x_1 - (1) + x_1(1) = 3x_1$

For $x_2 = 2$: $E(y) = 1 + 2x_1 - (2) + x_1(2) = -1 + 4x_1$

FIGURE 4.20

Graphs of $E(y) = 1 + 2x_1 - x_2 + x_1x_2$ for $x_2 = 0, 1, 2$

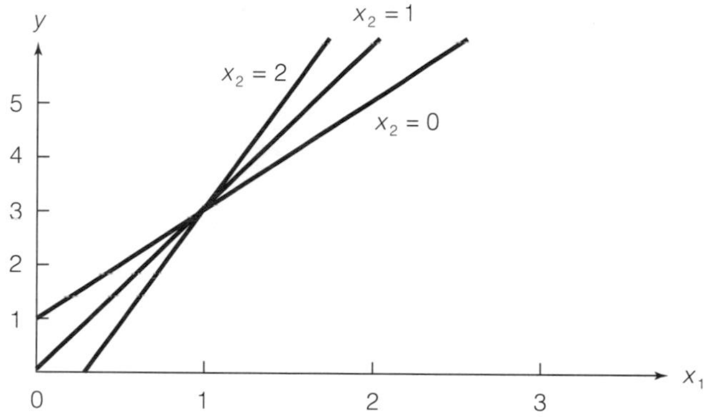

The effect of adding a term involving the cross-product x_1x_2 can be seen in Figure 4.20. In contrast to Figure 4.19, the lines relating $E(y)$ to x_1 are no longer parallel. The effect on $E(y)$ of a change in x_1 is now dependent on the value of x_2. When this situation occurs, we say that x_1 and x_2 **interact**. An **interaction model** is a model that contains first-order terms in the independent variables as well as two-way cross-product terms such as x_1x_2, x_1x_3, ... An interaction model with three quantitative independent variables is shown in the box.

An Interaction Model Relating $E(y)$ to Three Quantitative Independent Variables

$$E(y) = \beta_0 + \beta_1x_1 + \beta_2x_2 + \beta_3x_3 + \beta_4x_1x_2 + \beta_5x_1x_3 + \beta_6x_2x_3$$

Finally, consider relating the mean value $E(y)$ of a response y to two quantitative independent variables, x_1 and x_2, by the model

$$E(y) = 1 + 2x_1 - x_2 + x_1x_2 + x_1^2 + 3x_2^2$$

This model contains all of the terms contained in the interaction model plus the second-order terms x_1^2 and x_2^2. Figure 4.21 (page 214) shows a computer-generated graph of the relationship between $E(y)$ and x_1 for $x_2 = 0$, 1, and 2.

The response curves in Figure 4.21 rise (or fall) in the same manner as the lines shown in Figure 4.20. However, the graphs are curvilinear and the spacing

FIGURE 4.21 Computer graph of $E(y) = 1 + 2x_1 - x_2 + x_1x_2 + x_1^2 + 3x_2^2$ for $x_2 = 0, 1, 2$

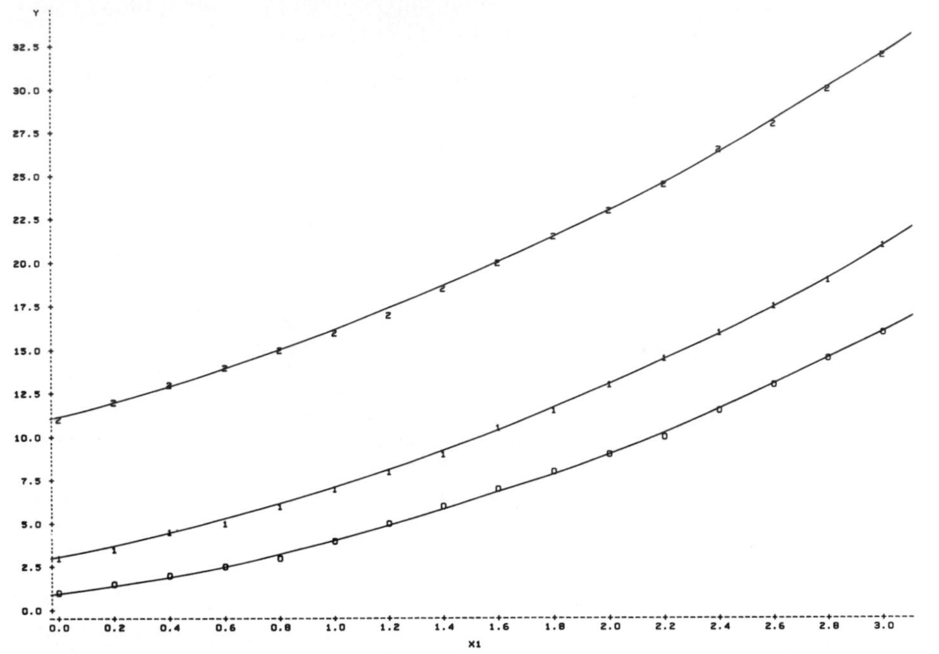

between the curves has changed. These changes were produced by adding the second-order terms (those involving x_1^2 and x_2^2) to the model.

The model $E(y) = 1 + 2x_1 - x_2 + x_1x_2 + x_1^2 + 3x_2^2$ is an example of a **second-order model** in two quantitative independent variables. A second-order model contains all of the terms in a first-order model and, in addition, the second-order terms involving cross-products (interaction terms) and squares of the independent variables. A second-order model with three quantitative independent variables is shown in the box. (Note that an interaction model is a special case of a second-order model, where the β coefficients of $x_1^2, x_2^2, \ldots$, are all equal to 0.)

A Second-Order Model with Three Quantitative Independent Variables

$$E(y) = \beta_0 + \beta_1x_1 + \beta_2x_2 + \beta_3x_3 + \beta_4x_1x_2 + \beta_5x_1x_3 + \beta_6x_2x_3 + \beta_7x_1^2 + \beta_8x_2^2 + \beta_9x_3^2$$

How can you choose an appropriate linear model to fit a set of data? Since most relationships in the real world are curvilinear (at least to some extent), a good first choice would be a second-order linear model. If you are fairly certain that the relationships between $E(y)$ and the individual independent variables are approximately first-order and that the independent variables do not interact, you could select a first-order model for the data. If you have prior information that suggests there is moderate or very little curvature over the region in which the independent variables are measured, you could use the interaction model described previously. However, keep in mind that for all multiple regression models, the number of data points must exceed the number of parameters in the model. Thus, you may be forced to use a first-order model rather than a second-order model simply because you do not have sufficient data to estimate all of the parameters in the second-order model.

A practical example of choosing and fitting a linear model with two quantitative independent variables follows.

EXAMPLE 4.4

Although a regional express delivery service bases the charge for shipping a package on the package weight and distance shipped, its profit per package depends on the package size (volume of space that it occupies) and the size and nature of the load on the delivery truck. The company recently conducted a study to investigate the relationship between the cost, y, of shipment (in dollars) and the variables that control the shipping charge—package weight, x_1 (in pounds), and distance shipped, x_2 (in miles). Twenty packages were randomly selected from among the large number received for shipment and a detailed analysis of the cost of shipment was made for each package, with the results shown in Table 4.3. The SAS printout is shown in Figure 4.22 on page 216.

TABLE 4.3 **Cost of Shipment Data for Example 4.4**

PACKAGE	x_1	x_2	y	PACKAGE	x_1	x_2	y
1	5.9	47	2.60	11	5.1	240	11.00
2	3.2	145	3.90	12	2.4	209	5.00
3	4.4	202	8.00	13	.3	160	2.00
4	6.6	160	9.20	14	6.2	115	6.00
5	.75	280	4.40	15	2.7	45	1.10
6	.7	80	1.50	16	3.5	250	8.00
7	6.5	240	14.50	17	4.1	95	3.30
8	4.5	53	1.90	18	8.1	160	12.10
9	.60	100	1.00	19	7.0	260	15.50
10	7.5	190	14.00	20	1.1	90	1.70

a. Give an appropriate linear model for the data.
b. Fit the model to the data and give the prediction equation.
c. Find the value of SSE and specify its number of degrees of freedom.
d. Find the value of R_a^2 and interpret it.
e. Is the model useful for the prediction of shipping cost y? Find the value of the F statistic on the printout and give the observed significance level (p-value) for the test.
f. Find a 95% prediction interval for the cost of shipping a 5-pound package a distance of 100 miles.

FIGURE 4.22
SAS printout for the multiple regression analysis of Example 4.4

Analysis of Variance

Source	DF	Sum of Squares	Mean Square	F Value	Prob>F
Model	5	449.34076	89.86815	458.388	0.0001
Error	14	2.74474	0.19605		
C Total	19	452.08550			

Root MSE	0.44278	R-square	0.9939
Dep Mean	6.33500	Adj R-sq	0.9918
C.V.	6.98940		

Parameter Estimates

Variable	DF	Parameter Estimate	Standard Error	T for H0: Parameter=0	Prob > |T|
INTERCEP	1	0.827016	0.70228935	1.178	0.2586
X1	1	-0.609137	0.17990408	-3.386	0.0044
X2	1	0.004021	0.00799842	0.503	0.6230
X1X2	1	0.007327	0.00063743	11.495	0.0001
X1SQ	1	0.089751	0.02020542	4.442	0.0006
X2SQ	1	0.000015070	0.00002243	0.672	0.5127

Obs	X1	X2	Dep Var Y	Predict Value	Std Err Predict	Lower95% Predict	Upper95% Predict	Residual
1	5.9	47	2.6000	2.6114	0.299	1.4655	3.7573	-0.0114
2	3.2	145	3.9000	4.0964	0.211	3.0443	5.1486	-0.1964
3	4.4	202	8.0000	7.8238	0.199	6.7823	8.8654	0.1762
4	6.6	160	9.2000	9.4828	0.182	8.4562	10.5093	-0.2828
5	0.75	280	4.4000	4.2666	0.399	2.9880	5.5452	0.1334
6	0.7	80	1.5000	1.2730	0.245	0.1874	2.3587	0.2270
7	6.5	240	14.5000	13.9229	0.213	12.8693	14.9764	0.5771
8	4.5	53	1.9000	1.9063	0.228	0.8378	2.9748	-0.00629
9	0.6	100	1.0000	1.4862	0.226	0.4202	2.5523	-0.4862
10	7.5	190	14.0000	13.0560	0.216	11.9998	14.1122	0.9440
11	5.1	240	11.0000	10.8562	0.196	9.8175	11.8949	0.1438
12	2.4	209	5.0000	5.0559	0.200	4.0140	6.0979	-0.0559
13	0.3	160	2.0000	2.0332	0.260	0.9316	3.1347	-0.0332
14	6.2	115	6.0000	6.3863	0.195	5.3482	7.4243	-0.3863
15	2.7	45	1.1000	0.9383	0.257	-0.1600	2.0366	0.1617
16	3.5	250	8.0000	8.1527	0.212	7.1001	9.2054	-0.1527
17	4.1	95	3.3000	3.2101	0.180	2.1847	4.2356	0.0899
18	8.1	160	12.1000	12.3066	0.301	11.1577	13.4555	-0.2066
19	7	260	15.5000	16.3603	0.311	15.1999	17.5207	-0.8603
20	1.1	90	1.7000	1.4749	0.199	0.4335	2.5163	0.2251
21	5	100	.	4.2414	0.184	3.2133	5.2695	.

Sum of Residuals	-1.04361E-14
Sum of Squared Residuals	2.7447
Predicted Resid SS (Press)	6.8568

Solution

a. Since we have no reason to expect that the relationship between y and x_1 and x_2 would be first-order, we will allow for curvature in the response surface and fit the second-order model

$$y = \beta_0 + \beta_1 x_1 + \beta_2 x_2 + \beta_3 x_1 x_2 + \beta_4 x_1^2 + \beta_5 x_2^2 + \varepsilon$$

The mean value of the random error term ε is assumed to equal 0. Therefore, the mean value of y is

$$E(y) = \beta_0 + \beta_1 x_1 + \beta_2 x_2 + \beta_3 x_1 x_2 + \beta_4 x_1^2 + \beta_5 x_2^2$$

b. The SAS printout for fitting the model to the $n = 20$ data points is shown in Figure 4.22. You can see from the printout that the parameter estimates (shaded in Figure 4.22) are

$$\hat{\beta}_0 = .827016 \qquad \hat{\beta}_1 = -.609137 \qquad \hat{\beta}_2 = .004021$$
$$\hat{\beta}_3 = .007327 \qquad \hat{\beta}_4 = .089751 \qquad \hat{\beta}_5 = .00001507$$

Therefore, the prediction equation that relates the predicted shipping cost, $\hat{y}$, to weight of package, x_1, and distance shipped, x_2, is

$$\hat{y} = .827016 - .609137x_1 + .004021x_2 + .007327x_1x_2 + .089751x_1^2 + .00001507x_2^2$$

c. The **Sum of Squares** for **Error**, shaded on the printout, is

$$\text{SSE} = 2.74474$$

based on 14 degrees of freedom (**DF** for **Error** in the printout). Recall that SSE has degrees of freedom equal to $n -$ (Number of estimated β parameters).

d. The value of R_a^2 shown in Figure 4.22 is **Adj R-sq** = .9918. This means that after adjusting for sample size and the number of model parameters, about 99% of the total variation, SS(Total) $= \text{SS}_{yy} = \Sigma\,(y - \bar{y})^2$, is explained by the model; the remainder is explained by random error.

e. The test statistic for testing whether the model is useful for predicting shipping cost is

$$F = \frac{\text{Mean square for model}}{\text{Mean square for error}} = \frac{\text{SS(Model)}/k}{\text{SSE}/[n - (k + 1)]}$$

where $n = 20$ is the number of data points and $k = 5$ is the number of parameters (excluding β_0) contained in the model.

This value of F has been computed for us as $F = 458.388$ and is shaded on the printout (Figure 4.22) in the row corresponding to **MODEL**. The observed significance level (p-value) for the test is shown to the right of the F value on the printout as **Prob > F** = .0001. This means that if the model contributed no information for the prediction of y, the probability of observing a value of the F statistic as large as 458.39 would be only .0001. Thus, we would reject the null hypothesis that the model contributes no information for the prediction of y for all values of α larger than .0001.

f. The predicted value of y for $x_1 = 5.0$ pounds and $x_2 = 100$ miles is

$$\hat{y} = .827016 - .609137(5.0) + .004021(100) + .007327(5.0)(100) + .089751(5.0)^2 + .00001507(100)^2$$

This quantity has been computed and is shown (shaded) on the printout as $\hat{y} = 4.2414$. The corresponding 95% prediction interval (shaded) is given as 3.2133 to 5.2695. Therefore, if we were to select a 5-pound package and ship it 100 miles, we would expect the actual cost to fall between \$3.21 and \$5.27.

Models with Qualitative x's

Linear models can also be written to include **qualitative** (or **categorical**) independent variables. Qualitative variables, unlike quantitative variables, cannot be measured on a numerical scale. Therefore, we need to code the values of the qualitative variable (called **levels**) as numbers before we can fit the model. These coded qualitative variables are called **dummy variables** since the numbers assigned to the various levels are arbitrarily selected.

For example, consider a salary discrimination case where there exists a claim of sex discrimination—specifically, the claim that male executives at a large company receive higher average salaries than female executives with the same credentials and qualifications.

To test this claim, we might propose a multiple regression model for executive salaries using the gender of an executive as one of the independent variables. The dummy variable used to describe gender may be coded as follows:

$$x_3 = \begin{cases} 1 & \text{if male} \\ 0 & \text{if female} \end{cases}$$

The advantage of using a 0–1 coding scheme is that the β coefficients associated with the dummy variables are easily interpreted. To illustrate, consider the following model for executive salary y:

$$E(y) = \beta_0 + \beta_1 x$$

where

$$x = \begin{cases} 1 & \text{if male} \\ 0 & \text{if female} \end{cases}$$

This model allows us to compare the mean executive salary $E(y)$ for males with the corresponding mean for females:

$$\textit{Males } (x = 1): \quad E(y) = \beta_0 + \beta_1(1) = \beta_0 + \beta_1$$
$$\textit{Females } (x = 0): \quad E(y) = \beta_0 + \beta_1(0) = \beta_0$$

First note that β_0 represents the mean salary for females (say, μ_F). When using a 0–1 coding convention, β_0 will always represent the mean response associated with the level of the qualitative variable assigned the value 0 (called the **base level**). The difference between the mean salary for males and the mean salary for females, $\mu_M - \mu_F$, is represented by β_1—that is,

$$\mu_M - \mu_F = (\beta_0 + \beta_1) - (\beta_0) = \beta_1$$

Therefore, with the 0–1 coding convention, β_1 will always represent the difference between the mean response for the level assigned the value 1 and the mean for the base level. Thus, for the executive salary model we have

$$\beta_0 = \mu_F$$
$$\beta_1 = \mu_M - \mu_F$$

If β_1 exceeds 0, then $\mu_M > \mu_F$ and evidence of sex discrimination at the company exists.

The model relating a mean response $E(y)$ to a qualitative independent variable at two levels is shown in the box.

A Model Relating $E(y)$ to a Qualitative Independent Variable with Two Levels

$$E(y) = \beta_0 + \beta_1 x$$

where

$$x = \begin{cases} 1 & \text{if level A} \\ 0 & \text{if level B} \end{cases}$$

Interpretation of β's:

$\beta_0 = \mu_B$ (Mean for base level)

$\beta_1 = \mu_A - \mu_B$

For models that involve qualitative independent variables at more than two levels, additional dummy variables must be created. In general, the number of dummy variables used to describe a qualitative variable will be one less than the number of levels of the qualitative variable. The next box presents a model that includes a qualitative independent variable at three levels.

A Model Relating $E(y)$ to a Qualitative Independent Variable with Three Levels

$$E(y) = \beta_0 + \beta_1 x_1 + \beta_2 x_2$$

where

$$x_1 = \begin{cases} 1 & \text{if level A} \\ 0 & \text{if not} \end{cases} \qquad x_2 = \begin{cases} 1 & \text{if level B} \\ 0 & \text{if not} \end{cases} \qquad \text{Base level} = \text{Level C}$$

Interpretation of β's:

$\beta_0 = \mu_C$ (Mean for base level)

$\beta_1 = \mu_A - \mu_C$

$\beta_2 = \mu_B - \mu_C$

EXAMPLE 4.5

Refer to the problem of modeling the shipment cost, y, of a regional express delivery service, described in Example 4.4. Suppose we want to model $E(y)$ as a function of cargo type, where cargo type has three levels—fragile, semifragile, and durable. Costs for 15 packages of approximately the same weight and same distance shipped, but of different cargo types, are listed in Table 4.4 (page 220).

TABLE 4.4 **Data for Example 4.4**

PACKAGE	COST, y	CARGO TYPE	x_1	x_2
1	$17.20	Fragile	1	0
2	11.10	Fragile	1	0
3	12.00	Fragile	1	0
4	10.90	Fragile	1	0
5	13.80	Fragile	1	0
6	6.50	Semifragile	0	1
7	10.00	Semifragile	0	1
8	11.50	Semifragile	0	1
9	7.00	Semifragile	0	1
10	8.50	Semifragile	0	1
11	2.10	Durable	0	0
12	1.30	Durable	0	0
13	3.40	Durable	0	0
14	7.50	Durable	0	0
15	2.00	Durable	0	0

a. Write a linear model relating $E(y)$ to cargo type.
b. Interpret the β coefficients in the model.
c. A MINITAB printout for the model, part **a**, is shown in Figure 4.23. Conduct the F test for overall model utility using $\alpha = .05$. Explain the practical significance of the result.

FIGURE 4.23
MINITAB printout for dummy variable regression, Example 4.5

```
The regression equation is
Y = 3.26 + 9.74 X1 + 5.44 X2

Predictor        Coef        Stdev      t-ratio        p
Constant        3.260        1.075         3.03    0.010
X1              9.740        1.521         6.41    0.000
X2              5.440        1.521         3.58    0.004

s = 2.404        R-sq = 77.4%        R-sq(adj) = 73.7%

Analysis of Variance

SOURCE        DF          SS          MS          F          p
Regression     2      238.25      119.13      20.61      0.000
Error         12       69.37        5.78
Total         14      307.62
```

Solution

a. Since the qualitative variable of interest, cargo type, has three levels, we must create $(3 - 1) = 2$ dummy variables. First, select (arbitrarily) one of the levels to be the base level—say, durable cargo. Then each of the remaining levels is assigned the value 1 in one of the two dummy variables as follows:

$$x_1 = \begin{cases} 1 & \text{if fragile} \\ 0 & \text{if not} \end{cases} \qquad x_2 = \begin{cases} 1 & \text{if semifragile} \\ 0 & \text{if not} \end{cases}$$

(Note that for the base level, durable cargo, $x_1 = x_2 = 0$.) The values of x_1 and x_2 for each package are given in Table 4.4. Then, the appropriate model is

$$E(y) = \beta_0 + \beta_1 x_1 + \beta_2 x_2$$

b. To interpret the β's, first write the mean shipment cost $E(y)$ for each of the three cargo types as a function of the β's:

Fragile ($x_1 = 1, x_2 = 0$):

$$E(y) = \beta_0 + \beta_1(1) + \beta_2(0) = \beta_0 + \beta_1 = \mu_F$$

Semifragile ($x_1 = 0, x_2 = 1$):

$$E(y) = \beta_0 + \beta_1(0) + \beta_2(1) = \beta_0 + \beta_2 = \mu_S$$

Durable ($x_1 = 0, x_2 = 0$):

$$E(y) = \beta_0 + \beta_1(0) + \beta_2(0) = \beta_0 = \mu_D$$

Then we have

$$\beta_0 = \mu_D \quad \text{(Mean of the base level)}$$

$$\beta_1 = \mu_F - \mu_D$$

$$\beta_2 = \mu_S - \mu_D$$

Note that the β's associated with the non–base levels of cargo type (fragile and semifragile) represent differences between a pair of means. As always, β_0 represents a single mean—the mean response for the base level (durable).

c. The F test for overall model utility tests the null hypothesis

$$H_0 = \beta_1 = \beta_2 = 0$$

Note that $\beta_1 = 0$ implies that $\mu_F = \mu_D$ and $\beta_2 = 0$ implies that $\mu_S = \mu_D$. Therefore, $\beta_1 = \beta_2 = 0$ implies that $\mu_F = \mu_S = \mu_D$. Thus, a test for model utility is equivalent to a test for equality of means, i.e.,

$$H_0: \ \mu_F = \mu_S = \mu_D$$

From the MINITAB printout, Figure 4.23, $F = 20.61$. Since the p-value of the test (.000) is less than $\alpha = .05$, the null hypothesis is rejected. Thus, there is evidence of a difference between any two of the three mean shipment costs; i.e., cargo type is a useful predictor of shipment cost y.

Multiplicative Models

In all the models presented so far, the random error component has been assumed to be *additive*. An additive error is one for which the response is equal to the mean $E(y)$ plus random error,

$$y = E(y) + \varepsilon$$

Another useful type of model for business and economic data is the **multiplicative model**. In this model, the response is written as a *product* of its mean and the random error component, i.e.,

$$y = [E(y)] \cdot \varepsilon$$

Researchers have found multiplicative models to be useful when the change in the response y for every 1-unit change in an independent variable x is better represented by a percentage increase (or decrease) rather than a constant amount increase (or decrease).* For example, economists often want to predict a percentage change in the price of a commodity or a percentage increase in the salary of a worker. Consequently, a multiplicative model is used rather than an additive model.

A multiplicative model in two independent variables can be specified as

$$y = (e^{\beta_0})(e^{\beta_1 x_1})(e^{\beta_2 x_2})(e^{\varepsilon})$$

where β_0, β_1, and β_2 are population parameters that must be estimated from the sample data and e^x is a notation for the antilogarithm of x. Note, however, that the multiplicative model is not a general linear model as defined in Section 4.1. To use the method of least squares to fit the model to the data, we must transform the model into the form of a linear model. Taking the natural logarithm of both sides of the equation, we obtain

$$\log(y) = \beta_0 + \beta_1 x_1 + \beta_2 x_2 + \varepsilon$$

which is now in the form of a general linear (additive) model.

When the dependent variable is $\log(y)$, rather than y, the β parameters and other key regression quantities have slightly different interpretations, as the next example illustrates.

EXAMPLE 4.6

Towers, Perrin, Forster & Crosby (TPF&C), an international management consulting firm, has developed a unique and interesting application of multiple regression analysis. Many firms are interested in evaluating their management salary structure, and TPF&C uses multiple regression models to accomplish this salary evaluation. The Compensation Management Service, as TPF&C calls it, measures both the internal and external consistency of a company's pay policies to determine whether they reflect the management's intent.

The dependent variable y used to measure executive compensation is annual salary. The independent variables used to explain salary structure include the variables listed in Table 4.5. The management at TPF&C has found that executive compensation models that use the logarithm of salary as the dependent variable are better predictors than models that use salary as the dependent variable. This is probably because salaries tend to be incremented in *percentages* rather than dollar values. Thus, the multiplicative model we propose (in its linear form) is

*Multiplicative models are also found to be useful when the standard regression assumption of equal variances is violated. We discuss this application of multiplicative models in Chapter 7.

$$\log(y) = \beta_0 + \beta_1 x_1 + \beta_2 x_2 + \beta_3 x_3 + \beta_4 x_4 + \beta_5 x_5 + \beta_6 x_1^2 + \beta_7 x_3 x_4 + \varepsilon$$

We have included a second-order term, x_1^2, to account for a possible curvilinear relationship between log(salary) and years of experience, x_1. Also, the interaction term $x_3 x_4$ is included to account for the fact that the relationship between the number of employees supervised, x_4, and corporate salary may depend on gender, x_3. For example, as the number of supervised employees increases, a male's salary (with all other factors being equal) might rise more rapidly than a female's. (If this is found to be true, the firm will take steps to remove the apparent discrimination against female executives.)

A sample of 100 executives is selected and the variables y and $x_1, x_2, \ldots, x_5$ are recorded. The sample is then used as input for a SAS regression routine; the output is shown in Figure 4.24.

TABLE 4.5 **List of Independent Variables for Executive Compensation Example**

INDEPENDENT VARIABLE	DESCRIPTION
x_1	Years of experience
x_2	Years of education
x_3	1 if male; 0 if female
x_4	Number of employees supervised
x_5	Corporate assets (millions of dollars)
x_6	x_1^2
x_7	$x_3 x_4$

FIGURE 4.24
Portion of the SAS printout for executive compensation example

```
                          Analysis of Variance

                          Sum of          Mean
Source          DF       Squares        Square      F Value        Prob>F

Model            7      27.06425       3.86632      1823.73        0.0001
Error           92       0.19551       0.00212
C Total         99      27.25976

          Root MSE        0.0461      R-square       0.9928
          Dep Mean        12.570      Adj R-sq       0.9923
          C.V.            0.3660

                          Parameter Estimates

                      Parameter      Standard     T for H0:
Variable     DF        Estimate         Error    Parameter=0    Prob > |T|

INTERCEP      1         8.87878       0.04612         192.49        0.0001
X1            1         0.04460       0.00166          26.83        0.0001
X2            1         0.03326       0.00270          12.31        0.0001
X3            1         0.11892       0.01724           6.89        0.0001
X4            1         0.00033       0.00001          19.97        0.0001
X5            1         0.00201       0.00002          73.25        0.0001
X1X1          1        -0.00071       0.00004         -15.11        0.0001
X3X4          1         0.00031       0.00002          16.16        0.0001

                               Dep Var  Predict   Std Err  Lower95%  Upper95%
Obs  X1   X2   X3   X4    X5         Y    Value   Predict   Predict   Predict  Residual

100  12   16    0  400  160.1        .  10.2977     .0483   10.2030   10.3924         .
```

TABLE 4.6 Values of Independent Variables for a Particular Executive

$x_1 =$	12 years of experience
$x_2 =$	16 years of education
$x_3 =$	0 (female)
$x_4 =$	400 employees supervised
$x_5 =$	\$160.1 million (the firm's asset value)
$x_1^2 =$	144
$x_3x_4 =$	0

a. Find the least squares prediction equation, and interpret the estimate of β_2.
b. Locate the estimate of s and interpret its value.
c. Locate R_a^2 and interpret its value.
d. Conduct a test of overall model utility.
e. Test for evidence of sex discrimination at the firm.
f. Use the model to predict the salary of an executive with the characteristics shown in Table 4.6.

Solution

a. The least squares model is

$$\widehat{\log(y)} = 8.88 + .045x_1 + .033x_2 + .119x_3 + .00033x_4 + .002x_5 - .00071x_6 + .00031x_7$$

Because we are using the logarithm of salary as the dependent variable, the β estimates have different interpretations than previously discussed. In general, a parameter β in a multiplicative (log) model represents the percentage increase (or decrease) in the dependent variable for a 1-unit increase in the corresponding independent variable. The percentage change is calculated by taking the antilogarithm of the β estimate and subtracting 1, i.e., $e^{\hat{\beta}} - 1$.* For example, the percentage change in executive compensation associated with a 1-unit (i.e., 1-year) increase in years of education x_2 is $(e^{\hat{\beta}_2} - 1) = (e^{.033} - 1) = .034$. Thus, when all other independent variables are held constant, we estimate executive salary to increase 3.4% for each additional year of education.

b. The estimate of the variance σ^2 is given in the SAS printout as

$$s^2 = \text{MSE} = \frac{\text{SSE}}{n - (k + 1)} = \frac{\text{SSE}}{10 - (7 + 1)} = .00212$$

and the estimate of the standard deviation σ, also given on the SAS printout as **Root MSE**, is $s = \sqrt{s^2} = .0461$. Our interpretation is that most of the observed $\log(y)$ values (logarithms of salaries) lie within $2s = 2(.0461) = .0922$ of their least squares predicted values, $\log(y)$. A more practical interpretation (in terms of salaries) is obtained, however, if we take the antilog of this value and subtract 1, similar to the manipulation in part **a**. That is,

*The result is derived by expressing the percentage change in salary y, as $(y_1 - y_0)/y_0$, where y_1 = the value of y when, say, $x = 1$, and y_0 = the value of y when $x = 0$. Now let $y^* = \log(y)$ and assume the log model is $y^* = \beta_0 + \beta_1 x$. Then

$$y = e^{y^*} = e^{\beta_0}e^{\beta_1 x} = \begin{cases} e^{\beta_0} & \text{when } x = 0 \\ e^{\beta_0}e^{\beta_1} & \text{when } x = 1 \end{cases}$$

Substituting, we have

$$\frac{y_1 - y_0}{y_0} = \frac{e^{\beta_0}e^{\beta_1} - e^{\beta_0}}{e^{\beta_0}} = e^{\beta_1} - 1$$

we expect most of the observed executive salaries to lie within $e^{2s} - 1 = e^{.0921} - 1 = .096$, or 9.6% of their respective least squares predicted values.

c. The adjusted R^2 value given on the SAS printout is $R_a^2 = .9923$. This implies that, after taking into account sample size and the number of independent variables, over 99% of the variation in the logarithm of salaries for these 100 sampled executives is accounted for by the model.

d. The test for overall model utility is conducted as follows:

H_0: $\beta_1 = \beta_2 = \cdots = \beta_7 = 0$

H_a: At least one of the model coefficients is nonzero.

Test statistic: $F = \dfrac{\text{Mean square for model}}{\text{MSE}} = 1{,}823.73$ (see Figure 4.24)

Rejection region: For $\alpha = .05$, $F > F_{.05}$
where $\nu_1 = k = 7$ and $\nu_2 = n - (k + 1) = 92$

where from Table 4 of Appendix C, $F_{.05} \approx 2.1$. Since $F = 1{,}823.73$ exceeds the tabulated value of F, we conclude that the model does contribute information for predicting executive salaries. It appears that at least one of the β parameters in the model differs from 0. Note that the observed significance level of the F test, $p = .0001$, confirms this result.

e. If the firm is (knowingly or unknowingly) discriminating against female executives, then the mean salary for females (denoted μ_F) will be less than the mean salary for males (denoted μ_M) with the same qualifications (e.g., years of experience, years of education, etc.) From our previous discussion of dummy variables, this difference will be represented by β_3, the β coefficient multiplied by x_3. Since $x_3 = 1$ if male, 0 if female, then $\beta_3 = (\mu_M - \mu_F)$ for fixed values of x_1, x_2 and x_5, and $x_4 = 0$. Consequently, a test of

H_0: $\beta_3 = 0$ versus H_a: $\beta_3 > 0$

is one way to test the discrimination hypothesis.* The p-value for this one-tailed test is one-half the p-value shown on the SAS printout, i.e., $.0001/2 = .00005$. With such a small p-value, there is strong evidence to reject H_0 and claim that some form of sex discrimination exists at the firm.

f. The least squares model can be used to obtain a predicted value for the logarithm of salary. Substituting the values of the x's shown in Table 4.6, we obtain

$$\widehat{\log(y)} = \hat{\beta}_0 + \hat{\beta}_1(12) + \hat{\beta}_2(16) + \hat{\beta}_3(0) + \hat{\beta}_4(400) + \hat{\beta}_5(160.1) + \hat{\beta}_6(144) + \hat{\beta}_7(0)$$

This predicted value is given at the bottom of the SAS printout, Figure 4.24, $\widehat{\log(y)} = 10.298$. The 95% prediction interval, from 10.203 to 10.392, is also

*A test for discrimination could also include testing the interaction term, $\beta_7 x_3 x_4$. If, as number of employees supervised (x_4) increases, the rate of increase in salary for males exceeds the rate for females, then $\beta_7 > 0$. Thus, rejecting H_0: $\beta_7 = 0$ in favor of H_a: $\beta_7 > 0$ would also suggest discrimination against female executives.

given. To predict the salary of an executive with these characteristics, we take the antilog of these values. That is, the predicted salary is $e^{10.298} = \$29{,}700$ (rounded to the nearest hundred) and the 95% prediction interval is from $e^{10.203}$ to $e^{10.392}$ (or from \$27,000 to \$32,600). Thus, an executive with the characteristics in Table 4.6 should be paid between \$27,000 and \$32,600 to be consistent with the sample data.

Warning: To decide whether a log transformation on the dependent variable is necessary, naive researchers sometimes compare the R^2 values for the two models

$$y = \beta_0 + \beta_1 x_1 + \cdots + \beta_k x_k + \varepsilon \quad \text{and} \quad \log(y) = \beta_0 + \beta_1 x_1 + \cdots + \beta_k x_k + \varepsilon$$

and choose the model with the larger R^2. But these R^2 values ***are not comparable*** since the dependent variables are not the same! One way to generate comparable R^2 values is to calculate the predicted values, $\widehat{\log(y)}$, for the log model and then compute the corresponding $\hat{y}$ values using the inverse transformation $\hat{y} = e^{\widehat{\log(y)}}$. A pseudo-$R^2$ for the log model can then be calculated in the usual way:

$$R^2_{\log(y)} = 1 - \frac{\Sigma\,(y_i - \hat{y}_i)^2}{\Sigma\,(y_i - \bar{y}_i)^2}$$

$R^2_{\log(y)}$ is now comparable to the R^2 for the untransformed model. See Maddala (1988) for a discussion of more formal methods for comparing the two models.

EXERCISES

4.21 Write a first-order linear model relating the mean value of y, $E(y)$, to
a. two quantitative independent variables
b. four quantitative independent variables

4.22 Write a second-order linear model relating the mean value of y, $E(y)$, to
a. two quantitative independent variables
b. three quantitative independent variables

4.23 Write a model relating $E(y)$ to a qualitative independent variable with
a. two levels, A and B
b. four levels, A, B, C, and D
Interpret the β parameters in each case.

4.24 Consider the first-order equation

$$y = 1 + 2x_1 + x_2$$

a. Graph the relationship between y and x_1 for $x_2 = 0$, 1, and 2.
b. Are the graphed curves in part **a** first-order or second-order?

c. How do the graphed curves in part **a** relate to each other?
d. If a linear model is first-order in two independent variables, what type of geometric relationship will you obtain when $E(y)$ is graphed as a function of one of the independent variables for various values of the other independent variable?

4.25 Consider the first-order equation

$$y = 1 + 2x_1 + x_2 - 3x_3$$

a. Graph the relationship between y and x_1 for $x_2 = 1$ and $x_3 = 3$.
b. Repeat part **a** for $x_2 = -1$ and $x_3 = 1$.
c. If a linear model is first-order in three independent variables, what type of geometric relationship will you obtain when $E(y)$ is graphed as a function of one of the independent variables for various values of the other independent variables?

4.26 Consider the second-order model

$$y = 1 + x_1 - x_2 + 2x_1^2 + x_2^2$$

a. Graph the relationship between y and x_1 for $x_2 = 0$, 1, and 2.
b. Are the graphed curves in part **a** first-order or second-order?
c. How do the graphed curves in part **a** relate to each other?
d. Do the independent variables x_1 and x_2 interact? Explain.

4.27 Consider the second-order model

$$y = 1 + x_1 - x_2 + x_1x_2 + 2x_1^2 + x_2^2$$

a. Graph the relationship between y and x_1 for $x_2 = 0$, 1, and 2.
b. Are the graphed curves in part **a** first-order or second-order?
c. How do the graphed curves in part **a** relate to each other?
d. Do the independent variables x_1 and x_2 interact? Explain.
e. Note that the model used in this exercise is identical to the noninteraction model of Exercise 4.26, except that it contains the term involving x_1x_2. What does the term x_1x_2 introduce into the model?

4.28 Personal computer (PC) technology is changing at a phenomenal rate. Consequently, the retail price of a PC may vary dramatically depending on when it is purchased and what features it includes. Retail price data were recently collected for IBM and IBM-compatible PCs. The data for $n = 60$ PCs, shown in the following table, were used to fit the multiple regression model

$$E(y) = \beta_0 + \beta_1x_1 + \beta_2x_2$$

where

y = Retail price (\$)

x_1 = Microprocessor speed (megahertz)

$$x_2 = \begin{cases} 1 & \text{if 386 CPU chip} \\ 0 & \text{if 286 CPU chip} \end{cases}$$

A MINITAB printout of the analysis follows the table.

RETAIL PRICE y	SPEED MHz	CHIP	RETAIL PRICE y	SPEED MHz	CHIP
$5099	33	386	$3249	25	386
3995	25	386	2995	20	386
2230	20	386	3419	20	386
4395	33	386	1590	20	386
6299	25	386	3899	20	386
2549	16	386	2249	12	286
3499	16	386	5796	25	386
2995	16	386	4330	16	286
1649	10	286	2699	16	386
5499	20	386	5579	20	386
1695	12	286	2095	16	386
2595	20	386	2695	25	386
3695	33	386	2295	20	386
3499	33	386	3445	25	386
2845	20	386	2445	16	386
4195	33	386	3795	25	386
2895	20	386	2395	16	386
2195	12	286	1595	12	286
5625	25	386	2095	16	386
2495	20	386	2995	25	386
3795	33	386	2895	20	386
3295	25	386	3995	33	386
1995	16	386	2595	20	386
2795	25	386	4995	25	386
5795	33	386	2695	25	386
3995	33	386	3990	33	386
1850	12	286	2795	20	386
1895	16	386	1995	20	286
1795	16	286	1595	16	286
2645	16	386	2875	20	386

Source: *Computer Monthly, Computer Shopper*, and IBM Corporation flyers. Data compiled by Jerasimos N. Mantas, University of South Florida business student.

MINITAB printout for Exercise 4.28

```
The regression equation is
Price = 648 + 105 Speed + 357 Chip

Predictor        Coef       Stdev    t-ratio        p
Constant        648.0       431.5       1.50    0.139
Speed          104.84       22.36       4.69    0.000
Chip            357.2       389.4       0.92    0.363

s = 953.7       R-sq = 40.0%      R-sq(adj) = 37.9%

Analysis of Variance

SOURCE        DF          SS          MS          F        p
Regression     2    34592104    17296052      19.02    0.000
Error         57    51840204      909477
Total         59    86432304

Unusual Observations
Obs.   Speed      Price       Fit  Stdev.Fit  Residual    St.Resid
  5     25.0       6299      3626        142      2673       2.83R
 10     20.0       5499      3102        151      2397       2.55R
 19     25.0       5625      3626        142      1999       2.12R
 37     25.0       5796      3626        142      2170       2.30R
 38     16.0       4330      2325        306      2005       2.22R
 40     20.0       5579      3102        151      2477       2.63R

R denotes an obs. with a large st. resid.
```

a. Write the least squares prediction equation.
b. Is the model adequate for predicting y? Test using $\alpha = .10$.
c. Construct a 90% confidence interval for β_1. Interpret the interval.
d. Is CPU chip (x_2) a useful predictor of price (y) in this model? Test using $\alpha = .10$.

4.29 A team of research physicians conducted a study to determine the effect of health education on the utilization of health services for hypertension patients (*Drug Topics*, Apr. 1993). Data collected for a sample of $n = 282$ new HMO enrollees with hypertension problems were used to fit the following regression model:

$$E(y) = \beta_0 + \beta_1 x_1 + \beta_2 x_2 + \beta_3 x_3 + \beta_4 x_4 + \beta_5 x_5$$

where

y = Annual health care expenditures (dollars)

x_1 = Age (years)

$$x_2 = \begin{cases} 1 & \text{if female} \\ 0 & \text{if male} \end{cases}$$

$$x_3 = \begin{cases} 1 & \text{if white} \\ 0 & \text{if nonwhite} \end{cases}$$

x_4 = Number of concomitant maintenance medications (regimen)

$$x_5 = \begin{cases} 1 & \text{if enrolled in a health education program} \\ 0 & \text{if not} \end{cases}$$

The regression results are summarized in the following table.

VARIABLE	β ESTIMATE	p-VALUE FOR TESTING H_0: $\beta_i = 0$
Intercept	64.82	$< .05$
Age (x_1)	1.05	$< .05$
Gender (x_2)	−10.53	nonsignificant
Race (x_3)	.27	nonsignificant
Regimen (x_4)	9.46	$< .05$
Health education (x_5)	−92.97	$< .001$
	$F = 37.84$, $R^2 = .4357$	

a. Write the least squares prediction equation for annual health care expenditures (y).
b. Interpret the estimates of β_1 and β_4.
c. Interpret the p-values shown in the table.
d. Interpret the F value.
e. Interpret the value of R^2.
f. Predict the annual health care expenditure of a 45-year-old male white hypertension patient who maintains three medications, but who has not enrolled in a health care education program.

4.30 One of the most promising methods for extracting crude oil employs a carbon dioxide (CO_2) flooding technique. When flooded into oil pockets, CO_2 enhances oil recovery by displacing the crude oil. In a microscopic investigation of the CO_2 flooding process, flow tubes were dipped into sample oil pockets containing a known amount of oil. The oil pockets were flooded with CO_2 and the percentage of oil displaced was recorded. The experiment was conducted at three different flow pressures and three different dipping angles. The displacement test data are recorded in the table.

PRESSURE x_1, pounds per square inch	DIPPING ANGLE x_2, degrees	OIL RECOVERY y, percentage
1,000	0	60.58
1,000	15	72.72
1,000	30	79.99
1,500	0	66.83
1,500	15	80.78
1,500	30	89.78
2,000	0	69.18
2,000	15	80.31
2,000	30	91.99

Source: Wang, G. C. "Microscopic investigation of CO_2 flooding process." *Journal of Petroleum Technology*, Vol. 34, No. 8, Aug. 1982, pp. 1789–1797. Copyright © 1982, Society of Petroleum Engineers, American Institute of Mining. First published in the *JPT* Aug. 1982.

a. Write the complete second-order model relating percentage oil recovery y to pressure x_1 and dipping angle x_2.
b. Plot the sample data on a scattergram, with percentage oil recovery y on the vertical axis and pressure x_1 on the horizontal axis. Connect the points corresponding to the same value of dipping angle x_2. Based on the scattergram, do you believe a complete second-order model is appropriate?
c. The SAS printout for the interaction model

$$y = \beta_0 + \beta_1 x_1 + \beta_2 x_2 + \beta_3 x_1 x_2 + \varepsilon$$

is provided here. Give the prediction equation for this model.

ANALYSIS OF VARIANCE

SOURCE	DF	SUM OF SQUARES	MEAN SQUARE	F VALUE	PROB>F
MODEL	3	843.19083	281.06361	44.670	0.0005
ERROR	5	31.45996667	6.29199333		
C TOTAL	8	874.65080			

ROOT MSE	2.508385	R-SQUARE	0.9640
DEP MEAN	76.90667	ADJ R-SQ	0.9425
C.V.	3.261596		

PARAMETER ESTIMATES

VARIABLE	DF	PARAMETER ESTIMATE	STANDARD ERROR	T FOR H0: PARAMETER=0	PROB > |T|
INTERCEP	1	54.50000000	5.03415841	10.826	0.0001
X1	1	0.007696667	0.003238311	2.377	0.0634
X2	1	0.55411111	0.25996282	2.132	0.0862
X1X2	1	0.000113333	0.000167226	0.678	0.5280

d. Construct a plot similar to the scattergram of part b, but use the predicted values from the interaction model on the vertical axis. Compare the two plots. Do you believe the interaction model will provide an adequate fit?
e. Check model adequacy using a statistical test with $\alpha = .05$.
f. Is there evidence of interaction between pressure x_1 and dipping angle x_2? Test using $\alpha = .05$.

4.31 *Environmental Science & Technology* (Oct. 1993) published an article that investigated the variables that affect the sorption of organic vapors on clay minerals. The independent variables and levels considered in the study are listed here. Identify the type (quantitative or qualitative) of each.
a. Temperature (50°, 60°, 75°, 90°)
b. Relative humidity (30%, 50%, 70%)
c. Organic compound (benzene, toluene, chloroform, methanol, anisole)
d. Refer to part c. Write a model for $E(y)$ as a function of organic compound at five levels.
e. Interpret the β parameters in the model, part d.
f. Explain how to test for differences among the mean retention coefficients of the five organic compounds.

4.32 Research has found that home ownership is a key factor in the exacerbation and perpetuation of racial/ethnic inequality. One study employed multiple regression to examine the variables that are related to differences in home ownership between the Hispanic and Anglo populations in the United States (*Social Problems*, Apr. 1986). The dependent variable in the analysis was the probability of home ownership, y, for a head of household.
a. One independent variable used to model y was the qualitative variable ethnic identity (Hispanic or Anglo). Write a model for $E(y)$ as a function of ethnic identity.
b. Interpret the β's in the model, part a.
c. A second independent variable used to model y was region of residence (Northeast, North Central, South, or West). Write a model for $E(y)$ as a function of region.
d. Interpret the β's in the model, part c.

4.33 Refer to the *Chemosphere* (1990) study of 103 production workers exposed to chemicals contaminated with the dioxin 2,3,7,8-TCDD, Exercise 1.51. Multiple regression analysis was used to relate the TCDD level (y) of a worker (measured in parts per trillion) to four independent variables in the model

$$E(y) = \beta_0 + \beta_1 x_1 + \beta_2 x_2 + \beta_3 x_3 + \beta_4 x_4$$

where

x_1 = Logarithm of years of exposure to TCDD

x_2 = Number of years since last exposure

x_3 = Age (in years)

x_4 = Body mass index

The results of the multiple regression analysis are summarized in the table on page 232. Interpret these results.

INDEPENDENT VARIABLE	PARAMETER ESTIMATE	STANDARD ERROR OF ESTIMATE	t VALUE	p-VALUE
Intercept	1.721	.770	2.24	—
x_1	.566	.054	10.48	< .001
x_2	−.085	.018	−4.72	< .001
x_3	.044	.010	4.40	< .001
x_4	.075	.021	3.57	< .001
$R^2 = .742$				

4.34 Refer to the study of Australian managers (*Organizational Behavior and Human Decision Processes*, Vol. 39, 1987), Exercise 4.14. Recall that a sample of 89 upper-level managers was asked to complete a questionnaire that measured the following (on a 7-point Likert scale):

y = Average performance of manager's subordinates (i.e., subordinate performance)

x_1 = Manager's preferred level of subordinate participation in decision making when conflict is present (i.e., group decision method)

x_2 = Average of subordinates' perceptions of manager's inclination to legitimize conflict (i.e., conflict legitimization)

a. Write a complete second-order model for x_1 and x_2.

b. In Exercise 4.14, the interaction model

$$E(y) = \beta_0 + \beta_1 x_1 + \beta_2 x_2 + \beta_3 x_1 x_2$$

was fitted to the 89 data points and yielded $R^2 = .22$. How will $R^2 = .22$ compare with the R^2 for the model, part **a**?

c. Which of the two models, parts **a** and **b**, will have a smaller value of s? Explain.

d. Suppose the marital status of each manager was measured at one of four levels: never married, married, divorced, widowed. Write a model for y as a function of marital status.

e. Interpret the β coefficients in the model, part **d**.

4.35 As a result of the U.S. surgeon general's warnings about the health hazards of smoking, Congress banned television and radio advertising of cigarettes in January 1971. The banning of prosmoking messages, however, also led to the virtual elimination of antismoking messages. In theory, if the pre-1971 antismoking commercials had been more effective than prosmoking commercials, the net effect of the Congressional ban should have been an increase in the consumption of cigarettes, thus benefiting the tobacco industry. To test this hypothesis, researchers at the University of Houston built a cigarette demand model based on data collected for 46 states over the 18-year period from 1963 to 1980 (*The Review of Economics and Statistics*, Feb. 1986). For each state–year, the following independent variables were recorded:

x_1 = Natural log of price of a carton of cigarettes

x_2 = Natural log of minimum price of a carton of cigarettes in any neighboring state (This variable was included to measure the effect of "bootlegging" cigarettes in nearby states with lower tax rates.)

x_3 = Natural log of real disposable income per capita

x_4 = Per capita index of expenditures for cigarette advertising on television and radio (This value is 0 for the years 1971–1980, when the ban was in effect.)

The dependent variable of interest is y, the natural log of per capita consumption of cigarettes by persons of smoking age (14 years and older). The multiple regression model

$$E(y) = \beta_0 + \beta_1 x_1 + \beta_2 x_2 + \beta_3 x_3 + \beta_4 x_4$$

was fitted to the $n = 828$ observations (48 states × 18 years) with the following results:

$$R^2 = .95$$
$$s = .047$$

a. Test the hypothesis that the model is useful for predicting y. Use $\alpha = .05$.
b. Interpret the value of s.
c. Give the null and alternative hypotheses appropriate for testing whether a decrease in per capita cigarette advertising expenditures is accompanied by an increase in per capita consumption of cigarettes over the period 1963–1980.
d. The value of $\hat{\beta}_4$ was determined to be .033. Interpret this value.
e. Does the value $\hat{\beta}_4 = .033$ support the alternative hypothesis in part c? Explain.

4.36 A study reported in *Human Factors* (Apr. 1990) investigated the effects of recognizer accuracy and vocabulary size on the performance of a computerized speech recognition device. Accuracy (x_1) of the device, measured as the percentage of correctly recognized spoken utterances, was set at three levels: 90%, 95%, and 99%. Vocabulary size (x_2), measured as the percentage of words needed for the task, was also set at three levels: 75%, 87.5%, and 100%. The dependent variable of primary interest was task completion time (y, in minutes), measured from when a user of the recognition device spoke the first input until the recognizer displayed the last spoken word of the task. Data collected for $n = 162$ trials were used to fit a complete second-order model for task completion time (y), as a function of the quantitative independent variables accuracy (x_1) and vocabulary (x_2). The coefficient of determination for the model was $R^2 = .75$.

a. Write the complete second-order model for $E(y)$.
b. Interpret the value of R^2.
c. Conduct a test of overall model adequacy. Use $\alpha = .05$.

4.10 A Test for Comparing Nested Models

In regression analysis, we often want to determine (with a high degree of confidence) which one among a set of candidate models best fits the data. In this section, we present such a method for **nested models**.

Definition 4.2

Two models are **nested** if one model contains all the terms of the second model and at least one additional term.

To illustrate, suppose you have collected data on a response, y, and two quantitative independent variables, x_1 and x_2, and you are considering the use of either a first-order or a second-order model to relate $E(y)$ to x_1 and x_2. Will the second-order model provide better predictions of y than the first-order model? To answer this question, examine the two models, and note that the second-order model contains all the terms in the first-order model plus three additional terms—those involving β_3, β_4, and β_5:

First-order model: $E(y) = \beta_0 + \beta_1 x_1 + \beta_2 x_2$

Second-order model: $E(y) = \beta_0 + \beta_1 x_1 + \beta_2 x_2 + \overbrace{\beta_3 x_1 x_2 + \beta_4 x_1^2 + \beta_5 x_2^2}^{\text{Second-order terms}}$

Consequently, these are nested models. Since the first-order model is the simpler of the two, we say that the *first-order model is nested within the more complex second-order model.*

In general, the more complex of two nested models is called the **complete** (or **full**) **model**, and the simpler of the two is called the **reduced model**. Asking whether the second-order (or *complete*) model contributes more information for the prediction of y than the first-order (or *reduced*) model is equivalent to asking whether at least one of the parameters, β_3, β_4, or β_5, differs from 0, i.e., whether the terms involving β_3, β_4, and β_5 should be retained in the model. Therefore, to test whether the second-order terms should be included in the model, we test the null hypothesis

H_0: $\beta_3 = \beta_4 = \beta_5 = 0$

(i.e, the second-order terms do not contribute information for the prediction of y) against the alternative hypothesis

H_a: At least one of the parameters, β_3, β_4, or β_5, differs from 0.

(i.e., at least one of the second-order terms contributes information for the prediction of y).

The procedure for conducting this test is intuitive: First, we use the method of least squares to fit the reduced model and calculate the corresponding sum of squares for error, SSE_R (the sum of squares of the deviations between observed and predicted y values). Next, we fit the complete model and calculate its sum of squares for error, SSE_C. Then, we compare SSE_R to SSE_C by calculating the difference $\text{SSE}_\text{R} - \text{SSE}_\text{C}$. If the second-order terms contribute to the model, then SSE_C should be much smaller than SSE_R, and the difference $\text{SSE}_\text{R} - \text{SSE}_\text{C}$ will be large. The larger the difference, the greater the weight of evidence that the complete model provides better predictions of y than does the reduced model.

The sum of squares for error will always decrease when new terms are added to the model since the total sum of squares, $SS_{yy} = \Sigma (y - \bar{y})^2$, remains the same. The question is whether this decrease is large enough to conclude that it is due to more than just an increase in the number of model terms and to chance. To test the null hypothesis that the curvature coefficients β_4 and β_5 simultaneously equal 0, we use an F statistic calculated as follows:

$$F = \frac{\text{Drop in SSE/Number of } \beta \text{ parameters being tested}}{s^2 \text{ for larger model}}$$

$$= \frac{(\text{SSE}_\text{R} - \text{SSE}_\text{C})/2}{\text{SSE}_\text{C}/[n - (5 + 1)]}$$

F Test for Comparing Nested Models

Reduced model: $E(y) = \beta_0 + \beta_1 x_1 + \cdots + \beta_g x_g$

Complete model: $E(y) = \beta_0 + \beta_1 x_1 + \cdots + \beta_g x_g + \beta_{g+1} x_{g+1} + \cdots + \beta_k x_k$

H_0: $\beta_{g+1} = \beta_{g+2} = \cdots = \beta_k = 0$

H_a: At least one of the β parameters being tested is nonzero.

Test statistic: $F = \dfrac{(\text{SSE}_\text{R} - \text{SSE}_\text{C})/(k - g)}{\text{SSE}_\text{C}/[n - (k + 1)]}$

$$= \frac{(\text{SSE}_\text{R} - \text{SSE}_\text{C})/\text{Number of } \beta\text{'s tested}}{\text{MSE}_\text{C}}$$

where

SSE_R = Sum of squared errors for the reduced model

SSE_C = Sum of squared errors for the complete model

MSE_C = Mean square error for the complete model

$k - g$ = Number of β parameters specified in H_0 (i.e., number of β's tested)

$k + 1$ = Number of β parameters in the complete model (including β_0)

n = Total sample size

Rejection region: $F > F_\alpha$

and

$\nu_1 = k - g$ = Degrees of freedom for the numerator

$\nu_2 = n - (k + 1)$ = Degrees of freedom for the denominator

When the assumptions listed in Sections 3.4 and 4.2 about the error term ε are satisfied and the β parameters for curvature are all 0 (H_0 is true), this F statistic has an F distribution with $\nu_1 = 2$ and $\nu_2 = n - 6$ df. Note that ν_1 is the number of β parameters being tested and ν_2 is the number of degrees of freedom associated with s^2 in the larger, second-order model.

If the quadratic terms *do* contribute to the model (H_a is true), we expect the F statistic to be large. Thus, we use a one-tailed test and reject H_0 if F exceeds some critical value, F_α, as shown in Figure 4.25.

FIGURE 4.25
Rejection region for the F test H_0: $\beta_4 = \beta_5 = 0$

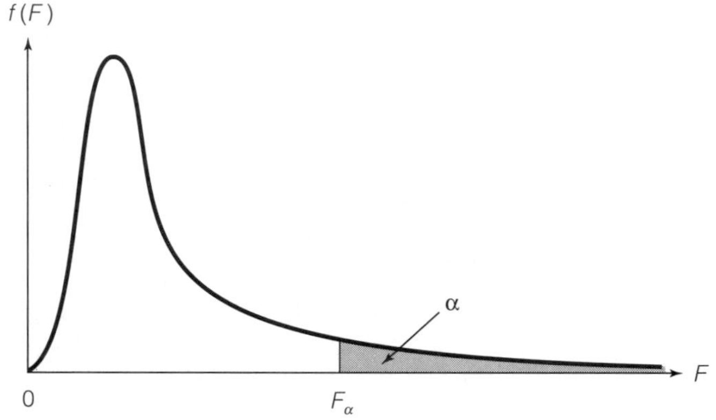

EXAMPLE 4.7

In Example 4.4, we fitted the second-order model for a set of $n = 20$ data points relating shipment cost to package weight and distance shipped. The SAS printout for this model, called the complete model, is shown in Figure 4.22. Figure 4.26 shows the SAS printout for the straight-line interaction model (the reduced model) fitted to the same $n = 20$ data points. Referring to the printouts, we find the following:

Straight-line interaction (reduced) model:

$\text{SSE}_\text{R} = 6.63330508$ (see Figure 4.26)

Second-order (complete) model:

$\text{SSE}_\text{C} = 2.74474$ (see Figure 4.22)

Test the hypothesis that the quadratic terms do not contribute information for the prediction of y.

Solution

The test statistic is

$$F = \frac{(\text{SSE}_\text{R} - \text{SSE}_\text{C})/2}{\text{SSE}_\text{C}/(20 - 6)}$$

$$= \frac{(6.63330508 - 2.74474)/2}{2.74474/14} = \frac{1.94428}{.19605} = 9.92$$

The critical value of F for $\alpha = .05$, $\nu_1 = 2$, and $\nu_2 = 14$ is found in Table 4 (Appendix C) to be

$$F_{.05} = 3.74$$

FIGURE 4.26 SAS printout for straight-line interaction model of Example 4.7

ANALYSIS OF VARIANCE

SOURCE	DF	SUM OF SQUARES	MEAN SQUARE	F VALUE	PROB>F
MODEL	3	445.45219	148.48406	358.154	0.0001
ERROR	16	6.63330508	0.41458157		
C TOTAL	19	452.08550			

ROOT MSE	0.6438801	R-SQUARE	0.9853
DEP MEAN	6.335	ADJ R-SQ	0.9826
C.V.	10.16385		

PARAMETER ESTIMATES

VARIABLE	DF	PARAMETER ESTIMATE	STANDARD ERROR	T FOR H0: PARAMETER=0	PROB > |T|
INTERCEP	1	-0.14050074	0.64810001	-0.217	0.8311
X1	1	0.01908803	0.15821160	0.121	0.9055
X2	1	0.77208456	0.39056785	1.977	0.0656
X1X2	1	0.77957444	0.08976644	8.684	0.0001

Since the calculated $F = 9.92$ exceeds 3.74, we are confident in concluding that the quadratic terms contribute to the prediction of y, shipment cost per package. The curvature terms should be retained in the model.

Suppose the F test in Example 4.7 yielded a test statistic that did not fall in the rejection region. That is, suppose there was insufficient evidence (at $\alpha = .05$) to say that the curvature terms contribute information for the prediction of product quality. As with any statistical test of hypothesis, we must be cautious about accepting H_0 since the probability of a Type II error is unknown. Nevertheless, most practitioners of regression analysis adopt the principle of **parsimony**. That is, in situations where two competing models are found to have essentially the same predictive power, the model with the lower number of β's (i.e., the more **parsimonious model**) is selected. The principle of parsimony would lead us to choose the simpler (reduced) model over the more complex complete model when we fail to reject H_0 in the F test for nested models.

Definition 4.3

A **parsimonious model** is a general linear model with a small number of β parameters. In situations where two competing models have essentially the same predictive power (as determined by an F test), choose the more parsimonious of the two.

When the candidate models in model building are nested models, the F test developed in this section is the appropriate procedure to apply to compare the models. However, if the models are not nested, this F test is not applicable. In this situation, the analyst must base the choice of the best model on statistics such as R_a^2 and s. It is important to remember that decisions based on these and other numerical descriptive measures of model adequacy cannot be supported with a measure of reliability and are often very subjective in nature.

EXERCISES

4.37 Determine which pairs of the following models are "nested" models. For each pair of nested models, identify the complete and reduced model.

a. $E(y) = \beta_0 + \beta_1 x_1 + \beta_2 x_2$
b. $E(y) = \beta_0 + \beta_1 x_1$
c. $E(y) = \beta_0 + \beta_1 x_1 + \beta_2 x_1^2$
d. $E(y) = \beta_0 + \beta_1 x_1 + \beta_2 x_2 + \beta_3 x_1 x_2$
e. $E(y) = \beta_0 + \beta_1 x_1 + \beta_2 x_2 + \beta_3 x_1 x_2 + \beta_4 x_1^2 + \beta_5 x_2^2$

4.38 Consider the second-order model relating $E(y)$ to three quantitative independent variables, x_1, x_2, and x_3:

$$E(y) = \beta_0 + \beta_1 x_1 + \beta_2 x_2 + \beta_3 x_3 + \beta_4 x_1 x_2 + \beta_5 x_1 x_3 + \beta_6 x_2 x_3 + \beta_7 x_1^2 + \beta_8 x_2^2 + \beta_9 x_3^2$$

a. Specify the parameters involved in a test of the hypothesis that no curvature exists in the response surface.
b. State the hypothesis of part **a** in terms of the model parameters.
c. What hypothesis would you test to determine whether x_3 is useful for the prediction of $E(y)$?

4.39 Refer to the *Journal of Personal Selling & Sales Management* (Summer 1990) study of gender differences in the industrial sales force, Exercise 3.40. Recall that a sample of 244 male sales managers and a sample of 153 female sales managers participated in the survey. One objective of the research was to assess how supervisory behavior affects intrinsic job satisfaction. Initially, the researchers fitted the following reduced model to the data on each gender group:

$$E(y) = \beta_0 + \beta_1 x_1 + \beta_2 x_2 + \beta_3 x_3 + \beta_4 x_4$$

where

y = Intrinsic job satisfaction (measured on a scale of 0 to 40)

x_1 = Age (years)

x_2 = Education level (years)

x_3 = Firm experience (months)

x_4 = Sales experience (months)

To determine the effects of supervisory behavior, four variables (all measured on a scale of 0 to 50) were added to the model: x_5 = contingent reward behavior, x_6 = noncontingent reward behavior,

x_7 = contingent punishment behavior, and x_8 = noncontingent punishment behavior. Thus, the complete model is

$$E(y) = \beta_0 + \beta_1 x_1 + \beta_2 x_2 + \beta_3 x_3 + \beta_4 x_4 + \beta_5 x_5 + \beta_6 x_6 + \beta_7 x_7 + \beta_8 x_8$$

a. For each gender, specify the null hypothesis and rejection region ($\alpha = .05$) for testing whether any of the four supervisory behavior variables affect intrinsic job satisfaction.

b. The R^2 values for the four models (reduced and complete model for both samples) are given in the accompanying table. Interpret the results. For each gender, does it appear that the supervisory behavior variables have an impact on intrinsic job satisfaction? Explain.

MODEL	R^2	
	Males	Females
Reduced	.218	.268
Complete	.408	.496

Source: Schul, et al. "Assessing gender differences in relationships between supervisory behaviors and job related outcomes in industrial sales force." *Journal of Personal Selling & Sales Management*, Vol. X, Summer 1990, p. 9 (Table 4).

c. The F statistics for comparing the two models are $F_{\text{males}} = 13.00$ and $F_{\text{females}} = 9.05$. Conduct the tests, part **a**, and interpret the results.

4.40 Refer to Exercise 4.39. One way to test for gender differences in the industrial sales force is to incorporate a dummy variable for gender into the model for intrinsic job satisfaction, y, and then fit the model to the data for the combined sample of males and females.

a. Write a model for y as a function of the independent variables, x_1 through x_8, and the gender dummy variable. Include interactions between gender and each of the other independent variables in the model.

b. Based on the model, part **a**, what is the null hypothesis for testing whether gender has an effect on job satisfaction?

c. Explain how to conduct the test, part **b**.

4.41 Refer to the *Motivation and Emotion* study on the relationship between cartoon funniness ratings (y) and pain (x_1) or aggression (x_2), Exercise 4.8. Since no evidence of an inverted-U relationship was found, the researchers fitted the following two first-order models to the $n = 32$ data points:

Model 1: $E(y) = \beta_0 + \beta_1 x_1$, SSE = 26.01

Model 2: $E(y) = \beta_0 + \beta_1 x_1 + \beta_2 x_2$, SSE = 25.44

a. What hypothesis would you test to determine whether the addition of the aggression (x_2) rating improves the predictive ability of the model?

b. Use the F test discussed in this section to test the hypothesis, part **a**. [Note that this test is equivalent to a t test on β_2.]

4.42 An exploration seismologist wants to develop a model that will allow him to estimate the average signal-to-noise ratio of an earthquake's seismic wave, y, as a function of two independent variables:

x_1 = Frequency (cycles per second)

x_2 = Amplitude of the wavelet

The model under consideration is a complete second-order model:

$$E(y) = \beta_0 + \beta_1 x_1 + \beta_2 x_2 + \beta_3 x_1 x_2 + \beta_4 x_1^2 + \beta_5 x_2^2$$

where

y = Signal-to-noise ratio

x_1 = Frequency of the wavelet

x_2 = Amplitude of wavelet

A portion of the computer printout that results from fitting this model to $n = 12$ data points follows:

SOURCE	DF	SUM OF SQUARES	MEAN SQUARE
Model	5	38638.97	7727.79
Error	6	159.94	26.66
Total	11	38798.91	R-SQUARE
			0.996

The reduced first-order model

$$E(y) = \beta_0 + \beta_1 x_1 + \beta_2 x_2$$

was also fitted to the same data; the resulting computer printout is partially reproduced here.

SOURCE	DF	SUM OF SQUARES	MEAN SQUARE
Model	2	36704.5	18352.2
Error	9	2094.4	232.7
Total	11	38798.9	R-SQUARE
			0.946

Is there sufficient evidence to conclude that a second-order model contributes more information for the prediction of y than does a first-order model? Test using $\alpha = .05$.

4.43 Research was conducted at Temple University to examine the effect of several factors on managerial performance (*Journal of Vocational Behavior*, Oct. 1986). A sample of 100 management personnel from several divisions within a government agency took part in the study. Each manager completed a questionnaire designed to measure the following variables:

y = Performance rating (1 = unacceptable, 5 = outstanding)

$$x_1 = \begin{cases} 1 & \text{if male} \\ 0 & \text{if female} \end{cases}$$

x_2 = Job tenure (years)

x_3 = Manager–subordinate work relationship rating (1 = unsatisfactory, 5 = excellent)

x_4 = Effort level (average number of hours per week invested in job)

$$x_5 = \begin{cases} 1 & \text{if middle/upper-level manager} \\ 0 & \text{if lower-level manager} \end{cases}$$

x_6 = Subordinate-related managerial behavior score (low scores indicate little or no effort spent on counseling, evaluating, and training subordinates)

The data collected on the 100 managers were then used to fit several regression models of managerial performance.

a. Initially, the model

$$E(y) = \beta_0 + \beta_1 x_1 + \beta_2 x_2 + \beta_3 x_3 + \beta_4 x_4$$

was considered to account for the influence of gender, job tenure, manager–subordinate work relationship, and effort level on performance rating. For this model, SSE = 352 and $R^2 = .11$. Calculate the F statistic for testing model adequacy. Is the model useful for predicting performance rating y? Use $\alpha = .05$.

b. Terms for managerial level and subordinate-related behavior (i.e., $\beta_5 x_5 + \beta_6 x_6$) were added to the model in part **a**, resulting in SSE = 341 and $R^2 = .14$. Do these terms contribute additional information for the prediction of performance rating y? Test using $\alpha = .05$.

c. A third model was also considered:

$$E(y) = \beta_0 + \beta_1 x_1 + \beta_2 x_2 + \beta_3 x_3 + \beta_4 x_4 + \beta_5 x_5 + \beta_6 x_6 + \beta_7 x_5 x_6$$

This model resulted in SSE = 321 and $R^2 = .19$. Test the hypothesis that the interaction between managerial level x_5 and subordinate-related behavior x_6 is not important; i.e., test H_0: $\beta_7 = 0$. Use $\alpha = .05$.

d. Interpret the result of part **c** in terms of the problem.

4.44 Since 1978, when the U.S. airline industry was deregulated, researchers have questioned whether the deregulation has ensured a truly competitive environment. If so, the profitability of any major airline would be related only to overall industry conditions (e.g., disposable income and market share) but not to any unchanging feature of that airline. This profitability hypothesis was tested in *Transportation Journal* (Winter 1990) using multiple regression. Data for $n = 234$ carrier-years were used to fit the model

$$E(y) = \beta_0 + \beta_1 x_1 + \beta_2 x_2 + \beta_3 x_3 + \cdots + \beta_{30} x_{30}$$

where

y = Profit rate

x_1 = Real personal disposable income

x_2 = Industry market share

x_3 through x_{30} = Dummy variables (coded 0–1) for the 29 air carriers investigated in the study

The results of the regression are summarized in the table. Interpret the results. Is the profitability hypothesis supported?

VARIABLE	β ESTIMATE	t VALUE	p-VALUE
Intercept	1.2642	.09	.9266
x_1	$-.0022$	$-.99$	.8392
x_2	4.8405	3.57	.0003
x_3–x_{30}	(not given)	—	—

$R^2 = .3402$
$F(\text{Model}) = 3.49$, p-value $= .0001$
$F(\text{Carrier dummies}) = 3.59$, p-value $= .0001$

Source: Leigh, L. E. "Contestability in deregulated airline markets: Some empirical tests." *Transportation Journal*, Winter 1990, p. 55 (Table 4).

4.11 Stepwise Regression

Refer to the problem of predicting executive salaries, Example 4.6. Perhaps the biggest problem in building a model to describe executive salaries is choosing the important independent variables to be included in the model. The list of potentially important independent variables is extremely long, and we need some objective method of screening out those that are not important.

The problem of deciding which of a large set of independent variables to include in a model is common, for instance, trying to determine which variables influence the profit of a firm, affect product quality, or reflect the state of the economy.

A systematic approach to building a model with a large number of independent variables is difficult because the interpretation of multivariable interactions and higher-order polynomials (squared terms, cubic terms, and so forth) is tedious. Therefore, we turn to a screening procedure known as **stepwise regression**.

The most commonly used stepwise regression procedure, available in most popular statistical software packages, works as follows. The user first identifies the response, y, and the set of potentially important independent variables, $x_1, x_2, \ldots, x_k$, where k is generally large. (Note that this set of variables could represent both first- and higher-order terms, as well as any interaction terms that might be important information contributors.) The response and independent variables are then entered into the computer, and the stepwise procedure begins.

STEP 1 The computer fits all possible one-variable models of the form

$$E(y) = \beta_0 + \beta_1 x_1$$

to the data. For each model, the test of the null hypothesis

$$H_0\colon \quad \beta_1 = 0$$

against the alternative hypothesis

$$H_a\colon \quad \beta_1 \neq 0$$

is conducted using the t (or the equivalent F) test for a single β parameter. The independent variable that produces the largest (absolute) t value is declared the best one-variable predictor of y.* Call this independent variable x_1.

STEP 2 The stepwise program now begins to search through the remaining $(k-1)$ independent variables for the best two-variable model of the form

$$E(y) = \beta_0 + \beta_1 x_1 + \beta_2 x_i$$

This is done by fitting all two-variable models containing x_1 and each of the other $(k-1)$ options for the second variable x_i. The t values for the test H_0: $\beta_2 = 0$ are computed for each of the $(k-1)$ models (corresponding to the remaining independent variables x_i, $i = 2, 3, \ldots, k$), and the variable having the largest t is retained. Call this variable x_2.

At this point, some software packages diverge in methodology. The better packages now go back and check the t value of $\hat{\beta}_1$ *after $\hat{\beta}_2 x_2$ has been added to the model*. If the t value has become nonsignificant at some specified α level (say, $\alpha = .10$), the variable x_1 is removed and a search is made for the independent variable with a β parameter that will yield the most significant t value in the presence of $\hat{\beta}_2 x_2$. Other packages do not recheck $\hat{\beta}_1$, but proceed directly to step 3.

The best-fitting model may yield a different value for $\hat{\beta}_1$ than that obtained in step 1, because $\hat{\beta}_1$ and $\hat{\beta}_2$ may be correlated. Thus, both the value of $\hat{\beta}_1$ and, therefore, its significance will usually change from step 1 to step 2. For this reason, the software packages that recheck the t values at each step are preferable.

STEP 3 The stepwise procedure now checks for a third independent variable to include in the model with x_1 and x_2. That is, we seek the best model of the form

$$E(y) = \beta_0 + \beta_1 x_1 + \beta_2 x_2 + \beta_3 x_i$$

To do this, we fit all the $(k-2)$ models using x_1, x_2, and each of the $(k-2)$ remaining variables, x_i, as a possible x_3. The criterion is again to include the independent variable with the largest t value. Call this best third variable x_3.

The better programs now recheck the t values corresponding to the x_1 and x_2 coefficients, replacing the variables that have t values that have become nonsignificant. This procedure is continued until no further independent variables can be found that yield significant t values (at the specified α level) in the presence of the variables already in the model.

The result of the stepwise procedure is a model containing only the main effects with t values that are significant at the specified α level. Thus, in most practical situations, only a portion of the large number of independent variables will remain. However, it is very important not to jump to the conclusion that all the independent variables important for predicting y have been identified or that the unimportant independent variables have been eliminated. Remember, the stepwise procedure is using only *sample estimates* of the true model coefficients

*Note that the variable with the largest t value will also be the one with the largest Pearson product moment correlation, r (Section 3.7), with y.

(β's) to select the important variables. An extremely large number of single β parameter t tests have been conducted, and the probability is very high that one or more errors have been made in including or excluding variables. That is, we have very probably included some unimportant independent variables in the model (Type I errors) and eliminated some important ones (Type II errors).

There is a second reason why we might not have arrived at a good model. When we choose the variables to be included in the stepwise regression, we may often omit high-order terms (to keep the number of variables manageable). Consequently, we may have initially omitted several important terms from the model. Thus, we should recognize stepwise regression for what it is—an objective screening procedure.

Now, we will consider interactions and quadratic terms (for quantitative variables) among variables screened by the stepwise procedure. It would be best to develop this response surface model with a second set of data independent of that used for the screening, so the results of the stepwise procedure can be partially verified with new data. However, this is not always possible, because in many business modeling situations only a small amount of data is available.

Remember, do not be deceived by the impressive-looking t values that result from the stepwise procedure—it has retained only the independent variables with the largest t values. Also, be certain to consider second-order terms in systematically developing the prediction model. The first-order model given by the stepwise procedure may be greatly improved by the addition of interaction and quadratic terms.

Warning

Be cautious when using the results of stepwise regression to make inferences about the relationship between $E(y)$ and the independent variables in the resulting first-order model. First, an extremely large number of t tests have been conducted, leading to a high probability of making either one or more Type I or Type II errors. Second, the stepwise model does not include any higher-order or interaction terms. Stepwise regression should be used only when necessary, i.e., when you want to determine which of a large number of potentially important independent variables should be used in the model-building process.

EXAMPLE 4.8

In Example 4.6, we fitted a multiple regression model for executive salaries as a function of experience, education, gender, etc. A preliminary step in the construction of this model was the determination of the most important independent variables. Ten independent variables (seven quantitative and three qualitative) were considered, as shown in Table 4.7. It would be very difficult to construct a second-order model with 10 independent variables. Therefore, we use the sample of 100 executives from Example 4.6 to decide which of the 10 variables should be included in the construction of the final model for executive salaries.

TABLE 4.7 **Independent Variables in the Executive Salary Example**

INDEPENDENT VARIABLE	DESCRIPTION
x_1	Experience (years)—quantitative
x_2	Education (years)—quantitative
x_3	Gender (1 if male, 0 if female)—qualitative
x_4	Number of employees supervised—quantitative
x_5	Corporate assets (millions of dollars)—quantitative
x_6	Board member (1 if yes, 0 if no)—qualitative
x_7	Age (years)—quantitative
x_8	Company profits (past 12 months, millions of dollars)—quantitative
x_9	International responsibility (1 if yes, 0 if no)—qualitative
x_{10}	Company's total sales (past 12 months, millions of dollars)—quantitative

Solution

We will use stepwise regression with the first-order terms of the seven quantitative independent variables and the main effects of the three qualitative independent variables to identify the most important variables. The dependent variable y is the natural logarithm of the executive salaries. The SAS stepwise regression printout is shown in Figure 4.27. The first variable included in the model is x_4, number of employees supervised by the executive. In the second step, x_5, corporate assets, is introduced in the model. In the sixth step, x_6, a dummy variable for the qualitative variable Board member, is introduced. However, because the significance (.2295) of the F statistic (SAS uses the $F = t^2$ statistic in the stepwise procedure rather than the t statistic) for x_6 exceeds the preassigned $\alpha = .10$, x_6 is then removed from the model. Thus, in step 7, the procedure indicates that the five-variable model including x_1, x_2, x_3, x_4, and x_5 is best. That is, none of the other independent variables can meet the $\alpha = .10$ criterion for admission to the model.

Thus, in our final modeling effort (Example 4.6) we concentrated on these five independent variables, and determined that several second-order terms were important in the prediction of executive salaries.

FIGURE 4.27
SAS stepwise regression printout for Example 4.8

```
STEP 1
   Variable X4 Entered          R-Square = 0.42071677        C(P) = 1274.7576

                          DF    Sum of Squares   Mean Square          F    Prob > F

   Regression              1       11.46854285   11.46854285      71.17      0.0001
   Error                  98       15.79113802    0.16113696
   Total                  99       27.25977087

                                       B Value     Std Error          F    Prob > F

   Intercept                       10.20077500
   X4                               0.00057284    0.00006790      71.17      0.0001
---------------------------------------------------------------------------------

STEP 2
   Variable X5 Entered          R-Square = 0.78299675        C(P) = 419.4947

                          DF    Sum of Squares   Mean Square          F    Prob > F

   Regression              2       21.34431198   10.67215599     175.00      0.0001
   Error                  97        5.91545889    0.06098411
   Total                  99       27.25977087
```

FIGURE 4.27 (*continued*)

	B Value	Std Error	F	Prob > F
Intercept	9.87702903			
X4	0.00058353	0.00004178	195.06	0.0001
X5	0.00183730	0.00014438	161.94	0.0001

STEP 3
Variable X1 Entered R-Square = 0.89667614 C(P) = 152.4952

	DF	Sum of Squares	Mean Square	F	Prob > F
Regression	3	24.44318616	8.14772872	277.71	0.0001
Error	96	2.81658471	0.02933942		
Total	99	27.25977087			

	B Value	Std Error	F	Prob > F
Intercept	9.66449288			
X4	0.00055251	0.00002914	359.59	0.0001
X5	0.00191195	0.00010041	362.60	0.0001
X1	0.01870784	0.00182032	105.62	0.0001

STEP 4
Variable X3 Entered R-Square = 0.94815717 C(P) = 32.6757

	DF	Sum of Squares	Mean Square	F	Prob > F
Regression	4	25.84654710	8.46163678	434.37	0.0001
Error	95	1.41322377	0.01487604		
Total	99	27.25977087			

	B Value	Std Error	F	Prob > F
Intercept	9.40077349			
X4	0.00055288	0.00002075	710.15	0.0001
X5	0.00190876	0.00007150	712.74	0.0001
X1	0.02074868	0.00131310	249.68	0.0001
X3	0.30011726	0.03089939	94.34	0.0001

STEP 5
Variable X2 Entered R-Square = 0.96039323 C(P) = 5.7215

	DF	Sum of Squares	Mean Square	F	Prob > F
Regression	5	26.18009940	5.23601988	455.87	0.0001
Error	94	1.07967147	0.01148587		
Total	99	27.25977087			

	B Value	Std Error	F	Prob > F
Intercept	8.85387930			
X4	0.00056061	0.00001829	939.84	0.0001
X5	0.00193684	0.00006304	943.98	0.0001
X1	0.02141724	0.00116047	340.61	0.0001
X3	0.31927842	0.02738298	135.95	0.0001
X2	0.03315807	0.00615303	29.04	0.0001

STEP 6
Variable X6 Entered R-Square = 0.96100666 C(P) = 6.2699

	DF	Sum of Squares	Mean Square	F	Prob > F
Regression	6	26.19682148	4.36613691	382.00	0.0001
Error	93	1.06294939	0.01142956		
Total	99	27.25977087			

	B Value	Std Error	F	Prob > F
Intercept	8.87509152			
X4	0.00055820	0.00001835	925.32	0.0001
X5	0.00193764	0.00006289	949.31	0.0001
X1	0.02133460	0.00115963	338.48	0.0001
X3	0.31093801	0.02817264	121.81	0.0001
X2	0.03272195	0.00614851	28.32	0.0001
X6	0.03866226	0.03196369	1.46	0.2295

FIGURE 4.27 (*continued*)

```
STEP 7
   Variable X6 Removed            R-Square = 0.96039323        C(P) = 5.7215

                           DF     Sum of Squares   Mean Square        F    Prob > F

   Regression               5        26.18009940    5.23601988   455.87      0.0001
   Error                   94         1.07967147    0.01148587
   Total                   99        27.25977087

                                         B Value     Std Error        F    Prob > F

   Intercept                          8.85387930
   X4                                 0.00056061    0.00001829   939.84      0.0001
   X5                                 0.00193684    0.00006304   943.98      0.0001
   X1                                 0.02141724    0.00116047   340.61      0.0001
   X3                                 0.31927842    0.02738298   135.95      0.0001
   X2                                 0.03315807    0.00615303    29.04      0.0001
```

There are several other stepwise regression techniques designed to select the most important independent variables. One of these, called **forward selection**, is nearly identical to the stepwise procedure previously outlined. The only difference is that the forward selection technique provides no option for rechecking the t values corresponding to the x's that have entered the model in an earlier step. Thus, stepwise regression is preferred to forward selection in practice.

Another technique, called **backward elimination**, initially fits a model containing terms for all potential independent variables. That is, for k independent variables, the model $E(y) = \beta_0 + \beta_1 x_1 + \beta_2 x_2 + \cdots + \beta_k x_k$ is fitted in step 1. The variable with the smallest t (or F) statistic for testing $H_0\colon \beta_i = 0$ is identified and dropped from the model if the t value is less than some specified critical value. The model with the remaining $(k - 1)$ independent variables is fitted in step 2, and again, the variable associated with the smallest nonsignificant t value is dropped. This process is repeated until no further nonsignificant independent variables can be found. The real disadvantage of using the backward elimination technique is that you need a sufficiently large number of data points to fit the initial model in step 1.

EXERCISES

4.45 There are six independent variables, x_1, x_2, x_3, x_4, x_5, and x_6, that might be useful in predicting a response y. A total of $n = 50$ observations are available, and it is decided to employ stepwise regression to help in selecting the independent variables that appear to be useful. The computer fits all possible one-variable models of the form

$$E(y) = \beta_0 + \beta_1 x_i$$

where x_i is the ith independent variable, $i = 1, 2, \ldots, 6$. The information in the table at the top of page 248 is provided from the computer printout.

INDEPENDENT VARIABLE	$\hat{\beta}_1$	$s_{\hat{\beta}_1}$
x_1	1.6	.42
x_2	−.9	.01
x_3	3.4	1.14
x_4	2.5	2.06
x_5	−4.4	.73
x_6	.3	.35

a. Which independent variable is declared the best one-variable predictor of y? Explain.
b. Would this variable be included in the model at this stage? Explain.
c. Describe the next phase that a stepwise procedure would execute.

4.46 Many power plants dump hot wastewater into nearby rivers, streams, and oceans, an action that may have an adverse effect on the aquatic organisms in the dumping areas. A marine biologist was hired by the EPA to determine whether the hot water runoff from a particular power plant located near a large gulf is having an adverse effect on the marine life in the area. In the initial phase of the study, the biologist's goal is to acquire a prediction equation for the number of marine animals located at certain predesignated areas, or stations, in the gulf. Based on past experience, the biologist considered the following environmental factors as predictors for the number of animals at a particular station:

x_1 = Temperature of water (TEMP)

x_2 = Salinity of water (SAL)

x_3 = Dissolved oxygen content of water (DO)

x_4 = Turbidity index, a measure of the turbidity of the water (TI)

x_5 = Depth of the water at the station (ST_DEPTH)

x_6 = Total weight of sea grasses in sample area (TGRSWT)

As a preliminary step in the construction of this model, the biologist used a stepwise regression procedure to identify the most important of these six variables. A total of 716 samples were taken at different stations in the gulf, producing the accompanying SAS printout. (The response measured was y, the log of the number of marine animals found in the sampled area.)

a. According to the SAS printout, which of the six independent variables should be used in the model? (Use $\alpha = .10$.)

```
STEP 1
   Variable ST_DEPTH Entered            R-Square = 0.1223

                          DF    Sum of Squares   Mean Square        F    Prob > F

   Regression              1             57.44         57.44    99.47      0.0001
   Error                 714            412.33          0.58
   Total                 715            469.77

                                   B Value       Std Error         F    Prob > F

   Intercept                       8.38559
   ST_DEPTH                       -0.43678         0.04379     99.47      0.0001
--------------------------------------------------------------------------------
```

SAS printout for Exercise 4.46 (*continued*)

```
STEP 2
   Variable TGRSWT Entered          R-Square = 0.1821

                             DF     Sum of Squares   Mean Square        F   Prob > F

   Regression                 2              85.55         42.78    79.38     0.0001
   Error                    713             384.22          0.54
   Total                    715             469.77

                                           B Value     Std Error        F   Prob > F

   Intercept                               8.07682
   ST_DEPTH                               -0.35355       0.04385    65.02     0.0001
   TGRSWT                                  0.00271       0.00038    52.16     0.0001
--------------------------------------------------------------------------------------
STEP 3
   Variable TI Entered              R-Square = 0.1870

                             DF     Sum of Squares   Mean Square        F   Prob > F

   Regression                 3              87.85         29.28    54.59     0.0001
   Error                    712             381.92          0.54
   Total                    715             469.77

                                           B Value     Std Error        F   Prob > F

   Intercept                               7.38864
   TI                                      0.65774       0.31783     4.28     0.0389
   ST_DEPTH                               -0.31451       0.47641    43.58     0.0001
   TGRSWT                                  0.00261       0.00038    47.73     0.0001
--------------------------------------------------------------------------------------
STEP 4
   Variable DO Entered              R-Square = 0.1889

                             DF     Sum of Squares   Mean Square        F   Prob > F

   Regression                 4              88.75         22.19    41.40     0.0001
   Error                    711             381.02          0.54
   Total                    715             469.77

                                           B Value     Std Error        F   Prob > F

   Intercept                               7.22576
   DO                                      0.01769       0.01363     1.69     0.1946
   TI                                      0.67347       0.31791     4.49     0.0345
   ST_DEPTH                               -0.30417       0.04828    39.69     0.0001
   TGRSWT                                  0.00267       0.00038    49.23     0.0001
--------------------------------------------------------------------------------------
STEP 5
   Variable DO Removed              R-Square = 0.1870

                             DF     Sum of Squares   Mean Square        F   Prob > F

   Regression                 3              87.85         29.28    54.59     0.0001
   Error                    712             381.92          0.54
   Total                    715             469.77

                                           B Value     Std Error        F   Prob > F

   Intercept                               7.38864
   TI                                      0.65774       0.31783     4.28     0.0389
   ST_DEPTH                               -0.31451       0.04764    43.58     0.0001
   TGRSWT                                  0.00261       0.00038    47.73     0.0001
```

b. Are we able to assume that the marine biologist has identified all the important independent variables for the prediction of y? Why?

c. Using the variables identified in part **a**, write the first-order model with interaction that may be used to predict y.

d. How would the marine biologist determine whether the model specified in part **c** was better than the first-order model?

e. Note the small value of R^2. What action might the biologist take to improve the model?

4.47 J. O. Wise and H. J. Dover employed stepwise regression to identify a number of important factors (variables) that can be used to predict rural property values. They obtained their results by analyzing a sample of 105 cases from seven counties in Georgia. Part of their findings are duplicated in the table. The variable names are listed in the order in which the stepwise regression procedure identified their importance, and the t values found at each step are given for each variable. Note that both qualitative and quantitative variables have been included. Since each qualitative variable is at two levels, only one main effect term (i.e., dummy variable) could be included in the model for each factor.

STEP	VARIABLE NAME	t VALUE
1	Residential land (yes–no)	10.466
2	Seedlings and saplings (number)	6.692
3	Percentage ponds (percent)	4.141
4	Distance to state park (miles)	3.985
5	Branches or springs (yes–no)	3.855
6	Site index (ratio)	3.160
7	Size (acres)	1.142
8	Farmland (yes–no)	2.288

Source: Wise, J. O., and Dover, H. J. "An evaluation of a statistical method of appraising rural property." *Appraisal Journal*, Vol. 42, Jan. 1974, pp. 103–113.

a. Which of the eight variables listed in the table would you use to model rural property value, y?

b. Based on your answer to part **a**, propose a complete model for $E(y)$.

4.48 In any production process in which one or more workers are engaged in a variety of tasks, the total time spent in production varies as a function of the size of the work pool and the level of output of the various activities. For example, in a large metropolitan department store, the number of hours worked (y) per day by the clerical staff may depend on the following variables:

x_1 = Number of pieces of mail processed (open, sort, etc.)

x_2 = Number of money orders and gift certificates sold

x_3 = Number of window payments (customer charge accounts) transacted

x_4 = Number of change order transactions processed

x_5 = Number of checks cashed

x_6 = Number of pieces of miscellaneous mail processed on an "as available" basis

x_7 = Number of bus tickets sold

The accompanying table of observations gives the output counts for these activities on each of 52 working days.

OBS.	DAY OF WEEK	y	x_1	x_2	x_3	x_4	x_5	x_6	x_7
1	M	128.5	7781	100	886	235	644	56	737
2	T	113.6	7004	110	962	388	589	57	1029
3	W	146.6	7267	61	1342	398	1081	59	830
4	Th	124.3	2129	102	1153	457	891	57	1468
5	F	100.4	4878	45	803	577	537	49	335
6	S	119.2	3999	144	1127	345	563	64	918
7	M	109.5	11777	123	627	326	402	60	335
8	T	128.5	5764	78	748	161	495	57	962
9	W	131.2	7392	172	876	219	823	62	665
10	Th	112.2	8100	126	685	287	555	86	577
11	F	95.4	4736	115	436	235	456	38	214
12	S	124.6	4337	110	899	127	573	73	484
13	M	103.7	3079	96	570	180	428	59	456
14	T	103.6	7273	51	826	118	463	53	907
15	W	133.2	4091	116	1060	206	961	67	951
16	Th	111.4	3390	70	957	284	745	77	1446
17	F	97.7	6319	58	559	220	539	41	440
18	S	132.1	7447	83	1050	174	553	63	1133
19	M	135.9	7100	80	568	124	428	55	456
20	T	131.3	8035	115	709	174	498	78	968
21	W	150.4	5579	83	568	223	683	79	660
22	Th	124.9	4338	78	900	115	556	84	555
23	F	97.0	6895	18	442	118	479	41	203
24	S	114.1	3629	133	644	155	505	57	781
25	M	88.3	5149	92	389	124	405	59	236
26	T	117.6	5241	110	612	222	477	55	616
27	W	128.2	2917	69	1057	378	970	80	1210
28	Th	138.8	4390	70	974	195	1027	81	1452
29	F	109.5	4957	24	783	358	893	51	616
30	S	118.9	7099	130	1419	374	609	62	957
31	M	122.2	7337	128	1137	238	461	51	968
32	T	142.8	8301	115	946	191	771	74	719
33	W	133.9	4889	86	750	214	513	69	489
34	Th	100.2	6308	81	461	132	430	49	341
35	F	116.8	6908	145	864	164	549	57	902
36	S	97.3	5345	116	604	127	360	48	126
37	M	98.0	6994	59	714	107	473	53	726
38	T	136.5	6781	78	917	171	805	74	1100
39	W	111.7	3142	106	809	335	702	70	1721
40	Th	98.6	5738	27	546	126	455	52	502
41	F	116.2	4931	174	891	129	481	71	737
42	S	108.9	6501	69	643	129	334	47	473
43	M	120.6	5678	94	828	107	384	52	1083
44	T	131.8	4619	100	777	164	834	67	841
45	W	112.4	1832	124	626	158	571	71	627
46	Th	92.5	5445	52	432	121	458	42	313
47	F	120.0	4123	84	432	153	544	42	654
48	S	112.2	5884	89	1061	100	391	31	280
49	M	113.0	5505	45	562	84	444	36	814
50	T	138.7	2882	94	601	139	799	44	907
51	W	122.1	2395	89	637	201	747	30	1666
52	Th	86.6	6847	14	810	230	547	40	614

Source: Adapted from *Work Measurement*, by G. L. Smith, Grid Publishing Co., Columbus, Ohio, 1978 (Table 3-1).

a. Conduct a stepwise regression analysis of the data using an available statistical software package.*
b. Interpret the β estimates in the resulting stepwise model.
c. What are the dangers associated with drawing inferences from the stepwise model?

4.12 Other Variable Selection Techniques (Optional)

In Section 4.11, we presented stepwise regression as an objective screening procedure for selecting the most important predictors of y. Other, more subjective, variable selection techniques have been developed in the literature for the purpose of identifying important independent variables. The most popular of these procedures are those that consider all possible regression models given the set of potentially important predictors. (Such a procedure is commonly known as an **all-possible-regressions selection procedure**.) The techniques differ with respect to the criteria for selecting the "best" subset of variables. In this section, we describe four criteria widely used in practice, then give an example illustrating the four techniques.

R^2 Criterion

Consider the set of potentially important variables, $x_1, x_2, x_3, \ldots, x_k$. We learned in Section 4.6 that the multiple coefficient of determination

$$R^2 = 1 - \frac{\text{SSE}}{\text{SS(Total)}}$$

will increase when independent variables are added to the model. Therefore, the model that includes all k independent variables

$$E(y) = \beta_0 + \beta_1 x_1 + \beta_2 x_2 + \cdots + \beta_k x_k$$

will yield the largest R^2. Yet, we have seen examples (in Section 4.11) where adding terms to the model does not yield a significantly better prediction equation. The objective of the R^2 criterion is to find a subset model (i.e., a model containing a subset of the k independent variables) so that adding more variables to the model will yield only small increases in R^2. In practice, the best model found by the R^2 criterion will rarely be the model with the largest R^2. Generally, you are looking for a simple model that is as good as, or nearly as good as, the model with all k independent variables. But unlike that in stepwise regression, the decision about when to stop adding variables to the model is a subjective one.

Adjusted R^2 or MSE Criterion

One drawback to using the R^2 criterion, you will recall, is that the value of R^2 does not account for the number of β parameters in the model. If enough variables are added to the model so that the sample size n equals the total number of β's in the model, you will force R^2 to equal 1. Alternatively, we can use the adjusted R^2. It is easy to show that R_a^2 is related to MSE as follows:

$$R_a^2 = 1 - (n - 1)\left[\frac{\text{MSE}}{\text{SS(Total)}}\right]$$

*The data are available, in ASCII form, on a 3½″ diskette from the publisher.

Note that R_a^2 increases only if MSE decreases [since SS(Total) remains constant for all models]. Thus, an equivalent procedure is to search for the model with the minimum, or near minimum, MSE.

C_p Criterion

A recently developed procedure, which is gaining increasing acceptance among regression analysts, is based on a quantity called the **total mean square error (TMSE)** for the fitted regression model:

$$\text{TMSE} = E\left\{\sum_{i=1}^{n} [\hat{y}_i - E(y_i)]^2\right\} = \sum_{i=1}^{n} [E(\hat{y}_i) - E(y_i)]^2 + \sum_{i=1}^{n} \text{Var}(\hat{y}_i)$$

where $E(\hat{y}_i)$ is the mean response for the subset (fitted) regression model and $E(y_i)$ is the mean response for the true model. The objective is to compare the TMSE for the subset regression model with σ^2, the variance of the random error for the true model, using the ratio

$$\Gamma = \frac{\text{TMSE}}{\sigma^2}$$

Small values of Γ imply that the subset regression model has a small total mean square error relative to σ^2. Unfortunately, both TMSE and σ^2 are unknown, and we must rely on sample estimates of these quantities. It can be shown (proof omitted) that an estimator of the ratio Γ is given by

$$C_p = \frac{\text{SSE}_p}{\text{MSE}_k} + 2(p + 1) - n$$

where n is the sample size, p is the number of independent variables in the subset model, k is the total number of potential independent variables, SSE_p is the SSE for the subset model, and MSE_k is the MSE for the model containing all k independent variables. In their latest releases, the statistical software packages discussed in this text have routines that calculate the C_p statistic. In fact, the C_p value is now automatically printed at each step in the SAS stepwise regression printout (see Figure 4.27).

The C_p criterion selects as the best model the subset model with (1) a small value of C_p (i.e., a small total mean square error) and (2) a value of C_p near $p + 1$, a property that indicates that slight or no bias exists in the subset regression model.*

Thus, the C_p criterion focuses on minimizing total mean square error and the regression bias. If you are mainly concerned with minimizing total mean square error, you will want to choose the model with the smallest C_p value, as long as the bias is not large. On the other hand, you may prefer a model that yields a C_p value slightly larger than the minimum but which has slight (or no) bias.

---

*A model is said to be *unbiased* if $E(\hat{y}) = E(y)$. We state (without proof) that for an unbiased regression model, $E(C_p) \approx p + 1$. In general, subset models will be biased since $k - p$ independent variables are omitted from the fitted model. However, when C_p is near $p + 1$, the bias is small and can essentially be ignored.

PRESS Criterion

A fourth criterion used to select the best subset regression model is related to $SSE = \sum_{i=1}^{n} (y_i - \hat{y}_i)^2$. The PRESS (prediction sum of squares) statistic for a model is calculated as follows:

$$\text{PRESS} = \sum_{i=1}^{n} [y_i - \hat{y}_{(i)}]^2$$

The symbol $\hat{y}_{(i)}$ denotes the predicted value for the ith observation obtained when the regression model is fitted with the data point for the ith observation omitted (or deleted) from the sample.* Thus, the candidate model is fitted to the sample data n times, each time omitting one of the data points and obtaining the predicted value of y for that data point. Since small differences $y_i - \hat{y}_{(i)}$ indicate that the model is predicting well, we desire a model with a small PRESS.

Computing the PRESS statistic may seem like a tiresome chore, since repeated regression runs (a total of n runs) must be made for each candidate model. However, most statistical software packages have options for computing PRESS automatically.†

Plots aid in the selection of the best subset regression model using the all-possible-regressions procedure. The criterion measure, either R^2, MSE, C_p, or PRESS, is plotted on the vertical axis against p, the number of independent variables in the subset model, on the horizontal axis. We illustrate all three variable selection techniques in Example 4.9.

EXAMPLE 4.9

In Example 4.8, we applied stepwise regression to identify the most important variables for predicting executive salary from the list of 10 variables given in Table 4.7. Since it is impractical to fit all possible regression models involving subsets of these independent variables (for $k = 10$, there exist 1,023 possible subset models), for this example we fit only the first-order models shown in Table 4.8. These models were selected based, in part, on the results of the stepwise regression. The values of R^2, MSE, C_p, and PRESS are calculated for each model and appear in the appropriate column in Table 4.8. The plots of each of these four quantities against p, the number of predictors in the subset model, are shown in Figure 4.28. Interpret the plots.

---

*The quantity $y_i - \hat{y}_{(i)}$ is called the "deleted" residual for the ith observation. We discuss deleted residuals in more detail in Chapter 7.

†PRESS can also be calculated using the results from a regression run on all n data points. The formula is

$$\text{PRESS} = \sum_{i=1}^{n} \left(\frac{y_i - \hat{y}_i}{1 - h_{ii}}\right)^2$$

where h_{ii} is a function of the independent variables in the model. In Chapter 7, we show how h_{ii} (called **leverage**) can be used to detect influential observations.

TABLE 4.8 Subset Models for the Executive Salary Example

NUMBER OF PREDICTORS, p	VARIABLES IN THE MODEL	R^2	MSE	C_p	PRESS
1	x_4	.421	.1611	1,339.6	17.62
2	x_4, x_5	.783	.0610	443.8	7.27
3	x_1, x_4, x_5	.897	.0293	164.1	3.45
4	x_1, x_3, x_4, x_5	.948	.0149	38.5	2.63
5	x_1, x_2, x_3, x_4, x_5	.960	.0115	10.2	2.24
6	$x_1, x_2, x_3, x_4, x_5, x_8$	.962	.0111	8.2	2.95
7	$x_1, x_2, x_4, x_5, x_8, x_9, x_{10}$	.963	.0110	7.7	3.01
8	$x_1, x_2, x_3, x_4, x_5, x_8, x_9, x_{10}$	.963	.0111	9.7	3.58
9	$x_1, x_2, x_3, x_4, x_5, x_6, x_8, x_9, x_{10}$	.964	.0109	9.2	3.55
10	$x_1, x_2, x_3, x_4, x_5, x_6, x_7, x_8, x_9, x_{10}$	.964	.0110	11.2	3.71

FIGURE 4.28
Plots of R^2, MSE, C_p, and PRESS for subset regression models of Example 4.9

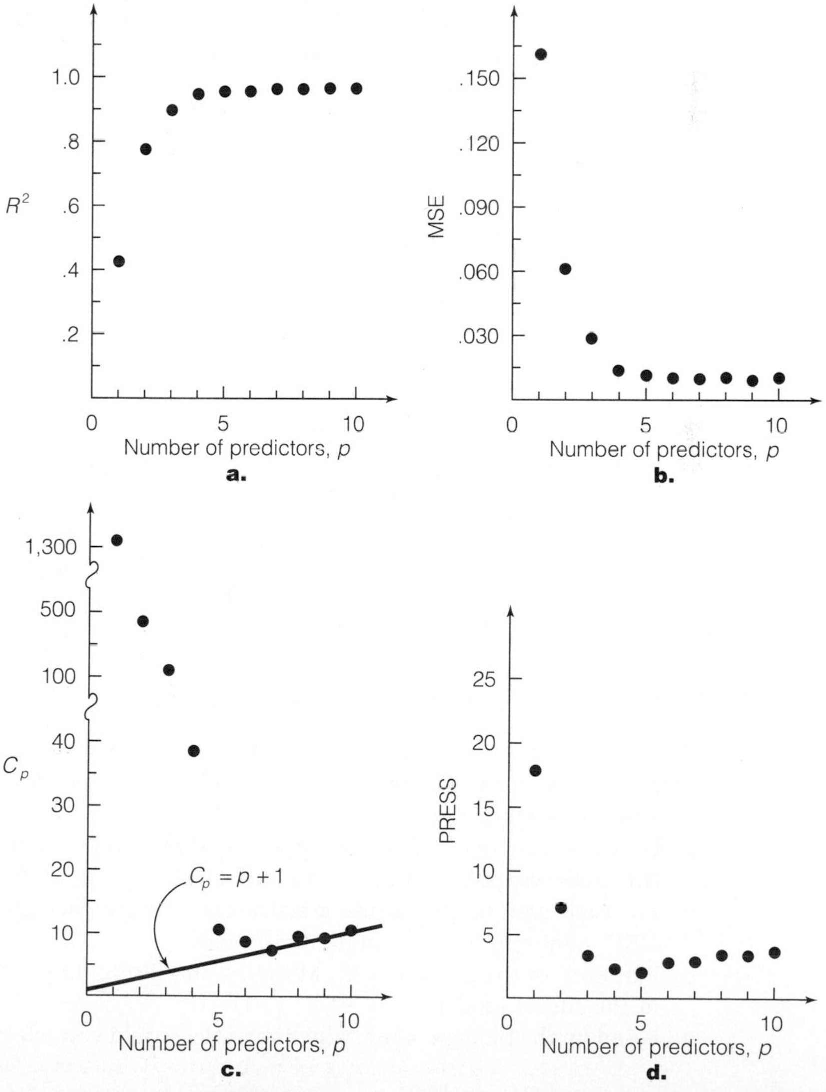

Solution

In Figure 4.28a, we see that the R^2 values tend to increase in very small amounts for models with more than $p = 4$ predictors. Similarly, Figure 4.28b shows that the MSE decreases by negligible amounts for models with more than $p = 4$ predictors. Thus, both the R^2 and MSE criteria suggest that the model containing the four predictors x_1, x_3, x_4, and x_5 is a good candidate for the best subset regression model.

Figure 4.28c shows the plotted C_p values and the line $C_p = p + 1$. Notice that the subset models with $p \geq 5$ independent variables all have relatively small C_p values and vary tightly about the line $C_p = p + 1$. This implies that these models have a small total mean square error and a negligible bias. The model corresponding to $p = 4$, although certainly outperforming the models $p \leq 3$, appears to fall short of the larger models according to the C_p criterion. The C_p value for this model is $C_p = 38.5$ (compared to C_p values ranging from 7.7 to 11.2 for models with $p \geq 5$), and the model has a slight bias. From Figure 4.28d you can see that the PRESS is smallest for the five-variable model with x_1, x_2, x_3, x_4, and x_5 (PRESS = 2.24).

According to all four criteria, the variables x_1, x_3, x_4, and x_5 should be included in the group of the most important predictors. The decision of whether to include another variable (e.g., x_2) in this group is left to the data analyst.

In summary, variable selection procedures based on the R^2, MSE, C_p, or PRESS criterion will assist you in identifying the most important independent variables for predicting y. Keep in mind, however, that these techniques lack the objectivity of a stepwise regression procedure. Furthermore, you should be wary of concluding that the best model for predicting y has been found, since, in practice, interactions and higher-order terms are typically omitted from the list of potential important predictors.

EXERCISE

4.49 Refer to the data on units of production and time worked for a department store clerical staff in Exercise 4.48. For this exercise, consider only the independent variables x_1, x_2, x_3, and x_4 in an all-possible-regressions select procedure.

a. How many models for $E(y)$ are possible, if the model includes (i) one variable, (ii) two variables, (iii) three variables, and (iv) four variables?

b. For each case in part **a**, use a statistical software package to find the maximum R^2, minimum MSE, minimum C_p, and minimum PRESS.

c. Plot each of the quantities R^2, MSE, C_p, and PRESS in part **b** against p, the number of predictors in the subset model.

d. Based on the plots in part **c**, which variables would you select for predicting total hours worked, y?

4.13 Multiple Regression: A Complete Example

The basic elements of multiple regression analysis have been presented in Sections 4.1–4.12. Now we assemble these elements by applying them to a practical problem.

In the United States, commercial contractors bid for the right to construct state highways and roads. A state government agency, usually the Department of Transportation (DOT), notifies various contractors of the state's intent to build a highway. Sealed bids are submitted by the contractors, and the contractor with the lowest bid (building cost) is awarded the road construction contract. The bidding process works extremely well in competitive markets, but has the potential to increase construction costs if the markets are noncompetitive or if collusive practices are present. The latter occurred in the 1970s and 1980s in Florida. Numerous contractors either admitted or were found guilty of price-fixing, i.e., setting the cost of construction above the fair, or competitive, cost through bid-rigging or other means.

In this section, we apply multiple regression to a data set obtained from the office of the Florida Attorney General. Our objective is to build and test the adequacy of a model designed to predict the cost y of a road construction contract awarded using the sealed-bid system in Florida.

STEP 1 Based on the opinions of several experts in road construction and bid-rigging, a list of potential predictors of contract cost y is obtained. This list is shown in Table 4.9. Data collected on these eight potential predictors and contract cost for a sample of $n = 235$ contracts are provided in Appendix H.

TABLE 4.9 **Description of Several Potential Predictors of Contract Cost: Data in Appendix H**

VARIABLE	DESCRIPTION
DOTEST (x_1)	DOT engineer's estimate of construction cost
B2B1RAT (x_2)	Ratio of second lowest bid to lowest bid
B3B1RAT (x_3)	Ratio of third lowest bid to lowest bid
BHB1RAT (x_4)	Ratio of highest bid to lowest bid
STATUS (x_5)	1 if fixed contract, 0 if competitive contract
DISTRICT (x_6)	1 if contract awarded in South Florida District, 0 if not
BTPRATIO (x_7)	Ratio of number of bidders to number of planholders
DAYSEST (x_8)	Engineer's estimate of number of workdays required

STEP 2 Since the number of potential predictors is large, we use stepwise regression to help us select the independent variables to include in the model. The SAS stepwise regression procedure applied to the sample data resulted in the printout shown in Figure 4.29 (page 258). You can see that only two of the eight variables—DOTEST (x_1) and STATUS (x_5)—were selected by the stepwise routine. Our modeling effort will focus on these two independent variables.

FIGURE 4.29

SAS stepwise regression printout for contract cost

```
                   Stepwise Procedure for Dependent Variable COST

Step 1    Variable DOTEST Entered      R-square = 0.97424702    C(p) = 15.18496446

                  DF         Sum of Squares        Mean Square            F    Prob>F

Regression         1     864035547.29525   864035547.29525     8814.50    0.0001
Error            233     22839676.680072    98024.36343379
Total            234     886875223.97532

                 Parameter          Standard            Type II
Variable          Estimate             Error    Sum of Squares            F    Prob>F

INTERCEP       20.90684416       24.36729323    72159.98186400         0.74    0.3918
DOTEST          0.92628789        0.00986614   864035547.29525      8814.50    0.0001

---------------------------------------------------------------------------------

Step 2    Variable STATUS Entered      R-square = 0.97545236    C(p) =  5.66262181

                  DF         Sum of Squares        Mean Square            F    Prob>F

Regression         2     865104526.39042   432552263.19521     4609.50    0.0001
Error            232     21770697.584902    93839.21372803
Total            234     886875223.97532

                 Parameter          Standard            Type II
Variable          Estimate             Error    Sum of Squares            F    Prob>F

INTERCEP      -20.53871363       26.81797336    55040.06386988         0.59    0.4445
DOTEST          0.93077968        0.00974453   856162794.59683      9123.72    0.0001
STATUS        166.35513274       49.28829319   1068979.0951699        11.39    0.0009

---------------------------------------------------------------------------------

All variables in the model are significant at the 0.1500 level.
No other variable met the 0.0500 significance level for entry into the model.

          Summary of Stepwise Procedure for Dependent Variable COST

      Variable           Number   Partial     Model
Step  Entered  Removed      In      R**2       R**2        C(p)           F    Prob>F

   1  DOTEST                 1    0.9742    0.9742     15.1850   8814.4979    0.0001
   2  STATUS                 2    0.0012    0.9755      5.6626     11.3916    0.0009
```

In Chapter 5, we will learn that a good initial choice is the complete second-order model. For one quantitative and one qualitative variable, the model has the following form:

$$E(y) = \beta_0 + \beta_1 x_1 + \beta_2 x_1^2 + \beta_3 x_5 + \beta_4 x_1 x_5 + \beta_5 x_1^2 x_5$$

where x_1 = DOTEST and x_5 = STATUS.

STEP 3 The SAS printout for the complete second-order model is shown in Figure 4.30. The β estimates, shaded on the printout, yield the following least squares prediction equation:

$$\hat{y} = -2.975 + .9155x_1 + .00000072x_1^2 - 36.725x_5 + .324x_1x_5 - .0000358x_1^2x_5$$

STEP 4 Before we can make inferences about model adequacy, we should be sure that the standard regression assumptions about the random error ε are satisfied. For given values of x_1 and x_5, the random errors ε have a normal distribution

FIGURE 4.30

SAS printout for complete second-order model

Dependent Variable: COST

Analysis of Variance

Source	DF	Sum of Squares	Mean Square	F Value	Prob>F
Model	5	866723465.17	173344693.03	1969.850	0.0001
Error	229	20151758.803	87998.94674		
C Total	234	886875223.98			

Root MSE	296.64616	R-square	0.9773
Dep Mean	1268.70217	Adj R-sq	0.9768
C.V.	23.38186		

Parameter Estimates

Variable	DF	Parameter Estimate	Standard Error	T for H0: Parameter=0	Prob > |T|
INTERCEP	1	-2.975454	30.89143173	-0.096	0.9234
DOTEST	1	0.915530	0.02917084	31.385	0.0001
DOTEST2	1	0.000000719	0.00000340	0.211	0.8330
STATUS	1	-36.724712	74.77308250	-0.491	0.6238
STA_DOT	1	0.324213	0.11917429	2.720	0.0070
STA_DOT2	1	-0.000035759	0.00002478	-1.443	0.1504

with mean 0, constant variance σ^2, and are independent. We learn how to check these assumptions in Chapter 7. For now, we are satisfied with estimating σ^2 and interpreting its value.

The value of MSE, shaded on Figure 4.30, is MSE $= s^2 = 87{,}998.9$. The value of **Root MSE** (also shaded) is $s = 296.65$. Our interpretation is that the complete second-order model can predict contract costs to within $2s = 593.3$ thousand dollars of its true value.

STEP 5 To check the adequacy of the complete second-order model, we conduct the analysis of variance F test. The elements of the test are as follows:

H_0: $\beta_1 = \beta_2 = \beta_3 = \beta_4 = \beta_5 = 0$

H_a: At least one $\beta \neq 0$

Test statistic: $F = 1{,}969.85$ (shaded in Figure 4.30)

p-value: $p = .0001$ (shaded in Figure 4.30)

Conclusion: The extremely small p-value indicates that the model is statistically adequate for predicting contract cost, y.

Are all the terms in the model statistically significant predictors? For example, is it necessary to include the curvilinear terms, $\beta_2 x_1^2$ and $\beta_5 x_1^2 x_5$, in the model? If not, the model can be simplified by dropping these curvature terms. The hypothesis we want to test is

H_0: $\beta_2 = \beta_5 = 0$

H_a: At least one of the curvature β's is nonzero.

To test this subset of β's, we need to fit a second (reduced) model. The reduced model takes the form

$$E(y) = \beta_0 + \beta_1 x_1 + \beta_3 x_5 + \beta_4 x_1 x_5$$

The SAS printout for the reduced model is shown in Figure 4.31. The SSE for the reduced model, $SSE_R = 20{,}334{,}954$ (shaded in Figure 4.31), is compared to the SSE for the complete model, $SSE_C = 20{,}151{,}759$ (shaded in Figure 4.30), using the test statistic computed here:

Test statistic:
$$F = \frac{(SSE_R - SSE_C)/\#\ \beta\text{'s tested}}{MSE_C} = \frac{(20{,}334{,}954 - 20{,}151{,}759)/2}{87{,}999} = 1.04$$

Rejection region: Using $\alpha = .01$, $F_{.01} \approx 4.61$ (based on 2 numerator and 229 denominator degrees of freedom)

Conclusion: Since $F = 1.04$ falls below the critical value of 4.61, we fail to reject H_0. That is, there is insufficient evidence (at $\alpha = .01$) to indicate that the curvature terms are useful predictors of construction cost, y.

The results of the partial F test lead us to select the reduced model as the better predictor of cost. The least squares prediction equation for the reduced model is

$$\hat{y} = -6.429 + .921x_1 + 28.671x_5 + .163x_1x_5$$

Note that we cannot simplify the model any further. The t test for the interaction term $\beta_3 x_1 x_5$ is highly significant (p-value $= .0001$, shaded on Figure 4.31). Thus, our best model for construction cost proposes interaction between the DOT estimate (x_1) and status (x_5) of the contract, but only a linear relationship between cost and DOT estimate.

FIGURE 4.31
SAS printout for reduced model

```
Dependent Variable: COST

                         Analysis of Variance

                           Sum of          Mean
Source          DF        Squares        Square       F Value        Prob>F

Model            3 866540269.49 288846756.50          3281.227        0.0001
Error          231 20334954.484   88030.10599
C Total        234 886875223.98

    Root MSE       296.69868      R-square        0.9771
    Dep Mean      1268.70217      Adj R-sq        0.9768
    C.V.            23.38600

                         Parameter Estimates

                        Parameter       Standard     T for H0:
Variable     DF          Estimate          Error   Parameter=0    Prob > |T|

INTERCEP      1         -6.428954    26.20854879        -0.245        0.8064
DOTEST        1          0.921336     0.00972347        94.754        0.0001
STATUS        1         28.670505    58.66231493         0.489        0.6255
STA_DOT       1          0.163282     0.04043122         4.039        0.0001
```

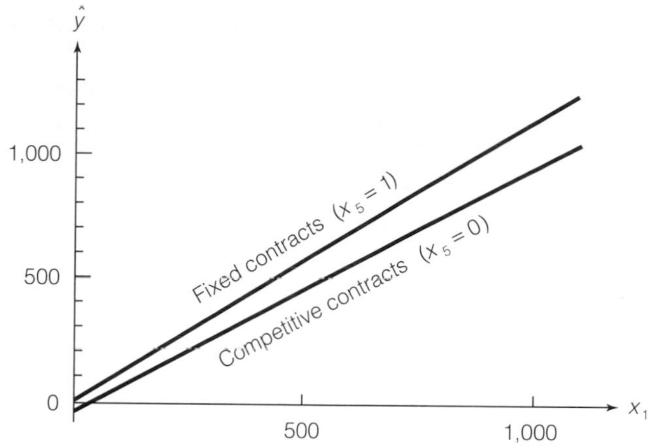

FIGURE 4.32
Plot of the least squares lines for the reduced model

A plot of the least squares lines for the reduced model is shown in Figure 4.32. You can see that the model proposes two straight lines (one for fixed contracts and one for competitive contracts) with different slopes. The estimated slopes of the y–x_1 lines are computed and interpreted as follows:

Competitive contracts ($x_5 = 0$): Estimated slope $= \hat{\beta}_1 = .921$
For every \$1,000 increase in DOT estimate, we estimate contract cost to increase \$921.

Fixed contracts ($x_5 = 1$): Estimated slope $= \hat{\beta}_1 + \hat{\beta}_4 = .921 + .163 = 1.084$
For every \$1,000 increase in DOT estimate, we estimate contract cost to increase \$1,084.

Before deciding to use the interaction model for estimation and/or prediction (step 6), we should check R^2 and s for the model. $R^2 = .9771$ (shaded on Figure 4.31) indicates that nearly 98% of the variation in the sample of construction costs can be "explained" by the model. The value of s (also shaded) implies that we can predict construction cost to within about $2s = 2(296.7) = 593.40$ thousand dollars of its true value using the model. Although the R^2 value is high, the large $2s$ value suggests that the predictive ability of the model might be improved by additional independent variables.

STEP 6 A portion of the SAS printout for the interaction (reduced) model not shown earlier is presented in Figure 4.33 on page 262. The printout gives predicted values and 95% prediction intervals for the first 10 contracts in the sample. The shaded portion gives the 95% prediction interval for contract cost when the DOT estimate is \$1,386,290 ($x_1 = 1,386.29$) and the contract is fixed ($x_2 = 1$). For a contract with these characteristics, we predict the cost to fall between 933.7 thousand dollars and 2,118.0 thousand dollars, with 95% confidence.

FIGURE 4.33
SAS printout of 95% prediction intervals for reduced model

Obs	DOTEST	STATUS	Dep Var COST	Predict Value	Std Err Predict	Lower95% Predict	Upper95% Predict	Residual
1	1386.293	1	1379.4	1525.8	47.792	933.7	2118.0	-146.4
2	85.712	1	134.0	115.2	50.533	-477.8	708.2	18.8263
3	248.892	0	202.3	222.9	24.949	-363.8	809.5	-20.5498
4	467.488	0	397.1	424.3	23.989	-162.2	1010.8	-27.1655
5	117.719	1	158.5	149.9	49.844	-442.9	742.7	8.6181
6	1008.908	1	1128.1	1116.5	42.729	525.9	1707.1	11.5835
7	472.9837	1	400.3	535.2	43.916	-55.7095	1126.2	-134.9
8	785.3859	0	581.6	717.2	22.876	130.9	1303.5	-135.5
9	370.022	0	354.0	334.5	24.399	-252.1	921.0	19.4725
10	174.255	0	138.7	154.1	25.309	-432.6	740.8	-15.4045

4.14 A Summary of the Steps to Follow in a Multiple Regression Analysis

We have discussed some of the methodology of **multiple regression analysis**, a technique for modeling a dependent variable y as a function of several independent variables $x_1, x_2, \ldots, x_k$. The steps we follow in constructing and using multiple regression models, which are much the same as those for the simple straight-line models, are listed here:

1. **The set of independent variables to be included in the model is identified.** If the number of independent variables is large, you may want to use a variable selection technique such as **stepwise regression** to screen out those that do not seem important for the prediction of y.
2. **The form of the probabilistic model is hypothesized.** The model may include **second-order** terms for quantitative variables, **interaction** terms, and **dummy variables** for qualitative variables. Remember that a model with no interaction terms implies that each of the independent variables affects the response y independently of the other independent variables. **Quadratic** (or **second-order**) terms add curvature to the response curve when $E(y)$ is plotted as a function of the quantitative independent variable. Dummy variables allow the mean response to differ for the different levels of the qualitative variable.
3. **The model coefficients are estimated using the method of least squares.**
4. **The probability distribution of ε is specified and σ^2 is estimated.**
5. **The utility of the model is checked using the analysis of variance F test and the multiple coefficient of determination R^2.** The F test for testing a partial set of β parameters and t tests on individual β parameters aid in deciding the final form of the model.
6. **If the model is deemed useful, it may be used to make estimates of $E(y)$ and to predict future values of y.**

Subsequent chapters extend the methods of this chapter to special applications and problems encountered during a regression analysis. One of the most common problems faced by regression analysts is the problem of multicollinearity, i.e., intercorrelations among the independent variables. Methods for detecting and overcoming multicollinearity, as well as other problems, are discussed in Chapter 6. Another aspect of regression analysis is the analysis of the residuals, i.e., the deviations between the observed and the predicted values of y. An analysis of residuals (Chapter 7) may indicate that the data do not comply with the assumptions of Section 4.2 and may suggest appropriate procedures for modifying the data analysis.

SUPPLEMENTARY EXERCISES

4.50 After a regression model is fitted to a set of data, a confidence interval for the mean value of y at a given setting of the independent variables will *always* be narrower than the corresponding prediction interval for a particular value of y at the same setting of the independent variables. Why?

4.51 Real estate appraisers rely heavily on multiple regression analysis in their evaluation of property. Typically, the sale price y of a home is modeled as a function of several home-related variables (e.g., home size, home condition, location, and so forth). For example, an article in *The Real Estate Appraiser and Analyst* (Spring 1986) considered the following regression model:

$$y = \beta_0 + \beta_1 x_1 + \beta_2 x_2 + \varepsilon$$

where

x_1 = Home size (in square feet)

x_2 = Home condition rating (1 = poor, ..., 10 = excellent)

Data collected for $n = 10$ recent home sales were used in the analysis. The data are reproduced in the table, and a SAS printout is provided on page 264.

SALE PRICE y, \$ thousands	HOME SIZE x_1, hundreds of sq. ft.	CONDITION RATING x_2, 1 to 10
60.0	23	5
32.7	11	2
57.7	20	9
45.5	17	3
47.0	15	8
55.3	21	4
64.5	24	7
42.6	13	6
54.5	19	7
57.5	25	2

Source: Andrews, R. L., and Ferguson, J. T. "Integrating judgment with a regression appraisal." *The Real Estate Appraiser and Analyst*, Vol. 52, No. 2, Spring 1986 (Table I).

a. Plot sale price y against home size x_1. Do you detect a linear relationship between the two variables? Is it positive or negative?
b. Plot sale price y against home condition x_2. Do you detect a linear relationship between the two variables? Is it positive or negative?
c. Is there evidence to indicate that sale price and home size are linearly related? Test using $\alpha = .01$.
d. Calculate a 99% confidence interval for β_2. Interpret the result.

SAS printout for Exercise 4.51

ANALYSIS OF VARIANCE

SOURCE	DF	SUM OF SQUARES	MEAN SQUARE	F VALUE	PROB>F
MODEL	2	819.32795	409.66398	350.866	0.0001
ERROR	7	8.17304573	1.16757796		
C TOTAL	9	827.50100			

ROOT MSE	1.080545	R-SQUARE	0.9901
DEP MEAN	51.73	ADJ R-SQ	0.9873
C.V.	2.088817		

PARAMETER ESTIMATES

VARIABLE	DF	PARAMETER ESTIMATE	STANDARD ERROR	T FOR H0: PARAMETER=0	PROB > |T|
INTERCEP	1	9.78227061	1.63048067	6.000	0.0005
X1	1	1.87093528	0.07617357	24.561	0.0001
X2	1	1.27814078	0.14440032	8.851	0.0001

OBS	ID	ACTUAL	PREDICT VALUE	STD ERR PREDICT	LOWER95% MEAN	UPPER95% MEAN	RESIDUAL
1	23	60.0000	59.2045	0.4714	58.0899	60.3191	0.7955
2	11	32.7000	32.9188	0.8200	30.9799	34.8578	-0.2188
3	20	57.7000	58.7042	0.6375	57.1969	60.2116	-1.0042
4	17	45.5000	45.4226	0.4919	44.2595	46.5857	0.0774
5	15	47.0000	48.0714	0.6019	46.6481	49.4948	-1.0714
6	21	55.3000	54.1845	0.4276	53.1735	55.1955	1.1155
7	24	64.5000	63.6317	0.5705	62.2826	64.9808	0.8683
8	13	42.6000	41.7733	0.5710	40.4231	43.1235	0.8267
9	19	54.5000	54.2770	0.4206	53.2824	55.2717	0.2230
10	25	57.5000	59.1119	0.7657	57.3013	60.9226	-1.6119

SUM OF RESIDUALS	6.75016E-14
SUM OF SQUARED RESIDUALS	8.173046
PREDICTED RESID SS (PRESS)	21.09523

4.52 In the mid-1800s, the U.S. census inquired about the real property and personal wealth of individual households. Using census information from 1860 and 1870, J. R. Kearl and C. L. Pope (Brigham Young University) examined the mobility of Utah households as measured by their wealth holdings (*The Review of Economics and Statistics*, May 1984). Holding occupation, time of entry into the economy, nativity, gender, place of residence, and internal migration constant, Kearl and Pope fitted the quadratic model $E(y) = \beta_0 + \beta_1 x + \beta_2 x^2$, where y is personal wealth (in dollars) of a Utah household and x is age (in years) of the head of household. The results of the regression are summarized as follows:

$$\hat{y} = 52.39 + 74.21x - .71x^2$$

$$s_{\hat{\beta}_1} = 5.38 \qquad s_{\hat{\beta}_2} = 4.73 \qquad n > 20{,}000$$

a. Graph the least squares prediction equation.

b. Is there evidence of a quadratic relationship in the wealth–age relationship for Utah households during 1860–1870? Test using $\alpha = .10$.

4.53 *Zoning* is defined as the distribution of vacant land to residential and nonresidential uses via policy set by local governments. Although the negative effects of zoning have been studied (e.g., distorting urban property markets, creating barriers to residential mobility, and impeding economic and social integration), little empirical evidence exists that identifies the factors that encourage restrictive zoning practices. A study reported in the *Journal of Urban Economics* (Vol. 21, 1987) developed a series of multiple regression models that hypothesize several determinants of zoning. One of the models studied took the form

$$E(y) = \beta_0 + \beta_1 x_1 + \beta_2 x_1^2 + \beta_3 x_2$$

where

y = Percentage of vacant land zoned for residential use

x_1 = Proportion of existing land in nonresidential use

x_2 = Proportion of total tax base derived from nonresidential property

The model was fitted to data collected for $n = 185$ municipal communities in northeastern New Jersey, with the following results:

INDEPENDENT VARIABLE	PARAMETER ESTIMATE	STANDARD ERROR OF ESTIMATE	t VALUE	p-VALUE
Intercept	92.26	3.07	30.05	$p < .01$
x_1	−96.35	46.59	−2.07	$p < .05$
x_1^2	166.80	120.88	1.38	$p > .10$
x_2	−75.51	13.35	−5.66	$p < .01$
Adjusted $R^2 = .25$	$F = 21.86$ $(p < .01)$			

Source: Rolleston, B. S. "Determinants of restrictive suburban zoning: An empirical analysis." *Journal of Urban Economics*, Vol. 21, 1987, p. 15, Table 4.

a. Construct a 95% confidence interval for β_3. Interpret the result.
b. Test the hypothesis that a curvilinear relationship exists between percentage (y) of land zoned for residential use and proportion (x_1) of existing land in nonresidential use.
c. Interpret the adjusted R^2 value.
d. Is the overall model statistically useful for predicting y?

4.54 An extensive study was undertaken at Utah State University to find the strongest predictor of a student-athlete's academic performance (*Sociology of Sport Journal*, Vol. 3, 1986). Based on data collected for a sample of $n = 519$ student-athletes, the following regression model was fitted:

$$y = \beta_0 + \beta_1 x_1 + \beta_2 x_2 + \beta_3 x_3 + \beta_4 x_4 + \beta_5 x_5$$

where

y = University grade point average

x_1 = Ratio of number of years the athlete lettered to number of years participated in sport

x_2 = Standardized score on college entrance exam (SAT or ACT)

x_3 = High school grade point average (GPA)

$$x_4 = \begin{cases} 1 & \text{if female} \\ 0 & \text{if male} \end{cases}$$

$$x_5 = \begin{cases} 1 & \text{if minority} \\ 0 & \text{if white} \end{cases}$$

The β estimates, standard errors, and corresponding t ratios are given in the table on page 266.

	VARIABLE	$\hat{\beta}$	$s_{\hat{\beta}}$	t
Letter ratio	x_1	.152	.05	3.04
College entrance score	x_2	1.653	22	7.51
High school GPA	x_3	.331	.06	5.52
Gender	x_4	.120	.05	2.40
Race	x_5	−.249	.06	−4.15

a. Interpret the β estimates in the model.
b. Construct a 95% confidence interval for β_3. Interpret the interval.
c. Test the hypothesis that letter ratio (x_1) is a useful predictor of university GPA (y). Use $\alpha = .05$.
d. The coefficient of determination for the model if $R^2 = .279$. Interpret this value.
e. Test the hypothesis that the overall model is useful for predicting university GPA (y). Use $\alpha = .05$.

4.55 A study was conducted at Union Carbide to identify the optimal catalyst preparation conditions in the conversion of monoethanolamine (MEA) to ethylenediamine (EDA), a substance used commercially in soaps.* For each of 10 selected catalysts, the following experimental variables were measured:

y = Rate of conversion of MEA to EDA

x_1 = Atom ratio of metal used in the experiment

x_2 = Reduction temperature

$$x_3 = \begin{cases} 1 & \text{if high-acidity support used} \\ 0 & \text{if low-acidity support used} \end{cases}$$

The data for the $n = 10$ experiments were used to fit the model $E(y) = \beta_0 + \beta_1 x_1 + \beta_2 x_2 + \beta_3 x_3$. The results are summarized here:

$$\hat{y} = 40.2 - .808x_1 - 6.38x_2 - 4.45x_3$$

$$R^2 = .899$$

$$s_{\hat{\beta}_1} = .231 \qquad s_{\hat{\beta}_2} = 1.93 \qquad s_{\hat{\beta}_3} = .99$$

a. Is there sufficient evidence to indicate that the model is useful for predicting rate of conversion y? Test using $\alpha = .01$.
b. Conduct a test to determine whether atom ratio x_1 is a useful predictor of rate of conversion y. Use $\alpha = .05$.
c. Construct a 95% confidence interval for β_2. Interpret the interval.

4.56 Many U.S. companies converted to the metric system of measurement during the 1970s. To quantify some of the characteristics of companies that converted to metric production, B. D. Phillips, H. A. G. Lakhani, and S. L. George analyzed data on 350 small manufacturers collected for a U.S. Metric Board study (*Technological Forecasting and Social Change*, Apr. 1984). One of the research objectives was to investigate the relationship between the percentage y of metric work performed by a company, age x_1 of the company (in years), and cost x_2 of metric conversion, where

$$x_2 = \begin{cases} 1 & \text{if cost over \$10,000} \\ 0 & \text{if not} \end{cases}$$

*Hansen, J. L., and Best, D. C. "How to pick a winner." Paper presented at Joint Statistical Meetings, American Statistical Association and Biometric Society, Aug. 1986, Chicago, Illinois.

A first-order linear model was fitted to the $n = 350$ data points with the following results:

$$\hat{y} = 70.9770 - .2167x_1 - 13.2768x_2$$
$$R^2 = .0576 \qquad t \text{ (for } H_0\text{: } \beta_1 = 0) = -1.56 \qquad t \text{ (for } H_0\text{: } \beta_2 = 0) = -2.71$$

a. Sketch the least squares relationship between $\hat{y}$ and x_1 for the two levels of metric conversion cost.
b. Is there evidence that the model is useful for predicting percentage y of metric work performed? Test using $\alpha = .01$.
c. Is there evidence that percentage y of metric work performed decreases as age x_1 of the company increases, for companies with the same cost x_2 of conversion? Test using $\alpha = .05$.
d. Write an interaction model for percentage y of metric work performed.
e. How will interaction between age x_1 and cost x_2, if determined to be significant, affect the graphs constructed in part a?

4.57 Researchers recently conducted an analysis of bus travel demand in Albuquerque, New Mexico, a city selected because of its unique multicentered "Sun Tran" public transit system. One aspect of the study involved the development of a multiple regression model for predicting y, the home-origin trip rate (that is, the number of home-origin trips per 1,000 residents) of a Sun Tran subzone urban area. The following five independent variables, all designed to measure transit level of service (travel time), were entered into the model:

x_1 = Composite in-vehicle travel time to reach major destination (minutes)

x_2 = Composite transit wait time (minutes)

x_3 = Composite number of transfers required to reach major destination

x_4 = Number of transit routes serving the Sun Tran zone

$$x_5 = \begin{cases} 1 & \text{if Sun Tran zone at end of major regional transportation corridor} \\ 0 & \text{if not} \end{cases}$$

Data collected from a survey of the city's bus passengers in each of 298 Sun Tran planning analysis zones were used to fit the first-order model

$$E(y) = \beta_0 + \beta_1x_1 + \beta_2x_2 + \beta_3x_3 + \beta_4x_4 + \beta_5x_5$$

with the results shown in the accompanying MINITAB printout.

```
The regression equation is
Y = 22.02 - .181 X1 - .250 X2 - 4.69 X3 + 3.67 X4 + 22.52 X5

Predictor       Coef        Stdev     t-ratio        p
Constant      22.019          *          *           *
X1            -0.181        0.039      -4.64     0.000
X2            -0.250        0.121      -2.07     0.038
X3            -4.691        1.702      -2.76     0.006
X4             3.674        0.403       9.12     0.000
X5            22.520        3.596       6.26     0.000

s = 8.657        R-sq = 59.9%       R-sq(adj) = 59.3%

Analysis of Variance

SOURCE        DF         SS          MS          F          P
Regression     5      32774      6554.8      87.45      0.000
Error        292      21886       74.95
Total        297      54660
```

Source: Adapted from Nelson, D., and O'Neil, K. "Analyzing demand for grid system transit." *Transportation Quarterly*, Vol. 37, No. 1, Jan. 1993, pp. 45–56.

a. Write the least squares prediction equation.
b. Compute and interpret the value of R^2.
c. Compute and interpret the value of s.
d. Is the model useful for predicting home-origin trip rate y? Test using $\alpha = .05$.
e. Is there evidence that home-origin trip rate y decreases as in-vehicle travel time x_1 increases and the remaining independent variables are held constant? Test using $\alpha = .05$.
f. Construct a 95% confidence interval for β_4. Interpret the interval.
g. Construct a 95% confidence interval for β_5. Interpret the interval.

4.58 To determine whether extra personnel are needed for the day, the owners of a water adventure park would like to find a model that would allow them to predict the day's attendance each morning before opening based on the day of the week and weather conditions. The model is of the form

$$E(y) = \beta_0 + \beta_1 x_1 + \beta_2 x_2 + \beta_3 x_3$$

where

$$y = \text{Daily admissions}$$

$$x_1 = \begin{cases} 1 & \text{if weekend} \\ 0 & \text{otherwise} \end{cases} \quad \text{(dummy variable)}$$

$$x_2 = \begin{cases} 1 & \text{if sunny} \\ 0 & \text{if overcast} \end{cases} \quad \text{(dummy variable)}$$

$$x_3 = \text{Predicted daily high temperature (°F)}$$

After collecting 30 days of data, the following least squares model is obtained:

$$\hat{y} = -105 + 25x_1 + 100x_2 + 10x_3$$

with $s_{\hat{\beta}_1} = 10$, $s_{\hat{\beta}_2} = 30$, and $s_{\hat{\beta}_3} = 4$. Also, $R^2 = .65$.
a. Interpret the model coefficients.
b. Is there sufficient evidence to conclude that this model is useful in the prediction of daily attendance? Use $\alpha = .05$.
c. Is there sufficient evidence to conclude that mean attendance increases on weekends? Use $\alpha = .10$.
d. Use the model to predict the attendance on a sunny weekday with a predicted high temperature of 95°F.
e. Suppose the 90% prediction interval for part **d** is (645, 1,245). Interpret this interval.

4.59 Refer to Exercise 4.58. The owners of the water adventure park are advised that the prediction model could probably be improved if interaction terms were added. In particular, it is thought that the *rate* of increase in mean attendance with increases in predicted high temperature will be greater on weekends than on weekdays. The following model is therefore proposed:

$$E(y) = \beta_0 + \beta_1 x_1 + \beta_2 x_2 + \beta_3 x_3 + \beta_4 x_1 x_3$$

The same 30 days of data used in Exercise 4.58 are again used to obtain the least squares model

$$\hat{y} = 250 - 700x_1 + 100x_2 + 5x_3 + 15x_1x_3$$

with $s_{\hat{\beta}_4} = 3.0$ and $R^2 = .96$.

a. Graph the predicted day's attendance, $\hat{y}$, against the day's predicted high temperature, x_3, for a sunny weekday and for a sunny weekend day. Plot both on the same graph for x_3 between 70°F and 100°F. Note the increase in slope for the weekend day.
b. Do the data indicate that the interaction term is a useful addition to the model? Use $\alpha = .05$.
c. Use this model to predict the attendance on a sunny weekday with a predicted high temperature of 95°F.
d. Suppose the 90% prediction interval for part **c** is (800, 850). Compare this with the prediction interval for the model without interaction in Exercise 4.58, part **e**. Do the relative widths of the confidence intervals support or refute your conclusion about the utility of the interaction term (part **b**)?
e. The owners, noting that the coefficient $\hat{\beta}_1 = -700$, conclude that the model is ridiculous because it seems to imply that the mean attendance will be 700 less on weekends than on weekdays. Refute their argument.

4.60 Refer to Exercise 4.59. Suppose the second-order model

$$E(y) = \beta_0 + \beta_1 x_1 + \beta_2 x_2 + \beta_3 x_3 + \beta_4 x_1 x_3 + \beta_5 x_3^2 + \beta_6 x_1 x_3^2$$

is fitted to the $n = 30$ observations on daily admissions.
a. What hypothesis would you test to determine whether the quadratic terms for predicted daily high temperature x_3 are important?
b. Use the SSEs for the interaction model (Exercise 4.59) and the second-order model given here to test the hypothesis of part **a**. Use $\alpha = .05$.

Interaction model: $SSE_1 = 585{,}000$
Second-order model: $SSE_2 = 530{,}000$

4.61 How satisfied are you with your auto repair service? G. J. Biehal (University of Houston) examined the factors that influence the satisfaction level for auto repair services in California. One objective of the study was to show that the extent of the information search conducted by the customer prior to selecting an auto repair service affects the customer's satisfaction with the service. A sample of 208 households in Palo Alto and Menlo Park, California, were questioned about their most recent auto repair experiences. All respondents reported at least one auto repair expense that exceeded $100 during the previous year. The dependent variable, level of dissatisfaction y, was measured on a 7-point Likert scale (0 = very satisfied to 7 = very dissatisfied). The following linear model was proposed:

$$E(y) = \beta_0 + \beta_1 x_1 + \beta_2 x_2 + \beta_3 x_3 + \beta_4 x_4 + \beta_5 x_5 + \beta_6 x_6$$

where

Level of external information search: x_1 (0 = none to 7 = very high)
Repair cost: x_2 (dollars)

Problem corrected: $x_3 = \begin{cases} 1 & \text{if more than one visit required to correct the problem} \\ 0 & \text{if the problem was corrected on the first visit} \end{cases}$

Prior experience with service:

$x_4 = \begin{cases} 1 & \text{if 1–2 times} \\ 0 & \text{if not} \end{cases}$ $x_5 = \begin{cases} 1 & \text{if 3–5 times} \\ 0 & \text{if not} \end{cases}$ $x_6 = \begin{cases} 1 & \text{if more than 5 times} \\ 0 & \text{if not} \end{cases}$

The results of the multiple regression analysis are summarized in the table.

PARAMETER	ESTIMATE	p-VALUE
β_0	2.14	—
β_1	−.15	$p < .05$
β_2	.03	$p > .05$
β_3	2.54	$p < .01$
β_4	−.34	$p > .05$
β_5	−.26	$p > .05$
β_6	−.72	$p < .05$
	$R^2 = .43$	

Source: Biehal, G. J. "Consumers' prior experiences and perceptions in auto repair choice." *Journal of Marketing*, Summer 1983, Vol. 47, No. 3, pp. 82–91. Reprinted by permission of the American Marketing Association.

a. Write the least squares prediction equation.
b. Is the model useful for predicting the dissatisfaction level for auto repair services? Test using $\alpha = .05$.
c. Is there evidence to indicate that the dissatisfaction level for auto repair service declines as the amount of external information search increases? Test using $\alpha = .05$.
d. Is there evidence to indicate that repair cost is a useful predictor of the dissatisfaction level for auto repair service? Test using $\alpha = .05$.
e. What hypothesis would you test to determine whether prior experience with service has no effect on the level of dissatisfaction?

4.62 R. N. Horn (James Madison University) and W. J. McGuire (Eastern Kentucky University) used multiple regression analysis to model academic year salaries for secondary-school teachers in Philadelphia during 1981–1982. Information on a sample of 4,316 secondary-school teachers was obtained from records compiled by the Pennsylvania Department of Education. The total sample was divided by race and gender to form four subsamples: black females, black males, white females, and white males. The data for each subsample were used to fit a multiple regression model of the form

$$E(y) = \beta_0 + \beta_1 x_1 + \beta_2 x_2 + \beta_3 x_3 + \cdots + \beta_{30} x_{30}$$

Years of experience, educational level, age, marital status, and major teaching field were among the 30 independent variables in the model. The results for each subsample are summarized in the table.

	BLACK MALES	BLACK FEMALES	WHITE MALES	WHITE FEMALES
n	526	862	1,848	1,080
R^2	.8074	.7674	.7724	.7879

Source: Horn, R. N., and McGuire, W. J. "Determinants of secondary school teacher salaries in a large urban school district." *Southern Economic Journal*, Oct. 1984, pp. 481–493.

a. Is there sufficient evidence to indicate that the model is useful for predicting academic year salaries for black male secondary-school teachers in Philadelphia? Test using $\alpha = .05$.

b. Is there sufficient evidence to indicate that the model is useful for predicting academic year salaries for black female secondary-school teachers in Philadelphia? Test using $\alpha = .05$.
c. Is there sufficient evidence to indicate that the model is useful for predicting academic year salaries for white male secondary-school teachers in Philadelphia? Test using $\alpha = .05$.
d. Is there sufficient evidence to indicate that the model is useful for predicting academic year salaries for white female secondary-school teachers in Philadelphia? Test using $\alpha = .05$.

4.63 Recent increases in gasoline prices have stimulated interest in modes of transportation other than the automobile. A metropolitan bus company wants to know whether changes in numbers of bus riders are related to changes in gasoline prices. By using information contained in the company files and gasoline price information obtained from fuel distributors, the company planned to fit the following model:

$$y = \beta_0 + \beta_1 x_1 + \beta_2 x_2 + \beta_3 x_1 x_2 + \varepsilon$$

where

$$x_1 = \text{Average wholesale price for regular gas in a given month}$$

$$x_2 = \begin{cases} 1 & \text{if the bus travels a city route only} \\ 0 & \text{if the bus travels a suburb–city route} \end{cases}$$

$$y = \text{Total number of riders per bus over 1 month}$$

a. For this model, how would you test to determine whether the relationship between gasoline price and the mean number of riders is different for the two different types of bus routes?
b. Suppose 12 months of data are kept, and the least squares model is

$$\hat{y} = 500 + 50x_1 + 5x_2 - 10x_1x_2$$

Graph the predicted relationship between number of riders and gas price for city buses and for suburb–city buses. Compare the slopes.
c. If $s_{\hat{\beta}_3} = 3.0$, do the data indicate that gas price affects the number of riders differently for city and suburb–city buses? Use $\alpha = .05$.

4.64 A naval base is considering modifying or adding to its fleet of 48 standard aircraft. The final decision regarding the type and number of aircraft to be added depends on a comparison of cost versus effectiveness of the modified fleet. Consequently, the naval base would like to model the projected percentage increase y in fleet effectiveness by the end of the decade as a function of the cost x of modifying the fleet. A first proposal is the quadratic model

$$E(y) = \beta_0 + \beta_1 x + \beta_2 x^2$$

The data provided in the table on page 272 were collected on 10 naval bases of similar size that recently expanded their fleets. The data were used to fit the model. The SAS printout of the multiple regression analysis is also reproduced on page 272.
a. Interpret the value of R_a^2 on the printout.
b. Find the value of s and interpret it.
c. Perform a test of overall model adequacy. Use $\alpha = .05$.
d. Is there sufficient evidence to conclude that the percentage improvement y increases more quickly for more costly fleet modifications than for less costly fleet modifications? Test with $\alpha = .05$.

PERCENTAGE IMPROVEMENT AT END OF DECADE y	COST OF MODIFYING FLEET x, millions of dollars
18	125
32	160
9	80
37	162
6	110
3	90
30	140
10	85
25	150
2	50

SAS printout for Exercise 4.64

ANALYSIS OF VARIANCE

SOURCE	DF	SUM OF SQUARES	MEAN SQUARE	F VALUE	PROB>F
MODEL	2	1368.77501	684.38750	33.079	0.0003
ERROR	7	144.82499	20.68928481		
C TOTAL	9	1513.60000			

ROOT MSE	4.548548	R-SQUARE	0.9043
DEP MEAN	17.2	ADJ R-SQ	0.8770
C.V.	26.44504		

PARAMETER ESTIMATES

VARIABLE	DF	PARAMETER ESTIMATE	STANDARD ERROR	T FOR H0: PARAMETER=0	PROB > |T|
INTERCEP	1	10.65903604	14.55009061	0.733	0.4876
X	1	-0.28160568	0.28087588	-1.003	0.3494
XX	1	0.002671936	0.001253832	2.131	0.0706

e. Now consider the model

$$E(y) = \beta_0 + \beta_1 x_1 + \beta_2 x_1^2 + \beta_3 x_2 + \beta_4 x_1 x_2$$

where

$$x_1 = \text{Cost of modifying the fleet} \qquad x_2 = \begin{cases} 1 & \text{if U.S. base} \\ 0 & \text{if foreign base} \end{cases}$$

The model is fitted to the $n = 10$ data points and results in SSE $= 97.645$. Is there sufficient evidence to indicate that type of base (U.S. or foreign) is a useful predictor of percentage improvement y? Test using $\alpha = .05$.

References

Draper, N., and Smith, H. *Applied Regression Analysis*, 3rd ed. New York: Wiley, 1989.

Maddala, G. S., *Introduction to Econometrics*. New York: Macmillan, 1988.

Montgomery, D. C., and Peck, E. A. *Introduction to Linear Regression Analysis*. New York: Wiley, 1982.

Neter, J., Wasserman, W., and Kutner, M. H. *Applied Linear Statistical Models*, 3rd ed. Homewood, Ill.: Richard D. Irwin, 1990.

Weisberg, S. *Applied Linear Regression*. New York: Wiley, 1980.

CHAPTER 5 Model Building

CONTENTS

OBJECTIVE

To show you why the choice of the deterministic portion of a linear model is crucial to the acquisition of a good prediction equation; to present some basic concepts and procedures for constructing good linear models

5.1 Introduction: Why Model Building Is Important

We have emphasized in both Chapters 3 and 4 that one of the first steps in the construction of a regression model is to hypothesize the form of the deterministic portion of the probabilistic model. This *model-building*, or model-construction, stage is the key to the success (or failure) of the regression analysis. If the hypothesized model does not reflect, at least approximately, the true nature of the relationship between the mean response $E(y)$ and the independent variables $x_1, x_2, \ldots, x_k$, the modeling effort will usually be unrewarded.

By **model building**, we mean writing a model that will provide a good fit to a set of data and that will give good estimates of the mean value of y and good predictions of future values of y for given values of the independent variables. To illustrate, several years ago, a nationally recognized educational research group issued a report concerning the variables related to academic achievement for a certain type of college student. The researchers selected a random sample of students and recorded a measure of academic achievement, y, at the end of the senior year together with data on an extensive list of independent variables, $x_1, x_2, \ldots, x_k$, that they thought were related to y. Among these independent variables were the student's IQ, scores on mathematics and verbal achievement examinations, rank in class, etc. They fitted the model

$$E(y) = \beta_0 + \beta_1 x_1 + \beta_2 x_2 + \cdots + \beta_k x_k$$

to the data, analyzed the results, and reached the conclusion that none of the independent variables was "significantly related" to y. The **goodness of fit** of the model, measured by the coefficient of determination R^2, was not particularly good, and t tests on individual parameters did not lead to rejection of the null hypotheses that these parameters equaled 0.

How could the researchers have reached the conclusion that there is no significant relationship, when it is evident, just as a matter of experience, that some of the independent variables studied are related to academic achievement? For example, achievement on a college mathematics placement test should be related to achievement in college mathematics. Certainly, many other variables will affect achievement—motivation, environmental conditions, and so forth—but generally speaking, there will be a positive correlation between entrance achievement test scores and college academic achievement. So, what went wrong with the educational researchers' study?

Although you can never discard the possibility of computing error as a reason for erroneous answers, most likely the difficulties in the results of the educational study were caused by the use of an improperly constructed model. For example, the model

$$E(y) = \beta_0 + \beta_1 x_1 + \beta_2 x_2 + \cdots + \beta_k x_k$$

assumes that the independent variables $x_1, x_2, \ldots, x_k$ affect mean achievement $E(y)$ independently of each other.* Thus, if you hold all the other independent variables constant and vary only x_1, $E(y)$ will increase by the amount β_1 for

*Keep in mind that we are discussing the deterministic portion of the model and that the word *independent* is used in a mathematical rather than a probabilistic sense.

every unit increase in x_1. A 1-unit change in any of the other independent variables will increase $E(y)$ by the value of the corresponding β parameter for that variable.

Do the assumptions implied by the model agree with your knowledge about academic achievement? First, is it reasonable to assume that the effect of time spent on study is independent of native intellectual ability? We think not. No matter how much effort some students invest in a particular subject, their rate of achievement is low. For others, it may be high. Therefore, assuming that these two variables—effort and native intellectual ability—affect $E(y)$ independently of each other is likely to be an erroneous assumption. Second, suppose that x_5 is the amount of time a student devotes to study. Is it reasonable to expect that a 1-unit increase in x_5 will always produce the same change β_5 in $E(y)$? The changes in $E(y)$ for a 1-unit increase in x_5 might depend on the value of x_5 (for example, the law of diminishing returns). Consequently, it is quite likely that the assumption of a constant rate of change in $E(y)$ for 1-unit increases in the independent variables will not be satisfied.

Clearly, the model

$$E(y) = \beta_0 + \beta_1 x_1 + \beta_2 x_2 + \cdots + \beta_k x_k$$

was a poor choice in view of the researchers' prior knowledge of some of the variables involved. Terms have to be added to the model to account for interrelationships among the independent variables and for curvature in the response function. Failure to include needed terms causes inflated values of SSE, nonsignificance in statistical tests, and, often, erroneous practical conclusions.

In this chapter, we discuss the most difficult part of a multiple regression analysis—the formulation of a good model for $E(y)$. Although many of the models presented in this chapter have already been introduced in Section 4.9, we assume the reader has little or no background in model building. This chapter serves as a basic reference guide to model building for teachers, students, and practitioners of multiple regression analysis.

5.2 The Two Types of Independent Variables: Quantitative and Qualitative

The independent variables that appear in a linear model can be one of two types—either **quantitative** or **qualitative**.

> Definition 5.1
>
> A **quantitative** independent variable is one that assumes numerical values corresponding to the points on a line. An independent variable that is not quantitative is called **qualitative**.

The nicotine content of a cigarette, prime interest rate, number of defects in a product, and IQ of a student are all examples of quantitative independent variables. On the other hand, suppose three different styles of packaging, A, B, and C, are used by a manufacturer. This independent variable, style of packaging, is qualitative, since it is not measured on a numerical scale. Certainly, style of packaging is an independent variable that may affect sales of a product, and we would want to include it in a model describing the product's sales, y.

Definition 5.2

The different intensity settings of an independent variable are called its **levels**.

For a quantitative variable, the levels correspond to the numerical values it assumes. For example, if the number of defects in a product ranges from 0 to 3, the independent variable assumes four levels: 0, 1, 2, and 3.

The levels of a qualitative variable are not numerical. They can be defined only by describing them. For example, the independent variable style of packaging was observed at three levels: A, B, and C.

EXAMPLE 5.1

In Chapter 4, we considered the problem of predicting executive salary as a function of several independent variables. Consider the following four independent variables that may affect executive salaries:

a. Years of experience
b. Gender of the employee
c. Firm's net asset value
d. Rank of the employee

For each of these independent variables, give its type and describe the nature of the levels you would expect to observe.

Solution

a. The independent variable for the number of years of experience is quantitative, since its values are numerical. We would expect to observe levels ranging from 0 to 40 (approximately) years.
b. The independent variable for gender is qualitative, since its levels can only be described by the nonnumerical labels "female" and "male."
c. The independent variable for the firm's net asset value is quantitative, with a very large number of possible levels corresponding to the range of dollar values representing various firms' net asset values.
d. Suppose the independent variable for the rank of the employee is observed at three levels: supervisor, assistant vice president, and vice president. Since we cannot assign a realistic measure of relative importance to each position, rank is a qualitative independent variable.

Quantitative and qualitative independent variables are treated differently in regression modeling. In the next section, we will see how quantitative variables are entered into a regression model.

EXERCISES

5.1 *Business Horizons* (Jan.–Feb. 1993) conducted a comprehensive study of 800 chief executive officers who run the country's largest global corporations. The purpose of the study was to build a profile of the CEOs based on characteristics of each CEO's social backgroiund. Several of the variables measured for each CEO are listed here. Classify each variable as quantitative or qualitative.

a. State of birth
b. Age
c. Education level
d. Tenure with firm
e. Total compensation
f. Area of expertise

5.2 Over the years, Graduate Record Examination (GRE) scores have been used to aid college administrators in the graduate school admission process. Some educators argue, however, that the GRE is biased against minority students, especially African Americans, who are often unfairly denied admission to graduate study on the basis of test scores alone. The *Journal of Negro Education* (Jan. 1985) reported on a study that used regression to model the GPA, y, of graduate students as a function of the independent variables GRE score (x_1) and race (x_2). Classify the independent variables as quantitative or qualitative.

5.3 The *Journal of Human Stress* (Summer 1987) reported on a study of "psychological response of firefighters to chemical fire." The researchers used multiple regression to predict emotional distress as a function of the following independent variables. Identify each independent variable as quantitative or qualitative. For qualitative variables, suggest several levels that might be observed. For quantitative variables, give a range of values (levels) for which the variable might be observed.

a. Number of preincident psychological symptoms
b. Years of experience
c. Cigarette smoking behavior
d. Level of social support
e. Marital status
f. Age
g. Ethnic status
h. Exposure to a chemical fire
i. Education level
j. Distance lived from site of incident
k. Gender

5.4 Which of the assumptions about ε (Section 4.2) prohibit the use of a qualitative variable as a dependent variable? (We present a technique for modeling a qualitative dependent variable in Chapter 8.)

5.3 Models with a Single Quantitative Independent Variable

To write a prediction equation that provides a good model for a response (one that will eventually yield good predictions), we have to know how the response might vary as the levels of an independent variable change. Then we have to know how to write a mathematical equation to model it. To illustrate (with a simple example), suppose we want to model a student's score on a statistics exam, y, as a function of the single independent variable x, the amount of study time invested. It may be that exam score, y, increases in a straight line as the amount of study time, x, varies from 1 hour to 6 hours, as shown in Figure 5.1a. If this were the entire range of x values for which you wanted to predict y, the model

$$E(y) = \beta_0 + \beta_1 x$$

would be appropriate.

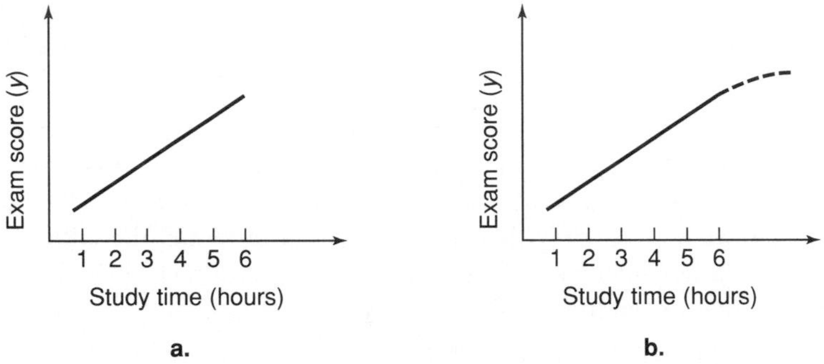

FIGURE 5.1
Modeling exam score, y, as a function of study time, x

Now, suppose you want to expand the range of values of x to $x = 8$ or $x = 10$ hours of studying. Will the straight-line model

$$E(y) = \beta_0 + \beta_1 x$$

be satisfactory? Perhaps, but making this assumption could be risky. As the amount of studying, x, is increased, sooner or later the point of diminishing returns will be reached. That is, the increase in exam score for a unit increase in study time will decrease, as shown by the dashed line in Figure 5.1b. To produce this type of curvature, you must know the relationship between models and graphs, and how types of terms will change the shape of the curve.

A response that is a function of a single quantitative independent variable can often be modeled by the first few terms of a polynomial algebraic function. The equation relating the mean value of y to a polynomial of order p in one independent variable x is shown in the box.

> **Formula for a pth-Order Polynomial with One Independent Variable**
>
> $$E(y) = \beta_0 + \beta_1 x + \beta_2 x^2 + \beta_3 x^3 + \cdots + \beta_p x^p$$
>
> where p is an integer and $\beta_0, \beta_1, \ldots, \beta_p$ are unknown parameters that must be estimated.

As we mentioned in Chapters 3 and 4, a **first-order polynomial** in x (i.e., $p = 1$),

$$E(y) = \beta_0 + \beta_1 x$$

graphs as a straight line. The β interpretations of this model are provided in the next box.

First-Order (Straight-Line) Model with One Independent Variable

$$E(y) = \beta_0 + \beta_1 x$$

INTERPRETATION OF MODEL PARAMETERS

β_0: y-intercept; the value of $E(y)$ when $x = 0$

β_1: Slope of the line; the change in $E(y)$ for a 1-unit increase in x

A **second-order polynomial** model ($p = 2$), called a **quadratic**, is given in the following box.

A Second-Order (Quadratic) Model with One Independent Variable

$$E(y) = \beta_0 + \beta_1 x + \beta_2 x^2$$

where β_0, β_1, and β_2 are unknown parameters that must be estimated.

INTERPRETATION OF MODEL PARAMETERS

β_0: y-intercept; the value of $E(y)$ when $x = 0$

β_1: Shift parameter; changing the value of β_1 shifts the parabola to the right or left (increasing the value of β_1 causes the parabola to shift to the right)

β_2: Rate of curvature

FIGURE 5.2

Graphs for two second-order polynomial models

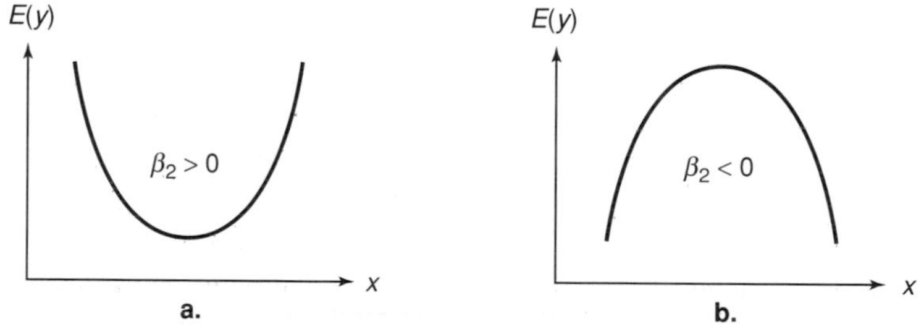

Graphs of two quadratic models are shown in Figure 5.2. The quadratic model is the equation of a **parabola** that opens either upward, as in Figure 5.2a, or downward, as in Figure 5.2b. (If the coefficient of x^2 is positive, it opens upward; if it is negative, it opens downward.) The parabola may be shifted upward or downward, left or right. The least squares procedure uses only the portion of the parabola that is needed to model the data. For example, if you fit a parabola to the data points shown in Figure 5.3, the portion shown as a solid curve passes through the data points. The outline of the unused portion of the parabola is indicated by a dashed curve.

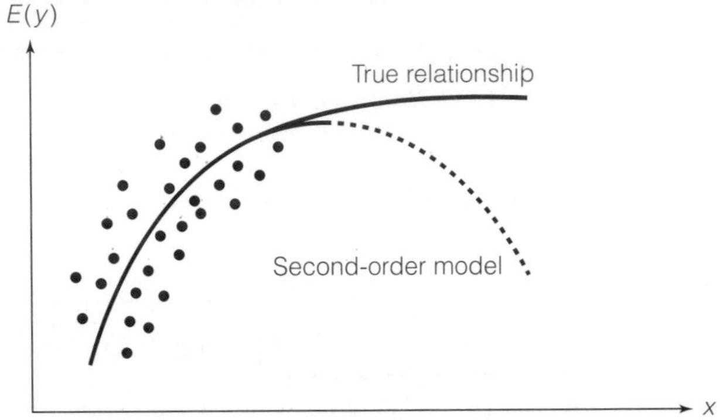

FIGURE 5.3
Example of the use of a quadratic model

Figure 5.3 illustrates an important limitation on the use of prediction equations: The model is valid only over the range of x values that were used to fit the model. For example, the response might rise, as shown in the figure, until it reaches a plateau. The second-order model might fit the data very well over the range of x values shown in Figure 5.3, but would provide a very poor fit if data were collected in the region where the parabola turns downward.

How do you decide the order of the polynomial you should use to model a response if you have no prior information about the relationship between $E(y)$ and x? If you have data, construct a scattergram of the data points, and see whether you can deduce the nature of a good approximating function. A pth-order polynomial, when graphed, will exhibit $(p - 1)$ peaks, troughs, or reversals in direction. Note that the graphs of the second-order model shown in Figure 5.2 each have $(p - 1) = 1$ peak (or trough). Likewise, a third-order model (shown in the box) will have $(p - 1) = 2$ peaks or troughs, as illustrated in Figure 5.4.

Third-Order Model with One Independent Variable

$$E(y) = \beta_0 + \beta_1 x + \beta_2 x^2 + \beta_3 x^3$$

INTERPRETATION OF MODEL PARAMETERS

β_0: y-intercept; the value of $E(y)$ when $x = 0$

β_3: The magnitude of β_3 controls the rate of reversal of curvature for the curve

FIGURE 5.4
Graphs of two third-order polynomial models

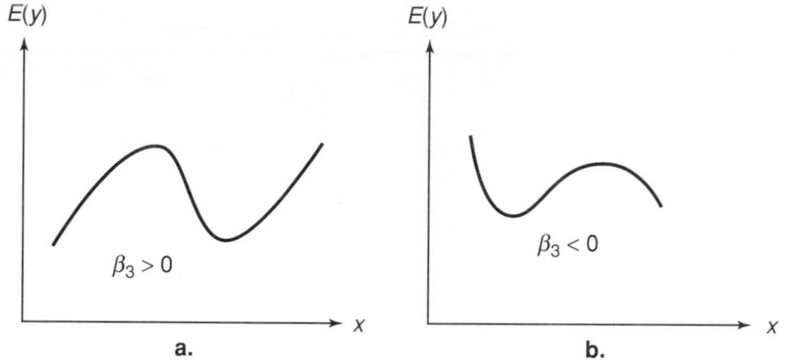

The graphs of most responses as a function of an independent variable x are, in general, curvilinear. Nevertheless, if the rate of curvature of the response curve is very small over the range of x that is of interest to you, a straight line might provide an excellent fit to the response data and serve as a very useful prediction equation. If the curvature is not (or may not be) slight, you should try a second-order model. Third- or higher-order models would be used only where you expect more than one reversal in the direction of the curve. These situations are rare, except where the response is a function of time. Models for forecasting over time are presented in Chapter 9.

EXAMPLE 5.2

To operate efficiently, power companies must be able to predict the peak power load at their various stations. The peak power load is the maximum amount of power that must be generated each day to meet demand.

Suppose a power company located in the southern part of the United States decides to model daily peak power load, y, as a function of the daily high temperature, x, and the model is to be constructed for the summer months when demand is greatest. Although we would expect the peak power load to increase as the high temperature increases, the *rate* of increase in $E(y)$ might also increase as x increases. That is, a 1-unit increase in high temperature from 100° to 101°F might result in a larger increase in power demand than would a 1-unit increase from 80° to 81°F. Therefore, we postulate the quadratic model

$$E(y) = \beta_0 + \beta_1 x + \beta_2 x^2$$

and we expect β_2 to be positive.

A random sample of 25 summer days is selected, and the data are shown in Table 5.1 at the top of page 282. Fit a second-order model using the data, and test the hypothesis that the power load increases at an increasing rate with temperature, i.e., that $\beta_2 > 0$.

Solution

The ASP printout shown in Figure 5.5 (also page 282) gives the least squares fit of the second-order model using the data in Table 5.1. The prediction equation is

$$\hat{y} = 385.048 - 8.293x + .05982x^2$$

TABLE 5.1 **Power Load Data**

TEMPERATURE °F	PEAK LOAD megawatts	TEMPERATURE °F	PEAK LOAD megawatts	TEMPERATURE °F	PEAK LOAD megawatts
94	136.0	106	178.2	76	100.9
96	131.7	67	101.6	68	96.3
95	140.7	71	92.5	92	135.1
108	189.3	100	151.9	100	143.6
67	96.5	79	106.2	85	111.4
88	116.4	97	153.2	89	116.5
89	118.5	98	150.1	74	103.9
84	113.4	87	114.7	86	105.1
90	132.0				

FIGURE 5.5
Portion of the ASP printout for the second-order model of Example 5.2

```
                QUADRATIC MODEL FOR PEAK POWER LOAD

MODEL:  Y = -8.29253X + 0.0598234XX + 385.048CNST

           COEF.        SD. ER.     t(22)     P-VALUE PT. R SQ.
        ----------- ----------- -------- ---------- ---------
   X   -8.29253     1.29905    -6.38356 2.00975E-6  0.649401
  XX    0.0598234   7.54855E-3  7.92514 6.8979E-8   0.74059
CNST  385.048      55.1724      6.97899 5.2661E-7   0.688854

R SQ. = 0.959363,   ADJ. R SQ. = 0.955668,   D. W. = 2.20408
SQ. ROOT MSE = 5.3762,   F(2/22) = 259.687 (P-VALUE = 4.99085E-16)
```

A plot of this equation and the observed values is given in Figure 5.6. Note that this curve passes through the data points and seems to produce (by visual examination) a set of deviations that are relatively small.

We now test to determine whether the sample value, $\hat{\beta}_2 = .05982$, is large enough to conclude in general that the power load increases at an increasing rate with temperature:

$$H_0\colon\ \beta_2 = 0$$
$$H_a\colon\ \beta_2 > 0$$

$$\textit{Test statistic:}\quad t = \frac{\hat{\beta}_2}{s_{\hat{\beta}_2}}$$

For $\alpha = .05$, $n = 25$, $k = 2$, and $\text{df} = n - (k + 1) = 22$, we reject H_0 if

$$t > t_{.05}$$

where $t_{.05} = 1.717$ (from Table 2 of Appendix C). From Figure 5.5, the calculated value of t is 7.92514. Since this value exceeds $t_{.05} = 1.717$, we reject H_0 and conclude that the mean power load increases at an increasing rate with temperature. Note that the observed significance level of the test, $p = .000000068979/2 \approx 0$ supports this conclusion.

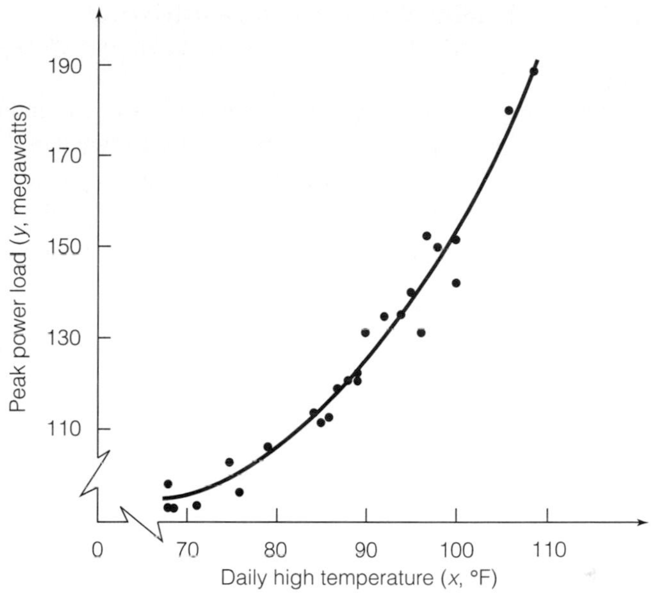

FIGURE 5.6
Plot of the observations and the second-order least squares fit

EXERCISES

5.5 The accompanying graphs depict pth-order polynomials for one independent variable.

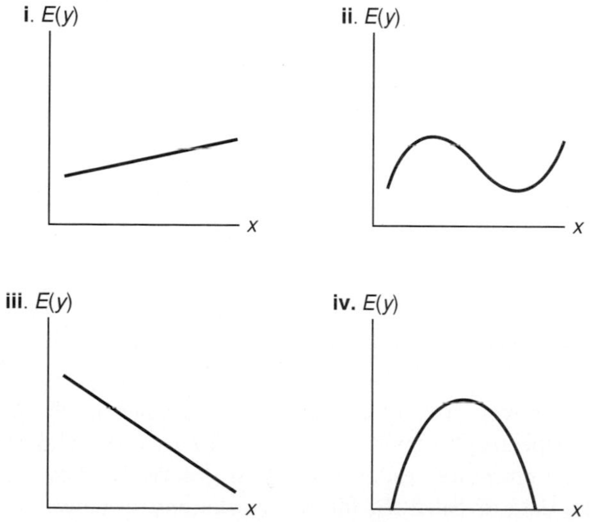

a. For each graph, identify the order of the polynomial.
b. Using the parameters β_0, β_1, β_2, etc., write an appropriate model relating $E(y)$ to x for each graph.
c. The signs (+ or −) of many of the parameters in the models of part **b** can be determined by examining the graphs. Give the signs of those parameters that can be determined.

5.6 In the pharmaceutical industry, a new chemical entity (NCE) is defined as a new chemical or biological compound tested in humans for therapeutic purposes for the first time. A study published in *Managerial & Decision Economics* (Sept. 3, 1988) reported that expenditures on research and development (R&D) of NCEs in the United Kingdom increased dramatically over the 20-year period 1964–1984. A plot of R&D expenditures (y) versus year (x) is shown here.

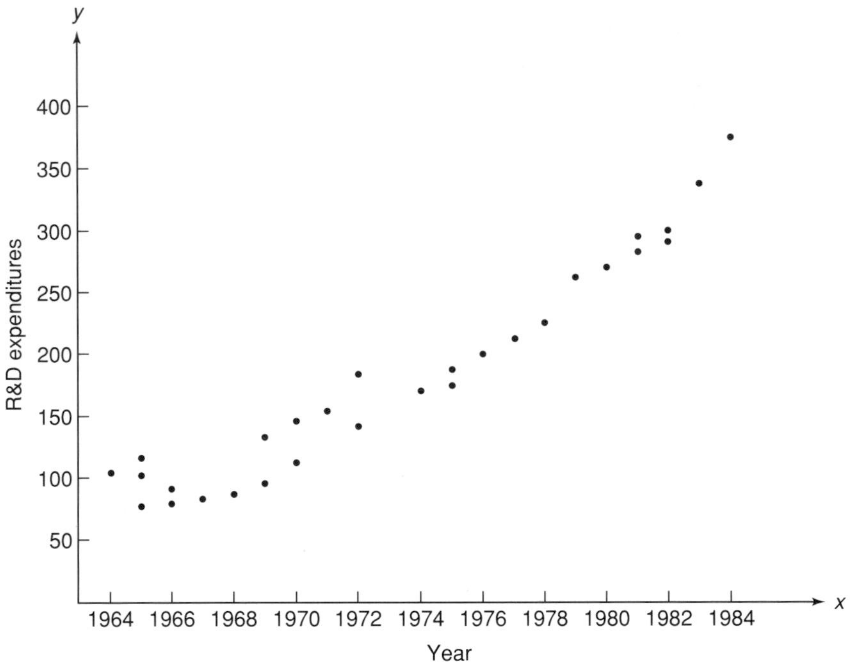

Source: Prentis, R. A., et al. "Pharmaceutical innovation and R&D investment in the UK." *Managerial & Decision Economics*, Sept. 3, 1988, p. 198 (Figure 1).

a Propose a model for $E(y)$ that would seem to fit the data well.
b. What are expected signs of the β's in the model, part **a**?

5.7 The optomotor responses of tree frogs were studied in the *Journal of Experimental Zoology* (Sept. 1993). Microspectrophotometry was used to measure the threshold quantal flux (the light intensity at which the optomotor response was first observed) of tree frogs tested at different spectral wavelengths. The data revealed the following relationship between the log of quantal flux (y) and wavelength (x). Hypothesize a model for $E(y)$ that corresponds to the following graph.

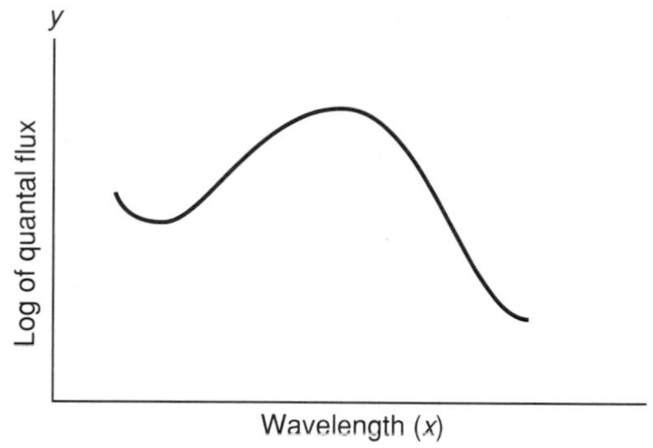

5.8 Underinflated or overinflated tires can increase tire wear and decrease gas mileage. A new tire was tested for wear at different pressures with the results shown in the table.

PRESSURE x, pounds per square inch	MILEAGE y, thousands
30	29
31	32
32	36
33	38
34	37
35	33
36	26

a. Plot the data on a scattergram.

b. If you were given the information for $x = 30, 31, 32, 33$ only, what kind of model would you suggest? For $x = 33, 34, 35, 36$? For all the data?

5.9 A company is considering having the employees on its assembly line work 4 10-hour days instead of 5 8-hour days. Management is concerned that the effect of fatigue as a result of longer afternoons of work might increase assembly times to an unsatisfactory level. An experiment with the 4-day week is planned in which time studies will be conducted on some of the workers during the afternoons. It is believed that an adequate model of the relationship between assembly time, y, and time since lunch, x, should allow for the average assembly time to decrease for a while after lunch before it starts to increase as the workers become tired. Write a model relating $E(y)$ and x that would reflect the management's belief, and sketch the hypothesized shape of the model.

5.4 First-Order Models with Two or More Quantitative Independent Variables

Like models for a single independent variable, models with two or more independent variables are classified as first-order, second-order, and so forth, but it is difficult (most often impossible) to graph the response because the plot is in a multidimensional space. For example, with one quantitative independent variable, x, the response y traces a curve. But for two quantitative independent variables, x_1 and x_2, the plot of y traces a surface over the x_1,x_2-plane (see Figure 5.7 on page 286). For three or more quantitative independent variables, the

FIGURE 5.7
Response surface for first-order model with two quantitative independent variables

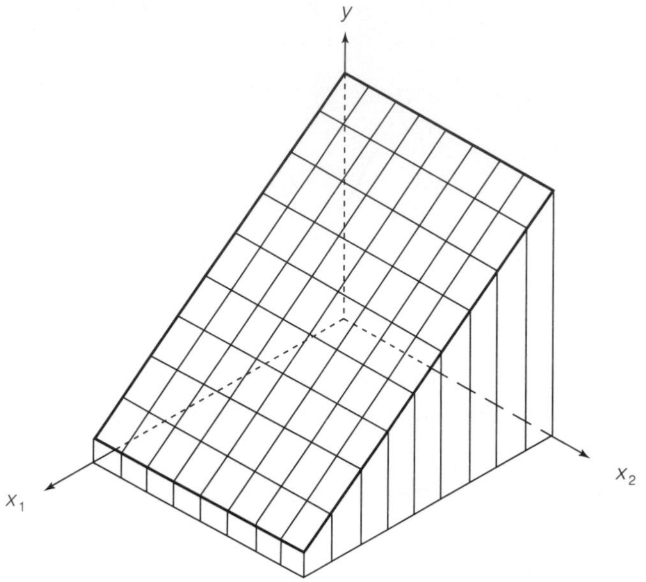

response traces a surface in a four- or higher-dimensional space. For these, we can construct two-dimensional contour curves for one independent variable or three-dimensional plots of response surfaces for two independent variables for fixed levels of the remaining independent variables, but this is the best we can do in providing a graphical description of a response.

A **first-order model** in k quantitative variables is a first-order polynomial in k independent variables. For $k = 1$, the graph is a straight line. For $k = 2$, the response surface is a plane (usually tilted) over the x_1,x_2-plane.

First-Order Model in k Quantitative Independent Variables

$$E(y) = \beta_0 + \beta_1 x_1 + \beta_2 x_2 + \cdots + \beta_k x_k$$

where $\beta_0, \beta_1, \ldots, \beta_k$ are unknown parameters that must be estimated.

INTERPRETATION OF MODEL PARAMETERS

β_0: y-intercept of $(k + 1)$-dimensional surface; the value of $E(y)$ when $x_1 = x_2 = \cdots = x_k = 0$

β_1: Change in $E(y)$ for a 1-unit increase in x_1, when $x_2, x_3, \ldots, x_k$ are held fixed

β_2: Change in $E(y)$ for a 1-unit increase in x_2, when $x_1, x_3, \ldots, x_k$ are held fixed

⋮

β_k: Change in $E(y)$ for a 1-unit increase in x_k, when $x_1, x_2, \ldots, x_{k-1}$ are held fixed

If we use a first-order polynomial to model a response, we are assuming that there is no curvature in the response surface and that the variables affect the response independently of each other. For example, suppose the true relationship between the mean response and the independent variables x_1 and x_2 is given by the equation

$$E(y) = 1 + 2x_1 + x_2$$

The response surface (a plane) corresponding to this equation is shown in Figure 5.8. The graphs of this expression for $x_2 = 1$, 2, and 3 (called **contour lines**), are shown in Figure 5.9 on page 288. You can see that when you substitute $x_2 = 1$ into the model, you obtain

$$\begin{aligned} E(y) &= 1 + 2x_1 + x_2 \\ &= 1 + 2x_1 + 1 \\ &= 2 + 2x_1 \end{aligned}$$

For $x_2 = 2$,

$$\begin{aligned} E(y) &= 1 + 2x_1 + 2 \\ &= 3 + 2x_1 \end{aligned}$$

And for $x_3 = 3$, $E(y) = 4 + 2x_1$. In other words, regardless of the value of x_2, $E(y)$ graphs as a straight line. Changing x_2 changes only the y-intercept (the constant in the equation). Consequently, assuming that a first-order model will adequately model a response is equivalent to assuming that a 1-unit change in one independent variable will have the same effect on the mean value of y regardless of the levels of the other independent variables. That is, *the contour lines will be parallel*. In Chapter 4, we stated that independent variables that have this property *do not interact*.

FIGURE 5.8
The plane $E(y) = 1 + 2x_1 + x_2$

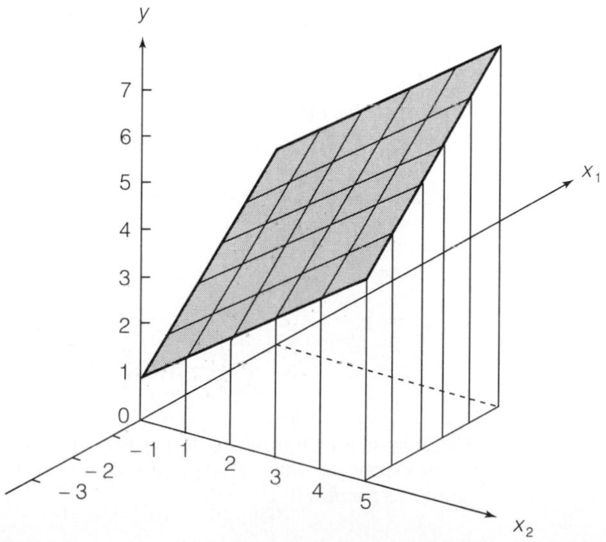

FIGURE 5.9
Contour lines of $E(y)$ for $x_2 = 1, 2, 3$ (first-order model)

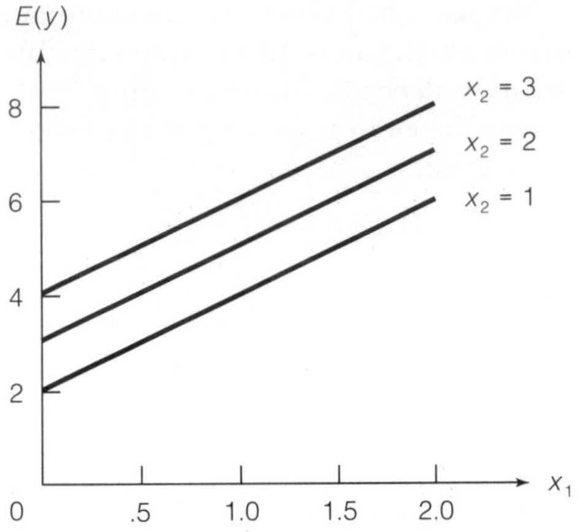

Except in cases where the ranges of levels for all independent variables are very small, the implication of no curvature in the response surface and the independence of variable effects on the response restrict the applicability of first-order models.

5.5 Second-Order Models with Two or More Quantitative Independent Variables

Second-order models with two or more independent variables permit curvature in the response surface. One important type of second-order term accounts for **interaction** between two variables.* To see the effect of interaction on the model, consider the two-variable model

$$E(y) = \beta_0 + \beta_1 x_1 + \beta_2 x_2 + \beta_3 x_1 x_2$$

This interaction model traces a ruled surface (twisted plane) in a three-dimensional space (see Figure 5.10). The second-order term $\beta_3 x_1 x_2$ is called the **interaction term**, and it permits the contour lines to be *nonparallel*. For example, suppose the true equation of the response surface is

$$E(y) = 1 + 2x_1 + x_2 - x_1 x_2$$

We graph the contour lines of this response for $x_2 = 1$, 2, and 3 in Figure 5.11. Note that when we substitute $x_2 = 1$ into the model, we get

$$\begin{aligned} E(y) &= 1 + 2x_1 + x_2 - x_1 x_2 \\ &= 1 + 2x_1 + 1 - x_1(1) \\ &= 2 + x_1 \end{aligned}$$

For $x_2 = 2$,

$$E(y) = 1 + 2x_1 + 2 - x_1(2) = 3$$

*The order of a term involving two or more *quantitative* independent variables is equal to the sum of their exponents. Thus, $\beta_3 x_1 x_2$ is a second-order term, as is $\beta_4 x_1^2$. A term of the form $\beta_i x_1 x_2 x_3$ is a third-order term.

FIGURE 5.10
Response surface for an interaction model (second-order)

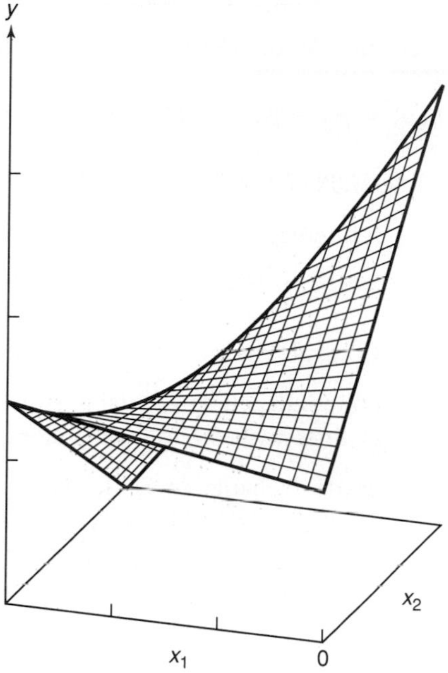

Similarly, when $x_2 = 3$, $E(y) = 4 - x_1$. Thus, when interaction is present in the model, both the *y-intercept and the slope change as* x_2 *changes. Consequently, the contour lines are not parallel. The presence of an interaction term implies that the effect of a 1-unit change in one independent variable will depend on the level of the other independent variable.* In our example (Figure 5.11), a 1-unit change in x_1 produces a 1-unit change in $E(y)$ when $x_2 = 1$, but a 1-unit change in x_1 produces *no* change in $E(y)$ when $x_2 = 2$ (i.e., the slope is 0).

FIGURE 5.11
Contour lines of $E(y)$ for $x_2 = 1, 2, 3$ (first-order model plus interaction)

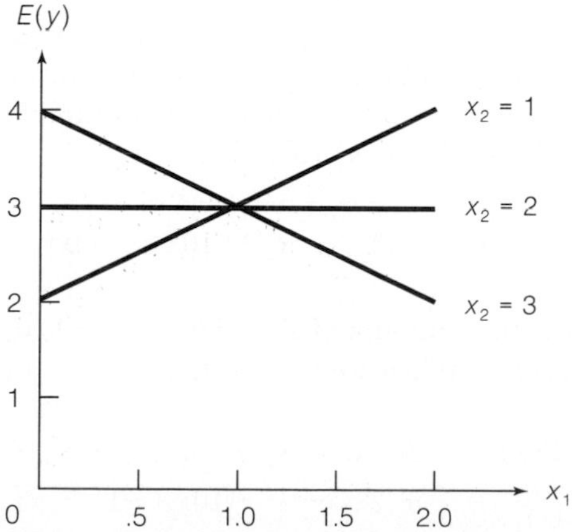

Interaction Model (Second-Order) with Two Independent Variables

$$E(y) = \beta_0 + \beta_1 x_1 + \beta_2 x_2 + \beta_3 x_1 x_2$$

INTERPRETATION OF MODEL PARAMETERS

β_0: y-intercept; the value of $E(y)$ when $x_1 = x_2 = 0$

β_1 and β_2: Changing β_1 and β_2 causes the surface to shift along the x_1 and x_2 axes

β_3: Controls the rate of twist in the ruled surface (see Figure 5.10)

When one independent variable is held fixed, the model produces straight lines with the following slopes:

$\beta_1 + \beta_3 x_2$: Change in $E(y)$ for a 1-unit increase in x_1, when x_2 is held fixed

$\beta_1 + \beta_3 x_1$: Change in $E(y)$ for a 1-unit increase in x_2, when x_1 is held fixed

Definition 5.3

Two variables x_1 and x_2 are said to **interact** if the change in $E(y)$ for a 1-unit change in x_1 (when x_2 is held fixed) is dependent on the value of x_2.

We can introduce even more flexibility into a model by the addition of quadratic terms. *The complete second-order model includes the constant β_0, all linear (first-order) terms, all two-variable interactions, and all quadratic terms.* This complete second-order model for two quantitative independent variables is shown in the box at the top of page 291.

The quadratic terms $\beta_4 x_1^2$ and $\beta_5 x_2^2$ in the second-order model imply that the response surface for $E(y)$ will possess curvature (see Figure 5.12). The interaction term $\beta_3 x_1 x_2$ allows the contours depicting $E(y)$ as a function of x_1 to have different shapes for various values of x_2. For example, suppose the complete second-order model relating $E(y)$ to x_1 and x_2 is

$$E(y) = 1 + 2x_1 + x_2 - 10x_1x_2 + x_1^2 - 2x_2^2$$

Then the contours of $E(y)$ for $x_2 = -1$, 0, and 1 are shown in Figure 5.13 on page 292. When we substitute $x_2 = -1$ into the model, we get

$$\begin{aligned} E(y) &= 1 + 2x_1 + x_2 - 10x_1x_2 + x_1^2 - 2x_2^2 \\ &= 1 + 2x_1 - 1 - 10x_1(-1) + x_1^2 - 2(-1)^2 \\ &= -2 + 12x_1 + x_1^2 \end{aligned}$$

Complete Second-Order Model with Two Independent Variables

$$E(y) = \beta_0 + \beta_1 x_1 + \beta_2 x_2 + \beta_3 x_1 x_2 + \beta_4 x_1^2 + \beta_5 x_2^2$$

INTERPRETATION OF MODEL PARAMETERS

β_0: y-intercept; the value of $E(y)$ when $x_1 = x_2 = 0$

β_1 and β_2: Changing β_1 and β_2 causes the surface to shift along the x_1 and x_2 axes

β_3: The value of β_3 controls the rotation of the surface

β_4 and β_5: Signs and values of these parameters control the type of surface and the rates of curvature

Three types of surfaces may be produced by a second-order model.*

A paraboloid that opens upward (Figure 5.12a)
A paraboloid that opens downward (Figure 5.12b)
A saddle-shaped surface (Figure 5.12c)

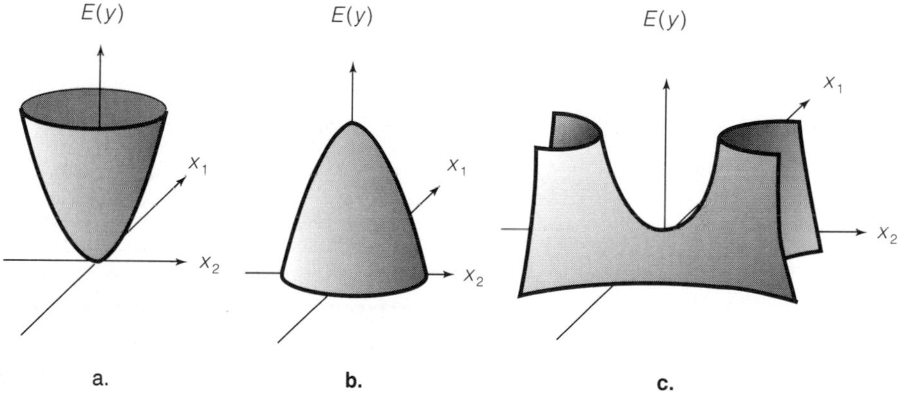

FIGURE 5.12
Graphs of three second-order surfaces

For $x_2 = 0$,

$$E(y) = 1 + 2x_1 + (0) - 10x_1(0) + x_1^2 - 2(0)^2$$
$$= 1 + 2x_1 + x_1^2$$

Similarly, for $x_2 = 1$,

$$E(y) = -8x_1 + x_1^2$$

*The saddle-shaped surface (Figure 5.12c) is produced when $\beta_3^2 > 4\beta_4\beta_5$. For $\beta_3^2 < 4\beta_4\beta_5$, the paraboloid opens upward (Figure 5.12a) when $\beta_4 + \beta_5 > 0$ and opens downward (Figure 5.12b) when $\beta_4 + \beta_5 < 0$.

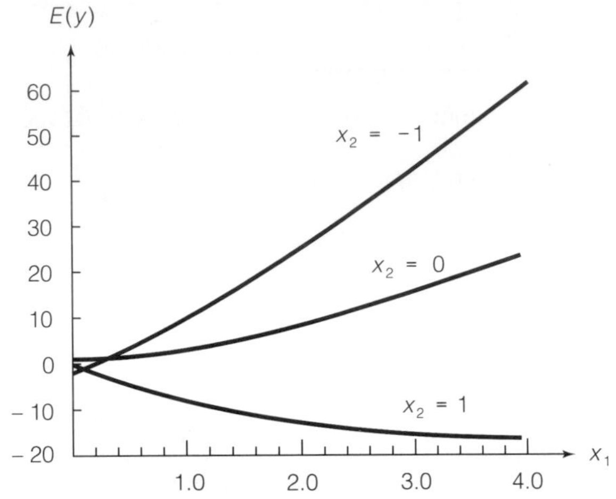

FIGURE 5.13
Contours of $E(y)$ for $x_2 = -1, 0, 1$ (complete second-order model)

Note how the shapes of the three contour curves in Figure 5.13 differ, indicating that the β parameter associated with the x_1x_2 (interaction) term differs from 0.

The complete second-order model for three independent variables is shown in the next box.

Complete Second-Order Model with Three Quantitative Independent Variables

$$E(y) = \beta_0 + \beta_1x_1 + \beta_2x_2 + \beta_3x_3 + \beta_4x_1x_2 + \beta_5x_1x_3 + \beta_6x_2x_3 + \beta_7x_1^2 + \beta_8x_2^2 + \beta_9x_3^2$$

where $\beta_0, \beta_1, \beta_2, \ldots, \beta_9$ are unknown parameters that must be estimated.

This second-order model in three independent variables demonstrates how you would write a second-order model for any number of independent variables. Always include the constant β_0 and then all first-order terms corresponding to $x_1, x_2, \ldots$. Then add the interaction terms for all pairs of independent variables $x_1x_2, x_1x_3, x_2x_3, \ldots$. Finally, include the second-order terms $x_1^2, x_2^2, \ldots$.

For any number, say, p, of quantitative independent variables, the response traces a surface in a $(p + 1)$-dimensional space, which is impossible to visualize. In spite of this handicap, the prediction equation can still tell us much about the phenomenon being studied.

EXAMPLE 5.3

Many companies manufacture products that are at least partially produced using chemicals (for example, steel, paint, gasoline). In many instances, the quality of the finished product is a function of the temperature and pressure at which the chemical reactions take place.

Suppose you wanted to model the quality, y, of a product as a function of the temperature, x_1, and the pressure, x_2, at which it is produced. Four inspectors independently assign a quality score between 0 and 100 to each product, and then the quality, y, is calculated by averaging the four scores. An experiment is conducted by varying temperature between 80° and 100°F and pressure between 50 and 60 pounds per square inch (psi). The resulting data ($n = 27$) are given in Table 5.2. Fit a complete second-order model to the data and sketch the response surface.

TABLE 5.2 **Temperature, Pressure, and Quality of the Finished Product**

x_1, °F	x_2, psi	y	x_1, °F	x_2, psi	y	x_1, °F	x_2, psi	y
80	50	50.8	90	50	63.4	100	50	46.6
80	50	50.7	90	50	61.6	100	50	49.1
80	50	49.4	90	50	63.4	100	50	46.4
80	55	93.7	90	55	93.8	100	55	69.8
80	55	90.9	90	55	92.1	100	55	72.5
80	55	90.9	90	55	97.4	100	55	73.2
80	60	74.5	90	60	70.9	100	60	38.7
80	60	73.0	90	60	68.8	100	60	42.5
80	60	71.2	90	60	71.3	100	60	41.4

Solution

The complete second-order model is

$$E(y) = \beta_0 + \beta_1 x_1 + \beta_2 x_2 + \beta_3 x_1 x_2 + \beta_4 x_1^2 + \beta_5 x_2^2$$

The data in Table 5.2 were used to fit this model. A portion of the SAS output is shown in Figure 5.14.

FIGURE 5.14 SAS printout for Example 5.3

Dependent Variable: Y

Analysis of Variance

Source	DF	Sum of Squares	Mean Square	F Value	Prob>F
Model	5	8402.26454	1680.45291	596.324	0.0001
Error	21	59.17843	2.81802		
C Total	26	8461.44296			

Root MSE	1.67870	R-square	0.9930
Dep Mean	66.96296	Adj R-sq	0.9913
C.V.	2.50690		

Parameter Estimates

Variable	DF	Parameter Estimate	Standard Error	T for H0: Parameter=0	Prob > |T|
INTERCEP	1	-5127.899074	110.29601493	-46.492	0.0001
X1	1	31.096389	1.34441322	23.130	0.0001
X2	1	139.747222	3.14005412	44.505	0.0001
X1X2	1	-0.145500	0.00969196	-15.012	0.0001
X1SQ	1	-0.133389	0.00685325	-19.464	0.0001
X2SQ	1	-1.144222	0.02741299	-41.740	0.0001

The least squares model is

$$\hat{y} = -5{,}127.90 + 31.10x_1 + 139.75x_2 - .146x_1x_2 - .133x_1^2 - 1.14x_2^2$$

A three-dimensional graph of this prediction model is shown in Figure 5.15. The mean quality seems to be greatest for temperatures of about 85°–90°F and for pressures of about 55–57 pounds per square inch.* Further experimentation in these ranges might lead to a more precise determination of the optimal temperature–pressure combination.

A look at the coefficient of determination, $R^2 = .993$, the F value for testing the entire model, $F = 596.32$, and the p-value for the test, $p = .0001$ (shaded in Figure 5.14), leaves little doubt that the complete second-order model is useful for explaining mean quality as a function of temperature and pressure. This, of course, will not always be the case. The additional complexity of second-order models is worthwhile only if a better model results. To determine whether the quadratic terms are important, we would test H_0: $\beta_4 = \beta_5 = 0$ using the partial F test outlined in Section 4.10.

FIGURE 5.15
Plot of second-order least squares model for Example 5.3

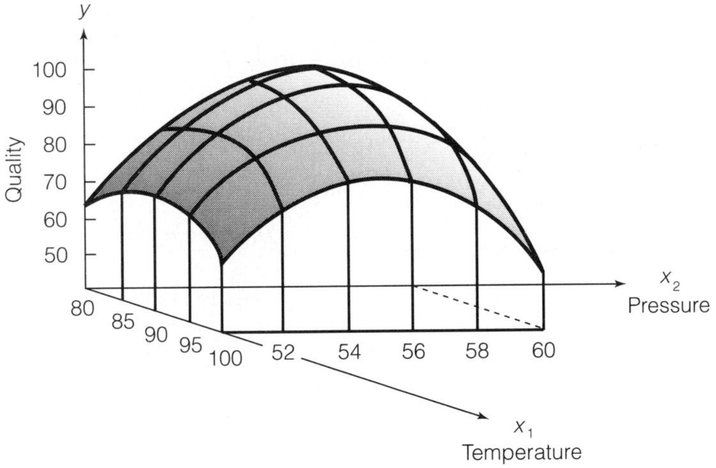

EXERCISES

5.10 An exploration seismologist wants to develop a model to estimate the average signal-to-noise ratio of an earthquake's seismic wave, y, as a function of two independent variables:

*Students with knowledge of calculus should note that we can determine the exact temperature and pressure that maximize quality in the least squares model by solving $\partial\hat{y}/\partial x_1 = 0$ and $\partial\hat{y}/\partial x_2 = 0$ for x_1 and x_2. These estimated optional values are $x_1 = 86.25$°F and $x_2 = 55.58$ pounds per square inch. Remember, however, that these are only sample estimates of the coordinates for the optional value.

x_1 = Frequency (cycles per second)

x_2 = Amplitude of the wavelet

a. Identify the independent variables as quantitative or qualitative.
b. Write the first-order model for $E(y)$.
c. Write a model for $E(y)$ that contains all first-order and interaction terms. Sketch typical response curves showing $E(y)$, the mean signal-to-noise ratio, versus x_2, the amplitude of the wavelet, for different values of x_1 (assume that x_1 and x_2 interact).
d. Write the complete second-order model for $E(y)$.

5.11 Refer to Exercise 5.10. Suppose the model from part **c** is fitted, with the following result:

$$\hat{y} = 1 + .05x_1 + x_2 + .05x_1x_2$$

Graph the estimated signal-to-noise ratio $\hat{y}$ as a function of the wavelet amplitude, x_2, over the range $x_2 = 10$ to $x_2 = 50$ for frequencies of $x_1 = 1, 5$, and 10. Do these functions agree (approximately) with the graphs you drew for Exercise 5.9, part **c**?

5.12 Refer to Exercise 5.10. Suppose an additional independent variable is considered, as follows:

x_3 = Time interval (seconds) between seismic waves

a. Write the first-order model plus interaction for $E(y)$ as a function of x_1, x_2, and x_3.
b. Write the complete second-order model plus interaction for $E(y)$ as a function of x_1, x_2, and x_3.

5.13 Researchers at the Upjohn Company utilized multiple regression analysis in the development of a sustained-release tablet.* One of the objectives of the research was to develop a model relating the dissolution y of a tablet (i.e., the percentage of the tablet dissolved over a specified period of time) to the following independent variables:

x_1 = Excipient level (i.e., amount of nondrug ingredient in the tablet)

x_2 = Process variable (e.g., machine setting under which tablet is processed)

a. Write the complete second-order model for $E(y)$.
b. Write a model that hypothesizes straight-line relationships between $E(y)$, x_1, and x_2. Assume that x_1 and x_2 do not interact.
c. Repeat part **b**, but add interaction to the model.
d. For the model in part **c**, what is the slope of the $E(y),x_1$ line for fixed x_2?
e. For the model in part **c**, what is the slope of the $E(y),x_2$ line for fixed x_1?

5.14 *Multinational* is the term given to an industry with foreign investors. A study of 216 manufacturing industries in Mexico found that multinational presence in a firm has a positive influence on market concentration (*World Development*, Vol. 14, 1986). The result was revealed in a multiple regression analysis on the dependent variable y, market concentration index, using the following quantitative independent variables:

x_1 = Market size

x_2 = Market rate of growth

---

*Klassen, R. A. "The application of response surface methods to a tablet formulation problem." Paper presented at Joint Statistical Meetings, American Statistical Association and Biometric Society, Aug. 1986, Chicago, Ill.

x_3 = Gross production in largest plants (expressed as a percentage of total gross production)

x_4 = Capital intensity (ratio of total assets to total number of employees)

x_5 = Advertising intensity (ratio of advertising to value added)

x_6 = Foreign share (i.e., gross output produced by foreign subsidiaries)

a. Write a first-order model for $E(y)$ as a function of x_1–x_6.
b. Interpret β_6 in the model in part **a**.
c. Based on the results of the study, is β_6 positive or negative?
d. Write a second-order model for $E(y)$ that proposes interaction between the independent variables but with no curvature.
e. Using the model in part **d**, how would you test the hypothesis that effect of a multinational presence on market concentration is independent of the other independent variables in the model?

5.6 Coding Quantitative Independent Variables (Optional)

In fitting higher-order polynomial regression models (e.g., second- or third-order models), it is often a good practice to code the quantitative independent variables. For example, suppose one of the independent variables in a regression analysis is level of competence in performing a task, C, measured on a 20-point scale, and C is observed at three levels: 5, 10, and 15. We can code (or transform) the competence measurements using the formula

$$x = \frac{C - 10}{5}$$

Then the coded levels $x = -1$, 0, and 1 correspond to the original C levels 5, 10, and 15.

In a general sense, *coding* means transforming a set of independent variables (qualitative or quantitative) into a new set of independent variables. For example, if we observe two independent variables,

C = Competence level

S = Satisfaction level

then we can transform C and S into two new coded variables, x_1 and x_2, where x_1 and x_2 are related to C and S by two functional equations:

$$x_1 = f_1(C, I) \qquad x_2 = f_2(S, I)$$

The functions f_1 and f_2, which are frequently expressed as equations, establish a one-to-one correspondence between combinations of levels of C and S with combinations of the coded values of x_1 and x_2.

Since qualitative independent variables are not numerical, it is necessary to code their values to fit the regression model. However, you might ask why we would bother to code the quantitative independent variables. There are two related reasons for coding quantitative variables. At first glance, it would appear that a computer would be oblivious to the values assumed by the independent variables in a regression analysis, but this is not the case. To calculate the estimates of the model parameters using the method of least squares, the computer must invert a matrix of numbers, called the **coefficient** (or **information) matrix** (see Appendix A). Considerable rounding error may occur during the inversion process if the numbers in the coefficient matrix vary greatly in absolute value. This can produce sizable errors in the computed values of the least squares estimates, $\hat{\beta}_0, \hat{\beta}_1, \hat{\beta}_2, \ldots$. Coding makes it computationally easier for the computer to invert the matrix, thus leading to more accurate estimates.

A second reason for coding quantitative variables pertains to a problem we will discuss in detail in Chapter 6: the problem of independent variables (x's) being intercorrelated (called **multicollinearity**). When polynomial regression models (e.g., second-order models) are fitted, the problem of multicollinearity is unavoidable, especially when higher-order terms are fitted. For example, consider the quadratic model

$$E(y) = \beta_0 + \beta_1 x + \beta_2 x^2$$

If the range of the values of x is narrow, then the two variables, $x_1 = x$ and $x_2 = x^2$, will generally be highly correlated. As we point out in Chapter 6, the likelihood of rounding errors in the regression coefficients is increased in the presence of these highly correlated independent variables.

The following procedure is the best way to cope with the problem of rounding error:

1. Code the quantitative variable so that the new coded origin is in the center of the coded values. For example, by coding competence level, C, as

$$x = \frac{C - 10}{5}$$

   we obtain coded values $-1, 0, 1$. This places the coded origin, 0, in the middle of the range of coded values (-1 to 1).
2. Code the quantitative variable so that the range of the coded values is approximately the same for all coded variables. You need not hold exactly to this requirement. The range of values for one independent variable could be double or triple the range of another without causing any difficulty, but it is not desirable to have a sizable disparity in the ranges, say, a ratio of 100 to 1.

When the data are observational (the values assumed by the independent variables are uncontrolled), the coding procedure described in the box at the top of page 298 satisfies, reasonably well, these two requirements. The coded variable u is similar to the standardized normal z statistic of Section 1.5. Thus, the u value is the deviation (the distance) between an x value and the mean of the x values, $\bar{x}$, expressed in units of s_x.* Since we know that most (approximately 95%) measurements in a set will lie within 2 standard deviations of their mean, it follows that most of the coded u values will lie in the interval -2 to $+2$.

*The divisor of the deviation, $x - \bar{x}$, need not equal s_x exactly. Any number approximately equal to s_x would suffice. Other candidate denominators are the range (R), $R/2$, and the interquartile range (IQR).

Coding Procedure for Observational Data

Let

x = Uncoded quantitative independent variable
u = Coded quantitative independent variable

Then if x takes values $x_1, x_2, \ldots, x_n$ for the n data points in the regression analysis, let

$$u_i = \frac{x_i - \bar{x}}{s_x}$$

where s_x is the standard deviation of the x values, i.e.,

$$s_x = \sqrt{\frac{\sum_{i=1}^{n} (x_i - \bar{x})^2}{n - 1}}$$

If you apply this coding to each quantitative variable, the range of values for each will be approximately -2 to $+2$. The variation in the absolute values of the elements of the coefficient matrix will be moderate, and rounding errors generated in finding the inverse of the matrix will be reduced. Additionally, the correlation between x and x^2 will be reduced.*

EXAMPLE 5.4

Table 5.3 gives observational data on the index of building construction costs per month as a function of the index of the cost of construction materials (other components of construction costs would be labor, the cost of money, etc.

TABLE 5.3 **Index of Building Construction Costs**

MONTH	CONSTRUCTION COST[a] y	INDEX OF ALL CONSTRUCTION MATERIALS[b] x
January	193.2	180.0
February	193.1	181.7
March	193.6	184.1
April	195.1	185.3
May	195.6	185.7
June	198.1	185.9
July	200.9	187.7
August	202.7	189.6

[a]*Source:* U.S. Department of Commerce, Bureau of the Census.
[b]*Source:* U.S. Department of Labor, Bureau of Labor Statistics.

*Another by-product of coding is that the β coefficients of the model have slightly different interpretations. For example, in the model $E(y) = \beta_0 + \beta_1 u$, where $u = (x - 10)/5$, the change in y for every 1-unit increase in x is not β_1, but $\beta_1/5$. In general, for first-order models with coded independent quantitative variables, the slope associated with x_i is represented by β_i/s_{x_i}, where s_{x_i} is the divisor of the coded x_i.

Suppose we are interested in relating monthly construction cost y to monthly index of construction materials x using a quadratic model.

a. Give the equation relating the coded variable u to the index of construction materials x using the coding system for observational data.
b. Calculate the coded values, u, for the eight x values.
c. Find the sum of the $n = 8$ values for u.

Solution

a. We first find $\bar{x}$ and s_x. From the MINITAB printout, Figure 5.16, which provides summary statistics for construction index, x, we obtain

$$\bar{x} = 185.0 \quad \text{and} \quad s_x = 3.08$$

FIGURE 5.16
MINITAB printout for Example 5.4

	N	MEAN	MEDIAN	TRMEAN	STDEV	SEMEAN
X	8	185.00	185.50	185.00	3.08	1.09

	MIN	MAX	Q1	Q3
X	180.00	189.60	182.30	187.25

Then the equation relating u and x is

$$u = \frac{x - 185.0}{3.08}$$

b. When $x = 180.0$,

$$u = \frac{x - 185.0}{3.08} = \frac{180.0 - 185.0}{3.08} = -1.62$$

Similarly, when $x = 181.7$,

$$u = \frac{x - 185.0}{3.08} = \frac{181.7 - 185.0}{3.08} = -1.07$$

Table 5.4 gives the coded values for all $n = 8$ observations. [*Note:* You can see that all the $n = 8$ values for u lie in the interval from -2 to $+2$.]

TABLE 5.4
Coded Values of x, Example 5.4

INDEX, x	CODED VALUES, u
180.0	−1.62
181.7	−1.07
184.1	−.29
185.3	.10
185.7	.23
185.9	.29
187.7	.88
189.6	1.49

c. If you ignore rounding error, the sum of the $n = 8$ values for u will equal 0. This is because the sum of the deviations of a set of measurements about their mean is always equal to 0.

To illustrate the advantage of coding, consider fitting the second-order model

$$E(y) = \beta_0 + \beta_1 x + \beta_2 x^2$$

to the data of Example 5.4. The coefficient of correlation between the two variables, x and x^2, shown on the MINITAB printout displayed in Figure 5.17, is $r = .999$. However, the coefficient of correlation between the corresponding coded values, u and u^2, shown in Figure 5.18, is only $r = -.203$. Thus, we can avoid potential rounding error caused by highly correlated x values by fitting, instead, the model

$$E(y) = \beta_0^* + \beta_1^* u + \beta_2^* u^2$$

FIGURE 5.17
MINITAB printout: Correlation between x and x^2

```
Correlation of X and X*X = 0.999
```

FIGURE 5.18
MINITAB printout: Correlation between u and u^2

```
Correlation of U and U*U = -0.203
```

Other methods of coding have been developed to reduce rounding errors and multicollinearity. One of the more complex coding systems involves fitting **orthogonal polynomials**. An orthogonal system of coding guarantees that the coded independent variables will be uncorrelated. For a discussion of orthogonal polynomials, consult the references given at the end of this chapter.

EXERCISES

5.15 Suppose you want to use the coding system for observational data to fit a second-order model to the tire pressure–automobile mileage data of Exercise 5.8, which are repeated in the table.

PRESSURE x, pounds per square inch	MILEAGE y, thousands
30	29
31	32
32	36
33	38
34	37
35	33
36	26

a. Give the equation relating the coded variable u to pressure, x, using the coding system for observational data.
b. Calculate the coded values, u.
c. Calculate the coefficient of correlation r between the variables x and x^2.
d. Calculate the coefficient of correlation r between the variables u and u^2. Compare this value to the value computed in part c.
e. Fit the model

$$E(y) = \beta_0 + \beta_1 u + \beta_2 u^2$$

using available statistical software. Interpret the results.

5.16 Refer to the *Journal of Applied Physics* (Sept. 1993) study of solar lighting with semiconductor lasers, Exercise 4.2. The data for the analysis are repeated here.

THRESHOLD CURRENT y, A/cm^2	WAVEGUIDE Al MOLE FRACTION x
273	.15
175	.20
146	.25
166	.30
162	.35
165	.40
245	.50
314	.60

Source: Unnikrishnan, S., and Anderson, N. G. "Quantum-well lasers for direct solar photopumping." *Journal of Applied Physics*, Vol. 74, No. 6, Sept. 15, 1993, p. 4226 (data adapted from Figure 2).

a. Give the equation relating the coded variable u to waveguide, x, using the coding system for observational data.
b. Calculate the coded values, u.
c. Calculate the coefficient of correlation r between the variables x and x^2.
d. Calculate the coefficient of correlation r between the variables u and u^2. Compare this value to the value computed in part c.
e. Fit the model

$$E(y) = \beta_0 + \beta_1 u + \beta_2 u^2$$

using available statistical software. Interpret the results.

5.17 As part of the first-year evaluation for new salespeople, a large food-processing firm projects the second-year sales for each salesperson based on his or her sales for the first year. Data for $n = 8$ salespeople are shown in the table at the top of page 302.
a. Give the equation relating the coded variable u to first-year sales, x, using the coding system for observational data.
b. Calculate the coded values, u.
c. Calculate the coefficient of correlation r between the variables x and x^2.
d. Calculate the coefficient of correlation r between the variables u and u^2. Compare this value to the value computed in part c.

FIRST-YEAR SALES x, thousands of dollars	SECOND-YEAR SALES y, thousands of dollars
75.2	99.3
91.7	125.7
100.3	136.1
64.2	108.6
81.8	102.0
110.2	153.7
77.3	108.8
80.1	105.4

e. Fit the model

$$E(y) = \beta_0 + \beta_1 u + \beta_2 u^2$$

using available statistical software. Interpret the results.

5.7 Models with One Qualitative Independent Variable

Suppose we want to write a model for the mean performance, $E(y)$, of a diesel engine as a function of type of fuel. (For the purpose of explanation, we will ignore other independent variables that might affect the response.) Further suppose there are three fuel types available: a petroleum-based fuel (P), a coal-based fuel (C), and a blended fuel (B). The fuel type is a single qualitative variable with three levels corresponding to fuels P, C, and B. Note that with a qualitative independent variable, we cannot attach a quantitative meaning to a given level. All we can do is describe it.

To simplify our notation, let μ_P be the mean performance for fuel P, and let μ_C and μ_B be the corresponding mean performances for fuels C and B. Our objective is to write a single prediction equation that will give the mean value of y for the three fuel types. This can be done as follows:

$$E(y) = \beta_0 + \beta_1 x_1 + \beta_2 x_2$$

where

$$x_1 = \begin{cases} 1 & \text{if fuel P is used} \\ 0 & \text{if not} \end{cases}$$

$$x_2 = \begin{cases} 1 & \text{if fuel C is used} \\ 0 & \text{if not} \end{cases}$$

The values of x_1 and x_2 for each of the three fuel types are shown in Table 5.5.

TABLE 5.5 **Mean Response for the Model with Three Diesel Fuel Types**

FUEL TYPE	x_1	x_2	MEAN RESPONSE, $E(y)$
Blended (B)	0	0	$\beta_0 = \mu_B$
Petroleum (P)	1	0	$\beta_0 + \beta_1 = \mu_P$
Coal (C)	0	1	$\beta_0 + \beta_2 = \mu_C$

The variables x_1 and x_2 are not meaningful independent variables as in the case of the models containing quantitative independent variables. Instead, they are **dummy (indicator) variables** that make the model work. To see how they work, let $x_1 = 0$ and $x_2 = 0$. This condition will apply when we are seeking the mean response for fuel B (neither fuel P nor C is used; hence, it must be B). Then the mean value of y when fuel B is used is

$$\mu_B = E(y) = \beta_0 + \beta_1(0) + \beta_2(0)$$
$$= \beta_0$$

This tells us that the mean performance level for fuel B is β_0. Or, it means that

$$\beta_0 = \mu_B.$$

Now suppose we want to represent the mean response, $E(y)$, when fuel P is used. Checking the dummy variable definitions, we see that we should let $x_1 = 1$ and $x_2 = 0$:

$$\mu_P = E(y) = \beta_0 + \beta_1(1) + \beta_2(0)$$
$$= \beta_0 + \beta_1$$

or, since $\beta_0 = \mu_B$,

$$\mu_P = \mu_B + \beta_1$$

Then it follows that the interpretation of β_1 is

$$\beta_1 = \mu_P - \mu_B$$

which is the difference in the mean performance levels for fuels P and B.

Finally, if we want the mean value of y when fuel C is used, we let $x_1 = 0$ and $x_2 = 1$:

$$\mu_C = E(y) = \beta_0 + \beta_1(0) + \beta_2(1)$$
$$= \beta_0 + \beta_2$$

or, since $\beta_0 = \mu_B$,

$$\mu_C = \mu_B + \beta_2$$

Then it follows that the interpretation of β_2 is

$$\beta_2 = \mu_C - \mu_B$$

Note that we were able to describe *three levels* of the qualitative variable with only *two dummy variables*, because the mean of the base level (fuel B, in this case) is accounted for by the intercept β_0.

Now, carefully examine the model for a single qualitative independent variable with three levels, because we will use exactly the same pattern for any number of levels. Arbitrarily select one level to be the base level, then set up 1–0 dummy variables for the remaining levels. This setup always leads to the interpretation of the parameters given in the box on page 304.

Procedure for Writing a Model with One Qualitative Independent Variable at k Levels (A, B, C, D, . . .)

$$E(y) = \beta_0 + \beta_1 x_1 + \beta_2 x_2 + \cdots + \beta_{k-1} x_{k-1}$$

where

x_i is the dummy variable for level $i + 1$ and

$$x_i = \begin{cases} 1 & \text{if } E(y) \text{ is the mean for level } i + 1 \\ 0 & \text{otherwise} \end{cases}$$

The number of dummy variables for a single qualitative variable is always 1 less than the number of levels for the variable. Then, assuming the base level is A, the mean for each level is

$$\begin{aligned} \mu_A &= \beta_0 \\ \mu_B &= \beta_0 + \beta_1 \\ \mu_C &= \beta_0 + \beta_2 \\ \mu_D &= \beta_0 + \beta_3 \\ &\vdots \end{aligned}$$

β Interpretations

$$\begin{aligned} \beta_0 &= \mu_A \\ \beta_1 &= \mu_B - \mu_A \\ \beta_2 &= \mu_C - \mu_A \\ \beta_3 &= \mu_D - \mu_A \\ &\vdots \end{aligned}$$

EXAMPLE 5.5

A large consulting firm markets a computerized system for monitoring road construction bids to various state departments of transportation. Since the high cost of maintaining the system is partially absorbed by the firm, the firm wants to compare the mean annual maintenance costs accrued by system users in three different states: Kansas, Kentucky, and Texas. A sample of 10 users is selected from each state installation and the maintenance cost accrued by each is recorded, as shown in Table 5.6. Do the data provide sufficient evidence (at $\alpha = .05$) to indicate that the mean annual maintenance costs accrued by system users differ for the three state installations?

Solution

The model relating $E(y)$ to the single qualitative variable, state installation, is

$$E(y) = \beta_0 + \beta_1 x_1 + \beta_2 x_2$$

TABLE 5.6 **Annual Maintenance Costs**

	STATE INSTALLATION		
	Kansas	Kentucky	Texas
	$ 198	$ 563	$ 385
	126	314	693
	443	483	266
	570	144	586
	286	585	178
	184	377	773
	105	264	308
	216	185	430
	465	330	644
	203	354	515
Totals	$2,796	$3,599	$4,778

where

$$x_1 = \begin{cases} 1 & \text{if Kentucky} \\ 0 & \text{if not} \end{cases} \qquad x_2 = \begin{cases} 1 & \text{if Texas} \\ 0 & \text{if not} \end{cases}$$

and

$$\beta_1 = \mu_2 - \mu_1$$
$$\beta_2 = \mu_3 - \mu_1$$

where μ_1, μ_2, and μ_3 are the mean responses for Kansas, Kentucky, and Texas, respectively. Testing the null hypothesis that the means for three states are equal, i.e., $\mu_1 = \mu_2 = \mu_3$, is equivalent to testing

$$H_0\text{:}\quad \beta_1 = \beta_2 = 0$$

because if $\beta_1 = \mu_2 - \mu_1 = 0$ and $\beta_2 = \mu_3 - \mu_1 = 0$, then μ_1, μ_2, and μ_3 must be equal. The alternative hypothesis is

H_a: At least one of the parameters, β_1 or β_2, differs from 0.

There are two ways to conduct this test. We can fit the complete model shown previously and the reduced model (discarding the terms involving β_1 and β_2),

$$E(y) = \beta_0$$

and conduct the F test described in the preceding section (we leave this as an exercise for you). Or, we can use the F test of the complete model (Section 4.10), which tests the null hypothesis that all parameters in the model, with the exception of β_0, equal 0. Either way you conduct the test, you will obtain the same computed value of F, the value shown on the SAS printout for a test of the complete model. The SAS printout for fitting the complete model,

$$E(y) = \beta_0 + \beta_1 x_1 + \beta_2 x_2$$

is shown in Figure 5.19. The value of the F statistic for testing the complete model (shaded on Figure 5.19) is $F = 3.482$; the p-value for the test (also shaded) is $p = .0452$. Since our choice of α, $\alpha = .05$, exceeds the p-value, we reject H_0 and conclude that at least one of the parameters, β_1 or β_2, differs from 0. Or equivalently, we conclude that the data provide sufficient evidence to indicate that the mean user maintenance cost does vary among the three state installations.

FIGURE 5.19
SAS printout for Example 5.5

```
Dependent Variable: Y

                         Analysis of Variance

                             Sum of          Mean
Source              DF      Squares        Square       F Value       Prob>F

Model                2 198772.46667   99386.23333         3.482       0.0452
Error               27 770670.90000   28543.36667
C Total             29 969443.36667

    Root MSE       168.94782      R-square         0.2050
    Dep Mean       372.43333      Adj R-sq         0.1462
    C.V.            45.36324

                         Parameter Estimates

                     Parameter         Standard     T for H0:
Variable   DF         Estimate            Error   Parameter=0     Prob > |T|

INTERCEP    1       279.600000      53.42599243         5.233         0.0001
X1          1        80.300000      75.55576307         1.063         0.2973
X2          1       198.200000      75.55576307         2.623         0.0141
```

5.8 Models with Two Qualitative Independent Variables

We will demonstrate how to write a model with two qualitative independent variables and then, in Section 5.9, we will explain how to use this technique to write models with any number of qualitative independent variables.

Let us return to the example used in Section 5.7, where we wrote a model for the mean performance, $E(y)$, of a diesel engine as a function of one qualitative independent variable, fuel type. Now suppose the performance is also a function of engine brand and we want to compare the top two brands. Therefore, this second qualitative independent variable, brand, will be observed at two levels. To simplify our notation, we will change the symbols for the three fuel types from B, D, C, to F_1, F_2, F_3, and we will let B_1 and B_2 represent the two brands. The six population means of performance measurements (measurements of y) are symbolically represented by the six cells in the two-way table shown in Table 5.7. Each μ subscript corresponds to one fuel type–brand combination.

TABLE 5.7 **The Six Combinations of Fuel Type and Diesel Engine Brand**

		BRAND	
		B_1	B_2
FUEL TYPE	F_1	μ_{11}	μ_{12}
	F_2	μ_{21}	μ_{22}
	F_3	μ_{31}	μ_{32}

First we will write a model in its simplest form—where the two qualitative variables affect the response independently of each other. To write the model for mean performance, $E(y)$, we start with a constant β_0 and then add *two* dummy variables for the three levels of fuel type in the manner explained in Section 5.7. These terms, which are called the **main effect terms** for fuel type, F, account for the effect of F on $E(y)$ when fuel type, F, and brand, B, affect $E(y)$ independently. Then,

$$E(y) = \beta_0 + \overbrace{\beta_1 x_1 + \beta_2 x_2}^{\substack{\text{Main effect} \\ \text{terms for } F}}$$

where

$$x_1 = \begin{cases} 1 & \text{if fuel type } F_2 \text{ was used} \\ 0 & \text{if not} \end{cases}$$

$$x_2 = \begin{cases} 1 & \text{if fuel type } F_3 \text{ was used} \\ 0 & \text{if not} \end{cases}$$

Now let level B_1 be the base level of the brand variable. Since there are two levels of this variable, we will need only one dummy variable to include the brand in the model:

$$E(y) = \beta_0 + \overbrace{\beta_1 x_1 + \beta_2 x_2}^{\substack{\text{Main effect} \\ \text{terms for } F}} + \overbrace{\beta_3 x_3}^{\substack{\text{Main effect} \\ \text{term for } B}}$$

where the dummy variables x_1 and x_2 are as defined previously and

$$x_3 = \begin{cases} 1 & \text{if engine brand } B_2 \text{ used} \\ 0 & \text{if engine brand } B_1 \text{ used} \end{cases}$$

If you check the model, you will see that by assigning specific values to x_1, x_2, and x_3, you create a model for the mean value of y corresponding to one of the cells of Table 5.7. We will illustrate with two examples.

EXAMPLE 5.6

Give the values of x_1, x_2, and x_3 and the model for the mean performance, $E(y)$, when using fuel type F_1 in engine brand B_1.

Solution

Checking the coding system, you will see that F_1 and B_1 occur when $x_1 = x_2 = x_3 = 0$. Then,

$$\begin{aligned} E(y) &= \beta_0 + \beta_1 x_1 + \beta_2 x_2 + \beta_3 x_3 \\ &= \beta_0 + \beta_1(0) + \beta_2(0) + \beta_3(0) \\ &= \beta_0 \end{aligned}$$

Therefore, the mean value of y at levels F_1 and B_1, which we represent as μ_{11}, is

$$\mu_{11} = \beta_0$$

EXAMPLE 5.7

Give the values of x_1, x_2, and x_3 and the model for the mean performance, $E(y)$, when using fuel type F_3 in engine brand B_2.

Solution

Checking the coding system, you will see that for levels F_3 and B_2,

$$x_1 = 0 \qquad x_2 = 1 \qquad x_3 = 1$$

Then, the mean performance for fuel F_3 used in engine brand B_2, represented by the symbol μ_{32} (see Table 5.7), is

$$\begin{aligned} \mu_{32} = E(y) &= \beta_0 + \beta_1 x_1 + \beta_2 x_2 + \beta_3 x_3 \\ &= \beta_0 + \beta_1(0) + \beta_2(1) + \beta_3(1) \\ &= \beta_0 + \beta_2 + \beta_3 \end{aligned}$$

Note that in the model described previously, we assumed the qualitative independent variables for fuel type and engine brand affect the mean response, $E(y)$, independently of each other. This type of model is called a **main effects model** and is shown in the box on page 309. Changing the level of one qualitative variable will have the same effect on $E(y)$ for any level of the second qualitative variable. In other words, the effect of one qualitative variable on $E(y)$ is independent (in a mathematical sense) of the level of the second qualitative variable.

When two independent variables affect the mean response independently of each other, you may obtain the pattern shown in Figure 5.20. Note that the difference in mean performance between any two fuel types (levels of F) is the same, *regardless* of the engine brand used. That is, the main effects model assumes that the relative effect of fuel type on performance is the same in both engine brands.

Main Effects Model with Two Qualitative Independent Variables, One at Three Levels (F_1, F_2, F_3) and the Other at Two Levels (B_1, B_2)

$$E(y) = \beta_0 + \overbrace{\beta_1 x_1 + \beta_2 x_2}^{\text{Main effect terms for } F} + \overbrace{\beta_3 x_3}^{\text{Main effect term for } B}$$

where

$$x_1 = \begin{cases} 1 & \text{if } F_2 \\ 0 & \text{if not} \end{cases} \qquad x_2 = \begin{cases} 1 & \text{if } F_3 \\ 0 & \text{if not} \end{cases} \qquad (F_1 \text{ is base level})$$

$$x_3 = \begin{cases} 1 & \text{if } B_2 \\ 0 & \text{if } B_1 \quad (\text{base level}) \end{cases}$$

INTERPRETATION OF MODEL PARAMETERS

β_0: μ_{11} (Mean of the combination of base levels)

β_1: $\mu_{2j} - \mu_{1j}$, for any level B_j $(j = 1, 2)$

β_2: $\mu_{3j} - \mu_{1j}$, for any level B_j $(j = 1, 2)$

β_3: $\mu_{i2} - \mu_{i1}$, for any level F_i $(i = 1, 2, 3)$

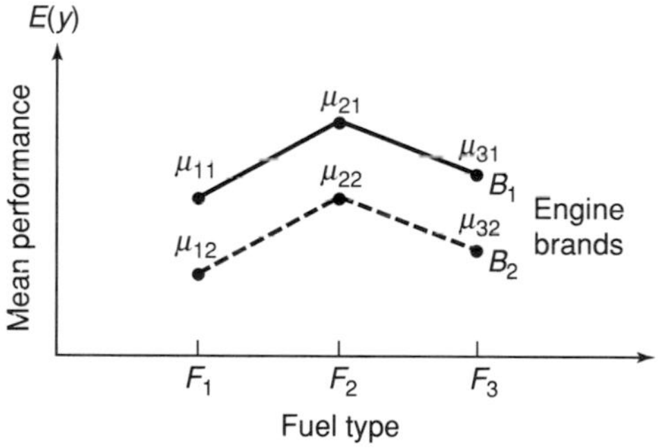

FIGURE 5.20
Main effects model: Mean response as a function of F and B when F and B affect $E(y)$ independently

If F and B do not affect $E(y)$ independently of each other, then the response function might appear as shown in Figure 5.21 (page 310). Note the difference between the mean response functions for Figures 5.20 and 5.21. When F and B affect the mean response in a dependent manner (Figure 5.21), the response functions differ for each brand. This means that you cannot study the effect of one variable on $E(y)$ without considering the level of the other. When this situation occurs, we say that the qualitative independent variables **interact**. The interaction model is shown in the box on page 310. In this example, interaction might be expected if one fuel type tends to perform better in engine B_1, whereas another performs better in engine B_2.

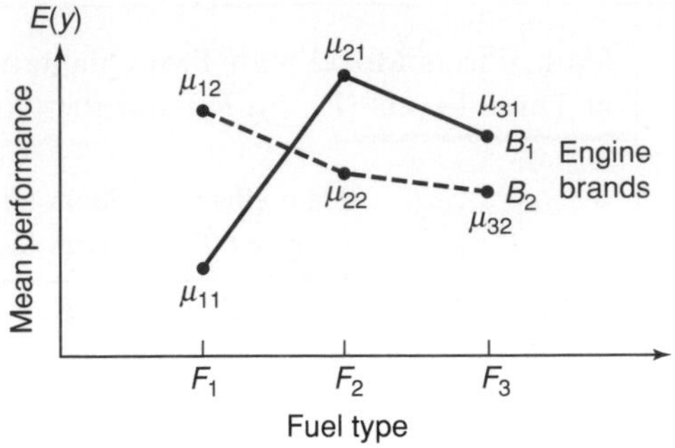

FIGURE 5.21
Interaction model: Mean response as a function of F and B when F and B interact to affect $E(y)$

Interaction Model with Two Qualitative Independent Variables, One at Three Levels (F_1, F_2, F_3) and the Other at Two Levels (B_1, B_2)

$$E(y) = \beta_0 + \overbrace{\beta_1 x_1 + \beta_2 x_2}^{\substack{\text{Main effect}\\ \text{terms for } F}} + \overbrace{\beta_3 x_3}^{\substack{\text{Main effect}\\ \text{term for } B}} + \overbrace{\beta_4 x_1 x_3 + \beta_5 x_2 x_3}^{\substack{\text{Interaction}\\ \text{terms}}}$$

where the dummy variables x_1, x_2, and x_3 are defined in the same way as for the main effects model.

INTERPRETATION OF MODEL PARAMETERS

β_0: μ_{11} (Mean of the combination of base levels)

β_1: $\mu_{21} - \mu_{11}$ (i.e., for base level B_1 only)

β_2: $\mu_{31} - \mu_{11}$ (i.e., for base level B_1 only)

β_3: $\mu_{12} - \mu_{11}$ (i.e., for base level F_1 only)

β_4: $(\mu_{22} - \mu_{12}) - (\mu_{21} - \mu_{11})$

β_5: $(\mu_{32} - \mu_{12}) - (\mu_{31} - \mu_{11})$

When qualitative independent variables interact, the model for $E(y)$ must be constructed so that it is able (if necessary) to give a different mean value, $E(y)$, for every cell in Table 5.7. We do this by adding **interaction terms** to the main effects model. These terms will involve all possible two-way cross-products between each of the two dummy variables for F, x_1, and x_2, and the one dummy variable for B, x_3. The number of interaction terms (for two independent variables) will equal the number of main effect terms for the one variable times the number of main effect terms for the other.

When F and B interact, the model contains six parameters: the two main effect terms for F, one main effect term for B, $(2)(1) = 2$ interaction terms, and β_0. This will make it possible, by assigning the various combinations of values to the dummy variables x_1, x_2, and x_3, to give six different values for $E(y)$ that will correspond to the means of the six cells of Table 5.7.

EXAMPLE 5.8

In Example 5.6, we gave the mean response when fuel F_1 was used in engine B_1, where we assumed that F and B affected $E(y)$ independently (no interaction). Now give the value of $E(y)$ for the model where F and B interact to affect $E(y)$.

Solution

When F and B interact,

$$E(y) = \beta_0 + \beta_1 x_1 + \beta_2 x_2 + \beta_3 x_3 + \beta_4 x_1 x_3 + \beta_5 x_2 x_3$$

For levels F_1 and B_1, we have agreed (according to our system of coding) to let $x_1 = x_2 = x_3 = 0$. Substituting into the equation for $E(y)$, we have

$$E(y) = \beta_0$$

(the same as for the main effects model).

EXAMPLE 5.9

In Example 5.7, we gave the mean response for fuel type F_3 and brand B_2, when F and B affected $E(y)$ independently. Now assume that F and B interact, and write a model for $E(y)$ when fuel F_3 is used in engine brand B_2.

Solution

When F and B interact,

$$E(y) = \beta_0 + \beta_1 x_1 + \beta_2 x_2 + \beta_3 x_3 + \beta_4 x_1 x_3 + \beta_5 x_2 x_3$$

To model $E(y)$ for F_3 and B_2, we set $x_1 = 0$, $x_2 = 1$, and $x_3 = 1$:

$$\begin{aligned} E(y) &= \beta_0 + \beta_1(0) + \beta_2(1) + \beta_3(1) + \beta_4(0)(1) + \beta_5(1)(1) \\ &= \beta_0 + \beta_2 + \beta_3 + \beta_5 \end{aligned}$$

This is the model for the value of μ_{32} in Table 5.7. Note the difference in $E(y)$ for the model assuming independence between F and B versus this model, which assumes interaction between F and B. The difference is β_5.

EXAMPLE 5.10

The performance, y (measured as mass burning rate per degree of crank angle), for the six combinations of fuel type and engine brand is shown in Table 5.8 (page 312). The number of test runs per combination varies from one for levels (F_1, B_2) to three for levels (F_1, B_1). A total of twelve test runs are sampled.

a. Assume the interaction between F and B is negligible. Fit the model $E(y)$ with interaction terms omitted.
b. Fit the complete model for $E(y)$ allowing for the fact that interactions might occur.
c. Use the prediction equation for the model, part **a**, to estimate the mean engine performance when fuel F_3 is used in brand B_2. Then calculate the sample

TABLE 5.8 Performance Data for Combinations of Fuel Type and Diesel Engine Brand

		BRAND	
		B_1	B_2
FUEL TYPE	F_1	65 73 68	36
	F_2	78 82	50 43
	F_3	48 46	61 62

mean for this cell of Table 5.8. Repeat for the model, part **b**. Explain the discrepancy between the sample mean for levels (F_3, B_2) and the estimate(s) obtained from one or both of the two prediction equations.

Solution

a. A portion of the SAS printout for main effects model

$$E(y) = \beta_0 + \overbrace{\beta_1x_1 + \beta_2x_2}^{\text{Main effect terms for } F} + \overbrace{\beta_3x_3}^{\text{Main effect term for } B}$$

is given in Figure 5.22. The least squares prediction equation is

$$\hat{y} = 64.5 + 6.7x_1 - 2.30x_2 - 15.8x_3$$

b. The SAS printout for the complete model is given in Figure 5.23. Recall that the complete model is

$$E(y) = \beta_0 + \beta_1x_1 + \beta_2x_2 + \beta_3x_3 + \beta_4x_1x_3 + \beta_5x_2x_3$$

The least squares prediction equation is

$$\hat{y} = 68.7 + 11.3x_1 - 21.7x_2 - 32.7x_3 - .8x_1x_3 + 47.2x_2x_3$$

c. To obtain the estimated mean response for cell (F_3, B_2), we let $x_1 = 0$, $x_2 = 1$, and $x_3 = 1$. Then, for the main effects model, we find

$$\hat{y} = 64.5 + 6.7(0) - 2.3(1) - 15.8(1) = 46.3$$

The 95% confidence interval for the true mean performance (shaded in Figure 5.22) is (27.8, 64.9).

For the complete model, we find

$$\bar{y} = 68.7 + 11.3(0) - 21.7(1) - 32.7(1) - .8(0)(1) + 47.2(1)(1)$$
$$= 61.5$$

FIGURE 5.22 SAS printout for main effects model of Example 5.10

Dependent Variable: Y

Analysis of Variance

Source	DF	Sum of Squares	Mean Square	F Value	Prob>F
Model	3	858.25758	286.08586	1.513	0.2838
Error	8	1512.40909	189.05114		
C Total	11	2370.66667			

Root MSE	13.74959	R-square	0.3620
Dep Mean	59.33333	Adj R-sq	0.1228
C.V.	23.17346		

Parameter Estimates

Variable	DF	Parameter Estimate	Standard Error	T for H0: Parameter=0	Prob > |T|
INTERCEP	1	64.454545	7.18048751	8.976	0.0001
X1	1	6.704545	9.94093481	0.674	0.5190
X2	1	-2.295455	9.94093481	-0.231	0.8232
X3	1	-15.818182	8.29131279	-1.908	0.0928

Obs	FUELBRND	Dep Var Y	Predict Value	Std Err Predict	Lower95% Mean	Upper95% Mean	Residual
1	F1B1	65.0000	64.4545	7.180	47.8962	81.0129	0.5455
2	F1B1	73.0000	64.4545	7.180	47.8962	81.0129	8.5455
3	F1B1	68.0000	64.4545	7.180	47.8962	81.0129	3.5455
4	F1B2	36.0000	48.6364	9.270	27.2596	70.0132	-12.6364
5	F2B1	78.0000	71.1591	8.028	52.6462	89.6719	6.8409
6	F2B1	82.0000	71.1591	8.028	52.6462	89.6719	10.8409
7	F2B2	50.0000	55.3409	8.028	36.8281	73.8538	-5.3409
8	F2B2	43.0000	55.3409	8.028	36.8281	73.8538	-12.3409
9	F3B1	48.0000	62.1591	8.028	43.6462	80.6719	-14.1591
10	F3B1	46.0000	62.1591	8.028	43.6462	80.6719	-16.1591
11	F3B2	61.0000	46.3409	8.028	27.8281	64.8538	14.6591
12	F3B2	62.0000	46.3409	8.028	27.8281	64.8538	15.6591

Sum of Residuals	2.131628E-14
Sum of Squared Residuals	1512.4091
Predicted Resid SS (Press)	3615.3752

The 95% confidence interval for true mean performance (shaded in Figure 5.23) is (55.7, 67.3). The mean for the cell (F_3, B_2) in Table 5.8 is

$$\bar{y}_{32} = \frac{61 + 62}{2} = 61.5$$

which is precisely what is estimated by the complete (interaction) model. However, the main effects model yields a different estimate, 46.4. The reason for the discrepancy is that the main effects model assumes the two qualitative independent variables affect $E(y)$ independently of each other. That is, the change in $E(y)$ produced by a change in levels of one variable is the same regardless of the level of the other variable. In contrast, the complete model contains six parameters $(\beta_0, \beta_1, \ldots, \beta_5)$ to describe the six cell populations, so that each population cell mean will be estimated by its sample mean. Thus, the complete model estimate for any cell mean is equal to the observed (sample) mean for that cell.

FIGURE 5.23 SAS printout for interaction model of Example 5.10

Dependent Variable: Y

Analysis of Variance

Source	DF	Sum of Squares	Mean Square	F Value	Prob>F
Model	5	2303.00000	460.60000	40.841	0.0001
Error	6	67.66667	11.27778		
C Total	11	2370.66667			

Root MSE	3.35824	R-square	0.9715
Dep Mean	59.33333	Adj R-sq	0.9477
C.V.	5.65996		

Parameter Estimates

Variable	DF	Parameter Estimate	Standard Error	T for H0: Parameter=0	Prob > |T|
INTERCEP	1	68.666667	1.93888093	35.416	0.0001
X1	1	11.333333	3.06563992	3.697	0.0101
X2	1	-21.666667	3.06563992	-7.068	0.0004
X3	1	-32.666667	3.87776186	-8.424	0.0002
X1X3	1	-0.833333	5.12979676	-0.162	0.8763
X2X3	1	47.166667	5.12979676	9.195	0.0001

Obs	FUELBRND	Dep Var Y	Predict Value	Std Err Predict	Lower95% Mean	Upper95% Mean	Residual
1	F1B1	65.0000	68.6667	1.939	63.9224	73.4109	-3.6667
2	F1B1	73.0000	68.6667	1.939	63.9224	73.4109	4.3333
3	F1B1	68.0000	68.6667	1.939	63.9224	73.4109	-0.6667
4	F1B2	36.0000	36.0000	3.358	27.7827	44.2173	-355E-16
5	F2B1	78.0000	80.0000	2.375	74.1895	85.8105	-2.0000
6	F2B1	82.0000	80.0000	2.375	74.1895	85.8105	2.0000
7	F2B2	50.0000	46.5000	2.375	40.6895	52.3105	3.5000
8	F2B2	43.0000	46.5000	2.375	40.6895	52.3105	-3.5000
9	F3B1	48.0000	47.0000	2.375	41.1895	52.8105	1.0000
10	F3B1	46.0000	47.0000	2.375	41.1895	52.8105	-1.0000
11	F3B2	61.0000	61.5000	2.375	55.6895	67.3105	-0.5000
12	F3B2	62.0000	61.5000	2.375	55.6895	67.3105	0.5000

Sum of Residuals	2.131628E-14
Sum of Squared Residuals	67.6667
Predicted Resid SS (Press)	213.5000

Example 5.10 demonstrates an important point. If we were to ignore the least squares analysis and calculate the six sample means of Table 5.8 directly, we would obtain estimates of $E(y)$ exactly the same as those obtained by a least squares analysis for the case where the interaction between F and B is assumed to exist. We would not obtain the same estimates if the model assumes that interaction does not exist.

Also, the estimates of means raise important questions. Do the data provide sufficient evidence to indicate that F and B interact? For our example, does the effect of fuel type on diesel engine performance depend on which engine brand is used? The plot of all six sample means, shown in Figure 5.24, seems to indicate interaction, since fuel types F_1 and F_2 appear to operate more effectively in engine brand B_1, whereas the mean performance of F_3 is higher in brand B_2. Can these sample facts be reliably generalized to conclusions about the populations?

To answer this question, we will want to perform a test for interaction between the two qualitative independent variables, fuel type and engine brand. Since allowance for interaction between fuel type and brand in the complete model was provided by the addition of the terms $\beta_4 x_1 x_3$ and $\beta_5 x_2 x_3$, it follows that the null hypothesis that the independent variables fuel type and brand do not interact is equivalent to the hypothesis that the terms $\beta_4 x_1 x_3$ and $\beta_5 x_2 x_3$ are not needed in the model for $E(y)$—or equivalently, that $\beta_4 = \beta_5 = 0$. Conversely, the alternative hypothesis that fuel type and brand do interact is equivalent to stating that at least one of the two parameters, β_4 or β_5, differs from 0.

FIGURE 5.24
Graph of sample means for engine performance example

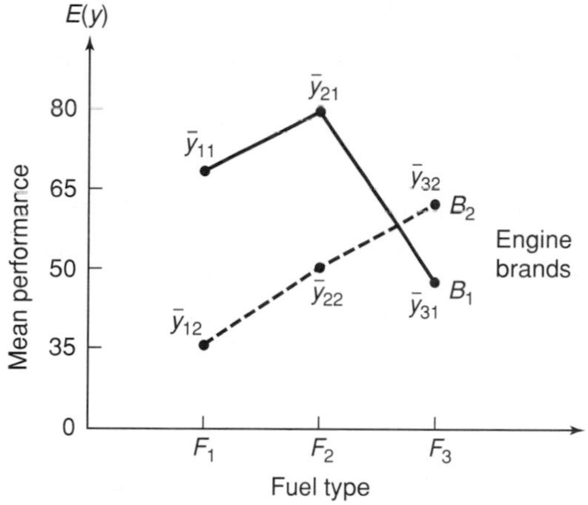

The appropriate procedure for testing a portion of the model parameters, a nested model F test, was discussed in Section 4.10. The F test is carried out as follows:

H_0: $\beta_4 = \beta_5 = 0$

H_a: At least one of β_4 and β_5 differs from 0.

Test statistic: $F = \dfrac{(\text{SSE}_R - \text{SSE}_C)/g}{\text{SSE}_C/[n - (k + 1)]}$

where

SSE_R = SSE for reduced model (main effects model)

SSE_C = SSE for complete model (interaction model)

g = Number of β's tested

= Numerator df for the F statistic

$n - (k + 1)$ = df for error for complete model

= Denominator df for the F statistic

For this example, we have

$$\text{SSE}_R = 1{,}512.41 \quad (\text{see Figure 5.22})$$
$$\text{SSE}_C = 67.67 \quad (\text{see Figure 5.23})$$
$$g = 2 \quad \text{and} \quad n - (k + 1) = 6$$

Then

$$\begin{aligned} F &= \frac{(1{,}512.41 - 67.67)/2}{67.67/6} \\ &= \frac{722.37}{11.28} \\ &= 64.04 \end{aligned}$$

The critical value of F for $\alpha = .05$, $\nu_1 = 2$, and $\nu_2 = 6$ is (from Table 4 of Appendix C) $F_{.05} = 5.14$. Therefore,

Rejection region: $F > 5.14$

Since the calculated $F = 64.04$ exceeds 5.14, we are confident (at $\alpha = .05$) in concluding that the interaction terms contribute to the prediction of y, engine performance. Equivalently, there is sufficient evidence to conclude that factors F and B do interact.

EXERCISES

5.18 Refer to the *Environmental Science & Technology* study of sorption of organic vapors, Exercise 4.31. Consider using the qualitative variable, organic compound, as a predictor of the retention coefficient y. Recall that five organic compounds were studied: benzene, toluene, chloroform, methanol, and anisole.

a. Write a model for $E(y)$ as a function of organic compound at two levels.

b. Interpret the β parameters in the model.

c. Explain how to test for differences among the mean retention coefficients of the five organic compounds.

5.19 According to the U.S. Department of Labor, the percentage of married women participating in the work force reached 56% in 1987. How does the employment status of wives affect their husbands' well-being? A study reported in the *Academy of Management* (Mar. 1989) addressed this issue by fitting the model $E(y) = \beta_0 + \beta_1 x$ to data collected for $n = 413$ professional accountants, where y = husband's job satisfaction (measured on a 5-point scale) and x is a dummy variable for employment status of wife (1 = employed, 0 = unemployed).

a. The estimate of β_1 was negative and statistically significant at $\alpha = .01$. Interpret these results.

b. The value of the coefficient of determination was $R^2 = .02$. Interpret this result.

5.20 Because of the hot, humid weather conditions in Florida, the growth rates of beef cattle and the milk production of dairy cows typically decline during the summer. However, agricultural and environmental engineers have found that a well-designed shade structure can significantly increase the milk production of dairy cows. In one experiment, 30 cows were selected and divided into three groups of 10 cows each. Group 1 cows were provided with a man-made shade structure, group 2 cows with tree shade, and group 3 cows with no shade. Of interest was the mean milk production (in gallons) of the cows in each group.

a. Identify the independent variables in the experiment.
b. Write a model relating the mean milk production, $E(y)$, to the independent variables. Identify and code all dummy variables.
c. Interpret the β parameters of the model.

5.21 Each semester, the University of Florida's Career Resource Center collects information on the job status and starting salary of graduating seniors. Data collected over the period 1989–1991 included 902 seniors who had found employment at the time of graduation. This information was used to model starting salary y as a function of two qualitative independent variables: college at five levels (Business Administration, Engineering, Liberal Arts & Sciences, Journalism, and Nursing) and gender at two levels (male and female). A main effects model relating starting salary, y, to both college and gender is

$$E(y) = \beta_0 + \beta_1 x_1 + \beta_2 x_2 + \beta_3 x_3 + \beta_4 x_4 + \beta_5 x_5$$

where

$$x_1 = \begin{cases} 1 & \text{if Business Administration} \\ 0 & \text{if not} \end{cases} \qquad x_2 = \begin{cases} 1 & \text{if Engineering} \\ 0 & \text{if not} \end{cases}$$

$$x_3 = \begin{cases} 1 & \text{if Liberal Arts \& Sciences} \\ 0 & \text{if not} \end{cases} \qquad x_4 = \begin{cases} 1 & \text{if Journalism} \\ 0 & \text{if not} \end{cases}$$

$$x_5 = \begin{cases} 1 & \text{if female} \\ 0 & \text{if male} \end{cases}$$

a. Write the equation relating mean starting salary, $E(y)$, to college, for male graduates only.
b. Interpret β_1 in the model, part **a**.
c. Interpret β_2 in the model, part **a**.
d. Interpret β_3 in the model, part **a**.
e. Interpret β_4 in the model, part **a**.
f. Write the equation relating mean starting salary, $E(y)$, to college, for female graduates only.
g. Interpret β_1 in the model, part **f**. Compare to your answer, part **b**.
h. Interpret β_2 in the model, part **f**. Compare to your answer, part **c**.
i. Interpret β_3 in the model, part **f**. Compare to your answer, part **d**.
j. Interpret β_4 in the model, part **f**. Compare to your answer, part **e**.
k. For a given college, interpret the value of β_5 in the model.
l. A SAS printout of the multiple regression analysis is displayed on page 318. Interpret the results. Part of your answer should include a statement about whether gender has an effect on average starting salary.

SAS printout for Exercise 5.21

```
Dependent Variable: SALARY

                         Analysis of Variance

                           Sum of         Mean
Source           DF       Squares        Square        F Value       Prob>F

Model             5   13609836905 2721967380.9          90.022       0.0001
Error           896   27092165483 30236791.833
C Total         901   40702002387

    Root MSE     5498.79913       R-square        0.3344
    Dep Mean    26020.20510       Adj R-sq        0.3307
    C.V.           21.13280

                         Parameter Estimates

                  Parameter        Standard     T for H0:
Variable  DF       Estimate           Error    Parameter=0    Prob > |T|

INTERCEP   1          29215    739.33031785         39.515        0.0001
X1         1   -3928.938467    731.13739384         -5.374        0.0001
X2         1    1845.020611    778.46344679          2.370        0.0180
X3         1   -8375.343226    902.00089218         -9.285        0.0001
X4         1   -7349.696165    795.38316872         -9.240        0.0001
X5         1   -1142.171471    419.57634068         -2.722        0.0066
```

5.22 Refer to Exercise 5.21.

a. Write an interaction model relating starting salary, y, to both college and gender. Use the dummy variables assignments made in Exercise 5.21.
b. Interpret β_1 in the model, part **a**.
c. Interpret β_2 in the model, part **a**.
d. Interpret β_3 in the model, part **a**.
e. Interpret β_4 in the model, part **a**.
f. Interpret β_5 in the model, part **a**.
g. Explain how to test to determine whether the difference between the mean starting salaries of male and female graduates depends on college.

5.23 The performance of an industry is often measured by the level of excess (or unutilized) capacity within the industry. Researchers examined the relationship between excess capacity y and several market variables in 273 U.S. manufacturing industries (*Quarterly Journal of Business and Economics*, Summer 1986). Two qualitative independent variables considered in the study were

Market concentration (low, moderate, and high)
Industry type (producer or consumer)

a. Write the main effects model for $E(y)$ as a function of the two qualitative variables.
b. Interpret the β coefficients in the main effects model.
c. Write the model for $E(y)$ that includes interaction between market concentration and industry type.
d. Interpret the β coefficients in the interaction model.
e. How would you test the hypothesis that the difference between the mean excess capacity levels of producer and consumer industry types is the same across all three market concentrations?

5.9 Models with Three or More Qualitative Independent Variables

We construct models with three or more qualitative independent variables in the same way that we construct models for two qualitative independent variables, except that we must add three-way interaction terms if we have three qualitative independent variables, three-way and four-way interaction terms for four independent variables, and so on. In this section, we will explain what we mean by three-way, four-way, etc., interactions, and we will demonstrate the procedure for writing the model for any number, say, k, of qualitative independent variables. The pattern used to write the model is shown in the box.

> **Pattern of the Model Relating $E(y)$ to k Qualitative Independent Variables**
>
> $E(y) = \beta_0$ + Main effect terms for all independent variables
> + All two-way interaction terms between pairs of independent variables
> + All three-way interaction terms between different groups of three independent variables
> +
> ⋮
> + All k-way interaction terms for the k independent variables

Recall that a two-way interaction term is formed by multiplying the dummy variable associated with one of the main effect terms of one (call it the first) independent variable by the dummy variable from a main effect term of another (the second) independent variable. Three-way interaction terms are formed in a similar way, by forming the product of three dummy variables, one from a main effect term from each of the three independent variables. Similarly, four-way interaction terms are formed by taking the product of four dummy variables, one from a main effect term from each of four independent variables. We will illustrate with three examples.

EXAMPLE 5.11

Suppose you have three qualitative independent variables, the first at three levels, A_1, A_2, and A_3, the second at three levels, B_1, B_2, and B_3, and the third at two levels, C_1 and C_2. Write a model for $E(y)$ that includes all main effect and interaction terms for the independent variables.

Solution

First write a model containing the main effect terms for the three variables:

$$E(y) = \beta_0 + \overbrace{\beta_1x_1 + \beta_2x_2}^{\text{Main effect terms for } A} + \overbrace{\beta_3x_3 + \beta_4x_4}^{\text{Main effect terms for } B} + \overbrace{\beta_5x_5}^{\text{Main effect term for } C}$$

where

$$x_1 = \begin{cases} 1 & \text{if level } A_2 \\ 0 & \text{if not} \end{cases} \qquad x_3 = \begin{cases} 1 & \text{if level } B_2 \\ 0 & \text{if not} \end{cases} \qquad x_5 = \begin{cases} 1 & \text{if level } C_2 \\ 0 & \text{if not} \end{cases}$$

$$x_2 = \begin{cases} 1 & \text{if level } A_3 \\ 0 & \text{if not} \end{cases} \qquad x_4 = \begin{cases} 1 & \text{if level } B_3 \\ 0 & \text{if not} \end{cases}$$

The next step is to add two-way interaction terms. These will be of three types—those for the interaction between A and B, between A and C, and between B and C. Thus,

$$E(y) = \beta_0 + \overbrace{\beta_1 x_1 + \beta_2 x_2}^{\substack{\text{Main effect} \\ A}} + \overbrace{\beta_3 x_3 + \beta_4 x_4}^{\substack{\text{Main effect} \\ B}} + \overbrace{\beta_5 x_5}^{\substack{\text{Main effect} \\ C}}$$
$$+ \overbrace{\beta_6 x_1 x_3 + \beta_7 x_1 x_4 + \beta_8 x_2 x_3 + \beta_9 x_2 x_4}^{AB \text{ interaction terms}}$$
$$+ \overbrace{\beta_{10} x_1 x_5 + \beta_{11} x_2 x_5}^{AC \text{ interaction terms}}$$
$$+ \overbrace{\beta_{12} x_3 x_5 + \beta_{13} x_4 x_5}^{BC \text{ interaction terms}}$$

Finally, since there are three independent variables, we must include terms for the interaction of A, B, and C. These terms are formed as the products of dummy variables, one from each of the A, B, and C main effect terms. The complete model for $E(y)$ is

$$E(y) = \beta_0 + \overbrace{\beta_1 x_1 + \beta_2 x_2}^{\substack{\text{Main effect} \\ A}} + \overbrace{\beta_3 x_3 + \beta_4 x_4}^{\substack{\text{Main effect} \\ B}} + \overbrace{\beta_5 x_5}^{\substack{\text{Main effect} \\ C}}$$
$$+ \overbrace{\beta_6 x_1 x_3 + \beta_7 x_1 x_4 + \beta_8 x_2 x_3 + \beta_9 x_2 x_4}^{AB \text{ interaction terms}}$$
$$+ \overbrace{\beta_{10} x_1 x_5 + \beta_{11} x_2 x_5}^{AC \text{ interaction terms}}$$
$$+ \overbrace{\beta_{12} x_3 x_5 + \beta_{13} x_4 x_5}^{BC \text{ interaction terms}}$$
$$+ \overbrace{\beta_{14} x_1 x_3 x_5 + \beta_{15} x_1 x_4 x_5 + \beta_{16} x_2 x_3 x_5 + \beta_{17} x_2 x_4 x_5}^{\text{Three-way } ABC \text{ interaction terms}}$$

Note that the complete model in Example 5.11 contains 18 parameters, one for each of the $3 \times 3 \times 2$ combinations of levels for A, B, and C. There are 18 linearly independent linear combinations of these parameters, *one corresponding to each of the means of the* $3 \times 3 \times 2$ *combinations of levels of A, B, and C.* We illustrate with an example.

EXAMPLE 5.12

Refer to Example 5.11 and give the expression for the mean value of y for observations taken at the second level of A, the first level of B, and the second level of C, i.e., at (A_2, B_1, C_2).

Solution

Check the coding for the dummy variables (given in Example 5.11) and you will see that they assume the following values:

$$\text{For level } A_2\text{:} \quad x_1 = 1, \quad x_2 = 0$$
$$\text{For level } B_1\text{:} \quad x_3 = 0, \quad x_4 = 0$$
$$\text{For level } C_2\text{:} \quad x_5 = 1$$

Substituting these values into the expression for $E(y)$, we obtain

$$\begin{aligned} E(y) = {} & \beta_0 + \beta_1(1) + \beta_2(0) + \beta_3(0) + \beta_4(0) + \beta_5(1) \\ & + \beta_6(1)(0) + \beta_7(1)(0) + \beta_8(0)(0) + \beta_9(0)(0) \\ & + \beta_{10}(1)(1) + \beta_{11}(0)(1) + \beta_{12}(0)(1) + \beta_{13}(0)(1) \\ & + \beta_{14}(1)(0)(1) + \beta_{15}(1)(0)(1) + \beta_{16}(0)(0)(1) + \beta_{17}(0)(0)(1) \\ = {} & \beta_0 + \beta_1 + \beta_5 + \beta_{10} \end{aligned}$$

Thus, the mean value of y observed at levels A_2, B_1, and C_2 is $\beta_0 + \beta_1 + \beta_5 + \beta_{10}$. You could find the mean values of y for the other 17 combinations of levels of A, B, and C by substituting the appropriate values of the dummy variables into the expression for $E(y)$ in the same manner. Each of the 18 means is a unique linear combination of the 18 β parameters in the model.

EXAMPLE 5.13

Suppose you want to test the hypothesis that the three qualitative independent variables discussed in Example 5.11 do not interact, i.e., the hypothesis that the effect of any one of the variables on $E(y)$ is independent of the level settings of the other two variables. Formulate the appropriate test of hypothesis about the model parameters.

Solution

No interaction among the three qualitative independent variables implies that the main effects model,

$$E(y) = \beta_0 + \overbrace{\beta_1 x_1 + \beta_2 x_2}^{\text{Main effect } A} + \overbrace{\beta_3 x_3 + \beta_4 x_4}^{\text{Main effect } B} + \overbrace{\beta_5 x_5}^{\text{Main effect } C}$$

is appropriate for modeling $E(y)$ or, equivalently, that all interaction terms should be excluded from the model. This situation will occur if

$$\beta_6 = \beta_7 = \cdots = \beta_{17} = 0$$

Consequently, we will test the null hypothesis

$$H_0: \quad \beta_6 = \beta_7 = \cdots = \beta_{17} = 0$$

against the alternative hypothesis that at least one of these β parameters differs from 0, or equivalently, that some interaction among the independent variables exists. This statistical test was described in Section 4.10.

Of what value is this section? If you are modeling a response, say, profit of a corporation, and you believe that several qualitative independent variables affect the response, then you must know how to enter these variables into your model. You must understand the implication of the interaction (or lack of it) among a subset of independent variables and how to write the appropriate terms in the model to account for it. Failure to write a good model for your response will usually lead to inflated values of the SSE and s^2 (with a consequent loss of information), and it also can lead to biased estimates of $E(y)$ and biased predictions of y.

5.10 Models with Both Quantitative and Qualitative Independent Variables

Perhaps the most interesting data analysis problems are those that involve both quantitative and qualitative independent variables. For example, suppose mean performance of a diesel engine is a function of one qualitative independent variable, fuel type at levels F_1 and F_2, and one quantitative independent variable, engine speed in revolutions per minute (rpm). We will proceed to build a model in stages, showing graphically the interpretation that we would give to the model at each stage. This will help you see the contribution of various terms in the model.

At first we assume that the qualitative independent variable has no effect on the response (i.e., the mean contribution to the response is the same for all three fuel types), but the mean performance, $E(y)$, is related to engine speed. In this case, one response curve, which might appear as shown in Figure 5.25, would be sufficient to characterize $E(y)$ for all three fuel types. The following second-order model would likely provide a good approximation to $E(y)$:

$$E(y) = \beta_0 + \beta_1 x_1 + \beta_2 x_1^2$$

where x_1 is speed in rpm. This model has some distinct disadvantages. If differences in mean performance exist for the three fuel types, they cannot be detected (because the model does not contain any parameters representing differences among fuel types). Also, the differences would inflate the SSE associated with the fitted model and consequently would increase errors of estimation and prediction.

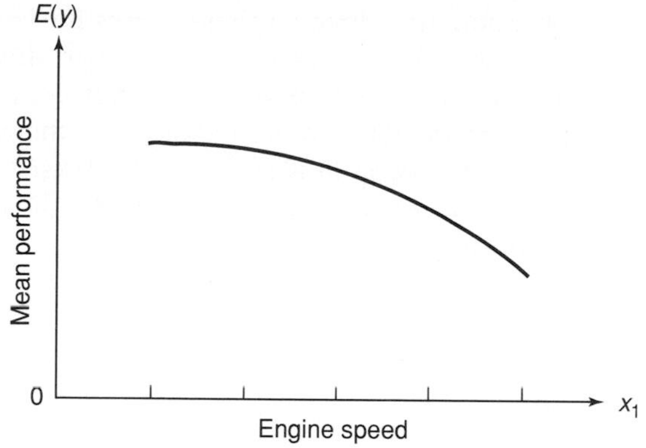

FIGURE 5.25
Model for $E(y)$ as a function of engine speed

The next stage in developing a model for $E(y)$ is to assume that the qualitative independent variable, fuel type, does affect mean performance, but the effect on $E(y)$ is independent of speed. In other words, the assumption is that the two independent variables do not interact. This model is obtained by adding main effect terms for fuel type to the second-order model we used in the first stage. Therefore, using the methods of Sections 5.7 and 5.8, we choose F_1 as the base level and add two terms to the model corresponding to levels F_2 and F_3:

$$E(y) = \beta_0 + \beta_1 x_1 + \beta_2 x_1^2 + \beta_3 x_2 + \beta_4 x_3$$

where

$$x_1 = \text{Engine speed} \qquad x_2 = \begin{cases} 1 & \text{if } F_2 \\ 0 & \text{if not} \end{cases} \qquad x_3 = \begin{cases} 1 & \text{if } F_3 \\ 0 & \text{if not} \end{cases}$$

What effect do these terms have on the graph for the response curve(s)? Suppose we want to model $E(y)$ for level E_1. Then we let $x_2 = 0$ and $x_3 = 0$. Substituting into the model equation, we have

$$\begin{aligned} E(y) &= \beta_0 + \beta_1 x_1 + \beta_2 x_1^2 + \beta_3(0) + \beta_4(0) \\ &= \beta_0 + \beta_1 x_1 + \beta_2 x_1^2 \end{aligned}$$

which would graph as a second-order curve similar to the one shown in Figure 5.25.

Now suppose that we use one of the other two fuel types, for example, F_2. Then $x_2 = 1$, $x_3 = 0$, and

$$\begin{aligned} E(y) &= \beta_0 + \beta_1 x_1 + \beta_2 x_1^2 + \beta_3(1) + \beta_4(0) \\ &= (\beta_0 + \beta_3) + \beta_1 x_1 + \beta_2 x_1^2 \end{aligned}$$

This is the equation of exactly the same parabola that we obtained for fuel type F_1 except that the y-intercept has changed from β_0 to $(\beta_0 + \beta_3)$. Similarly, the response curve for F_3 is

$$E(y) = (\beta_0 + \beta_4) + \beta_1 x_1 + \beta_2 x_1^2$$

Therefore, the three response curves for levels F_1, F_2, and F_3 (shown in Figure 5.26) are identical except that they are shifted vertically upward or downward in relation to each other. The curves depict the situation when the two independent variables do not interact; i.e., the effect of speed on mean performance is the same regardless of the fuel type used, and the effect of fuel type on mean performance is the same for all speeds (the relative distances between the curves is constant).

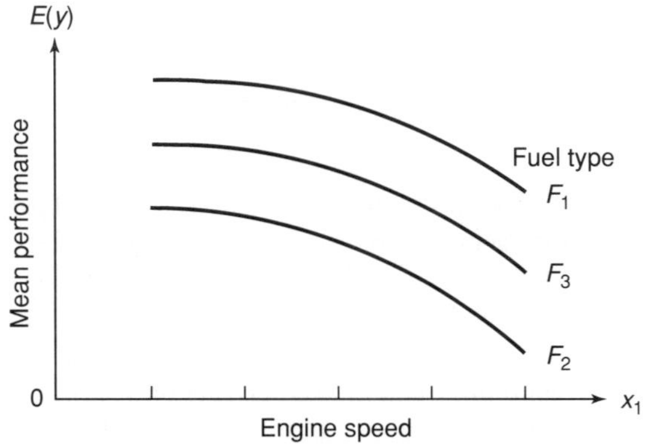

FIGURE 5.26
Model for $E(y)$ as a function of fuel type and engine speed (no interaction)

This noninteractive second-stage model has drawbacks similar to those of the simple first-stage model. It is highly unlikely that the response curves for the three fuel types would be identical except for differing y-intercepts. Because the model does not contain parameters that measure interaction between engine speed and fuel type, we cannot test to see whether a relationship exists. Also, if interaction does exist, it will cause the SSE for the fitted model to be inflated and will consequently increase the errors of estimating model parameters $E(y)$.

This leads us to the final stage of the model-building process—adding interaction terms to allow the three response curves to differ in shape:

$$E(y) = \beta_0 + \overbrace{\beta_1 x_1 + \beta_2 x_1^2}^{\substack{\text{Main effect} \\ \text{terms for} \\ \text{engine speed}}} + \overbrace{\beta_3 x_2 + \beta_4 x_3}^{\substack{\text{Main effect} \\ \text{terms for} \\ \text{fuel type}}}$$
$$+ \overbrace{\beta_5 x_1 x_2 + \beta_6 x_1 x_3 + \beta_7 x_1^2 x_2 + \beta_8 x_1^2 x_3}^{\text{Interaction terms}}$$

where

$$x_1 = \text{Engine speed} \qquad x_2 = \begin{cases} 1 & \text{if } E_2 \\ 0 & \text{if not} \end{cases} \qquad x_3 = \begin{cases} 1 & \text{if } E_3 \\ 0 & \text{if not} \end{cases}$$

Notice that this model graphs as three different second-order curves.* If fuel type F_1 is used, we substitute $x_2 = x_3 = 0$ into the formula for $E(y)$, and all but the first three terms equal 0. The result is

$$E(y) = \beta_0 + \beta_1 x_1 + \beta_2 x_1^2$$

If F_2 is used, $x_2 = 1$, $x_3 = 0$, and

$$\begin{aligned} E(y) &= \beta_0 + \beta_1 x_1 + \beta_2 x_1^2 + \beta_3(1) + \beta_4(0) \\ &\quad + \beta_5 x_1(1) + \beta_6 x_1(0) + \beta_7 x_1^2(1) + \beta_8 x_1^2(0) \\ &= (\beta_0 + \beta_3) + (\beta_1 + \beta_5)x_1 + (\beta_2 + \beta_7)x_1^2 \end{aligned}$$

The y-intercept, the coefficient of x_1, and the coefficient of x_1^2 differ from the corresponding coefficients in $E(y)$ at level F_1. Finally, when F_3 is used, $x_2 = 0$, $x_3 = 1$, and the result is

$$E(y) = (\beta_0 + \beta_4) + (\beta_1 + \beta_6)x_1 + (\beta_2 + \beta_8)x_1^2$$

A graph of the model for $E(y)$ might appear as shown in Figure 5.27. Compare this figure with Figure 5.25, where we assumed the response curves were identical for all three fuel types, and with Figure 5.26, where we assumed no interaction between the independent variables. Note in Figure 5.27 that the second-order curves may be completely different.

FIGURE 5.27
Graph of $E(y)$ as a function of fuel type and engine speed (interaction)

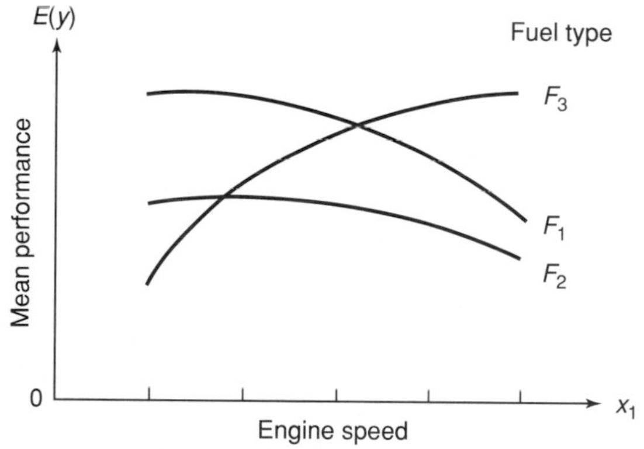

Now that you know how to write a model for two independent variables—one qualitative and one quantitative—we ask a question. Why do it? Why not write a separate second-order model for each level of fuel type where $E(y)$ is a function of engine speed only? *One reason we write the single model representing all three response curves is so that we can test to determine whether the curves are different.* For example, we might want to know whether the effect of fuel type

*Note that the model remains a second-order model for the quantitative independent variable x_1. The terms involving $x_1^2 x_2$ and $x_1^2 x_3$ appear to be third-order terms, but they are not because x_2 and x_3 are dummy variables.

depends on engine speed. Thus, one fuel type might be especially efficient at low engine speeds, but less so at high speeds. The reverse might be true for one of the other two fuel types. The hypothesis that the independent variables, fuel type and engine speed, affect the response independently of one another (a case of no interaction) is equivalent to testing the hypothesis that $\beta_5 = \beta_6 = \beta_7 = \beta_8 = 0$ [i.e., that the model in Figure 5.26 adequately characterizes $E(y)$] using the F test discussed in Section 4.10. *A second reason for writing a single model is that we obtain a pooled estimate of σ^2, the variance of the random error component ε.* If the variance of ε is truly the same for each fuel type, the pooled estimate is superior to calculating three estimates by fitting a separate model for each fuel type.

In conclusion, suppose you want to write a model relating $E(y)$ to several quantitative and qualitative independent variables. Proceed in exactly the same manner as for two independent variables, one qualitative and one quantitative. First, write the model (using the methods of Sections 5.4 and 5.5) that you want to use to describe the quantitative independent variables. Then introduce the main effect and interaction terms for the qualitative independent variables. This gives a model that represents a set of identically shaped response surfaces, one corresponding to each combination of levels of the qualitative independent variables. If you could visualize surfaces in a multidimensional space, their appearance would be analogous to the response curves of Figure 5.26. To complete the model, add terms for the interaction between the quantitative and qualitative variables. This is done by interacting *each* qualitative variable term with *every* quantitative variable term. We will demonstrate with an example.

EXAMPLE 5.14

A marine biologist wished to investigate the effects of three factors on the level of the contaminant DDT found in fish inhabiting a polluted lake. The factors were

1. Species of fish (two levels)
2. Location of capture (two levels)
3. Fish length (centimeters)

Write a model for the DDT level, y, found in contaminated fish.

Solution

The response y is affected by two qualitative factors (species and location), each at two levels, and one quantitative factor (length). Fish of each of the two species, S_1 and S_2, could be captured at each of the two locations, L_1 and L_2, giving $2 \times 2 = 4$ possible combinations—call them (S_1, L_1), (S_1, L_2), (S_2, L_1), (S_2, L_2). For each of these combinations, you would obtain a curve that graphs DDT level as a function of the quantitative factor x_1, fish length (see Figure 5.28). The stages in writing the model for the response y shown in Figure 5.28 are listed here.

STAGE 1 *Write a model relating y to the quantitative factor(s).* It is likely that an increase in the value of the single quantitative factor x_1, length, will yield an increase in DDT level. However, this increase is likely to be slower for larger

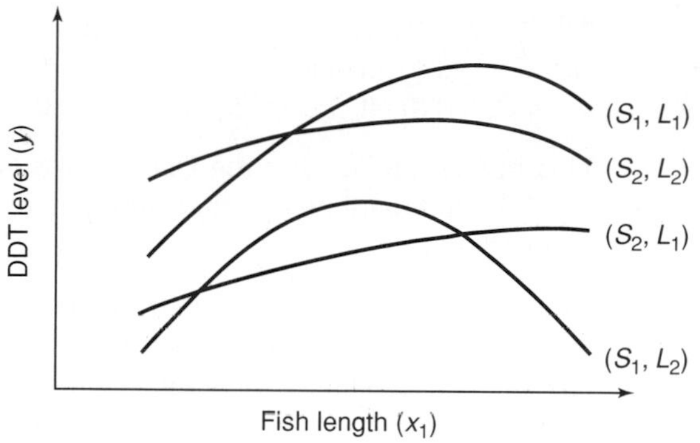

FIGURE 5.28
A graphical portrayal of three factors—two qualitative and one quantitative—on DDT level

fish, and will eventually level off once a fish reaches a certain length, thus producing the curvature shown in Figure 5.28. Consequently, we will model the mean DDT level, $E(y)$, with the second-order model

$$E(y) = \beta_0 + \beta_1 x_1 + \beta_2 x_1^2$$

This is the model we would use if we were certain that the DDT curves were identical for all species–location combinations (S_i, L_j). The model would appear as shown in Figure 5.29a.

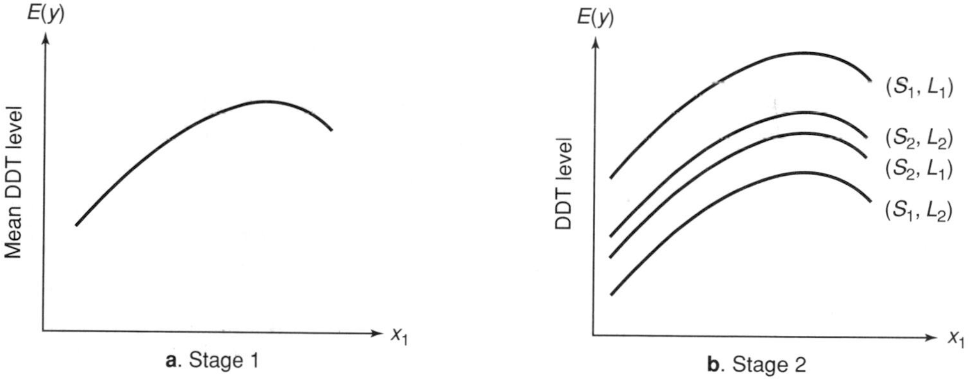

FIGURE 5.29
DDT curves for stages 1 and 2

STAGE 2 *Add the terms, both main effect and interaction, for the qualitative factors.* Thus,

$$E(y) = \beta_0 + \overbrace{\beta_1 x_1 + \beta_2 x_1^2}^{\text{Terms for quantitative factor}}$$

$$+ \overbrace{\beta_3 x_2}^{\substack{\text{Main effect}\\ S}} + \overbrace{\beta_4 x_3}^{\substack{\text{Main effect}\\ L}} + \overbrace{\beta_5 x_2 x_3}^{SL \text{ interaction}}$$

where

$$x_2 = \begin{cases} 1 & \text{if species } S_2 \\ 0 & \text{if species } S_1 \end{cases} \qquad x_3 = \begin{cases} 1 & \text{if location } L_2 \\ 0 & \text{if location } L_1 \end{cases}$$

This model implies that the DDT curves are identically shaped for each of the (S_i, L_j) combinations but that they possess different y-intercepts, as shown in Figure 5.29b.

STAGE 3 *Add terms to allow for interaction between the quantitative and qualitative factors.* This is done by interacting every pair of terms—one quantitative and one qualitative. Thus, the complete model, which graphs as four different-shaped second-order curves (see Figure 5.28), is

$$E(y) = \overbrace{\beta_0 + \beta_1 x_1 + \beta_2 x_1^2}^{\text{First-stage terms}}$$
$$+ \overbrace{\beta_3 x_2 + \beta_4 x_3 + \beta_5 x_2 x_3}^{\text{Second-stage terms}}$$
$$+ \overbrace{\beta_6 x_1 x_2 + \beta_7 x_1 x_3 + \beta_8 x_1 x_2 x_3 + \beta_9 x_1^2 x_2 + \beta_{10} x_1^2 x_3 + \beta_{11} x_1^2 x_2 x_3}^{\text{Third-stage terms}}$$

EXAMPLE 5.15

Use the model of Example 5.14 to find the equation relating $E(y)$ to x_1 for species S_1 and location L_2.

Solution

Checking the coding for the model, we see (noted at the second stage) that when DDT level y is measured on a fish of species S_1 captured at location L_2, we set $x_2 = 0$ and $x_3 = 1$. Substituting these values into the complete model, we obtain

$$\begin{aligned} E(y) &= \beta_0 + \beta_1 x_1 + \beta_2 x_1^2 \\ &\quad + \beta_3 x_2 + \beta_4 x_3 + \beta_5 x_2 x_3 \\ &\quad + \beta_6 x_1 x_2 + \beta_7 x_1 x_3 + \beta_8 x_1 x_2 x_3 + \beta_9 x_1^2 x_2 + \beta_{10} x_1^2 x_3 + \beta_{11} x_1^2 x_2 x_3 \\ &= \beta_0 + \beta_1 x_1 + \beta_2 x_1^2 \\ &\quad + \beta_3(0) + \beta_4(1) + \beta_5(0)(1) \\ &\quad + \beta_6 x_1(0) + \beta_7 x_1(1) + \beta_8 x_1(0)(1) \\ &\quad + \beta_9 x_1^2(0) + \beta_{10} x_1^2(1) + \beta_{11} x_1^2(0)(1) \\ &= (\beta_0 + \beta_4) + (\beta_1 + \beta_7)x_1 + (\beta_2 + \beta_{10})x_1^2 \end{aligned}$$

Note that this equation graphs as a portion of a parabola with y-intercept equal to $(\beta_0 + \beta_4)$. The coefficient of x_1 is $(\beta_1 + \beta_7)$, and the curvature coefficient (the coefficient of x_1^2) is $(\beta_2 + \beta_{10})$.

EXAMPLE 5.16

Suppose you have two qualitative independent variables, A and B, and A is at two levels and B is at three levels. You also have two quantitative independent variables, C and D, each at three levels. Further suppose you plan to fit a second-order response surface as a function of the quantitative independent variables C and D, and that you want your model for $E(y)$ to allow for different shapes of the second-order surfaces for the six (2×3) combinations of levels corresponding to the qualitative independent variables A and B. Write a model for $E(y)$.

Solution

STAGE 1 *Write the second-order model corresponding to the two quantitative independent variables.* If we let

$$x_1 = \text{Level for independent variable } C$$
$$x_2 = \text{Level for independent variable } D$$

then

$$E(y) = \beta_0 + \beta_1 x_1 + \beta_2 x_2 + \beta_3 x_1 x_2 + \beta_4 x_1^2 + \beta_5 x_2^2$$

This is the model you would use if you believed that the six response surfaces, corresponding to the six combinations of levels of A and B, were identical.

STAGE 2 *Add the main effect and interaction terms for the qualitative independent variables.* These are

$$\overbrace{\beta_6 x_6}^{\substack{\text{Main effect term}\\ \text{for } A}} + \overbrace{\beta_7 x_7 + \beta_8 x_8}^{\substack{\text{Main effect terms}\\ \text{for } B}} + \overbrace{\beta_9 x_6 x_7 + \beta_{10} x_6 x_8}^{\substack{AB \text{ interaction}\\ \text{terms}}}$$

$$x_6 = \begin{cases} 1 & \text{if at level } A_2 \\ 0 & \text{if not} \end{cases} \quad x_7 = \begin{cases} 1 & \text{if at level } B_2 \\ 0 & \text{if not} \end{cases} \quad x_8 = \begin{cases} 1 & \text{if at level } B_3 \\ 0 & \text{if not} \end{cases}$$

The addition of these terms to the model produces six identically shaped second-order surfaces, one corresponding to each of the six combinations of levels of A and B. They differ only in their y-intercepts.

STAGE 3 *Add terms that allow for interaction between the quantitative and qualitative independent variables.* This is done by interacting each of the five qualitative independent variable terms (both main effect and interaction) with each term (except β_0) of the quantitative first-stage model. Thus,

$$E(y) = \beta_0 + \beta_1 x_1 + \beta_2 x_2 + \beta_3 x_1 x_2 + \beta_4 x_1^2 + \beta_5 x_2^2 \quad \Big\} \text{ First-stage model}$$

$$+ \overbrace{\beta_6 x_6}^{\substack{\text{Main effect}\\ A}} + \overbrace{\beta_7 x_7 + \beta_8 x_8}^{\substack{\text{Main effect}\\ B}} + \overbrace{\beta_9 x_6 x_7 + \beta_{10} x_6 x_8}^{AB \text{ interaction}} \quad \Big\} \text{ Portion added to form second-stage model}$$

$$+ \beta_{11} x_6 x_1 + \beta_{12} x_6 x_2 + \beta_{13} x_6 x_1 x_2 + \beta_{14} x_6 x_1^2 + \beta_{15} x_6 x_2^2 \quad \Big\} \text{ Interacting } x_6 \text{ with the quantitative terms}$$

$$+ \beta_{16} x_7 x_1 + \beta_{17} x_7 x_2 + \beta_{18} x_7 x_1 x_2 + \beta_{19} x_7 x_1^2 + \beta_{20} x_7 x_2^2 \quad \Big\} \text{ Interacting } x_7 \text{ with the quantitative terms}$$

$$+ \cdots \qquad \cdots$$

$$+ \beta_{31}x_6x_8x_1 + \beta_{32}x_6x_8x_2 + \beta_{33}x_6x_8x_1x_2 + \beta_{34}x_6x_8x_1^2 + \beta_{35}x_6x_8x_2^2 \Bigg\} \begin{array}{l}\text{Interacting} \\ x_6x_8 \text{ with the} \\ \text{quantitative terms}\end{array}$$

Note that the complete model contains 36 terms, one for β_0, five needed to complete the second-order model in the two quantitative variables, five for the two qualitative variables, and $5 \times 5 = 25$ terms for the interactions between the quantitative and qualitative variables.

To see how the model gives different second-order surfaces—one for each combination of the levels of variables A and B—consider the next example.

EXAMPLE 5.17

Refer to Example 5.16. Find the response surface that portrays $E(y)$ as a function of the two quantitative independent variables C and D for the (A_1, B_2) combination of levels of the qualitative independent variables.

Solution

Checking the coding, we see that when y is observed at the first level of A (level A_1) and the second level of B (level B_2), the dummy variables take the following values: $x_6 = 0$, $x_7 = 1$, $x_8 = 0$. Substituting these values into the formula for the complete model (and deleting the terms that equal 0), we obtain

$$\begin{aligned} E(y) &= \beta_0 + \beta_1x_1 + \beta_2x_2 + \beta_3x_1x_2 + \beta_4x_1^2 + \beta_5x_2^2 + \beta_7 + \beta_{16}x_1 + \beta_{17}x_2 + \beta_{18}x_1x_2 + \beta_{19}x_1^2 + \beta_{20}x_2^2 \\ &= (\beta_0 + \beta_7) + (\beta_1 + \beta_{16})x_1 + (\beta_2 + \beta_{17})x_2 + (\beta_3 + \beta_{18})x_1x_2 + (\beta_4 + \beta_{19})x_1^2 + (\beta_5 + \beta_{20})x_2^2 \end{aligned}$$

Note that this is the equation of a second-order model for $E(y)$. It graphs the response surface for $E(y)$ when the qualitative independent variables A and B are at levels A_1 and B_2.

EXERCISES

5.24 Refer to the *Environmental Science & Technology* study of sorption of organic vapors, Exercise 5.18. The independent variables used to model the retention coefficient y are as follows:

x_1 = Temperature (degrees)

x_2 = Relative humidity (percent)

Organic compound = (benzene, toluene, chloroform, methanol, and anisole)

a. Write a first-order, main effects model for $E(y)$ as a function of temperature and organic compound. Sketch the model.

b. Interpret the β parameters of the model, part **a**.

c. Write a model for $E(y)$ as a function of relative humidity and organic compound that hypothesizes different retention–relative humidity slopes for the five compounds. Sketch the model.

d. Give the slopes of the five compounds (in terms of the β's) for the model, part **c**.

5.25 Refer to Exercise 5.24. Consider using the quantitative variable, relative humidity, and the qualitative variable, organic compound (at five levels), to model the retention coefficient y.

a. Write a complete second-order model that relates $E(y)$ to relative humidity.
b. Add the main effect terms for organic compound to the model of part **a**.
c. Add terms to the model of part **b** to allow for interaction between relative humidity and organic compound.
d. Under what circumstances will the response curves of the model of part **c** possess the same shape but have different y-intercepts?
e. Under what circumstances will the response curves of the model of part **c** be parallel lines?
f. Under what circumstances will the response curves of the model of part **c** be identical?

5.26 Eli Lilly and Company has developed three methods (G, R_1, and R_2) for estimating the shelf life of its drug products based on potency.* One way to compare the three methods is to build a regression model for the dependent variable, estimated shelf life y (as a percentage of true shelf life), with potency of the drug (x_1) as a quantitative predictor and method as a qualitative predictor.
a. Write a first-order, main effects model for $E(y)$ as a function of potency (x_1) and method.
b. Interpret the β coefficients of the model, part **a**.
c. Write a first-order model for $E(y)$ that will allow the slopes to differ for the three methods.
d. Refer to part **c**. For each method, write the slope of the y–x_1 line in terms of the β's.

5.27 An experiment was conducted to evaluate the performances of a diesel engine run on synthetic (coal-derived) and petroleum-derived fuel oil (*Journal of Energy Resources Technology*, Mar. 1990). The petroleum-derived fuel used was a number 2 diesel fuel (DF-2) obtained from Phillips Chemical Company. Two synthetic fuels were used: a blended fuel (50% coal-derived and 50% DF-2) and a blended fuel with advanced timing. The brake power (kilowatts) and fuel type were varied in test runs, and engine performance was measured. The following table gives the experimental results for the performance measure, mass burning rate per degree of crank angle.

BRAKE POWER, x_1	FUEL TYPE	MASS BURNING RATE, y
4	DF-2	13.2
4	Blended	17.5
4	Advanced Timing	17.5
6	DF-2	26.1
6	Blended	32.7
6	Advanced Timing	43.5
8	DF-2	25.9
8	Blended	46.3
8	Advanced Timing	45.6
10	DF-2	30.7
10	Blended	50.8
10	Advanced Timing	68.9
12	DF-2	32.3
12	Blended	57.1

Source: Litzinger, T. A., and Buzza, T. G. "Performance and emissions of a diesel engine using a coal-derived fuel." *Journal of Energy Resources Technology*, Vol. 112, Mar. 1990, p. 32, Table 3.

*Murphy, J. R., and Weisman, D. "Using random slopes for estimating shelf life." Paper presented at Joint Statistical Meetings, Anaheim, Calif., Aug. 1990.

a. Initially, the researchers fitted the first-order, main effects model

$$E(y) = \beta_0 + \beta_1 x_1 + \beta_2 x_2 + \beta_3 x_3$$

where

$$y = \text{Mass burning rate}$$
$$x_1 = \text{Brake power (kW)}$$
$$x_2 = \begin{cases} 1 & \text{if DF-2 fuel} \\ 0 & \text{if not} \end{cases}$$
$$x_3 = \begin{cases} 1 & \text{if blended fuel} \\ 0 & \text{if not} \end{cases}$$

Interpret the results shown in the MINITAB printout.

First-order main effects model

```
The regression equation is
Y = 13.3 + 4.36 X1 - 22.6 X2 - 7.36 X3

Predictor        Coef       Stdev    t-ratio        p
Constant       13.320       6.931       1.92    0.084
X1             4.3650      0.8057       5.42    0.000
X2            -22.600       5.464      -4.14    0.002
X3             -7.360       5.464      -1.35    0.208

s = 8.057        R-sq = 81.2%      R-sq(adj) = 75.6%

Analysis of Variance

SOURCE       DF          SS          MS          F        p
Regression    3     2807.90      935.97      14.42    0.001
Error        10      649.09       64.91
Total        13     3456.99

SOURCE       DF      SEQ SS
X1            1     1603.93
X2            1     1086.22
X3            1      117.76

Unusual Observations
Obs.       X1          Y        Fit Stdev.Fit   Residual    St.Resid
  3       4.0      17.50      30.78      4.70     -13.28      -2.03R

R denotes an obs. with a large st. resid.
```

b. The interaction model

$$E(y) = \beta_0 + \beta_1 x_1 + \beta_2 x_2 + \beta_3 x_3 + \beta_4 x_1 x_2 + \beta_5 x_1 x_3$$

was fitted using MINITAB, with the results shown in the following printout. Conduct a test to determine whether brake power and fuel type interact. Test using $\alpha = .01$.

c. Refer to the model, part **b**. Give the estimates of the slope of the y–x_1 line for each of the three fuel types.

Interaction model

```
The regression equation is
Y = - 10.8 + 7.82 X1 + 19.4 X2 + 12.8 X3 - 5.68 X1X2 - 2.95 X1X3

Predictor        Coef        Stdev    t-ratio        p
Constant      -10.830        8.277      -1.31    0.227
X1              7.815        1.126       6.94    0.000
X2              19.35        10.69       1.81    0.108
X3              12.79        10.69       1.20    0.266
X1X2           -5.675        1.380      -4.11    0.003
X1X3           -2.950        1.380      -2.14    0.065

s = 5.037        R-sq = 94.1%      R-sq(adj) = 90.5%

Analysis of Variance

SOURCE        DF          SS          MS          F        p
Regression     5     3253.98      650.80      25.65    0.000
Error          8      203.01       25.38
Total         13     3456.99

SOURCE        DF      SEQ SS
X1             1     1603.93
X2             1     1086.22
X3             1      117.76
X1X2           1      330.04
X1X3           1      116.03
```

5.28 Refer to the *Journal of Human Stress* study of firefighters, Exercise 5.3. It is thought that the following complete second-order model will be adequate to describe the relationship between emotional distress and years of experience for two groups of firefighters—those exposed to a chemical fire and those unexposed.*

$$E(y) = \beta_0 + \beta_1 x_1 + \beta_2 x_1^2 + \beta_3 x_2 + \beta_4 x_1 x_2 + \beta_5 x_1^2 x_2$$

where

y = Emotional distress

x_1 = Experience (years)

$$x_2 = \begin{cases} 1 & \text{if exposed to chemical fire} \\ 0 & \text{if not} \end{cases}$$

a. What hypothesis would you test to determine whether the *rate* of increase of emotional distress with experience is different for the two groups of firefighters?

b. What hypothesis would you test to determine whether there are differences in mean emotional distress levels that are attributable to exposure group?

c. A portion of the SAS printout that results from fitting the second-order model to a sample of 200 firefighters is shown at the top of page 334.

*In practice, we would include other variables in the model. We include only two here to simplify the exercise.

Second-order model

Analysis of Variance

Source	DF	Sum of Squares	Mean Square	F Value	Prob>F
Model	5	2351.70	470.34	116.42	0.0001
Error	194	783.90	4.04		
C Total	199	3135.60			

Root MSE	2.0102	R-square	0.7500
Dep Mean	24.221	Adj R-sq	0.7436
C.V.	8.299		

The reduced model $E(y) = \beta_0 + \beta_1 x_1 + \beta_2 x_1^2$ is fitted to the same data, and the resulting computer printout is reproduced here. Is there sufficient evidence to support the claim that the mean emotional distress levels differ for the two groups of firefighters? Use $\alpha = .05$.

Reduced model

Analysis of Variance

Source	DF	Sum of Squares	Mean Square	F Value	Prob>F
Model	2	2340.37	1170.185	289.87	0.0001
Error	197	795.23	4.037		
C Total	199	3135.60			

Root MSE	2.0092	R-square	0.7464
Dep Mean	24.221	Adj R-sq	0.7438
C.V.	8.295		

5.29 Research conducted at Ohio State University focused on the factors that influence the allocation of black and white men in labor market positions (*American Sociological Review*, June 1986). Data collected for each of 837 labor market positions were used to build a regression model for y, defined as the natural logarithm of the ratio of the proportion of blacks employed in a labor market position to the corresponding proportion of whites employed (called the *black–white log odds ratio*). Positive values of y indicate that blacks have a greater likelihood of employment than whites. Several independent variables were considered, including the following:

x_1 = Market power (a quantitative measure of the size and visibility of firms in the labor market)

x_2 = Percentage of workers in the labor market who are union members

$$x_3 = \begin{cases} 1 & \text{if labor market position includes craft occupations} \\ 0 & \text{if not} \end{cases}$$

a. Write the first-order main effects model for $E(y)$ as a function of x_1, x_2, and x_3.

b. One theory hypothesized by the researchers is that the mean log odds ratio $E(y)$ is smaller for craft occupations than for noncraft occupations. (That is, the likelihood of black employment is less for craft occupations.) Explain how to test this hypothesis using the model in part **a**.

c. Write the complete second-order model for $E(y)$ as a function of x_1, x_2, and x_3.

d. Using the model in part **c**, explain how to test the hypothesis that level of market power x_1 has no effect on black–white log odds ratio y.

e. Consider the model

$$E(y) = \beta_0 + \beta_1 x_1 + \beta_2 x_2 + \beta_3 x_3 + \beta_4 x_1 x_3 + \beta_5 x_2 x_3$$

Holding the percentage of union members x_2 fixed, sketch the proposed contour lines for the relationship between log odds ratio y and market power x_1.

5.30 Since glass is not subject to radiation damage, encapsulation of waste in glass is considered to be one of the most promising solutions to the problem of low-level nuclear waste in the environment. However, glass undergoes chemical changes when exposed to extreme environmental conditions, and certain of its constituents can leach into the surroundings. In addition, these chemical reactions may weaken the glass. These concerns led to a study undertaken jointly by the Department of Materials Science and Engineering at the University of Florida and the U.S. Department of Energy to assess the utility of glass as a waste encapsulant material.* Corrosive chemical solutions (called corrosion baths) were prepared and applied directly to glass samples containing one of three types of waste (TDS-3A, FE, and AL); the chemical reactions were observed over time. A few of the key variables measured were

y = Amount of silicon (in parts per million) found in solution at end of experiment. (This is both a measure of the degree of breakdown in the glass and a proxy for the amount of radioactive species released into the environment.)

x_1 = Temperature (°C) of the corrosion bath

$$x_2 = \begin{cases} 1 & \text{if waste type TDS-3A} \\ 0 & \text{if not} \end{cases} \qquad x_3 = \begin{cases} 1 & \text{if waste type FE} \\ 0 & \text{if not} \end{cases}$$

Waste type AL is the base level. Suppose we want to model amount y of silicon as a function of temperature (x_1) and type of waste (x_2, x_3).

a. Write a model that proposes parallel straight-line relationships between amount of silicon and temperature, one line for each of the three waste types.

b. Add terms for the interaction between temperature and waste type to the model of part **a**.

c. Refer to the model of part **b**. For each waste type, give the slope of the line relating amount of silicon to temperature.

d. Explain how you could test for the presence of temperature–waste type interaction.

5.11 Model Building: An Example

We illustrate the modeling techniques outlined in this chapter with an example based, in part, on an actual trucking deregulation study. Consider the problem of modeling the price charged for motor transport service (such as trucking) in a particular state. In the early 1980s, several states removed regulatory constraints on the rate charged for intrastate trucking services. (Florida was the first state to embark on a deregulation policy, on July 1, 1980.) One of the goals of the regression analysis is to assess the impact of state deregulation on the supply price y charged per ton-mile.

Suppose that after a careful variable-screening process (for example, stepwise regression), the following independent variables were selected as the best predictors of supply price:

1. Distance shipped (hundreds of miles)
2. Weight of product shipped (thousands of pounds)

*The background information for this exercise was provided by Dr. David Clark, Department of Materials Science and Engineering, University of Florida.

3. Deregulation in effect (yes or no)
4. Size of market destination (large or small)

Distance shipped and weight of product are quantitative variables since they each assume numerical values (miles and pounds, respectively) corresponding to the points on a line. Deregulation and market size are qualitative, or categorical, variables that we must describe with dummy (or coded) variables. The variable assignments are given as follows:

$$x_1 = \text{Distance shipped}$$
$$x_2 = \text{Weight of product}$$
$$x_3 = \begin{cases} 1 & \text{if deregulation in effect} \\ 0 & \text{if not} \end{cases}$$
$$x_4 = \begin{cases} 1 & \text{if large market} \\ 0 & \text{if small market} \end{cases}$$

Note that in defining the dummy variables, we have arbitrarily chosen "no" and "small" to be the base levels of deregulation and market size, respectively.

We will begin the model-building process by specifying the three models shown here. Notice that the first model specified is the complete second-order model. Recall from Section 5.10 that the complete second-order model contains quadratic (curvature) terms for quantitative variables and interactions among the quantitative and qualitative terms. For this example, the complete second-order model (model 1) traces a parabolic surface for mean price $E(y)$ as a function of distance (x_1) and weight (x_2), and the response surfaces differ for the $2 \times 2 = 4$ combinations of the levels of deregulation and market size. Generally, the complete second-order model is a good place to start the model-building process since most real-world relationships are curvilinear. (Keep in mind, however, that you must have a sufficient number of data points to find estimates of all the parameters in the model.)

MODEL 1
$$\begin{aligned} E(y) = \beta_0 &+ \beta_1x_1 + \beta_2x_2 + \beta_3x_1x_2 + \beta_4x_1^2 + \beta_5x_2^2 \quad \} \text{ Stage 1 terms} \\ &+ \beta_6x_3 + \beta_7x_4 + \beta_8x_3x_4 \quad \} \text{ Stage 2 terms} \\ &\left.\begin{aligned} &+ \beta_9x_1x_3 + \beta_{10}x_1x_4 + \beta_{11}x_1x_3x_4 \\ &+ \beta_{12}x_2x_3 + \beta_{13}x_2x_4 + \beta_{14}x_2x_3x_4 \\ &+ \beta_{15}x_1x_2x_3 + \beta_{16}x_1x_2x_4 + \beta_{17}x_1x_2x_3x_4 \\ &+ \beta_{18}x_1^2x_3 + \beta_{19}x_1^2x_4 + \beta_{20}x_1^2x_3x_4 \\ &+ \beta_{21}x_2^2x_3 + \beta_{22}x_2^2x_4 + \beta_{23}x_2^2x_3x_4 \end{aligned}\right\} \text{ Stage 3 terms} \end{aligned}$$

MODEL 2
$$\begin{aligned} E(y) = \beta_0 &+ \beta_1x_1 + \beta_2x_2 + \beta_3x_1x_2 \quad \} \text{ Stage 1 terms} \\ &+ \beta_4x_3 + \beta_5x_4 + \beta_6x_3x_4 \quad \} \text{ Stage 2 terms} \\ &\left.\begin{aligned} &+ \beta_7x_1x_3 + \beta_8x_1x_4 + \beta_9x_1x_3x_4 \\ &+ \beta_{10}x_2x_3 + \beta_{11}x_2x_4 + \beta_{12}x_2x_3x_4 \\ &+ \beta_{13}x_1x_2x_3 + \beta_{14}x_1x_2x_4 + \beta_{15}x_1x_2x_3x_4 \end{aligned}\right\} \text{ Stage 3 terms} \end{aligned}$$

Model 2 contains all the terms of model 1 (the complete second-order model), except that the quadratic terms (terms involving x_1^2 and x_2^2) are dropped. This model also proposes four different response surfaces for the combinations of levels of deregulation and market size, but the surfaces are twisted planes (see Figure 5.10) rather than paraboloids. A direct comparison of models 1 and 2 will allow us to test for the importance of the curvature terms.

MODEL 3 $E(y) = \beta_0 + \beta_1 x_1 + \beta_2 x_2 + \beta_3 x_1 x_2 + \beta_4 x_3 + \beta_5 x_4 + \beta_6 x_3 x_4$

Model 3 is a reduction of model 2, with the quantitative–qualitative interaction terms omitted. This model assumes that the four response surfaces corresponding to the four deregulation–market size combinations, which are twisted planes, differ only with respect to the y-intercept in the space.

Data collected for $n = 132$ shipments were used to fit the models. The results are summarized in Table 5.9.

TABLE 5.9 **Trucking Deregulation Regression Results**

MODEL	SSE	R^2	df(ERROR)
1	203,570	.83	108
2	227,520	.81	116
3	395,165	.67	125

To determine whether the quadratic terms for distance (x_1) and weight (x_2), i.e., those involving x_1^2 and x_2^2, contribute information for predicting the mean supply price $E(y)$, we compare models 1 and 2 using the partial F test given in Section 4.10. If the quadratic terms are unimportant, then the β coefficients involving the x_1^2 and x_2^2 terms in model 1 (i.e., $\beta_4, \beta_5, \beta_{18}, \beta_{19}, \ldots, \beta_{23}$) will all equal 0. Thus, we test

H_0: $\beta_4 = \beta_5 = \beta_{18} = \beta_{19} = \beta_{20} = \beta_{21} = \beta_{22} = \beta_{23} = 0$

H_a: At least one of the quadratic β's differs from 0.

where the complete model is model 1 and the reduced model is model 2. The test statistic is

$$F = \frac{(\text{SSE}_2 - \text{SSE}_1)/\text{Number of } \beta \text{ parameters being tested}}{\text{SSE}_1/\text{df(Error) for model 1}}$$

$$= \frac{(227{,}520 - 203{,}570)/8}{203{,}570/108}$$

$$= \frac{2{,}993.75}{1{,}884.91} = 1.59$$

For $\alpha = .05$, $\nu_1 =$ number of β's tested (8), and $\nu_2 =$ df(Error) for model 1 (108), the critical value (from Table 4 of Appendix C) is approximately $F_{.05} = 2.02$.

Since the calculated value $F = 1.59$ does not exceed this critical value, we have insufficient evidence (at $\alpha = .05$) to conclude that the curvature terms are important predictors of supply price y. We could collect more data and retest to determine whether x_1^2 and x_2^2 contribute information for the prediction of supply price. Lacking this additional information, we will simplify our model by dropping the terms involving x_1^2 and x_2^2.*

Can we simplify the model even further by dropping the terms involving quantitative–qualitative interactions? That is, do the response surfaces for the four combinations of deregulation and market size differ only with respect to the y-intercept? If so, then the β coefficients involving the quantitative–qualitative interaction terms in model 2 ($\beta_7, \beta_8, \ldots, \beta_{15}$) will all equal 0.

We compare model 2 (now called the *complete* model) and model 3 (the *reduced* model) with another partial F test:

H_0: $\beta_7 = \beta_8 = \cdots = \beta_{15} = 0$

H_a: At least one of the quantitative–qualitative interaction β parameters differs from 0.

Test statistic:

$$F = \frac{(\text{SSE}_3 - \text{SSE}_2)/\text{Number of } \beta \text{ parameters being tested}}{\text{SSE}_2/\text{df(Error)}} = \frac{(395{,}165 - 227{,}520)/9}{227{,}520/116} = \frac{18{,}627.22}{1{,}961.38} = 9.50$$

Rejection region: $F > F_{.05} = 1.96$ (from Table 4 of Appendix C) where $\nu_1 =$ number of β's tested (9) and $\nu_2 =$ df(Error) for model 2 (116).

Since the calculated value $F = 9.50$ exceeds the critical value $F_{.05} = 1.96$, there is sufficient evidence (at $\alpha = .05$) to indicate that the quantitative–qualitative interaction terms are important. We should retain these terms in the model.

The results of the previous tests suggest that of the three models, model 2 is the best for modeling the mean supply price $E(y)$. Further testing may lead to a simpler model, however. For example, we might want to test the importance of the quantitative–quantitative interaction (x_1x_2) terms. If a partial F test reveals no evidence of interaction between x_1 and x_2, we may wish to drop terms involving x_1x_2 from the model.

A note of caution: Just as with t tests on individual β parameters, you should avoid conducting too many partial F tests. Regardless of the type of test (t test

*There is always danger in dropping terms from the model. Essentially, we are accepting H_0: $\beta_4 = \beta_5 = \beta_{18} = \cdots = \beta_{23} = 0$ when P(Type II error) $= P$(Accepting H_0 when H_0 is false) $= \beta$ is unknown. In practice, however, many researchers are willing to risk making a Type II error rather than use a more complex model for $E(y)$ when simpler models that are nearly as good as predictors (and easier to apply and interpret) are available. Note that we used a relatively large amount of data ($n = 132$) in fitting our models and that R^2 for model 2 is only 2% less than R^2 for model 1. If the quadratic terms are, in fact, important (i.e., we have made a Type II error), there is little lost in terms of explained variability in using model 2.

or F test), the more tests that are performed, the higher the overall Type I error rate will be. In practice, you should limit the number of models that you propose for $E(y)$ so that the overall Type I error rate α for conducting partial F tests remains reasonably small.*

Summary

Although this chapter on **model building** covered many topics, only experience can make you competent in this fascinating area of statistics. Successful model building requires a delicate blend of knowledge of the process being modeled, geometry, and formal statistical testing.

1. Identify the **response variable** y and the **set of independent variables**.
2. Classify each independent variable as either **quantitative** or **qualitative**.
3. Define **dummy variables** to represent the qualitative independent variables.

When the number of independent variables is manageable, we are ready to consider what level of complexity is appropriate.

4. Consider **second-order models**—those containing **two-way interactions** and **quadratic terms** in the quantitative variables. Remember that a model with no interaction terms implies that each of the independent variables affects the response independently of the other independent variables.
5. Consider **quadratic terms that add curvature** to the contour curves when $E(y)$ is plotted as a function of the independent variable.
6. Consider **coding the quantitative independent variables** in higher-order models, thereby reducing rounding error and the built-in multicollinearity problem.

Many problems can arise in regression modeling, and the intermediate steps are often tedious and frustrating. However, the end result of a careful and determined modeling effort is very rewarding—you will have a better understanding of the process and will have a predictive model for the dependent variable y.

SUPPLEMENTARY EXERCISES

[Exercises from the optional section are identified by an asterisk (*).]

5.31 Psychiatrists keep personnel files that contain important information on each client's background. The data in these files could be used to predict the probability that therapy will be successful. Identify the independent variables listed here as qualitative or quantitative.

a. Age
b. Years in therapy
c. Highest educational degree
d. Job classification
e. Marital status
f. Religious preference
g. IQ
h. Gender

*A technique suggested by Bonferroni is often applied to maintain control of the overall Type I error rate α. If p tests are to be performed, then conduct each individual test at significance level α/p. This will guarantee an overall Type I error rate less than or equal to α. For example, conducting each of $p = 5$ tests at the $.05/5 = .01$ level of significance guarantees an overall $\alpha \le .05$.

5.32 Each year *Business Week* reports the total cash compensations (salary plus bonus) for the top corporate executives in the United States. The data in the table (in thousands of dollars) were extracted from *Business Week*'s 1990 Executive Compensation Scoreboard. To compare the mean 1990 cash compensation, $E(y)$, of executives in the four groups, the following model was fitted to the data:

$$E(y) = \beta_0 + \beta_1 x_1 + \beta_2 x_2 + \beta_3 x_3$$

where

$$x_1 = \begin{cases} 1 & \text{if consumer products} \\ 0 & \text{if not} \end{cases} \qquad x_2 = \begin{cases} 1 & \text{if utilities} \\ 0 & \text{if not} \end{cases}$$

$$x_3 = \begin{cases} 1 & \text{if industrial–high tech} \\ 0 & \text{if not} \end{cases}$$

Base level = Financial services

The MINITAB printout follows the data.

CONSUMER PRODUCTS	UTILITIES	INDUSTRIAL–HIGH TECH	FINANCIAL SERVICES
1,567	1,862	2,925	3,125
3,313	1,390	3,409	4,143
2,058	1,115	1,767	4,013
25,216	1,105	4,097	6,583
4,634	1,272	3,196	3,169
5,214	2,849	4,042	5,217
20,795	1,732	2,601	3,447
9,162	1,474	8,286	4,469

Source: "Executive compensation scoreboard." *Business Week*, May 7, 1990, pp. 65–108.

```
The regression equation is
Y = 4271 + 4724 X1 - 2671 X2 - 480 X3

Predictor        Coef       Stdev    t-ratio        p
Constant         4271        1651       2.59    0.015
X1               4724        2334       2.02    0.053
X2              -2671        2334      -1.14    0.262
X3               -480        2334      -0.21    0.838

s = 4669         R-sq = 27.6%      R-sq(adj) = 19.8%

Analysis of Variance

SOURCE        DF          SS            MS          F         p
Regression     3   232505648      77501880       3.56     0.027
Error         28   610272512      21795446
Total         31   842778176

SOURCE        DF      SEQ SS
X1             1   200071984
X2             1    31510622
X3             1      923041

Unusual Observations
Obs.      X1          Y         Fit Stdev.Fit   Residual    St.Resid
  4     1.00      25216        8995      1651      16221       3.71R
  7     1.00      20795        8995      1651      11800       2.70R

R denotes an obs. with a large st. resid.
```

a. Is there sufficient evidence to indicate that the model is useful for predicting cash compensation?
b. What does the result from part **a** imply about the mean cash compensation for the four groups of executives?
c. Find a 99% confidence interval for the difference between the mean 1990 cash compensation of executives in the consumer products and financial services industries.

5.33 As a result of the dramatic decline in the cost of computer hardware, it is becoming economically feasible to build computers with thousands of processors. However, the scheduling of computer jobs on these advanced computers can be a difficult task. Parallel scheduling algorithms have been designed to solve this problem. A *parallel algorithm* is a set of scheduling instructions designed to minimize the number of tardy jobs in the system and to minimize the mean finish time of the entire job stream. Suppose three different scheduling algorithms (A, B, and C) have been proposed for minimizing the mean finish time of *n* jobs in a system with a large number of processors.

a. Write a main effects model with interaction to relate the mean finish time, $E(y)$, the number of jobs (x_1) and scheduling algorithm (A, B, or C).
b. The model of part **a** was fitted to data collected on 12 simulated systems (four systems for each of the three algorithms) with the results shown in the accompanying SAS printout. Test whether the model is useful in predicting mean finish time. Use $\alpha = .05$.

Analysis of Variance

Source	DF	Sum of Squares	Mean Square	F Value	Prob>F
Model	5	87.473	17.495	4.895	0.0394
Error	6	21.443	3.574		
C Total	11	108.916			

Root MSE	1.8905	R-square	0.8031
Dep Mean	12.604	Adj R-sq	0.6390
C.V.	14.999		

c. Write the main effects model (with no interaction) relating mean finish time to number of jobs and scheduling algorithm.
d. The main effects (reduced) model was fitted to the data and produced SSE = 38.289. Does this provide sufficient evidence at the $\alpha = .05$ level of significance to indicate that the interaction terms should be kept in the model?

5.34 During the 1970s, several industries, including the airline, trucking, natural gas, and cable television industries, were deregulated as a result of pressure from special interest groups and legislators. In the case of the airline industry, federal regulations on fares, schedules, and routes were thought to protect the airlines from price competition and generally prohibit new entry into the market. Thus, in theory, deregulation was expected to benefit consumers while having a negative impact on the airlines and their shareholders.

To test this theory, economists analyzed the impact of the airline Deregulation Act of 1978 on the security returns in the airline industry (*Quarterly Journal of Business and Economics*, Autumn 1984). Specifically, the researchers examined the daily rates of returns of a sample of airline common stocks both prior to and following deregulation.

Thirty-two airlines engaged in air transportation for at least 1 year and listed on either the New York or the American Stock Exchange were selected for analysis. For each airline, daily stock returns were recorded for each of 120 days prior to deregulation and 120 days after deregulation. Data for the total of $n = 240$ observations (days) were then used to fit the model

$$E(y) = \beta_0 + \beta_1 x_1 + \beta_2 x_2 + \beta_3 x_1 x_2$$

where

y = Daily rate of return on the airline stock

x_1 = Average daily rate of return on the market

$$x_2 = \begin{cases} 1 & \text{if after deregulation} \\ 0 & \text{if prior to deregulation} \end{cases}$$

Thus, 32 regression analyses were conducted, one for each airline in the sample.

a. Write the equation of the line relating daily stock return y to average daily market return x_1 prior to deregulation (i.e., when $x_2 = 0$). Identify the y-intercept and slope of the line. [The slope is used to measure the stock's systematic risk and is often called the **β risk index** or **β value** for the stock. When the β value is greater than 1, the stock is classified as an *aggressive* or *risky* security since its daily rate of return is expected to move (upward or downward) faster than the market rate of return. In contrast, when the β value is less than 1, the stock is classified as a *defensive* or *stable* security since its daily rate of return moves slower than the market. A stock with a β value near 1 is called a *neutral* security, for its daily rate of return mirrors the market.]

b. Write the equation of the line relating daily stock return y to average daily market return x_1 after deregulation (i.e., when $x_2 = 1$). Identify the y-intercept and slope of the line.

c. What hypothesis would you test to determine whether the model is adequate for predicting y?

d. What hypothesis would you test to determine whether deregulation had an effect on the measure of systematic risk (i.e., β value) associated with the airline stock? [*Hint:* Use your answers to parts **a** and **b**.]

e. Of the 32 airline stocks analyzed, 26 had significant regressions (i.e., we could reject H_0: $\beta_1 = \beta_2 = \beta_3 = 0$) at $\alpha = .10$. The least squares prediction equations for these stocks are given in the table. Identify those stocks that have significant (at $\alpha = .10$) interaction between average market rate of return x_1 and deregulation x_2. For each of these stocks, how has deregulation affected the stock's β value?

STOCK	$\hat{\beta}_0$	$\hat{\beta}_1$	$\hat{\beta}_2$	$\hat{\beta}_3$
AMR Corporation	.0005	2.8852*	−.0031	−.4106
Airborne Freight	.0024	.9748*	−.0012	−.6367*
Braniff International	.0007	1.4487*	−.0022	.5717
Canadian Pacific	.0011	.7687*	.0003	.3906
Continental Airlines	−.0021	2.1702*	.0004	−.7175*
Delta Airlines	−.0002	1.8557*	−.0005	−.6667*
Eastern Airlines	.0037	1.6353*	−.0069*	.9261*
Frontier	.0006	2.2188*	−.0033	−1.0355*
Greyhound	.0000	.3830*	.0020	.2163
Royal Dutch Airlines	.0004	1.3281	−.0024	−.5674
Lockheed Corporation	.0042	1.9337*	−.0053*	.6399
Northwest Airlines	−.0009	2.6056*	−.0005	−.1698

STOCK	$\hat{\beta}_0$	$\hat{\beta}_1$	$\hat{\beta}_2$	$\hat{\beta}_3$
Ozark Airlines	.0032	1.1591*	−.0017	−.2921
PSA Airlines	.0033	.2555*	−.0036	1.4888*
Pan American	.0012	1.2136*	−.0025	−.0146
Piedmont	.0012	1.2138*	−.0025	−.0146
Purolator, Inc.	.0009	.6829*	.0002	−.3787
Republic Airlines	.0023	.9524*	−.0031	1.3359*
Southwest Airlines	.0030	.8600*	.0016	−.2357
Tiger International	.0003	2.4979*	−.0009	−.7462*
Trans World Corp.	.0007	2.6399*	.0000	.1699
United Airlines	.0023	1.8137*	−.0039	.1444
US Air, Inc.	.0041	.8628	−.0029	1.4039*
W.A.F., Inc.	.0024	1.9271*	.0035	1.7067*
Western Airlines	.0012	1.5750*	−.0014	−.3987
World Airways	−.0014	3.2765*	.0015	−1.4218*

*Asterisk identifies β coefficients significant at $\alpha = .10$.

Source: Davidson, W. N., Chandy, P. R., and Walker, M. "The stock market effects of airline deregulation." *Quarterly Journal of Business and Economics*, Autumn 1984, Vol. 23, No. 4, pp. 31–45.

5.35 A company wants to model the total weekly sales, y, of its product as a function of the variables packaging and location. Two types of packaging, P_1 and P_2, are used in each of four locations, L_1, L_2, L_3, and L_4.

a. Write a main effects model to relate $E(y)$ to packaging and location. What implicit assumption are we making about the interrelationships between sales, packaging, and location when we use this model?

b. Now write a model for $E(y)$ that includes interaction between packaging and location. How many parameters are in this model (remember to include β_0)? Compare this number to the number of packaging–location combinations being modeled.

c. Suppose the main effects and interaction models are fitted for 40 observations on weekly sales. The values of SSE are

SSE for main effects model = 422.36

SSE for interaction model = 346.65

Determine whether the data indicate that the interaction between location and packaging is important in estimating mean weekly sales. Use $\alpha = .05$. What implications does your conclusion have for the company's marketing strategy?

5.36 To make a product more appealing to the consumer, an automobile manufacturer is experimenting with a new type of paint that is supposed to help the car maintain its new-car look. The durability of this paint depends on the length of time the car body is in the oven after it has been painted. In the initial experiment, three groups of 10 car bodies each were baked for three different lengths of time—12, 24, and 36 hours—at the standard temperature setting. Then, the paint finish of each of the 30 cars was analyzed to determine a durability rating, y.

a. Write a quadratic model relating the mean durability, $E(y)$, to the length of baking.

b. Could a cubic model be fitted to the data? Explain.

c. Suppose the research and development department develops three new types of paint to be tested. Thus, 90 cars are to be tested—30 for each type of paint. Write the complete second-order model for $E(y)$ as a function of the type of paint and bake time.

5.37 Economic research has established evidence of a positive correlation between earnings and educational attainment (*Economic Inquiry*, Jan. 1984). However, it is unclear whether higher wage rates for better educated workers reflect an individual's added value or merely the employer's use of higher education as a screening device in the recruiting process. One version of this "sheepskin screening" hypothesis supported by many economists is that wages will rise faster with extra years of education when the extra years culminate in a certificate (e.g., master's or Ph.D. degree, CPA certificate, or actuarial degree).

a. Write a first-order, main effects model for mean wage rate $E(y)$ of an employer as a function of employee's years of education and whether or not the employee is certified.
b. Write a first-order model for $E(y)$ that corresponds to the "sheepskin screening" hypothesis.
c. Write the complete second-order model for $E(y)$ as a function of the two independent variables.

*5.38 Use the coding system for observational data to fit a second-order model to the data on demand y and price p given in the following table. Show that the inherent multicollinearity problem with fitting a polynomial model is reduced when the coded values of p are used.

DEMAND y, pounds	1,120	999	932	884	807	760	701	688
PRICE p, dollars	3.00	3.10	3.20	3.30	3.40	3.50	3.60	3.70

5.39 One factor that must be considered in developing a shipping system that is beneficial to both the customer and the seller is time of delivery. A manufacturer of farm equipment can ship its products by either rail or truck. Quadratic models are thought to be adequate in relating time of delivery to distance to be shipped for both modes of transportation. Consequently, it has been suggested that the following model be fitted to begin the model-building process:

$$E(y) = \beta_0 + \beta_1 x_1 + \beta_2 x_1^2 + \beta_3 x_2 + \beta_4 x_1 x_2 + \beta_5 x_1^2 x_2$$

where

$$y = \text{Time of delivery}$$

$$x_1 = \text{Distance to be shipped}$$

$$x_2 = \begin{cases} 1 & \text{if rail} \\ 0 & \text{if truck} \end{cases}$$

a. Sketch the proposed relationships between delivery time y and distance x_1 for both modes of transportation.
b. What hypothesis would you test to determine whether the data indicate that the quadratic distance terms are useful in the model, i.e., whether curvature is present in the relationship between mean delivery time and distance?
c. What hypothesis would you test to determine whether there is a difference in mean delivery time by rail and by truck?

5.40 Suppose an oil company wants to model the mean monthly gasoline sales, $E(y)$, of its affiliated stations as a function of type of gasoline purchased—regular, premium, or lead-free—and of type of service—self-service or full-service.

a. How many dummy variables will be needed to describe each of the qualitative variables, type of gasoline and type of service?

b. Write the main effects model relating $E(y)$ to type of gasoline and type of service. Be sure to code the dummy variables.

c. Write a model for $E(y)$ that includes interaction between type of gasoline and type of service.

d. Do you think interaction would be important in this model? A plot of your intuitive estimates of the mean will help you decide.

5.41 Suppose the interaction model of Exercise 5.40, part c, is used and the following least squares model is obtained (units of sales, y, are millions of dollars):

$$\hat{y} = 4 - 2x_1 - x_2 - x_3 + 2x_1x_3 + 3x_2x_3$$

where

$$x_1 = \begin{cases} 1 & \text{if premium} \\ 0 & \text{otherwise} \end{cases} \qquad x_2 = \begin{cases} 1 & \text{if lead-free} \\ 0 & \text{otherwise} \end{cases} \qquad x_3 = \begin{cases} 1 & \text{if full-service} \\ 0 & \text{if self-service} \end{cases}$$

a. What is the estimate of mean sales for lead-free gasoline at the full-service pumps?

b. What is the estimated difference between mean sales of regular gasoline at full-service and self-service pumps?

c. To see the effects of interaction, compare the difference between the regular self-service and full-service mean sales to the difference between the premium self-service and full-service mean sales.

5.42 Use the coding system for observational data to fit a complete second-order model to the data of Example 5.3, which are repeated here.

x_1, °F	x_2, pounds per square inch	y	x_1, °F	x_2, pounds per square inch	y	x_1, °F	x_2, pounds per square inch	y
80	50	50.8	90	50	63.4	100	50	46.6
80	50	50.7	90	50	61.6	100	50	49.1
80	50	49.4	90	50	63.4	100	50	46.4
80	55	93.7	90	55	93.8	100	55	69.8
80	55	90.9	90	55	92.1	100	55	72.5
80	55	90.9	90	55	97.4	100	55	73.2
80	60	74.5	90	60	70.9	100	60	38.7
80	60	73.0	90	60	68.8	100	60	42.5
80	60	71.2	90	60	71.3	100	60	41.4

a. Give the coded values u_1 and u_2 for x_1 and x_2, respectively.

b. Compare the coefficient of correlation between x_1 and x_1^2 with the coefficient of correlation between u_1 and u_1^2.

c. Compare the coefficient of correlation between x_2 and x_2^2 with the coefficient of correlation between u_2 and u_2^2.

d. Give the prediction equation.

5.43 One of the provisions of the Rehabilitation Act of 1973 is that programs offered by colleges and universities that receive federal funds must be readily available to severely disabled students. Researchers conducted a study to determine the variables related to disabled college students' achievement in terms of grade point average (GPA) (*Journal of Rehabilitation*, Apr./May/June 1985). The following independent variables were measured on each of 60 disabled college students and used to model college GPA, y:

x_1 = High school GPA

$$x_2 = \begin{cases} 1 & \text{if severely disabled} \\ 0 & \text{if nonseverely disabled} \end{cases}$$

x_3 = Internal–External Scale score (a measure of the degree to which the disabled student believes that life events are controlled internally or externally)

x_4 = Counseling Relationship Inventory Scale score (a measure of the overall quality of the counseling relationship as perceived by the disabled student)

a. Write a complete second-order model relating college GPA (y) to high school GPA (x_1) and disability (x_2). Sketch the relationships hypothesized by the model.
b. Write a complete second-order model relating college GPA (y) to Internal–External Scale (x_3) and Counseling Relationship Inventory Scale (x_4). Sketch the relationships hypothesized by the model.
c. Write a first-order model relating college GPA (y) to all four independent variables, x_1–x_4. Assume that a college student's disability does not affect the linear relationship between GPA and the three quantitative independent variables.
d. Repeat part c but assume that disability does affect the linear relationships between GPA (y) and the three quantitative independent variables.

References

Draper, N., and Smith, H. *Applied Regression Analysis*, 3rd ed. New York: Wiley, 1989.

Graybill, F. A. *Theory and Application of the Linear Model*. North Scituate, Mass.: Duxbury, 1976.

Mendenhall, W. *Introduction to Linear Models and the Design and Analysis of Experiments*. Belmont, Calif.: Wadsworth, 1968.

Neter, J., Wasserman, W., and Kutner, M. H. *Applied Linear Statistical Models*, 3rd ed. Homewood, Ill.: Richard D. Irwin, 1988.

CHAPTER 6

Some Regression Pitfalls

CONTENTS

OBJECTIVE

To identify several potential problems you may encounter when constructing a model for a response y; to help you recognize when these problems exist so that you can avoid some of the pitfalls of multiple regression analysis

6.1 Introduction

Multiple regression analysis is recognized by practitioners as a powerful tool for modeling a response y and is therefore widely used. But it is also one of the most abused statistical techniques. The ease with which a multiple regression analysis can be run on the computer has opened the door to many data analysts who have but a limited knowledge of multiple regression and statistics. In practice, building a model for some response y is rarely a simple, straightforward process. There are a number of pitfalls that trap the unwary analyst. In this chapter, we discuss several problems that you should be aware of when constructing a multiple regression model.

6.2 Observational Data Versus Designed Experiments

One problem encountered in using a regression analysis is caused by the type of data that the analyst is often forced to collect. Recall, from Section 2.4, that the data for regression can be either *observational* (where the values of the independent variables are uncontrolled) or *experimental* (where the x's are controlled via a designed experiment). Whether data are observational or experimental is important for the following reasons. First, as you will subsequently learn in Chapter 10, the quantity of information in an experiment is controlled not only by the *amount of data*, but also by the *values of the predictor variables* $x_1, x_2, \ldots, x_k$. Consequently, if you can design the experiment (sometimes this is physically impossible), you may be able to increase greatly the amount of information in the data at no additional cost.

Second, the use of observational data creates a problem involving randomization. When an experiment has been designed and we have decided on the various settings of the independent variables to be used, the experimental units are then randomly assigned in such a way that each combination of the independent variables has an equal chance of receiving experimental units with unusually high (or low) readings. (We will illustrate this method of randomization in Chapter 11.) This procedure tends to average out any variation within the experimental units. The result is that if the difference between two sample means is statistically significant, then you can infer (with probability of Type I error equal to α) that the population means differ. But more important, you can infer that this difference was due to the settings of the predictor variables, which is what you did to make the two populations different. Thus, you can infer a cause-and-effect relationship.

If the data are observational, a statistically significant relationship between a response y and a predictor variable x does not imply a cause-and-effect relationship. It simply means that x contributes information for the prediction of y, and nothing more. This point is aptly illustrated in the following example.

EXAMPLE 6.1

The *Orlando Sentinel Star* (February 28, 1979) reported on a socioeconomic research project in an article entitled "Couples who marry with child on way end up far poorer." The article states that "White suburban couples beginning marriage with the bride already pregnant face lower income and living standards and 22 percent fewer assets by age 40 than couples with no premarital pregnancy." This conclusion was based on interviews with approximately 1,000 randomly selected white suburban married women over the period 1962–1977. The two variables measured in the study—financial reward (income) at age 40, y, and premarital pregnancy, x (where $x = 1$ if premarital pregnancy and $x = 0$ if no premarital pregnancy)—were found to be negatively correlated. Note that although the quotation does not use the word *cause*, it certainly implies that the researchers have concluded that lower income can be expected to follow premarital pregnancy.

a. Are the data for the research project observational or experimental?
b. Identify any weaknesses in the study.

Solution

a. The women in the study (the experimental units) were randomly selected and no attempt was made to control the value of x, premarital pregnancy; hence, the data are observational.
b. The pitfalls provided by the researcher's observational data are apparent. The response y (income) is related to a single variable, the presence or absence of premarital pregnancy, x. Since the women questioned in the experiment were *not* randomly assigned to the two groups—an obviously impossible task—a real possibility exists that lower prospective economic achievers tended to fall in the premarital pregnancy group and higher prospective economic achievers tended to fall in the non–premarital pregnancy group. In other words, perhaps the survey is showing that women from lower socioeconomic groups are more likely to be subject to both premarital pregnancy *and* lower long-term economic rewards. Whether this explanation or the researcher's explanation of the relationship between long-term economic gain and premarital pregnancy is valid is impossible to decide based on observational data. This demonstrates the primary weakness of observation experiments.

The point of the previous example is twofold. If you can control the values of the independent variables in an experiment, it pays to do so. If you cannot control them, you can still learn much from a regression analysis about the relationship between a response y and a set of predictors. In particular, a prediction equation that provides a good fit to your data will almost always be useful. But, **you must be careful about deducing cause-and-effect relationships between the response and the predictors in an observational experiment**.

Warning

With observational data, a statistically significant relationship between a response y and a predictor variable x *does not necessarily* imply a cause-and-effect relationship.

Learning about the design of experiments is useful even if most of your applications of regression analysis involve observational data. Learning how to design an experiment and control the information in the data will improve your ability to assess the quality of observational data. We introduce experimental design in Chapter 10 and present methods for analyzing the data in a designed experiment in Chapter 11.

6.3 Deviating from the Assumptions

When we apply a regression analysis to a set of data, we never know for certain that the assumptions about the random error term ε are satisfied. How far can we deviate from the assumptions and still expect a multiple regression analysis to yield results that will have the reliability stated in Chapter 4? How can we detect departures (if they exist) from the assumptions, and what can we do about them? We will provide some partial answers to these questions in this section and direct you to further discussion in succeeding chapters.

Remember (from Section 4.2) that for a given set of values of $x_1, x_2, \ldots, x_k$,

$$y = \beta_0 + \beta_1 x_1 + \beta_2 x_2 + \cdots + \beta_k x_k + \varepsilon$$

where ε is a random error. The first assumption we made was that the mean value of the random error for *any* given set of values of $x_1, x_2, \ldots, x_k$ is $E(\varepsilon) = 0$.

One consequence of this assumption is that the mean $E(y)$ for a specific set of values of $x_1, x_2, \ldots, x_k$ is

$$E(y) = \beta_0 + \beta_1 x_1 + \beta_2 x_2 + \cdots + \beta_k x_k$$

That is,

$$y = \overbrace{E(y)}^{\substack{\text{Mean value of } y \\ \text{for specific values} \\ \text{of } x_1,\, x_2,\, \ldots,\, x_k}} + \overbrace{\varepsilon}^{\substack{\text{Random} \\ \text{error}}}$$

The second consequence of this assumption (which we state without proof) is that the least squares estimators of the model parameters $\beta_0, \beta_1, \beta_2, \ldots, \beta_k$, will be unbiased regardless of the remaining assumptions that we attribute to the random errors and their probability distributions.

The properties of the sampling distributions of the parameter estimators $\hat{\beta}_0, \hat{\beta}_1, \ldots, \hat{\beta}_k$ will depend on the remaining assumptions that we specify concerning the probability distributions of the random errors. You will recall that we assumed that for any given set of values of $x_1, x_2, \ldots, x_k$, ε has a normal probability distribution with mean equal to 0 and variance equal to σ^2. Also, we assumed that the random errors are independent (in a probabilistic sense).

It is unlikely that the assumptions stated above are satisfied exactly for many practical situations. If departures from the assumptions are not too great, experience has shown that a least squares regression analysis produces estimates—predictions and statistical test results—that have, for all practical purposes, the properties specified in Chapter 4. On the other hand, if the assumptions are flagrantly violated, any inferences derived from the regression analysis are suspect.

If the observations are likely to be correlated (as in the case of **time series data**—that is, data collected over time), we must check for correlation between the random errors (a topic to be discussed in Chapter 7) and we may have to modify our methodology if correlation exists. The solution to this problem is to construct a time series model; this will be the subject of Chapter 9. If the variance of the random error ε changes from one setting of the independent x variables to another, we can sometimes transform the data so that the standard least squares methodology will be appropriate. Some techniques for detecting nonhomogeneous variances of the random errors (a condition called **heteroscedasticity**) and some methods for treating this type of data are discussed in Chapter 7. The normality assumption is the least restrictive of the assumptions when regression analysis is applied in practice. However, nonnormality can result in predicted values that deviate greatly from the observed values. A careful analysis of these extreme values, or **outliers**, is an important component of regression analysis. In Chapter 7, we give some methods for detecting outliers and determining their influence on the prediction equation.

Frequently, the data $(y, x_1, x_2, \dots, x_k)$ are observational; i.e., we just observe an experimental unit and record values for $y, x_1, x_2, \dots, x_k$. Do these data violate the assumption that $x_1, x_2, \dots, x_k$ are fixed? For this particular case, if we can assume that $x_1, x_2, \dots, x_k$ are *measured without error*, the mean value $E(y)$ can be viewed as a conditional mean. That is, it gives the mean value of y, *given* that the x variables assume a specific set of values. With this modification in our thinking, the least squares regression analysis is applicable to observational data. Keep in mind, however, that inferences about $E(y)$ have the reliability stated in Chapter 4 only for the given set of x values.

To conclude, remember that when you perform a regression analysis, the reliability you can place in your inferences depends on having satisfied the assumptions prescribed in Section 4.2. We will never know for certain that the random errors satisfy these assumptions, but we will examine the residuals [the deviations $(y_i - \hat{y}_i)$ between the observed and the corresponding predicted values of y] in Chapter 7 to see whether we can discover patterns that suggest correlation, heteroscedasticity, nonnormality, or an improper choice for the deterministic portion of the model. An examination of the residuals will also have another beneficial effect: The magnitudes of the residuals will give you an idea of how well the model is predicting. This should convince you that, although the assumptions may not always be satisfied exactly, a multiple regression analysis is a powerful statistical tool.

6.4 Parameter Estimability and Interpretation

Suppose we want to fit the first-order model

$$E(y) = \beta_0 + \beta_1 x$$

to relate a developmentally challenged child's creativity score y to the child's flexibility score x. Now, suppose we collect data for three such challenged children, and each child has a flexibility score of 5. The data are shown in Figure 6.1 on page 352. You can see the problem: The parameters of the straight-line model cannot be estimated when all the data are concentrated at a single x value. Recall that it takes two points (x values) to fit a straight line. Thus, the parameters are not estimable when only one x value is observed.

FIGURE 6.1
Creativity and flexibility data for three children

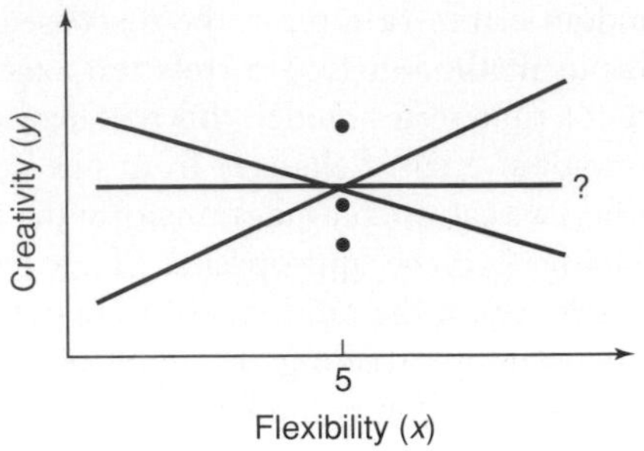

A similar problem would occur if we attempted to fit the second-order model

$$E(y) = \beta_0 + \beta_1 x + \beta_2 x^2$$

to a set of data for which only one *or two* different x values were observed (see Figure 6.2). At least three different x values must be observed before a second-order model can be fitted to a set of data (that is, before all three parameters are estimable). In general, the number of levels of a quantitative independent variable x must be at least one more than the order of the polynomial in x that you want to fit. If two values of x are too close together, you may not be able to estimate a parameter because of rounding error encountered in fitting the model. Remember, also, that the sample size n must be sufficiently large to allow degrees of freedom for estimating σ^2. The requirements for fitting a pth-order polynomial regression model are shown in the box.

FIGURE 6.2
Only two different x values observed—the second-order model is not estimable

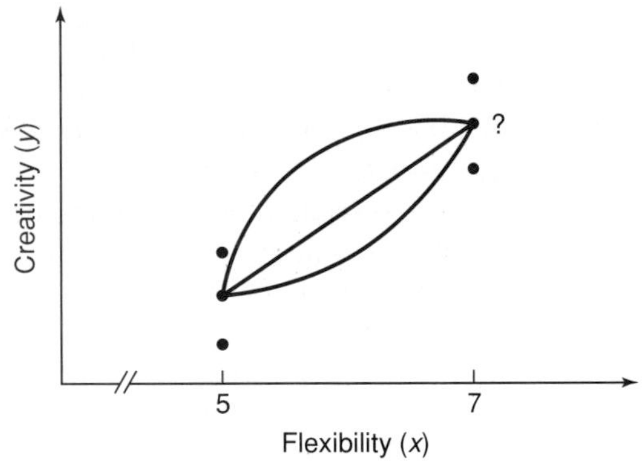

Requirements for Fitting a pth-Order Polynomial Regression Model

$$E(y) = \beta_0 + \beta_1 x + \beta_2 x^2 + \cdots + \beta_p x^p$$

1. The number of levels of x must be greater than or equal to $(p + 1)$.
2. The sample size n must be greater than $(p + 1)$ to allow sufficient degrees of freedom for estimating σ^2.

Most variables are not controlled by the researcher, but the independent variables are usually observed at a sufficient number of levels to permit estimation of the model parameters. However, when the computer program you use suddenly refuses to fit a model, the problem is probably inestimable parameters.

Given that the parameters of the model are estimable, it is important to interpret the parameter estimates correctly. A typical misconception is that $\hat{\beta}_i$ always measures the effect of x_i on $E(y)$, *independently* of the other x variables in the model. This may be true for some models, but it is not true in general. We will see in Section 6.5 that when the independent variables are correlated, the values of the estimated β coefficients are often misleading. Even if the independent variables are uncorrelated, the presence of interaction changes the meaning of the parameters. For example, the underlying assumption of the first-order model

$$E(y) = \beta_0 + \beta_1 x_1 + \beta_2 x_2$$

is, in fact, that x_1 and x_2 affect the mean response $E(y)$ independently. Recall from Sections 4.5 and 5.4 that the slope parameter β_1 measures the rate of change of y for a 1-unit increase in x_1, for any given value of x_2. However, if the relationship between $E(y)$ and x_1 depends on x_2 (i.e., if x_1 and x_2 interact), then the interaction model

$$E(y) = \beta_0 + \beta_1 x_1 + \beta_2 x_2 + \beta_3 x_1 x_2$$

is more appropriate. For the interaction model, we showed that the effect of x_1 on $E(y)$, i.e., the slope, is not measured by a single β parameter, but by $\beta_1 + \beta_3 x_2$.

Generally, the interpretation of an individual β parameter becomes increasingly difficult as the model becomes more complex. As we learned in Chapter 5, the individual β's of higher-order models usually have no practical interpretation.

Another misconception about the parameter estimates is that the magnitude of $\hat{\beta}_i$ determines the importance of x_i; that is, the larger (in absolute value) the $\hat{\beta}_i$, the more important the independent variable x_i is as a predictor of y. We learned in Chapter 4, however, that the standard error of the estimate $s_{\hat{\beta}_i}$ is critical in making inferences about the true parameter value. To reliably assess the importance of an individual term in the model, we conduct a test of H_0: $\beta_i = 0$ or construct a confidence interval for β_i using formulas that reflect the magnitude of $s_{\hat{\beta}_i}$.

In addition to the parameter estimates, $\hat{\beta}_i$, some statistical software packages report the **standardized regression coefficients**,

$$\hat{\beta}_i^* = \hat{\beta}_i\left(\frac{s_{x_i}}{s_y}\right)$$

where s_{x_i} and s_y are the standard deviations of the x_i and y values, respectively, in the sample. Unlike $\hat{\beta}_i$, $\hat{\beta}_i^*$ is scaleless. These standardized regression coefficients make it more feasible to compare parameter estimates since the units are the same. However, the problems with interpreting standardized regression coefficients are much the same as those mentioned previously. Therefore, you should be wary of using a standardized regression coefficient as the sole determinant of an x variable's importance. The next example illustrates this point.

EXAMPLE 6.2

Refer to the problem of modeling the auction price y of antique grandfather clocks, Examples 4.1 and 4.2. In Example 4.1, we fitted the model

$$E(y) = \beta_0 + \beta_1 x_1 + \beta_2 x_2$$

where x_1 = age of the clock and x_2 = number of bidders. The SPSS printout for the regression analysis is shown in Figure 6.3. Locate the standardized β coefficients on the printout and interpret them.

FIGURE 6.3
SPSS printout for Example 6.2

```
Equation Number 1    Dependent Variable..   Y


Multiple R              .94464
R Square                .89234
Adjusted R Square       .88492
Standard Error       133.48467

Analysis of Variance
                       DF       Sum of Squares       Mean Square
Regression              2       4283062.96010     2141531.48005
Residual               29        516726.53990       17818.15655

F =      120.18816        Signif F =   .0000

------------------ Variables in the Equation ------------------

Variable                B          SE B         Beta          T   Sig T

X2              85.952984      8.728523      .620287      9.847   .0000
X1              12.740574       .904740      .887029     14.082   .0000
(Constant)   -1338.951340    173.809471                  -7.704   .0000
```

Solution

The standardized β coefficients are given on the SPSS printout in the column labeled **Beta**. These values, shaded in Figure 6.3, are

$$\hat{\beta}_1^* = .887 \quad \text{and} \quad \hat{\beta}_2^* = .620$$

Compare these values to the unstandardized β coefficients (in the **B** column):

$$\hat{\beta}_1 = 12.74 \quad \text{and} \quad \hat{\beta}_2 = 85.95$$

Based on the fact that $\hat{\beta}_2$ is nearly seven times larger than $\hat{\beta}_1$, we might be tempted to say that number of bidders (x_2) is a more important predictor of auction price than age of the clock (x_1). Once we standardize the β's (i.e., take the units of measurement and variation into account), we see that the opposite may, in fact, be true since $\hat{\beta}_1^*$ exceeds $\hat{\beta}_2^*$. Of course, from Example 4.2 we know that the two independent variables, x_1 and x_2, interact to affect y. Consequently, both age and number of bidders are important for predicting auction price and we should resist inferring that one of the variables is more important than the other.

6.5 Multicollinearity

Often, two or more of the independent variables used in the model for $E(y)$ will contribute redundant information. That is, the independent variables will be correlated with each other. For example, suppose we want to construct a model to predict the gasoline mileage rating, y, of a truck as a function of its load, x_1, and the horsepower, x_2, of its engine. In general, you would expect heavier loads to require greater horsepower and to result in lower mileage ratings. Thus, although both x_1 and x_2 contribute information for the prediction of mileage rating, some of the information is overlapping, because x_1 and x_2 are correlated. When the independent variables are correlated, we say that **multicollinearity** exists. In practice, it is not uncommon to observe correlations among the independent variables. However, a few problems arise when serious multicollinearity is present in the regression analysis.

> **Definition 6.1**
>
> **Multicollinearity** exists when two or more of the independent variables used in regression are correlated.

First, high correlations among the independent variables increase the likelihood of rounding errors in the calculations of the β estimates, standard errors, and so forth.* Second, the regression results may be confusing and misleading.

To illustrate, if the gasoline mileage rating model

$$E(y) = \beta_0 + \beta_1 x_1 + \beta_2 x_2$$

were fitted to a set of data, we might find that the t values for both $\hat{\beta}_1$ and $\hat{\beta}_2$ (the least squares estimates) are nonsignificant. However, the F test for H_0: $\beta_1 = \beta_2 = 0$ would probably be highly significant. The tests may seem to be contradictory, but really they are not. The t tests indicate that the contribution of one variable, say, x_1 = load, is not significant after the effect of x_2 = horsepower has been discounted (because x_2 is also in the model). The significant F test, on the other hand, tells us that at least one of the two variables is making a contribution to the prediction of y (i.e., β_1, β_2, or both differ from 0). In fact, both are probably contributing, but the contribution of one overlaps with that of the other.

Multicollinearity can also have an effect on the signs of the parameter estimates. More specifically, a value of $\hat{\beta}_i$ may have the opposite sign from what is expected. For example, we expect the signs of both of the parameter estimates for the gasoline mileage rating model to be negative, yet the regression analysis for the model might yield the estimates $\hat{\beta}_1 = .2$ and $\hat{\beta}_2 = -.7$. The positive value of $\hat{\beta}_1$ seems to contradict our expectation that heavy loads will result in lower mileage ratings. We mentioned in the previous section, however, that it is dan-

*The result is due to the fact that, in the presence of severe multicollinearity, the computer has difficulty inverting the information matrix $(X'X)$. See Appendix A for a discussion of the $(X'X)$ matrix and the mechanics of a regression analysis.

gerous to interpret a β coefficient when the independent variables are correlated. Because the variables contribute redundant information, the effect of load x_1 on mileage rating is measured only partially by $\hat{\beta}_1$. Also, we warned in Section 6.2 that we cannot establish a cause-and-effect relationship between y and the predictor variables based on observational data. By attempting to interpret the value $\hat{\beta}_1$, we are really trying to establish a cause-and-effect relationship between y and x_1 (by suggesting that a heavy load x_1 will *cause* a lower mileage rating y).

How can you avoid the problems of multicollinearity in regression analysis? One way is to conduct a designed experiment so that the levels of the x variables are uncorrelated (see Section 6.2). Unfortunately, time and cost constraints may prevent you from collecting data in this manner. For these and other reasons, much of the data collected in scientific studies are observational. Since observational data frequently consist of correlated independent variables, you will need to recognize when multicollinearity is present and, if necessary, make modifications in the analysis.

Several methods are available for detecting multicollinearity in regression. A simple technique is to calculate the coefficient of correlation r between each pair of independent variables in the model and use the procedure outlined in Section 3.7 to test for evidence of positive or negative correlation. If one or more of the r values is statistically different from 0, the variables in question are correlated and a severe multicollinearity problem may exist.* Other indications of the presence of multicollinearity include those mentioned in the beginning of this section—namely, nonsignificant t tests for the individual β parameters when the F test for overall model adequacy is significant, and estimates with opposite signs from what is expected.

A more formal method for detecting multicollinearity involves the calculation of **variance inflation factors** for the individual β parameters. One reason why the t tests on the individual β parameters are nonsignificant is that the standard errors of the estimates, $s_{\hat{\beta}_i}$, are inflated in the presence of multicollinearity. When the dependent and independent variables are appropriately transformed,† it can be shown that

$$s^2_{\hat{\beta}_i} = s^2\left(\frac{1}{1 - R_i^2}\right)$$

where s^2 is the estimate of σ^2, the variance of ε, and R_i^2 is the multiple coefficient of determination for the model that regresses the independent variable x_i on the remaining independent variables $x_1, x_2, \ldots, x_{i-1}, x_{i+1}, \ldots, x_k$. The quantity

*Remember that r measures only the pairwise correlation between x values. Three variables, x_1, x_2, and x_3, may be highly correlated as a group, but may not exhibit large pairwise correlations. Thus, multicollinearity may be present even when all pairwise correlations are not significantly different from 0.

†The transformed variables are obtained as

$$y_i^* = (y_i - \bar{y})/s_y \qquad x_{1i}^* = (x_{1i} - \bar{x}_1)/s_1 \qquad x_{2i}^* = (x_{2i} - \bar{x}_2)/s_2$$

and so on, where $\bar{y}, \bar{x}_1, \bar{x}_2, \ldots,$ and $s_y, s_1, s_2, \ldots,$ are the sample means and standard deviations, respectively, of the original variables.

$1/(1 - R_i^2)$ is called the *variance inflation factor* for the parameter β_i, denoted $(\text{VIF})_i$. Note that $(\text{VIF})_i$ will be large when R_i^2 is large—that is, when the independent variable x_i is strongly related to the other independent variables.

Various authors maintain that, in practice, a severe multicollinearity problem exists if the largest of the variance inflation factors for the β's is greater than 10 or, equivalently, if the largest multiple coefficient of determination, R_i^2, is greater than .90.* Several of the statistical software packages discussed in this text have options for calculating variance inflation factors.†

The methods for detecting multicollinearity are summarized in the accompanying box. We illustrate the use of these statistics in Example 6.3.

Detecting Multicollinearity in the Regression Model

$$E(y) = \beta_0 + \beta_1 x_1 + \beta_2 x_2 + \cdots + \beta_k x_k$$

The following are indicators of multicollinearity:

1. Significant correlations between pairs of independent variables in the model
2. Nonsignificant t tests for all (or nearly all) the individual β parameters when the F test for overall model adequacy H_0: $\beta_1 = \beta_2 = \cdots = \beta_k = 0$ is significant
3. Opposite signs (from what is expected) in the estimated parameters
4. A variance inflation factor (VIF) for a β parameter greater than 10, where

$$(\text{VIF})_i = \frac{1}{1 - R_i^2}, \quad i = 1, 2, \ldots, k$$

and R_i^2 is the multiple coefficient of determination for the model

$$E(x_i) = \alpha_0 + \alpha_1 x_1 + \alpha_2 x_2 + \cdots + \alpha_{i-1} x_{i-1} + \alpha_{i+1} x_{i+1} + \cdots + \alpha_k x_k$$

EXAMPLE 6.3

The Federal Trade Commission (FTC) annually ranks varieties of domestic cigarettes according to their tar, nicotine, and carbon monoxide contents. The U.S. surgeon general considers each of these three substances hazardous to a smoker's health. Past studies have shown that increases in the tar and nicotine contents

*See, for example, Montgomery and Peck (1982) or Neter, Wasserman, and Kutner (1990).

†Some software packages calculate an equivalent statistic, called the **tolerance**. The tolerance for a β coefficient is the reciprocal of the variance inflation factor, i.e.,

$$(\text{TOL})_i = \frac{1}{(\text{VIF})_i} = 1 - R_i^2$$

For $R_i^2 > .90$ (the extreme multicollinearity case), $(\text{TOL})_i < .10$. These computer packages allow the user to set tolerance limits, so that any independent variable with a value of $(\text{TOL})_i$ below the tolerance limit will not be allowed to enter into the model.

of a cigarette are accompanied by an increase in the carbon monoxide emitted from the cigarette smoke. Table 6.1 lists tar, nicotine, and carbon monoxide contents (in milligrams) and weight (in grams) for a sample of 25 (filter) brands tested in a recent year. Suppose we want to model carbon monoxide content, y, as a function of tar content, x_1, nicotine content, x_2, and weight, x_3, using the model

$$E(y) = \beta_0 + \beta_1 x_1 + \beta_2 x_2 + \beta_3 x_3$$

The model is fitted to the 25 data points in Table 6.1. A portion of the resulting SAS printout is shown in Figure 6.4. Examine the printout. Do you detect any signs of multicollinearity?

TABLE 6.1 **FTC Cigarette Data for Example 6.3**

BRAND	TAR x_1, milligrams	NICOTINE x_2, milligrams	WEIGHT x_3, grams	CARBON MONOXIDE y, milligrams
Alpine	14.1	.86	.9853	13.6
Benson & Hedges	16.0	1.06	1.0938	16.6
Bull Durham	29.8	2.03	1.1650	23.5
Camel Lights	8.0	.67	.9280	10.2
Carlton	4.1	.40	.9462	5.4
Chesterfield	15.0	1.04	.8885	15.0
Golden Lights	8.8	.76	1.0267	9.0
Kent	12.4	.95	.9225	12.3
Kool	16.6	1.12	.9372	16.3
L&M	14.9	1.02	.8858	15.4
Lark Lights	13.7	1.01	.9643	13.0
Marlboro	15.1	.90	.9316	14.4
Merit	7.8	.57	.9705	10.0
Multifilter	11.4	.78	1.1240	10.2
Newport Lights	9.0	.74	.8517	9.5
Now	1.0	.13	.7851	1.5
Old Gold	17.0	1.26	.9186	18.5
Pall Mall Light	12.8	1.08	1.0395	12.6
Raleigh	15.8	.96	.9573	17.5
Salem Ultra	4.5	.42	.9106	4.9
Tareyton	14.5	1.01	1.0070	15.9
True	7.3	.61	.9806	8.5
Viceroy Rich Lights	8.6	.69	.9693	10.6
Virginia Slims	15.2	1.02	.9496	13.9
Winston Lights	12.0	.82	1.1184	14.9

Source: Federal Trade Commission.

Solution

First, notice that a test of

$$H_0\colon \ \beta_1 = \beta_2 = \beta_3 = 0$$

is highly significant. The F value (shaded on the printout) is very large ($F = 78.984$), and the observed significance level of the test (also shaded) is small ($p = .0001$). Therefore, we can reject H_0 for any α greater than .0001 and conclude that at least one of the parameters, β_1, β_2, and β_3, is nonzero. The t tests for two of the three individual β's, however, are nonsignificant. (The p-values for these tests are shaded on the printout.) Unless tar is the only one of the three variables useful for predicting carbon monoxide content, these results are the first indication of a potential multicollinearity problem.

A second clue to the presence of multicollinearity is the negative value for $\hat{\beta}_2$ and $\hat{\beta}_3$ (shaded on the printout),

$$\hat{\beta}_2 = -2.63 \qquad \hat{\beta}_3 = -.13$$

From past studies, the FTC expects carbon monoxide content y to increase when either nicotine content x_2 or weight x_3 increases—that is, the FTC expects *positive* relationships between y and x_2, and y and x_3, not negative ones.

FIGURE 6.4 Portion of the SAS printout for Example 6.3

DEP VARIABLE: CO

ANALYSIS OF VARIANCE

SOURCE	DF	SUM OF SQUARES	MEAN SQUARE	F VALUE	PROB>F
MODEL	3	495.25781	165.08594	78.984	0.0001
ERROR	21	43.89258562	2.09012312		
C TOTAL	24	539.15040			

ROOT MSE	1.445726	R-SQUARE	0.9186
DEP MEAN	12.528	ADJ R-SQ	0.9070
C.V.	11.53996		

PARAMETER ESTIMATES

VARIABLE	DF	PARAMETER ESTIMATE	STANDARD ERROR	T FOR H0: PARAMETER=0	PROB > |T|	TOLERANCE	VARIANCE INFLATION
INTERCEP	1	3.20219002	3.46175473	0.925	0.3655		0
TAR	1	0.96257386	0.24224436	3.974	0.0007	0.04623058	21.63070592
NICOTINE	1	-2.63166111	3.90055745	-0.675	0.5072	0.04566227	21.89991722
WEIGHT	1	-0.13048185	3.88534182	-0.034	0.9735	0.74970451	1.33385886

A more formal procedure for detecting multicollinearity is to examine the variance inflation factors. Figure 6.4 shows the variance inflation factors (shaded) for each of the three parameters under the column labeled **VARIANCE INFLATION**. Note that the variance inflation factors for both the tar and nicotine parameters are greater than 10. The variance inflation factor for the tar parameter, $(\text{VIF})_1 = 21.63$, implies that a model relating tar content x_1 to the remaining two independent variables, nicotine content x_2 and weight x_3, resulted in a coefficient of determination

$$R_1^2 = 1 - \frac{1}{(\text{VIF})_1}$$

$$= 1 - \frac{1}{21.63} = .954$$

TABLE 6.2 **Correlation Coefficients for the Three Pairs of Independent Variables in Example 6.3**

PAIR	r
x_1, x_2	.977
x_1, x_3	.491
x_2, x_3	.500

All signs indicate that a serious multicollinearity problem exists. To confirm our suspicions, we calculated the coefficient of correlation r for each of the three pairs of independent variables in the model. These values are given in Table 6.2. You can see that tar content x_1 and nicotine content x_2 appear to be highly correlated ($r = .977$), whereas weight x_3 appears to be moderately correlated with both tar content ($r = .491$) and nicotine content ($r = .500$). In fact, all three sample correlations have test statistics that exceed the critical t value, for a two-tailed test of H_0: $\rho = 0$ conducted at $\alpha = .05$ with $n - 2 = 23$ df (see Section 3.7).

Once you have detected that a multicollinearity problem exists, there are several alternative measures available for solving the problem. The appropriate measure to take depends on the severity of the multicollinearity and the ultimate goal of the regression analysis.

Some researchers, when confronted with highly correlated independent variables, choose to include only one of the correlated variables in the final model. One way of deciding which variable to include is to use **stepwise regression**, a topic discussed in Chapter 4. Generally, only one (or a small number) of a set of multicollinear independent variables will be included in the regression model by the stepwise regression procedure since this procedure tests the parameter associated with each variable in the presence of all the variables already in the model. For example, in fitting the gasoline mileage rating model introduced earlier, if at one step the variable representing truck load is included as a significant variable in the prediction of the mileage rating, the variable representing horsepower will probably never be added in a future step. Thus, if a set of independent variables is thought to be multicollinear, some screening by stepwise regression may be helpful.

If you are interested only in using the model for estimation and prediction, you may decide not to drop any of the independent variables from the model. In the presence of multicollinearity, we have seen that it is dangerous to interpret the individual β's for the purpose of establishing cause and effect. However, confidence intervals for $E(y)$ and prediction intervals for y generally remain unaffected *as long as the values of the independent variables used to predict y follow the same pattern of multicollinearity exhibited in the sample data*. That is, you must take strict care to ensure that the values of the x variables fall within the experimental region. (We discuss this problem in further detail in Section 6.6.) Alternatively, if your goal is to establish a cause-and-effect relationship between y and the independent variables, you will need to conduct a designed experiment to break up the pattern of multicollinearity.

When fitting a polynomial regression model [e.g., the second-order model $E(y) = \beta_0 + \beta_1 x + \beta_2 x^2$], the independent variables $x_1 = x$ and $x_2 = x^2$ will often be correlated. If the correlation is high, the computer solution may result in extreme rounding errors. For this model, the solution is not to drop one of the independent variables but to transform the x variable in such a way that the correlation between the coded x and x^2 values is substantially reduced. Coding the independent quantitative variables as described in optional Section 5.6 is a useful technique for reducing the multicollinearity inherent with polynomial regression models.

Another, more complex, procedure for reducing the rounding errors caused by multicollinearity involves a modification of the least squares method, called **ridge regression**. In ridge regression, the estimates of the β coefficients are biased [that is, $E(\hat{\beta}_i) \neq \beta_i$] but have significantly smaller standard errors than the unbiased β estimates yielded by the least squares method. Thus, the β estimates for the ridge regression are more stable than the corresponding least squares estimates. Ridge regression is a topic discussed in optional Chapter 8.

Solutions to Some Problems Created by Multicollinearity

1. Drop one or more of the correlated independent variables from the final model. A screening procedure such as stepwise regression is helpful in determining which variables to drop.
2. If you decide to keep all the independent variables in the model:
   a. Avoid making inferences about the individual β parameters (such as establishing a cause-and-effect relationship between y and the predictor variables).
   b. Restrict inferences about $E(y)$ and future y values to values of the independent variables that fall within the experimental region (see Section 6.6).
3. If your ultimate objective is to establish a cause-and-effect relationship between y and the predictor variables, use a designed experiment (see Chapters 10 and 11).
4. To reduce rounding errors in polynomial regression models, code the independent variables so that first-, second-, and higher-order terms for a particular x variable are not highly correlated (see Section 5.6).
5. To reduce rounding errors and stabilize the regression coefficients, use ridge regression to estimate the β parameters (see Section 8.7).

6.6 Extrapolation: Predicting Outside the Experimental Region

By the late 1960s many research economists had developed highly technical models to relate the state of the economy to various economic indices and other independent variables. Many of these models were multiple regression models, where, for example, the dependent variable y might be next year's growth in GNP and the independent variables might include this year's rate of inflation, this year's Consumer Price Index, and so forth. In other words, the model might be constructed to predict next year's economy using this year's knowledge.

Unfortunately, these models were almost unanimously unsuccessful in predicting the recession in the early 1970s. What went wrong? Well, one of the problems was that regression models were used to predict y for values of the independent variables that were outside the region in which the model was developed. For example, the inflation rate in the late 1960s, when the models were developed, ranged from 6% to 8%. When the double-digit inflation of the early 1970s became a reality, some researchers attempted to use the same models to predict the growth in GNP 1 year hence. As you can see in Figure 6.5, the model may be very accurate for predicting y when x is in the range of experimentation, but the use of the model outside that range is a dangerous (although sometimes unavoidable) practice. A $100(1 - \alpha)\%$ prediction interval for GNP when the inflation rate is, say, 10%, will be less reliable than the stated confidence coefficient $(1 - \alpha)$. How much less is unknown.

FIGURE 6.5
Using a regression model outside the experimental region

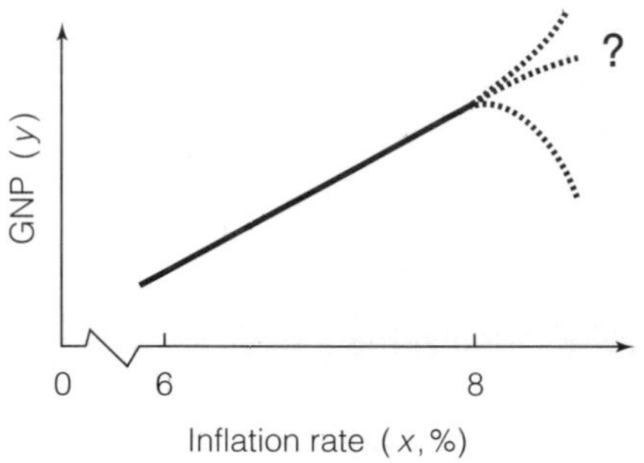

For a single independent variable x, the experimental region is simply the range of the values of x in the sample. Establishing the experimental region for a multiple regression model that includes a number of independent variables may be more difficult. For example, consider a model for GNP (y) using inflation rate (x_1) and prime interest rate (x_2) as predictor variables. Suppose a sample of size $n = 5$ was observed, and the values of x_1 and x_2 corresponding to the five values for GNP were (6, 10), (6.25, 12), (7.25, 10.25), (7.5, 13), and (8, 11.5). Notice that x_1 ranges from 6% to 8% and x_2 ranges from 10% to 13% in the sample data. You may think that the experimental region is defined by the ranges of the individual variables, i.e., $6 \le x_1 \le 8$ and $10 \le x_2 \le 13$. However, the levels of x_1 and x_2 *jointly* define the region. Figure 6.6 shows the experimental region for our hypothetical data. You can see that an observation with levels $x_1 = 8$ and $x_2 = 10$ clearly falls outside the experimental region, yet is within the ranges of the individual x values. Using the model to predict GNP for this observation may lead to unreliable results.

FIGURE 6.6
Experimental region for modeling GNP (y) as a function of inflation rate (x_1) and prime interest rate (x_2)

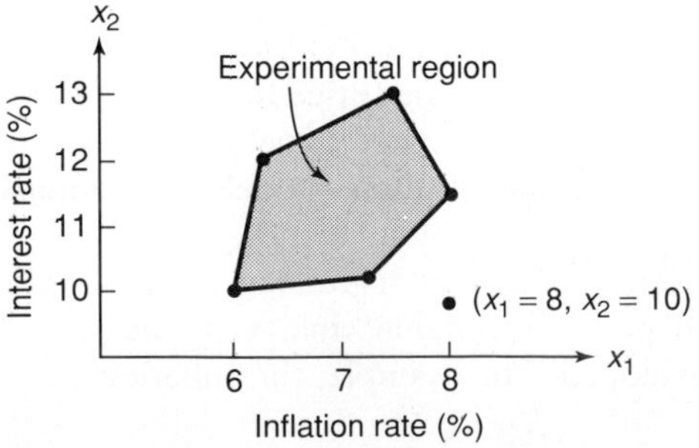

6.7 Data Transformations

The word *transform* means to change the form of some object or thing. Consequently, the phrase *data transformation* means that we have done, or plan to do, something to change the form of the data. For example, if one of the independent variables in a model is the price p of a commodity, we might choose to introduce this variable into the model as $x = 1/p$, $x = \sqrt{p}$, or $x = e^{-p}$. Thus, if we were to let $x = \sqrt{p}$, we would compute the square root of each price value, and these square roots would be the values of x that would be used in the regression analysis.

Data transformations are performed on the y values to make them more nearly satisfy the assumptions of Section 4.2 and, sometimes, to make the deterministic portion of the model a better approximation to the mean value of the transformed response. Transformations of the values of the independent variables are performed solely for the latter reason—that is, to achieve a model that provides a better approximation to $E(y)$. In this section, we discuss transformations on the dependent and independent variables to achieve a good approximation to $E(y)$. (Transformations on the y values for the purpose of satisfying the assumptions will be discussed in Chapter 7.)

Suppose you want to fit a model relating the demand y for a product to its price p. Also, suppose the product is a nonessential item, and you expect the mean demand to decrease as price p increases and then to decrease more slowly as p gets larger (see Figure 6.7). What function of p will provide a good approximation to $E(y)$?

FIGURE 6.7
Hypothetical relation between demand y and price p

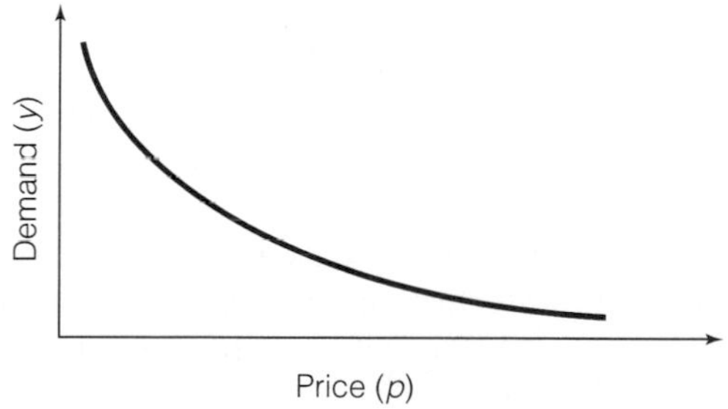

To answer this question, you need to know the graphs of some elementary mathematical functions—there is a one-to-one relationship between mathematical functions and graphs. If we want to model a relationship similar to the one indicated in Figure 6.7, we need to be able to select a mathematical function that will possess a graph similar to the curve shown.

Portions of some curves corresponding to mathematical functions that decrease as p increases are shown in Figure 6.8 on pages 364 and 365. Of the seven models shown, the curves in Figures 6.8c, 6.8d, 6.8f, and 6.8g will probably provide the best approximations to $E(y)$. These four graphs all show $E(y)$ decreasing and approaching (but never reaching) 0 as p increases. Figures 6.8c and 6.8d suggest that the independent variable, price, should be transformed using either $x = 1/p$ or $x = e^{-p}$. Then you might try fitting the model

$$E(y) = \beta_0 + \beta_1 x$$

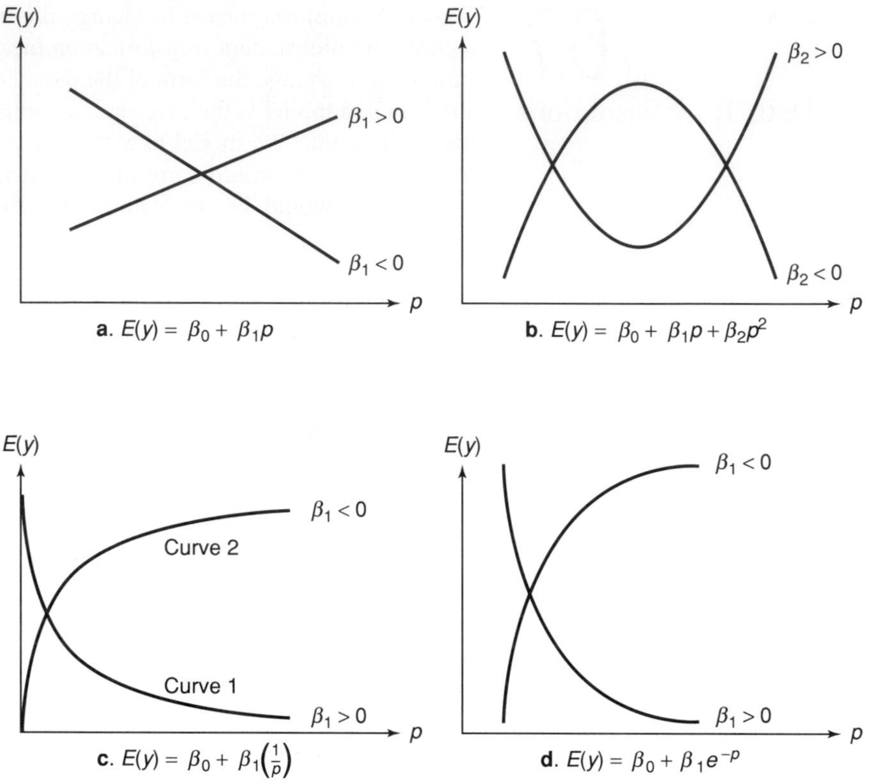

FIGURE 6.8 Graphs of some mathematical functions relating $E(y)$ to p

using the transformed data. Or, as suggested by Figures 6.8f and 6.8g, you might try the transformation $x = \log(p)$ and fit either of the models

$$E(y) = \beta_0 + \beta_1 x$$

or

$$E\{\log(y)\} = \beta_0 + \beta_1 x$$

The functions shown in Figure 6.8 produce curves that either rise or fall depending on the sign of the parameter β_1 in parts **a**, **c**, **d**, **e**, **f**, and **g**, and on β_2 and the portion of the curve used in part **b**. When you choose a model for a regression analysis, you do not have to specify the sign of the parameter(s). The least squares procedure will choose as estimates of the parameters those that minimize the sum of squares of the residuals. Consequently, if you were to fit the model shown in Figure 6.8c to a set of y values that increase in value as p increases, your least squares estimate of β_1 would be negative, and a graph of y would produce a curve similar to curve 2 in Figure 6.8c. If the y values decrease as p increases, your estimate of β_1 will be positive and the curve will be similar

Figure 6.8 (*continued*)

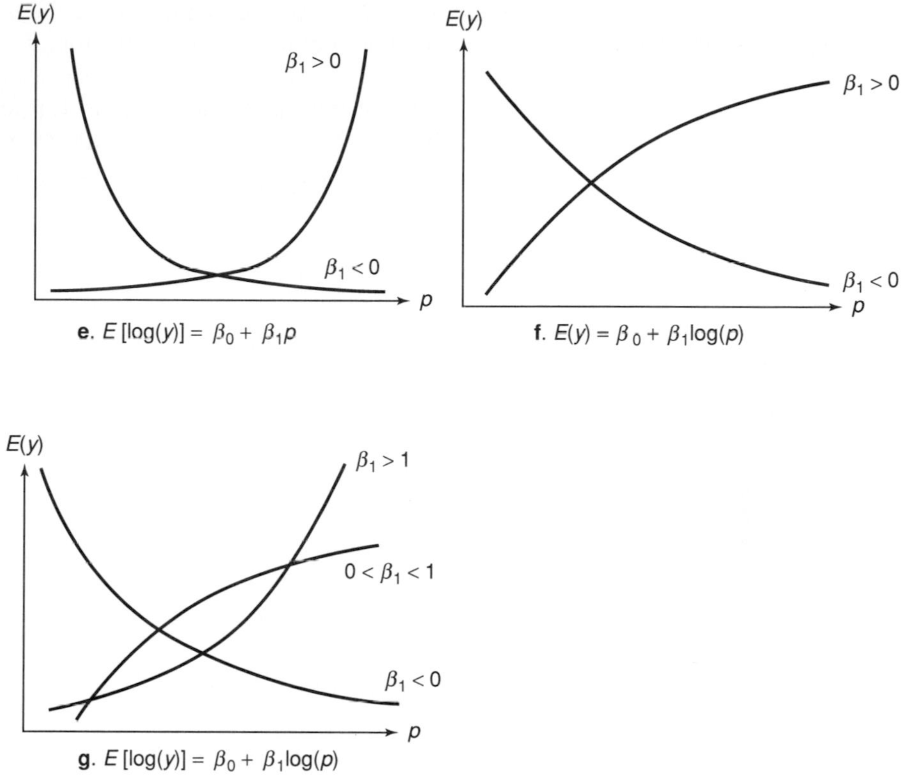

e. $E[\log(y)] = \beta_0 + \beta_1 p$

f. $E(y) = \beta_0 + \beta_1 \log(p)$

g. $E[\log(y)] = \beta_0 + \beta_1 \log(p)$

to curve 1 in Figure 6.8c. All the curves in Figure 6.8 shift upward or downward depending on the value of β_0.

EXAMPLE 6.4

A supermarket chain conducted an experiment to investigate the effect of price p on the weekly demand (in pounds) for a house brand of coffee. Eight supermarket stores that had nearly equal past records of demand for the product were used in the experiment. Eight prices were randomly assigned to the stores and were advertised using the same procedures. The number of pounds of coffee sold during the following week was recorded for each of the stores and is shown in the table.

DEMAND y, pounds	PRICE p, dollars
1,120	3.00
999	3.10
932	3.20
884	3.30
807	3.40
760	3.50
701	3.60
688	3.70

a. Fit the model

$$E(y) = \beta_0 + \beta_1 x$$

to the data, letting $x = 1/p$.

b. Do the data provide sufficient evidence to indicate that the model contributes information for the prediction of demand?

c. Find a 90% confidence interval for the mean demand when the price is set at \$3.20 per pound. Interpret this interval.

Solution

y	$x = 1/p$
1,120	.3333
999	.3226
932	.3125
884	.3030
807	.2941
760	.2857
701	.2778
688	.2703

a. The first step is to calculate $x = 1/p$ for each data point. These values are given in the table. The ASP computer printout* (Figure 6.9) gives

$$\hat{\beta}_0 = -1{,}180.48 \qquad \hat{\beta}_1 = 6{,}808.11$$

and

$$\hat{y} = -1{,}180.48 + 6{,}808.11x$$
$$= -1{,}180.48 + 6{,}808.11\left(\frac{1}{p}\right)$$

(You can verify that the formulas of Section 3.3 give the same answers.) A graph of this prediction equation is shown in Figure 6.10.

FIGURE 6.9

ASP printout for Example 6.4

```
                  DEMAND-TRANSFORMED PRICE MODEL

MODEL:   Demand(y) = 6808.11x + -1180.48CNST

          COEF.  SD. ER.     t(6)      P-VALUE  PT. R SQ.
        -------- -------  --------- ----------- ---------
   x    6808.11 358.353   18.9983  1.37472E-6   0.983648
CNST   -1180.48 107.729  -10.9578  3.4303E-5    0.952409

R SQ. = 0.983648,    ADJ. R SQ. = 0.980923,    D. W. = 1.68056
SQ. ROOT MSE = 20.9038,    F(1/6) = 360.936  (P-VALUE = 1.37472E-6)


FORECAST OF Demand(y) WHERE:

                    x = 0.3125
                 CNST = 1

                    FORECASTED VALUE:    947.051
           SD. ER. OF FORECASTED VALUE:    22.6258
        SD. ER. OF E(FORECASTED VALUE):     8.65785

90% CONFIDENCE INTERVALS:
                            LOWER LIMIT   FORECAST   UPPER LIMIT
                            -----------   --------   -----------
   FORECASTED VALUE:          903.085     947.051       991.017
E(FORECASTED VALUE):          930.228     947.051       963.875
```

b. To determine whether x contributes information for the prediction of y, we test H_0: $\beta_1 = 0$ against the alternative hypothesis H_a: $\beta_1 \neq 0$. The test statistic, shaded in Figure 6.9, is $t = 18.9983$. We wish to detect either $\beta_1 > 0$ or $\beta_1 < 0$, thus we will use a two-tailed test. Since the two-tailed p-value shown on the ASP printout, $p = .00000137472$, is less than $\alpha = .05$, we reject H_0: $\beta_1 = 0$ and conclude that $x = 1/p$ contributes information for the prediction of demand y.

c. For price $p = 3.20$, $x = 1/p = .3125$. The bottom of the ASP printout gives a 90% confidence interval for the mean demand $E(y)$ when price is $p = \$3.20$

*The ASP program uses full decimal accuracy for $x = 1/p$. Hence, the results shown in Figure 6.9 differ from results that would be calculated using the four-decimal values for $x = 1/p$ shown in the table.

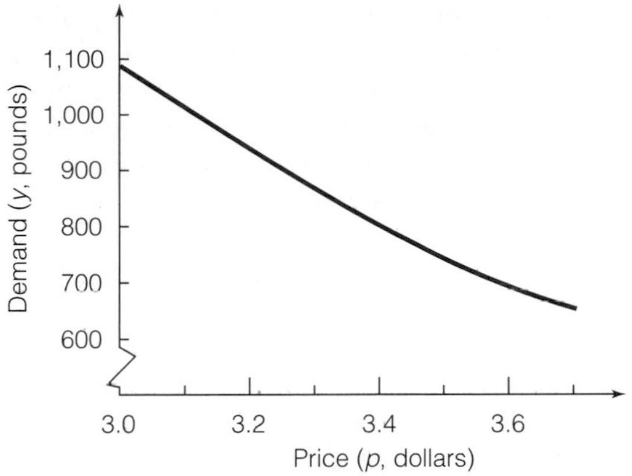

FIGURE 6.10
Graph of the demand–price curve for Example 6.4

(i.e., $x = .3125$). The interval (shaded) is (930.228, 963.875). Thus, we are 90% confident that mean demand will fall between 930 and 964 pounds when the price is set at \$3.20.

This discussion is intended to emphasize the importance of data transformation and to explain its role in model building. Keep in mind that the symbols, $x_1, x_2, \ldots, x_k$ that appear in the linear models of this text can be transformations on the independent variables you have observed. These transformations, coupled with the methods of Chapter 5, allow you to use a great variety of mathematical functions to model the mean $E(y)$ for data.

Summary

There are several problems that you should be aware of when constructing a model for a response y. In this chapter we have identified a few of the most important of these problem areas, as follows:

1. *Establishing cause and effect* When the data used in the regression analysis are observational (i.e., uncontrolled), it is dangerous to deduce a cause-and-effect relationship between y and the independent (predictor) variables. Only when the experiment has been designed properly can you be certain that any changes in y are due solely to the different settings of the predictor variables.
2. *Departures from the assumptions* In a practical setting, it is unlikely that the standard least squares assumptions about the error term are satisfied exactly. When departures from the assumptions are slight, the model remains a powerful predictor of the response y. On the other hand, the model performs poorly when the assumptions of equal variances and uncorrelated errors are violated.
3. *Parameter estimability and interpretation* To estimate all the parameters in a pth-order model, the number of levels of x must be greater than or equal to $(p + 1)$. For any model, the sample size n must be sufficiently large to allow degrees of freedom for estimating σ^2 so that a test of model adequacy can be

performed. Be wary of interpreting the individual β parameters in the presence of interaction or highly correlated independent variables.

4. *Multicollinearity* When highly correlated independent variables are present in a regression model, the results may be confusing: The t tests on the individual β's may be nonsignificant even though the F test for overall model adequacy is significant, and the β's may have signs opposite from what is expected. Also, there may be extreme rounding errors in the computation of the β estimates. Variance inflation factors aid in determining whether a serious multicollinearity problem exists. The solution to the problem depends on the severity of the multicollinearity and the ultimate goal of the regression analyst.
5. *Extrapolation* Predicting y when the x values are outside the range of experimentation is a dangerous practice. The level of reliability associated with any inference derived from the model will be less than the stated level of confidence $(1 - \alpha)$ since the adequacy of the model outside the experimental region is unknown.
6. *Data transformations* To achieve a model that provides a better approximation to $E(y)$, you may need to transform the values of the independent variables or the value of y. The type of transformation you should make depends on the theoretical relationships between $E(y)$ and the independent variables.

EXERCISES

6.1 Discuss the consequences of fitting multiple regression models when the assumptions of Section 4.2 are violated.

6.2 Why is it dangerous to predict y for values of independent variables that fall outside the experimental region?

6.3 Discuss the problems that result when multicollinearity is present in a regression analysis.

6.4 How can you detect multicollinearity?

6.5 What remedial measures are available when multicollinearity is detected?

6.6 Refer to Example 6.4. Can you think of any other transformations on price that might provide a good fit to the data? Try them and answer the questions of Example 6.4 again.

6.7 To meet the increasing demand for new software products, many systems development experts have adopted a prototyping methodology. The effects of prototyping on the system development life cycle (SDLC) were investigated in the *Journal of Computer Information Systems* (Spring 1993). A survey of 500 randomly selected corporate level MIS managers was conducted. Three potential independent variables were (1) *importance* of prototyping to each phase of the SDLC, (2) degree of *support* prototyping provides for the SDLC, and (3) degree to which prototyping *replaces* each phase of the SDLC. The accompanying table gives the pairwise correlations of the three variables in the survey data for one particular phase of the SDLC. Use this information to assess the degree of multicollinearity in the survey data. Would you recommend using all three independent variables in a regression analysis? Explain.

VARIABLE PAIRS	CORRELATION COEFFICIENT, r
Importance—Replace	.2682
Importance—Support	.6991
Replace—Support	−.0531

Source: Hardgrave, B. C., Doke, E. R., and Swanson, N. E. "Prototyping effects of the system development life cycle: An empirical study." *Journal of Computer Information Systems*, Vol. 33, No. 3, Spring 1993, p. 16 (Table 1).

6.8 A bioengineer wants to model the amount (y) of carbohydrate solubilized during steam processing of peat as a function of temperature (x_1), exposure time (x_2), and pH value (x_3). Data collected for each of 15 peat samples were used to fit the model

$$E(y) = \beta_0 + \beta_1 x_1 + \beta_2 x_2 + \beta_3 x_3$$

A summary of the regression results follows:

$$\hat{y} = -3{,}000 + 3.2x_1 - .4x_2 - 1.1x_3 \qquad R^2 = .93$$

$$s_{\hat{\beta}_1} = 2.4 \qquad s_{\hat{\beta}_2} = .6 \qquad s_{\hat{\beta}_3} = .8$$

$$r_{12} = .92 \qquad r_{13} = .87 \qquad r_{23} = .81$$

Based on these results, the bioengineer concludes that none of the three independent variables, x_1, x_2, and x_3, is a useful predictor of carbohydrate amount, y. Do you agree with this statement? Explain.

6.9 The provost of a top research university wants to know what salaries should be paid to the college's top researchers, based on years of experience. An independent consultant has proposed the quadratic model

$$E(y) = \beta_0 + \beta_1 x + \beta_2 x^2$$

where

y = Annual salary (thousands of dollars)

x = Years of experience

To fit the model, the consultant randomly sampled three researchers at other research universities and recorded the information given in the accompanying table. Give your opinion regarding the adequacy of the proposed model.

	y	x
Researcher 1	60	2
Researcher 2	45	1
Researcher 3	82	5

6.10 A particular meat-processing plant slaughters steers and cuts and wraps the beef for its customers. Suppose a complaint has been filed with the Food and Drug Administration (FDA) against the processing plant. The complaint alleges that the consumer does not get all the beef from the steer he purchases. In particular, one consumer purchased a 300-pound steer but received only 150 pounds of cut and wrapped beef. To settle the complaint, the FDA collected data on the live weights and dressed weights of nine steers processed by a reputable meat-processing plant (not the firm in question). The results are listed in the table.

LIVE WEIGHT x, pounds	DRESSED WEIGHT y, pounds
420	280
380	250
480	310
340	210
450	290
460	280
430	270
370	240
390	250

a. Fit the model $E(y) = \beta_0 + \beta_1 x$ to the data.
b. Construct a 95% prediction interval for the dressed weight y of a 300-pound steer.
c. Would you recommend that the FDA use the interval obtained in part **b** to determine whether the dressed weight of 150 pounds is a reasonable amount to receive from a 300-pound steer? Explain.

6.11 Refer to the FTC cigarette data of Example 6.3. The data of Table 6.1 are reproduced here for convenience.

BRAND	TAR x_1, milligrams	NICOTINE x_2, milligrams	WEIGHT x_3, grams	CARBON MONOXIDE y, milligrams
Alpine	14.1	.86	.9853	13.6
Benson & Hedges	16.0	1.06	1.0938	16.6
Bull Durham	29.8	2.03	1.1650	23.5
Camel Lights	8.0	.67	.9280	10.2
Carlton	4.1	.40	.9462	5.4
Chesterfield	15.0	1.04	.8885	15.0
Golden Lights	8.8	.76	1.0267	9.0
Kent	12.4	.95	.9225	12.3
Kool	16.6	1.12	.9372	16.3
L&M	14.9	1.02	.8858	15.4
Lark Lights	13.7	1.01	.9643	13.0
Marlboro	15.1	.90	.9316	14.4
Merit	7.8	.57	.9705	10.0
Multifilter	11.4	.78	1.1240	10.2
Newport Lights	9.0	.74	.8517	9.5
Now	1.0	.13	.7851	1.5
Old Gold	17.0	1.26	.9186	18.5
Pall Mall Light	12.8	1.08	1.0395	12.6
Raleigh	15.8	.96	.9573	17.5
Salem Ultra	4.5	.42	.9106	4.9
Tareyton	14.5	1.01	1.0070	15.9
True	7.3	.61	.9806	8.5
Viceroy Rich Lights	8.6	.69	.9693	10.6
Virginia Slims	15.2	1.02	.9496	13.9
Winston Lights	12.0	.82	1.1184	14.9

Source: Federal Trade Commission.

a. Fit the model $E(y) = \beta_0 + \beta_1 x_1$ to the data. Is there evidence that tar content x_1 is useful for predicting carbon monoxide content y?
b. Fit the model $E(y) = \beta_0 + \beta_2 x_2$ to the data. Is there evidence that nicotine content x_2 is useful for predicting carbon monoxide content y?
c. Fit the model $E(y) = \beta_0 + \beta_3 x_3$ to the data. Is there evidence that weight x_3 is useful for predicting carbon monoxide content y?
d. Compare the signs of $\hat{\beta}_1$, $\hat{\beta}_2$, and $\hat{\beta}_3$ in the models of parts **a**, **b**, and **c**, respectively, to the signs of the $\hat{\beta}$'s in the multiple regression model fit in Example 6.3. Is the fact that the $\hat{\beta}$'s change dramatically when the independent variables are removed from the model an indication of a serious multicollinearity problem?

6.12 An economist wants to model annual per capita demand, y, for passenger car motor fuel in the United States as a function of the two quantitative independent variables, average real weekly earnings (x_1) and average price of regular gasoline (x_2). Data on these three variables for the years 1965–1980 are shown in the table. Suppose the economist fits the model $E(y) = \beta_0 + \beta_1 x_1 + \beta_2 x_2$ to the data for the years 1965–1979. Would you recommend that the economist use the least squares prediction equation to predict per capita consumption of motor fuel in 1980? Explain.

YEAR	PER CAPITA CONSUMPTION OF MOTOR FUEL y, gallons	AVERAGE REAL WEEKLY EARNINGS x_1, 1967 dollars	AVERAGE PRICE OF GASOLINE x_2, dollars
1965	258.88	101.01	.32
1966	271.16	101.67	.33
1967	277.35	101.84	.34
1968	291.58	103.39	.34
1969	308.09	104.38	.36
1970	320.82	103.04	.36
1971	335.63	104.96	.36
1972	350.17	109.26	.37
1973	368.10	109.23	.40
1974	346.89	104.78	.53
1975	354.17	101.45	.57
1976	361.47	102.90	.59
1977	366.49	104.13	.62
1978	376.46	104.30	.63
1979	356.29	101.02	.86
1980	323.67	95.18	1.19

Source: Per capita consumption and average price of gasoline from *Statistical Abstract of the United States*. Average real weekly earnings from *Employment and Earnings*, U.S. Department of Labor, Bureau of Labor Statistics, Oct. 1983, p. 109.

6.13 A firm wants to use multiple regression in a cost analysis of its shipping department. Since most of the costs incurred by shipping result from direct labor, the firm will model weekly hours of labor (y) as a function of total weight shipped (x_1), percentage of units shipped by truck (x_2), and average weight per shipment (x_3). Data collected for a 20-week period and the SAS computer printout for the model $E(y) = \beta_0 + \beta_1 x_1 + \beta_2 x_2 + \beta_3 x_3$ are shown on page 372. The firm is concerned about the problems that occur in regression analysis when multicollinearity is present. Examine the SAS printout. Do you detect any signs of multicollinearity?

WEEK	HOURS OF LABOR y	THOUSANDS OF POUNDS SHIPPED x_1	PERCENTAGE OF UNITS SHIPPED BY TRUCK x_2	AVERAGE NUMBER OF POUNDS PER SHIPMENT x_3
1	100	5.1	90	20
2	85	3.8	99	22
3	108	5.3	58	19
4	116	7.5	16	15
5	92	4.5	54	20
6	63	3.3	42	26
7	79	5.3	12	25
8	101	5.9	32	21
9	88	4.0	56	24
10	71	4.2	64	29
11	122	6.8	78	10
12	85	3.9	90	30
13	50	3.8	74	28
14	114	7.5	89	14
15	104	4.5	90	21
16	111	6.0	40	20
17	110	8.1	55	16
18	100	2.9	64	19
19	82	4.0	35	23
20	85	4.8	58	25

DEP VARIABLE: LABOR

ANALYSIS OF VARIANCE

SOURCE	DF	SUM OF SQUARES	MEAN SQUARE	F VALUE	PROB>F
MODEL	3	5158.31383	1719.43794	17.866	0.0001
ERROR	16	1539.88617	96.24288576		
C TOTAL	19	6698.20000			

ROOT MSE	9.810346	R-SQUARE	0.7701
DEP MEAN	93.3	ADJ R-SQ	0.7270
C.V.	10.51484		

PARAMETER ESTIMATES

VARIABLE	DF	PARAMETER ESTIMATE	STANDARD ERROR	T FOR H0: PARAMETER=0	PROB > |T|	TOLERANCE	VARIANCE INFLATION
INTERCEP	1	131.92425	25.69321439	5.135	0.0001	.	0
WEIGHT	1	2.72608977	2.27500488	1.198	0.2483	0.44435417	2.25045709
TRUCK	1	0.04721841	0.09334856	0.506	0.6199	0.91496179	1.09294182
AVGSHIP	1	-2.58744391	0.64281819	-4.025	0.0010	0.46162372	2.16626650

6.14 How many levels of x are required to fit the model $E(y) = \beta_0 + \beta_1 x + \beta_2 x^2$? How large a sample size is required to have sufficient degrees of freedom for estimating σ^2?

6.15 How many levels of x_1 and x_2 are required to fit the model $E(y) = \beta_0 + \beta_1 x_1 + \beta_2 x_2 + \beta_3 x_1 x_2$? How large a sample size is required to have sufficient degrees of freedom for estimating σ^2?

6.16 How many levels of x_1 and x_2 are required to fit the model $E(y) = \beta_0 + \beta_1 x_1 + \beta_2 x_2 + \beta_3 x_1 x_2 + \beta_4 x_1^2 + \beta_5 x_2^2$? How large a sample is required to have sufficient degrees of freedom for estimating σ^2?

6.17 A physiologist wanted to investigate the relationship between the physical characteristics of preadolescent boys and their maximal oxygen uptake (measured in milliliters of oxygen per kilogram of body weight). The data shown in the table were collected on a random sample of 10 preadolescent boys. As a first step in the data analysis, the researcher fitted the regression model

$$y = \beta_0 + \beta_1 x_1 + \beta_2 x_2 + \beta_3 x_3 + \beta_4 x_4 + \varepsilon$$

to the data. The output for a SAS regression analysis follows.

MAXIMAL OXYGEN UPTAKE y	AGE x_1, years	HEIGHT x_2, centimeters	WEIGHT x_3, kilograms	CHEST DEPTH x_4, centimeters
1.54	8.4	132.0	29.1	14.4
1.74	8.7	135.5	29.7	14.5
1.32	8.9	127.7	28.4	14.0
1.50	9.9	131.1	28.8	14.2
1.46	9.0	130.0	25.9	13.6
1.35	7.7	127.6	27.6	13.9
1.53	7.3	129.9	29.0	14.0
1.71	9.9	138.1	33.6	14.6
1.27	9.3	126.6	27.7	13.9
1.50	8.1	131.8	30.8	14.5

```
Dependent Variable: Y

                         Analysis of Variance

                            Sum of          Mean
 Source            DF      Squares        Square       F Value       Prob>F

 Model              4      0.20604       0.05151        37.204       0.0007
 Error              5      0.00692       0.00138
 C Total            9      0.21296

     Root MSE          0.03721     R-square        0.9675
     Dep Mean          1.49200     Adj R-sq        0.9415
     C.V.              2.49391

                         Parameter Estimates

                   Parameter       Standard      T for H0:
Variable  DF        Estimate          Error    Parameter=0    Prob > |T|

INTERCEP   1       -4.774739     0.86281773         -5.534        0.0026
X1         1       -0.035214     0.01538630         -2.289        0.0708
X2         1        0.051637     0.00621522          8.308        0.0004
X3         1       -0.023417     0.01342835         -1.744        0.1416
X4         1        0.034489     0.08523877          0.405        0.7025
```

a. Is the model adequate for predicting maximal oxygen uptake?

b. It seems reasonable to assume that the greater a child's age, the greater should be the maximal oxygen uptake. But note that $\hat{\beta}_1$, the estimated coefficient of age, x_1, is negative. Give an explanation for this result.

c. It would seem that the weight of a child should be positively correlated to lung volume and hence to maximal oxygen uptake. Can you explain the small t value associated with $\hat{\beta}_3$?

d. Calculate the coefficient of correlation r for each pair of independent variables. Does this information confirm your suspicions in parts **b** and **c**?

6.18 Consider the data shown in the table.

x	54	42	28	38	25	70	48	41	20	52	65
y	6	16	33	18	41	3	10	14	45	9	5

a. Plot the points on a scattergram. What type of relationship appears to exist between x and y?
b. For each observation calculate $\log x$ and $\log y$. Plot the log-transformed data points on a scattergram. What type of relationship appears to exist between $\log x$ and $\log y$?
c. The scattergram from part **b** suggests that the transformed model

$$\log y = \beta_0 + \beta_1 \log x + \varepsilon$$

may be appropriate. Fit the transformed model to the data. Is the model adequate? Test using $\alpha = .05$.
d. Use the transformed model to predict the value of y when $x = 30$. [*Hint:* Use the inverse transformation $y = e^{\log y}$.]

6.19 D. Hamilton illustrated the multicollinearity problem with an example using the data shown in the accompanying table. The values of x_1, x_2, and y in the table represent appraised land value, appraised improvements value, and sale price, respectively, of a randomly selected residential property. (All measurements are in thousands of dollars.)

x_1	x_2	y	x_1	x_2	y
22.3	96.6	123.7	30.4	77.1	128.6
25.7	89.4	126.6	32.6	51.1	108.4
38.7	44.0	120.0	33.9	50.5	112.0
31.0	66.4	119.3	23.5	85.1	115.6
33.9	49.1	110.6	27.6	65.9	108.3
28.3	85.2	130.3	39.0	49.0	126.3
30.2	80.4	131.3	31.6	69.6	124.6
21.4	90.5	114.4			

Source: Hamilton, D. "Sometimes $R^2 > r^2_{yx_1} + r^2_{yx_2}$: Correlated variables are not always redundant." *The American Statistician*, Vol. 41, No. 2, May 1987, pp. 129–132.

a. Calculate the coefficient of correlation between y and x_1. Is there evidence of a linear relationship between sale price and appraised land value?
b. Calculate the coefficient of correlation between y and x_2. Is there evidence of a linear relationship between sale price and appraised improvements?
c. Based on the results in parts **a** and **b**, do you think the model $E(y) = \beta_0 + \beta_1 x_1 + \beta_2 x_2$ will be useful for predicting sale price?
d. Use a statistical computer software package to fit the model in part **c**, and conduct a test of model adequacy. In particular, note the value of R^2. Does the result agree with your answer to part **c**?
e. Calculate the coefficient of correlation between x_1 and x_2. What does the result imply?
f. Many researchers avoid the problems of multicollinearity by always omitting all but one of the "redundant" variables from the model. Would you recommend this strategy for this example? Explain. (Hamilton notes that, in this case, such a strategy "can amount to throwing out the baby with the bathwater.")

6.20 Neil A. Palomba used multiple regression to relate the strike activity in a state (the percentage y of total working hours lost due to strikes) to three independent variables:

x_1 = Percentage of union members in nonagricultural establishments

x_2 = Percentage of all nonagricultural employment that is manufacturing

x_3 = Hourly earnings of workers on manufacturing payrolls

The data for the analysis are reproduced in the table.

STATE	y	x_1	x_2	x_3	STATE	y	x_1	x_2	x_3
Alabama	.14	18.0	30.5	2.17	Nebraska	.05	19.3	16.6	2.36
Alaska	.11	32.2	8.9	3.54	Nevada	.36	32.8	4.6	3.16
Arizona	.09	20.08	15.3	2.72	New Hampshire	.03	20.9	40.9	2.00
Arkansas	.10	26.2	29.2	1.78	New Jersey	.27	37.7	37.1	2.67
California	.16	33.8	24.9	2.96	New Mexico	.09	13.4	6.8	2.29
Colorado	.04	21.6	15.8	2.74	New York	.11	39.4	28.2	2.60
Connecticut	.08	24.6	42.5	2.62	North Carolina	.01	6.7	41.6	1.75
Delaware	.41	21.5	36.1	2.65	North Dakota	.03	14.8	5.8	2.28
Florida	.20	13.1	15.5	2.11	Ohio	.38	35.7	39.0	2.91
Georgia	.13	12.7	31.8	1.92	Oklahoma	.01	13.7	15.5	2.35
Hawaii	.02	24.2	12.1	2.14	Oregon	.12	34.8	26.5	2.85
Idaho	.11	19.2	18.8	2.50	Pennsylvania	.14	38.4	37.8	2.55
Illinois	.18	37.9	33.5	2.76	Rhode Island	.09	29.6	38.2	2.11
Indiana	.16	34.1	40.8	2.81	South Carolina	.01	7.9	42.7	1.80
Iowa	.16	20.8	25.4	2.71	South Dakota	.16	9.5	8.8	2.34
Kansas	.11	18.8	20.6	2.65	Tennessee	.23	17.6	34.6	2.03
Kentucky	.17	25.7	26.6	2.43	Texas	.06	13.3	19.4	2.42
Louisiana	.10	17.1	17.8	2.49	Utah	.66	19.7	17.6	2.77
Maine	.15	20.3	36.6	2.00	Vermont	.26	19.3	30.9	2.08
Massachusetts	.07	29.1	33.0	2.37	Virginia	.04	15.5	26.5	2.04
Michigan	.83	38.9	40.7	3.11	Washington	.16	43.1	25.6	2.98
Minnesota	.02	33.0	24.0	2.64	West Virginia	.45	42.0	27.4	2.67
Mississippi	.14	11.6	30.5	1.76	Wisconsin	.21	31.5	37.0	2.66
Missouri	.14	39.8	28.5	2.53	Wyoming	.01	19.2	7.7	2.82
Montana	.28	36.2	12.2	2.71	Maryland	—	—	—	—

Source: Palomba, N. A. "Strike activity and union membership: An empirical approach." *University of Washington Business Review*, Winter 1969.

a. Palomba initially considered the straight-line model

$$y = \beta_0 + \beta_1 x_1 + \varepsilon$$

Fit the model to the data and give your opinion on the adequacy of the model. In particular, interpret the value of $\hat{\beta}_1$.

b. Now consider the first-order model

$$y = \beta_0 + \beta_1 x_1 + \beta_2 x_2 + \beta_3 x_3 + \varepsilon$$

Fit the model to the data using an available multiple regression package, and give your opinion on the adequacy of the model.

c. Refer to part **b**. Conduct a test to determine whether the percentage of union members x_1 has a positive effect on the level of strike activity (when the other independent variables, x_2 and x_3, are held constant). Does this result contradict your result in part **a**? Explain.

d. Calculate the variance inflation factor (VIF) for β_1. [*Hint*: You will need to fit the model $x_1 = \alpha_0 + \alpha_1 x_2 + \alpha_2 x_3 + \varepsilon$.] Interpret your result.

6.21 To model the relationship between y, a dependent variable, and x, an independent variable, a researcher has taken one measurement on y at each of five different x values. Drawing on his mathematical expertise, the researcher realizes that he can fit the fourth-order polynomial model

$$E(y) = \beta_0 + \beta_1 x + \beta_2 x^2 + \beta_3 x^3 + \beta_4 x^4$$

and it will pass exactly through all five points, yielding SSE = 0. The researcher, delighted with the "excellent" fit of the model, eagerly sets out to use it to make inferences. What problems will the researcher encounter in attempting to make inferences?

References

Draper, N., and Smith, H. *Applied Regression Analysis*, 2nd ed. New York: Wiley, 1981.

Montgomery, D. C., and Peck, E. A. *Introduction to Linear Regression Analysis*. New York: Wiley, 1982.

Mosteller, F., and Tukey, J. W. *Data Analysis and Regression: A Second Course in Statistics*. Reading, Mass.: Addison-Wesley, 1977.

Neter, J., Wasserman, W., and Kutner, M. H. *Applied Linear Statistical Models*, 3rd ed. Homewood, Ill.: Richard D. Irwin, 1990.

CHAPTER 7 Residual Analysis

CONTENTS

OBJECTIVE

To show how residuals can be used to detect departures from the model assumptions and to suggest some procedures for coping with these problems

7.1 Introduction

We have repeatedly stated that the validity of many of the inferences associated with a regression analysis depends on the error term, ε, satisfying certain assumptions. Thus, when we test a hypothesis about a regression coefficient or a set of regression coefficients, or when we form a prediction interval for a future value of y, we must assume that (1) ε is normally distributed with a mean of 0, (2) the variance σ^2 is constant, and (3) all pairs of error terms are uncorrelated.* The objective of this chapter is to provide you with both graphical tools and statistical tests that will aid in checking the validity of these assumptions. In addition, these tools will help you evaluate the utility of the model and, in some cases, may suggest modifications to the model that will allow you to better describe the mean response.

In Section 7.2, we will show how to plot the residuals to reveal model inadequacies. In Section 7.3, we examine the use of these plots and a simple test to detect unequal variances at different levels of the independent variable(s). A graphical analysis of residuals for checking the normality assumption is the topic of Section 7.4. In Section 7.5, residual plots are used to detect outliers, i.e., observations that are unusually large or small relative to the others; procedures for measuring the influence these outliers may have on the fitted regression model are also presented. Finally, we discuss the use of residuals to test for time series correlation of the error term in Section 7.6.

7.2 Plotting Residuals and Detecting Lack of Fit

The error term in a multiple regression model is, in general, not observable. To see this, consider the model

$$y = \beta_0 + \beta_1 x_1 + \cdots + \beta_k x_k + \varepsilon$$

and solve for the error term:

$$\varepsilon = y - (\beta_0 + \beta_1 x_1 + \cdots + \beta_k x_k)$$

Although you will observe values of the dependent variable and the independent variables $x_1, x_2, \ldots, x_k$, you will not know the true values of the regression coefficients $\beta_0, \beta_1, \ldots, \beta_k$. Therefore, the exact value of ε cannot be calculated.

After we use the data to obtain least squares estimates $\hat{\beta}_0, \hat{\beta}_1, \ldots, \hat{\beta}_k$ of the regression coefficients, we can estimate the value of ε associated with each y value using the corresponding **regression residual**, i.e., the deviation between the observed and the predicted value of y:

$$\hat{\varepsilon}_i = y_i - \hat{y}_i$$

To accomplish this, we must substitute the values of $x_1, x_2, \ldots, x_k$ into the prediction equation for each data point to obtain $\hat{y}$, and then this value must be subtracted from the observed value of y. Remember that you encountered the

*We assumed (Section 4.2) that the random errors associated with the linear model were independent. If two random variables are independent, it follows (proof omitted) that they will be uncorrelated. The reverse is generally untrue, except for normally distributed random variables. If two normally distributed random variables are uncorrelated, it can be shown that they are also independent.

regression residual in Chapters 3 and 4. In particular, the least squares estimates of $\beta_0, \beta_1, \beta_2, \ldots, \beta_k$ are those that minimize the sum of squares of the residuals,

$$\sum_{i=1}^{n} \hat{\varepsilon}_i^2 = \sum_{i=1}^{n} (y_i - \hat{y}_i)^2$$

Definition 7.1

The **regression residual** is the observed value of the dependent variable minus the predicted value, or

$$\hat{\varepsilon} = y - \hat{y} = y - (\hat{\beta}_0 + \hat{\beta}_1 x_1 + \cdots + \hat{\beta}_k x_k)$$

EXAMPLE 7.1

The data in Table 7.1 represent the level of cholesterol (in milligrams per liter) and average daily intake of saturated fat (in milligrams) for a sample of 10 Olympic athletes. Consider a regression model relating cholesterol level y to fat intake x. Calculate the regression residuals for

a. the straight-line (first-order) model
b. the quadratic (second-order) model

TABLE 7.1 **Data for Example 7.1**

ATHLETE	FAT INTAKE x, milligrams	CHOLESTEROL y, milligrams/liter
1	1,290	1,182
2	1,350	1,172
3	1,470	1,264
4	1,600	1,493
5	1,710	1,571
6	1,840	1,711
7	1,980	1,804
8	2,230	1,840
9	2,400	1,956
10	2,930	1,954

Solution

a. The SAS printout for the regression analysis of the first-order model,

$$y = \beta_0 + \beta_1 x + \varepsilon$$

is shown in Figure 7.1 on page 380. The least squares model is

$$\hat{y} = 578.928 + .540304x$$

Thus, the residual for the first observation, $x = 1{,}290$ and $y = 1{,}182$, is obtained by first calculating the predicted value

$$\hat{y} = 578.928 + .540304(1{,}290) = 1{,}275.92$$

FIGURE 7.1
SAS printout for first-order model: Example 7.1a

```
Dependent Variable: Y

                         Analysis of Variance

                            Sum of         Mean
      Source          DF   Squares        Square       F Value      Prob>F

      Model            1 703957.18342 703957.18342      39.536      0.0002
      Error            8 142444.91658  17805.61457
      C Total          9 846402.10000

          Root MSE     133.43768      R-square       0.8317
          Dep Mean    1594.70000      Adj R-sq       0.8107
          C.V.           8.36757

                         Parameter Estimates

                       Parameter       Standard    T for H0:
    Variable  DF        Estimate          Error  Parameter=0    Prob > |T|

    INTERCEP   1      578.927752   166.96805715        3.467        0.0085
    X          1        0.540304     0.08592981        6.288        0.0002

Sum of Residuals                            0
Sum of Squared Residuals          142444.9166
Predicted Resid SS (Press)        361206.7384
```

and then subtracting from the observed value:

$$\begin{aligned}\hat{\varepsilon} &= y - \hat{y} = 1{,}182 - 1{,}275.92\\ &= -93.92\end{aligned}$$

Similar calculations for the other nine observations produce the residuals shown in Table 7.2.

b. The SAS printout for the second-order model

$$y = \beta_0 + \beta_1 x + \beta_2 x^2 + \varepsilon$$

is shown in Figure 7.2. The least squares model is

$$\hat{y} = -1{,}216.14 + 2.39893x - .000450x^2$$

For the first observation, $x = 1{,}290$ and $y = 1{,}182$, the predicted cholesterol level is

$$\begin{aligned}\hat{y} &= -1{,}216.14 + 2.39893(1{,}290) - .000450(1{,}290)^2\\ &= 1{,}129.56^*\end{aligned}$$

and the regression residual is

$$\begin{aligned}\hat{\varepsilon} &= y - \hat{y} = 1{,}182 - 1{,}129.56\\ &= 52.44\end{aligned}$$

All the regression residuals for the second-order model are given in Table 7.3.

---

*The residuals in Tables 7.2 and 7.3 have been generated using a computer program. Therefore, the results reported here will differ slightly from hand-calculated residuals because of rounding error.

TABLE 7.2 **Regression Residuals for First-Order Model: Example 7.1a**

x	y	$\hat{y}$	$\hat{\varepsilon} = y - \hat{y}$
1,290	1,182	1,275.92	−93.92
1,350	1,172	1,308.34	−136.34
1,470	1,264	1,373.18	−109.18
1,600	1,493	1,443.41	49.59
1,710	1,571	1,502.85	68.15
1,840	1,711	1,573.09	137.91
1,980	1,804	1,648.73	155.27
2,230	1,840	1,783.81	56.19
2,400	1,956	1,875.66	80.34
2,930	1,954	2,162.02	−208.02

TABLE 7.3 **Regression Residuals for Second-Order Model: Example 7.1b**

x	y	$\hat{y}$	$\hat{\varepsilon} = y - \hat{y}$
1,290	1,182	1,129.56	52.44
1,350	1,172	1,202.21	−30.21
1,470	1,264	1,337.79	−73.79
1,600	1,493	1,470.04	22.96
1,710	1,571	1,570.06	.94
1,840	1,711	1,674.23	36.77
1,980	1,804	1,769.40	34.60
2,230	1,840	1,895.47	−55.47
2,400	1,956	1,949.06	6.94
2,930	1,954	1,949.17	4.83

FIGURE 7.2
SAS regression printout for second-order model: Example 7.1b

```
Dependent Variable: Y

                          Analysis of Variance

                             Sum of          Mean
      Source        DF      Squares        Square       F Value       Prob>F

      Model          2 831069.54637 415534.77319        189.710       0.0001
      Error          7  15332.55363   2190.36480
      C Total        9 846402.10000

          Root MSE      46.80133      R-square         0.9819
          Dep Mean    1594.70000      Adj R-sq         0.9767
          C.V.           2.93480

                          Parameter Estimates

                      Parameter        Standard      T for H0:
    Variable  DF       Estimate           Error    Parameter=0     Prob > |T|

    INTERCEP   1   -1216.143887    242.80636850         -5.009         0.0016
    X          1       2.398930      0.24583560          9.758         0.0001
    XX         1      -0.000450      0.00005908         -7.618         0.0001

Sum of Residuals                 -2.95586E-12
Sum of Squared Residuals           15332.5536
Predicted Resid SS (Press)         31308.3032
```

Graphical displays of regression residuals are useful aids to their interpretation. For example, the regression residual can be plotted on the vertical axis against one of the independent variables on the horizontal axis, or against the predicted value $\hat{y}$ (which is a linear function of the independent variables). If the assumptions concerning the error term ε are satisfied, we expect to see residual plots that have no trends, no dramatic increases or decreases in variability, and only a few residuals (about 5%) more than 2 estimated standard deviations ($2s$) of ε above or below 0. It is a property of the least squares prediction equation that the mean of the regression residuals is always 0. (This property applies only to models that include an intercept term, β_0.) Thus, the least squares prediction equation not only minimizes the SSE, the sum of squared errors (residuals), but also produces residuals whose mean is 0.

To illustrate, the residuals $\hat{\varepsilon}$ obtained by fitting the second-order model to the cholesterol data of Table 7.3 are plotted against fat intake, x, in Figure 7.3. The middle, upper, and lower horizontal lines in Figure 7.3 locate the mean (0), $+2s$, and $-2s$, respectively, for the residuals. We detect no distinctive patterns or trends in this plot. All the residuals lie within $2s$ of the mean (0), and the variability around the mean is consistent for small and large values of x.

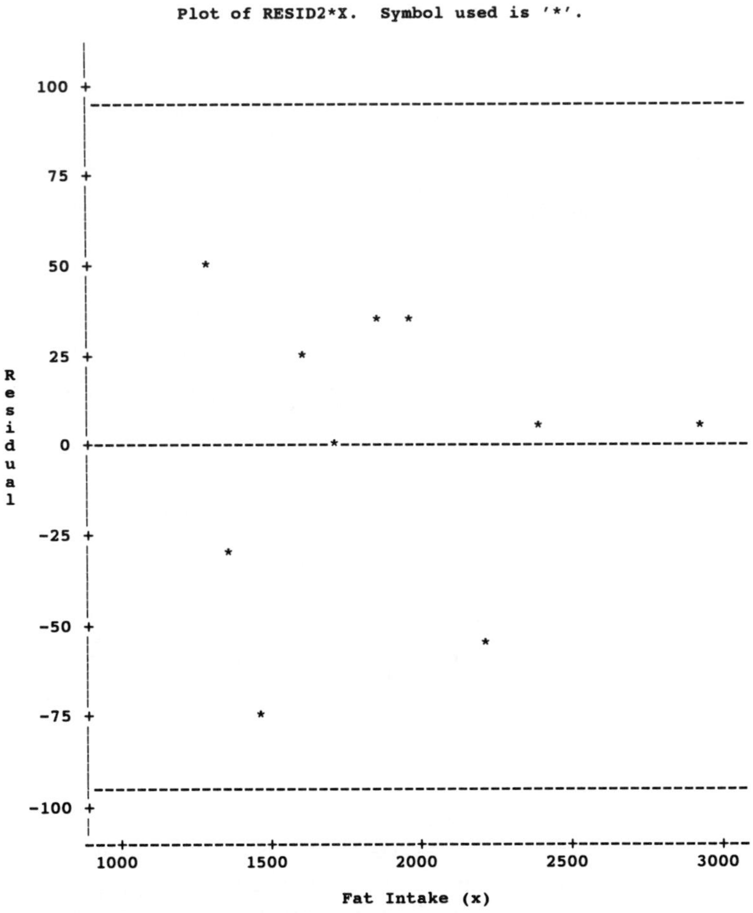

FIGURE 7.3
SAS plot of regression residuals for the second-order model of Example 7.1b

EXAMPLE 7.2

Example 7.1a gives the residuals obtained from fitting a first-order model to the cholesterol data. Plot the residuals obtained in this regression analysis against the fat intake, x (x is recorded on the horizontal axis). Does the plot suggest model inadequacy or departure from the usual assumptions made about the error term ε?

Solution

The residuals for the first-order model were given in Table 7.2. The plot of these residuals versus fat intake is shown in Figure 7.4. The distinctive aspect of this plot is the parabolic distribution of the residuals about their mean; i.e., all residuals tend to be positive for athletes with intermediate levels of fat intake x and negative for the athletes with either relatively high or low levels of fat intake. This parabolic appearance of the trend in the residuals suggests that a second-order term may improve the model. In fact, the addition of a second-order term does improve the model: The quadratic (β_2) term in the model is highly significant (see the SAS printout, Figure 7.2), and the residual plot for the second-order model no longer shows an observable pattern (see Figure 7.3).

FIGURE 7.4

SAS plot of regression residuals for the first-order model of Example 7.1a

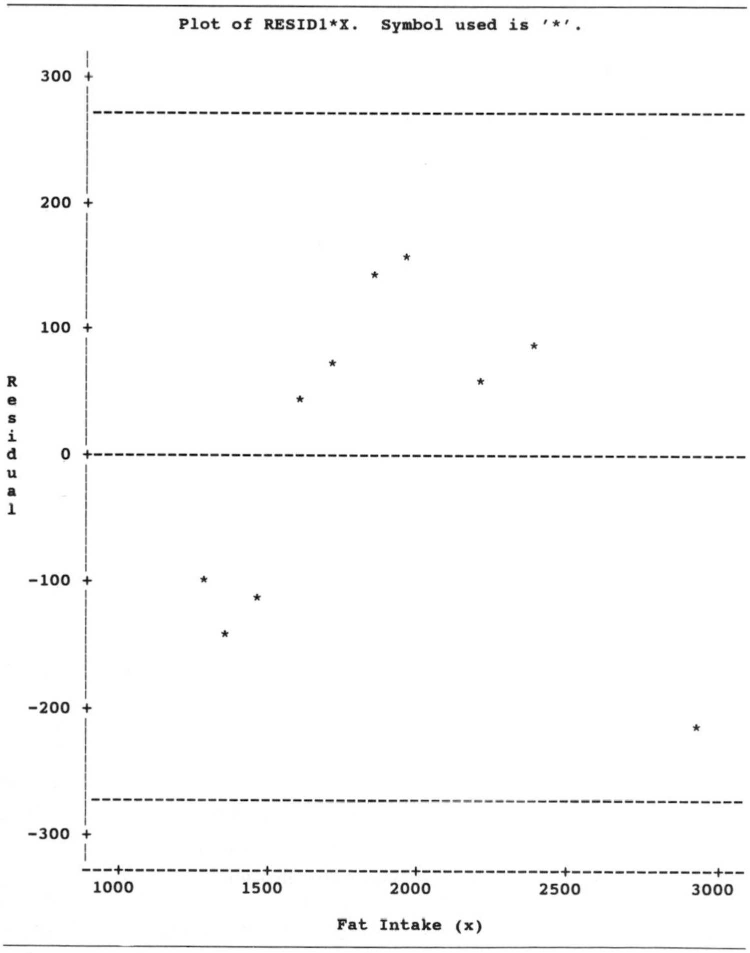

An alternative method of detecting lack of fit in models with more than one independent variable is to construct a partial residual plot. The **partial residuals** for the jth independent variable, x_j, in the model are calculated as follows:

$$\begin{aligned}\hat{\varepsilon}^* &= y - (\hat{\beta}_0 + \hat{\beta}_1 x_1 + \hat{\beta}_2 x_2 + \cdots + \hat{\beta}_{j-1} x_{j-1} + \hat{\beta}_{j+1} x_{j+1} + \cdots + \hat{\beta}_k x_k) \\ &= \hat{\varepsilon} + \hat{\beta}_j x_j\end{aligned}$$

where $\hat{\varepsilon}$ is the usual regression residual.

Partial residuals measure the influence of x_j on the independent variable y *after the effects of the other independent variables* $(x_1, x_2, \ldots, x_{j-1}, x_{j+1}, \ldots, x_k)$ *have been removed or accounted for*. If the partial residuals $\hat{\varepsilon}^*$ are regressed against x_j in a straight-line model, the resulting least squares slope is equal to $\hat{\beta}_j$—the β estimate obtained from the full model. Therefore, when the partial residuals are plotted against x_j, the points are scattered around a line with slope equal to $\hat{\beta}_j$. Unusual deviations or patterns around this line indicate lack of fit for the variable x_j.

A plot of the partial residuals versus x_j often reveals more information about the relationship between y and x_j than the usual residual plot. In particular, a partial residual plot usually indicates more precisely how to modify the model,† as the next example illustrates.

Definition 7.2

The set of **partial regression residuals** for the jth independent variable x_j is calculated as follows:

$$\begin{aligned}\hat{\varepsilon}^* &= y - (\hat{\beta}_0 + \hat{\beta}_1 x_1 + \hat{\beta}_2 x_2 + \cdots \\ &\qquad + \hat{\beta}_{j-1} x_{j-1} + \hat{\beta}_{j+1} x_{j+1} + \cdots + \hat{\beta}_k x_k) \\ &= \hat{\varepsilon} + \hat{\beta}_j x_j\end{aligned}$$

where $\hat{\varepsilon} = y - \hat{y}$ is the usual regression residual (see Definition 7.1).

EXAMPLE 7.3

Refer to the supermarket chain experiment in Example 6.4. Recall that the chain wanted to investigate the effect of price x_1 on the weekly demand y for a house brand of coffee at eight of its stores. Eight prices were randomly assigned to the stores and were advertised using the same procedures. A few weeks later, the chain conducted the same experiment using no advertisements. The data for the entire study are shown in Table 7.4.

Consider the model

$$E(y) = \beta_0 + \beta_1 p + \beta_2 x_2$$

†Partial residual plots display the correct functional form of the predictor variables across the relevant range of interest, except in cases where severe multicollinearity exists. See Mansfield and Conerly (1987) for an excellent discussion of the use of residual and partial residual plots.

where

$$x_2 = \begin{cases} 1 & \text{if advertisement used} \\ 0 & \text{if not} \end{cases}$$

TABLE 7.4 **Data for Example 7.3**

WEEKLY DEMAND y, pounds	PRICE p, dollars per pound	ADVERTISEMENT x_2
1,120	3.00	1
999	3.10	1
932	3.20	1
884	3.30	1
807	3.40	1
760	3.50	1
701	3.60	1
688	3.70	1
1,037	3.00	0
962	3.10	0
904	3.20	0
827	3.30	0
775	3.40	0
715	3.50	0
666	3.60	0
607	3.70	0

a. Fit the model to the data. Is the model adequate for predicting weekly demand y?
b. Calculate and plot the residuals versus p. Do you detect any trends?
c. Calculate the partial residuals for the independent variable p, and construct the corresponding partial residual plot. What does the plot reveal?
d. Fit the model $E(y) = \beta_0 + \beta_1 x_1 + \beta_2 x_2$, where $x_1 = 1/p$. Has the predictive ability of the model improved?

Solution

a. The SAS printout for the regression analysis is shown in Figure 7.5 on page 386. The F value for testing model adequacy, i.e., H_0: $\beta_1 = \beta_2 = 0$, is given on the printout (shaded) as $F = 368.298$ with a corresponding p-value (also shaded) of $p = .0001$. Thus, there is sufficient evidence (at any α of .0001 or greater) that the model contributes information for the prediction of weekly demand, y. Also, the coefficient of determination is $R^2 = .9827$, meaning that the model explains approximately 98% of the sample variation in weekly demand.

Recall from Example 6.4, however, that we fitted a model with the transformed independent variable $x_1 = 1/p$. That is, we expect the relationship between weekly demand y and price p to be decreasing in a curvilinear fashion and approaching (but never reaching) 0 as p increases. (See curve 1 in Figure 6.8c.) If such a relationship exists, the model (with untransformed price), although statistically useful for predicting demand y, will be inadequate in a practical setting.

FIGURE 7.5
SAS printout for Example 7.3

```
Dependent Variable: Y

                          Analysis of Variance

                             Sum of          Mean
Source              DF      Squares        Square      F Value       Prob>F

Model                2 320515.29762 160257.64881       368.298       0.0001
Error               13   5656.70238    435.13095
C Total             15 326172.00000

     Root MSE       20.85979     R-square       0.9827
     Dep Mean      836.50000     Adj R-sq       0.9800
     C.V.            2.49370

                          Parameter Estimates

                  Parameter         Standard     T for H0:
Variable   DF      Estimate            Error    Parameter=0      Prob > |T|

INTERCEP    1   2848.744048      76.60151888         37.189          0.0001
P           1   -608.095238      22.75989979        -26.718          0.0001
X2          1     49.750000      10.42989636          4.770          0.0004

                               Dep Var     Predict
             Obs       P          Y         Value    Residual

               1       3      1120.0       1074.2     45.7917
               2     3.1       999.0       1013.4    -14.3988
               3     3.2       932.0        952.6    -20.5893
               4     3.3       884.0        891.8     -7.7798
               5     3.4       807.0        831.0    -23.9702
               6     3.5       760.0        770.2    -10.1607
               7     3.6       701.0        709.4     -8.3512
               8     3.7       688.0        648.5     39.4583
               9       3      1037.0       1024.5     12.5417
              10     3.1       962.0        963.6     -1.6488
              11     3.2       904.0        902.8      1.1607
              12     3.3       827.0        842.0    -15.0298
              13     3.4       775.0        781.2     -6.2202
              14     3.5       715.0        720.4     -5.4107
              15     3.6       666.0        659.6      6.3988
              16     3.7       607.0        598.8      8.2083

Sum of Residuals                 -5.22959E-12
Sum of Squared Residuals            5656.7024
Predicted Resid SS (Press)          9753.5574
```

b. The regression residuals for the model in part **a** are shown in the bottom portion of Figure 7.5. Figure 7.6 is a computer-generated (SAS) plot of these residuals against price p. Notice that the plot reveals a parabolic trend, implying a lack of fit. Thus, the residual plot supports our hypothesis that the weekly demand–price relationship is curvilinear, not linear. However, the appropriate transformation on price (i.e., $1/p$) is not evident from the plot. In fact, the nature of the curvature in Figure 7.6 may lead you to conclude that the addition of the quadratic term, $\beta_3 p^2$, to the model will solve the problem. In general, a residual plot will detect curvature if it exists, but may not reveal the appropriate transformation.

c. The partial residuals (denoted $\hat{\varepsilon}^*$) for the independent variable p are calculated using the formula given in Definition 7.2:

$$\hat{\varepsilon}^* = \hat{\varepsilon} + \hat{\beta}_1 p$$

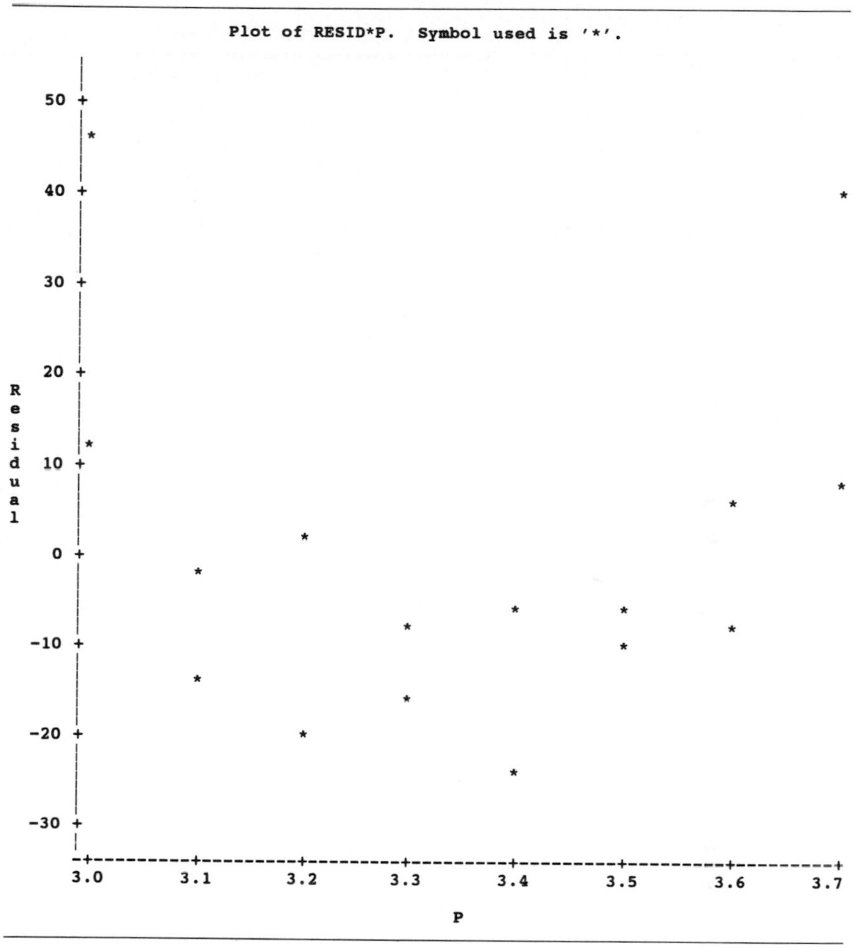

FIGURE 7.6
SAS printout of residuals against price for Example 7.3

where $\hat{\beta}_1 = -608.1$ (from Figure 7.5). For example, the partial residual for the first observation is calculated by substituting $\hat{\varepsilon} = 45.79$ and $p = 3.00$ into the equation:

$$\begin{aligned}\hat{\varepsilon}^* &= \hat{\varepsilon} - 608.1p \\ &= 45.79 - 608.1(3) = -1{,}778.5\end{aligned}$$

The complete set of partial residuals for p, Table 7.5, and a computer-generated (SAS) partial residual plot, Figure 7.7, are shown on page 388.

You can see that the partial residual plot also reveals a curvilinear trend but, in addition, displays the correct functional form of weekly demand–price relationship. Notice that the curve is decreasing and approaching (but never reaching) 0 as p increases. This suggests that the appropriate transformation on price is either $1/p$ or e^{-p} (see Figures 6.8c and 6.8d).

TABLE 7.5 **Partial Residuals for Price p in First-Order Model for Example 7.3**

PRICE p	RESIDUAL $\hat{\varepsilon}$	PARTIAL RESIDUAL $\hat{\varepsilon}^*$	PRICE p	RESIDUAL $\hat{\varepsilon}$	PARTIAL RESIDUAL $\hat{\varepsilon}^*$
3.0	45.792	−1,778.5	3.0	12.542	−1,811.7
3.1	−14.399	−1,899.5	3.1	−1.649	−1,886.7
3.2	−20.589	−1,966.5	3.2	1.161	−1,944.7
3.3	−7.780	−2,014.5	3.3	−15.030	−2,021.7
3.4	−23.970	−2,091.5	3.4	−6.220	−2,073.7
3.5	−10.161	−2,138.5	3.5	−5.411	−2,133.7
3.6	−8.351	−2,197.5	3.6	6.399	−2,182.7
3.7	39.458	−2,210.5	3.7	8.208	−2,241.7

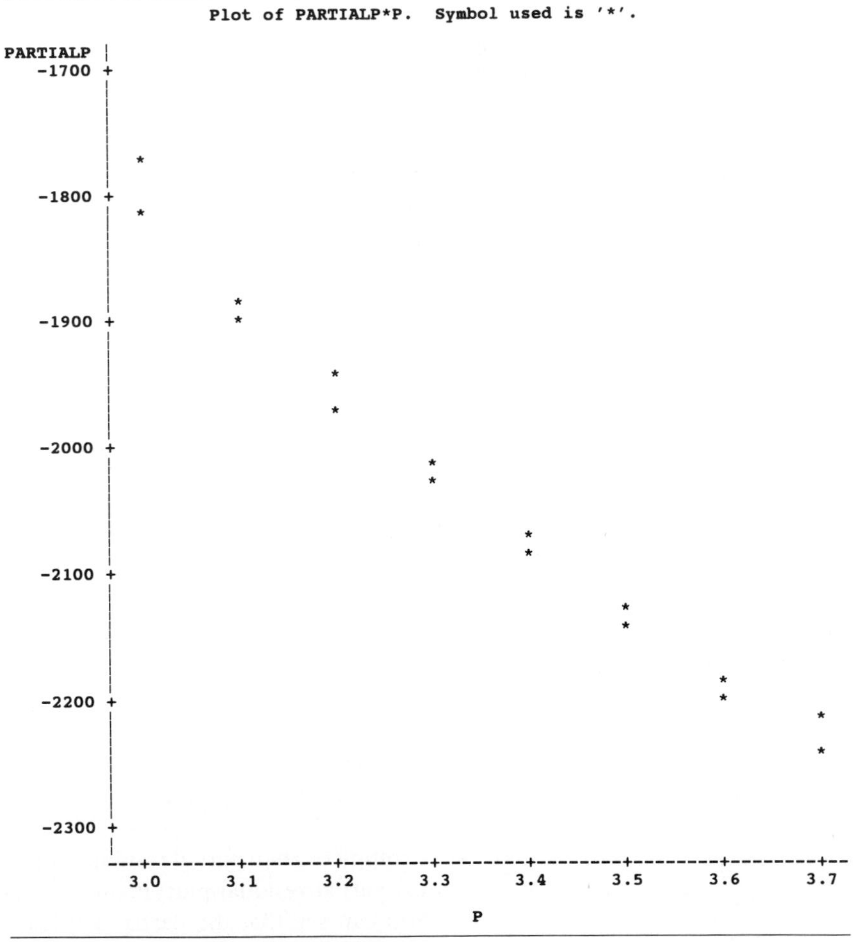

FIGURE 7.7
SAS printout of partial residuals against price for Example 7.3

d. Using the transformation $x_1 = 1/p$, we refit the model to the data, and the resulting SAS printout is shown in Figure 7.8. The small p-value ($p = .0001$) for testing H_0: $\beta_1 = \beta_2 = 0$ indicates that the model is adequate for predicting y. Although the coefficient of determination increased only slightly (from $R^2 = .9827$ to $R^2 = .9915$), the model standard deviation (**Root MSE**) decreased significantly (from $s = 20.85979$ to $s = 14.56978$). Thus, whereas the model with untransformed price can predict weekly demand for coffee to within $2s = 2(20.9) = 41.8$ pounds, the transformed model can predict demand to within $2(14.6) = 29.2$ pounds.

FIGURE 7.8
SAS printout for Example 7.3

```
Dependent Variable: Y

                         Analysis of Variance

                          Sum of          Mean
Source          DF       Squares        Square       F Value       Prob>F

Model            2  323412.38092  161706.19046       761.765       0.0001
Error           13    2759.61908     212.27839
C Total         15  326172.00000

      Root MSE      14.56978       R-square         0.9915
      Dep Mean     836.50000       Adj R-sq         0.9902
      C.V.           1.74175

                         Parameter Estimates

                  Parameter         Standard     T for H0:
Variable   DF      Estimate            Error   Parameter=0     Prob > |T|

INTERCEP    1  -1223.995202      53.21896999       -22.999         0.0001
X1          1   6787.311692     176.61334352        38.430         0.0001
X2          1     49.750000       7.28488832         6.829         0.0001
```

Residual (or partial residual) plots are useful for indicating potential model improvements, but they are no substitute for formal statistical tests of model terms to determine their importance. Thus, a true test of whether the second-order term contributes to the cholesterol model (Example 7.1) is the t test of the null hypothesis H_0: $\beta_2 = 0$. The appropriate test statistic, shown in the printout of Figure 7.2, indicates that the second-order term does contribute information for the prediction of cholesterol level y. We have confidence in this statistical inference because we know the probability α of committing a Type I error (concluding a term is important when, in fact, it is not). In contrast, decisions based on residual plots are subjective, and their reliability cannot be measured. Therefore, we suggest that such plots be used only as indicators of *potential* problems. The final judgment on model adequacy should be based on appropriate statistical tests.*

*A more general procedure for determining whether the straight-line model adequately fits the data tests the null hypothesis H_0: $E(y) = \beta_0 + \beta_1 x$ against the alternative H_a: $E(y) \neq \beta_0 + \beta_1 x$. You can see that this test, called a test for *lack of fit*, does not restrict the alternative hypothesis to second-order models. Lack-of-fit tests are appropriate when the x values are replicated, i.e., when the sample data include two or more observations for several different levels of x. When the data are observational, however, replication rarely occurs. (Note that none of the values of x is repeated in Table 7.1.) For details on how to conduct tests for lack of fit, consult the references given at the end of this chapter.

EXERCISES

7.1 A first-order model is fitted to the data shown in the table with the following result:

$$\hat{y} = 2.588 + .541x$$

x	−2	−2	−1	−1	0	0	1	1	2	2	3	3
y	1.1	1.3	2.0	2.1	2.7	2.8	3.4	3.6	4.0	3.9	3.8	3.6

a. Calculate the residuals for the model.
b. Plot the residuals versus x. Do you detect any trends? If so, what does the pattern suggest about the model?

7.2 A first-order model is fitted to the data shown in the table with the following result:

$$\hat{y} = -3.179 + 2.491x$$

x	2	4	7	10	12	15	18	20	21	25
y	5	10	12	22	25	27	39	50	47	65

a. Calculate the residuals for the model.
b. Plot the residuals versus x. Do you detect any trends? If so, what does the pattern suggest about the model?

7.3 Refer to Example 3.2. Recall that a manufacturer of a new tire tested the tire for wear at different pressures with the results shown in the table.

PRESSURE x, pounds per sq. inch	MILEAGE y, thousands
30	29.5
30	30.2
31	32.1
31	34.5
32	36.3
32	35.0
33	38.2
33	37.6
34	37.7
34	36.1
35	33.6
35	34.2
36	26.8
36	27.4

a. Fit the straight-line model $y = \beta_0 + \beta_1 x + \varepsilon$ to the data.
b. Calculate the residuals for the model.

c. Plot the residuals versus x. Do you detect any trends? If so, what does the pattern suggest about the model?

d. Fit the quadratic model $y = \beta_0 + \beta_1 x + \beta_2 x^2 + \varepsilon$ to the data using an available statistical software package. Has the addition of the quadratic term improved model adequacy?

7.4 Moissanite is a popular abrasive material because of its extreme hardness. Another important property of moissanite is elasticity. The elastic properties of the material were investigated in the *Journal of Applied Physics* (Sept. 1993). A diamond anvil cell was used to compress a mixture of moissanite, sodium chloride, and gold in a ratio of 33:99:1 by volume. The compressed volume, y, of the mixture (relative to the zero-pressure volume) was measured at each of 11 different pressures (GPa). The results are displayed in the table, followed by a MINITAB printout for the straight-line regression model $E(y) = \beta_0 + \beta_1 x$.

COMPRESSED VOLUME y, %	PRESSURE x, GPa	COMPRESSED VOLUME y, %	PRESSURE x, GPa
100	0	85.2	51.6
96	9.4	83.3	60.1
93.8	15.8	82.9	62.6
90.2	30.4	82.9	62.6
87.7	41.6	81.7	68.4
86.2	46.9		

Source: Bassett, W. A., Weathers, M. S., and Wu, T. C. "Compressibility of SiC up to 68.4 GPa." *Journal of Applied Physics*, Vol. 74, No. 6, Sept. 15, 1993, p. 3825 (Table I).

```
The regression equation is
Volume = 98.6 - 0.256 Pressure

Predictor        Coef        Stdev     t-ratio        p
Constant      98.6149       0.4037      244.26    0.000
Pressure    -0.255594     0.008646      -29.56    0.000

s = 0.6484         R-sq = 99.0%       R-sq(adj) = 98.9%

Analysis of Variance

SOURCE        DF          SS          MS         F         p
Regression     1      367.34      367.34    873.87     0.000
Error          9        3.78        0.42
Total         10      371.12

Unusual Observations
Obs.Pressure     Volume        Fit Stdev.Fit  Residual    St.Resid
  1      0.0    100.000     98.615     0.404     1.385       2.73R

R denotes an obs. with a large st. resid.
```

a. Calculate the regression residuals.

b. Plot the residuals against x. Do you detect a trend?

c. Propose an alternative model based on the plot, part **b**.

d. Fit and analyze the model, part **c**.

7.5 The real estate data for Exercise 4.51 are reproduced on page 392. Recall that the property appraisers fitted the model

$$E(y) = \beta_0 + \beta_1 x_1 + \beta_2 x_2$$

SALE PRICE y, \$ thousands	HOME SIZE x_1, hundreds of sq. ft.	CONDITION RATING x_2, 1 to 10
60.0	23	5
32.7	11	2
57.7	20	9
45.5	17	3
47.0	15	8
55.3	21	4
64.5	24	7
42.6	13	6
54.5	19	7
57.5	25	2

Source: Andrews, R. L., and Ferguson, J. T. "Integrating judgment with a regression appraisal." *The Real Estate Appraiser and Analyst*, Vol. 52, No. 2, Spring 1986 (Table I).

where

$$y = \text{Sale price (in \$ thousands)}$$
$$x_1 = \text{Home size (in square feet)}$$
$$x_2 = \text{Condition rating (1 to 10)}$$

The resulting least squares prediction equation is

$$\hat{y} = 9.782 + 1.871x_1 + 1.278x_2$$

a. Calculate the residuals for the model.
b. Plot the residuals versus x_1. Do you detect any trends? If so, what does the pattern suggest about the model?
c. Plot the residuals versus x_2. Do you detect any trends? If so, what does the pattern suggest about the model?
d. Calculate and plot the partial residuals for x_1. Interpret the result.
e. Calculate and plot the partial residuals for x_2. Interpret the result.

7.6 A certain type of rare gem serves as a status symbol for many of its owners. In theory, then, the demand for the gem would increase as the price increases, decreasing at low prices, leveling off at moderate prices, and increasing at high prices, because obtaining the gem at a high price confers high status on the owner. Although a quadratic model would seem to match the theory, the model proposed to explain the demand for the gem by its price is the first-order model

$$y = \beta_0 + \beta_1 x + \varepsilon$$

where y is the demand (in thousands) and x is the retail price per carat (dollars). This model was fitted to the 12 data points given in the table, and the results of the analysis are shown in the accompanying SPSS printout.

x	100	700	450	150	500	800	70	50	300	350	750	700
y	130	150	60	120	50	200	150	160	50	40	180	130

```
Multiple R              .23064
R Square                .05319
Adjusted R Square      -.04149
Standard Error        56.20658

Analysis of Variance
                   DF      Sum of Squares        Mean Square
Regression          1          1774.86785         1774.86785
Residual           10         31591.79882         3159.17988

F =         .56181        Signif F =  .4708

----------------- Variables in the Equation -----------------

Variable             B          SE B          Beta          T   Sig T

X               .04516        .06025        .23064       .750   .4708
(Constant)    99.81690      29.55565                    3.377   .0070
```

a. Use the least squares prediction equation to calculate the regression residuals.
b. Plot the residuals against retail price per carat, x.
c. Can you detect any trends in the residual plot? What does this imply?

7.7 Refer to *The New England Journal of Medicine* study of passive exposure to environmental tobacco smoke in children with cystic fibrosis, Exercise 3.34. Recall that the researchers investigated the correlation between a child's weight percentile (y) and the number of cigarettes smoked per day in the child's home (x). The accompanying table lists the data for the 25 boys. A SAS regression printout for the straight-line model relating y to x is shown on page 394.

WEIGHT PERCENTILE, y	NO. OF CIGARETTES SMOKED PER DAY, x	WEIGHT PERCENTILE, y	NO. OF CIGARETTES SMOKED PER DAY, x
6	0	43	0
6	15	49	0
2	40	50	0
8	23	49	22
11	20	46	30
17	7	54	0
24	3	58	0
25	0	62	0
17	25	66	0
25	20	66	23
25	15	83	0
31	23	87	44
35	10		

Source: Rubin, B. K. "Exposure of children with cystic fibrosis to environmental tobacco smoke." *The New England Journal of Medicine*, Sept. 20, 1990, Vol. 323, No. 12, p. 785 (data extracted from Figure 3).

a. Verify that the sum of the residuals is 0.
b. Plot the residuals against the number of cigarettes smoked per day, x.
c. Do you detect any patterns in the plot, part **b**? What does this imply?

SAS printout for Exercise 7.7

```
Dependent Variable: Y

                        Analysis of Variance

                               Sum of          Mean
Source              DF        Squares        Square       F Value       Prob>F

Model                1      304.88209     304.88209         0.500       0.4864
Error               23    14011.11791     609.17904
C Total             24    14316.00000

     Root MSE         24.68155      R-square        0.0213
     Dep Mean         37.80000      Adj R-sq       -0.0213
     C.V.             65.29511

                        Parameter Estimates

                     Parameter        Standard     T for H0:
Variable   DF         Estimate           Error   Parameter=0    Prob > |T|

INTERCEP    1        41.152655      6.84296599         6.014        0.0001
X           1        -0.261926      0.37024180        -0.707        0.4864

                              (continued)
       Dep Var   Predict   Std Err             Std Err   Student                  Cook's
Obs          Y     Value   Predict  Residual  Residual  Residual  -2-1-0 1 2           D

  1     6.0000   41.1527     6.843  -35.1527    23.714    -1.482 |    **|     |   0.091
  2    43.0000   41.1527     6.843    1.8473    23.714     0.078 |      |     |   0.000
  3     6.0000   37.2238     5.003  -31.2238    24.169    -1.292 |    **|     |   0.036
  4    49.0000   41.1527     6.843    7.8473    23.714     0.331 |      |     |   0.005
  5     2.0000   30.6756    11.215  -28.6756    21.986    -1.304 |    **|     |   0.221
  6    50.0000   41.1527     6.843    8.8473    23.714     0.373 |      |     |   0.006
  7     8.0000   35.1284     6.215  -27.1284    23.886    -1.136 |    **|     |   0.044
  8    49.0000   35.3903     5.997   13.6097    23.942     0.568 |      |*    |   0.010
  9    11.0000   35.9141     5.610  -24.9141    24.036    -1.037 |    **|     |   0.029
 10    46.0000   33.2949     8.057   12.7051    23.329     0.545 |      |*    |   0.018
 11    17.0000   39.3192     5.383  -22.3192    24.087    -0.927 |     *|     |   0.021
 12    54.0000   41.1527     6.843   12.8473    23.714     0.542 |      |*    |   0.012
 13    24.0000   40.3669     6.126  -16.3669    23.909    -0.685 |     *|     |   0.015
 14    58.0000   41.1527     6.843   16.8473    23.714     0.710 |      |*    |   0.021
 15    25.0000   41.1527     6.843  -16.1527    23.714    -0.681 |     *|     |   0.019
 16    62.0000   41.1527     6.843   20.8473    23.714     0.879 |      |*    |   0.032
 17    17.0000   34.6045     6.691  -17.6045    23.757    -0.741 |     *|     |   0.022
 18    66.0000   41.1527     6.843   24.8473    23.714     1.048 |      |**   |   0.046
 19    25.0000   35.9141     5.610  -10.9141    24.036    -0.454 |      |     |   0.006
 20    66.0000   35.1284     6.215   30.8716    23.886     1.292 |      |**   |   0.057
 21    25.0000   37.2238     5.003  -12.2238    24.169    -0.506 |     *|     |   0.005
 22    83.0000   41.1527     6.843   41.8473    23.714     1.765 |      |***  |   0.130
 23    31.0000   35.1284     6.215   -4.1284    23.886    -0.173 |      |     |   0.001
 24    87.0000   29.6279    12.562   57.3721    21.246     2.700 |      |*****|   1.275
 25    35.0000   38.5334     5.044   -3.5334    24.161    -0.146 |      |     |   0.000
```

7.3 Detecting Unequal Variances

Recall that one of the assumptions necessary for the validity of regression inferences is that the error term ε have constant variance σ^2 for all levels of the independent variable(s). Variances that satisfy this property are called **homoscedastic**. Unequal variances for different settings of the independent variable(s) are said to be **heteroscedastic**. Various statistical tests for heteroscedasticity have been developed. However, plots of the residuals will frequently reveal the presence of heteroscedasticity. In this section we will show how residual plots can be used to detect departures from the assumption of equal variances, and then give a simple test for heteroscedasticity. In addition, we will suggest some modifications to the model that may remedy the situation.

When data fail to be homoscedastic, the reason is often that the variance of the response y is a function of its mean $E(y)$. Some examples follow:

1. If the response y is a count that has a Poisson distribution, the variance will be equal to the mean $E(y)$. Poisson data are usually counts per unit volume, area, time, etc. For example, the number of sick days per month for an employee would very likely be a Poisson random variable. If the variance of a response is proportional to $E(y)$, the regression residuals produce a pattern about $\hat{y}$, the least squares estimate of $E(y)$, like that shown in Figure 7.9.

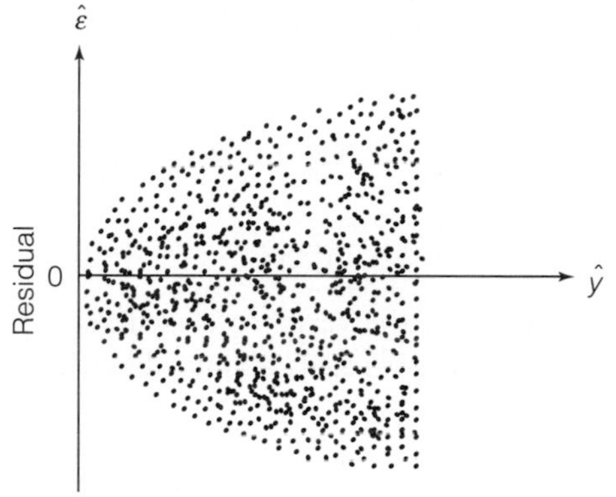

FIGURE 7.9
A plot of residuals for Poisson data

2. Many responses are proportions (or percentages) generated by **binomial experiments**. For instance, the proportion of a random sample of 100 convicted felons who are repeat offenders is an example of a binomial response. Binomial proportions have variances that are functions of both the true proportion (the mean) and the sample size. In fact, if the observed proportion $y_i = \hat{p}_i$ is generated by a binomial distribution with sample size n_i and true probability p_i, the variance of y_i is

$$\text{Var}(y_i) = \frac{p_i(1 - p_i)}{n_i} = \frac{E(y_i)[1 - E(y_i)]}{n_i}$$

Residuals for binomial data produce a pattern about $\hat{y}$ like that shown in Figure 7.10.

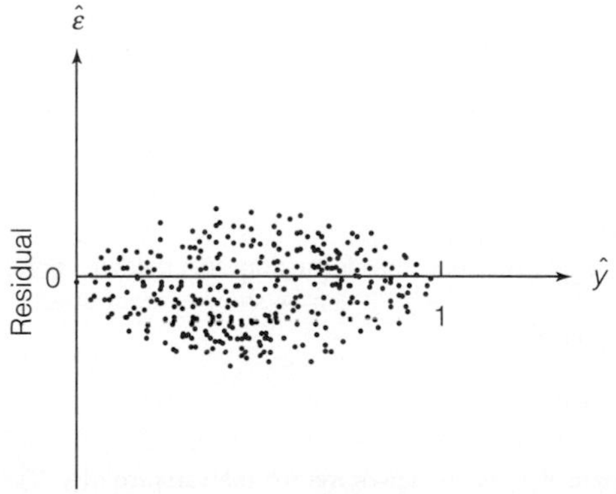

FIGURE 7.10
A plot of residuals for binomial data (proportions or percentages)

3. The random error component has been assumed to be **additive** in all the models we have constructed. An additive error is one for which the response is equal to the mean $E(y)$ *plus* random error,

$$y = E(y) + \varepsilon$$

Another useful type of model, especially for business and economic data, is the **multiplicative** model. In this model, the response is written as the *product* of its mean and the random error component, i.e.,

$$y = [E(y)]\varepsilon$$

The variance of this response will grow proportionally to the *square* of the mean, i.e.,

$$\text{Var}(y) = [E(y)]^2\sigma^2$$

where σ^2 is the variance of ε. Data subject to multiplicative errors produce a pattern of residuals about $\hat{y}$ like that shown in Figure 7.11.

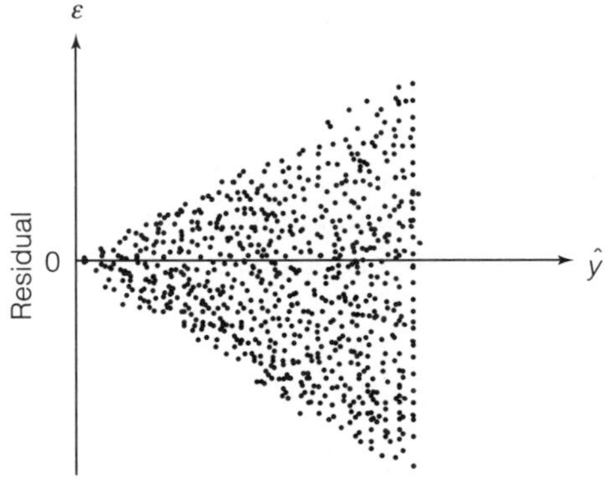

FIGURE 7.11
A plot of residuals for data subject to multiplicative errors

When the variance of y is a function of its mean, we can often satisfy the least squares assumption of homoscedasticity by transforming the response to some new response that has a constant variance. These are called **variance-stabilizing transformations**. For example, if the response y is a count that follows a Poisson distribution, the square root transform $\sqrt{y}$ can be shown to have approximately constant variance.† Consequently, if the response is a Poisson random variable, we would let

$$y^* = \sqrt{y}$$

†The square root transformation for Poisson responses is derived by finding the integral of $1/\sqrt{E(y)}$. In general, it can be shown (proof omitted) that the appropriate transformation for any response y is

$$y^* = \int \frac{1}{\sqrt{V(y)}}\,dy$$

where $V(y)$ is an expression for the variance of y.

and fit the model

$$y^* = \beta_0 + \beta_1 x_1 + \cdots + \beta_k x_k + \varepsilon$$

This model will satisfy approximately the least squares assumption of homoscedasticity.

Similar transformations that are appropriate for percentages and proportions (binomial data) or for data subject to multiplicative errors are shown in Table 7.6. The transformed responses will satisfy (at least approximately) the assumption of homoscedasticity.

TABLE 7.6 **Stabilizing Transformations for Heteroscedastic Responses**

TYPE OF RESPONSE	VARIANCE	STABILIZING TRANSFORMATION
Poisson	$E(y)$	$\sqrt{y}$
Binomial proportion	$\frac{E(y)[1 - E(y)]}{n}$	$\sin^{-1}\sqrt{y}$
Multiplicative	$[E(y)]^2\sigma^2$	$\log y$[a]

[a]Unless otherwise noted, natural logarithms (to the base e) will be used.

The data in Table 7.7 are the executive salaries, y, and years of experience, x, for a sample of 50 executives from a major industry. If we fit the second-order model $E(y) = \beta_0 + \beta_1 x + \beta_2 x^2$ to the data, we obtain the MINITAB computer

TABLE 7.7 **Salary and Experience Data for 50 Executives from a Major Industry**

YEARS OF EXPERIENCE x	SALARY y	YEARS OF EXPERIENCE x	SALARY y	YEARS OF EXPERIENCE x	SALARY y
7	$26,075	21	$43,628	28	$99,139
28	79,370	4	16,105	23	52,624
23	65,726	24	65,644	17	50,594
18	41,983	20	63,022	25	53,272
19	62,309	20	47,780	26	65,343
15	41,154	15	38,853	19	46,216
24	53,610	25	66,537	16	54,288
13	33,697	25	67,447	3	20,844
2	22,444	28	64,785	12	32,586
8	32,562	26	61,581	23	71,235
20	43,076	27	70,678	20	36,530
21	56,000	20	51,301	19	52,745
18	58,667	18	39,346	27	67,282
7	22,210	1	24,833	25	80,931
2	20,521	26	65,929	12	32,303
18	49,727	20	41,721	11	38,371
11	33,233	26	82,641		

FIGURE 7.12
MINITAB regression analysis printout for second-order model: Executive salaries

```
The regression equation is
Y = 20242 + 522 X + 53.0 XX

Predictor        Coef       Stdev    t-ratio        p
Constant        20242        4423       4.58    0.000
X               522.4       616.7       0.85    0.401
XX              53.00       19.57       2.71    0.009

s = 8123        R-sq = 81.6%       R-sq(adj) = 80.8%

Analysis of Variance

SOURCE       DF           SS          MS         F        p
Regression    2  13722605568  6861302784    103.98    0.000
Error        47   3101243136    65983896
Total        49  16823848960

SOURCE       DF       SEQ SS
X             1  13238774784
XX            1    483829792

Unusual Observations
Obs.        X          Y        Fit  Stdev.Fit   Residual    St.Resid
  9       2.0      22444      21499       3453        945      0.13 X
 15       2.0      20521      21499       3453       -978     -0.13 X
 31       1.0      24833      20817       3911       4016      0.56 X
 35      28.0      99139      76421       2663      22718      2.96R

R denotes an obs. with a large st. resid.
X denotes an obs. whose X value gives it large influence.
```

printout for the regression analysis shown in Figure 7.12 and the prediction equation

$$\hat{y} = 20{,}242 + 522x + 53x^2$$

The computer printout suggests that the second-order model provides an adequate fit to the data. The R^2 value, .816, indicates that the model explains almost 82% of the total variation of the y values about $\bar{y}$. The global F value, $F = 103.98$, is highly significant ($p \approx 0$), indicating that the model contributes information for the prediction of y. However, an examination of the salary residuals plotted against the estimated mean salary, $\hat{y}$, as shown in Figure 7.13, reveals a potential problem. Note the "cone" shape of the residual variability; the size of the residuals* increases as the estimated mean salary increases. This residual plot indicates that a multiplicative model may be appropriate. We will explore this possibility further in Example 7.4.

*The vertical axis of the MINITAB residual plot in Figure 7.13 represents the standardized residuals, $\hat{\varepsilon}^*$. MINITAB computes the standardized residuals as follows:

$$\hat{\varepsilon}_i^* = \frac{\hat{\varepsilon}_i}{s\sqrt{1 - h_i}}$$

where s is the standard deviation of the model and h_i is the "leverage" value for observation i. We discuss leverage in Section 7.5.

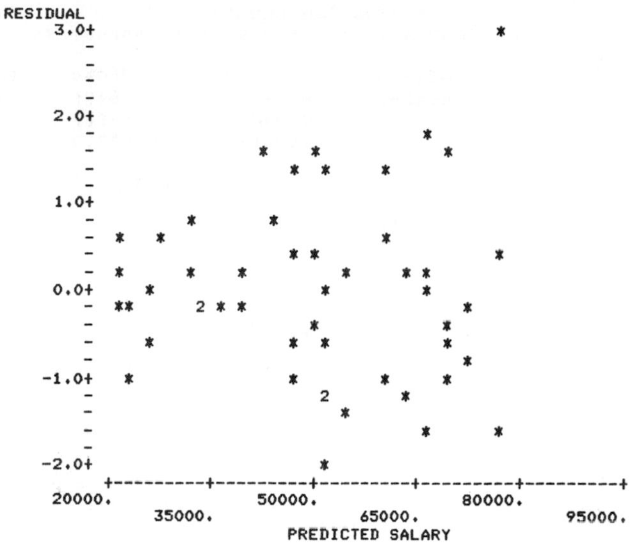

FIGURE 7.13
Executive salary versus experience example: MINITAB residual plot for second-order model with dependent variable Salary

EXAMPLE 7.4

Consider the salary and experience data in Table 7.7. Use the logarithmic transformation on the dependent variable, and relate log y to years of experience, x, using the second-order model

$$\widehat{\log y} = \beta_0 + \beta_1 x + \beta_2 x^2 + \varepsilon$$

Evaluate the adequacy of the model.

Solution

The MINITAB computer printout in Figure 7.14 on page 400 gives the regression analysis for the $n = 50$ measurements. The prediction equation used in computing the residuals is

$$\widehat{\log y} = 9.84289 + .04969x + .0000093x^2$$

The residual plot in Figure 7.15 (also on page 400) indicates that the logarithmic transformation has significantly reduced the heteroscedasticity.* Note that the cone shape is gone; there is no apparent tendency of the residual variance to increase as mean salary increases. We therefore are confident that inferences using the logarithmic model are more reliable than those using the untransformed model.

To evaluate model adequacy, we first note that $R^2 = .864$ and that about 86% of the variation in log(salary) is accounted for by the model. The global F value ($F = 148.66$) and its associated p-value ($p \approx 0$) indicate that the model significantly improves upon the sample mean as a predictor of log(salary).

*A printout of the residuals is omitted.

FIGURE 7.14
MINITAB regression analysis for logarithmic transform of salary data: Second-order model

```
The regression equation is
LOGY = 9.84 + 0.0497 X +0.000009 XX

Predictor        Coef         Stdev     t-ratio         p
Constant      9.84289       0.08479      116.08     0.000
X             0.04969       0.01182        4.20     0.000
XX          0.0000093     0.0003753        0.02     0.980

s = 0.1557        R-sq = 86.4%        R-sq(adj) = 85.8%

Analysis of Variance

SOURCE        DF          SS          MS          F         p
Regression     2      7.2119      3.6059     148.66     0.000
Error         47      1.1400      0.0243
Total         49      8.3519
```

FIGURE 7.15
Executive salary versus experience example: MINITAB residual plot for second-order model with dependent variable, log(salary)

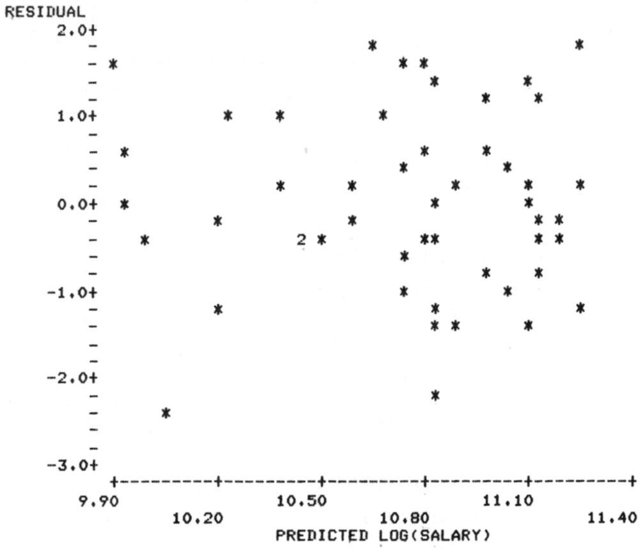

Although the estimate $\hat{\beta}_2$ of β_2 is very small, we should check to determine whether the data provide sufficient evidence to indicate that the second-order term contributes information for the prediction of log(salary). The test of

$$H_0: \beta_2 = 0$$
$$H_a: \beta_2 \neq 0$$

is conducted using the t statistic shown in Figure 7.14, $t = .02$. The absolute value of this computed t value is extremely small and, clearly, does not exceed the tabulated t value for any reasonable value of α ($t_{.05} \approx 1.645$). Consequently, there is insufficient evidence to indicate that the second-order term contributes to the prediction of log(salary). There is no indication that the second-order model is an improvement over the straight-line model,

$$\widehat{\log y} = \beta_0 + \beta_1 x + \varepsilon$$

for predicting log(salary).

The MINITAB computer printout for the first-order model (Figure 7.16) shows that the prediction equation for the first-order model is

$$\widehat{\log y} = 9.84133 + .049978x$$

The value of R^2, .863, is approximately the same as the value of R^2 obtained for the second-order model. The F statistic, computed from the mean squares in Figure 7.16, $F = 303.65$, indicates that the model contributes significantly to the prediction of log y.

FIGURE 7.16
MINITAB regression analysis for logarithmic transform of salary data: First-order model

```
The regression equation is
LOGY = 9.84 + 0.0500 X

Predictor        Coef        Stdev      t-ratio        p
Constant      9.84133      0.05636       174.63    0.000
X            0.049978     0.002868        17.43    0.000

s = 0.1541      R-sq = 86.3%      R-sq(adj) = 86.1%

Analysis of Variance

SOURCE        DF           SS           MS         F         p
Regression     1       7.2118       7.2118    303.65     0.000
Error         48       1.1400       0.0238
Total         49       8.3519

Unusual Observations
Obs.         X       LOGY        Fit Stdev.Fit  Residual    St.Resid
 19        4.0     9.6869    10.0412    0.0460   -0.3544      -2.41R
 31        1.0    10.1199     9.8913    0.0537    0.2286       1.58 X
 45       20.0    10.5059    10.8409    0.0225   -0.3350      -2.20R

R denotes an obs. with a large st. resid.
X denotes an obs. whose X value gives it large influence.
```

When the transformed model of Example 7.4 is used to predict the value of log y, the predicted value of y is the antilog, $\hat{y} = e^{\widehat{\log y}}$. The endpoints of the prediction interval are similarly transformed back to the original scale, and the interval will retain its meaning. In repeated use, the intervals will contain the observed y value $100(1 - \alpha)\%$ of the time.

Unfortunately, you cannot take antilogs to find the confidence interval for the mean value $E(y)$. The reason for this is that the mean value of log y is not equal to the logarithm of the mean of y. In fact, the antilog of the logarithmic mean of a random variable y is called its **geometric mean**. Thus, the antilogs of the endpoints of the confidence interval for the mean of the transformed response will give a confidence interval for the geometric mean. Similar care must be exercised with other types of transformations. In general, prediction intervals can be transformed back to the original scale without losing their meaning, but confidence intervals for the mean of a transformed response cannot.

The preceding examples illustrate that, in practice, residual plots can be a powerful technique for detecting heteroscedasticity. Furthermore, the pattern of the residuals often suggests the appropriate variance-stabilizing transformation to use. Keep in mind, however, that no measure of reliability can be attached to inferences derived from a graphical technique. For this reason, you may want to rely on a statistical test.

Various tests for heteroscedasticity in regression have been developed. One of the simpler techniques utilizes the F test (discussed in Chapter 1) for comparing population variances. The procedure requires that you divide the sample data in half and fit the regression model to each half. If the regression model fitted to one-half the observations yields a significantly smaller or larger MSE than the model fitted to the other half, there is evidence that the assumption of equal variances for all levels of the x variables in the model is being violated. (Recall that MSE, or mean square for error, estimates σ^2, the variance of the random error term.) Where you divide the data depends on where you suspect the differences in variances to be. We illustrate this procedure with an example.

EXAMPLE 7.5

Refer to Example 7.4, which compared executive salary (y) versus years of experience (x). The residual plot for the quadratic model

$$E(y) = \beta_0 + \beta_1 x + \beta_2 x^2$$

indicates that the assumption of equal variances may be violated (see Figure 7.13). Conduct a statistical test of hypothesis to determine whether heteroscedasticity exists. Use $\alpha = .05$.

Solution

The residual plot shown in Figure 7.13 reveals that the residuals associated with larger values of predicted salary tend to be more variable than the residuals associated with smaller values of predicted salary. Therefore, we will divide the sample observations based on the values of $\hat{y}$, or, equivalently, the value of x (since, for the fitted model, $\hat{y}$ increases as x increases). An examination of the data in Table 7.7 reveals that approximately one-half of the 50 observed values of years of experience, x, fall below $x = 20$. Thus, we will divide the data into two subsamples as follows:

SUBSAMPLE 1	SUBSAMPLE 2
$x < 20$	$x \geq 20$
$n_1 = 24$	$n_2 = 26$

Figures 7.17a and 7.17b give the SAS printouts for the quadratic model fit to subsample 1 and subsample 2, respectively. The value of MSE is shaded in each printout.

The null and alternative hypotheses to be tested are

$$H_0\colon \frac{\sigma_1^2}{\sigma_2^2} = 1 \quad \text{(Assumption of equal variances satisfied)}$$

$$H_a\colon \frac{\sigma_1^2}{\sigma_2^2} \neq 1 \quad \text{(Assumption of equal variances violated)}$$

where

σ_1^2 = Variance of the random error term, ε, for subpopulation 1 (i.e., $x < 20$)

σ_2^2 = Variance of the random error term, ε, for subpopulation 2 (i.e., $x \geq 20$)

The test statistic for a two-tailed test is given by:

$$F = \frac{\text{Larger } s^2}{\text{Smaller } s^2} = \frac{\text{Larger MSE}}{\text{Smaller MSE}} \quad \text{(see Section 1.10)}$$

where the distribution of F is based on ν_1 = df(error) associated with the larger MSE and ν_2 = df(error) associated with the smaller MSE. Recall that for a quadratic model, df(error) $= n - 3$.

From the printouts shown in Figures 7.17a and 7.17b, we have

$$\text{MSE}_1 = 31{,}577{,}876 \quad \text{and} \quad \text{MSE}_2 = 94{,}708{,}058$$

FIGURE 7.17

a. SAS regression analysis for second-order model: Subsample 1 (years of experience < 20)

ANALYSIS OF VARIANCE

SOURCE	DF	SUM OF SQUARES	MEAN SQUARE	F VALUE	PROB>F
MODEL	2	3231228653	1615614327	51.163	0.0001
ERROR	21	663135395	31577875.97		
C TOTAL	23	3894364049			

ROOT MSE	5619.42	R-SQUARE	0.8297
DEP MEAN	37152.75	ADJ R-SQ	0.8135
C.V.	15.12518		

PARAMETER ESTIMATES

VARIABLE	DF	PARAMETER ESTIMATE	STANDARD ERROR	T FOR H0: PARAMETER=0	PROB > |T|
INTERCEP	1	20372.31906	3817.93090	5.336	0.0001
X	1	263.14290	861.88016	0.305	0.7631
XX	1	76.77081657	40.01457868	1.919	0.0687

b. SAS regression analysis for second-order model: Subsample 2 (years of experience ≥ 20)

ANALYSIS OF VARIANCE

SOURCE	DF	SUM OF SQUARES	MEAN SQUARE	F VALUE	PROB>F
MODEL	2	2930533276	1465266638	15.471	0.0001
ERROR	23	2178285323	94708057.53		
C TOTAL	25	5108818599			

ROOT MSE	9731.806	R-SQUARE	0.5736
DEP MEAN	62185.85	ADJ R-SQ	0.5365
C.V.	15.64955		

PARAMETER ESTIMATES

VARIABLE	DF	PARAMETER ESTIMATE	STANDARD ERROR	T FOR H0: PARAMETER=0	PROB > |T|
INTERCEP	1	-19228.62348	168795.40	-0.114	0.9103
X	1	2996.18859	14415.13670	0.208	0.8372
XX	1	17.03645465	304.21753	0.056	0.9558

Therefore, the test statistic is

$$F = \frac{\text{MSE}_2}{\text{MSE}_1} = \frac{94{,}708{,}058}{31{,}577{,}876} = 3.00$$

Since the MSE for subsample 2 is placed in the numerator of the test statistic, this F value is based on $n_2 - 3 = 26 - 3 = 23$ numerator df and $n_1 - 3 = 24 - 3 = 21$ denominator df. For a two-tailed test at $\alpha = .05$, the critical value for $\nu_1 = 23$ and $\nu_2 = 21$ (found in Table 5 of Appendix C) is approximately $F_{.025} = 2.37$.

Since the observed value, $F = 3.00$, exceeds the critical value, there is sufficient evidence (at $\alpha = .05$) to indicate that the error variances differ.* Thus, this test supports the conclusions reached by using the residual plots in the preceding examples.

The test for heteroscedasticity outlined in Example 7.5 is easy to apply when only a single independent variable appears in the model. For a multiple regression model that contains several different independent variables, the choice of the levels of the x variables for dividing the data is more difficult, if not impossible. If you require a statistical test for heteroscedasticity in a multiple regression model, you may need to resort to other, more complex, tests.† Consult the references at the end of this chapter for details on how to conduct these tests.

EXERCISES

7.8 Refer to Exercise 7.1. Plot the residuals for the first-order model versus $\hat{y}$. Do you detect any trends? If so, what does the pattern suggest about the model?

7.9 Refer to Exercise 7.2. Plot the residuals for the first-order model versus $\hat{y}$. Do you detect any trends? If so, what does the pattern suggest about the model?

7.10 Chemical engineers at Tokyo Metropolitan University analyzed urban air specimens for the presence of low-molecular-weight dicarboxylic acids (*Environmental Science & Engineering*, Oct. 1993). The dicarboxylic acid (as a percentage of total carbon) and oxidant concentrations (in ppm) for 19 air specimens collected from urban Tokyo are listed in the accompanying table. SAS printouts for the straight-line model relating dicarboxylic acid percentage (y) to oxidant concentration (x) are shown on pages 405 and 406. Use the information in the SAS printouts to assess the validity of the assumption of equal error variances.

*Most statistical tests require that the observations in the sample be independent. For this F test, the observations are the residuals. Even if the standard least squares assumption of independent errors is satisfied, the regression residuals will be correlated. Fortunately, when n is large compared to the number of β parameters in the model, the correlation among the residuals is reduced and, in most cases, can be ignored.

†For example, consider fitting the absolute values of the residuals as a function of the independent variables in the model; i.e., fit the regression model $E\{\,|\hat{\varepsilon}|\,\} = \beta_0 + \beta_1x_1 + \beta_2x_2 + \cdots + \beta_kx_k$. A nonsignificant global F implies that the assumption of homoscedasticity is satisfied. A significant F, however, indicates that changing the values of the x's will lead to a larger (or smaller) residual variance.

DICARBOXYLIC ACID, %	OXIDANT, ppm	DICARBOXYLIC ACID, %	OXIDANT, ppm
.85	78	.50	32
1.45	80	.38	28
1.80	74	.30	25
1.80	78	.70	45
1.60	60	.80	40
1.20	62	.90	45
1.30	57	1.22	41
.20	49	1.00	34
.22	34	1.00	25
.40	36		

Source: Kawamura, K., and Ikushima, K. "Seasonal changes in the distribution of dicarboxylic acids in the urban atmosphere." *Environmental Science & Technology*, Vol. 27, No. 10, Oct. 1993, p. 2,232 (data extracted from Figure 4).

SAS printout for Exercise 7.10

```
Model: MODEL1
Dependent Variable: DICARBOX

                          Analysis of Variance

                             Sum of          Mean
      Source        DF      Squares        Square      F Value       Prob>F

      Model          1      2.41362       2.41362       17.080       0.0007
      Error         17      2.40234       0.14131
      C Total       18      4.81597

          Root MSE       0.37592     R-square       0.5012
          Dep Mean       0.92737     Adj R-sq       0.4718
          C.V.          40.53600

                          Parameter Estimates

                      Parameter       Standard     T for H0:
    Variable  DF       Estimate          Error   Parameter=0     Prob > |T|

    INTERCEP   1      -0.023737     0.24576577        -0.097         0.9242
    OXIDANT    1       0.019579     0.00473739         4.133         0.0007

         Dep Var   Predict   Std Err             Std Err   Student                      Cook's
    Obs DICARBOX     Value   Predict   Residual  Residual  Residual    -2-1-0 1 2            D

      1   0.8500    1.5034     0.164    -0.6534     0.338    -1.931   |   ***|      |    0.438
      2   0.5000    0.6028     0.117    -0.1028     0.357    -0.288   |      |      |    0.004
      3   1.4500    1.5425     0.172    -0.0925     0.334    -0.277   |      |      |    0.010
      4   0.3800    0.5245     0.130    -0.1445     0.353    -0.410   |      |      |    0.011
      5   1.8000    1.4251     0.148     0.3749     0.346     1.085   |      |**    |    0.108
      6   0.3000    0.4657     0.141    -0.1657     0.348    -0.476   |      |      |    0.019
      7   1.8000    1.5034     0.164     0.2966     0.338     0.877   |      |*     |    0.090
      8   0.7000    0.8573     0.088    -0.1573     0.365    -0.430   |      |      |    0.005
      9   1.6000    1.1510     0.102     0.4490     0.362     1.241   |      |**    |    0.061
     10   0.8000    0.7594     0.095     0.0406     0.364     0.112   |      |      |    0.000
     11   1.2000    1.1901     0.107     0.0099     0.360     0.027   |      |      |    0.000
     12   0.9000    0.8573     0.088     0.0427     0.365     0.117   |      |      |    0.000
     13   1.3000    1.0922     0.095     0.2078     0.364     0.571   |      |*     |    0.011
     14   1.2200    0.7790     0.093     0.4410     0.364     1.211   |      |**    |    0.048
     15   0.2000    0.9356     0.086    -0.7356     0.366    -2.010   |  ****|      |    0.112
     16   1.0000    0.6419     0.110     0.3581     0.359     0.997   |      |*     |    0.047
     17   0.2200    0.6419     0.110    -0.4219     0.359    -1.174   |    **|      |    0.065
     18   1.0000    0.4657     0.141     0.5343     0.348     1.533   |      |***   |    0.193
     19   0.4000    0.6811     0.105    -0.2811     0.361    -0.779   |     *|      |    0.026

Sum of Residuals                 1.110223E-15
Sum of Squared Residuals               2.4023
Predicted Resid SS (Press)             3.0590
```

SAS printout for Exercise 7.10

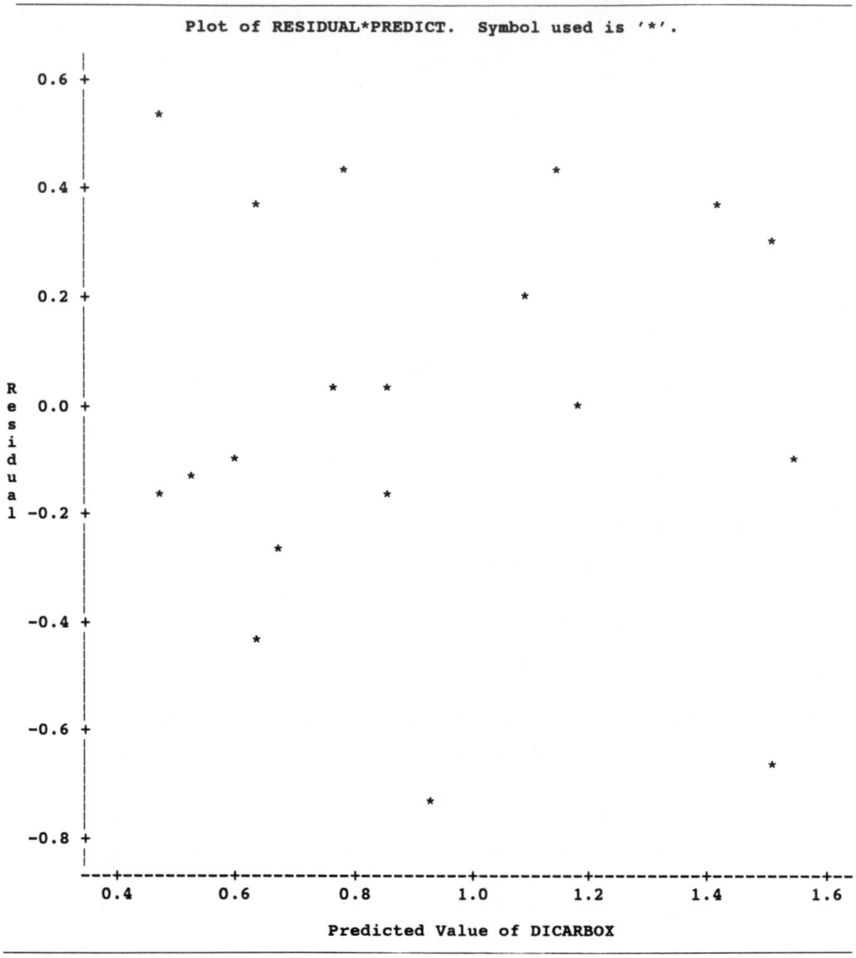

7.11 Breakdowns of machines that produce steel cans are very costly. The more breakdowns, the fewer cans produced, and the smaller the company's profits. To help anticipate profit loss, the owners of a can company would like to find a model that will predict the number of breakdowns on the assembly line. The model proposed by the company's statisticians is the following:

$$y = \beta_0 + \beta_1 x_1 + \beta_2 x_2 + \beta_3 x_3 + \beta_4 x_4 + \varepsilon$$

where y is the number of breakdowns per 8-hour shift,

$$x_1 = \begin{cases} 1 & \text{if afternoon shift} \\ 0 & \text{otherwise} \end{cases} \qquad x_2 = \begin{cases} 1 & \text{if midnight shift} \\ 0 & \text{otherwise} \end{cases}$$

x_3 is the temperature of the plant (°F), and x_4 is the number of inexperienced personnel working on the assembly line. After the model is fitted using the least squares procedure, the residuals are plotted against $\hat{y}$, as shown in the accompanying figure.

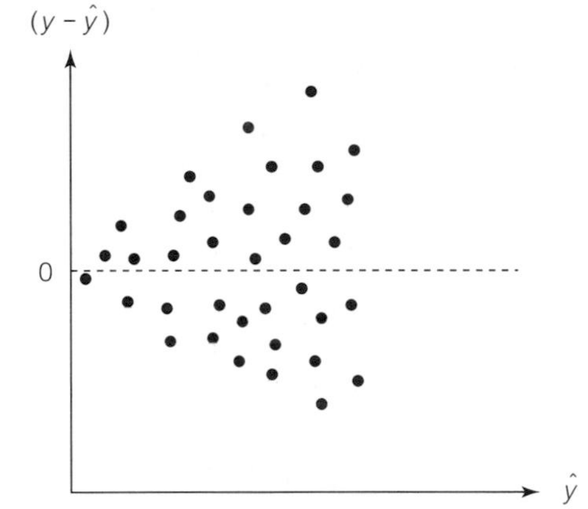

a. Do you detect a pattern in the residual plot? What does this suggest about the least squares assumptions?
b. Given the nature of the response variable y and the pattern detected in part **a**, what model adjustments would you recommend?

7.12 Refer to Exercise 7.11. The regression analysis for the transformed model

$$y^* = \sqrt{y} = \beta_0 + \beta_1 x_1 + \beta_2 x_2 + \beta_3 x_3 + \beta_4 x_4 + \varepsilon$$

produces the prediction equation

$$\hat{y}^* = 1.3 + .008x_1 - .13x_2 + .0025x_3 + .26x_4$$

a. Use the equation to predict the number of breakdowns during the midnight shift if the temperature of the plant at that time is 87°F and if there is only one inexperienced worker on the assembly line.
b. A 95% prediction interval for y^* when $x_1 = 0$, $x_2 = 0$, $x_3 = 90$°F, and $x_4 = 2$ is (1.965, 2.125). For those same values of the independent variables, find a 95% prediction interval for y, the number of breakdowns per 8-hour shift.
c. A 95% confidence interval for $E(y^*)$ when $x_1 = 0$, $x_2 = 0$, $x_3 = 90$°F, and $x_4 = 2$ is (1.987, 2.107). Using only the information given in this problem, is it possible to find a 95% confidence interval for $E(y)$? Explain.

7.13 The manager of a retail appliance store wants to model the proportion of appliance owners who decide to purchase a service contract for a specific major appliance. Since the manager believes that the proportion y decreases with age x of the appliance (in years), he will fit the first-order model

$$E(y) = \beta_0 + \beta_1 x$$

A sample of 50 purchasers of new appliances are contacted about the possibility of purchasing a service contract. Fifty owners of 1-year-old machines, and 50 owners each of 2-, 3-, and 4-year-old machines are also contacted. One year later, another survey is conducted in a similar manner. The proportion y of owners deciding to purchase the service policy is shown in the table on page 408.

a. Fit the first-order model to the data.
b. Calculate the residuals and construct a residual plot versus $\hat{y}$.
c. What does the plot from part **b** suggest about the variance of y?

AGE OF APPLIANCE x, years	0	0	1	1	2	2	3	3	4	4
PROPORTION BUYING SERVICE CONTRACT, y	.94	.96	.7	.76	.6	.4	.24	.3	.12	.1

d. Explain how you could stabilize the variances.

e. Refit the model using the appropriate variance-stabilizing transformation. Plot the residuals for the transformed model and compare to the plot obtained in part **b**. Does the assumption of homoscedasticity appear to be satisfied?

7.14 Prior to 1980, private homeowners in Hawaii had to lease the land their homes were built on because the law (dating back to the islands' feudal period) required that land be owned only by the big estates. After 1980, however, a new law instituted condemnation proceedings so that citizens could buy their own land. To comply with the 1980 law, one large Hawaiian estate wanted to use regression analysis to estimate the fair market value of its land. Its first proposal was the quadratic model

$$E(y) = \beta_0 + \beta_1 x + \beta_2 x^2$$

where

y = Leased fee value (i.e., sale price of property)

x = Size of property in square feet

Data collected for 20 property sales in a particular neighborhood, given in the accompanying table, were used to fit the model. The least squares prediction equation is

$$\hat{y} = -44.0947 + 11.5339x - .06378x^2$$

PROPERTY	LEASED FEE VALUE y, thousands of dollars	SIZE x, thousands	PROPERTY	LEASED FEE VALUE y, thousands of dollars	SIZE x, thousands
1	70.7	13.5	11	148.0	14.5
2	52.7	9.6	12	85.0	10.2
3	87.6	17.6	13	171.2	18.7
4	43.2	7.9	14	97.5	13.2
5	103.8	11.5	15	158.1	16.3
6	45.1	8.2	16	74.2	12.3
7	86.8	15.2	17	47.0	7.7
8	73.3	12.0	18	54.7	9.9
9	144.3	13.8	19	68.0	11.2
10	61.3	10.0	20	75.2	12.4

a. Calculate the predicted values and corresponding residuals for the model.

b. Plot the residuals versus $\hat{y}$. Do you detect any trends? If so, what does the pattern suggest about the model?

c. Conduct a test for heteroscedasticity. [*Hint:* Divide the data into two subsamples, $x \leq 12$ and $x > 12$, and fit the model to both subsamples.]

d. Based on your results from parts **b** and **c**, how should the estate proceed?

7.4 Checking the Normality Assumption

Recall from Section 4.2 that all the inferential procedures associated with a regression analysis are based on the assumptions that, for any setting of the independent variables, the random error ε is normally distributed with mean 0 and variance σ^2, and all pairs of errors are independent. Of these assumptions, the normality assumption is the least restrictive when we apply regression analysis in practice. That is, moderate departures from the assumption of normality have very little effect on error rates associated with the statistical tests and on the confidence coefficients associated with the confidence intervals.

Although tests are available to check the normality assumption (see, for example, Stephens, 1974), we discuss only graphical techniques in this section. The simplest way to determine whether the data violate the assumption of normality is to construct a frequency or relative frequency distribution for the residuals using the computer. If this distribution is not badly skewed, you can feel reasonably confident that the measures of reliability associated with your inferences are as stated in Chapter 4. This visual check is not foolproof because we are lumping the residuals together for all settings of the independent variables. It is conceivable (but not likely) that the distribution of residuals might be skewed to the left for some values of the independent variables and skewed to the right for others. Combining these residuals into a single relative frequency distribution could produce a distribution that is relatively symmetric. But, as noted above, we think that this situation is unlikely and that this graphical check is very useful.

To illustrate, a computer-generated frequency distribution for the $n = 50$ residuals of Example 7.4* is shown in Figure 7.18 on page 410. You can see that this distribution is mound-shaped and reasonably symmetric. Consequently, it is unlikely that the normality assumption would be violated using these data.

If the number of observations is small or if you do not have access to a computer, you may want to construct a stem-and-leaf display for the residuals (see Section 1.3). Figure 7.19 (page 410) shows a stem-and-leaf display for the 50 residuals of Example 7.4. For our display, we chose the *stem* portion of a residual as the first digit to the right of the decimal point. The remaining portion of the residual, to the right of the stem, is the *leaf*. (For example, a residual value of .13 has a stem of .1 and a leaf of 3.) If you turn the stem-and-leaf display (Figure 7.19) on its side, it will look very much like the relative frequency distribution (Figure 7.18), mound-shaped and reasonably symmetric.

A third graphical technique for checking the assumption of normality is to construct a **normal probability plot**. In a normal probability plot, the residuals are graphed against the expected values of the residuals under the assumption of normality. When the errors are, in fact, normally distributed, a residual value will approximately equal its expected value. Thus, a linear trend on the normal probability plot suggests that the normality assumption is nearly satisfied, whereas a nonlinear trend indicates that the assumption is most likely violated.

Most computer packages have procedures for constructing normal probability plots. Figure 7.20 (page 410) shows the SAS normal probability plot for the

*A printout of the residuals is omitted.

FIGURE 7.18 A relative frequency distribution for the $n = 50$ residuals of Example 7.4

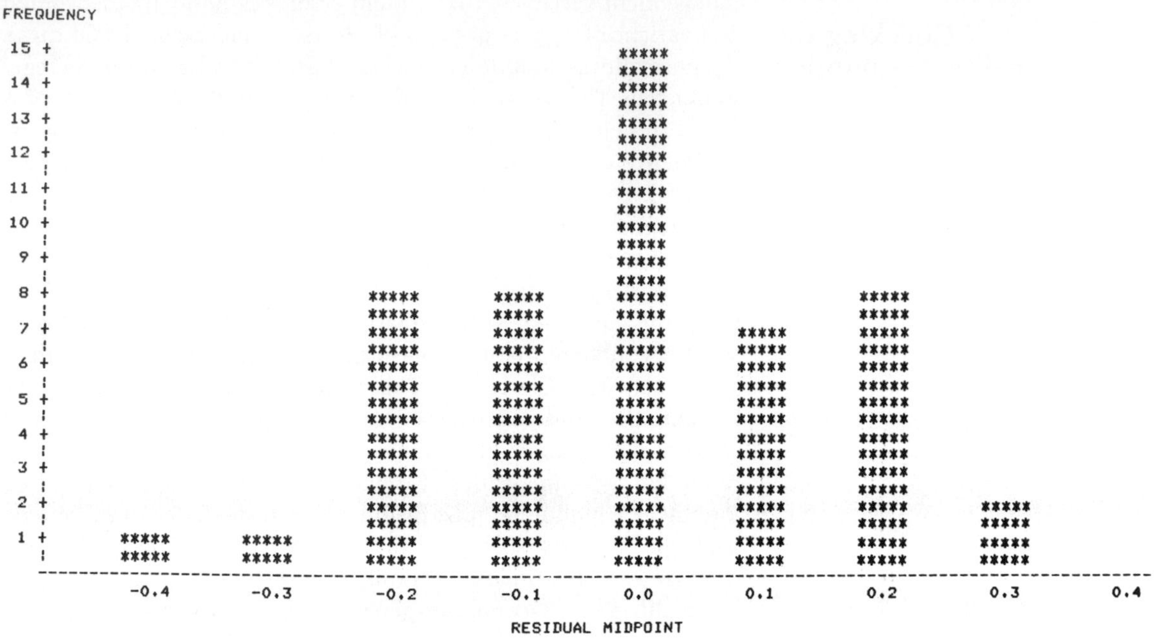

FIGURE 7.19

Stem-and-leaf display for the $n = 50$ residuals of Example 7.4

STEM	LEAF
−.3	3, 5
−.2	0, 1, 1
−.1	0, 1, 2, 5, 6, 6, 7, 8
−.0	0, 1, 2, 2, 3, 5, 5, 5, 5, 5, 6, 7, 7, 8
.0	1, 2, 3, 3, 4, 4, 5, 7, 8, 8
.1	0, 4, 5, 6, 8, 8
.2	1, 1, 3, 4, 5, 6, 6

FIGURE 7.20

SAS normal probability plot for the $n = 50$ residuals of Example 7.4

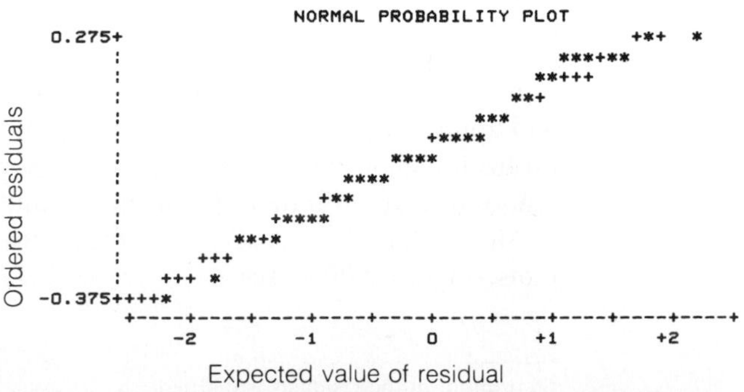

residuals of Example 7.4.* Notice that the points (represented by the plotting symbol "*") fall reasonably close to a straight line (plotting symbol "+"), indicating that the normality assumption is most likely satisfied. If you do not have access to a computer package that contains a normal probability plot option, you can calculate the expected values of the residuals (under normality) using the procedure outlined in the next box.

Constructing a Normal Probability Plot for Regression Residuals

1. List the residuals in ascending order, where $\hat{\varepsilon}_i$ represents the ith ordered residual.
2. For each residual, calculate the corresponding tail area (of the standard normal distribution),

$$A = \frac{i - .375}{n + .25}$$

where n is the sample size.

3. Calculate the estimated value of $\hat{\varepsilon}_i$ under normality using the following formula:

$$E(\hat{\varepsilon}_i) \approx \sqrt{\text{MSE}}\,[Z(A)]$$

where

MSE = Mean square error for the fitted model
$Z(A)$ = Value of the standard normal distribution (z value) that cuts off an area of A in the lower tail of the distribution

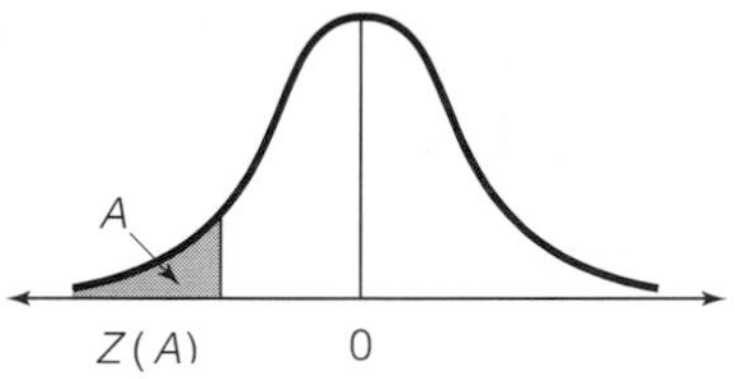

4. Plot the residuals $\hat{\varepsilon}_i$ against the estimated expected residuals, $i = 1, 2, \ldots, n$.

Nonnormality of the distribution of the random error ε is often accompanied by heteroscedasticity. Both these situations can frequently be rectified by applying the variance-stabilizing transformations of Section 7.3. For example, if the relative frequency distribution (or stem-and-leaf display) of the residuals is highly skewed

*The horizontal axis of the SAS normal probability plot (Figure 7.20) gives the expected values of the residuals in terms of number of standard deviations (positive or negative) from the mean 0.

to the right (as it would be for Poisson data), the square-root transformation on y will stabilize (approximately) the variance and, at the same time, will reduce skewness in the distribution of the residuals. Thus, for any given setting of the independent variables, the square-root transformation will reduce the larger values of y to a greater extent than the smaller ones. This has the effect of reducing or eliminating the positive skewness.

For situations in which the errors are homoscedastic but nonnormal, normalizing transformations are available. This family of transformations on the dependent variable includes $\sqrt{y}$ and $\log(y)$ (Section 7.3), as well as such simple transformations as y^2, $1/\sqrt{y}$, and $1/y$. Box and Cox (1964) have developed a procedure for selecting the appropriate transformation to use. Consult the references to learn details of the Box–Cox approach. Keep in mind, however, that regression is extremely *robust* with respect to nonnormal errors. That is, the inferences derived from the regression analysis tend to remain valid even when the assumption of normal errors is violated. Consequently, you may want to search for a normalizing transformation only when the distribution of the regression residuals is highly skewed.

EXERCISES

7.15 Refer to the *Environmental Science & Technology* regression model for dicarboxylic acid percentage, Exercise 7.10. Additional SAS printouts of the residual analysis are shown here. Comment on the validity of the assumption of normal errors.

```
Stem Leaf                    #             Boxplot
   4 453                     3                |
   2 1067                    4             +-----+
   0 144                     3             *--+--*
  -0 76409                   5             +-----+
  -2 8                       1                |
  -4 2                       1                |
  -6 45                      2                |
     ----+----+----+----+
 Multiply Stem.Leaf by 10**-1
```

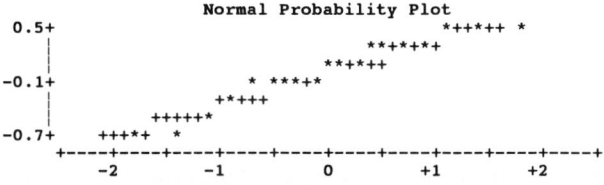

```
                    Normal Probability Plot
 0.5+                                     *++*++ *
    |                               **+*+*+
    |                           **+*++
-0.1+                     * ***++
    |                  +*+++
    |            +++++*
-0.7+       +++*+   *
     +----+----+----+----+----+----+----+----+----+----+
         -2        -1         0        +1        +2
```

7.16 Refer to Exercise 4.48. Use one of the graphical techniques described in this section to check the normality assumption.

7.17 Refer to Exercise 7.14. Use one of the graphical techniques described in this section to check the normality assumption.

7.18 In the 1980s, L. De Cola conducted an extensive investigation of the geopolitical and socioeconomic processes that shape the urban size distributions of the world's nations. One of the goals of the study was to determine the factors that influence population size in each nation's largest city. Using data collected for a sample of 126 countries, De Cola fitted the following log model:

$$E(y) = \beta_0 + \beta_1 x_1 + \beta_2 x_2 + \beta_3 x_3 + \beta_4 x_4 + \beta_5 x_5 + \beta_6 x_6 + \beta_7 x_7 + \beta_8 x_8 + \beta_9 x_9 + \beta_{10} x_{10}$$

where

y = Log of population (in thousands) of largest city in country

x_1 = Log of area (in thousands of square kilometers) of country

x_2 = Log of radius (in hundreds of kilometers) of country

x_3 = Log of national population (in thousands)

x_4 = Percentage annual change in national population (1960–1970)

x_5 = Log of energy consumption per capita (in kilograms of coal equivalent)

x_6 = Percentage of nation's population in urban areas

x_7 = Log of population (in thousands) of second largest city in country

$$x_8 = \begin{cases} 1 & \text{if seaport city} \\ 0 & \text{if not} \end{cases}$$

$$x_9 = \begin{cases} 1 & \text{if capital city} \\ 0 & \text{if not} \end{cases}$$

$$x_{10} = \begin{cases} 1 & \text{if city data are for metropolitan area} \\ 0 & \text{if not} \end{cases}$$

[*Note:* All logarithms are to the base 10.]

The regression resulted in

$R^2 = .879$ and MSE $= .036$

a. Conduct a test for model adequacy. Use $\alpha = .05$.

b. The residuals for five cities selected from the total sample are given in the table. For each of these cities, calculate the estimated expected residuals under the assumption of normality.

CITY	RESIDUAL	RANK
Bangkok	.510	126
Paris	.228	110
London	.033	78
Warsaw	−.132	32
Lagos	−.392	2

Source: De Cola, L. "Statistical determinants of the population of a nation's largest city." *Economic Development and Cultural Change*, Vol. 3, No. 1, Oct. 1984, pp. 71–98.

c. A computer-generated (SAS) stem-and-leaf plot of all the residuals is shown on page 414. Does it appear that the assumption of normal errors is satisfied?

SAS stem-and-leaf plot of residuals for Exercise 7.18

```
STEM LEAF                     #
   5 1                        1
   4 5                        1
   4
   3 79                       2
   3 1224                     4
   2 5899                     4
   2 000012233344            12
   1 5789                     4
   1 00001113444             11
   0 5566888                  7
   0 11111122223334          14
  -0 4433333322111000        16
  -0 9999988665              10
  -1 44433332221110          14
  -1 88865                    5
  -2 444443100                9
  -2 77665                    5
  -3 3000                     4
  -3 97                       2
  -4
  -4 6                        1
     ----+----+----+----+
  MULTIPLY STEM.LEAF BY 10**-01
```

7.5 Detecting Outliers and Identifying Influential Observations

Although we expect almost all the regression residuals to fall within 3 standard deviations of their mean (0), sometimes one or several residuals fall outside this interval. Observations with residuals that are extremely large or small (say, more than 3 standard deviations from 0) are called **outliers**.

Outliers are usually attributable to one of several causes. The measurement associated with the outlier may be invalid. For example, the experimental procedure used to generate the measurement may have malfunctioned, the experimenter may have misrecorded the measurement, or the data may have been coded incorrectly for entry into the computer. Careful checks of the experimental and coding procedures should reveal this type of problem if it exists, so that we can eliminate erroneous observations from a data set.

For example, Table 7.8 presents the sales, y, in thousands of dollars per week, for fast-food outlets in each of four cities. The objective is to model sales, y, as a function of traffic flow, adjusting for city-to-city variations that might be due

TABLE 7.8 **Data for Fast-Food Sales**

CITY	TRAFFIC FLOW thousands of cars	WEEKLY SALES y, thousands of dollars	CITY	TRAFFIC FLOW thousands of cars	WEEKLY SALES y, thousands of dollars
1	59.3	6.3	3	75.8	8.2
1	60.3	6.6	3	48.3	5.0
1	82.1	7.6	3	41.4	3.9
1	32.3	3.0	3	52.5	5.4
1	98.0	9.5	3	41.0	4.1
1	54.1	5.9	3	29.6	3.1
1	54.4	6.1	3	49.5	5.4
1	51.3	5.0	4	73.1	8.4
1	36.7	3.6	4	81.3	9.5
2	23.6	2.8	4	72.4	8.7
2	57.6	6.7	4	88.4	10.6
2	44.6	5.2	4	23.2	3.3

to size or other market conditions. We expect a first-order (linear) relationship to exist between mean sales, $E(y)$, and traffic flow. Further, we believe that the level of mean sales will differ from city to city, but that the change in mean sales per unit increase in traffic flow will remain the same for all cities, i.e., that the factors Traffic flow and City do not interact. The model is therefore

$$E(y) = \beta_0 + \beta_1 x_1 + \beta_2 x_2 + \beta_3 x_3 + \beta_4 x_4$$

where

$$x_1 = \begin{cases} 1 & \text{if city 1} \\ 0 & \text{other} \end{cases} \qquad x_2 = \begin{cases} 1 & \text{if city 2} \\ 0 & \text{other} \end{cases}$$

$$x_3 = \begin{cases} 1 & \text{if city 3} \\ 0 & \text{other} \end{cases} \qquad x_4 = \text{Traffic flow}$$

The SAS printout for the regression analysis is shown in Figure 7.21 on page 416. The regression analysis indicates that the first-order model in traffic flow is inadequate for explaining mean sales. The coefficient of determination, R^2, is .2595, indicating that only 26.0% of the total sum of squares of deviations of the sales y about their mean $\bar{y}$ is accounted for by the model. The F value, 1.665, which tests the adequacy of the model, does not indicate that the model is useful for predicting sales. The observed significance level is only .1996.

Plots of the residuals against traffic flow and city are shown in Figures 7.22 and 7.23 on pages 417 and 418, respectively. The dashed horizontal lines locate the mean (0), $+2s$, and $-2s$ for the residuals. As you can see, the plots of the residuals are very revealing. Both the plot of residuals against traffic flow in Figure 7.22 and the plot of residuals against city in Figure 7.23 indicate the presence of an outlier. One observation in city 3, (observation 13), with traffic flow of 75.8, is approximately 4 standard deviations from 0. (Note in Figure 7.21 that the standard deviation is 14.85762, and the outlier residual is 56.4638.) A further check of the observation associated with this residual reveals that the sales value entered into the computer, 82.0, does not agree with the corresponding value of sales, 8.2, that appears in Table 7.8. The decimal point was evidently dropped when the data were entered into the computer.

If the correct y value, 8.2, is substituted for the 82.0, we obtain the regression analysis shown in Figure 7.24 on page 419. Plots of the residuals against traffic flow and city are respectively shown in Figures 7.25 and 7.26 (pages 420 and 421). The corrected computer printout indicates the dramatic effect that a single outlier can have on a regression analysis. The value of R^2 is now .9791, and the F value that tests the adequacy of the model, 222.173, verifies the strong predictive capability of the model. Further analysis reveals that significant differences exist in the mean sales among cities, and that the estimated mean weekly sales increase by \$104 for every 1,000-car increase in traffic flow ($\hat{\beta}_4 = .104$). The 95% confidence interval for β_4 is

$$\hat{\beta}_4 \pm t_{.025} s_{\hat{\beta}_4} = .104 \pm (2.093)(.004094) = .104 \pm .009$$

Thus, a 95% confidence interval for the mean increase in sales per 1,000-car increase in traffic flow is \$95 to \$113.

FIGURE 7.21
SAS regression printout for model of fast-food sales

Analysis of Variance

Source	DF	Sum of Squares	Mean Square	F Value	Prob>F
Model	4	1469.76287	367.44072	1.665	0.1996
Error	19	4194.22671	220.74877		
C Total	23	5663.98958			

Root MSE	14.85762	R-square	0.2595
Dep Mean	9.07083	Adj R-sq	0.1036
C.V.	163.79550		

Parameter Estimates

Variable	DF	Parameter Estimate	Standard Error	T for H0: Parameter=0	Prob > |T|
INTERCEP	1	-16.459248	13.16399794	-1.250	0.2264
X1	1	1.106092	8.42256884	0.131	0.8969
X2	1	6.142771	11.67996860	0.526	0.6050
X3	1	14.489623	9.28839086	1.560	0.1353
X4	1	0.362873	0.16790819	2.161	0.0437

Obs	CITY	X4	Dep Var Y	Predict Value	Residual
1	1	59.3	6.3000	6.1652	0.1348
2	1	60.3	6.6000	6.5281	0.0719
3	1	82.1	7.6000	14.4387	-6.8387
4	1	32.3	3.0000	-3.6324	6.6324
5	1	98	9.5000	20.2084	-10.7084
6	1	54.1	5.9000	4.2783	1.6217
7	1	54.4	6.1000	4.3871	1.7129
8	1	51.3	5.0000	3.2622	1.7378
9	1	36.7	3.6000	-2.0357	5.6357
10	2	23.6	2.8000	-1.7527	4.5527
11	2	57.6	6.7000	10.5850	-3.8850
12	2	44.6	5.2000	5.8677	-0.6677
13	3	75.8	82.0000	25.5362	56.4638
14	3	48.3	5.0000	15.5571	-10.5571
15	3	41.4	3.9000	13.0533	-9.1533
16	3	52.5	5.4000	17.0812	-11.6812
17	3	41	4.1000	12.9082	-8.8082
18	3	29.6	3.1000	8.7714	-5.6714
19	3	49.5	5.4000	15.9926	-10.5926
20	4	73.1	8.4000	10.0668	-1.6668
21	4	81.3	9.5000	13.0423	-3.5423
22	4	72.4	8.7000	9.8128	-1.1128
23	4	88.4	10.6000	15.6187	-5.0187
24	4	23.2	3.3000	-8.0406	11.3406

Sum of Residuals	1.261213E-13
Sum of Squared Residuals	4194.2267
Predicted Resid SS (Press)	7303.4839

Outliers cannot always be explained by computer or recording errors. Extremely large or small residuals may be attributable to skewness (nonnormality) of the probability distribution of the random error, chance, or unassignable causes. Although some analysts advocate elimination of outliers, regardless of whether cause can be assigned, others encourage the correction of only those outliers that can be traced to specific causes. The best philosophy is probably a compromise between these extremes. For example, before deciding the fate of an outlier, you may want to determine how much influence it has on the regression analysis. When an accurate outlier (i.e., an outlier that is not due to recording or measurement error) is found to have a dramatic effect on the regression

FIGURE 7.22
SAS plot of residuals versus traffic flow

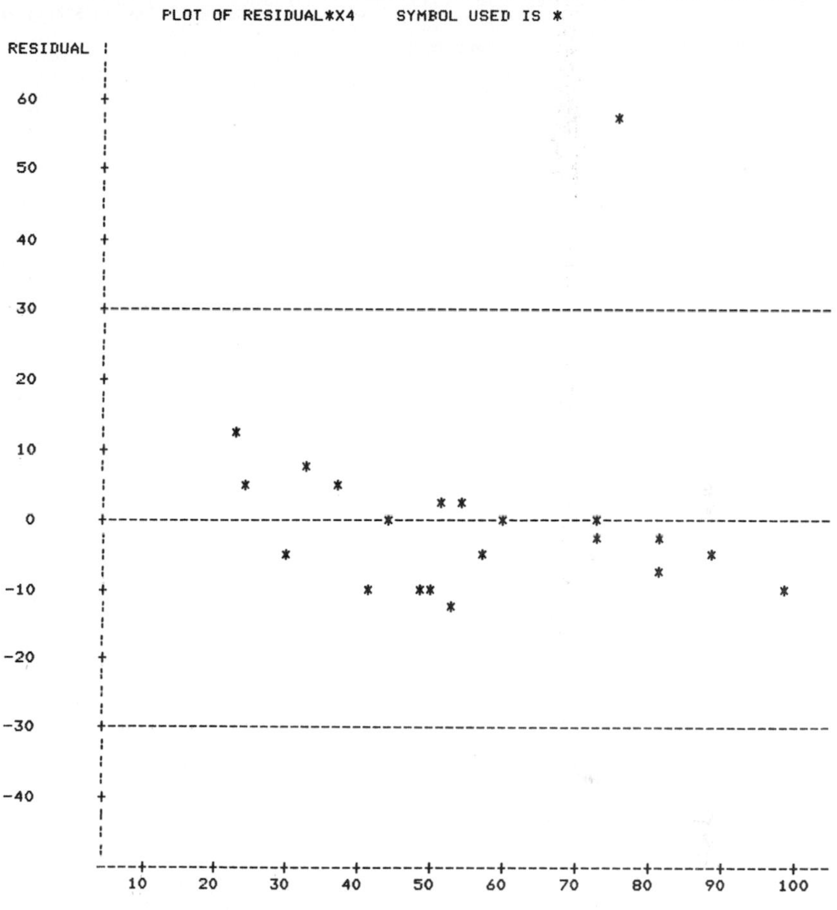

NOTE: THREE OBSERVATIONS ARE NOT SHOWN BECAUSE THEY COINCIDED WITH OTHERS THAT APPEAR ON THE PLOT. THEIR OMISSION DOES NOT DETRACT FROM THE INFORMATION CONTRIBUTED BY THE PLOT.

analysis, it may be the model and not the outlier that is suspect. Omission of important independent variables or higher-order terms could be the reason why the model is not predicting well for the outlying observation. Several sophisticated numerical techniques are available for identifying outlying influential observations. We conclude this section with a brief discussion of some of these methods and an example.

Leverage

This procedure is based on a result (proof omitted) in regression analysis that states that the predicted value for the ith observation, $\hat{y}_i$, can be written as a linear combination of the n observed values $y_1, y_2, \ldots, y_n$:

$$\hat{y}_i = h_1 y_1 + h_2 y_2 + \cdots + h_i y_i + \cdots + h_n y_n, \quad i = 1, 2, \ldots, n$$

where the weights $h_1, h_2, \ldots, h_n$ of the observed values are functions of the independent variables. In particular, the coefficient h_i measures the influence of

FIGURE 7.23
SAS plot of residuals versus city

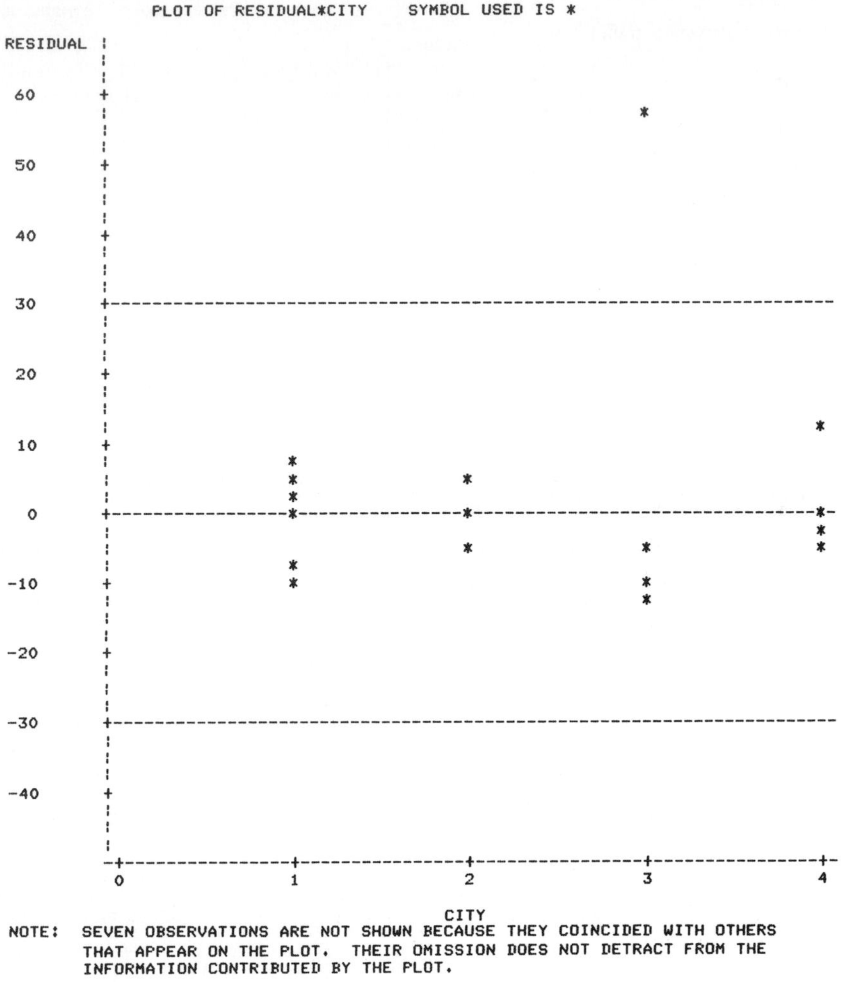

the observed value y_i on its own predicted value $\hat{y}_i$. This value, h_i, is called the **leverage** of the *i*th observation (with respect to the values of the independent variables). Thus, leverage values can be used to identify influential observations—the larger the leverage value, the more influence the observed y value has on its predicted value.

Leverage values are extremely difficult to calculate without the aid of a computer.* Fortunately, most of the statistical software packages discussed in this text have options that give the leverage associated with each observation. The

*In matrix notation, the leverage values are the diagonals of the **H** matrix (called the "hat" matrix), where $\mathbf{H} = \mathbf{X}(\mathbf{X}'\mathbf{X})^{-1}\mathbf{X}'$. See Appendix A for details on matrix multiplication and definition of the **X** matrix in regression.

FIGURE 7.24
Corrected SAS regression printout for model of fast-food sales

Analysis of Variance

Source	DF	Sum of Squares	Mean Square	F Value	Prob>F
Model	4	116.65552	29.16388	222.173	0.0001
Error	19	2.49407	0.13127		
C Total	23	119.14958			

Root MSE	0.36231	R-square	0.9791
Dep Mean	5.99583	Adj R-sq	0.9747
C.V.	6.04265		

Parameter Estimates

Variable	DF	Parameter Estimate	Standard Error	T for H0: Parameter=0	Prob > |T|
INTERCEP	1	1.083388	0.32100795	3.375	0.0032
X1	1	-1.215762	0.20538681	-5.919	0.0001
X2	1	-0.530757	0.28481946	-1.863	0.0779
X3	1	-1.076525	0.22650014	-4.753	0.0001
X4	1	0.103673	0.00409449	25.320	0.0001

Obs	CITY	X4	Dep Var Y	Predict Value	Residual
1	1	59.3	6.3000	6.0155	0.2845
2	1	60.3	6.6000	6.1191	0.4809
3	1	82.1	7.6000	8.3792	-0.7792
4	1	32.3	3.0000	3.2163	-0.2163
5	1	98	9.5000	10.0276	-0.5276
6	1	54.1	5.9000	5.4764	0.4236
7	1	54.4	6.1000	5.5075	0.5925
8	1	51.3	5.0000	5.1861	-0.1861
9	1	36.7	3.6000	3.6724	-0.0724
10	2	23.6	2.8000	2.9993	-0.1993
11	2	57.6	6.7000	6.5242	0.1758
12	2	44.6	5.2000	5.1765	0.0235
13	3	75.8	8.2000	7.8653	0.3347
14	3	48.3	5.0000	5.0143	-0.0143
15	3	41.4	3.9000	4.2989	-0.3989
16	3	52.5	5.4000	5.4497	-0.0497
17	3	41	4.1000	4.2575	-0.1575
18	3	29.6	3.1000	3.0756	0.0244
19	3	49.5	5.4000	5.1387	0.2613
20	4	73.1	8.4000	8.6619	-0.2619
21	4	81.3	9.5000	9.5120	-0.0120
22	4	72.4	8.7000	8.5893	0.1107
23	4	88.4	10.6000	10.2481	0.3519
24	4	23.2	3.3000	3.4886	-0.1886

Sum of Residuals	1.332268E-14
Sum of Squared Residuals	2.4941
Predicted Resid SS (Press)	3.8772

leverage value for an observation is usually compared with the average leverage value of all n observations, $\bar{h}$, where

$$\bar{h} = \frac{k+1}{n} = \frac{\text{Number of } \beta \text{ parameters in the model, including } \beta_0{}^*}{n}$$

*The proof of this result is beyond the scope of this text. Consult the references given at the end of this chapter. [See Neter, Wasserman, and Kutner (1990).]

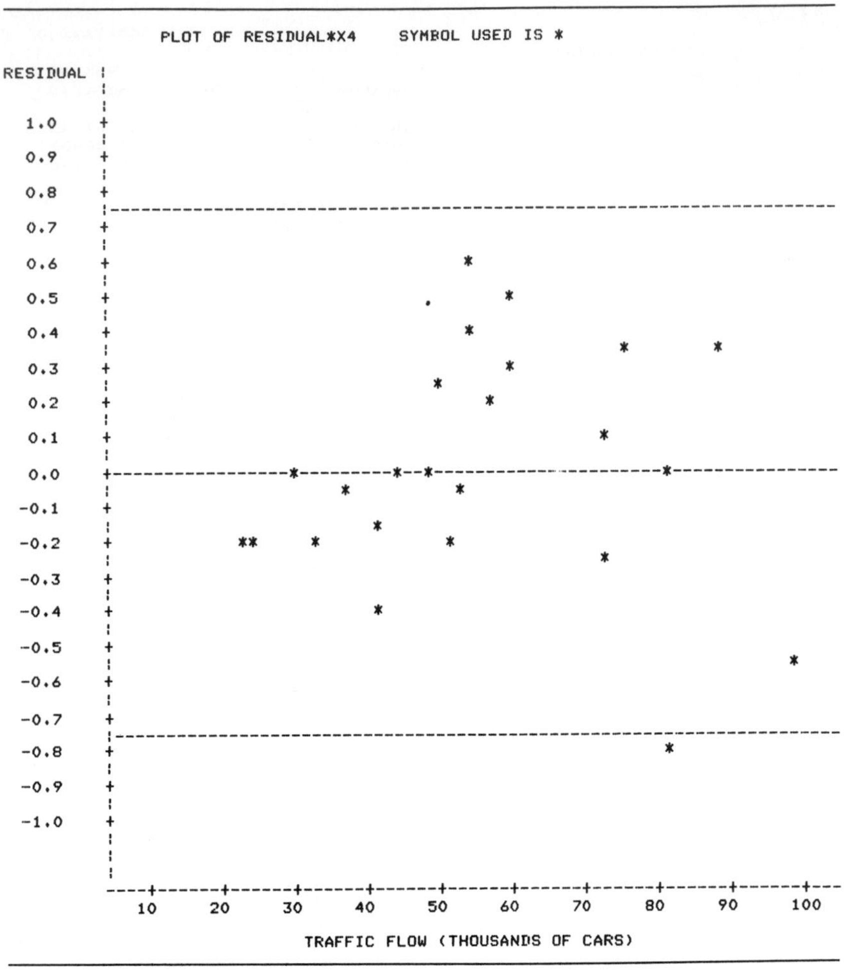

FIGURE 7.25
Corrected SAS plot of residuals versus traffic flow

A good rule of thumb identifies an observation y_i as influential if its leverage value h_i is more than twice as large as $\bar{h}$, that is, if

$$h_i > \frac{2(k+1)}{n}$$

The Jackknife

Another technique for identifying influential observations requires that you delete the observations one at a time, each time refitting the regression model based on only the remaining $n - 1$ observations. This method is based on a statistical procedure, called the **jackknife**,* that is gaining increasing acceptance among practitioners. The basic principle of the jackknife when applied to regression is

*The procedure derives its name from the Boy Scout jackknife, which serves as a handy tool in a variety of situations when specialized techniques may not be applicable. [See Belsley, Kuh, and Welsch (1980).]

FIGURE 7.26
Corrected SAS plot of residuals versus city

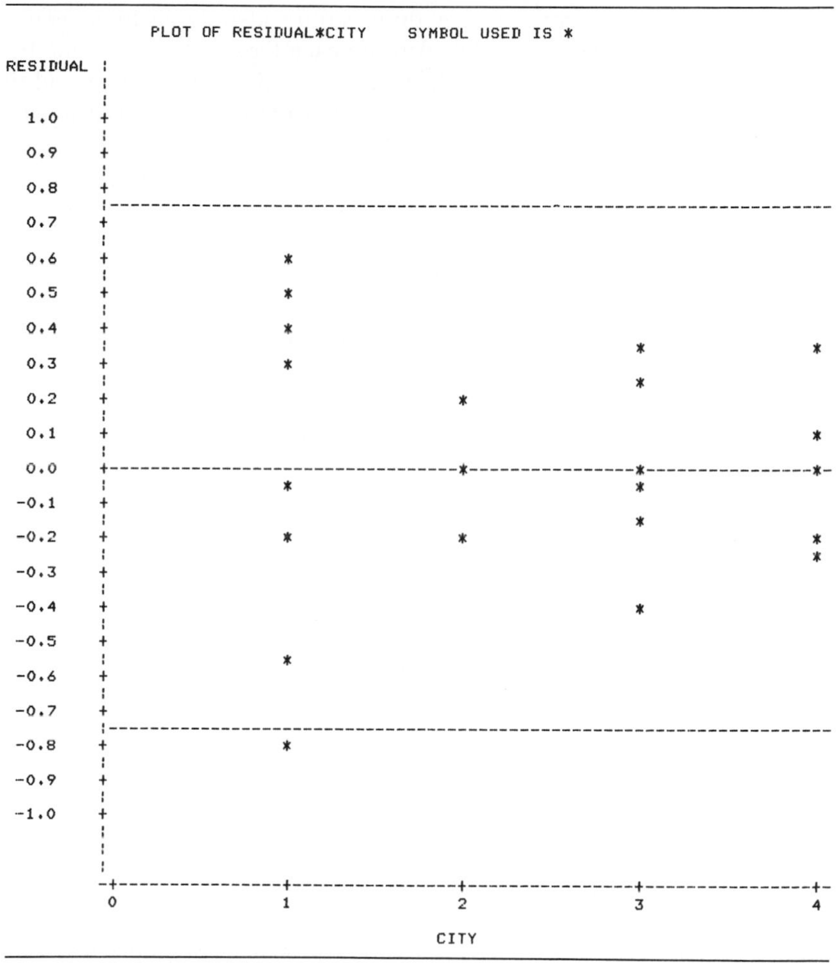

to compare the regression results using all n observations to the results with the ith observation deleted to ascertain how much influence a particular observation has on the analysis. Using the jackknife, several alternative influence measures can be calculated.

The **deleted residual**, $d_i = y_i - \hat{y}_{(i)}$, measures the difference between the observed value y_i and the predicted value $\hat{y}_{(i)}$ based on the model with the ith observation deleted. [The notation (i) is generally used to indicate that the observed value y_i was deleted from the regression analysis.] An observation with an unusually large (in absolute value) deleted residual is considered to have large influence on the fitted model.

A measure closely related to the deleted residual is the difference between the predicted value based on the model fitted to all n observations and the predicted value obtained when y_i is deleted, i.e., $\hat{y}_i - \hat{y}_{(i)}$. When the difference $\hat{y}_i - \hat{y}_{(i)}$ is large relative to the predicted value $\hat{y}_i$, the observation y_i is said to influence the regression fit.

A third way to identify an influential observation using the jackknife is to calculate, for each β parameter in the model, the difference between the parameter estimate based on all n observations and that based on only $n - 1$ observations (with the observation in question deleted). Consider, for example, the straight-line model $E(y) = \beta_0 + \beta_1 x$. The differences $\hat{\beta}_0 - \hat{\beta}_0^{(i)}$ and $\hat{\beta}_1 - \hat{\beta}_1^{(i)}$ measure how influential the ith observation y_i is on the parameter estimates. [Using the (i) notation defined previously, $\hat{\beta}^{(i)}$ represents the estimate of the β coefficient when the ith observation is omitted from the analysis.] If the parameter estimates change drastically, i.e., if the absolute differences are large, y_i is deemed an influential observation.

Each of the statistical software packages discussed in this text has a jackknife routine that produces one or more of the measures we described.

Cook's Distance

A measure of the overall influence an outlying observation has on the estimated β coefficients was proposed by R. D. Cook (1979). Cook's distance, D_i, is calculated for the ith observation as follows:

$$D_i = \frac{(y_i - \hat{y}_i)^2}{(k + 1)\text{MSE}}\left[\frac{h_i}{(1 - h_i)^2}\right]$$

Note that D_i depends on both the residual $(y_i - \hat{y}_i)$ and the leverage h_i for the ith observation. A large value of D_i indicates that the observed y_i value has strong influence on the estimated β coefficients (since the residual, the leverage, or both will be large). Values of D_i can be compared to the values of the F distribution with $\nu_1 = k + 1$ and $\nu_2 = n - (k + 1)$ degrees of freedom. Usually, an observation with a value of D_i that falls at or above the 50th percentile of the F distribution is considered to be an influential observation. Like the other numerical measures of influence, options for calculating Cook's distance are available in most statistical software packages.

EXAMPLE 7.6

We now return to the fast-food sales example in which we detected an outlier using residual plots. Recall that the outlier was due to an error in coding the weekly sales value for observation 13 (denoted y_{13}). The SAS regression analysis is rerun with options for producing influence diagnostics. (An **influence diagnostic** is a number that measures how much influence an observation has on the regression analysis.) The resulting SAS printout is shown in Figure 7.27. Locate and interpret the measures of influence for y_{13} on the printout.

FIGURE 7.27 SAS regression analysis with influence diagnostics

```
                          Analysis of Variance

                                Sum of          Mean
Source              DF         Squares        Square       F Value       Prob>F

Model                4      1469.76287     367.44072         1.665       0.1996
Error               19      4194.22671     220.74877
C Total             23      5663.98958

     Root MSE        14.85762      R-square       0.2595
     Dep Mean         9.07083      Adj R-sq       0.1036
     C.V.           163.79550
```

(*continued*)

FIGURE 7.27 *(continued)*

Parameter Estimates

Variable	DF	Parameter Estimate	Standard Error	T for H0: Parameter=0	Prob > |T|
INTERCEP	1	-16.459248	13.16399794	-1.250	0.2264
X1	1	1.106092	8.42256884	0.131	0.8969
X2	1	6.142771	11.67996860	0.526	0.6050
X3	1	14.489623	9.28839086	1.560	0.1353
X4	1	0.362873	0.16790819	2.161	0.0437

Obs	Dep Var Y	Predict Value	Std Err Predict	Residual	Std Err Residual	Student Residual	-2-1-0 1 2	Cook's D
1	6.3000	6.1652	4.953	0.1348	14.008	0.010		0.000
2	6.6000	6.5281	4.960	0.0719	14.005	0.005		0.000
3	7.6000	14.4387	6.319	-6.8387	13.447	-0.509	*	0.011
4	3.0000	-3.6324	6.649	6.6324	13.287	0.499		0.012
5	9.5000	20.2084	8.248	-10.7084	12.358	-0.866	*	0.067
6	5.9000	4.2783	5.013	1.6217	13.986	0.116		0.000
7	6.1000	4.3871	5.005	1.7129	13.989	0.122		0.000
8	5.0000	3.2622	5.107	1.7378	13.952	0.125		0.000
9	3.6000	-2.0357	6.181	5.6357	13.511	0.417		0.007
10	2.8000	-1.7527	9.114	4.5527	11.734	0.388		0.018
11	6.7000	10.5850	8.972	-3.8850	11.843	-0.328		0.012
12	5.2000	5.8677	8.590	-0.6677	12.123	-0.055		0.000
13	82.0000	25.5362	7.270	56.4638	12.957	4.358	******	1.196
14	5.0000	15.5571	5.616	-10.5571	13.755	-0.767	*	0.020
15	3.9000	13.0533	5.734	-9.1533	13.707	-0.668	*	0.016
16	5.4000	17.0812	5.660	-11.6812	13.737	-0.850	*	0.025
17	4.1000	12.9082	5.748	-8.8082	13.701	-0.643	*	0.015
18	3.1000	8.7714	6.434	-5.6714	13.392	-0.423		0.008
19	5.4000	15.9926	5.619	-10.5926	13.754	-0.770	*	0.020
20	8.4000	10.0668	6.707	-1.6668	13.258	-0.126		0.001
21	9.5000	13.0423	7.027	-3.5423	13.091	-0.271		0.004
22	8.7000	9.8128	6.692	-1.1128	13.265	-0.084		0.000
23	10.6000	15.6187	7.500	-5.0187	12.826	-0.391		0.010
24	3.3000	-8.0406	9.996	11.3406	10.992	1.032	**	0.176

Obs	Rstudent	Hat Diag H	Cov Ratio	Dffits	INTERCEP Dfbetas	X1 Dfbetas	X2 Dfbetas	X3 Dfbetas	X4 Dfbetas
1	0.0094	0.1112	1.4742	0.0033	-0.0001	0.0020	0.0000	0.0000	0.0001
2	0.0050	0.1114	1.4747	0.0018	-0.0001	0.0011	0.0000	0.0000	0.0001
3	-0.4984	0.1809	1.4939	-0.2342	0.1256	-0.1339	-0.0539	-0.0510	-0.1455
4	0.4891	0.2003	1.5339	0.2447	0.1410	0.0780	-0.0604	-0.0572	-0.1633
5	-0.8606	0.3081	1.5482	-0.5743	0.3965	-0.2848	-0.1700	-0.1609	-0.4592
6	0.1129	0.1138	1.4735	0.0405	0.0054	0.0224	-0.0023	-0.0022	-0.0063
7	0.1192	0.1135	1.4724	0.0427	0.0053	0.0237	-0.0023	-0.0022	-0.0062
8	0.1213	0.1181	1.4799	0.0444	0.0094	0.0234	-0.0040	-0.0038	-0.0108
9	0.4079	0.1731	1.5134	0.1866	0.0964	0.0680	-0.0413	-0.0391	-0.1116
10	0.3791	0.3763	2.0190	0.2945	0.0859	-0.0178	0.1667	-0.0348	-0.0995
11	-0.3202	0.3647	2.0048	-0.2426	0.0614	-0.0127	-0.1967	-0.0249	-0.0711
12	-0.0536	0.3342	1.9667	-0.0380	0.0017	-0.0004	-0.0286	-0.0007	-0.0020
13	179.3101	0.2394	0.0000	100.6096	-55.1618	11.4109	23.6508	69.3701	63.8990
14	-0.7589	0.1429	1.3061	-0.3098	-0.0000	0.0000	0.0000	-0.1873	0.0000
15	-0.6578	0.1489	1.3673	-0.2752	-0.0480	0.0099	0.0206	-0.1435	0.0556
16	-0.8439	0.1451	1.2625	-0.3477	0.0374	-0.0077	-0.0160	-0.2237	-0.0433
17	-0.6327	0.1497	1.3806	-0.2654	-0.0489	0.0101	0.0209	-0.1370	0.0566
18	-0.4141	0.1875	1.5381	-0.1990	-0.0838	0.0173	0.0359	-0.0710	0.0971
19	-0.7616	0.1430	1.3049	-0.3111	0.0096	-0.0020	-0.0041	-0.1919	-0.0112
20	-0.1224	0.2038	1.6389	-0.0619	-0.0237	0.0469	0.0318	0.0409	-0.0084
21	-0.2639	0.2237	1.6557	-0.1417	-0.0278	0.0974	0.0591	0.0797	-0.0461
22	-0.0817	0.2028	1.6408	-0.0412	-0.0164	0.0314	0.0215	0.0276	-0.0049
23	-0.3824	0.2548	1.6888	-0.2236	-0.0104	0.1378	0.0743	0.1054	-0.1037
24	1.0336	0.4527	1.7946	0.9400	0.9216	-0.6183	-0.6154	-0.6930	-0.7023

Sum of Residuals	1.261213E-13
Sum of Squared Residuals	4194.2267
Predicted Resid SS (Press)	7303.4839

Solution The influence diagnostics are shown in the last portion of the SAS printout in Figure 7.27. Leverage values for each observation are given under the column heading **Hat Diag H**. The leverage value for y_{13} (shaded on the printout) is $h_{13} = .2394$, whereas the average leverage for all $n = 24$ observations is

$$\bar{h} = \frac{k+1}{n} = \frac{5}{24} = .2083$$

Since the leverage value .2394 does not exceed $2\bar{h} = .4166$, we would not identify y_{13} as an influential observation. At first, this result may seem confusing since we already know the dramatic effect the incorrectly coded value of y_{13} had on the regression analysis. Remember, however, that the leverage values, $h_1, h_2, \ldots, h_{24}$, are functions of the independent variables only. Since we know the values of x_1, x_2, x_3, and x_4 were coded correctly, the relatively small leverage value of .2394 simply indicates that observation 13 is not an outlier with respect to the values of the independent variables.

A better overall measure of the influence of y_{13} on the fitted regression model is Cook's distance, D_{13}. Recall that Cook's distance is a function of both leverage and the magnitude of the residual. This value, $D_{13} = 1.196$ (shaded) is given in the column labeled **Cook's D** located on the right side of the printout. You can see that the value is extremely large relative to the other values of D_i in the printout. [In fact, $D_{13} = 1.196$ falls in the 65th percentile of the F distribution with $\nu_1 = k + 1 = 5$ and $\nu_2 = n - (k + 1) = 24 - 5 = 19$ degrees of freedom.] This implies that the observed value y_{13} has substantial influence on the estimates of the model parameters.

A statistic related to the deleted residual of the jackknife procedure is the **Studentized deleted residual** given under the column heading **Rstudent**. The Studentized deleted residual, denoted d_i^*, is calculated by dividing the deleted residual d_i by its standard error s_{d_i}:

$$d_i^* = \frac{d_i}{s_{d_i}}$$

The Studentized deleted residual for y_{13} (shaded on the printout) is $d_{13}^* = 179.3101$. This extremely large value† is another indication that y_{13} is an influential observation.

The **Dffits** column gives the difference between the predicted value when all 24 observations are used and when the ith observation is deleted. The difference, $\hat{y}_i - \hat{y}_{(i)}$, is divided by its standard error so that the differences can be compared more easily. For observation 13, this scaled difference (shaded on the printout)

---

†Under the assumptions of Section 4.2, the Studentized deleted residual d_i^* has a sampling distribution that is approximated by a Student's t distribution with $(n - 1) - (k + 1)$ df.

is 100.6096, an extremely large value relative to the other differences in predicted values. Similarly, the changes in the parameter estimates when observation 13 is deleted are given in the **Dfbetas** columns (shaded) immediately to the right of **Dffits** on the printout. (Each difference is also divided by the appropriate standard error.) The large magnitude of these differences provides further evidence that y_{13} is very influential on the regression analysis.

Several techniques designed to limit the influence an outlying observation has on the regression analysis are available. One method produces estimates of the β's that minimize the sum of the absolute deviations, $\Sigma_{i=1}^{n} |y_i - \hat{y}_i|$.* Because the deviations $(y_i - \hat{y}_i)$ are not squared, this method places less emphasis on outliers than the method of least squares. Regardless of whether you choose to eliminate an outlier or dampen its influence, careful study of residual plots and influence diagnostics are essential for outlier detection.

EXERCISES

7.19 Refer to the data and model of Exercise 7.1. The MSE for the model is .1267. Plot the residuals versus $\hat{y}$. Identify any outliers on the plot.

7.20 Refer to the data and model of Exercise 7.2. The MSE for the model is 17.2557. Plot the residuals versus $\hat{y}$. Identify any outliers on the plot.

7.21 Refer to the *Environmental Quality* regression model relating PCB concentration of a bay in 1985 (y) to the PCB concentration in 1984 (x), Exercise 4.20. A SAS printout of the straight-line model with residuals is shown here.

```
                     Analysis of Variance

                         Sum of          Mean
Source            DF    Squares        Square      F Value      Prob>F

Model              1 462349.85512 462349.85512      21.772      0.0001
Error             35 743254.18292  21235.83380
C Total           36 1205604.0380

      Root MSE     145.72520      R-square       0.3835
      Dep Mean     107.13351      Adj R-sq       0.3659
      C.V.         136.02205

                     Parameter Estimates

                 Parameter       Standard    T for H0:
Variable  DF      Estimate          Error  Parameter=0    Prob > |T|

INTERCEP   1     85.013798    24.42159452        3.481        0.0014
PCB84      1      0.040454     0.00866978        4.666        0.0001
```

(continued)

*The method of absolute deviations requires linear programming techniques that are beyond the scope of this text. Consult the references given at the end of the chapter for details on how to apply this method.

SAS printout for Exercise 7.21
(continued)

Obs	BAY	PCB84	Dep Var PCB85	Predict Value	Residual
1	Casco	95.28	77.5500	88.8682	-11.3182
2	Merrmack	52.97	29.2300	87.1566	-57.9266
3	Salem	533.58	403.1	106.6	296.5
4	Boston	17104.86	736.0	777.0	-40.9695
5	Buzzards	308.46	192.2	97.5	94.7
6	Narragan	159.96	220.6	91.4848	129.1
7	ELongIsl	10	8.6200	85.4183	-76.7983
8	WLongIsl	234.43	174.3	94.5	79.8126
9	Raritan	443.89	529.3	103.0	426.3
10	Delaware	2.5	130.7	85.1149	45.5551
11	LChesapk	51	39.7400	87.0769	-47.3369
12	Pamilico	0	0	85.0138	-85.0138
13	Charlest	9.1	8.4300	85.3819	-76.9519
14	Sapelo	0	0	85.0138	-85.0138
15	StJohns	140	120.0	90.6773	29.3627
16	Tampa	0	0	85.0138	-85.0138
17	Apalach	12	11.9300	85.4992	-73.5692
18	Mobile	0	0	85.0138	-85.0138
19	RoundIsl	0	0	85.0138	-85.0138
20	MissRiv	34	30.1400	86.3892	-56.2492
21	Baratara	0	0	85.0138	-85.0138
22	SanAnton	0	0	85.0138	-85.0138
23	CorpusCh	0	0	85.0138	-85.0138
24	SDiegoHa	422.1	531.7	102.1	429.6
25	SDiegoBa	6.74	9.3000	85.2865	-75.9865
26	DanaPt	7.06	5.7400	85.2994	-79.5594
27	SealBch	46.71	46.4700	86.9034	-40.4334
28	SanPedro	159.56	176.9	91.4686	85.4314
29	SantaMon	14	13.6900	85.5802	-71.8902
30	Bodega	4.18	4.8900	85.1829	-80.2929
31	Coos	3.19	6.6000	85.1428	-78.5428
32	Columbia	8.77	6.7300	85.3686	-78.6386
33	Nisquall	4.23	4.2800	85.1849	-80.9049
34	Commence	20.6	20.5000	85.8471	-65.3471
35	Elliot	329.97	414.5	98.4	316.1
36	Lutak	5.5	5.8000	85.2363	-79.4363
37	Nahku	6.6	5.0800	85.2808	-80.2008

a. Is the model adequate for predicting y? Explain.

b. Refer to part **a**. The Environmental Protection Agency believes San Diego Harbor has a strong influence on the regression because of its large residual value. Remove the observation for San Diego Harbor (observation 24) from the data and refit the model. Has model adequacy improved?

c. An alternative approach is to use the log transformations $y^* =$ natural $\log(y + 1)$ and $x^* =$ natural $\log(x + 1)$ and fit the model $E(y^*) = \beta_0 + \beta_1 x^*$. A SAS printout for this model follows. Conduct a test for model adequacy and perform a residual analysis. Interpret the results. In particular, comment on the residual value for San Diego.

Analysis of Variance

Source	DF	Sum of Squares	Mean Square	F Value	Prob>F
Model	1	145.58169	145.58169	251.172	0.0001
Error	35	20.28631	0.57961		
C Total	36	165.86800			

Root MSE	0.76132	R-square	0.8777
Dep Mean	2.94451	Adj R-sq	0.8742
C.V.	25.85556		

(continued)

Parameter Estimates

Variable	DF	Parameter Estimate	Standard Error	T for H0: Parameter=0	Prob > |T|
INTERCEP	1	0.425110	0.20232699	2.101	0.0429
LNPCB84	1	0.850826	0.05368523	15.848	0.0001

Obs	BAY	LNPCB84	Dep Var LNPCB85	Predict Value	Residual
1	Casco	4.567261	4.3637	4.3111	0.0527
2	Merrmack	3.988428	3.4088	3.8186	-0.4097
3	Salem	6.281481	6.0017	5.7696	0.2321
4	Boston	9.747176	6.6026	8.7183	-2.1157
5	Buzzards	5.734829	5.2635	5.3045	-0.0410
6	Narragan	5.081156	5.4009	4.7483	0.6526
7	ELongIsl	2.397895	2.2638	2.4653	-0.2015
8	WLongIsl	5.461414	5.1666	5.0718	0.0947
9	Raritan	6.097827	6.2734	5.6133	0.6601
10	Delaware	1.252763	4.8803	1.4910	3.3893
11	LChesapk	3.951244	3.7072	3.7869	-0.0797
12	Pamilico	0	0	0.4251	-0.4251
13	Charlest	2.312535	2.2439	2.3927	-0.1488
14	Sapelo	0	0	0.4251	-0.4251
15	StJohns	4.94876	4.7961	4.6356	0.1605
16	Tampa	0	0	0.4251	-0.4251
17	Apalach	2.564949	2.5596	2.6074	-0.0479
18	Mobile	0	0	0.4251	-0.4251
19	RoundIsl	0	0	0.4251	-0.4251
20	MissRiv	3.555348	3.4385	3.4501	-0.0116
21	Baratara	0	0	0.4251	-0.4251
22	SanAnton	0	0	0.4251	-0.4251
23	CorpusCh	0	0	0.4251	-0.4251
24	SDiegoHa	6.047609	6.2779	5.5706	0.7073
25	SDiegoBa	2.046402	2.3321	2.1662	0.1659
26	DanaPt	2.086914	1.9081	2.2007	-0.2926
27	SealBch	3.865141	3.8601	3.7137	0.1464
28	SanPedro	5.078668	5.1812	4.7462	0.4351
29	SantaMon	2.70805	2.6872	2.7292	-0.0420
30	Bodega	1.644805	1.7733	1.8246	-0.0513
31	Coos	1.432701	2.0281	1.6441	0.3841
32	Columbia	2.279316	2.0451	2.3644	-0.3193
33	Nisquall	1.654411	1.6639	1.8327	-0.1688
34	Commence	3.072693	3.0681	3.0394	0.0286
35	Elliot	5.802028	6.0295	5.3616	0.6679
36	Lutak	1.871802	1.9169	2.0177	-0.1008
37	Nahku	2.028148	1.8050	2.1507	-0.3457

7.22 Refer to the grandfather clock example, Example 4.1. The least squares model used to predict auction price, y, from age of the clock, x_1, and number of bidders, x_2, was determined to be

$$\hat{y} = -1{,}336.722 + 12.7362x_1 + 85.8151x_2$$

a. Use this equation to calculate the residuals of each of the prices given in Table 4.2.
b. Calculate the mean and the variance of the residuals. The mean should equal 0, and the variance should be close to the value of MSE given in the MINITAB printout shown in Figure 4.7.
c. Find the proportion of the residuals that fall outside 2 estimated standard deviations ($2s$) of 0.
d. If you have access to a multiple regression computer package, rerun the analysis and request influence diagnostics. Interpret the measures of influence given on the printout.

7.23 Refer to the study of the population of the world's largest cities in Exercise 7.18. A multiple regression model for log of the population (in thousands) of each country's largest city was fitted to data collected on 126 nations and resulted in MSE = .036. A computer-generated (SAS) plot of the regression residuals versus $\hat{y}$ is shown on page 428. Identify any outliers on the plot.

SAS printout for Exercise 7.23

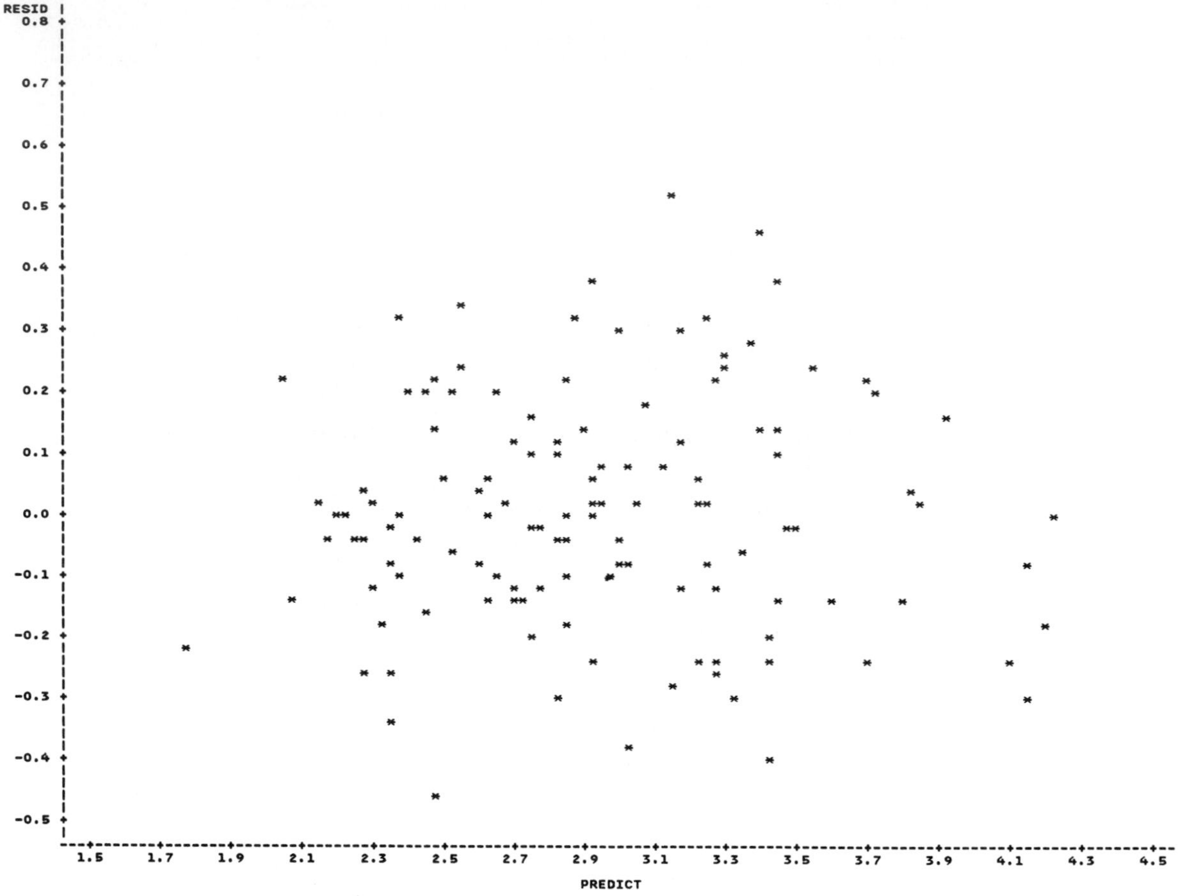

NOTE: 2 OBS HIDDEN

7.24 A large manufacturing firm wants to determine whether a relationship exists between the number of work-hours an employee misses per year and the employee's annual wages. A sample of 15 employees produced the data in the accompanying table. A first-order model was fitted to the data with the following results:

$$\hat{y} = 222.64 - 9.60x$$

$$r^2 = .073$$

a. Interpret the value of r^2.
b. Calculate and plot the regression residuals. What do you notice?
c. After searching through its employees' files, the firm has found that employee #13 had been fired but that his name had not been removed from the active employee payroll. This explains the large accumulation of work-hours missed (543) by that employee. In view of this fact, what is your recommendation concerning this outlier?

EMPLOYEE	WORK-HOURS MISSED y	ANNUAL WAGES x, thousands of dollars	EMPLOYEE	WORK-HOURS MISSED y	ANNUAL WAGES x, thousands of dollars
1	49	12.8	9	191	7.8
2	36	14.5	10	6	15.8
3	127	8.3	11	63	10.8
4	91	10.2	12	79	9.7
5	72	10.0	13	543	12.1
6	34	11.5	14	57	21.2
7	155	8.8	15	82	10.9
8	11	17.2			

d. Use an available multiple regression program to measure how influential the observation for employee #13 is on the regression analysis.

e. Refit the model to the data, excluding the outlier, and find the least squares line. Calculate r^2 and comment on model adequacy.

7.25 Refer to *The New England Journal of Medicine* regression model relating a child's weight percentile, y, and the number of cigarettes smoked per day in the child's home (x), Exercise 7.7. A SAS regression printout (with residuals) for the straight-line model relating y to x is shown here.

```
Dependent Variable: Y

                         Analysis of Variance

                          Sum of          Mean
Source           DF      Squares        Square      F Value       Prob>F

Model             1    304.88209     304.88209        0.500       0.4864
Error            23  14011.11791     609.17904
C Total          24  14316.00000

      Root MSE       24.68155     R-square       0.0213
      Dep Mean       37.80000     Adj R-sq      -0.0213
      C.V.           65.29511

                        Parameter Estimates

                    Parameter        Standard     T for H0:
Variable  DF         Estimate           Error    Parameter=0      Prob > |T|

INTERCEP   1        41.152655      6.84296599          6.014          0.0001
X          1        -0.261926      0.37024180         -0.707          0.4864

     Dep Var   Predict   Std Err             Std Err   Student                    Cook's
Obs       Y      Value   Predict  Residual  Residual  Residual   -2-1-0 1 2            D

  1   6.0000   41.1527    6.843  -35.1527    23.714    -1.482  |    **|      |     0.091
  2  43.0000   41.1527    6.843    1.8473    23.714     0.078  |      |      |     0.000
  3   6.0000   37.2238    5.003  -31.2238    24.169    -1.292  |    **|      |     0.036
  4  49.0000   41.1527    6.843    7.8473    23.714     0.331  |      |      |     0.005
  5   2.0000   30.6756   11.215  -28.6756    21.986    -1.304  |    **|      |     0.221
  6  50.0000   41.1527    6.843    8.8473    23.714     0.373  |      |      |     0.006
  7   8.0000   35.1284    6.215  -27.1284    23.886    -1.136  |    **|      |     0.044
  8  49.0000   35.3903    5.997   13.6097    23.942     0.568  |      |*     |     0.010
  9  11.0000   35.9141    5.610  -24.9141    24.036    -1.037  |    **|      |     0.029
 10  46.0000   33.2949    8.057   12.7051    23.329     0.545  |      |*     |     0.018
 11  17.0000   39.3192    5.383  -22.3192    24.087    -0.927  |     *|      |     0.021
 12  54.0000   41.1527    6.843   12.8473    23.714     0.542  |      |*     |     0.012
 13  24.0000   40.3669    6.126  -16.3669    23.909    -0.685  |     *|      |     0.015
 14  58.0000   41.1527    6.843   16.8473    23.714     0.710  |      |*     |     0.021
 15  25.0000   41.1527    6.843  -16.1527    23.714    -0.681  |     *|      |     0.019
 16  62.0000   41.1527    6.843   20.8473    23.714     0.879  |      |*     |     0.032
 17  17.0000   34.6045    6.691  -17.6045    23.757    -0.741  |     *|      |     0.022
 18  66.0000   41.1527    6.843   24.8473    23.714     1.048  |      |**    |     0.046
 19  25.0000   35.9141    5.610  -10.9141    24.036    -0.454  |      |      |     0.006
 20  66.0000   35.1284    6.215   30.8716    23.886     1.292  |      |**    |     0.057
 21  25.0000   37.2238    5.003  -12.2238    24.169    -0.506  |     *|      |     0.005
 22  83.0000   41.1527    6.843   41.8473    23.714     1.765  |      |***   |     0.130
 23  31.0000   35.1284    6.215   -4.1284    23.886    -0.173  |      |      |     0.001
 24  87.0000   29.6279   12.562   57.3721    21.246     2.700  |      |***** |     1.275
 25  35.0000   38.5334    5.044   -3.5334    24.161    -0.146  |      |      |     0.000
```

(continued)

SAS printout for Exercise 7.25 (*continued*)

Obs	Rstudent	Hat Diag H	Cov Ratio	Dffits	INTERCEP Dfbetas	X Dfbetas
1	-1.5244	0.0769	0.9686	-0.4399	-0.4399	0.3046
2	0.0762	0.0769	1.1834	0.0220	0.0220	-0.0152
3	-1.3120	0.0411	0.9804	-0.2716	-0.1627	-0.0442
4	0.3244	0.0769	1.1727	0.0936	0.0936	-0.0648
5	-1.3255	0.2065	1.1812	-0.6762	0.2058	-0.6072
6	0.3660	0.0769	1.1697	0.1056	0.1056	-0.0731
7	-1.1433	0.0634	1.0398	-0.2975	-0.0453	-0.1808
8	0.5599	0.0590	1.1292	0.1403	0.0281	0.0797
9	-1.0383	0.0517	1.0474	-0.2424	-0.0741	-0.1152
10	0.5361	0.1066	1.1920	0.1852	-0.0195	0.1463
11	-0.9236	0.0476	1.0635	-0.2064	-0.1936	0.0823
12	0.5333	0.0769	1.1540	0.1539	0.1539	-0.1066
13	-0.6764	0.0616	1.1178	-0.1733	-0.1718	0.1027
14	0.7026	0.0769	1.1326	0.2027	0.2027	-0.1404
15	-0.6730	0.0769	1.1367	-0.1942	-0.1942	0.1345
16	0.8746	0.0769	1.1058	0.2524	0.2524	-0.1748
17	-0.7335	0.0735	1.1240	-0.2066	-0.0134	-0.1395
18	1.0501	0.0769	1.0737	0.3030	0.3030	-0.2099
19	-0.4461	0.0517	1.1319	-0.1041	-0.0318	-0.0495
20	1.3126	0.0634	1.0036	0.3415	0.0520	0.2075
21	-0.4974	0.0411	1.1146	-0.1030	-0.0617	-0.0168
22	1.8561	0.0769	0.8851	0.5356	0.5356	-0.3709
23	-0.1691	0.0634	1.1639	-0.0440	-0.0067	-0.0267
24	3.1959	0.2590	0.6880	1.8896	-0.6678	1.7376
25	-0.1431	0.0418	1.1385	-0.0299	-0.0253	0.0061

a. Examine the residuals in the printout. Do you detect any outliers?

b. Influence diagnostics are also given on the SAS printout. Interpret these results.

7.6 Detecting Residual Correlation: The Durbin–Watson Test

Many types of business data are observed at regular time intervals. The Consumer Price Index (CPI) is computed and published monthly, the profits of most major corporations are published quarterly, and the *Fortune* 500 list of largest corporations is published annually. Data like these, which are observed over time, are called **time series**. We will often want to construct regression models where the data for the dependent and independent variables are time series.

Regression models of time series may pose a special problem. Because business time series tend to follow economic trends and seasonal cycles, the value of a time series at time t is often indicative of its value at time $(t + 1)$. That is, the value of a time series at time t is **correlated** with its value at time $(t + 1)$. If such a series is used as the dependent variable in a regression analysis, the result is that the random errors are correlated, and this violates one of the assumptions basic to the least squares inferential procedures. Consequently, we cannot apply the standard least squares inference-making tools and have confidence in their validity. Modifications of the methods, which allow for correlated residuals in time series regression models, will be presented in Chapter 9. In this section, we present a method of testing for the presence of residual correlation.

Consider the time series data in Table 7.9, which gives sales data for the 35-year history of a company. The computer printout shown in Figure 7.28 gives the regression analysis for the first-order linear model

$$y = \beta_0 + \beta_1 t + \varepsilon$$

This model seems to fit the data very well, since $R^2 = .98$ and the F value (1,615.72) that tests the adequacy of the model is significant. The hypothesis that the coefficient β_1 is positive is accepted at almost any α level ($t = 40.2$ with 33 df).

The residuals $\hat{\varepsilon} = y - (\hat{\beta}_0 + \hat{\beta}_1 t)$ are plotted in Figure 7.29 on page 433. Note that there is a distinct tendency for the residuals to have long positive and negative runs. That is, if the residual for year t is positive, there is a tendency for the residual for year $(t + 1)$ to be positive. These cycles are indicative of possible positive correlation between residuals.

TABLE 7.9 **A Firm's Annual Sales Revenue (thousands of dollars)**

YEAR t	SALES y	YEAR t	SALES y	YEAR t	SALES y
1	4.8	13	48.4	25	100.3
2	4.0	14	61.6	26	111.7
3	5.5	15	65.6	27	108.2
4	15.6	16	71.4	28	115.5
5	23.1	17	83.4	29	119.2
6	23.3	18	93.6	30	125.2
7	31.4	19	94.2	31	136.3
8	46.0	20	85.4	32	146.8
9	46.1	21	86.2	33	146.1
10	41.9	22	89.9	34	151.4
11	45.5	23	89.2	35	150.9
12	53.5	24	99.1		

FIGURE 7.28
SAS printout for regression analysis of annual sales model

```
                          Analysis of Variance

                              Sum of          Mean
Source              DF       Squares        Square      F Value       Prob>F

Model                1   65875.20817   65875.20817     1615.724       0.0001
Error               33    1345.45355      40.77132
C Total             34   67220.66171

     Root MSE          6.38524      R-square        0.9800
     Dep Mean         77.72286      Adj R-sq        0.9794
     C.V.              8.21540

                          Parameter Estimates

                     Parameter        Standard     T for H0:
Variable    DF        Estimate           Error   Parameter=0     Prob > |T|

INTERCEP     1        0.401513      2.20570829         0.182         0.8567
T            1        4.295630      0.10686692        40.196         0.0001

Durbin-Watson D                 0.821
(For Number of Obs.)               35
1st Order Autocorrelation       0.590
```

(continued)

FIGURE 7.28 *(continued)*

Obs	T	Dep Var Y	Predict Value	Residual
1	1	4.8000	4.6971	0.1029
2	2	4.0000	8.9928	-4.9928
3	3	5.5000	13.2884	-7.7884
4	4	15.6000	17.5840	-1.9840
5	5	23.1000	21.8797	1.2203
6	6	23.3000	26.1753	-2.8753
7	7	31.4000	30.4709	0.9291
8	8	46.0000	34.7666	11.2334
9	9	46.1000	39.0622	7.0378
10	10	41.9000	43.3578	-1.4578
11	11	45.5000	47.6534	-2.1534
12	12	53.5000	51.9491	1.5509
13	13	48.4000	56.2447	-7.8447
14	14	61.6000	60.5403	1.0597
15	15	65.6000	64.8360	0.7640
16	16	71.4000	69.1316	2.2684
17	17	83.4000	73.4272	9.9728
18	18	93.6000	77.7229	15.8771
19	19	94.2000	82.0185	12.1815
20	20	85.4000	86.3141	-0.9141
21	21	86.2000	90.6097	-4.4097
22	22	89.9000	94.9	-5.0054
23	23	89.2000	99.2	-10.0010
24	24	99.1	103.5	-4.3966
25	25	100.3	107.8	-7.4923
26	26	111.7	112.1	-0.3879
27	27	108.2	116.4	-8.1835
28	28	115.5	120.7	-5.1792
29	29	119.2	125.0	-5.7748
30	30	125.2	129.3	-4.0704
31	31	136.3	133.6	2.7339
32	32	146.8	137.9	8.9383
33	33	146.1	142.2	3.9427
34	34	151.4	146.5	4.9471
35	35	150.9	150.7	0.1514

Sum of Residuals	-8.10019E-13
Sum of Squared Residuals	1345.4535
Predicted Resid SS (Press)	1484.2108

For most economic time series models, we want to test the null hypothesis

H_0: No residual correlation

against the alternative

H_a: Positive residual correlation

since the hypothesis of positive residual correlation is consistent with economic trends and seasonal cycles.

The **Durbin–Watson *d* statistic** is used to test for the presence of residual correlation. This statistic is given by the formula

$$d = \frac{\sum_{t=2}^{n} (\hat{\varepsilon}_t - \hat{\varepsilon}_{t-1})^2}{\sum_{t=1}^{n} \hat{\varepsilon}_t^2}$$

FIGURE 7.29
SAS plot of residuals for the sales data: Least squares model

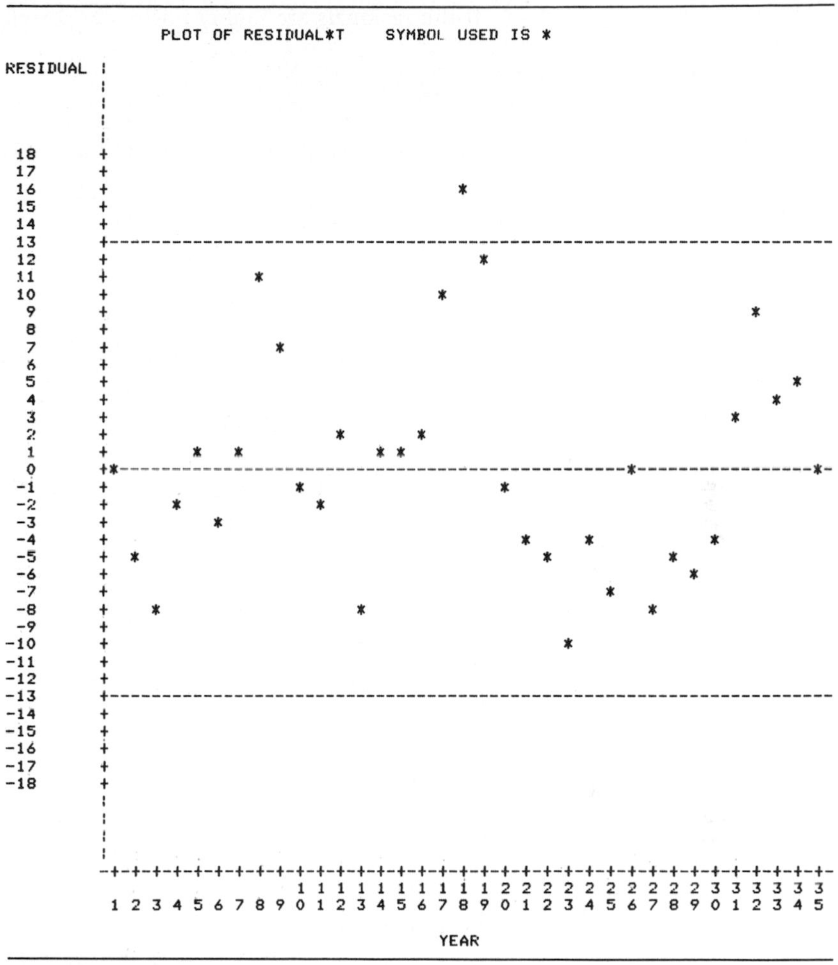

where n is the number of observations and $(\hat{\varepsilon}_t - \hat{\varepsilon}_{t-1})$ represents the difference between a pair of successive residuals. By expanding the numerator of d, we can also write

$$d = \frac{\sum_{t=2}^{n} \hat{\varepsilon}_t^2}{\sum_{t=1}^{n} \hat{\varepsilon}_t^2} + \frac{\sum_{t=2}^{n} \hat{\varepsilon}_{t-1}^2}{\sum_{t=1}^{n} \hat{\varepsilon}_t^2} - \frac{2\sum_{t=2}^{n} \hat{\varepsilon}_t\hat{\varepsilon}_{t-1}}{\sum_{t=1}^{n} \hat{\varepsilon}_t^2} \approx 2 - \frac{2\sum_{t=2}^{n} \hat{\varepsilon}_t\hat{\varepsilon}_{t-1}}{\sum_{t=1}^{n} \hat{\varepsilon}_t^2}$$

If the residuals are uncorrelated,

$$\sum_{t=2}^{n} \hat{\varepsilon}_t\hat{\varepsilon}_{t-1} \approx 0$$

indicating no relationship between $\hat{\varepsilon}_t$ and $\hat{\varepsilon}_{t-1}$, the value of d will be close to 2.

If the residuals are highly positively correlated,

$$\sum_{t=2}^{n} \hat{\varepsilon}_t \hat{\varepsilon}_{t-1} \approx \sum_{t=2}^{n} \hat{\varepsilon}_t^2$$

(since $\hat{\varepsilon}_t \approx \hat{\varepsilon}_{t-1}$), and the value of d will be near 0:

$$d \approx 2 - \frac{2\sum_{t=2}^{n} \hat{\varepsilon}_t \hat{\varepsilon}_{t-1}}{\sum_{t=1}^{n} \hat{\varepsilon}_t^2} \approx 2 - \frac{2\sum_{t=2}^{n} \hat{\varepsilon}_t^2}{\sum_{t=1}^{n} \hat{\varepsilon}_t^2} \approx 2 - 2 = 0$$

If the residuals are very negatively correlated, then $\hat{\varepsilon}_t \approx -\hat{\varepsilon}_{t-1}$, so that

$$\sum_{t=2}^{n} \hat{\varepsilon}_t \hat{\varepsilon}_{t-1} \approx -\sum_{t=2}^{n} \hat{\varepsilon}_t^2$$

and d will be approximately equal to 4. Thus, d ranges from 0 to 4, with interpretations as summarized in the box.

Interpretation of Durbin–Watson d Statistic

DEFINITION

$$d = \frac{\sum_{t=2}^{n} (\hat{\varepsilon}_t - \hat{\varepsilon}_{t-1})^2}{\sum_{t=1}^{n} \hat{\varepsilon}_t^2}$$

Range of d: $0 \le d \le 4$

1. If residuals are uncorrelated, $d \approx 2$.
2. If residuals are positively correlated, $d < 2$, and if the correlation is very strong, $d \approx 0$.
3. If residuals are negatively correlated, $d > 2$, and if the correlation is very strong, $d \approx 4$.

Durbin and Watson (1951) have given tables for the lower-tail values of the d statistic, which we show in Table 8 ($\alpha = .05$) and Table 9 ($\alpha = .01$) of Appendix C.

Part of Table 8 is reproduced in Table 7.10. For the sales example, we have $k = 1$ independent variable and $n = 35$ observations. Using $\alpha = .05$ for the one-tailed test for positive residual correlation, the table values are $d_L = 1.40$ and $d_U = 1.52$. The meaning of these values is illustrated in Figure 7.30. Because of the complexity of the sampling distribution of d, it is not possible to specify a single point that acts as a boundary between the rejection and nonrejection regions, as we did for the z, t, F, and other test statistics. Instead, an upper (d_U)

and lower (d_L) bound are specified so that a d value less than d_L definitely *does* provide strong evidence of positive residual correlation at $\alpha = .05$ (recall that small d values indicate positive correlation), a d value greater than d_U *does not* provide evidence of positive correlation at $\alpha = .05$, but a value of d between d_L and d_U *might* be significant at the $\alpha = .05$ level. If $d_L < d < d_U$, more information is needed before we can reach any conclusion about the presence of residual correlation. A summary of the Durbin–Watson d test is given in the box on page 436.

TABLE 7.10 **Reproduction of Part of Table 8 of Appendix C ($\alpha = .05$)**

n	k = 1		k = 2		k = 3		k = 4		k = 5	
	d_L	d_U	d_L	d_U	d_L	d_U	d_L	d_U	d_L	d_U
31	1.36	1.50	1.30	1.57	1.23	1.65	1.16	1.74	1.09	1.83
32	1.37	1.50	1.31	1.57	1.24	1.65	1.18	1.73	1.11	1.82
33	1.38	1.51	1.32	1.58	1.26	1.65	1.19	1.73	1.13	1.81
34	1.39	1.51	1.33	1.58	1.27	1.65	1.21	1.73	1.15	1.81
35	1.40	1.52	1.34	1.58	1.28	1.65	1.22	1.73	1.16	1.80
36	1.41	1.52	1.35	1.59	1.29	1.65	1.24	1.73	1.18	1.80
37	1.42	1.53	1.36	1.59	1.31	1.66	1.25	1.72	1.19	1.80
38	1.43	1.54	1.37	1.59	1.32	1.66	1.26	1.72	1.21	1.79
39	1.43	1.54	1.38	1.60	1.33	1.66	1.27	1.72	1.22	1.79
40	1.44	1.54	1.39	1.60	1.34	1.66	1.29	1.72	1.23	1.79

FIGURE 7.30
Rejection region for the Durbin–Watson d test: Sales example

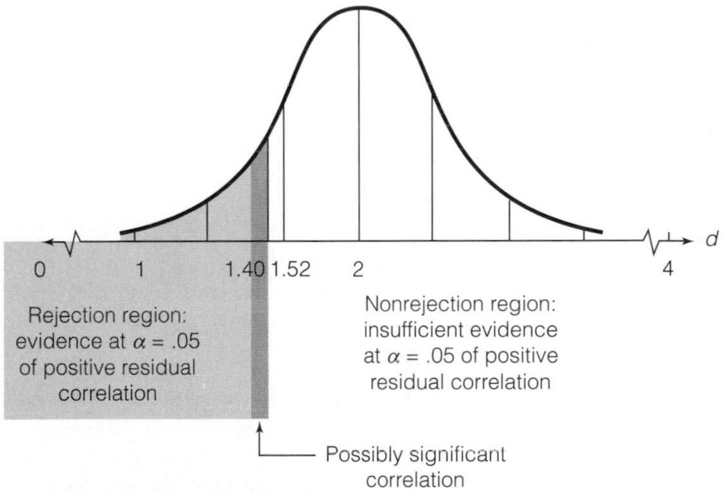

As indicated in the printout for the sales example (Figure 7.28), the computed value of d, .821, is less than the tabulated value of d_L, 1.40. Thus, we conclude that the residuals of the straight-line model for sales are positively correlated.

Tests for negative correlation and two-tailed tests can be conducted by making use of the symmetry of the sampling distribution of the d statistic about its mean, 2 (see Figure 7.30). That is, we compare $(4 - d)$ to d_L and d_U and conclude that the residuals are negatively correlated if $(4 - d) < d_L$, that there is insufficient

Durbin–Watson *d* Test

ONE-TAILED TEST	TWO-TAILED TEST
H_0: No residual correlation H_a: Positive residual correlation [or H_a: Negative residual correlation]	H_0: No residual correlation H_a: Positive or negative residual correlation

Test statistic:

$$d = \frac{\sum_{t=2}^{n} (\hat{\varepsilon}_t - \hat{\varepsilon}_{t-1})^2}{\sum_{t=1}^{n} \hat{\varepsilon}_t^2}$$

ONE-TAILED TEST	TWO-TAILED TEST
Rejection region: $d < d_{L,\alpha}$ [or $(4 - d) < d_{L,\alpha}$ if H_a: Negative residual correlation]	*Rejection region:* $d < d_{L,\alpha/2}$ or $(4 - d) < d_{L,\alpha/2}$
Nonrejection region: $d > d_{U,\alpha}$ [or $(4 - d) > d_{U,\alpha}$ if H_a: Negative residual correlation]	*Nonrejection region:* $d > d_{U,\alpha/2}$ or $(4 - d) > d_{U,\alpha/2}$
Inconclusive ("possibly significant") region: $d_{L,\alpha} \le d \le d_{U,\alpha}$ (see Figure 7.30) [or $d_{L,\alpha} \le (4 - d) \le d_{U,\alpha}$ if H_a: Negative residual correlation]	*Inconclusive ("possibly significant") region:* Any other result
where $d_{L,\alpha}$ and $d_{U,\alpha}$ are the lower and upper tabulated values, respectively, corresponding to k independent variables and n observations.	where $d_{L,\alpha/2}$ and $d_{U,\alpha/2}$ are the lower and upper tabulated values, respectively, corresponding to k independent variables and n observations.

Assumption: The residuals are normally distributed.

evidence to conclude that the residuals are negatively correlated if $(4 - d) > d_U$, and that the test for negative residual correlation is *possibly* significant if $d_L < (4 - d) < d_U$.

Once strong evidence of residual correlation has been established, as in the case of the sales example, doubt is cast on the least squares results and any inferences drawn from them. In Chapter 9, we present a time series model that accounts for the correlation of the random errors. The residual correlation can be taken into account in a time series model, thereby improving both the fit of the model and the reliability of model inferences.

EXERCISES

7.26 Find the values of d_L and d_U from Tables 8 and 9 of Appendix C for each of the following situations:

a. $n = 30, \quad k = 3, \quad \alpha = .05$
b. $n = 40, \quad k = 1, \quad \alpha = .01$
c. $n = 35, \quad k = 5, \quad \alpha = .05$

7.27 Exploratory research published in the *Journal of Professional Services Marketing* (Vol. 5, 1990) examined the relationship between deposit share of a retail bank and several marketing variables. Quarterly deposit share data were collected for the years 1981–1985 for each of nine retail banking institutions. The model analyzed took the following form:

$$y_t = \beta_0 + \beta_1 P_{t-1} + \beta_2 S_{t-1} + \beta_3 D_{t-1} + \varepsilon_t$$

where

y_t = Deposit share of bank in quarter t, $t = 1, 2, \ldots, 20$
P_{t-1} = Expenditures on promotion-related activities in quarter $t - 1$
S_{t-1} = Expenditures on service-related activities in quarter $t - 1$
D_{t-1} = Expenditures on distribution-related activities in quarter $t - 1$

A separate model was fitted for each bank with the results shown in the table.

BANK	R^2	p-VALUE FOR GLOBAL F	DURBIN–WATSON d[a]
1	.914	.000	1.3
2	.721	.004	3.4
3	.926	.000	2.7
4	.827	.000	1.9
5	.270	.155	.85
6	.616	.012	1.8
7	.962	.000	2.5
8	.495	.014	2.3
9	.500	.011	1.1

[a]*Note:* The values of d shown are approximated based on other information provided in the article.

a. Interpret the value of R^2 for each bank.
b. Test the overall adequacy of the model for each bank.
c. Conduct the Durbin–Watson d test for each bank. Interpret the practical significance of the tests.

7.28 Forecasts of automotive vehicle sales in the United States provide the basis for financial and strategic planning of large automotive corporations. Olson and Janakiraman* developed a forecasting model for y, total monthly passenger car and light truck sales (in thousands):

$$E(y) = \beta_0 + \beta_1 x_1 + \beta_2 x_2 + \beta_3 x_3 + \beta_4 x_4 + \beta_5 x_5$$

*Olson, S. J., and Janakiraman, J. "Proposed U.S. passenger car and light truck sales forecast model." Paper presented at SAS User's Group International Conference, Reno, Nevada, 1985.

where

x_1 = Average monthly retail price of regular gasoline

x_2 = Annual percentage change in GNP per quarter

x_3 = Monthly consumer confidence index

x_4 = Total number of vehicles scrapped (millions) per month

x_5 = Vehicle seasonality

The model was fitted to monthly data collected over a 12-year period (i.e., $n = 144$ months) with the following results:

$$\hat{y} = -676.42 - 1.93x_1 + 6.54x_2 + 2.02x_3 + .08x_4 + 9.82x_5$$

$$R^2 = .856$$

Durbin–Watson $d = 1.01$

a. Is there sufficient evidence to indicate that the model contributes information for the prediction of y? Test using $\alpha = .05$.

b. Is there sufficient evidence to indicate that the regression errors are positively correlated? Test using $\alpha = .05$.

c. Comment on the validity of the inference concerning model adequacy in light of the result of part **b**.

7.29 The consumer purchasing value of the dollar from 1970 to 1993 is illustrated by the data in the accompanying table, where the purchasing power of the dollar (compared to 1982) is listed for each year. The first-order model $E(y_t) = \beta_0 + \beta_1 t$ was fitted to the data using SAS. The SAS printout is displayed on page 439.

YEAR, t	VALUE, y	YEAR, t	VALUE, y
1970	$2.55	1982	$1.00
1971	2.47	1983	.98
1972	2.39	1984	.96
1973	2.19	1985	.95
1974	1.90	1986	.97
1975	1.72	1987	.95
1976	1.65	1988	.93
1977	1.55	1989	.88
1978	1.43	1990	.84
1979	1.29	1991	.82
1980	1.14	1992	.81
1981	1.04	1993	.79

Source: *Statistical Abstract of the U.S.*, 1994.

a. Plot the regression residuals (shown on the printout) against t. Is there a tendency for the residuals to have long positive and negative runs? How do you account for this?

b. Locate the Durbin–Watson d statistic for this model on the printout. Test the hypothesis that the time series residuals are positively correlated. Test at $\alpha = .05$.

SAS printout for Exercise 7.29

```
Model: MODEL1
Dependent Variable: Y

                         Analysis of Variance

                               Sum of          Mean
       Source          DF     Squares        Square       F Value       Prob>F

       Model            1     6.44178       6.44178       120.391       0.0001
       Error           22     1.17716       0.05351
       C Total         23     7.61893

           Root MSE        0.23132      R-square         0.8455
           Dep Mean        1.34167      Adj R-sq         0.8385
           C.V.           17.24094

                         Parameter Estimates

                      Parameter       Standard     T for H0:
     Variable  DF      Estimate          Error    Parameter=0     Prob > |T|

     INTERCEP   1    149.644019    13.51615991         11.071         0.0001
     T          1     -0.074843     0.00682113        -10.972         0.0001


Durbin-Watson D                  0.106
(For Number of Obs.)                24
1st Order Autocorrelation        0.855


                                  Dep Var    Predict
                Obs       T            Y      Value   Residual

                  1    1970       2.5500     2.2024     0.3476
                  2    1971       2.4700     2.1275     0.3425
                  3    1972       2.3900     2.0527     0.3373
                  4    1973       2.1900     1.9778     0.2122
                  5    1974       1.9000     1.9030   -0.00299
                  6    1975       1.7200     1.8281    -0.1081
                  7    1976       1.6500     1.7533    -0.1033
                  8    1977       1.5500     1.6785    -0.1285
                  9    1978       1.4300     1.6036    -0.1736
                 10    1979       1.2900     1.5288    -0.2388
                 11    1980       1.1400     1.4539    -0.3139
                 12    1981       1.0400     1.3791    -0.3391
                 13    1982       1.0000     1.3042    -0.3042
                 14    1983       0.9800     1.2294    -0.2494
                 15    1984       0.9600     1.1546    -0.1946
                 16    1985       0.9500     1.0797    -0.1297
                 17    1986       0.9700     1.0049    -0.0349
                 18    1987       0.9500     0.9300     0.0200
                 19    1988       0.9300     0.8552     0.0748
                 20    1989       0.8800     0.7803     0.0997
                 21    1990       0.8400     0.7055     0.1345
                 22    1991       0.8200     0.6307     0.1893
                 23    1992       0.8100     0.5558     0.2542
                 24    1993       0.7900     0.4810     0.3090
```

7.30 The table on page 440 gives the factory sales (in thousands) of passenger cars in the United States for the years 1992 and 1993. The straight-line model $E(y_t) = \beta_0 + \beta_1 t$ is fitted to the data using the method of least squares, with the following results:

$\hat{y}_t = 467.78 - 1.31t$

Durbin–Watson $d = 1.58$

a. Calculate and plot the regression residuals against t. Is there a tendency for the residuals to have long positive and negative runs?

b. Is there evidence at $\alpha = .05$ level of significance that the residuals are autocorrelated?

MONTH	TIME, t	1992 SALES, y	TIME, t	1993 SALES, y
January	1	404	13	440
February	2	444	14	479
March	3	506	15	596
April	4	506	16	539
May	5	548	17	545
June	6	572	18	562
July	7	362	19	305
August	8	418	20	426
September	9	474	21	459
October	10	529	22	547
November	11	458	23	543
December	12	464	24	495

Source: *Survey of Current Business*, U.S. Dept. of Commerce.

7.31 B. N. Song compared annual consumption for two lower developed countries (LDCs)—Korea, a poor LDC, and Italy, a rich LDC (*Economic Development and Cultural Change*, Apr. 1981). Using data from the post–Korean War period, Song modeled annual consumption y_t as a function of total labor income x_{1t} and total property income x_{2t}, with the following results (assume data for $n = 40$ years were used in the analysis):

Korea: $\hat{y}_t = 7.81 + .91x_{1t} + .57x_{2t}$

$s = 1.29$

$d = 2.09$

Italy: $\hat{y}_t = 1{,}043.4 + .85x_{1t} + .40x_{2t}$

$s = 290.5$

$d = 1.07$

a. Is there evidence of positively correlated residuals in the consumption model for Korea? Test using $\alpha = .05$.

b. Is there evidence of positively correlated residuals in the consumption model for Italy? Test using $\alpha = .05$.

7.32 T. C. Chiang considered several time series forecasting models of future foreign exchange rates for U.S. currency (*The Journal of Financial Research*, Summer 1986). One popular theory among financial analysts is that the forward (90-day) exchange rate is a useful predictor of the future spot exchange rate. Using monthly data on exchange rates for the British pound for $n = 81$ months, Chiang fitted the model

$$E(y_t) = \beta_0 + \beta_1 x_{t-1}$$

where

$y = \ln$ (spot rate) in month t

$x_t = \ln$ (forward rate) in month t

The method of least squares yielded the following results:

$\hat{y}_t = -.009 + .986x_{t-1} \quad (t = 47.9)$

$s = .0249 \qquad R^2 = .957 \qquad$ Durbin–Watson $d = .962$

a. Is the model useful for predicting future spot exchange rates for the British pound? Test using $\alpha = .05$.
b. Interpret the values of s and R^2.
c. Is there evidence of positive autocorrelation among the residuals? Test using $\alpha = .05$.
d. Based on the results of parts **a–c**, would you recommend using the least squares model to forecast spot exchange rates?

Summary

An analysis of regression **residuals** can play an important role in the modeling process. Plots of the residuals against the independent variables can suggest modifications that will improve the model. These include the **addition of quadratic terms to allow for curvature** in the response surface and **transforming the dependent variable to stabilize its variance. Histograms, stem-and-leaf displays**, and **normal probability plots** of residuals give visual clues as to whether the normality assumption is satisfied. **Plots of residuals** are also helpful for identification of **outliers**, which can then be traced to determine the cause of an unusually large or small observation. The influence the outlying observation has on the regression analysis can be measured using **leverage**, **Cook's distance** D, and **deleted residuals**.

When you use residual plots, you should always be aware that conclusions drawn from them are subjective. Therefore, they cannot substitute for formal tests to detect model inadequacies.

The F test (Section 1.9) can be used to detect differences in pairs of variances, and F tests for sets of parameters (Section 4.10) can be used to detect factor interactions and curvature in a response surface. The **Durbin–Watson** d **test** can be used to test for the presence of **residual correlation**. We will present methods for constructing time series models that allow for correlation of the random errors in Chapter 9.

SUPPLEMENTARY EXERCISES

7.33 Identify the problem(s) in each of the following residual plots:

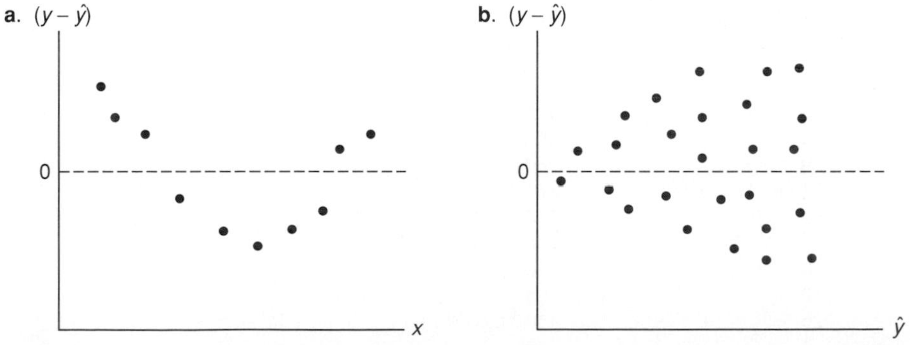

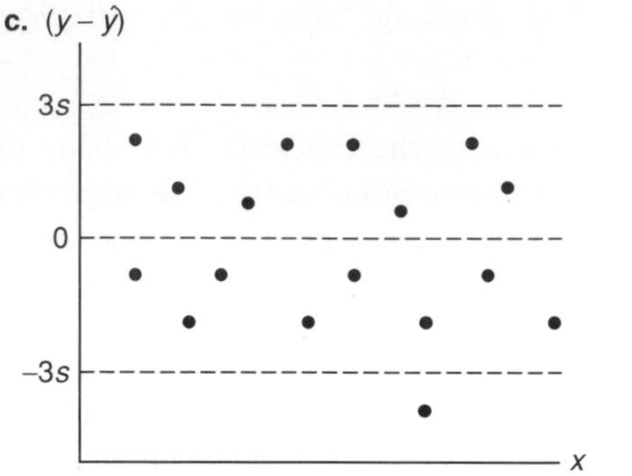

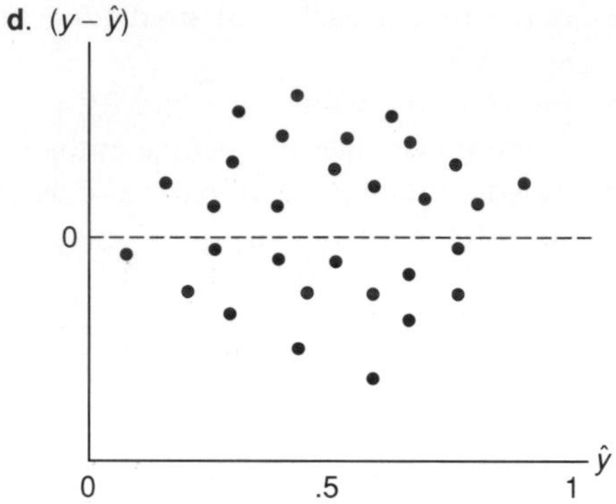

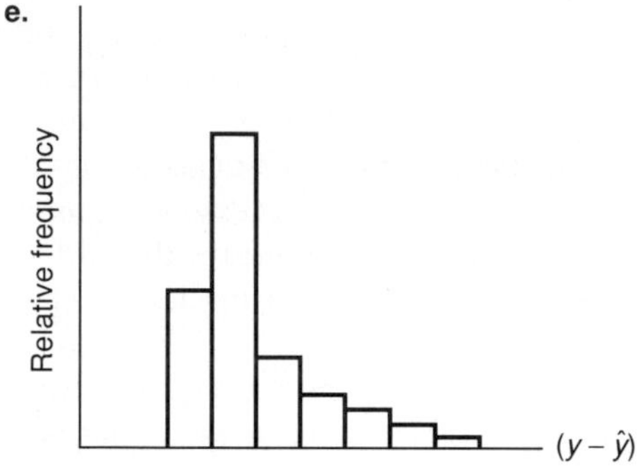

7.34 A naval base is considering modifying or adding to its fleet of 48 standard aircraft. The final decision regarding the type and number of aircraft to be added depends on a comparison of cost versus effectiveness of the modified fleet. Consequently, the naval base would like to model the projected percentage increase y in fleet effectiveness by the end of the decade as a function of the cost x of modifying the fleet. A first proposal is the quadratic model

$$E(y) = \beta_0 + \beta_1 x + \beta_2 x^2$$

The data provided in the accompanying table were collected on 10 naval bases of a similar size that recently expanded their fleets. The data were used to fit the model, and the SAS printout of the multiple regression analysis is reproduced on page 443.

PERCENTAGE IMPROVEMENT AT END OF DECADE y	COST OF MODIFYING FLEET x, millions of dollars
18	125
32	160
9	80
37	162
6	110
3	90
30	140
10	85
25	150
2	50

SAS printout for Exercise 7.34

```
DEP VARIABLE: Y
                              ANALYSIS OF VARIANCE

                              SUM OF         MEAN
          SOURCE     DF      SQUARES        SQUARE      F VALUE      PROB>F

          MODEL       2    1368.77501     684.38750      33.079      0.0003
          ERROR       7     144.82499   20.68928481
          C TOTAL     9    1513.60000

             ROOT MSE       4.548548      R-SQUARE       0.9043
             DEP MEAN           17.2      ADJ R-SQ       0.8770
             C.V.           26.44504

                              PARAMETER ESTIMATES

                          PARAMETER        STANDARD      T FOR H0:
      VARIABLE  DF         ESTIMATE           ERROR    PARAMETER=0     PROB > |T|

      INTERCEP   1      10.65903604     14.55009061          0.733         0.4876
      X          1      -0.28160568      0.28087588         -1.003         0.3494
      XX         1      0.002671936     0.001253832          2.131         0.0706


                          PREDICT    STD ERR               STD ERR    STUDENT                      COOK'S
OBS        ACTUAL          VALUE    PREDICT   RESIDUAL   RESIDUAL   RESIDUAL     -2-1-0 1 2              D

   1      18.0000        17.2073     2.0627     0.7927     4.0539     0.1955   :      :     :       0.003
   2      32.0000        34.0037     2.6525    -2.0037     3.6951    -0.5423   :     *:     :       0.051
   3       9.0000         5.2310     2.0601     3.7690     4.0553     0.9294   :      :*    :       0.074
   4      37.0000        35.1612     2.8397     1.8388     3.5532     0.5175   :      :*    :       0.057
   5       6.0000        12.0128     2.2177    -6.0128     3.9713    -1.5141   :   ***:     :       0.238
   6       3.0000         6.9572     2.0835    -3.9572     4.0433    -0.9787   :     *:     :       0.085
   7      30.0000        23.6042     1.8468     6.3958     4.1568     1.5387   :      :***  :       0.156
   8      10.0000         6.0273     2.0492     3.9727     4.0608     0.9783   :      :*    :       0.081
   9      25.0000        28.5367     2.0070    -3.5367     4.0818    -0.8665   :     *:     :       0.060
  10       2.0000         3.2586     4.1920    -1.2586     1.7654    -0.7129   :     *:     :       0.955

SUM OF RESIDUALS               4.97380E-14
SUM OF SQUARED RESIDUALS           144.825
PREDICTED RESID SS (PRESS)         301.668

                                       HAT DIAG        COV                 INTERCEP    X           XX
   OBS    RESIDUAL     RSTUDENT             H         RATIO      DFFITS     DFBETAS     DFBETAS     DFBETAS

     1      0.7927       0.1815        0.2057        1.9665      0.0924     -0.0594      0.0657     -0.0639
     2     -2.0037      -0.5129        0.3401        2.1156     -0.3682     -0.1192      0.1505     -0.1871
     3      3.7690       0.9190        0.2051        1.3457      0.4669      0.0286      0.0632     -0.1088
     4      1.8388       0.4886        0.3898        2.3148      0.3904      0.1473     -0.1817      0.2199
     5     -6.0128      -1.7093        0.2377        0.6336     -0.9545      0.5920     -0.7014      0.7211
     6     -3.9572      -0.9753        0.2098        1.2924     -0.5025      0.1474     -0.2357      0.2724
     7      6.3958       1.7511        0.1649        0.5511      0.7780     -0.3140      0.3143     -0.2585
     8      3.9727       0.9748        0.2030        1.2818      0.4919     -0.0653      0.1582     -0.2007
     9     -3.5367      -0.8490        0.1947        1.4030     -0.4174      0.0129      0.0093     -0.0503
    10     -1.2586      -0.6854        0.8494        8.4082     -1.6276     -1.4594      1.2838     -1.1539
```

a. Calculate the regression residuals and construct a residual plot versus x. Do you detect any trends? Any outliers?

b. Interpret the influence diagnostics shown on the printout. Are there any observations that have large influence on the analysis?

7.35 In 1974 the federal government limited highway speeds to 55 miles per hour (mph) in an effort to conserve gasoline. Several years after this limit was imposed, it was observed that traffic fatalities had apparently declined, as well as gas consumption. University of Colorado Professors T. H. Ferrester, R. F. McNown, and L. D. Singell conducted an analysis to estimate the effect of the 55-mph speed limit on traffic fatalities (*Southern Economic Journal*, Jan. 1984). Time series data for the United States from 1952 to 1979 ($n = 28$ years) were used to fit a regression model relating traffic fatalities y_t at time t to $k = 7$ independent variables:

x_{1t} = Real earned income

x_{2t} = Vehicle miles

x_{3t} = Ratio of number of youths to number of adults

x_{4t} = Percentage of all car purchases that are imported cars

x_{5t} = Average highway speed

x_{6t} = Percentage of cars traveling between 45 and 60 mph

$$x_{7t} = \begin{cases} 0 & \text{if 55-mph speed limit imposed} \\ 1 & \text{otherwise} \end{cases}$$

The results of the multiple regression are summarized as follows:

$$\hat{y}_t = -20{,}016.4 + 7{,}544.85x_{1t} - .01046x_{2t} - 36{,}758.0x_{3t} - 117.609x_{4t} + 1{,}325.22x_{5t} - 415.742x_{6t} + 9{,}678.08x_{7t}$$

$R^2 = .987 \qquad F = 217.23 \qquad d = 1.97$

a. Is there evidence that the model is useful for predicting annual traffic fatalities? Test using $\alpha = .05$.

b. Is there evidence that the regression residuals are positively correlated? Test using $\alpha = .05$.

7.36 A leading pharmaceutical company that produces a new hypertension pill would like to model annual revenue generated by this product. Company researchers utilized data collected over the previous 15 years to fit the model

$$E(y_t) = \beta_0 + \beta_1 x_t + \beta_2 t$$

where

y_t = Revenue in year t (in millions of dollars)

x_t = Cost per pill in year t

t = Year (1, 2, . . . , 15)

The SAS printout for the regression analysis is reproduced here. A company statistician suspects that the assumption of independent errors may be violated and that, in fact, the regression residuals are positively correlated. Test this claim using $\alpha = .05$.

DEP VARIABLE: Y — ANALYSIS OF VARIANCE

SOURCE	DF	SUM OF SQUARES	MEAN SQUARE	F VALUE	PROB>F
MODEL	2	48.82325339	24.41162670	206.187	0.0001
ERROR	12	1.42074661	0.11839555		
C TOTAL	14	50.24400000			

ROOT MSE	0.3440865	R-SQUARE	0.9717
DEP MEAN	7.32	ADJ R-SQ	0.9670
C.V.	4.700636		

(continued)

PARAMETER ESTIMATES

VARIABLE	DF	PARAMETER ESTIMATE	STANDARD ERROR	T FOR H0: PARAMETER=0	PROB > |T|
INTERCEP	1	3.26119109	1.87880228	1.736	0.1082
T	1	0.39158795	0.07045937	5.558	0.0001
X	1	1.58760907	4.12905034	0.384	0.7073

OBS	ID	ACTUAL	PREDICT VALUE	RESIDUAL
1	0.48	5.0000	4.4148	0.5852
2	0.45	4.9000	4.7588	0.1412
3	0.5	5.3000	5.2298	0.0702
4	0.5	5.7000	5.6213	0.0787
5	0.55	5.9000	6.0923	-0.1923
6	0.57	6.1000	6.5157	-0.4157
7	0.6	6.9000	6.9549	-0.0549
8	0.6	7.0000	7.3465	-0.3465
9	0.62	7.5000	7.7698	-0.2698
10	0.6	7.8000	8.1296	-0.3296
11	0.6	8.3000	8.5212	-0.2212
12	0.62	8.9000	8.9446	-0.0446
13	0.65	9.6000	9.3838	0.2162
14	0.7	10.5000	9.8547	0.6453
15	0.71	10.4000	10.2622	0.1378

```
SUM OF RESIDUALS                    1.82077E-14
SUM OF SQUARED RESIDUALS               1.420747

DURBIN-WATSON D                 0.776
(FOR NUMBER OF OBS.)               15
1ST ORDER AUTOCORRELATION       0.485
```

7.37 Finding the cost of driving to campus increasingly prohibitive, students at one large university are buying inexpensive used bikes for their daily commute, thus saving on gas. Because of this increased demand, the owner of a nearby bicycle shop is having difficulty determining the quantity of used bicycles she should stock. To solve this problem, it is essential that the owner be able to predict the monthly demand for the bikes. The owner proposes the following model:

$$y = \beta_0 + \beta_1 x_1 + \beta_2 x_2 + \beta_3 x_3 + \beta_4 x_4 + \beta_5 x_5 + \varepsilon$$

where

y = Monthly demand for used bikes

x_1 = Selling price of used bikes

x_2 = Average price of lead-free gasoline

$$x_3 = \begin{cases} 1 & \text{if fall quarter (September–November)} \\ 0 & \text{if not} \end{cases}$$

$$x_4 = \begin{cases} 1 & \text{if winter quarter (December–February)} \\ 0 & \text{if not} \end{cases}$$

$$x_5 = \begin{cases} 1 & \text{if spring quarter (March–May)} \\ 0 & \text{if not} \end{cases}$$

Data obtained from past records (given in the table on page 446) were used to fit the first-order model. A portion of the SAS printout is also shown.

a. Construct and interpret plots of residuals against each of the independent variables, x_1 and x_2.
b. Calculate and plot the partial residuals for x_1. Interpret the plot.
c. Calculate and plot the partial residuals for x_2. Interpret the plot.
d. Check the plots in part a for residuals that lie more than 2 estimated standard deviations of ε away from the mean of 0. Can you classify any of the residuals as outliers?

YEAR	MONTH	DEMAND y	SELLING PRICE x_1, dollars	AVERAGE PRICE OF LEAD-FREE GASOLINE x_2, dollars	YEAR	MONTH	DEMAND y	SELLING PRICE x_1, dollars	AVERAGE PRICE OF LEAD-FREE GASOLINE x_2, dollars
1994	May	50	93	1.22	1995	January	51	105	1.20
	June	31	95	1.21		February	30	105	1.21
	July	16	85	1.21		March	22	115	1.22
	August	22	83	1.19		April	37	120	1.24
	September	99	95	1.18		May	47	115	1.26
	October	80	103	1.16		June	28	110	1.27
	November	37	100	1.17		July	20	110	1.28
	December	39	105	1.20					

SAS printout for Exercise 7.37

```
                         Analysis of Variance

                            Sum of           Mean
Source          DF         Squares          Square       F Value         Prob>F

Model            5      4773.85553       954.77111         3.383         0.0538
Error            9      2539.74447       282.19383
C Total         14      7313.60000

     Root MSE        16.79863     R-square        0.6527
     Dep Mean        40.60000     Adj R-sq        0.4598
     C.V.            41.37593

                         Parameter Estimates

                    Parameter        Standard     T for H0:
Variable  DF         Estimate           Error   Parameter=0     Prob > |T|

INTERCEP   1    -252.617103    308.22378892        -0.820         0.4336
X1         1      -0.789823      0.76446032        -1.033         0.3285
X2         1     285.969152    292.73703924         0.977         0.3542
X3         1      68.488937     23.28222353         2.942         0.0164
X4         1      31.432295     18.55433765         1.694         0.1245
X5         1      25.918087     15.17546604         1.708         0.1218

Durbin-Watson D               2.269
(For Number of Obs.)             15
1st Order Autocorrelation    -0.143

                         Dep Var    Predict
            Obs   MONTH        Y      Value   Residual

              1   MAY94   50.0000   48.7298     1.2702
              2   JUN94   31.0000   18.3724    12.6276
              3   JUL94   16.0000   26.2706   -10.2706
              4   AUG94   22.0000   22.1309    -0.1309
              5   SEP94      99.0   78.2823    20.7177
              6   OCT94   80.0000   66.2443    13.7557
              7   NOV94   37.0000   71.4735   -34.4735
              8   DEC94   39.0000   39.0468    -0.0468
              9   JAN95   51.0000   39.0468    11.9532
             10   FEB95   30.0000   41.9065   -11.9065
             11   MAR95   22.0000   31.3537    -9.3537
             12   APR95   37.0000   33.1240     3.8760
             13   MAY95   47.0000   42.7925     4.2075
             14   JUN95   28.0000   23.6832     4.3168
             15   JUL95   20.0000   26.5429    -6.5429

Sum of Residuals             1.090683E-12
Sum of Squared Residuals        2539.7445
Predicted Resid SS (Press)      6522.8552
```

e. Would you recommend that the owner use this model to predict monthly bicycle demand? If not, suggest an alternative model.

7.38 The foreman of a printing shop is scheduling his work load for 1996, and he must estimate the number of employees available for work. He asks the company statistician to forecast the absentee rate for 1996. Since it is known that quarterly fluctuations exist, the following model is proposed:

$$y = \beta_0 + \beta_1 x_1 + \beta_2 x_2 + \beta_3 x_3 + \varepsilon$$

where

$$y = \text{Absentee rate} = \frac{\text{Total employees absent}}{\text{Total employees}}$$

$$x_1 = \begin{cases} 1 & \text{if quarter 1 (January–March)} \\ 0 & \text{if not} \end{cases}$$

$$x_2 = \begin{cases} 1 & \text{if quarter 2 (April–June)} \\ 0 & \text{if not} \end{cases}$$

$$x_3 = \begin{cases} 1 & \text{if quarter 3 (July–September)} \\ 0 & \text{if not} \end{cases}$$

YEAR	QUARTER 1	QUARTER 2	QUARTER 3	QUARTER 4
1991	.06	.13	.28	.07
1992	.12	.09	.19	.09
1993	.08	.18	.41	.07
1994	.05	.13	.23	.08
1995	.06	.07	.30	.05

a. Fit the model to the data given in the table.
b. Consider the nature of the response variable, y. Do you think that there may be possible violations of the usual assumptions about ε? Explain.
c. Suggest an alternative model that will approximately stabilize the variance of the error term ε.
d. Fit the alternative model. Check R^2 to determine whether model adequacy has improved.

7.39 The data in the accompanying table are the amounts of crude oil (millions of barrels) imported into the United States from the Organization of Petroleum Exporting Countries (OPEC) for the years 1974–1993.

YEAR	t	IMPORTS, y_t	YEAR	t	IMPORTS, y_t
1974	1	926	1984	11	553
1975	2	1,171	1985	12	479
1976	3	1,663	1986	13	771
1977	4	2,058	1987	14	876
1978	5	1,892	1988	15	987
1979	6	1,866	1989	16	1,232
1980	7	1,414	1990	17	1,282
1981	8	1,067	1991	18	1,233
1982	9	633	1992	19	1,247
1983	10	540	1993	20	1,339

Source: *Statistical Abstracts of the United States*, U. S. Bureau of the Census, 1994.

a. Fit the model $E(y) = \beta_0 + \beta_1 t$.
b. Calculate the residuals for the model and plot the residuals against t. Do you detect any trends?
c. Test for correlated residuals using $\alpha = .01$.

7.40 The breeding ability of a thoroughbred horse is sometimes a more important consideration to prospective buyers than racing ability. Usually, the longer a horse lives, the greater its value for breeding purposes. Before marketing a group of horses, a breeder would like to be able to predict their life spans. The breeder believes that the gestation period of a thoroughbred horse may be an indicator of its life span. The information in the table was supplied to the breeder by various stables in the area. (Note that the horse has the greatest variation of gestation period of any species due to seasonal and feed factors.) The first-order (linear) model

$$y = \beta_0 + \beta_1 x + \varepsilon$$

was fitted to the data. A portion of the SAS printout is shown here.

HORSE	GESTATION PERIOD x, days	LIFE SPAN y, years
1	403	30
2	279	22
3	307	7
4	416	31
5	265	21
6	356	27
7	298	25

```
                              ANALYSIS OF VARIANCE

                        SUM OF          MEAN
SOURCE        DF       SQUARES        SQUARE          F VALUE        PROB>F

MODEL          1     146.31556     146.31556            2.960        0.1459
ERROR          5     247.11301   49.42260285
C TOTAL        6     393.42857

      ROOT MSE        7.030121      R-SQUARE           0.3719
      DEP MEAN        23.28571      ADJ R-SQ           0.2463
      C.V.             30.1907

                              PARAMETER ESTIMATES

                    PARAMETER          STANDARD       T FOR H0:
VARIABLE   DF        ESTIMATE             ERROR     PARAMETER=0      PROB > |T|

INTERCEP    1     -3.94341407       16.04679821          -0.246          0.8156
X           1      0.08201545        0.04766649           1.721          0.1459

                                                   PREDICT
        OBS                ID        ACTUAL          VALUE       RESIDUAL

               1          403       30.0000        29.1088         0.8912
               2          279       22.0000        18.9389         3.0611
               3          307        7.0000        21.2353       -14.2353
               4          416       31.0000        30.1750         0.8250
               5          265       21.0000        17.7907         3.2093
               6          356       27.0000        25.2541         1.7459
               7          298       25.0000        20.4972         4.5028

SUM OF RESIDUALS                 7.10543E-15
SUM OF SQUARED RESIDUALS             247.113
```

a. Check model adequacy by interpreting the F and R^2 statistics.
b. Construct a plot of the residuals versus x, gestation period.
c. Check for residuals that lie outside the interval $0 \pm 2s$ or $0 \pm 3s$.
d. The breeder has been informed that the short life span of horse #3 (7 years) was due to a very rare disease. Omit the data for horse #3 and refit the least squares line. Has the omission of this observation improved the model?

7.41 Suppose you were to fit the time series model

$$E(y_t) = \beta_0 + \beta_1 t + \beta_2 t^2$$

to quarterly time series data collected over a 10-year period ($n = 40$ quarters), where t = quarter ($t = 1, 2, 3, \ldots, 40$).
a. Set up the test of hypothesis for positively correlated residuals. Specify H_0, H_a, the test statistic, and the rejection region.
b. Suppose the Durbin–Watson d statistic is calculated to be 1.14. What is the appropriate conclusion?

7.42 The data in the table are the monthly market shares for a product over most of the past year. The least squares line relating market share to television advertising expenditure is found to be

$$\hat{y} = -1.56 + .687x$$

MONTH	MARKET SHARE y, %	TELEVISION ADVERTISING EXPENDITURE x, thousands of dollars
January	15	23
February	17	27
March	17	25
May	13	21
June	12	20
July	14	24
September	16	26
October	14	23
December	15	25

a. Calculate and plot the regression residuals in the manner outlined in this section.
b. The response variable y, market share, is recorded as a percentage. What does this lead you to believe about the least squares assumption of homoscedasticity? Does the residual plot substantiate this belief?
c. What variance-stabilizing transformation is suggested by the trend in the residual plot? If you have access to a computer package, refit the first-order model using the transformed responses. Calculate and plot these new regression residuals. Is there evidence that the transformation has been successful in stabilizing the variance of the error term, ε?

References

Barnett, V., and Lewis, T. *Outliers in Statistical Data*. New York: Wiley, 1978.

Belsley, D. A., Kuh, E., and Welsch, R. E. *Regression Diagnostics: Identifying Influential Data and Sources of Collinearity*. New York: Wiley, 1980.

Box, G. E. P., and Cox, D. R. "An analysis of transformations." *Journal of the Royal Statistical Society, Series B*, 1964, Vol. 26, pp. 211–243.

Cook, R. D. "Influential observations in linear regression." *Journal of the American Statistical Association*, 1979, Vol. 74, pp. 169–174.

Draper, N., and Smith, H. *Applied Regression Analysis*, 2nd ed. New York: Wiley, 1981.

Durbin, J., and Watson, G. S. "Testing for serial correlation in least squares regression, I." *Biometrika*, 1950, Vol. 37, pp. 409–428.

Durbin, J., and Watson, G. S. "Testing for serial correlation in least squares regression, II." *Biometrika*, 1951, Vol. 38, pp. 159–178.

Durbin, J., and Watson, G. S. "Testing for serial correlation in least squares regression, III." *Biometrika*, 1971, Vol. 58, pp. 1–19.

Granger, C. W. J., and Newbold, P. *Forecasting Economic Time Series*. New York: Academic Press, 1977.

Larsen, W. A., and McCleary, S. J. "The use of partial residual plots in regression analysis." *Technometrics*, Vol. 14, 1972, pp. 781–790.

Mansfield, E. R., and Conerly, M. D. "Diagnostic value of residual and partial residual plots." *The American Statistician*, Vol. 41, No. 2, May 1987, pp. 107–116.

Mendenhall, W. *Introduction to Linear Models and the Design and Analysis of Experiments*. Belmont, Calif.: Wadsworth, 1968.

Montgomery, D. C., and Peck, E. A. *Introduction to Linear Regression Analysis*. New York: Wiley, 1982.

Neter, J., Wasserman, W., and Kutner, M. H. *Applied Linear Statistical Models*, 3rd ed. Homewood, Ill.: Richard D. Irwin, 1990.

Stephens, M. A. "EDF statistics for goodness of fit and some comparisons." *Journal of the American Statistical Association*, 1974, Vol. 69, pp. 730–737.

CHAPTER 8 Special Topics in Regression (Optional)

CONTENTS

OBJECTIVE

To introduce a number of special regression techniques for problems that require more advanced methods of analysis

8.1 Introduction

The procedures presented in Chapters 3–7 provide the tools basic to a regression analysis. An understanding of these techniques will enable you to successfully apply regression analysis to a variety of problems encountered in practice. For some studies, however, you may require more sophisticated techniques. In this chapter, we introduce several special topics in regression for the advanced student.

8.2 Piecewise Linear Regression

Occasionally, the linear relationship between a dependent variable y and an independent variable x may differ for different intervals over the range of x. For example, it is known that the compressive strength y of concrete depends on the proportion x of water mixed with the cement. A certain type of concrete, when mixed in batches with varying water/cement ratios (measured as a percentage), may yield compressive strengths (measured in pounds per square inch) that follow the pattern shown in Figure 8.1. Note that the compressive strength decreases at a much faster rate for batches with water/cement ratios greater than 70%. That is, the slope of the relationship between compressive strength (y) and water/cement ratio (x) changes when $x = 70$.

FIGURE 8.1
Relationship between compressive strength (y) and water/cement ratio (x)

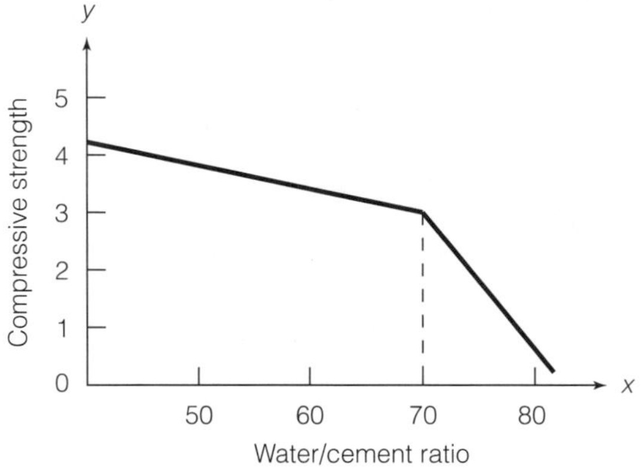

A model that proposes different straight-line relationships for different intervals over the range of x is called a **piecewise linear regression model**. As its name suggests, the linear regression model is fitted in pieces. For the concrete example, the piecewise model would consist of two pieces, $x \leq 70$ and $x > 70$. The model can be expressed as follows:

$$y = \beta_0 + \beta_1 x_1 + \beta_2(x_1 - 70)x_2 + \varepsilon$$

where

$$x_1 = \text{Water/cement ratio } (x)$$

$$x_2 = \begin{cases} 1 & \text{if } x_1 > 70 \\ 0 & \text{if } x_1 \leq 70 \end{cases}$$

The value of the dummy variable x_2 controls the values of the slope and y-intercept for each piece. For example, when $x_1 \leq 70$, then $x_2 = 0$ and the equation is given by

$$y = \beta_0 + \beta_1 x_1 + \beta_2(x_1 - 70)(0) + \varepsilon$$
$$= \underbrace{\beta_0}_{y\text{-intercept}} + \underbrace{\beta_1 x_1}_{\text{Slope}} + \varepsilon$$

Conversely, if $x_1 > 70$, then $x_2 = 1$ and we have

$$y = \beta_0 + \beta_1 x_1 + \beta_2(x_1 - 70)(1) + \varepsilon$$
$$= \beta_0 + \beta_1 x_1 + \beta_2 x_1 - 70\beta_2 + \varepsilon$$

or

$$y = \underbrace{(\beta_0 - 70\beta_2)}_{y\text{-intercept}} + \underbrace{(\beta_1 + \beta_2)}_{\text{Slope}} x_1 + \varepsilon$$

Thus, β_1 and $(\beta_1 + \beta_2)$ represent the slopes of the lines for the two intervals of x, $x \leq 70$ and $x > 70$, respectively. Similarly, β_0 and $(\beta_0 - 70\beta_2)$ represent the respective y-intercepts. The slopes and y-intercepts of the two lines are illustrated graphically in Figure 8.2. [*Note*: The value at which the slope changes, 70 in this example, is often referred to as a **knot value**. Usually, the knot values of a piecewise regression are unknown and must be estimated from the sample data. This is often accomplished by visually inspecting the scattergram for the data and locating the points on the x-axis at which the slope appears to change.]

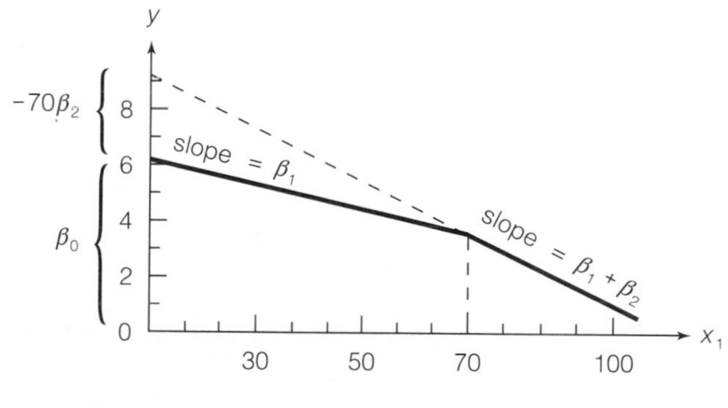

FIGURE 8.2
Slopes and y-intercepts for piecewise linear regression

We can fit piecewise regression models by using the standard multiple regression routines of most computer packages to make the appropriate transformations on the independent variables. For example, consider the data on compressive strength (y) and water/cement ratio (x) for 18 batches of concrete recorded in Table 8.1 on page 454. (The water/cement ratio is computed by dividing the weight of water used in the mix by the weight of the cement.) To obtain the least squares fit of the piecewise linear regression model for the data of Table 8.1, we specify the model

$$E(y) = \beta_0 + \beta_1 x_1 + \beta_2 x_2^*$$

TABLE 8.1 **Data on Compressive Strength and Water/Cement Ratios for 18 Batches of Cement**

BATCH	COMPRESSIVE STRENGTH y, pounds per square inch	WATER/CEMENT RATIO x_1, percent	BATCH	COMPRESSIVE STRENGTH y, pounds per square inch	WATER/CEMENT RATIO x_1, percent
1	4.67	47	10	2.21	73
2	3.54	68	11	4.10	60
3	2.25	75	12	1.13	85
4	3.82	65	13	1.67	80
5	4.50	50	14	1.59	75
6	4.07	55	15	3.91	63
7	.76	82	16	3.15	70
8	3.01	72	17	4.37	50
9	4.29	52	18	3.75	57

where

$$x_2^* = (x_1 - 70)x_2 \quad \text{and} \quad x_2 = \begin{cases} 1 & \text{if } x_1 > 70 \\ 0 & \text{if } x_1 \le 70 \end{cases}$$

The SAS printout for the piecewise linear regression is shown in Figure 8.3. From the printout we obtain the least squares prediction equation:

$$\hat{y} = 7.791983 - .066331x_1 - .101186x_2^*$$

Note that the estimated mean change in compressive strength for a 1% increase in water/cement ratio is $\hat{\beta}_1 = -.06633$ for ratios less than or equal to 70% and $\hat{\beta}_1 + \hat{\beta}_2 = -.06633 + (-.10119) = -.16752$ for ratios greater than 70%.

FIGURE 8.3
SAS printout for piecewise linear regression of data in Table 8.1

```
Dependent Variable: Y
                          Analysis of Variance

                            Sum of         Mean
Source            DF       Squares       Square      F Value      Prob>F

Model              2      24.71775     12.35888      114.441      0.0001
Error             15       1.61990      0.10799
C Total           17      26.33765

    Root MSE        0.32862     R-square        0.9385
    Dep Mean        3.15500     Adj R-sq        0.9303
    C.V.           10.41595

                          Parameter Estimates

                     Parameter       Standard    T for H0:
Variable    DF       Estimate          Error    Parameter=0    Prob > |T|

INTERCEP     1       7.791983     0.67696058         11.510        0.0001
X1           1      -0.066331     0.01123476         -5.904        0.0001
X2STAR       1      -0.101186     0.02812449         -3.598        0.0026
```

Piecewise regression is not limited to two pieces, nor is it limited to straight lines. One or more of the pieces may require a quadratic or higher-order fit. Also, piecewise regression models can be proposed to allow for discontinuities or jumps in the regression function. Such models require additional dummy variables to be introduced. Several different piecewise linear regression models relating y to an independent variable x are shown in the following box.

Piecewise Linear Regression Models Relating y to an Independent Variable x_1

TWO STRAIGHT LINES (CONTINUOUS)

$$E(y) = \beta_0 + \beta_1 x_1 + \beta_2(x_1 - k)x_2$$

where

k = Knot value (i.e., the value of the independent variable x_1 at which the slope changes)

$$x_2 = \begin{cases} 1 & \text{if } x_1 > k \\ 0 & \text{if not} \end{cases}$$

	$x_1 \le k$	$x_1 > k$
y-intercept	β_0	$\beta_0 - k\beta_2$
Slope	β_1	$\beta_1 + \beta_2$

THREE STRAIGHT LINES (CONTINUOUS)

$$E(y) = \beta_0 + \beta_1 x_1 + \beta_2(x_1 - k_1)x_2 + \beta_3(x_1 - k_2)x_3$$

where k_1 and k_2 are knot values of the independent variable x_1, $k_1 < k_2$, and

$$x_2 = \begin{cases} 1 & \text{if } x_1 > k_1 \\ 0 & \text{if not} \end{cases} \qquad x_3 = \begin{cases} 1 & \text{if } x_1 > k_2 \\ 0 & \text{if not} \end{cases}$$

	$x_1 \le k_1$	$k_1 < x_1 \le k_2$	$x_1 > k_2$
y-intercept	β_0	$\beta_0 - k_1\beta_2$	$\beta_0 - k_1\beta_2 - k_2\beta_3$
Slope	β_1	$\beta_1 + \beta_2$	$\beta_1 + \beta_2 + \beta_3$

TWO STRAIGHT LINES (DISCONTINUOUS)

$$E(y) = \beta_0 + \beta_1 x_1 + \beta_2(x_1 - k)x_2 + \beta_3 x_2$$

where

k = Knot value (i.e., the value of the independent variable x_1 at which the slope changes—also the point of discontinuity)

$$x_2 = \begin{cases} 1 & \text{if } x_1 > k \\ 0 & \text{if not} \end{cases}$$

	$x_1 \le k$	$x_1 > k$
y-intercept	β_0	$\beta_0 - k\beta_2 + \beta_3$
Slope	β_1	$\beta_1 + \beta_2$

Tests of model adequacy, tests and confidence intervals on individual β parameters, confidence intervals for $E(y)$, and prediction intervals for y for piecewise regression models are conducted in the usual manner.

EXERCISES

8.1 Consider a two-piece linear relationship between y and x with no discontinuity and a slope change at $x = 15$.

a. Specify the appropriate piecewise linear regression model for y.

b. In terms of the β coefficients, give the y-intercept and slope for observations with $x \leq 15$; for observations with $x > 15$.

c. Explain how you could determine whether the two slopes proposed by the model are, in fact, different.

8.2 Consider a three-piece linear relationship between y and x with no discontinuity and slope changes at $x = 1.45$ and $x = 5.20$.

a. Specify the appropriate piecewise linear regression model for y.

b. In terms of the β coefficients, give the y-intercept and slope for each of the following intervals: $x \leq 1.45$, $1.45 < x \leq 5.20$, and $x > 5.20$.

c. Explain how you could determine whether at least two of the three slopes proposed by the model are, in fact, different.

8.3 Consider a two-piece linear relationship between y and x with discontinuity and slope change at $x = 320$.

a. Specify the appropriate piecewise linear regression model for y.

b. In terms of the β coefficients, give the y-intercept and slope for observations with $x \leq 320$; for observations with $x > 320$.

c. Explain how you could determine whether the two straight lines proposed by the model are, in fact, different.

8.4 The total amount y of corn produced in the United States is recorded (in millions of bushels) for the years 1950–1986 in the accompanying table.

a. Plot the annual corn production y against year x. Note that corn production appears to increase at a much faster rate over the period 1971–1986.

b. Propose a piecewise linear model for annual corn production y with a knot at $x = 1970$.

c. If you have access to a computer software package, fit the model proposed in part **b**. Give the least squares prediction equation.

d. Is the model adequate for predicting annual corn production y? Test using $\alpha = .05$.

e. Give the estimates of the expected annual increases in corn production over the two periods, 1950–1970 and 1971–1986.

f. Is there sufficient evidence to indicate that annual corn production increases at a faster rate after 1970? Test using $\alpha = .05$.

YEAR x	PRODUCTION y	YEAR x	PRODUCTION y	YEAR x	PRODUCTION y
1950	3,075	1963	4,019	1976	6,289
1951	2,926	1964	3,484	1977	6,505
1952	3,292	1965	4,084	1978	7,268
1953	3,210	1966	4,117	1979	7,928
1954	3,058	1967	4,760	1980	6,639
1955	3,220	1968	4,450	1981	8,119
1956	3,445	1969	4,687	1982	8,235
1957	3,400	1970	4,152	1983	4,175
1958	3,725	1971	5,646	1984	7,674
1959	4,197	1972	5,580	1985	8,865
1960	4,314	1973	5,671	1986	8,253
1961	3,598	1974	4,701		
1962	3,606	1975	5,841		

Sources: *Agricultural Statistics*, 1984, U.S. Department of Agriculture (1968–1982); *Historical Statistics of the U.S., Colonial Times to 1970*, U.S. Department of Commerce, Bureau of the Census (1950–1967); *Commodity Year Book 1986*, *Commodity Research Bureau* (1983–1985); *Survey of Current Business*, U.S. Department of Commerce.

8.5 The manager of a packaging plant wants to model the unit cost y of shipping lots of a semifragile product as a linear function of lot size x. Because of economies of scale, the manager believes that the cost per unit will decrease at a faster rate for lot sizes of more than 1,000. Data collected on unit cost and lot size for 15 recent shipments are given in the table.

SHIPPING COST y, \$ per unit	LOT SIZE x	SHIPPING COST y, \$ per unit	LOT SIZE x
1.29	1,150	2.90	520
2.20	840	2.63	670
2.26	900	.55	1,420
2.38	800	2.31	850
1.77	1,070	1.90	1,000
1.25	1,220	2.15	910
1.87	980	1.20	1,230
.71	1,300		

a. Specify the appropriate piecewise linear model for y.
b. If you have access to a computer program package, fit the model to the data. Give the least squares prediction equation.
c. Is the model adequate for predicting unit cost y? Test using $\alpha = .10$.
d. Give a 90% confidence interval for the mean increase in shipping cost per unit for every unit increase in lot size for lots with 1,000 or fewer units.

8.3 Inverse Prediction

Often, the goal of regression is to predict the value of one variable when another variable takes on a specified value. For most simple linear regression problems, we are interested in predicting y for a given x. We provided a formula for a prediction interval for y when $x = x_p$ in Section 3.9. In this section, we discuss

inverse prediction—that is, predicting x for a given value of the dependent variable y.

Inverse prediction has many applications in the engineering and physical sciences, in medical research, and in business. For example, when calibrating a new instrument, scientists often search for approximate measurements y, which are easy and inexpensive to obtain and which are related to the precise, but more expensive and time-consuming measurements x. If a regression analysis reveals that x and y are highly correlated, then the scientist could choose to use the quick and inexpensive approximate measurement value, say, $y = y_{\text{p}}$, to estimate the unknown precise measurement x. (In this context, the problem of inverse prediction is sometimes referred to as a **linear calibration** problem.) Physicians often use inverse prediction to determine the required dosage of a drug. Suppose a regression analysis conducted on patients with high blood pressure showed that a linear relationship exists between decrease in blood pressure y and dosage x of a new drug. Then a physician treating a new patient may want to determine what dosage x to administer to reduce the patient's blood pressure by an amount $y = y_{\text{p}}$. To illustrate inverse prediction in a business setting, consider a firm that sells a particular product. Suppose the firm's monthly market share y is linearly related to its monthly television advertising expenditure x. For a particular month, the firm may want to know how much it must spend on advertising x to attain a specified market share $y = y_{\text{p}}$.

The classical approach to inverse prediction is first to fit the familiar straight-line model

$$y = \beta_0 + \beta_1 x + \varepsilon$$

to a sample of n data points and obtain the least squares prediction equation

$$\hat{y} = \hat{\beta}_0 + \hat{\beta}_1 x$$

Solving the least squares prediction equation for x, we have

$$x = \frac{\hat{y} - \hat{\beta}_0}{\hat{\beta}_1}$$

Now let y_{p} be an observed value of y in the future with unknown x. Then a point estimate of x is given by

$$\hat{x} = \frac{y_{\text{p}} - \hat{\beta}_0}{\hat{\beta}_1}$$

Although no exact expression for the standard error of $\hat{x}$ (denoted $s_{\hat{x}}$) is known, we can algebraically manipulate the formula for a prediction interval for y given x (see Section 3.9) to form a prediction interval for x given y. It can be shown (proof omitted) that an approximate $(1 - \alpha)100\%$ prediction interval for x when $y = y_{\text{p}}$ is

$$\hat{x} \pm t_{\alpha/2} s_{\hat{x}} \approx \hat{x} \pm t_{\alpha/2}\left(\frac{s}{\hat{\beta}_1}\right)\sqrt{1 + \frac{1}{n} + \frac{(\hat{x} - \bar{x})^2}{\text{SS}_{xx}}}$$

where the distribution of t is based on $(n - 2)$ degrees of freedom, $s = \sqrt{\text{MSE}}$, and

$$\text{SS}_{xx} = \sum x^2 - n(\bar{x})^2$$

This approximation is appropriate as long as the quantity

$$D = \left(\frac{t_{\alpha/2}s}{\hat{\beta}_1}\right)^2 \cdot \frac{1}{\text{SS}_{xx}}$$

is small. The procedure for constructing an approximate confidence interval for x in inverse prediction is summarized in the box.

Inverse Prediction: Approximate $(1 - \alpha)100\%$ Prediction Interval for x When $y = y_p$ in Simple Linear Regression

$$\hat{x} \pm t_{\alpha/2}\left(\frac{s}{\hat{\beta}_1}\right)\sqrt{1 + \frac{1}{n} + \frac{(\hat{x} - \bar{x})^2}{\text{SS}_{xx}}}$$

where

$$\hat{x} = \frac{y_p - \hat{\beta}_0}{\hat{\beta}_1}$$

$\hat{\beta}_0$ and $\hat{\beta}_1$ are the y-intercept and slope, respectively, of the least squares line

$$n = \text{Sample size}$$

$$\bar{x} = \frac{\sum x}{n}$$

$$\text{SS}_{xx} = \sum x^2 - n(\bar{x})^2$$

$$s = \sqrt{\text{MSE}}$$

and the distribution of t is based on $(n - 2)$ degrees of freedom.

The approximation is appropriate when the quantity

$$D = \left(\frac{t_{\alpha/2}s}{\hat{\beta}_1}\right)^2 \cdot \frac{1}{\text{SS}_{xx}}$$

is small.*

EXAMPLE 8.1

A firm that sells copiers advertises regularly on television. One goal of the firm is to determine the amount it must spend on television advertising in a single month to gain a market share of 10%. For one year, the firm varied its monthly

*Neter, Wasserman, and Kutner (1990) and others suggest using the approximation when D is less than .1.

television advertising expenditures (x) and at the end of each month determined its market share (y). The data for the 12 months are recorded in Table 8.2.

TABLE 8.2 **A Firm's Market Share and Television Advertising Expenditure for 12 Months, Example 8.1**

MONTH	MARKET SHARE y, percent	TELEVISION ADVERTISING EXPENDITURE x, \$ thousands
January	7.5	23
February	8.5	25
March	6.5	21
April	7.0	24
May	8.0	26
June	6.5	22
July	9.5	27
August	10.0	31
September	8.5	28
October	11.0	32
November	10.5	30
December	9.0	29

a. Fit the straight-line model $y = \beta_0 + \beta_1 x + \varepsilon$ to the data.

b. Is there evidence that television advertising expenditure x is linearly related to market share y? Test using $\alpha = .05$.

c. Use inverse prediction to estimate the amount that must be spent on television advertising in a particular month for the firm to gain a market share of $y =$ 10%. Construct an approximate 95% prediction interval for monthly television advertising expenditure x.

Solution

a. The ASP printout for the simple linear regression is shown in Figure 8.4. From the printout, we obtain the least squares line

$$\hat{y} = -1.97494 + .396853x$$

The least squares line is plotted along with 12 data points in Figure 8.5.

b. To determine whether television advertising expenditure x is linearly related to market share y, we test the hypothesis

$$H_0: \ \beta_1 = 0$$

against

$$H_a: \ \beta_1 \neq 0$$

The value of the test statistic, shaded on the printout, is $t = 9.11997$, and the associated p-value of the test is $p = .00000367298$ (also shaded). Thus, there is sufficient evidence, at any value of α greater than .0000037, to indicate that television advertising expenditure x and market share y are linearly related.

Caution: You should avoid using inverse prediction when there is insufficient evidence to reject the null hypothesis H_0: $\beta_1 = 0$. Inverse predictions made when x and y are *not* linearly related may lead to nonsensical results. Therefore, you should always conduct a test of model adequacy to be sure that x and y are linearly related before you carry out an inverse prediction.

FIGURE 8.4
ASP printout of straight-line model, Example 8.1

```
                    Straight-Line Model for Market Share

MODEL:  y (MarketShare) = 0.396853x (TVAdExpend) + -1.97494CNST

                      COEF.     SD. ER.      t(10)     P-VALUE  PT. R SQ.
                    --------- ---------  ---------- ----------  ---------
x (TVAdExpend)      0.396853 0.0435147   9.11997 3.67298E-6   0.892674
           CNST    -1.97494  1.16288    -1.69831 0.120294     0.22386

R SQ. = 0.892674,   ADJ. R SQ. = 0.881941,   D. W. = 1.91517
SQ. ROOT MSE = 0.520361,   F(1/10) = 83.1739 (P-VALUE = 3.67298E-6)
```

FIGURE 8.5
Scattergram of data and least squares line, Example 8.1

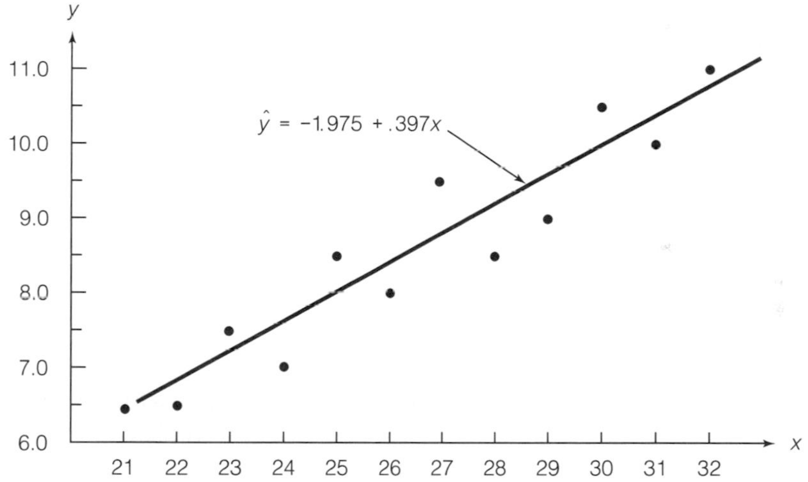

c. Since the model is found to be adequate, we can use the model to predict x from y. For this example, we want to estimate the television advertising expenditure x that yields a market share of $y_p = 10\%$.

Substituting $y_p = 10$, $\hat{\beta}_0 = -1.975$, and $\hat{\beta}_1 = .397$ into the formula for $\hat{x}$ given in the box on page 459, we have

$$\hat{x} = \frac{y_p - \hat{\beta}_0}{\hat{\beta}_1}$$

$$= \frac{10 - (-1.975)}{.397}$$

$$= 30.16$$

Thus, we estimate that the firm must spend \$30,160 on television advertising in a particular month to gain a market share of 10%.

Before we construct an approximate 95% prediction interval for x, we check to determine whether the approximation is appropriate, that is, whether the quantity

$$D = \left(\frac{t_{\alpha/2}s}{\hat{\beta}_1}\right)^2 \cdot \frac{1}{\text{SS}_{xx}}$$

is small. For $\alpha = .05$, $t_{\alpha/2} = t_{.025} = 2.228$ for $n - 2 = 12 - 2 = 10$ degrees of freedom. From the printout (Figure 8.4), $s =$ **SQ. ROOT MSE** $= .5204$ and $\hat{\beta}_1 = .396853$. The value of SS_{xx} is not shown on the printout and must be calculated as follows:

$$\begin{aligned}\text{SS}_{xx} &= \sum x^2 - n(\bar{x})^2\\ &= 8{,}570 - 12\left(\frac{318}{12}\right)^2\\ &= 8{,}570 - 8{,}427\\ &= 143\end{aligned}$$

Substituting these values into the formula for D, we have

$$\begin{aligned}D &= \left(\frac{t_{\alpha/2}s}{\hat{\beta}_1}\right)^2 \cdot \frac{1}{\text{SS}_{xx}}\\ &= \left[\frac{(2.228)(.5204)}{.397}\right]^2 \cdot \frac{1}{143}\\ &= \frac{8.5295}{143}\\ &= .0596\end{aligned}$$

Since the value of D is small (i.e., less than .1), we may use the formula for the approximate 95% prediction interval given in the box on page 459:

$$\hat{x} \pm t_{\alpha/2}\left(\frac{s}{\hat{\beta}_1}\right)\sqrt{1 + \frac{1}{n} + \frac{(\hat{x} - \bar{x})^2}{\text{SS}_{xx}}}$$

$$30.16 \pm (2.228)\,\frac{(.5204)}{.397}\sqrt{1 + \frac{1}{12} + \frac{\left(30.16 - \frac{318}{12}\right)^2}{143}}$$

$$30.16 \pm (2.9205)(1.0849)$$

$$30.16 \pm 3.17$$

or (26.99, 33.33). Therefore, using the 95% prediction interval, we estimate that the amount of monthly television advertising expenditure required to gain a market share of 10% falls between \$26,999 and \$33,330.

Another approach to the inverse prediction problem is to regress x on y, i.e., fit the model (called the **inverse estimator model**)

$$x = \beta_0 + \beta_1 y + \varepsilon$$

and then use the standard formula for a prediction interval given in Section 3.9. However, in theory this method requires that x be a random variable. In many business applications, the value of x is set in advance (i.e., controlled) and therefore is *not* a random variable. (For example, the firm in Example 8.1 selected the amount x spent on advertising *prior* to each month.) Thus, the inverse model above may violate the standard least squares assumptions given in Chapter 4. Some researchers advocate the use of the inverse model despite this caution, whereas others have developed different estimators of x using a modification of the classical approach. Consult the references given at the end of this chapter for details on the various alternative methods of inverse prediction.

EXERCISES

8.6 Some economists fear that the current unemployment compensation system in the United States distorts the number of layoffs in a downturn of the business cycle. The hypothesis is that unemployment compensation subsidy causes firms to lay off more people than they would if they knew those laid off would receive no outside subsidy. The accompanying table gives the unemployment compensation subsidy rate x (as a percentage of total revenues) and the layoff rate y (number of workers per 1,000) for 11 industries. Use inverse prediction to estimate the subsidy rate x for a particular industry that laid off workers at a rate of $y = 6.50$ workers per 1,000. Construct an approximate 99% prediction interval for x.

INDUSTRY	SUBSIDY RATE x	LAYOFF RATE y
Apparel	57%	12.54
Chemicals	32	1.78
Construction	31	7.10
Electrical machinery	29	8.38
Fabricated metals	27	11.72
Food	36	5.10
Machinery	32	4.44
Miscellaneous manufacturing	61	9.82
Primary metals	23	7.34
Retail	27	1.98
Wholesale trade	33	1.86

Source: Tropel, R. H. "On layoffs and unemployment insurance." *American Economic Review*, 1983. Vol. 83, pp. 541–559.

8.7 Starting salary is considered to be an important indicator of success in the job market by many graduating MBAs. The factors that influence starting salary are many and varied, but one variable intrinsically interesting to MBA students is their Graduate Management Aptitude Test (GMAT) score.

The starting salaries and GMAT scores for a sample of 10 MBAs who recently graduated from the University of Florida's MBA program are given in the table.

STARTING SALARY y	GMAT x
\$40,000	510
33,000	510
40,000	550
35,000	600
28,000	600
28,000	520
34,000	560
30,000	530
32,500	530
31,000	590

Source: Graduate College of Business Administration, University of Florida.

a. Use inverse prediction to estimate the GMAT score x of a former University of Florida MBA student with a starting salary of $y = \$35{,}000$. Construct an approximate 95% prediction interval for x.

b. Explain why the interval of part **a** is so wide.

8.8 The data in Table 3.8 are reproduced here. Use inverse prediction to estimate the distance from nearest fire station, x, for a residential fire that caused \$18,200 in damages. Construct a 90% prediction interval for x.

DISTANCE FROM FIRE STATION x, miles	FIRE DAMAGE y, thousands of dollars
3.4	26.2
1.8	17.8
4.6	31.3
2.3	23.1
3.1	27.5
5.5	36.0
.7	14.1
3.0	22.3
2.6	19.6
4.3	31.3
2.1	24.0
1.1	17.3
6.1	43.2
4.8	36.4
3.8	26.1

8.9 A pharmaceutical company has developed a new drug designed to reduce a smoker's reliance on tobacco. Since certain dosages of the drug may reduce one's pulse rate to dangerously low levels, the product-testing division of the pharmaceutical company wants to model the relationship between decrease in pulse rate y (beats/minute) and dosage x (cubic centimeters). Different dosages of the drug were administered to eight randomly selected patients, and 30 minutes later the decrease in each patient's pulse rate was recorded, with the results given in the table.

PATIENT	DOSAGE x, cubic centimeters	DECREASE IN PULSE RATE y, beats/minute
1	2.0	12
2	4.0	20
3	1.5	6
4	1.0	3
5	3.0	16
6	3.5	20
7	2.5	13
8	3.0	18

a. Fit the straight-line model $E(y) = \beta_0 + \beta_1 x$ to the data.
b. Conduct a test for model adequacy. Use $\alpha = .05$.
c. Use inverse prediction to estimate the appropriate dosage x to administer to reduce a patient's pulse rate $y = 10$ beats per minute. Construct an approximate 95% prediction interval for x.

8.4 Weighted Least Squares

Consider the general linear model

$$y = \beta_0 + \beta_1 x_1 + \beta_2 x_2 + \cdots + \beta_k x_k + \varepsilon$$

To obtain the least squares estimates of the unknown β parameters, recall (from Section 4.3) that we minimize the quantity

$$\text{SSE} = \sum_{i=1}^{n} (y_i - \hat{y}_i)^2 = \sum_{i=1}^{n} [y_i - (\hat{\beta}_0 + \hat{\beta}_1 x_{1i} + \hat{\beta}_2 x_{2i} + \cdots + \hat{\beta}_k x_{ki})]^2$$

with respect to $\hat{\beta}_0, \hat{\beta}_1, \ldots, \hat{\beta}_k$.

The least squares criterion weighs each observation equally in determining the estimates of the β's. Sometimes we will want to weigh some observations more heavily than others. To do this we minimize

$$\begin{aligned} \text{WSSE} &= \sum_{i=1}^{n} w_i (y_i - \hat{y}_i)^2 \\ &= \sum_{i=1}^{n} w_i [y_i - (\hat{\beta}_0 + \hat{\beta}_1 x_{1i} + \hat{\beta}_2 x_{2i} + \cdots + \hat{\beta}_k x_{ki})]^2 \end{aligned}$$

where w_i is the weight assigned to the ith observation. This procedure is known as **weighted least squares** and the resulting parameter estimates are called **weighted least squares estimates**. [Note that the ordinary least squares procedure assigns a weight of $w_i = 1$ to each observation.]

Weighted least squares has applications in the following two areas:

1. Stabilizing the variance of ε to satisfy the standard regression assumption of homoscedasticity
2. Limiting the influence of outlying observations on the regression analysis

Although the two applications are related, our discussion of weighted least squares in this section is directed toward the first application.

The regression routines of most statistical software packages have options for conducting a weighted least squares analysis. However, the weights w_i must be specified. When using weighted least squares as a variance-stabilizing technique, the weight for the ith observation should be the reciprocal of the variance of that observation's error term, σ_i^2, i.e.,

$$w_i = \frac{1}{\sigma_i^2}$$

In this manner, observations with larger error variances will receive less weight (and hence have less influence on the analysis) than observations with smaller error variances.

In practice, the actual variances σ_i^2 will usually be unknown. Fortunately, in many applications, the error variance σ_i^2 is proportional to one or more of the levels of the independent variables. This fact will allow us to determine the appropriate weights to use. For example, in a simple linear regression problem, suppose we know that the error variance σ_i^2 increases proportionally with the value of the independent variable x_i, i.e.,

$$\sigma_i^2 = kx_i$$

where k is some unknown constant. Then the appropriate (albeit unknown) weight to use is

$$w_i = \frac{1}{kx_i}$$

Fortunately, it can be shown (proof omitted) that k can be ignored and the weights can be assigned as follows:

$$w_i = \frac{1}{x_i}$$

If the functional relationship between σ_i^2 and x_i is not known prior to conducting the analysis, the weights can be estimated based on the results of an ordinary (unweighted) least squares fit. For example, in simple linear regression, one approach is to divide the regression residuals into several groups of approximately equal size based on the value of the independent variable x and calculate the variance of the observed residuals in each group. An examination of the relationship between the residual variances and several different functions of x (such as x, x^2, and $\sqrt{x}$) may reveal the appropriate weights to use.

EXAMPLE 8.2

A Department of Transportation (DOT) official is investigating the possibility of collusive bidding among the state's road construction contractors. One aspect of the investigation involves a comparison of the winning (lowest) bid price y on a job with the length x of new road construction, a measure of job size. The data listed in Table 8.3 were supplied by the DOT for a sample of 11 new road construction jobs with approximately the same number of bidders.

TABLE 8.3 Sample Data for New Road Construction Jobs, Example 8.2

JOB	LENGTH OF ROAD x, miles	WINNING BID PRICE y, \$ thousands	JOB	LENGTH OF ROAD x, miles	WINNING BID PRICE y, \$ thousands
1	2.0	10.1	7	7.0	71.1
2	2.4	11.4	8	11.5	132.7
3	3.1	24.2	9	10.9	108.0
4	3.5	26.5	10	12.2	126.2
5	6.4	66.8	11	12.6	140.7
6	6.1	53.8			

a. Use the method of least squares to fit the straight-line model

$$E(y) = \beta_0 + \beta_1 x$$

b. Calculate and plot the regression residuals against x. Do you detect any evidence of heteroscedasticity?

c. Use the method described in the preceding paragraph to find the approximate weights necessary to stabilize the error variances with weighted least squares.

d. Carry out the weighted least squares analysis using the weights determined in part c.

e. The **weighted least squares residuals** are defined as

$$\sqrt{w_i}(y_i - \hat{y}_i)$$

where $\hat{y}_i$ is the predicted value from the weighted least squares fit and w_i is the weight. Plot the weighted least squares residuals against x to determine whether the variances have stabilized.

Solution

a. The simple linear regression analysis was conducted using the MINITAB regression package. The MINITAB printout is given in Figure 8.6 on page 468. The least squares line, obtained from the printout, is

$$\hat{y} = -15.112 + 12.0687x$$

Note that the model is statistically useful (reject H_0: $\beta_1 = 0$) at $p = .000$.

b. The regression residuals are calculated and reported in the bottom portion of the MINITAB printout. A plot of the residuals against the predictor variable x is shown in Figure 8.7 (also on page 468). The residual plot clearly shows that the residual variance increases as length of road x increases, strongly suggesting the presence of heteroscedasticity. A procedure such as weighted least squares is needed to stabilize the variances.

c. To apply weighted least squares, we must first determine the weights. Since it is not clear what function of x the error variance is proportional to, we will apply the procedure described previously to estimate the weights.

First, we must divide the data into several groups according to the value of the independent variable x. Ideally, we want to form one group of data points for each different value of x. However, unless each value of x is rep-

FIGURE 8.6

MINITAB printout for least squares fit of straight-line model, Example 8.2

```
The regression equation is
Y = - 15.1 + 12.1 X

Predictor        Coef        Stdev     t-ratio        p
Constant      -15.112        3.342       -4.52    0.000
X             12.0687       0.4138       29.16    0.000

s = 5.374        R-sq = 99.0%       R-sq(adj) = 98.8%

Analysis of Variance

SOURCE        DF          SS          MS          F         p
Regression     1       24558       24558     850.45     0.000
Error          9         260          29
Total         10       24818

Obs.         X          Y        Fit  Stdev.Fit   Residual    St.Resid
  1        2.0      10.10       9.02       2.65       1.08        0.23
  2        2.4      11.40      13.85       2.52      -2.45       -0.52
  3        3.1      24.20      22.30       2.31       1.90        0.39
  4        3.5      26.50      27.13       2.19      -0.63       -0.13
  5        6.4      66.80      62.13       1.64       4.67        0.91
  6        6.1      53.80      58.51       1.67      -4.71       -0.92
  7        7.0      71.10      69.37       1.62       1.73        0.34
  8       11.5     132.70     123.68       2.45       9.02        1.89
  9       10.9     108.00     116.44       2.27      -8.44       -1.73
 10       12.2     126.20     132.13       2.67      -5.93       -1.27
 11       12.6     140.70     136.95       2.81       3.75        0.82
```

FIGURE 8.7

Plot of least squares residuals versus x, Example 8.2

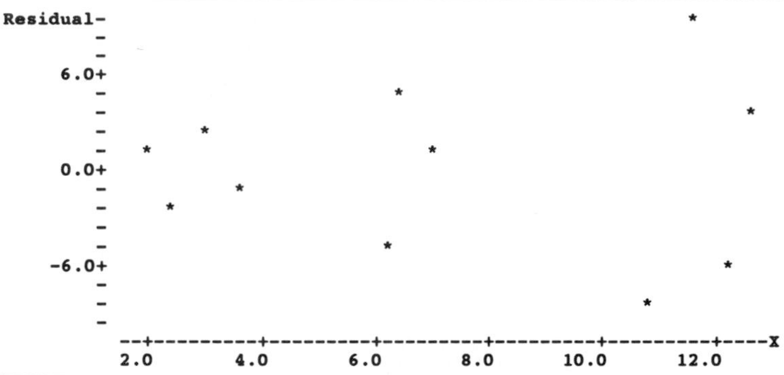

licated, not all of the group residual variances can be calculated. Therefore, we resort to grouping the data according to "nearest neighbors." One choice would be to use three groups, $2 \le x \le 4$, $6 \le x \le 7$, and $10 \le x \le 13$. These groups have approximately the same numbers of observations (namely, 4, 3, and 4 observations, respectively).

Next, we calculate the sample variance s_j^2 of the residuals included in each group. The three residual variances are given in Table 8.4. These variances are compared to three different functions of $\bar{x}$ ($\bar{x}$, $\bar{x}^2$, and $\sqrt{\bar{x}}$), as shown in Table 8.4, where $\bar{x}_j$ is the mean road length x for group j, $j = 1, 2, 3$.

Note that the ratio $s_j^2/\bar{x}_j^2$ yields a value near .5 for each of the three groups. This result suggests that the residual variance of each group is proportional to $\bar{x}^2$, i.e.,

$$\sigma_j^2 = k\bar{x}_j^2, \quad j = 1, 2, 3$$

TABLE 8.4 **Comparison of Residual Variances to Three Functions of $\bar{x}$, Example 8.2**

GROUP	RANGE OF x	$\bar{x}_j$	s_j^2	$s_j^2/\bar{x}_j$	$s_j^2/\bar{x}_j^2$	$s_j^2/\sqrt{\bar{x}_j}$
1	$2 \le x \le 4$	2.75	3.722	1.353	.492	2.244
2	$6 \le x \le 7$	6.5	23.016	3.541	.545	9.028
3	$10 \le x \le 13$	11.8	67.031	5.681	.481	19.514

where k is approximately .5. Thus, a reasonable approximation to the weight for each group is

$$w_j = \frac{1}{\bar{x}_j^2}$$

With this weighting scheme, observations associated with large values of length of road x will have less influence on the regression residuals than observations associated with smaller values of x.

d. A weighted least squares analysis was conducted on the data in Table 8.3 using the weights

$$w_{ij} = \frac{1}{\bar{x}_j^2}$$

where w_{ij} is the weight for observation i in group j. The weighted least squares estimates are shown in the MINITAB printout reproduced in Figure 8.8. The prediction equation is

$$\hat{y} = -15.274 + 12.1204x$$

Note that the test of model adequacy, H_0: $\beta_1 = 0$, is significant at $p = .000$. Also, the standard error of the model, s, is significantly smaller than the value

FIGURE 8.8
MINITAB printout of weighted least squares fit for straight-line model, Example 8.2

```
The regression equation is
Y = - 15.3 + 12.1 X

Predictor        Coef       Stdev     t-ratio        p
Constant      -15.274       1.601       -9.54    0.000
X             12.1204      0.3792       31.97    0.000

s = 0.669       R-sq = 99.1%      R-sq(adj) = 99.0%

Analysis of Variance

SOURCE        DF          SS          MS          F         p
Regression     1      457.48      457.48    1021.77     0.000
Error          9        4.03        0.45
Total         10      461.51

Obs.       X          Y        Fit  Stdev.Fit   Residual    St.Resid
  1      2.0     10.100      8.966      1.037      1.134        0.75
  2      2.4     11.400     13.815      0.956     -2.415       -1.54
  3      3.1     24.200     22.299      0.864      1.901        1.17
  4      3.5     26.500     27.147      0.845     -0.647       -0.40
  5      6.4     66.800     62.296      1.360      4.504        1.09
  6      6.1     53.800     58.660      1.273     -4.860       -1.17
  7      7.0     71.100     69.568      1.545      1.532        0.38
  8     11.5    132.700    124.110      3.117      8.590        1.18
  9     10.9    108.000    116.838      2.898     -8.838       -1.20
 10     12.2    126.200    132.594      3.373     -6.394       -0.90
 11     12.6    140.700    137.442      3.520      3.258        0.46
```

of s for the unweighted least squares analysis (.669 compared to 5.37). This last result is expected because, in the presence of heteroscedasticity, the unweighted least squares estimates are subject to greater sampling error than the weighted least squares estimates.

e. A plot of the weighted least squares residuals against x is shown in Figure 8.9. The lack of a discernible pattern in the residual plot suggests that the weighted least squares procedure has corrected the problem of unequal variances.

FIGURE 8.9
Plot of weighted residuals versus x, Example 8.2

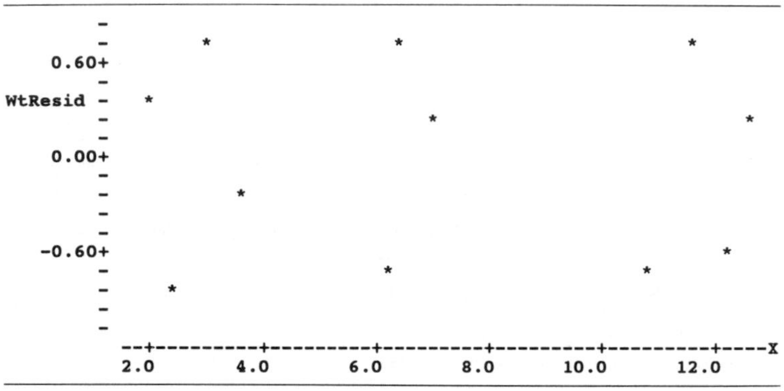

Before concluding this section, we mention that the "nearest neighbor" technique, illustrated in Example 8.2, will not always be successful in finding the optimal or near-optimal weights in weighted least squares. First, it may not be easy to identify the appropriate groupings of data points, especially if more than one independent variable is included in the regression. Second, the relationship between the residual variance and some preselected function of the independent variables may not reveal a consistent pattern over groups. In other words, unless the right function (or approximate function) of x is examined, the weights will be difficult to determine. More sophisticated techniques for choosing the weights in weighted least squares are available. Consult the references given at the end of this chapter for details on how to use these techniques.

EXERCISES

8.10 Consider the straight-line model $y_i = \beta_0 + \beta_1 x_i + \varepsilon_i$. Give the appropriate weights w_i to use in a weighted least squares regression if the variance of the random error ε_i, i.e., σ_i^2, is proportional to

a. x_i^2 b. $\sqrt{x_i}$ c. x_i

d. $\frac{1}{n_i}$, where n_i is the number of observations at level x_i e. $\frac{1}{x_i}$

8.11 A machine that mass produces rubber gaskets can be set at one of three different speeds: 100, 150, or 200 gaskets per minute. As part of a quality control study, the machine was monitored several different times at each of the three speeds, and the number of defectives produced per hour was recorded. The data are provided in the accompanying table. Since the number of defectives (y) is thought to be linearly related to speed (x), the following straight-line model is proposed:

$$y = \beta_0 + \beta_1 x + \varepsilon$$

MACHINE SPEED x, gaskets per minute	NUMBER OF DEFECTIVES y	MACHINE SPEED x, gaskets per minute	NUMBER OF DEFECTIVES y
100	15	150	35
100	23	150	24
100	11	200	26
100	14	200	48
100	18	200	27
150	19	200	38
150	29	200	39
150	20		

a. Fit the model using the method of least squares. Is there evidence that the model is useful for predicting y? Test using $\alpha = .05$.
b. Plot the residuals from the least squares model against x. What does the plot reveal about the standard least squares assumption of homoscedasticity?
c. Estimate the appropriate weights to use in a weighted least squares regression. [*Hint*: Calculate the variance of the least squares residuals at each level of x.]
d. Refit the model using weighted least squares. Compare the standard deviation of the weighted least squares slope to the standard deviation of the unweighted least squares slope.
e. Plot the weighted residuals against x to determine whether using weighted least squares has corrected the problem of unequal variances.

8.12 Refer to the data on salary (y) and years of experience (x) for 50 executives, given in Table 7.7. (The data are reproduced here for convenience.) Recall that the least squares fit of the quadratic model $E(y) = \beta_0 + \beta_1 x + \beta_2 x^2$ yielded regression residuals with unequal variances (see Figure 7.13). Apply the method of weighted least squares to correct this problem. [*Hint*: Estimate the weights using the "nearest neighbor" technique outlined in this section.]

YEARS OF EXPERIENCE x	SALARY y	YEARS OF EXPERIENCE x	SALARY y	YEARS OF EXPERIENCE x	SALARY y	YEARS OF EXPERIENCE x	SALARY y
7	$26,075	28	$64,785	7	$22,210	26	$65,343
28	79,370	26	61,581	2	20,521	19	46,216
23	65,726	27	70,678	18	49,727	16	54,288
18	41,983	20	51 301	11	33,233	3	20,844
19	62,309	18	39,346	21	43,628	12	32,586
15	41,154	1	24,833	4	16,105	23	71,235
24	53,610	26	65,929	24	65,644	20	36,530
13	33,697	20	41,721	20	63,022	19	52,745
2	22,444	26	82,641	20	47,780	27	67,282
8	32,562	28	99,139	15	38,853	25	80,931
20	43,076	23	52,624	25	66,537	12	32,303
21	56,000	17	50,594	25	67,447	11	38,371
18	58,667	25	53,272				

8.5 Modeling Qualitative Dependent Variables

For all models discussed in the previous sections of this text, the response (dependent) variable y is a *quantitative* variable. In this section, we consider models for which the response y is a **qualitative variable at two levels**, or, as it is sometimes called, a **binary variable**.

For example, an entrepreneur may want to relate the success or failure of a new business to the characteristics (such as age, years of experience, and years of education) of the owner. The value of the response of interest to the entrepreneur is either *yes*, the new business is a success, or *no*, the new business is a failure. (A success implies the business did not fail.) Similarly, a state attorney general investigating collusive practices among bidders for road construction contracts may want to determine which contract-related variables (such as number of bidders, bid amount, and cost of materials) are useful indicators of whether a bid is fixed (i.e., whether the bid price is intentionally set higher than the fair market value). Here, the value of the response variable is either *fixed* bid or *competitive* bid.

Just as with qualitative independent variables, we use **dummy** (i.e., coded 0–1) **variables** to represent the qualitative response variable. For example, the response of interest to the entrepreneur is recorded as

$$y = \begin{cases} 1 & \text{if new business a success} \\ 0 & \text{if new business a failure} \end{cases}$$

where the assignment of 0 and 1 to the two levels is arbitrary. The general linear model takes the usual form

$$y = \beta_0 + \beta_1 x_1 + \beta_2 x_2 + \cdots + \beta_k x_k + \varepsilon$$

However, when the response is binary, the expected response

$$E(y) = \beta_0 + \beta_1 x_1 + \beta_2 x_2 + \cdots + \beta_k x_k$$

has a special meaning. It can be shown* that $E(y) = \pi$, where π is the probability that $y = 1$ for given values of $x_1, x_2, \ldots, x_k$. Thus, for the entrepreneur, the mean response $E(y)$ represents the probability that a new business with certain owner-related characteristics will be a success.

When the ordinary least squares approach is used to fit models with a binary response, several well-known problems are encountered. A discussion of these problems and their solutions follows.

Problem 1

Nonnormal errors The standard least squares assumption of normal errors is violated since the response y and, hence, the random error ε can take on only

*The result is a straightforward application of the expectation theorem for a random variable. Let $\pi = P(y = 1)$ and $1 - \pi = P(y = 0)$, $0 \leq \pi \leq 1$. Then, by definition, $E(y) = \Sigma_y\, y_i \cdot p(y) = (1)P(y = 1) + (0)P(y = 0) = P(y = 1) = \pi$. Students familiar with discrete random variables will recognize y as the **Bernoulli random variable**, i.e., a binomial random variable with $n = 1$.

two values. To see this, consider the simple model $y = \beta_0 + \beta_1 x + \varepsilon$. Then we can write

$$\varepsilon = y - (\beta_0 + \beta_1 x)$$

Thus, when $y = 1$, $\varepsilon = 1 - (\beta_0 + \beta_1 x)$ and when $y = 0$, $\varepsilon = -\beta_0 - \beta_1 x$.

When the sample size n is large, however, any inferences derived from the least squares prediction equation remain valid in most practical situations even though the errors are nonnormal.*

Problem 2

Unequal variances It can be shown† that the variance σ^2 of the random error is a function of π, the probability that the response y equals 1. Specifically,

$$\sigma^2 = V(\varepsilon) = \pi(1 - \pi)$$

Since, for the general linear model,

$$\pi = E(y) = \beta_0 + \beta_1 x_1 + \beta_2 x_2 + \cdots + \beta_k x_k$$

this implies that σ^2 is not constant and, in fact, depends on the values of the independent variables; hence, the standard least squares assumption of equal variances is also violated. One solution to this problem is to use weighted least squares (see Section 8.4), where the weights are inversely proportional to σ^2, i.e.,

$$w_i = \frac{1}{\sigma_i^2} = \frac{1}{\pi_i(1 - \pi_i)}$$

Unfortunately, the true proportion

$$\pi_i = E(y_i) = \beta_0 + \beta_1 x_{1i} + \beta_2 x_{2i} + \cdots + \beta_k x_{ki}$$

is unknown since $\beta_0, \beta_1, \ldots, \beta_k$ are unknown population parameters. However, a technique called **two-stage least squares** can be applied to circumvent this difficulty. Two-stage least squares, as its name implies, involves conducting an analysis in two steps:

STAGE 1 Fit the regression model using the *ordinary least squares* procedure and obtain the predicted values $\hat{y}_i$, $i = 1, 2, \ldots, n$. Recall that $\hat{y}_i$ estimates π_i for the binary model.

*This property is due to the asymptotic normality of the least squares estimates of the model parameters under very general conditions.

†Using the properties of expected values with the Bernoulli random variable, we obtain $V(y) = E(y^2) - [E(y)]^2 = \Sigma y^2 \cdot p(y) - (\pi)^2 = (1)^2 P(y = 1) + (0)^2 P(y = 0) - \pi^2 = \pi - \pi^2 = \pi(1 - \pi)$. Since in regression, $V(\varepsilon) = V(y)$, the result follows.

STAGE 2 Refit the regression model using *weighted least squares*, where the estimated weights are calculated as follows:

$$w_i = \frac{1}{\hat{y}_i(1 - \hat{y}_i)}$$

Further iterations—revising the weights at each step—can be performed if desired. In most practical problems, however, the estimates of π_i obtained in stage 1 are adequate for use in weighted least squares.

Problem 3

Restricting the predicted response to be between 0 and 1 Since the predicted value $\hat{y}$ estimates $E(y) = \pi$, the probability that the response y equals 1, we would like $\hat{y}$ to have the property that $0 \le \hat{y} \le 1$. There is no guarantee, however, that the regression analysis will always yield predicted values in this range. Thus, the regression may lead to nonsensical results, i.e., negative estimated probabilities or predicted probabilities greater than 1. To avoid this problem, you may want to fit a model with a mean response function $E(y)$ that automatically falls between 0 and 1. (We consider one such model in the next section.)

In summary, the purpose of this section has been to identify some of the problems resulting from fitting a linear model with a binary response and to suggest ways in which to circumvent these problems. Another approach is to fit a model specially designed for a binary response, called a **logistic model**. Logistic models are the subject of Section 8.6.

EXERCISES

8.13 Discuss the problems associated with fitting a model where the response y is recorded as 0 or 1.

8.14 A retailer of home personal computers (PCs) conducted a study to relate PC ownership with annual income of heads of households. Data collected for a random sample of 20 households were used to fit the straight-line model $E(y) = \beta_0 + \beta_1 x$, where

$$y = \begin{cases} 1 & \text{if own PC} \\ 0 & \text{if not} \end{cases}$$

x = Annual income (in dollars)

The data are shown in the accompanying table. Fit the model using two-stage least squares. Is the model useful for predicting y? Test using $\alpha = .05$.

HOUSEHOLD	y	x	HOUSEHOLD	y	x
1	0	$16,300	11	1	$22,400
2	0	11,200	12	0	10,600
3	0	36,500	13	0	21,400
4	1	21,700	14	0	8,300
5	1	40,200	15	1	27,500
6	0	12,400	16	0	15,700
7	0	15,000	17	0	12,100
8	0	9,200	18	1	59,600
9	1	36,700	19	1	20,200
10	0	62,000	20	0	33,100

8.15 Suppose you are investigating allegations of sex discrimination in the hiring practices of a particular firm. An equal-rights group claims that females are less likely to be hired than males with the same background, experience, and other qualifications. Data (shown in the table) collected on 28 former applicants will be used to fit the model $E(y) = \beta_0 + \beta_1 x_1 + \beta_2 x_2 + \beta_3 x_3$, where

$$y = \begin{cases} 1 & \text{if hired} \\ 0 & \text{if not} \end{cases}$$

x_1 = Years of higher education (4, 6, or 8)

x_2 = Years of experience

$$x_3 = \begin{cases} 1 & \text{if male applicant} \\ 0 & \text{if female applicant} \end{cases}$$

HIRING STATUS y	EDUCATION x_1, years	EXPERIENCE x_2, years	GENDER x_3	HIRING STATUS y	EDUCATION x_1, years	EXPERIENCE x_2, years	GENDER x_3
0	6	2	0	1	4	5	1
0	4	0	1	0	6	4	0
1	6	6	1	0	8	0	1
1	6	3	1	1	6	1	1
0	4	1	0	0	4	7	0
1	8	3	0	0	4	1	1
0	4	2	1	0	4	5	0
0	4	4	0	0	6	0	1
0	6	1	0	1	8	5	1
1	8	10	0	0	4	9	0
0	4	2	1	0	8	1	0
0	8	5	0	0	6	1	1
0	4	2	0	1	4	10	1
0	6	7	0	1	6	12	0

a. Interpret each of the β's in the multiple regression model.
b. If you have access to a statistical software package, fit the multiple regression model using two-stage least squares.

c. Conduct a test of model adequacy. Use $\alpha = .05$.
d. Is there sufficient evidence to indicate that gender is an important predictor of hiring status? Test using $\alpha = .05$.
e. Calculate a 95% confidence interval for the mean response $E(y)$ when $x_1 = 4$, $x_2 = 3$, and $x_3 = 0$. Interpret the interval.

8.6 Logistic Regression

Often, the relationship between a qualitative binary response y and a single predictor variable x is curvilinear. One particular curvilinear pattern frequently encountered in practice is the S-shaped curve shown in Figure 8.10. Points on the curve represent $\pi = P(y = 1)$ for each value of x. A model that accounts for this type of curvature is the **logistic** (or **logit**) **model**,

$$E(y) = \frac{\exp(\beta_0 + \beta_1 x)}{1 + \exp(\beta_0 + \beta_1 x)}$$

FIGURE 8.10
Graph of $E(y)$ for the logistic model

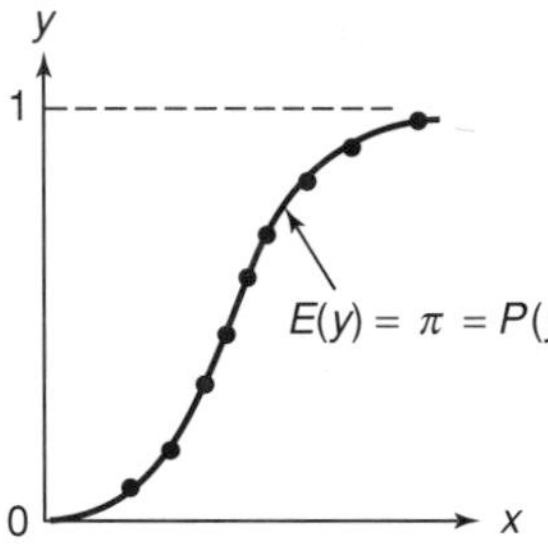

The logistic model was originally developed for use in **survival analysis**, where the response y is typically measured as 0 or 1, depending on whether the experimental unit (for example, a patient) "survives." Note that the curve shown in Figure 8.10 has asymptotes at 0 and 1—that is, the mean response $E(y)$ can never fall below 0 or above 1. Thus, the logistic model ensures that the estimated response $\hat{y}$ (i.e., the estimated probability that $y = 1$) lies between 0 and 1.

In general, the logistic model can be written as shown in the box.

Logistic Regression Model for a Binary Dependent Variable

$$E(y) = \frac{\exp(\beta_0 + \beta_1 x_1 + \beta_2 x_2 + \cdots + \beta_k x_k)}{1 + \exp(\beta_0 + \beta_1 x_1 + \beta_2 x_2 + \cdots + \beta_k x_k)}$$

where

$$y = \begin{cases} 1 & \text{if category A occurs} \\ 0 & \text{if category B occurs} \end{cases}$$

$E(y) = P(\text{Category A occurs}) = \pi$

$x_1, x_2, \ldots, x_k$ are quantitative or qualitative independent variables

Note that the general logistic model is not a linear function of the β parameters (see Section 4.1). Obtaining the parameter estimates of a **nonlinear regression model**, such as the logistic model, is a numerically tedious process and often requires sophisticated computer programs. In this section we briefly discuss two approaches to the problem, and give an example of a computer printout for the second.

1. *Least squares estimation using a transformation* One method of fitting the model involves a transformation on the mean response $E(y)$. Recall (from Section 8.5) that for a binary response, $E(y) = \pi$, where π denotes the probability that $y = 1$. Then the logistic model

$$\pi = \frac{\exp(\beta_0 + \beta_1 x_1 + \cdots + \beta_k x_k)}{1 + \exp(\beta_0 + \beta_1 x_1 + \cdots + \beta_k x_k)}$$

implies (proof omitted) that

$$\ln\left(\frac{\pi}{1 - \pi}\right) = \beta_0 + \beta_1 x_1 + \cdots + \beta_k x_k$$

Set

$$\pi^* = \ln\left(\frac{\pi}{1 - \pi}\right)$$

The transformed logistic model

$$\pi^* = \beta_0 + \beta_1 x_1 + \cdots + \beta_k x_k$$

is now linear in the β's and the method of least squares can be applied.

Note: Since $\pi = P(y = 1)$, then $1 - \pi = P(y = 0)$. The ratio

$$\frac{\pi}{1 - \pi} = \frac{P(y = 1)}{P(y = 0)}$$

is known as the **odds** of the event, $y = 1$, occurring. (For example, if $\pi = .8$, then the odds of $y = 1$ occurring are $.8/.2 = 4$, or 4 to 1.) The transformed model, π^*, then, is a model for the log of the odds of $y = 1$ occurring and is often called the **log-odds model**.

Definition 8.1

In logistic regression with a binary response y, we define the **odds of the event (y = 1) occurring** as follows:

$$\text{Odds} = \frac{\pi}{1 - \pi} = \frac{P(y = 1)}{P(y = 0)}$$

Although the transformation succeeds in linearizing the response function, two other problems remain. First, since the true probability π is unknown, the values of the log-odds π^*, necessary for input into the regression, are also unknown. To carry out the least squares analysis, we must obtain estimates of π^* for each combination of the independent variables. A good choice is the estimator

$$\pi^* = \ln\left(\frac{\hat{\pi}}{1 - \hat{\pi}}\right)$$

where $\hat{\pi}$ is the sample proportion of 1's for the particular combination of x's. To obtain these estimates, however, *we must have replicated observations of the response y at each combination of the levels of the independent variables.* Thus, the least squares transformation approach is limited to replicated experiments, which occur infrequently in a practical business setting.

The second problem is associated with unequal variances. The transformed logistic model yields error variances that are inversely proportional to $\pi(1 - \pi)$. Since π, or $E(y)$, is a function of the independent variables, the regression errors are heteroscedastic. To stabilize the variances, weighted least squares should be used. This technique also requires that replicated observations be available for each combination of the x's and, in addition, that the number of observations at each combination be relatively large. If the experiment is replicated, with n_j (large) observations at each combination of the levels of the independent variables, then the appropriate weights to use are

$$w_j = n_j\hat{\pi}_j(1 - \hat{\pi}_j)$$

where

$$\hat{\pi}_j = \frac{\text{Number of 1's for combination } j \text{ of the } x\text{'s}}{n_j}$$

2. *Maximum likelihood estimation* Estimates of the β parameters in the logistic model also can be obtained by applying a common statistical technique, called **maximum likelihood estimation**. Like the least squares estimators, the maximum likelihood estimators have certain desirable properties.† (In fact, when the errors of a linear regression model are normally distributed, the least squares estimates and maximum likelihood estimates are equivalent.) Many of the available statistical computer software packages use maximum likelihood estimation to fit logistic regression models. Therefore, one practical advantage of using the maximum likelihood method (rather than the transformation approach) to fit logistic regression models is that computer programs are readily available. Another advantage is that the data need not be replicated to apply maximum likelihood estimation.

†For details on how to obtain maximum likelihood estimators and what their distributional properties are, consult the references given at the end of the chapter.

The maximum likelihood estimates of the parameters of a logistic model have distributional properties that are different from the standard F and t distributions of least squares regression. Under certain conditions, the test statistics for testing individual parameters and overall model adequacy have approximate **chi-square (χ^2) distributions**. The χ^2 distribution is similar to the F distribution in that it depends on degrees of freedom and is nonnegative, as shown in Figure 8.11. (Critical values of the χ^2 distribution for various values of α and degrees of freedom are given in Table 10, Appendix C.) We illustrate the application of maximum likelihood estimation for logistic regression with an example.

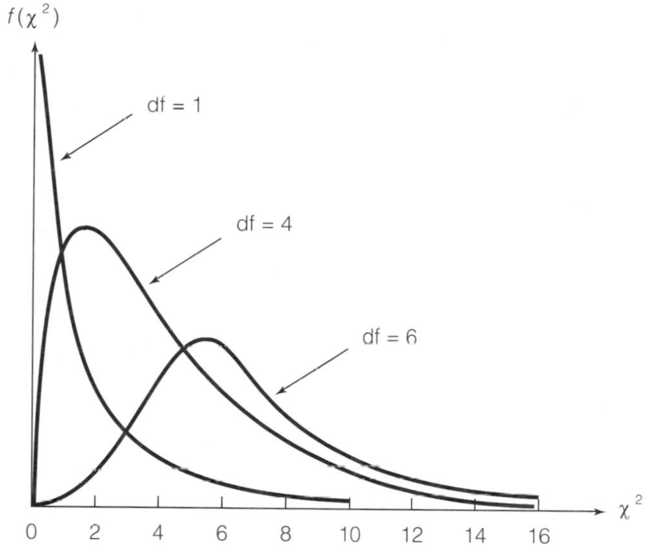

FIGURE 8.11
Several chi-square probability distributions

EXAMPLE 8.3

Consider the problem of collusive (i.e., noncompetitive) bidding among road construction contractors. Recall (from Section 8.5) that contractors sometimes scheme to set bid prices higher than the fair market (or competitive) price. Suppose an investigator has obtained information on the bid status (fixed or competitive) for a sample of 31 contracts. In addition, two variables thought to be related to bid status are also recorded for each contract: number of bidders x_1 and the difference between the winning (lowest) bid and the estimated competitive bid (called the engineer's estimate) x_2, measured as a percentage of the estimate. The data appear in Table 8.5 on page 480, with the response y recorded as follows:

$$y = \begin{cases} 1 & \text{if fixed bid} \\ 0 & \text{if competitive bid} \end{cases}$$

An appropriate model for $E(y)$ is the logistic model

$$E(y) = \frac{\exp(\beta_0 + \beta_1 x_1 + \beta_2 x_2)}{1 + \exp(\beta_0 + \beta_1 x_1 + \beta_2 x_2)}$$

TABLE 8.5 **Data for a Sample of 31 Road Construction Bids**

CONTRACT	BID STATUS y	NUMBER OF BIDDERS x_1	DIFFERENCE BETWEEN WINNING BID AND ENGINEER'S ESTIMATE x_2, %	CONTRACT	BID STATUS y	NUMBER OF BIDDERS x_1	DIFFERENCE BETWEEN WINNING BID AND ENGINEER'S ESTIMATE x_2, %
1	1	4	19.2	17	0	10	6.6
2	1	2	24.1	18	1	5	−2.5
3	0	4	−7.1	19	0	13	24.2
4	1	3	3.9	20	0	7	2.3
5	0	9	4.5	21	1	3	36.9
6	0	6	10.6	22	0	4	−11.7
7	0	2	−3.0	23	1	2	22.1
8	0	11	16.2	24	1	3	10.4
9	1	6	72.8	25	0	2	9.1
10	0	7	28.7	26	0	5	2.0
11	1	3	11.5	27	0	6	12.6
12	1	2	56.3	28	1	5	18.0
13	0	5	−.5	29	0	3	1.5
14	0	3	−1.3	30	1	4	27.3
15	0	3	12.9	31	0	10	−8.4
16	0	8	34.1				

The model was fitted to the data using the logistic regression option of SAS. The resulting printout is shown in Figure 8.12. Interpret the results.

Solution

The maximum likelihood estimates of β_0, β_1, and β_2 are given in Figure 8.12 under the column heading **Parameter Estimate**. These estimates (shaded in the printout) are $\hat{\beta}_0 = 1.4212$, $\hat{\beta}_1 = -.7553$, and $\hat{\beta}_2 = .1122$. Therefore, the prediction equation for the probability of a fixed bid [i.e., $\pi = P(y = 1)$] is

$$\hat{y} = \frac{\exp(1.4212 - .7553x_1 + .1122x_2)}{1 + \exp(1.4212 - .7553x_1 + .1122x_2)}$$

FIGURE 8.12
SAS printout for logistic regression on bid status

Criteria for Assessing Model Fit

Criterion	Intercept Only	Intercept and Covariates	Chi-Square for Covariates
AIC	43.381	28.843	.
SC	44.815	33.145	.
-2 LOG L	41.381	22.843	18.538 with 2 DF (p=0.0001)
Score	.	.	13.466 with 2 DF (p=0.0012)

Analysis of Maximum Likelihood Estimates

Variable	Parameter Estimate	Standard Error	Wald Chi-Square	Pr > Chi-Square	Standardized Estimate
INTERCPT	1.4212	1.2867	1.2199	0.2694	.
NUMBIDS	-0.7553	0.3388	4.9708	0.0258	-1.231128
DOTEST	0.1122	0.0514	4.7670	0.0290	1.143067

(continued)

FIGURE 8.12 *(continued)*

Predicted Probabilities and 95% Confidence Limits

OBS	NUMBIDS	DOTEST	STATUS	PRED	CLLOWER	CLUPPER
1	4	19.2	1	0.63510	0.32984	0.86023
2	2	24.1	1	0.93180	0.53648	0.99384
3	4	-7.1	0	0.08342	0.01043	0.44010
4	3	3.9	1	0.39958	0.15868	0.70132
5	9	4.5	0	0.00760	0.00016	0.26825
6	6	10.6	0	0.12770	0.02582	0.44708
7	2	-3.0	0	0.39506	0.10273	0.78836
8	11	16.2	0	0.00624	0.00007	0.36810
9	6	72.8	1	0.99368	0.35201	0.99998
10	7	28.7	0	0.34391	0.06138	0.80776
11	3	11.5	1	0.60958	0.31579	0.84081
12	2	56.3	1	0.99803	0.69696	0.99999
13	5	-0.5	0	0.08229	0.01253	0.38782
14	3	-1.3	0	0.27078	0.07452	0.63131
15	3	12.9	0	0.64626	0.34076	0.86589
16	8	34.1	0	0.31103	0.03168	0.86168
17	10	6.6	0	0.00453	0.00006	0.26602
18	5	-2.5	1	0.06686	0.00852	0.37403
19	13	24.2	0	0.00339	0.00001	0.45712
20	7	2.3	0	0.02639	0.00166	0.30640
21	3	36.9	1	0.96428	0.54751	0.99834
22	4	-11.7	0	0.05152	0.00412	0.41602
23	2	22.1	1	0.91608	0.51886	0.99103
24	3	10.4	1	0.57984	0.29466	0.82011
25	2	9.1	0	0.71740	0.33904	0.92627
26	5	2.0	0	0.10611	0.02005	0.40784
27	6	12.6	0	0.15485	0.03485	0.48180
28	5	18.0	1	0.41683	0.17873	0.70127
29	3	1.5	0	0.33704	0.11480	0.66587
30	4	27.3	1	0.81200	0.40060	0.96541
31	10	-8.4	0	0.00085	0.00000	0.15843

In general, the coefficient $\hat{\beta}_i$ in the logistic model estimates the change in the log-odds when x_i is increased by 1 unit, holding all other x's in the model fixed. The antilog of the coefficient, $e^{\hat{\beta}_i}$, then estimates the odds-ratio

$$\frac{\pi_{x+1}/(1 - \pi_{x+1})}{\pi_x/(1 - \pi_x)}$$

where π_x is the value of $P(y = 1)$ for a fixed value x.[†] Typically analysts compute $(e^{\hat{\beta}_i}) - 1$, which is an estimate of the percentage increase (or decrease) in the odds $\pi = P(y = 1)/P(y = 0)$ for every 1-unit increase in x_i, holding the other x's fixed.

This leads to the following interpretations of the β estimates:

$\hat{\beta}_1 = -.7553$; $e^{\hat{\beta}_1} = .47$; $e^{\hat{\beta}_1} - 1 = -.53$: For each additional bidder (x_1), we estimate the odds of a fixed contract to *decrease* by 53%, holding **DOTEST** (x_2) fixed.

[†]To see this, consider the model $\pi^* = \beta_0 + \beta_1 x$, where $x = 1$ or $x = 0$. When $x = 1$, we have $\pi_1^* = \beta_0 + \beta_1$; when $x = 0$, $\pi_0^* = \beta_0$. Now replace π_i^* with $\log[\pi_i/(1 + \pi_i)]$, and take the antilog of each side of the equation. Then we have $\pi_1/(1 - \pi_1) = e^{\beta_0}e^{\beta_1}$ and $\pi_0/(1 - \pi_0) = e^{\beta_0}$. Consequently, the odds-ratio is

$$\frac{\pi_1/(1 - \pi_1)}{\pi_0/(1 - \pi_0)} = e^{\beta_1}$$

Interpretations of β parameters in the logistic model

$$\pi^* = \beta_0 + \beta_1 x_1 + \beta_2 x_2 + \cdots + \beta_k x_k$$

where

$$\pi^* = \ln\left(\frac{\pi}{1-\pi}\right)$$

$$\pi = P(y = 1)$$

β_i = Change in log-odds π^* for every 1-unit increase in x_i, holding all other x's fixed

$e^{\beta_i} - 1$ = Percentage change in odds $\pi/(1-\pi)$ for every 1-unit increase in x_i, holding all other x's fixed

$\hat{\beta}_2 = .1122$ $e^{\hat{\beta}_2} = 1.12$; $e^{\hat{\beta}_2} - 1 = .12$: For every 1% increase in **DOTEST** (x_2), we estimate the odds of a fixed contract to *increase* by 12%, holding **NUMBIDS** (x_1) fixed.

The standard errors of the β estimates are given under the column **Standard Error**, and the (squared) ratios of the β estimates to their respective standard errors are given under the column **Wald Chi-Square**. As in regression with a linear model, this ratio provides a test statistic for testing the contribution of each variable to the model (i.e., for testing H_0: $\beta_i = 0$).† The observed significance levels of the tests (i.e., the p-values) are given under the column **Pr > Chi-Square**. Note that both independent variables, **NUMBIDS** (x_1) and **DOTEST** (x_2), have p-values less than .03 (implying that we would reject H_0: $\beta_1 = 0$ and H_0: $\beta_2 = 0$ for $\alpha = .03$).

The test statistic for testing the overall adequacy of the logistic model, i.e., for testing H_0: $\beta_1 = \beta_2 = 0$, is given in the upper portion of the printout (shaded) as $\chi^2 = 18.538$, with observed significance level (shaded) $p = .0001$.‡ Based on the p-value of the test, we can reject H_0 and conclude that at least one of the β coefficients is nonzero. Thus, the model is adequate for predicting bid status y.

Finally, the bottom portion of the printout gives predicted values and lower and upper 95% prediction limits for each observation used in the analysis in the columns titled **PRED**, **CLLOWER**, and **CLUPPER**, respectively. The 95% prediction interval for π for a contract with $x_1 = 3$ bidders and winning bid amount $x_2 = 11.5\%$ above the engineer's estimate is shaded on the printout. We estimate π, the probability of this particular contract being fixed, to fall between .3158 and .8408. Note that all the predicted values and limits lie between 0 and 1, a property of the logistic model.

†In the logistic regression model, the ratio $(\hat{\beta}_i/s_{\hat{\beta}_i})^2$ has an approximate χ^2 distribution with 1 degree of freedom. Consult the references for more details about the χ^2 distribution and its use in logistic regression.

‡The test statistic has an approximate χ^2 distribution with $k = 2$ degrees of freedom, where k is the number of β parameters in the model (excluding β_0).

In summary, we have presented two approaches to fitting logistic regression models. If the data are replicated, you may want to apply the transformation approach. The maximum likelihood estimation approach can be applied to any data set, but you need access to a statistical software package (such as SAS or SPSS) with logistic regression procedures.

This section should be viewed only as an overview of logistic regression. Many of the details of fitting logistic regression models using either technique have been omitted. Before conducting a logistic regression analysis, we strongly recommend that you consult the references given at the end of this chapter.

EXERCISES

8.16 Refer to Exercise 8.14. The data for the random sample of 20 households were used to fit the logit model

$$E(y) = \frac{\exp(\beta_0 + \beta_1 x)}{1 + \exp(\beta_0 + \beta_1 x)}$$

An SPSS printout of the logistic regression is presented here. Interpret the results.

```
Dependent Variable..   Y

                        Chi-Square     df Significance
 -2 Log Likelihood         22.969      18        .1918
 Model Chi-Square           2.929       1        .0870
 Improvement                2.929       1        .0870
 Goodness of Fit           19.343      18        .3710

Classification Table for Y
                        Predicted
                      .00       1.00      Percent Correct
                       0    |    1
Observed            +-------+-------+
   .00         0    |   12  |    1  |    92.31%
                    +-------+-------+
  1.00         1    |    5  |    2  |    28.57%
                    +-------+-------+
                            Overall      70.00%

---------------------- Variables in the Equation -----------------------

Variable             B      S.E.      Wald     df       Sig        R    Exp(B)

X             5.47E-05 3.491E-05    2.4533      1     .1173    .1323    1.0001
Constant       -2.0188    1.0314    3.8314      1     .0503
---------------------------------------------------------------------------
```

8.17 Refer to Exercise 8.15. The data collected on the 28 former applicants were used to fit the logit model

$$E(y) = \frac{\exp(\beta_0 + \beta_1 x_1 + \beta_2 x_2 + \beta_3 x_3)}{1 + \exp(\beta_0 + \beta_1 x_1 + \beta_2 x_2 + \beta_3 x_3)}$$

where

$$y = \begin{cases} 1 & \text{if hired} \\ 0 & \text{if not} \end{cases}$$

x_1 = Years of higher education (4, 6, or 8)

x_2 = Years of experience

$$x_3 = \begin{cases} 1 & \text{if male applicant} \\ 0 & \text{if female applicant} \end{cases}$$

A SAS printout of the logistic regression is shown here.

Criteria for Assessing Model Fit

Criterion	Intercept Only	Intercept and Covariates	Chi-Square for Covariates
AIC	37.165	22.735	.
SC	38.497	28.064	.
-2 LOG L	35.165	14.735	20.430 with 3 DF (p=0.0001)
Score	.	.	15.032 with 3 DF (p=0.0018)

Analysis of Maximum Likelihood Estimates

Variable	Parameter Estimate	Standard Error	Wald Chi-Square	Pr > Chi-Square	Standardized Estimate
INTERCPT	-14.2483	6.0805	5.4909	0.0191	.
EDUC	1.1549	0.6023	3.6767	0.0552	1.001936
EXP	0.9098	0.4293	4.4919	0.0341	1.690596
SEX	5.6037	2.6028	4.6352	0.0313	1.569063

Predicted Probabilities and 95% Confidence Limits

OBS	EDUC	EXP	SEX	HIRED	PRED	CLL	CLU
1	6	6	1	1	0.97688	0.42319	0.99959
2	6	3	1	1	0.73385	0.26804	0.95405
3	8	3	0	1	0.09282	0.00485	0.68232
4	8	10	0	1	0.98352	0.27405	0.99989
5	4	5	1	1	0.62813	0.11439	0.95669
6	6	1	1	1	0.30886	0.07490	0.71155
7	8	5	1	1	0.99420	0.50305	0.99997
8	4	10	1	1	0.99378	0.29208	0.99998
9	6	12	0	1	0.97338	0.19876	0.99981
10	6	2	0	0	0.00407	0.00005	0.27086
11	4	0	1	0	0.01755	0.00048	0.40027
12	4	1	0	0	0.00016	0.00000	0.15324
13	4	2	1	0	0.09927	0.00894	0.57370
14	4	4	0	0	0.00250	0.00002	0.24465
15	6	1	0	0	0.00164	0.00001	0.24049
16	4	2	1	0	0.09927	0.00894	0.57370
17	8	5	0	0	0.38699	0.04394	0.89661
18	4	2	0	0	0.00041	0.00000	0.17559
19	6	7	0	0	0.27888	0.04027	0.78091
20	6	4	0	0	0.02461	0.00108	0.37067
21	8	0	1	0	0.64439	0.11457	0.96209
22	4	7	0	0	0.03698	0.00141	0.50996
23	4	1	1	0	0.04248	0.00221	0.47030
24	4	5	0	0	0.00618	0.00009	0.30151
25	6	0	1	0	0.15248	0.02129	0.59808
26	4	9	0	0	0.19153	0.01081	0.83708
27	8	1	0	0	0.01631	0.00026	0.51595
28	6	1	1	0	0.30886	0.07490	0.71155

a. Conduct a test of model adequacy. Use $\alpha = .05$.

b. Is there sufficient evidence to indicate that gender is an important predictor of hiring status? Test using $\alpha = .05$.

c. Calculate a 95% confidence interval for the mean response $E(y)$ when $x_1 = 4$, $x_2 = 0$, and $x_3 = 1$. Interpret the interval.

8.7 Ridge Regression

When the sample data for regression exhibit multicollinearity, the least squares estimates of the β coefficients may be subject to extreme roundoff error as well as inflated standard errors (see Section 6.5). Since their magnitudes and signs may change considerably from sample to sample, the least squares estimates are said to be *unstable*. A technique developed for stabilizing the regression coefficients in the presence of multicollinearity is **ridge regression**.

Ridge regression is a modification of the method of least squares to allow *biased* estimators of the regression coefficients. At first glance, the idea of biased estimation may not seem very appealing. But consider the sampling distributions of two different estimators of a regression coefficient β, one unbiased and the other biased, shown in Figure 8.13.

FIGURE 8.13

Sampling distributions of two estimators of a regression coefficient β

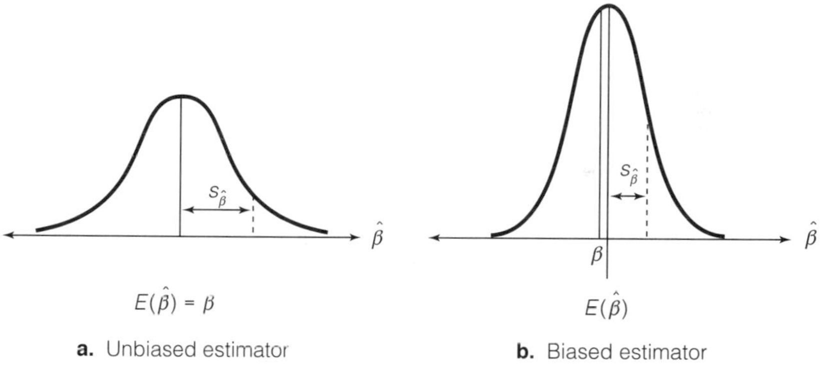

Figure 8.13a shows an unbiased estimator of β with a fairly large variance. In contrast, the estimator shown in Figure 8.13b has a slight bias but is much less variable. In this case, we would prefer the biased estimator over the unbiased estimator since it will lead to more precise estimates of the true β (i.e., narrower confidence intervals for β). One way to measure the "goodness" of an estimator of β is to calculate the **mean square error** of $\hat{\beta}$, denoted by $\text{MSE}(\hat{\beta})$, where $\text{MSE}(\hat{\beta})$ is defined as

$$\begin{aligned}\text{MSE}(\hat{\beta}) &= E[(\hat{\beta} - \beta)^2] \\ &= V(\hat{\beta}) + [E(\hat{\beta}) - \beta]^2\end{aligned}$$

The difference $E(\hat{\beta}) - \beta$ is called the **bias** of $\hat{\beta}$. Therefore, $\text{MSE}(\hat{\beta})$ is just the sum of the variance of $\hat{\beta}$ and the squared bias:

$$\text{MSE}(\hat{\beta}) = V(\hat{\beta}) + (\text{Bias in } \hat{\beta})^2$$

Let $\hat{\beta}_{\text{LS}}$ denote the least squares estimate of β. Then, since $E(\hat{\beta}_{\text{LS}}) = \beta$, the bias is 0 and

$$\text{MSE}(\hat{\beta}_{\text{LS}}) = V(\hat{\beta}_{\text{LS}})$$

We have previously stated that the variance of the least squares regression coefficient, and hence $\text{MSE}(\hat{\beta}_{\text{LS}})$, will be quite large in the presence of multicollinearity. The idea behind ridge regression is to introduce a small amount of bias in the ridge estimator of β, denoted by $\hat{\beta}_R$, so that its mean square error is considerably smaller than the corresponding mean square error for least squares, i.e.,

$$\text{MSE}(\hat{\beta}_R) < \text{MSE}(\hat{\beta}_{LS})$$

In this manner, ridge regression will lead to narrower confidence intervals for the β coefficients, and hence, more stable estimates.

Although the mechanics of a ridge regression are beyond the scope of this text, we point out that some of the more sophisticated software packages (including SAS) are now capable of conducting this type of analysis. To obtain the ridge regression coefficients, the user must specify the value of a biasing constant c, where $c \geq 0$.* Researchers have shown that as the value of c increases, the bias in the ridge estimates increases while the variance decreases. The idea is to choose c so that the total mean square error for the ridge estimators is smaller than the total mean square error for the least squares estimates. Although such a c exists, the optimal value, unfortunately, is unknown.

Various methods for choosing the value of c have been proposed. One commonly used graphical technique employs a **ridge trace**. Values of the estimated ridge regression coefficients are calculated for different values of c ranging from 0 to 1 and are plotted. The plots for each of the independent variables in the model are overlaid to form the ridge trace. An example of ridge trace for a model with three independent variables is shown in Figure 8.14. Initially, the estimated coefficients may fluctuate dramatically as c is increased from 0 (especially if severe multicollinearity is present). Eventually, however, the ridge estimates will sta-

FIGURE 8.14
Ridge trace of β coefficients of a model with three independent variables

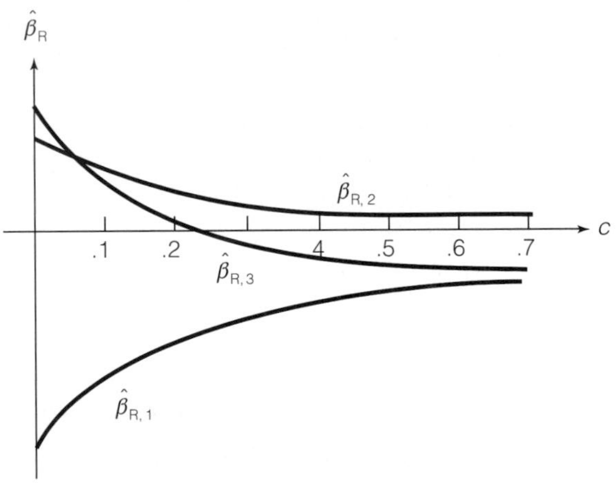

*In matrix notation, the ridge estimator $\hat{\beta}_R$ is calculated as follows:

$$\hat{\beta}_R = (\mathbf{X}'\mathbf{X}) + c\mathbf{I})^{-1}\mathbf{X}'\mathbf{Y}$$

When $c = 0$, the least squares estimator

$$\hat{\beta}_{LS} = (\mathbf{X}'\mathbf{X})^{-1}\mathbf{X}'\mathbf{Y}$$

is obtained. See Appendix A for details on the matrix mechanics of a regression analysis.

bilize. After careful examination of the ridge trace, the analyst chooses the smallest value of c for which it appears that all the ridge estimates are stable. The choice of c, therefore, is subjective.

Once the value of c has been determined (using the ridge trace or some other analytical technique), the corresponding ridge estimates may be used in place of the least squares estimates. If the optimal (or near-optimal) value of c has been selected, the new estimates will have reduced variances (which lead to narrower confidence intervals for the β's). Also, some of the other problems associated with multicollinearity (e.g., incorrect signs on the β's) should have been corrected.

In conclusion, we caution that you should not assume that ridge regression is a panacea for multicollinearity or poor data. Although there are probably ridge regression estimates that are better than the least squares estimates when multicollinearity is present, the choice of the biasing constant c is crucial. Unfortunately, much of the controversy in ridge regression centers on how to find the optimal value of c. In addition, the exact distributional properties of the ridge estimators are unknown when c is estimated from the data. For these reasons, some statisticians recommend that ridge regression be used only as an exploratory data analysis tool for identifying unstable regression coefficients, and not for estimating parameters and testing hypotheses in a linear regression model.

8.8 Robust Regression

Consider the problem of fitting the linear regression model

$$y = \beta_0 + \beta_1 x_1 + \beta_2 x_2 + \cdots + \beta_k x_k + \varepsilon$$

by the method of least squares when the errors ε are nonnormal. In practice, moderate departures from the assumption of normality tend to have minimal effect on the validity of the least squares results (see Section 7.4). However, when the distribution of ε is **heavy-tailed** (longer-tailed) compared to the normal distribution, the method of least squares may not be appropriate. For example, the heavy-tailed error distribution shown in Figure 8.15 will most likely produce outliers with strong influence on the regression analysis. Furthermore, since they tend to "pull" the least squares fit too much in their direction, these outliers will have smaller than expected residuals and, consequently, are more difficult to detect.

FIGURE 8.15

Probability distribution of ε: Normal versus heavy-tailed

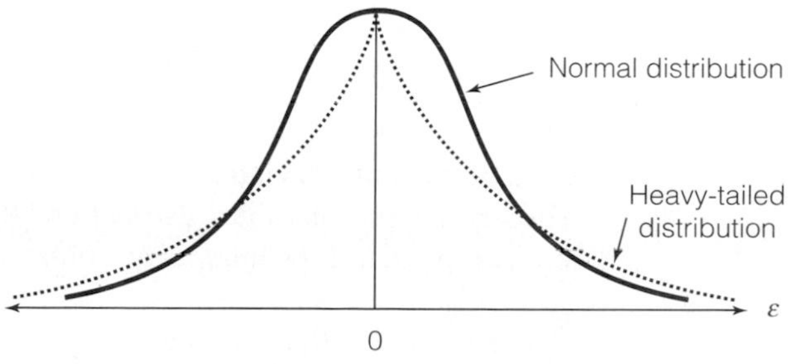

Robust regression procedures are available for errors that follow a nonnormal distribution. In the context of regression, the term *robust* describes a technique

that yields estimates for the β's that are nearly as good as the least squares estimates when the assumption of normality is satisfied, and significantly better for a heavy-tailed distribution. Robust regression is designed to dampen the effect of outlying observations that otherwise would exhibit strong influence on the analysis. This has the effect of leaving the residuals of influential observations large so that they may be more easily identified.

A number of different robust regression procedures exist. They fall into one of three general classes: **M estimators**, **R estimators**, and **L estimators**. Of the three, robust techniques that produce *M* estimates of the β coefficients receive the most attention in the literature.

The *M* estimates of the β coefficients are obtained by minimizing the quantity

$$\sum_{i=1}^{n} f(\hat{\varepsilon}_i)$$

where

$$\hat{\varepsilon}_i = y_i - (\hat{\beta}_0 + \hat{\beta}_1 x_{1i} + \hat{\beta}_2 x_{2i} + \cdots + \hat{\beta}_k x_{ki})$$

are the unobservable residuals and $f(\hat{\varepsilon}_i)$ is some function of the residuals. Note that since we are minimizing

$$\begin{aligned}\sum_{i=1}^{n} f(\hat{\varepsilon}_i) &= \sum_{i=1}^{n} \hat{\varepsilon}_i^2 \\ &= \sum_{i=1}^{n} [y_i - (\hat{\beta}_0 + \hat{\beta}_1 x_{1i} + \hat{\beta}_2 x_{2i} + \cdots + \hat{\beta}_k x_{ki})]^2 \\ &= \text{SSE}\end{aligned}$$

the function $f(\hat{\varepsilon}_i) = \hat{\varepsilon}_i^2$ yields the ordinary least squares estimates and, therefore, is appropriate when the errors are normal. For errors with heavier-tailed distributions, the analyst chooses some other function $f(\hat{\varepsilon}_i)$ that places less weight on the errors in the tails of the distribution. For example, the function $f(\hat{\varepsilon}_i) = |\hat{\varepsilon}_i|$ is appropriate when the errors follow the heavy-tailed distribution pictured in Figure 8.15. Since we are minimizing

$$\begin{aligned}\sum_{i=1}^{n} f(\hat{\varepsilon}_i) &= \sum_{i=1}^{n} |\hat{\varepsilon}_i| \\ &= \sum_{i=1}^{n} |y_i - (\hat{\beta}_0 + \hat{\beta}_1 x_{1i} + \hat{\beta}_2 x_{2i} + \cdots + \hat{\beta}_k x_{ki})|\end{aligned}$$

the *M* estimators of robust regression yield the estimates obtained from the **method of absolute deviations** (see Section 7.5).

The other types of robust estimation, *R* estimation and *L* estimation, take a different approach. *R* estimators are obtained by minimizing the quantity

$$\sum_{i=1}^{n} [y_i - (\hat{\beta}_0 + \hat{\beta}_1 x_{1i} + \hat{\beta}_2 x_{2i} + \cdots + \hat{\beta}_k x_{ki})]R_i$$

where R_i is the rank of the *i*th residual when the residuals are placed in ascending order. *L* estimation is similar to *R* estimation because it involves ordering of the data, but it uses measures of location (such as the sample median) to estimate the regression coefficients.

The numerical techniques for obtaining robust estimates (*M*, *R*, or *L* estimates) are quite complex and require sophisticated computer programs. At present, statistical software packages for robust regression are not widely available. However, the growing demand for packaged robust regression programs, especially *M* estimation procedures, leads us to believe that these programs will be available in the near future.

Much of the current research in the area of robust regression is focused on the distributional properties of the robust estimators of the β coefficients. At present, there is little information available on robust confidence intervals, prediction intervals, and hypothesis testing procedures. For this reason, some researchers recommend that robust regression be used in conjunction with and as a check on the method of least squares. If the results of the two procedures are substantially the same, use the least squares fit since confidence intervals and tests on the regression coefficients can be made. On the other hand, if the two analyses yield quite different results, use the robust fit to identify any influential observations. A careful examination of these data points may reveal the problem with the least squares fit.

8.9 Model Validation

Regression analysis is one of the most widely used statistical tools for estimation and prediction in the business world. All too frequently, however, a regression model deemed to be an adequate predictor of some response y performs poorly when applied in practice. For example, a model developed for forecasting new housing starts, although found to be statistically useful based on a test for overall model adequacy, may fail to take into account any extreme changes in future home mortgage rates generated by new government policy. This points out an important problem. **Models that fit the sample data well may not be successful predictors of y when applied to new data**. For this reason, it is important to assess the **validity** of the regression model in addition to its **adequacy** before using it in practice.

In the preceding chapters, we have presented several techniques for checking *model adequacy* (for example, tests of overall model adequacy, partial F tests, residual analysis, influence diagnostics). In short, checking model adequacy involves determining whether the regression model adequately fits the *sample data*. **Model validation**, however, involves an assessment of how the fitted regression model will perform in practice—that is, how successful it will be when applied to new or future data. A number of different model validation techniques have been proposed, several of which are briefly discussed in this section. You will need to consult the references for more details on how to apply these techniques.

1. *Examining the predicted values* Sometimes, the predicted values $\hat{y}$ of the fitted regression model can help to identify an invalid model. Nonsensical or unrea-

sonable predicted values may indicate that the form of the model is incorrect or that the β coefficients are poorly estimated. For example, a binary response model may yield predicted probabilities that are negative or greater than 1. In this case, the user may want to consider a model that produces predicted values between 0 and 1 (such as a logistic model) in practice. On the other hand, if the predicted values of the fitted model all seem reasonable, the user should refrain from using the model in practice until further checks of model validity are carried out.

2. *Examining the estimated model parameters* Typically, the user of a regression model has some knowledge of the relative size and sign (positive or negative) of the model parameters. This information should be used as a check on the estimated β coefficients. Coefficients with signs opposite to what is expected or with unusually small or large values, or unstable coefficients (i.e., coefficients with large standard errors) forewarn that the final model may perform poorly when applied to new or different data.

3. *Collecting new data for prediction* One of the most effective ways of validating a regression model is to use the model to predict y for a new sample. By directly comparing the predicted values to the observed values of the new data, we can determine the accuracy of the predictions and use this information to assess how well the model performs in practice.

   Several measures of model validity have been proposed for this purpose. One simple technique is to calculate the percentage of variability in the new data explained by the model, denoted $R^2_{\text{prediction}}$, and compare it to the coefficient of determination R^2 for the least squares fit. Let $y_1, y_2, \ldots, y_{n_1}$ represent the n_1 observations used to fit the final regression model and $y_{n_1+1}, y_{n_1+2}, \ldots, y_{n_1+n_2}$ represent the n_2 observations in the new data set. Then

$$R^2_{\text{prediction}} = 1 - \frac{\sum_{i=n_1+1}^{n_1+n_2} (y_i - \hat{y}_i)^2}{\sum_{i=n_1+1}^{n_1+n_2} (y_i - \bar{y})^2}$$

   where $\hat{y}_i$ is the predicted value for the ith observation using the β estimates from the fitted model and $\bar{y}$ is the sample mean of the original data.* If $R^2_{\text{prediction}}$ compares favorably to R^2 from the least squares fit, we will have increased confidence in the usefulness of the model. However, if a significant drop in R^2 is observed, we should be cautious about using the model for prediction in practice.

   A similar type of comparison can be made between the mean square error, MSE, for the least squares fit and the mean squared prediction error

$$\text{MSE}_{\text{prediction}} = \frac{\sum_{i=n_1+1}^{n_1+n_2} (y_i - \hat{y}_i)^2}{n_2 - (k + 1)}$$

*Alternatively, the sample mean of the new data may be used.

where k is the number of β coefficients (excluding β_0) in the model. Whichever measure of model validity you decide to use, the number of observations in the new data set should be large enough to reliably assess the model's prediction performance. Montgomery and Peck (1982), for example, recommend 15–20 new observations.

4. *Data-splitting (cross-validation)* For those applications where it is impossible or impractical to collect new data, the original sample data can be split into two parts, with one part used to estimate the model parameters and the other part used to assess the fitted model's predictive ability. **Data-splitting** (or **cross-validation**, as it is sometimes known) can be accomplished in a variety of ways. A common technique is to randomly assign half the observations to the estimation data set and the other half to the prediction data set.* Measures of model validity, such as $R^2_{\text{prediction}}$ or $\text{MSE}_{\text{prediction}}$ can then be calculated. Of course, a sufficient number of observations must be available for data-splitting to be effective. For the estimation and prediction data sets of equal size, it has been recommended that the entire sample consist of at least $n = 2k + 25$ observations, where k is the number of β parameters in the model [see Snee (1977)].

5. *Jackknifing* Recall (from Section 7.5) that the jackknife method is a *leave-one-observation-out-at-a-time* approach to finding influential observations in regression. Jackknifing can also be used for model validation in situations where the sample data set is too small to apply data-splitting.

   Recall that $y_{(i)}$ denotes the predicted value for the ith observation obtained when the regression model is fitted with the data point for y_i omitted (or deleted) from the sample. The jackknife method involves calculating the deleted residuals, $y_i - \hat{y}_{(i)}$, for all n observations in the data set. Measures of model validity, such as R^2 and MSE, are then calculated:

$$R^2_{\text{jackknife}} = \frac{\Sigma\,(y_i - \hat{y}_{(i)})^2}{\Sigma\,(y_i - \bar{y})^2}$$

$$\text{MSE}_{\text{jackknife}} = \frac{\Sigma\,(y_i - \hat{y}_{(i)})^2}{n - (k + 1)}$$

   Note that the numerator of both $R^2_{\text{jackknife}}$ and $\text{MSE}_{\text{jackknife}}$ is the PRESS statistic of Section 4.12. In general, PRESS will be larger than the SSE of the fitted model. Consequently, R^2_{jacknife} will be smaller than the R^2 of the fitted model and $\text{MSE}_{\text{jackknife}}$ will be larger than the MSE of the fitted model. These jackknife measures, then, give a more conservative (and more realistic) assessment of the ability of the model to predict future observations than the usual measures of model adequacy.

   The appropriate model validation technique(s) will vary from application to application. Keep in mind that a favorable result is still no guarantee that the model will always perform successfully in practice. However, we have

*Random splits are usually applied in cases where there is no logical basis for dividing the data. Consult the references for other, more formal, data-splitting techniques.

much greater confidence in a validated model than in one that simply fits the sample data well.

Summary

A number of special topics in regression have been introduced in this chapter. **Piecewise linear regression** can be employed when the theoretical relationship between the dependent variable y and a single independent variable x differs for different intervals over the range of x. **Inverse prediction** is a technique used for predicting a value of x for a given value of y. When the response y is **binary** (i.e., takes on only two values, 0 or 1), a **logistic regression model** may be more appropriate than a linear regression model.

Several methods are available for situations when the standard least squares assumptions about the random errors are violated. **Weighted least squares** is a variance-stabilizing technique that can also be used to limit the influence of outlying observations. When the distribution of the errors is nonnormal, **robust regression** yields estimates of the β's with certain optimal properties. **Ridge regression** was developed to stabilize the estimated β coefficients in the presence of multicollinearity.

Finally, it is often important to assess a model's predictive performance before releasing it for use in the real world. Several **model validation techniques** are available for this purpose.

References

Agresti, A. *Categorical Data Analysis*. New York: Wiley, 1990.

Andrews, D. F. "A robust method for multiple linear regression." *Technometrics*, Vol. 16, 1974, pp. 523–531.

Cox, D. R. *The Analysis of Binary Data*. London: Methuen, 1970.

Draper, N. R., and Van Nostrand, R. C. "Ridge regression and James–Stein estimation: Review and comments." *Technometrics*. Vol. 21, 1979, p. 451.

Geisser, S. "The predictive sample reuse method with applications." *Journal of the American Statistical Association*, Vol. 70, 1975, pp. 320–328.

Graybill, F. A. *Theory and Application of the Linear Model*. North Scituate, Mass.: Duxbury Press, 1976.

Halperin, M., Blackwelder, W. C., and Verter, J. I. "Estimation of the multivariate logistic risk function: A comparison of the discriminant function and maximum likelihood approaches." *Journal of Chronic Diseases*, Vol. 24, 1971, pp. 125–158.

Hauck, W. W., and Donner, A. "Wald's test as applied to hypotheses in logit analysis." *Journal of the American Statistical Association*, Vol. 72, 1977, pp. 851–853.

Hill, R. W., and Holland, P. W. "Two robust alternatives to least squares regression." *Journal of the American Statistical Association*, Vol. 72, 1977, pp. 828–833.

Hoerl, A. E., and Kennard, R. W. "Ridge regression: Biased estimation for nonorthogonal problems." *Technometrics*, Vol. 12, 1970, pp. 55–67.

Hoerl, A. E., Kennard, R. W., and Baldwin, K. F. "Ridge regression: Some simulations." *Communications in Statistics*, Vol. A5, 1976, pp. 77–88.

Hogg, R. V. "Statistical robustness: One view of its use in applications today." *The American Statistician*, Vol. 33, 1979, pp. 108–115.

Hosmer, D. W., and Lemeshow, S. *Applied Logistic Regression*. New York: Wiley, 1989.

Montgomery, D. C., and Peck, E. A. *Introduction to Linear Regression Analysis*. New York: Wiley, 1982.

Mosteller, F., and Tukey, J. W. *Data Analysis and Regression: A Second Course in Statistics*. Reading, Mass.: Addison-Wesley, 1977.

Neter, J., Wasserman, W., and Kutner, M. H. *Applied Linear Statistical Models*, 3rd ed. Homewood, Ill.: Richard D. Irwin, 1990.

Obenchain, R. L. "Classical *F*-tests and confidence intervals for ridge regression." *Technometrics*, Vol. 19, 1977, pp. 429–439.

Snee, R. D. "Validation of regression models: Methods and examples." *Technometrics*, Vol. 19, 1977, pp. 415–428.

Tsiatis, A. A. "A note on the goodness-of-fit test for the logistic regression model." *Biometrika*, Vol. 67, 1980, pp. 250–251.

Walker, S. H., and Duncan, D. B. "Estimation of the probability of an event as a function of several independent variables." *Biometrika*, Vol. 54, 1967, pp. 167–179.

CHAPTER 9 Time Series Modeling and Forecasting

CONTENTS

OBJECTIVE

To present models that allow for the correlation between observations taken sequentially over time; to show how these models can be used to forecast a future response

9.1 What Is a Time Series?

In many business and economic studies, the response variable y is measured sequentially in time. For example, we might record the number y of new housing starts for each month in a particular region. This collection of data is called a **time series**. Other examples of time series are data collected on the quarterly number of highway deaths in the United States, the annual sales for a corporation, and the recorded month-end values of the prime interest rate.

Definition 9.1

A **time series** is a collection of data obtained by observing a response variable at periodic points in time.

Definition 9.2

If repeated observations on a variable produce a time series, the variable is called a **time series variable**. We use y_t to denote the value of the variable at time t.

If you were to develop a model relating the number of new housing starts to the prime interest rate over time, the model would be called a **time series model**, because both the dependent variable, new housing starts, and the independent variable, prime interest rate, are measured sequentially over time. Furthermore, time itself would probably play an important role in such a model, because the economic trends and seasonal cycles associated with different points in time would almost certainly affect both time series.

The construction of time series models is an important aspect of business and economic analyses, because many of the variables of most interest to business and economic researchers are time series. This chapter is an introduction to the very complex and voluminous body of material concerned with time series modeling and forecasting future values of a time series.

9.2 Time Series Components

Researchers often approach the problem of describing the nature of a time series y_t by identifying four kinds of change, or variation, in the time series values. These four components are commonly known as (1) secular trend, (2) cyclical effect, (3) seasonal variation, and (4) residual effect. The components of a time series are most easily identified and explained pictorially.

Figure 9.1a (page 496) shows a **secular trend** in the time series values. The secular component describes the tendency of the value of the variable to increase or decrease over a long period of time. Thus, this type of change or variation is also known as the **long-term trend**. In Figure 9.1a, the long-term trend is of an increasing nature. However, this does not imply that the time series has always moved upward from month to month and from year to year. You can see that although the series fluctuates, the trend has been an increasing one over that period of time.

FIGURE 9.1 The components of a time series

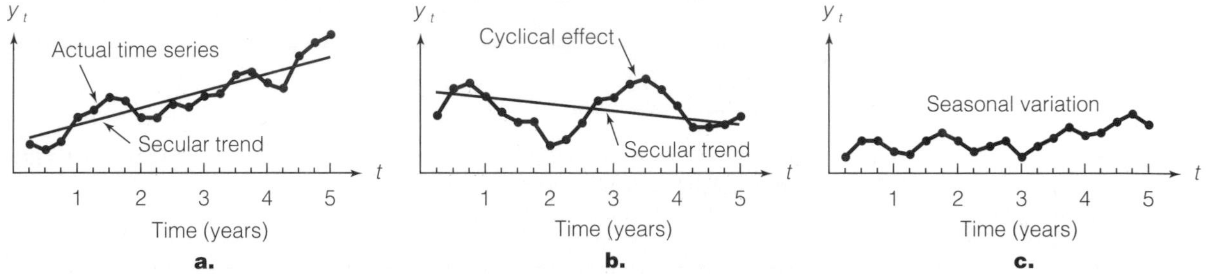

The **cyclical effect** in a time series, as shown in Figure 9.1b, generally describes the fluctuation about the secular trend that is attributable to business and economic conditions at the time. These fluctuations are sometimes called **business cycles**. During a period of general economic expansion, the business cycle lies above the secular trend, whereas during a recession, when business activity is likely to slump, the cycle lies below the secular trend. You can see that the cyclical variation does not follow any definite trend, but moves rather unpredictably.

The **seasonal variation** in a time series describes the fluctuations that recur during specific portions of each year (e.g., monthly or seasonally). In Figure 9.1c, you can see that the pattern of change in the time series within a year tends to be repeated from year to year, producing a wavelike or oscillating curve.

The final component, the **residual effect**, is what remains after the secular, cyclical, and seasonal components have been removed. This component is not systematic and may be attributed to unpredictable influences such as wars and political unrest, hurricanes and droughts, and the randomness of human actions. Thus, the residual effect represents the random error component of a time series.

Definition 9.3

The **secular trend** (T_t) of a time series is the tendency of the series to increase or decrease over a long period of time. It is also known as the **long-term trend**.

Definition 9.4

The **cyclical fluctuation** (C_t) of a time series is the wavelike or oscillating pattern about the secular trend that is attributable to business and economic conditions at the time. It is also known as a **business cycle**.

Definition 9.5

The **seasonal variation** (S_t) of a time series describes the fluctuations that recur during specific portions of the year (e.g., monthly or seasonally).

Definition 9.6

The **residual effect** (R_t) of a time series is what remains after the secular, cyclical, and seasonal components have been removed.

In many practical applications of time series, the objective is to *forecast* (predict) some *future value or values* of the series. To obtain forecasts, some type of model that can be projected into the future must be used to describe the time series. One of the most widely used models is the **additive model***

$$y_t = T_t + C_t + S_t + R_t$$

where T_t, C_t, S_t, and R_t represent the secular trend, cyclical effect, seasonal variation, and residual effect, respectively, of the time series variable y_t. Various methods exist for estimating the components of the model and forecasting the time series. These range from simple **descriptive techniques**, which rely on smoothing the pattern of the time series, to complex **inferential models**, which combine regression analysis with specialized time series models. Several descriptive forecasting techniques are presented in Section 9.3, and forecasting using the general linear regression model of Chapter 4 is discussed in Section 9.4. The remainder of the chapter is devoted to the more complex and more powerful time series models.

9.3 Forecasting Using Smoothing Techniques (Optional)

Various descriptive methods are available for identifying and characterizing a time series. Generally, these methods attempt to remove the rapid fluctuations in a time series so that the secular trend can be seen. For this reason, they are sometimes called **smoothing techniques**. Once the secular trend is identified, forecasts for future values of the time series are easily obtained. In this section, we present three of the more popular smoothing techniques.

Moving Average Method

A widely used smoothing technique is the **moving average method**. A moving average, M_t, at time t is formed by averaging the time series values over adjacent time periods. Moving averages aid in identifying the secular trend of a time series

*Another useful model is the **multiplicative model** $y_t = T_tC_tS_tR_t$. Recall (Section 4.9) that this model can be written in the form of an additive model by taking natural logarithms:

$$\ln y_t = \ln T_t + \ln C_t + \ln S_t + \ln R_t$$

because the averaging modifies the effect of short-term (cyclical or seasonal) variation. That is, a plot of the moving averages yields a "smooth" time series curve that clearly depicts the long-term trend.

For example, consider the 1991–1994 quarterly power loads for a utility company located in a southern part of the United States, given in Table 9.1.

TABLE 9.1 **Quarterly Power Loads, 1991–1994**

YEAR	QUARTER	TIME t	POWER LOAD y_t, megawatts
1991	I	1	103.5
	II	2	94.7
	III	3	118.6
	IV	4	109.3
1992	I	5	126.1
	II	6	116.0
	III	7	141.2
	IV	8	131.6
1993	I	9	144.5
	II	10	137.1
	III	11	159.0
	IV	12	149.5
1994	I	13	166.1
	II	14	152.5
	III	15	178.2
	IV	16	169.0

A graph of the quarterly time series, Figure 9.2, shows the pronounced seasonal variation, i.e., the fluctuation that recurs from year to year. The quarterly power loads are highest in the summer months (quarter III) with another smaller peak in the winter months (quarter I), and lowest during the spring and fall (quarters II and IV). To clearly identify the long-term trend of the series, we need to average, or "smooth out," these seasonal fluctuations. We will apply the moving average method for this purpose.

The first step in calculating a moving average for quarterly data is to sum the observed time values y_t—in this example, quarterly power loads—for the four quarters during the initial year 1991. Summing the values from Table 9.1, we have

$$\begin{aligned} y_1 + y_2 + y_3 + y_4 &= 103.5 + 94.7 + 118.6 + 109.3 \\ &= 426.1 \end{aligned}$$

This sum is called a **4-point moving total**, which we denote by the symbol L_t. It is customary to use a subscript t to represent the time period at the midpoint of the four quarters in the total. Since for this sum, the midpoint is between $t = 2$ and $t = 3$, we will use the conventional procedure of "dropping it down one line" to $t = 3$. Thus, our first 4-point moving total is $L_3 = 426.1$.

FIGURE 9.2
Graph of quarterly power loads, Table 9.1

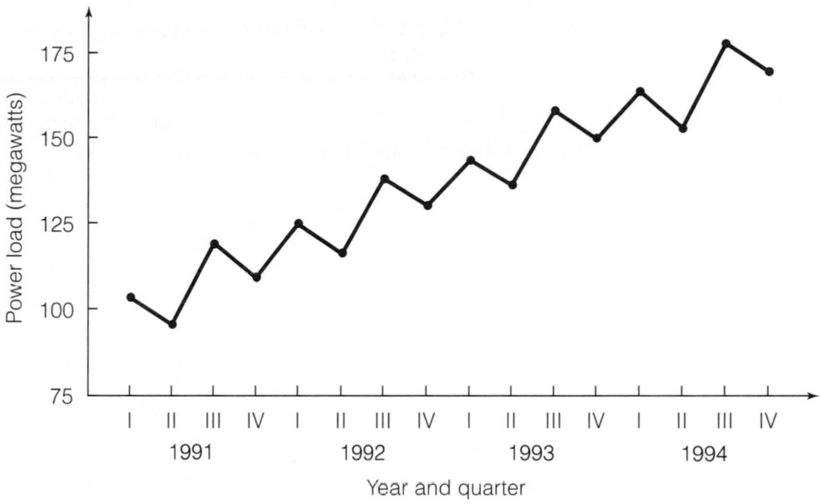

We find the next moving total by eliminating the first quantity in the sum, $y_1 = 103.5$, and adding the next value in the time series sequence, $y_5 = 126.1$. This enables us to keep four quarters in the total of adjacent time periods. Thus, we have

$$L_4 = y_2 + y_3 + y_4 + y_5 = 94.7 + 118.6 + 109.3 + 126.1 = 448.7$$

Continuing this process of "moving" the 4-point total over the time series until we have included the last value, we find

$$\begin{aligned}
L_5 &= y_3 + y_4 + y_5 + y_6 &&= 118.6 + 109.3 + 126.1 + 116.0 = 470.0\\
L_6 &= y_4 + y_5 + y_6 + y_7 &&= 109.3 + 126.1 + 116.0 + 141.2 = 492.6\\
&\vdots &&\vdots \qquad\qquad\qquad\qquad\qquad\qquad \vdots \quad \vdots\\
L_{15} &= y_{13} + y_{14} + y_{15} + y_{16} &&= 166.1 + 152.5 + 178.2 + 169.0 = 665.8
\end{aligned}$$

The complete set of 4-point moving totals is given in the appropriate column of Table 9.2 on page 500. Notice that three data points will be "lost" in forming the moving totals.

After the 4-point moving totals are calculated, the second step is to determine the **4-point moving average**, denoted by M_t, by dividing each of the moving totals by 4. For example, the first three values of the 4-point moving average for the quarterly power load data are

$$M_3 = \frac{y_1 + y_2 + y_3 + y_4}{4} = \frac{L_3}{4} = \frac{426.1}{4} = 106.5$$

$$M_4 = \frac{y_2 + y_3 + y_4 + y_5}{4} = \frac{L_4}{4} = \frac{448.7}{4} = 112.2$$

$$M_5 = \frac{y_3 + y_4 + y_5 + y_6}{4} = \frac{L_5}{4} = \frac{470.0}{4} = 117.5$$

TABLE 9.2 **4-Point Moving Average for the Quarterly Power Load Data**

YEAR	QUARTER	TIME t	POWER LOAD y_t	4-POINT MOVING TOTAL L_t	4-POINT MOVING AVERAGE M_t	RATIO y_t/M_t
1991	I	1	103.5	—	—	—
	II	2	94.7	—	—	—
	III	3	118.6	426.1	106.5	1.113
	IV	4	109.3	448.7	112.2	.974
1992	I	5	126.1	470.0	117.5	1.073
	II	6	116.0	492.6	123.2	.942
	III	7	141.2	514.9	128.7	1.097
	IV	8	131.6	533.3	133.3	.987
1993	I	9	144.5	554.4	138.6	1.043
	II	10	137.1	572.2	143.1	.958
	III	11	159.0	590.1	147.5	1.078
	IV	12	149.5	611.7	152.9	.978
1994	I	13	166.1	627.1	156.8	1.059
	II	14	152.5	646.3	161.6	.944
	III	15	178.2	665.8	166.5	1.071
	IV	16	169.0	—	—	—

All of the 4-point moving averages are given in the appropriate column of Table 9.2.

Both the original power load time series and the 4-point moving average are graphed in Figure 9.3. Notice that the moving average has smoothed the time series; i.e., the averaging has modified the effects of the short-term or seasonal variation. The plot of the 4-point moving average clearly depicts the secular (long-term) trend component of the time series.

FIGURE 9.3 Quarterly power loads and 4-point moving average

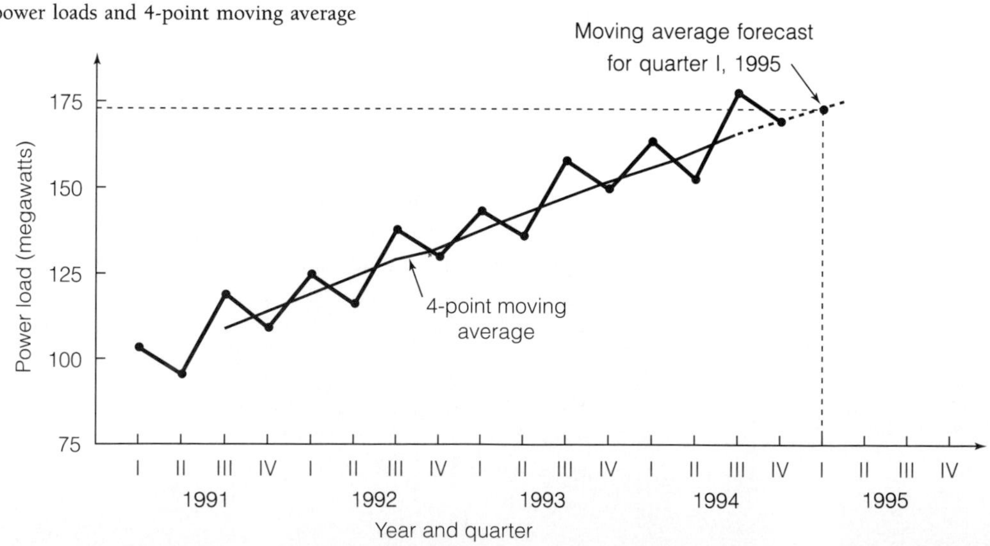

In addition to identifying a long-term trend, moving averages provide us with a measure of the seasonal effects in a time series. The ratio between the observed power load y_t and the 4-point moving average M_t for each quarter measures the seasonal effect (primarily attributable to temperature differences) for that quarter. The ratios y_t/M_t are shown in the last column of Table 9.2. Note that the ratio is always greater than 1 in quarters I and III, and always less than 1 in quarters II and IV. The average of the ratios for a particular quarter, multiplied by 100, can be used to form a **seasonal index** for that quarter. For example, the seasonal index for quarter I is

$$100\left(\frac{1.073 + 1.043 + 1.059}{3}\right) = 105.8$$

implying that the time series value in quarter I is, on the average, 105.8% of the moving average value for that time period.

To forecast a future value of the time series, simply extend the moving average M_t on the graph to the future time period. For example, a graphical extension of the moving average for the quarterly power loads to quarter I of 1995 (t = 17) yields a moving average of approximately $M_{17} = 172$ (see Figure 9.3). Thus, if there were no seasonal variation in the time series, we would expect the power load for quarter I of 1995 to be approximately 172 megawatts. To adjust the forecast for seasonal variation, multiply the future moving average value M_{17} = 172 by the seasonal index for quarter I, then divide by 100:

$$\begin{aligned} F_{17} &= M_{17}\left(\frac{\text{Seasonal index for quarter I}}{100}\right) \\ &= 172\left(\frac{105.8}{100}\right) \\ &\approx 182 \end{aligned}$$

where F_{17} is the forecast of y_{17}. Therefore, the moving average forecast for the power load in quarter I of 1995 is approximately 182 megawatts.

Moving averages are not restricted to 4 points. For example, you may wish to calculate a 7-point moving average for daily data, a 12-point moving average for monthly data, or a 5-point moving average for yearly data. Although the choice of the number of points is arbitrary, you should search for the number N that yields a smooth series, but is not so large that many points at the end of the series are "lost." The method of forecasting with a general N-point moving average is outlined in the box on page 502.

Exponential Smoothing

One problem with using a moving average to forecast future values of a time series is that values at the ends of the series are lost, thereby requiring that we subjectively extend the graph of the moving average into the future. No exact calculation of a forecast is available since the moving average at a future time period t requires that we know one or more future values of the series. **Expo-**

Forecasting Using an N-Point Moving Average

1. Select N, the number of consecutive time series values $y_1, y_2, \ldots, y_n$ that will be averaged. (The time series values must be equally spaced.)
2. Calculate the N-point moving total, L_t, by summing the time series values over N adjacent time periods, where

$$L_t = \begin{cases} y_{t-(N-1)/2} + \cdots + y_t + \cdots + y_{t+(N-1)/2} & \text{if } N \text{ is odd} \\ y_{t-N/2} + \cdots + y_t + \cdots + y_{t+N/2-1} & \text{if } N \text{ is even} \end{cases}$$

3. Compute the N-point moving average, M_t, by dividing the corresponding moving total by N:

$$M_t = \frac{L_t}{N}$$

4. Graph the moving average M_t on the vertical axis with time t on the horizontal axis. (This plot should reveal a smooth curve that identifies the long-term trend of the time series.*) Extend the graph to a future time period to obtain the forecasted value of M_t.
5. For a future time period t, the forecast of y_t is

$$F_t = \begin{cases} M_t & \text{if little or no seasonal variation exists in the time series} \\ M_t\left(\dfrac{\text{Seasonal index}}{100}\right) & \text{otherwise} \end{cases}$$

where the seasonal index for a particular quarter (or month) is the average of past values of the ratios

$$\frac{Y_t}{M_t}(100)$$

for that quarter (or month).

nential smoothing is a technique that leads to forecasts that can be explicitly calculated. Like the moving average method, exponential smoothing deemphasizes (or smooths) most of the residual effects. However, exponential smoothing averages only past and current values of the time series.

To obtain an exponentially smoothed time series, we first need to choose a weight w, between 0 and 1, called the **exponential smoothing constant**. The exponentially smoothed series, denoted E_t, is then calculated as follows:

*When the number N of points is small, the plot may not yield a very smooth curve. However, the moving average will be smoother (or less variable) than the plot of the original time series values.

$$E_1 = y_1$$
$$E_2 = wy_2 + (1 - w)E_1$$
$$E_3 = wy_3 + (1 - w)E_2$$
$$\vdots \quad \vdots$$
$$E_t = wy_t + (1 - w)E_{t-1}$$

You can see that the exponentially smoothed value at time t is simply a weighted average of the current time series value, y_t, and the exponentially smoothed value at the previous time period, E_{t-1}. Smaller values of w give less weight to the current value, y_t, whereas larger values give more weight to y_t.

For example, suppose we want to smooth the quarterly power loads given in Table 9.1 using an exponential smoothing constant of $w = .7$. Then we have

$$E_1 = y_1 = 103.5$$
$$E_2 = .7y_2 + (1 - .7)E_1$$
$$= .7(94.7) + .3(103.5) = 97.3$$
$$E_3 = .7y_3 + (1 - .7)E_2$$
$$= .7(118.6) + .3(97.3) = 112.2$$
$$\vdots$$

The exponentially smoothed values (using $w = .7$) for all the quarterly power loads are given in Table 9.3. Both the actual and the smoothed time series values are graphed in Figure 9.4 on page 504.

Exponential smoothing forecasts are obtained by taking a weighted average of the most recent value of the time series, y_t, and the most recent exponentially smoothed value, E_t. If n is the last time period in which y_t is observed, then the forecast for a future time period t is given by

$$F_t = wy_n + (1 - w)E_n \quad \text{(see the box on page 505)}$$

TABLE 9.3 **Quarterly Power Load with Exponential Smoothing**

YEAR	QUARTER	TIME t	POWER LOAD y_t	EXPONENTIALLY SMOOTHED POWER LOAD E_t
1991	I	1	103.5	103.5
	II	2	94.7	97.3
	III	3	118.6	112.2
	IV	4	109.3	110.2
1992	I	5	126.1	121.3
	II	6	116.0	117.6
	III	7	141.2	134.1
	IV	8	131.6	132.4

(continued)

TABLE 9.3 *(continued)*

YEAR	QUARTER	TIME t	POWER LOAD y_t	EXPONENTIALLY SMOOTHED POWER LOAD E_t
1993	I	9	144.5	140.9
	II	10	137.1	138.2
	III	11	159.0	152.8
	IV	12	149.5	150.5
1994	I	13	166.1	161.4
	II	14	152.5	155.2
	III	15	178.2	171.3
	IV	16	169.0	169.7

FIGURE 9.4
Plot of exponentially smoothed power loads

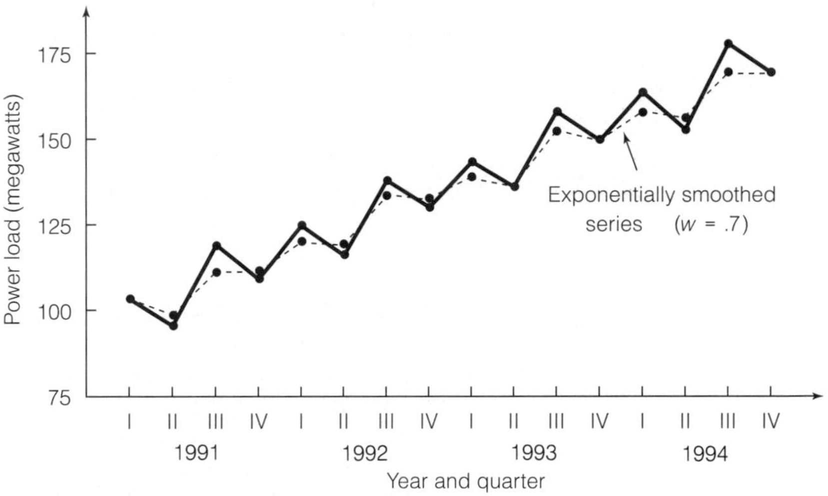

The right-hand side of the forecast equation does not depend on t; hence, F_t is used to forecast *all* future values of y_t. For example, the forecast for the power load in quarter I of 1995 ($t = 17$) is calculated as follows:

$$\begin{aligned} F_{17} &= wy_{16} + (1 - w)E_{16} \\ &= .7(169.0) + .3(169.7) \\ &= 169.2 \end{aligned}$$

The forecasts for quarter II of 1995 ($t = 18$), quarter III of 1995 ($t = 19$), and all other future time periods will be the same:

$$\begin{aligned} F_{18} &= 169.2 \\ F_{19} &= 169.2 \\ F_{20} &= 169.2 \\ &\vdots \end{aligned}$$

This points out one disadvantage of the exponential smoothing forecasting technique. Since the exponentially smoothed forecast is constant for all future values, any changes in trend and/or seasonality are not taken into account. Therefore, exponentially smoothed forecasts are appropriate only when the trend and seasonal components of the time series are relatively insignificant.

Forecasting Using Exponential Smoothing

1. The data consist of n equally spaced time series values, $y_1, y_2, \ldots, y_n$.
2. Select a smoothing constant, w, between 0 and 1. (Smaller values of w give less weight to the current value of the series and yield a smoother series. Larger values of w give more weight to the current value of the series and yield a more variable series.)
3. Calculate the exponentially smoothed series, E_t, as follows:

$$E_1 = y_1$$
$$E_2 = wy_2 + (1 - w)E_1$$
$$E_3 = wy_3 + (1 - w)E_2$$
$$\vdots$$
$$E_n = wy_n + (1 - w)E_{n-1}$$

4. Calculate the forecast for any future time period t as follows:

$$F_t = wy_n + (1 - w)E_n, \quad t = n + 1, n + 2, \ldots$$

Holt–Winters Forecasting Model

One drawback to the exponential smoothing forecasting method is that the secular trend and seasonal components of a time series are not taken into account. The **Holt–Winters forecasting model** is an extension of the exponential smoothing method that explicitly recognizes the trend and seasonal variation in a time series.

Consider a time series with a trend component, but little or no seasonal variation. Then the Holt–Winters model for y_t is

$$E_t = wy_t + (1 - w)(E_{t-1} + T_{t-1})$$
$$T_t = v(E_t - E_{t-1}) + (1 - v)T_{t-1}$$

where E_t is the exponentially smoothed series, T_t is the trend component, and w and v are smoothing constants between 0 and 1. Note that the trend component T_t is a weighted average of the most recent change in the smoothed value (measured by the difference $E_t - E_{t-1}$) and the trend estimate of the previous time period (T_{t-1}). When seasonal variation is present in the time series, the Holt–Winters model takes the form

$$E_t = w(y_t/S_{t-P}) + (1 - w)(E_{t-1} + T_{t-1})$$
$$T_t = v(E_t - E_{t-1}) + (1 - v)T_{t-1}$$
$$S_t = u(y_t/E_t) + (1 - u)S_{t-P}$$

where S_t is the seasonal component, u is a constant between 0 and 1, and P is the number of time periods in a cycle (usually a year). The seasonal component S_t is a weighted average of the ratio y_t/E_t (i.e., the ratio of the actual time series value to the smoothed value) and the seasonal component for the previous cycle. For example, for the quarterly power loads, $P = 4$ (four quarters in a year) and the seasonal component for, say, quarter III of 1992 ($t = 7$) is a weighted average of the ratio y_7/E_7 and the seasonal component for quarter III of 1991 ($t = 3$). That is,

$$S_7 = u(y_7/E_7) + (1 - u)S_3$$

Forecasts for future time periods, $t = n + 1, n + 2, \ldots$, using the Holt–Winters models are obtained by summing the most recent exponentially smoothed component with an estimate of the expected increase (or decrease) attributable to trend. For seasonal models, the forecast is multiplied by the most recent estimate of the seasonal component (similar to the moving average method).

The Holt–Winters forecasting methodology is summarized in the accompanying box.

EXAMPLE 9.1

Refer to the 1991–1994 quarterly power loads listed in Table 9.1. Use the Holt–Winters forecasting model with both trend and seasonal components to forecast the utility company's quarterly power loads in 1995. Use the smoothing constants $w = .7$, $v = .5$, and $u = .5$.

Solution

First note that $P = 4$ for the quarterly time series. Following the formulas for E_t, T_t, and S_t given in the box, we calculate

$$E_2 = y_2 = 94.7$$
$$T_2 = y_2 - y_1 = 94.7 - 103.5 = -8.8$$
$$S_2 = y_2/E_2 = 94.7/94.7 = 1$$
$$E_3 = .7y_3 + (1 - .7)(E_2 + T_2)$$
$$= .7(118.6) + .3(94.7 - 8.8) = 108.8$$
$$T_3 = .5(E_3 - E_2) + (1 - .5)T_2$$
$$= .5(108.8 - 94.7) + .5(-8.8) = 2.6$$
$$S_3 = y_3/E_3 = 118.6/108.8 = 1.090$$
$$E_4 = .7y_4 + (1 - .7)(E_3 + T_3)$$
$$= .7(109.3) + .3(108.8 + 2.6) = 109.9$$
$$T_4 = .5(E_4 - E_3) + (1 - .5)T_3$$
$$= .5(109.9 - 108.8) + .5(2.6) = 1.9$$
$$S_4 = y_4/E_4 = 109.3/109.9 = .994$$
$$\vdots$$

Forecasting Using the Holt–Winters Model

TREND COMPONENT ONLY

1. The data consist of n equally spaced time series values, $y_1, y_2, \ldots, y_n$.
2. Select smoothing constants w and v, where $0 \leq w \leq 1$ and $0 \leq v \leq 1$.
3. Calculate the exponentially smoothed component, E_t, and the trend component, T_t, for $t = 2, 3, \ldots, n$ as follows:

$$E_t = \begin{cases} y_2, & t = 2 \\ wy_t + (1 - w)(E_{t-1} + T_{t-1}), & t > 2 \end{cases}$$

$$T_t = \begin{cases} y_2 - y_1, & t = 2 \\ v(E_t - E_{t-1}) + (1 - v)T_{t-1}, & t > 2 \end{cases}$$

[*Note:* E_1 and T_1 are not defined.]

4. The forecast for a future time period t is given by

$$F_t = \begin{cases} E_n + T_n, & t = n + 1 \\ E_n + 2T_n, & t = n + 2 \\ \vdots & \\ E_n + kT_n, & t = n + k \end{cases}$$

TREND AND SEASONAL COMPONENTS

1. The data consist of n equally spaced time series values, $y_1, y_2, \ldots, y_n$.
2. Select smoothing constants w, v, and u, where $0 \leq w \leq 1$, $0 \leq v \leq 1$, and $0 \leq u \leq 1$.
3. Determine P, the number of time periods in a cycle. Usually, $P = 4$ for quarterly data and $P = 12$ for monthly data.
4. Calculate the exponentially smoothed component, E_t, the trend component, T_t, and the seasonal component, S_t, for $t = 2, 3, \ldots, n$ as follows:

$$E_t = \begin{cases} y_2, & t = 2 \\ wy_t + (1 - w)(E_{t-1} + T_{t-1}), & t = 3, 4, \ldots, P + 2 \\ w(y_t/S_{t-P}) + (1 - w)(E_{t-1} + T_{t-1}), & t > P + 2 \end{cases}$$

$$T_t = \begin{cases} y_2 - y_1, & t = 2 \\ v(E_t - E_{t-1}) + (1 - v)T_{t-1}, & t > 2 \end{cases}$$

$$S_t = \begin{cases} y_t/E_t, & t = 2, 3, \ldots, P + 2 \\ u(y_t/E_t) + (1 - u)S_{t-P}, & t > P + 2 \end{cases}$$

[*Note:* E_1, T_1, and S_1 are not defined.]

5. The forecast for a future time period t is given by

$$F_t = \begin{cases} (E_n + T_n)S_{n+1-P}, & t = n + 1 \\ (E_n + 2T_n)S_{n+2-P}, & t = n + 2 \\ \vdots & \\ (E_n + kT_n)S_{n+k-P}, & t = n + k \end{cases}$$

The forecast for quarter I of 1995 (i.e., y_{17}) is given by

$$\begin{aligned} F_{17} &= (E_{16} + T_{16})S_{17-4} \\ &= (E_{16} + T_{16})S_{13} = (168.7 + 4.7)(1.044) \\ &= 181.0 \end{aligned}$$

(Remember that beginning with $t = P + 3 = 7$, the formulas for E_t and S_t, shown in the box, are slightly different.) All the values of E_t, T_t, and S_t are given in Table 9.4.

TABLE 9.4 **Holt–Winters Components for Quarterly Power Load Data**

YEAR	QUARTER	TIME t	POWER LOAD y_t	E_t ($w = .7$)	T_t ($v = .5$)	S_t ($u = .5$)
1991	I	1	103.5	—	—	—
	II	2	94.7	94.7	−8.8	1.000
	III	3	118.6	108.8	2.6	1.090
	IV	4	109.3	109.9	1.9	.994
1992	I	5	126.1	121.8	6.9	1.035
	II	6	116.0	119.8	2.5	.968
	III	7	141.2	127.4	5.1	1.100
	IV	8	131.6	132.3	5.0	.995
1993	I	9	144.5	138.9	5.8	1.038
	II	10	137.1	142.6	4.8	.965
	III	11	159.0	145.4	3.8	1.097
	IV	12	149.5	149.9	4.2	.996
1994	I	13	166.1	158.2	6.3	1.044
	II	14	152.5	160.0	4.1	.959
	III	15	178.2	162.9	3.5	1.095
	IV	16	169.0	168.7	4.7	.999

Similarly, the forecasts for y_{18}, y_{19}, and y_{20} (quarters II, III, and IV, respectively) are

$$\begin{aligned} F_{18} &= (E_{16} + 2T_{16})S_{18-4} \\ &= (E_{16} + 2T_{16})S_{14} = [168.7 + 2(4.7)](.959) \\ &= 170.8 \end{aligned}$$

$$\begin{aligned} F_{19} &= (E_{16} + 3T_{16})S_{19-4} \\ &= (E_{16} + 3T_{16})S_{15} = [168.7 + 3(4.7)](1.095) \\ &= 200.2 \end{aligned}$$

$$\begin{aligned} F_{20} &= (E_{16} + 4T_{16})S_{20-4} \\ &= (E_{16} + 4T_{16})S_{16} = [168.7 + 4(4.7)](.999) \\ &= 187.3 \end{aligned}$$

With any of these forecasting methods, forecast errors can be computed once the future values of the time series have been observed. Forecast error is defined as the difference between the predicted and actual future value at time t, $F_i - y_r$. Aggregating the forecast errors into a summary statistic is useful for assessing the overall accuracy of the forecasting method. Formulas for two popular measures of forecast accuracy, the **mean absolute deviation** (**MAD**) and **root mean squared error** (**RMSE**), are given in the accompanying box.

Measures of Overall Forecast Accuracy for m Forecasts

Mean absolute deviation: $$\text{MAD} = \frac{\sum_{t=1}^{m} |F_t - y_t|}{m}$$

Root mean square error: $$\text{RMSE} = \sqrt{\frac{\sum_{t=1}^{m} (F_t - y_t)^2}{m}}$$

EXAMPLE 9.2

Refer to the quarterly power load data, Table 9.1. The exponential smoothing and Holt–Winters forecasts for the four quarters of 1995 are listed in Table 9.5, as are the actual quarterly power loads (not previously given) for the year. Compute MAD and RMSE for each of the two forecasting methods. Which method yields more accurate forecasts?

Solution

The first step is to calculate the forecast errors, $F_t - y_t$, for each method. For example, for the exponential smoothing forecast of quarter I ($t = 17$), $y_{17} = 181.5$ and $F_{17} = 169.2$. Thus, the forecast error is $F_{17} - y_{17} = 169.2 - 181.5 = -12.3$. The forecast errors for the remaining exponential smoothing forecasts and the Holt–Winters forecasts are also shown in Table 9.5.

TABLE 9.5 **Forecasts and Actual Quarterly Power Loads for 1995**

QUARTER	TIME t	ACTUAL POWER LOAD y_t	EXPONENTIAL SMOOTHING Forecast F_t	EXPONENTIAL SMOOTHING Error $(F_t - y_t)$	HOLT–WINTERS Forecast F_t	HOLT–WINTERS Error $(F_t - y_t)$
I	17	181.5	169.2	−12.3	181.0	−.5
II	18	175.2	169.2	−6.0	170.8	−4.4
III	19	195.0	169.2	−25.8	200.2	5.2
IV	20	189.3	169.2	−20.1	187.3	−2.0

The MAD and RMSE calculations for each method are as follows:

Exponential smoothing:

$$\text{MAD} = \frac{|-12.3| + |-6.0| + |-25.8| + |-20.1|}{4} = 16.05$$

$$\text{RMSE} = \sqrt{\frac{(-12.3)^2 + (-6.0)^2 + (-25.8)^2 + (-20.1)^2}{4}} = 17.73$$

Holt–Winters:

$$\text{MAD} = \frac{|-.5| + |-4.4| + |-5.2| + |-2.0|}{4} = 3.03$$

$$\text{RMSE} = \sqrt{\frac{(-.5)^2 + (-4.4)^2 + (-5.2)^2 + (-2.0)^2}{4}} = 3.56$$

The Holt–Winters values of MAD and RMSE are about one-fifth of the corresponding exponential smoothed values. Overall, the Holt–Winters method clearly leads to more accurate forecasts than exponential smoothing. This, of course, is expected since the Holt–Winters method accounts for both long-term and seasonal variation in the power loads, whereas exponentially smoothing does not.

We conclude this section with a comment. A major disadvantage of forecasting with smoothing techniques (the moving average method, exponential smoothing, or the Holt–Winters models) is that no measure of the forecast error (or reliability) is known *prior to* observing the future value. Although forecast errors can be calculated *after* the future values of the time series have been observed (as in Example 9.2), we prefer to have some measure of the accuracy of the forecast *before* the actual values are observed. For this reason, smoothing techniques are generally regarded as descriptive rather than as inferential procedures. On the other hand, forecasts with inferential models (such as regression models) are accompanied by measures of the *standard error of the forecast*, which allow us to construct prediction intervals for the future time series value. We discuss inferential time series forecasting models in the remaining sections of this chapter.

EXERCISES

9.1 The quarterly numbers of housing starts (in thousands of dwellings) in the United States from 1989 through 1993 are recorded in the accompanying table.

YEAR	QUARTER	HOUSING STARTS	YEAR	QUARTER	HOUSING STARTS
1989	I	290.6	1992	I	262.0
	II	390.9		II	340.6
	III	346.2		III	322.1
	IV	303.6		IV	276.7
1990	I	300.8	1993	I	240.6
	II	320.8		II	367.2
	III	307.1		III	355.6
	IV	233.0		IV	322.0
1991	I	185.4			
	II	300.8			
	III	284.8			
	IV	152.0			

Source: *Standard & Poor's Statistical Service: Current Statistics*, Jan. 1995, New York, Standard & Poor's Corporation.

a. Plot the quarterly time series. Can you detect a long-term trend? Can you detect any seasonal variation?

b. Calculate the 4-point moving average for the quarterly housing starts.

c. Graph the 4-point moving average on the same set of axes you used for the graph in part **a**. Is the long-term trend more evident? What effects has the moving average method removed or smoothed?
d. Calculate the seasonal index for the number of housing starts in quarter I.
e. Calculate the seasonal index for the number of housing starts in quarter II.
f. Use the moving average method to forecast the number of housing starts in quarters I and II of 1994.

9.2 Refer to the quarterly housing starts data in Exercise 9.1.
a. Calculate the exponentially smoothed series for housing starts using a smoothing constant of $w = .2$.
b. Use the exponentially smoothed series from part **a** to forecast the number of housing starts in the first two quarters of 1994.
c. Use the Holt–Winters forecasting model with both trend and seasonal components to forecast the number of housing starts in the first two quarters of 1994. Use smoothing constants $w = .2$, $v = .5$, and $u = .7$.

9.3 Refer to Exercises 9.1 and 9.2. Suppose the actual numbers of housing starts (in thousands) for quarters I and II of 1994 are 293.9 and 421.6, respectively.
a. Compare the accuracy of the moving average, exponential smoothing, and Holt–Winters forecasts using MAD.
b. Repeat part **a** using RMSE.
c. Comment on which forecasting method is more accurate.

9.4 The data in the accompanying table are the amounts of crude oil (millions of barrels) imported into the United States from the Organization of Petroleum Exporting Countries (OPEC) for the years 1974–1993.

YEAR	t	IMPORTS, y_t	YEAR	t	IMPORTS, y_t
1974	1	926	1984	11	553
1975	2	1,171	1985	12	479
1976	3	1,663	1986	13	771
1977	4	2,058	1987	14	876
1978	5	1,892	1988	15	987
1979	6	1,866	1989	16	1,232
1980	7	1,414	1990	17	1,282
1981	8	1,067	1991	18	1,233
1982	9	633	1992	19	1,247
1983	10	540	1993	20	1,339

Source: *Statistical Abstracts of the United States*, U.S. Bureau of the Census, 1994.

a. Plot the yearly time series. Can you detect a long-term trend?
b. Calculate and plot a 3-point moving average for annual OPEC oil imports.
c. Calculate and plot the exponentially smoothed series for annual OPEC oil imports using a smoothing constant of $w = .3$.
d. Forecast OPEC oil imports in 1994 using the moving average method.
e. Forecast OPEC oil imports in 1994 using exponential smoothing with $w = .3$.

f. Forecast OPEC oil imports in 1994 using the Holt–Winters forecasting model with trend. Use smoothing constants $w = .3$ and $v = .8$.

g. Actual OPEC crude oil imports in 1994 totaled 1,400 million barrels. Calculate the errors of the forecast, parts **d–f**. Which method yields the most accurate short-term forecast?

9.5 The Consumer Price Index (CPI) measures the increase (or decrease) in the prices of goods and services relative to a base year. The CPI for the years 1980–1993 (using 1967 as a base period) is shown in the table.

YEAR	CPI	YEAR	CPI
1980	246.8	1987	340.1
1981	272.4	1988	354.2
1982	289.1	1989	371.3
1983	298.4	1990	391.3
1984	311.1	1991	401.6
1985	322.2	1992	413.2
1986	328.4	1993	425.6

Source: *Survey of Current Business*, U.S. Department of Commerce, Bureau of Economic Analysis.

a. Graph the time series. Do you detect a long-term trend?

b. Calculate and plot a 5-point moving average for the CPI. Use the moving average to forecast the CPI in 1995.

c. Calculate and plot the exponentially smoothed series for the CPI using a smoothing constant of $w = .4$. Use the exponentially smoothed values to forecast the CPI in 1995.

d. Use the Holt–Winters forecasting model with trend to forecast the CPI in 1995. Use smoothing constants $w = .4$ and $v = .5$.

9.6 Standard & Poor's 500 Composite Stock Index (S&P 500) is a stock market index. Like the Dow Jones Industrial Average, it is an indicator of stock market activity. The accompanying table contains end-of-quarter values of the S&P 500 for the years 1985–1992.

YEAR	QUARTER	S&P 500	YEAR	QUARTER	S&P 500
1985	I	180.6	1989	I	294.8
	II	191.8		II	317.9
	III	182.0		III	349.1
	IV	211.2		IV	353.4
1986	I	232.3	1990	I	339.9
	II	245.3		II	358.0
	III	238.2		III	306.0
	IV	248.6		IV	330.2
1987	I	291.7	1991	I	372.2
	II	304.0		II	378.3
	III	321.8		III	387.2
	IV	247.0		IV	388.5
1988	I	258.8	1992	I	407.4
	II	273.5		II	408.3
	III	271.9		III	418.5
	IV	277.7		IV	435.6

Source: *Standard & Poor's Statistical Service: Current Statistics*, Jan. 1993, New York, Standard & Poor's Corporation.

a. Calculate a 4-point moving average for the quarterly S & P 500.
b. Plot the quarterly index and the 4-point moving average on the same graph. Can you identify the long-term trend of the time series? Can you identify any seasonal variations about the secular trend?
c. Use the moving average method to forecast the quarterly S&P 500 for 1994.
d. Calculate and plot the exponentially smoothed series for the quarterly S&P 500 using a smoothing constant of $w = .3$.
e. Use the exponential smoothing technique with $w = .3$ to forecast the quarterly S&P 500 for 1994.
f. Use the Holt–Winters forecasting model with trend and seasonal components to forecast the quarterly S&P 500 for 1994. Use smoothing constants $w = .3$, $v = .8$, and $u = .5$.

9.7 Consider the time series of gold prices recorded in the table. (Gold prices are given in dollars per troy ounce.)

YEAR	PRICE OF GOLD	YEAR	PRICE OF GOLD	YEAR	PRICE OF GOLD
1971	41.25	1978	193.50	1985	317.30
1972	58.61	1979	307.80	1986	367.87
1973	97.81	1980	606.01	1987	408.91
1974	159.70	1981	450.63	1988	436.93
1975	161.40	1982	374.18	1989	381.21
1976	124.80	1983	449.03	1990	384.07
1977	148.30	1984	360.29		

Source: *Survey of Current Business*, U.S. Department of Commerce.

a. Calculate a 3-point moving average for the gold price time series. Plot the gold prices and the 3-point moving average on the same graph. Can you detect the long-term trend and any cyclical patterns in the time series?
b. Use the moving averages to forecast the price of gold in 1991, 1992, and 1993.
c. Calculate and plot the exponentially smoothed gold price series using a smoothing constant of $w = .8$.
d. Use the exponentially smoothed series to forecast the price of gold in 1991, 1992, and 1993.
e. Use the Holt–Winters forecasting model with trend to forecast the price of gold, 1991–1993. Use smoothing constants $w = .8$ and $v = .4$.
f. The actual gold prices in 1991, 1992, and 1993 were \$362.04, \$344.50, and \$383.69, respectively. Use these values to assess the accuracy of the three forecasting methods, parts **b**, **d**, and **e**.

9.4 Forecasting: The Regression Approach

Many firms use past sales to forecast future sales. Suppose a wholesale distributor of sporting goods is interested in forecasting its sales revenue for each of the next 5 years. Since an inaccurate forecast may have dire consequences to the distributor, some measure of the forecast's reliability is required. To make such forecasts and assess their reliability, an **inferential time series forecasting model** must be constructed. The familiar general linear regression model of Chapter 4 represents one type of inferential model since it allows us to calculate prediction intervals for the forecasts.

To illustrate the technique of forecasting with regression, consider the data in Table 9.6 (page 514). The data are annual sales (in thousands of dollars) for a firm (say, the sporting goods distributor) in each of its 35 years of operation. A plot of the data (Figure 9.5) reveals a linearly increasing trend, so the first-order (straight-line) model

$$E(y_t) = \beta_0 + \beta_1 t$$

seems plausible for describing the secular trend. The SAS printout for the model is shown in Figure 9.6. The model apparently provides an excellent fit to the data, with $R^2 = .98$, $F = 1{,}615.724$ (p-value $< .0001$), and $s = 6.38524$. The least squares prediction equation, whose coefficients are shaded in Figure 9.6, is

$$\hat{y}_t = \hat{\beta}_0 + \hat{\beta}_1 t = .401513 + 4.295630t$$

TABLE 9.6 **A Firm's Yearly Sales Revenue (thousands of dollars)**

t	y_t	t	y_t	t	y_t
1	4.8	13	48.4	25	100.3
2	4.0	14	61.6	26	111.7
3	5.5	15	65.6	27	108.2
4	15.6	16	71.4	28	115.5
5	23.1	17	83.4	29	119.2
6	23.3	18	93.6	30	125.2
7	31.4	19	94.2	31	136.3
8	46.0	20	85.4	32	146.8
9	46.1	21	86.2	33	146.1
10	41.9	22	89.9	34	151.4
11	45.5	23	89.2	35	150.9
12	53.5	24	99.1		

FIGURE 9.5
Plot of sales data

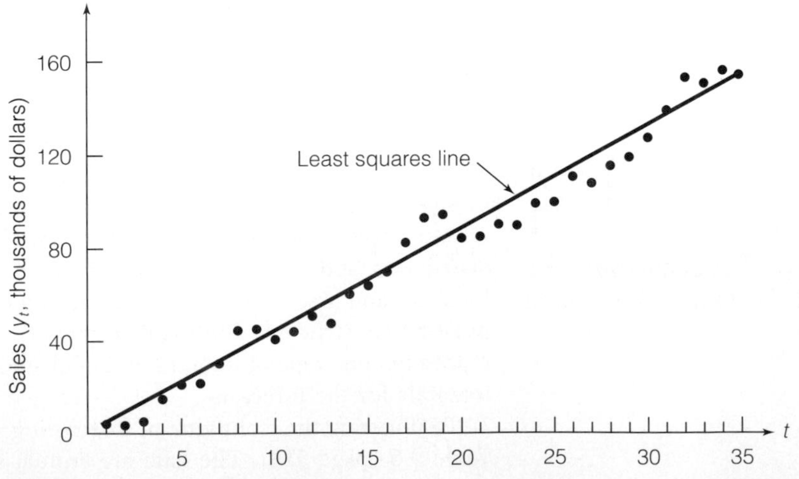

FIGURE 9.6
SAS printout for the straight-line model of yearly sales revenue

Analysis of Variance

Source	DF	Sum of Squares	Mean Square	F Value	Prob>F
Model	1	65875.20817	65875.20817	1615.724	0.0001
Error	33	1345.45355	40.77132		
C Total	34	67220.66171			

Root MSE	6.38524	R-square	0.9800
Dep Mean	77.72286	Adj R-sq	0.9794
C.V.	8.21540		

Parameter Estimates

Variable	DF	Parameter Estimate	Standard Error	T for H0: Parameter=0	Prob > |T|
INTERCEP	1	0.401513	2.20570829	0.182	0.8567
T	1	4.295630	0.10686692	40.196	0.0001

Obs	Dep Var Y	Predict Value	Std Err Predict	Lower95% Predict	Upper95% Predict	Residual
1	4.8000	4.6971	2.113	-8.9866	18.3809	0.1029
2	4.0000	8.9928	2.022	-4.6338	22.6194	-4.9928
3	5.5000	13.2884	1.932	-0.2843	26.8611	-7.7884
4	15.6000	17.5840	1.845	4.0619	31.1061	-1.9840
5	23.1000	21.8797	1.759	8.4048	35.3545	1.2203
6	23.3000	26.1753	1.676	12.7444	39.6062	-2.8753
7	31.4000	30.4709	1.596	17.0805	43.8613	0.9291
8	46.0000	34.7666	1.519	21.4133	48.1198	11.2334
9	46.1000	39.0622	1.446	25.7426	52.3818	7.0378
10	41.9000	43.3578	1.377	30.0684	56.6472	-1.4578
11	45.5000	47.6534	1.313	34.3908	60.9161	-2.1534
12	53.5000	51.9491	1.255	38.7096	65.1886	1.5509
13	48.4000	56.2447	1.204	43.0249	69.4645	-7.8447
14	61.6000	60.5403	1.161	47.3366	73.7441	1.0597
15	65.6000	64.8360	1.126	51.6448	78.0272	0.7640
16	71.4000	69.1316	1.100	55.9494	82.3138	2.2684
17	83.4000	73.4272	1.085	60.2504	86.6041	9.9728
18	93.6000	77.7229	1.079	64.5478	90.8979	15.8771
19	94.2000	82.0185	1.085	68.8416	95.2	12.1815
20	85.4000	86.3141	1.100	73.1319	99.5	-0.9141
21	86.2000	90.6097	1.126	77.4185	103.8	-4.4097
22	89.9000	94.9	1.161	81.7016	108.1	-5.0054
23	89.2000	99.2	1.204	85.9812	112.4	-10.0010
24	99.1	103.5	1.255	90.2571	116.7	-4.3966
25	100.3	107.8	1.313	94.5	121.1	-7.4923
26	111.7	112.1	1.377	98.8	125.4	-0.3879
27	108.2	116.4	1.446	103.1	129.7	-8.1835
28	115.5	120.7	1.519	107.3	134.0	-5.1792
29	119.2	125.0	1.596	111.6	138.4	-5.7748
30	125.2	129.3	1.676	115.8	142.7	-4.0704
31	136.3	133.6	1.759	120.1	147.0	2.7339
32	146.8	137.9	1.845	124.3	151.4	8.9383
33	146.1	142.2	1.932	128.6	155.7	3.9427
34	151.4	146.5	2.022	132.8	160.1	4.9471
35	150.9	150.7	2.113	137.1	164.4	0.1514
36	.	155.0	2.206	141.3	168.8	.
37	.	159.3	2.300	145.5	173.1	.
38	.	163.6	2.394	149.8	177.5	.
39	.	167.9	2.490	154.0	181.9	.
40	.	172.2	2.587	158.2	186.2	.

Sum of Residuals	-8.10019E-13
Sum of Squared Residuals	1345.4535
Predicted Resid SS (Press)	1484.2108

We can obtain sales forecasts and corresponding 95% prediction intervals for years 36–40 by using the formulas given in Section 3.9. However, these values are given in the bottom portion of the SAS printout shown in Figure 9.6. For example, for $t = 36$, we have $\hat{y}_{36} = 155.0$ with the 95% prediction interval (141.3, 168.8). That is, we predict that sales revenue in year $t = 36$ will fall between \$141,300 and \$168,800 with 95% confidence.

Note that the prediction intervals for $t = 36, 37, \ldots, 40$ widen as we attempt to forecast farther into the future. Intuitively, we know that the farther into the future we forecast, the less certain we are of the accuracy of the forecast since some unexpected change in business and economic conditions may make the model inappropriate. Since we have less confidence in the forecast for, say, $t = 40$ than for $t = 36$, it follows that the prediction interval for $t = 40$ must be wider to attain a 95% level of confidence. For this reason, time series forecasting (regardless of the forecasting method) is generally confined to the short term.

Multiple regression models can also be used to forecast future values of a time series with seasonal variation. We illustrate with an example.

EXAMPLE 9.3

Refer to the 1991–1994 quarterly power loads listed in Table 9.1.

a. Propose a model for quarterly power load, y_t, that will account for both the secular trend and seasonal variation present in the series.
b. Fit the model to the data, and use the least squares prediction equation to forecast the utility company's quarterly power loads in 1995. Construct 95% prediction intervals for the forecasts.

Solution

a. A common way to describe seasonal differences in a time series is with dummy variables.* For quarterly data, a model that includes both trend and seasonal components is

$$E(y_t) = \beta_0 + \underbrace{\beta_1 t}_{\substack{\text{Secular}\\ \text{trend}}} + \underbrace{\beta_2 Q_1 + \beta_3 Q_2 + \beta_4 Q_3}_{\text{Seasonal component}}$$

where

t = Time period, ranging from $t = 1$ for quarter I of 1991 to $t = 16$ for quarter IV of 1994

y_t = Power load (megawatts) in time t

$$Q_1 = \begin{cases} 1 & \text{if quarter I} \\ 0 & \text{if not} \end{cases} \qquad Q_2 = \begin{cases} 1 & \text{if quarter II} \\ 0 & \text{if not} \end{cases}$$

$$Q_3 = \begin{cases} 1 & \text{if quarter III} \\ 0 & \text{if not} \end{cases} \qquad \text{Base level} = \text{quarter IV}$$

The β coefficients associated with the seasonal dummy variables determine the mean increase (or decrease) in power load for each quarter, relative to the base level quarter, quarter IV.

b. The model is fitted to the data from Table 9.1 using the SAS multiple regression routine. The resulting SAS printout is shown in Figure 9.7. Note that the model appears to fit the data quite well: $R^2 = .9972$, indicating that the model

*Another way to account for seasonal variation is with trigonometric (sine and cosine) terms. We discuss seasonal models with trigonometric terms in Section 9.7.

FIGURE 9.7

SAS printout of least squares fit to quarterly power loads

```
Dependent Variable: Y

                          Analysis of Variance

                                Sum of           Mean
Source              DF         Squares         Square       F Value        Prob>F

Model                4      9101.67800     2275.41950       968.962        0.0001
Error               11        25.83138        2.34831
C Total             15      9127.50938

      Root MSE        1.53242      R-square          0.9972
      Dep Mean      137.30625      Adj R-sq          0.9961
      C.V.            1.11606

                          Parameter Estimates

                        Parameter         Standard      T for H0:
Variable   DF            Estimate            Error     Parameter=0     Prob > |T|

INTERCEP    1           90.206250       1.14931396          78.487         0.0001
T           1            4.964375       0.08566480          57.951         0.0001
Q1          1           10.093125       1.11364246           9.063         0.0001
Q2          1           -4.846250       1.09704478          -4.418         0.0010
Q3          1           14.364375       1.08696452          13.215         0.0001

                        Dep Var    Predict    Std Err   Lower95%   Upper95%
Obs         ID                Y      Value    Predict    Predict    Predict    Residual

  1     1991_1            103.5      105.3      0.923      101.3      109.2     -1.7637
  2     1991_2             94.7       95.3      0.923    91.3518       99.2     -0.5887
  3     1991_3            118.6      119.5      0.923      115.5      123.4     -0.8637
  4     1991_4            109.3      110.1      0.923      106.1      114.0     -0.7637
  5     1992_1            126.1      125.1      0.785      121.3      128.9      0.9788
  6     1992_2            116.0      115.1      0.785      111.4      118.9      0.8538
  7     1992_3            141.2      139.3      0.785      135.5      143.1      1.8788
  8     1992_4            131.6      129.9      0.785      126.1      133.7      1.6788
  9     1993_1            144.5      145.0      0.785      141.2      148.8     -0.4787
 10     1993_2            137.1      135.0      0.785      131.2      138.8      2.0963
 11     1993_3            159.0      159.2      0.785      155.4      163.0     -0.1787
 12     1993_4            149.5      149.8      0.785      146.0      153.6     -0.2787
 13     1994_1            166.1      164.8      0.923      160.9      168.8      1.2637
 14     1994_2            152.5      154.9      0.923      150.9      158.8     -2.3612
 15     1994_3            178.2      179.0      0.923      175.1      183.0     -0.8363
 16     1994_4            169.0      169.6      0.923      165.7      173.6     -0.6362
 17     1995_1                .      184.7      1.149      180.5      188.9           .
 18     1995_2                .      174.7      1.149      170.5      178.9           .
 19     1995_3                .      198.9      1.149      194.7      203.1           .
 20     1995_4                .      189.5      1.149      185.3      193.7           .

Sum of Residuals                   6.252776E-13
Sum of Squared Residuals                25.8314
Predicted Resid SS (Press)              55.6184
```

accounts for 99.7% of the sample variation in power loads over the 4-year period; $F = 968.962$ strongly supports the hypothesis that the model has predictive utility (p-value $= .0001$); and the standard deviation, **Root MSE** $= 1.53242$, implies that the model predictions will usually be accurate to within approximately $\pm 2(1.53)$, or about ± 3.06 megawatts.

Forecasts and corresponding 95% prediction intervals for the 1995 power loads are reported in the bottom portion of the printout in Figure 9.7. For example, the forecast for power load in quarter I of 1995 is 184.7 megawatts with the 95% prediction interval (180.5, 188.9). Therefore, using a 95% prediction interval, we expect the power load in quarter I of 1995 to fall between 180.5 and 188.9 megawatts. Recall from Table 9.5 in Example 9.2 that the actual 1995 quarterly power loads are 181.5, 175.2, 195.0 and 189.3, respectively. Note that each of these falls within its respective 95% prediction interval shown in Figure 9.7.

Many descriptive forecasting techniques have proved their merit by providing good forecasts for particular applications. Nevertheless, the advantage of forecasting using the regression approach is clear: Regression analysis provides us with a measure of reliability for each forecast through prediction intervals. However, there are two problems associated with forecasting time series using a multiple regression model.

PROBLEM 1 We are using the least squares prediction equation to forecast values outside the region of observation of the independent variable, t. For example, in Example 9.3, we are forecasting for values of t between 17 and 20 (the four quarters of 1995), even though the observed power loads are for t values between 1 and 16. As noted in Chapter 6, it is risky to use a least squares regression model for prediction outside the range of the observed data because some unusual change— economic, political, etc.—may make the model inappropriate for predicting future events. Because forecasting always involves predictions about future values of a time series, this problem obviously cannot be avoided. However, it is important that the forecaster recognize the dangers of this type of prediction.

PROBLEM 2 Recall the standard assumptions made about the random error component of a multiple regression model (Section 4.2). We assume that the errors have mean 0, constant variance, normal probability distributions, and are *independent*. The latter assumption is often violated in time series that exhibit short-term trends. As an illustration, refer to the plot of the sales revenue data shown in Figure 9.5. Notice that the observed sales tend to deviate about the least squares line in positive and negative runs. That is, if the difference between the observed sales and predicted sales in year t is positive (or negative), the difference in year $t + 1$ tends to be positive (or negative). Since the variation in the yearly sales is systematic, the implication is that the errors are correlated. (We gave a formal statistical test for correlated errors in Section 7.6.) Violation of this standard regression assumption could lead to unreliable forecasts.

Time series models have been developed specifically for the purpose of making forecasts when the errors are known to be correlated. These models include an **autoregressive term** for the correlated errors that result from cyclical, seasonal, or other short-term effects. Time series autoregressive models are the subject of Sections 9.5–9.11.

EXERCISES

9.8 The accompanying table records the volume of wheat (in thousands of bushels) harvested by members of a farmers' marketing cooperative for the period 1981–1994. The cooperative is interested in detecting the long-term trend of the wheat harvest.

YEAR	TIME	WHEAT HARVESTED	YEAR	TIME	WHEAT HARVESTED
1981	1	75	1988	8	91
1982	2	78	1989	9	92
1983	3	82	1990	10	92
1984	4	82	1991	11	93
1985	5	84	1992	12	96
1986	6	85	1993	13	101
1987	7	87	1994	14	102

a. Graph the wheat harvest time series.
b. Propose a model for the long-term linear trend of the time series.
c. Fit the model, using the method of least squares. Plot the least squares line on the graph of part **a**. Can you identify the long-term trend?
d. How well does the linear model describe the long-term trend? [*Hint:* Check the value of R^2.]
e. Use the least squares model to forecast the volume of wheat harvested in 1995. Construct a 95% prediction interval for the forecast.

9.9 A realtor working in a large city wants to identify the secular trend in the weekly number of single-family houses sold by her firm. For the past 15 weeks she has collected data on her firm's home sales, as shown in the table.

WEEK t	HOMES SOLD y_t	WEEK t	HOMES SOLD y_t	WEEK t	HOMES SOLD y_t
1	59	6	137	11	88
2	73	7	106	12	75
3	70	8	122	13	62
4	82	9	93	14	44
5	115	10	86	15	45

a. Plot the time series. Is there visual evidence of a quadratic trend?
b. The realtor hypothesizes the model $E(y_t) = \beta_0 + \beta_1 t + \beta_2 t^2$ for the secular trend of the weekly time series. Fit the model to the data, using the method of least squares. (You will need access to a statistical software package.)
c. Plot the least squares model on the graph of part **a**. How well does the quadratic model describe the secular trend?
d. Use the model to forecast home sales in week 16 with a 95% prediction interval.

9.10 Refer to the quarterly S&P 500 values given in Exercise 9.6.
a. Hypothesize a time series model to account for trend and seasonal variation.
b. Fit the model in part **a** to the data.
c. Use the least squares model from part **b** to forecast the S&P 500 for all four quarters of 1994. Obtain 95% prediction intervals for the forecasts.

9.11 Information on intercity passenger traffic (excluding travel by private automobiles) from 1940 to 1985 is given in the table at the top of page 520. The data are recorded as percentages of total passenger-miles traveled.

YEAR	TIME	RAILROADS	BUSES	AIR CARRIERS
1940	1	67.1	26.5	2.8
1945	2	74.3	21.4	2.7
1950	3	46.3	37.7	14.3
1955	4	36.5	32.4	28.9
1960	5	28.6	25.7	42.1
1965	6	17.9	24.2	54.7
1970	7	7.3	16.9	73.1
1975	8	5.8	14.2	77.7
1980	9	4.7	11.4	83.9
1985	10	3.6	7.9	88.4

Source: *Statistical Abstract of the United States*, 1987. Interstate Commerce Commission, Civil Aeronautics Board.

a. Let y_t be the percentage of total passenger-miles at time t for a particular mode of transportation. Consider the linear model $E(y_t) = \beta_0 + \beta_1 t$. Which modes of transportation do you think have a secular trend adequately represented by this model?

b. Fit the model in part **a** to the data for each mode of transportation, using the method of least squares.

c. Plot the data and the least squares line for each mode of transportation. Which models adequately describe the secular trend of percentage of total passenger-miles traveled? Does this agree with your answer to part **a**?

d. Refer to your answer for part **c**. Use the least squares prediction equations to forecast the percentage of total passenger-miles to be traveled for the respective modes of transportation in 1995. Obtain 95% prediction intervals. What are the risks associated with this forecasting procedure?

9.12 The annual price (in cents per pound) of galvanized steel from 1971 to 1989 is shown in the table.

YEAR	t	y_t	YEAR	t	y_t	YEAR	t	y_t
1971	1	9.61	1978	8	20.47	1985	15	30.30
1972	2	10.88	1979	9	22.32	1986	16	30.30
1973	3	10.59	1980	10	23.88	1987	17	30.49
1974	4	12.39	1981	11	26.88	1988	18	31.05
1975	5	14.80	1982	12	26.75	1989	19	31.05
1976	6	16.07	1983	13	28.43			
1977	7	18.10	1984	14	30.30			

Source: *Standard & Poor's Trade and Securities Statistics* (Annual), New York, Standard & Poor's Corporation.

a. Plot the time series. Is there visual evidence of a linear trend? A quadratic trend? Propose a regression model that is likely to fit the data well.

b. Fit the model, part **a**, to the data, using the method of least squares.

c. Plot the least squares prediction equation on the graph of part **a**. How well does the model describe the time series?

d. Use the fitted least squares model to forecast the price of galvanized steel for the years 1990–1995. Obtain 95% prediction intervals for the forecasts and verify that the width of the interval increases the farther you forecast into the future.

9.13 An analysis of seasonality in returns of stock traded on the London Stock Exchange was published in the *Journal of Business* (Vol. 60, 1987). One of the objectives was to determine whether the introduction of a capital gains tax in 1965 affected rates of return. The following model was fitted to data collected over the years 1956–1980:

$$y_t = \beta_0 + \beta_1 D_1 + \varepsilon_t$$

where y_t is the difference between the April rates of return of the two stocks on the exchange with the largest and smallest returns in year t, and D_t is a dummy variable that takes on the value 1 in the posttax period (1966–1980) and the value 0 in the pretax period (1956–1965).

a. Interpret the value of β_1.
b. Interpret the value of β_0.
c. The least squares prediction equation was found to be $\hat{y}_t = -.55 + 3.08D_t$. Use the equation to estimate the mean difference in April rates of returns of the two stocks during the pretax period.
d. Repeat part c for the posttax period.
e. Obtain a forecast of the difference in April rates of return of the two stocks in 1995.

9.14 A traditional indicator of the economic health of the accommodations (hotel–motel) industry is the trend in room occupancy. Average monthly occupancies for 2 recent years are given in the accompanying table for hotels and motels in the cities of Atlanta, Georgia, and Phoenix, Arizona. Let y_t = occupancy rate for Phoenix in month t.

YEAR ONE	PERCENTAGE OF ROOMS OCCUPIED		YEAR TWO	PERCENTAGE OF ROOMS OCCUPIED	
Month	Atlanta	Phoenix	Month	Atlanta	Phoenix
January	59	67	January	64	72
February	63	85	February	69	91
March	68	83	March	73	87
April	70	69	April	67	75
May	63	63	May	68	70
June	59	52	June	71	61
July	68	49	July	67	46
August	64	49	August	71	44
September	62	56	September	65	63
October	73	69	October	72	73
November	62	63	November	63	71
December	47	48	December	47	51

Source: *Trends in the Hotel Industry.*

a. Propose a model for $E(y_t)$ that accounts for possible seasonal variation in the monthly series. [*Hint:* Consider a model with dummy variables for the 12 months, January, February, etc.]
b. Fit the model of part **a** to the data.
c. Test the hypothesis that the monthly dummy variables are useful predictors of occupancy rate. [*Hint:* Conduct a partial F test.]
d. Use the fitted least squares model from part **b** to forecast the Phoenix occupancy rate in January of year 3 with a 95% prediction interval.
e. Repeat parts **a–d** for the Atlanta monthly occupancy rates.

9.15 The Employee Retirement Income Security Act (ERISA) of 1974 was originally established to enhance retirement security income. J. Ledolter (University of Iowa) and M. L. Power (Iowa State University) investigated the effects of ERISA on the growth in the number of private retirement plans (*Journal of Risk and Insurance*, Dec. 1983). Using quarterly data from 1956 through the third quarter of 1982 ($n = 107$ quarters), Ledolter and Power fitted quarterly time series models for the number of pension qualifications and the number of profit-sharing plan qualifications. One of several models investigated was the quadratic model $E(y_t) = \beta_0 + \beta_1 t + \beta_2 t^2$, where y_t is the logarithm of the dependent variable (number of pension or number of profit-sharing qualifications) in quarter t. The results (modified for the purpose of this exercise) are summarized here:

Pension plan qualifications:

$$\hat{y}_t = 6.19 + .039t - .00024t^2$$
$$t \text{ (for } H_0\text{: } \beta_2 = 0) = -1.39$$

Profit-sharing plan qualifications:

$$\hat{y}_t = 6.22 + .035t - .00021t^2$$
$$t \text{ (for } H_0\text{: } \beta_2 = 0) = -1.61$$

a. Is there evidence that the quarterly number of pension plan qualifications increases at a decreasing rate over time? Test using $\alpha = .05$. [*Hint:* Test H_0: $\beta_2 = 0$ against H_a: $\beta_2 < 0$.]
b. Forecast the number of pension plan qualifications for the fourth quarter of 1982 (i.e., $t = 108$). [*Hint:* Since y_t is the logarithm of the number of pension plan qualifications, to obtain the forecast you must take the antilogarithm of $\hat{y}_{108}$, i.e., $e^{\hat{y}_{108}}$.]
c. Is there evidence that the quarterly number of profit-sharing plan qualifications increases at a decreasing rate over time? Test using $\alpha = .05$. [*Hint:* Test H_0: $\beta_2 = 0$ against H_a: $\beta_2 < 0$.]
d. Forecast the number of profit-sharing plan qualifications for the fourth quarter of 1982 (i.e., $t = 108$). [*Hint:* Since y_t is the logarithm of the number of profit-sharing plan qualifications, to obtain the forecast you must take the antilogarithm of $\hat{y}_{108}$, i.e., $e^{\hat{y}_{108}}$.]

9.5 Autocorrelation and Autoregressive Error Models

In Chapter 7, we presented the Durbin–Watson test for detecting correlated residuals in a regression analysis. Correlated residuals are quite common when the response is a *time series* variable. Correlation of residuals for a regression model with a time series response is called **autocorrelation**, because the correlation is between residuals from the *same* time series model at different points in time.

A special case of autocorrelation that has many applications to business and economic phenomena is the case in which neighboring residuals one time period apart (say, at times t and $t + 1$) are correlated. This type of correlation is called **first-order autocorrelation**. In general, correlation between time series residuals m time periods apart is mth-order autocorrelation.

Definition 9.7

Autocorrelation is the correlation between time series residuals at different points in time. The special case in which neighboring residuals one time period apart (at times t and $t + 1$) are correlated is called **first-order autocorrelation**.

To see how autocorrelated residuals affect the regression model, we will assume a model similar to the general linear model of Chapter 4,

$$y_t = E(y_t) + R_t$$

where $E(y_t)$ is the regression model

$$E(y_t) = \beta_0 + \beta_1 x_1 + \cdots + \beta_k x_k$$

and R_t represents the random residual. We assume that the residual R_t has mean 0 and constant variance σ^2, but that it is autocorrelated. The effect of autocorrelation on the general linear model depends on the pattern of the autocorrelation. One of the most common patterns is that the autocorrelation between residuals at consecutive time points is positive. Thus, when the residual at time t, R_t, indicates that the observed value y_t is more than the mean value $E(y_t)$, then the residual at time $(t + 1)$ will have a tendency (probability greater than .5) to be positive. This would occur, for example, if you were to model a monthly economic index (e.g., the Consumer Price Index) with a straight-line model. In times of recession, the observed values of the index will tend to be less than the predictions of a straight line for most or all of the months during the period. Similarly, in extremely inflationary periods, the residuals are likely to be positive because the observed value of the index will lie above the straight-line model. In either case, the fact that residuals at consecutive time points tend to have the same sign implies that they are **positively correlated**.

A second property commonly observed for autocorrelated residuals is that the size of the autocorrelation between values of the residual R at two different points in time diminishes rapidly as the distance between the time points increases. Thus, the autocorrelation between R_t and R_{t+m} becomes smaller (i.e., weaker) as the distance m between the time points becomes larger.

A residual model that possesses this property—positive autocorrelation diminishing rapidly as distance between time points increases—is the **first-order autoregressive error model**:

$$R_t = \phi R_{t-1} + \varepsilon_t, \quad -1 < \phi < 1$$

where ε_t, a residual called **white noise**, is uncorrelated with any and all other residual components. Thus, the value of the residual R_t is equal to a constant multiple, ϕ (Greek letter "phi"), of the previous residual, R_{t-1}, plus random error. In general, the constant ϕ is between -1 and $+1$, and the numerical value of ϕ determines the sign (positive or negative) and strength of the autocorrelation. In fact, it can be shown (proof omitted) that the autocorrelation (abbreviated AC) between two residuals that are m time units apart, R_t, and R_{t+m}, is

$$\text{AC}(R_t, R_{t+m}) = \phi^m$$

Since the absolute value of ϕ will be less than 1, the autocorrelation between R_t and R_{t+m}, ϕ^m, will decrease as m increases. This means that neighboring values of R_t, i.e., $m = 1$, will have the highest correlation, and the correlation diminishes rapidly as the distance m between time points is increased. This points to an interesting property of the autoregressive time series model. The autocorrelation function depends only on the distance m between R values, and not on the time t. Time series models that possess this property are said to be **stationary**.

Definition 9.8

A **stationary time series model** for regression residuals is one that has mean 0, constant variance, and autocorrelations that depend only on the distance between time points.

The autocorrelation function of first-order autoregressive models is shown for several values of ϕ in Figure 9.8. Note that positive values of ϕ yield positive autocorrelation for all residuals, whereas negative values of ϕ imply negative correlation for neighboring residuals, positive correlation between residuals two time points apart, negative correlation for residuals three time points apart, and so forth. The appropriate pattern will, of course, depend on the particular application, but the occurrence of a positive autocorrelation pattern is more common.

Although the first-order autoregressive error model provides a good representation for many autocorrelation patterns, more complex patterns can be described by higher-order autoregressive models. The general form of a pth-order autoregressive error model is

$$R_t = \phi_1 R_{t-1} + \phi_2 R_{t-2} + \cdots + \phi_p R_{t-p} + \varepsilon_t$$

The inclusion of p parameters, $\phi_1, \phi_2, \ldots, \phi_p$, permits more flexibility in the pattern of autocorrelations exhibited by a residual time series. When an autoregressive model is used to describe residual autocorrelations, the observed autocorrelations are used to estimate these parameters. Methods for estimating these parameters will be presented in Section 9.8.

FIGURE 9.8

Autocorrelation functions for several first-order autoregressive error models: $R_t = \phi_1 R_{t-1} + \varepsilon_t$

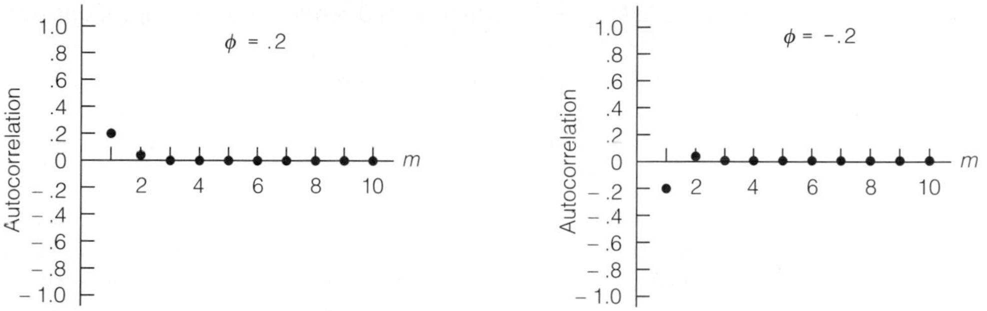

a. Weak autocorrelation

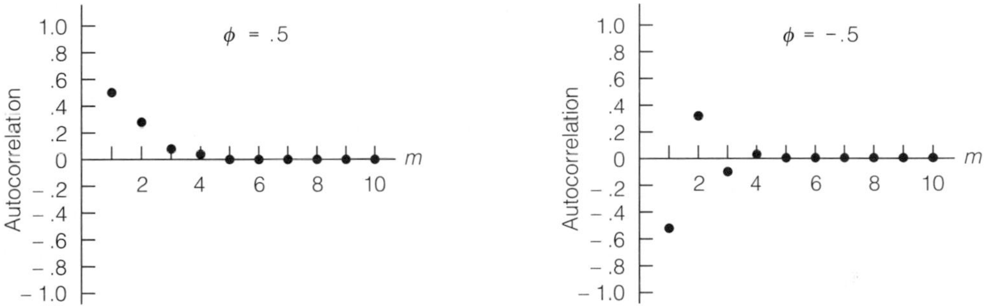

b. Moderate autocorrelation

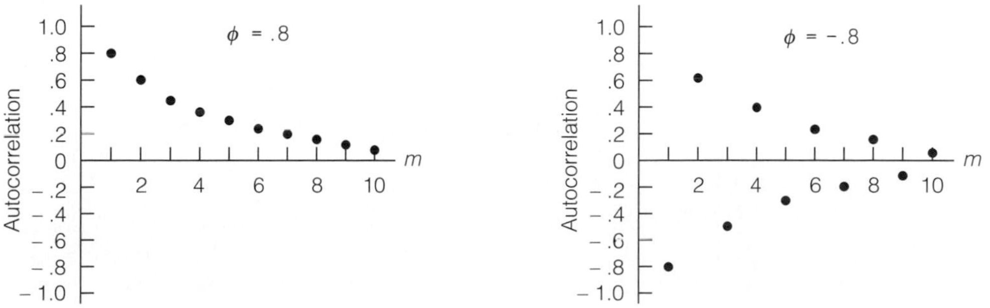

c. Strong autocorrelation

EXERCISES

9.16 Suppose that the random component of a time series model follows the first-order autoregressive model $R_t = \phi R_{t-1} + \varepsilon_t$, where ε_t is a white-noise process. Consider four versions of this model: $\phi = .9$, $\phi = -.9$, $\phi = .2$, and $\phi = -.2$.

a. Calculate the first 10 autocorrelations, $AC(R_t, R_{t+m})$, $m = 1, 2, 3, \ldots, 10$, for each of the four models.

b. Plot the autocorrelations against the distance in time separating the R values (m) for each case.

c. Examine the rate at which the correlation diminishes in each plot. What does this imply?

9.17 When using time series to analyze quarterly data (data in which seasonal effects are present), it is highly possible that the random component of the model R_t also exhibits the same seasonal variation as the dependent variable. In these cases, the following non–first-order autoregressive model is sometimes postulated for the correlated error term, R_t:

$$R_t = \phi R_{t-4} + \varepsilon_t$$

where $|\phi| < 1$ and ε_t is a white-noise process. The autocorrelation function for this model is given by

$$AC(R_t, R_{t+m}) = \begin{cases} \phi^{m/4} & \text{if } m = 4, 8, 12, 16, 20, \ldots \\ 0 & \text{if otherwise} \end{cases}$$

a. Calculate the first 20 autocorrelations ($m = 1, 2, \ldots, 20$) for the model with constant coefficient $\phi = .5$.

b. Plot the autocorrelations against m, the distance in time separating the R values. Compare the rate at which the correlation diminishes with the first-order model $R_t = .5R_{t-1} + \varepsilon_t$.

9.18 Consider the autocorrelation pattern shown in the figure. Write a first-order autoregressive model that exhibits this pattern.

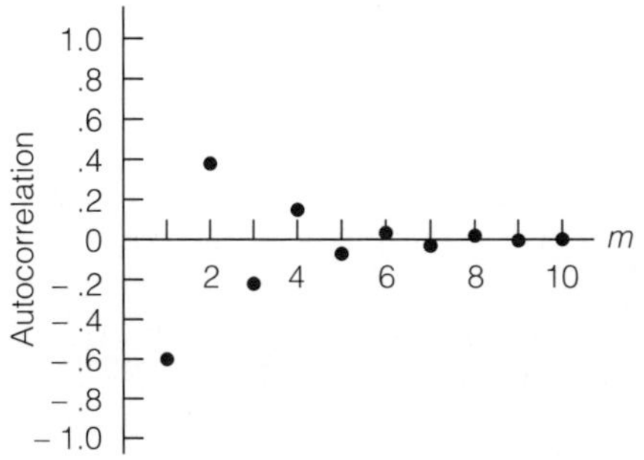

9.19 Write the general form for a fourth-order autoregressive model.

9.6 Other Models for Autocorrelated Errors (Optional)

There are many models for autocorrelated residuals in addition to the autoregressive model, but the autoregressive model provides a good approximation for the autocorrelation pattern in many applications. Recall that the autocorrelations for autoregressive models diminish rapidly as the time distance m between the residuals increases. Occasionally, residual autocorrelations appear to change abruptly from nonzero for small values of m to 0 for larger values of m. For example, neighboring residuals ($m = 1$) may be correlated, whereas residuals that are farther apart ($m > 1$) are uncorrelated. This pattern can be described by the **first-order moving average model**

$$R_t = \varepsilon_t + \theta\varepsilon_{t-1}$$

Note that the residual R_t is a linear combination of the current and previous *uncorrelated* (white-noise) residuals. It can be shown that the autocorrelations for this model are

$$\text{AC}(R_t, R_{t+m}) = \begin{cases} \dfrac{\theta}{1 + \theta^2} & \text{if } m = 1 \\ 0 & \text{if } m > 1 \end{cases}$$

This pattern is shown in Figure 9.9.

FIGURE 9.9

Autocorrelations for the first-order moving average model: $R_t = \varepsilon_t + \theta\varepsilon_{t-1}$

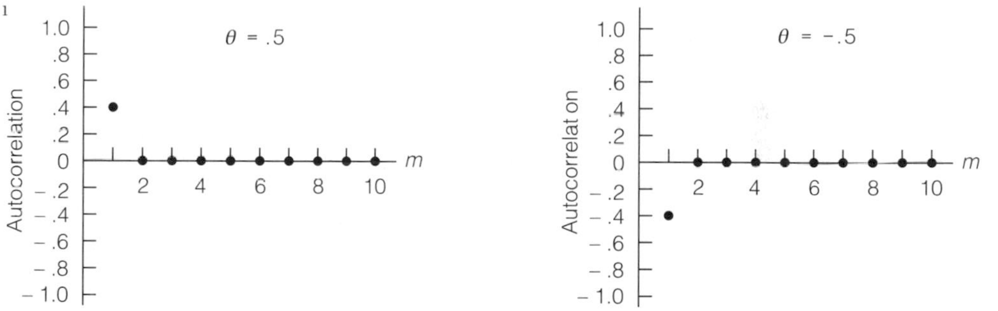

More generally, a qth-order moving average model is given by

$$R_t = \varepsilon_t + \theta\varepsilon_{t-1} + \theta_2\varepsilon_{t-2} + \cdots + \theta_q\varepsilon_{t-q}$$

Residuals within q time points are correlated, whereas those farther than q time points apart are uncorrelated. For example, a regression model for the quarterly earnings per share for a company may have residuals that are autocorrelated when within 1 year ($m = 4$ quarters) of one another, but uncorrelated when farther apart. An example of this pattern is shown in Figure 9.10 on page 528.

Some autocorrelation patterns require even more complex residual models. A more general model is a combination of the **autoregressive–moving average (ARMA) models,**

$$R_t = \phi_1 R_{t-1} + \cdots + \phi_p R_{t-p} + \varepsilon_t + \theta_1\varepsilon_{t-1} + \cdots + \theta_q\varepsilon_{t-q}$$

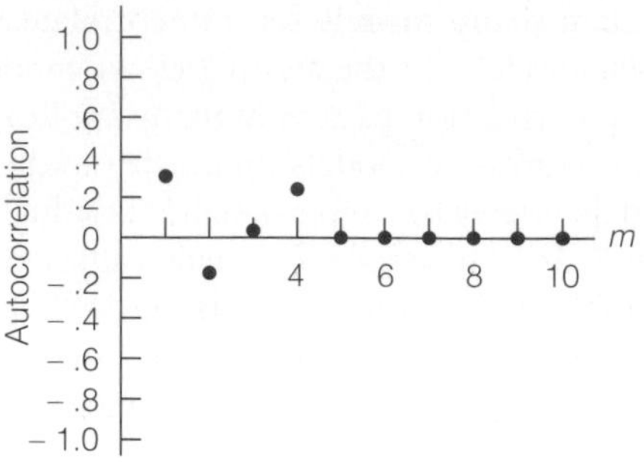

FIGURE 9.10
Autocorrelations for a fourth-order moving average model

Like the autoregressive model, the ARMA model has autocorrelations that diminish as the distance m between residuals increases. However, the patterns that can be described by ARMA models are more general than those of either autoregressive or moving average models.

In Section 9.8, we present a method for estimating the parameters of an autoregressive residual model. The method for fitting time series models when the residual is either moving average or ARMA is more complicated, however. Consult the references at the end of the chapter for details of these methods.

9.7 Constructing Time Series Models

Recall that the general form of the times series model is

$$y_t = E(y_t) + R_t$$

We are assuming that the expected value of y_t is

$$E(y_t) = \beta_0 + \beta_1 x_1 + \beta_2 x_2 + \cdots + \beta_k x_k$$

where $x_1, x_2, \ldots, x_k$ are independent variables, which themselves may be time series, and the residual component, R_t, accounts for the pattern of autocorrelation in the residuals. Thus, a time series model consists of a pair of models: one model for the deterministic component $E(y_t)$ and one model for the autocorrelated residuals R_t.

Choosing the Deterministic Component

The deterministic portion of the model is chosen in exactly the same manner as the regression models of the preceding chapters except that some of the independent variables might be time series variables or might be trigonometric functions of time (such as sin t or cos t). It is helpful to think of the deterministic component as consisting of the trend (T_t), cyclical (C_t), and seasonal (S_t) effects described in Section 9.2.

For example, we may want to model the number of new housing starts, y_t, as a function of the prime interest rate, x_t. Then, one model for the mean of y_t is

$$E(y_t) = \beta_0 + \beta_1 x_t$$

for which the mean number of new housing starts is a multiple β_1 of the prime interest rate, plus a constant β_0. Another possibility is a second-order relationship,

$$E(y_t) = \beta_0 + \beta_1 x_t + \beta_2 x_t^2$$

which permits the *rate* of increase in the mean number of housing starts to increase or decrease with the prime interest rate.

Yet another possibility is to model the mean number of new housing starts as a function of both the prime interest rate and the year, t. Thus, the model

$$E(y_t) = \beta_0 + \beta_1 x_t + \beta_2 t + \beta_3 x_t t$$

implies that the mean number of housing starts increases linearly in x_t, the prime interest rate, but the rate of increase depends on the year t. If we wanted to adjust for seasonal (cyclical) effects due to t, we might introduce time into the model using trigonometric functions of t. This topic will be explained subsequently in greater detail.

Another important type of model for $E(y_t)$ is the **lagged independent variable model**. *Lagging* means that we are pairing observations on a dependent variable and independent variable at two different points in time, with the time corresponding to the independent variable lagging behind the time for the dependent variable. Suppose, for example, we believe that the monthly mean number of new housing starts is a function of the *previous* month's prime interest rate. Thus, we model y_t as a linear function of the lagged independent variable, prime interest rate, x_{t-1},

$$E(y_t) = \beta_0 + \beta_1 x_{t-1}$$

or, alternatively, as the second-order function,

$$E(y_t) = \beta_0 + \beta_1 x_{t-1} + \beta_2 x_{t-1}^2$$

For this example, the independent variable, prime interest rate x_t, is lagged 1 month behind the response y_t.

Many time series have distinct seasonal patterns. Retail sales are usually highest around Christmas, spring, and fall, with relative lulls in the winter and summer periods. Energy usage is highest in summer and winter, and lowest in spring and fall. Teenage unemployment rises in the summer months when schools are not in session, and falls near Christmas when many businesses hire part-time help.

When a time series' seasonality is exhibited in a relatively consistent pattern from year to year, we can model the pattern using trigonometric terms in the model for $E(y_t)$. For example, the model of a monthly series with mean $E(y_t)$ might be

$$E(y_t) = \beta_0 + \beta_1\left(\cos\frac{2\pi}{12}t\right) + \beta_2\left(\sin\frac{2\pi}{12}t\right)$$

This model would appear as shown in Figure 9.11 on page 530. Note that the model is **cyclic**, with a **period** of 12 months. That is, the mean $E(y_t)$ completes a cycle every 12 months and then repeats the same cycle over the next 12 months. Thus, the **expected peaks and valleys** of the series remain the same from year to year. The coefficients β_1 and β_2 determine the **amplitude** and **phase shift** of the model. The amplitude is the magnitude of the seasonal effect, whereas the phase shift locates the peaks and valleys in time. For example, if we assume month 1 is January, the mean of the time series depicted in Figure 9.11 has a peak each April and a valley each October.

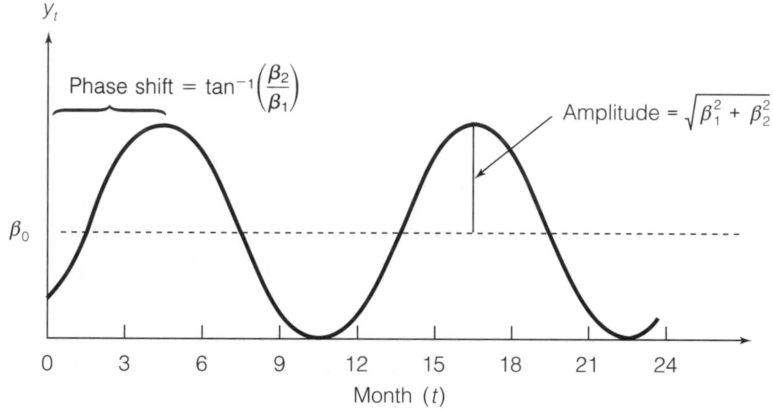

FIGURE 9.11
A seasonal time series model

If the data are monthly or quarterly, we can treat the season as a qualitative independent variable (see Example 9.3), and write the model

$$E(y_t) = \beta_0 + \beta_1 S_1 + \beta_2 S_2 + \beta_3 S_3$$

where

$$S_1 = \begin{cases} 1 & \text{if season is spring (II)} \\ 0 & \text{otherwise} \end{cases} \qquad S_2 = \begin{cases} 1 & \text{if season is summer (III)} \\ 0 & \text{otherwise} \end{cases}$$

$$S_3 = \begin{cases} 1 & \text{if season is fall (IV)} \\ 0 & \text{otherwise} \end{cases}$$

Thus, S_1, S_2, and S_3 are dummy variables that describe the four levels of season, letting winter (I) be the base level. The β coefficients determine the mean value of y_t for each season, as shown in Figure 9.12. Note that for the dummy variable model and the trigonometric model, we assume the seasonal effects are approximately the same from year to year. If they tend to increase or decrease with time, an interaction of the seasonal effect with time may be necessary. (An example will be given in Section 9.10.)

The appropriate form of the deterministic time series model will depend on both theory and data. Economic theory often provides several plausible models relating the mean response to one or more independent variables. The data can then be used to determine which, if any, of the models is best supported. The process is often an iterative one, beginning with preliminary models based on theoretical notions, using data to refine and modify these notions, collecting additional data to test the modified theories, and so forth.

FIGURE 9.12
Seasonal model for quarterly data using dummy variables

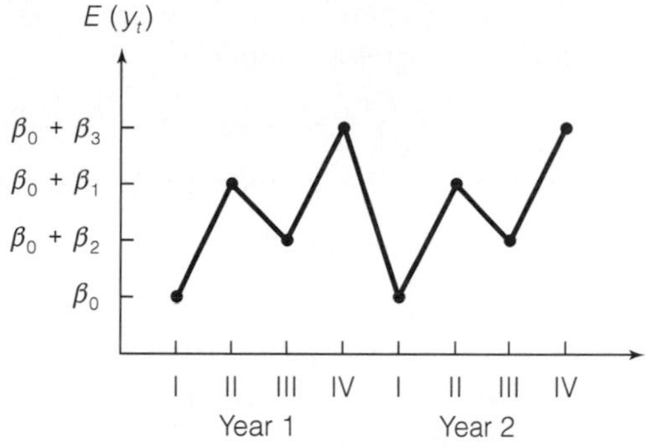

Choosing the Residual Component

The appropriate form of the residual component R_t will depend on the pattern of autocorrelation in the residuals (see Sections 9.5 and 9.6). The autoregressive model of Section 9.5 is very useful for this aspect of time series modeling. The general form of an autoregressive model of order p is

$$R_t = \phi_1 R_{t-1} + \phi_2 R_{t-2} + \cdots + \phi_p R_{t-p} + \varepsilon_t$$

where ε_t is white noise (uncorrelated error). Recall that the name *autoregressive* comes from the fact that R_t is regressed on its own past values. As the order p is increased, more complex autocorrelation functions can be modeled. There are several other types of models that can be used for the random component, but the autoregressive model is very flexible and receives more application in business forecasting than the other models.

The simplest autoregressive error model is the **first-order autoregressive model**

$$R_t = \phi R_{t-1} + \varepsilon_t$$

Recall that the autocorrelation between residuals at two different points in time diminishes as the distance between the time points increases. Since many business and economic time series exhibit this property, the first-order autoregressive model is a popular choice for the residual component.

To summarize, we describe a general approach for constructing a time series:

1. Construct a regression model for the trend, seasonal, and cyclical components of $E(y_t)$. This model may be a polynomial in t for the trend (usually a straight-line or quadratic model) with trigonometric terms or dummy variables for the seasonal (cyclical) effects. The model may also include other time series variables as independent variables. For example, last year's rate of inflation may be used as a predictor of this year's Gross Domestic Product (GDP).
2. Next, construct a model for the random component (residual effect) of the model. A model that is widely used in practice is the first-order autoregressive error model

$$R_t = \phi R_{t-1} + \varepsilon_t$$

When the pattern of autocorrelation is more complex, use the general pth-order autoregressive model

$$R_t = \phi_1 R_{t-1} + \phi_2 R_{t-2} + \cdots + \phi_p R_{t-p} + \varepsilon_t$$

3. Combine the two components so that the model can be used for forecasting:

$$y_t = E(y_t) + R_t$$

Prediction intervals are calculated to measure the reliability of the forecasts. In the following two sections, we will demonstrate how time series models are fitted to data and used for forecasting. In Section 9.10, we will present an example in which we fit a seasonal time series model to a set of data.

EXERCISES

9.20 Suppose you are interested in buying stock in the Pepsi Company (PepsiCo). Your broker has advised you that your best strategy is to sell the stock at the first substantial jump in price. Hence, you are interested in a short-term investment. Before buying, you would like to model the closing price of PepsiCo, y_t, over time (in days), t.

a. Write a first-order model for the deterministic portion of the model, $E(y_t)$.

b. If a plot of the daily closing prices for the past month reveals a quadratic trend, write a plausible model for $E(y_t)$.

c. Since the closing price of PepsiCo on day $(t + 1)$ is very highly correlated with the closing price on day t, your broker suggests that the random error components of the model are not white noise. Given this information, postulate a model for the error term, R_t.

9.21 An economist wishes to model the Gross Domestic Product (GDP) over time (in years) and also as a function of certain personal consumption expenditures. Let t = time in years and let

y_t = GDP at time t

x_{1t} = Durable goods at time t

x_{2t} = Nondurable goods at time t

x_{3t} = Services at time t

a. The economist believes that y_t is linearly related to the independent variables x_{1t}, x_{2t}, x_{3t}, and t. Write the first-order model for $E(y_t)$.

b. Rewrite the model if interaction between the independent variables and time is present.

c. Postulate a model for the random error component, R_t. Explain why this model is appropriate.

9.22 Airlines sometimes overbook flights because of "no-show" passengers, i.e., passengers who have purchased a ticket but fail to board the flight. An airline supervisor wishes to be able to predict, for a flight from Miami to New York, the monthly accumulation of no-show passengers during the upcoming year, using data from the past 3 years. Let y_t = Number of no-shows during month t.

a. Using dummy variables, propose a model for $E(y_t)$ that will take into account the seasonal (fall, winter, spring, summer) variation that may be present in the data.

b. Postulate a model for the error term R_t.

c. Write the full time series model for y_t (include random error terms).

d. Suppose the airline supervisor believes that the seasonal variation in the data is not constant from year to year, in other words, that there exists interaction between time and season. Rewrite the full model with the interaction terms added.

9.23 A farmer is interested in modeling the daily price of hogs at a livestock market. The farmer knows that the price varies over time (days) and also is reasonably confident that a seasonal effect is present.

a. Write a seasonal time series model with trigonometric terms for $E(y_t)$, where y_t = Selling price (in dollars) of hogs on day t.

b. Interpret the β parameters.

c. Include in the model an interaction between time and the trigonometric components. What does the presence of interaction signify?

d. Is it reasonable to assume that the random error component of the model, R_t, is white noise? Explain. Postulate a more appropriate model for R_t.

9.24 Numerous studies have been conducted to examine the relationship between seniority and productivity in business. A problem encountered in such studies is that individual output is often difficult to measure. G. A. Krohn developed a technique for estimating the experience–productivity relationship when such a measure is available (*Journal of Business & Economic Statistics*, Oct. 1983). Krohn modeled the batting average of a major league baseball player in year t (y_t) as a function of the player's age in year t (x_t) and an autoregressive error term (R_t).

a. Write a model for $E(y_t)$ that hypothesizes, as did Krohn, a curvilinear relationship with x_t.

b. Write a first-order autoregressive model for R_t.

c. Use the models from parts **a** and **b** to write the full time series autoregressive model for y_t.

9.8 Fitting Time Series Models with Autoregressive Errors

We have proposed a general form for a time series model:

$$y_t = E(y_t) + R_t$$

where

$$E(y_t) = \beta_0 + \beta_1 x_1 + \cdots + \beta_k x_k$$

and, using an autoregressive model for R_t,

$$R_t = \phi R_{t-1} + \phi_2 R_{t-2} + \cdots + \phi_p R_{t-p} + \varepsilon_t$$

We now want to develop estimators for the parameters $\beta_0, \beta_1, \ldots, \beta_k$ of the regression model, and for the parameters $\phi_1, \phi_2, \ldots, \phi_p$ of the autoregressive model. The ultimate objective is to use the model to obtain forecasts (predictions) of future values of y_t, as well as to make inferences about the structure of the model itself.

We will introduce the techniques of fitting a time series model with a simple example. Refer to the data in Table 9.6, the annual sales for a firm in each of its 35 years of operation. Recall that the objective is to forecast future sales in years 36–40. In Section 9.4, we used a simple straight-line model for the mean sales

$$E(y_t) = \beta_0 + \beta_1 t$$

to make the forecasts.

The SAS printout showing the least squares estimates of β_0 and β_1 is reproduced in Figure 9.13. Although the model is useful for predicting annual sales (p-value for H_0: $\beta_1 = 0$ is less than .0001), the Durbin–Watson statistic is $d = .821$, which is less than the tabulated value, $d_L = 1.40$ (Table 8 of Appendix C), for $\alpha = .05$, $n = 35$, and $k = 1$ independent variable. Thus, there is evidence that the residuals are positively correlated. The plot of the least squares residuals over time, in Figure 9.14, shows the pattern of positive autocorrelation. The residuals tend to cluster in positive and negative runs; if the residual at time t is positive, the residual at time $(t + 1)$ tends to be positive.

FIGURE 9.13

SAS printout: Regression analysis for least squares sales data

```
Dependent Variable: Y

                              Analysis of Variance

                                Sum of          Mean
        Source          DF     Squares        Square       F Value        Prob>F

        Model            1  65875.20817  65875.20817      1615.724        0.0001
        Error           33   1345.45355     40.77132
        C Total         34  67220.66171

            Root MSE       6.38524     R-square       0.9800
            Dep Mean      77.72286     Adj R-sq       0.9794
            C.V.           8.21540

                              Parameter Estimates

                         Parameter        Standard     T for H0:
      Variable  DF        Estimate           Error   Parameter=0    Prob > |T|

      INTERCEP   1        0.401513      2.20570829         0.182        0.8567
      T          1        4.295630      0.10686692        40.196        0.0001

Durbin-Watson D                0.821
(For Number of Obs.)              35
1st Order Autocorrelation      0.590
```

What are the consequences of fitting the least squares model when autocorrelated residuals are present? Although *the least squares estimators of* β_0 *and* β_1 *remain unbiased* even if the residuals are autocorrelated, i.e., $E(\hat{\beta}_0) = \beta_0$ and $E(\hat{\beta}_1) = \beta_1$, the *standard errors given by least squares theory are usually smaller than the true standard errors* when the residuals are positively autocorrelated. Consequently, t values computed by the methods of Chapter 4 (which apply when the errors are uncorrelated) will usually be inflated and will lead to a higher Type I error rate (α) than the value of α selected for a test. Thus, the application of standard least squares techniques to time series often produces misleading statistical test results that result in overoptimistic evaluations of a model's predictive ability. There is a second reason for seeking methods that specifically take into account the autocorrelated residuals. If we can successfully model the residual autocorrelation, we should achieve a smaller MSE and correspondingly narrower prediction intervals than those given by the least squares model.

To account for the autocorrelated residual, we postulate a first-order autoregressive model,

$$R_t = \phi R_{t-1} + \varepsilon_t$$

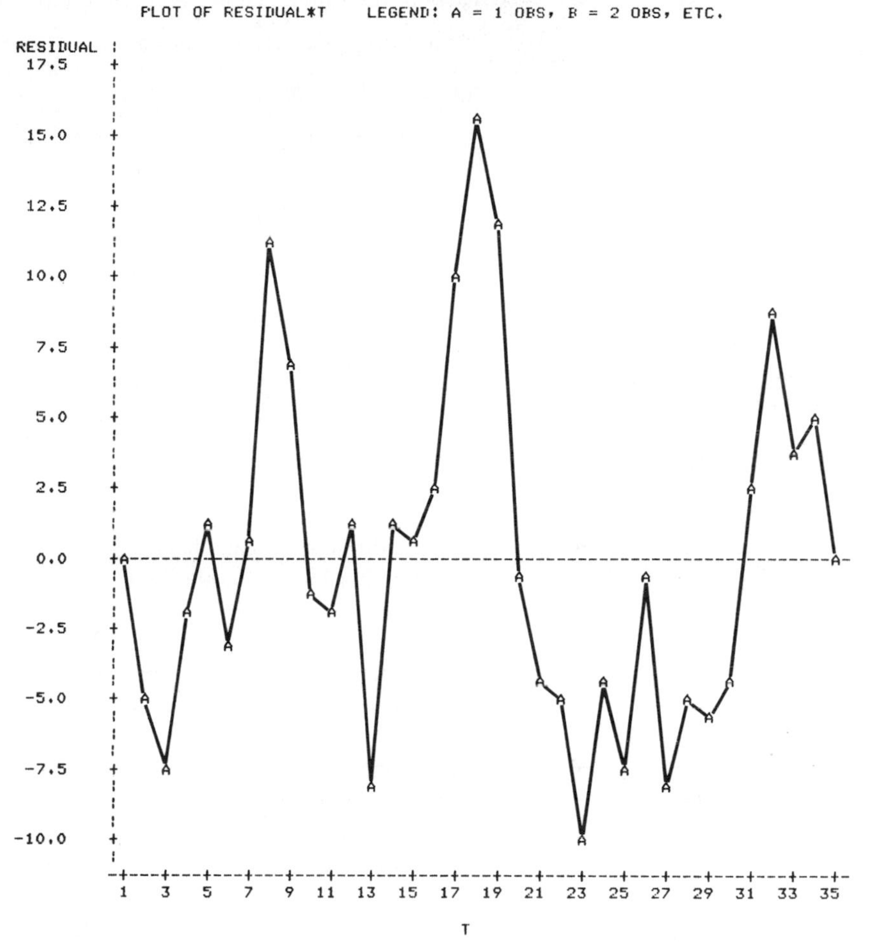

FIGURE 9.14
Annual sales time series example: Least squares residual plot

Thus, we use the pair of models

$$y_t = \beta_0 + \beta_1 t + R_t$$
$$R_t = \phi R_{t-1} + \varepsilon_t$$

to describe the yearly sales of the firm. To estimate the parameters of the time series model (β_0, β_1, and ϕ), a modification of the least squares method is required. To do this, we use a *transformation* that is much like the variance-stabilizing transformations discussed in Chapter 7.

First, we multiply the model

$$y_t = \beta_0 + \beta_1 t + R_t \tag{1}$$

by ϕ at time $(t - 1)$ to obtain

$$\phi y_{t-1} = \phi\beta_0 + \phi\beta_1(t - 1) + \phi R_{t-1} \tag{2}$$

Taking the difference between equations (1) and (2), we have

$$y_t - \phi y_{t-1} = \beta_0(1 - \phi) + \beta_1[t - \phi(t - 1)] + (R_t - \phi R_{t-1})$$

or, since $R_t = \phi R_{t-1} + \varepsilon_t$, then

$$y_t^* = \beta_0^* + \beta_1 t^* + \varepsilon_t$$

where $y_t^* = y_t - \phi y_{t-1}$, $t^* = t - \phi(t - 1)$, and $\beta_0^* = \beta_0(1 - \phi)$. Thus, we can use the transformed dependent variable y_t^* and transformed independent variable t^* to obtain least squares estimates of β_0^* and β_1. The residual ε_t is uncorrelated, so that the assumptions necessary for the least squares estimators are all satisfied. The estimator of the original intercept, β_0, can be calculated by

$$\hat{\beta}_0 = \frac{\hat{\beta}_0^*}{1 - \phi}$$

This transformed model appears to solve the problem of first-order autoregressive residuals. However, making the transformation requires knowing the value of the parameter ϕ. Also, we lose the initial observation, since the values of y_t^* and t^* can be calculated only for $t \geq 2$. The methods for estimating ϕ and adjustments for the values at $t = 1$ will not be detailed here. Instead, we will present output from the SAS computer package, which both performs the transformation and estimates the model parameters, β_0, β_1, and ϕ.

The SAS printout of the straight-line, autoregressive time series model fitted to the sales data is shown in Figure 9.15. Note that the format of the time series printout is different from that of the standard regression printout. The estimates of β_0 and β_1 in the deterministic component $E(y_t)$ appear at the bottom of the printout under the column heading **B Value**. The estimate of the first-order autoregressive parameter ϕ is given in the middle portion of the printout titled **Estimates of the Autoregressive Parameters** beneath the column heading **Coefficient**.

The interpretations of two quantities shown on the SAS printout for the time series procedure differ from those described in the preceding sections. First, the quantity printed as **Reg Rsq** (in the lower portion of the printout) is not the value of R^2 based on the values of y_t. Instead, it is based on the values of the transformed variable, y_t^*. When we refer to R^2 in this chapter, we will always mean the value R^2 based on the original time series variable y_t. This value, which will usually be larger than the **Reg Rsq** value, is given on the printout as **Total Rsq** (shaded). Second, the SAS time series model is defined so that ϕ takes the *opposite* sign from the value contained in our model. Consequently, you must multiply the estimate of ϕ shown in the printout by (-1) to obtain the estimate of ϕ for our model.

Therefore, the fitted models are

$$\hat{y}_t = .40575699 + 4.29593038t + \hat{R}_t \qquad \hat{R}_t = .58962415\hat{R}_{t-1}$$

with

$$\text{MSE} = 27.42767$$

FIGURE 9.15

SAS printout for the combined straight-line autoregressive residual fit to the sales data

```
                              Autoreg Procedure

Dependent Variable = Y

                       Ordinary Least Squares Estimates

            SSE              1345.454      DFE                  33
            MSE              40.77132      Root MSE       6.385242
            SBC              234.1562      AIC            231.0455
            Reg Rsq            0.9800      Total Rsq        0.9800
            Durbin-Watson      0.8207

   Variable       DF         B Value     Std Error     t Ratio Approx Prob

   Intercept       1      0.40151261        2.2057       0.182      0.8567
   T               1      4.29563025        0.1069      40.196      0.0001

                        Estimates of Autocorrelations

Lag  Covariance  Correlation -1 9 8 7 6 5 4 3 2 1 0 1 2 3 4 5 6 7 8 9 1

 0    38.44153      1.000000 |                   |********************|
 1    22.66605      0.589624 |                   |************        |

                         Preliminary MSE = 25.07708

                  Estimates of the Autoregressive Parameters

            Lag      Coefficient      Std Error          t Ratio
              1      -0.58962415     0.14277861        -4.129639

                            Yule-Walker Estimates

            SSE              877.6854      DFE                  32
            MSE              27.42767      Root MSE       5.237143
            SBC              223.1868      AIC            218.5208
            Reg Rsq            0.9412      Total Rsq        0.9869

   Variable       DF         B Value     Std Error     t Ratio Approx Prob

   Intercept       1      0.40575699        3.9970       0.102      0.9198
   T               1      4.29593038        0.1898      22.630      0.0001
```

and

$R^2 = .9869$ (**Total Rsq** on the printout, Figure 9.15)

A comparison of the least squares (Figure 9.6) and autoregressive (Figure 9.15) computer printouts is given in Table 9.7 on page 538. Note that the autoregressive model reduces MSE and increases R^2. The values of the estimators β_0 and β_1 change very little, but the estimated standard errors are considerably increased, thereby decreasing the t value for testing H_0: $\beta_1 = 0$. The implication that the linear relationship between sales y_t and year t is of significant predictive value is the same using either method. However, you can see that the underestimation of standard errors by using least squares in the presence of residual autocorrelation could result in the inclusion of unimportant independent variables in the model, since the t values will usually be inflated.

TABLE 9.7 **Comparison of Least Squares and Time Series Results**

	LEAST SQUARES	AUTOREGRESSIVE
R^2	.98	.99
MSE	40.77	27.43
$\hat{\beta}_0$	.4015	.4058
$\hat{\beta}_1$	4.2956	4.2959
Standard error ($\hat{\beta}_0$)	2.2057	3.9970
Standard error ($\hat{\beta}_1$)	.1069	.1898
t statistic for H_0: $\beta_1 = 0$	40.20 ($p < .0001$)	22.63 ($p < .0001$)
$\hat{\phi}$	—	.5896
t statistic for H_0: $\phi = 0$	—	4.13

The estimated value of ϕ is .5896, and an approximate t test* of the hypothesis H_0: $\phi = 0$ yields a t value of 4.13. With 32 df, this value is significant at less than $\alpha = .01$. Thus, the result of the Durbin–Watson d test is confirmed: There is adequate evidence of positive residual autocorrelation.† Furthermore, the first-order autoregressive model appears to describe this residual correlation well.

The steps for fitting a time series model to a set of data are summarized in the box. Once the model is estimated, the model can be used to forecast future values of the time series y_t.

Steps for Fitting Time Series Models

1. Use the least squares approach to obtain initial estimates of the β parameters. Do *not* use the t or F tests to assess the importance of the parameters, since the estimates of their standard errors may be biased (often underestimated).
2. Analyze the residuals to determine whether they are autocorrelated. The Durbin–Watson test is one technique for making this determination.
3. If there is evidence of autocorrelation, construct a model for the residuals. The autoregressive model is one useful model. Consult the references at the end of the chapter for more types of residual models and for methods of identifying the most suitable model.
4. Reestimate the β parameters, taking the residual model into account. This involves a simple transformation if an autoregressive model is used; several statistical software packages have computer routines to accomplish this.

*An explanation of this t test has been omitted. Consult the references at the end of the chapter for details of this test.

†This result is to be expected since it can be shown (proof omitted) that $\hat{\phi} \approx 1 - d/2$, where d is the value of the Durbin–Watson statistic.

EXERCISES

9.25 The Gross Domestic Product (GDP) is a measure of total U.S. output and is, therefore, an important indicator of the U.S. economy. The quarterly GDP values (in billions of dollars) from 1990 to 1993 are given in the table. Let y_t be the GDP in quarter t, $t = 1, 2, 3, \ldots, 16$.

YEAR	QUARTER			
	I	II	III	IV
1990	4,881	4,900	4,903	4,855
1991	4,824	4,841	4,832	4,838
1992	4,874	4,892	4,998	5,068
1993	5,078	5,102	5,139	5,218

Source: *Survey of Current Business.*

a. Hypothesize a time series model for quarterly GDP that includes a straight-line long-term trend and autocorrelated residuals.
b. The SAS printout for the time series model $y_t = \beta_0 + \beta_1 t + \phi R_{t-1} + \varepsilon_t$ is shown here. Write the least squares prediction equation.
c. Interpret the estimates of the model parameters, β_0, β_1, and ϕ.
d. Interpret the values of R^2 and Root MSE.

```
                      Ordinary Least Squares Estimates

            SSE               78083.02     DFE                  14
            MSE               5577.359     Root MSE       74.68171
            SBC               186.8382     AIC            185.2931
            Reg Rsq             0.6813     Total Rsq        0.6813
            Durbin-Watson       0.2883

     Variable      DF        B Value     Std Error     t Ratio Approx Prob

     Intercept      1     4764.35000        39.163     121.653      0.0001
     T              1       22.15735         4.050       5.471      0.0001

                        Estimates of Autocorrelations

 Lag  Covariance  Correlation -1 9 8 7 6 5 4 3 2 1 0 1 2 3 4 5 6 7 8 9 1

  0    4880.189     1.000000 |                    |********************|
  1    3590.525     0.735735 |                    |***************     |

                         Preliminary MSE = 2238.515

                   Estimates of the Autoregressive Parameters

            Lag     Coefficient        Std Error          t Ratio
              1     -0.73573478       0.18784084        -3.916799

                            Yule-Walker Estimates

            SSE               24720.72     DFE                  13
            MSE               1901.593     Root MSE       43.60726
            SBC               171.9881     AIC            169.6703
            Reg Rsq             0.5335     Total Rsq        0.8991

     Variable      DF        B Value     Std Error     t Ratio Approx Prob

     Intercept      1     4787.81640        60.725      78.844      0.0001
     T              1       22.33703         5.794       3.855      0.0020
```

9.26 Refer to Exercise 9.8.

a. Hypothesize a time series model for annual volume of wheat harvested, y_t, that takes into account the residual autocorrelation.

b. Fit the autoregressive time series model, part a. Interpret the estimates of the model parameters.

9.27 The Dow Jones Industrial Average (DJIA) is a widely followed stock market indicator. The values of the DJIA from 1971 to 1990 are given in the accompanying table. Suppose we want to model the yearly DJIA, y_t, as a function of t, where t is the number of years since 1970 (i.e., $t = 1$ for 1971, $t = 2$ for 1972, . . . , $t = 20$ for 1990). A time series model that includes a long-term trend and autocorrelated residuals is the following regression–autoregression pair.

$$y_t = \beta_0 + \beta_1 t + R_t$$
$$R_t = \phi R_{t-1} + \varepsilon_t$$

The SAS printout for the time series model is shown on page 541.

YEAR	DJIA	YEAR	DJIA
1971	885	1981	899
1972	951	1982	1,047
1973	924	1983	1,259
1974	759	1984	1,212
1975	802	1985	1,547
1976	975	1986	1,896
1977	835	1987	2,276
1978	805	1988	2,061
1979	839	1989	2,508
1980	964	1990	2,679

Source: *The Wall Street Journal.*

a. Identify and interpret estimates of the model parameters.

b. Interpret the value of R^2.

9.28 Refer to Exercise 9.15 and the study on the long-term effects of the Employment Retirement Income Security Act (ERISA). Ledolter and Power also fitted quarterly time series models for the number of pension plan terminations and the number of profit-sharing plan terminations from the first quarter of 1956 through the third quarter of 1982 ($n = 107$ quarters). To account for residual correlation, they fitted straight-line autoregressive models of the form

$$y_t = \beta_0 + \beta_1 t + \phi R_{t-1} + \varepsilon_t$$

The results were as follows:

Pension plan terminations: $\hat{y}_t = 3.54 + .039t + .40\hat{R}_{t-1}$

Profit-sharing plan terminations: $\hat{y}_t = 3.45 + .038t + .22\hat{R}_{t-1}$

a. Interpret the estimates of the model parameters for pension plan terminations.

b. Interpret the estimates of the model parameters for profit-sharing plan terminations.

SAS printout for Exercise 9.27

```
                         Autoreg Procedure

Dependent Variable = DJA

                  Ordinary Least Squares Estimates

              SSE              1998865    DFE               18
              MSE               111048    Root MSE    333.2387
              SBC             292.9962    AIC         291.0047
              Reg Rsq           0.7303    Total Rsq     0.7303
              Durbin-Watson     0.3298

      Variable      DF       B Value    Std Error   t Ratio Approx Prob

      Intercept      1    358.931579       154.80     2.319      0.0324
      T              1     90.211278        12.92     6.981      0.0001

                     Estimates of Autocorrelations

   Lag  Covariance  Correlation -1 9 8 7 6 5 4 3 2 1 0 1 2 3 4 5 6 7 8 9 1

    0    99943.24     1.000000 |                    |********************|
    1    72059.18     0.721001 |                    |**************      |

                     Preliminary MSE = 47988.51

              Estimates of the Autoregressive Parameters

              Lag     Coefficient        Std Error         t Ratio
                1     -0.72100099       0.16806119       -4.290110

                        Yule-Walker Estimates

              SSE             703545.1    DFE               17
              MSE                41385    Root MSE     203.433
              SBC             275.8415    AIC         272.8543
              Reg Rsq           0.5519    Total Rsq     0.9051

      Variable      DF       B Value    Std Error   t Ratio Approx Prob

      Intercept      1    434.929919       256.82     1.694      0.1086
      T              1     92.279852        20.17     4.576      0.0003
```

9.9 Forecasting with Time Series Autoregressive Models

Often, the ultimate objective of fitting a time series model is to forecast future values of the series. We will demonstrate the techniques for the simple model

$$y_t = \beta_0 + \beta_1 x_t + R_t$$

with the first-order autoregressive residual

$$R_t = \phi R_{t-1} + \varepsilon_t$$

Suppose we use the data $(y_1, x_1), (y_2, x_2), \ldots, (y_n, x_n)$ to obtain estimates of β_0, β_1, and ϕ, using the method presented in Section 9.8. We now want to forecast the value of y_{n+1}. From the model,

$$y_{n+1} = \beta_0 + \beta_1 x_{n+1} + R_{n+1}$$

where

$$R_{n+1} = \phi R_n + \varepsilon_{n+1}$$

Combining these, we obtain

$$y_{n+1} = \beta_0 + \beta_1 x_{n+1} + \phi R_n + \varepsilon_{n+1}$$

From this equation, we obtain the forecast of y_{n+1}, denoted F_{n+1}, by estimating each of the unknown quantities and setting ε_{n+1} to its expected value of 0:*

$$F_{n+1} = \hat{\beta}_0 + \hat{\beta}_1 x_{n+1} + \hat{\phi}\hat{R}_n$$

where $\hat{\beta}_0$, $\hat{\beta}_1$, and $\hat{\phi}$ are the estimates based on the time series model-fitting approach presented in Section 9.8. The estimate $\hat{R}_n$ of the residual R_n is obtained by noting that

$$R_n = y_n - (\beta_0 + \beta_1 x_n)$$

so that

$$\hat{R}_n = y_n - (\hat{\beta}_0 + \hat{\beta}_1 x_n)$$

The two-step-ahead forecast of y_{n+2} is similarly obtained. The true value of y_{n+2} is

$$\begin{aligned} y_{n+2} &= \beta_0 + \beta_1 x_{n+2} + R_{n+2} \\ &= \beta_0 + \beta_1 x_{n+2} + \phi R_{n+1} + \varepsilon_{n+2} \end{aligned}$$

and the forecast at $t = n + 2$ is

$$F_{n+2} = \hat{\beta}_0 + \hat{\beta}_1 x_{n+2} + \hat{\phi}\hat{R}_{n+1}$$

The residual R_{n+1} (and all future residuals) can now be obtained from the recursive relation

$$R_{n+1} = \phi R_n + \varepsilon_{n+1}$$

so that

$$\hat{R}_{n+1} = \hat{\phi}\hat{R}_n$$

Thus, the forecasting of future y values is an iterative process, with each new forecast making use of the previous residual to obtain the estimated residual for the future time period. The general forecasting procedure using time series models with first-order autoregressive residuals is outlined in the box on page 543.

EXAMPLE 9.4

Suppose we want to forecast the sales of the company for the data analyzed in Section 9.8. Recall that we fitted the regression–autoregression pair of models

$$y_t = \beta_0 + \beta_1 t + R_t \qquad R_t = \phi R_{t-1} + \varepsilon_t$$

Using 35 years of sales data, we obtained the estimated models

$$\hat{y}_t = .4058 + 4.2959t + \hat{R}_t \qquad \hat{R}_t = .5896\hat{R}_{t-1}$$

*Note that the forecast requires the value of x_{n+1}. When x_t is itself a time series, the future value x_{n+1} will generally be unknown and must also be estimated. Often, $x_t = t$ (as in Example 9.4). In this case, the future time period (e.g., $t = n + 1$) is known and no estimate is required.

Forecasting Using Time Series Models with First-Order Autoregressive Residuals

$$y_t = \beta_0 + \beta_1 x_{1t} + \beta_2 x_{2t} + \cdots + \beta_k x_{kt} + R_t$$
$$R_t = \phi R_{t-1} + \varepsilon_t$$

STEP 1 Use a statistical software package to obtain the estimated model

$$\hat{y}_t = \hat{\beta}_0 + \hat{\beta}_1 x_{1t} + \hat{\beta}_2 x_{2t} + \cdots + \hat{\beta}_k x_{kt} + \hat{R}_t, \quad t = 1, 2, \ldots, n$$
$$\hat{R}_t = \hat{\phi}\hat{R}_{t-1}$$

STEP 2 Compute the estimated residual for the last time period in the data (i.e., $t = n$) as follows:

$$\hat{R}_n = y_n - \hat{y}_n$$
$$= y_n - (\hat{\beta}_0 + \hat{\beta}_1 x_{1n} + \hat{\beta}_2 x_{2n} + \cdots + \hat{\beta}_k x_{kn})$$

STEP 3 The forecast of the value y_{n+1} (i.e., the one-step-ahead forecast) is

$$F_{n+1} = \hat{\beta}_0 + \hat{\beta}_1 x_{1n+1} + \hat{\beta}_2 x_{2,n+1} + \cdots + \hat{\beta}_k x_{k,n+1} + \hat{\phi}\hat{R}_n$$

where $\hat{R}_n$ is obtained from step 2.

STEP 4 The forecast of the value y_{n+2} (i.e., the two-step-ahead forecast) is

$$F_{n+2} = \hat{\beta}_0 + \hat{\beta}_1 x_{1,n+2} + \hat{\beta}_2 x_{2,n+2} + \cdots + \hat{\beta}_k x_{k,n+2} + (\hat{\phi})^2\hat{R}_n$$

where $\hat{R}_{n+1}$ is obtained from step 3.

In general, the m-step-ahead forecast is

$$F_{n+m} = \hat{\beta}_0 + \hat{\beta}_1 x_{1,n+m} + \hat{\beta}_2 x_{2,n+m} + \cdots + \hat{\beta}_k x_{k,n+m} + (\hat{\phi})^m\hat{R}_n$$

Combining these, we have

$$\hat{y}_t = .4058 + 4.2959t + .5896\hat{R}_{t-1}$$

a. Use the fitted model to forecast sales in years $t = 36$, 37, and 38.
b. Calculate approximate 95% prediction intervals for the forecasts.

Solution

a. The forecast for the 36th year requires an estimate of the last residual R_{35},

$$\hat{R}_{35} = y_{35} - [\hat{\beta}_0 + \hat{\beta}_1(35)]$$
$$= 150.9 - [.4058 + 4.2959(35)]$$
$$= .1377$$

Then the one-step-ahead forecast (i.e., the sales forecast for year 36) is

$$F_{36} = \hat{\beta}_0 + \hat{\beta}_1(36) + \hat{\phi}\hat{R}_{35}$$
$$= .4058 + 4.2959(36) + (.5896)(.1377)$$
$$= 155.14$$

Using the formula in the box on page 543, the two-step-ahead forecast (i.e., the sales forecast for year 37) is

$$\begin{aligned} F_{37} &= \hat{\beta}_0 + \hat{\beta}_1(37) + (\hat{\phi})^2\hat{R}_{35} \\ &= .4058 + 4.2959(37) + (.5896)^2(.1377) \\ &= 159.40 \end{aligned}$$

Similarly, the three-step-ahead forecast (i.e., the sales forecast for year 38) is

$$\begin{aligned} F_{38} &= \hat{\beta}_0 + \hat{\beta}_1(38) + (\hat{\phi})^3\hat{R}_{35} \\ &= .4058 + 4.2959(38) + (.5896)^3(.1377) \\ &= 163.68 \end{aligned}$$

We can proceed in this manner to generate sales forecasts as far into the future as desired. However, the potential for error increases as the distance into the future increases. Forecast errors are traceable to three primary causes, as follows:

1. The form of the model may change at some future time. This is an especially difficult source of error to quantify, since we will not usually know when or if the model changes, or the extent of the change. The possibility of a change in the model structure is the primary reason we have consistently urged you to avoid predictions outside the observed range of the independent variables. However, time series forecasting leaves us little choice—by definition, the forecast will be a prediction at a future time.
2. A second source of forecast error is the uncorrelated residual, ε_t, with variance σ^2. For a first-order autoregressive residual, the forecast variance of the one-step-ahead prediction is σ^2, whereas that for the two-step-ahead prediction is $\sigma^2(1 + \phi^2)$, and, in general, for m steps ahead, the forecast variance* is $\sigma^2(1 + \phi^2 + \phi^4 + \cdots + \phi^{2(m-1)})$. Thus, the forecast variance increases as the distance is increased. These variances allow us to form approximate 95% prediction intervals for the forecasts (see the next box).
3. A third source of variability is that attributable to the error of estimating the model parameters. This is generally of less consequence than the others, and is usually ignored in forming prediction intervals.

b. To obtain a prediction interval, we first estimate σ^2 by the MSE, the mean square for error from the time series regression analysis. For the sales data, we form an approximate 95% prediction interval for the sales in year 36:

$$\begin{aligned} &F_{36} \pm 2\sqrt{\text{MSE}} \\ &155.1 \pm 2\sqrt{27.42767} \\ &155.1 \pm 10.1 \end{aligned}$$

or (144.8, 165.4). Thus, we forecast that the sales in year 36 will be between \$145,000 and \$165,000.

*See Fuller (1976).

Approximate 95% Forecasting Limits Using Time Series Models with First-Order Autoregressive Residuals

One-Step-Ahead Forecast

$$\hat{y}_{n+1} \pm 2\sqrt{\text{MSE}}$$

Two-Step-Ahead Forecast

$$\hat{y}_{n+2} \pm 2\sqrt{\text{MSE}(1 + \hat{\phi}^2)}$$

Three-Step-Ahead Forecast

$$\hat{y}_{n+3} \pm 2\sqrt{\text{MSE}(1 + \hat{\phi}^2 + \hat{\phi}^4)}$$

$$\vdots$$

***m*-Step-Ahead Forecast**

$$\hat{y}_{n+m} \pm 2\sqrt{\text{MSE}(1 + \hat{\phi}^2 + \hat{\phi}^4 + \cdots + \hat{\phi}^{2(m-1)})}$$

[*Note:* MSE estimates σ^2, the variance of the uncorrelated residual ε_t.]

The approximate 95% prediction interval for year 37 is

$$F_{37} \pm 2\sqrt{\text{MSE}(1 + \phi^2)}$$

$$159.4 \pm 2\sqrt{27.42767[1 + (.5896)^2]}$$

$$159.4 \pm 11.9$$

or (147.5, 171.3). Note that this interval is wider than that for the one-step-ahead forecast. The intervals will continue to widen as we attempt to forecast farther ahead.

The forecasts and prediction intervals for years 36–40 are shown in Figure 9.16 on page 546. We again stress that the accuracy of these forecasts and intervals depends on the assumption that the model structure does not change during the forecasting period. If, for example, the company merges with another company during year 37, the structure of the sales model will almost surely change, and therefore, prediction intervals past year 37 are probably useless.

It is important to note that the forecasting procedure makes explicit use of the residual autocorrelation. The result is a better forecast than would be obtained using the standard least squares procedure of Chapter 4 (which ignores residual correlation). Generally, this is reflected by narrower prediction intervals for the time series forecasts than for the least squares prediction.* The end result, then,

*When n is large, approximate 95% prediction intervals obtained from the standard least squares procedure reduce to $\hat{y}_t \pm 2\sqrt{\text{MSE}}$ for *all* future values of the time series. These intervals may actually be narrower than the more accurate prediction intervals produced from the time series analysis.

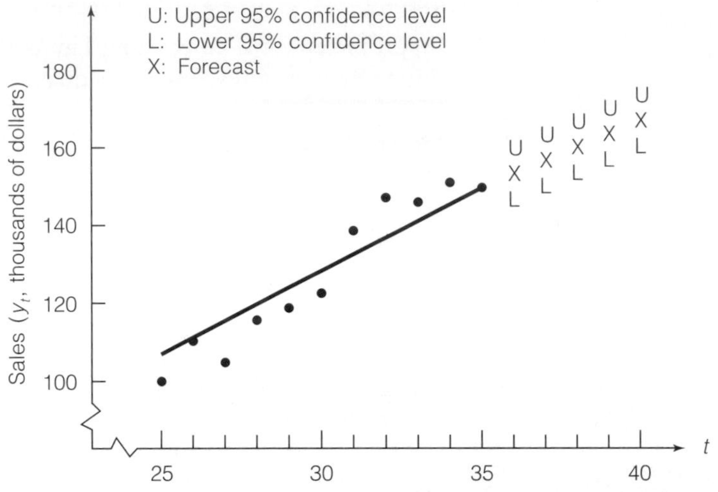

FIGURE 9.16
Forecasts and prediction intervals for years 36–40: Straight-line model with autoregressive residual

of using a time series model when autocorrelation is present is that you obtain more reliable estimates of the β coefficients, smaller residual variance, and more accurate prediction intervals for future values of the time series.

EXERCISES

9.29 The quarterly time series model $y_t = \beta_0 + \beta_1 t + \beta_2 t^2 + \phi R_{t-1} + \varepsilon_t$ was fit to data collected for $n = 48$ quarters, with the following results:

$$\hat{y}_t = 220 + 17t - .3t^2 + .82\hat{R}_{t-1}$$

$$y_{48} = 350 \qquad \text{MSE} = 10.5$$

a. Calculate forecasts for y_t for $t = 49$, $t = 50$, and $t = 51$.

b. Construct approximate 95% prediction intervals for the forecasts obtained in part **a**.

9.30 The annual time series model $y_t = \beta_0 + \beta_1 t + \phi R_{t-1} + \varepsilon_t$ was fit to data collected for $n = 30$ years with the following results:

$$\hat{y}_t = 10 + 2.5t + .64\hat{R}_{t-1}$$

$$y_{30} = 82 \qquad \text{MSE} = 4.3$$

a. Calculate forecasts for y_t for $t = 31$, $t = 32$, and $t = 33$.

b. Construct approximate 95% prediction intervals for the forecasts obtained in part **a**.

9.31 Use the fitted time series model of Exercise 9.25 to forecast GDP for the first three quarters of 1994 and calculate approximate 95% forecast limits. Do these bounds contain the actual 1994 GDP values shown in the accompanying table?

QUARTER	1994 GDP
1	5,261
2	5,314
3	5,359

9.32 Use the fitted time series model of Exercise 9.26 to forecast annual volume of wheat harvest for 1995. Place approximate 95% confidence bounds on the forecast.

9.33 Use the fitted time series model of Exercise 9.27 to forecast the DJIA for the years 1991–1993 (i.e., $t = 21$, 22, and 23). Calculate approximate 95% prediction intervals for the forecast. Do these intervals contain the actual 1991–1993 DJIA values shown in the accompanying table? If not, give a plausible explanation.

YEAR	DJIA
1991	3,015
1992	3,160
1993	3,520

9.34 Refer to the gold price series, 1971–1993, Exercise 9.7. The time series is reproduced in the table.

YEAR	PRICE OF GOLD	YEAR	PRICE OF GOLD	YEAR	PRICE OF GOLD
1971	41.25	1978	193.50	1985	317.30
1972	58.61	1979	307.80	1986	367.87
1973	97.81	1980	606.01	1987	408.91
1974	159.70	1981	450.63	1988	436.93
1975	161.40	1982	374.18	1989	381.21
1976	124.80	1983	449.03	1990	384.07
1977	148.30	1984	360.29	1991	362.04
				1992	344.50
				1993	383.69

a. Hypothesize a deterministic model for $E(y_t)$ based on a plot of the time series.
b. Do you expect the random error term of the model, part **a**, to be uncorrected? Explain.
c. Hypothesize a model for the correlated error term, R_t.
d. Combine the two models, parts **a** and **c**, to form a time series forecasting model.
e. Fit the time series model, part **d**, to the data.
f. Use the fitted time series model from part **e** to forecast the gold price in 1994. Place an approximate 95% prediction interval around the forecast.

9.35 Refer to Exercise 9.28. The values of MSE for the quarterly time series models of retirement plan terminations are as follows:

Pension plan termination: MSE = .0440
Profit-sharing plan termination: MSE = .0402

a. Forecast the number of pension plan terminations for the fourth quarter of 1982 (i.e., $t = 108$). Assume that $y_{107} = 7.5$. [*Hint:* Remember that the forecasted number of pension plan terminations is $e^{\hat{y}_{108}}$.]
b. Place approximate 95% confidence bounds on the forecast obtained in part **a**. [*Hint:* First, calculate upper and lower confidence limits for y_{108}, then take antilogarithms.]
c. Repeat parts **a** and **b** for the number of profit-sharing plan terminations in the fourth quarter of 1982. Assume that $y_{107} = 7.6$.

9.10 Seasonal Time Series Models: An Example

We have used a simple regression model to illustrate the methods of model estimation and forecasting when the residuals are autocorrelated. In this section, we present a more realistic example that requires a seasonal model for $E(y_t)$, as well as an autoregressive model for the residual.

Critical water shortages have dire consequences for both business and private sectors of communities. Forecasting water usage for months in advance is essential to avoid such shortages. Suppose a community has monthly water usage records over the past 15 years. A plot of the last 6 years of the time series, y_t, is shown in Figure 9.17. Note that both an increasing trend and a seasonal pattern appear prominent in the data. The water usage seems to peak during the summer months and decline during the winter months. Thus, we might propose the following model:

$$E(y_t) = \beta_0 + \beta_1 t + \beta_2\left(\cos \frac{2\pi}{12}t\right) + \beta_3\left(\sin \frac{2\pi}{12}t\right)$$

Since the amplitude of the seasonal effect (that is, the magnitude of the peaks and valleys) appears to increase with time, we include in the model an interaction between time and trigonometric components, to obtain

$$E(y_t) = \beta_0 + \beta_1 t + \beta_2\left(\cos \frac{2\pi}{12}t\right) + \beta_3\left(\sin \frac{2\pi}{12}t\right) + \beta_4 t\left(\cos \frac{2\pi}{12}t\right) + \beta_5 t\left(\sin \frac{2\pi}{12}t\right)$$

FIGURE 9.17
Water usage time series

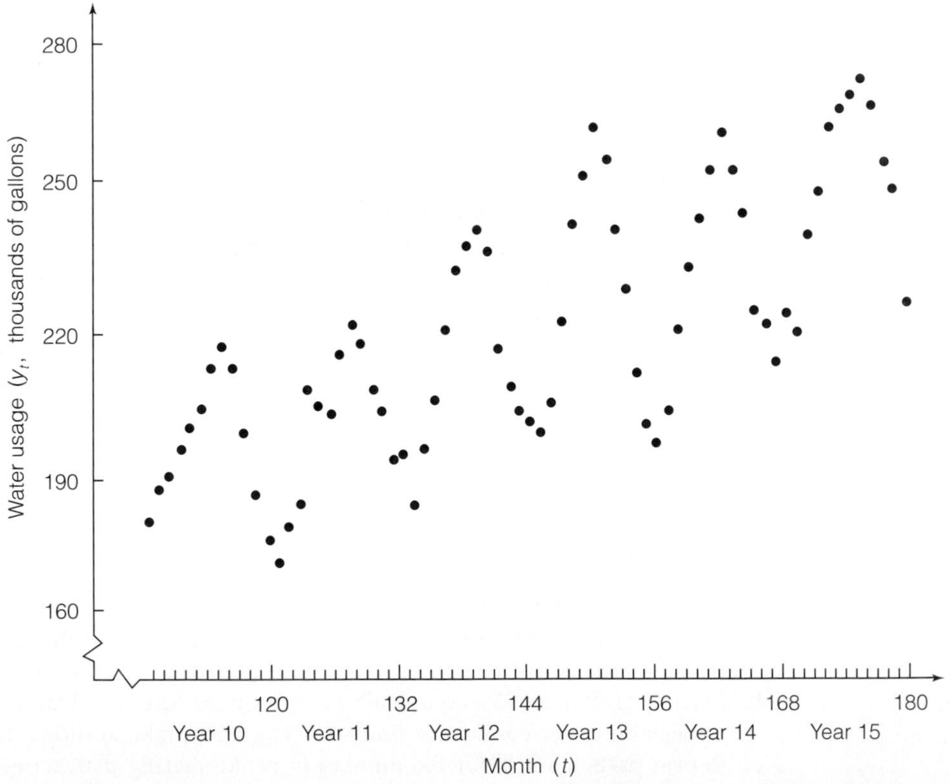

The model for the random component R_t must allow for short-term cyclic effects. For example, in an especially hot summer, if the water usage, y_t, exceeds the expected usage, $E(y_t)$, for July, we would expect the same thing to happen in August. Thus, we propose a first-order autoregressive model* for the random component:

$$R_t = \phi R_{t-1} + \varepsilon_t$$

We now fit the models to the time series y_t, where y_t is expressed in thousands of gallons. The SAS printout is shown in Figure 9.18. The estimated models are given by

$$\hat{y}_t = 100.083 + .826t - 10.801\left(\cos\frac{2\pi}{12}t\right) - 7.086\left(\sin\frac{2\pi}{12}t\right) - .0556t\left(\cos\frac{2\pi}{12}t\right) - .0296t\left(\sin\frac{2\pi}{12}t\right) + \hat{R}_t$$

$$\hat{R}_t = .6617\hat{R}_{t-1}$$

with MSE = 23.135. The R^2 value of .99 (**TOTAL RSQ**) indicates that the models provide a good fit to the data.

FIGURE 9.18
SAS computer printout for water usage models

ESTIMATES OF THE AUTOREGRESSIVE PARAMETERS

LAG	COEFFICIENT	STD ERROR	T RATIO
1	-0.66167894	0.055886	-11.839831

YULE-WALKER ESTIMATES

SSE	4025.513	DFE	174
MSE	23.135	ROOT MSE	4.810
REG RSQ	0.9431	TOTAL RSQ	0.9900

VARIABLE	DF	B VALUE	STD ERROR	T RATIO	APPROX PROB
INTERCEP	1	100.083218977	2.07617706007	48.206	0.0001
T	1	0.826274293	0.01979498750	41.742	0.0001
CS	1	-10.801144	1.85586558083	-5.820	0.0001
SN	1	-7.0857642	1.89574083666	-3.738	0.0003
CST	1	-0.055634923	0.01771077652	-3.141	0.0020
SNT	1	-0.029630055	0.01820045673	-1.628	0.1053

We now use the models to forecast water usage for the next 12 months. The forecast for the first month is obtained as follows. The last residual value (obtained from a portion of the printout not shown) is $\hat{R}_{180} = -1.3247$. Then the formula for the one-step-ahead forecast is

$$F_{181} = \hat{\beta}_0 + \hat{\beta}_1(181) + \hat{\beta}_2\left(\cos\frac{2\pi}{12}181\right) + \hat{\beta}_3\left(\sin\frac{2\pi}{12}181\right) + \hat{\beta}_4(181)\left(\cos\frac{2\pi}{12}181\right) + \hat{\beta}_5(181)\left(\sin\frac{2\pi}{12}181\right) + \hat{\phi}\hat{R}_{180}$$

*A more complex time series model may be more appropriate. We use the simple first-order autoregressive model so you can follow the modeling process more easily.

Substituting the values of $\hat{\beta}_0, \hat{\beta}_1, \ldots, \hat{\beta}_5$, and $\hat{\phi}$ shown in Figure 9.18, we obtain $F_{181} = 238.0$. Approximate 95% prediction bounds on this forecast are given by $\pm 2\sqrt{\text{MSE}} = \pm 2\sqrt{23.135} = \pm 9.6$.* That is, we expect our forecast for 1 month ahead to be within 9,600 gallons of the actual water usage. This forecasting process is then repeated for the next 11 months. The forecasts and their bounds are shown in Figure 9.19. Also shown are the actual values of water usage during year 16. Note that the forecast prediction intervals widen as we attempt to forecast farther into the future. This property of the prediction intervals makes long-term forecasts very unreliable.

FIGURE 9.19
Forecasts of water usage

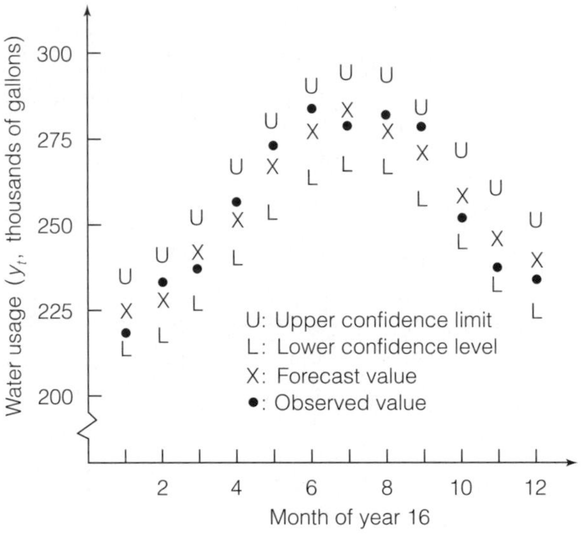

The variety and complexity of time series modeling techniques are overwhelming. We have barely scratched the surface here. However, if we have convinced you that time series modeling is a useful and powerful tool for business forecasting, we have accomplished our purpose. The successful construction of time series models requires much experience, and entire texts are devoted to the subject (see the references at the end of the chapter).

We conclude with a warning: Many oversimplified forecasting methods have been proposed. They usually consist of graphical extensions of a trend or seasonal pattern to future time periods. Although such pictorial techniques are easy to understand and therefore are intuitively appealing, they should be avoided. There is no measure of reliability for these forecasts, and thus the risk associated with making decisions based on them is very high.

---

*We are ignoring the errors in the parameter estimates in calculating the forecast reliability. These errors should be small for a series of this length.

9.11 Forecasting Using Lagged Values of the Dependent Variable (Optional)

In Section 9.7, we discussed a variety of choices for the deterministic component, $E(y_t)$, of the time series models. All these models were functions of independent variables, such as t, x_t, x_{t-1}, and seasonal dummy variables. Often, the forecast of y_t can be improved by adding *lagged values of the dependent variable* to the model. For example, since the price y_t of a stock on day t is highly correlated with the price on the previous day, (i.e., on day $t - 1$), a useful model for $E(y_t)$ is

$$E(y_t) = \beta_0 + \beta_1 y_{t-1}$$

Models with lagged values of y_t tend to violate the standard regression assumptions outlined in Section 4.2; thus, they must be fitted using specialized methods.

Box and Jenkins (1977) developed a method of analyzing time series models based on past values of y_t and past values of the random error ε_t. The general model, denoted **ARMA(*p*, *q*)**, takes the form

$$y_t + \phi_1 y_{t-1} + \phi_2 y_{t-2} + \cdots + \phi_p y_{t-p} = \varepsilon_t + \theta_1 \varepsilon_{t-1} + \theta_2 \varepsilon_{t-2} + \cdots + \theta_q \varepsilon_{t-q}$$

Note that the left side of the equation is a **pth-order autoregressive model** for y_t (see Section 9.5), whereas the right side of the equation is a **qth-order moving average model** for the random error ε_t (see Section 9.6).

The analysis of an ARMA(p, q) model is divided into three stages: (1) identification, (2) estimation, and (3) forecasting. In the identification stage, the values of p and q are determined from the sample data. That is, the order of both the autoregressive portion and the moving average portion of the model are identified.* For example, the analyst may find the best fit to be an ARMA model with $p = 2$ and $q = 0$. Substituting $p = 2$ and $q = 0$ into the previous equation, we obtain the ARMA(2, 0) model

$$y_t + \phi_1 y_{t-1} + \phi_2 y_{t-2} = \varepsilon_t$$

Note that since $q = 0$, there is no moving average component to the model.

Once the model is identified, the second stage involves obtaining estimates of the model's parameters. In the case of the ARMA(2, 0) model, we require estimates of the autoregressive parameters ϕ_1 and ϕ_2. Tests for model adequacy are conducted, and, if the model is deemed adequate, the estimated model is used to forecast future values of y_t in the third stage.

Analysis of ARMA(p, q) models for y_t requires a level of expertise that is beyond the scope of this text. Even with this level of expertise, the analyst cannot hope to proceed without the aid of a sophisticated computer program. Procedures for identifying, estimating, and forecasting with ARMA(p, q) models are available in ASP, SAS, SPSS, and MINITAB. Before attempting to run these procedures, however, you should consult the references provided at the end of this chapter.

---

*This step involves a careful examination of a plot of the sample autocorrelations. Certain patterns in the plot (such as those shown in Figures 9.8–9.10) allow the analyst to identify p and q.

Summary

Time series are often modeled as a combination of four components: **secular**, **seasonal**, **cyclical**, and **residual**. Both descriptive and inferential techniques are available for **estimating** the time series components and **forecasting** future values of the time series. The **moving average method** is a smoothing technique that uses estimates of the secular and seasonal components to forecast future values of a time series. However, the method requires you to extrapolate the moving average into the future to obtain the forecasts. Two alternative smoothing techniques that lead to explicit forecasts are **exponential smoothing** and the **Holt–Winters model**. Exponential smoothing is an adaptive forecasting method for time series with little or no secular or seasonal trends. The Holt–Winters model is an extension of the exponential smoothing technique that allows for trend and seasonal components.

One type of **inferential time series model** employs a combination of the **deterministic component** $E(y_t)$ of the typical multiple regression model with an autoregressive model for the **autocorrelated residual**. The deterministic portion of the model accounts for the trend and seasonal components, and the autocorrelated residual deals with the problem of correlated errors.

The forecaster should be very careful to **distinguish between descriptive and inferential time series models**. If descriptive models (e.g., smoothing techniques) are used to predict future values of the series, no assessment of forecast reliability is possible. Only when a probabilistic model (e.g., a time series autoregressive model) is constructed can a prediction interval be used to evaluate the reliability of the forecast. Even then, if the structure of the model changes at some future time, forecasts beyond that point are probably useless. Careful application of time series modeling and forecasting will usually be rewarded with a better understanding of the phenomenon and with useful forecasts that assist in planning future strategy.

SUPPLEMENTARY EXERCISES

9.36 The level at which commercial lending institutions set mortgage interest rates has a significant effect on the volume of buying, selling, and construction of residential and commercial real estate. The data in the table are the annual average mortgage interest rates for the period 1980–1993. Forecast the 1994 average mortgage interest rate using each of the methods listed here.

YEAR	INTEREST RATE, %	YEAR	INTEREST RATE, %
1980	14.30	1987	10.46
1981	16.54	1988	10.86
1982	16.83	1989	12.07
1983	13.92	1990	11.78
1984	13.71	1991	11.14
1985	12.91	1992	9.29
1986	11.33	1993	8.09

Source: *Statistical Abstract of the United States*, U.S. Bureau of the Census, 1994.

a. A 3-point moving average
b. The exponential smoothing technique ($w = .2$)
c. The Holt–Winters model with trend ($w = .2$ and $v = .5$)
d. Simple linear regression (Obtain a 95% prediction interval.)
e. A straight-line, first-order autoregressive model (Obtain an approximate 95% prediction interval.)

9.37 The accompanying table records the monthly number of mortgage applications (in thousands) for new home construction processed by the Federal Housing Administration (FHA) for the period 1991–1993.

	MORTGAGE APPLICATIONS Thousands		
	1991	1992	1993
January	8.0	7.2	5.7
February	6.7	7.5	7.0
March	8.2	10.1	7.7
April	9.4	9.4	8.2
May	10.5	7.9	7.7
June	8.8	7.7	8.4
July	10.1	8.8	8.3
August	7.4	7.5	8.6
September	7.1	7.1	7.4
October	8.7	7.3	8.8
November	6.6	7.1	9.2
December	6.5	6.5	7.1

Source: *Survey of Current Business*, U.S. Department of Commerce, Bureau of Economic Analysis.

a. Calculate and plot a 12-point moving average for the mortgage applications time series. Can you detect the secular trend? Does there appear to be a seasonal pattern?
b. Use the moving average from part **a** to forecast mortgage applications in January 1994.
c. Calculate and plot the exponentially smoothed series using $w = .6$.
d. Obtain the forecast for January 1994 using the exponential smoothing technique.
e. Obtain the forecast for January 1994 using the Holt–Winters model with trend and seasonal components and smoothing constants $w = .6$, $v = .7$, and $u = .5$.
f. Propose a time series model for monthly mortgage applications that accounts for secular trend, seasonal variation, and residual autocorrelation.
g. Fit the time series model specified in part f, using an available software package.
h. Use the time series model to forecast mortgage applications in January 1994. Obtain an approximate 95% prediction interval for the forecast.

9.38 Refer to the data on average monthly occupancies of hotels and motels in the cities of Atlanta and Phoenix, Exercise 9.14. The data are reproduced in the table on page 554. In part **a** of Exercise 9.14, you hypothesized a model for mean occupancy (y_t) that accounted for seasonal variation in the series.

MONTH	PERCENTAGE OF ROOMS OCCUPIED YEAR 1		YEAR 2	
	Atlanta	Phoenix	Atlanta	Phoenix
January	59	67	64	72
February	63	85	69	91
March	68	83	73	87
April	70	69	67	75
May	63	63	68	70
June	59	52	71	61
July	68	49	67	46
August	64	49	71	44
September	62	56	65	63
October	73	69	72	73
November	62	63	63	71
December	47	48	47	51

Source: *Trends in the Hotel Industry*.

a. Modify the model of part **a** of Exercise 9.14 to account for first-order residual correlation.
b. Fit the model in part **a** to the data for each city. Interpret the results.
c. Would you recommend using the model to forecast monthly occupancy rates in year 3? Explain.

9.39 In May 1978, the first casino (Resorts International Hotel and Casino) opened in Atlantic City, New Jersey. In the first few years following the casino opening, employment in hotels and other lodging places accelerated along Atlantic City's boardwalk, as shown in the table.

YEAR	QUARTER	EMPLOYMENT IN ATLANTIC CITY HOTELS
1978	I	1,711
	II	4,065
	III	5,787
	IV	5,019
1979	I	5,459
	II	9,184
	III	12,168
	IV	11,842
1980	I	13,730
	II	14,964
	III	18,058
	IV	21,393

Source: *Business Review*, Jan.–Feb. 1982.

a. Use a smoothing technique to forecast employment in Atlantic City hotels in quarter I, 1981. Comment on the reliability of this forecast.
b. Propose a time series model for the quarterly series that will account for secular trend, seasonal variation, and residual autocorrelation. If you have access to a software package with a modified least squares routine, fit the model.
c. Use the fitted time series model of part **b** to forecast employment in quarter I, 1981. Place an approximate 95% prediction interval about the forecast.

d. Actual employment in quarter I of 1981 was 22,772. Check to see whether the forecasting technique of part **c** has captured this value.
e. Would you recommend using the fitted model in part **b** for forecasting quarterly employment in 1995? Explain.

9.40 Suppose you were to fit the time series model

$$E(y_t) = \beta_0 + \beta_1 t + \beta_2 t^2$$

to quarterly time series data collected over a 10-year period ($n = 40$ quarters).
a. Set up the test of hypothesis for positively autocorrelated residuals. Specify H_0, H_a, the test statistic, and the rejection region. Use $\alpha = .05$.
b. Suppose the Durbin–Watson *d* statistic is calculated to be 1.14. What is the appropriate conclusion?

9.41 The accompanying table shows U.S. beer production for the years 1973–1993. Suppose you are interested in forecasting U.S. beer production in 1994. Since a plot of the time series y_t reveals a linearly increasing trend, you hypothesize the model

$$E(y_t) = \beta_0 + \beta_1 t$$

for the secular trend.

YEAR	t	U.S. BEER PRODUCTION y_t, millions of barrels	YEAR	t	U.S. BEER PRODUCTION y_t, millions of barrels
1973	1	149	1984	12	193
1974	2	156	1985	13	194
1975	3	161	1986	14	197
1976	4	164	1987	15	195
1977	5	171	1988	16	197
1978	6	179	1989	17	199
1979	7	184	1990	18	204
1980	8	194	1991	19	202
1981	9	194	1992	20	202
1982	10	196	1993	21	207
1983	11	196			

Source: *Standard & Poor's Statistical Service: Current Statistics*, New York, Standard & Poor's Corporation, Jan. 1995.

a. Fit the model to the data using the method of least squares.
b. Plot the least squares model from part **a** and extend the line to forecast y_{22}, the U.S. beer production (in millions of barrels) in 1994. How reliable do you think this forecast is?
c. Calculate and plot the residuals for the model obtained in part **a**. Is there visual evidence of residual autocorrelation?
d. How could you test to determine whether residual autocorrelation exists? If you have access to a computer package, carry out the test. Use $\alpha = .05$.
e. Hypothesize a time series model that will account for the residual autocorrelation. Fit the model to the data and interpret the results.
f. Compute a 95% prediction interval for y_{22}, the U.S. beer production in 1994. Why is this forecast preferred to that of part **b**?

9.42 Suppose a CPA firm wants to model its monthly income, y_t. The firm is growing at an increasing rate, so that the mean income will be modeled as a second-order function of t. In addition, the mean monthly income increases significantly each year from January through April because of processing tax returns.

a. Write a model for $E(y_t)$ to reflect both the second-order function of time, t, and the January–April jump in mean income.

b. Suppose the size of the January–April jump grows each year. How could this information be included in the model? Assume that 5 years of monthly data are available.

9.43 The data on annual OPEC oil imports, Exercise 9.4, are reproduced in the accompanying table.

YEAR	t	IMPORTS, y_t
1974	1	926
1975	2	1,171
1976	3	1,663
1977	4	2,058
1978	5	1,892
1979	6	1,866
1980	7	1,414
1981	8	1,067
1982	9	633
1983	10	540
1984	11	553
1985	12	479
1986	13	771
1987	14	876
1988	15	987
1989	16	1,232
1990	17	1,282
1991	18	1,233
1992	19	1,247
1993	20	1,339

Source: *Statistical Abstracts of the United States*, U.S. Bureau of the Census, 1994.

a. Plot the time series.

b. Hypothesize a straight-line autoregressive time series model for annual amount of imported crude oil, y_t.

c. Fit the proposed model to the data. Interpret the results.

d. From the output, write the modified least squares prediction equation for y_t.

e. Forecast the amount of foreign crude oil imported into the United States from OPEC in 1994. Place approximate 95% prediction bounds on the forecast value.

References

Anderson, T. W. *The Statistical Analysis of Time Series*. New York: Wiley, 1971.

Box, G. E. P., and Jenkins, G. M. *Time Series Analysis: Forecasting and Control*, 2nd ed. San Francisco: Holden-Day, 1977.

Fuller, W. A. *Introduction to Statistical Time Series*. New York: Wiley, 1976.

Granger, C. W. J. *Spectral Analysis of Economic Time Series*. Princeton: Princeton University Press, 1964.

Granger, C. W. J., and Newbold, P. *Forecasting Economic Time Series*. New York: Academic Press, 1977.

Makridakis, S. et al. *The Forecasting Accuracy of Major Time Series Methods*. New York: Wiley, 1984.

Nelson, C. R. *Applied Time Series Analysis for Managerial Forecasting*. San Francisco: Holden-Day, 1973.

Seitz, N. *Business Forecasting: Concepts and Microcomputer Applications*. Reston, Va.: Reston Publishing Company, 1984.

CHAPTER 10 Principles of Experimental Design

CONTENTS

OBJECTIVE

To present an overview of experiments designed to compare two or more population means; to explain the statistical principles of experimental design

10.1 Introduction

In Chapter 6, we learned that a regression analysis of observational data has some limitations. In particular, establishing a cause-and-effect relationship between an independent variable x and the response y is difficult since the values of other relevant independent variables—both those in the model and those omitted from the model—are not controlled. Recall that experimental data are data collected with the values of the x's set in advance of observing y (i.e., the values of the x's are controlled). With experimental data, we usually select the x's so that we can compare the mean responses, $E(y)$, for several different combinations of the x values.

The procedure for selecting sample data with the x's set in advance is called the **design of the experiment**. The statistical procedure for comparing the population means is called an **analysis of variance**. The objective of this chapter is to introduce some key aspects of experimental design. The analysis of the data from such experiments using an analysis of variance is the topic of Chapter 11.

10.2 Experimental Design Terminology

The study of experimental design originated in England and, in its early years, was associated solely with agricultural experimentation. The need for experimental design in agriculture was very clear: It takes a full year to obtain a single observation on the yield of a new variety of most crops. Consequently, the need to save time and money led to a study of ways to obtain more information using smaller samples. Similar motivations led to its subsequent acceptance and wide use in all fields of scientific experimentation. Despite this fact, the terminology associated with experimental design clearly indicates its early association with the biological sciences.

We will call the process of collecting sample data an **experiment** and the (dependent) variable to be measured, the **response** y. The planning of the sampling procedure is called the **design** of the experiment. The object upon which the response measurement y is taken is called an **experimental unit**.

Definition 10.1

The process of collecting sample data is called an **experiment**.

Definition 10.2

The plan for collecting the sample is called the **design** of the experiment.

Definition 10.3

The variable measured in the experiment is called the **response variable**.

Definition 10.4

The object upon which the response y is measured is called an **experimental unit**.

Independent variables that may be related to a response variable y are called **factors**. The value—that is, the intensity setting—assumed by a factor in an experiment is called a **level**. The combinations of levels of the factors for which the response will be observed are called **treatments**.

Definition 10.5

The independent variables, quantitative or qualitative, that are related to a response variable y are called **factors**.

Definition 10.6

The intensity setting of a factor (i.e., the value assumed by a factor in an experiment) is called a **level**.

Definition 10.7

A **treatment** is a particular combination of levels of the factors involved in an experiment.

EXAMPLE 10.1

A designed experiment. A marketing study is conducted to investigate the effects of brand and shelf location on weekly coffee sales. Coffee sales are recorded for each of two brands (brand A and brand B) at each of three shelf locations (bottom, middle, and top). The $2 \times 3 = 6$ combinations of brand and shelf location were varied each week for a period of 18 weeks. Figure 10.1 is a layout of the design. For this experiment, identify

a. the experimental unit
b. the response, y
c. the factors
d. the factor levels
e. the treatments

FIGURE 10.1
Layout for designed experiment of Example 10.1

		SHELF LOCATION		
		Bottom	Middle	Top
BRAND	A	Week 1 9 14	Week 2 7 16	Week 4 12 17
	B	Week 5 10 13	Week 3 8 18	Week 6 11 15

Solution

a. Since the data will be collected each week for a period of 18 weeks, the experimental unit is 1 week.
b. The variable of interest, i.e., the response, is y = weekly coffee sales. Note that weekly coffee sales is a quantitative variable.
c. Since we are interested in investigating the effect of brand and shelf location on sales, brand and shelf location are the factors. Note that both factors are qualitative variables, although, in general, they may be quantitative or qualitative.
d. For this experiment, brand is measured at two levels (A and B) and shelf location at three levels (bottom, middle, and top).
e. Since coffee sales are recorded for each of the six brand–shelf location combinations (brand A, bottom), (brand A, middle), (brand A, top), (brand B, bottom), (brand B, middle), and (brand B, top), then the experiment involves six treatments (see Figure 10.1). The term *treatments* is used to describe the factor level combinations to be included in an experiment because many experiments involve "treating" or doing something to alter the nature of the experimental unit. Thus, we might view the six brand–shelf location combinations as treatments on the experimental units in the marketing study involving coffee sales.

Now that you understand some of the terminology, it is helpful to think of the design of an experiment in four steps.

STEP 1 Select the factors to be included in the experiment, and identify the parameters that are the object of the study. Usually, the target parameters are the population means associated with the factor level combinations (i.e., treatments).

STEP 2 Choose the treatments (the factor level combinations to be included in the experiment).

STEP 3 Determine the number of observations (sample size) to be made for each treatment. [This will usually depend on the standard error(s) that you desire.]

STEP 4 Plan how the treatments will be assigned to the experimental units. That is, decide on which design to use.

By following these steps, you can control the quantity of information in an experiment. We shall explain how this is done in Section 10.3.

10.3 Controlling the Information in an Experiment

The problem of acquiring good experimental data is analogous to the problem faced by a communications engineer. The receipt of any signal, verbal or otherwise, depends on the volume of the signal and the amount of background noise. The greater the volume of the signal, the greater will be the amount of information transmitted to the receiver. Conversely, the amount of information transmitted is reduced when the background noise is great. These intuitive thoughts about the factors that affect the information in an experiment are supported by the following fact: The standard errors of most estimators of the target parameters are proportional to σ (a measure of data variation or noise) and inversely proportional to the sample size (a measure of the volume of the signal). To illustrate, take the simple case where we wish to estimate a population mean μ by the sample mean $\bar{y}$. The standard error of the sampling distribution of $\bar{y}$ is

$$\sigma_{\bar{y}} = \frac{\sigma}{\sqrt{n}} \quad \text{(see Section 1.6)}$$

For a fixed sample size n, the smaller the value of σ, which measures the **variability (noise)** in the population of measurements, the smaller will be the standard error $\sigma_{\bar{y}}$. Similarly, by increasing the sample size n (**volume of the signal**) in a given experiment, you decrease $\sigma_{\bar{y}}$.

The first three steps in the design of an experiment—selecting the factors and treatments to be included in an experiment and specifying the sample sizes—determine the volume of the signal. You must select the treatments so that the observed values of y provide information on the parameters of interest. Then the larger the treatment sample sizes, the greater will be the quantity of information in the experiment. We present an example of a volume-increasing experiment in Section 10.5.

Is it possible to observe y and obtain no information on a parameter of interest? The answer is yes. To illustrate, suppose that you attempt to fit a first-order model

$$E(y) = \beta_0 + \beta_1 x$$

to a set of $n = 10$ data points, all of which were observed for a single value of x, say, $x = 5$. The data points might appear as shown in Figure 10.2. Clearly, there is no possibility of fitting a line to these data points. The only way to obtain information on β_0 and β_1 is to observe y for *different* values of x. Consequently, the $n = 10$ data points in this example contain absolutely no information on the parameters β_0 and β_1.

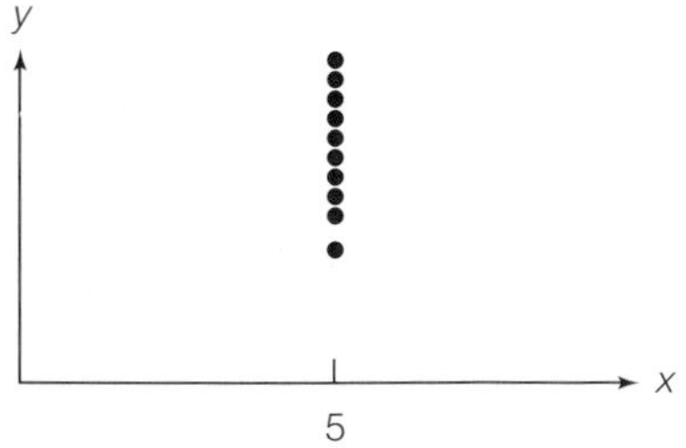

FIGURE 10.2
Data set with $n = 10$ responses, all at $x = 5$

Step 4 in the design of an experiment provides an opportunity to reduce the noise (or experimental error) in an experiment. As we illustrate in Section 10.4, known sources of data variation can be reduced or eliminated by **blocking**—that is, observing all treatments within relatively homogeneous **blocks** of experimental material. When the treatments are compared within each block, any background noise produced by the block is canceled, or eliminated, allowing us to obtain better estimates of treatment differences.

Summary of Steps in Experimental Design

Volume-increasing: 1. Select the factors.
2. Choose the treatments (factor level combinations).
3. Determine the sample size for each treatment.

Noise-reducing: 4. Assign the treatments to the experimental units.

In summary, it is useful to think of experimental designs as being either "noise reducers" or "volume increasers." We will learn, however, that most designs are multifunctional. That is, they tend to both reduce the noise and increase the volume of the signal at the same time. Nevertheless, we will find that specific designs lean heavily toward one or the other objective.

10.4 Noise-Reducing Designs

Noise reduction in an experimental design, i.e., the removal of extraneous experimental variation, can be accomplished by an appropriate assignment of treatments to the experimental units. The idea is to compare treatments within blocks of relatively homogeneous experimental units. The most common design of this type is called a **randomized block design**.

To illustrate, suppose we want to compare the mean performance times of female long-distance runners using three different training liquids (e.g., fructose drinks, glucose drinks, and water) 1 hour prior to running a race. Thus, we want to compare the three means μ_A, μ_B, and μ_C, where μ_i is the mean processing time for liquid i. One way to design the experiment is to select 15 female runners (where the runners are the experimental units) and randomly assign one of the three liquids (treatments) to each runner. A diagram of this design, called a **completely randomized design** (since the treatments are randomly assigned to the experimental units), is shown in Table 10.1.

TABLE 10.1 **Completely Randomized Design with $p = 3$ Treatments**

RUNNER	TREATMENT (LIQUID) ASSIGNED
1	B
2	A
3	B
4	C
5	C
6	A
7	B
8	C
9	A
10	A
11	C
12	A
13	B
14	C
15	B

Definition 10.8

A **completely randomized design** to compare p treatments is one in which the treatments are randomly assigned to the experimental units.

This design has the obvious disadvantage that the performance times would vary greatly from runner to runner depending on the fitness level of the athlete, the athlete's age, etc. A better design—one that contains more information on the mean performance times—would be to use only five runners and require each athlete to run three long-distance races, drinking a different liquid before each race. This *randomized block* procedure acknowledges the fact that performance time in a long-distance race varies substantially from runner to runner. By comparing the three performance times for each runner, we eliminate runner-to-runner variation from the comparison.

The randomized block design that we have just described is diagrammed in Figure 10.3. The figure shows that there are five runners. Each runner can be viewed as a **block** of three experimental units—one corresponding to the use of each of the training liquids, A, B, and C. The blocks are said to be **randomized** because the treatments (liquids) are randomly assigned to the experimental units within a block. For our example, the liquids drunk prior to a race would be assigned in random order to avoid bias introduced by other unknown and unmeasured variables that may affect a runner's performance time.

In general, a randomized block design to compare p treatments will contain b relatively homogeneous blocks, with each block containing p experimental units. Each treatment appears once in every block, with the p treatments randomly assigned to the experimental units within each block.

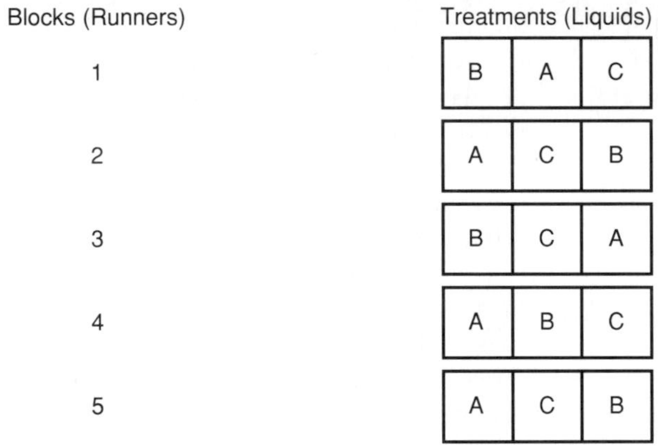

FIGURE 10.3
Diagram for a randomized block design containing $b = 5$ blocks and $p = 3$ treatments

Definition 10.9

A **randomized block design** to compare p treatments involves b blocks, each containing p relatively homogeneous experimental units. The p treatments are randomly assigned to the experimental units within each block, with one experimental unit assigned per treatment.

EXAMPLE 10.2

Suppose you want to compare the abilities of four real estate appraisers, A, B, C, and D. One way to make the comparison would be to randomly allocate a number of pieces of real estate—say, 40—ten to each of the four appraisers. Each appraiser would appraise the property, and you would record y, the difference between the appraised and selling prices expressed as a percentage of the selling price. Thus, y measures the appraisal error expressed as a percentage of selling price, and the treatment allocation to experimental units that we have described is a completely randomized design.

a. Discuss the problems with using a completely randomized design for this experiment.
b. Explain how you could employ a randomized block design.

Solution

a. The problem with using a completely randomized design for the appraisal experiment is that the comparison of mean percentage errors will be influenced by the nature of the properties. Some properties will be easier to appraise than others, and the variation in percentage errors that can be attributed to this fact will make it more difficult to compare the treatment means.
b. To eliminate the effect of property-to-property variability in comparing appraiser means, you could select only 10 properties and require each appraiser to appraise the value of each of the 10 properties. Although in this case there is probably no need for randomization, it might be desirable to randomly assign the order (in time) of the appraisals. This randomized block design, consisting of $p = 4$ treatments and $b = 10$ blocks would appear as shown in Figure 10.4.

FIGURE 10.4
Diagram for a randomized block design: Example 10.2

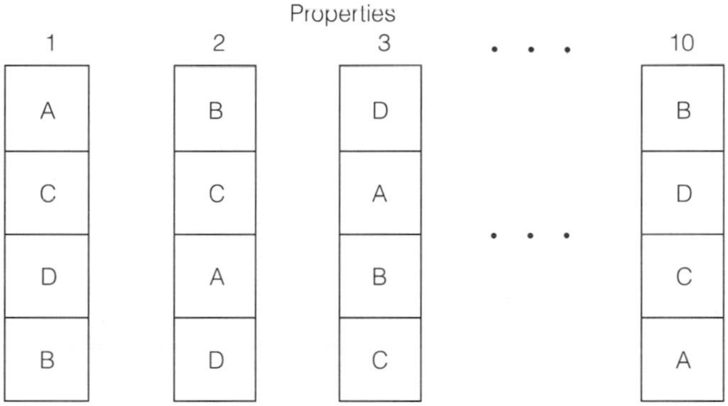

Each experimental design can be represented by a general linear model relating the response y to the factors (treatments, blocks, etc.) in the experiment. When the factors are qualitative in nature (as is often the case), the model includes dummy variables. For example, consider the completely randomized design portrayed in Table 10.1. Since the experiment involves three treatments (liquids), we require two dummy variables. The model for this completely randomized design would appear as follows:

$$y = \beta_0 + \beta_1 x_1 + \beta_2 x_2 + \varepsilon$$

where

$$x_1 = \begin{cases} 1 & \text{if liquid A} \\ 0 & \text{if not} \end{cases} \qquad x_2 = \begin{cases} 1 & \text{if liquid B} \\ 0 & \text{if not} \end{cases}$$

We have arbitrarily selected program C as the base level. From our discussion of dummy-variable models in Chapter 5, we know that the mean responses for the three liquids are

$$\mu_A = \beta_0 + \beta_1$$
$$\mu_B = \beta_0 + \beta_2$$
$$\mu_C = \beta_0$$

Recall that $\beta_1 = \mu_A - \mu_C$ and $\beta_2 = \mu_B - \mu_C$. Thus, to estimate the differences between the treatment means, we require estimates of β_1 and β_2.

Similarly, we can write the model for the randomized block design in Figure 10.3 as follows:

$$y = \beta_0 + \underbrace{\beta_1 x_1 + \beta_2 x_2}_{\text{Treatment effects}} + \underbrace{\beta_3 x_3 + \beta_4 x_4 + \beta_5 x_5 + \beta_6 x_6}_{\text{Block effects}} + \varepsilon$$

where

$$x_1 = \begin{cases} 1 & \text{if liquid A} \\ 0 & \text{if not} \end{cases} \quad x_2 = \begin{cases} 1 & \text{if liquid B} \\ 0 & \text{if not} \end{cases} \quad x_3 = \begin{cases} 1 & \text{if runner 1} \\ 0 & \text{if not} \end{cases}$$

$$x_4 = \begin{cases} 1 & \text{if runner 2} \\ 0 & \text{if not} \end{cases} \quad x_5 = \begin{cases} 1 & \text{if runner 3} \\ 0 & \text{if not} \end{cases} \quad x_6 = \begin{cases} 1 & \text{if runner 4} \\ 0 & \text{if not} \end{cases}$$

In addition to the treatment terms, the model includes four dummy variables representing the five blocks (runners). Note that we have arbitrarily selected runner 5 as the base level. Using this model, we can write each response y in the experiment of Figure 10.3 as a function of β's, as shown in Table 10.2.

TABLE 10.2 **The Response for the Randomized Block Design Shown in Figure 10.3**

BLOCKS (RUNNERS)	TREATMENTS (LIQUIDS)		
	A ($x_1 = 1, x_2 = 0$)	B ($x_1 = 0, x_2 = 1$)	C ($x_1 = 0, x_2 = 0$)
1 ($x_3 = 1, x_4 = x_5 = x_6 = 0$)	$y_{A1} = \beta_0 + \beta_1 + \beta_3 + \varepsilon_{A1}$	$y_{B1} = \beta_0 + \beta_2 + \beta_3 + \varepsilon_{B1}$	$y_{C1} = \beta_0 + \beta_3 + \varepsilon_{C1}$
2 ($x_4 = 1, x_3 = x_5 = x_6 = 0$)	$y_{A2} = \beta_0 + \beta_1 + \beta_4 + \varepsilon_{A2}$	$y_{B2} = \beta_0 + \beta_2 + \beta_4 + \varepsilon_{B2}$	$y_{C2} = \beta_0 + \beta_4 + \varepsilon_{C2}$
3 ($x_5 = 1, x_3 = x_4 = x_6 = 0$)	$y_{A3} = \beta_0 + \beta_1 + \beta_5 + \varepsilon_{A3}$	$y_{B3} = \beta_0 + \beta_2 + \beta_5 + \varepsilon_{B3}$	$y_{C3} = \beta_0 + \beta_5 + \varepsilon_{C3}$
4 ($x_6 = 1, x_3 = x_4 = x_5 = 0$)	$y_{A4} = \beta_0 + \beta_1 + \beta_6 + \varepsilon_{A4}$	$y_{B4} = \beta_0 + \beta_2 + \beta_6 + \varepsilon_{B4}$	$y_{C4} = \beta_0 + \beta_6 + \varepsilon_{C4}$
5 ($x_3 = x_4 = x_5 = x_6 = 0$)	$y_{A5} = \beta_0 + \beta_1 + \varepsilon_{A5}$	$y_{B5} = \beta_0 + \beta_2 + \varepsilon_{B5}$	$y_{C5} = \beta_0 + \varepsilon_{C5}$

For example, to obtain the model for the response y for treatment A in block 1 (denoted y_{A1}), we substitute $x_1 = 1$, $x_2 = 0$, $x_3 = 1$, $x_4 = 0$, $x_5 = 0$, and $x_6 = 0$ into the equation. The resulting model is

$$y_{A1} = \beta_0 + \beta_1 + \beta_3 + \varepsilon_{A1}$$

Now we will use Table 10.2 to illustrate how a randomized block design reduces experimental noise. Since each treatment appears in each of the five blocks, there are five measured responses per treatment. Averaging the five responses for treatment A shown in Table 10.2, we obtain

$$\begin{aligned}\bar{y}_A &= \frac{y_{A1} + y_{A2} + y_{A3} + y_{A4} + y_{A5}}{5} \\ &= [(\beta_0 + \beta_1 + \beta_3 + \varepsilon_{A1}) + (\beta_0 + \beta_1 + \beta_4 + \varepsilon_{A2}) + (\beta_0 + \beta_1 + \beta_5 + \varepsilon_{A3}) \\ &\quad + (\beta_0 + \beta_1 + \beta_6 + \varepsilon_{A4}) + (\beta_0 + \beta_1 + \varepsilon_{A5})]/5 \\ &= \frac{5\beta_0 + 5\beta_1 + (\beta_3 + \beta_4 + \beta_5 + \beta_6) + (\varepsilon_{A1} + \varepsilon_{A2} + \varepsilon_{A3} + \varepsilon_{A4} + \varepsilon_{A5})}{5} \\ &= \beta_0 + \beta_1 + \frac{(\beta_3 + \beta_4 + \beta_5 + \beta_6)}{5} + \bar{\varepsilon}_A\end{aligned}$$

Similarly, the mean responses for treatments B and C are obtained:

$$\begin{aligned}\bar{y}_B &= \frac{y_{B1} + y_{B2} + y_{B3} + y_{B4} + y_{B5}}{5} \\ &= \beta_0 + \beta_2 + \frac{(\beta_3 + \beta_4 + \beta_5 + \beta_6)}{5} + \bar{\varepsilon}_B \\ \bar{y}_C &= \frac{y_{C1} + y_{C2} + y_{C3} + y_{C4} + y_{C5}}{5} \\ &= \beta_0 + \frac{(\beta_3 + \beta_4 + \beta_5 + \beta_6)}{5} + \bar{\varepsilon}_C\end{aligned}$$

Since the objective is to compare treatment means, we are interested in the differences $\bar{y}_A - \bar{y}_B$, $\bar{y}_A - \bar{y}_C$, and $\bar{y}_B - \bar{y}_C$, which are calculated as follows:

$$\begin{aligned}\bar{y}_A - \bar{y}_B &= [\beta_0 + \beta_1 + (\beta_3 + \beta_4 + \beta_5 + \beta_6)/5 + \bar{\varepsilon}_A] \\ &\quad - [\beta_0 + \beta_2 + (\beta_3 + \beta_4 + \beta_5 + \beta_6)/5 + \bar{\varepsilon}_B] \\ &= (\beta_1 - \beta_2) + (\bar{\varepsilon}_A - \bar{\varepsilon}_B) \\ \bar{y}_A - \bar{y}_C &= [\beta_0 + \beta_1 + (\beta_3 + \beta_4 + \beta_5 + \beta_6)/5 + \bar{\varepsilon}_A] \\ &\quad - [\beta_0 + (\beta_3 + \beta_4 + \beta_5 + \beta_6)/5 + \bar{\varepsilon}_C] \\ &= \beta_1 + (\bar{\varepsilon}_A - \bar{\varepsilon}_C) \\ \bar{y}_B - \bar{y}_C &= [\beta_0 + \beta_2 + (\beta_3 + \beta_4 + \beta_5 + \beta_6)/5 + \bar{\varepsilon}_B] \\ &\quad - [\beta_0 + (\beta_3 + \beta_4 + \beta_5 + \beta_6)/5 + \bar{\varepsilon}_C] \\ &= \beta_2 + (\bar{\varepsilon}_B - \bar{\varepsilon}_C)\end{aligned}$$

For each pairwise comparison, the block β's (β_3, β_4, β_5, and β_6) cancel out, leaving only the treatment β's (β_1 and β_2). That is, the experimental noise resulting from differences between blocks is eliminated when treatment means are compared. The quantities $\bar{\varepsilon}_A - \bar{\varepsilon}_B$, $\bar{\varepsilon}_A - \bar{\varepsilon}_C$, and $\bar{\varepsilon}_B - \bar{\varepsilon}_C$ are the errors of estimation and represent the noise that tends to obscure the true differences between the treatment means.

What would occur if we employed the completely randomized design of Table 10.1 rather than the randomized block design? Since each runner is assigned to drink a single liquid, each treatment does not appear in each block. Consequently, when we compare the treatment means, the runner-to-runner variation (i.e., the block effects) will not cancel. For example, the difference between $\bar{y}_A$ and $\bar{y}_C$ would be

$$\bar{y}_A - \bar{y}_C = \beta_1 + \underbrace{(\text{Block } \beta\text{'s that do not cancel}) + (\bar{\varepsilon}_A - \bar{\varepsilon}_C)}_{\text{Error of estimation}}$$

Thus, for the completely randomized design, the error of estimation will be increased by an amount involving the block effects (β_3, β_4, β_5, and β_6) that do not cancel. These effects, which inflate the error of estimation, cancel out for the randomized block design, thereby reducing the noise in the experiment.

EXAMPLE 10.3

Refer to Example 10.2 and the randomized block design employed to compare the mean percentage error rates for the four appraisers. The design is illustrated in Figure 10.4.

a. Write the model for the randomized block design.
b. Interpret the β parameters of the model, part **a**.
c. How can we use the model, part **a**, to test for differences among the mean percentage error rates of the four appraisers?

Solution

a. The experiment involves a qualitative factor (Appraisers) at four levels, which represent the treatments. The blocks for the experiment are the 10 properties. Therefore, the model is

$$E(y) = \beta_0 + \underbrace{\beta_1x_1 + \beta_2x_2 + \beta_3x_3}_{\substack{\text{Treatments} \\ \text{(Appraisers)}}} + \underbrace{\beta_4x_4 + \beta_5x_5 + \cdots + \beta_{12}x_{12}}_{\substack{\text{Blocks} \\ \text{(Properties)}}}$$

where

$$x_1 = \begin{cases} 1 & \text{if appraiser A} \\ 0 & \text{if not} \end{cases} \quad x_2 = \begin{cases} 1 & \text{if appraiser B} \\ 0 & \text{if not} \end{cases} \quad x_3 = \begin{cases} 1 & \text{if appraiser C} \\ 0 & \text{if not} \end{cases}$$

$$x_4 = \begin{cases} 1 & \text{if property 1} \\ 0 & \text{if not} \end{cases} \quad x_5 = \begin{cases} 1 & \text{if property 2} \\ 0 & \text{if not} \end{cases}, \ldots, x_{12} = \begin{cases} 1 & \text{if property 9} \\ 0 & \text{if not} \end{cases}$$

b. Note that we have arbitrarily selected appraiser D and property 10 as the base levels. Following our discussion in Section 5.8, the interpretations of the β's are

$$\begin{aligned}
\beta_1 &= \mu_A - \mu_D && \text{for a given property} \\
\beta_2 &= \mu_B - \mu_D && \text{for a given property} \\
\beta_3 &= \mu_C - \mu_D && \text{for a given property} \\
\beta_4 &= \mu_1 - \mu_{10} && \text{for a given appraiser} \\
\beta_5 &= \mu_2 - \mu_{10} && \text{for a given appraiser} \\
&\vdots \\
\beta_{12} &= \mu_9 - \mu_{10} && \text{for a given appraiser}
\end{aligned}$$

c. One way to determine whether the means for the four appraisers differ is to test the null hypothesis

$$H_0: \mu_A = \mu_B = \mu_C = \mu_D$$

From our β interpretations in part **b**, this hypothesis is equivalent to testing

$$H_0: \beta_1 = \beta_2 = \beta_3 = 0$$

To test this hypothesis, we drop the treatment β's (β_1, β_2, and β_3) from the complete model and fit the reduced model

$$E(y) = \beta_0 + \beta_4 x_4 + \beta_5 x_5 + \cdots + \beta_{12} x_{12}$$

Then we conduct the nested model partial F test (see Section 4.10), where

$$F = \frac{(\text{SSE}_{\text{Reduced}} - \text{SSE}_{\text{Complete}})/3}{\text{MSE}_{\text{Complete}}}$$

The randomized block design represents one of the simplest types of noise-reducing designs. Other, more complex designs that employ the principle of blocking remove trends or variation in two or more directions. The **Latin square design** is useful when you want to eliminate two sources of variation, i.e., when you want to block in two directions. **Latin cube designs** allow you to block in three directions. A further variation in blocking occurs when the block contains fewer experimental units than the number of treatments. By properly assigning the treatments to a specified number of blocks, you can still obtain an estimate of the difference between a pair of treatments free of block effects. These are known as **incomplete block designs**. Consult the references for details on how to set up these more complex block designs.

EXERCISES

10.1 What two factors affect the quantity of information in an experiment?

10.2 How do block designs increase the quantity of information in an experiment?

10.3 Researchers recently conducted an experiment to compare the mean job satisfaction rating $E(y)$ of workers using three types of work scheduling: flextime (which allows workers to set their individual work schedules), staggered starting hours, and fixed hours.

a. Identify the treatments in the experiment.
b. Suppose 60 workers are available for the study. Explain how you would employ a completely randomized design for this experiment.
c. Write the linear model for the completely randomized design.

10.4 A commonly used index to estimate the reliability of a building subjected to lateral loads is the drift ratio. Sophisticated computer programs such as STAAD-III have been developed to estimate the drift ratio based on variables such as beam stiffness, column stiffness, story height, moment of inertia, etc. Civil engineers at SUNY, Buffalo, and the University of Central Florida performed an experiment to compare drift ratio estimates using STAAD-III with the estimates produced by a new, simpler microcomputer program called DRIFT (*Microcomputers in Civil Engineering*, 1993). Data for a 21-story building were used as input to the programs. Two runs were made with STAAD-III: Run 1 considered axial deformation of the building columns, and run 2 neglected this information. The goal of the analysis was to compare the mean drift ratios (where drift is measured as lateral displacement) estimated by the three computer runs.

a. Identify the treatments in the experiment.
b. Because lateral displacement will vary greatly across building levels (floors), a randomized block design will be used to reduce the level-to-level variation in drift. Explain, diagrammatically, the set-up of the design if all 21 levels are to be included in the study.
c. Write the linear model for the randomized block design.

10.5 Refer to the randomized block design of Examples 10.2 and 10.3.

a. Write the model for each observation of percentage appraisal error y for appraiser B. Sum the observations to obtain the average for appraiser B.
b. Repeat part **a** for appraiser D.
c. Show that $(\bar{y}_B - \bar{y}_D) = \beta_2 + (\bar{\varepsilon}_B - \bar{\varepsilon}_D)$. Note that the β's for blocks cancel when computing this difference.

10.5 Volume-Increasing Designs

In this section, we focus on how the proper choice of the treatments associated with two or more factors can increase the "volume" of information extracted from the experiment. The volume-increasing designs we will discuss are commonly known as **factorial designs** because they involve careful selection of the combinations of **factor levels** (i.e., treatments) in the experiment.

Consider a utility company that charges its customers a lower rate for using electricity during off-peak (less demanded) hours. The company is experimenting with several time-of-day pricing schedules. Two factors (i.e., independent variables) that the company can manipulate to form the schedule are price ratio, x_1, measured as the ratio of peak to off-peak prices, and peak period length, x_2, measured in hours. Suppose the utility company wants to investigate pricing ratio at two levels, 200% and 400%, and peak period length at two levels, 6 and 9 hours. The company will measure customer satisfaction, y, for several different schedules (i.e., combinations of x_1 and x_2) with the goal of comparing the mean satisfaction levels of the schedules. How should the company select the treatments for the experiment?

One method of selecting the price ratio–peak period length levels to be assigned to the experimental units (customers) would be to use the "one-at-a-time" approach. According to this procedure, one independent variable is varied while the remaining independent variables are held constant. This process is repeated for each of the independent variables in the experiment. This plan would *appear* to be extremely logical and consistent with the concept of blocking introduced in Section 10.4—that is, making comparisons within relatively homogeneous conditions—but this is not the case, as we will demonstrate.

The one-at-a-time approach applied to price ratio (x_1) and peak period length (x_2) is illustrated in Figure 10.5. When length is held constant at $x_2 = 6$ hours, we will observe the response y at a ratio of $x_1 = 200\%$ and $x_1 = 400\%$, thus yielding one pair of y values to estimate the average change in customer satisfaction as a result of changing the pricing ratio (x_1). Also, when pricing ratio is held constant at $x_1 = 200\%$, we observe the response y at a peak period length of $x_2 = 9$ hours. This observation, along with the one at (200%, 6 hours), allows us to estimate the average change in customer satisfaction due to a change in peak period length (x_2). The three treatments just described, (200%, 6 hours), (400%, 6 hours), and (200%, 9 hours), are indicated as points in Figure 10.5. The figure shows two measurements (points) for each treatment. This is necessary to obtain an estimate of the standard deviation of the differences of interest.

A second method of selecting the factor level combinations would be to choose the same three treatments as implied by the one-at-a-time approach and then to choose the fourth treatment at (400%, 9 hours) as shown in Figure 10.6. In other words, we have varied both variables, x_1 and x_2, at the same time.

FIGURE 10.5
One-at-a-time approach to selecting treatments

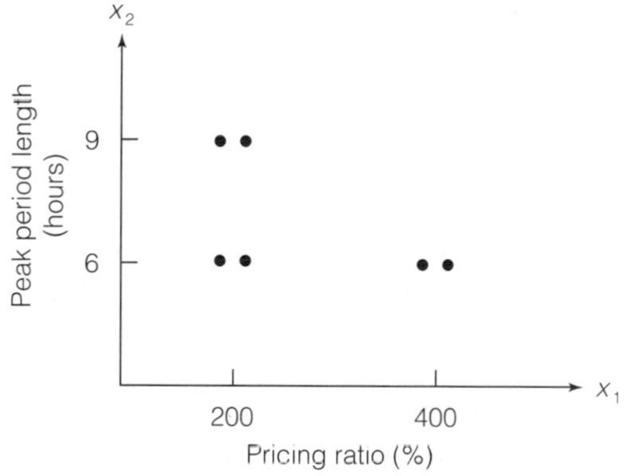

FIGURE 10.6
Selecting all possible treatments

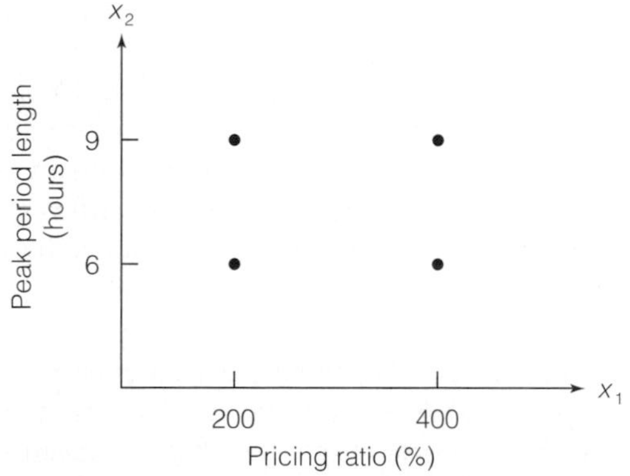

Which of the two designs yields more information about the treatment differences? Surprisingly, the design of Figure 10.6, with only four observations, yields more accurate information than the one-at-a-time approach with its six observations. First, note that both designs yield two estimates of the difference between the mean response y at $x_1 = 200\%$ and $x_1 = 400\%$ when peak period length (x_2) is held constant, and both yield two estimates of the difference between the mean response y at $x_2 = 6$ hours and $x_2 = 9$ hours when pricing ratio (x_1) is held constant. But what if the difference between the mean response y at $x_1 = 200\%$ and at $x_1 = 400\%$ depends on which level of x_2 is held fixed? That is, what if pricing ratio (x_1) and peak period length (x_2) *interact*? Then, we require estimates of the mean difference $(\mu_{200} - \mu_{400})$ when $x_2 = 6$ and the mean difference $(\mu_{200} - \mu_{400})$ when $x_2 = 9$. Estimates of both these differences are obtainable from the second design, Figure 10.6. However, since no estimate of the mean response for $x_1 = 400$ and $x_2 = 9$ is available from the one-at-a-time method, the interaction will go undetected for this design!

The importance of interaction between independent variables was emphasized in Section 4.9 and Chapter 5. If interaction is present, we cannot study the effect of one variable (or factor) on the response y independent of the other variable. Consequently, we require experimental designs that provide information on factor interaction.

Designs that accomplish this objective are called **factorial experiments**. A **complete factorial experiment** is one that includes all possible combinations of the levels of the factors as treatments. For the experiment on time-of-day pricing, we have two levels of pricing ratio (200% and 400%) and two levels of peak period length (6 and 9 hours). Hence, a complete factorial experiment will include $(2 \times 2) = 4$ treatments, as shown in Figure 10.6, and is called a **2 × 2 factorial design**.

Definition 10.10

A **factorial design** is a method for selecting the treatments (that is, the factor level combinations) to be included in an experiment. A complete factorial experiment is one in which the treatments consist of all factor level combinations.

If we were to include a third factor, say, season, at four levels, then a complete factorial experiment would include all $2 \times 2 \times 4 = 16$ combinations of pricing ratio, peak period length, and season. The resulting collection of data would be called a **2 × 2 × 4 factorial design**.

EXAMPLE 10.4

Suppose you plan to conduct an experiment to compare the yield strengths of nickel alloy tensile specimens charged in a sulfuric acid solution. In particular, you want to investigate the effect on mean strength of three factors: nickel composition at three levels (A_1, A_2, and A_3), charging time at three levels (B_1, B_2, and B_3), and alloy type at two levels (C_1 and C_2). Consider a complete factorial experiment. Identify the treatments for this $3 \times 3 \times 2$ factorial design.

Solution

The complete factorial experiment includes all possible combinations of nickel composition, charging time, and alloy type. We therefore would include the following treatments: $A_1B_1C_1$, $A_1B_1C_2$, $A_1B_2C_1$, $A_1B_2C_2$, $A_1B_3C_1$, $A_1B_3C_2$,

$A_2B_1C_1$, $A_2B_1C_2$, $A_2B_2C_1$, $A_2B_2C_2$, $A_2B_3C_1$, $A_2B_3C_2$, $A_3B_1C_1$, $A_3B_1C_2$, $A_3B_2C_1$, $A_3B_2C_2$, $A_3B_3C_1$, $A_3B_3C_2$. These 18 treatments are diagrammed in Figure 10.7.

FIGURE 10.7
The 18 treatments for the 3 × 3 × 2 factorial of Example 10.4

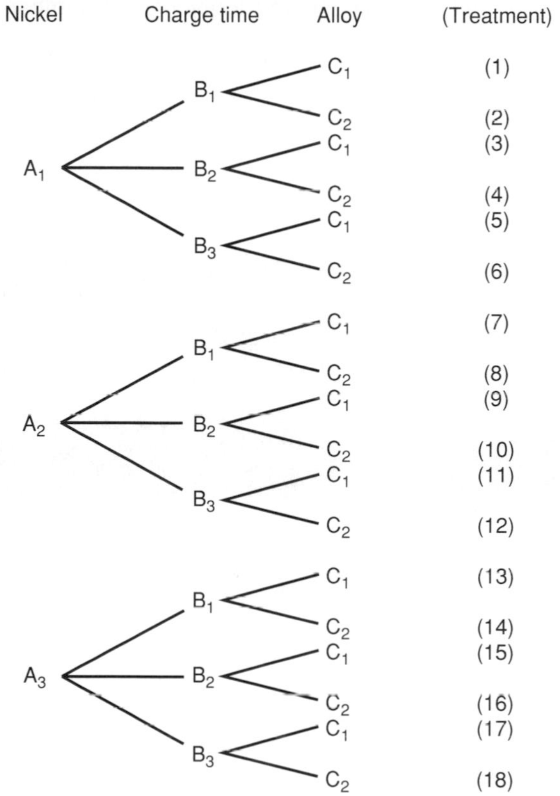

The linear model for a factorial design includes terms for each of the factors in the experiment—called **main effects**—and terms for factor interactions. For example, the model for the 2 × 2 factorial for the time-of-day pricing experiment includes a first-order term for the quantitative factor, pricing ratio (x_1); a first-order term for the quantitative factor, peak period length (x_2); and an interaction term:

$$y = \beta_0 + \underbrace{\beta_1 x_1 + \beta_2 x_2}_{\text{Main effects}} + \underbrace{\beta_3 x_1 x_2}_{\text{Interaction}} + \varepsilon$$

In general, the linear model for a complete factorial design for k factors contains terms for the following:

The main effects for each of the k factors

Two-way interaction terms for all pairs of factors

Three-way interaction terms for all combinations of three factors

⋮

k-way interaction terms of all combinations of k factors

If the factors are qualitative, then we set up dummy variables and proceed as in the next example.

EXAMPLE 10.5 Write the model for the $3 \times 3 \times 2$ factorial experiment of Example 10.4.

Solution Since the factors are qualitative, we set up dummy variables as follows:

$$x_1 = \begin{cases} 1 & \text{if nickel } A_1 \\ 0 & \text{if not} \end{cases} \qquad x_2 = \begin{cases} 1 & \text{if nickel } A_2 \\ 0 & \text{if not} \end{cases}$$

$$x_3 = \begin{cases} 1 & \text{if charge } B_1 \\ 0 & \text{if not} \end{cases} \qquad x_4 = \begin{cases} 1 & \text{if charge } B_2 \\ 0 & \text{if not} \end{cases}$$

$$x_5 = \begin{cases} 1 & \text{if alloy } C_1 \\ 0 & \text{if alloy } C_2 \end{cases}$$

Then the appropriate model is

$$y = \beta_0 + \underbrace{\beta_1 x_1 + \beta_2 x_2}_{\substack{\text{Nickel main} \\ \text{effects}}} + \underbrace{\beta_3 x_3 + \beta_4 x_4}_{\substack{\text{Charge main} \\ \text{effects}}} + \underbrace{\beta_5 x_5}_{\substack{\text{Alloy main} \\ \text{effect}}}$$
$$+ \underbrace{\beta_6 x_1 x_3 + \beta_7 x_1 x_4 + \beta_8 x_2 x_3 + \beta_9 x_2 x_4}_{\text{Nickel} \times \text{Charge}} + \underbrace{\beta_{10} x_1 x_5 + \beta_{11} x_2 x_5}_{\text{Nickel} \times \text{Alloy}}$$
$$+ \underbrace{\beta_{12} x_3 x_5 + \beta_{13} x_4 x_5}_{\text{Charge} \times \text{Alloy}}$$
$$+ \underbrace{\beta_{14} x_1 x_3 x_5 + \beta_{15} x_1 x_4 x_5 + \beta_{16} x_2 x_3 x_5 + \beta_{17} x_2 x_4 x_5}_{\text{Nickel} \times \text{Charge} \times \text{Alloy}}$$

Note that the number of parameters in the model for the $3 \times 3 \times 2$ factorial design of Example 10.5 is 18, which is equal to the number of treatments contained in the experiment. This is always the case for a complete factorial experiment. Consequently, if we fit the complete model to a single replication of the factorial treatments (i.e., one y observation measured per treatment), we will have no degrees of freedom available for estimating the error variance, σ^2. One way to solve this problem is to add additional data points to the sample. Researchers usually accomplish this by *replicating* the complete set of factorial treatments. That is, we collect two or more observed y values for each treatment in the experiment. This provides sufficient degrees of freedom for estimating σ^2.

One potential disadvantage of a complete factorial experiment is that it may require a large number of treatments. For example, an experiment involving 10 factors each at two levels would require $2^{10} = 1{,}024$ treatments! This might occur in an exploratory study where we are attempting to determine which of a large set of factors affect the response y. Several volume-increasing designs are available that employ only a fraction of the total number of treatments in a complete factorial experiment. For this reason, they are called **fractional factorial experiments**. Fractional factorials permit the estimation of the β parameters of lower-order terms (e.g., main effects and two-way interactions); however, β estimates of certain higher-order terms (e.g., three-way and four-way interactions) will be the same as some lower-order terms, thus confounding the results of the experiment. Consequently, a great deal of expertise is required to run and interpret fractional factorial experiments. Consult the references for details on fractional factorials and other more complex, volume-increasing designs.

EXERCISES

10.6 In what sense does a factorial experiment increase the quantity of information in an experiment?

10.7 Suppose you plan to investigate the effect of hourly pay rate and length of workday on some measure y of worker productivity. Both pay rate and length of workday will be set at three levels, and y will be observed for all combinations of these factors.

a. What type of experiment is this?
b. Identify the factors and state whether they are quantitative or qualitative.
c. Identify the treatments to be employed in the experiment.

10.8 Many cognitively demanding jobs (e.g., air traffic controller, radar/sonar operator) require efficient processing of visual information. Researchers at Georgia Tech investigated the variables that affect the reaction time of subjects performing a visual search task. (*Human Factors*, June 1993.) College students were trained on microcomputers using one of two methods: continuously consistent or adjusted consistent. Each student was then assigned to one of six different practice sessions. Finally, the consistency of the search task was manipulated at four degrees: 100%, 67%, 50%, or 33%. The goal of the researcher was to compare the mean reaction times of students assigned to each of the (training method) $\times$ (practice session) $\times$ (task consistency) $= 2 \times 6 \times 4 = 48$ experimental conditions.

a. List the factors involved in the experiment.
b. For each factor, state whether it is quantitative or qualitative.
c. How many treatments are involved in this experiment? List them.

10.9 Consider a factorial design with two factors, A and B, each at three levels. Suppose we select the following treatment (factor level) combinations to be included in the experiment: A_1B_1, A_2B_1, A_3B_1, A_1B_2, and A_1B_3.

a. Is this a complete factorial experiment? Explain.
b. Explain why it is impossible to investigate AB interaction in this experiment.

10.10 Write the complete factorial model for a 2×3 factorial experiment where both factors are qualitative.

10.11 Write the complete factorial model for a $2 \times 3 \times 3$ factorial experiment where the factor at two levels is quantitative and the other two factors are qualitative.

10.12 Suppose you wish to investigate the effect of three factors on a response y. Explain why a factorial selection of treatments is better than varying each factor, one at a time, while holding the remaining two factors constant.

10.13 Why is the randomized block design a poor design to use to investigate the effect of two qualitative factors on a response y?

10.6 Selecting the Sample Size

We demonstrated how to select the sample size for estimating a single population mean or comparing two population means in Sections 1.7 and 1.9. We now show you how this problem can be solved for designed experiments.

As mentioned in Section 10.3, a measure of the quantity of information in an experiment that is pertinent to a particular population parameter is the standard error of the estimator of the parameter. A more practical measure is the half-width of the parameter's confidence interval, which will, of course, be a function of the standard error. For example, the half-width of a confidence interval for a population mean (given in Section 1.7) is

$$t_{\alpha/2}s_{\bar{y}} = t_{\alpha/2}\left(\frac{s}{\sqrt{n}}\right)$$

Similarly, the half-width of a confidence interval for the slope β_1 of a straight-line model relating y to x (given in Section 3.6) is

$$(t_{\alpha/2})s_{\hat{\beta}_1} = t_{\alpha/2}\left(\frac{s}{\sqrt{SS_{xx}}}\right) = t_{\alpha/2}\left(\sqrt{\frac{SSE}{n-2}}\right)\left(\frac{1}{\sqrt{SS_{xx}}}\right)$$

In both cases, the half-width is a function of the total number of data points in the experiment; each interval half-width gets smaller as the total number of data points n increases. The same is true for a confidence interval for a parameter β_i of a general linear model, for a confidence interval for $E(y)$, and for a prediction interval for y. Since each designed experiment can be represented by a linear model, this result can be used to select, approximately, the number of replications (i.e., the number of observations measured for each treatment) in the experiment.

For example, consider a designed experiment consisting of three treatments, A, B, and C. Suppose we want to estimate $(\mu_B - \mu_C)$, the difference between the treatment means for B and C. From our knowledge of linear models for designed experiments, we know this difference will be represented by one of the β parameters in the model, say, β_2. The confidence interval for β_2 for a single replication of the experiment is

$$\hat{\beta}_2 \pm (t_{\alpha/2})s_{\hat{\beta}_2}$$

If we repeat exactly the same experiment r times (we call this r **replications**), it can be shown (proof omitted) that the confidence interval for β_2 will be

$$\hat{\beta}_2 \pm B \qquad \text{where } B = t_{\alpha/2}\left(\frac{s_{\hat{\beta}_2}}{\sqrt{r}}\right)$$

To find r, we first set the half-width of the interval to the largest value, B, we are willing to tolerate. Then we approximate $(t_{\alpha/2})$ and $s_{\hat{\beta}_2}$ and solve for the number of replications r.

EXAMPLE 10.6

Consider a 2 × 2 factorial experiment to investigate the effect of two factors on the light output y of flashbulbs used in cameras. The two factors (and their levels) are: x_1 = Amount of foil contained in the bulb (100 and 200 milligrams) and

x_2 = Speed of sealing machine (1.2 and 1.3 revolutions per minute). The complete model for the 2 × 2 factorial experiment is

$$E(y) = \beta_0 + \beta_1 x_1 + \beta_2 x_2 + \beta_3 x_1 x_2$$

How many replicates of the 2 × 2 factorial are required to estimate β_3, the interaction β, to within .3 of its true value using a 95% confidence interval?

Solution

To solve for the number of replicates, r, we want to solve the equation

$$t_{\alpha/2}\left(\frac{s_{\hat{\beta}_3}}{\sqrt{r}}\right) = B$$

You can see that we need to have an estimate of $s_{\hat{\beta}_3}$, the standard error of $\hat{\beta}_3$ for a single replication. Suppose it is known from a previous experiment conducted by the manufacturer of the flashbulbs that $s_{\hat{\beta}_3} \approx .2$. For a 95% confidence interval, $\alpha = .05$ and $\alpha/2 = .025$. Since we want the half-width of the interval to be $B = .3$, we have

$$t_{.025}\left(\frac{.2}{\sqrt{r}}\right) = .3$$

The degrees of freedom for $t_{.025}$ will depend on the sample size $n = (2 \times 2)r = 4r$; consequently, we must approximate its value. In fact, since the model includes four parameters, the degrees of freedom for t will be df(Error) $= n - 4 = 4r - 4 = 4(r - 1)$. At minimum, we require two replicates; hence, we will have at least $4(2 - 1) = 4$ df. In Table 2 of Appendix C, we find $t_{.025} = 2.776$ for df = 4. We will use this conservative estimate of t in our calculations.

Substituting $t = 2.776$ into the equation, we have

$$\frac{2.776(.2)}{\sqrt{r}} = .3$$

$$\sqrt{r} = \frac{(2.776)(.2)}{.3} = 1.85$$

$$r = 3.42$$

Since we can run either three or four replications (but not 3.42), we should choose four replications to be reasonably certain that we will be able to estimate the interaction parameter, β_3, to within .3 of its true value. The 2 × 2 factorial with four replicates would be laid out as shown in Table 10.3.

TABLE 10.3 **2 × 2 Factorial, with Four Replicates**

		AMOUNT OF FOIL, x_1	
		100	200
MACHINE SPEED, x_2	1.2	4 observations on y	4 observations on y
	1.3	4 observations on y	4 observations on y

EXERCISES

10.14 Why is replication important in a complete factorial experiment?

10.15 Consider a 2×2 factorial. How many replications are required to estimate the interaction β to within two units with a 90% confidence interval? Assume that the standard error of the estimate of the interaction β (based on a single replication) is approximately 3.

10.16 For a randomized block design with b blocks, the estimated standard error of the estimated difference between any two treatment means is $s\sqrt{2/b}$. Use this formula to determine the number of blocks required to estimate $(\mu_A - \mu_B)$, the difference between two treatment means, to within 10 units using a 95% confidence interval. Assume $s \approx 15$.

10.7 The Importance of Randomization

All the basic designs presented in this chapter involve randomization of some sort. In a completely randomized design and a basic factorial experiment, the treatments are randomly assigned to the experimental units. In a randomized block design, the blocks are randomly selected and the treatments within each block are assigned in random order. Why randomize? The answer is related to the assumptions we make about the random error ε in the linear model. Recall (Section 4.2) our assumption that ε follows a normal distribution with mean 0 and constant variance σ^2 for fixed settings of the independent variables (i.e., for each of the treatments). Further, we assume that the random errors associated with repeated observations are independent of each other in a probabilistic sense.

Experimenters rarely know all of the important variables in a process, nor do they know the true functional form of the model. Hence, the functional form chosen to fit the true relation is only an approximation, and the variables included in the experiment form only a subset of the total. The random error, ε, is thus a composite error caused by the failure to include all of the important factors as well as the error in approximating the function.

Although many unmeasured and important independent variables affecting the response y do not vary in a completely random manner during the conduct of a designed experiment, we hope their behavior is such that their cumulative effect varies in a random manner and satisfies the assumptions upon which our inferential procedures are based. *The randomization in a designed experiment has the effect of randomly assigning these error effects to the treatments and assists in satisfying the assumptions on* ε.

Summary

Regression analysis based on observational data has at least one limitation: Even when the independent variables in a model are highly significant, we cannot infer a cause-and-effect relationship between the x's and y. The focus of this chapter was on data collected from a designed experiment in which the values of the independent variables are set in advance of observing y. By controlling the values of the x's, we hope to increase the amount of information extracted from the data.

Experimental design is a plan (or strategy) for collecting the experimental data. The goal is to increase the amount of information by controlling two factors:

1. **Volume** of the signal contained in the data
2. **Noise** or random variation in the data that is measured by σ^2

The first three steps in designing an experiment are as follows:

STEP 1 Select the **factors** (i.e., the independent variables) to be investigated.

STEP 2 Choose the factor level combinations (**treatments**).

STEP 3 Determine the number of observations for each treatment (i.e., the number of **replications** of the experiment).

These steps affect the volume of the signal contained in the data because they enable us to shift the information in the experiment so that it focuses on the parameter(s) of interest. An example of a volume-increasing design is a **factorial experiment**, in which all possible treatments (factor level combinations) are selected. With factorial designs, we shift the focus of the experiment to an investigation of factor interaction.

The fourth step in designing an experiment is

STEP 4 Decide how to assign the treatments to the experimental units.

Two basic methods of assigning treatments to the experimental units are the **completely randomized design** and the **randomized block design**. The latter is a noise-reducing design; by assigning treatments to relatively homogeneous blocks of experimental units, we can reduce the variation of treatment differences. The net effect of this action is to reduce experimental noise, measured by the variance of the random error ε that appears in the linear model.

The choice of design, noise-reducing or volume-increasing, will depend on your experimental objectives. In practice, researchers will attempt to employ both principles of design to increase the quantity of information in the experiment. For example, the treatments of a 2×2 factorial could be laid out in blocks to eliminate or reduce an unwanted source of variation. (An example of such a design is given in the next chapter.)

This chapter introduced the key principles of experimental design and presented some basic methods of collecting data in a designed experiment. Other, more complex designs, although beyond the scope of this text, may be more appropriate for your research problem. Consult the references listed at the end of the chapter to learn more about these designs. In Chapter 11, we demonstrate how to analyze experimental data using an **analysis of variance**.

SUPPLEMENTARY EXERCISES

10.17 How do you measure the quantity of information in a sample that is pertinent to a particular population parameter?

10.18 What steps in the design of an experiment affect the volume of the signal pertinent to a particular population parameter?

10.19 In what step in the design of an experiment can you possibly reduce the variation produced by extraneous and uncontrolled variables?

10.20 Explain the difference between a completely randomized design and a randomized block design. When is a randomized block design more advantageous?

10.21 Consider a two-factor factorial experiment where one factor is set at two levels and the other factor is set at four levels. How many treatments are included in the experiment? List them.

10.22 Write the complete factorial model for a $2 \times 2 \times 4$ factorial experiment where both factors at two levels are quantitative and the third factor at four levels is qualitative. If you conduct one replication of this experiment, how many degrees of freedom will be available for estimating σ^2?

10.23 Refer to Exercise 10.22. Write the model for y assuming that you wish to enter main-effect terms for the factors, but no terms for factor interactions. How many degrees of freedom will be available for estimating σ^2?

10.24 Retail store audits are periodic audits of a sample of retail sales to monitor inventory and purchases of a particular product. Such audits are often used by marketing researchers to estimate market share. A study was conducted to compare market shares of beer brands estimated by two different auditing methods.

a. Identify the treatments in the experiment.

b. Because of brand-to-brand variation in estimated market share, a randomized block design will be used. Explain how the treatments might be assigned to the experimental units if 10 beer brands are to be included in the study.

c. Write the linear model for the randomized block design.

10.25 Researchers investigated the effect of gender (male or female) and weight (light or heavy) on the length of time required by firefighters to perform a particular firefighting task (*Human Factors*, 1982). Eight firefighters were selected in each of the four gender–weight categories. Each firefighter was required to perform a certain task. The time (in minutes) needed to perform the task was recorded for each.

a. List the factors involved in the experiment.

b. For each factor, state whether it is quantitative or qualitative.

c. How many treatments are involved in this experiment? List them.

References

Box, G. E. P., Hunter, W. G., and Hunter, J. S. *Statistics for Experimenters*. New York: Wiley, 1957.

Cochran, W. G., and Cox, G. M. *Experimental Designs*, 2nd ed. New York: Wiley, 1957.

Davies, O. L. *The Design and Analysis of Industrial Experiments*. New York: Hafner, 1956.

Kirk, R. E. *Experimental Design: Procedures for the Behavioral Sciences*. Pacific Grove, Calif.: Brooks/Cole, 1968.

Mendenhall, W. *Introduction to Linear Models and the Design and Analysis of Experiments*. Belmont, Calif.: Wadsworth, 1968.

Neter, J., Wasserman, W., and Kutner, M. H. *Applied Linear Statistical Models*, 3rd ed. Homewood, Ill.: Richard D. Irwin, 1988.

Winer, B. J. *Statistical Principles in Experimental Design*. New York: McGraw-Hill, 1962.

CHAPTER 11

The Analysis of Variance for Designed Experiments

CONTENTS

OBJECTIVE

To present a method for analyzing data collected from designed experiments for comparing two or more population means; to define the relationship of the analysis of variance to regression analysis and to identify their common features

11.1 Introduction

Once the data for a designed experiment have been collected, we will want to use the sample information to make inferences about the population means associated with the various treatments. The method used to compare the treatment means is traditionally known as **analysis of variance**, or **ANOVA**. The analysis of variance procedure provides a set of formulas that enable us to compute test statistics and confidence intervals required to make these inferences.

The formulas—one set for each experimental design—were developed in the early 1900s, well before the invention of computers. The formulas are easy to use, although the calculations can become quite tedious. However, you will recall from Chapter 10 that a linear model is associated with each experimental design. Consequently, the same inferences derived from the ANOVA calculation formulas can be obtained by properly analyzing the model using a regression analysis and the computer.

In this chapter, the main focus is on the regression approach to analyzing data from a designed experiment. Several common experimental designs—some of which were presented in Chapter 10—are analyzed. We also provide the ANOVA calculation formulas for each design and show their relationship to regression. First, we provide the logic behind an analysis of variance and these formulas in Section 11.2.

11.2 The Logic Behind an Analysis of Variance

The concept behind an analysis of variance can be explained using the following simple example.

Consider an experiment with a single factor at two levels (that is, two treatments). Suppose we want to decide whether the two treatment means differ based on the means of two independent random samples, each containing $n_1 = n_2 = 5$ measurements, and that the y values appear as in Figure 11.1. Note that the five circles on the left are plots of the y values for sample 1 and the five solid dots on the right are plots of the y values for sample 2. Also, observe the horizontal lines that pass through the means for the two samples $\bar{y}_1$ and $\bar{y}_2$. Do you think the plots provide sufficient evidence to indicate a difference between the corresponding population means?

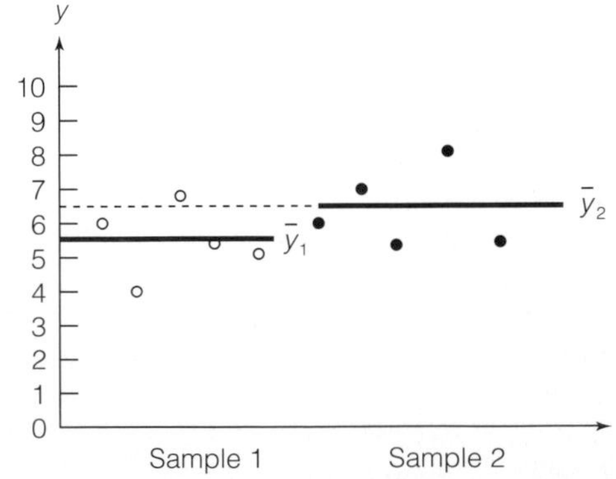

FIGURE 11.1
Plots of data for two samples

If you are uncertain whether the population means differ for the data in Figure 11.1, examine the situation for two different samples in Figure 11.2a. We think that you will agree that for these data, it appears that the population means differ. Examine a third case in Figure 11.2b. For these data, it appears that there is little or no difference between the population means.

FIGURE 11.2

Plots of data for two cases

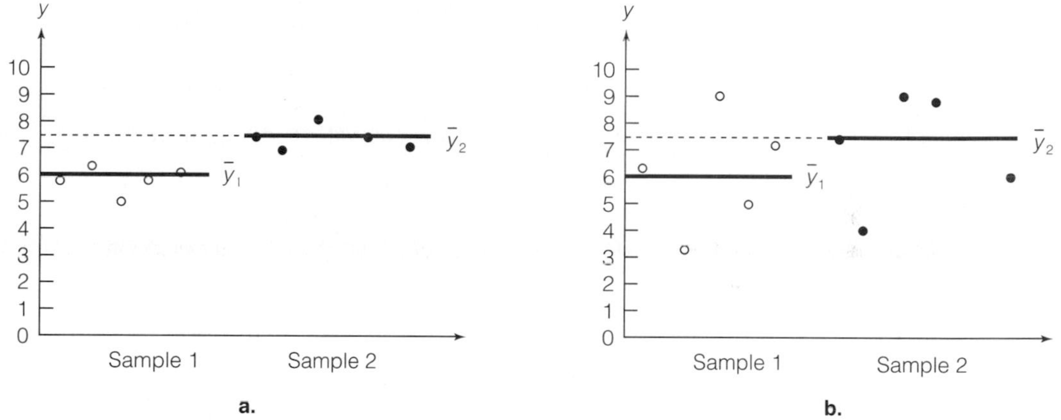

What elements of Figures 11.1 and 11.2 did we intuitively use to decide whether the data indicate a difference between the population means? The answer to the question is that we visually compared the distance (the variation) *between* the sample means to the variation *within* the y values for each of the two samples. Since the difference between the sample means in Figure 11.2a is large relative to the within-sample variation, we inferred that the population means differ. Conversely, in Figure 11.2b, the variation between the sample means is small relative to the within-sample variation, and therefore there is little evidence to imply that the means are significantly different.

The variation within samples is measured by the pooled s^2 that we computed for the independent random samples t test of Section 1.8, namely,

$$\textit{Within-sample variation:}\quad s^2 = \frac{\sum_{i=1}^{n_1} (y_{i1} - \bar{y}_1)^2 + \sum_{i=1}^{n_2} (y_{i2} - \bar{y}_2)^2}{n_1 + n_2 - 2} = \frac{\text{SSE}}{n_1 + n_2 - 2}$$

where y_{i1} is the ith observation in sample 1 and y_{i2} is the ith observation in sample 2. The quantity in the numerator of s^2 is often denoted **SSE**, the **sum of squared errors**. As with regression analysis, SSE measures unexplained variability. But in this case, it measures variability *unexplained* by the differences between the sample means.

A measure of the between-sample variation is given by the weighted sum of squares of deviations of the individual sample means about the mean for all 10 observations, $\bar{y}$, divided by the number of samples minus 1, i.e.,

Between-sample variation: $$\frac{n_1(\bar{y}_1 - \bar{y})^2 + n_2(\bar{y}_2 - \bar{y})^2}{2 - 1} = \frac{\text{SST}}{1}$$

The quantity in the numerator is often denoted SST, the **sum of squares for treatments**, since it measures the variability *explained* by the differences between the sample means of the two treatments.

For this experimental design, SSE and SST sum to a known total, namely,

$$\text{SS(Total)} = \sum (y_i - \bar{y})^2$$

[*Note:* SS(Total) is equivalent to SS_{yy} in regression.] Also, the ratio

$$F = \frac{\text{Between-sample variation}}{\text{Within-sample variation}} = \frac{\text{SST}/1}{\text{SSE}/(n_1 + n_2 - 2)}$$

has an F distribution with $\nu_1 = 1$ and $\nu_2 = n_1 + n_2 - 2$ degrees of freedom (df) and therefore can be used to test the null hypothesis of no difference between the treatment means. The additivity property of the sums of squares led early researchers to view this analysis as a **partitioning** of $\text{SS(Total)} = \Sigma (y_i - \bar{y})^2$ into sources corresponding to the factors included in the experiment and to SSE. The simple formulas for computing the sums of squares, the additivity property, and the form of the test statistic made it natural for this procedure to be called **analysis of variance**. We demonstrate the analysis of variance procedure and its relation to regression for several common experimental designs in Sections 11.3–11.6.

11.3 Completely Randomized Designs

Recall (Section 10.2) the first two steps in designing an experiment: (1) decide on the factors to be investigated and (2) select the factor level combinations (treatments) to be included in the experiment. For example, suppose you wish to compare the length of time to assemble a device in a manufacturing operation for workers who have completed one of three training programs, A, B, and C. Then this experiment involves a single factor, training program, at three levels, A, B, and C. Since training program is the only factor, these levels (A, B, and C) represent the treatments. Now we must decide the sample size for each treatment (step 3) and figure out how to assign the treatments to the experimental units, namely, the specific workers (step 4).

As we learned in Chapter 10, the most common assignment of treatments to experimental units is called a **completely randomized design**. To illustrate, suppose we wish to obtain equal amounts of information on the mean assembly times for the three training procedures; i.e., we decide to assign equal numbers of workers to each of the three training programs. Also, suppose we use the procedure of Section 1.7 (Example 1.11) to select the sample size and determine the number of workers in each of the three samples to be $n_1 = n_2 = n_3 = 10$. Then a completely randomized design is one in which the $n_1 + n_2 + n_3 = 30$ workers are **randomly assigned**, 10 to each of the three treatments. *A random assignment is one in which any one assignment is as probable as any other*. This eliminates the possibility of bias that might occur if the workers were assigned in some systematic manner. For example, a systematic assignment might accidentally assign most of the manually dexterous workers to training program A, thus underestimating the true mean assembly time corresponding to A.

Example 11.1 illustrates how a **random number table** can be used to assign the 30 workers to the three treatments.

EXAMPLE 11.1

Use the random number table, Table 7 in Appendix C, to assign $n = 30$ experimental units to three treatment groups.

Solution

The first step is to number the 30 workers from 1 to 30. We will then use Table 7 in Appendix C to select two-digit numbers, discarding those that are larger than 30 or are identical, until we have a total of 20 two-digit numbers. We will then have 20 of the integers between 1 and 30 arranged in random order. The workers who have been assigned the first 10 numbers in the sequence are assigned to training program A, the second group of 10 workers are assigned to B, and the remaining workers are assigned to C.

To illustrate, suppose we start with the two-digit random number in row 5, column 6 of Table 7 and proceed down the column, selecting only two-digit numbers (the first two digits) less than or equal to 30 and deleting those that repeat. The first 20 are: 20, 18, 13, 16, 19, 04, 14, 06, 30, 25, 27, 17, 24, 21, 22, 02, 15, 05, 09, 08. The workers with the first 10 numbers are assigned to program A, the second 10 to B, and the remaining 10 to C. So the workers are assigned to the training program as shown in Table 11.1.

TABLE 11.1 **Random Assignment of Workers to Treatments**

A	B	C
20, 18, 13, 16, 19, 4, 14, 6, 30, 25	27, 17, 24, 21, 22, 2, 15, 5, 9, 8	1, 3, 7, 10, 11, 12, 23, 26, 28, 29

EXAMPLE 11.2

Suppose a beverage bottler wished to compare the effect of three different advertising displays on the sales of a beverage in supermarkets. Identify the experimental units you would use for the experiment, and explain how you would employ a completely randomized design to collect the sales data.

Solution

Presumably, the bottler has a list of supermarkets that market the beverage in a number of different cities. If we decide to measure the sales increase (or decrease) as the monthly dollar increase in sales (over the previous month) for a given supermarket, then the experimental unit is a 1-month unit of time in a specific supermarket. Thus, we would randomly select a 1-month period of time for each of $n_1 + n_2 + n_3$ supermarkets and assign n_1 supermarkets to receive display D_1, n_2 to receive D_2, and n_3 to receive display D_3.

In some experimental situations, we are unable to assign the treatment to the experimental units randomly because of the nature of the experimental units themselves. For example, suppose we want to compare the mean annual salaries of professors in three College of Liberal Arts departments: chemistry, mathematics, and sociology. Then the treatments—chemistry, mathematics, and sociology—cannot be "assigned" to the professors (experimental units). A professor is a member of the chemistry, mathematics, or sociology (or some other) department and cannot be arbitrarily assigned one of the treatments. Rather, we view the treatments (departments) as populations from which we will select independent random samples of experimental units (professors). A completely randomized design involves a comparison of the means for a number, say, p, of treatments, based on independent random samples of $n_1, n_2, \ldots, n_p$ observations, drawn from populations associated with treatments $1, 2, \ldots, p$, respectively. We repeat our definition of a completely randomized design (given in Section 10.4) with this modification. The general layout for a completely randomized design is shown in Figure 11.3.

FIGURE 11.3
Layout for a completely randomized design

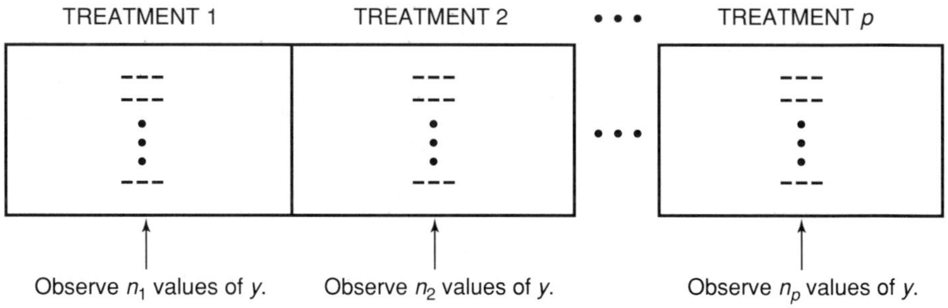

Definition 11.1

A **completely randomized design** to compare p treatment means is one in which the treatments are randomly assigned to the experimental units, or in which independent random samples are drawn from each of the p populations.

After collecting the data from a completely randomized design, we want to make inferences about p population means where μ_i is the mean of the population of measurements associated with treatment i, for $i = 1, 2, \ldots, p$. The null hypothesis to be tested is that the p treatment means are equal, i.e., H_0: $\mu_1 = \mu_2 = \cdots = \mu_p$, and the alternative hypothesis we wish to detect is that at least two of the treatment means differ. The appropriate linear model for the response y is

$$E(y) = \beta_0 + \beta_1 x_1 + \beta_2 x_2 + \cdots + \beta_{p-1} x_{p-1}$$

where

$$x_1 = \begin{cases} 1 & \text{if treatment 2} \\ 0 & \text{if not} \end{cases} \quad x_2 = \begin{cases} 1 & \text{if treatment 3} \\ 0 & \text{if not} \end{cases} \quad \cdots \quad x_{p-1} = \begin{cases} 1 & \text{if treatment } p \\ 0 & \text{if not} \end{cases}$$

and (arbitrarily) treatment 1 is the base level. Recall that this 0–1 system of coding implies that

$$\begin{aligned} \beta_0 &= \mu_1 \\ \beta_1 &= \mu_2 - \mu_1 \\ \beta_2 &= \mu_3 - \mu_1 \\ &\vdots \\ \beta_{p-1} &= \mu_p - \mu_1 \end{aligned}$$

The null hypothesis that the p population means are equal is equivalent to the null hypothesis that all the treatment differences equal 0, i.e.,

$$H_0: \quad \beta_1 = \beta_2 = \cdots = \beta_{p-1} = 0$$

To test this hypothesis using regression, we use the technique of Section 4.10; that is, we compare the sum of squares for error, SSE_R, for the nested *reduced* model

$$E(y) = \beta_0$$

to the sum of squares for error, SSE_C, for the *complete* model

$$E(y) = \beta_0 + \beta_1 x_1 + \beta_2 x_2 + \cdots + \beta_{p-1} x_{p-1}$$

using the F statistic

$$\begin{aligned} F &= \frac{(SSE_R - SSE_C)/\text{Number of } \beta \text{ parameters in } H_0}{SSE_C/[n - (\text{Number of } \beta \text{ parameters in the complete model})]} \\ &= \frac{(SSE_R - SSE_C)/(p-1)}{SSE_C/(n-p)} \\ &= \frac{(SSE_R - SSE_C)/(p-1)}{MSE_C} \end{aligned}$$

where F is based on $\nu_1 = (p - 1)$ and $\nu_2 = (n - p)$ df. If F exceeds the upper critical value, F_α, we reject H_0 and conclude that at least one of the treatment differences, $\beta_1, \beta_2, \ldots, \beta_{p-1}$, differs from zero; i.e., we conclude that at least two treatment means differ.

EXAMPLE 11.3

Show that the F statistic for testing the equality of treatment means in a completely randomized design is equivalent to a global F test of the complete model.

Solution

Since the reduced model contains only the β_0 term, the least squares estimate of β_0 is $\bar{y}$, and it follows that

$$\text{SSE}_\text{R} = \sum (y - \bar{y})^2 = \text{SS}_{yy}$$

We called this quantity the sum of squares for total in Chapter 4. The difference $(\text{SSE}_\text{R} - \text{SSE}_\text{C})$ is simply $(\text{SS}_{yy} - \text{SSE})$ for the complete model. Since in regression $(\text{SS}_{yy} - \text{SSE}) = \text{SS(Model)}$, and the complete model has $(p - 1)$ terms (excluding β_0),

$$F = \frac{(\text{SSE}_\text{R} - \text{SSE}_\text{C})/(p-1)}{\text{MSE}_\text{C}} = \frac{\text{SS(Model)}/(p-1)}{\text{MSE}} = \frac{\text{MS(Model)}}{\text{MSE}}$$

Thus, it follows that the test statistic for testing the null hypothesis,

$$H_0\text{: } \mu_1 = \mu_2 = \cdots = \mu_p$$

in a completely randomized design is the same as the F statistic for testing the global utility of the complete model for this design.

The regression approach to analyzing data from a completely randomized design is summarized in the box on page 589. Note that the test requires several assumptions about the distributions of the response y for the p treatments and that these *assumptions are necessary regardless of the sizes of the samples*. (We have more to say about these assumptions in Section 11.9.)

EXAMPLE 11.4

Sociologists often conduct experiments to investigate the relationship between socioeconomic status and college performance. Socioeconomic status is generally partitioned into three groups: lower class, middle class, and upper class. Consider the problem of comparing the mean grade point average of those college freshmen associated with the lower class, those associated with the middle class, and those associated with the upper class. The grade point averages (GPAs) for random samples of seven college freshmen associated with each of the three socioeconomic classes were selected from a university's files at the end of the academic year. The data are recorded in Table 11.2. Do the data provide sufficient evidence to indicate a difference among the mean freshmen GPAs for the three socioeconomic classes? Test using $\alpha = .05$.

Model and F Test for a Completely Randomized Design with p Treatments

Complete model: $E(y) = \beta_0 + \beta_1 x_1 + \beta_2 x_2 + \cdots + \beta_{p-1} x_{p-1}$

where

$$x_1 = \begin{cases} 1 & \text{if treatment 2} \\ 0 & \text{if not} \end{cases} \qquad x_2 = \begin{cases} 1 & \text{if treatment 3} \\ 0 & \text{if not} \end{cases}, \ldots,$$

$$x_{p-1} = \begin{cases} 1 & \text{if treatment } p \\ 0 & \text{if not} \end{cases}$$

H_0: $\beta_1 = \beta_2 = \cdots = \beta_{p-1} = 0$ (i.e., H_0: $\mu_1 = \mu_2 = \cdots = \mu_p$)

H_a: At least one of the β parameters listed in H_0 differs from 0 (i.e., H_a: At least two means differ.).

Test statistic: $F = \dfrac{\text{MS(Model)}}{\text{MSE}}$

Rejection region: $F > F_\alpha$, where the distribution of F is based on $\nu_1 = p - 1$ and $\nu_2 = n - p$ degrees of freedom.

Assumptions:
1. All p population probability distributions corresponding to the p treatments are normal.
2. The population variances of the p treatments are equal.

TABLE 11.2 **Grade Point Averages for Three Socioeconomic Groups**

	LOWER CLASS	MIDDLE CLASS	UPPER CLASS
	2.87	3.23	2.25
	2.16	3.45	3.13
	3.14	2.78	2.44
	2.51	3.77	2.54
	1.80	2.97	3.27
	3.01	3.53	2.81
	2.16	3.01	1.36
Sample means:	$\bar{y}_1 = 2.52$	$\bar{y}_2 = 3.25$	$\bar{y}_3 = 2.54$

Solution

This experiment involves a single factor, socioeconomic class, at three levels. Thus, we have a completely randomized design with $p = 3$ treatments. Let μ_L, μ_M, and μ_U represent the mean GPAs for students in the lower, middle, and upper socioeconomic classes, respectively. Then we want to test

$$H_0: \mu_L = \mu_M = \mu_U$$

against

H_a: At least two of the three treatment means differ.

The appropriate linear model for $p = 3$ treatments is

Complete model: $E(y) = \beta_0 + \beta_1 x_1 + \beta_2 x_2$

where

$$x_1 = \begin{cases} 1 & \text{if middle socioeconomic class} \\ 0 & \text{if not} \end{cases}$$

$$x_2 = \begin{cases} 1 & \text{if upper socioeconomic class} \\ 0 & \text{if not} \end{cases}$$

Thus, we want to test H_0: $\beta_1 = \beta_2 = 0$.

The SAS regression analysis for the complete model is shown in Figure 11.4. The F statistic for testing the overall adequacy of the model (shaded on the printout) is $F = 4.579$, where the distribution of F is based on $\nu_1 = (p - 1) = 3 - 1 = 2$ and $\nu_2 = (n - p) = 21 - 3 = 18$ df. For $\alpha = .05$, the critical value (obtained from Table 4 of Appendix C) is $F_{.05} = 3.55$ (see Figure 11.5).

FIGURE 11.4
SAS printout for the completely randomized design, Example 11.4

Dependent Variable: GPA

Analysis of Variance

Source	DF	Sum of Squares	Mean Square	F Value	Prob>F
Model	2	2.39687	1.19843	4.579	0.0247
Error	18	4.71111	0.26173		
C Total	20	7.10798			

Root MSE	0.51159	R-square	0.3372
Dep Mean	2.77095	Adj R-sq	0.2636
C.V.	18.46275		

Parameter Estimates

Variable	DF	Parameter Estimate	Standard Error	T for H0: Parameter=0	Prob > |T|
INTERCEP	1	2.521429	0.19336441	13.040	0.0001
X1	1	0.727143	0.27345857	2.659	0.0160
X2	1	0.021429	0.27345857	0.078	0.9384

Since the computed value of F, 4.579, exceeds the critical value, $F_{.05} = 3.55$, we reject H_0 and conclude (at the $\alpha = .05$ level of significance) that the mean GPA for college freshmen differs in at least two of the three socioeconomic classes. We can arrive at the same conclusion by noting that $\alpha = .05$ is greater than the p-value (.0247) shaded on the printout.

The analysis of the data in Example 11.4 can also be accomplished using ANOVA computing formulas. In Section 11.2, we learned that an analysis of variance partitions SS(Total) $= \Sigma (y - \bar{y})^2$ into two components, SSE and SST (see Figure 11.6).

FIGURE 11.5
Rejection region for Example 11.4; numerator df = 2, denominator df = 18, $\alpha = .05$

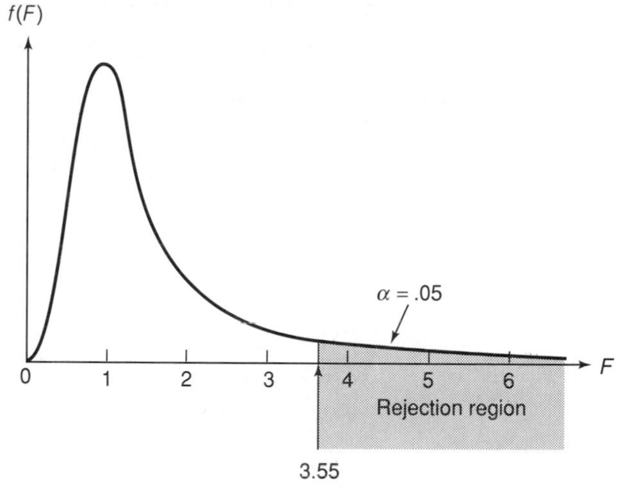

FIGURE 11.6
Partitioning of SS(Total) for a completely randomized design

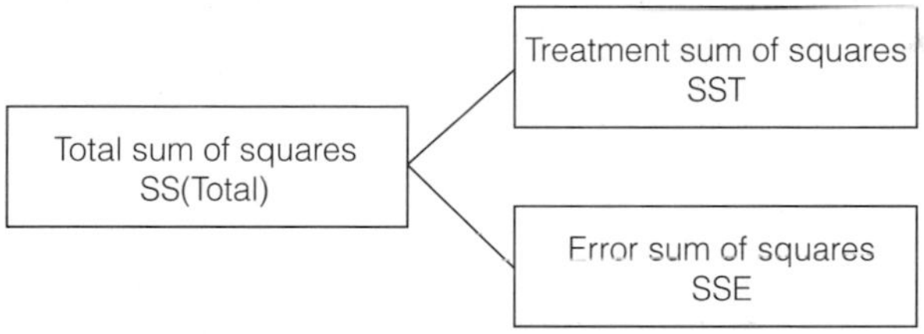

Recall that the quantity SST denotes the sum of squares for treatments and measures the variation explained by the differences between the treatment means. The sum of squares for error, SSE, is a measure of the unexplained variability, obtained by calculating a pooled measure of the variability *within* the p samples. If the treatment means truly differ, then SSE should be substantially smaller than SST. We compare the two sources of variability by forming an F statistic:

$$F = \frac{\text{SST}/(p-1)}{\text{SSE}/(n-p)} = \frac{\text{MST}}{\text{MSE}}$$

where n is the total number of measurements. The numerator of the F statistic, $\text{MST} = \text{SST}/(p-1)$, denotes **mean square for treatments** and is based on $(p-1)$ degrees of freedom—one for each of the p treatments minus one for the estimation of the overall mean. The denominator of the F statistic, $\text{MSE} = \text{SSE}/(n-p)$, denotes **mean square for error** and is based on $(n-p)$ degrees of freedom—one for each of the n measurements minus one for each of the p treatment means being estimated. We have already demonstrated that this F statistic is identical to the global F value for the regression model specified previously.

For completeness, we provide the computing formulas for an analysis of variance in the box on page 592.

Computing Formulas for the Analysis of Variance for a Completely Randomized Design

$$\text{Sum of all } n \text{ measurements} = \sum_{i=1}^{n} y_i$$

$$\text{Mean of all } n \text{ measurements} = \bar{y}$$

$$\text{Sum of squares of all } n \text{ measurements} = \sum_{i=1}^{n} y_i^2$$

$$\begin{aligned}
\text{CM} &= \text{Correction for mean} \\
&= \frac{(\text{Total of all observations})^2}{\text{Total number of observations}} = \frac{\left(\sum_{i=1}^{n} y_i\right)^2}{n} \\
\text{SS(Total)} &= \text{Total sum of squares} \\
&= (\text{Sum of squares of all observations}) - \text{CM} \\
&= \sum_{i=1}^{n} y_i^2 - \text{CM} \\
\text{SST} &= \text{Sum of squares for treatments} \\
&= \left(\begin{array}{c}\text{Sum of squares of treatment totals with} \\ \text{each square divided by the number of} \\ \text{observations for that treatment}\end{array}\right) - \text{CM} \\
&= \frac{T_1^2}{n_1} + \frac{T_2^2}{n_2} + \cdots + \frac{T_p^2}{n_p} - \text{CM} \\
\text{SSE} &= \text{Sum of squares for error} \\
&= \text{SS(Total)} - \text{SST} \\
\text{MST} &= \text{Mean square for treatments} \\
&= \frac{\text{SST}}{p-1} \\
\text{MSE} &= \text{Mean square for error} \\
&= \frac{\text{SSE}}{n-p} \\
F &= \frac{\text{MST}}{\text{MSE}}
\end{aligned}$$

EXAMPLE 11.5

Refer to Example 11.4. Analyze the data of Table 11.2 using the ANOVA approach. Use $\alpha = .05$.

Solution

Rather than performing the tedious calculations by hand (we leave this for the student as an exercise), we use a statistical software package with an ANOVA routine. All four of the software packages discussed in this text (ASP, SAS,

MINITAB, and SPSS) have procedures that automatically compute the ANOVA sums of squares and the ANOVA F statistic.

The MINITAB ANOVA printout is shown in Figure 11.7. The value of the test statistic (shaded on the printout) is $F = 4.58$. Note that this is identical to the F value obtained using the regression approach in Example 11.4. The p-value of the test (also shaded) is $p = .025$. (Likewise, this quantity is identical to that in Example 11.4.) Since $\alpha = .05$ exceeds this p-value, we have sufficient evidence to conclude that the treatments differ.

FIGURE 11.7
MINITAB ANOVA printout for Example 11.5

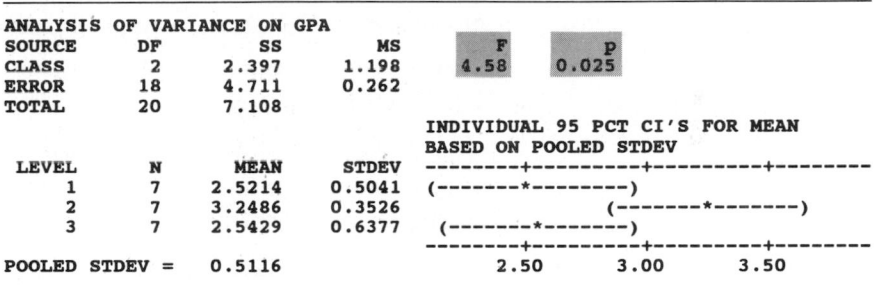

```
ANALYSIS OF VARIANCE ON GPA
SOURCE      DF        SS         MS          F         P
CLASS        2     2.397      1.198       4.58     0.025
ERROR       18     4.711      0.262
TOTAL       20     7.108
                                       INDIVIDUAL 95 PCT CI'S FOR MEAN
                                       BASED ON POOLED STDEV
  LEVEL      N      MEAN      STDEV    --------+---------+---------+--------
      1      7    2.5214     0.5041    (-------*--------)
      2      7    3.2486     0.3526                 (-------*-------)
      3      7    2.5429     0.6377     (-------*-------)
                                       --------+---------+---------+--------
POOLED STDEV =    0.5116                      2.50      3.00      3.50
```

The results of an analysis of variance are often summarized in tabular form. The general form of an ANOVA table for a completely randomized design is shown in the next box. The column head **SOURCE** refers to the source of variation, and for each source, **df** refers to the degrees of freedom, **SS** to the sum of squares, **MS** to the mean square, and **F** to the F statistic comparing the treatment mean square to the error mean square. Table 11.3 (page 594) is the ANOVA summary table corresponding to the analysis of variance data for Example 11.5, obtained from the MINITAB printout.

ANOVA Summary Table for a Completely Randomized Design

SOURCE	df	SS	MS	F
Treatments	$p - 1$	SST	$\text{MST} = \frac{\text{SST}}{p-1}$	$F = \frac{\text{MST}}{\text{MSE}}$
Error	$n - p$	SSE	$\text{MSE} = \frac{\text{SSE}}{n-p}$	
Total	$n - 1$	SS(Total)		

TABLE 11.3 **ANOVA Summary Table for Example 11.5**

SOURCE	df	SS	MS	F
Socioeconomic class	2	2.40	1.198	4.58
Error	18	4.71	.262	
Total	20	7.11		

Because the completely randomized design involves the selection of independent random samples, we can find a confidence interval for a single treatment mean using the method of Section 1.7 or for the difference between two treatment means using the methods of Section 1.9. The estimate of σ^2 will be based on the pooled sum of squares within all p samples; that is,

$$\text{MSE} = s^2 = \frac{\text{SSE}}{n - p}$$

This is the same quantity that is used as the denominator for the analysis of variance F test. The formulas for the confidence intervals of Sections 1.7 and 1.9 are reproduced in the box.

Confidence Intervals for Means: Completely Randomized Design

Single treatment mean (say, treatment i): $\bar{y}_i \pm t_{\alpha/2}\left(\frac{s}{\sqrt{n_i}}\right)$

Difference between two treatment means (say, treatments i and j):

$$(\bar{y}_i - \bar{y}_j) \pm t_{\alpha/2}s\sqrt{\frac{1}{n_i} + \frac{1}{n_j}}$$

where $\bar{y}_i$ is the sample mean response for population (treatment) i, $s = \sqrt{\text{MSE}}$, and $t_{\alpha/2}$ is the tabulated value of t (Table 2 of Appendix C) that locates $\alpha/2$ in the upper tail of the t distribution with $(n - p)$ df (the degrees of freedom associated with error in the ANOVA).

EXAMPLE 11.6

Refer to Example 11.4. Find a 95% confidence interval for μ_L, the mean GPA of freshmen from the lower socioeconomic class.

Solution

From Table 11.3, MSE = .262. Then

$$s = \sqrt{\text{MSE}} = \sqrt{.262} = .512$$

The sample mean GPA for freshmen students from the lower class is

$$\bar{y}_L = \frac{17.64}{7} = 2.52$$

where 17.64 is the total of GPAs for the lower socioeconomic class obtained from Table 11.2. The tabulated value of $t_{.025}$ for 18 df (the same as for MSE) is 2.101. Therefore, a 95% confidence interval for μ_L, the mean GPA of college freshmen in the lower class, is

$$\bar{y}_L \pm t_{\alpha/2}\frac{s}{\sqrt{n}} = 2.52 \pm 2.101\frac{.512}{\sqrt{10}}$$
$$= 2.52 \pm .41$$

or (2.11, 2.93).

Note that this confidence interval is relatively wide—probably too wide to be of any practical value (considering that GPA is measured on a 4-point scale). The interval is this wide because of the large amount of variation within each socioeconomic class. For example, the GPA for freshmen in the lower class varies from 1.8 to 3.01. The more variable the data, the larger the value of s in the confidence interval and the wider the confidence interval. Consequently, if you want to obtain a more accurate estimate of treatment means with a narrower confidence interval, you will have to select larger samples of freshmen from within each socioeconomic class.

Although we can use the formula given in the box to compare two treatment means in ANOVA, unless the two treatments are selected a priori (i.e., prior to conducting the ANOVA), it is more appropriate to apply one of the methods for comparing means presented in Sections 11.7 and 11.8.

EXERCISES

11.1 Refer to the completely randomized design of Exercise 10.3. Recall that the researchers want to compare the mean job satisfaction rating of workers using three types of work scheduling: flextime, staggered starting hours, and fixed hours. Use the random number table (Table 7 in Appendix C) to randomly assign the workers to the three work schedules.

11.2 A partially completed ANOVA table for a completely randomized design is shown here.

SOURCE	df	SS	MS	F
Treatments	4	24.7	____	____
Error	____	____	____	
Total	34	62.4		

a. Complete the ANOVA table.
b. How many treatments are involved in the experiment?
c. Do the data provide sufficient evidence to indicate a difference among the treatment means? Test using $\alpha = .10$.

11.3 The data for a completely randomized design with two treatments are shown in the accompanying table.

TREATMENT 1	TREATMENT 2
10	12
7	8
8	13
11	10
10	10
9	11
9	

a. Give the linear model appropriate for analyzing the data using regression.

b. Fit the model, part **a**, to the data and conduct the analysis. [*Hint:* You do not need a computer to fit the model. Use the formulas provided in Chapter 3.]

11.4 Refer to Exercise 11.3.

a. Calculate MST for the data using the ANOVA formulas. What type of variability is measured by this quantity?

b. Calculate MSE for the data using the ANOVA formulas. What type of variability is measured by this quantity?

c. How many degrees of freedom are associated with MST?

d. How many degrees of freedom are associated with MSE?

e. Compute the test statistic appropriate for testing H_0: $\mu_1 = \mu_2$ against the alternative that the two treatment means differ, using a significance level of $\alpha = .05$. (Compare the value to the test statistic obtained using regression in part **b**, Exercise 11.3.)

f. Summarize the results from parts **a–e** in an ANOVA table.

g. Specify the rejection region, using a significance level of $\alpha = .05$.

h. State the proper conclusion.

11.5 Exercises 11.3 and 11.4 involve a test of the null hypothesis H_0: $\mu_1 = \mu_2$ based on independent random sampling (recall the definition of a completely randomized design). This test was conducted in Section 1.9 using a Student's t statistic.

a. Use the Student's t test to test the hypothesis H_0: $\mu_1 = \mu_2$ against the alternative hypothesis H_a: $\mu_1 \neq \mu_2$. Test using $\alpha = .05$.

b. It can be shown (proof omitted) that an F statistic with $\nu_1 = 1$ numerator degree of freedom and ν_2 denominator degrees of freedom is equal to t^2, where t is a Student's t statistic based on ν_2 degrees of freedom. Square the value of t calculated in part **a**, and show that it is equal to the value of F calculated in Exercises 11.3**b** and 11.4**e**.

c. Is the analysis of variance F test for comparing two population means a one- or a two-tailed test of H_0: $\mu_1 = \mu_2$? [*Hint:* Although the t test can be used to test either for H_a: $\mu_1 > \mu_2$ or for H_a: $\mu_1 < \mu_2$, the alternative hypothesis for the F test is H_a: The two means are different.]

11.6 The *Journal of Testing and Evaluation* (July 1992) published an investigation of the mean compression strength of corrugated fiberboard shipping containers. Comparisons were made for boxes of five different sizes: A, B, C, D, and E. Twenty identical boxes of each size were tested and the peak compression strength (pounds) recorded for each box. The accompanying figure shows the sample means for the five box types as well as the variation around each sample mean.

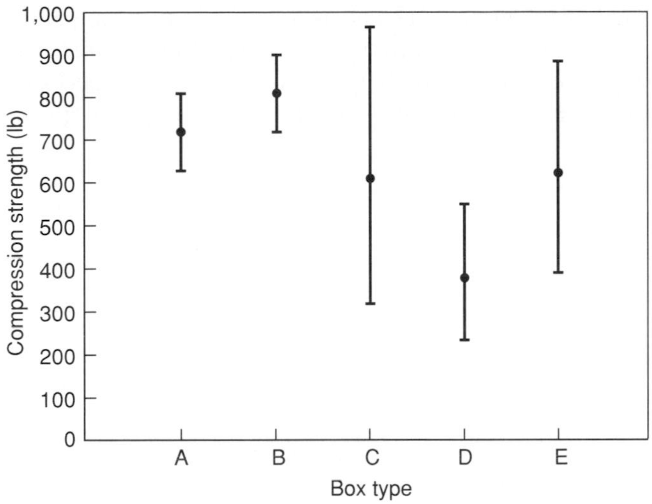

Source: Singh, S. P., et al. "Compression of single-wall corrugated shipping containers using fixed and floating test platens." *Journal of Testing and Evaluation*, Vol. 20, No. 4, July 1992, p. 319 (Figure 3).

a. Explain why the data are collected as a completely randomized design.

b. Refer to box types B and D. Based on the graph, does it appear that the mean compression strengths of these two box types are significantly different? Explain.

c. Based on the graph, does it appear that the mean compression strengths of all five box types are significantly different? Explain.

11.7 Anorexia nervosa and bulimia are two major eating disorders that afflict women. Researchers have found that patients with eating disorders have lower self-esteem than normal eaters. However, it is unclear whether the low self-esteem results directly from the eating disorder, from possible depression, or from both the eating disorder and depression. To clarify this issue, a designed experiment was conducted in which patients with eating disorders were compared to depressed female psychiatric patients having no history of eating disturbance (*Journal of Abnormal Psychology*, Vol. 97, 1987). The study included three age-matched groups of women: 37 eating-disorder patients, 12 depressed patients, and 34 normal eaters. All 83 participants were administered the Bern Sex Role Inventory (BSRI), a questionnaire designed to measure self-esteem. The scores were subjected to an analysis of variance to compare the mean self-esteem ratings of the three groups of women.

a. Identify the treatments in this experiment.

b. Give the null hypothesis of interest to the researchers.

c. Give the degrees of freedom associated with the sources of variation in the ANOVA.

d. The researchers reported the test statistic for testing the null hypothesis, part **b**, as $F = 11.5$. Interpret this result. (Use $\alpha = .01$.)

11.8 Speech recognition technology has advanced to the point that it is now possible to communicate with a computer through verbal commands. A study was conducted to evaluate the value of speech recognition in human interactions with computer systems (*Special Interest Group on Computer–Human Interaction Bulletin*, July 1993). A sample of 45 subjects was randomly divided into three groups (15 subjects per group), and each subject was asked to perform tasks on a basic voice mail system. A different interface was used in each group: (1) touch-tone, (2) human operator, or (3) simulated speech recognition. One of the variables measured was overall time (in seconds) to perform the assigned tasks. An analysis was conducted to compare the mean overall performance times of the three groups. The sample mean performance times for the three groups are given in the table.

GROUP	MEAN PERFORMANCE TIME, seconds
Touch-tone	1,400
Human operator	1,030
Speech recognition	1,040

a. Identify the experimental design used in this study.
b. Propose a regression model that will allow you to compare the three means.
c. In terms of means, give the appropriate null hypothesis to be tested.
d. In terms of the β's of the model, part **b**, give the appropriate null hypothesis to be tested.
e. Despite differences among the sample means, the null hypothesis of part **c** could not be rejected at $\alpha = .05$. Explain how this is possible.

11.9 Objectivity is an essential characteristic of auditing. A study was conducted to investigate whether prior involvement in audit program design impairs an external auditor's objectivity in making decisions about that program (*Accounting and Finance*, Nov. 1993). A sample of 45 auditors was randomly divided into three equal-size groups, designated A/R, A/P, and Control. The A/R group designed an audit program for accounts receivable and evaluated an audit program for accounts payable designed by someone else. The A/P group did the reverse. Finally, the control group merely evaluated the audit programs for both accounts. All 45 auditors were then requested to allocate an additional 15 hours to investigate suspected irregularities in either one or both audit programs. The objective of the experiment was to compare the mean number of hours allocated to the accounts receivable for the three groups.
a. What type of design is used in this study?
b. Identify the treatments for this design.
c. A partial ANOVA table is shown here. Complete the table.

SOURCE	df	SS	MS	F	p-VALUE
Groups	____	71.51	____	____	.01
Error	____	____	7.65		
Total	____	392.98			

d. Based on the results of the analysis, what inference can the researchers make?

11.10 Vanadium (V) is an essential trace element found in living organisms. An experiment was conducted to compare the concentrations of V in biological materials using isotope dilution mass spectrometry (*Analytical Chemistry*, Nov. 1985). The accompanying table gives the quantities of V (measured in nanograms per gram) in dried samples of oyster tissue, citrus leaves, bovine liver, and human serum. The data were used to fit the linear model

$$E(y) = \beta_0 + \beta_1 x_1 + \beta_2 x_2 + \beta_3 x_3$$

where

$$x_1 = \begin{cases} 1 & \text{if oyster tissue} \\ 0 & \text{if not} \end{cases} \qquad x_2 = \begin{cases} 1 & \text{if citrus leaves} \\ 0 & \text{if not} \end{cases}$$

$$x_3 = \begin{cases} 1 & \text{if bovine liver} \\ 0 & \text{if not} \end{cases}$$

OYSTER TISSUE	CITRUS LEAVES	BOVINE LIVER	HUMAN SERUM
2.35	2.32	.39	.10
1.30	3.07	.54	.17
.34	4.09	.30	.14
			.16
			.16

Dependent Variable: V

Analysis of Variance

Source	DF	Sum of Squares	Mean Square	F Value	Prob>F
Model	3	18.86832	6.28944	17.314	0.0003
Error	10	3.63252	0.36325		
C Total	13	22.50084			

Root MSE	0.60270	R-square	0.8386
Dep Mean	1.10214	Adj R-sq	0.7901
C.V.	54.68474		

Parameter Estimates

Variable	DF	Parameter Estimate	Standard Error	T for H0: Parameter=0	Prob > |T|
INTERCEP	1	0.146000	0.26953738	0.542	0.5999
X1	1	1.184000	0.44015270	2.690	0.0227
X2	1	3.014000	0.44015270	6.848	0.0001
X3	1	0.264000	0.44015270	0.600	0.5620

a. Identify the treatments in this experiment.
b. Is there sufficient evidence (at $\alpha = .05$) to indicate that the mean V concentrations differ among the four biological materials?
c. Use the β estimates of the model to estimate the mean V concentrations in each of the four biological materials.

11.11 The display consoles of modern computer-based systems use many abbreviated words to accommodate the large volume of information to be displayed. Therefore, operators must learn to decode each abbreviation quickly and accurately. An experiment was conducted to determine the optimal method for abbreviating any specific set of words on the sonar consoles used at the Naval Submarine Medical Research Laboratory in Groton, Connecticut (*Human Factors*, Feb. 1984). Of the 20 Navy and civilian personnel who took part in the study, five were highly familiar with the sonar system. The 15 subjects unfamiliar with the system were randomly divided into three groups of five. Thus, the study consisted of a total of four groups (one experienced and three inexperienced groups), with five subjects per group. The experienced group and one inexperienced group (denoted TE and TI, respectively) were assigned the simple method of abbreviation. One of the remaining inexperienced groups was assigned the conventional single abbreviation method (denoted CS), whereas the other was assigned the conventional multiple abbreviation method (denoted CM). Each subject was then given a list of 75 abbreviations to learn, one at a time, through the display console of a minicomputer. The number of trials until the subject accurately decoded at least 90% of the words on the list was recorded. Do the data provide sufficient evidence to indicate differences among the mean numbers of trials required for the four groups? Test using $\alpha = .05$. (Use the SAS printout to solve this problem.)

CM	CS	TE	TI
4	6	5	8
7	9	5	4
5	5	7	8
6	7	8	10
8	6	7	3

Source: Data are simulated values based on the group means reported in *Human Factors*, Feb. 1984. Copyright 1984 by the Human Factors Society, Inc. and reproduced by permission.

Analysis of Variance Procedure

Dependent Variable: TRIALS

Source	DF	Sum of Squares	Mean Square	F Value	Pr > F
Model	3	1.20000000	0.40000000	0.10	0.9566
Error	16	61.60000000	3.85000000		
Corrected Total	19	62.80000000			

R-Square	C.V.	Root MSE	TRIALS Mean
0.019108	30.658464	1.9621417	6.40000000

Source	DF	Anova SS	Mean Square	F Value	Pr > F
GROUP	3	1.20000000	0.40000000	0.10	0.9566

11.12 In the past decade, many county-run local jails have acquired major responsibility for treating mentally ill patients. Historically, state mental hospitals have experienced conflicts between the correctional and mental health staffs. A study reported in *Criminology* was conducted to determine whether the conflict between correctional and mental health staffs found in state mental hospitals also exists in local jails. Staff members at 43 jails with mental health programs were mailed questionnaires addressing the conflict in the day-to-day delivery of mental health services in the jails. A total of $n = 167$ questionnaires were returned. In one portion of the study, respondents were classified into one of four groups according to staff affiliation: (1) jail correctional, (2) jail mental health, (3) county mental health, and (4) other mental health. The variable in question was "perceived level of conflict in providing treatment to inmates/patients," measured on a scale of 1 (little or no conflict) to 7 (extreme conflict). The data were subjected to a one-way analysis of variance on staff affiliation with the results shown in the accompanying ANOVA summary table.

SOURCE	df	SS	MS	F
Staff affiliation	_____	21.31	7.10	_____
Error	163	_____	_____	
Total	_____	120.62		

Source: Steadman, H. J., Morrissey, J. P., and Robbins, P. C. "Reevaluating the custody–therapy conflict paradigm in correctional mental health settings." *Criminology*, Vol. 23, No. 1, 1985, pp. 165–179.

a. Complete the ANOVA table.
b. Is there sufficient evidence of a difference among the mean levels of conflict perceived by the four groups of jail staff members? Test using $\alpha = .05$.

11.13 Bell Communications Research (Bellcore) publishes, on average, 150 technical memos (TMs) each month. Since not all TMs are relevant to all employees, Bellcore recognizes that "information filtering" will naturally occur—each employee will retain only the information that is relevant to him or her. Bellcore researchers recently conducted a study of four automated information filtering methods (*Communications of the Association for Computing Machinery*, Dec. 1992). These methods are (1) keyword match-word profile, (2) latent semantic indexing (LSI)-word profile, (3) keyword match-document profile, and (4) LSI-document profile. A sample of TM abstracts were filtered by each method, and the relevance of the filtered abstracts was rated on a 7-point scale by a panel of Bellcore employees. In addition, a subset of TM abstracts were randomly selected and rated by the panel. The mean relevance ratings of the five filtering methods (four automated methods plus the random selection method) were compared using an analysis of variance for a completely randomized design.
a. Identify the treatments in the experiment.
b. Identify the response variable.
c. The ANOVA resulted in a test statistic of $F = 117.5$, based on 4 numerator degrees of freedom and 132 denominator degrees of freedom. Interpret this result at a significance level of $\alpha = .05$.

11.14 A study was conducted to determine whether entrepreneurs, newly hired (transferred) managers, and newly promoted managers differ in their risk-taking propensities (*Academy of Management Journal*, Sept. 1980). For the purposes of this study, entrepreneurs were defined as individuals who, within 3 months before the study, had ceased working for their employers and begun their own business ventures. Thirty-one individuals from each of the three groups were randomly selected to participate in the study. Each was administered a questionnaire that required the respondent to choose between a safe alternative and a more attractive but risky one. Test scores were designed to measure risk-taking propensity. (Lower scores are associated with greater conservatism in risk-taking situations.) The test scores for the three groups are summarized in the table. [*Note:* Although the individual scores are not provided, there is sufficient information in the table to conduct the analysis for this completely randomized design.]

GROUP	SAMPLE SIZE	SAMPLE MEAN	STANDARD DEVIATION	GROUP TOTALS
Entrepreneurs	31	71.00	11.94	2,201
Transferred managers	31	72.52	12.19	2,248
Promoted managers	31	66.97	10.84	2,076
	93			6,525

Source: Brockhaus, R. H. "Risk-taking propensity of entrepreneurs." *Academy of Management Journal*, Sept. 1980, Vol. 23, pp. 509–520.

a. Use the sum of the group totals and the total sample size to compute CM.
b. Use the individual group totals and sample sizes to compute SST.
c. Compute SSE using the pooled sum of squares formula:

$$\text{SSE} = \sum (y_{i1} - \bar{y}_1)^2 + \sum (y_{i2} - \bar{y}_2)^2 + \sum (y_{i3} - \bar{y}_3)^2$$
$$= (n_1 - 1)s_1^2 + (n_2 - 1)s_2^2 + (n_3 - 1)s_3^2$$

d. Find SS(Total).
e. Construct an ANOVA table for the data.
f. Do the data provide sufficient evidence to indicate differences in the mean risk-taking propensities among the three groups? Test using $\alpha = .05$.

11.15 Refer to Exercise 11.14

a. Give the linear model appropriate for analyzing the data using regression.
b. Use the information in the table of Exercise 11.14 to find the least squares prediction equation.

11.16 Epidemiologists have theorized that the risk of coronary heart disease can be reduced by an increased consumption of fish. One study, begun in 1960, monitored the diet and health of a random sample of middle-aged Dutch men. The men were divided into five groups according to the numbers of grams of fish consumed per day: 0, 1–14, 15–29, 30–44, and 45 or more. One of the many variables measured on each subject was intake of polysaccharides (a substance linked to coronary heart disease.) An analysis of variance on the levels of polysaccharides (measured as a percentage of energy) in the five groups of men resulted in the partial ANOVA table given here.

SOURCE	df	SS	MS	F
Groups	____	534.97	____	____
Error	____	23,659.45	____	
Total	851	24,194.42		

Source: Kromhout, D., Bosschieter, E. B., and Coulander, C. D. L. "The inverse relation between fish consumption and 20-year mortality from coronary heart disease." *New England Journal of Medicine*, May 9, 1985, Vol. 312, No. 19, pp. 1205–1209. Reprinted by permission.

a. Give the total number of Dutch men included in this portion of the study.
b. Complete the ANOVA summary table.
c. Is there sufficient evidence of differences among the mean levels of polysaccharides in the five groups of men? Test using $\alpha = .01$.

11.17 When marketing its products in a foreign country, should a company use its own salespeople or salespeople from the target market country? To answer this question, a study was designed to investigate the effect of salesperson nationality on buyer attitudes (*Journal of Business Research*, Vol. 22, 1991). A sample of U.S. MBA students was divided into two groups and shown a videotape of an advertisement for forklift trucks made in India. For group 1, an Indian sales representative made the presentation; for group 2, a U.S. sales representative made the presentation. After viewing the tape, the subjects were asked whether the salesperson was trustworthy (measured on a 5-point scale). The mean scores were compared using an ANOVA.

a. The ANOVA resulted in an F value of 2.32, with an observed significance level of .13. Is there evidence of a difference between the mean trustworthiness scores of the two groups of MBA students? Use $\alpha = .10$.
b. The sample mean scores for the two groups are $\bar{y}_1 = 3.12$ and $\bar{y}_2 = 3.49$. Suppose you were to test H_0: $\mu_1 = \mu_2$ against H_a: $\mu_1 < \mu_2$ at $\alpha = .10$. Use the result, part a, to make the proper conclusion. [*Hint*: Use Exercise 11.5 and the fact that the p-value for a two-tailed t test is double the p-value for a one-tailed test.]

11.4 Randomized Block Designs

Randomized block design is a commonly used noise-reducing design. Recall (Definition 10.9) that a randomized block design employs groups of homogeneous experimental units (matched as closely as possible) to compare the means of the populations associated with p treatments. The general layout of a randomized block design is shown in Figure 11.8. Note that there are b blocks of relatively homogeneous experimental units. Since each treatment must be represented in each block, the blocks each contain p experimental units. Although Figure 11.8 shows the p treatments in order within the blocks, in practice they would be assigned to the experimental units in random order (hence the name **randomized block design**).

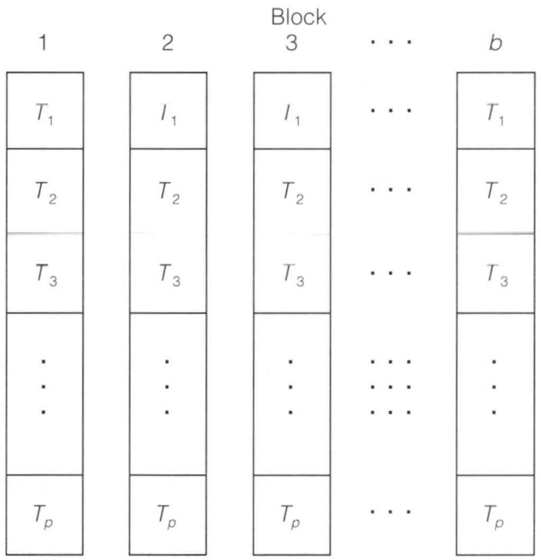

FIGURE 11.8
General form of a randomized block design (treatment is denoted by T_p)

The complete model for a randomized block design contains $(p - 1)$ dummy variables for treatments and $(b - 1)$ dummy variables for blocks. Therefore, the total number of terms in the model, excluding β_0, is $(p - 1) + (b - 1) = p + b - 2$, as shown here.

Complete model:

$$E(y) = \beta_0 + \underbrace{\beta_1 x_1 + \beta_2 x_2 + \cdots + \beta_{p-1} x_{p-1}}_{\text{Treatment effects}} + \underbrace{\beta_p x_p + \cdots + \beta_{p+b-2} x_{p+b-2}}_{\text{Block effects}}$$

where

$$x_1 = \begin{cases} 1 & \text{if treatment 2} \\ 0 & \text{if not} \end{cases}, \quad x_2 = \begin{cases} 1 & \text{if treatment 3} \\ 0 & \text{if not} \end{cases}, \quad \ldots, \quad x_{p-1} = \begin{cases} 1 & \text{if treatment } p \\ 0 & \text{if not} \end{cases},$$

$$x_p = \begin{cases} 1 & \text{if block 2} \\ 0 & \text{if not} \end{cases}, \quad x_{p+1} = \begin{cases} 1 & \text{if block 3} \\ 0 & \text{if not} \end{cases}, \quad \ldots, \quad x_{p+b-2} = \begin{cases} 1 & \text{if block } b \\ 0 & \text{if not} \end{cases}$$

Note that the model does *not* include terms for treatment–block interaction. The reasons are twofold. First, the addition of these terms would leave 0 degrees of freedom for estimating σ^2. Second, the failure of the mean difference between a pair of treatments to remain the same from block to block is, by definition, experimental error. In other words, in a randomized block design, treatment–block interaction and experimental error are synonymous.

The primary objective of the analysis is to compare the p treatment means, $\mu_1, \mu_2, \ldots, \mu_p$. That is, we want to test the null hypothesis

$$H_0\text{:} \quad \mu_1 = \mu_2 = \mu_3 = \cdots = \mu_p$$

Recall (Section 10.3) that this is equivalent to testing whether all the treatment parameters in the complete model are equal to 0, i.e.,

$$H_0\text{:} \quad \beta_1 = \beta_2 = \cdots = \beta_{p-1} = 0$$

To perform this test using regression, we drop the treatment terms and fit the reduced model:

Reduced model for testing treatments

$$E(y) = \beta_0 + \beta_p x_p + \underbrace{\beta_{p+1} x_{p+1} + \cdots + \beta_{p+b-2} x_{p+b-2}}_{\text{Block effects}}$$

Then we compare the SSEs for the two models, SSE_R and SSE_C, using the "partial" F statistic:

$$F = \frac{(\text{SSE}_\text{R} - \text{SSE}_\text{C})/\text{Number of } \beta\text{'s tested}}{\text{MSE}_\text{C}} = \frac{(\text{SSE}_\text{R} - \text{SSE}_\text{C})/(p-1)}{\text{MSE}_\text{C}}$$

A significant F value implies that the treatment means differ.

Occasionally, experimenters want to determine whether blocking was effective in removing the extraneous source of variation, i.e., whether there is evidence of a difference among block means. In fact, if there are no differences among block means, the experimenter will lose information by blocking because blocking reduces the number of degrees of freedom associated with the estimated variance of the model, s^2. If blocking is *not* effective in reducing the variability, then the block parameters in the complete model will all equal 0 (i.e., there will be no differences among block means). Thus, we want to test

$$H_0\text{:} \quad \beta_p = \beta_{p+1} = \cdots = \beta_{p+b-2} = 0$$

Another reduced model, with the block β's dropped, is fitted:

Reduced model for testing blocks

$$E(y) = \beta_0 + \underbrace{\beta_1 x_1 + \beta_2 x_2 + \cdots + \beta_{p-1}x_{p-1}}_{\text{Treatment effects}}$$

The SSE for this second reduced model is compared to the SSE for the complete model in the usual fashion. A significant F test implies that blocking is effective in removing (or reducing) the targeted extraneous source of variation.

These two tests are summarized in the following box.

Models and ANOVA F Tests for a Randomized Block Design with p Treatments and b Blocks

Complete model:

$$E(y) = \beta_0 + \overbrace{\beta_1 x_1 + \cdots + \beta_{p-1}x_{p-1}}^{(p-1)\text{ treatment terms}} + \overbrace{\beta_p x_p + \cdots + \beta_{p+b-2}x_{p+b-2}}^{(b-1)\text{ block terms}}$$

where

$$x_1 = \begin{cases} 1 & \text{if treatment 2} \\ 0 & \text{if not} \end{cases} \quad \cdots \quad x_{p-1} = \begin{cases} 1 & \text{if treatment } p \\ 0 & \text{if not} \end{cases}$$

$$x_p = \begin{cases} 1 & \text{if block 2} \\ 0 & \text{if not} \end{cases} \quad \cdots \quad x_{p+b-2} = \begin{cases} 1 & \text{if block } b \\ 0 & \text{if not} \end{cases}$$

TEST FOR COMPARING TREATMENT MEANS

H_0: $\beta_1 = \beta_2 = \cdots = \beta_{p-1} = 0$
(i.e., H_0: The p treatment means are equal.)

H_a: At least one of the β parameters listed in H_0 differs from 0.
(i.e., H_a: At least two treatment means differ.)

Reduced model: $E(y) = \beta_0 + \beta_p x_p + \cdots + \beta_{p+b-2}x_{p+b-2}$

Test statistic:

$$F = \frac{(\text{SSE}_\text{R} - \text{SSE}_\text{C})/(p-1)}{\text{SSE}_\text{C}/(n-p-b+1)} = \frac{(\text{SSE}_\text{R} - \text{SSE}_\text{C})/(p-1)}{\text{MSE}_\text{C}}$$

where

SSE_R = SSE for reduced model
SSE_C = SSE for complete model
MSE_C = MSE for complete model

Rejection region: $F > F_\alpha$ where F is based on $\nu_1 = (p-1)$ and $\nu_2 = (n-p-b+1)$ degrees of freedom

(continued)

TEST FOR COMPARING BLOCK MEANS

H_0: $\beta_p = \beta_{p+1} = \cdots = \beta_{p+b-2} = 0$
(i.e., H_0: The b block means are equal.)

H_a: At least one of the β parameters listed in H_0 differs from 0.
(i.e., H_a: At least two block means differ.)

Reduced model: $E(y) = \beta_0 + \beta_1 x_1 + \beta_2 x_2 + \cdots + \beta_{p-1} x_{p-1}$

Test statistic:
$$F = \frac{(\text{SSE}_\text{R} - \text{SSE}_\text{C})/(b-1)}{\text{SSE}_\text{C}/(n-p-b+1)} = \frac{(\text{SSE}_\text{R} - \text{SSE}_\text{C})/(b-1)}{\text{MSE}_\text{C}}$$

where

SSE_R = SSE for reduced model
SSE_C = SSE for complete model
MSE_C = MSE for complete model

Rejection region: $F > F_\alpha$ where F is based on $\nu_1 = (b-1)$ and $\nu_2 = (n-p-b+1)$ degrees of freedom

Assumptions:

1. The probability distribution of the difference between any pair of treatment observations within a block is approximately normal.
2. The variance of the difference is constant and the same for all pairs of observations.

EXAMPLE 11.7

Prior to submitting a bid for a construction job, cost engineers prepare a detailed analysis of the estimated labor and materials costs required to complete the job. This estimate will depend on the engineer who performs the analysis. An overly large estimate will reduce the chance of acceptance of a company's bid price, whereas an estimate that is too low will reduce the profit or even cause the company to lose money on the job. A company that employs three job cost engineers wanted to compare the mean level of the engineers' estimates. This was done by having each engineer estimate the cost of the same four jobs. The data (in hundreds of thousands of dollars) are shown in Table 11.4.

a. Perform an analysis of variance on the data, and test to determine whether there is sufficient evidence to indicate differences among treatment means. Test using $\alpha = .05$.
b. Test to determine whether blocking on jobs was successful in reducing the job-to-job variation in the estimates. Use $\alpha = .05$.

TABLE 11.4 **Data for the Randomized Block Design of Example 11.7**

		JOB 1	2	3	4	TREATMENT MEANS
ENGINEER	1	4.6	6.2	5.0	6.6	5.60
	2	4.9	6.3	5.4	6.8	5.85
	3	4.4	5.9	5.4	6.3	5.50
BLOCK MEANS		4.63	6.13	5.27	6.57	

Solution

a. The data for this experiment were collected according to a randomized block design because estimates of the same job were expected to be more nearly alike than estimates between jobs. Thus, the experiment involves three treatments (engineers) and four blocks (jobs).

The complete model for this design is

$$E(y) = \beta_0 + \underbrace{\beta_1 x_1 + \beta_2 x_2}_{\text{Treatments (engineers)}} + \underbrace{\beta_3 x_3 + \beta_4 x_4 + \beta_5 x_5}_{\text{Blocks (jobs)}}$$

where

$$y = \text{Cost estimate}$$

$$x_1 = \begin{cases} 1 & \text{if engineer 2} \\ 0 & \text{if not} \end{cases} \qquad x_2 = \begin{cases} 1 & \text{if engineer 3} \\ 0 & \text{if not} \end{cases}$$

Base level = Engineer 1

$$x_3 = \begin{cases} 1 & \text{if block 2} \\ 0 & \text{if not} \end{cases} \qquad x_4 = \begin{cases} 1 & \text{if block 3} \\ 0 & \text{if not} \end{cases} \qquad x_5 = \begin{cases} 1 & \text{if block 4} \\ 0 & \text{if not} \end{cases}$$

Base level = Block 1

The SAS printout for the complete model is shown in Figure 11.9 on page 608. Note that $SSE_C = .18667$ and $MSE_C = .03111$ (shaded on the printout).

To test for differences among the treatment means, we will test

$$H_0\colon \quad \mu_1 = \mu_2 = \mu_3$$

where μ_i = mean cost estimate of engineer i. This is equivalent to testing

$$H_0\colon \quad \beta_1 = \beta_2 = 0$$

in the complete model. We fit the reduced model

$$E(y) = \beta_0 + \underbrace{\beta_3 x_3 + \beta_4 x_4 + \beta_5 x_5}_{\text{Blocks (jobs)}}$$

The SAS printout for this reduced model is shown in Figure 11.10 on page 608. Note that $SSE_R = .44667$ (shaded on the printout).

FIGURE 11.9
SAS printout for complete model of Example 11.7

```
Dependent Variable: ESTCOST

                          Analysis of Variance

                            Sum of          Mean
Source              DF     Squares        Square      F Value        Prob>F

Model                5     7.02333       1.40467       45.150        0.0001
Error                6     0.18667       0.03111
C Total             11     7.21000

     Root MSE        0.17638      R-square         0.9741
     Dep Mean        5.65000      Adj R-sq         0.9525
     C.V.            3.12183

                          Parameter Estimates

                  Parameter        Standard     T for H0:
Variable   DF      Estimate           Error    Parameter=0     Prob > |T|

INTERCEP    1      4.583333      0.12472191         36.748         0.0001
X1          1      0.250000      0.12472191          2.004         0.0919
X2          1     -0.100000      0.12472191         -0.802         0.4533
X3          1      1.500000      0.14401646         10.415         0.0001
X4          1      0.633333      0.14401646          4.398         0.0046
X5          1      1.933333      0.14401646         13.424         0.0001
```

FIGURE 11.10
SAS printout for reduced model for testing treatments, Example 11.7

```
Dependent Variable: ESTCOST

                          Analysis of Variance

                            Sum of          Mean
Source              DF     Squares        Square      F Value        Prob>F

Model                3     6.76333       2.25444       40.378        0.0001
Error                8     0.44667       0.05583
C Total             11     7.21000

     Root MSE        0.23629      R-square         0.9380
     Dep Mean        5.65000      Adj R-sq         0.9148
     C.V.            4.18214

                          Parameter Estimates

                  Parameter        Standard     T for H0:
Variable   DF      Estimate           Error    Parameter=0     Prob > |T|

INTERCEP    1      4.633333      0.13642255         33.963         0.0001
X3          1      1.500000      0.19293062          7.775         0.0001
X4          1      0.633333      0.19293062          3.283         0.0111
X5          1      1.933333      0.19293062         10.021         0.0001
```

The remaining elements of the test follow.

Test statistic:

$$F = \frac{(\text{SSE}_\text{R} - \text{SSE}_\text{C})/(p-1)}{\text{MSE}_\text{C}} = \frac{(.44667 - .18667)/2}{.03111} = 4.18$$

Rejection region: $F > 5.14$, where $F_{.05} = 5.14$ (from Table 4, Appendix C) is based on $\nu_1 = (p-1) = 2$ df and $\nu_2 = (n-p-b+1) = 6$ df.

Conclusion: Since $F = 4.18$ is less than the critical value, 5.14, there is insufficient evidence, at the $\alpha = .05$ level of significance, to indicate differences among the mean estimates for the three cost engineers.

b. To test for the effectiveness of blocking on jobs, we test

$$H_0\colon \quad \beta_3 = \beta_4 = \beta_5 = 0$$

in the complete model specified in part **a**. The reduced model is

$$E(y) = \beta_0 + \underbrace{\beta_1 x_1 + \beta_2 x_2}_{\text{Treatments (engineers)}}$$

The SAS printout for this second reduced model is shown in Figure 11.11. Note that $SSE_R = 6.95$ (shaded on the printout). The elements of the test follow.

FIGURE 11.11
SAS printout for reduced model for testing blocks, Example 11.7

Dependent Variable: ESTCOST

Analysis of Variance

Source	DF	Sum of Squares	Mean Square	F Value	Prob>F
Model	2	0.26000	0.13000	0.168	0.8477
Error	9	6.95000	0.77222		
C Total	11	7.21000			

Root MSE	0.87876	R-square	0.0361
Dep Mean	5.65000	Adj R-sq	-0.1781
C.V.	15.55331		

Parameter Estimates

Variable	DF	Parameter Estimate	Standard Error	T for H0: Parameter=0	Prob > |T|
INTERCEP	1	5.600000	0.43938088	12.745	0.0001
X1	1	0.250000	0.62137840	0.402	0.6968
X2	1	-0.100000	0.62137840	-0.161	0.8757

Test statistic:

$$F = \frac{(SSE_R - SSE_C)/(b-1)}{MSE_C} = \frac{(6.95 - .18667)/3}{.03111} = 72.46$$

Rejection region: $F > 4.76$, where $F_{.05} = 4.76$ (from Table 4, Appendix C) is based on $\nu_1 = (b-1) = 3$ df and $\nu_2 = (n - p - b + 1) = 6$ df.

Conclusion: Since $F = 72.46$ exceeds the critical value 4.76, there is sufficient evidence (at $\alpha = .05$) to indicate differences among the block (job) means. It appears that blocking on jobs was effective in reducing the job-to-job variation in cost estimates.

Caution: The result of the test for the equality of block means must be interpreted with care, especially when the calculated value of the F test statistic does not fall in the rejection region. This does not necessarily imply that the block means are the same, i.e., that blocking is unimportant. Reaching this conclusion would be equivalent to accepting the null hypothesis, a practice we have carefully avoided because of the unknown probability of committing a Type II error (that is, of accepting H_0 when H_a is true). In other words, even when a test for block differences is inconclusive, we may still want to use the randomized block design in similar future experiments. If the experimenter believes that the experimental units are more homogeneous within blocks than among blocks, he or she should use the randomized block design regardless of whether the test comparing the block means shows them to be different.

The traditional analysis of variance approach to analyzing the data collected from a randomized block design is similar to the completely randomized design. The partitioning of SS(Total) for the randomized block design is most easily seen by examining Figure 11.12. Note that SS(Total) is now partitioned into *three* parts:

$$\text{SS(Total)} = \text{SSB} + \text{SST} + \text{SSE}$$

The formulas for calculating SST and SSB follow the same pattern as the formula for calculating SST for the completely randomized design.

FIGURE 11.12
Partitioning of the total sum of squares for the randomized block design

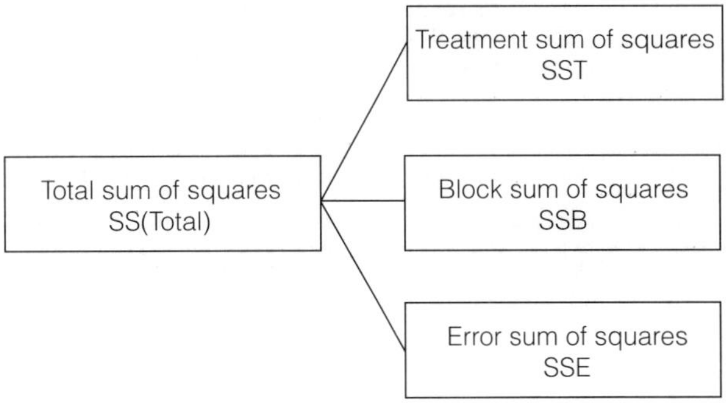

From these quantities, we obtain mean square for treatments, MST, mean square for blocks, MSB, and mean square for error, MSE, as shown in the box opposite. The test statistics are

$$F = \frac{\text{MST}}{\text{MSE}} \quad \text{for testing treatments}$$

$$F = \frac{\text{MSB}}{\text{MSE}} \quad \text{for testing blocks}$$

These F values are equivalent to the "partial" F statistics of the regression approach.

Computing Formulas for the Analysis of Variance for a Randomized Block Design

$$\sum_{i=1}^{n} y_i = \text{Sum of all } n \text{ measurements}$$

$$\sum_{i=1}^{n} y_i^2 = \text{Sum of squares of all } n \text{ measurements}$$

$$\text{CM} = \text{Correction for mean}$$

$$= \frac{(\text{Total of all measurements})^2}{\text{Total number of measurements}} = \frac{\left(\sum_{i=1}^{n} y_i\right)^2}{n}$$

$$\text{SS(Total)} = \text{Total sum of squares}$$

$$= (\text{Sum of squares of all measurements}) - \text{CM}$$

$$= \sum_{i=1}^{n} y_i^2 - \text{CM}$$

$$\text{SST} = \text{Sum of squares for treatments}$$

$$= \begin{pmatrix} \text{Sum of squares of treatment totals with} \\ \text{each square divided by } b\text{, the number of} \\ \text{measurements for that treatment} \end{pmatrix} - \text{CM}$$

$$= \frac{T_1^2}{b} + \frac{T_2^2}{b} + \cdots + \frac{T_p^2}{b} - \text{CM}$$

$$\text{SSB} = \text{Sum of squares for blocks}$$

$$= \begin{pmatrix} \text{Sum of squares for block totals with} \\ \text{each square divided by } p\text{, the number} \\ \text{of measurements in that block} \end{pmatrix} - \text{CM}$$

$$= \frac{B_1^2}{p} + \frac{B_2^2}{p} + \cdots + \frac{B_b^2}{p} - \text{CM}$$

$$\text{SSE} = \text{Sum of squares for error} = \text{SS(Total)} - \text{SST} - \text{SSB}$$

$$\text{MST} = \text{Mean square for treatments} = \frac{\text{SST}}{p-1}$$

$$\text{MSB} = \text{Mean square for blocks} = \frac{\text{SSB}}{b-1}$$

$$\text{MSE} = \text{Mean square for error} = \frac{\text{SSE}}{n-p-b+1}$$

$$F = \frac{\text{MST}}{\text{MSE}} \quad \text{for testing treatments}$$

$$F = \frac{\text{MSB}}{\text{MSE}} \quad \text{for testing blocks}$$

EXAMPLE 11.8

Refer to Example 11.7. Perform an analysis of variance of the data in Table 11.4 using the ANOVA approach.

Solution

Rather than perform the calculations by hand (again, we leave this as an exercise for the student), we utilize a computer software package. The SPSS printout of the ANOVA is displayed in Figure 11.13. The F value for testing treatments, $F = 4.179$, and the F value for testing blocks, $F = 72.464$, are both shaded on the printout. Note that these values are identical to the F values computed using the regression approach, Example 11.8. The p-values of the tests (also shaded) lead to the same conclusions reached in Example 11.7. For example, the p-value for the test of treatment differences, $p = .073$, exceeds $\alpha = .05$; thus, there is insufficient evidence of differences among the treatment means.

FIGURE 11.13
SPSS printout for ANOVA of data in Table 11.4

Source of Variation	Sum of Squares	DF	Mean Square	F	Signif of F
Main Effects	7.023	5	1.405	45.150	.000
ENGINEER	.260	2	.130	4.179	.073
JOB	6.763	3	2.254	72.464	.000
Explained	7.023	5	1.405	45.150	.000
Residual	.187	6	.031		
Total	7.210	11	.655		

As with a completely randomized design, the sources of variation and their respective degrees of freedom, sums of squares, and mean squares for a randomized block design are shown in an ANOVA summary table. The general format of such a table for a randomized block design is shown in the box; the ANOVA table for the data of Table 11.4 is shown in Table 11.5. (These quantities were obtained from the SPSS printout, Figure 11.13.) Note that the degrees of freedom for the three sources of variation, treatments, blocks, and error, sum to the degrees of freedom for SS(Total). Similarly, the sums of squares for the three sources will always sum to SS(Total).

General Format of ANOVA Table for a Randomized Block Design

SOURCE	df	SS	MS	F
Treatments	$p-1$	SST	$MST = \frac{SST}{p-1}$	$F = \frac{MST}{MSE}$
Blocks	$b-1$	SSB	$MSB = \frac{SSB}{b-1}$	$F = \frac{MSB}{MSE}$
Error	$n-p-b+1$	SSE	$MSE = \frac{SSE}{n-p-b+1}$	
Total	$n-1$	SS(Total)		

TABLE 11.5 **ANOVA Summary Table for Example 11.8**

SOURCE	df	SS	MS	F
Treatments (Engineers)	2	.260	.130	4.18
Blocks (Jobs)	3	6.763	2.254	72.46
Error	6	.187	.031	
Total	11	7.210		

Confidence intervals for the difference between a pair of treatment means or block means for a randomized block design are shown in the following box.

Confidence Intervals for the Difference ($\mu_i - \mu_j$) Between a Pair of Treatment Means or Block Means

Treatment means: $(\overline{T}_i - \overline{T}_j) \pm t_{\alpha/2}s\sqrt{\frac{2}{b}}$

Block means: $(\overline{B}_i - \overline{B}_j) \pm t_{\alpha/2}s\sqrt{\frac{2}{p}}$

where

b = Number of blocks

p = Number of treatments

$s = \sqrt{\text{MSE}}$

$\overline{T}_i$ = Sample mean for treatment i

$\overline{B}_i$ = Sample mean for block i

and $t_{\alpha/2}$ is based on $(n - p - b + 1)$ degrees of freedom

EXAMPLE 11.9

Refer to Example 11.7. Find a 90% confidence interval for the difference between the mean level of estimates for engineers 1 and 2.

Solution

From Example 11.7, we know that $b = 4$, $\overline{T}_1 = 5.60$, $\overline{T}_2 = 5.85$, and $s^2 = \text{MSE}_C = .03111$. The degrees of freedom associated with s^2 (and, therefore, with $t_{\alpha/2}$) is 6. Therefore, $s = \sqrt{s^2} = \sqrt{.03111} = .176$ and $t_{\alpha/2} = t_{.05} = 1.943$. Substituting these values into the formula for the confidence interval for $(\mu_1 - \mu_2)$, we obtain

$$(\overline{T}_1 - \overline{T}_2) \pm t_{\alpha/2}s\sqrt{\frac{2}{b}}$$

$$(5.60 - 5.85) \pm 1.943(.176)\sqrt{\frac{2}{4}}$$

$$-.25 \pm .24$$

or, $-.49$ to $-.01$. Since each unit represents \$100,000, we estimate the difference between the mean level of job estimates for estimators 1 and 2 to be enclosed by the interval, $-\$49,000$ to $-\$1,000$. [*Note*: At first glance, this result may appear to contradict the result of the F test for comparing treatment means. However, the observed significance level of the F test (.07) implies that significant differences exist between the means at $\alpha = .10$, which is consistent with the fact that 0 is not within the 90% confidence interval.]

There is one very important point to note when you block the treatments in an experiment. Recall from Section 10.3 that the block effects cancel. This fact enables us to calculate confidence intervals for the difference between treatment means using the formulas given in the box on page 613. But, if a sample treatment mean is used to estimate a *single treatment mean*, the block effects do not cancel. *Therefore, the only way that you can obtain an unbiased estimate of a single treatment mean (and corresponding confidence interval) in a blocked design is to randomly select the blocks from a large collection (population) of blocks and to treat the block effect as a second random component, in addition to random error.* Designs that contain two or more random components are called *nested designs* and are beyond the scope of this text. For more information on this topic, see the references at the end of this chapter.

EXERCISES

11.18 Do managers make inferences about an employee based on the employee's absenteeism? This question was researched in the *Journal of Management* (Vol. 18, 1992). A sample of 33 managers, all of whom were active members of a local association of human resources administrators, participated in the study. Each manager was presented with a booklet describing the absenteeism of three hypothetical employees. One employee was described as having an "excellent" record of attendance, the second an "average" record, and the third was described as being "absence-prone." The managers then estimated the total number of days each employee was absent during a 2-year period. The goal of the study was to compare the mean number of absences for the three hypothetical employees.

a. Identify the treatments and the blocks for this randomized block design.
b. Identify the response variable.
c. Specify the null hypothesis to be tested by the ANOVA.
d. Explain why a randomized block design is used in this study rather than a completely randomized design.

11.19 *Physical Therapy* (Aug. 1986) reported on a study to "determine whether the medial rotation that accompanies flexion of the shoulder took place during the performance of the flexion/abduction/lateral-rotation proprioceptive neuromuscular facilitation pattern (D_2F)." Ten college students, who exhibited no evidence of disease or limitation of movement in their shoulders, served as the subjects for the study. For each subject, the medial rotation was measured (in degrees) at each of three positions in the D_2F pattern: (1) beginning position, (2) point at which rotation changed directions, and (3) ending position. The goal of the analysis is to compare the mean medial rotation measurements of the three positions.

a. Identify the treatments in this experiment.
b. Identify the blocks in this experiment.

c. Identify the response variable.
d. Explain why a randomized block design is appropriate for this experiment.
e. Give the linear model appropriate for analyzing the data.

11.20 The analysis of variance for a randomized block design produced the ANOVA table entries shown here.

SOURCE	df	SS	MS	F
Treatments	3	27.1	____	____
Blocks	5	____	14.90	____
Error	____	33.4	____	
Total	____	____		

The sample means for the four treatments are as follows:

$\bar{y}_A = 9.7 \qquad \bar{y}_B = 12.1 \qquad \bar{y}_C = 6.2 \qquad \bar{y}_D = 9.3$

a. Complete the ANOVA table.
b. Do the data provide sufficient evidence to indicate a difference among the treatment means? Test using $\alpha = .01$.
c. Do the data provide sufficient evidence to indicate that blocking was a useful design strategy to employ for this experiment? Explain.
d. Find a 95% confidence interval for $(\mu_A - \mu_B)$.
e. Find a 95% confidence interval for $(\mu_B - \mu_D)$.

11.21 Early full-screen video display terminals presented the viewer with white characters on a black background. Initially, viewers found the high degree of contrast easy on the eyes. However, after an extended period of use, black and white displays were frequently found to cause temporary eye irritations. Experimentation with other colors revealed that yellow/amber displays may be the easiest on the eyes. In one German study, video display terminals were produced with white/black and six different symbol colors. Thirty test subjects were asked to specify which color combination they preferred by ranking each of the seven color combinations on a scale from 0 (no preference) to 10. Based on the mean preference scores for each color provided by the researchers, we have simulated the individual preference scores for 10 subjects in the accompanying table. The data were subjected to an ANOVA for a randomized block design using MINITAB; the results are shown in the printout on page 616.

SUBJECT	GREEN/ BLACK	WHITE/ BLACK	YELLOW/ WHITE	ORANGE/ WHITE	YELLOW/ BLACK	YELLOW/ AMBER	YELLOW/ ORANGE
1	7	6	7	2	8	9	3
2	8	6	9	4	9	8	1
3	5	5	7	1	6	8	2
4	3	4	2	0	2	6	0
5	9	8	8	3	9	9	2
6	7	5	6	2	7	7	1
7	6	7	8	4	6	9	5
8	6	5	8	1	8	9	1
9	9	9	8	2	9	8	0
10	9	8	8	3	9	10	1

Source: Adapted from Solomon, L., and Burawa, A. "Maximize your computing comfort and efficiency." *Computers & Electronics*, Apr. 1983, pp. 35–40.

MINITAB printout for Exercise 11.21

ANALYSIS OF VARIANCE SCORE

SOURCE	DF	SS	MS
COLOR	6	421.34	70.22
SUBJECT	9	114.30	12.70
ERROR	54	71.80	1.33
TOTAL	69	607.44	

a. Do the data provide sufficient evidence of a difference among the mean preference scores for the seven video display color combinations? Test using $\alpha = .05$.

b. Perform the analysis, part **a**, by fitting and comparing the appropriate linear models. Verify that the results agree.

11.22 A commonly used index to estimate the reliability of a building subjected to lateral loads is the drift ratio. Sophisticated computer programs such as STAAD-III have been developed to estimate the drift ratio based on variables such as beam stiffness, column stiffness, story height, moment of inertia, and so on. Civil engineers at the State University of New York at Buffalo and the University of Central Florida performed an experiment to compare drift ratio estimates using STAAD-III with the estimates produced by a new, simpler microcomputer program called DRIFT (*Microcomputers in Civil Engineering*, 1993). Data for a 21-story building were used as input to the programs. Two runs were made with STAAD-III: Run 1 considered axial deformation of the building columns, and run 2 neglected this information. The goal of the analysis is to compare the mean drift ratios (where drift is measured as lateral displacement) estimated by the three computer runs (the two STAAD-III runs and DRIFT). The lateral displacements (in inches) estimated by the three programs are recorded in the table for each of five building levels (1, 5, 10, 15, and 21). A MINITAB printout of the analysis of variance for the data is also shown.

a. Identify the treatments in the experiment.

LEVEL	STAAD-III (1)	STAAD-III (2)	DRIFT
1	.17	.16	.16
5	1.35	1.26	1.27
10	3.04	2.76	2.77
15	4.54	3.98	3.99
21	5.94	4.99	5.00

Source: Valles, R. E., et al. "Simplified drift evaluation of wall-frame structures." *Microcomputers in Civil Engineering*, Vol. 8, 1993, p. 242 (Table 2).

Analysis of Variance for DftRatio

Source	DF	SS	MS	F	P
Program	2	0.4664	0.2332	4.79	0.043
Level	4	52.1812	13.0453	267.74	0.000
Error	8	0.3898	0.0487		
Total	14	53.0374			

b. Because lateral displacement will vary greatly across building levels (floors), a randomized block design will be used to reduce the level-to-level variation in drift. Explain, diagramatically, the set-up of the design if all 21 levels are to be included in the study.

c. Using the information in the printout, compare the mean drift ratios estimated by the three programs.

11.23 Plant therapists believe that plants can reduce the stress levels of humans. A Kansas State University study was conducted to investigate this phenomenon. Two weeks before final exams, 10 undergraduate students took part in an experiment to determine what effect the presence of a live plant, a photo of a plant, or absence of a plant has on the student's ability to relax while isolated in a dimly lit room. Each student participated in three sessions—one with a live plant, one with a plant photo, and one with no plant (control).* During each session, finger temperature was measured at 1-minute intervals for 20 minutes. Since increasing finger temperature indicates an increased level of relaxation, the maximum temperature (in degrees) was used as the response variable. The data for the experiment, provided in the table, were analyzed using the ANOVA procedure of SPSS. Use the accompanying SPSS printout to make the proper inference.

STUDENT	LIVE PLANT	PLANT PHOTO	NO PLANT (CONTROL)
1	91.4	93.5	96.6
2	94.9	96.6	90.5
3	97.0	95.8	95.4
4	93.7	96.2	96.7
5	96.0	96.6	93.5
6	96.7	95.5	94.8
7	95.2	94.6	95.7
8	96.0	97.2	96.2
9	95.6	94.8	96.0
10	95.6	92.6	96.6

Source: Elizabeth Schreiber, Department of Statistics, Kansas State University, Manhattan, Kansas.

```
        * * *  A N A L Y S I S   O F   V A R I A N C E  * * *

              TEMP
         BY   PLANT
              STUDENT

                            Sum of              Mean              Signif
Source of Variation         Squares     DF      Square        F     of F

Main Effects                 18.537     11       1.685      .523    .863
  PLANT                        .122      2        .061      .019    .981
  STUDENT                    18.415      9       2.046      .635    .754

  Explained                  18.537     11       1.685      .523    .863

  Residual                   58.038     18       3.224

  Total                      76.575     29       2.641

       30 Cases were processed.
        0 Cases (   .0 PCT) were missing.
```

*The experiment is simplified for this exercise. The actual experiment involved 30 students who participated in 12 sessions.

11.24 Runzheimer International, a Wisconsin-based management consulting firm specializing in travel and living costs, recently conducted a worldwide study of prices of goods and services. The data in the table, extracted from *Consumer's Digest* (Dec. 1993), lists the prices (in U.S. dollars) of seven products sold in major cities of 15 different countries. Use the accompanying ASP printout to compare the average prices in the 15 countries with an analysis of variance.

CITY	CHICKEN, WHOLE (1 lb)	TUNA, CANNED (6.5 oz)	EGGS, LARGE (1 dozen)	SOFT DRINK (2 liters)	VODKA (1 liter)	MAN'S DRESS SHIRT	RAZOR BLADE (5 count)
Caracas	$ .70	$ .77	$1.12	$1.18	$ 6.77	$45.93	$ 4.75
Frankfurt	1.64	1.45	1.81	2.19	15.42	40.93	2.12
Hong Kong	2.70	1.27	1.36	1.77	21.89	41.92	3.04
London	1.29	.67	1.98	1.51	22.82	27.41	3.08
Los Angeles	.99	.85	1.94	1.33	10.12	32.54	3.48
Madrid	1.24	1.38	2.09	1.53	9.89	46.32	3.62
Mexico City	1.05	.77	1.22	2.17	7.10	25.87	2.70
Milan	1.47	1.60	2.51	1.46	9.12	71.44	2.87
Paris	2.69	1.84	2.48	1.49	13.68	52.94	3.53
Sao Paulo	.38	1.64	1.40	1.02	4.65	35.50	2.64
Singapore	1.75	1.67	1.41	1.31	35.54	35.52	3.25
Stockholm	2.95	1.17	2.67	3.13	34.35	68.67	5.33
Sydney	1.73	1.31	1.64	1.57	23.16	22.49	3.54
Tokyo	4.28	2.40	2.35	5.73	24.27	51.62	4.54
Toronto	1.85	1.51	1.17	1.42	16.69	28.12	3.05

```
                        RANDOM BLOCK ANALYSIS

DEP. VAR.:  Price
  FACTORS:  Product    Country

        ---------------- ANALYSIS OF VARIANCE TABLE ----------------

             SUM OF SQ'S D.F.     MEAN SQ.    F(D.F./84)     P-VALUE
             ----------- ----    ---------    ----------  ----------
   Product     20654.6      6    3442.43        81.3421  7.0608E-33
   Country     858.827     14     61.3448       1.44953  0.149068
     ERROR     3554.91     84     42.3204
        ------------------------------------------------------------
     TOTAL     25068.3    104
```

11.25 The "in-tray" exercise aids in assessing the management potential of future administrators and executives. Trainees are provided with the typical contents of an executive's in-tray with a variety of everyday problems in written form—letters, memoranda, notes, reports, and telephone messages—requiring decisions and action. After the tasks are completed, the trainees' performances are assessed by one or more expert raters, usually on a scale of 1 (high performance) to 6 (low performance). However, the reliability of the assessors' ratings should be determined before using the in-tray measure of managerial effectiveness. The phenomenon of rater reliability was investigated in the *Journal of Occupational Psychology*. Seven subjects, all candidates for a general management position in a manufacturing company in the British motor industry, were given the in-tray test. Overall in-tray performance of each candidate was assessed by three different raters. The results are given in the accompanying table. Note that each of the three raters judged the overall performance of all seven candidates.

CANDIDATE	RATER 1	RATER 2	RATER 3
A	4.5	4.5	5.0
B	2.5	4.5	4.5
C	5.0	3.0	4.0
D	4.0	4.5	4.5
E	1.5	2.0	4.5
F	3.5	4.5	4.5
G	4.0	4.0	4.0

Source: Gill, R. W. T. "The in-tray (in-basket) exercise as a measure of management potential." *Journal of Occupational Psychology*, 1979, Vol. 52, pp. 185–195.

a. Give the complete model appropriate for this design.
b. Give the reduced model appropriate for testing for differences in the mean scores given by the three raters.
c. Give the reduced model appropriate for determining whether blocking by candidates was effective in removing an unwanted source of variability.

11.26 Refer to Exercise 11.25. The models of parts a, b, and c were fitted to data in the table using MINITAB. The MINITAB printouts are displayed here and on page 620.

MINITAB printout for complete model, Exercise 11.25a

```
The regression equation is
SCORE = 4.48 - 0.857 R1 - 0.571 R2
        + 0.667 C1 - 0.167 C2 + 0.000 C3 + 0.333 C4 - 1.33 C5 + 0.167 C6

Predictor       Coef       Stdev    t-ratio        p
Constant      4.4762      0.5401       8.29    0.000
R1           -0.8571      0.4410      -1.94    0.076
R2           -0.5714      0.4410      -1.30    0.219
C1            0.6667      0.6736       0.99    0.342
C2           -0.1667      0.6736      -0.25    0.809
C3            0.0000      0.6736       0.00    1.000
C4            0.3333      0.6736       0.49    0.630
C5           -1.3333      0.6736      -1.98    0.071
C6            0.1667      0.6736       0.25    0.809

s = 0.8250       R-sq = 54.5%     R-sq(adj) = 24.2%

Analysis of Variance

SOURCE        DF          SS          MS          F        p
Regression     8      9.7857      1.2232       1.80    0.174
Error         12      8.1667      0.6806
Total         20     17.9524
```

MINITAB printout for reduced model, Exercise 11.25b

```
The regression equation is
SCORE = 4.00 + 0.667 C1 - 0.167 C2 + 0.000 C3 + 0.333 C4 - 1.33 C5 + 0.167 C6

Predictor       Coef       Stdev    t-ratio        p
Constant      4.0000      0.5079       7.88    0.000
C1            0.6667      0.7182       0.93    0.369
C2           -0.1667      0.7182      -0.23    0.820
C3            0.0000      0.7182       0.00    1.000
C4            0.3333      0.7182       0.46    0.650
C5           -1.3333      0.7182      -1.86    0.085
C6            0.1667      0.7182       0.23    0.820

s = 0.8797       R-sq = 39.7%     R-sq(adj) = 13.8%

Analysis of Variance

SOURCE        DF          SS          MS          F        p
Regression     6      7.1190      1.1865       1.53    0.238
Error         14     10.8333      0.7738
Total         20     17.9524
```

MINITAB printout for reduced model, Exercise 11.25c

```
The regression equation is
SCORE = 4.43 - 0.857 R1 - 0.571 R2

Predictor        Coef        Stdev     t-ratio       p
Constant       4.4286       0.3483       12.71   0.000
R1            -0.8571       0.4926       -1.74   0.099
R2            -0.5714       0.4926       -1.16   0.261

s = 0.9215       R-sq = 14.9%       R-sq(adj) = 5.4%

Analysis of Variance

SOURCE        DF          SS          MS          F        p
Regression     2      2.6667      1.3333       1.57    0.235
Error         18     15.2857      0.8492
Total         20     17.9524
```

a. Construct an ANOVA summary table.

b. Is there evidence of a difference among the mean performance scores assessed by the three raters? Use $\alpha = .05$.

c. Is there evidence of a difference among the mean performance scores of the candidates? That is, is there evidence that blocking by candidates was effective in removing an unwanted source of variability? Use $\alpha = .05$.

11.27 A simulation study was conducted to investigate the machine performance of several new algorithms for functions in the FORTRAN computer program library (*IBM Journal of Research and Development*, Mar. 1986). The accompanying table gives the time per call (in microseconds) for several randomly selected scalar functions (averaged over 10,000 random arguments) on each of three different IBM System/370 machines. Treating the functions as blocks, the data were subjected to an ANOVA for a randomized block design using SAS. Use the accompanying SAS printout to answer the following questions.

FUNCTION	IBM 4331	IBM 4361	IBM 4341
EDUM	9.90	3.07	4.88
ACOS CIRC(O, PI)	179.62	33.28	33.23
SIN LINEAR(−PI, PI)	105.72	24.13	27.08
EXP LINEAR(−16, 16)	254.82	39.14	37.46
D2DUM	13.47	4.63	5.72

Source: Agarwal, R. C., et al. "New scalar and vector elementary functions for the IBM System/370" *IBM Journal of Research and Development*, Vol. 30, No. 2, Mar. 1986, p. 139 (Table 4). Copyright 1986 by International Business Machines Corporation, reprinted with permission.

```
                     Analysis of Variance Procedure

Dependent Variable: TIME
                                   Sum of            Mean
Source                  DF        Squares          Square   F Value      Pr > F

Model                    6    53025.20409      8837.53402      3.21      0.0653
Error                    8    22016.91424      2752.11428
Corrected Total         14    75042.11833

                  R-Square           C.V.        Root MSE             TIME Mean

                  0.706606       101.3862        52.46060            51.7433333


Source                  DF       Anova SS     Mean Square   F Value      Pr > F

MACHINE                  2    27875.04789     13937.52395      5.06      0.0379
FUNCTION                 4    25150.15620      6287.53905      2.28      0.1487
```

a. Is there sufficient evidence to indicate that the mean function call times differ for the three IBM System/370 machines? Test using $\alpha = .10$.
b. Conduct a test to determine whether blocking on functions was effective in removing an extraneous source of variation. Use $\alpha = .10$.

11.5 Two-Factor Factorial Experiments

In Section 10.4, we learned that factorial experiments are volume-increasing designs conducted to investigate the effect of two or more independent variables (factors) on the mean value of the response y. In this section, we focus on the analysis of two-factor factorial experiments.

Suppose, for example, we want to relate the mean number of defects on a finished item—say, a new desk top—to two factors, type of nozzle for the varnish spray gun and length of spraying time. Suppose further that we want to investigate the mean number of defects per desk for three types (three levels) of nozzles (N_1, N_2, and N_3) and for two lengths (two levels) of spraying time (S_1 and S_2). If we choose the treatments for the experiment to include all combinations of the three levels of nozzle type with the two levels of spraying time (i.e., we observe the number of defects for the factor level combinations N_1S_1, N_1S_2, N_2S_1, N_2S_2, N_3S_1, N_3S_2), our design is called a **complete 3 × 2 factorial experiment**. Note that the design will contain $3 \times 2 = 6$ treatments.

Factorial experiments, you will recall, are useful methods for selecting treatments because they permit us to make inferences about factor interactions. The complete model for the 3×2 factorial experiment contains $(3 - 1) = 2$ main effect terms for nozzles, $(2 - 1) = 1$ main effect term for spray time, and $(3 - 1)(2 - 1) = 2$ nozzle–spray time interaction terms:

$$E(y) = \beta_0 + \underbrace{\beta_1 x_1 + \beta_2 x_2}_{\substack{\text{Main effects} \\ \text{Nozzle}}} + \underbrace{\beta_3 x_3}_{\substack{\text{Main effect} \\ \text{Spray time}}} + \underbrace{\beta_4 x_1 x_2 + \beta_5 x_1 x_3}_{\substack{\text{Interaction} \\ \text{Nozzle} \times \text{Spray time}}}$$

The independent variables (factors) in the model can be either quantitative or qualitative. If they are quantitative, the main effects are represented by terms such as x, x^2, x^3, etc.; if qualitative, the main effects are represented by dummy variables. In our 3×2 factorial experiment, nozzle type is qualitative and spraying time is quantitative; hence, the x variables in the model are defined as follows:

$$x_1 = \begin{cases} 1 & \text{if nozzle } N_1 \\ 0 & \text{if not} \end{cases} \qquad x_2 = \begin{cases} 1 & \text{if nozzle } N_2 \\ 0 & \text{if not} \end{cases} \qquad \text{Base level} = N_3$$

$$x_3 = \text{Length of spraying time (in minutes)}$$

Note that the model for the 3×2 factorial contains a total of $3 \times 2 = 6$ β parameters. If we observe only a single value of the response y for each of the $3 \times 2 = 6$ treatments, then $n = 6$ and df(Error) for the complete model is $(n - 6) = 0$. Consequently, for a factorial experiment, *the number r of observations per factor level combination (i.e., the number of replications of the factorial experiment) must always be 2 or more.* Otherwise, no degrees of freedom are available for estimating σ^2.

To test for factor interaction, we drop the interaction terms and fit the reduced model:

$$E(y) = \beta_0 + \underbrace{\beta_1 x_1 + \beta_2 x_2}_{\substack{\text{Main effects} \\ \text{Nozzle}}} + \underbrace{\beta_3 x_3}_{\substack{\text{Main effect} \\ \text{Spray time}}}$$

The null hypothesis of no interaction, H_0: $\beta_4 = \beta_5 = 0$, is tested by comparing the SSEs for the two models in a partial F statistic. This test for interaction is summarized, in general, in the box.

Tests for factor main effects are conducted in a similar manner. The main effect terms of interest are dropped from the complete model and the reduced model is fitted. The SSEs for the two models are compared in the usual fashion.

Before we work through a numerical example of an analysis of variance for a factorial experiment, we must understand the practical significance of the tests for factor interaction and factor main effects. We illustrate these concepts in Example 11.10.

Models and ANOVA F Test for Interaction in a Two-Factor Factorial Experiment with Factor A at a Levels and Factor B at b Levels

Complete model:

$$E(y) = \beta_0 + \overbrace{\beta_1 x_1 + \cdots + \beta_{a-1} x_{a-1}}^{\text{Main effect } A \text{ terms}} + \overbrace{\beta_a x_a + \cdots + \beta_{a+b-2} x_{a+b-2}}^{\text{Main effect } B \text{ terms}}$$

$$+ \overbrace{\beta_{a+b-1} x_1 x_a + \beta_{a+b} x_1 x_{a+1} + \cdots + \beta_{ab-1} x_{a-1} x_{a+b-2}}^{AB \text{ interaction terms}}$$

where*

$$x_1 = \begin{cases} 1 & \text{if level 2 of factor } A \\ 0 & \text{if not} \end{cases} \quad \cdots$$

$$x_{a-1} = \begin{cases} 1 & \text{if level } a \text{ of factor } A \\ 0 & \text{if not} \end{cases}$$

$$x_a = \begin{cases} 1 & \text{if level 2 of factor } B \\ 0 & \text{if not} \end{cases} \quad \cdots$$

$$x_{a+b-2} = \begin{cases} 1 & \text{if level } b \text{ of factor } B \\ 0 & \text{if not} \end{cases}$$

H_0: $\beta_{a+b-1} = \beta_{a+b} = \cdots = \beta_{ab-1} = 0$
(i.e., H_0: No interaction between factors A and B.)

H_a: At least one of the β parameters listed in H_0 differs from 0.
(i.e., H_a: Factors A and B interact.)

Reduced model:

$$E(y) = \beta_0 + \overbrace{\beta_1 x_1 + \cdots + \beta_{a-1}x_{a-1}}^{\text{Main effect } A \text{ terms}} + \overbrace{\beta_a x_a + \cdots + \beta_{a+b-2}x_{a+b-2}}^{\text{Main effect } B \text{ terms}}$$

Test statistic: $F = \dfrac{(\text{SSE}_R - \text{SSE}_C)/[(a-1)(b-1)]}{\text{SSE}_C/[ab(r-1)]}$

$= \dfrac{(\text{SSE}_R - \text{SSE}_C)/[(a-1)(b-1)]}{\text{MSE}_C}$

where

SSE_R = SSE for reduced model

SSE_C = SSE for complete model

MSE_C = MSE for complete model

r = Number of replications (i.e., number of y measurements per cell of the $a \times b$ factorial)

Rejection region: $F > F_\alpha$, where F is based on $\nu_1 = (a-1)(b-1)$ and $\nu_2 = ab(r-1)$ df

Assumptions:
1. The population probability distribution of the observations for any factor level combination is approximately normal.
2. The variance of the probability distribution is constant and the same for all factor level combinations.

**Note:* The independent variables, $x_1, x_2, \ldots, x_{a+b-2}$, are defined for an experiment in which both factors represent *qualitative* variables. When a factor is *quantitative*, you may choose to represent the main effects with quantitative terms such as x, x^2, x^3, and so forth.

EXAMPLE 11.10

A company that stamps gaskets out of sheets of rubber, plastic, and other materials wants to compare the mean number of gaskets produced per hour for two different types of stamping machines. Practically, the manufacturer wants to determine whether one machine is more productive than the other. Even more important is determining whether one machine is more productive in making rubber gaskets while the other is more productive in making plastic gaskets. To answer these questions, the manufacturer decides to conduct a 2×3 factorial experiment using three types of gasket material, B_1, B_2, and B_3, with each of the two types of stamping machines, A_1 and A_2. Each machine is operated for three 1-hour time periods for each of the gasket materials, with the eighteen 1-hour time periods assigned to the six machine–material combinations in random order. (The purpose of the randomization is to eliminate the possibility that uncontrolled environmental factors might bias the results.) Suppose we have calculated and plotted the six treatment means. Two hypothetical plots of the six means are shown in Figures 11.14a and 11.14b. The three means for stamping machine A_1 are connected by solid line segments and the corresponding three means for machine A_2 by dashed line segments. What do these plots imply about the productivity of the two stamping machines?

FIGURE 11.14

Hypothetical plot of the means for the six machine–material combinations

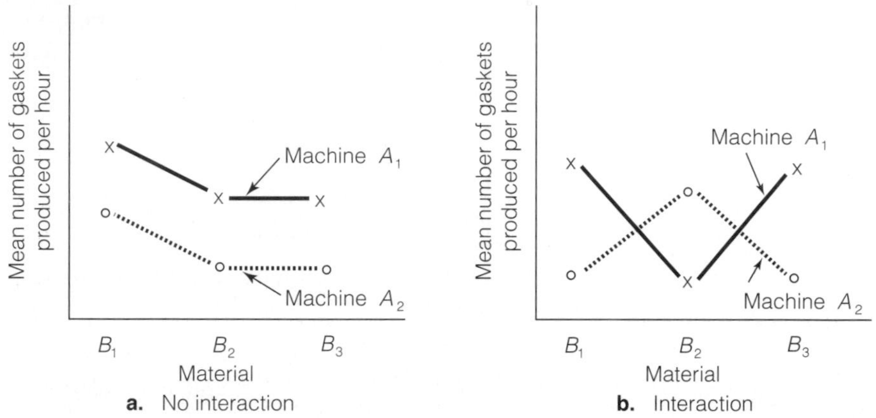

Solution

Figure 11.14a suggests that machine A_1 produces a larger number of gaskets per hour, regardless of the gasket material, and is therefore superior to machine A_2. On the average, machine A_1 stamps more cork (B_1) gaskets per hour than rubber or plastic, but the *difference* in the mean numbers of gaskets produced by the two machines remains approximately the same, regardless of the gasket material. Thus, the difference in the mean number of gaskets produced by the two machines is *independent* of the gasket material used in the stamping process.

In contrast to Figure 11.14a, Figure 11.14b shows the productivity for machine A_1 to be greater than that for machine A_2, when the gasket material is cork (B_1) or plastic (B_3). But the means are reversed for rubber (B_2) gasket material. For this material, machine A_2 produces, on the average, more gaskets per hour than machine A_1. Thus, Figure 11.14b illustrates a situation where the mean value of the response variable *depends* on the combination of the factor levels. When this situation occurs, we say that the factors *interact*. Thus, one of the most important objectives of a factorial experiment is to detect factor interaction if it exists.

Definition 11.2

In a factorial experiment, when the difference in the mean levels of factor A depends on the different levels of factor B, we say that the factors A and B **interact**. If the difference is independent of the levels of B, then there is **no interaction** between A and B.

Tests for main effects are relevant only when no interaction exists between factors. Generally, the test for interaction is performed first. *If there is evidence of factor interaction, then we will not perform the tests on the main effects.* Rather, we will want to focus attention on the individual cell (treatment) means, perhaps locating one that is the largest or the smallest.

EXAMPLE 11.11

A manufacturer, whose daily supply of raw materials is variable and limited, can use the material to produce two different products in various proportions. The profit per unit of raw material obtained by producing each of the two products depends on the length of a product's manufacturing run and, hence, on the amount of raw material assigned to it. Other factors, such as worker productivity and machine breakdown, affect the profit per unit as well, but their net effect on profit is random and uncontrollable. The manufacturer has conducted an experiment to investigate the effect of the level of supply of raw materials, S, and the ratio of its assignment, R, to the two product manufacturing lines on the profit y per unit of raw material. The ultimate goal would be to be able to choose the best ratio R to match each day's supply of raw materials, S. The levels of supply of the raw material chosen for the experiment were 15, 18, and 21 tons; the levels of the ratio of allocation to the two product lines were $\frac{1}{2}$, 1, and 2. The response was the profit (in dollars) per unit of raw material supply obtained from a single day's production. Three replications of a complete 3×3 factorial experiment were conducted in a random sequence (i.e., a completely randomized design). The data for the 27 days are shown in Table 11.6.

TABLE 11.6 **Data for Example 11.11**

		RAW MATERIAL SUPPLY (S), tons		
		15	18	21
RATIO OF RAW MATERIAL ALLOCATION (R)	$\frac{1}{2}$	23, 20, 21	22, 19, 20	19, 18, 21
	1	22, 20, 19	24, 25, 22	20, 19, 22
	2	18, 18, 16	21, 23, 20	20, 22, 24

a. Write the complete model for the experiment.
b. Do the data present sufficient evidence to indicate an interaction between supply S and ratio R? Use $\alpha = .05$.
c. Based on the result, part **b**, should we perform tests for main effects?

Solution

a. Both factors, supply and ratio, are quantitative. Accordingly, when the factors in a factorial experiment are quantitative, the main effects can be represented by terms such as x, x^2, x^3, and so forth. Since each factor has three levels, we require two main effects, x and x^2, for each factor. (In general, the number of main effect terms will be one less than the number of levels for a factor.) Consequently, the complete factorial model for this 3×3 factorial experiment is

$$y = \beta_0 + \underbrace{\beta_1 x_1 + \beta_2 x_1^2}_{\text{Supply main effects}} + \underbrace{\beta_3 x_2 + \beta_4 x_2^2}_{\text{Ratio main effects}}$$

$$+ \underbrace{\beta_5 x_1 x_2 + \beta_6 x_1 x_2^2 + \beta_7 x_1^2 x_2 + \beta_8 x_1^2 x_2^2}_{\text{Supply} \times \text{Ratio interaction}} + \varepsilon$$

where

x_1 = Supply of raw material (in tons)

x_2 = Ratio of allocation

Note that the interaction terms for the model are constructed by taking the products of the various main effect terms, one from each factor. For example, we included terms involving the products of x_1 with x_2 and x_2^2. The remaining interaction terms were formed by multiplying x_1^2 by x_2 and by x_2^2.

b. To test the null hypothesis that supply and ratio do not interact, we must test the null hypothesis that the interaction terms are not needed in the linear model of part **a**:

$$H_0\colon \quad \beta_5 = \beta_6 = \beta_7 = \beta_8 = 0$$

This requires that we fit the reduced model

$$y = \beta_0 + \beta_1 x_1 + \beta_2 x_1^2 + \beta_3 x_2 + \beta_4 x_2^2$$

and perform the partial F test outlined in Section 4.10. The test statistic is

$$F = \frac{(\text{SSE}_\text{R} - \text{SSE}_\text{C})/4}{\text{MSE}_\text{C}}$$

where

SSE_R = SSE for reduced model

SSE_C = SSE for complete model

MSE_C = MSE for complete model

The complete model of part **a** and the reduced model here were fitted to the data in Table 11.6 using SAS. The SAS printouts are displayed in Figures 11.15a and 11.15b. The pertinent quantities, shaded on the printouts, are

SSE_C = 43.33333 (see Figure 11.15a)

MSE_C = 2.40741 (see Figure 11.15a)

SSE_R = 89.55556 (see Figure 11.15b)

Substituting these values into the formula for the test statistic, we obtain

$$F = \frac{(\text{SSE}_\text{R} - \text{SSE}_\text{C})/4}{\text{MSE}_\text{C}} = \frac{(89.55556 - 43.33333)/4}{2.40741} = 4.80$$

FIGURE 11.15a
SAS printout for complete factorial model

Analysis of Variance

Source	DF	Sum of Squares	Mean Square	F Value	Prob>F
Model	8	74.66667	9.33333	3.877	0.0081
Error	18	43.33333	2.40741		
C Total	26	118.00000			

Root MSE	1.55158	R-square	0.6328
Dep Mean	20.66667	Adj R-sq	0.4696
C.V.	7.50766		

Parameter Estimates

Variable	DF	Parameter Estimate	Standard Error	T for H0: Parameter=0	Prob > |T|
INTERCEP	1	245.333333	130.49665074	1.880	0.0764
X1	1	-25.074074	14.71842356	-1.704	0.1057
X1SQ	1	0.679012	0.40837272	1.663	0.1137
X2	1	-534.333333	252.45534989	-2.117	0.0485
X2SQ	1	192.666667	97.17010948	1.983	0.0629
X1X2	1	60.555556	28.47387077	2.127	0.0475
X1X2SQ	1	-22.148148	10.95959797	-2.021	0.0584
X1SQX2	1	-1.666667	0.79002700	-2.110	0.0492
X1SQX2SQ	1	0.617284	0.30408153	2.030	0.0574

FIGURE 11.15b
SAS printout for reduced factorial model

Analysis of Variance

Source	DF	Sum of Squares	Mean Square	F Value	Prob>F
Model	4	28.44444	7.11111	1.747	0.1757
Error	22	89.55556	4.07071		
C Total	26	118.00000			

Root MSE	2.01760	R-square	0.2411
Dep Mean	20.66667	Adj R-sq	0.1031
C.V.	9.76258		

Parameter Estimates

Variable	DF	Parameter Estimate	Standard Error	T for H0: Parameter=0	Prob > |T|
INTERCEP	1	-43.481481	29.32960686	-1.483	0.1524
X1	1	6.814815	3.29853705	2.066	0.0508
X1SQ	1	-0.185185	0.09152016	-2.023	0.0553
X2	1	5.666667	4.35851270	1.300	0.2070
X2SQ	1	-2.296296	1.67759232	-1.369	0.1849

The rejection region for the test is $F > F_{.05}$, where $\nu_1 = 4$ df (the number of β's tested in H_0), $\nu_2 = 18$ df (the degrees of freedom for error for the complete model), and $F_{.05} = 2.93$ (obtained from Table 4, Appendix C). Since the computed test statistic, $F = 4.80$, exceeds $F_{.05}$, we reject H_0 and conclude that supply and ratio interact.

c. The presence of interaction tells you that the mean profit depends on the particular combination of levels of supply S and ratio R. Consequently, there is little point in checking to see whether the means differ for the three levels of supply or whether they differ for the three levels of ratio (i.e., we will not perform the tests for main effects). For example, the supply level that gave the highest mean profit (over all levels of R) might not be the same supply–ratio level combination that produces the largest mean profit per unit of raw material.

The traditional analysis of variance approach to analyzing a complete two-factor factorial with factor A at a levels and factor B at b levels utilizes the fact that the total sum of squares, SS(Total), can be partitioned into four parts, SS(A), SS(B), SS(AB), and SSE (see Figure 11.16). The first two sums of squares, SS(A) and SS(B), are called **main effect sums of squares** to distinguish them from the **interaction sum of squares**, SS(AB).

FIGURE 11.16
Partitioning of the total sum of squares for a complete two-factor factorial experiment

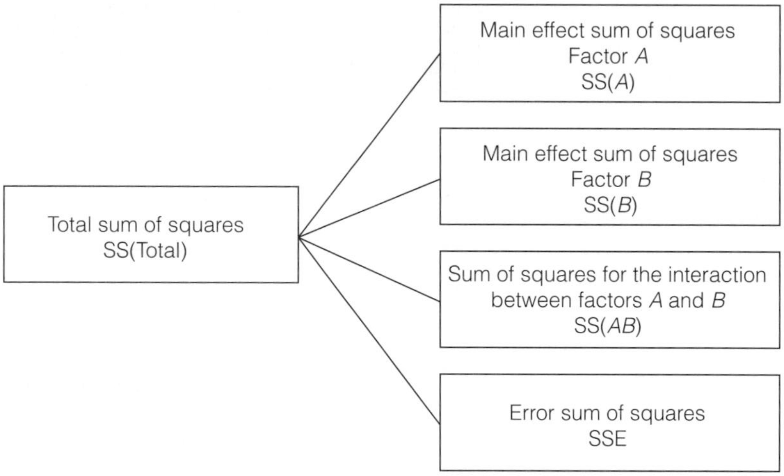

Since the sums of squares and the degrees of freedom for the analysis of variance are additive, the ANOVA table appears as shown in the following box.

ANOVA Table for an $a \times b$ Factorial Design with r Observations per Cell

SOURCE	df	SS	MS	F
Main effects A	$(a-1)$	SS(A)	$MS(A) = SS(A)/(a-1)$	$MS(A)/MSE$
Main effects B	$(b-1)$	SS(B)	$MS(B) = SS(B)/(b-1)$	$MS(B)/MSE$
AB interaction	$(a-1)(b-1)$	SS(AB)	$MS(AB) = SS(AB)/[(a-1)(b-1)]$	$MS(AB)/MSE$
Error	$ab(r-1)$	SSE	$MSE = SSE/[ab(r-1)]$	
Total	$abr-1$	SS(Total)		

(*Note:* $n = abr$)

Note that the F statistics for testing factor main effects and factor interaction are obtained by dividing the appropriate mean square by MSE. The numerator df for the test of interest will equal the df of the source of variation being tested; the denominator df will always equal df(Error). These F tests are equivalent to the F tests obtained by fitting complete and reduced models in regression.*

For completeness, the formulas for calculating the ANOVA sums of squares for a complete two-factor factorial experiment are given in the next box.

Computing Formulas for the Analysis of Variance for a Two-Factor Factorial Experiment

$$\text{CM} = \text{Correction for the mean} = \frac{(\text{Total of all } n \text{ measurements})^2}{n} = \frac{\left(\sum_{i=1}^{n} y_i\right)^2}{n}$$

$$\text{SS(Total)} = \text{Total sum of squares} = \text{Sum of squares of all } n \text{ measurements} - \text{CM} = \sum_{i=1}^{n} y_i^2 - \text{CM}$$

$$\text{SS}(A) = \text{Sum of squares for main effects, independent variable 1} = \begin{pmatrix}\text{Sum of squares of the totals } A_1, A_2, \ldots, A_a \\ \text{divided by the number of measurements} \\ \text{in a single total, namely, } br\end{pmatrix} - \text{CM} = \frac{\sum_{i=1}^{a} A_i^2}{br} - \text{CM}$$

(continued)

*The ANOVA F tests for main effects shown in the ANOVA summary table are equivalent to those of the regression approach only when the reduced model includes interaction terms. Since we usually test for main effects only after determining that interaction is nonsignificant, some statisticians favor dropping the interaction terms from both the complete and reduced models prior to conducting the main effect tests. For example, to test for main effect A, the complete model includes terms for main effects A and B, whereas the reduced model includes terms for main effect B only. To obtain the equivalent result using the ANOVA approach, the sums of squares for AB interaction and error are "pooled" and a new MSE computed, where

$$\text{MSE} = \frac{\text{SS}(AB) + \text{SSE}}{n - a - b + 1}$$

$$\text{SS}(B) = \text{Sum of squares for main effects, independent variable 2}$$
$$= \begin{pmatrix} \text{Sum of squares of the totals } B_1, B_2, \ldots, B_b \\ \text{divided by the number of measurements} \\ \text{in a single total, namely, } ar \end{pmatrix} - \text{CM}$$
$$= \frac{\sum_{i=1}^{b} B_i^2}{ar} - \text{CM}$$

$$\text{SS}(AB) = \text{Sum of squares for } AB \text{ interaction}$$
$$= \begin{pmatrix} \text{Sum of squares of the cell totals} \\ AB_{11}, AB_{12}, \ldots, AB_{ab} \text{ divided by} \\ \text{the number of measurements} \\ \text{in a single total, namely, } r \end{pmatrix} - \text{SS}(A) - \text{SS}(B) - \text{CM}$$
$$= \frac{\sum_{i=1}^{b}\sum_{i=1}^{a} AB_{ij}^2}{r} - \text{SS}(A) - \text{SS}(B) - \text{CM}$$

where

a = Number of levels of independent variable 1

b = Number of levels of independent variable 2

r = Number of measurements for each pair of levels of independent variables 1 and 2

n = Total number of measurements $= a \times b \times r$

A_i = Total of all measurements of independent variable 1 at level i $(i = 1, 2, \ldots, a)$

B_j = Total of all measurements of independent variable 2 at level j $(j = 1, 2, \ldots, b)$

AB_{ij} = Total of all measurements at the ith level of independent variable 1 and at the jth level of independent variable 2 $(i = 1, 2, \ldots, a;\ j = 1, 2, \ldots, b)$

EXAMPLE 11.12

Refer to Example 11.11.

a. Construct an ANOVA summary table for the analysis.

b. Conduct the test for supply × ratio interaction using the traditional analysis of variance approach.

Solution

a. Although the formulas given in the previous box are straightforward, they can become quite tedious to use. Therefore, we use a statistical software package to conduct the ANOVA. A SAS printout of the ANOVA is displayed in Figure 11.17. The value of SS(Total), given in the SAS printout under **Sum**

of Squares in the **Corrected Total** row, is SS(Total) $= 118$. The sums of squares, mean squares, and F values for the factors S, R, and $S \times R$ interaction are given under the **Anova SS**, **Mean Square**, and **F Value** columns, respectively, in the bottom portion of the printout. These values are shown in Table 11.7.

FIGURE 11.17
SAS printout for ANOVA of data in Example 11.12

```
                         Analysis of Variance Procedure

Dependent Variable: PROFIT
                                      Sum of             Mean
Source                     DF        Squares           Square    F Value      Pr > F

Model                       8    74.66666667       9.33333333       3.88      0.0081
Error                      18    43.33333333       2.40740741
Corrected Total            26   118.00000000

                     R-Square           C.V.         Root MSE            PROFIT Mean

                     0.632768       7.507656         1.551582             20.6666667


Source                     DF       Anova SS      Mean Square    F Value      Pr > F

SUPPLY                      2    20.22222222      10.11111111       4.20      0.0318
RATIO                       2     8.22222222       4.11111111       1.71      0.2094
SUPPLY*RATIO                4    46.22222222      11.55555556       4.80      0.0082
```

TABLE 11.7 **ANOVA Table for Example 11.12**

SOURCE	df	SS	MS
Supply	2	20.22	10.11
Ratio	2	8.22	4.11
Supply $\times$ Ratio interaction	4	46.22	11.56
Error	18	43.33	2.41
Total	26	118.00	

b. To test the hypothesis that supply and ratio interact, we use the test statistic

$$F = \frac{\text{MS}(SR)}{\text{MSE}} = \frac{11.56}{2.41} = 4.80 \quad \text{(shaded on the SAS printout)}$$

Note that this value is identical to the test statistic obtained in Example 11.11 using regression. The p-value of the test (also shaded on the SAS printout) is .0082. Since this value is less than the selected value of $\alpha = .05$, we conclude that supply and ratio interact.

Confidence intervals for a single treatment mean and for the difference between two treatment means in a factorial experiment are provided in the boxes on page 632.

$100(1 - \alpha)\%$ Confidence Interval for the Mean of a Single Treatment: Factorial Experiment

$$\bar{y}_{ij} \pm t_{\alpha/2}\left(\frac{s}{\sqrt{r}}\right)$$

where

$\bar{y}_{ij}$ = Sample mean for the treatment identified by level i of the first factor and level j of the second factor

r = Number of measurements per treatment

$s = \sqrt{\text{MSE}}$

and $t_{\alpha/2}$ is based on $ab(r - 1)$ df.

$100(1 - \alpha)\%$ Confidence Interval for the Difference Between a Pair of Treatment Means: Factorial Experiment

Let

$\bar{y}_1$ = Sample mean of the r measurements for the first treatment

$\bar{y}_2$ = Sample mean of the r measurements for the second treatment

Then, the $100(1 - \alpha)\%$ confidence interval for the difference between the treatment means is

$$(\bar{y}_1 - \bar{y}_2) \pm t_{\alpha/2}s\sqrt{\frac{2}{r}}$$

where $s = \sqrt{\text{MSE}}$ and $t_{\alpha/2}$ is based on $ab(r - 1)$ df.

EXAMPLE 11.13

Refer to Examples 11.11 and 11.12.

a. Find a 95% confidence interval to estimate the mean profit per unit of raw materials when $S = 18$ tons and the ratio of production is $R = 1$.

b. Find a 95% confidence interval to estimate the difference in mean profit per unit of raw materials when $\left(S = 18, R = \frac{1}{2}\right)$ and $(S = 18, R = 1)$.

Solution

a. A 95% confidence interval for the mean $E(y)$ when supply $S = 18$ and $R = 1$ is

$$\bar{y}_{18,1} \pm t_{.025}\left(\frac{s}{\sqrt{r}}\right)$$

where $\bar{y}_{18,1}$ is the mean of the $r = 3$ values of y for $S = 18$, $R = 1$ (obtained from Table 11.7), and $t_{.025} = 2.101$ is based on 18 df. Substituting, we obtain

$$\frac{71}{3} \pm 2.101\left(\frac{1.55}{\sqrt{3}}\right)$$

$$23.67 \pm 1.88$$

Therefore, our interval estimate for the mean profit per unit of raw material where $S = 18$ and $R = 1$ is \$21.79 to \$25.55.

b. A 95% confidence interval for the difference in mean profit per unit of raw material for two different combinations of levels of S and R is

$$(\bar{y}_1 - \bar{y}_2) \pm t_{.025}s\sqrt{\frac{2}{r}}$$

where $\bar{y}_1$ and $\bar{y}_2$ represent the means of the $r = 3$ replications for the factor level combinations $\left(S = 18, R = \frac{1}{2}\right)$ and $(S = 18, R = 1)$, respectively. From Table 11.7, the sums of the three measurements for these two treatments are 61 and 71. Substituting, we obtain

$$\left(\frac{61}{3} - \frac{71}{3}\right) \pm (2.101)(1.55)\sqrt{\frac{2}{3}}$$

$$-3.33 \pm 2.66$$

Therefore, the interval estimate for the difference in mean profit per unit of raw material for the two factor level combinations is (−\$5.99, −\$.67). The negative values indicate that we estimate the mean for $\left(S = 18, R = \frac{1}{2}\right)$ to be less than the mean for $(S = 18, R = 1)$ by between \$.67 and \$5.99.

Throughout this chapter, we have presented two methods for analyzing data from a designed experiment: the regression approach and the traditional ANOVA approach. In a factorial experiment, the two methods yield identical results when both factors are qualitative; however, regression will provide more information when at least one of the factors is quantitative. For example, the analysis of variance in Example 11.12 enables us to estimate the mean profit per unit of supply for *only* the nine combinations of supply–ratio levels. It will not permit us to estimate the mean response for some other combination of levels of the independent variables not included among the nine used in the factorial experiment. Alternatively, the prediction equation obtained from the regression analysis in Example 11.11 enables us to estimate the mean profit per unit of supply when $(S = 17, R = 1)$. We could not obtain this estimate from the analysis of variance in Example 11.12.

The prediction equation found by regression analysis also contributes other information not provided by traditional analysis of variance. For example, we might wish to estimate the rate of change in the mean profit, $E(y)$, for unit changes in S, R, or both for specific values of S and R. Or, we might want to determine whether the third- and fourth-order terms in the complete model of

Example 11.11 really contribute additional information for the prediction of profit, y.

We illustrate some of these applications in the next two examples.

EXAMPLE 11.14

Do the data provide sufficient information to indicate that third- and fourth-order terms in the complete factorial model given in Example 11.11 contribute information for the prediction of y? Use $\alpha = .05$.

Solution

If the response to the question is yes, then at least one of the parameters, β_6, β_7, or β_8, of the complete factorial model differs from 0 (i.e., they are needed in the model). Consequently, the null hypothesis is

$$H_0\text{:}\quad \beta_6 = \beta_7 = \beta_8 = 0$$

and the alternative hypothesis is

$$H_a\text{:}\quad \text{At least one of the three } \beta\text{'s is nonzero.}$$

To test this hypothesis, we compute the drop in SSE between the appropriate reduced and complete model.

For this application the complete model is the complete factorial model of Example 11.11:

$$\textit{Complete model:}\quad E(y) = \beta_0 + \beta_1 x_1 + \beta_2 x_1^2 + \beta_3 x_2 + \beta_4 x_2^2 + \beta_5 x_1 x_2 + \beta_6 x_1 x_2^2 + \beta_7 x_1^2 x_2 + \beta_8 x_1^2 x_2^2$$

The reduced model is this complete model minus the third- and fourth-order terms; i.e., the reduced model is the second-order model shown here:

$$\textit{Reduced model:}\quad E(y) = \beta_0 + \beta_1 x_1 + \beta_2 x_1^2 + \beta_3 x_2 + \beta_4 x_2^2 + \beta_5 x_1 x_2$$

Recall (from Figure 11.15a) that the SSE and MSE for the complete model are $SSE_C = 43.3333$ and $MSE_C = 2.4704$. A SAS printout of the regression analysis of the reduced model is shown in Figure 11.18. The SSE for the reduced model (shaded) is $SSE_R = 54.49206$.

Consequently, the test statistic required to conduct the test is

Test statistic:

$$F = \frac{(SSE_R - SSE_C)/(\text{Number of } \beta\text{'s tested})}{MSE_C} = \frac{(54.49206 - 43.3333)/3}{2.4704} = 1.54$$

The F statistic is based on $\nu_1 = 3$ numerator df, $\nu_2 = 18$ denominator df, and the critical value (obtained from Table 4 of Appendix C) is $F_{.05} = 3.16$. Thus, the rejection region is

Rejection region: $F > 3.16$

Conclusion: Since the computed value of F (1.54) is less than the critical value, $F_{.05} = 3.16$, we cannot reject the null hypothesis that $\beta_6 = \beta_7 = \beta_8 = 0$. That is, there is insufficient evidence (at $\alpha = .05$) to indicate that the third- and fourth-order terms associated with β_6, β_7, and β_8 contribute information

FIGURE 11.18
SAS printout for the reduced (second-order) model

Dependent Variable: PROFIT

Analysis of Variance

Source	DF	Sum of Squares	Mean Square	F Value	Prob>F
Model	5	63.50794	12.70159	4.895	0.0040
Error	21	54.49206	2.59486		
C Total	26	118.00000			

Root MSE	1.61086	R-square	0.5382
Dep Mean	20.66667	Adj R-sq	0.4283
C.V.	7.79447		

Parameter Estimates

Variable	DF	Parameter Estimate	Standard Error	T for H0: Parameter=0	Prob > |T|
INTERCEP	1	-27.814815	23.80152168	-1.169	0.2557
S	1	5.944444	2.64418353	2.248	0.0354
R	1	-7.761905	5.04522969	-1.538	0.1389
SR	1	0.746032	0.20294890	3.676	0.0014
SS	1	-0.185185	0.07306996	-2.534	0.0193
RR	1	-2.296296	1.33939441	-1.714	0.1012

for the prediction of y. Since the complete factorial model contributes no more information about y than the reduced (second-order) model, we recommend using the second-order model in practice.

EXAMPLE 11.15

Use the second-order model of Example 11.14 and find a 95% confidence interval for the mean profit per unit supply of raw material when $S = 17$ and $R = 1$.

Solution

The portion of the SAS printout for the second-order model with 95% confidence intervals for $E(y)$ is shown in Figure 11.19.

FIGURE 11.19
SAS printout of confidence intervals for mean profit

Obs	S	R	Dep Var PROFIT	Predict Value	Std Err Predict	Lower95% Mean	Upper95% Mean	Residual
1	15	0.5	23.0000	20.8254	0.803	19.1549	22.4959	2.1746
2	15	0.5	20.0000	20.8254	0.803	19.1549	22.4959	-0.8254
3	15	0.5	21.0000	20.8254	0.803	19.1549	22.4959	0.1746
4	18	0.5	22.0000	21.4444	0.693	20.0029	22.8860	0.5556
5	18	0.5	19.0000	21.4444	0.693	20.0029	22.8860	-2.4444
6	18	0.5	20.0000	21.4444	0.693	20.0029	22.8860	-1.4444
7	21	0.5	19.0000	18.7302	0.803	17.0596	20.4007	0.2698
8	21	0.5	18.0000	18.7302	0.803	17.0596	20.4007	-0.7302
9	21	0.5	21.0000	18.7302	0.803	17.0596	20.4007	2.2698
10	15	1	22.0000	20.8175	0.701	19.3605	22.2744	1.1825
11	15	1	20.0000	20.8175	0.701	19.3605	22.2744	-0.8175
12	15	1	19.0000	20.8175	0.701	19.3605	22.2744	-1.8175
13	18	1	24.0000	22.5556	0.693	21.1140	23.9971	1.4444
14	18	1	25.0000	22.5556	0.693	21.1140	23.9971	2.4444
15	18	1	22.0000	22.5556	0.693	21.1140	23.9971	-0.5556
16	21	1	20.0000	20.9603	0.701	19.5034	22.4173	-0.9603
17	21	1	19.0000	20.9603	0.701	19.5034	22.4173	-1.9603
18	21	1	22.0000	20.9603	0.701	19.5034	22.4173	1.0397
19	15	2	18.0000	17.3571	0.859	15.5707	19.1436	0.6429
20	15	2	18.0000	17.3571	0.859	15.5707	19.1436	0.6429
21	15	2	16.0000	17.3571	0.859	15.5707	19.1436	-1.3571
22	18	2	21.0000	21.3333	0.693	19.8918	22.7749	-0.3333
23	18	2	23.0000	21.3333	0.693	19.8918	22.7749	1.6667
24	18	2	20.0000	21.3333	0.693	19.8918	22.7749	-1.3333
25	21	2	20.0000	21.9762	0.859	20.1897	23.7627	-1.9762
26	21	2	22.0000	21.9762	0.859	20.1897	23.7627	0.0238
27	21	2	24.0000	21.9762	0.859	20.1897	23.7627	2.0238
28	17	1	.	22.3466	0.663	20.9687	23.7244	.

The confidence interval for $E(y)$ when $S = 17$ and $R = 1$ is given in the last row of the printout. You can see that the interval is (20.9687, 23.7244). Thus, we estimate (with confidence coefficient equal to .95) that the mean profit per unit of supply will lie between \$20.97 and \$23.72 when $S = 17$ tons and $R = 1$. Beyond this immediate result, this example illustrates the power and versatility of a regression analysis. In particular, there is no way to obtain this estimate from the analysis of variance in Example 11.12. However, a computerized regression package can be easily programmed to include the confidence interval automatically.

EXERCISES

11.28 The analysis of variance for a 3×2 factorial experiment, with four observations per treatment, produced the ANOVA summary table entries shown here.

SOURCE	df	SS	MS	F
A	____	100	____	____
B	1	____	____	____
AB	2	____	2.5	____
Error	____	____	2.0	
Total	____	700		

a. Complete the ANOVA summary table.
b. Test for interaction between factor A and factor B. Use $\alpha = .05$.
c. Test for differences in main effect means for factor A. Use $\alpha = .05$.
d. Test for differences in main effect means for factor B. Use $\alpha = .05$.

11.29 Many temperate-zone animal species exhibit physiological and morphological changes when the hours of daylight begin to decrease during autumn months. A study was conducted to investigate the "short day" traits of collared lemmings (*The Journal of Experimental Zoology*, Sept. 1993). A total of 124 lemmings were bred in a colony maintained with a photoperiod of 22 hours of light per day. At weaning (19 days of age), the lemmings were weighed and randomly assigned to live under one of two photoperiods: (1) 16 hours or less of light per day, and (2) more than 16 hours light per day. (Each group was assigned the same number of males and females.) After 10 weeks, the lemmings were weighed again. The response variable of interest was the gain in body weight (measured in grams) over the 10-week experimental period. The researchers analyzed the data using an ANOVA for a 2×2 factorial design, where the two factors are photoperiod (at two levels) and gender (at two levels).

a. Construct an ANOVA table for the experiment, listing the sources of variation and associated degrees of freedom.
b. Give the models that will enable the researchers to test for photoperiod by gender interaction.
c. The F test for interaction was not significant. Interpret this result practically.
d. The p-values for testing for photoperiod and gender main effects were both smaller than .001. Interpret these results practically.

11.30 Turnover among truck drivers is a major problem for both carriers and shippers. Since knowledge of driver-related job attitudes is valuable for predicting and controlling future turnover, a study of the work-related attitudes of truck drivers was conducted (*Transportation Journal*, Fall 1993). The two factors considered in the study were career stage and time spent on road. Career stage was set at three levels: early (less than 2 years), mid-career (between 3 and 10 years), and late (more than 10 years). Road time was dichotomized as short (gone for one weekend or less) and long (gone for longer than one weekend). Data were collected on job satisfaction for drivers sampled in each of the $3 \times 2 = 6$ combinations of career stage and road time. [Job satisfaction was measured on a 5-point scale, where 1 = really dislike and 5 = really like.]

a. Identify the response variable for this experiment.
b. Identify the factors for this experiment.
c. Identify the treatments for this experiment.
d. The ANOVA table for the analysis is shown here. Fully interpret the results.

SOURCE	*F* VALUE	*p*-VALUE
Career stage (*CS*)	26.67	$p \leq .001$
Road time (*RT*)	.19	$p > .05$
$CS \times RT$	1.59	$p < .05$

Source: McElroy, J. C., et al. "Career stage, time spent on the road, and truckload driver attitudes." *Transportation Journal*, Vol. 33, No. 1, Fall 1993, p. 10 (Table 2).

e. The researchers theorized that the impact of road time on job satisfaction may be different depending on the career stage of the driver. Do the results support this theory?
f. The researchers also theorized that career stage affects the job satisfaction of truck drivers. Do the results support this theory?

11.31 *The American Journal of Psychology* (Winter 1991) reported on a study designed to investigate the way in which adolescents with low reading ability comprehend simple text-based problems. Fourteen-year-old students from New York City schools participated in the experiment. Based on expert evaluation, the students were divided into four groups: (1) learning-disabled, low socioeconomic status; (2) nondisabled, low socioeconomic status; (3) learning-disabled, high socioeconomic status; and (4) nondisabled, high socioeconomic status. Each student was asked to read and retell a "story problem"; however, the way in which the problem was presented was varied. Some students read a "no-priority" problem (i.e., a problem with no clear goals and/or objectives), whereas others read a "priority" problem (i.e., a problem with a clear statement of the character's priority). The experiment was designed as a 4×2 factorial, with group at four levels and problem type (priority or no-priority) at two levels. One of the dependent variables measured was proportion of ideas recalled correctly.

a. The test for group by problem type interaction was nonsignificant at $\alpha = .01$. Interpret this result.
b. The test for problem type main effects was nonsignificant at $\alpha = .01$. Interpret this result.
c. The test for group main effects was statistically significant at $\alpha = .01$. Interpret this result.

11.32 Video games have revolutionized children's leisure time activities. However, many parents believe that video games are a bad influence on their children. A study was conducted to examine the effect of playing video games on fifth-graders' free play (*Journal of Applied Social Psychology*, Vol. 16, 1986). Eighty-four fifth-graders were paired randomly, and then each pair was randomly assigned to one of three types of games, an aggressive video game (Missile Command), a nonaggressive video game

(Pac-Man), or a pen-and-paper maze-solving game (control) in equal numbers. One member of each pair was then randomly chosen to play the designated game (player) for 8 minutes, whereas the other member watched (observer). Thus, 14 fifth-graders were assigned to each of the $3 \times 2 = 6$ experimental conditions. After video play was concluded, the children were sent to a toy room for free play. The goal of the experiment was to investigate the effect of type of game (Missile Command, Pac-Man, and control) and position (player or observer) on degree of aggressive play in the toy room.

a. Identify the factors in this factorial experiment.
b. Identify the levels of the factors.
c. What are the treatments?
d. Give the sources of variation and their respective degrees of freedom in an ANOVA table for this experiment.
e. Give the complete model appropriate for analyzing the data for this experiment.
f. A significant interaction was found between type of game and position (p-value $< .01$). Interpret this result in the words of the problem.

11.33 The chemical element antimony is sometimes added to tin–lead solder to replace the more expensive tin and to reduce the cost of soldering. A factorial experiment was conducted to determine how antimony affects the strength of the tin–lead solder joint (*Journal of Materials Science*, May 1986). Tin–lead solder specimens were prepared using one of four possible cooling methods (water-quenched, WQ; oil-quenched, OQ; air-blown, AB; and furnace-cooled, FC) and with one of four possible amounts of antimony (0%, 3%, 5%, and 10%) added to the composition. Three solder joints were randomly assigned to each of the $4 \times 4 = 16$ treatments and the shear strength of each measured. The experimental results, shown in the accompanying table, were subjected to an ANOVA using SAS. The SAS printout is also shown.

AMOUNT OF ANTIMONY % weight	COOLING METHOD	SHEAR STRENGTH, MPa		
0	WQ	17.6	19.5	18.3
0	OQ	20.0	24.3	21.9
0	AB	18.3	19.8	22.9
0	FC	19.4	19.8	20.3
3	WQ	18.6	19.5	19.0
3	OQ	20.0	20.9	20.4
3	AB	21.7	22.9	22.1
3	FC	19.0	20.9	19.9
5	WQ	22.3	19.5	20.5
5	OQ	20.9	22.9	20.6
5	AB	22.9	19.7	21.6
5	FC	19.6	16.4	20.5
10	WQ	15.2	17.1	16.6
10	OQ	16.4	19.0	18.1
10	AB	15.8	17.3	17.1
10	FC	16.4	17.6	17.6

Source: Tomlinson, W. J., and Cooper, G. A. "Fracture Mechanism of brass/Sn-Pb-Sb solder joints and the effect of production variables on the joint strength." *Journal of Materials Science*, Vol. 21, No. 5, May 1986, p. 1731 (Table II). Copyright 1986 Chapman and Hall.

SAS Printout for Exercise 11.33

```
                       Analysis of Variance Procedure

Dependent Variable: STRENGTH
                                   Sum of           Mean
Source                    DF      Squares         Square     F Value      Pr > F

Model                     15  157.95250000    10.53016667       6.10      0.0001

Error                     32   55.24666667     1.72645833

Corrected Total           47  213.19916667

                    R-Square         C.V.       Root MSE          STRENGTH Mean

                    0.740868    6.7195275      1.3139476            19.55416667


Source                    DF      Anova SS    Mean Square     F Value      Pr > F

AMOUNT                     3    104.194167      34.731389       20.12      0.0001
METHOD                     3     28.627500       9.542500        5.53      0.0036
AMOUNT*METHOD              9     25.130833       2.792315        1.62      0.1523
```

a. Construct an ANOVA summary table for the experiment.

b. Conduct a test to determine whether the two factors, amount of antimony and cooling method, interact. Use $\alpha = .01$.

c. Interpret the result obtained in part **b**.

d. If appropriate, conduct the tests for main effects. Use $\alpha = .01$.

11.34 What is the optimal method of directing newcomers to a specific location in a complex building? Researchers at Ball State University (Indiana) investigated this "wayfinding" problem and reported their results in *Human Factors* (Mar. 1993). Subjects met in a starting room on a multilevel building and were asked to locate the "goal" room as quickly as possible. (Some of the subjects were provided directional aids, whereas others were not.) Upon reaching their destination, the subjects returned to the starting room and were given a second room to locate. (One of the goal rooms was located in the east end of the building, the other in the west end.) The experimentally controlled variables in the study were aid type at three levels (signs, map, no aid) and room order at two levels (east/west, west/east). Subjects were randomly assigned to each of the $3 \times 2 = 6$ experimental conditions and the travel time (in seconds) recorded. The results of the analysis of the east room data for this 3×2 factorial design are provided in the table. Interpret the results.

SOURCE	df	MS	F	p-VALUE
Aid type	2	511,323.06	76.67	$p < .0001$
Room order	1	13,005.08	1.95	$p > .10$
Aid × Order	2	8,573.13	1.29	$p < .10$
Error	46	6,668.94		

Source: Butler, D. L., et al. "Wayfinding by newcomers in a complex building." *Human Factors*, Vol. 35, No. 1, Mar. 1993, p. 163 (Table 2).

11.35 The *Accounting Review* (Jan. 1991) reported on a study of the effect of two factors, confirmation of accounts receivable and verification of sales transactions, on account misstatement risk by auditors. Both factors were held at the same two levels: completed or not completed. Thus, the experimental design is a 2×2 factorial design.

a. Identify the factors, factor levels, and treatments for this experiment.

b. Explain what factor interaction means for this experiment.

c. A graph of the hypothetical mean misstatement risks for each of the 2 × 2 = 4 treatments is shown here. In this hypothetical case, does it appear that interaction exists?

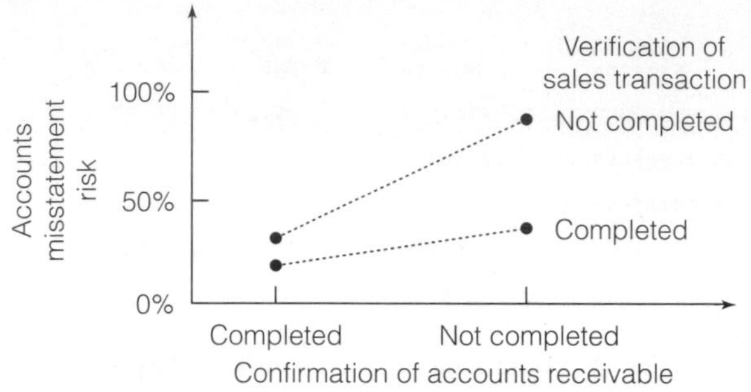

Source: Brown, C. E. and Solomon, I. "Configural information processing in auditing: The role of domain-specific knowledge." *The Accounting Review,* Vol. 66, No. 1, Jan. 1991, p. 105 (Figure 1).

11.36 *Time-of-day pricing* is a plan by which customers are charged a lower rate for using electricity during off-peak (less demanded) hours. One experiment (reported in the *Journal of Consumer Research*, June 1982) was conducted to measure customer satisfaction with several time-of-day pricing schemes. The experiment consisted of two factors, price ratio (the ratio of peak to off-peak prices) and peak period length, each at three levels. The 3 × 3 = 9 combinations of price ratio and peak period length represent the nine time-of-day pricing schemes. For each pricing scheme, customers were randomly selected and asked to rate satisfaction with the plan using an index from 10 to 38, with 38 indicating extreme satisfaction. Suppose four customers were sampled for each pricing scheme. The table gives the satisfaction scores for these customers. [*Note:* The data are based on mean scores provided in the *Journal of Consumer Research* article.]

		PRICING RATIO					
		2:1		4:1		8:1	
PEAK PERIOD LENGTH	6 hours	25	28	31	29	24	28
		26	27	26	27	25	26
	9 hours	26	27	25	24	33	28
		29	30	30	26	25	27
	12 hours	22	20	33	27	30	31
		25	21	25	27	26	27

a. The data were subjected to an analysis of variance using MINITAB. Use the accompanying MINITAB printout to construct an ANOVA table for the data.

```
ANALYSIS OF VARIANCE  SATSCORE

SOURCE          DF         SS         MS
PERIOD           2      10.67       5.33
RATIO            2      32.00      16.00
INTERACTION      4      95.33      23.83
ERROR           27     161.00       5.96
TOTAL           35     299.00
```

b. Compute the nine customer satisfaction index means.
c. Plot the nine means from part **b** on a graph similar to Figure 11.14. Does it appear that the two factors, price ratio and peak period length, interact? Explain.
d. Do the data provide sufficient evidence of interaction between price ratio and peak period length? Test using $\alpha = .05$.
e. Do the data provide sufficient evidence that mean customer satisfaction differs for the three peak period lengths? Test using $\alpha = .05$.
f. When is the test of part **e** appropriate?
g. Find a 90% confidence interval for the mean customer satisfaction rating of a pricing scheme with a peak period length of 9 hours and pricing ratio of 2:1.
h. Find a 95% confidence interval for the difference between the mean customer satisfaction ratings of pricing schemes 9 hours, 8:1 ratio and 6 hours, 8:1 ratio. Interpret the interval.

11.37 Refer to Exercise 11.21. Another important concern of designers and users of computer display monitors is readability of the text on the screen. Two factors thought to affect readability of scrolling texts is window size (i.e., number of characters displayed per line) and jump length (i.e., number of characters advanced per jump). To investigate this phenomenon, a 2×3 factorial experiment was conducted, with window size at two levels (20 and 40 characters) and jump length at three levels (1, 5, and 9 characters). The response variable of interest was reading rate (measured as number of words per minute) of Chinese college students who participated in the study (*Human Factors*, June 1988).
a. The ANOVA F test for interaction between the two factors resulted in a p-value exceeding .10. Interpret this result.
b. The ANOVA F test for the main effect of window size resulted in a p-value exceeding .10. Interpret this result.
c. The ANOVA F test for the main effect of jump length resulted in a p-value less than .05. Interpret this result.

11.38 Computer-based management information systems (MIS) is one of the fastest growing industries in the United States, yet little is known about the ethical decision-making processes of persons involved in creating and maintaining these systems. An empirical investigation was conducted to determine whether MIS majors, on average, exhibit ethical decision-making processes that differ from other business students (*Journal of Business Ethics*, Vol. 10, 1991). A large sample of business students were divided into two groups based on their major (MIS or non-MIS). Within each group, half of the students were administered the regular form of the Defining Issues Test (DIT) and the other half a form of the DIT modified to incorporate MIS. Thus, a 2×2 factorial experimental design was used, with the two factors, major and form. The dependent (response) variable measured was the "principled morality," or P score, expressed as a percentage. (High scores indicate morally conscious decisions.) The results are shown in the ANOVA summary table.

SOURCE	df	SS	MS	F	p-VALUE
Form	1	.13	.13	.00	.98
Major	1	1,290.10	1,290.10	6.25	.01
Form × Major	1	56.38	56.38	.27	.60
Error	233	48,120.15	206.52		
Total	236	49,466.76			

Source: Paradice, D. B., and Dejoie, R. M. "The ethical decision-making processes of information systems workers." *Journal of Business Ethics*, Vol. 10, 1991, p. 9 (Table V).

a. Write the complete model for this 2×2 factorial design.
b. Interpret the results of the ANOVA summary table.

11.39 A trade-off study regarding the inspection and test of transformer parts was conducted by the quality department of a major defense contractor. The investigation was structured to examine the effects of varying inspection levels and incoming test times to detect early part failure or fatigue. The levels of inspection selected were full military inspection (A), reduced military specification level (B), and commercial grade (C). Operational burn-in test times chosen for this study were at 1-hour increments from 1 hour to 9 hours. The response was failures per thousand pieces obtained from samples taken from lot sizes inspected to a specified level and burned-in over a prescribed time length. Three replications were randomly sequenced under each condition, making this a complete 3×9 factorial experiment (a total of 81 observations). The data for the study (shown in the table) were subjected to an ANOVA using SAS. The SAS printout follows. Analyze and interpret the results.

	INSPECTION LEVELS								
BURN-IN, hours	Full Military Specification, *A*			Reduced Military Specification, *B*			Commercial, *C*		
1	7.60	7.50	7.67	7.70	7.10	7.20	6.16	6.13	6.21
2	6.54	7.46	6.84	5.85	6.15	6.15	6.21	5.50	5.64
3	6.53	5.85	6.38	5.30	5.60	5.80	5.41	5.45	5.35
4	5.66	5.98	5.37	5.38	5.27	5.29	5.68	5.47	5.84
5	5.00	5.27	5.39	4.85	4.99	4.98	5.65	6.00	6.15
6	4.20	3.60	4.20	4.50	4.56	4.50	6.70	6.72	6.54
7	3.66	3.92	4.22	3.97	3.90	3.84	7.90	7.47	7.70
8	3.76	3.68	3.80	4.37	3.86	4.46	8.40	8.60	7.90
9	3.46	3.55	3.45	5.25	5.63	5.25	8.82	9.76	9.52

Source: Danny La Nuez, College of Business Administration, graduate student, University of South Florida, 1989–1990.

```
                    Analysis of Variance Procedure

Dependent Variable: FAILURES
                                     Sum of          Mean
Source                   DF         Squares        Square    F Value      Pr > F

Model                    26     168.6120667     6.4850795     101.31      0.0001
Error                    54       3.4565333     0.0640099
Corrected Total          80     172.0686000

               R-Square              C.V.      Root MSE          FAILURE Mean

               0.979912          4.405990      0.253002            5.74222222

Source                   DF         Anova SS   Mean Square   F Value      Pr > F

BURNIN                    8      27.97440000    3.49680000     54.63      0.0001
INSLEVEL                  2      43.08411852   21.54205926    336.54      0.0001
BURNIN*INSLEVEL          16      97.55354815    6.09709676     95.25      0.0001
```

11.40 As part of a study on the rate of combustion of artificial graphite in humid air flow, researchers conducted an experiment to investigate oxygen diffusivity through a water vapor mixture. A 3×9

factorial experiment was conducted with mole fraction of water (H_2O) at three levels and temperature of the nitrogen–water mixture at nine levels. The data are shown in the table.

TEMPERATURE °K	MOLE FRACTION OF H_2O .0022	.017	.08
1,000	1.68	1.69	1.72
1,100	1.98	1.99	2.02
1,200	2.30	2.31	2.35
1,300	2.64	2.65	2.70
1,400	3.00	3.01	3.06
1,500	3.38	3.39	3.45
1,600	3.78	3.79	3.85
1,700	4.19	4.21	4.27
1,800	4.63	4.64	4.71

Source: Matsui, K., Tsuji, H., and Makino, A. "The effects of water vapor concentration on the rate of combustion of an artificial graphite in humid air flow." *Combustion and Flame*, Vol. 50, 1983, pp. 107–118. Copyright 1983 by The Combustion Institute. Reprinted by permission of Elsevier Science Publishing Co., Inc.

a. Explain why the traditional analysis of variance (using the ANOVA formulas) is inappropriate for the analysis of these data.

b. Write a second-order model relating mean oxygen diffusivity, $E(y)$, to temperature x_1 (in hundreds) and mole fraction x_2 (in thousandths).

c. The SAS computer printout for the regression analysis is shown on page 644. Find SSE, s^2, and SS(Total).

d. Find R^2 and verify that

$$R^2 = \frac{\text{SSE}}{\text{SS(Total)}}$$

Interpret the value of R^2.

e. Suppose that temperature and mole fraction of H_2O do not interact. What does this imply about the relationship between $E(y)$ and x_1 and x_2?

f. Do the data provide sufficient information to indicate that temperature and mole fraction of H_2O interact? Test using $\alpha = .05$.

g. Give the least squares prediction equation for $E(y)$.

h. Substitute into the prediction equation to predict the mean diffusivity when the temperature of the process is 1,300°K and the mole fraction of water is .017.

i. The printout shows 95% confidence intervals for each of the 3×9 factor level combinations. Find the 95% confidence interval for mean diffusivity when the temperature of the process is 1,300°K and the mole fraction of water is .017.

SAS printout for Exercise 11.39

Dependent Variable: Y

Analysis of Variance

Source	DF	Sum of Squares	Mean Square	F Value	Prob>F
Model	5	24.85819	4.97164	696562.744	0.0001
Error	21	0.00015	0.00001		
C Total	26	24.85834			

Root MSE	0.00267	R-square	1.0000
Dep Mean	3.08852	Adj R-sq	1.0000
C.V.	0.08650		

Parameter Estimates

Variable	DF	Parameter Estimate	Standard Error	T for H0: Parameter=0	Prob > |T|
INTERCEP	1	-0.280150	0.01712523	-16.359	0.0001
X1	1	0.001000	0.00002477	40.388	0.0001
X2	1	-0.285549	0.13650623	-2.092	0.0488
X1X2	1	0.000733	0.00005903	12.411	0.0001
X1SQ	1	0.000000959	0.00000001	109.060	0.0001
X2SQ	1	0.551414	1.24232481	0.444	0.6617

Obs	X1	X2	Dep Var Y	Predict Value	Std Err Predict	Lower95% Mean	Upper95% Mean	Residual
1	1000	0.0022	1.6800	1.6796	0.002	1.6762	1.6830	0.000382
2	1000	0.017	1.6900	1.6864	0.001	1.6833	1.6895	0.00361
3	1000	0.08	1.7200	1.7179	0.002	1.7141	1.7217	0.00207
4	1100	0.0022	1.9800	1.9811	0.001	1.9786	1.9836	-0.00109
5	1100	0.017	1.9900	1.9890	0.001	1.9866	1.9913	0.00105
6	1100	0.08	2.0200	2.0251	0.001	2.0223	2.0280	-0.00511
7	1200	0.0022	2.3000	2.3017	0.001	2.2995	2.3040	-0.00174
8	1200	0.017	2.3100	2.3107	0.001	2.3086	2.3128	-0.00068
9	1200	0.08	2.3500	2.3515	0.001	2.3491	2.3538	-0.00145
10	1300	0.0022	2.6400	2.6416	0.001	2.6394	2.6438	-0.00156
11	1300	0.017	2.6500	2.6516	0.001	2.6494	2.6538	-0.00158
12	1300	0.08	2.7000	2.6970	0.001	2.6947	2.6992	0.00303
13	1400	0.0022	3.0000	3.0005	0.001	2.9983	3.0028	-0.00054
14	1400	0.017	3.0100	3.0117	0.001	3.0094	3.0139	-0.00165
15	1400	0.08	3.0600	3.0617	0.001	3.0594	3.0639	-0.00165
16	1500	0.0022	3.3800	3.3787	0.001	3.3765	3.3809	0.00130
17	1500	0.017	3.3900	3.3909	0.001	3.3887	3.3931	-0.0009
18	1500	0.08	3.4500	3.4455	0.001	3.4433	3.4477	0.00449
19	1600	0.0022	3.7800	3.7760	0.001	3.7738	3.7782	0.00397
20	1600	0.017	3.7900	3.7893	0.001	3.7872	3.7914	0.000692
21	1600	0.08	3.8500	3.8485	0.001	3.8462	3.8509	0.00146
22	1700	0.0022	4.1900	4.1925	0.001	4.1900	4.1951	-0.00253
23	1700	0.017	4.2100	4.2069	0.001	4.2045	4.2092	0.00311
24	1700	0.08	4.2700	4.2707	0.001	4.2679	4.2736	-0.00074
25	1800	0.0022	4.6300	4.6282	0.002	4.6248	4.6316	0.00181
26	1800	0.017	4.6400	4.6436	0.001	4.6405	4.6468	-0.00364
27	1800	0.08	4.7100	4.7121	0.002	4.7083	4.7159	-0.00210

11.6 More Complex Factorial Designs (Optional)

In this optional section, we present some useful factorial designs that are more complex than the basic two-factor factorial of Section 11.5. These designs fall under the general category of a **k-way classification of data**. A k-way classification of data arises when we run all combinations of the levels of k independent variables. These independent variables can be factors or blocks.

For example, consider a replicated $2 \times 3 \times 3$ factorial experiment in which the $2 \times 3 \times 3 = 18$ treatments are assigned to the experimental units according to a completely randomized design. Since every combination of the three factors (a total of 18) is examined, the design is often called a three-way classification of data, Similarly, a k-way classification of data would result if we randomly assign the treatments of a $(k - 1)$-factor factorial experiment to the experimental units of a randomized block design. For example, if we assigned the $2 \times 3 = 6$ treatments of a complete 2×3 factorial experiment to blocks containing six experimental units each, the data would be arranged in a three-way classification, i.e., according to the two factors and the blocks.

The formulas required for calculating the sums of squares for main effects and interactions for an analysis of variance for a k-way classification of data are complicated and are, therefore, not given here. If you are interested in the computational formulas, see the references. As with the designs in the previous three sections, we provide the appropriate linear model for these more complex designs and use either regression or the standard ANOVA output of a statistical software package to analyze the data.

EXAMPLE 11.16

Consider a $2 \times 3 \times 3$ factorial experiment with qualitative factors and $r = 3$ experimental units randomly assigned to each treatment.

a. Write the appropriate linear model for the design.
b. Indicate the sources of variation and their associated degrees of freedom in a partial ANOVA table.

Solution

a. Denote the three qualitative factors as A, B, and C, with A at two levels, and B and C at three levels. Then the linear model for the experiment will contain one parameter corresponding to main effects for A, two each for B and C, $(1)(2) = 2$ each for the AB and AC interactions, $(2)(2) = 4$ for the BC interaction, and $(1)(2)(2) = 4$ for the three-way ABC interaction. Three-way interaction terms measure the failure of two-way interaction effects to remain the same from one level to another level of the third factor.

$$
\begin{aligned}
E(y) = \beta_0 &+ \underbrace{\beta_1 x_1}_{\substack{\text{Main effect}\\ A}} + \underbrace{\beta_2 x_2 + \beta_3 x_3}_{\substack{\text{Main effects}\\ B}} + \underbrace{\beta_4 x_4 + \beta_5 x_5}_{\substack{\text{Main effects}\\ C}} \\
&+ \underbrace{\beta_6 x_1 x_2 + \beta_7 x_1 x_3}_{A \times B \text{ interaction}} + \underbrace{\beta_8 x_1 x_4 + \beta_9 x_1 x_5}_{A \times C \text{ interaction}} \\
&+ \underbrace{\beta_{10} x_2 x_4 + \beta_{11} x_2 x_5 + \beta_{12} x_3 x_4 + \beta_{13} x_3 x_5}_{B \times C \text{ interaction}} \\
&+ \underbrace{\beta_{14} x_1 x_2 x_4 + \beta_{15} x_1 x_3 x_4 + \beta_{16} x_1 x_2 x_5 + \beta_{17} x_1 x_3 x_5}_{A \times B \times C \text{ interaction}}
\end{aligned}
$$

where

$$x_1 = \begin{cases} 1 & \text{if level 1 of } A \\ 0 & \text{if level 2 of } A \end{cases} \qquad x_2 = \begin{cases} 1 & \text{if level 1 of } B \\ 0 & \text{if not} \end{cases}$$

$$x_3 = \begin{cases} 1 & \text{if level 2 of } B \\ 0 & \text{if not} \end{cases} \qquad x_4 = \begin{cases} 1 & \text{if level 1 of } C \\ 0 & \text{if not} \end{cases}$$

$$x_5 = \begin{cases} 1 & \text{if level 2 of } C \\ 0 & \text{if not} \end{cases}$$

b. The sources of variation and the respective degrees of freedom corresponding to these sets of parameters are shown in Table 11.8.

TABLE 11.8 **Table of Sources and Degrees of Freedom for Example 11.16**

SOURCE	df
Main effect A	1
Main effect B	2
Main effect C	2
AB interaction	2
AC interaction	2
BC interaction	4
ABC interaction	4
Error	36
Total	53

The degrees of freedom for SS(Total) will always equal $(n - 1)$—that is, n minus 1 degree of freedom for β_0. Since the degrees of freedom for all sources must sum to the degrees of freedom for SS(Total), it follows that the degrees of freedom for error will equal the degrees of freedom for SS(Total), minus the sum of the degrees of freedom for main effects and interactions, i.e., $(n - 1) - 17$. Our experiment will contain three observations for each of the $2 \times 3 \times 3 = 18$ treatments; therefore, $n = (18)(3) = 54$, and the degrees of freedom for error will equal $53 - 17 = 36$.

If data for this experiment were analyzed on a computer, the computer printout would show the analysis of variance table that we have constructed and would include the associated mean squares, values of the F test statistics, and their observed significance levels. Each F statistic would represent the ratio of the source mean square to $\text{MSE} = s^2$.

EXAMPLE 11.17

A transistor manufacturer conducted an experiment to investigate the effects of three factors on productivity (measured in thousands of dollars of items produced) per 40-hour week. The factors were as follows:

1. Length of work week (two levels): five consecutive 8-hour days or four consecutive 10-hour days
2. Shift (two levels): day or evening shift
3. Number of coffee breaks (three levels): 0, 1, or 2

The experiment was conducted over a 24-week period with the $2 \times 2 \times 3 = 12$ treatments assigned randomly to the 24 weeks. The data for this completely randomized design are shown in Table 11.9. Perform an analysis of variance for the data.

TABLE 11.9 **Data for Example 11.17**

		DAY SHIFT			NIGHT SHIFT		
		COFFEE BREAKS			COFFEE BREAKS		
		0	1	2	0	1	2
LENGTH OF WORK WEEK	4 days	94	105	96	90	102	103
		97	106	91	89	97	98
	5 days	96	100	82	81	90	94
		92	103	88	84	92	96

Solution

The data were subjected to an analysis of variance. The SAS printout is shown in Figure 11.20.

FIGURE 11.20
SAS printout for ANOVA of data in Table 11.9

Analysis of Variance Procedure

Dependent Variable: DOLLARS

Source	DF	Sum of Squares	Mean Square	F Value	Pr > F
Model	11	1009.833333	91.803030	13.43	0.0001
Error	12	82.000000	6.833333	(1)	
Corrected Total	23	1091.833333			

R-Square	C.V.	Root MSE	DOLLARS Mean
(4) 0.924897	2.768647	(3) 2.614065	94.4166667

Source	DF	Anova SS	Mean Square	F Value	Pr > F
SHIFT	1	48.1666667	48.1666667	7.05	0.0210
DAYS	1	204.1666667	204.1666667	29.88 (2)	0.0001
SHIFT*DAYS	1	8.1666667	8.1666667	1.20	0.2958
BREAKS	2	334.0833333	167.0416667	24.45	0.0001
SHIFT*BREAKS	2	385.5833333	192.7916667	28.21	0.0001
DAYS*BREAKS	2	8.0833333	4.0416667	0.59	0.5689
SHIFT*DAYS*BREAKS	2	21.5833333	10.7916667	1.58	0.2461

Pertinent sections of the SAS printout are boxed and numbered, as follows:

1. The value of SS(Total), shown in the **Corrected Total** row of box 1, is 1,091.833333. The number of degrees of freedom associated with this quantity is $(n - 1) = (24 - 1) = 23$. Box 1 gives the partitioning (the analysis of variance) of this quantity into two sources of variation. The first source, **Model**, corresponds to the 11 parameters (all except β_0) in the model. The second source is **Error**. The degrees of freedom, sums of squares, and mean squares for these quantities are shown in their respective columns. For example, MSE = 6.833333. The F statistic for testing

$$H_0\text{:}\quad \beta_1 = \beta_2 = \cdots = \beta_{11} = 0$$

is based on $\nu_1 = 11$ and $\nu_2 = 12$ degrees of freedom and is shown on the printout as $F = 13.43$. The observed significance level, shown under **Pr > F**, is .0001. This small observed significance level presents ample evidence to indicate that at least one of the three independent variables—shifts, number of days in a work week, or number of coffee breaks per day—contributes information for the prediction of mean productivity.

2. To determine which sets of parameters are actually contributing information for the prediction of y, we examine the breakdown (box 2) of SS(Model) into components corresponding to the sets of parameters for main effects **SHIFT**, **DAYS**, and **BREAKS**, and parameters for two-way interactions, **SHIFT*DAYS**, **SHIFT*BREAKS**, and **DAYS*BREAKS**. The last **Model** source of variation corresponds to the set of all three-way **SHIFT*DAYS*BREAKS** parameters. Note that the degrees of freedom for these sources sum to 11, the number of degrees of freedom for **Model**. Similarly, the sum of the component sums of squares is equal to SS(Model). Box 2 does not give the mean squares associated with the sources, but it does give the F values associated with testing hypotheses concerning the set of parameters associated with each source. Box 2 also gives the observed significance levels of these tests. You can see that there is ample evidence to indicate the presence of a **SHIFT*BREAKS** interaction. The F tests associated with all three main effect parameter sets are also statistically significant at the $\alpha = .05$ level of significance. The practical implication of these results is that there is evidence to indicate that all three independent variables, shift, number of work days per week, and number of coffee breaks per day, contribute information for the prediction of productivity. The presence of a **SHIFT*BREAKS** interaction means that the effect of the number of breaks on productivity is not the same from shift to shift. Thus, the specific number of coffee breaks that might achieve maximum productivity on one shift might be different from the number of breaks that would achieve maximum productivity on the other shift.

3. Box 3 gives the value of $s = \sqrt{\text{MSE}} = 2.614065$. This value would be used to construct a confidence interval to compare the difference between 2 of the 12 treatment means. The confidence interval for the difference between a pair of means, $(\mu_i - \mu_j)$, would be

$$(\bar{y}_i - \bar{y}_j) \pm t_{\alpha/2} s \sqrt{\frac{2}{r}}$$

where r is the number of replications of the factorial experiment within a completely randomized design. There were $r = 2$ observations for each of the 12 treatments (factor level combinations) in this example.

4. Box 4 gives the value of R^2, a measure of how well the model fits the experimental data. It is of value primarily when the number of degrees of freedom for error is large—say, at least 5 or 6. The larger the number of degrees of freedom for error, the greater will be its practical importance. The value of R^2 for this analysis, .924897, indicates that the model provides a fairly good fit to the data. It also suggests that the model could be improved by adding new predictor variables or, possibly, by including higher-order terms in the variables originally included in the model.

EXAMPLE 11.18

In a manufacturing process, a plastic rod is produced by heating a granular plastic to a molten state and then extruding it under pressure through a nozzle. An experiment was conducted to investigate the effect of two factors, extrusion temperature (°F) and pressure (pounds per square inch), on the rate of extrusion (inches per second) of the molded rod. A complete 2×2 factorial experiment (that is, with each factor at two levels) was conducted. Three batches of granular plastic were used for the experiment, with each batch (viewed as a block) divided into four equal parts. The four portions of granular plastic for a given batch were randomly assigned to the four treatments; this was repeated for each of the three batches, resulting in a 2×2 factorial experiment laid out in three blocks. The data are shown in Table 11.10. Perform an analysis of variance for these data.

TABLE 11.10 **Data for Example 11.18**

		BATCH (BLOCK)					
		1		2		3	
		PRESSURE		PRESSURE		PRESSURE	
		40	60	40	60	40	60
TEMPERATURE	200°	1.35	1.74	1.31	1.67	1.40	1.86
	300°	2.48	3.63	2.29	3.30	2.14	3.27

Solution

This experiment consists of a three-way classification of the data corresponding to batches (blocks), pressure, and temperature. The analysis of variance for this 2×2 factorial experiment (four treatments) laid out in a randomized block design (three blocks) yields the sources and degrees of freedom shown in Table 11.11.

TABLE 11.11 **Table of Sources and Degrees of Freedom for Example 11.18**

SOURCE	df
Pressure (P)	1
Temperature (T)	1
Blocks	2
Pressure × Temperature interaction	1
Error	6
Total	11

The linear model for the experiment is

$$E(y) = \beta_0 + \underbrace{\beta_1 x_1}_{\text{Main effect } P} + \underbrace{\beta_2 x_2}_{\text{Main effect } T} + \underbrace{\beta_3 x_1 x_2}_{PT \text{ interaction}} + \underbrace{\beta_4 x_3 + \beta_5 x_4}_{\text{Block terms}}$$

where

$$x_1 = \text{Pressure} \qquad x_2 = \text{Temperature}$$

$$x_3 = \begin{cases} 1 & \text{if block 2} \\ 0 & \text{otherwise} \end{cases} \qquad x_4 = \begin{cases} 1 & \text{if block 3} \\ 0 & \text{otherwise} \end{cases}$$

The SAS printout for the analysis of variance is shown in Figure 11.21 on page 650. You can see from the printout that the F test for the model was highly significant (observed significance level is .0001). Thus, there is ample evidence to indicate differences among the block means or the treatment means or both. Proceeding to the breakdown of the model sources, you can see that the values of the F statistics for pressure, temperature, and the temperature × pressure interaction are all highly significant (that is, their observed significance levels are very small). Therefore, all of the terms ($\beta_1 x_1$, $\beta_2 x_2$, and $\beta_3 x_1 x_2$) contribute information for the prediction of y.

FIGURE 11.21
SAS printout for ANOVA of data in Table 11.10

```
                         Analysis of Variance Procedure

Dependent Variable: RATE
                                        Sum of            Mean
Source                      DF         Squares          Square    F Value        Pr > F

Model                        5      7.14938333      1.42987667      83.23        0.0001
Error                        6      0.10308333      0.01718056
Corrected Total             11      7.25246667

                      R-Square            C.V.        Root MSE                RATE Mean

                      0.985786        5.948924        0.131075               2.20333333


Source                      DF        Anova SS     Mean Square    F Value        Pr > F

PRESSURE                     1      1.68750000      1.68750000      98.22        0.0001
TEMP                         1      5.04403333      5.04403333     293.59        0.0001
PRESSURE*TEMP                1      0.36053333      0.36053333      20.98        0.0038
BATCH                        2      0.05731667      0.02865833       1.67        0.2654
```

The treatments in the experiment were assigned according to a randomized block design. Thus, we expected the extrusion of the plastic to vary from batch to batch. Because the F test for testing differences among block means was not statistically significant (the observed significance level, **Pr > F**, was as large as .2654), there is insufficient evidence to indicate a difference in the mean extrusion of the plastic from batch to batch. Blocking does not appear to have increased the amount of information in the experiment.

Many other complex designs, such as fractional factorials, Latin square designs, and incomplete blocks designs, fall under the general k-way classification of data. Consult the references for the layout of these designs and the linear models appropriate for analyzing them.

EXERCISES

11.41 An experiment was conducted to investigate the effects of three factors—paper stock, bleaching compound, and coating type—on the whiteness of fine bond paper. Three paper stocks (factor A), four types of bleaches (factor B), and two types of coatings (factor C) were used for the experiment. Six paper specimens were prepared for each of the $3 \times 4 \times 2$ stock–bleach–coating combinations and a measure of whiteness was recorded.

a. Construct an analysis of variance table showing the sources of variation and the respective degrees of freedom.

b. Suppose MSE $= .14$, MS(AB) $= .39$, and the mean square for all interactions combined is .73. Do the data provide sufficient evidence to indicate any interactions among the three factors? Test using $\alpha = .05$.

c. Do the data present sufficient evidence to indicate an AB interaction? Test using $\alpha = .05$. From a practical point of view, what is the significance of an AB interaction?
d. Suppose SS(A) = 2.35, SS(B) = 2.71, and SS(C) = .72. Find SS(Total). Then find R^2 and interpret its value.

11.42 In increasingly severe oil-well environments, oil producers are interested in high-strength nickel alloys that are corrosion-resistant. Since nickel alloys are especially susceptible to hydrogen embrittlement, an experiment was conducted to compare the yield strengths of nickel alloy tensile specimens cathodically charged in a 4% sulfuric acid solution saturated with carbon disulfide, a hydrogen recombination poison. Two alloys were combined: inconel alloy (75% nickel composition) and incoloy (30% nickel composition). The alloys were tested under two material conditions (cold rolled and cold drawn), each at three different charging times (0, 25, and 50 days). Thus, a $2 \times 2 \times 3$ factorial experiment was conducted, with alloy type at two levels, material condition at two levels, and charging time at three levels. Two hydrogen-charged tensile specimens were prepared for each of the $2 \times 2 \times 3 = 12$ factor level combinations. Their yield strengths (kilograms per square inch) are recorded in the table. The SAS analysis of variance printout for the data is also shown here.

		ALLOY TYPE							
		INCONEL				INCOLOY			
		Cold rolled		Cold drawn		Cold rolled		Cold drawn	
CHARGING TIME	0 days	53.4	52.6	47.1	49.3	50.6	49.9	30.9	31.4
	25 days	55.2	55.7	50.8	51.4	51.6	53.2	31.7	33.3
	50 days	51.0	50.5	45.2	44.0	50.5	50.2	29.7	28.1

```
Dependent Variable: YIELD
                                    Sum of            Mean
Source                    DF       Squares          Square    F Value      Pr > F

Model                     11   1931.734583      175.612235     258.73      0.0001
Error                     12      8.145000        0.678750
Corrected Total           23   1939.879583

                    R-Square          C.V.        Root MSE              YIELD Mean

                    0.995801      1.801942        0.823863              45.7208333

Source                    DF       Anova SS     Mean Square   F Value      Pr > F

ALLOY                      1    552.0004167     552.0004167    813.26      0.0001
MATCOND                    1    956.3437500     956.3437500   1408.98      0.0001
ALLOY*MATCOND              1    339.7537500     339.7537500    500.56      0.0001
TIME                       2     71.0408333      35.5204167     52.33      0.0001
ALLOY*TIME                 2      7.9858333       3.9929167      5.88      0.0166
MATCOND*TIME               2      4.1725000       2.0862500      3.07      0.0836
ALLOY*MATCOND*TIME         2      0.4375000       0.2187500      0.32      0.7306
```

a. Is there evidence of any interactions among the three factors? Test using $\alpha = .05$. [*Note:* This means that you must test all the interaction parameters. The drop in SSE appropriate for the test would be the sum of all interaction sums of squares.]
b. Now examine the F tests shown on the printout for the individual interactions. Which, if any, of the interactions are statistically significant at the .05 level of significance?

11.43 Refer to Exercise 11.42. Since charging time is a quantitative factor, we could plot the strength y versus charging time x_1 for each of the four combinations of alloy type and material condition. This suggests that a prediction equation relating mean strength $E(y)$ to charging time x_1 may be useful. Consider the model

$$E(y) = \beta_0 + \beta_1 x_1 + \beta_2 x_1^2 + \beta_3 x_2 + \beta_4 x_3 + \beta_5 x_2 x_3 + \beta_6 x_1 x_2 + \beta_7 x_1 x_3 + \beta_8 x_1 x_2 x_3 + \beta_9 x_1^2 x_2 + \beta_{10} x_1^2 x_3 + \beta_{11} x_1^2 x_2 x_3$$

where

x_1 = Charging time

$$x_2 = \begin{cases} 1 & \text{if inconel alloy} \\ 0 & \text{if incoloy alloy} \end{cases} \qquad x_3 = \begin{cases} 1 & \text{if cold rolled} \\ 0 & \text{if cold drawn} \end{cases}$$

a. Using the model shown above, give the relationship between mean strength $E(y)$ and charging time x_1 for cold-drawn incoloy alloy.
b. Using the model shown above, give the relationship between mean strength $E(y)$ and charging time x_1 for cold-drawn inconel alloy.
c. Using the model shown above, give the relationship between mean strength $E(y)$ and charging time x_1 for cold-rolled inconel alloy.
d. The SAS multiple regression analysis for fitting the model to the data is shown here. Find the prediction equation.

Dependent Variable: YIELD

Analysis of Variance

Source	DF	Sum of Squares	Mean Square	F Value	Prob>F
Model	11	1931.73458	175.61223	258.729	0.0001
Error	12	8.14500	0.67875		
C Total	23	1939.87958			

Root MSE	0.82386	R-square	0.9958
Dep Mean	45.72083	Adj R-sq	0.9920
C.V.	1.80194		

Parameter Estimates

Variable	DF	Parameter Estimate	Standard Error	T for H0: Parameter=0	Prob > |T|
INTERCEP	1	31.150000	0.58255901	53.471	0.0001
X1	1	0.153000	0.05940960	2.575	0.0243
X1SQ	1	-0.003960	0.00114158	-3.469	0.0046
X2	1	17.050000	0.82386285	20.695	0.0001
X3	1	19.100000	0.82386285	23.183	0.0001
X2X3	1	-14.300000	1.16511802	-12.273	0.0001
X1X2	1	0.151000	0.08401786	1.797	0.0975
X1X3	1	0.017000	0.08401786	0.202	0.8430
X1X2X3	1	-0.080000	0.11881919	-0.673	0.5135
X1SQX2	1	-0.003560	0.00161443	-2.205	0.0477
X1SQX3	1	0.000600	0.00161443	0.372	0.7166
X1SQX2X3	1	0.001200	0.00228316	0.526	0.6087

e. Refer to part d. Find the prediction equations for each of the four combinations of alloy type and material condition.

f. Refer to part **d**. Plot the data points for each of the four combinations of alloy type and material condition. Graph the respective prediction equations.

11.44 Refer to Exercises 11.42–11.43. If the relationship between mean strength $E(y)$ and charging time x_1 is the same for all four combinations of alloy type and material condition, the appropriate model for $E(y)$ is

$$E(y) = \beta_0 + \beta_1 x_1 + \beta_2 x_1^2$$

Use the following SAS printout for fitting this model to the data, together with the information in the printout of Exercise 11.43, to decide whether the data provide sufficient evidence to indicate differences among the second-order models relating $E(y)$ to x_1 for the four categories of alloy type and material condition. Test using $\alpha = .05$.

```
Dependent Variable: YIELD

                         Analysis of Variance

                          Sum of          Mean
Source           DF      Squares        Square       F Value       Prob>F

Model             2     71.04083      35.52042         0.399       0.6759
Error            21   1868.83875      88.99232
C Total          23   1939.87958

    Root MSE        9.43357     R-square        0.0366
    Dep Mean       45.72083     Adj R-sq       -0.0551
    C.V.           20.63299

                         Parameter Estimates

                      Parameter      Standard     T for H0:
Variable   DF          Estimate         Error    Parameter=0    Prob > |T|

INTERCEP    1         45.650000    3.33527213         13.687        0.0001
X1          1          0.217000    0.34013235          0.638        0.5304
X1SQ        1         -0.005140    0.00653577         -0.786        0.4404
```

11.45 A study was conducted to evaluate the use of computer-assisted instruction (CAI) in teaching an introductory FORTRAN programming course (GE 102) in the College of Engineering at Oregon State University (*Engineering Education*, Feb. 1986). One of the objectives was to investigate the effect of four factors on a student's final exam score (y) in the course. The factors and their respective levels are as follows.

Group (3 levels):
Control group (student receives no CAI)
Guided CAI (student receives CAI, but proceeds at same pace as normal class)
Self-paced CAI (student receives CAI and proceeds at his or her own pace)

Math background (4 levels):
High school algebra
Trigonometry
Differential calculus
Integral calculus

Computer background (3 levels):
None (little or no exposure)
Some (one programming language)
Extensive (more than one programming language)

Grade in prerequisite course, GE 101 (3 levels):
A, B, or C

a. How many treatments are associated with this four-way factorial experiment?
b. Write the complete factorial model for this experiment. [*Hint:* Use dummy variables to represent the factors.]
c. What hypothesis would you test to determine whether interaction exists among the four factors?

11.46 A 2 × 2 factorial experiment was conducted for each of 3 weeks to determine the effect of two factors, temperature and pressure, on the yield of a chemical. Temperature was set at 300° and 500°. The pressure maintained in the reactor was set at 100 and 200 pounds per square inch. Four days were randomly selected within each week and the four factor level combinations were randomly assigned to them.

a. What type of design was used for this experiment?
b. Construct an analysis of variance table showing all sources and their respective degrees of freedom.

11.7 Follow-Up Analysis: Tukey's Multiple Comparisons of Means

Many practical experiments are conducted to determine the largest (or the smallest) mean in a set. For example, suppose a chemist has developed five chemical solutions for removing a corrosive substance from metal. The chemist would want to determine which solution will remove the greatest amount of corrosive substance in a single application. Similarly, a production engineer might want to determine which among six machines or which among three foremen achieves the highest mean productivity per hour. A stockbroker might want to choose one stock, from among four, that yields the highest mean return, and so on.

Once differences among, say, five treatment means have been detected in an ANOVA, choosing the treatment with the largest mean might appear to be a simple matter. We could, for example, obtain the sample means $\bar{y}_1, \bar{y}_2, \ldots, \bar{y}_5$, and compare them by constructing a $(1 - \alpha)100\%$ confidence interval for the difference between each pair of treatment means. However, there is a problem associated with this procedure: **A confidence interval for $\mu_i - \mu_j$, with its corresponding value of α, is valid only when the two treatments (i and j) to be compared are selected prior to experimentation**. After you have looked at the data, you cannot use a confidence interval to compare the treatments for the largest and smallest sample means because they will always be farther apart, on the average, than any pair of treatments selected at random. Furthermore, if you construct a series of confidence intervals, each with a chance α of indicating a difference between a pair of means if no difference exists, then the risk of making *at least one* Type I error in the series of inferences will be larger than the value of α specified for a single interval.

There are a number of procedures for comparing and ranking a group of treatment means as part of a **follow-up analysis** to the ANOVA. The one that we present in this section, known as **Tukey's method for multiple comparisons**, utilizes the Studentized range

$$q = \frac{\bar{y}_{\text{max}} - \bar{y}_{\text{min}}}{s/\sqrt{n}}$$

(where $\bar{y}_{\text{max}}$ and $\bar{y}_{\text{min}}$ are the largest and smallest sample means, respectively) to determine whether the difference in any pair of sample means implies a difference in the corresponding treatment means. The logic behind this **multiple comparisons procedure** is that if we determine a critical value for the difference between the largest and smallest sample means, $|\bar{y}_{\text{max}} - \bar{y}_{\text{min}}|$, one that implies a difference in their respective treatment means, then any other pair of sample means that differ by as much as or more than this critical value would also imply a difference in the corresponding treatment means. Tukey's (1949) procedure selects this critical distance, ω, so that the probability of making one or more Type I errors (concluding that a difference exists between a pair of treatment means if, in fact, they are identical) is α. Therefore, the risk of making a Type I error applies to the whole procedure, i.e., to the comparisons of all pairs of means in the experiment, rather than to a single comparison. Consequently, the value of α selected by the researchers is called an **experimentwise error rate** (in contrast to a **comparisonwise error rate**).

Tukey's procedure relies on the assumption that the p sample means are based on independent random samples, *each containing an equal number n_t of observations*. Then if $s = \sqrt{\text{MSE}}$ is the computed standard deviation for the analysis, the distance ω is

$$\omega = q_{\alpha}(p, \nu)\frac{s}{\sqrt{n_t}}$$

The tabulated statistic $q_{\alpha}(p, \nu)$ is the critical value of the Studentized range, the value that locates α in the upper tail of the q distribution. This critical value depends on α, the number of treatment means involved in the comparison, and ν, the number of degrees of freedom associated with MSE, as shown in the box on page 656. Values of $q_{\alpha}(p, \nu)$ for $\alpha = .05$ and $\alpha = .01$ are given in Tables 11 and 12, respectively, of Appendix C.

EXAMPLE 11.19

Refer to the ANOVA for the completely randomized design, Examples 11.4 and 11.5. Recall that we rejected the null hypothesis of no differences among the mean GPAs for the three socioeconomic groups of college freshmen. Use Tukey's method to compare the three treatment means.

Solution

STEP 1 For this follow-up analysis, we will select an experimentwise error rate of $\alpha = .05$.

STEP 2 From previous examples, we have $(p - 3)$ treatments, $\nu = 18$ df for error, $s = \sqrt{\text{MSE}} = .512$, and $n_t = 7$ observations per treatment. The critical value of

Tukey's Multiple Comparisons Procedure: Equal Sample Sizes

1. Select the desired experimentwise error rate, α.
2. Calculate

$$\omega = q_{\alpha}(p, \nu)\frac{s}{\sqrt{n_t}}$$

where

p = Number of sample means (i.e., number of treatments)
$s = \sqrt{\text{MSE}}$
ν = Number of degrees of freedom associated with MSE
n_t = Number of observations in each of the p samples (i.e., number of observations per treatment)
$q_{\alpha}(p, \nu)$ = Critical value of the Studentized range (Tables 11 and 12 of Appendix C)

3. Calculate and rank the p sample means.
4. Place a bar over those pairs of treatment means that differ by less than ω. A pair of treatments not connected by an overbar (i.e., differing by more than ω) implies a difference in the corresponding population means.

Note: The confidence level associated with all inferences drawn from the analysis is $(1 - \alpha)$.

the Studentized range (obtained from Table 11, Appendix C) is $q_{.05}(3, 18) = 3.61$. Substituting these values into the formula for ω, we obtain

$$\omega = q_{.05}(3, 18)\left(\frac{s}{\sqrt{n_t}}\right) = 3.61\left(\frac{.512}{\sqrt{7}}\right) = .70$$

STEP 3 The sample means for the three socioeconomic groups (obtained from Table 11.12) are

$$\bar{y}_{\text{L}} = 2.52 \qquad \bar{y}_{\text{M}} = 3.25 \qquad \bar{y}_{\text{U}} = 2.54$$

STEP 4 Based on the critical difference $\omega = .70$, the three treatment means are ranked as follows:

Sample means	2.52	2.54	3.25
Treatments	Lower	Upper	Middle

The same information can be obtained using a statistical software package. The SAS printout of the Tukey analysis is shown in Figure 11.22. Tukey's critical difference, $\omega = .6979$, is shaded on the printout. (This value differs slightly from our calculated value because of rounding.) Note that SAS lists the treatment means vertically in descending order. Treatment means connected by the same letter (A, B, C, etc.) are *not* significantly different.

FIGURE 11.22
SAS printout of Tukey analysis, Example 11.19

```
                    Analysis of Variance Procedure

     Tukey's Studentized Range (HSD) Test for variable: GPA

NOTE: This test controls the type I experimentwise error rate, but
      generally has a higher type II error rate than REGWQ.

              Alpha= 0.05  df= 18  MSE= 0.261729
          Critical Value of Studentized Range= 3.609
           Minimum Significant Difference= 0.6979

Means with the same letter are not significantly different.

        Tukey Grouping              Mean      N  CLASS

                     A             3.249      7  MIDDLE

                     B             2.543      7  UPPER
                     B
                     B             2.521      7  LOWER
```

From the information in Figure 11.22, we infer that the mean freshman GPA for the middle class is significantly larger than the means for the other classes, since $\bar{y}_M$ exceeds both $\bar{y}_L$ and $\bar{y}_U$ by more than the critical value. However, the lower and upper classes are connected by a bar (or the same letter) since $(\bar{y}_U - \bar{y}_L)$ is less than ω. This indicates that the means for these treatments are not significantly different. These inferences are made with an overall confidence level of $(1 - \alpha) = .95$.

EXAMPLE 11.20

A transistor manufacturer conducted an experiment to investigate the effects of two factors on productivity (measured in thousands of dollars of items produced) per 40-hour week. The factors were:

Length of work week (two levels): five consecutive 8-hour days or four consecutive 10-hour days

Number of coffee breaks (three levels): 0, 1, or 2

The experiment was conducted over a 12-week period with the $2 \times 3 = 6$ treatments assigned in a random manner to the 12 weeks. The data for this two-factor factorial experiment are shown in Table 11.12. (This experiment is a simpler version of the design used in Example 11.17.)

a. Perform an analysis of variance for the data.
b. Compare the six population means using Tukey's multiple comparisons procedure. Use $\alpha = .05$.

TABLE 11.12 **Data for Example 11.20**

		COFFEE BREAKS		
		0	1	2
LENGTH OF WORK WEEK	4 days	101 102	104 107	95 92
	5 days	95 93	109 110	83 87

Solution

a. The SAS printout of the ANOVA for the 2×3 factorial is shown in Figure 11.23. Note that the test for interaction between the two factors, length (L) and breaks (B), is significant at $\alpha = .01$. (The p-value, .0051, is shaded on the printout.) Since interaction implies that the level of length (L) that yields the highest mean productivity may differ across different levels of breaks (B), we ignore the tests for main effects and focus our investigation on the individual treatment means.

FIGURE 11.23
SAS ANOVA printout for Example 11.20

```
                        Analysis of Variance Procedure

Dependent Variable: PRODUCT
                                     Sum of             Mean
Source                    DF        Squares           Square   F Value      Pr > F

Model                      5    811.6666667      162.3333333     48.70      0.0001
Error                      6     20.0000000        3.3333333
Corrected Total           11    831.6666667

                    R-Square           C.V.         Root MSE           PRODUCT Mean

                    0.975952       1.859839         1.825742             98.1666667


Source                    DF       Anova SS      Mean Square   F Value      Pr > F

LENGTH                     1     48.0000000       48.0000000     14.40      0.0090
BREAKS                     2    667.1666667      333.5833333    100.07      0.0001
LENGTH*BREAKS              2     96.5000000       48.2500000     14.48      0.0051
```

b. The sample means for the six factor level combinations are shown in Table 11.13. Since the sample means in the table represent measures of productivity in the manufacture of transistors, we want to find the length of work week and number of coffee breaks that yield the highest mean productivity.

TABLE 11.13 **Sample Means for the $p = 6$ Treatments of Example 11.20**

		COFFEE BREAKS, B		
		0	1	2
LENGTH OF WORK WEEK, L	4 days	101.5	105.5	93.5
	5 days	94.0	109.5	85.0

The first step in the ranking procedure is to calculate ω for $p = 6$ (we are ranking six treatment means), $n_t = 2$ (two observations per treatment), $\alpha = .05$, and $s = \sqrt{\text{MSE}} = \sqrt{3.33} = 1.83$ (where MSE is given in Figure 11.23). Since MSE is based on $\nu = 6$ degrees of freedom, we have

$$q_{.05}(6, 6) = 5.63$$

and

$$\omega = q_{.05}(6, 6)\left(\frac{s}{\sqrt{n_t}}\right)$$

$$= (5.63)\left(\frac{1.83}{\sqrt{2}}\right)$$

$$= 7.27$$

Therefore, population means corresponding to pairs of sample means that differ by more than $\omega = 7.27$ will be judged to be different. The six sample means are ranked as follows:

Sample means	85.0	93.5	94.0	101.5	105.5	109.5
Treatments (Length, Breaks)	(5, 2)	(4, 2)	(5, 0)	(4, 0)	(4, 1)	(5, 1)

Using $\omega = 7.27$ as a yardstick to determine differences between pairs of treatments, we have placed connecting bars over those means that *do not* significantly differ. The following conclusions can be drawn:

1. There is evidence of a difference between the population mean of the treatment corresponding to a 5-day work week with two coffee breaks (with the smallest sample mean of 85.0) and every other treatment mean. Therefore, we can conclude that the 5-day, 2-break work week yields the lowest mean productivity among all length–break combinations.
2. The population mean of the treatment corresponding to a 5-day, 1-break work week (with the largest sample mean of 109.5) is significantly larger than the treatments corresponding to the four smallest sample means. However, there is no evidence of a difference between the 5-day, 1-break treatment mean and the 4-day, 1-break treatment mean (with a sample mean of 105.5).
3. There is no evidence of a difference between the 4-day, 1-break treatment mean (with a sample mean of 105.5) and the 4-day, 0-break treatment mean (with a sample mean of 101.5). Both these treatments, though, have significantly larger means than the treatments corresponding to the three smallest sample means.
4. There is no evidence of a difference among the treatments corresponding to the sample means 93.5 and 94.0. Further experimentation would be required to determine whether the observed differences in these means really imply a difference in the corresponding sample means.

In summary, the treatment means appear to fall into four groups, as follows:

	Treatments (Length, Breaks)
Group 1 (lowest mean productivity)	(5, 2)
Group 2	(4, 2) and (5, 0)
Group 3	(4, 0) and (4, 1)
Group 4 (highest mean productivity)	(4, 1) and (5, 1)

Notice that it is unclear where we should place the treatment corresponding to a 4-day, 1-break work week because of the overlapping bars above its sample mean, 105.5. That is, although there is sufficient evidence to indicate that treatments (4, 0) and (5, 1) differ, neither has been shown to differ significantly from treatment (4, 1). Tukey's method guarantees that the probability of making one or more Type I errors in these pairwise comparisons is only $\alpha = .05$.

Remember that Tukey's multiple comparisons procedure requires the sample sizes associated with the treatments to be equal. This, of course, will be satisfied for the randomized block designs and factorial experiments described in Sections 11.4 and 11.5, respectively. The sample sizes, however, may not be equal in a completely randomized design (Section 11.3). In this case a modification of Tukey's method (sometimes called the Tukey–Kramer method) is necessary, as described in the accompanying box. The technique requires that the critical difference ω_{ij} be calculated for each pair of treatments (i, j) in the experiment and pairwise comparisons made based on the appropriate value of ω_{ij}. However, when Tukey's method is used with unequal sample sizes, the value of α selected a priori by the researcher only approximates the true experimentwise error rate. In fact, when applied to unequal sample sizes, the procedure has been found to

Tukey's Approximate Multiple Comparisons Procedure for Unequal Sample Sizes

1. Calculate for each treatment pair (i, j)

$$\omega_{ij} = q_\alpha(p, \nu)\frac{s}{\sqrt{2}}\sqrt{\frac{1}{n_i} + \frac{1}{n_j}}$$

where

p = Number of sample means

$s = \sqrt{\text{MSE}}$

ν = Number of degrees of freedom associated with MSE

n_i = Number of observations in sample for treatment i

n_j = Number of observations in sample for treatment j

$q_\alpha(p, \nu)$ = Critical value of the Studentized range (Tables 11 and 12 of Appendix C)

2. Rank the p sample means and place a bar over any treatment pair (i, j) that differs by less than ω_{ij}. Any pair of sample means not connected by an overbar (i.e., differing by more than ω) implies a difference in the corresponding population means.

Note: This procedure is approximate, i.e., the value of α selected by the researcher approximates the true probability of making at least one Type I error.

be more conservative, i.e., less likely to detect differences between pairs of treatment means when they exist, than in the case of equal sample sizes. For this reason, researchers sometimes look to alternative methods of multiple comparisons when the sample sizes are unequal. Two of these methods are presented in optional Section 11.8.

In general, multiple comparisons of treatment means should be performed only as a follow-up analysis to the ANOVA, i.e., only after we have conducted the appropriate analysis of variance F test(s) and determined that sufficient evidence exists of differences among the treatment means. Be wary of conducting multiple comparisons when the ANOVA F test indicates no evidence of a difference among a small number of treatment means—this may lead to confusing and contradictory results.*

Warning

In practice, it is advisable to avoid conducting multiple comparisons of a small number of treatment means when the corresponding ANOVA F test is nonsignificant; otherwise, confusing and contradictory results may occur.

EXERCISES

11.47 Are all videocassette recorder (VCR) users alike, or can they be segmented into subgroups with different motivations and behaviors? This question was the topic of research reported in the *Journal of Advertising Research* (Apr./May 1988). A sample of 371 members of a large videotape rental club in a southeastern city were surveyed about their VCR use. Based on their responses, each member was categorized into one of five groups as follows:

GROUP	CHARACTERISTICS	NUMBER IN SAMPLE
(1) *Videophile*	Record TV programs often, and rent/buy videotapes often	61
(2) *Time shifter*	Record TV programs often, rarely rent/buy videotapes	74
(3) *Source shifter*	Rarely record TV programs, rent/buy videotapes often	50
(4) *Low user*	Rarely record TV programs or rent/buy videotapes	58
(5) *Regular user*	Periodically record TV programs and/or rent/buy videotapes	128
		371

One of the dependent variables measured was degree to which the user "zapped" (i.e., fast-forwarded through commercials) while replaying a taped TV program. This "ad avoidance" variable was measured on a 7-point scale, where 1 = almost always and 7 = never.

*When a large number of treatments are to be compared, a borderline, nonsignificant F value (e.g., $.05 < p\text{-value} < .10$) may mask differences between some of the means. In this situation, it is better to ignore the F test and proceed directly to a multiple comparisons procedure.

a. The F value for testing the hypothesis H_0: $\mu_1 = \mu_2 = \mu_3 = \mu_4 = \mu_5$ is $F = 5.4$. Interpret this value (use $\alpha = .05$).

b. The mean ad avoidance levels of the five groups are listed here, as well as the results of a multiple comparisons analysis (at $\alpha = .05$). Interpret the results.

		‾‾‾‾‾‾	‾‾‾‾‾‾	‾‾‾‾‾‾	‾‾‾‾‾‾
Mean ad avoidance	1.8	2.6	2.8	2.9	3.4
VCR user segment	Time shifter	Videophile	Regular	Low user	Source shifter

11.48 Refer to the *Journal of Abnormal Psychology* study of self-esteem, eating disorders, and depression in women described in Exercise 11.7. A follow-up analysis, using Tukey's multiple comparisons procedure, was conducted on the three group means. The ranked means are listed here, with an overbar connecting the means that are not significantly different at $\alpha = .01$. Interpret the results.

	‾‾‾‾‾‾	‾‾‾‾‾‾	
Mean self-esteem rating	3.6	3.9	4.9
Group	Depression	Eating disorders	Normal

11.49 In business, the prevailing theory is that companies can be categorized into one of four types based on their strategic profile: *reactors*, which are dominated by industry forces; *defenders*, which specialize in lowering costs for established products while maintaining quality; *prospectors*, which develop new/improved products; and *analyzers*, which operate in two product areas—one stable, and the other dynamic. The *American Business Review* (Jan. 1990) reported on a study that proposes a fifth organization type, *balancers*, which operate in three product spheres—one stable and two dynamic. Each firm in a sample of 78 glassware firms was categorized as one of these five types, and the level of performance (process research and development ratio) of each was measured.

a. A completely randomized design ANOVA of the data resulted in a significant (at $\alpha = .05$) F value for treatments (organization types). Interpret this result.

b. Multiple comparisons of the five mean performance levels (using Tukey's procedure at $\alpha = .05$) are summarized in the following table. Interpret the results.

			‾‾‾‾‾‾	‾‾‾‾‾‾	
				‾‾‾‾‾‾	‾‾‾‾‾‾
Mean	.138	.235	.820	.826	.911
Type	Reactor	Prospector	Defender	Analyzer	Balancer

Source: Wright, P., et al. "Business performance and conduct of organization types: A study of select special-purpose and laboratory glassware firms." *American Business Review*, Jan. 1990, p. 95 (Table 4).

11.50 Refer to the *Accounting and Finance* (Nov. 1993) study of auditors' objectivity, Exercise 11.9. The means of the three groups of auditors were ranked using a Tukey multiple comparisons procedure at $\alpha = .05$, as shown here:

	‾‾‾‾‾‾	‾‾‾‾‾‾	
Mean number of hours allocated to receivables	6.7	7.6	9.7
Group	A/R	C	A/P

At the beginning of the study, the researchers theorized that the A/R group would allocate the least audit effort to receivables and that the A/P group would allocate the most. Formally stated, the researchers believed that $\mu_{AR} < \mu_C < \mu_{AP}$. Do the results support this theory? Explain.

11.51 Refer to the *Human Factors* (Apr. 1990) study of the performance of a computerized speech recognizer, Exercise 4.36. Accuracy was measured at three levels (90%, 95%, and 99%) and vocabulary size at three levels (75%, 87.5%, and 100%). The data on task completion times (minutes) were subjected to an analysis of variance for a 3 × 3 factorial design. The F test for accuracy–vocabulary interaction resulted in a p-value less than .0003.

a. Interpret the result of the test for interaction.

b. As a follow-up to the test for interaction, the mean task completion times for the three levels of accuracy were compared under each level of vocabulary. Do you agree with this method of analysis? Explain.

c. Refer to part **b**. Tukey's multiple comparisons method was used to compare the three accuracy means within each level of vocabulary at an experimentwise error rate of $\alpha = .05$. The results are summarized in the table. Interpret these results.

VOCABULARY SIZE	ACCURACY LEVEL		
	99%	95%	90%
75%	15.49	19.29	22.19
87.5%	12.77	14.31	16.48
100%	8.67	9.68	11.88

Source: Casali, S. P., Williges, B. H., and Dryden, R. D. "Effects of recognition accuracy and vocabulary size of a speech recognition system on task performance and user acceptance." *Human Factors*, Vol. 32, No. 2, Apr. 1990, p. 190 (Figure 2).

11.52 Refer to Exercise 11.16. The mean levels of polysaccharides found in the five groups of Dutch men are provided in the accompanying table. Use Tukey's method to rank the group means. Use $\alpha = .05$.

FISH CONSUMPTION grams/day	SAMPLE SIZE	MEAN LEVEL OF POLYSACCHARIDES percentage of energy
0	159	27.0
1–14	283	27.0
15–29	215	26.6
30–44	116	25.7
45 or more	79	24.4

11.53 Refer to the *Journal of Computer Information Systems* (Spring 1993) study of end-user computing, Exercise 1.76. Data on the ratings of 18 specific end-user computing (EUC) policies were obtained for each of 82 managers. (Managers rated policies on a 5-point scale, where 1 = no value and 5 = necessity.) The goal was to compare the mean ratings of the 18 EUC policies; thus, a randomized block design with 18 treatments (policies) and 82 blocks (managers) was used. Since the ANOVA F test for treatments was significant at $\alpha = .01$, a follow-up analysis was conducted. The mean ratings for the 18 EUC policies are reported in the table on page 664. Using an overall significance level of $\alpha = .05$, the Tukey critical difference for comparing the 18 means was determined to be $\omega = .32$.

a. Determine the pairs of EUC policy means that are significantly different.

b. According to the researchers, the group of policies receiving the highest rated values have mean ratings of 4.0 and above. Do you agree with this assessment?

EUC POLICY	MEAN RATING
1. Organizational value	2.439
2. Training	2.683
3. Goals	2.854
4. Justify applications	3.098
5. Relation with MIS	3.293
6. Hardware movement	3.366
7. Accountability	3.390
8. Justify data	3.561
9. Ownership of files	3.756
10. In-house software	3.854
11. Copyright infringement	3.878
12. Compatibility	4.000
13. Document files	4.000
14. Role of networking	4.049
15. Data confidentiality	4.073
16. Data security	4.219
17. Hardware standards	4.293
18. Software purchases	4.317

Source: Mitchell, R. B., and Neal, R. "Status of planning and control systems in the end-user computing environment." *Journal of Computer Information Systems*, Vol. 33, No. 3, Spring 1993, p. 29 (Table 4).

11.54 Refer to Exercise 11.25. Use Tukey's multiple comparisons procedure to compare the mean in-tray performance scores assessed by the three raters. Identify the means that appear to differ. Use $\alpha = .05$.

11.55 Refer to Exercise 11.33. Use Tukey's multiple comparisons procedure to compare the mean shear strengths for the four antimony amounts. Identify the means that appear to differ. Use $\alpha = .01$.

11.56 Refer to Exercise 11.36. Use Tukey's multiple comparisons procedure to compare the mean satisfaction scores for the three peak period lengths under each of the three pricing ratios. Identify the means that appear to differ under each pricing ratio. Use $\alpha = .01$.

11.8 Other Multiple Comparisons Methods (Optional)

In this optional section, we present two alternatives to Tukey's method of multiple comparisons of treatment means. The choice of methods will depend on the type of experimental design used and the particular error rate that the researcher wants to control.

Scheffé Method

Recall that Tukey's method of multiple comparisons is designed to control the experimentwise error rate, i.e., the probability of making at least one Type I error in the comparison of *all pairs* of treatment means in the experiment. Therefore, Tukey's method should be applied when you are interested in pairwise comparisons only.

Scheffé (1953) developed a more general procedure for comparing all possible linear combinations of the treatment means, called **contrasts**.

Definition 11.3

A **contrast** L is a linear combination of the p treatment means in a designed experiment, i.e.,

$$L = \sum_{i=1}^{p} c_i \mu_i$$

where the constants $c_1, c_2, \ldots, c_p$ sum to 0, i.e., $\sum_{i=1}^{p} c_i = 0$.

For example, in an experiment with four treatments (A, B, C, D), you might want to compare the following contrasts, where μ_i represents the population mean for treatment i:

$$L_1 = \frac{\mu_A + \mu_B}{2} - \frac{\mu_C + \mu_D}{2}$$

$$L_2 = \mu_A - \mu_D$$

$$L_3 = \frac{\mu_B + \mu_C + \mu_D}{3} - \mu_A$$

The contrast L_2 involves a comparison of a pair of treatment means, whereas L_1 and L_3 are more complex comparisons of the treatments. Thus, pairwise comparisons are special cases of general contrasts.

As in Tukey's method, the value of α selected by the researcher using Scheffé's method applies to the procedure as a whole, i.e., to the comparisons of all possible contrasts (not just those considered by the researcher). Unlike Tukey's method, however, the probability of at least one Type I error, α, is exact regardless of whether the sample sizes are equal. For this reason, some researchers prefer Scheffé's method to Tukey's method in the case of unequal samples, even if only pairwise comparisons of treatment means are made. The Scheffé method for general contrasts is outlined in the box on page 666.

In the special case of all pairwise comparisons in an experiment with four treatments, the relevant contrasts reduce to $L_1 = \mu_A - \mu_B$, $L_2 = \mu_A - \mu_C$, $L_3 = \mu_A - \mu_D$, and so forth. Notice that for each of these contrasts $\Sigma\, c_i^2/n_i$ reduces to $(1/n_i + 1/n_j)$, where n_i and n_j are the sizes of treatments i and j, respectively. [For example, for contrast L_1, $c_1 = 1$, $c_2 = -1$, $c_3 = c_4 = 0$, and $\Sigma\, c_i^2/n_i = (1/n_1 + 1/n_2)$.] Consequently, the formula for S in the general contrast method can be simplified and pairwise comparisons made using the technique of Section 11.7. The Scheffé method for pairwise comparisons of treatment means is shown in the box on page 667.

EXAMPLE 11.21

Refer to the 2×3 factorial experiment to investigate the effects of length of work week and number of coffee breaks on mean productivity in Example 11.20. Compare the population means corresponding to the six length–break combinations (treatments) using the Scheffé method of multiple comparisons. Use $\alpha = .05$.

Scheffé's Multiple Comparisons Procedure for General Contrasts

1. For each contrast $L = \sum_{i=1}^{p} c_i \mu_i$, calculate

$$\hat{L} = \sum_{i=1}^{p} c_i \bar{y}_i$$

and

$$S = \sqrt{(p-1)F_{\alpha}(p-1, \nu)\text{MSE} \sum_{i=1}^{p} \left(\frac{c_i^2}{n_i}\right)}$$

where

p = Number of sample (treatment) means
MSE = Mean squared error
n_i = Number of observations in sample for treatment i
$\bar{y}_i$ = Sample mean for treatment i
$F_{\alpha}(p-1, \nu)$ = Critical value of F distribution with $\nu_1 = p - 1$ numerator df and $\nu_2 = \nu$ denominator df (Tables 3, 4, 5, and 6 of Appendix C)
ν = Number of degrees of freedom associated with MSE

2. Calculate the confidence interval $\hat{L} \pm S$ for each contrast. The confidence coefficient, $1 - \alpha$, applies to the procedure as a whole, i.e., to the entire set of confidence intervals for all possible contrasts.

Solution

From Figure 11.23 in Example 11.20, we have MSE = 3.33, $p = 6$, and ν = df(Error) = 6. Also, there are two observations per treatment, $n_i = n_j = 2$, for all treatment pairs. Consequently, the critical difference S_{ij} will be the same for all treatment pairs (i, j). From Table 4 in Appendix C, we have $F_{.05} = 4.39$ (based on $p - 1 = 5$ numerator df and $\nu = 6$ denominator df). Then, Scheffé's critical difference S_{ij} is

$$S_{ij} = \sqrt{(p-1)F_{.05}\text{MSE}\left(\frac{1}{n_i} + \frac{1}{n_j}\right)}$$

$$= \sqrt{(5)(4.39)(3.33)\left(\frac{1}{2} + \frac{1}{2}\right)} = 8.55$$

Treatment means differing by more than $S = 8.55$ will imply a significant difference between the corresponding population means. The rankings of the treatment means, with overbars indicating "no evidence of a difference," are shown here:

Scheffé's Multiple Comparisons Procedure for Pairwise Comparisons of Treatment Means

1. Calculate Scheffé's critical difference for each pair of treatments (i, j):

$$S_{ij} = \sqrt{(p - 1)F_\alpha(p-1, \nu)\text{MSE}\left(\frac{1}{n_i} + \frac{1}{n_j}\right)}$$

where

p = Number of sample (treatment) means
MSE = Mean squared error
n_i = Number of observations in sample for treatment i
n_j = Number of observations in sample for treatment j
$F_\alpha(p - 1, \nu)$ = Critical value of F distribution with $\nu_1 = p - 1$ numerator df and $\nu_2 = \nu$ denominator df (Tables 3, 4, 5, and 6 of Appendix C)
ν = Number of degrees of freedom associated with MSE

2. Rank the p sample means and place a bar over any treatment pair (i, j) that differs by less than S_{ij}. Any pair of sample means not connected by an overbar implies a difference in the corresponding population means.

Sample means	85.0	93.5	94.0	101.5	105.5	109.5
Treatments (Length, Breaks)	(5, 2)	(4, 2)	(5, 0)	(4, 0)	(4, 1)	(5, 1)

Recall that the manufacturer's goal is to determine the treatment(s) yielding the highest mean productivity. Based on this result, the six means can be grouped as follows:

	TREATMENTS (LENGTH, BREAKS)
Group 1 (lowest mean productivity)	(5, 2) and (4, 2)
Group 2	(4, 2), (5, 0), and (4, 0)
Group 3 (highest mean productivity)	(4, 0), (4, 1), and (5, 1)

You can see that the treatments corresponding to 5-day, 1-break and 4-day, 1-break work weeks produce the highest mean productivity. The Scheffé method did not detect a significant difference between these treatments and treatment (4, 0), or a significant difference between treatment (4, 0) and either treatment

(4, 2) or (5, 0). Thus, we are not certain where to place treatment (4, 0)—in the group with the highest mean productivity (group 3) or in the middle group (group 2).

Note that in Example 11.21, the Scheffé method produced a critical difference of $S = 8.55$—a value larger than Tukey's critical difference of $\omega = 7.27$ (Example 11.20). This implies that Tukey's method produces narrower confidence intervals than Scheffé's method for differences in pairs of treatment means. Therefore, if only pairwise comparisons of treatments are to be made, Tukey's is the preferred method as long as the sample sizes are equal. The Scheffé method, on the other hand, yields narrower confidence intervals (i.e., smaller critical differences) for situations in which the goal of the researchers is to make comparisons of general contrasts.

Bonferroni Approach

As noted previously, Tukey's multiple comparisons procedure is approximate in the case of unequal sample sizes. That is, the value of α selected a priori only approximates the true probability of making at least one Type I error. The Bonferroni approach is an exact method that is applicable in either the equal or the unequal sample size case. Furthermore, Bonferroni's procedure covers all possible comparisons of treatments, including pairwise comparisons, general contrasts, or combinations of pairwise comparisons and more complex contrasts.

The Bonferroni approach is based on the following result (proof omitted): If g comparisons are to be made, each with confidence coefficient $1 - \alpha/g$, then the overall probability of making one or more Type I errors (i.e., the experimentwise error rate) is at most α. That is, the set of intervals constructed using the Bonferroni method yields an overall confidence level of at least $1 - \alpha$. For example, if you want to construct $g = 2$ confidence intervals with an experimentwise error rate of at most $\alpha = .05$, then each individual interval must be constructed using a confidence level of $1 - .05/2 = .975$.

The Bonferroni approach for general contrasts is shown in the next box. When applied only to pairwise comparisons of treatments, the Bonferroni approach can be carried out as shown in the box on page 670.

EXAMPLE 11.22

Refer to the two-factor factorial experiment in Example 11.20. Use Bonferroni's method to perform pairwise comparisons of the six treatment means. Use $\alpha = .05$.

Solution

From Examples 11.20 and 11.21, we have $p = 6$, $s = \sqrt{\text{MSE}} = 1.83$, $\nu = 6$, and $n_i = n_j = 2$ for all treatment pairs (i, j). For $p = 6$ means, the number of pairwise comparisons to be made is

$$g = \frac{p(p-1)}{2} = \frac{6(5)}{2} = 15$$

Bonferroni Multiple Comparisons Procedure for General Contrasts

1. For each contrast $L = \sum_{i=1}^{p} c_i \mu_i$, calculate

$$\hat{L} = \sum_{i=1}^{p} c_i \bar{y}_i$$

and

$$B = t_{\alpha/(2g)} s \sqrt{\sum_{i=1}^{p} \left(\frac{c_i^2}{n_i}\right)}$$

where

p = Number of sample (treatment) means
g = Number of contrasts
$s = \sqrt{\text{MSE}}$
ν = Number of degrees of freedom associated with MSE
n_i = Number of observations in sample for treatment i
$\bar{y}_i$ = Sample mean for treatment i
$t_{\alpha/(2g)}$ = Critical value of t distribution with ν df and tail area $\alpha/(2g)$ (Table 2 in Appendix C)

2. Calculate the confidence interval $\hat{L} \pm B$ for each contrast. The confidence coefficient for the procedure as a whole, i.e., for the entire set of confidence intervals, is *at least* $1 - \alpha$.

Thus, we need to find the critical value, $t_{\alpha/(2g)} = t_{.05/[2(15)]} = t_{.0017}$, for the t distribution based on $\nu = 6$ df. This value, although not shown in Table 2 in Appendix C, is approximately 4.7.* Substituting $t_{.0017} \approx 4.7$ into the equation for Bonferroni's critical difference B_{ij}, we have

$$B_{ij} \approx t_{.0017} s \sqrt{\frac{1}{n_i} + \frac{1}{n_j}} = (4.7)(1.83)\sqrt{\frac{1}{2} + \frac{1}{2}} = 8.60$$

for any treatment pair (i, j).

Using the value $B_{ij} = 8.60$ to detect significant differences between treatment means, we obtain the following results:

Sample means	85.0	93.5	94.0	101.5	105.5	109.5
Treatments (Length, Breaks)	(5, 2)	(4, 2)	(5, 0)	(4, 0)	(4, 1)	(5, 1)

*We obtained the value using the SAS probability generating function for a Student's t distribution.

Bonferroni Multiple Comparisons Procedure for Pairwise Comparisons of Treatment Means

1. Calculate for each treatment pair (i, j)

$$B_{ij} = t_{\alpha/(2g)}s\sqrt{\frac{1}{n_i} + \frac{1}{n_j}}$$

where

p = Number of sample (treatment) means in the experiment

g = Number of pairwise comparisons
[*Note:* If all pairwise comparisons are to be made, then $g = p(p - 1)/2$]

$s = \sqrt{\text{MSE}}$

ν = Number of degrees of freedom associated with MSE

n_i = Number of observations in sample for treatment i

n_j = Number of observations in sample for treatment j

$t_{\alpha/(2g)}$ = Critical value of t distribution with ν df and tail area $\alpha/(2g)$ (Table 2 in Appendix C)

2. Rank the sample means and place a bar over any treatment pair (i, j) whose sample means differ by less than B_{ij}. Any pair of means not connected by an overbar implies a difference in the corresponding population means.

Note: The level of confidence associated with all inferences drawn from the analysis is at least $(1 - \alpha)$.

You can see that the group of treatments with the highest mean productivity includes treatments (4, 0), (4, 1), and (5, 1). The bar over these three means, however, indicates that we are unable to detect differences between any pair of these treatments. All inferences derived from this analysis can be made at an overall confidence level of at least $1 - \alpha = .95$.

When applied to pairwise comparisons of treatments, the Bonferroni method, like the Scheffé procedure, produces wider confidence intervals (reflected by the magnitude of the critical difference) than Tukey's method. (In Example 11.22, Bonferroni's critical difference is $B \approx 8.60$ compared to Tukey's $\omega = 7.27$.) Therefore, if only pairwise comparisons are of interest, Tukey's procedure is again superior. However, if the sample sizes are unequal or more complex contrasts are to be compared, the Bonferroni technique may be preferred. Unlike the Tukey and Scheffé methods, however, Bonferroni's procedure requires that you know in advance how many contrasts are to be compared. Also, the value needed to calculate the critical difference B, $t_{\alpha/(2g)}$, may not be available in the t tables provided in most texts, and you will have to estimate it.

In this section, we have presented two alternatives to Tukey's multiple comparisons procedure. The technique you select will depend on several factors, including the sample sizes and the type of comparisons to be made. Keep in mind, however, that many other methods of making multiple comparisons are available, and one or more of these techniques may be more appropriate to use in your particular application. Consult the references given at the end of this chapter for details on other techniques.

EXERCISES

11.57 Refer to the *Criminology* study described in Exercise 11.12. The mean levels of conflict perceived by the four groups of jail staff members are provided in the table. Compare the means (at $\alpha = .06$) using Bonferroni's procedure. Interpret the result.

STAFF AFFILIATION	SAMPLE SIZE	MEAN LEVEL OF CONFLICT
Jail correctional	58	1.81
Jail mental health	29	2.32
County mental health	52	2.32
Other mental health	28	2.84

11.58 Refer to the *Transportation Journal* (Fall 1993) study of truck driver job satisfaction, Exercise 11.30. Since career stage was found to be the only significant factor in the 3 × 2 factorial ANOVA, the mean job satisfaction levels of the three career stages (early, middle, and late) were compared using the Bonferroni method.

a. Find the adjusted α level to use in the analysis, if the researchers desire an overall significance level of $\alpha = .09$.

b. The sample mean job satisfaction levels for the three career stages are given here. Assuming equal sample sizes for each stage and a Bonferroni critical difference of $B = .06$, rank the means.

Mean job satisfaction	3.47	3.38	3.36
Career stage	Early	Middle	Late

11.59 As oil drilling costs rise at unprecedented rates, the task of measuring drilling performance becomes essential to a successful oil company. One method of lowering drilling costs is to increase drilling speed. Researchers at Cities Service Co. have developed a drill bit, called the PD-1, which they believe penetrates rock at a faster rate than any other bit on the market. It is decided to compare the speed of the PD-1 with the two fastest drill bits known, the IADC 1-2-6 and the IADC 5-1-7, at 12 drilling locations in Texas. Four drilling sites were randomly assigned to each bit, and the rate of penetration (RoP) in feet per hour (fph) was recorded after drilling 3,000 feet at each site. The table giving the data and the MINITAB ANOVA printout are shown on page 672.

PD-1	IADC 1-2-6	IADC 5-1-7
35.2	25.8	14.7
30.1	29.7	28.9
37.6	26.6	23.3
34.3	30.1	16.2

MINITAB printout for Exercise 11.59

```
ANALYSIS OF VARIANCE ON ROP
SOURCE       DF        SS        MS         F        p
DRILLBIT      2     366.6     183.3      9.50    0.006
ERROR         9     173.7      19.3
TOTAL        11     540.2
                                    INDIVIDUAL 95 PCT CI'S FOR MEAN
                                    BASED ON POOLED STDEV
 LEVEL        N      MEAN     STDEV  --------+---------+---------+--------
     1        4    34.300     3.127                      (------*------)
     2        4    28.050     2.167                (------*------)
     3        4    20.775     6.589   (------*------)
                                     --------+---------+---------+--------
POOLED STDEV =      4.393                  21.0      28.0      35.0
```

a. Based on this information, can Cities Service Co. conclude that the mean RoP differs for at least two of the three drill bits? Test at the $\alpha = .05$ level of significance.
b. Use Tukey's method to perform all pairwise comparisons of the mean RoP for the three types of drill bits. Use $\alpha = .05$.
c. Use the Scheffé method to perform all pairwise comparisons of the mean RoP for the three types of drill bits. Use $\alpha = .05$.
d. Use the Bonferroni approach to perform all pairwise comparisons of the means RoP for the three types of drill bits. Use $\alpha = .05$.
e. Compare the results, parts **b–d**.

11.60 A field experiment was conducted at a not-for-profit research and development organization to examine the expectations, attitudes, and decisions of employees with regard to training programs (*Academy of Management Journal*, Sept. 1987). In particular, the study was aimed at determining how managers' evaluations of a training program were affected by the prior information they received and by the degree of choice they had in entering the program. These two factors, prior information and degree of choice, were each varied at two levels. The prior information managers received about the training program was either a realistic preview of the program and its benefits or a traditional announcement that tended to exaggerate the workshop's benefits. Degree of choice was either low (mandatory attendance) or high (little pressure from supervisors to attend). Twenty-one managers were randomly assigned to each of the $2 \times 2 = 4$ experimental conditions; thus, a 2×2 factorial design was employed. At the end of the training program, each manager was asked to rate his or her satisfaction with the workshop on a 7-point scale (1 = no satisfaction, 7 = extremely satisfied). The ratings were subjected to an analysis of variance, with the results shown in the partial ANOVA summary table at the top of page 673.

a. Complete the ANOVA summary table.
b. Conduct the appropriate ANOVA F tests (use $\alpha = .05$). Interpret the results.
c. The sample mean satisfaction ratings of managers for the four combinations of prior information and degree of choice are shown in the accompanying table. Use Tukey's method to rank the four means. Use. $\alpha = .06$.

SOURCE	df	SS	MS	F
Prior information (*P*)	1	_____	1.55	_____
Degree of choice (*D*)	1	_____	22.26	_____
PD interaction	1	_____	.61	_____
Error	80	_____	1.43	
Total	83	_____		

Source: Hicks, W. D., and Klimoski, R. J. "Entry into training programs and its effects on training outcomes: A field experiment." *Academy of Management Journal*, Vol. 30, No. 3, Sept. 1987, p. 548.

		PRIOR INFORMATION	
		Realistic Preview	Traditional Announcement
DEGREE OF CHOICE	High	6.20	6.06
	Low	5.33	4.82

Source: Hicks, W. D., and Klimoski, R. J. "Entry into training programs and its effects on training outcomes: A field experiment." *Academy of Management Journal*, Vol. 30, No. 3, Sept. 1987, p. 548.

d. Use the Scheffé method to perform all pairwise comparisons of the four treatment means. Use $\alpha = .05$.

e. Use the Bonferroni approach to perform all pairwise comparisons of the four treatment means. Use $\alpha = .05$.

f. Compare the results, parts **c–e**.

11.9 Checking ANOVA Assumptions

For each of the experiments and designs discussed in this chapter, we listed in the relevant boxes the assumptions underlying the analysis in the terminology of ANOVA. For example, in the box on page 589, the assumptions for a completely randomized design are that (1) the p probability distributions of the response y corresponding to the p treatments are normal and (2) the population variances of the p treatments are equal. Similarly, for randomized block designs and factorial designs, the data for the treatments must come from normal probability distributions with equal variances.

These assumptions are equivalent to those required for a regression analysis (see Section 4.2). The reason, of course, is that the probabilistic model for the response y that underlies each design is the familiar general linear regression model of Chapter 4. Consequently, checks on the ANOVA assumptions can be performed by examining the regression residuals, as described in Chapter 7. A brief overview of these techniques follows.

Detecting Nonnormal Populations

1. For each treatment, construct a histogram or stem-and-leaf display of the residuals. Look for highly skewed distributions. (Remember that ANOVA, like regression, is robust with respect to the normality assumption. That is, slight departures from normality will have little impact on the validity of the inferences derived from the analysis.) [*Note:* If the sample size for each treatment is small, then these graphs will probably be of limited use.]

2. Formal statistical tests of normality (such as the Shapiro–Wilk test) are also available. The null hypothesis is that the probability distribution of the response is normal. These tests, however, are sensitive to slight departures from normality. Since in most scientific applications the normality assumption will not be satisfied exactly, these tests will likely result in a rejection of the null hypothesis and, consequently, are of limited use in practice. Consult the references for more information on these formal tests.
3. If the distribution of the residuals departs greatly from normality, a *normalizing transformation* may be necessary. For example, for highly skewed distributions, transformations on the response y such as $\log(y)$ or $\sqrt{y}$ tend to "normalize" the data since these functions "pull" the observations in the tail of the distribution back toward the mean.

Detecting Unequal Variances

1. For each treatment, construct a **residual frequency** plot and look for differences in the spread (variability) of the residuals shown in the plots. Residual frequency plots for the three socioeconomic classes (treatments) in the completely randomized design ANOVA of Example 11.4 are shown in Figure 11.24. Note that the variability of the residuals in each plot is about the same; thus, the assumption of equal variances appears to be satisfied.

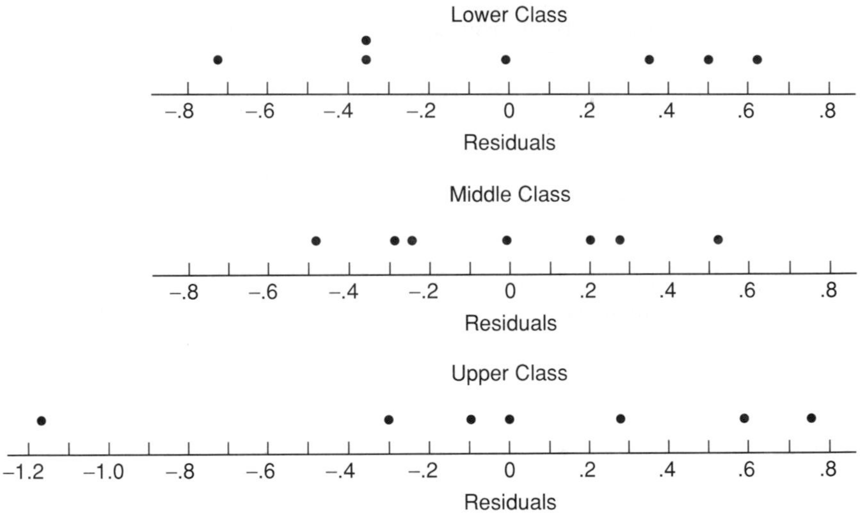

FIGURE 11.24
Residual frequency plot for ANOVA of Example 11.4

2. When the sample sizes are small for each treatment, only a few points are plotted on the residual frequency plots, making it difficult to detect differences in variation. In this situation, you may want to use one of several formal statistical tests of homogeneity of variances that are available. For p treatments, the null hypothesis is H_0: $\sigma_1^2 = \sigma_2^2 = \cdots = \sigma_p^2$, where σ_i^2 is the population variance of the response y corresponding to the ith treatment. If all p populations are approximately normal, **Bartlett's test for homogeneity of variances** can be applied. The elements of the test are shown in the accompanying box. Note that the test statistic depends on whether the sample sizes are equal or unequal.

We apply Bartlett's test to the ANOVA of Example 11.4. The null hypothesis is

$$H_0: \ \sigma_L^2 = \sigma_M^2 = \sigma_U^2$$

where σ_L^2, σ_M^2 and σ_U^2 are the population GPA variances for freshmen in the lower, middle, and upper socioeconomic classes, respectively. Since the sample sizes are the same ($n_L = n_M = n_U = 7$), the formula for the test statistic is

Bartlett's Test of Homogeneity of Variance

H_0: $\sigma_1^2 = \sigma_2^2 = \cdots = \sigma_p^2$

H_a: At least two variances differ.

Test statistic (equal sample sizes):

$$B = \frac{(n-1)[p \ln \bar{s}^2 - \Sigma \ln s_i^2]}{1 + \dfrac{p+1}{3p(n-1)}}$$

where

$n = n_1 = n_2 = \cdots = n_p$

s_i^2 = Sample variance for sample i

$\bar{s}^2$ = Average of the p sample variances = $(\Sigma\, s_i^2)/p$

$\ln x$ = Natural logarithm (i.e., log to the base e) of the quantity x

Test statistic (unequal sample sizes):

$$B = \frac{[\Sigma(n_i - 1)]\ln \bar{s}^2 - \Sigma(n_i - 1)\ln s_i^2}{1 + \dfrac{1}{3(p-1)}\left\{\Sigma \dfrac{1}{(n_i - 1)} - \dfrac{1}{\Sigma\,(n_i - 1)}\right\}}$$

where

n_i = Sample size for sample i

s_i^2 = Sample variance for sample i

$\bar{s}^2$ = Weighted average of the p sample variances = $\dfrac{\Sigma\,(n_i - 1)\, s_i^2}{\Sigma\,(n_i - 1)}$

$\ln x$ = Natural logarithm (i.e., log to the base e) of the quantity x

Rejection region: $B > \chi_\alpha^2$, where χ_α^2, locates an area α in the upper tail of a χ^2 distribution with $(p - 1)$ degrees of freedom

Assumptions:
1. Independent random samples are selected from the p populations.
2. All p populations are normally distributed.

$$B = \frac{(n-1)[p \ln \bar{s}^2 - \Sigma \ln s_i^2]}{1 + \left(\dfrac{p+1}{3p(n-1)}\right)}$$

To obtain B, we first compute the sample variances, s_L^2, s_M^2, and s_U^2, and their average, $\bar{s}^2$. The sample variances, shown (shaded) on the SAS printout displayed in Figure 11.25, are $s_L^2 = .254$, $s_M^2 = .124$, and $s_U^2 = .407$. Then, the average sample variance is $\bar{s}^2 = (.254 + .124 + .407)/3 = .262$. Substituting these values into the formula, we obtain

$$B = \frac{(7-1)\{3 \ln(.262) - [\ln(.254) + \ln(.124) + \ln(.407)]\}}{1 + \dfrac{(3+1)}{3(3)(7-1)}} = 1.89$$

FIGURE 11.25
SAS descriptive statistics for residuals of Example 11.4

```
Analysis Variable : RESID

-------------------------------- CLASS=LOWER --------------------------------

N Obs          Mean       Variance        Std Dev
--------------------------------------------------
    7  9.516197E-17      0.2541143      0.5040975
--------------------------------------------------

-------------------------------- CLASS=MIDDLE -------------------------------

N Obs          Mean       Variance        Std Dev
--------------------------------------------------
    7  -1.26883E-16      0.1243476      0.3526296
--------------------------------------------------

-------------------------------- CLASS=UPPER --------------------------------

N Obs          Mean       Variance        Std Dev
--------------------------------------------------
    7  -2.85486E-16      0.4067238      0.6377490
--------------------------------------------------
```

Since this value is less than the critical value, $\chi^2_{.05} = 5.99147$ (based on $p - 1 = 2$ degrees of freedom), we fail to reject the null hypothesis of equal variances; there is insufficient evidence (at $\alpha = .05$) of differences among the variances in GPA for the three socioeconomic classes. This result supports the conclusion we derived from the residual frequency plots of Figure 11.24.

Bartlett's test works well when the data come from normal (or near normal) distributions. The results, however, can be misleading for nonnormal data. In this case, we can apply a test that is much less sensitive to nonnormality in the data. See the references at the end of this chapter for more information on alternative tests.

3. When unequal variances are detected, use one of the **variance-stabilizing transformations** of the response y discussed in Section 7.3.

In most applications, the assumptions will not be satisfied exactly. These analysis of variance procedures are flexible, however, in the sense that slight departures from the assumptions will not significantly affect the analysis or the validity of the resulting inferences. On the other hand, gross violations of the assumptions (e.g., a nonconstant variance) will cast doubt on the validity of the inferences. Therefore, you should make it standard practice to conduct an analysis of the residuals from the ANOVA using the techniques of Chapter 7 to verify that the assumptions are (approximately) satisfied.

EXERCISES

[*Note:* These exercises require the use of a computer to calculate and plot residuals.]

11.61 Check the assumptions for the completely randomized design ANOVA of Exercise 11.10.

11.62 Check the assumptions for the completely randomized design ANOVA of Exercise 11.11.

11.63 Check the assumptions for the randomized block design ANOVA of Exercise 11.21.

11.64 Check the assumptions for the factorial design ANOVA of Exercise 11.36.

11.65 Check the assumptions for the factorial design ANOVA of Exercise 11.39.

Summary

In this chapter, we demonstrated how to analyze data collected from a designed experiment using either regression analysis or **analysis of variance (ANOVA)**. An analysis of variance partitions the total sum of squares, SS(Total), into SSE and, depending on the design, sums of squares for treatments (SST), blocks (SSB), and factor main effects and interaction. Tests for treatment means, block means, factor interactions, and so forth are obtained by calculating the ratio of the appropriate mean square to MSE and conducting an F test. These F tests can also be conducted by fitting the appropriate linear models to the data using regression. The models differ depending on the specific design employed.

Throughout this chapter we showed that an ANOVA and a regression analysis yield equivalent results. But an analysis of variance possesses both advantages and disadvantages compared with a regression analysis. One major advantage of an analysis of variance is that it is easy to perform on a pocket or desk calculator. Second, when y is affected by more than one source of random variation, an analysis of variance permits us to separate these sources and to estimate the variances of their respective random components. (A discussion of these models is not included in this text.) The disadvantages are its restrictions and limitations, as follows:

1. **The set of analysis of variance formulas appropriate for a particular experimental design applies only to that design.** If the data collected are observational (i.e., the independent variables are uncontrolled), an analysis of variance is inappropriate. No deviations from the design are permitted. Consequently, the method is of value only for special types of designed experiments.
2. **In contrast to a regression analysis, the analysis of variance formulas change from one design to another.** (There is a pattern, as indicated in Section 11.3, but the pattern is usually not apparent to a beginner.)

3. **The ANOVA formulas for a factorial experiment and many other experimental designs can be used only when the sample sizes are equal.** However, the regression approach applies to both equal and unequal sample sizes for the various factor level combinations.
4. **An analysis of variance does not give you a prediction equation.** This is a great handicap when one (or more) of the independent variables is quantitative.
5. **Although a linear model is always implied in an analysis of variance, it is rarely presented or discussed when analyses of data have been performed.** Consequently, the thrust of an analysis of variance is often counter (although it need not be) to the notion of modeling, which is the modern quantitative way of analyzing real-world phenomena.

In conclusion, perhaps the most important point for you to note in this chapter is the following: **If your data can be modeled using a linear model that contains a single random error component (which is the model used throughout this text), then a regression analysis can do everything that an analysis of variance can do and it can do more!** But you will probably need a computer to do it. Regression analysis is simple, it uses the same formulas for all analyses, it is programmed for both mainframe and personal computers, and it can be used to analyze data obtained from both designed and undesigned experiments. Consequently, a beginner may be advised to stick to regression analyses for analyzing the relationship between a set of independent variables and a response y if a computer is available to perform the computations.

SUPPLEMENTARY EXERCISES

[*Note:* Exercises marked with an asterisk(*) are from the optional sections in this chapter.]

11.66 Each year *Business Week* reports the total cash compensations (salary plus bonus) for the top corporate executives. The data in the accompanying table (in thousands of dollars) were extracted from *Business Week*'s 1990 Executive Compensation Scoreboard. To compare the mean cash compensation, $E(y)$, of executives in the four groups, the following model was fitted to the data:

$$E(y) = \beta_0 + \beta_1 x_1 + \beta_2 x_2 + \beta_3 x_3$$

where

$$x_1 = \begin{cases} 1 & \text{if consumer products} \\ 0 & \text{if not} \end{cases} \qquad x_2 = \begin{cases} 1 & \text{if utilities} \\ 0 & \text{if not} \end{cases}$$

$$x_3 = \begin{cases} 1 & \text{if industrial–high tech} \\ 0 & \text{if not} \end{cases}$$

Base level = financial services

The MINITAB printout is also presented here.

CONSUMER PRODUCTS	UTILITIES	INDUSTRIAL–HIGH TECH	FINANCIAL SERVICES
1,567	1,862	2,925	3,125
3,313	1,390	3,409	4,143
2,058	1,115	1,767	4,013
25,216	1,105	4,097	6,583
4,634	1,272	3,196	3,169
5,214	2,849	4,042	5,217
20,795	1,732	2,601	3,447
9,162	1,474	8,286	4,469

Source: "Executive compensation scoreboard." *Business Week*, May 3, 1990, pp. 65–108.

```
The regression equation is
Y = 4271 + 4724 X1 - 2671 X2 - 480 X3

Predictor        Coef       Stdev     t-ratio        p
Constant         4271        1651        2.59    0.015
X1               4724        2334        2.02    0.053
X2              -2671        2334       -1.14    0.262
X3               -480        2334       -0.21    0.838

s = 4669         R-sq = 27.6%      R-sq(adj) = 19.8%

Analysis of Variance

SOURCE        DF          SS           MS          F        p
Regression     3   232505648     77501880       3.56    0.027
Error         28   610272512     21795446
Total         31   842778176

SOURCE        DF      SEQ SS
X1             1   200071984
X2             1    31510622
X3             1      923041

Unusual Observations
Obs.      X1          Y        Fit  Stdev.Fit  Residual   St.Resid
  4     1.00      25216       8995       1651     16221      3.71R
  7     1.00      20795       8995       1651     11800      2.70R

R denotes an obs. with a large st. resid.
```

a. Is there sufficient evidence to indicate that the model is useful for predicting cash compensation? Test using $\alpha = .01$.

b. What does the result from part a imply about the mean cash compensation for the four groups of executives?

c. Conduct a follow-up analysis to compare the means of the four groups of executives. Use $\alpha = .05$.

d. Check whether the assumptions required for the ANOVA are valid.

11.67 A recent supermarket advertisement states: "Winn Dixie offers you the lowest total food bill! Here's the proof!" The "proof" (shown in the table on page 680) is a side-by-side listing of the prices of 60 grocery items purchased at Winn Dixie and two other supermarkets, Publix and Kash 'N Karry, on the same day. The SAS printout of the ANOVA is also shown on page 680.

ITEM	WINN-DIXIE	PUBLIX	KASH N' KARRY	ITEM	WINN-DIXIE	PUBLIX	KASH N' KARRY
Big Thirst Towel	1.21	1.49	1.59	Keb Graham Crust	.79	1.29	1.28
Camp Crm/Broccoli	.55	.67	.67	Spiffits Glass	1.98	2.19	2.59
Royal Oak Charcoal	2.99	3.59	3.39	Prog Lentil Soup	.79	1.13	1.12
Combo Chdr/Chz Snk	1.29	1.29	1.39	Lipton Tea Bags	2.07	2.17	2.17
Sure Sak Trash Bag	1.29	1.79	1.89	Carnation Hot Coco	1.59	1.89	1.99
Dow Handi Wrap	1.59	2.39	2.29	Crystal Hot Sauce	.70	.87	.89
White Rain Shampoo	.96	.97	1.39	C/F/N/ Coffee Bag	1.17	1.15	1.55
Post Golden Crisp	2.78	2.99	3.35	Soup Start Bf Veg	1.39	2.03	1.94
Surf Detergent	2.29	1.89	1.89	Camp Pork & Beans	.44	.49	.58
Sacramento T/Juice	.79	.89	.99	Sunsweet Pit Prune	.98	1.33	1.10
SS Prune Juice	1.36	1.61	1.48	DM Vgcls Grdn Duet	1.07	1.13	1.29
V-8 Cocktail	1.18	1.29	1.28	Argo Corn Starch	.69	.89	.79
Rodd Kosher Dill	1.39	1.79	1.79	Sno Drop Bowl Clnr	.53	1.15	.99
Bisquick	2.09	2.19	2.09	Cadbury Milk Choc	.79	1.29	1.28
Kraft Italian Drs	.99	1.19	1.00	Andes Crm/De Ment	1.09	1.30	1.09
BC Hamburger Helper	1.46	1.75	1.75	Combat Ant & Roach	2.33	2.39	2.79
Comstock Chrry Pie	1.29	1.69	1.69	Joan/Arc Kid Bean	.45	.56	.38
Dawn Liquid King	2.59	2.29	2.58	La Vic Salsa Pican	1.22	1.75	1.49
DelMonte Ketchup	1.05	1.25	.59	Moist N Beef/Chz	2.39	3.19	2.99
Silver Floss Kraut	.77	.81	.69	Ortega Taco Shells	1.08	1.33	1.09
Trop Twist Beverag	1.74	2.15	2.25	Fresh Step Cat Lit	3.58	3.79	3.81
Purina Kitten Chow	1.09	1.05	1.29	Field Trial Dg/Fd	3.49	3.79	3.49
Niag Spray Starch	.89	.99	1.39	Tylenol Tablets	5.98	5.29	5.98
Soft Soap Country	.97	1.19	1.19	Rolaids Tablets	1.88	2.20	2.49
Northwood Syrup	1.13	1.37	1.37	Plax Rinse	2.88	3.14	2.53
Bumble Bee Tuna	.58	.65	.65	Correctol Laxative	3.44	3.98	3.59
Mueller Elbow/Mac	2.09	2.69	2.69	Tch Scnt Potpourri	1.50	1.89	1.89
Kell Nut Honey Crn	2.95	3.25	3.23	Chld Enema 2.250	.98	1.15	1.19
Cutter Spray	3.09	3.95	3.69	Gillette Atra Plus	5.00	5.24	5.59
Lawry Season Salt	2.28	2.97	2.85	Colgate Shave	.94	1.10	1.19

SAS printout for Exercise 11.67

```
                        Analysis of Variance Procedure

Dependent Variable: PRICE
                                        Sum of            Mean
Source                      DF         Squares          Square    F Value      Pr > F

Model                       61     218.2361989       3.5776426     106.27      0.0001
Error                      118       3.9725322       0.0336655
Corrected Total            179     222.2087311

                      R-Square            C.V.        Root MSE             PRICE Mean

                      0.982123        9.989324        0.183482             1.83677778


Source                      DF         Anova SS     Mean Square   F Value      Pr > F

SUPERMKT                     2        2.6412678       1.3206339     39.23      0.0001
ITEM                        59      215.5949311       3.6541514    108.54      0.0001

                Level of          ------------PRICE------------
                SUPERMKT    N          Mean               SD

                KNKarry    60     1.92533333       1.14118503
                Publix     60     1.91950000       1.10339142
                WinnDix    60     1.66550000       1.09622376
```

a. Suppose we want to use the data to compare the mean prices of grocery items at the three supermarkets. Identify the treatments for this design.
b. Give the complete model appropriate for analyzing the data.
c. Give the reduced model for testing for differences among the mean prices at the three supermarkets.
d. Fit the two models, parts **b** and **c**. Conduct the test for treatments.
e. Use the information in the SAS printout to construct an ANOVA table for the data. Verify that the F value on the printout agrees with the F value computed in part **d**.
f. Test to determine whether blocking on grocery items was effective in reducing an extraneous source of variation.
g. Use Tukey's multiple comparisons procedure to compare the mean prices of grocery items for the three supermarkets. Identify the means that appear to differ. Use $\alpha = .01$.

11.68 In social psychology, researchers have found that, under certain circumstances, a less credible source can have a higher impact on positive attitude change than a highly credible source. Does this phenomenon exist in a personal selling situation? The *Journal of Personal Selling & Sales Management* (Fall 1990) reported on a study to examine the effects of salesperson credibility on buyer persuasion. The experiment involved two factors, each at two levels: brand quality (high versus low) and salesperson credibility (high versus low). Each of 64 undergraduate students was randomly assigned to one of the $2 \times 2 = 4$ experimental treatments (8 students per treatment). After viewing a presentation on laptop computers, the students' intentions to buy were measured with a questionnaire.

*a. Treating intention to buy as the dependent variable, write the appropriate model for this experiment.
b. A portion of the ANOVA table for this experiment is shown here. Interpret the results.

SOURCE OF VARIATION	df	SS	MS	F	p-VALUE
Brand quality (A)	1	59.30	59.30	39.74	.001
Salesperson credibility (B)	1	3.51	3.51	2.35	.130
$A \times B$	1	15.13	15.13	10.14	.002

Source: Sharma, A. "The persuasive effect of salesperson credibility: Conceptual and empirical examination." *Journal of Personal Selling & Sales Management*, Fall 1990, Vol. 10, pp. 71–80 (Table 2).

11.69 A fast-food chain that specializes in Mexican food (tacos, burritos, etc.) is opening a new franchise in a university town. An important consideration in determining where the franchise will be located is traffic density. Five possible locations (each near a major intersection) are under consideration by the chain. To compare the average density of traffic at the possible sites, company employees are placed at each of the five locations to count the number of cars passing each location daily for a period of 10 randomly selected days. (At location IV, the counter assigned to record traffic density became ill and could obtain data for only eight of the days.) The results are listed in the table on page 682. Assuming the samples of days were independently selected, conduct a complete analysis of the data using an available statistical software package.

LOCATION				
I	II	III	IV	V
344	412	237	518	367
382	441	390	501	445
353	607	365	577	480
395	531	355	642	323
207	486	217	489	366
312	508	268	475	325
407	337	117	532	316
421	419	273	540	381
366	499	288		407
222	387	351		339

11.70 A nuclear power plant, which uses water from the surrounding bay for cooling its condensers, is required by the Environmental Protection Agency (EPA) to determine whether discharging its heated water into the bay has a detrimental effect on the plant life in the water. The EPA requests that the power plant investigate three strategically chosen locations, called *stations*. Stations 1 and 2 are located near the plant's discharge tubes, whereas station 3 is located farther out in the bay. During one randomly selected day in each of six months, a diver descends to each of the stations, randomly samples a square meter area of the bottom, and counts the number of blades of the different types of grasses present. The results for one important grass type are listed in the table.

MONTH	STATION		
	1	2	3
April	32	40	30
May	28	31	53
June	25	22	61
July	37	30	56
August	20	26	48
September	18	21	30

The goal of the study is to determine whether the mean number of blades found per square meter per month differs for at least two of the three stations. Use an available statistical software package to conduct an ANOVA of the data.

11.71 Refer to the *Industrial Marketing Management* (1993) study of humor in trade magazine advertisements, Exercise 1.20. A sample of 665 ads were categorized according to nationality (U.S., British, or German) and industry (29 categories, ranging from accounting to travel). Then a panel of judges determined the degree of humor in each ad using a 5-point scale (where 1 = not at all humorous and 5 = very humorous). The data were analyzed using a 3×29 factorial ANOVA, where the factors were nationality (at 3 levels) and industry (at 29 levels). The results of the ANOVA are reported in the accompanying table.*

*As a result of missing data, the number of degrees of freedom for Nationality × Industry interaction is less than $2 \times 28 = 56$.

SOURCE	df	SS	MS	F	p-VALUE
Nationality (N)	2	1.44	.72	2.40	.087
Industry (I)	28	48.00	1.71	5.72	.000
$N \times I$	49	20.28	.41	1.38	.046

Source: McCullough, L. S., and Taylor, R. K. "Humor in American, British, and German ads." *Industrial Marketing Management*, Vol. 22, 1993, p. 21 (Table 1).

a. Using $\alpha = .05$, interpret the ANOVA results. Comment on the order in which the ANOVA F tests should be conducted and whether any of the tests should be ignored.

b. According to the researchers, "British ads were more likely to be humorous than German or U.S. ads in the Graphics industry. German ads were least humorous in the Grocery and Mining industries, but funnier than U.S. ads in the Medical industry and funnier than British ads in the Packaging industry." Do these inferences agree or conflict with the conclusions reached in part **a**? Explain.

11.72 Patients recovering from myocardial infarctions (i.e., heart attacks) and other cardiovascular diseases frequently undergo cardiac rehabilitation during their hospital stay. The rehabilitation usually involves supervised low-intensity exercise. A clinical trial was conducted to study the physiological effects on patients of five active exercises used in the earliest stages of cardiac rehabilitation (*Physical Therapy*, Aug. 1986). Twelve healthy female physical therapy students participated in the study, performing each of the five exercises (exercises A, B, C, D, E) in a randomized order. Thus, the experiment was set up as a randomized block design, with the subjects representing the blocks and the exercises the treatments. After each exercise set, the subject's heart rate (in beats per minute) was recorded. The results of the ANOVA on heart rate are summarized in the table. [*Note:* In addition to the five exercises, the heart rate was also measured when the students were at rest. Thus, the experiment involves a total of six treatments: rest and the five exercises.] Interpret the results.

SOURCE	df	SS	MS	F
Exercises	5	873	174.60	30.21
Subjects	11	3,963	360.27	62.33
Error	55	318	5.78	
Total	71	5,154		

Source: Dehne, P. R., and Protas, E. J. "Oxygen consumption and heart rate responses during five exercises." *Physical Therapy*, Vol. 66, No. 8, Aug. 1986, pp. 1215–1219 (Table 2). Reprinted with the permission of the American Physical Therapy Association.

11.73 Refer to the *Physical Therapy* study of heart rates after exercise in Exercise 11.72. A follow-up analysis using Tukey's multiple comparisons procedure was conducted on the six treatment means. The ranked treatment means are listed here, with overbars connecting the means that are not significantly different at $\alpha = .02$. Interpret the results.

Mean heart rate (beats per minute)	61	62	66	68	69	69
Treatment	Rest	A	B	C	D	E

11.74 A company conducted an experiment to determine the effects of three types of incentive pay plans on worker productivity for both union and non-union workers. The company used plants in adjacent towns; one was unionized and the other was not. One-third of the production workers in each plant were assigned to each incentive plan. Then six workers were randomly selected from each group, and their productivity (in number of items produced) was measured for a 1-week period. The six productivity measures for the 2 × 3 factor combinations are listed in the accompanying table. Conduct the analysis for the company using an available statistical software package.

		INCENTIVE PLAN					
		A		B		C	
UNION AFFILIATION	Union	337	328	346	373	317	341
		362	319	351	338	335	329
		305	344	355	365	310	315
	Nonunion	359	346	371	377	350	336
		345	396	352	401	349	351
		381	373	399	378	374	340

11.75 The steam explosion of peat yields fermentable carbohydrates that have a number of potentially important industrial uses. A study of the steam explosion process was initiated to determine the optimum conditions for the release of fermentable carbohydrate (*Biotechnology and Bioengineering*, Feb. 1986). Triplicate samples of peat were treated for .5, 1.0, 2.0, 3.0, and 5.0 minutes at 170°, 200°, and 215°C, in the steam explosion process. Thus, the experiment consists of two factors—temperature at three levels and treatment time at five levels. The accompanying table gives the percentage of carbohydrate solubilized for each of the 3 × 5 = 15 peat samples.

TEMPERATURE °C	TIME minutes	CARBOHYDRATE SOLUBILIZED %
170	.5	1.3
170	1.0	1.8
170	2.0	3.2
170	3.0	4.9
170	5.0	11.7
200	.5	9.2
200	1.0	17.3
200	2.0	18.1
200	3.0	18.1
200	5.0	18.8
215	.5	12.4
215	1.0	20.4
215	2.0	17.3
215	3.0	16.0
215	5.0	15.3

Source: Forsberg, C. W., et al. "The release of fermentable carbohydrate from peat by steam explosion and its use in the microbial production of solvents." *Biotechnology and Bioengineering*, Vol. 28, No. 2, Feb. 1986, p. 179 (Table 1). Copyright 1986.

a. What type of experimental design was used?
b. Explain why the traditional analysis of variance formulas are inappropriate for the analysis of these data.
c. Write a second-order model relating mean amount of carbohydrate solubilized, $E(y)$, to temperature (x_1) and time (x_2).
d. Explain how you could test the hypothesis that the two factors, temperature (x_1) and time (x_2), interact.
e. If you have access to a statistical software package, fit the model and perform the test for interaction.

11.76 In the late 1970s and 1980s, environmental scientists hypothesized that *acid rain* could be a serious environmental problem. It is formed by the combination of water vapor in clouds with nitrous oxide and sulfur dioxide, which are among the emissions products of coal and oil combustion. The pH of rain in central and northern Florida consistently ranges from 4.5 to 5, indicating an acidic condition. (On the 14-point pH scale, any value below 7 is considered acidic, whereas values above 7 are considered alkaline.) To determine the effects of acid rain on soil pH in a natural ecosystem, engineers at the University of Florida's Institute of Food and Agricultural Sciences irrigated experimental plots near Gainesville, Florida, with rainwater at two pH levels, 3.7 and 4.5. The acidity of the soil was then measured at three different depths, 0–15, 15–30, and 30–46 centimeters. Tests were conducted during three different time periods. The resulting soil pH values are shown in the table.

		APRIL 3 ACID RAIN pH		JUNE 16 ACID RAIN pH		JUNE 30 ACID RAIN pH	
		3.7	4.5	3.7	4.5	3.7	4.5
SOIL DEPTH, cm	0–15	5.33	5.33	5.47	5.47	5.20	5.13
	15–30	5.27	5.03	5.50	5.53	5.33	5.20
	30–46	5.37	5.40	5.80	5.60	5.33	5.17

Source: "Acid rain linked to growth of coal-fired power." *Florida Agricultural Research*, 83, Vol. 2, No. 1, Winter 1983.

Suppose we treat the experiment as a 2 × 3 factorial laid out in three blocks, where the factors are acid rain at two pH levels and soil depth at three levels, and the blocks are the three time periods. The SAS printout for the analysis of variance is provided here.

```
                    Analysis of Variance Procedure

Dependent Variable: SOILPH
                                   Sum of            Mean
Source                   DF       Squares          Square    F Value      Pr > F

Model                     7    0.48685556      0.06955079       6.99      0.0034
Error                    10    0.09952222      0.00995222
Corrected Total          17    0.58637778

                   R-Square          C.V.        Root MSE           SOILPH Mean

                   0.830276      1.861595       0.0997608             5.35888889


Source                   DF      Anova SS     Mean Square    F Value      Pr > F

DEPTH                     2    0.06714444      0.03357222       3.37      0.0759
RAINPH                    1    0.03042222      0.03042222       3.06      0.1110
RAINPH*DEPTH              2    0.00781111      0.00390556       0.39      0.6854
DATE                      2    0.38147778      0.19073889      19.17      0.0004
```

a. Is there evidence of an interaction between pH level of acid rain and soil depth? Test using $\alpha = .05$.
b. Conduct a test to determine whether blocking over time was effective in removing an extraneous source of variation. Use $\alpha = .05$.

11.77 How likely is a firm to hire a disabled, but rehabilitated, worker? Billions of dollars are spent annually in the United States on training disabled persons for the workplace, yet only 25% of all disabled people served by vocational rehabilitation are gainfully employed. A study reported in the *Journal of Rehabilitation* (Apr./May/June 1986) investigated the low placement of disabled persons in the work force. Each employer in a sample of 124 companies located in central Kentucky was asked to rate the employability of an individual with a physical handicap in his or her company, using a 5-point scale (1 = cannot accommodate, 5 = can accommodate quite easily). One goal of the study was to determine whether company size (measured by the number of employees) affects the employability ratings of disabled people. To accomplish this, the companies were divided into three groups according to size—small (1–15 employees), medium (16–55 employees), and large (over 55 employees)—and the mean employability ratings compared.

a. Give the appropriate linear model for this study.
b. Give the appropriate null and alternative hypotheses for this study.
c. A partial ANOVA table for the data is shown here. Complete the table.

SOURCE	df	SS	MS	F
Company size	_____	_____	_____	4.93
Error	_____	190	_____	
Total	123			

Source: Combs, I. H., and Omvig, C. P. "Accommodation of disabled people into employment: Perceptions of employers." *Journal of Rehabilitation*, Vol. 52, No. 2, Apr./May/June 1986, pp. 42–45.

d. Is there sufficient evidence to indicate that the mean employability ratings of physically handicapped persons differ among the three groups? Test using $\alpha = .05$.

11.78 Refer to the *American Journal of Psychology* 4×2 factorial experiment, Exercise 11.31. Recall that group was the only significant factor. The mean proportions of ideas recalled correctly for the four groups were compared with a multiple comparisons procedure (at $\alpha = .05$) with the results shown here. Interpret the results.

Mean	.252	.361	.379	.589
Group	LD-Low SES	ND-Low SES	LD-High SES	ND-High SES

11.79 The traditional retail store audit is one of the most widely used marketing research tools among consumer package goods companies. It involves periodic audits of a sample of retail outlets to monitor inventory and purchases of a particular product. V. K. Prasad, W. R. Casper, and R. J. Schieffer conducted a study to compare market data yielded by retail store audits with alternative, less costly auditing procedures—weekend selldown audits and store purchases audits (*Journal of Marketing*, Winter 1984). The market shares of six major brands of beer distributed in eastern cities were estimated using each of the three store audit methods. The data are provided in the accompanying table, followed by a MINITAB printout of the analysis of variance.

BRAND	TRADITIONAL STORE AUDIT	WEEKEND SELLDOWN AUDIT	STORE PURCHASES AUDIT
1	18.0	19.0	20.7
2	15.3	17.3	14.0
3	8.9	8.5	10.1
4	6.5	4.9	6.1
5	5.3	6.1	4.6
6	3.4	3.0	3.1

Source: Prasad, V. K., Casper, W. R., and Schieffer, R. J. "Alternatives to the traditional retail store audit: A field study." *Journal of Marketing*, Winter 1984, 48, pp. 54–61. Reprinted by permission of the American Marketing Association.

MINITAB printout for Exercise 11.79

```
ANALYSIS OF VARIANCE   SHARE

SOURCE          DF        SS          MS
METHOD           2      0.19        0.10
BRAND            5    605.70      121.14
ERROR           10     13.05        1.30
TOTAL           17    618.94
```

a. Use the information in the MINITAB printout to construct an ANOVA summary table for the data.
b. Verify the entries in the table, part **a**, using the ANOVA formulas.
c. Is there sufficient evidence to indicate a difference in the mean estimates of beer-brand market shares produced by the three auditing methods? Test using $\alpha = .05$.
d. Estimate the difference between the mean estimates of beer-brand market shares produced by the traditional store audit and the weekend selldown audit using a 95% confidence interval.

11.80 The percentage of water removed from paper as it passes through a dryer depends on the temperature of the dryer and the speed of the paper passing through it. A laboratory experiment was conducted to investigate the relationship between dryer temperature T at three levels (100°, 120°, and 140°F) and exposure time E (which is related to speed) also at three levels (10, 20, and 30 seconds). Four paper specimens were prepared for each of the $3 \times 3 = 9$ conditions. The data (percentage of water removed) are shown in the accompanying table. Carry out a complete analysis of the data using an available statistical software package.

		TEMPERATURE (T)		
		100	120	140
EXPOSURE TIME (E)	10	24 26 21 25	33 33 36 32	45 49 44 45
	20	39 34 37 40	51 50 47 52	67 64 68 65
	30	58 55 56 53	75 71 70 73	89 87 86 83

11.81 Researchers at the University of Iowa conducted a study to evaluate the effectiveness of performance appraisal training in an organizational setting (*Personnel Psychology*, Autumn 1984). Each member of a sample of 345 middle-level managers was randomly assigned to one of three training conditions: no training ($n_1 = 122$), computer-assisted instruction ($n_2 = 135$), and computer-assisted training plus a behavior modeling workshop ($n_3 = 88$). After formal training, the managers were administered a 25-question multiple choice test of managerial knowledge, and the number of correct answers was recorded for each. The data are summarized in the table. Analyze the data for the researchers. [*Hint:* Use the technique outlined in Exercise 11.14.]

TRAINING GROUP	SAMPLE SIZE	SAMPLE MEAN	STANDARD DEVIATION
No training	122	16.75	1.37
Computer-assisted training	135	18.35	1.33
Computer training plus workshop	88	18.88	1.20

Source: Davis, B. L., and Mount, M. K. "Effectiveness of performance appraisal training using computer-assisted instruction and modeling behavior." *Personnel Psychology*, Autumn 1984, Vol. 37, pp. 439–451.

11.82 A production manager who supervises an assembly operation wants to investigate the effect of the incoming rate (parts per minute) x_1 of components and room temperature x_2 on the productivity (number of items produced per minute) y. The component parts approach the worker on a belt and return to the worker if not selected on the first trip past the assembly point. It is thought that an increase in the arrival rate of components has a positive effect on the assembly rate, up to a point, after which increases may annoy the assembler and reduce productivity. Similarly, it is suspected that lowering the room temperature is beneficial to a point, after which reductions may reduce productivity. The experimenter used the same assembly position for each worker. Thirty-two workers were used for the experiment, two each assigned to the 16 factor level combinations of a 4×4 factorial experiment. The data, in parts per minute averaged over a 5-minute period, are shown in the table.

		RATE OF INCOMING COMPONENTS (x_1), parts per minute			
		40	50	60	70
ROOM TEMPERATURE (x_2), °F	65	24.0, 23.8	25.6, 25.4	29.2, 29.4	28.4, 27.6
	70	25.0, 26.0	28.8, 28.8	31.6, 32.0	30.2, 30.0
	75	25.6, 25.0	27.6, 28.0	29.8, 28.6	28.0, 27.0
	80	24.0, 24.6	27.6, 26.2	27.6, 28.6	26.0, 24.4

a. Perform an analysis of variance for the data. Display the computed quantities in an ANOVA table.
b. Write the linear model implied by the analysis of variance. [*Hint:* For a quantitative variable recorded at four levels, main effects include terms for x, x^2, and x^3.]
c. Do the data provide sufficient evidence to indicate differences among the mean responses for the 16 treatments of the 4×4 factorial experiment? Test using $\alpha = .05$.
d. Do the data provide sufficient evidence to indicate an interaction between arrival rate x_1 and room temperature x_2 on worker productivity? Test using $\alpha = .05$.

e. Find the value of R^2 that would be obtained if you were to fit the linear model in part **b** to the data.
f. Explain why a regression analysis would be a useful addition to the inferential methods used in parts **a–e**.

11.83 A second-order model would be a reasonable choice to model the data of Exercise 11.82. To simplify the analysis, we will code the arrival rate and temperature values as follows:

$$x_1 = \frac{\text{Arrival rate} - 55}{5} \qquad x_2 = \frac{\text{Temperature} - 72.5}{2.5}$$

A printout of the SAS regression analysis is shown here.

ANALYSIS OF VARIANCE

SOURCE	DF	SUM OF SQUARES	MEAN SQUARE	F VALUE	PROB>F
MODEL	5	130.80680	26.16136000	27.726	0.0001
ERROR	26	24.53320000	0.94358462		
C TOTAL	31	155.34000			

ROOT MSE	0.9713828	R-SQUARE	0.8421
DEP MEAN	27.325	ADJ R-SQ	0.8117
C.V.	3.554923		

PARAMETER ESTIMATES

VARIABLE	DF	PARAMETER ESTIMATE	STANDARD ERROR	T FOR H0: PARAMETER=0	PROB > |T|
INTERCEP	1	29.85625000	0.34876060	85.607	0.0001
X1	1	0.56000000	0.07679456	7.292	0.0001
X2	1	-0.16250000	0.07679456	-2.116	0.0441
X1X2	1	-0.11350000	0.03434357	-3.305	0.0028
X1X1	1	-0.27500000	0.04292946	-6.406	0.0001
X2X2	1	-0.23125000	0.04292946	-5.387	0.0001

a. Write the second-order model for the response. Note the difference between this model and the ANOVA model in Exercise 11.82, part **a**.
b. Give the prediction relating the response y to the coded independent variables x_1 and x_2.
c. Why does the SSE given in the computer printout differ from the SSE obtained in Exercise 11.82?
d. Find the value of R^2 appropriate for your second-order model and interpret its value.
e. Do the data provide sufficient evidence to indicate that the complete factorial model provides more information for predicting y than a second-order model?

*11.84 Suppose you want to investigate the effect of two factors—arrival rate of product components, A, and temperature of the room, T—on the length of time, y, required by individual workers to perform a product assembly operation. Each factor will be held at two levels: arrival rate at .5 and 1.0 component per second, and temperature at 70° and 80°F. Thus, a 2×2 factorial experiment will be employed. To block out worker-to-worker variability, each of 10 randomly selected workers will be required to assemble the product under all four experimental conditions. Therefore, the four treatments (working conditions) will be assigned to the experimental units (workers) using a randomized block design, where the workers represent the blocks. The appropriate complete model for the randomized block design is

$$\textit{Complete model:}\quad E(y) = \beta_0 + \overbrace{\beta_1x_1 + \beta_2x_2 + \beta_3x_1x_2}^{\text{Treatment effects (main effects and interaction terms for arrival rate and temperature)}}$$

$$+ \overbrace{\beta_4x_3 + \beta_5x_4 + \cdots + \beta_{12}x_{11}}^{\text{Block (worker) effects}}$$

where

x_1 = Arrival rate x_2 = Temperature

$$x_3 = \begin{cases} 1 & \text{if worker 1} \\ 0 & \text{if not} \end{cases}$$

$$x_4 = \begin{cases} 1 & \text{if worker 2} \\ 0 & \text{if not} \end{cases}$$

$$\vdots$$

$$x_{11} = \begin{cases} 1 & \text{if worker 9} \\ 0 & \text{if not} \end{cases}$$

[Note that $x_3 = x_4 = \cdots = x_{11} = 0$ if worker (block) 10 is the assembler.]

The assembly time data for the 2 × 2 factorial experiment with a randomized block design are given in the table. The SAS printouts for the complete model and the reduced model,

$$\textit{Reduced model:}\quad E(y) = \beta_0 + \overbrace{\beta_4x_3 + \beta_5x_4 + \cdots + \beta_{12}x_{11}}^{\text{Workers}}$$

are also provided.

				WORKER									
				1	2	3	4	5	6	7	8	9	10
ROOM TEMPERATURE	70°F	ARRIVAL RATE component per second	.5	1.7	1.3	1.7	2.0	2.0	2.3	2.0	2.8	1.5	1.6
			1.0	.8	.8	1.5	1.2	1.2	1.7	1.1	1.5	.5	1.0
	80°F		.5	1.3	1.5	2.3	1.6	2.2	2.1	1.8	2.4	1.3	1.8
			1.0	1.8	1.5	2.3	2.0	2.7	2.2	2.3	2.6	1.3	1.8

a. Do the data provide sufficient evidence to indicate a difference among the four treatment means?
b. Does the effect of a change in arrival rate on assembly time depend on temperature (i.e., do arrival rate and temperature interact)?
c. Estimate the mean loss (or gain) in assembly time as arrival rate is increased from .5 to 1.0 component per second and temperature is held at 70°F. What inference can you make based on this estimate?

SAS printout: Complete model for Exercise 11.84

ANALYSIS OF VARIANCE

SOURCE	DF	SUM OF SQUARES	MEAN SQUARE	F VALUE	PROB>F
MODEL	12	10.17400000	0.84783333	21.176	0.0001
ERROR	27	1.08100000	0.04003704		
C TOTAL	39	11.25500000			

ROOT MSE	0.2000926	R-SQUARE	0.9040
DEP MEAN	1.725	ADJ R-SQ	0.8613
C.V.	11.59957		

PARAMETER ESTIMATES

VARIABLE	DF	PARAMETER ESTIMATE	STANDARD ERROR	T FOR H0: PARAMETER=0	PROB > |T|
INTERCEP	1	9.75500000	1.50701723	6.473	0.0001
X1	1	-15.24000000	1.90245845	-8.011	0.0001
X2	1	-0.10400000	0.02000926	-5.198	0.0001
X1X2	1	0.19600000	0.02530993	7.744	0.0001
X3	1	-0.15000000	0.14148681	-1.060	0.2985
X4	1	-0.27500000	0.14148681	-1.944	0.0624
X5	1	0.40000000	0.14148681	2.827	0.0087
X6	1	0.15000000	0.14148681	1.060	0.2985
X7	1	0.47500000	0.14148681	3.357	0.0024
X8	1	0.52500000	0.14148681	3.711	0.0010
X9	1	0.25000000	0.14148681	1.767	0.0885
X10	1	0.77500000	0.14148681	5.478	0.0001
X11	1	-0.40000000	0.14148681	-2.827	0.0087

SAS printout: Reduced model for Exercise 11.84

ANALYSIS OF VARIANCE

SOURCE	DF	SUM OF SQUARES	MEAN SQUARE	F VALUE	PROB>F
MODEL	9	5.19500000	0.57722222	2.858	0.0147
ERROR	30	6.06000000	0.20200000		
C TOTAL	39	11.25500000			

ROOT MSE	0.4494441	R-SQUARE	0.4616
DEP MEAN	1.725	ADJ R-SQ	0.3000
C.V.	26.05473		

PARAMETER ESTIMATES

VARIABLE	DF	PARAMETER ESTIMATE	STANDARD ERROR	T FOR H0: PARAMETER=0	PROB > |T|
INTERCEP	1	1.55000000	0.22472205	6.897	0.0001
X3	1	-0.15000000	0.31780497	-0.472	0.6404
X4	1	-0.27500000	0.31780497	-0.865	0.3937
X5	1	0.40000000	0.31780497	1.259	0.2179
X6	1	0.15000000	0.31780497	0.472	0.6404
X7	1	0.47500000	0.31780497	1.495	0.1455
X8	1	0.52500000	0.31780497	1.652	0.1090
X9	1	0.25000000	0.31780497	0.787	0.4377
X10	1	0.77500000	0.31780497	2.439	0.0209
X11	1	-0.40000000	0.31780497	-1.259	0.2179

11.85 Researchers conducted a study to determine what effects contingent and noncontingent pay systems might have on bargaining behavior and outcomes (*Journal of Purchasing and Materials Management*, Summer 1983). They employed a 2 × 2 factorial experiment with two factors (buyer condition and seller condition), each at two levels (contingent and noncontingent reward). A sample of 160 industrial purchasers was randomly divided into two groups of buyers and sellers, with 80 subjects in each group. Each buyer was matched with a seller to form one of 80 different bargaining "dyads." The dyads were then divided equally among the $2 \times 2 = 4$ buyer–seller reward conditions. Thus, 20 bargaining dyads were assigned to each of the four "treatments" of the experiment.

All subjects participated in a game in which the sellers were told they represented an individual who wanted to sell an office building (for no less than $100,000) and buyers were informed they represented an individual interested in purchasing the building (for no more than $150,000). Sellers in the contingent reward group (SC) were told that they would be rewarded in cash in proportion to the final negotiated price, whereas sellers in the noncontingent reward group (SNC) were told they would be paid a fixed fee. Similarly, buyers in the contingent reward group (BC) were led to believe that they would be compensated according to the final price, whereas buyers in the noncontingent reward group (BNC) received a fixed sum regardless of the outcome. One of the key bargaining variables recorded in the experiment was seller's initial offer. The accompanying table gives the means of the seller's initial offer (in thousands of dollars) for each of the four buyer–seller reward conditions.

		BUYER CONDITION	
		Contingent (BC)	Noncontingent (BNC)
SELLER CONDITION	Contingent (SC)	160.3	173.05
	Noncontingent (SNC)	155.5	149.50

Source: McFillen, J. M., Reck, R. R., and Benton, W. C. "An experiment in purchasing negotiations." *Journal of Purchasing and Materials Management*, Summer 1983, Vol. 19, No. 1, pp. 2–8.

a. Construct an ANOVA table for the 2×2 factorial experiment. (For this experiment, $s = \sqrt{\text{MSE}} \approx 21.00$.)
b. Plot the four cell means on the same graph. Does it appear that the two factors, buyer condition and seller condition, interact?
c. Test for interaction between the two factors, buyer condition and seller condition. Use $\alpha = .10$.
d. Give the complete and reduced models appropriate for testing for interaction using the regression approach.
e. Assuming that contingently rewarded sellers open with higher initial offers than noncontingently rewarded sellers, the researchers hypothesized that this difference is due to reward manipulation and therefore that the means for BC/SC and BNC/SC will not differ significantly. Construct a 90% confidence interval for the difference between mean seller's initial offer for the BC/SC and BNC/SC groups. Does the result refute or support the researchers' hypothesis?

11.86 Suppose you plan to investigate the effect of hourly pay rate and length of workday on some measure y of worker productivity. Both pay rate and length of workday will be set at three levels, and y will be observed for all combinations of these factors. Thus, a 3×3 factorial experiment will be employed.

a. Identify the factors and state whether they are quantitative or qualitative.
b. Identify the treatments to be employed in the experiment.
c. Write a complete factorial model for the experiment. [*Hint:* When the factors are quantitative, main effect terms include x and x^2 terms for each factor.]

d. What is the order of the model specified in part c?
e. Suppose you want to fit a second-order model to the data. Give the appropriate model.
f. If you have only one observation for each combination and you fit a complete factorial model to the data, how many degrees of freedom will be available for estimating σ^2?
g. Refer to part f. If you fit a second-order model to the data, how many degrees of freedom will be available for estimating σ^2?
h. Suppose you replicated the experiment and hence obtained two observations for each treatment. How many degrees of freedom would be available for estimating σ^2 if you fit (1) the complete factorial model? (2) a second-order model?
i. Which model—complete factorial or second-order—do you think would be more appropriate for this experiment?
j. Explain how to conduct a test for interaction between pay rate and length of workday using the complete factorial model.
k. Explain how to conduct a test for interaction between pay rate and length of workday using the second-order model.

11.87 The data for the 3 × 3 factorial experiment described in Exercise 11.86 are shown in the accompanying table. The SAS computer printout of the regression analysis for the second-order model is also shown.

		HOURLY PAY RATE (x_1), dollars		
		6.50	7.00	7.50
LENGTH OF WORKDAY (x_2), hours	8	350 377	375 390	402 411
	9	398 386	423 424	434 429
	10	345 351	377 381	394 389

```
                              ANALYSIS OF VARIANCE

                          SUM OF           MEAN
SOURCE        DF         SQUARES          SQUARE          F VALUE        PROB>F

MODEL          5     11355.01389      2271.00278           33.863        0.0001
ERROR         12       804.76389     67.06365741
C TOTAL       17     12159.77778

        ROOT MSE         8.18924        R-SQUARE           0.9338
        DEP MEAN        390.8889        ADJ R-SQ           0.9062
        C.V.             2.09503

                              PARAMETER ESTIMATES

                      PARAMETER          STANDARD        T FOR H0:
VARIABLE    DF         ESTIMATE             ERROR      PARAMETER=0       PROB > |T|

INTERCEP     1     -4026.63889         939.43751           -4.286           0.0011
X1           1       385.08333         235.19426            1.637           0.1275
X1X1         1    -24.66666667       16.37848069           -1.506           0.1579
X2           1       661.58333       84.14751627            7.862           0.0001
X2X2         1    -37.16666667        4.09462017           -9.077           0.0001
X1X2         1      0.25000000        5.79066738            0.043           0.9663
```

a. Do the data provide sufficient evidence to indicate that the model contributes information for the prediction of y?
b. Find R^2 and interpret its meaning.
c. Does a large value for R^2 imply that the second-order model is a good predictor of productivity?
d. If the value for R^2 were small, would this imply that the model is inadequate, i.e., that we need to change the form of the model and/or add other independent variables to the model that may be related to worker productivity?
e. Is there evidence of interaction between the two factors, pay rate and length of workday? Test using $\alpha = .05$.
f. Extract the parameter estimates from the computer printout and give the prediction equation.
g. Graph the predicted productivity $\hat{y}$ as a function of pay rate x_1 for $x_2 = 8$ hours. Then obtain the predicted productivity curves for $x_2 = 9$ and $x_2 = 10$ hours.

*11.88 A $2 \times 2 \times 2 \times 2 = 2^4$ factorial experiment was conducted to investigate the effect of four factors on the light output, y, of flashbulbs. Two observations were taken for each of the factorial treatments. The factors are amount of foil contained in a bulb (100 and 120 milligrams); speed of sealing machine (1.2 and 1.3 revolutions per minute); shift (day or night); and machine operator (A or B). The data for the two replications of the 2^4 factorial experiment are shown in the table, and the SAS computer printout for the regression analysis follows on the opposite page.

		AMOUNT OF FOIL			
		100 milligrams		120 milligrams	
		SPEED OF MACHINE			
		1.2 rpm	1.3 rpm	1.2 rpm	1.3 rpm
DAY SHIFT	Operator B	6; 5	5; 4	16; 14	13; 14
	Operator A	7; 5	6; 5	16; 17	16; 15
NIGHT SHIFT	Operator B	8; 6	7; 5	15; 14	17; 14
	Operator A	5; 4	4; 3	15; 13	13; 14

To simplify computations, we let

$$x_1 = \frac{\text{Amount of foil} - 110}{10} \qquad x_2 = \frac{\text{Speed of machine} - 1.25}{.05}$$

so that x_1 and x_2 will take values -1 and $+1$. Also,

$$x_3 = \begin{cases} -1 & \text{if night shift} \\ 1 & \text{if day shift} \end{cases} \qquad x_4 = \begin{cases} -1 & \text{if machine operator B} \\ 1 & \text{if machine operator A} \end{cases}$$

a. Do the data provide sufficient evidence to indicate that any of the factors contribute information for the prediction of y? Give the results of a statistical test to support your answer.
b. Identify the factors that appear to affect the amount of light y in the flashbulbs.
c. Give the complete factorial model for y.
d. How many degrees of freedom will be available for estimating σ^2?

SAS printout for Exercise 11.88

ANALYSIS OF VARIANCE

SOURCE	DF	SUM OF SQUARES	MEAN SQUARE	F VALUE	PROB>F
MODEL	15	745.46875	49.69791667	40.778	0.0001
ERROR	16	19.50000000	1.21875000		
C TOTAL	31	764.96875			

ROOT MSE	1.10397	R-SQUARE	0.9745
DEP MEAN	10.03125	ADJ R-SQ	0.9506
C.V.	11.00531		

PARAMETER ESTIMATES

VARIABLE	DF	PARAMETER ESTIMATE	STANDARD ERROR	T FOR H0: PARAMETER=0	PROB > |T|
INTERCEP	1	10.03125000	0.19515619	51.401	0.0001
X1	1	4.71875000	0.19515619	24.179	0.0001
X2	1	-0.34375000	0.19515619	-1.761	0.0973
X3	1	0.21875000	0.19515619	1.121	0.2789
X4	1	-0.15625000	0.19515619	-0.801	0.4351
X1X2	1	0.09375000	0.19515619	0.480	0.6375
X1X3	1	0.15625000	0.19515619	0.801	0.4351
X1X4	1	0.28125000	0.19515619	1.441	0.1688
X2X3	1	-0.15625000	0.19515619	-0.801	0.4351
X2X4	1	-0.03125000	0.19515619	-0.160	0.8748
X3X4	1	0.78125000	0.19515619	4.003	0.0010
X1X2X3	1	-0.21875000	0.19515619	-1.121	0.2789
X1X2X4	1	-0.09375000	0.19515619	-0.480	0.6375
X1X3X4	1	-0.03125000	0.19515619	-0.160	0.8748
X2X3X4	1	0.15625000	0.19515619	0.801	0.4351
X1X2X3X4	1	0.09375000	0.19515619	0.480	0.6375

References

Box, G. E. P., Hunter, W. G., and Hunter, J. S. *Statistics for Experimenters*. New York: Wiley, 1978.

Cochran, W. G., and Cox, G. M. *Experimental Designs*, 2nd ed. New York: Wiley, 1957.

Davies, O. L. *The Design and Analysis of Industrial Experiments*. New York: Hafner, 1956.

Kirk, R. E. *Experimental Design: Procedures for the Behavioral Sciences*. Monterey, Calif.: Brooks/Cole, 1968.

Kramer, C. Y. "Extension of multiple range tests to group means with unequal number of replications." *Biometrics*, Vol. 12, 1956, pp. 307–310.

Mendenhall, W. *Introduction to Linear Models and the Design and Analysis of Experiments*. Belmont, Calif.: Wadsworth, 1968.

Miller, R. G. *Simultaneous Statistical Inference*, 2nd ed. New York: Springer-Verlag, 1981.

Neter, J., Wasserman, W., and Kutner, M. H. *Applied Linear Statistical Models*, 3rd ed. Homewood, Ill.: Richard D. Irwin, 1990.

Scheffé, H. "A method for judging all contrasts in the analysis of variance." *Biometrika*, Vol. 40, 1953, pp. 87–104.

Scheffé, H. *The Analysis of Variance*. New York: Wiley, 1959.

Tukey, J. W. "Comparing individual means in the analysis of variance." *Biometrics*, Vol. 5, 1949, pp. 99–114.

Winer, B. J. *Statistical Principles in Experimental Design*. New York: McGraw-Hill, 1962.

CASE STUDY 12

Modeling the Sale Prices of Residential Properties in Four Neighborhoods

CONTENTS

OBJECTIVE

To demonstrate how regression analysis can be used to model and compare the relationship between the sale prices and assessed values of residential properties for four different city neighborhoods

12.1 The Problem

This case study concerns a problem of interest to real estate appraisers, tax assessors, real estate investors, and home buyers—namely, the relationship between the appraised value of a property and its sale price. The sale price for any given property will vary depending on the price set by the seller, the strength of appeal of the property to a specific buyer, and the state of the money and real estate markets. Therefore, we can think of the sale price of a specific property as possessing a relative frequency distribution. The mean of this distribution might be regarded as a measure of the fair value of the property. Presumably, this is the value that a property appraiser or a tax assessor would like to attach to a given property.

The purpose of this case study is to examine the relationship between the mean sale price $E(y)$ of a property and the following independent variables:

1. Appraised land value of the property
2. Appraised value of the improvements on the property
3. Neighborhood in which the property is listed

The objectives of the study are twofold:

1. To determine whether the data indicate that appraised values of land and improvements are related to sale prices. That is, do the data supply sufficient evidence to indicate that these variables contribute information for the prediction of sale price?
2. To acquire the prediction equation relating appraised value of land and improvements to sale price and to determine whether this relationship is the same for a variety of neighborhoods. In other words, do the appraisers use the same appraisal criteria for various types of neighborhoods?

12.2 The Data

The data for the study were supplied by the property appraiser's office of Hillsborough County, Florida, and consist of the appraised land and improvement values and sale prices for residential properties sold in the city of Tampa, Florida, during 1993. Four neighborhoods (Carrollwood Village, Tampa Palms, Town & Country, and Ybor City), each relatively homogeneous but differing sociologically and in property types and values, were identified within the city and surrounding area. The subset of sales and appraisal data pertinent to these four neighborhoods—a total of 448 observations— was used to develop a prediction equation relating sale prices to appraised land and improvement values. The data (recorded in thousands of dollars) are given in Appendix I. For the purpose of this case study, we use the symbols A, B, C, and D to represent the four neighborhoods.

12.3 The Models

If the mean sale price $E(y)$ of a property were, in fact, equal to its appraised value x, the relationship between $E(y)$ and x would be a straight line with slope equal to 1, as shown in Figure 12.1 on page 698. But it is unlikely that this ideal situation will exist. The property appraiser's data could be several years old and consequently may represent (because of inflation) only a percentage of the actual mean sale price. In fact, it is common for realtors and real estate appraisers to

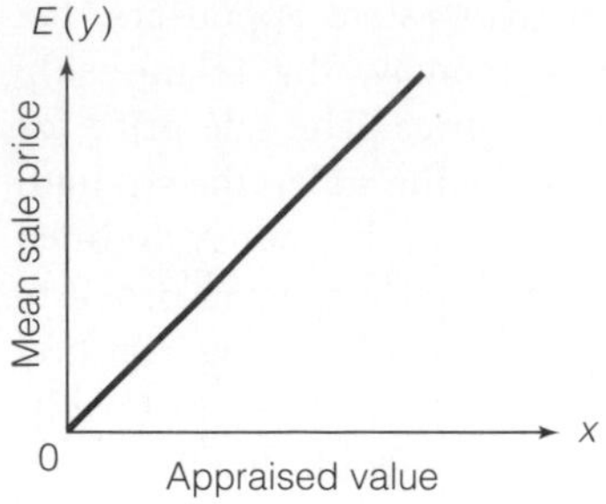

FIGURE 12.1
The theoretical relationship between mean sale price and appraised value x

model the natural logarithm of sales price, $\log(y)$, as a function of appraised value, x. We know (Section 4.9) that the antilogarithm of the slope of the log model represents a percentage change in sale price y for every 1-unit increase in appraised value x. Also, experience has shown that the relationship between $E(y)$ and x is usually not a straight line, but curvilinear. One reason is that appraisers have a tendency to overappraise or underappraise properties in specific price ranges, say, very low-priced or very high-priced properties. Recall (Section 6.7) that modeling $\log(y)$ as a linear function of x introduces a curvilinear relationship between y and x. Consequently, we will use $y^* = \log(y)$ as the dependent variable.

Recall that we want to relate y^* to three independent variables: the qualitative factor, neighborhood (four levels), and the two quantitative factors, appraised land value and appraised improvement value. We consider the following four models as candidates for this relationship.

Model 1

Model 1 is a first-order log model that will trace a response plane for mean log of sale price, $E(y^*)$, as a function of x_1 = appraised land value and x_2 = appraised improvement value. This model will assume that the response planes are identical for all four neighborhoods, i.e., that a first-order log model is appropriate for relating y^* to x_1 and x_2 and that the relationship between the sale price and the appraised value of a property is the same for all neighborhoods. This model is

MODEL 1
First-order log model, identical for all neighborhoods

$$E(y^*) = \beta_0 + \overbrace{\beta_1 x_1}^{\text{Appraised land value}} + \overbrace{\beta_2 x_2}^{\text{Appraised improvement value}}$$

In Model 1, we are assuming that the percentage change in sale price y for every \$1,000 (1-unit) increase in appraised land value x_1 (represented by $e^{\beta_1} - 1$) is constant for a fixed appraised improvements value, x_2. Likewise, the percentage change in y for every \$1,000 increase in x_2 (represented by $e^{\beta_2} - 1$) is constant for fixed x_1.

Model 2

Model 2 will assume that the relationship between $E(y^*)$ and x_1 and x_2 is first-order (a planar response surface), but that the planes' y^*-intercepts differ depending on the neighborhood. This model would be appropriate if the appraiser's procedure for establishing appraised values produced a relationship between mean sale price and x_1 and x_2 that differed in at least two neighborhoods, but the differences remained constant for different values of x_1 and x_2. Model 2 is

MODEL 2
First-order log model, constant differences between neighborhoods

$$E(y^*) = \beta_0 + \overbrace{\beta_1 x_1}^{\text{Appraised land value}} + \overbrace{\beta_2 x_2}^{\text{Appraised improvement value}} + \overbrace{\beta_3 x_3 + \beta_4 x_4 + \beta_5 x_5}^{\text{Main effect terms for neighborhoods}}$$

where

x_1 = Appraised land value

x_2 = Appraised improvement value

$$x_3 = \begin{cases} 1 & \text{if neighborhood A} \\ 0 & \text{if not} \end{cases} \qquad x_4 = \begin{cases} 1 & \text{if neighborhood B} \\ 0 & \text{if not} \end{cases}$$

$$x_5 = \begin{cases} 1 & \text{if neighborhood C} \\ 0 & \text{if not} \end{cases}$$

The fourth neighborhood, neighborhood D, was chosen as the base level. Consequently, the model will predict $E(y^*)$ for neighborhood D when $x_3 = x_4 = x_5 = 0$.

Although it allows for neighborhood differences, Model 2 assumes that percentage change in sale price y for every \$1,000 increase in either x_1 or x_2 does not depend on neighborhood.

Model 3

Model 3 is similar to Model 2 except that we will add interaction terms between the neighborhood dummy variables and x_1 and between the neighborhood dummy variables and x_2. These interaction terms allow the percentage change in y for increases in x_1 or x_2 to vary depending on the neighborhood. The equation of Model 3 is

MODEL 3

First-order log model, no restrictions on neighborhood differences

$$E(y^*) = \beta_0 + \overbrace{\beta_1 x_1}^{\text{Appraised land value}} + \overbrace{\beta_2 x_2}^{\text{Appraised improvement value}}$$

$$+ \overbrace{\beta_3 x_3 + \beta_4 x_4 + \beta_5 x_5}^{\text{Main effect terms for neighborhoods}}$$

$$+ \overbrace{\beta_6 x_1 x_3 + \beta_7 x_1 x_4 + \beta_8 x_1 x_5}^{\text{Interaction, appraised land by neighborhood}}$$

$$+ \overbrace{\beta_9 x_2 x_3 + \beta_{10} x_2 x_4 + \beta_{11} x_2 x_5}^{\text{Interaction, appraised improvement by neighborhood}}$$

Note that for Model 3, the percentage change in sale price y for every \$1,000 increase in appraised land value x_1 (holding x_2 fixed) is $(e^{\beta_1} - 1)$ in neighborhood D and $(e^{\beta_1+\beta_6} - 1)$ in neighborhood A.

Model 4

Model 4 differs from the previous three models by the addition of terms for x_1,x_2-interaction. Thus, Model 4 is a second-order (interaction) model that will trace (geometrically) a second-order response surface, one for each neighborhood. The interaction model follows:

MODEL 4

Interaction model in x_1 and x_2 that differs from one neighborhood to another

$$E(y^*) = \overbrace{\beta_0 + \beta_1 x_1 + \beta_2 x_2 + \beta_3 x_1 x_2}^{\text{Interaction model in } x_1 \text{ and } x_2} + \overbrace{\beta_4 x_3 + \beta_5 x_4 + \beta_6 x_5}^{\text{Main effect terms for neighborhoods}}$$

$$\left.\begin{array}{l} + \beta_7 x_1 x_3 + \beta_8 x_1 x_4 + \beta_9 x_1 x_5 + \beta_{10} x_2 x_3 \\ + \beta_{11} x_2 x_4 + \beta_{12} x_2 x_5 + \beta_{13} x_1 x_2 x_3 \\ + \beta_{14} x_1 x_2 x_4 + \beta_{15} x_1 x_2 x_5 \end{array}\right\} \text{Interaction terms: } x_1, x_2, \text{ and } x_1x_2 \text{ terms by neighborhood}$$

Unlike Models 1–3, Model 4 allows the percentage change in y for increases in x_1 to depend on x_2, and vice versa. For example, the percentage change in sale price for a \$1,000 increase in appraised land value in neighborhood D is $(e^{\beta_1+\beta_3 x_2} - 1)$.

We will fit Models 1–4 to the data. Then, we will compare the models using the partial F test outlined in Section 4.10.

12.4 Model Comparisons

The SAS printouts for Models 1–4 are shown in Figures 12.2, 12.3, 12.4, and 12.5, respectively. Checking these printouts, you will note that the sum of squares for error, the mean square for error, R^2, s, and degrees of freedom for error for each of the four models are as listed in Table 12.1.

TABLE 12.1 **Summary of Regressions of the Models**

MODEL	SSE	MSE	R^2	s	df(Error)
1	91.74	.206	.675	.454	.445
2	35.16	.080	.875	.282	.442
3	27.75	.064	.902	.252	.436
4	26.56	.061	.906	.248	.432

FIGURE 12.2
Model 1: First-order log model in land and improvements appraised values, identical for all neighborhoods

```
Model: MODEL1
Dependent Variable: LNSALES
                          Analysis of Variance

                               Sum of          Mean
   Source           DF        Squares        Square       F Value        Prob>F

   Model             2      190.26816      95.13408       461.442        0.0001
   Error           445       91.74428       0.20617
   C Total         447      282.01244

      Root MSE        0.45406       R-square       0.6747
      Dep Mean        4.35493       Adj R-sq       0.6732
      C.V.           10.42626

                          Parameter Estimates

                   Parameter       Standard      T for H0:
  Variable  DF      Estimate          Error    Parameter=0     Prob > |T|

  INTERCEP   1      3.506587     0.03522502         99.548         0.0001
  LAND       1      0.004877     0.00254387          1.917         0.0559
  IMP        1      0.011885     0.00105968         11.215         0.0001
```

TEST #1
Model 1 versus Model 2

To test the hypothesis that a single first-order log model is appropriate for all neighborhoods, we wish to test the null hypothesis that the neighborhood parameters in Model 2 are all equal to 0, i.e.,

$$H_0: \beta_3 = \beta_4 = \beta_5 = 0$$

FIGURE 12.3
Model 2: First-order log model, constant differences between neighborhoods

```
Model: MODEL2
Dependent Variable: LNSALES

                          Analysis of Variance

                              Sum of         Mean
        Source       DF      Squares       Square      F Value       Prob>F

        Model         5    246.85718     49.37144      620.737       0.0001
        Error       442     35.15526      0.07954
        C Total     447    282.01244

            Root MSE       0.28202     R-square       0.8753
            Dep Mean       4.35493     Adj R-sq       0.8739
            C.V.           6.47595

                          Parameter Estimates

                       Parameter       Standard    T for H0:
      Variable  DF      Estimate          Error   Parameter=0    Prob > |T|

      INTERCEP   1      2.974798     0.03101350        95.919        0.0001
      LAND       1      0.006394     0.00160193         3.992        0.0001
      IMP        1      0.006016     0.00070200         8.569        0.0001
      NA         1      1.158494     0.04566920        25.367        0.0001
      NB         1      1.169420     0.06471783        18.070        0.0001
      NC         1      0.909529     0.04008817        22.688        0.0001

Test: M1_M2     Numerator:      18.8630  DF:     3   F value: 237.1608
                Denominator:   0.079537  DF:   442   Prob>F:    0.0001
```

FIGURE 12.4
Model 3: First-order log model, no restriction on differences between neighborhoods

```
Model: MODEL3
Dependent Variable: LNSALES

                          Analysis of Variance

                              Sum of         Mean
        Source       DF      Squares       Square      F Value       Prob>F

        Model        11    254.25998     23.11454      363.137       0.0001
        Error       436     27.75246      0.06365
        C Total     447    282.01244

            Root MSE       0.25229     R-square       0.9016
            Dep Mean       4.35493     Adj R-sq       0.8991
            C.V.           5.79331

                          Parameter Estimates

                       Parameter       Standard    T for H0:
      Variable  DF      Estimate          Error   Parameter=0    Prob > |T|

      INTERCEP   1      2.665707     0.07548643        35.314        0.0001
      LAND       1      0.028730     0.00815835         3.522        0.0005
      IMP        1      0.014972     0.00322223         4.646        0.0001
      NA         1      1.143270     0.09321119        12.265        0.0001
      NB         1      1.855434     0.10433578        17.783        0.0001
      NC         1      0.909214     0.11365981         7.999        0.0001
      LAND_NA    1     -0.025230     0.00834982        -3.022        0.0027
      LAND_NB    1     -0.024610     0.00883438        -2.786        0.0056
      LAND_NC    1     -0.013588     0.01082764        -1.255        0.2102
      IMP_NA     1     -0.003919     0.00337608        -1.161        0.2463
      IMP_NB     1     -0.011143     0.00344158        -3.238        0.0013
      IMP_NC     1     -0.004542     0.00379759        -1.196        0.2324

Test: M2_M3     Numerator:       1.2338  DF:     6   F value:   19.3834
                Denominator:   0.063652  DF:   436   Prob>F:    0.0001
```

FIGURE 12.5
Model 4: Log model with (land × improvements) interaction, different for all neighborhoods

```
Model: MODEL4
Dependent Variable: LNSALES

                         Analysis of Variance

                          Sum of          Mean
Source          DF       Squares        Square      F Value        Prob>F

Model           15     255.45575      17.03038      277.035        0.0001
Error          432      26.55669       0.06147
C Total        447     282.01244

    Root MSE        0.24794     R-square        0.9058
    Dep Mean        4.35493     Adj R-sq        0.9026
    C.V.            5.69330

                        Parameter Estimates

                     Parameter       Standard      T for H0:
Variable    DF        Estimate          Error    Parameter=0     Prob > |T|

INTERCEP     1        2.472132     0.12987419         19.035         0.0001
LAND         1        0.054449     0.01627497          3.346         0.0009
IMP          1        0.025110     0.00641875          3.912         0.0001
LAND_IMP     1       -0.001275     0.00070213         -1.816         0.0701
NA           1        1.139930     0.16096417          7.082         0.0001
NB           1        1.676795     0.19008650          8.821         0.0001
NC           1        1.037488     0.23533367          4.409         0.0001
LAND_NA      1       -0.042363     0.01672197         -2.533         0.0116
LAND_NB      1       -0.047328     0.01664016         -2.844         0.0047
LAND_NC      1       -0.035276     0.02083240         -1.693         0.0911
IMP_NA       1       -0.012334     0.00653086         -1.889         0.0596
IMP_NB       1       -0.017502     0.00663945         -2.636         0.0087
IMP_NC       1       -0.013238     0.00777765         -1.702         0.0895
L_I_NA       1        0.001205     0.00070269          1.714         0.0872
L_I_NB       1        0.001245     0.00070219          1.773         0.0770
L_I_NC       1        0.001192     0.00073786          1.615         0.1071

Test: M3_M4    Numerator:      0.2989  DF:    4   F value:    4.8629
               Denominator:  0.061474  DF:  432   Prob>F:     0.0008
```

That is, we want to compare the complete model, Model 2, to the reduced model, Model 1. The test statistic is

$$F = \frac{(\text{SSE}_\text{R} - \text{SSE}_C)/\text{Number of } \beta \text{ parameters in } H_0}{\text{MSE}_\text{C}}$$

$$= \frac{(\text{SSE}_1 - \text{SSE}_2)/3}{\text{MSE}_2}$$

where the mean square for the numerator is based on $\nu_1 = 3$ df, and MSE_2, the estimate of σ^2 using Model 2, is based on $\nu_2 = 442$ df. Substituting SSE_1, SSE_2, and MSE_2 into the formula for F, we obtain

$$F = \frac{(\text{SSE}_1 - \text{SSE}_2)/3}{\text{MSE}_2} = \frac{(91.74 - 35.16)/3}{.080} = 237.16$$

The tabulated critical value of F for $\alpha = .01$ and $\nu_1 = 3$ df and $\nu_2 = 442$ df is not shown in Table 6 of Appendix C, but you can see that it is approximately equal to 3.78. Since the computed value of F, 237.16, exceeds this value, we have evidence to indicate that the addition of the neighborhood dummy variables in Model 2 contributes significantly to the prediction of y^*. (Note that the p-value of the test, .0001, is shown at the bottom of the SAS printout, Figure 12.3.) The practical implication of this result is that the appraiser is not assigning appraised values to properties in such a way that the first-order relationship between log(sales), y^*, and appraised values x_1 and x_2 is the same for all neighborhoods.

TEST # 2

Model 2 versus Model 3

Can the prediction equation be improved by the addition of interactions between neighborhood and x_1 and neighborhood and x_2? That is, do the data provide sufficient evidence to indicate that Model 3 is a better predictor of sale price than Model 2? To answer this question, we will test the null hypothesis that the parameters associated with all neighborhood interaction terms in Model 3 equal 0. Thus, Model 2 is now the reduced model and Model 3 is the complete model.

Checking the equation of Model 3, you will see that there are six neighborhood interaction terms and that the parameters included in H_0 will be

$$H_0\colon \quad \beta_6 = \beta_7 = \beta_8 = \beta_9 = \beta_{10} = \beta_{11} = 0$$

To test H_0, we form the test statistics

$$F = \frac{(\text{SSE}_\text{R} - \text{SSE}_\text{C})/\text{Number of } \beta \text{ parameters in } H_0}{\text{MSE}_\text{C}} = \frac{(\text{SSE}_2 - \text{SSE}_3)/6}{\text{MSE}_3}$$

where MSE_3 is the estimate of σ^2 obtained from the complete second-order model (Model 3). Substituting the values of SSE_2, SSE_3, and MSE_3 into the formula for F, we obtain

$$F = \frac{(35.16 - 27.75)/6}{.064} = 19.38$$

The degrees of freedom for F are $\nu_1 = 6$ and $\nu_2 = 436$ (the degrees of freedom for MSE_3 are given on the computer printout, Figure 12.4) and the tabulated F value for $\alpha = .01$ (Table 6 of Appendix C) is approximately 2.80. Since the computed value of F, 19.38, exceeds the critical value, $F_{.01} = 2.80$, there is sufficient evidence to indicate that the neighborhood interaction terms of Model 3 contribute information for the prediction of y^*. (The p-value for this test, .0001, is also given at the bottom of the SAS printout, Figure 12.4.) Practically, this test implies that the rate of change (measured as a percentage) of sale price y with either appraised value, x_1 or x_2, differs for each of the four neighborhoods.

TEST # 3

Model 3 versus Model 4

We have already shown that the first-order prediction equations vary among neighborhoods. To determine whether the (second-order) interaction terms involving the appraised values, x_1 and x_2, contribute significantly to the prediction of y^*, we test the hypothesis that the four parameters involving x_1x_2 in Model 4 all equal 0. The null hypothesis is

$$H_0\colon \quad \beta_3 = \beta_{13} = \beta_{14} = \beta_{15} = 0$$

and the alternative hypothesis is that at least one of these parameters does not equal 0. Using Model 4 as the complete model and Model 3 as the reduced model, the F statistic is

$$F = \frac{(\text{SSE}_{\text{R}} - \text{SSE}_{\text{C}})/\text{Number of } \beta \text{ parameters in } H_0}{\text{MSE}_{\text{C}}} = \frac{(\text{SSE}_3 - \text{SSE}_4)/4}{\text{MSE}_4}$$

$$= \frac{(27.75 - 26.56)/4}{.061} = 4.86$$

Again, the tabulated value of $F_{.01}$ for $\nu_1 = 4$ df and $\nu_2 = 432$ df is not given in the $F_{.01}$ table, but you can see that it is approximately equal to 3.32. The computed F value, 4.86, exceeds this critical value, supporting the alternative hypothesis that the x_1x_2 interaction terms of Model 4 contribute significantly to the prediction of y^*. [*Note:* The p-value of the test, .0008, is shown at the bottom of the SAS printout, Figure 12.5.]

The results of the preceding tests suggest that Model 4 is the best of the four models for modeling sale price y. The global F value for testing

$$H_0\text{:} \quad \beta_1 = \beta_2 = \cdots = \beta_{15} = 0$$

is highly significant ($F = 277.035$, p-value $< .0001$); the R^2 value indicates that the model explains almost 90% of the variability in the log of sale prices. Although a few of the t tests involving the individual β parameters in Model 4 are nonsignificant, this does not imply that these terms should be dropped from the model.

Whenever a model includes a large number of interactions (as in Model 4) and/or squared terms, several t tests will often be nonsignificant even if the global F test is highly significant. This result is due partly to the unavoidable intercorrelations among the main effects for a variable, its interactions, and its squared terms (see the discussion on multicollinearity in Section 6.5). We warned in Chapter 4 of the dangers of conducting a series of t tests to determine model adequacy. For a model with a large number of β's, such as Model 4, you should avoid conducting any t tests at all and rely on the global F test and partial F tests to determine the important terms for predicting y.

12.5 Interpreting the Prediction Equation

Substituting the estimates of the Model 4 parameters (Figure 12.5) into the prediction equation, we have

$$\begin{aligned}\hat{y}^* = {} & 2.4721 + .0544x_1 + .0251x_2 - .00127x_1x_2 + 1.1399x_3 + 1.6768x_4 \\ & + 1.0375x_5 - .0424x_1x_3 - .0473x_1x_4 - .0353x_1x_5 - .0123x_2x_3 \\ & - .0175x_2x_4 - .0132x_2x_5 + .0012x_1x_2x_3 + .00125x_1x_2x_4 \\ & + .0012x_1x_2x_5\end{aligned}$$

We have noted that the model yields four response surfaces, one for each neighborhood. One way to interpret the prediction equation is to first find the equation of the response surface for each neighborhood. Substituting the appropriate values of the neighborhood dummy variables, x_3, x_4, and x_5, into the equation and combining like terms, we obtain the following:

Neighborhood A: $(x_3 = 1, x_4 = x_5 = 0)$

$$\hat{y}^* = (2.4721 + 1.1399) + (.0544 - .0424)x_1 + (.0251 - .0123)x_2 + (-.00127 + .00120)x_1x_2$$
$$= \mathbf{3.612 + .012x_1 + .0128x_2 - .00007x_1x_2}$$

Neighborhood B: $(x_3 = 0, x_4 = 1, x_5 = 0)$

$$\hat{y}^* = (2.4721 + 1.6768) + (.0544 - .0473)x_1 + (.0251 - .0175)x_2 + (-.00127 + .00125)x_1x_2$$
$$= \mathbf{4.1489 + .0071x_1 + .0076x_2 - .00002x_1x_2}$$

Neighborhood C: $(x_3 = x_4 = 0, x_5 = 1)$

$$\hat{y}^* = (2.4721 + 1.0375) + (.0544 - .0353)x_1 + (.0251 - .0132)x_2 + (-.00127 + .00120)x_1x_2$$
$$= \mathbf{3.5096 + .0191x_1 + .0119x_2 - .00007x_1x_2}$$

Neighborhood D: $(x_3 = x_4 = x_5 = 0)$

$$\hat{y}^* = \mathbf{2.4721 + .0544x_1 + .0251x_2 - .00127x_1x_2}$$

Note that each equation is in the form of an interaction model involving appraised land value x_1 and appraised improvements x_2. To interpret the β estimates of each interaction equation, we hold one independent variable fixed, say, x_1, and focus on the slope of the line relating y^* to x_2. For example, holding appraised land value constant at \$10,000 ($x_1 = 10$), the slope of the y^*–x_2 line for neighborhood D is

$$\hat{\beta}_2 + \hat{\beta}_3 x_1 = .0251 - .00127(10) = .0124$$

Since the dependent variable, y^*, is a log of sales price, the antilog of the slope minus 1 represents the percentage change in sale price y. Since $e^{.0234} - 1 = .0125$, for residential properties in neighborhood D with appraised land value of \$10,000, the sale price will increase 1.25% for every \$1,000 increase in appraised improvements.

Similar interpretations can be made for the slopes for other combinations of neighborhoods and appraised land value x_1. The estimated slopes for several of these combinations are computed and shown in Table 12.2.

TABLE 12.2 **Estimated Percentage Increase in Sale Price for \$1,000 Increase in Appraised Improvements**

		NEIGHBORHOOD			
		A	B	C	D
APPRAISED LAND VALUE	\$10,000	1.21	.74	1.12	1.25
	\$15,000	1.18	.73	1.09	.61
	\$20,000	1.14	.72	1.05	.03

Because of the interaction terms in the model, the percentage increases in sale price for a \$1,000 increase in appraised improvements, x_2, differ for each neighborhood and for different levels of land value, x_1.

Some trends are evident from Table 12.2. For fixed appraised land value, x_1, the percentage increase in sales price for every \$1,000 increase in appraised improvements is smallest for neighborhood B. For a given neighborhood, the percentage increase decreases as appraised land value increases.

Another way to describe the prediction equation would be to graph predicted sale price for each neighborhood as a function of appraised improvements value x_2 for different levels of appraised land value x_1. The curves (one curve for each neighborhood) are shown in Figure 12.6 for appraised land value $x_1 = \$10{,}000$. Similar sets of curves are shown in Figures 12.7 and 12.8 (pages 708 and 709) for $x_1 = \$25{,}000$ and \$50,000, respectively.* Note that not all figures have curves corresponding to all four neighborhoods. This is because the appraised land values for sales in some neighborhoods might not have been as low as \$10,000 or as high as \$50,000. Some curves are shortened for similar reasons; i.e., the appraised improvements values for some neighborhoods might not span the range shown on the x_2-axis.

Before we examine the curves in Figures 12.6–12.8, we want some information concerning the nature of the neighborhoods. Figure 12.9 on page 710 gives the means, standard deviations, and other descriptive statistics for the sale price y and the appraised values x_1 and x_2 for each of the four neighborhoods. The mean sale prices confirm what the authors know to be true, i.e., that neighborhoods A and B (Carrollwood Village and Tampa Palms, respectively) are two of the relatively expensive residential areas in the city. Most of the inhabitants are older, established professional or business people. In contrast, neighborhood C (Town & Country) is a less expensive residential area inhabited primarily by young married couples who are starting their careers. Neighborhood D (Ybor City) is considered to be one of the least expensive residential areas in the city and is inhabited by mostly low-income families.

In Figures 12.6–12.8, the estimated mean sale price $\hat{y}$ increases as the appraised improvements value x_2 increases, but the increase is not always linear. The relationship appears to be nearly a straight line for some neighborhoods (for example, neighborhood A) but is curvilinear for other neighborhoods.

There are some other interesting features to note. For example, in Figure 12.7, observe the different predicted sale prices for an appraised improvement value of \$40,000. You can see that properties in neighborhood C (a lower-priced neighborhood) sell at a higher predicted price than those in the more expensive neighborhood A when the appraised land value is low, i.e., $x_1 = \$25{,}000$. This would suggest that the appraised values of properties in this price range in

*The curves for predicted sale price, $\hat{y}$, were obtained as follows: First, the predicted log of sale price, $\hat{y}^*$, was obtained from the fitted regression equation for each combination of x_1, x_2, and neighborhood. Then, antilogs of the predicted log sale price were computed to obtain $\hat{y}$, i.e., $\hat{y} = e^{\hat{y}*}$. The predicted value, $\hat{y}$, was then plotted against x_2 for the different levels of x_1 using neighborhood as a plotting symbol.

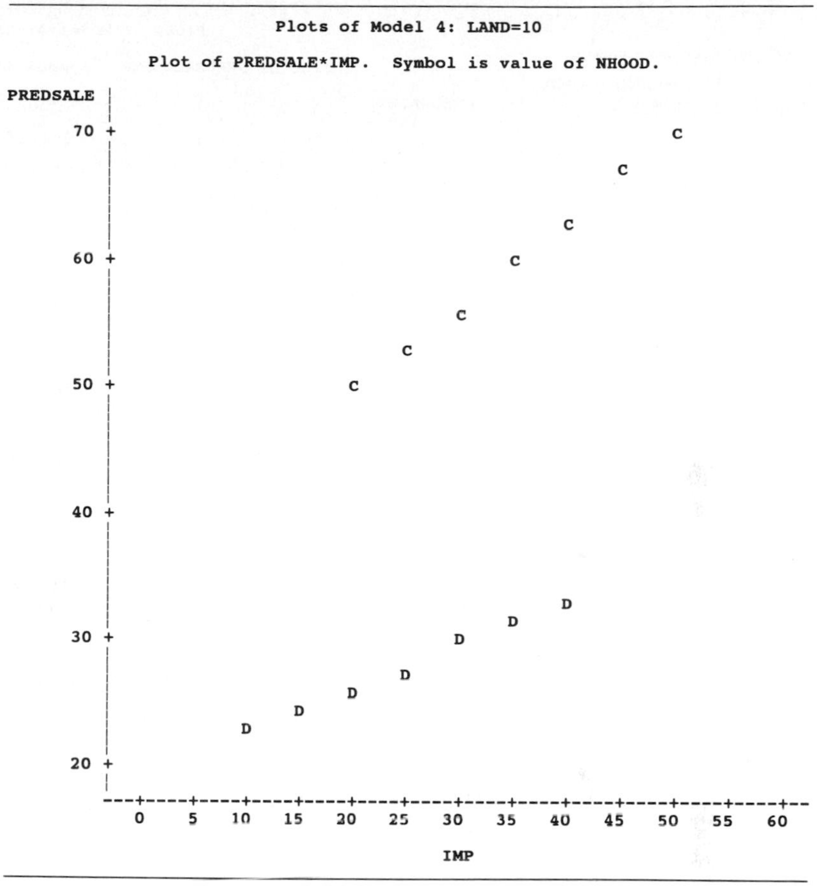

FIGURE 12.6
Graph of predicted sale price versus appraised improvements (x_2) when appraised land value $(x)_2$ is \$10,000

neighborhood A are too high compared with similar properties in neighborhood C. Perhaps a low appraised property value in neighborhood A corresponds to a very small lot; this might have a strong depressive effect on sale prices. In contrast, you can see in Figure 12.7 that properties in neighborhood A bring higher prices for an appraised home value of \$70,000 than for similarly appraised homes in neighborhood C. Thus, neighborhood A homes are appraised at a lower value than homes in neighborhood C that sell for the same price.

The three major points to be derived from an analysis of the sale price–appraised value curves are as follows:

1. The percentage rate at which sale price increases with appraised value differs for different neighborhoods. This percentage increase is smallest for the most expensive neighborhood, neighborhood B.
2. The curves for neighborhoods A and B frequently lie above those for neighborhoods C and D, indicating that properties in the higher-priced neighborhoods are being underappraised relative to sale price compared with properties in the lower-priced neighborhoods.

FIGURE 12.7
Graph of predicted sale price versus appraised value of improvements when appraised land value is $25,000

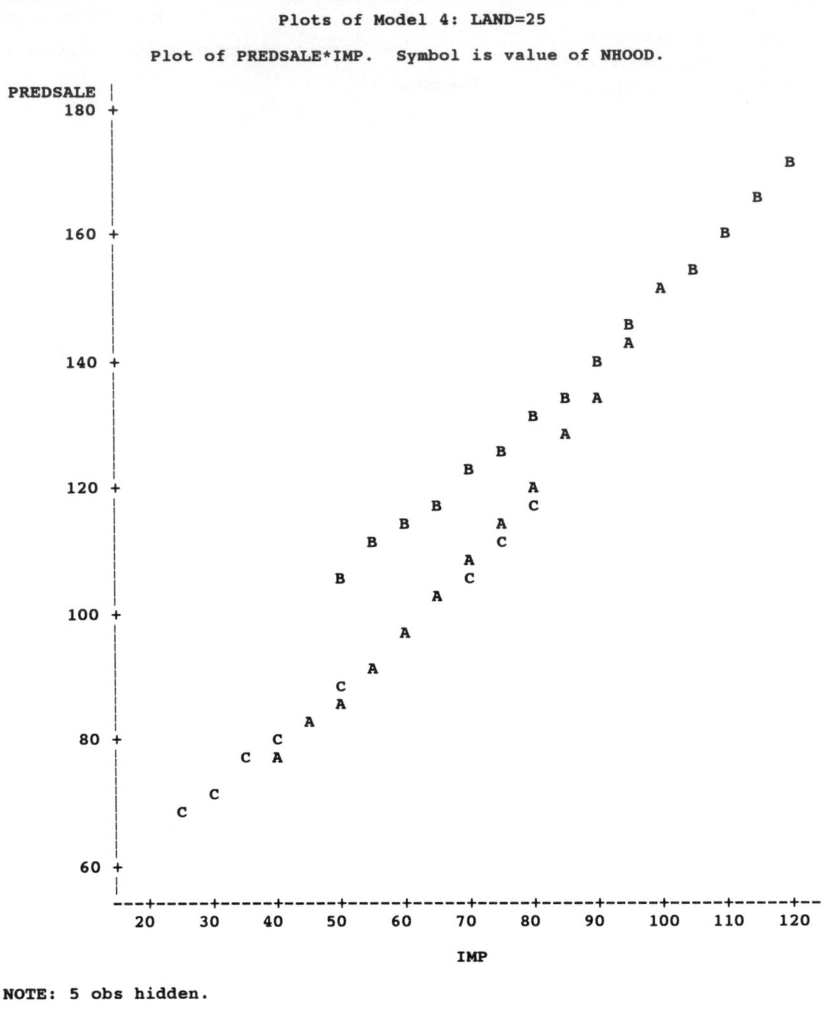

3. For most neighborhoods, the graphs curve upward as the appraised improvements value increases, indicating that more expensive properties within most neighborhoods are underappraised in comparison with the appraised values of less expensive properties.

12.6 Predicting the Sale Price of a Property

How well do appraised land value x_1 and appraised improvements value x_2 predict residential property sale price? Recall that from Model 4 (Figure 12.5), we obtained $R^2 = .906$, indicating that the model accounts for approximately 90% of the sample variability in the log sale price values, y^*. This seems to indicate that the model provides a reasonably good fit to the data, but note that $s = .248$ (see Figure 12.5). Our interpretation is that approximately 95% of the predicted

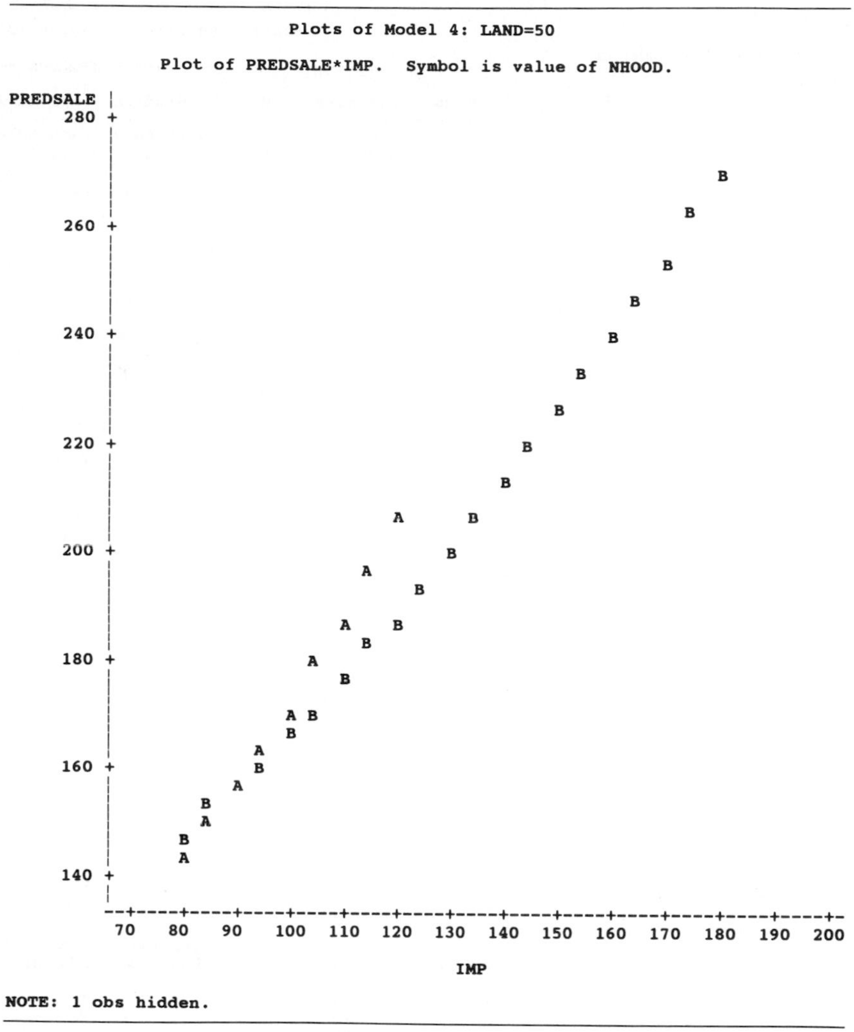

FIGURE 12.8
Graph of predicted sale price versus appraised value of improvements when appraised land value is $50,000

sale price values will fall within $(e^{2s} - 1)100\% = 64\%$ of their actual values. This relatively large standard deviation may lead to large errors of prediction for some residential properties if the model is used in practice.

Figure 12.10 on page 710 is a portion of a SAS printout showing 95% prediction intervals for the log sale price of several residential properties from each neighborhood. By taking antilogs of the endpoints of each interval, we obtain 95% prediction intervals for sale price, y. For example, the last row of the printout gives the 95% prediction interval for $\log(y)$ for a property in neighborhood D with an appraised land value of $10,000 and an appraised improvements value of $20,000. The interval is (2.7094, 3.6947). Taking antilogs of the endpoints, we obtain

$$e^{2.7094} = 15.020$$
$$e^{3.6947} = 40.233$$

FIGURE 12.9
Real estate analyses: 1993 sales in four neighborhoods

Descriptive Statistics for Four Neighborhoods

NHOOD=A

N Obs	Variable	N	Minimum	Maximum	Mean	Std Dev
169	SALES	169	59.0000000	375.0000000	137.4923077	62.8275607
	LNSALES	169	4.0775374	5.9269260	4.8302534	0.4274563
	LAND	169	11.7410000	129.3600000	31.4333964	18.1721574
	IMP	169	30.9480000	167.8380000	82.4475799	32.0649255

NHOOD=B

N Obs	Variable	N	Minimum	Maximum	Mean	Std Dev
54	SALES	54	95.0000000	805.0000000	198.4277778	115.6730321
	LNSALES	54	4.5538769	6.6908423	5.1877051	0.4177129
	LAND	54	24.5380000	166.5440000	48.5539259	26.6469484
	IMP	54	49.7600000	502.5850000	121.8540926	74.7016009

NHOOD=C

N Obs	Variable	N	Minimum	Maximum	Mean	Std Dev
138	SALES	138	36.1000000	169.0000000	70.4768116	18.6849262
	LNSALES	138	3.5862929	5.1298987	4.2263969	0.2346653
	LAND	138	3.9100000	31.9430000	14.3948333	3.8833211
	IMP	138	14.1650000	93.5630000	41.5632101	13.7558156

NHOOD=D

N Obs	Variable	N	Minimum	Maximum	Mean	Std Dev
87	SALES	87	8.5000000	70.0000000	25.7641149	13.1730216
	LNSALES	87	2.1400662	4.2484952	3.1185658	0.5241121
	LAND	87	3.5340000	24.0840000	7.4160690	3.4163850
	IMP	87	1.0000000	44.4620000	16.0164253	8.6499344

FIGURE 12.10
95% prediction intervals for four residential properties

95% Prediction Intervals: Model 4

Obs	NHOOD	LAND	IMP	Dep Var LNSALES	Predict Value	Std Err Predict	Lower95% Predict	Upper95% Predict	Residual
1	A	30	150	.	5.5741	0.072	5.0670	6.0813	.
2	B	50	120	.	5.2361	0.038	4.7431	5.7291	.
3	C	15	40	.	4.2221	0.023	3.7326	4.7116	.
4	D	10	15	.	3.2020	0.037	2.7094	3.6947	.

Because y is recorded in thousands of dollars, a 95% prediction interval for the sale price of this particular residential property is (\$15,020, \$40,233).

Such a wide prediction interval casts doubt on whether the prediction equation could be of practical value in predicting property sale prices. We feel certain that a much more accurate predictor of sale price could be developed by relating y to the variables that describe the property (such as location, square footage, and number of bedrooms) and those that describe the market (mortgage interest rates, availability of money, and so forth).

12.7 Conclusions

The results of the regression analyses described in Section 12.4 indicate that the relationships between property sale prices and appraised values are not consistent from one neighborhood to another. Further, the widths of the prediction intervals in Section 12.6 are rather sizable, indicating that there is room for improvement in the methods used to determine appraised property values.

EXERCISES

12.1 Explain why the tests of model adequacy conducted in Section 12.4 give no assurance that Model 4 will be a successful predictor of sale price in the future.

12.2 If you have access to a statistical computer package, use the data-splitting technique of Section 8.9 to assess the validity of Model 4.

12.3 Recall that the data for this case study are given in Appendix I.* The full data set contains sale price information for the four neighborhoods (A, B, C, and D) compared in this case study, as well as sale price information for two additional neighborhoods (E and F). Use the full data set to build a regression model for sale price of a residential property. Part of your analysis will involve a comparison of the six neighborhoods.

*This data set, as well as all appendix data sets, can be obtained in ASCII format on a $3\frac{1}{2}''$ diskette by contacting the publisher.

CASE STUDY 13 An Analysis of Rain Levels in California

CONTENTS

OBJECTIVE

To illustrate how a residual analysis can be used to detect an important omitted variable in regression

13.1 The Problem

The problem of describing interrelationships among variables is one that arises in almost all fields of research. Consequently, it is not surprising that multiple regression analysis is one of the most frequently used (and abused) statistical tools. For this case study, we focus on an application of regression analysis in the science of geography.

Writing in the journal *Geography* (July 1980), P. J. Taylor sought to describe the method of multiple regression to the research geographer "in a completely nontechnical manner." Taylor chose to investigate the variation in average annual precipitation in California—"a typical research problem that would be tackled using multiple regression analysis." In this chapter, we use Taylor's data to build a model for average annual precipitation, y. Then we examine the residuals, the deviations between the predicted and the actual precipitation levels, to detect (as did Taylor) an important independent variable omitted from the regression model.

13.2 The Data

The state of California operates numerous meteorological stations. One of the many functions of each station is to monitor rainfall on a daily basis. This information is then used to produce an average annual precipitation level for each station.

Table 13.1 on page 714 lists average annual precipitation levels (in inches) for a sample of 30 meteorological stations scattered throughout the state. (These are the data analyzed by Taylor.) In addition to average annual precipitation (y), the table lists three independent variables that are believed (by California geographers) to have the most impact on the amount of rainfall at each station, as follows:

1. Altitude of the station (x_1, feet)
2. Latitude of the station (x_2, degrees)
3. Distance of the station from the Pacific coast (x_3, miles)

13.3 A Model for Average Annual Precipitation

As an initial attempt in explaining the average annual precipitation in California, Taylor considered the following first-order model:

Model 1

$$E(y) = \beta_0 + \beta_1 x_1 + \beta_2 x_2 + \beta_3 x_3$$

Model 1 assumes that the relationship between average annual precipitation y and each independent variable is linear, and the effect of each x on y is independent of the other x's (i.e., no interaction).

The model is fitted to the data of Table 13.1, resulting in the SPSS printout shown in Figure 13.1 on page 715. The key numbers on the printout are shaded and interpreted as follows.

Global $F = 13.01951$ (p-value $= .0000$): At any significance level $\alpha > .0001$, we reject the null hypothesis H_0: $\beta_1 = \beta_2 = \beta_3 = 0$. Thus, there is sufficient evidence to indicate that the model is "statistically" useful for predicting average annual precipitation, y.

TABLE 13.1 **Data for 30 Meteorological Stations in California**

STATION	AVERAGE ANNUAL PRECIPITATION y, inches	ALTITUDE x_1, feet	LATITUDE x_2, degrees	DISTANCE FROM COAST x_3, miles
1. Eureka	39.57	43	40.8	1
2. Red Bluff	23.27	41	40.2	97
3. Thermal	18.20	4,152	33.8	70
4. Fort Bragg	37.48	74	39.4	1
5. Soda Springs	49.26	6,752	39.3	150
6. San Francisco	21.82	52	37.8	5
7. Sacramento	18.07	25	38.5	80
8. San Jose	14.17	95	37.4	28
9. Giant Forest	42.63	6,360	36.6	145
10. Salinas	13.85	74	36.7	12
11. Fresno	9.44	331	36.7	114
12. Pt. Piedras	19.33	57	35.7	1
13. Paso Robles	15.67	740	35.7	31
14. Bakersfield	6.00	489	35.4	75
15. Bishop	5.73	4,108	37.3	198
16. Mineral	47.82	4,850	40.4	142
17. Santa Barbara	17.95	120	34.4	1
18. Susanville	18.20	4,152	40.3	198
19. Tule Lake	10.03	4,036	41.9	140
20. Needles	4.63	913	34.8	192
21. Burbank	14.74	699	34.2	47
22. Los Angeles	15.02	312	34.1	16
23. Long Beach	12.36	50	33.8	12
24. Los Banos	8.26	125	37.8	74
25. Blythe	4.05	268	33.6	155
26. San Diego	9.94	19	32.7	5
27. Daggett	4.25	2,105	34.09	85
28. Death Valley	1.66	−178	36.5	194
29. Crescent City	74.87	35	41.7	1
30. Colusa	15.95	60	39.2	91

$R^2_{\text{adj}} = .55425$: After accounting for sample size and number of β parameters in the model, approximately 55% of the sample variation in average annual precipitation levels is explained by the first-order model with altitude (x_1), latitude (x_2), and distance from Pacific coast (x_3).

$s = 11.09709$: Approximately 95% of the actual average annual precipitation levels at the stations will fall within $2s = 22.2$ inches of the values predicted by the first-order model.

$\hat{\beta}_1 = .00409$: Holding latitude (x_2) and distance from coast (x_3) constant, we estimate average annual precipitation (y) of a station to increase .0041 inch for every 1-foot increase in the station's altitude (x_1).

$\hat{\beta}_2 = 3.450911$: Holding altitude (x_1) and distance from coast (x_3) constant, we estimate average annual precipitation (y) of a station to increase 3.45 inches for every 1-degree increase in the station's latitude (x_2).

FIGURE 13.1
SPSS printout for Model 1

```
        * * * *  M U L T I P L E   R E G R E S S I O N  * * * *

Equation Number 1    Dependent Variable..   RAIN

Variable(s) Entered on Step Number
   1..    COAST
   2..    LATITUDE
   3..    ALTITUDE

Multiple R            .77483
R Square              .60036
Adjusted R Square     .55425
Standard Error      11.09709

Analysis of Variance
                    DF        Sum of Squares       Mean Square
Regression           3           4809.87539        1603.29180
Residual            26           3201.77820         123.14532

F =       13.01951       Signif F =  .0000

------------------ Variables in the Equation ------------------

Variable               B          SE B        Beta           T   Sig T

COAST           -.142860       .036337    -.595647      -3.932   .0006
LATITUDE        3.450911       .794671     .553704       4.343   .0002
ALTITUDE         .004091       .001218     .516052       3.358   .0024
(Constant)   -102.350243     29.198238                  -3.505   .0017
```

$\hat{\beta}_3 = -.142860$: Holding altitude (x_1) and latitude (x_2) constant, we estimate average annual precipitation (y) of a station to decrease .143 inch for every 1-mile increase in the station's distance from the Pacific coast (x_3).

Note also that t tests for the three independent variables in the model are all highly significant (p-value $< .01$). Therefore, it appears that the first-order model is adequate for predicting a meteorological station's average annual precipitation.

Can we be certain that additional independent variables or higher-order terms will not improve the prediction equation? The answer, of course, is no. In the next section, we use a residual analysis to help guide us to a better model.

13.4 A Residual Analysis of the Model

The residuals of Model 1 are analyzed using the graphs discussed in Chapter 7. The SPSS printout in Figure 13.2 on page 716 shows both a histogram and a normal probability plot for the standardized residuals. Both graphs appear to support the regression assumption of normally distributed errors.

The SPSS printouts shown in Figure 13.3 on page 717 are plots of the residuals against each of the independent variables. Other than one or two unusual observations (outliers), the plots exhibit no distinctive patterns or trends. Consequently, transformations on the independent variables for the purposes of improving the fit of the model do not seem to be necessary.

Figure 13.4 on page 718 is an SPSS plot of the residuals against predicted precipitation, $\hat{y}$. Again, except for one or two outliers, no clear pattern can be detected. Thus, it appears that the regression assumption of constant error variance is approximately satisfied.

FIGURE 13.2
SPSS plots of residuals for Model 1: Normality check

```
Histogram - Standardized Residual

NExp N        (* = 1 Cases,     . : = Normal Curve)
0   .02    Out
1   .05   3.00 *
0   .12   2.67
0   .27   2.33
0   .55   2.00 .
0 1.00    1.67 .
1 1.65    1.33 *.
4 2.42    1.00 *:**
1 3.19     .67 * .
2 3.76     .33 ** .
9 3.97     .00 ***:*****
4 3.76    -.33 ***:
6 3.19    -.67 **:***
1 2.42   -1.00 *.
0 1.65   -1.33  .
0 1.00   -1.67 .
0   .55  -2.00 .
0   .27  -2.33
1   .12  -2.67 *
0   .05  -3.00
0   .02    Out
```

Normal Probability (P-P) Plot
Standardized Residual

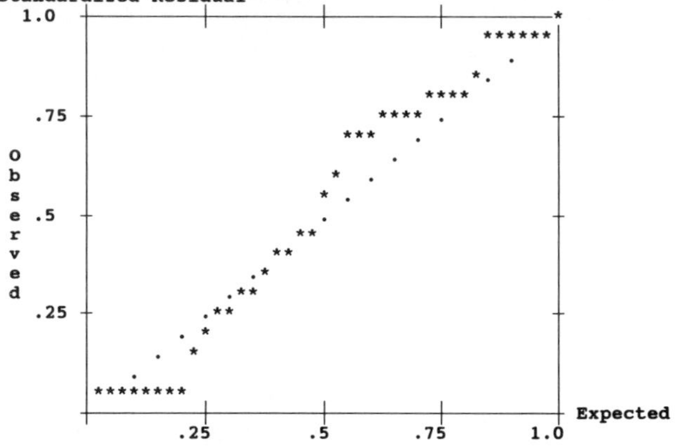

On the surface, the residual plots (Figures 13.2–13.4) seem to imply that no adjustments to the first-order model can be made to improve the prediction equation. Taylor, however, used his knowledge of geography and regression to examine Figure 13.4 more closely. He found that the residuals shown in Figure 13.4 actually exhibit a fairly consistent pattern. Taylor noticed that stations located on the west-facing slopes of the California mountains invariably had positive residuals whereas stations on the leeward side of the mountains had negative residuals.

To see what Taylor observed more clearly, we plotted the residuals of Model 1 against $\hat{y}$ using either "W" or "L" as a plotting symbol. Stations numbered 1, 4, 5, 6, 9, 12, 16, 17, 21, 22, 23, 26, and 29 in Table 13.1 were assigned a "W" since they all are located on west-facing slopes, whereas the remaining stations were assigned an "L" since they are leeward-facing. The revised residual plot is shown in the SAS printout, Figure 13.5 on page 719. You can see that with few

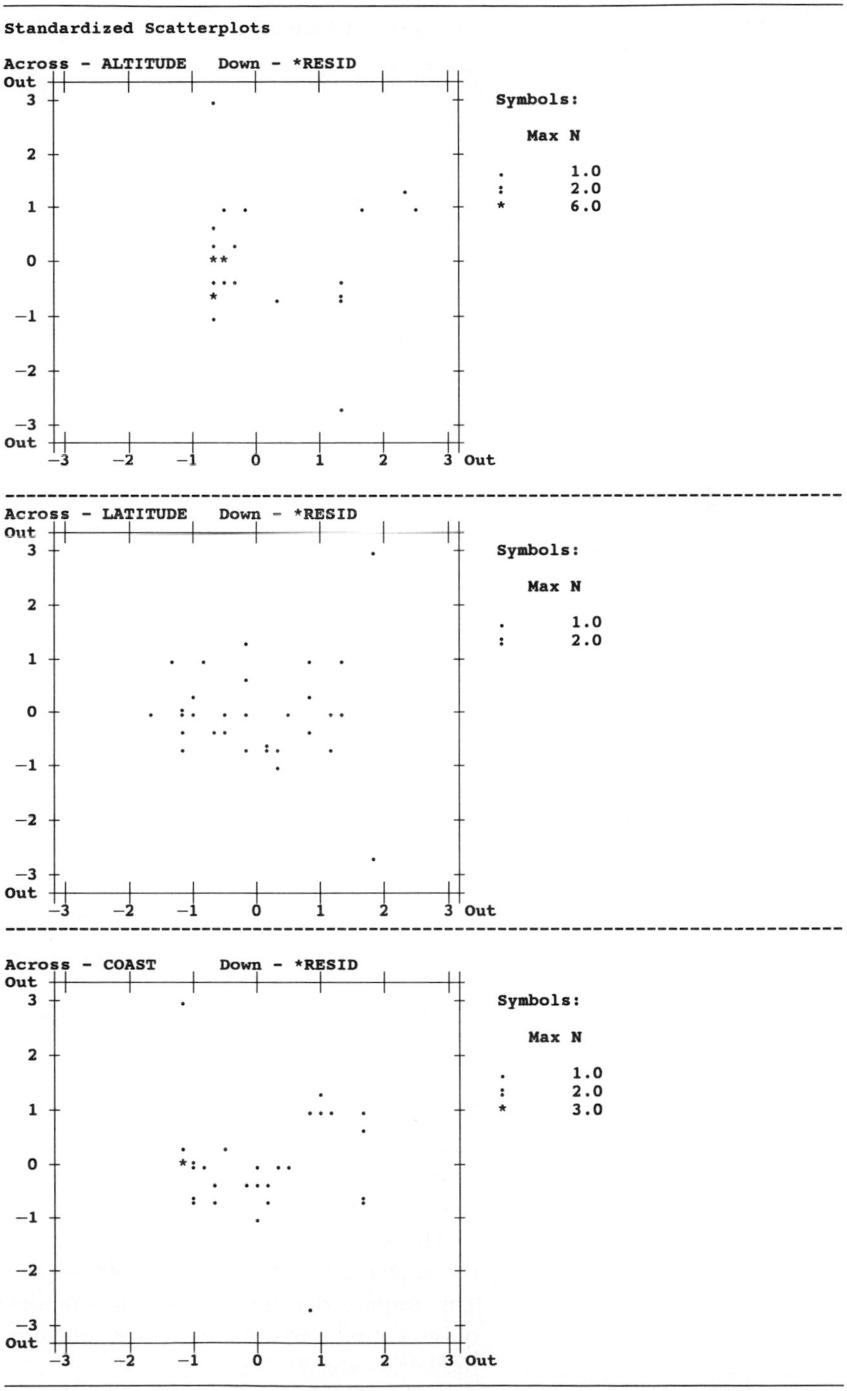

FIGURE 13.3

SPSS plots of residuals of Model 1 versus independent variables

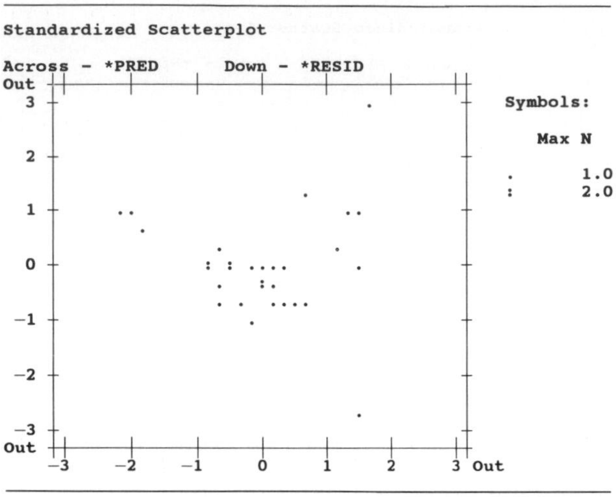

FIGURE 13.4
SPSS plot of residuals for Model 1 versus predicted values

exceptions, the "W" points have positive residuals (implying that the least squares model underpredicted the level of precipitation), whereas the "L" points have negative residuals (implying that the least squares model overpredicted the level of precipitation). In Taylor's words, the results shown in Figure 13.5 "suggest a very clear shadow effect of the mountains, for which California is known." Thus, it appears we can improve the fit of the model by adding a variable that represents the shadow effect.

13.5 Adjustments to the Model

To account for the shadow effect of the California mountains, consider the dummy variable

$$\text{Shadow:} \quad x_4 = \begin{cases} 1 & \text{if station on the leeward side} \\ 0 & \text{if station on the westward side} \end{cases}$$

Model 2

The model with the shadow effect takes the form

$$E(y) = \beta_0 + \beta_1 x_1 + \beta_2 x_2 + \beta_3 x_3 + \beta_4 x_4$$

Model 2, like Model 1, allows for straight-line relationships between precipitation and altitude (x_1), precipitation and latitude (x_2), and precipitation and distance from coast (x_3). The y-intercepts of these lines, however, will depend on the shadow effect (i.e., whether the station is leeward or westward).

The SAS printout for Model 2 is shown in Figure 13.6 on page 720. Note that the adjusted R^2 for Model 2 is .6963—an increase of about 15% from Model 1. This implies that the shadow-effect model (Model 2) explains about 15% more of the sample variation in average annual precipitation than the no-shadow-effect model (Model 1).

Is this increase a statistically significant one? To answer this question, we test the contribution for the shadow effect by testing

$$H_0\colon \ \beta_4 = 0 \qquad \text{against} \qquad H_a\colon \ \beta_4 \neq 0$$

FIGURE 13.5
SAS plot of residuals for Model 1 versus predicted variables: Shadow effect

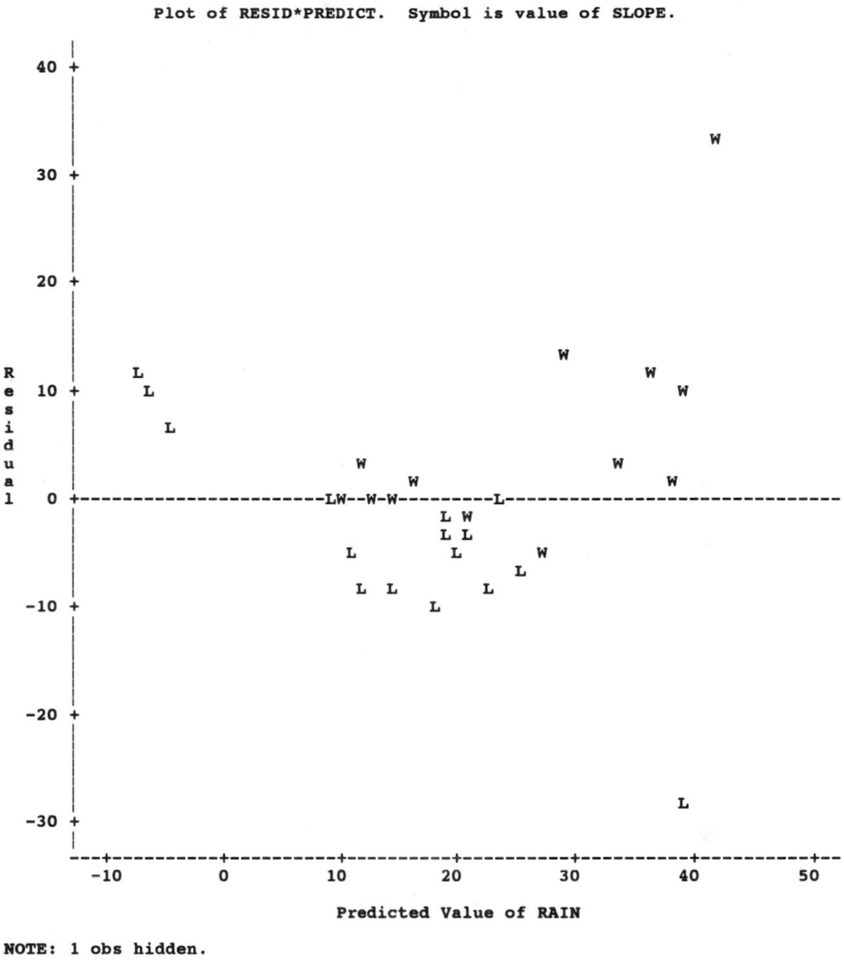

The test statistic, shaded on Figure 13.6, is $t = -3.627$ and the two-tailed p-value (also shaded) is $p = .0013$. Thus, there is sufficient evidence (at $\alpha = .01$) to conclude that $\beta_4 \neq 0$; i.e., the shadow-effect term contributes to the prediction of average annual precipitation.

Can Model 2 be improved by adding interaction terms? Consider Model 3:

Model 3

$$E(y) = \beta_0 + \beta_1 x_1 + \beta_2 x_2 + \beta_3 x_3 + \beta_4 x_4 + \beta_5 x_1 x_4 + \beta_6 x_2 x_4 + \beta_7 x_3 x_4$$

Note that Model 3 includes interactions between the shadow effect (x_4) and each of the quantitative independent variables. This model allows the slopes of the lines relating y to x_1, y to x_2, and y to x_3 to depend on the shadow effect (x_4). The SAS printout for Model 3 is given in Figure 13.7 on page 720.

FIGURE 13.6
SAS printout for Model 2

```
Model: MODEL2
Dependent Variable: RAIN

                         Analysis of Variance

                              Sum of         Mean
Source           DF          Squares       Square      F Value       Prob>F

Model             4       5913.80591   1478.45148       17.619       0.0001
Error            25       2097.84768     83.91391
C Total          29       8011.65359

     Root MSE          9.16045      R-square        0.7382
     Dep Mean         19.80733      Adj R-sq        0.6963
     C.V.             46.24779

                         Parameter Estimates

                    Parameter        Standard      T for H0:
Variable    DF       Estimate           Error    Parameter=0    Prob > |T|

INTERCEP     1     -97.878183     24.13415893         -4.056        0.0004
ALTITUDE     1       0.002206      0.00113193          1.949        0.0626
LATITUDE     1       3.453198      0.65598748          5.264        0.0001
COAST        1      -0.053670      0.03878696         -1.384        0.1787
SHADOW       1     -15.853894      4.37101246         -3.627        0.0013
```

FIGURE 13.7
SAS printout for Model 3

```
Model: MODEL3
Dependent Variable: RAIN

                         Analysis of Variance

                              Sum of         Mean
Source           DF          Squares       Square      F Value       Prob>F

Model             7       6921.77656    988.82522       19.960       0.0001
Error            22       1089.87703     49.53986
C Total          29       8011.65359

     Root MSE          7.03846      R-square        0.8640
     Dep Mean         19.80733      Adj R-sq        0.8207
     C.V.             35.53460

                         Parameter Estimates

                    Parameter        Standard      T for H0:
Variable    DF       Estimate           Error    Parameter=0    Prob > |T|

INTERCEP     1    -160.703577     25.77904593         -6.234        0.0001
ALTITUDE     1       0.004533      0.00417845          1.085        0.2897
LATITUDE     1       5.141276      0.69807118          7.365        0.0001
COAST        1      -0.130082      0.17569908         -0.740        0.4669
SHADOW       1     127.142280     37.56760493          3.384        0.0027
SHAD_ALT     1      -0.003722      0.00432984         -0.860        0.3992
SHAD_LAT     1      -3.787036      1.01885898         -3.717        0.0012
SHAD_CST     1       0.070779      0.17841202          0.397        0.6954

Test: SHADINT  Numerator:     335.9902  DF:    3   F value:    6.7822
               Denominator:   49.53986  DF:   22   Prob>F:     0.0021
```

To determine whether these interaction terms are important, we test

H_0: $\beta_5 = \beta_6 = \beta_7 = 0$

H_a: At least one of the β's $\neq 0$

The test is carried out by comparing Models 2 and 3 with the nested model partial F test of Section 4.10. The F test statistic, shaded at the bottom of Figure 13.7, is $F = 6.7822$ and the associated p-value (also shaded) is $p = .0021$.

Consequently, there is sufficient evidence (at $\alpha = .01$) to reject H_0 and conclude that at least one of the interaction β's is nonzero. This implies that Model 3, with the interaction terms, is a better predictor of average annual precipitation than Model 2.

The improvement of Model 3 over the other two models can be seen practically by examining R^2_{adj} and s on the printout, Figure 13.7. For Model 3, $R^2_{\text{adj}} = .8207$, an increase of about 12% from Model 2 and 27% from Model 1. The standard deviation of Model 3 is $s = 7.03$, compared to $s = 9.16$ for Model 2 and $s = 11.1$ for Model 1. Thus, in practice, we expect Model 3 to predict average annual precipitation of a meteorological station to within about 14 inches of its true value. (This is compared to a bound on the error of prediction of about 22 inches for Model 1 and 18 inches for Model 2.) Clearly, a model that incorporates the shadow effect and its interactions with altitude, latitude, and distance from coast is a more useful predictor of average annual precipitation, y.

13.6 Conclusions

We have demonstrated how a residual analysis can help the analyst find important independent variables that were originally omitted from the regression model. This technique, however, requires substantial knowledge of the problem, data, and potentially important predictor variables. Without knowledge of the presence of a shadow effect in California, the geographer Taylor could not have enhanced the residual plot, Figure 13.4, and consequently would not have seen its potential for improving the fit of the model.

EXERCISES

13.1. Conduct an outlier analysis of the residuals for Model 1. Identify any influential observations, and suggest how to handle these observations. (The data are available on a $3\frac{1}{2}''$ diskette from the publisher.)

13.2 Determine whether interactions between the quantitative variables, altitude (x_1), latitude (x_2), and distance from coast (x_3) will improve the fit of the model.

Reference

Taylor, P. J. "A pedagogic application of multiple regression analysis." *Geography*, July 1980, Vol. 65, pp. 203–212.

CASE STUDY 14

Reluctance to Transmit Bad News: The MUM Effect

CONTENTS

OBJECTIVE

To present a designed experiment that investigates the effects of two manipulated factors on the reluctance of human subjects to transmit bad news to others

14.1 The Problem

In a 1970 experiment, psychologists S. Rosen and A. Tesser found that people were reluctant to transmit bad news to peers in a nonprofessional setting. Rosen and Tesser termed this phenomenon the "MUM effect."* Since that time, numerous studies have investigated the impact of the MUM effect in a professional setting, e.g., on doctor–patient relationships, organizational functioning, and group psychotherapy. The consensus: The reluctance to transmit bad news continues to be a major professional concern.

Why do people keep mum when given an opportunity to transmit bad news to others? Two theories have emerged from this research. The first maintains that the MUM effect is an *aversion to private discomfort*. To avoid discomforts such as empathy with the victim's distress or guilt feelings for their own good fortune, would-be communicators of bad news keep mum. The second theory is that the MUM effect is a *public display*. People experience little or no discomfort when transmitting bad news, but keep mum to avoid an unfavorable impression or to pay homage to a social norm.

The subject of this case study is an article by C. F. Bond and E. L. Anderson (*Journal of Experimental Social Psychology*, Vol. 23, 1987). Bond and Anderson conducted a controlled experiment to determine which of the two explanations for the MUM effect is more plausible. "If the MUM effect is an aversion to private discomfort," they state, "subjects should show the effect whether or not they are visible [to the victim]. If the effect is a public display, it should be stronger if the subject is visible than if the subject cannot be seen."

14.2 The Design

Forty undergraduates (25 males and 15 females) at Duke University participated in the experiment to fulfill an introductory psychology course requirement. Each subject was asked to administer an IQ test to another student and then provide the test taker with his or her percentile score. Unknown to the subject, the test taker was a confederate student working with the researchers.

The experiment manipulated two factors, *subject visibility* and *confederate success*, each at two levels. Subject visibility was manipulated by written instructions that told some subjects that they were *visible* to the test taker through a glass plate and the others that they were *not visible* through a one-way mirror. Confederate success was manipulated by supplying the subject with one of two bogus answer keys. With one answer key, the confederate would always seem to succeed at the test, placing him or her in the top 20% of all Duke undergraduates; when the other answer key was used, the confederate would always seem to fail, ranking in the bottom 20%.

Ten subjects were randomly assigned to each of the $2 \times 2 = 4$ experimental conditions; thus, a 2×2 factorial design with 10 replications was employed. The design is diagrammed in Table 14.1 on page 724.

*Rosen, S., and Tesser, A. "On reluctance to communicate undesirable information: The MUM effect." *Journal of Communication*, Vol. 22, 1970, pp. 124–141.

TABLE 14.1 **2 × 2 Factorial Design**

		CONFEDERATE SUCCESS: Success	CONFEDERATE SUCCESS: Failure
SUBJECT VISIBILITY	Visible	Subject 1 2 ⋮ 10	Subject 21 22 ⋮ 30
	Not Visible	Subject 11 12 ⋮ 20	Subject 31 32 ⋮ 40

One of several behavioral variables that were measured during the experiment was *latency to feedback*, defined as time (in seconds) between the end of the test and delivery of feedback (i.e., the percentile score) from the subject to the test taker. This case focuses on an analysis of variance of the dependent variable, latency to feedback. The longer it takes the subject to deliver the score, presumably the greater the MUM effect. With this analysis, the researchers hope to determine whether either one of the two factors, subject visibility or confederate success, has an impact on the MUM effect, and, if so, whether the factors are independent.

14.3 Analysis of Variance Models and Results

Since both factors, subject visibility and confederate success, are qualitative, the complete model for this 2 × 2 factorial experiment is written as follows.

Complete model: $$E(y) = \beta_0 + \underbrace{\beta_1 x_1}_{\substack{\text{Visibility}\\ \text{main}\\ \text{effect}}} + \underbrace{\beta_2 x_2}_{\substack{\text{Success}\\ \text{main}\\ \text{effect}}} + \underbrace{\beta_3 x_1 x_2}_{\substack{\text{Visibility} \times \text{Success}\\ \text{interaction}}}$$

where

$$y = \text{Latency to feedback}$$

$$x_1 = \begin{cases} 1 & \text{if subject visible} \\ 0 & \text{if not} \end{cases} \qquad x_2 = \begin{cases} 1 & \text{if confederate success} \\ 0 & \text{if confederate failure} \end{cases}$$

To test for factor interaction, we can compare the complete model to the reduced model

Reduced model: $E(y) = \beta_0 + \beta_1 x_1 + \beta_2 x_2$

using the partial F test, or, equivalently, we can conduct a t test on the interaction parameter, β_3. Either way, the null hypothesis to be tested is

$$H_0: \quad \beta_3 = 0$$

Although the raw data for the experiment were not provided in the journal article, the results were given in the form of an ANOVA table, which is reproduced in Table 14.2.

TABLE 14.2 **ANOVA Table for the 2 × 2 Factorial Experiment**

SOURCE	df	SS	MS	F
Subject visibility	1	1,380.24	1,380.24	4.26
Confederate success	1	1,325.16	1,325.16	4.09
Visibility × Success	1	3,385.80	3,385.80	10.45
Error	36	11,664.00	324.00	
Total	39	17,755.20		

The F statistic for testing the visibility–success interaction reported in the table is $F = 10.45$. Since the p-value of the test is not provided, we are required to find the rejection region for a given value of α. The critical F value depends on $\nu_1 = 1$ numerator degree of freedom (i.e., df for visibility × success) and $\nu_2 = 36$ denominator degrees of freedom (i.e., df for error). Using $\alpha = .05$, the critical F value (found in Table 4, Appendix C) is $F_{.05} \approx 4.12$. Thus, the rejection region is

Rejection region: $F > 4.12$

Since the calculated F (10.45) falls into the rejection region, we reject H_0 at $\alpha = .05$ and conclude that the two factors, subject visibility and confederate success, interact.

Practically, this result implies that the effect of confederate success on mean latency to feedback, $E(y)$, depends on whether the subject is visible. Similarly, the effect of subject visibility on $E(y)$ depends on the success or failure of the confederate student. In other words, we cannot examine the effect of one factor on latency to feedback without knowing the level of the second factor. Consequently, we ignore the F test for factor main effects and focus on the nature of the differences among the means of the $2 \times 2 = 4$ experimental conditions.

14.4 Follow-up Analysis

The sample latency to feedback means (in seconds) for each of the four experimental conditions are provided in Table 14.3. These four means are plotted in Figure 14.1 on page 726.

TABLE 14.3 **Sample Means for the Four Experimental Conditions**

		CONFEDERATE SUCCESS	
		Success	Failure
SUBJECT	Visible	73.1	147.2
	Not visible	89.6	72.5

We will conduct a follow-up analysis of the ANOVA by comparing the two confederate success means within each level of subject visibility. Since a balanced design is employed ($n = 10$ subjects per treatment), Tukey's method of multiple comparisons of means will be used.

FIGURE 14.1
Plot of sample means for 2 × 2 factorial

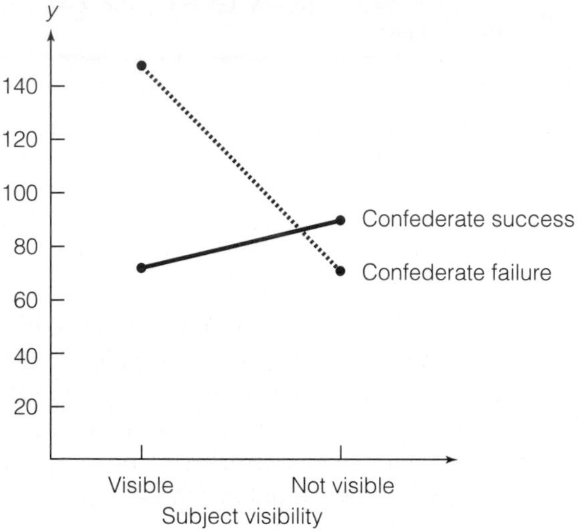

Recall (Section 11.7) that Tukey's method requires that we find the critical value of the Studentized range, $q_\alpha(p, \nu)$, where p is the number of means to be compared and ν is the degrees of freedom associated with MSE (i.e., df for error). Since we want to compare two means at each level of visibility, $p = 2$; also, from Table 14.2, $\nu = 36$ df. Using $\alpha = .05$, the critical value of q (obtained from Table 11, Appendix C) is $q_{.05}(2, 36) \approx 2.87$.

Tukey's critical difference is

$$\omega = q_\alpha(p, \nu)\frac{s}{\sqrt{n_t}}$$

where $s = \sqrt{\text{MSE}}$ and n_t is the number of observations per treatment. Substituting the appropriate values into the formula for ω, we have

$$\omega = q_{.05}(2, 36)\sqrt{\frac{3{,}385.80}{10}} = (2.87)\sqrt{338.58} = 52.81$$

Consequently, the difference between the two sample means must exceed 52.81 for the corresponding population means to be considered different.

In Table 14.3, we observe that the two confederate success means for nonvisible subjects, $\bar{y}_{\text{success}} = 89.6$ and $\bar{y}_{\text{failure}} = 72.5$, are not significantly different (at $\alpha = .05$) since their difference is less than 52.81 in absolute value. Alternatively, the two confederate success means for visible subjects, $\bar{y}_{\text{success}} = 73.1$ and $\bar{y}_{\text{failure}} = 147.2$, are significantly different at $\alpha = .05$. Thus, only when the subject is visible can we conclude that confederate success has an effect on the mean latency to feedback. Furthermore, since $\bar{y}_{\text{failure}} = 147.2$ is over twice as large as $\bar{y}_{\text{success}} = 73.1$ at this level of subject visibility, the researchers conclude that "subjects appear reluctant to transmit bad news—but only when they are visible to the news recipient."

14.5 Conclusions

In their discussion of these results, the researchers conclude:

> In this experiment, subjects were required to give a test taker either success or failure feedback. While doing so, they presumed themselves to be visible to the test taker or visible to no one. Subjects who were visible took twice as long to deliver failure feedback as success feedback; those who were not visible delivered failure and success feedback with equal speed.
>
> These results are not consistent with the discomfort explanation as originally conceived. We had imagined that subjects might empathize with another's failure, that mere observation of the failure would be sufficient to arouse vicarious distress. We found no behavioral evidence of such discomfort. . . . We also imagined that subjects would be reluctant to induce discomfort by announcing a poor intelligence performance, and that they would defer the announcement while checking the IQ test score. We found evidence of this deferral—but only when the subject could be seen. In private, subjects seemed blithe to others' misfortune—as quick to relay bad as good news. As the latency results suggest, there is no inherent discomfort in the transmission of bad news.

EXERCISES

14.1 Use Table 14.2 to determine SSEs for the complete and reduced ANOVA models. Then use these values to obtain the F statistic for testing interaction.

14.2 The journal article made no mention of an analysis of the ANOVA residuals. Discuss the potential problems of an ANOVA when no residual analysis is conducted.

14.3 A second dependent variable measured in the study was *gaze*, defined as the proportion of time the subject was looking toward the confederate test taker on the other side of the glass plate. Gaze was measured at four points in time using videotape segments: early in the test, late in the test, during the wait for feedback, and after the feedback. Construct a complete model for analyzing gaze as a function of subject visibility, confederate success, and videotape segment. Identify the important tests to conduct.

Reference

Bond, C. F., and Anderson, E. L. "The reluctance to transmit bad news: Private discomfort or public display?" *Journal of Experimental Social Psychology*, Vol. 23, 1987, pp. 176–187.

CASE STUDY 15 An Investigation of Factors Affecting the Sale Price of Condominium Units Sold at Public Auction

CONTENTS

OBJECTIVE

To show how regression analysis can be used to develop a model relating sale price of condominium units to a set of independent variables and, particularly, to show how the model can be used to reveal some interesting relationships among these variables

15.1 The Problem

This chapter contains a partial investigation of the factors that affect the sale price of oceanside condominium units. It represents an extension of an analysis of the same data by Herman Kelting (1979). Because there are many different theories (and models) that might be proposed in this type of study, we present the complete data set for further analysis in Appendix J.

The sales data were obtained for a new oceanside condominium complex consisting of two adjacent and connected eight-floor buildings. The complex contains 200 units of equal size (approximately 500 square feet each). The locations of the buildings relative to the ocean, the swimming pool, the parking lot, etc., are shown in Figure 15.1. There are several features of the complex that you should note. The units facing south, called *ocean-view*, face the beach and ocean. In addition, units in building 1 have a good view of the pool. Units to the rear of the building, called *bay-view*, face the parking lot and an area of land that ultimately borders a bay. The view from the upper floors of these units is primarily of wooded, sandy terrain. The bay is very distant and barely visible.

The only elevator in the complex is located at the east end of building 1, as are the office and the game room. People moving to or from the higher-floor units in building 2 would likely use the elevator and move through the passages to their units. Thus, units on the higher floors and at a greater distance from the

FIGURE 15.1 Layout of condominium complex

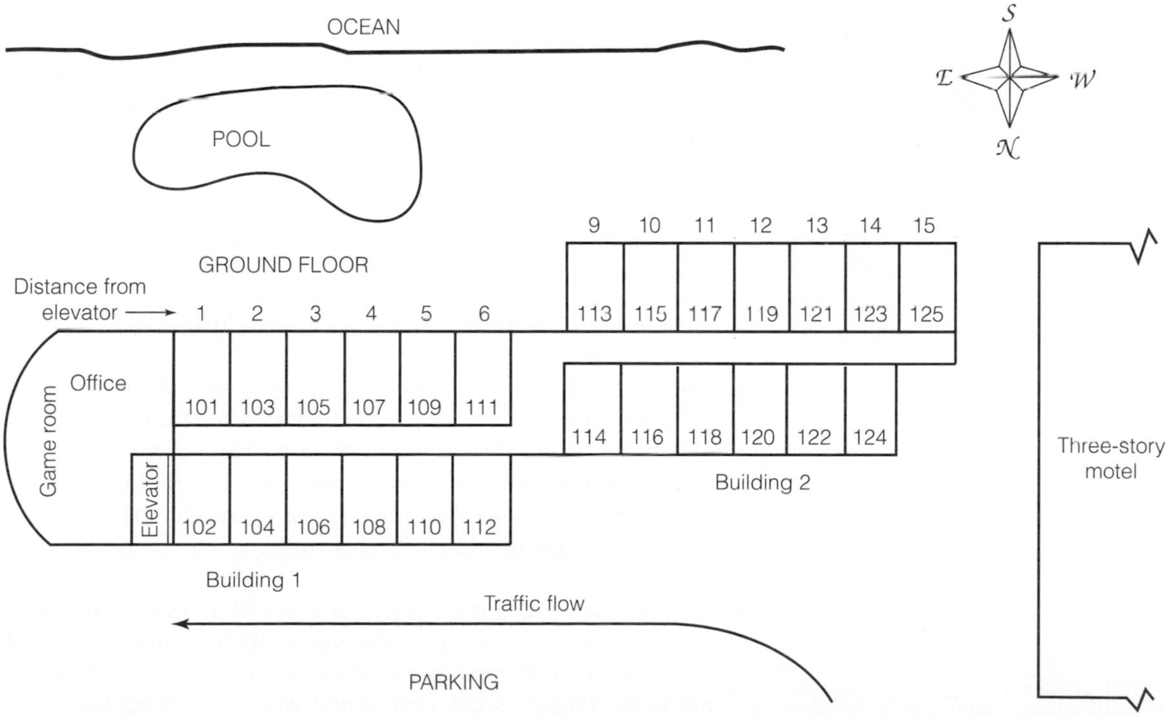

elevator would be less convenient; they would require greater effort in moving baggage, groceries, etc., and would be farther from the game room, the office, and the swimming pool. These units also possess an advantage: There would be the least amount of traffic through the hallways in the area, and hence they are the most private.

Lower-floor oceanside units are most suited to active people; they open onto the beach, ocean, and pool. They are within easy reach of the game room and they are easily reached from the parking area.

Checking Figure 15.1, you will see that some of the units in the center of the complex, units numbered __11 and __14, have part of their view blocked. We would expect this to be a disadvantage. We will show you later that this expectation is true for the ocean-view units and that these units sold at a lower price than adjacent ocean-view units.

The condominium complex was completed at the time of the 1975 recession; sales were slow and the developer was forced to sell most of the units at auction approximately 18 months after opening. Many unsold units were furnished by the developer and rented prior to the auction.

This condominium complex was particularly suited to our study. The single elevator located at one end of the complex produces a remarkably high level of both inconvenience and privacy for the people occupying units on the top floors in building 2. Consequently, the data provide a good opportunity to investigate the relationship between sale price, height of the unit (floor number), distance of the unit from the elevator, and presence or absence of an ocean view. The presence or absence of furniture in each of the units also enables us to investigate the effect of the availability of furniture on sale price. Finally, the auction data are completely buyer-specified and hence consumer-oriented in contrast to most other real estate sales data, which are, to a high degree, seller- and broker-specified.

15.2 The Data

In addition to the sale price, the following data were recorded for each of the 106 units sold at the auction:

1. *Floor height* The floor location of the unit; this variable, x_1, could take values 1, 2, . . . , 8.
2. *Distance from elevator* This distance, measured along the length of the complex, was expressed in number of condominium units. An additional two units of distance was added to the units in building 2 to account for the walking distance in the connecting area between the two buildings. Thus, the distance of unit 105 from the elevator would be 3, and the distance between unit 113 and the elevator would be 9. This variable, x_2, could take values 1, 2, . . . , 15.
3. *View of ocean* The presence or absence of an ocean view was recorded for each unit and entered into the model with a dummy variable, x_3, where $x_3 = 1$ if the unit possessed an ocean view and $x_3 = 0$ if not. Note that units not possessing an ocean view would face the parking lot.

4. *End unit* We expected the partial reduction of view of end units on the ocean side (numbers ending in 11) to reduce their sale price. The ocean view of these end units is partially blocked by building 2. This qualitative variable was entered into the model with a dummy variable, x_4, where $x_4 = 1$ if the unit has a unit number ending in 11 and $x_4 = 0$ if not.
5. *Furniture* The presence or absence of furniture was recorded for each unit. This qualitative variable was entered into the model using a single dummy variable, x_5, where $x_5 = 1$ if the unit was furnished and $x_5 = 0$ if not.

The raw data used in this analysis are presented in Appendix J.

15.3 The Models

We recorded data on five independent variables, two quantitative (floor height x_1 and distance from elevator x_2) and three qualitative (view of ocean, end unit, and furniture). We postulated four models relating mean sale price to these five factors. The models, numbered 1–4, are developed in sequence, Model 1 being the simplest and Model 4, the most complex. Each of Models 2 and 3 contains all the terms of the preceding models along with new terms that we think will improve their predictive ability. Thus, Model 2 contains all the terms contained in Model 1 plus some new terms, and hence it should predict mean sale price as well as or better than Model 1. Similarly, Model 3 should predict as well as or better than Model 2. Model 4 does not contain all the terms contained in Model 3, but that is only because we have entered floor height into Model 4 as a qualitative independent variable. Consequently, Model 4 contains all the predictive ability of Model 3, and it could be an improvement over Model 3 if our theory is correct. The logic employed in this sequential model-building procedure will be explained in the following discussion.

The simplest theory that we might postulate is that the five factors affect the price in an independent manner and that the effect of the two quantitative factors on sale price is linear. Thus, we envision a set of planes, each identical except for their y-intercepts. We would expect sale price planes for ocean-view units to be higher than those with a bay view, those corresponding to end units (__11) would be lower than for non–end units, and those with furniture would be higher than those without.

Model 1

$$E(y) = \beta_0 + \beta_1 x_1 + \beta_2 x_2 + \beta_3 x_3 + \beta_4 x_4 + \beta_5 x_5$$

where

x_1 = Floor height $(x_1 = 1, 2, \ldots, 8)$

x_2 = Distance from elevator $(x_2 = 1, 2, \ldots, 15)$

$$x_3 = \begin{cases} 1 & \text{if an ocean view} \\ 0 & \text{if not} \end{cases} \qquad x_4 = \begin{cases} 1 & \text{if an end unit} \\ 0 & \text{if not} \end{cases} \qquad x_5 = \begin{cases} 1 & \text{if furnished} \\ 0 & \text{if not} \end{cases}$$

The second theory that we considered was that the effects on sale price of floor height and distance from elevator might not be linear. Consequently, we constructed Model 2, which is similar to Model 1 except that second-order terms are included for x_1 and x_2. This model envisions a single second-order response surface for $E(y)$ in x_1 and x_2 that possesses identically the same shape, regardless of the view, whether the unit is an end unit, and whether the unit is furnished. Expressed in other terminology, Model 2 assumes that there is no interaction between any of the qualitative factors (view of ocean, end unit, and furniture) and the quantitative factors (floor height and distance from elevator).

Model 2

$$E(y) = \beta_0 + \overbrace{\beta_1 x_1 + \beta_2 x_2 + \beta_3 x_1 x_2 + \beta_4 x_1^2 + \beta_5 x_2^2}^{\text{Second-order model in } x_1 \text{ and } x_2}$$

$$+ \overbrace{\beta_6 x_3}^{\text{View of ocean}} + \overbrace{\beta_7 x_4}^{\text{End unit}} + \overbrace{\beta_8 x_5}^{\text{Furniture}}$$

Model 2 may possess a serious shortcoming. It assumes that the shape of the second-order response surface relating mean sale price $E(y)$ to x_1 and x_2 is identical for ocean-view and bay-view units. Since we think that there is a strong possibility that completely different preference patterns may govern the purchase of these two groups of units, we will construct a model that provides for two completely different second-order response surfaces—one for ocean-view units and one for bay-view units. Further, we will assume that the effects of the two qualitative factors, end unit and furniture, are additive; i.e., their presence or absence will simply shift the mean sale price response surface up or down by a fixed amount. Thus, Model 3 is given as follows:

Model 3

$$E(y) = \beta_0 + \overbrace{\beta_1 x_1 + \beta_2 x_2 + \beta_3 x_1 x_2 + \beta_4 x_1^2 + \beta_5 x_2^2}^{\text{Second-order model in } x_1 \text{ and } x_2}$$

$$+ \overbrace{\beta_6 x_3}^{\text{View of ocean}} + \overbrace{\beta_7 x_4}^{\text{End unit}} + \overbrace{\beta_8 x_5}^{\text{Furniture}}$$

$$+ \overbrace{\beta_9 x_1 x_3 + \beta_{10} x_2 x_3 + \beta_{11} x_1 x_2 x_3 + \beta_{12} x_1^2 x_3 + \beta_{13} x_2^2 x_3}^{\text{Interaction of the second-order model with view of ocean}}$$

As a fourth possibility, we constructed a model similar to Model 3 but entered floor height as a qualitative factor at eight levels. The reasons for doing this are

1. Higher-floor units have better views but less accessibility to the outdoors. This latter characteristic could be a particularly undesirable feature for these units.
2. The views of some lower-floor bayside units were blocked by a nearby three-story motel.

If our supposition is correct and if these features would have a depressive effect on the sale price of these units, then the relationship between floor height and mean sale price would not be second-order (a smooth curvilinear relationship).

Entering floor height as a qualitative factor would permit a better fit to this irregular relationship and improve the prediction equation. Thus, Model 4 is identical to Model 3 except that Model 4 contains seven main effect terms for floor height (in contrast to two for Model 3), and it also contains the corresponding interactions of these variables with the other variables included in Model 3. We will subsequently show that there was no evidence to indicate that Model 4 contributes more information for the prediction of y than Model 3. For this reason and also because Model 4 contains so many terms (49), we will not give the formula for this model.*

15.4 The Regression Analyses

This section gives the regression analyses for the four models described in Section 15.3. You will see that our approach is to build the model in a sequential manner. In each case, we use an F test to see whether a particular model contributes more information for the prediction of sale price than its predecessor.

This procedure is more conservative than a step-down procedure. In a step-down approach you would assume Model 4 to be the appropriate model, then test and possibly delete terms. But deleting terms can be particularly risky because, in doing so, you are tacitly accepting the null hypothesis. Thus, you risk deleting important terms from the model and do so with an unknown probability of committing a Type II error.

Do not be unduly influenced by the individual t tests associated with an analysis. As you will see, it is possible for a set of terms to contribute information for the prediction of y when none of their respective t values are statistically significant. This is because the t test focuses on the contribution of a single term, given that all the other terms are retained in the model. Therefore, if a set of terms contributes overlapping information, it is possible that none of the terms individually would be statistically significant, even when the set as a whole contributes information for the prediction of y.

The SAS regression analysis computer printouts for fitting Models 1, 2, 3, and 4 to the data are shown in Figures 15.2, 15.3, 15.4, and 15.5 (pages 734 and 735), respectively. A summary containing SSE values for these models, their respective degrees of freedom, and R^2 values is provided in Table 15.1 (page 734).

Examining the computer printout for the first-order model (Model 1) in Figure 15.2, you can see that the value of the F statistic for testing the null hypothesis

$$H_0\colon\ \beta_1 = \beta_2 = \cdots = \beta_5 = 0$$

is 48.42. This is statistically significant at a level of $\alpha = .0001$. Consequently, there is ample evidence to indicate that the overall model contributes information for the prediction of y. At least one of the five factors contributes information for the prediction of sale price.

*Some of these terms were not estimable because sales were not consummated for some combinations of the independent variables. This is why the computer printout in Figure 15.5 shows only 41 df for the model.

FIGURE 15.2
SAS regression analysis: Model 1

ANALYSIS OF VARIANCE

SOURCE	DF	SUM OF SQUARES	MEAN SQUARE	F VALUE	PROB>F
MODEL	5	236620761	47324152.11	48.419	0.0001
ERROR	100	97737975.28	977379.75		
C TOTAL	105	334358736			

ROOT MSE	988.6252	R-SQUARE	0.7077
DEP MEAN	19176.04	ADJ R-SQ	0.6931
C.V.	5.155524		

PARAMETER ESTIMATES

VARIABLE	DF	PARAMETER ESTIMATE	STANDARD ERROR	T FOR H0: PARAMETER=0	PROB > |T|
INTERCEP	1	17770.00813	416.07044	42.709	0.0001
X1	1	-73.68311471	52.97836340	-1.391	0.1674
X2	1	-86.41176445	24.44923524	-3.534	0.0006
X3	1	3136.59235	222.70788	14.084	0.0001
X4	1	-1781.05526	397.45816	-4.481	0.0001
X5	1	986.99033	204.77016	4.820	0.0001

FIGURE 15.3
SAS regression analysis: Model 2

ANALYSIS OF VARIANCE

SOURCE	DF	SUM OF SQUARES	MEAN SQUARE	F VALUE	PROB>F
MODEL	8	244325938	30540742.24	32.904	0.0001
ERROR	97	90032797.92	928173.17		
C TOTAL	105	334358736			

ROOT MSE	963.4174	R-SQUARE	0.7307
DEP MEAN	19176.04	ADJ R-SQ	0.7085
C.V.	5.024069		

PARAMETER ESTIMATES

VARIABLE	DF	PARAMETER ESTIMATE	STANDARD ERROR	T FOR H0: PARAMETER=0	PROB > |T|
INTERCEP	1	19461.81838	764.78661	25.447	0.0001
X1	1	-683.94788	245.08261	-2.791	0.0063
X2	1	-264.54977	122.58866	-2.158	0.0334
X1X2	1	4.81613443	13.54099144	0.356	0.7229
X1X1	1	57.93750913	23.74605653	2.440	0.0165
X2X2	1	11.33982388	7.70152793	1.472	0.1441
X3	1	3051.55998	219.25992	13.918	0.0001
X4	1	-1680.93326	409.72999	-4.103	0.0001
X5	1	1114.78991	205.04676	5.437	0.0001

TABLE 15.1 **A Summary of the Values (Rounded) of SSE, MSE, and R^2 for Models 1, 2, 3, and 4**

MODEL	SSE	df(Error)	MSE	R^2
1	97,737,975	100	977,380	.7077
2	90,032,798	97	928,173	.7307
3	78,428,545	92	852,484	.7654
4	51,647,128	64	806,986	.8455

If you examine the t tests for the individual parameters, you will see that they are all statistically significant except the test for β_1, the parameter associated with floor height x_1 (p-value = .1674). The failure of floor height x_1 to reveal itself as an important information contributor goes against our intuition, and it

FIGURE 15.4
SAS regression analysis: Model 3

ANALYSIS OF VARIANCE

SOURCE	DF	SUM OF SQUARES	MEAN SQUARE	F VALUE	PROB>F
MODEL	13	255930191	19686937.74	23.094	0.0001
ERROR	92	78428545.24	852484.19		
C TOTAL	105	334358736			

ROOT MSE	923.3007	R-SQUARE	0.7654
DEP MEAN	19176.04	ADJ R-SQ	0.7323
C.V.	4.814867		

PARAMETER ESTIMATES

VARIABLE	DF	PARAMETER ESTIMATE	STANDARD ERROR	T FOR H0: PARAMETER=0	PROB > |T|
INTERCEP	1	14412.04197	2795.75178	5.155	0.0001
X1	1	819.81446	941.47799	0.871	0.3861
X2	1	-413.28219	303.20570	-1.363	0.1762
X1X2	1	33.53465808	34.14413805	0.982	0.3286
X1X1	1	-54.41406576	80.65633152	-0.675	0.5016
X2X2	1	11.87166612	16.59695367	0.715	0.4762
X3	1	8247.71451	2885.53387	2.858	0.0053
X4	1	-1632.24166	400.11602	-4.079	0.0001
X5	1	1242.52585	204.36346	6.080	0.0001
X1X3	1	-1350.92966	974.75335	-1.386	0.1691
X2X3	1	50.74158830	334.14998	0.152	0.8796
X1X2X3	1	-29.98215571	37.25553940	-0.805	0.4230
X1X1X3	1	91.37334655	84.49650785	1.081	0.2824
X2X2X3	1	5.55440578	19.06625192	0.291	0.7715

FIGURE 15.5
SAS regression analysis: Model 4

ANALYSIS OF VARIANCE

SOURCE	DF	SUM OF SQUARES	MEAN SQUARE	F VALUE	PROB>F
MODEL	41	282711608	6895405.07	8.545	0.0001
ERROR	64	51647128.00	806986.37		
C TOTAL	105	334358736			

ROOT MSE	898.3242	R-SQUARE	0.8455
DEP MEAN	19176.04	ADJ R-SQ	0.7466
C.V.	4.684618		

demonstrates the pitfalls that can attend an unwary attempt to interpret the results of t tests in a regression analysis. Intuitively, we would expect floor height to be an important factor. You might argue that units on the higher floors possess a better view and hence should command a higher mean sale price. Or, you might argue that units on the lower floors have greater accessibility to the pool and ocean and, consequently, should be in greater demand. Why, then, is the t test for floor height not statistically significant? The answer is that both of the preceding arguments are correct, one for the oceanside and one for the bayside. Thus, you will subsequently see that there is an interaction between floor height and view of ocean. Ocean-view units on the lower floors sell at higher prices than ocean-view units on the higher floors. In contrast, bay-view units on the higher floors command higher prices than bay-view units on the lower floors. These two contrasting effects tend to cancel (because we have not included interaction terms in the model) and thereby give the false impression that floor height is not an important variable for predicting mean sale price.

But, of course, we are looking ahead. Our next step is to determine whether Model 2 is better than Model 1.

Are floor height x_1 and distance from elevator x_2 related to sale price in a curvilinear manner; i.e., should we be using a second-order response surface instead of a first-order surface to relate $E(y)$ to x_1 and x_2? To answer this question, we will examine the drop in SSE from Model 1 to Model 2. The null hypothesis "Model 2 contributes no more information for the prediction of y than Model 1" is equivalent to testing

$$H_0\colon \quad \beta_3 = \beta_4 = \beta_5 = 0$$

where β_3, β_4, and β_5 appear in Model 2. The F statistic for the test, based on 3 and 97 df, is

$$F = \frac{\dfrac{\text{SSE}_1 - \text{SSE}_2}{\text{Number of } \beta \text{ parameters in } H_0}}{\text{MSE}_2} = \frac{\dfrac{97{,}737{,}975 - 90{,}032{,}798}{3}}{928{,}173.17}$$

$$= 2.77$$

An approximate value for $F_{.05}$ based on 3 and 97 df, obtained from Table 4 in Appendix C, is 2.70. Since the computed F value exceeds the tabulated value, $F_{.05} = 2.70$, we reject H_0. There is evidence to indicate that Model 2 contributes more information for the prediction of y than Model 1. This tells us that there is evidence of curvature in the response surfaces relating mean sale price, $E(y)$, to floor height x_1 and distance from elevator x_2.

You will recall that the difference between Models 2 and 3 is that Model 3 allows for two differently shaped second-order surfaces, one for ocean-view units and another for bay-view units; Model 2 employs a single surface to represent both types of units. Consequently, we wish to test the null hypothesis that "a single second-order surface adequately characterizes the relationship between $E(y)$, floor height x_1, and distance from elevator x_2 for both ocean-view and bay-view units" [i.e., Model 2 adequately models $E(y)$] against the alternative hypothesis that you need two different second-order surfaces [i.e, you need Model 3]. Thus,

$$H_0\colon \quad \beta_9 = \beta_{10} = \cdots = \beta_{13} = 0$$

where $\beta_9, \beta_{10}, \ldots, \beta_{13}$ are parameters in Model 3. The F statistic for this test, based on 5 and 92 df, is

$$F = \frac{\dfrac{\text{SSE}_2 - \text{SSE}_3}{\text{Number of } \beta \text{ parameters in } H_0}}{\text{MSE}_3}$$

$$= \frac{\dfrac{90{,}032{,}798 - 78{,}428{,}545}{5}}{852{,}484.19}$$

$$= 2.72$$

An approximate value for $F_{.05}$ based on 5 and 92 df, obtained from Table 4 in Appendix C, is 2.33. Since the computed F value exceeds this tabulated value, we reject H_0 and conclude that there is evidence to indicate that we need two different second-order surfaces to relate $E(y)$ to x_1 and x_2, one each for ocean-view and bay-view units.

Finally, we question whether Model 4 will provide an improvement over Model 3; i.e., will we gain information for predicting y by entering floor height into the model as a qualitative factor at eight levels? The F statistic to test the null hypothesis "Model 4 contributes no more information for predicting y than does Model 3" compares the drop in SSE from Model 3 to Model 4 with s_4^2. This F statistic, based on 28 df (the difference in the numbers of parameters in Models 4 and 3) and 64 df, is

$$F = \frac{\dfrac{\text{SSE}_3 - \text{SSE}_4}{\text{Number of } \beta \text{ parameters in } H_0}}{\text{MSE}_4}$$

$$= \frac{\dfrac{78{,}428{,}545 - 51{,}647{,}128}{28}}{806{,}986}$$

$$= 1.19$$

Checking Table 4 in Appendix C, you will find that the value for $F_{.05}$, based on 28 and 64 df, is approximately 1.65. Since the computed F is less than this value, there is not sufficient evidence to indicate that Model 4 is a significant improvement over Model 3.

Having checked the four theories of Section 15.3, we have evidence to indicate that Model 2 is significantly better than Model 1 and that Model 3 is better than Model 2. We will examine the prediction equation for Model 3 and see what it tells us about the relationship between the mean sale price $E(y)$ and the five factors used in our study, but first, it is important that we examine the residuals for Model 3 to determine whether the standard least squares assumptions about the random error term are satisfied.

15.5 An Analysis of the Residuals from Model 3

The four standard least squares assumptions about the random error term ε are (from Chapter 4) the following:

1. The mean is 0.
2. The variance (σ^2) is constant for all settings of the independent variables.
3. The errors follow a normal distribution.
4. The errors are independent.

If one or more of these assumptions are violated, any inferences derived from the Model 3 regression analysis are suspect. It is unlikely that assumption 1 (0 mean) is violated because the method of least squares guarantees that the mean of the residuals is 0. The same can be said for assumption 4 (independent errors) since the sale price data are not a time series. However, verifying assumptions 2 and 3 requires a thorough examination of the residuals from Model 3.

Recall that we can check for heteroscedastic errors (i.e., errors with unequal variances) by plotting the residuals against the predicted values. This residual plot is shown in Figure 15.6. If the variances were not constant, we would expect to see a cone-shaped pattern (since the response is sale price) in Figure 15.6, with the spread of the residuals increasing as $\hat{y}$ increases. Note, however, that the residuals appear to be randomly scattered around 0. Therefore, assumption 2 (constant variance) appears to be satisfied.

To check the normality assumption (assumption 3), we have generated a histogram of the residuals in Figure 15.7 on page 740. It is very evident that the distribution of residuals is not normal, but skewed to the right. At this point, we could opt to use a transformation on the response (similar to the variance-stabilizing transformations discussed in Section 7.3) to normalize the residuals. However, a nonnormal error distribution is often due to the presence of a single outlier. If this outlier is eliminated (or corrected), the normality assumption may then be satisfied.

We can use the residual plot in Figure 15.6 to detect outliers in the analysis. In Section 7.4, we defined outliers to be residuals that exceed $3s$ (in absolute value) and suspect outliers as residuals that fall between $2s$ and $3s$ away from 0. The $\pm 2s$ and $\pm 3s$ lines are marked on Figure 15.6 (where $s = 923$ from Figure 15.4). Note that there is one outlier and one suspect outlier, both with large *positive* residuals (approximately 5,500 and 2,500, respectively). Should we automatically eliminate these two observations from the analysis and refit Model 3? Although many analysts adopt such an approach, we should carefully examine the observations before deciding to eliminate them. We may discover a correctable recording (or coding) error, or we may find that the outliers are very influential and are due to an inadequate model (in which case, it is the model that needs fixing, not the data).

An examination of the SAS printout of the Model 3 residuals (not shown) reveals that the two observations in question are identified by observation numbers 35 and 49 (where the observations are numbered from 1 to 106). The sale prices, floor heights, and so forth, for these two data points were found to be recorded and coded correctly. To determine how influential these outliers are on the analysis, influence diagnostics (i.e., Cook's D and leverage) were generated using SAS. The results are summarized in Table 15.2.

TABLE 15.2 **Influence Diagnostics for Two Outliers in Model 3**

OBSERVATION	RESPONSE y	PREDICTED VALUE $\hat{y}$	RESIDUAL $y - \hat{y}$	LEVERAGE h	COOK'S DISTANCE D
35	26,500	21,070.4	5,429.6	.0605	.169
49	21,000	18,414.3	2,585.7	.1607	.128

Based on the "rules of thumb" given in Section 7.5, neither observation has strong influence on the analysis. Both leverage (h) values fall below $2(k + 1)/n = 2(14)/106 = .264$, indicating that the observations are not influential with respect to their x values; and both Cook's D values fall below .96 [the 50th percentile of an F distribution with $\nu_1 = k + 1 = 14$ and $\nu_2 = n - (k + 1) =$

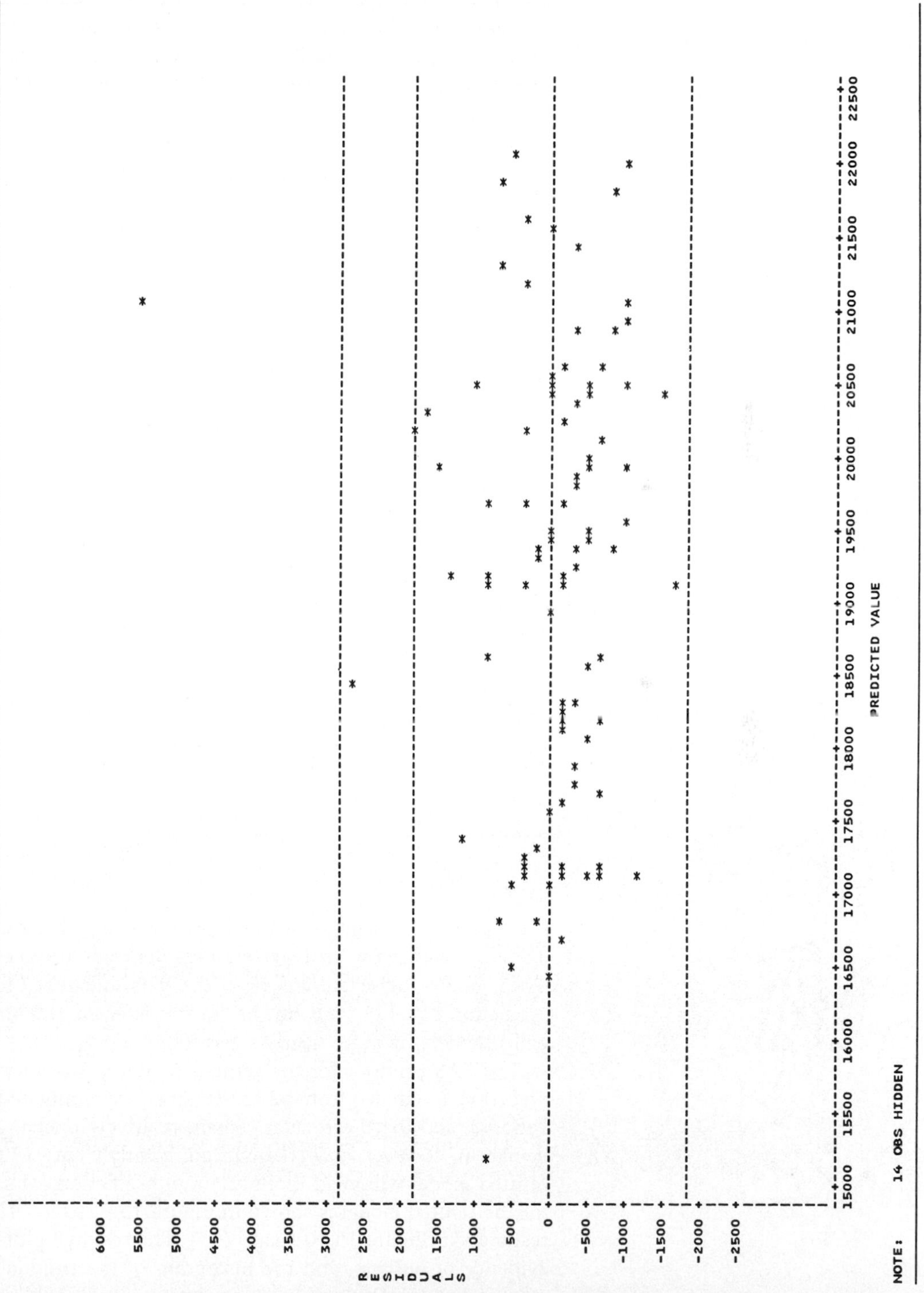

FIGURE 15.6
Plot of residuals versus $\hat{y}$ for Model 3

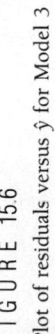

FIGURE 15.7
Histogram of residuals from Model 3

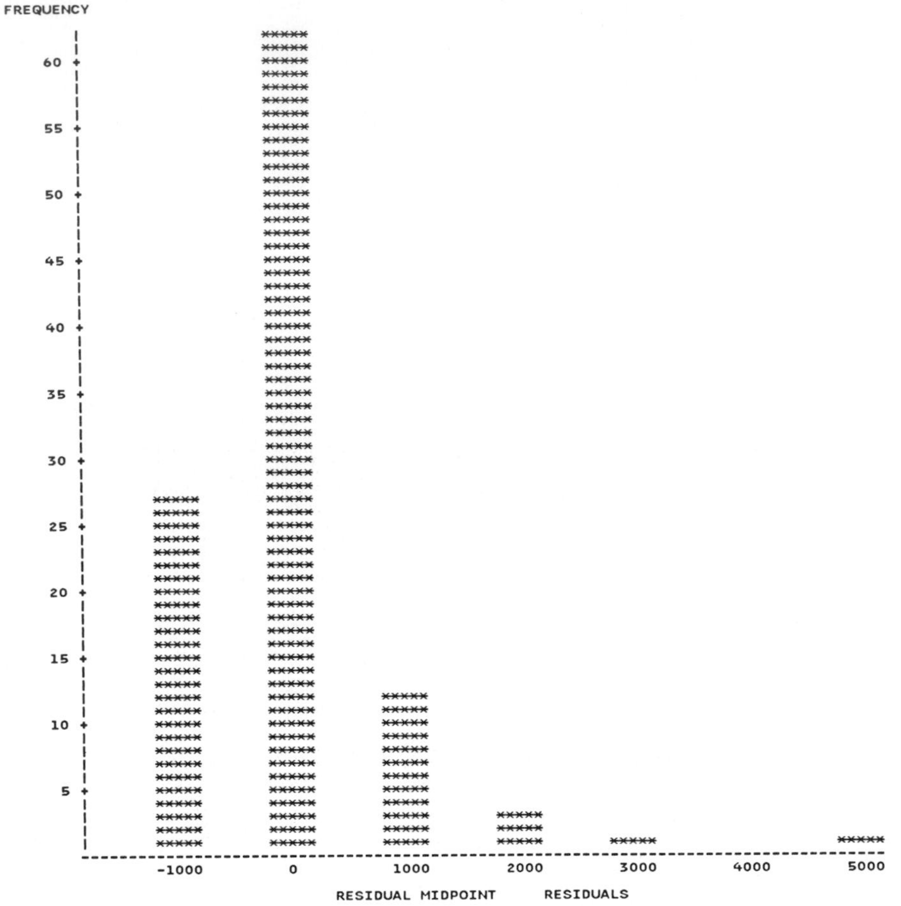

106 − 14 = 92 degrees of freedom], implying that they do not exhibit strong overall influence on the regression results (e.g., the β estimates). Consequently, if we remove these outliers from the data and refit Model 3, the least squares prediction equation will not be greatly affected and the normality assumption will probably be more nearly satisfied.

The SAS printout for the refitted model is shown in Figure 15.8. Note that df(Error) is reduced from 92 to 90 (since we eliminated the two outlying observations), and the β estimates remain relatively unchanged. The model standard deviation, however, is decreased significantly from 923 to 658, implying that the refitted model will yield more accurate predictions of sale price. A residual plot for the refitted model is shown in Figure 15.9 (page 742) and a histogram of the residuals in Figure 15.10 (page 743). The residual plot (Figure 15.9) reveals no evidence of outliers, and the histogram of the residuals (Figure 15.10) is now approximately normal.

FIGURE 15.8
SAS printout for Model 3 with outliers deleted

ANALYSIS OF VARIANCE

SOURCE	DF	SUM OF SQUARES	MEAN SQUARE	F VALUE	PROB>F
MODEL	13	237649572	18280736.29	42.254	0.0001
ERROR	90	38937243.63	432636.04		
C TOTAL	103	276586815			

ROOT MSE	657.7507	R-SQUARE	0.8592
DEP MEAN	19088.08	ADJ R-SQ	0.8389
C.V.	3.445872		

PARAMETER ESTIMATES

VARIABLE	DF	PARAMETER ESTIMATE	STANDARD ERROR	T FOR H0: PARAMETER=0	PROB > |T|
INTERCEP	1	15390.19258	2002.11309	7.687	0.0001
X1	1	310.30678	682.48668	0.455	0.6504
X2	1	-203.35236	222.11810	-0.916	0.3624
X1X2	1	26.08674126	24.39118628	1.070	0.2877
X1X1	1	-10.85790288	58.55677607	-0.185	0.8533
X2X2	1	1.09206281	12.11658757	0.090	0.9284
X3	1	7537.23222	2065.74801	3.649	0.0004
X4	1	-1500.60982	285.47441	-5.257	0.0001
X5	1	1075.38112	146.64993	7.333	0.0001
X1X3	1	-1024.61067	706.31066	-1.451	0.1504
X2X3	1	-167.24636	243.44976	-0.687	0.4939
X1X2X3	1	-25.43791062	26.60757746	-0.956	0.3416
X1X1X3	1	67.67866117	61.32668383	1.104	0.2727
X2X2X3	1	19.21642228	13.82949599	1.390	0.1681

15.6 What the Model 3 Regression Analysis Tells Us

We have settled on Model 3 (with two observations deleted) as our choice to relate mean sale price $E(y)$ to five factors: the two quantitative factors, floor height x_1 and distance from elevator x_2; and the three qualitative factors, view of ocean, end unit, and furniture. This model postulates two different second-order surfaces relating mean sale price $E(y)$ to x_1 and x_2, one for ocean-view units and one for bay-view units. The effect of each of the two qualitative factors, end unit (numbered __11) and furniture, is to produce a change in mean sale price that is identical for all combinations of values of x_1 and x_2. In other words, assigning a value of 1 to one of the dummy variables increases (or decreases) the estimated mean sale price by a fixed amount. The net effect is to push the second-order surface upward or downward, with the direction depending on the level of the specific qualitative factor. The estimated increase (or decrease) in mean sale price because of a given qualitative factor is given by the estimated value of the β parameter associated with its dummy variable.

For example, the prediction equation (with rounded values given for the parameter estimates) obtained from Figure 15.8 is

$$\begin{aligned}\hat{y} = 15{,}390.2 &+ 310.3x_1 - 203.4x_2 \\ &+ 26.1x_1x_2 - 10.9x_1^2 + 1.1x_2^2 \\ &+ 7{,}537.2x_3 - 1{,}500.6x_4 + 1{,}075.4x_5 \\ &- 1{,}024.6x_1x_3 - 167.2x_2x_3 - 25.4x_1x_2x_3 \\ &+ 67.7x_1^2x_3 + 19.2x_2^2x_3\end{aligned}$$

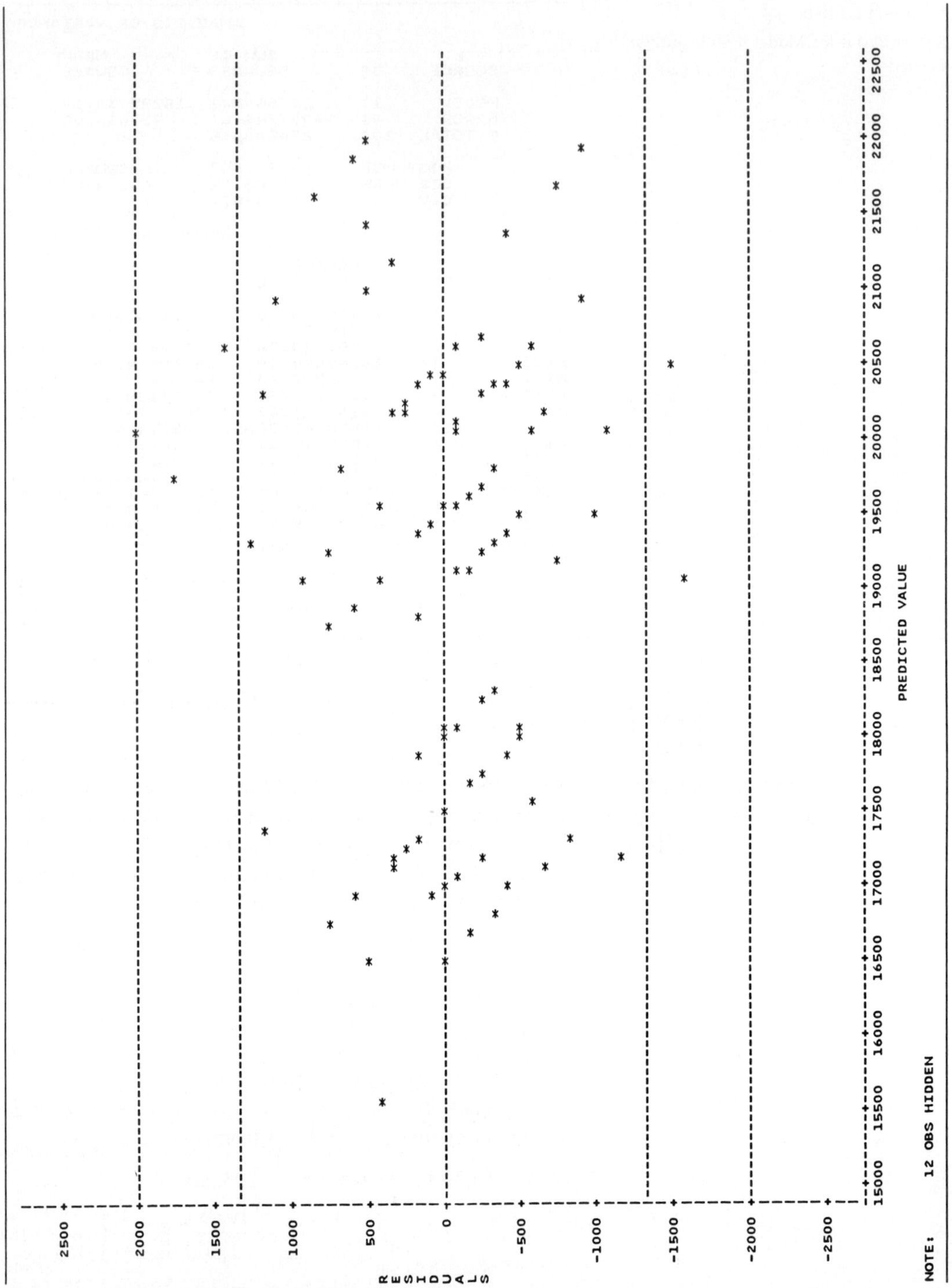

FIGURE 15.9
Plot of residuals versus $\hat{y}$ for Model 3 with outliers deleted

FIGURE 15.10 Histogram of residuals from Model 3 with outliers deleted

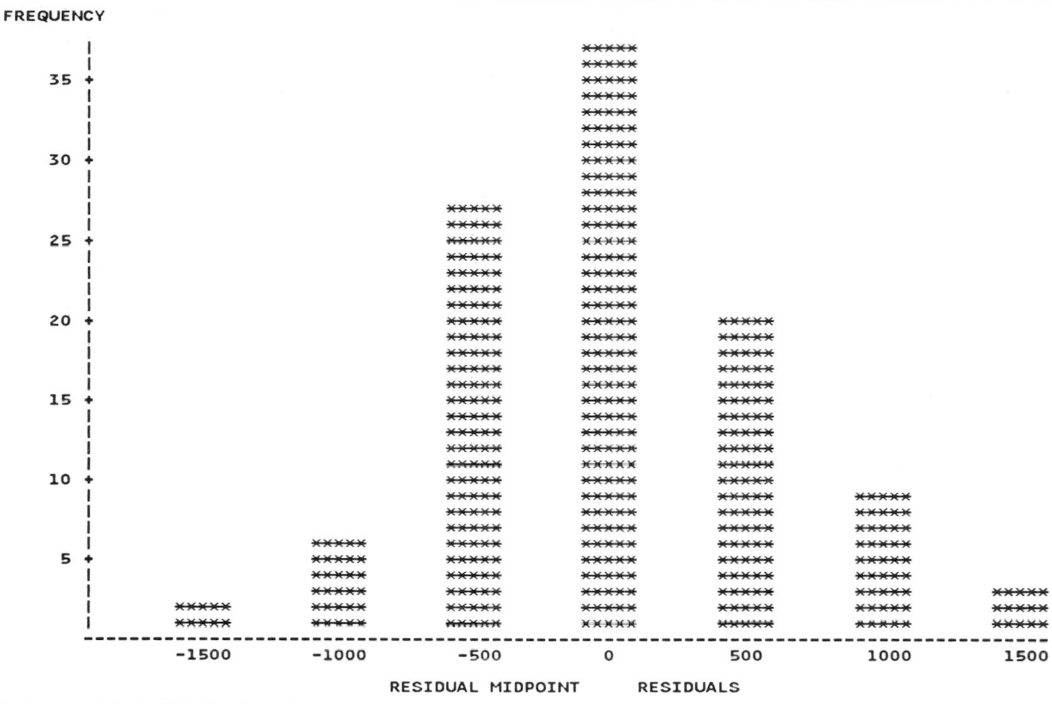

Since the dummy variables for end unit and furniture are, respectively, x_4 and x_5, the estimated changes in mean sale price for these qualitative factors are

$$\text{End unit } (x_4 = 1)\text{:} \quad \hat{\beta}_7 = -\$1{,}500.6$$

$$\text{Furnished } (x_5 = 1)\text{:} \quad \hat{\beta}_8 = +\$1{,}075.4$$

Thus, if you substitute $x_4 = 1$ into the prediction equation, the estimated mean decrease in sale price for an end unit is \$1,500.6, regardless of the view, floor, and whether it is furnished.

The effect of floor height x_1 and distance from elevator x_2 can be determined by plotting $\hat{y}$ as a function of one of the variables for given values of the other. For example, suppose we wish to examine the relationship between $\hat{y}$, x_1, and x_2 for bay-view ($x_3 = 0$), non–end units ($x_4 = 0$) with no furniture ($x_5 = 0$). The prediction curve relating $\hat{y}$ to distance from elevator x_2 can be graphed for each floor by first setting $x_1 = 1$, then $x_1 = 2, \ldots, x_1 = 8$. The graphs of these curves are shown in Figure 15.11 on page 744. The 1's indicate the curve for the first floor, the 2's the curve for the second floor, and so forth. In Figure 15.11, we can also see some interesting patterns in the estimated mean sale prices:

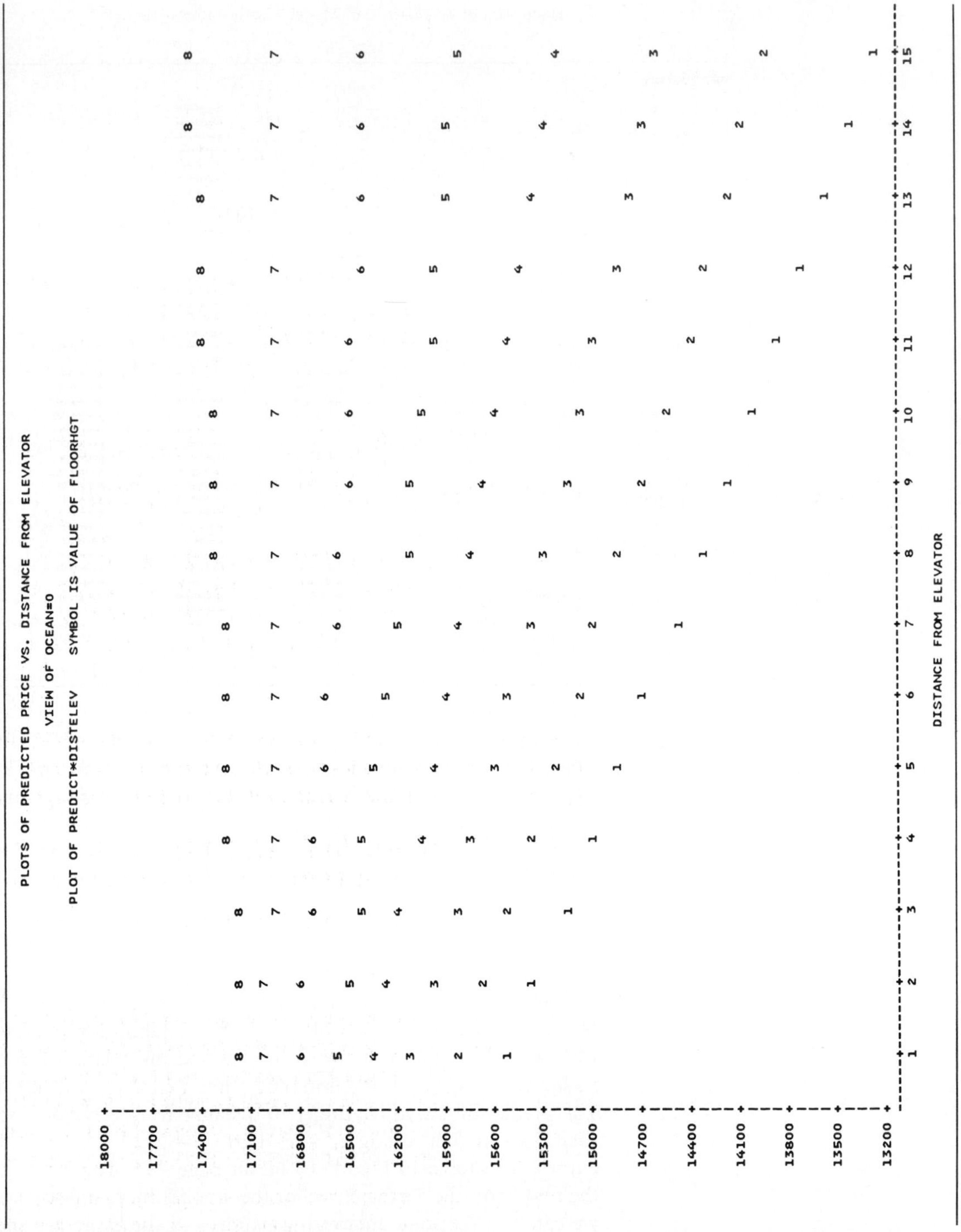

FIGURE 15.11 Plot of predicted price versus distance from elevator: Bay-view units

1. The higher the floor of a bay-view unit, the higher will be the mean sale price. Low floors look out onto the parking lot and, all other variables held constant, are least preferred.
2. The relationship is curvilinear and is not the same for each floor.
3. Units on the first floor near the office have a higher estimated mean sale price than second- or third-floor units located in the west end of the complex. Perhaps the reason for this is that these units are close to the pool and the game room, and these advantages outweigh the disadvantage of a poor view.
4. The mean sale price decreases as the distance from the elevator and center of activity increases for the lower floors, but the decrease is less as you move upward, floor to floor. Finally, note that the estimated mean sale price increases substantially for units on the highest floor that are farthest away from the elevator. These units are subjected to the least human traffic and are, therefore, the most private. Consequently, a possible explanation for their high price is that buyers place a higher value on the privacy provided by the units than the negative value that they assign to their inconvenience. One additional explanation for the generally higher estimated sale price for units at the ends of the complex may be that they possess more windows.

A similar set of curves is shown in Figure 15.12 on page 746 for ocean-view units ($x_3 = 1$). You will note some amazing differences between these curves and those for the bay-view units in Figure 15.11 (these differences explain why we needed two separate second-order surfaces to describe these two sets of units). The preference for floors is completely reversed on the ocean side of the complex: the lower the floor, the higher the estimated mean sale price. Apparently, people selecting the ocean-view units are primarily concerned with accessibility to the ocean, pool, beach, and game room. Note that the estimated mean sale price is highest near the elevator. It drops and then rises as you reach the units farthest from the elevator. An explanation for this phenomenon is similar to the one that we used for the bayside units. Units near the elevator are more accessible and nearer to the recreational facilities. Those farthest from the elevators afford the greatest privacy. Units near the center of the complex offer reduced amounts of both accessibility *and* privacy. Notice that units adjacent to the elevator command a higher estimated mean sale price than those near the west end of the complex, suggesting that accessibility has a greater influence on price than privacy.

Rather than examine the graphs of $\hat{y}$ as a function of distance from elevator x_2, you may want to see how $\hat{y}$ behaves as a function of floor height x_1 for units located at various distances from the elevator. These estimated mean sale price curves are shown for bay-view units in Figure 15.13 (page 747) and for ocean-view units in Figure 15.14 (page 748). To avoid congestion in the graphs, we have shown only the curves for distances $x_2 = 1, 3, 5, \ldots, 13, 15$. A curve traced by a sequence of 1's indicates that it applies to units located a distance of 1 from the elevator. Similarly, a curve traced by a sequence of 5's applies to units located a distance of 5 from the elevator. We leave it to you and to the real estate experts to deduce the practical implications of these curves.

FIGURE 15.12 Plot of predicted price versus distance from elevator: Ocean-view units

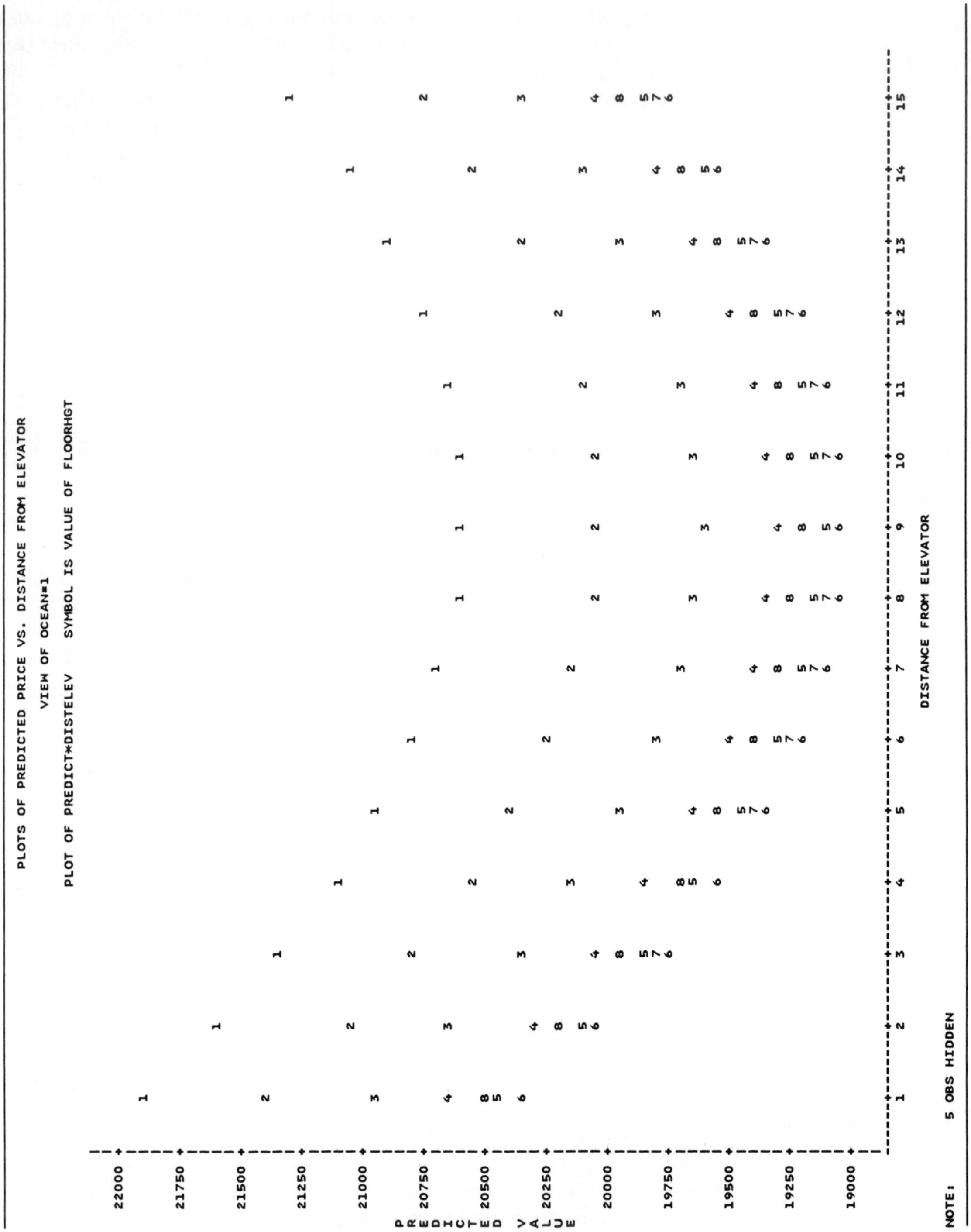

FIGURE 15.13 Plot of predicted price versus floor height: Bay-view units

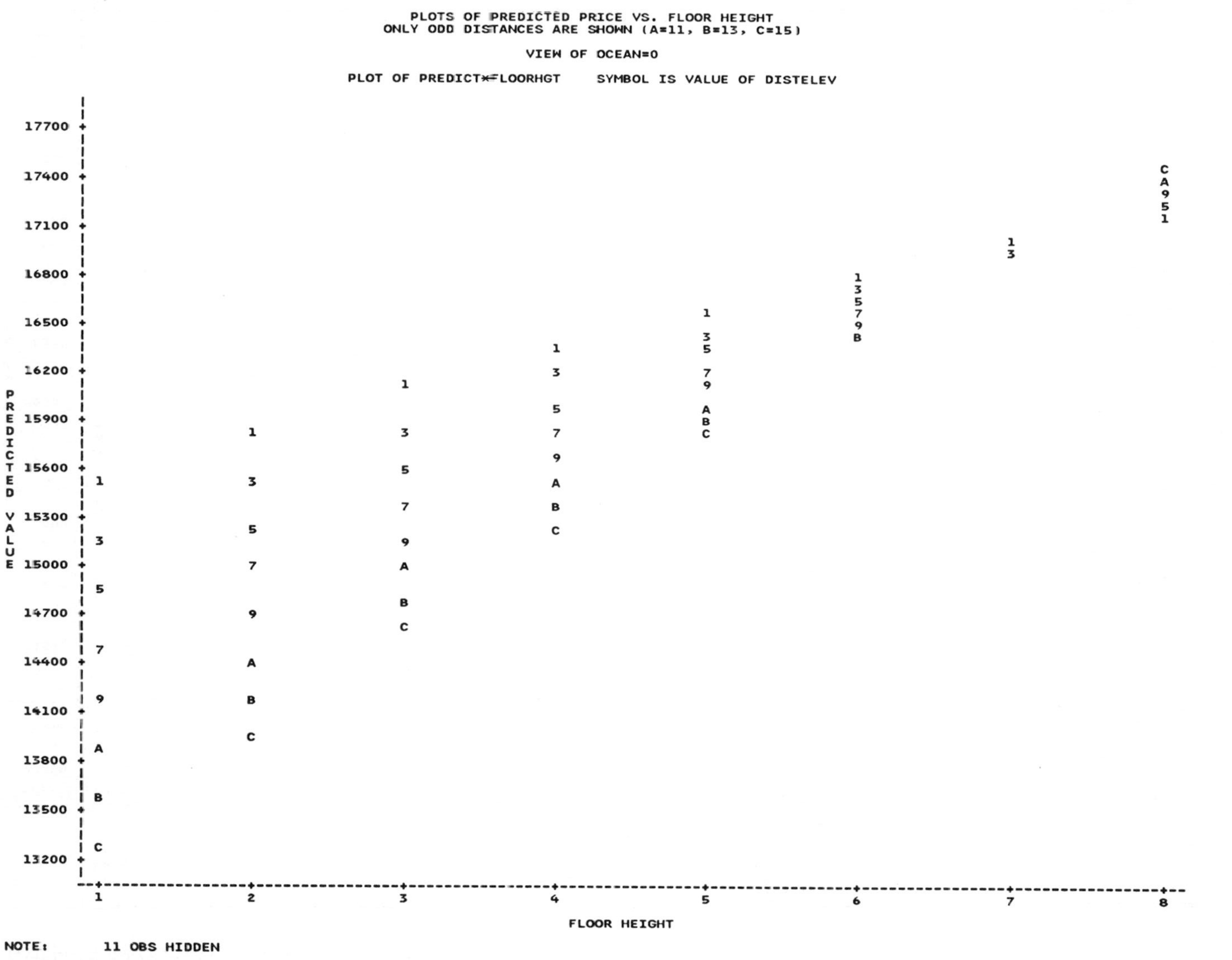

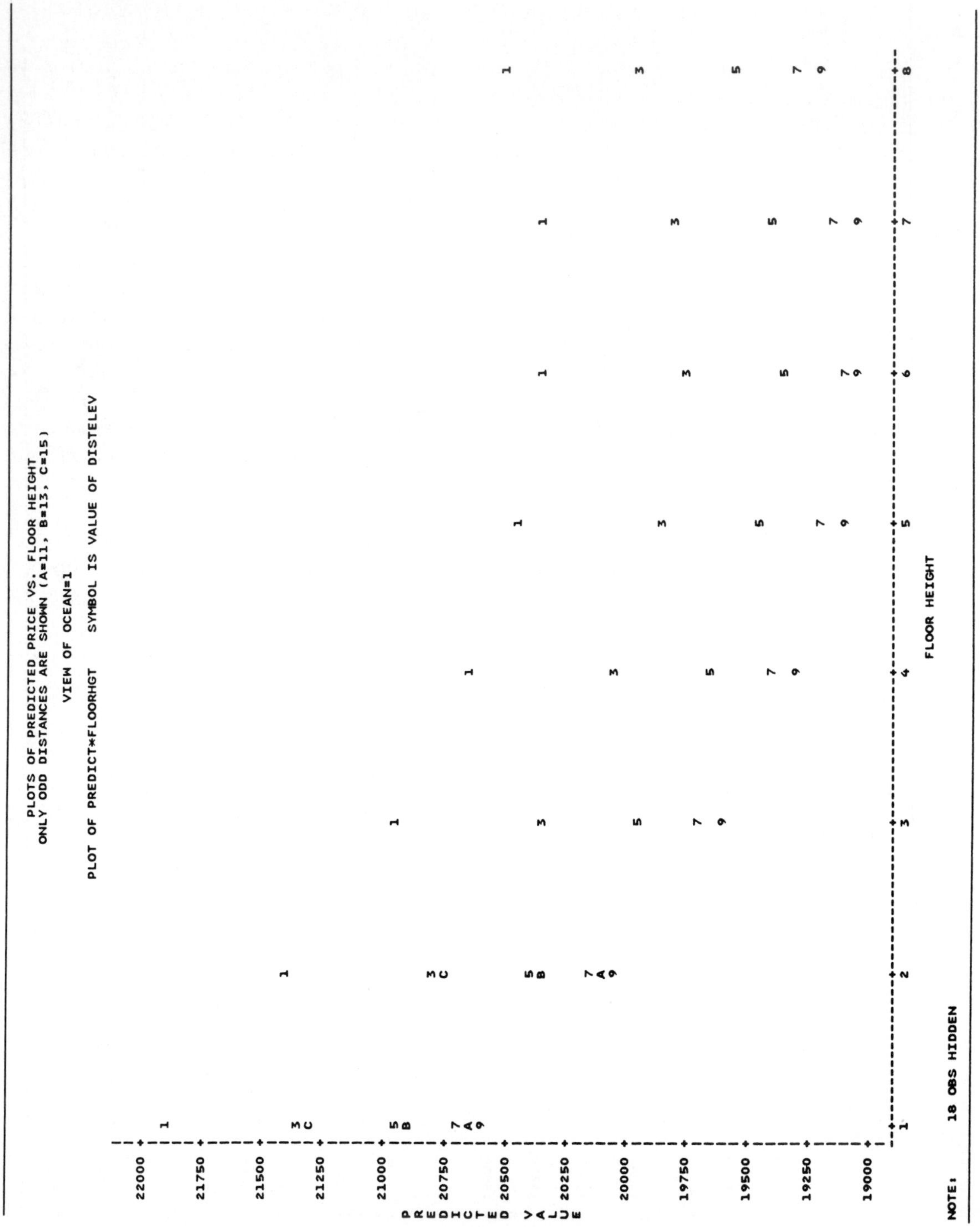

FIGURE 15.14 Plot of predicted price versus floor height: Ocean-view units

15.7 Comparing the Mean Sale Price for Two Types of Units (Optional)

[*Note:* This section requires an understanding of the mechanics of a multiple regression analysis presented in Appendix A.]

Comparing the mean sale price for two types of units might seem a useless endeavor, considering that all the units have been sold and that we will never be able to sell the units in the same economic environment that existed at the time the data were collected. Nevertheless, this information might be useful to a real estate appraiser or to a developer who is pricing units in a new and similar condominium complex. We will assume that a comparison is useful and show you how it can be accomplished.

Suppose you want to estimate the difference in mean sale price for units in two different locations and with or without furniture. For example, suppose you wish to estimate the difference in mean sale price between the first-floor ocean-view and bay-view units located at the east end of building 1 (units 101 and 102 in Figure 15.1). Both these units afford a maximum of accessibility, but they possess different views. We assume that both are furnished. The estimate of the mean sale price $E(y)$ for the first-floor, bay-view unit will be the value of $\hat{y}$ when $x_1 = 1$, $x_2 = 1$, $x_3 = 0$, $x_4 = 0$, $x_5 = 1$. Similarly, the estimated value of $E(y)$ for the first-floor, ocean-view unit is obtained by substituting $x_1 = 1$, $x_2 = 1$, $x_3 = 1$, $x_4 = 0$, and $x_5 = 1$ into the prediction equation.

We will let $\hat{y}_o$ and $\hat{y}_b$ represent the estimated mean sale prices for the first-floor ocean-view and bay-view units, respectively. Then the estimator of the difference in mean sale prices for the two units is

$$\ell = \hat{y}_o - \hat{y}_b$$

We represent this estimator by the symbol ℓ, because it is a linear function of the parameter estimators $\hat{\beta}_0, \hat{\beta}_1, \ldots, \hat{\beta}_{13}$; i.e.,

$$\begin{aligned}\hat{y}_o = \hat{\beta}_0 &+ \hat{\beta}_1(1) + \hat{\beta}_2(1) + \hat{\beta}_3(1)(1) + \hat{\beta}_4(1)^2 + \hat{\beta}_5(1)^2 \\ &+ \hat{\beta}_6(1) + \hat{\beta}_7(0) + \hat{\beta}_8(1) + \hat{\beta}_9(1)(1) + \hat{\beta}_{10}(1)(1) \\ &+ \hat{\beta}_{11}(1)(1)(1) + \hat{\beta}_{12}(1)^2(1) + \hat{\beta}_{13}(1)^2(1) \\ \hat{y}_b = \hat{\beta}_0 &+ \hat{\beta}_1(1) + \hat{\beta}_2(1) + \hat{\beta}_3(1)(1) + \hat{\beta}_4(1)^2 + \hat{\beta}_5(1)^2 \\ &+ \hat{\beta}_6(0) + \hat{\beta}_7(0) + \hat{\beta}_8(1) + \hat{\beta}_9(1)(0) + \hat{\beta}_{10}(1)(0) \\ &+ \hat{\beta}_{11}(1)(1)(0) + \hat{\beta}_{12}(1)^2(0) + \hat{\beta}_{13}(1)^2(0)\end{aligned}$$

then

$$\ell = \hat{y}_o - \hat{y}_b = \hat{\beta}_6 + \hat{\beta}_9 + \hat{\beta}_{10} + \hat{\beta}_{11} + \hat{\beta}_{12} + \hat{\beta}_{13}$$

A 95% confidence interval for the mean value of a linear function of the estimators $\hat{\beta}_0, \hat{\beta}_1, \ldots, \hat{\beta}_k$, given in Section A.7 of Appendix A, is

$$\ell \pm t_{.025} s \sqrt{\mathbf{a}'(\mathbf{X}'\mathbf{X})^{-1}\mathbf{a}}$$

where in our case, $\ell = \hat{y}_o - \hat{y}_b$ is the estimate of the difference in mean values for the two units, $E(y_o) - E(y_b)$; s is the least squares estimate of the standard deviation from the regression analysis of Model 3 (Figure 15.8); and $(\mathbf{X}'\mathbf{X})^{-1}$, the inverse matrix for the Model 3 regression analysis, is shown in Figure 15.15. The **a** matrix is a column matrix containing elements $a_0, a_1, a_2, \ldots a_{13}$, where $a_0, a_1, a_2, \ldots, a_{13}$ are the coefficients of $\hat{\beta}_0, \hat{\beta}_1, \ldots, \hat{\beta}_{13}$ in the linear function ℓ, i.e.,

$$\ell = a_0\hat{\beta}_0 + a_1\hat{\beta}_1 + \cdots + a_{13}\hat{\beta}_{13}$$

Since our linear function is

$$\ell = \hat{\beta}_6 + \hat{\beta}_9 + \hat{\beta}_{10} + \hat{\beta}_{11} + \hat{\beta}_{12} + \hat{\beta}_{13}$$

it follows that $a_6 = a_9 = a_{10} = a_{11} = a_{12} = a_{13} = 1$ and $a_0 = a_1 = a_2 = a_3 = a_4 = a_5 = a_7 = a_8 = 0$.

Substituting the values of $\hat{\beta}_6, \hat{\beta}_9, \hat{\beta}_{10}, \ldots, \hat{\beta}_{13}$ (given in Figure 15.8) into ℓ, we have

$$\begin{aligned}\ell = \hat{y}_o - \hat{y}_b &= \hat{\beta}_6 + \hat{\beta}_9 + \hat{\beta}_{10} + \hat{\beta}_{11} + \hat{\beta}_{12} + \hat{\beta}_{13} \\ &= 7{,}537.23 - 1{,}024.61 - 167.25 - 25.44 + 67.68 + 19.22 \\ &= \$6{,}406.83\end{aligned}$$

The value of $t_{.025}$ needed for the confidence interval is approximately equal to 1.96 (because of the large number of degrees of freedom), and the value of s, given in Figure 15.8, is $s = 657.75$. Finally, the matrix product $\mathbf{a}'(\mathbf{X}'\mathbf{X})^{-1}\mathbf{a}$ can be obtained by multiplying the **a** matrix (described in the preceding paragraph) and the $(\mathbf{X}'\mathbf{X})^{-1}$ matrix given in Figure 15.15. Substituting these values into the formula for the confidence interval, we obtain (using a computer):

$$\overbrace{\hat{y}_o - \hat{y}_b}^{\ell} \pm t_{.025}s\sqrt{\mathbf{a}'(\mathbf{X}'\mathbf{X})^{-1}\mathbf{a}}$$

$$\$6{,}406.83 \pm \$2{,}733.46$$

Therefore, we estimate the difference in the mean sale prices of first-floor ocean-view and bay-view units (units 101 and 102) to lie within the interval \$3,673.37 to \$9,140.29.

You can use the technique described above to compare the mean sale prices for any pair of units.

15.8 Conclusions

You may be able to propose a better model for mean sale price than Model 3, but we think that Model 3 provides a good fit to the data. Further, it reveals some interesting information on the preferences of buyers of oceanside condominium units.

Lower floors are preferred on the ocean side; the closer the units lie to the elevator and pool, the higher the estimated price. Some preference is given to the privacy of units located in the upper floor west-end.

Higher floors are preferred on the bay-view side (the side facing away from the ocean), with maximum preference given to units near the elevator (convenient and close to activities) and, to a lesser degree, to the privacy afforded by the west-end units.

FIGURE 15.15 SAS printout of the $(X'X)^{-1}$ matrix for Model 3

INVERSE	INTERCEP	X1	X2	X1X2	X1X1	X2X2	X3	X4
INTERCEP	9.265194	-2.99228	-0.25651	0.01708831	0.2368571	0.01335886	-9.26105	-0.00350909
X1	-2.99228	1.076628	-0.00585467	0.002321133	-0.090368	-0.00156845	2.993569	-0.00109312
X2	-0.25651	-0.00585467	0.1140368	-0.00896821	0.004048291	-0.00445162	0.2560235	0.000412168
X1X2	0.01708831	0.002321133	-0.00896821	0.001375128	-0.000755996	.00003112222	-0.0170757	-.0000107253
X1X1	0.2368571	-0.090368	0.004048291	-0.000755996	0.00792559	0.0001270988	-0.23705	0.0001635619
X2X2	0.01335886	-0.00156845	-0.00445162	.00003112222	0.0001270988	0.0003393423	-0.0133355	-0.000019801
X3	-9.26105	2.993569	0.2560235	-0.0170757	-0.23705	-0.0133355	9.863521	-0.00346016
X4	-0.00350909	-0.00109312	0.000412168	-.0000107253	0.0001635619	-0.000019801	-0.00346016	0.18837
X5	-0.0362161	-0.0112817	0.00425385	-0.000110692	0.001688068	-0.00020436	0.03053109	0.004816517
X1X3	2.99394	-1.07611	0.005659513	-0.00231605	0.09029058	0.001577825	-3.16263	0.01236905
X2X3	0.2609271	0.007230662	-0.114556	0.008981714	-0.00425418	0.004476544	-0.325309	-0.020075
X1X2X3	-0.0168751	-0.00225471	0.008943169	-0.00137448	0.0007460576	-.0000299191	0.02213208	-0.000318277
X1X1X3	-0.237302	0.09022947	-0.00399605	0.0007546363	-0.00790486	-0.000129609	0.2497183	-0.000886821
X2X2X3	-0.0137351	0.00145126	0.004495806	-0.000032272	-0.000109564	-0.000341465	0.01594939	0.001543755
PRICPAID	15390.19	310.3068	-203.352	26.08674	-10.8579	1.092063	7537.232	-1500.61

INVERSE	X5	X1X3	X2X3	X1X2X3	X1X1X3	X2X2X3	PRICPAID
INTERCEP	-0.0362161	2.99394	0.2609271	-0.0168751	-0.237302	-0.0137351	15390.19
X1	-0.0112817	-1.07611	0.007230662	-0.00225471	0.09022947	0.00145126	310.3068
X2	0.00425385	0.005659513	-0.114556	0.008943169	-0.00399605	0.004495806	-203.352
X1X2	-0.000110692	-0.00231605	0.008981714	-0.00137448	0.0007546363	-0.000032272	26.08674
X1X1	0.001688068	0.09029058	-0.00425418	0.0007460576	-0.00790486	-0.000109564	-10.8579
X2X2	-0.00020436	0.001577825	0.004476544	-.0000299191	-0.000129609	-0.000341465	1.092063
X3	0.03053109	-3.16263	-0.325309	0.02213208	0.2497183	0.01594939	7537.232
X4	0.004816517	0.01236905	-0.020075	-0.000318277	-0.000886821	0.001543755	-1500.61
X5	0.04970968	0.009001128	-0.0103167	-0.000181965	-0.00107756	0.0007207221	1075.381
X1X3	0.009001128	1.153105	-0.00425868	0.001544672	-0.0973915	-0.00145736	-1024.61
X2X3	-0.0103167	-0.00425868	0.1369923	-0.00972204	0.004412018	-0.00567736	-167.246
X1X2X3	-0.000181965	0.001544672	-0.00972204	0.001636394	-0.000836949	-.0000172506	-25.4379
X1X1X3	-0.00107756	-0.0973915	0.004412018	-0.000836949	0.008693132	0.0001387393	67.67866
X2X2X3	0.0007207221	-0.00145736	-0.00567736	-.0000172506	0.0001387393	0.0004420689	19.21642
PRICPAID	1075.381	-1024.61	-167.246	-25.4379	67.67866	19.21642	38937244

EXERCISES

15.1 The data used in this study are presented in Appendix J.* If you have access to a computer, fit Models 1, 2, and 3 to the data set.

15.2 Postulate some models that you think might be an improvement over Model 3. Fit these models to the data set in Appendix J. Test to see whether they do, in fact, contribute more information for predicting sale price than Model 3.

Reference

Kelting, H. "Investigation of condominium sale prices in three market scenarios: Utility of stepwise, interactive, multiple regression analysis and implications for design and appraisal methodology." Unpublished paper, University of Florida, Gainesville, 1979.

*Of the 200 units in the condominium complex, 106 were sold at auction and the remainder were sold (some more than once) at the developer's fixed price. The 106 units analyzed in this study are identified by observation (OBS) numbers 77–182 in Appendix J.

CASE STUDY 16 Modeling Daily Peak Electricity Demands

CONTENTS

OBJECTIVE

To present a time series approach to modeling daily peak electricity demands on a power company and to show how to use the time series model for short-term forecasting

16.1 The Problem

To operate effectively, power companies must be able to predict daily peak demand for electricity. *Demand* (or *load*) is defined as the rate (measured in megawatts) at which electric energy is delivered to customers. Since demand is normally recorded on an hourly basis, daily peak demand refers to the maximum hourly demand in a 24-hour period. Power companies are continually developing and refining statistical models of daily peak demand.

Models of daily peak demand serve a twofold purpose. First, the models provide short-term *forecasts* that will assist in the economic planning and dispatching of electric energy. Second, models that relate peak demand to one or more weather variables provide estimates of historical peak demands under a set of alternative weather conditions. That is, since changing weather conditions represent the primary source of variation in peak demand, the model can be used to answer the often-asked question, "What would the peak daily demand have been had normal weather prevailed?" This second application, commonly referred to as *weather normalization*, is mainly an exercise in *backcasting* (i.e., adjusting historical data) rather than forecasting (Jacob, 1985).

Since peak demand is recorded over time (days), the dependent variable is a time series and one approach to modeling daily peak demand is to use a time series model. This chapter presents key results of a study designed to compare several alternative methods of modeling 1983 daily peak demand for the Florida Power Corporation (FPC). For this case study, we focus on two time series models and a multiple regression model proposed in the original FPC study. Then we demonstrate how to forecast daily peak demand using one of the time series models. (We leave the problem of backcasting as an exercise.)

16.2 The Data

The data for the study consist of daily observations on peak demand recorded by the FPC for the period beginning November 1, 1982, and ending October 31, 1983, and several factors that are known to influence demand. It is typically assumed that demand consists of two components, a non–weather-sensitive "base" demand that is not influenced by temperature changes and a weather-sensitive demand that is highly responsive to changes in temperature.

The principal factor that affects the usage of non–weather-sensitive appliances (such as refrigerators, generators, lights, and computers) is the *day of the week*. Typically, Saturdays have lower peak demands than weekdays due to decreased commercial and industrial activity, whereas Sundays and holidays exhibit even lower peak demand levels as commercial and industrial activity declines even further.

The single most important factor affecting the usage of weather-sensitive appliances (such as heaters and air conditioners) is *temperature*. During the winter months, as temperatures drop below comfortable levels, customers begin to operate their electric heating units, thereby increasing the level of demand placed on the system. Similarly, during the summer months, as temperatures climb above comfortable levels, the use of air conditioning drives demand upward. Since the FPC serves 32 counties along west-central and northern Florida, it was necessary to obtain temperature conditions from multiple weather stations. This was accomplished by identifying three primary weather stations within the FPC service area and recording the temperature value at the hour of peak demand each day at each station. A weighted average of these three daily temperatures was used to represent coincident temperature (i.e., temperature at the hour of peak demand) for the entire FPC service area, where the weights were proportional to the percentage of total electricity sales attributable to the weather zones surrounding each of the three weather stations.

To summarize, the independent variable (y_t) and the independent variables recorded for each of the 365 days of the November 1982–October 1983 year were as follows:

Dependent Variable:

y_t = Peak demand (in megawatts) observed on day t

Independent Variables:

Day of the week: Weekday, Saturday, or Sunday/holiday

Temperature: Coincident temperature (in degrees), i.e., the temperature recorded at the hour of the peak demand on day t, calculated as a weighted average of three daily temperatures

16.3 The Models

In any modeling procedure, it is often helpful to plot the data in a scattergram. Figure 16.1 on page 756 shows a graph of the daily peak demand (y_t) from November 1982 through October 1983. The effects of seasonal weather on peak demand are readily apparent from the figure. One way to account for this seasonal variation is to include dummy variables for months or trigonometric terms in the model (refer to Section 9.6). However, since temperature is such a strong indicator of the weather, the FPC chose a simpler model with temperature as the sole seasonal weather variable.

Figure 16.2 on page 757 is a scatterplot of daily peak demands versus coincident temperature. Note the nonlinear relationship that exists between the two variables. During the cool winter months, peak demand is inversely related to temperature; lower temperatures cause increased usage of heating equipment, which in turn causes higher peak demands. In contrast, the summer months reveal a positive relationship between peak demand and temperature; higher temperatures yield higher peak demands because of greater usage of air conditioners. You might think that a second-order (quadratic) model would be a good choice to account for the U-shaped distribution of peak demands shown in Figure 16.2. The FPC, however, rejected such a model for two reasons:

1. A quadratic model yields a symmetrical shape (i.e., a parabola) and would, therefore, not allow independent estimates of the winter and summer peak demand–temperature relationship.
2. In theory, there exists a mild temperature range where peak demand is assumed to consist solely of the non–weather-sensitive base demand component. For this range, a temperature change will not spur any additional heating or cooling and, consequently, has no impact on demand. The lack of linearity in the bottom portion of the U-shaped parabola fitted by the quadratic model would

FIGURE 16.1 Daily peak megawatt demands, November 1982–October 1983

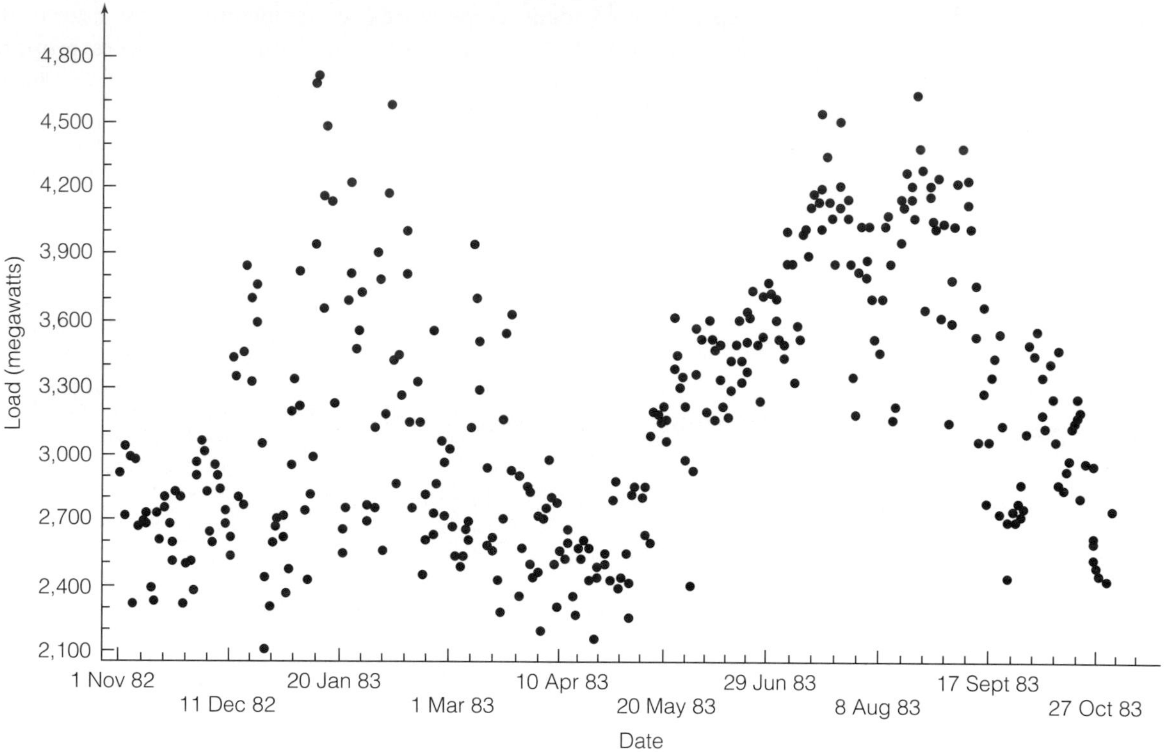

Source: Florida Power Corporation.

yield overestimates of peak demand at the extremes of the mild temperature range and underestimates for temperatures in the middle of this range (see Figure 16.3).

The solution was to model daily peak demand with a piecewise linear regression model (see Section 8.2). This approach has the advantage of allowing the peak demand–temperature relationship to vary between some prespecified temperature ranges, as well as providing a mechanism for joining the separate pieces.

Using the piecewise linear specification as the basic model structure, the following model of daily peak demand was proposed:

Model 1

$$y_t = \beta_0 + \underbrace{\beta_1(x_{1t} - 59)x_{2t} + \beta_2(x_{1t} - 78)x_{3t}}_{\text{Temperature}} + \underbrace{\beta_3 x_{4t} + \beta_4 x_{5t}}_{\text{Day of the week}} + \varepsilon_t$$

where

x_{1t} = Coincident temperature on day t

$$x_{2t} = \begin{cases} 1 & \text{if } x_{1t} < 59 \\ 0 & \text{if not} \end{cases} \qquad x_{3t} = \begin{cases} 1 & \text{if } x_{1t} > 78 \\ 0 & \text{if not} \end{cases}$$

FIGURE 16.2 Daily peak demand versus temperature, November 1982–October 1983

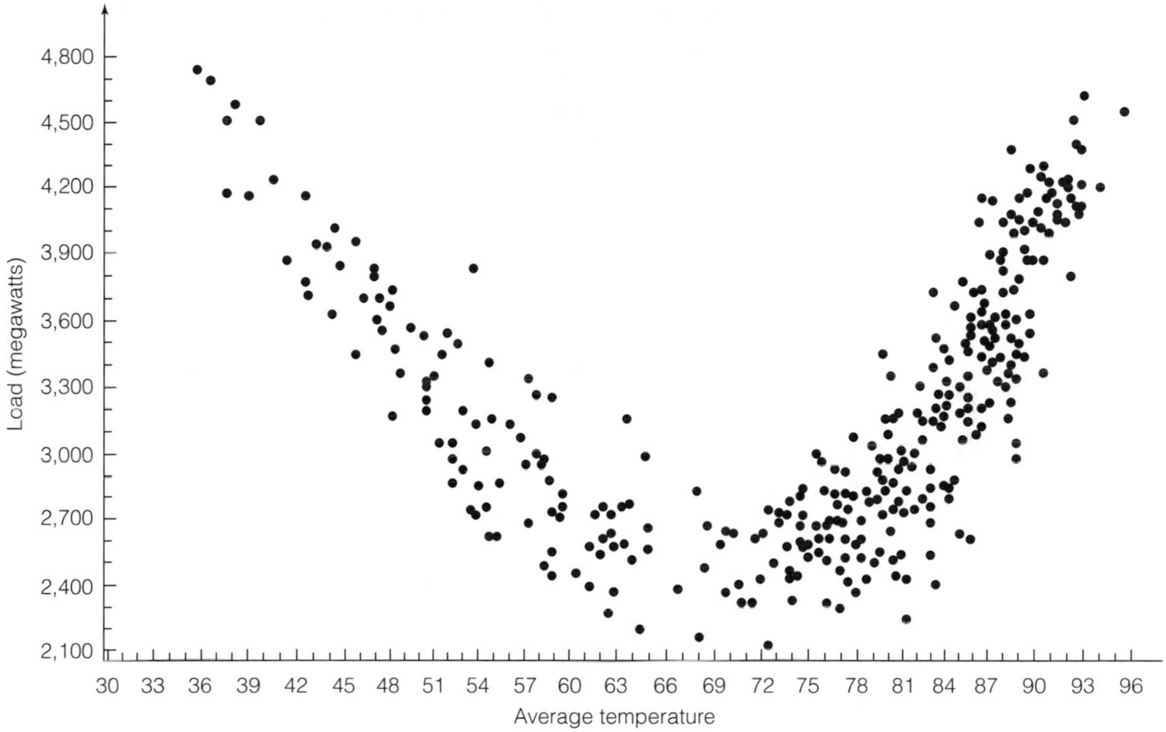

Source: Florida Power Corporation.

FIGURE 16.3
Theoretical relationship between daily peak demand and temperature

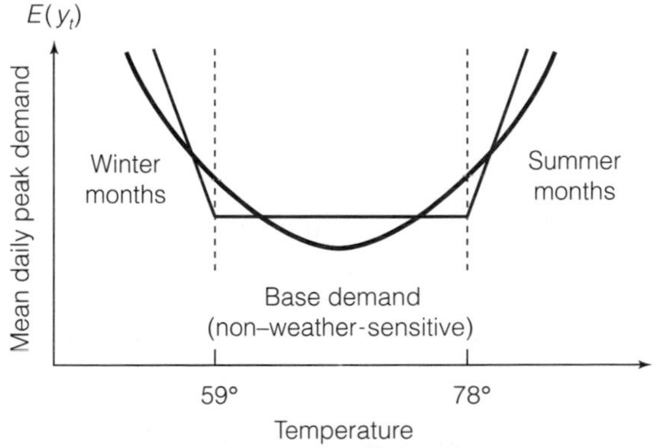

$$x_{4t} = \begin{cases} 1 & \text{if Saturday} \\ 0 & \text{if not} \end{cases} \qquad x_{5t} = \begin{cases} 1 & \text{if Sunday or holiday} \\ 0 & \text{if not} \end{cases} \quad \text{(Base level = Weekday)}$$

$$\varepsilon_t = \text{Uncorrelated error term}$$

Model 1 proposes three different straight-line relationships between peak demand (y_t) and coincident temperature x_{1t}, one for each of the three temperature ranges corresponding to winter months (less than 59°), non–weather-sensitive months (between 59° and 78°), and summer months (greater than 78°).* The model also allows for variations in demand because of day of the week (Saturday, Sunday/holiday, or weekday). Since interaction between temperature and day of the week is omitted, the model is assuming that the differences between mean peak demand for weekdays and weekends/holidays is constant for the winter-sensitive, summer-sensitive, and non–weather-sensitive months.

We will illustrate the mechanics of the piecewise linear terms by finding the equations of the three demand–temperature lines for weekdays (i.e., $x_{4t} = x_{5t} = 0$). Substituting $x_{4t} = 0$ and $x_{5t} = 0$ into the model, we have

Winter-sensitive months ($x_{1t} < 59°$, $x_{2t} = 1$, $x_{3t} = 0$):

$$\begin{aligned} E(y_t) &= \beta_0 + \beta_1(x_{1t} - 59)(1) + \beta_2(x_{1t} - 78)(0) + \beta_3(0) + \beta_4(0) \\ &= \beta_0 + \beta_1(x_{1t} - 59) \\ &= (\beta_0 - 59\beta_1) + \beta_1 x_{1t} \end{aligned}$$

Summer-sensitive months ($x_{1t} > 78°$, $x_{2t} = 0$, $x_{3t} = 1$):

$$\begin{aligned} E(y_t) &= \beta_0 + \beta_1(x_{1t} - 59)(0) + \beta_2(x_{1t} - 78)(1) + \beta_3(0) + \beta_4(0) \\ &= \beta_0 + \beta_2(x_{1t} - 78) \\ &= (\beta_0 - 78\beta_2) + \beta_2 x_{1t} \end{aligned}$$

Non–weather-sensitive months ($59° \le x_{1t} \le 78°$, $x_{2t} = x_{3t} = 0$):

$$\begin{aligned} E(y_t) &= \beta_0 + \beta_1(x_{1t} - 59)(0) + \beta_2(x_{1t} - 78)(0) + \beta_3(0) + \beta_4(0) \\ &= \beta_0 \end{aligned}$$

Note that the slope of the demand–temperature line for winter-sensitive months (when $x_{1t} < 59$) is β_1 (which we expect to be negative), whereas the slope for summer-sensitive months (when $x_{1t} > 78$) is β_2 (which we expect to be positive). The intercept term β_0 represents the mean daily peak demand observed in the non–weather-sensitive period (when $59 \le x_{1t} \le 78$). Notice also that the peak demand during non–weather-sensitive days does not depend on temperature (x_{1t}).

Model 1 is a multiple regression model that relies on the standard regression assumptions of independent errors (ε_t uncorrelated). This may be a serious shortcoming in view of the fact that the data are in the form of a time series. To account for possible autocorrelated residuals, two time series models were proposed:

Model 2

$$\begin{aligned} y_t &= \beta_0 + \beta_1(x_{1t} - 59)x_{2t} + \beta_2(x_{1t} - 78)x_{3t} + \beta_3 x_{4t} + \beta_4 x_{5t} + R_t \\ R_t &= \phi_1 R_{t-1} + \varepsilon_t \end{aligned}$$

*The temperature values, 59° and 78°, identify where the winter- and summer-sensitive portions of demand join the base demand component. These "knot values" were determined from visual inspection of the graph in Figure 16.2.

Model 2 proposes a regression–autoregression pair of models for daily peak demand (y_t). The deterministic component, $E(y_t)$, is identical to the deterministic component of Model 1; however, a first-order autoregressive model is chosen for the random error component. Recall (from Section 9.5) that a first-order autoregressive model is appropriate when the correlation between residuals diminishes as the distance between time periods (in this case, days) increases.

Model 3

$$y_t = \beta_0 + \beta_1(x_{1t} - 59)x_{2t} + \beta_2(x_{1t} - 78)x_{3t} + \beta_3 x_{4t} + \beta_4 x_{5t} + R_t$$
$$R_t = \phi_1 R_{t-1} + \phi_2 R_{t-2} + \phi_5 R_{t-5} + \phi_7 R_{t-7} + \varepsilon_t$$

Model 3 extends the first-order autoregressive error model of Model 2 to a seventh-order autoregressive model with lags at 1, 2, 5, and 7. In theory, the peak demand on day t will be highly correlated with the peak demand on day $t + 1$. However, there also may be significant correlation between demand 2 days, 5 days, and/or 1 week (7 days) apart. This more general error model is proposed to account for any residual correlation that may occur as a result of the week-to-week variation in peak demand, in addition to the day-to-day variation.

16.4 The Regression and Autoregression Analyses

The multiple regression computer printout for Model 1 is shown in Figure 16.4, and a plot of the least squares fit is shown in Figure 16.5 (page 760). The model appears to provide a good fit to the data, with $R^2 = .8307$ and $F = 441.729$ (significant at $p = .0001$). The value of **ROOT MSE**, $s = 245.585$, implies that we can expect to predict daily peak demand accurate to within $2s \approx 491$ megawatts of its true value. However, we must be careful not to conclude at this point that the model is useful for predicting peak demand. Recall that in the presence

FIGURE 16.4
SAS printout for multiple regression model of daily peak demand, Model 1

DEP VARIABLE: LOAD

SOURCE	DF	SUM OF SQUARES	MEAN SQUARE	F VALUE	PROB > F
MODEL	4	106565982	26641496	441.729	0.0001
ERROR	360	21712247	60311.797		
C TOTAL	364	128278229			

ROOT MSE	245.585	R-SQUARE	0.8307
DEP MEAN	3191.863	ADJ R-SQ	0.8289
C.V.	7.694083		

VARIABLE	DF	PARAMETER ESTIMATE	STANDARD ERROR	T FOR H0: PARAMETER = 0	PROB > |T|
INTERCEP	1	2670.171	21.251829	125.644	0.0001
AVTW	1	-82.039853	2.941928	-27.886	0.0001
AVTS	1	114.443	3.050468	37.516	0.0001
SAT	1	-164.932	37.990216	-4.341	0.0001
SUN	1	-285.114	35.328293	-8.070	0.0001

DURBIN-WATSON D	0.705
(NUMBER OF OBS)	365
1ST ORDER AUTOCORRELATION	0.648

FIGURE 16.5 Daily peak demand versus temperature: Actual versus fitted piecewise linear model

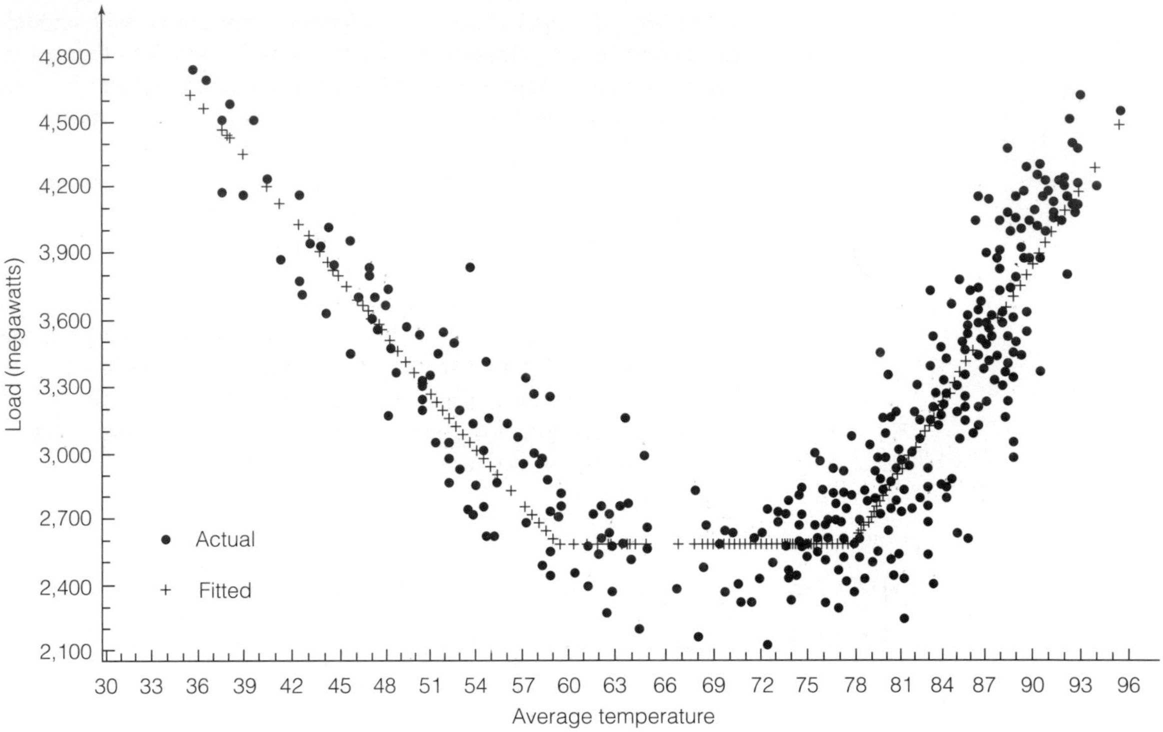

Source: Florida Power Corporation.

of autocorrelated residuals, the standard errors of the regression coefficients are underestimated, thereby inflating the corresponding t statistics for testing H_0: $\beta_i = 0$. At worst, this could lead to the false conclusion that a β parameter is significantly different from 0; at best, the results, although significant, give an overoptimistic view of the predictive ability of the model.

To determine whether the residuals of the multiple regression model are positively autocorrelated, we conduct the Durbin–Watson test:

H_0: Uncorrelated residuals

H_a: Positive residual correlation

Recall that the Durbin–Watson test is designed specifically for detecting first-order autocorrelation in the residuals, R_t. Thus, we can write the null and alternative hypotheses as

H_0: $\phi_1 = 0$

H_a: $\phi_1 > 0$

where $R_t = \phi_1 R_{t-1} + \varepsilon_t$, and ε_t = uncorrelated error (white noise).

The test statistic, given at the bottom of the printout in Figure 16.4, is $d = .705$. Recall that small values of d lead us to reject H_0: $\phi_1 = 0$ in favor of the alternative H_a: $\phi_1 > 0$. For $\alpha = .01$, $n = 365$, and $k = 4$ (the number of β parameters in the model, excluding β_0), the lower bound on the critical value (obtained from Table 9 of Appendix C) is approximately $d_L = 1.46$. Since the value of the test statistic, $d = .705$, falls well below the lower bound, there is strong evidence at $\alpha = .01$ of positive (first-order) autocorrelated residuals. Thus, we need to incorporate terms for residual autocorrelation into the model.

The time series printouts for Models 2 and 3 are shown in Figures 16.6 and 16.7 (page 762), respectively. A summary of the results for all three models is given in Table 16.1.

TABLE 16.1 **Summary of Results for Models 1, 2, and 3**

	MODEL 1	MODEL 2	MODEL 3
R^2	.8307	.9225	.9351
MSE	60,311.797	27,687.44	23,398.43
s	245.585	166.394	152.966

FIGURE 16.6 SAS printout for first-order autoregressive time series model of daily peak demand, Model 2

```
                              DEPENDENT VARIABLE = LOAD

                           ORDINARY LEAST SQUARES ESTIMATES

                              VARIABLE DF        B VALUE
                               INTERCPT 1       2670.171
                               AVTW       1     -82.0399
                               AVTS       1     114.4427
                               SAT        1     -164.932
                               SUN        1     -285.114

                            ESTIMATES OF AUTOCORRELATIONS

LAG     COVARIANCE     CORRELATION     -1 9 8 7 6 5 4 3 2 1  0 1 2 3 4 5 6 7 8 9 1
  0       59485.6        1.000000       |                    |********************|
  1       38519.4        0.647541       |                    |*************       |

                           PRELIMINARY MSE =        34542.75

                       ESTIMATES OF THE AUTOREGRESSIVE PARAMETERS

                    LAG     COEFFICIENT          STD ERROR       T RATIO
                      1     -0.64754083          0.039887     -16.234581
                             YULE-WALKER ESTIMATES
               SSE                9939789                DFE                 359
               MSE                27687.44               ROOT MSE       166.3943
               REG RSQ              0.7626               TOTAL RSQ        0.9225

VARIABLE  DF        B VALUE         STD ERROR        T RATIO     APPROX PROB
INTERCPT   1    2812.96710162    29.8790879359        94.145          0.0001
AVTW       1      -65.337453      2.6639248330       -24.527          0.0001
AVTS       1     83.45523858      3.8531993234        21.659          0.0001
SAT        1      -130.82831     22.4136023517        -5.837          0.0001
SUN        1      -275.55071     21.3736779578       -12.892          0.0001
```

FIGURE 16.7

SAS printout for seventh-order autoregressive time series model of daily peak demand, Model 3

```
                         DEPENDENT VARIABLE = LOAD

                       ORDINARY LEAST SQUARES ESTIMATES

                         VARIABLE DF        B VALUE
                         INTERCPT 1        2670.171
                         AVTW      1       -82.0399
                         AVTS      1       114.4427
                         SAT       1       -164.932
                         SUN       1       -285.114

                         ESTIMATES OF AUTOCORRELATIONS

LAG   COVARIANCE    CORRELATION   -1 9 8 7 6 5 4 3 2 1 0 1 2 3 4 5 6 7 8 9 1
  0      59485.6       1.000000    |                    |********************|
  1      38519.4       0.647541    |                    |*************       |
  2        35741       0.600834    |                    |************        |
  3      32868.2       0.552540    |                    |***********         |
  4      29917.9       0.502943    |                    |**********          |
  5      31340.9       0.526865    |                    |***********         |
  6      30061.9       0.505364    |                    |**********          |
  7        31508       0.529674    |                    |***********         |

                      PRELIMINARY MSE =       28841.4

                 ESTIMATES OF THE AUTOREGRESSIVE PARAMETERS

        LAG    COEFFICIENT        STD ERROR        T RATIO
          1    -0.36793644         0.049902      -7.373164
          2    -0.20702784         0.051722      -4.002705
          3     0.00000000         0.000000
          4     0.00000000         0.000000
          5    -0.13526445         0.049072      -2.756459
          6     0.00000000         0.000000
          7    -0.15338478         0.048430      -3.167144

                         EXPECTED AUTOCORRELATIONS

                              LAG  AUTOCORR
                                0    0.9668
                                1    0.6117
                                2    0.5640
                                3    0.4794
                                4    0.4494
                                5    0.4819
                                6    0.4469
                                7    0.4888

                          YULE-WALKER ESTIMATES
           SSE                  8329842      DFE                356
           MSE                 23398.43      ROOT MSE      152.9655
           REG RSQ               0.8112      TOTAL RSQ       0.9351

VARIABLE DF        B VALUE        STD ERROR      T RATIO    APPROX PROB
INTERCPT  1  2809.95021301    58.2345577940       48.252         0.0001
AVTW      1     -71.28248      2.2620998226      -31.512         0.0001
AVTS      1    79.12014515     4.1805721109       18.926         0.0001
SAT       1    -150.52375     23.4727721121       -6.413         0.0001
SUN       1    -262.27342     21.6832940758      -12.096         0.0001
```

The addition of the first-order autoregressive error term in Model 2 yielded a drastic improvement to the fit of the model. The value of R^2 (i.e., **TOTAL RSQ**) increased from .83 for Model 1 to .92, and the standard deviation s (i.e., **ROOT MSE**) decreased from 245.6 to 166.4. These results support the conclusion reached by the Durbin–Watson test—namely, that the first-order autoregressive lag parameter ϕ_1 is significantly different from 0.

Does the more general autoregressive error model (Model 3) provide a better approximation to the pattern of correlation in the residuals than the first-order autoregressive model (Model 2)? To test this hypothesis, we would need to test H_0: $\phi_2 = \phi_5 = \phi_7 = 0$. Although we omit discussion of tests on autoregressive parameters in this text,* we can arrive at a decision from a pragmatic point of view by again comparing the values of R^2 and s for the two models. The more complex autoregressive model proposed by Model 3 yields a slight increase in R^2 (.935 compared to .923 for Model 2) and a slight decrease in the value of s (153.00 compared to 166.4 for Model 2). The additional lag parameters, although they may be statistically significant, may not be practically significant. The practical analyst may decide that the first-order autoregressive process proposed by Model 2 is the more desirable option since it is easier to use to forecast peak daily demand (and therefore more explainable to managers) while yielding approximate prediction errors (as measured by $2s$) that are only slightly larger than those for Model 3.

For the purposes of illustration, we use Model 2 to forecast daily peak demand in the following section.

16.5 Forecasting Daily Peak Electricity Demand

Suppose the FPC decided to use Model 2 to forecast daily peak demand for the first seven days of November 1983. The estimated model,† obtained from Figure 16.6, is given by

$$\hat{y}_t = 2{,}812.967 - 65.337(x_{1t} - 59)x_{2t} + 83.455(x_{1t} - 78)x_{3t} - 130.828x_{4t} - 275.551x_{5t} + \hat{R}_t$$

$$\hat{R}_t = .6475\hat{R}_{t-1}$$

The forecast for November 1, 1983 ($t = 366$), requires an estimate of the residual R_{365}, where $\hat{R}_{365} = y_{365} - \hat{y}_{365}$. The last day of the November 1982–October 1983 time period ($t = 365$) was October 31, 1983, a Monday. On this day the peak demand was recorded as $y_{365} = 2{,}752$ megawatts and the coincident temperature as $x_{1,365} = 77°$. Substituting the appropriate values of the dummy variables into the equation for $\hat{y}_t$ (i.e., $x_{2t} = 0$, $x_{3t} = 0$, $x_{4t} = 0$, and $x_{5t} = 0$),

*For details of tests on autoregressive parameters, see Fuller (1976).

†Remember that the estimate of ϕ_1 is obtained by multiplying the value reported on the SAS printout by (-1).

we have

$$\begin{aligned}\hat{R}_{365} &= y_{365} - \hat{y}_{365}\\ &= 2{,}752 - [2{,}812.967 - 65.337(77 - 59)(0) + 83.455(77 - 78)(0)\\ &\qquad - 130.828(0) - 275.551(0)]\\ &= 2{,}752 - 2{,}812.967 = -60.967\end{aligned}$$

Then the formula for calculating the forecast for Tuesday, November 1, 1983, is

$$\begin{aligned}\hat{y}_{366} = 2{,}812.967 &- 65.337(x_{1,366} - 59)x_{2,366} + 83.455(x_{1,366} - 78)x_{3,366}\\ &- 130.828x_{4,366} - 275.551x_{5,366} + \hat{R}_{366}\end{aligned}$$

where

$$\hat{R}_{366} = \hat{\phi}_1\hat{R}_{365} = (.6475)(-60.967) = -39.476$$

Note that the forecast requires an estimate of coincident temperature on that day, $\hat{x}_{1,366}$. If the FPC wants to forecast demand under normal weather conditions, then this estimate can be obtained from historical data for that day. Or, the FPC may choose to rely on a meteorologist's weather forecast for that day. For this example, assume that $\hat{x}_{1,366} = 76°$ (the actual temperature recorded by the FPC). Then $x_{2,366} = x_{3,366} = 0$ (since $59 \le \hat{x}_{1,366} \le 78$) and $x_{4,366} = x_{5,366} = 0$ (since the target day is a Tuesday). Substituting these values and the value of $\hat{R}_{366}$ into the equation, we have

$$\begin{aligned}\hat{y}_{366} &= 2{,}812.967 - 65.337(76 - 59)(0) + 83.455(76 - 78)(0)\\ &\qquad - 130.828(0) - 275.551(0) - 39.476\\ &= 2{,}773.49\end{aligned}$$

Similarly, a forecast for Wednesday, November 2, 1983 (i.e., $t = 367$), can be obtained:

$$\begin{aligned}\hat{y}_{367} = 2{,}812.967 &- 65.337(x_{1,367} - 59)x_{2,367} + 83.455(x_{1,367} - 78)x_{3,367}\\ &- 130.828x_{3,367} - 275.551x_{4,367} + \hat{R}_{367}\end{aligned}$$

where $\hat{R}_{367} = \hat{\phi}_1\hat{R}_{366} = (.6475)(-39.476) = -25.561$, and $x_{3,367} = x_{4,367} = 0$. For an estimated coincident temperature of $\hat{x}_{1,367} = 77°$ (again, this is the actual temperature recorded on that day), we have $x_{2,367} = 0$ and $x_{3,367} = 0$. Substituting these values into the prediction equation, we obtain

$$\begin{aligned}\hat{y}_{367} &= 2{,}812.967 - 65.337(77 - 59)(0) + 83.455(77 - 78)(0)\\ &\qquad - 130.828(0) - 275.551(0) - 25.561\\ &= 2{,}812.967 - 25.561\\ &= 2{,}787.41\end{aligned}$$

Approximate 95% prediction intervals for the two forecasts are calculated as follows:

Tuesday, Nov. 1, 1983:

$$\hat{y}_{366} \pm 1.96\sqrt{\text{MSE}}$$

$$= 2{,}773.49 \pm 1.96\sqrt{27{,}687.44}$$
$$= 2{,}773.49 \pm 326.14 \quad \text{or} \quad (2{,}447.35,\ 3{,}099.63)$$

Wednesday, Nov. 2, 1983:

$$\hat{y}_{367} \pm 1.96\sqrt{\text{MSE}(1 + \hat{\phi}_1^2)}$$
$$= 2{,}787.41 \pm 1.96\sqrt{(27{,}687.44)[1 + (.6475)^2]}$$
$$= 2{,}787.41 \pm 388.53 \quad \text{or} \quad (2{,}398.88,\ 3{,}175.94)$$

The forecasts, approximate 95% prediction intervals, and actual daily peak demands (recorded by the FPC) for the first seven days of November 1983 are given in Table 16.2. Note that actual peak demand y_t falls within the corresponding prediction interval for all seven days. Thus, the model appears to be useful for making short-term forecasts of daily peak demand. Of course, if the prediction intervals were extremely wide, this result would be of no practical value. For example, the forecast error $y_t - \hat{y}_t$, measured as a percentage of the actual value y_t, may be large even when y_t falls within the prediction interval. Various techniques, such as the percent forecast error, are available for evaluating the accuracy of forecasts. Consult the references given at the end of Chapter 9 for details on these techniques.

TABLE 16.2 **Forecasts and Actual Peak Demands for the First Seven Days of November 1983**

DATE	DAY t	FORECAST $\hat{y}_t$	APPROXIMATE 95% PREDICTION INTERVAL	ACTUAL DEMAND y_t	ACTUAL TEMPERATURE x_{1t}
Tues., Nov. 1	366	2,773.49	(2,447.35, 3,099.63)	2,799	76
Wed., Nov. 2	367	2,787.41	(2,398.88, 3,175.94)	2,784	77
Thurs., Nov. 3	368	2,796.42	(2,384.53, 3,208.31)	2,845	77
Fri., Nov. 4	369	2,802.25	(2,380.92, 3,223.58)	2,701	76
Sat., Nov. 5	370	2,675.20	(2,249.97, 3,100.43)	2,512	72
Sun., Nov. 6	371	2,532.92	(2,106.07, 2,959.77)	2,419	71
Mon., Nov. 7	372	2,810.06	(2,382.59, 3,237.53)	2,749	68

16.6 Conclusions

This case study presents a time series approach to modeling and forecasting daily peak demand observed at Florida Power Corporation. A graphical analysis of the data provided the means of identifying and formulating a piecewise linear regression model relating peak demand to temperature and day of the week. The multiple regression model, although providing a good fit to the data, exhibited strong signs of positive residual autocorrelation.

Two autoregressive time series models were proposed to account for the autocorrelated errors. Both models were shown to provide a drastic improvement in model adequacy. Either could be used to provide reliable short-term forecasts of daily peak demand or for weather normalization (i.e., estimating the peak demand if normal weather conditions had prevailed).

EXERCISES

16.1 All three models discussed in this case study make the underlying assumption that the peak demand–temperature relationship is independent of day of the week. Write a model that includes interaction between temperature and day of the week. Show the effect the interaction has on the straight-line relationships between peak demand and temperature. Explain how you could test the significance of the interaction terms.

16.2 Consider the problem of using Model 2 for weather normalization. Suppose the temperature on Saturday, March 5, 1983 (i.e., $t = 125$), was $x_{1,125} = 25°$, unusually cold for that day. Normally, temperatures range from 40° to 50° on March 5 in the FPC service area. Substitute $x_{1,125} = 45°$ into the prediction equation to obtain an estimate of the peak demand expected if normal weather conditions had prevailed on March 5, 1983. Calculate an approximate 95% prediction interval for the estimate. [*Hint*: Use $\hat{y}_{125} \pm 1.96\sqrt{\text{MSE}}$.]

References

Fuller, W. A. *Introduction to Statistical Time Series*. New York: Wiley, 1976.

Jacob, M. F. "A time series approach to modeling daily peak electricity demands." Paper presented at the SAS Users Group International Annual Conference, Reno, Nevada, 1985.

APPENDIX A

The Mechanics of a Multiple Regression Analysis

CONTENTS

A.1 Introduction

The rationale behind a multiple regression analysis and the types of inferences it permits you to make are the subjects of Chapter 4. We noted that the method of least squares most often leads to a very difficult computational problem—namely, the solution of a set of $(k + 1)$ simultaneous linear equations in the unknown values of the estimates $\hat{\beta}_0, \hat{\beta}_1, \ldots, \hat{\beta}_k$—and that the formulas for the estimated standard errors $s_{\hat{\beta}_0}, s_{\hat{\beta}_1}, \ldots, s_{\hat{\beta}_k}$ are too complicated to express as ordinary algebraic formulas. We circumvented both these problems easily. We relied on the least squares estimates, confidence intervals, tests, etc., provided by a standard regression analysis software package. Thus, Chapter 4 provides a basic working knowledge of the types of inferences you might wish to make from a multiple regression analysis and explains how to interpret the results. If we can do this, why would we wish to know the actual process performed by the computer?

There are several answers to this question:

1. Some multiple regression statistical software packages do not print all the information you may want. As one illustration, we noted in Chapter 4 that very often the objective of a regression analysis is to develop a prediction equation that can be used to estimate the mean value of y (say, mean profit or mean yield) for given values of the predictor variables $x_1, x_2, \ldots, x_k$. Some software packages do not give the confidence interval for $E(y)$ or a prediction interval for y. Thus, you might need to know how to find the necessary quantities from the analysis and perform the computations yourself.
2. A multiple regression software package may possess the capability of computing some specific quantity that you desire, but you may find the instructions on how to "call" for this special calculation difficult to understand. It may be easier to identify the components required for your computation and do it yourself.
3. For some designed experiments, finding the least squares equations and solving them is a trivial operation. Understanding the process by which the least squares equations are generated and understanding how they are solved will help you understand how experimental design affects the results of a regression analysis. Thus, a knowledge of the computations involved in performing a regression analysis will help you to better understand the contents of Chapters 10 and 11.

To summarize, "knowing how it is done" is not essential for performing an ordinary regression analysis or interpreting its results. But "knowing how" helps, and it is essential for an understanding of many of the finer points associated with a multiple regression analysis. This appendix explains "how it is done" without getting into the unpleasant task of performing the computations for solving the least squares equations. This mechanical and tedious procedure can be left to a computer (the solutions are verifiable). We illustrate the procedure in Appendix B.

A.2 Matrices and Matrix Multiplication

Although it is very difficult to give the formulas for the multiple regression least squares estimators and for their estimated standard errors in ordinary algebra, it is easy to do so using **matrix algebra**. Thus, by arranging the data in particular rectangular patterns called **matrices** and by performing various operations with them, we can obtain the least squares estimates and their estimated standard errors. In this section and Sections A.3 and A.4, we will define what we mean by a matrix and explain various operations that can be performed with matrices. We will explain how to use this information to conduct a regression analysis in Section A.5.

Three matrices, **A**, **B**, and **C**, are shown here. Note that each matrix is a rectangular arrangement of numbers with one number in every row–column position.

$$\mathbf{A} = \begin{bmatrix} 2 & 3 \\ 0 & 1 \\ -1 & 6 \end{bmatrix} \qquad \mathbf{B} = \begin{bmatrix} 3 & 0 & 1 \\ -1 & 0 & 1 \\ 4 & 2 & 0 \end{bmatrix} \qquad \mathbf{C} = \begin{bmatrix} 1 \\ 2 \\ 1 \end{bmatrix}$$

Definition A.1

A **matrix** is a rectangular array of numbers.*

The numbers that appear in a matrix are called **elements** of the matrix. If a matrix contains r rows and c columns, there will be an element in each of the row–column positions of the matrix, and the matrix will have $r \times c$ elements. For example, the matrix **A** shown previously contains $r = 3$ rows, $c = 2$ columns, and $rc = (3)(2) = 6$ elements, one in each of the six row–column positions.

Definition A.2

A number in a particular row–column position is called an **element** of the matrix.

Notice that the matrices **A**, **B**, and **C** contain different numbers of rows and columns. The numbers of rows and columns give the **dimensions** of a matrix.

*For our purpose, we assume that the numbers are real.

When we give a formula in matrix notation, the elements of a matrix will be represented by symbols. For example, if we have a matrix

$$\mathbf{A} = \begin{bmatrix} a_{11} & a_{12} & a_{13} \\ a_{21} & a_{22} & a_{23} \end{bmatrix}$$

the symbol a_{ij} will denote the element in the ith row and jth column of the matrix. The first subscript always identifies the row and the second identifies the column in which the element is located. For example, the element a_{12} is in the first row and second column of the matrix **A**. The rows are always numbered from top to bottom, and the columns are always numbered from left to right.

Definition A.3

A matrix containing r rows and c columns is said to be an **$r \times c$ matrix** where r and c are the **dimensions** of the matrix.

Definition A.4

If $r = c$, a matrix is said to be a **square matrix**.

Matrices are usually identified by capital letters, such as **A**, **B**, **C**, corresponding to the letters of the alphabet employed in ordinary algebra. The difference is that in ordinary algebra, a letter is used to denote a single real number, whereas in matrix algebra, *a letter denotes a rectangular array of numbers*. The operations of matrix algebra are very similar to those of ordinary algebra—you can add matrices, subtract them, multiply them, and so on. But since we are concerned only with the applications of matrix algebra to the solution of the least squares equations, we will define only the operations and types of matrices that are pertinent to that subject.

The most important operation for us is matrix multiplication, which requires **row–column multiplication**. To illustrate this process, suppose we wish to find the product **AB**, where

$$\mathbf{A} = \begin{bmatrix} 2 & 1 \\ 4 & -1 \end{bmatrix} \qquad \mathbf{B} = \begin{bmatrix} 2 & 0 & 3 \\ -1 & 4 & 0 \end{bmatrix}$$

We will always multiply the rows of **A** (the matrix on the left) by the columns of **B** (the matrix on the right). The product formed by the first row of **A** times the first column of **B** is obtained by multiplying the elements in corresponding positions and summing these products. Thus, the first row, first column product, shown diagrammatically here, is

$$(2)(2) + (1)(-1) = 4 - 1 = 3$$

$$\mathbf{AB} = \begin{bmatrix} 2 & 1 \\ 4 & -1 \end{bmatrix} \begin{bmatrix} 2 & 0 & 3 \\ -1 & 4 & 0 \end{bmatrix} = \begin{bmatrix} 3 & & \\ & & \end{bmatrix}$$

Similarly, the first row, second column product is

$$(2)(0) + (1)(4) = 0 + 4 = 4$$

So far we have

$$\mathbf{AB} = \begin{bmatrix} 3 & 4 & \\ & & \end{bmatrix}$$

To find the complete matrix product **AB**, all we need to do is find each element in the **AB** matrix. Thus, we will define an element in the *i*th row, *j*th column of **AB** as the product of the *i*th row of **A** and the *j*th column of **B**. We complete the process in Example A.1.

EXAMPLE A.1

Find the product **AB**, where

$$\mathbf{A} = \begin{bmatrix} 2 & 1 \\ 4 & -1 \end{bmatrix} \qquad \mathbf{B} = \begin{bmatrix} 2 & 0 & 3 \\ -1 & 4 & 0 \end{bmatrix}$$

Solution

If we represent the product **AB** as

$$\mathbf{C} = \begin{bmatrix} c_{11} & c_{12} & c_{13} \\ c_{21} & c_{22} & c_{23} \end{bmatrix}$$

we have already found $c_{11} = 3$ and $c_{12} = 4$. Similarly, the element c_{21}, the element in the second row, first column of **AB**, is the product of the second row of **A** and the first column of **B**:

$$(4)(2) + (-1)(-1) = 8 + 1 = 9$$

Proceeding in a similar manner to find the remaining elements of **AB**, we have

$$\mathbf{AB} = \begin{bmatrix} 2 & 1 \\ 4 & -1 \end{bmatrix} \begin{bmatrix} 2 & 0 & 3 \\ -1 & 4 & 0 \end{bmatrix} = \begin{bmatrix} 3 & 4 & 6 \\ 9 & -4 & 12 \end{bmatrix}$$

Now, try to find the product **BA**, using matrices **A** and **B** from Example A.1. You will observe two very important differences between multiplication in matrix algebra and multiplication in ordinary algebra:

1. You cannot find the product **BA** because you cannot perform row–column multiplication. You can see that the dimensions do not match by placing the matrices side by side.

   BA does not exist

   $2 \times 3 \quad 2 \times 2$

   The number of elements (3) in a row of **B** (the matrix on the left) does not match the number of elements (2) in a column of **A** (the matrix on the right). Therefore, you cannot perform row–column multiplication, and the matrix product **BA** does not exist. The point is, not all matrices can be multiplied. You can find products for matrices **A** and **B** only when **A** is $r \times d$ and **B** is $d \times c$. That is:

Requirement for Multiplication

AB

$r \times d \quad d \times c$

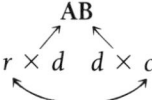

The two inner dimension numbers must be equal. The dimensions of the product will always be given by the outer dimension numbers:

Dimensions of AB Are $r \times c$

AB

$r \times d \quad d \times c$

2. The second difference between ordinary and matrix multiplication is that in ordinary algebra, $ab = ba$. In matrix algebra, **AB** usually does not equal **BA**. In fact, as noted in item 1, **BA** may not even exist.

Definition A.5

The product **AB** of an $r \times d$ matrix **A** and a $d \times c$ matrix **B** is an $r \times c$ matrix **C**, where the element c_{ij} $(i = 1, 2, \ldots, r; j = 1, 2, \ldots, c)$ of **C** is the product of the ith row of **A** and the jth column of **B**.

EXAMPLE A.2

Given the matrices below, find **IA** and **IB**.

$$\mathbf{A} = \begin{bmatrix} 2 \\ 1 \\ 3 \end{bmatrix} \qquad \mathbf{B} = \begin{bmatrix} 3 & 0 \\ 1 & 2 \\ 4 & -1 \end{bmatrix} \qquad \mathbf{I} = \begin{bmatrix} 1 & 0 & 0 \\ 0 & 1 & 0 \\ 0 & 0 & 1 \end{bmatrix}$$

Solution

Notice that the product

IA

$3 \times 3 \quad 3 \times 1$

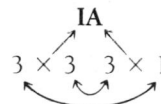

exists and that it will be of dimensions 3×1. Performing the row–column multiplication yields

$$\mathbf{IA} = \begin{bmatrix} 1 & 0 & 0 \\ 0 & 1 & 0 \\ 0 & 0 & 1 \end{bmatrix} \begin{bmatrix} 2 \\ 1 \\ 3 \end{bmatrix} = \begin{bmatrix} 2 \\ 1 \\ 3 \end{bmatrix}$$

Similarly,

IB

$3 \times 3 \quad 3 \times 2$

exists and is of dimensions 3×2. Performing the row–column multiplications, we obtain

$$\mathbf{IB} = \begin{bmatrix} 1 & 0 & 0 \\ 0 & 1 & 0 \\ 0 & 0 & 1 \end{bmatrix} \begin{bmatrix} 3 & 0 \\ 1 & 2 \\ 4 & -1 \end{bmatrix} = \begin{bmatrix} 3 & 0 \\ 1 & 2 \\ 4 & -1 \end{bmatrix}$$

Notice that the **I** matrix possesses a special property. We have **IA** = **A** and **IB** = **B**. We will comment further on this property in Section A.3.

EXERCISES

A.1 Given the matrices **A**, **B**, and **C**:

$$\mathbf{A} = \begin{bmatrix} 3 & 0 \\ -1 & 4 \end{bmatrix} \qquad \mathbf{B} = \begin{bmatrix} 2 & 1 \\ 0 & -1 \end{bmatrix} \qquad \mathbf{C} = \begin{bmatrix} 1 & 0 & 3 \\ -2 & 1 & 2 \end{bmatrix}$$

a. Find **AB**. b. Find **AC**. c. Find **BA**.

A.2 Given the matrices **A**, **B**, and **C**:

$$\mathbf{A} = \begin{bmatrix} 3 & 1 & 3 \\ 2 & 0 & 4 \\ -4 & 1 & 2 \end{bmatrix} \qquad \mathbf{B} = [1 \quad 0 \quad 2] \qquad \mathbf{C} = \begin{bmatrix} 3 \\ 0 \\ 2 \end{bmatrix}$$

a. Find **AC**. b. Find **BC**.
c. Is it possible to find **AB**? Explain.

A.3 Suppose **A** is a 3 × 2 matrix and **B** is a 2 × 4 matrix.
a. What are the dimensions of **AB**?
b. Is it possible to find the product **BA**? Explain.

A.4 Suppose matrices **B** and **C** are of dimensions 1 × 3 and 3 × 1, respectively.
a. What are the dimensions of the product **BC**?
b. What are the dimensions of **CB**?
c. If **B** and **C** are the matrices shown in Exercise A.2, find **CB**.

A.5 Given the matrices **A**, **B**, and **C**:

$$\mathbf{A} = \begin{bmatrix} 1 & 0 & 0 \\ 0 & 3 & 0 \\ 0 & 0 & 2 \end{bmatrix} \qquad \mathbf{B} = \begin{bmatrix} 2 & 3 \\ -3 & 0 \\ 4 & -1 \end{bmatrix} \qquad \mathbf{C} = [3 \quad 0 \quad 2]$$

a. Find **AB**. b. Find **CA**. c. Find **CB**.

A.6 Given the matrices:

$$\mathbf{A} = [3 \quad 0 \quad -1 \quad 2] \qquad \mathbf{B} = \begin{bmatrix} 2 \\ -1 \\ 0 \\ 3 \end{bmatrix}$$

a. Find **AB**. b. Find **BA**.

A.3 Identity Matrices and Matrix Inversion

In ordinary algebra, the number 1 is the identity element for the multiplication operation. That is, 1 is the element such that any other number, say, c, multiplied by the identity element is equal to c. Thus, $4(1) = 4$, $(-5)(1) = -5$, and so forth.

The corresponding identity element for multiplication in matrix algebra, identified by the symbol **I**, is a matrix such that

$$\mathbf{AI} = \mathbf{IA} = \mathbf{A} \quad \text{for any matrix } \mathbf{A}$$

The difference between identity elements in ordinary algebra and matrix algebra is that in ordinary algebra there is only one identity element, the number 1. In matrix algebra, the identity matrix must possess the correct dimensions for the product **IA** to exist. Consequently, there is an infinitely large number of identity matrices—all square and possessing the same pattern. The 1×1, 2×2, and 3×3 identity matrices are

$$\underset{1\times 1}{\mathbf{I}} = [1] \qquad \underset{2\times 2}{\mathbf{I}} = \begin{bmatrix} 1 & 0 \\ 0 & 1 \end{bmatrix} \qquad \underset{3\times 3}{\mathbf{I}} = \begin{bmatrix} 1 & 0 & 0 \\ 0 & 1 & 0 \\ 0 & 0 & 1 \end{bmatrix}$$

In Example A.2, we demonstrated the fact that this matrix satisfies the property

$$\mathbf{IA} = \mathbf{A}$$

Definition A.6

If $\mathbf{A}$ is any matrix, then a matrix $\mathbf{I}$ is defined to be an **identity matrix** if $\mathbf{AI} = \mathbf{IA} = \mathbf{A}$. The matrices that satisfy this definition possess the pattern

$$\mathbf{I} = \begin{bmatrix} 1 & 0 & 0 & \dots & 0 \\ 0 & 1 & 0 & \dots & 0 \\ 0 & 0 & 1 & \dots & 0 \\ \cdot & \cdot & \cdot & \cdots & \cdot \\ \cdot & \cdot & \cdot & \cdots & \cdot \\ \cdot & \cdot & \cdot & \cdots & \cdot \\ 0 & 0 & 0 & \dots & 1 \end{bmatrix}$$

EXAMPLE A.3

If $\mathbf{A}$ is the matrix shown here, find $\mathbf{IA}$ and $\mathbf{AI}$.

$$\mathbf{A} = \begin{bmatrix} 3 & 4 & -1 \\ 1 & 0 & 2 \end{bmatrix}$$

Solution

$$\underset{2\times 2 \quad 2\times 3}{\mathbf{IA}} = \begin{bmatrix} 1 & 0 \\ 0 & 1 \end{bmatrix} \begin{bmatrix} 3 & 4 & -1 \\ 1 & 0 & 2 \end{bmatrix} = \begin{bmatrix} 3 & 4 & -1 \\ 1 & 0 & 2 \end{bmatrix} = \mathbf{A}$$

$$\underset{2\times 3 \quad 3\times 3}{\mathbf{AI}} = \begin{bmatrix} 3 & 4 & -1 \\ 1 & 0 & 2 \end{bmatrix} \begin{bmatrix} 1 & 0 & 0 \\ 0 & 1 & 0 \\ 0 & 0 & 1 \end{bmatrix} = \begin{bmatrix} 3 & 4 & -1 \\ 1 & 0 & 2 \end{bmatrix} = \mathbf{A}$$

Notice that the identity matrices used to find the products $\mathbf{IA}$ and $\mathbf{AI}$ were of different dimensions. This was necessary for the products to exist.

The identity element assumes importance when we consider the process of division and its role in the solution of equations. In ordinary algebra, division is essentially multiplication using the reciprocals of elements. For example, the equation

$$2X = 6$$

can be solved by dividing both sides of the equation by 2, *or* it can be solved by *multiplying* both sides of the equation by $\frac{1}{2}$, which is the reciprocal of 2. Thus,

$$\left(\frac{1}{2}\right)2X = \frac{1}{2}(6)$$
$$X = 3$$

What is the reciprocal of an element? It is the element such that the reciprocal times the element is equal to the identity element. Thus, the reciprocal of 3 is $\frac{1}{3}$ because

$$3\left(\frac{1}{3}\right) = 1$$

The identity matrix plays the same role in matrix algebra. Thus, the reciprocal of a matrix **A**, called the **inverse of A** and denoted by the symbol $\mathbf{A}^{-1}$, is a matrix such that $\mathbf{AA}^{-1} = \mathbf{A}^{-1}\mathbf{A} = \mathbf{I}$.

Inverses are defined only for square matrices, but not all square matrices possess inverses. Those that do have inverses play an important role in solving the least squares equations and in other aspects of a regression analysis. We will show you one important application of the inverse matrix in Section A.4. The procedure for finding the inverse of a matrix is demonstrated in Appendix B.

Definition A.7

The square matrix $\mathbf{A}^{-1}$ is said to be the **inverse** of the square matrix **A** if

$$\mathbf{A}^{-1}\mathbf{A} = \mathbf{AA}^{-1} = \mathbf{I}$$

The procedure for finding an inverse matrix is computationally quite tedious and is performed most often using a computer. There are several exceptions. For example, finding the inverse of one type of matrix, called a **diagonal matrix**, is easy. A diagonal matrix is one that has nonzero elements down the **main diagonal** (running from top left of the matrix to bottom right) and 0 elements elsewhere. Thus, the identity matrix is a diagonal matrix (with 1's along the main diagonal), as are the following matrices:

$$\mathbf{A} = \begin{bmatrix} 3 & 0 & 0 \\ 0 & 1 & 0 \\ 0 & 0 & 2 \end{bmatrix} \qquad \mathbf{B} = \begin{bmatrix} 5 & 0 & 0 & 0 \\ 0 & 2 & 0 & 0 \\ 0 & 0 & 1 & 0 \\ 0 & 0 & 0 & 5 \end{bmatrix}$$

Definition A.8

A **diagonal matrix** is one that contains nonzero elements on the main diagonal and 0 elements elsewhere.

You can verify that the inverse of

$$\mathbf{A} = \begin{bmatrix} 3 & 0 & 0 \\ 0 & 1 & 0 \\ 0 & 0 & 2 \end{bmatrix} \quad \text{is} \quad \mathbf{A}^{-1} = \begin{bmatrix} \frac{1}{3} & 0 & 0 \\ 0 & 1 & 0 \\ 0 & 0 & \frac{1}{2} \end{bmatrix}$$

That is, $\mathbf{AA}^{-1} = \mathbf{I}$. In general, the inverse of a diagonal matrix is given by the following theorem, which is stated without proof:

Theorem A.1

The **inverse of a diagonal matrix**

$$\mathbf{D} = \begin{bmatrix} d_{11} & 0 & 0 & \cdots & 0 \\ 0 & d_{22} & 0 & \cdots & 0 \\ 0 & 0 & d_{33} & \cdots & 0 \\ \vdots & \vdots & \vdots & \cdots & \vdots \\ 0 & 0 & 0 & \cdots & d_{nn} \end{bmatrix} \quad \text{is} \quad \mathbf{D}^{-1} = \begin{bmatrix} 1/d_{11} & 0 & 0 & \cdots & 0 \\ 0 & 1/d_{22} & 0 & \cdots & 0 \\ 0 & 0 & 1/d_{33} & \cdots & 0 \\ \vdots & \vdots & \vdots & \cdots & \vdots \\ 0 & 0 & 0 & \cdots & 1/d_{nn} \end{bmatrix}$$

A second type of matrix that is easy to invert is a 2×2 matrix. The following theorem shows how to find the inverse of this type of matrix.

Theorem A.2

The **inverse of a 2×2 matrix**

$$\mathbf{A} = \begin{bmatrix} a & b \\ c & d \end{bmatrix} \quad \text{is} \quad \mathbf{A}^{-1} = \begin{bmatrix} \dfrac{d}{ad - bc} & \dfrac{-b}{ad - bc} \\ \dfrac{-c}{ad - bc} & \dfrac{a}{ad - bc} \end{bmatrix}$$

You can verify that the inverse of

$$\mathbf{A} = \begin{bmatrix} 1 & -2 \\ -2 & 6 \end{bmatrix} \quad \text{is} \quad \mathbf{A}^{-1} = \begin{bmatrix} 3 & 1 \\ 1 & \frac{1}{2} \end{bmatrix}$$

We demonstrate another technique for finding $\mathbf{A}^{-1}$ in Appendix B.

EXERCISES

A.7 Let $\mathbf{A} = \begin{bmatrix} 3 & 0 & 2 \\ -1 & 1 & 4 \end{bmatrix}$.

a. Give the identity matrix that will be used to obtain the product **IA**.
b. Show that **IA** = **A**.
c. Give the identity matrix that will be used to find the product **AI**.
d. Show that **AI** = **A**.

A.8 Given the following matrices **A** and **B**, show that **AB** = **I**, that **BA** = **I**, and consequently, verify that **B** = $\mathbf{A}^{-1}$.

$$\mathbf{A} = \begin{bmatrix} 1 & 0 & 0 \\ 0 & 2 & 0 \\ 0 & 0 & 3 \end{bmatrix} \qquad \mathbf{B} = \begin{bmatrix} 1 & 0 & 0 \\ 0 & \frac{1}{2} & 0 \\ 0 & 0 & \frac{1}{3} \end{bmatrix}$$

A.9 If

$$\mathbf{A} = \begin{bmatrix} 12 & 0 & 0 & 8 \\ 0 & 12 & 0 & 0 \\ 0 & 0 & 8 & 0 \\ 8 & 0 & 0 & 8 \end{bmatrix}$$

verify that

$$\mathbf{A}^{-1} = \begin{bmatrix} \frac{1}{4} & 0 & 0 & -\frac{1}{4} \\ 0 & \frac{1}{12} & 0 & 0 \\ 0 & 0 & \frac{1}{8} & 0 \\ -\frac{1}{4} & 0 & 0 & \frac{3}{8} \end{bmatrix}$$

A.10 If

$$\mathbf{A} = \begin{bmatrix} 3 & 0 & 0 \\ 0 & 5 & 0 \\ 0 & 0 & 7 \end{bmatrix}$$

show that

$$\mathbf{A}^{-1} = \begin{bmatrix} \frac{1}{3} & 0 & 0 \\ 0 & \frac{1}{5} & 0 \\ 0 & 0 & \frac{1}{7} \end{bmatrix}$$

A.11 Verify Theorem A.1.

A.12 Verify Theorem A.2.

A.13 Find the inverse of

$$\mathbf{A} = \begin{bmatrix} 2 & -1 \\ 2 & 3 \end{bmatrix}$$

A.4 Solving Systems of Simultaneous Linear Equations

Consider the following set of simultaneous linear equations in two unknowns:

$$2v_1 + v_2 = 7$$
$$v_1 - v_2 = 2$$

Note that the solution for these equations is $v_1 = 3$, $v_2 = 1$.

Now define the matrices

$$\mathbf{A} = \begin{bmatrix} 2 & 1 \\ 1 & -1 \end{bmatrix} \quad \mathbf{V} = \begin{bmatrix} v_1 \\ v_2 \end{bmatrix} \quad \mathbf{G} = \begin{bmatrix} 7 \\ 2 \end{bmatrix}$$

Thus, **A** is the matrix of coefficients of v_1 and v_2, **V** is a column matrix containing the unknowns (written in order, top to bottom), and **G** is a column matrix containing the numbers on the right-hand side of the equal signs.

Now, the given system of simultaneous equations can be rewritten as a **matrix equation**:

$$\mathbf{AV} = \mathbf{G}$$

By a matrix equation, we mean that the product matrix, **AV**, is equal to the matrix **G**. *Equality of matrices means that corresponding elements are equal.* You can see that this is true for the expression **AV** = **G**, since

$$\underset{2 \times 2 \quad 2 \times 1}{\mathbf{AV}} = \begin{bmatrix} 2 & 1 \\ 1 & -1 \end{bmatrix} \begin{bmatrix} v_1 \\ v_2 \end{bmatrix} = \begin{bmatrix} (2v_1 + v_2) \\ (v_1 - v_2) \end{bmatrix} = \underset{2 \times 1}{\mathbf{G}}$$

The matrix procedure for expressing a system of two simultaneous linear equations in two unknowns can be extended to express a set of k simultaneous equations in k unknowns. If the equations are written in the orderly pattern

$$\begin{aligned} a_{11}v_1 + a_{12}v_2 + \cdots + a_{1k}v_k &= g_1 \\ a_{21}v_1 + a_{22}v_2 + \cdots + a_{2k}v_k &= g_2 \\ \vdots \qquad \vdots \qquad\qquad \vdots \quad &\quad \vdots \\ a_{k1}v_1 + a_{k2}v_2 + \cdots + a_{kk}v_k &= g_k \end{aligned}$$

then the set of simultaneous linear equations can be expressed as the matrix equation **AV** = **G**, where

$$\mathbf{A} = \begin{bmatrix} a_{11} & a_{12} & \cdots & a_{1k} \\ a_{21} & & \cdots & a_{2k} \\ \vdots & & & \vdots \\ a_{k1} & & \cdots & a_{kk} \end{bmatrix} \quad \mathbf{V} = \begin{bmatrix} v_1 \\ v_2 \\ \vdots \\ v_k \end{bmatrix} \quad \mathbf{G} = \begin{bmatrix} g_1 \\ g_2 \\ \vdots \\ g_k \end{bmatrix}$$

Now let us solve this system of simultaneous equations. (If they are uniquely solvable, it can be shown that $\mathbf{A}^{-1}$ exists.) Multiplying both sides of the matrix equation by $\mathbf{A}^{-1}$, we have

$$(\mathbf{A}^{-1})\mathbf{A}\mathbf{V} = (\mathbf{A}^{-1})\mathbf{G}$$

But since $\mathbf{A}^{-1}\mathbf{A} = \mathbf{I}$, we have

$$(\mathbf{I})\mathbf{V} = \mathbf{A}^{-1}\mathbf{G}$$
$$\mathbf{V} = \mathbf{A}^{-1}\mathbf{G}$$

In other words, if we know $\mathbf{A}^{-1}$, we can find the solution to the set of simultaneous linear equations by obtaining the product $\mathbf{A}^{-1}\mathbf{G}$.

Matrix Solution to a Set of Simultaneous Linear Equations, $\mathbf{AV} = \mathbf{G}$

Solution: $\mathbf{V} = \mathbf{A}^{-1}\mathbf{G}$

EXAMPLE A.4

Apply the result from the box to find the solution to the set of simultaneous linear equations

$$2v_1 + v_2 = 7$$
$$v_1 - v_2 = 2$$

Solution

The first step is to obtain the inverse of the coefficient matrix,

$$\mathbf{A} = \begin{bmatrix} 2 & 1 \\ 1 & -1 \end{bmatrix}$$

namely,

$$\mathbf{A}^{-1} = \begin{bmatrix} \frac{1}{3} & \frac{1}{3} \\ \frac{1}{3} & -\frac{2}{3} \end{bmatrix}$$

(This matrix can be found using a packaged computer program for matrix inversion or, for this simple case, you could use the procedure explained in Appendix B.) As a check, note that

$$\mathbf{A}^{-1}\mathbf{A} = \begin{bmatrix} \frac{1}{3} & \frac{1}{3} \\ \frac{1}{3} & -\frac{2}{3} \end{bmatrix} \begin{bmatrix} 2 & 1 \\ 1 & -1 \end{bmatrix} = \begin{bmatrix} 1 & 0 \\ 0 & 1 \end{bmatrix} = \mathbf{I}$$

The second step is to obtain the product $\mathbf{A}^{-1}\mathbf{G}$. Thus,

$$\mathbf{V} = \mathbf{A}^{-1}\mathbf{G} = \begin{bmatrix} \frac{1}{3} & \frac{1}{3} \\ \frac{1}{3} & -\frac{2}{3} \end{bmatrix} \begin{bmatrix} 7 \\ 2 \end{bmatrix} = \begin{bmatrix} 3 \\ 1 \end{bmatrix}$$

Since

$$\mathbf{V} = \begin{bmatrix} v_1 \\ v_2 \end{bmatrix} = \begin{bmatrix} 3 \\ 1 \end{bmatrix}$$

it follows that $v_1 = 3$ and $v_2 = 1$. You can see that these values of v_1 and v_2 satisfy the simultaneous linear equations and are the values that we specified as a solution at the beginning of this section.

EXERCISES

A.14 Suppose the simultaneous linear equations

$$3v_1 + v_2 = 5$$
$$v_1 - v_2 = 3$$

are expressed as a matrix equation,

$$\mathbf{AV} = \mathbf{G}$$

a. Find the matrices **A**, **V**, and **G**.
b. Verify that

$$\mathbf{A}^{-1} = \begin{bmatrix} \frac{1}{4} & \frac{1}{4} \\ \frac{1}{4} & -\frac{3}{4} \end{bmatrix}$$

[*Note*: A procedure for finding $\mathbf{A}^{-1}$ is given in Appendix B.]
c. Solve the equations by finding $\mathbf{V} = \mathbf{A}^{-1}\mathbf{G}$.

A.15 For the simultaneous linear equations

$$10v_1 + 20v_3 - 60 = 0$$
$$20v_2 - 60 = 0$$
$$20v_1 + 68v_3 - 176 = 0$$

a. Find the matrices **A**, **V**, and **G**.
b. Verify that

$$\mathbf{A}^{-1} = \begin{bmatrix} \frac{17}{70} & 0 & -\frac{1}{14} \\ 0 & \frac{1}{20} & 0 \\ -\frac{1}{14} & 0 & \frac{1}{28} \end{bmatrix}$$

c. Solve the equations by finding $\mathbf{V} = \mathbf{A}^{-1}\mathbf{G}$.

A.5 The Least Squares Equations and Their Solutions

To apply matrix algebra to a regression analysis, we must place the data in matrices in a particular pattern. We will suppose that the linear model is

$$y = \beta_0 + \beta_1 x_1 + \beta_2 x_2 + \cdots + \beta_k x_k + \varepsilon$$

where (from Chapter 4) $x_1, x_2, \ldots, x_k$ could actually represent the squares, cubes, cross products, or other functions of predictor variables, and ε is a random error. We will assume that we have collected n data points, i.e., n values of y and corresponding values of $x_1, x_2, \ldots, x_k$, and that these are denoted as shown in the table:

DATA POINT	y Value	x_1	x_2	$\cdots$	x_k
1	y_1	x_{11}	x_{21}		x_{k1}
2	y_2	x_{12}	x_{22}		x_{k2}
$\vdots$	$\vdots$	$\vdots$	$\vdots$		$\vdots$
n	y_n	x_{1n}	x_{2n}		x_{kn}

Then the two data matrices **Y** and **X** are as shown in the next box.

The Data Matrices Y and X and the $\hat{\boldsymbol{\beta}}$ Matrix

$$\mathbf{Y} = \begin{bmatrix} y_1 \\ y_2 \\ y_3 \\ \vdots \\ y_n \end{bmatrix} \qquad \mathbf{X} = \begin{bmatrix} 1 & x_{11} & x_{21} & \cdots & x_{k1} \\ 1 & x_{12} & x_{22} & \cdots & x_{k2} \\ 1 & x_{13} & x_{23} & \cdots & x_{k3} \\ \vdots & \vdots & \vdots & & \vdots \\ 1 & x_{1n} & x_{2n} & \cdots & x_{kn} \end{bmatrix} \qquad \hat{\boldsymbol{\beta}} = \begin{bmatrix} \hat{\beta}_0 \\ \hat{\beta}_1 \\ \hat{\beta}_2 \\ \vdots \\ \hat{\beta}_k \end{bmatrix}$$

Notice that the first column in the **X** matrix is a column of 1's. Thus, we are inserting a value of x, namely, x_0, as the coefficient of β_0, where x_0 is a variable always equal to 1. Therefore, there is one column in the **X** matrix for each β parameter. Also, remember that a particular data point is identified by specific rows of the **Y** and **X** matrices. For example, the y value y_3 for data point 3 is in the third row of the **Y** matrix, and the corresponding values of $x_1, x_2, \ldots, x_k$ appear in the third row of the **X** matrix.

The $\hat{\boldsymbol{\beta}}$ matrix shown in the box contains the least squares estimates (which we are attempting to obtain) of the coefficients $\beta_0, \beta_1, \ldots, \beta_k$ of the linear model

$$y = \beta_0 + \beta_1 x_1 + \beta_2 x_2 + \cdots + \beta_k x_k + \varepsilon$$

To write the least squares equation, we need to define what we mean by the **transpose of a matrix**. If

$$\mathbf{Y} = \begin{bmatrix} 5 \\ 1 \\ 0 \\ 4 \\ 2 \end{bmatrix} \qquad \mathbf{X} = \begin{bmatrix} 1 & 0 \\ 1 & 1 \\ 1 & 4 \\ 1 & 2 \\ 1 & 6 \end{bmatrix}$$

then the transpose matrices of the **Y** and **X** matrices, denoted as **Y′** and **X′**, respectively, are

$$\mathbf{Y}' = [5 \quad 1 \quad 0 \quad 4 \quad 2] \qquad \mathbf{X}' = \begin{bmatrix} 1 & 1 & 1 & 1 & 1 \\ 0 & 1 & 4 & 2 & 6 \end{bmatrix}$$

Definition A.9

The **transpose of a matrix A**, denoted as **A′**, is obtained by interchanging corresponding rows and columns of the **A** matrix. That is, the ith row of the **A** matrix becomes the ith column of the **A′** matrix.

Using the **Y** and **X** data matrices, their transposes, and the $\hat{\boldsymbol{\beta}}$ matrix, we can write the least squares equations (proof omitted) as:

Least Squares Matrix Equation

$$(\mathbf{X}'\mathbf{X})\hat{\boldsymbol{\beta}} = \mathbf{X}'\mathbf{Y}$$

Thus, $(\mathbf{X}'\mathbf{X})$ is the coefficient matrix of the least squares estimates $\hat{\beta}_0$, $\hat{\beta}_1, \ldots, \hat{\beta}_k$, and $\mathbf{X}'\mathbf{Y}$ gives the matrix of constants that appear on the right-hand side of the equality signs. In the notation of Section A.4,

$$\mathbf{A} = \mathbf{X}'\mathbf{X} \qquad \mathbf{V} = \hat{\boldsymbol{\beta}} \qquad \mathbf{G} = \mathbf{X}'\mathbf{Y}$$

The solution, which follows from Section A.4, is

Least Squares Solution

$$\hat{\boldsymbol{\beta}} = (\mathbf{X}'\mathbf{X})^{-1}\mathbf{X}'\mathbf{Y}$$

Thus, to solve the least squares matrix equation, the computer calculates $(\mathbf{X'X})$, $(\mathbf{X'X})^{-1}$, $\mathbf{X'Y}$, and, finally, the product $(\mathbf{X'X})^{-1}\mathbf{X'Y}$. We will illustrate this process using the data for the advertising example from Section 3.3.

EXAMPLE A.5

Find the least squares line for the data given in Table A.1.

TABLE A.1

MONTH	ADVERTISING EXPENDITURE x, hundreds of dollars	SALES REVENUE y, thousands of dollars
1	1	1
2	2	1
3	3	2
4	4	2
5	5	4

Solution

The model is

$$y = \beta_0 + \beta_1 x_1 + \varepsilon$$

and the $\mathbf{Y}$, $\mathbf{X}$, and $\hat{\boldsymbol{\beta}}$ matrices are

$$\mathbf{Y} = \begin{bmatrix} 1 \\ 1 \\ 2 \\ 2 \\ 4 \end{bmatrix} \qquad \mathbf{X} = \begin{matrix} x_0 & x_1 \\ \end{matrix} \begin{bmatrix} 1 & 1 \\ 1 & 2 \\ 1 & 3 \\ 1 & 4 \\ 1 & 5 \end{bmatrix} \qquad \hat{\boldsymbol{\beta}} = \begin{bmatrix} \hat{\beta}_0 \\ \hat{\beta}_1 \end{bmatrix}$$

Then,

$$\mathbf{X'X} = \begin{bmatrix} 1 & 1 & 1 & 1 & 1 \\ 1 & 2 & 3 & 4 & 5 \end{bmatrix} \begin{bmatrix} 1 & 1 \\ 1 & 2 \\ 1 & 3 \\ 1 & 4 \\ 1 & 5 \end{bmatrix} = \begin{bmatrix} 5 & 15 \\ 15 & 55 \end{bmatrix}$$

$$\mathbf{X'Y} = \begin{bmatrix} 1 & 1 & 1 & 1 & 1 \\ 1 & 2 & 3 & 4 & 5 \end{bmatrix} \begin{bmatrix} 1 \\ 1 \\ 2 \\ 2 \\ 4 \end{bmatrix} = \begin{bmatrix} 10 \\ 37 \end{bmatrix}$$

The last matrix that we need is $(\mathbf{X}'\mathbf{X})^{-1}$. This matrix, which can be found by using Theorem A.2 (or by using the method of Appendix B), is

$$(\mathbf{X}'\mathbf{X})^{-1} = \begin{bmatrix} 1.1 & -.3 \\ -.3 & .1 \end{bmatrix}$$

Then the solution to the least squares equation is

$$\hat{\boldsymbol{\beta}} = (\mathbf{X}'\mathbf{X})^{-1}\mathbf{X}'\mathbf{Y} = \begin{bmatrix} 1.1 & -.3 \\ -.3 & .1 \end{bmatrix}\begin{bmatrix} 10 \\ 37 \end{bmatrix} = \begin{bmatrix} -.1 \\ .7 \end{bmatrix}$$

Thus, $\hat{\beta}_0 = -.1$, $\hat{\beta}_1 = .7$, and the prediction equation is

$$\hat{y} = -.1 + .7x$$

You can verify that this is the same answer as obtained in Section 3.3.

EXAMPLE A.6

Table A.2 contains data on monthly electrical power usage and home size for a sample of $n = 10$ homes. Find the least squares solution for fitting the monthly power usage y to size of home x for the model

$$y = \beta_0 + \beta_1 x + \beta_2 x^2 + \varepsilon$$

TABLE A.2 **Data for Power Usage Study**

SIZE OF HOME x, square feet	MONTHLY USAGE y, kilowatt-hours	SIZE OF HOME x, square feet	MONTHLY USAGE y, kilowatt-hours
1,290	1,182	1,840	1,711
1,350	1,172	1,980	1,804
1,470	1,264	2,230	1,840
1,600	1,493	2,400	1,956
1,710	1,571	2,930	1,954

Solution

The $\mathbf{Y}$, $\mathbf{X}$, and $\hat{\boldsymbol{\beta}}$ matrices are as follows:

$$\mathbf{Y} = \begin{bmatrix} 1{,}182 \\ 1{,}172 \\ 1{,}264 \\ 1{,}493 \\ 1{,}571 \\ 1{,}711 \\ 1{,}804 \\ 1{,}840 \\ 1{,}956 \\ 1{,}954 \end{bmatrix}$$

$$
\mathbf{X} = \begin{array}{c}
\begin{array}{ccc} x_0 & \quad x & \qquad x^2 \end{array} \\
\begin{bmatrix}
1 & 1{,}290 & 1{,}664{,}100 \\
1 & 1{,}350 & 1{,}822{,}500 \\
1 & 1{,}470 & 2{,}160{,}900 \\
1 & 1{,}600 & 2{,}560{,}000 \\
1 & 1{,}710 & 2{,}924{,}100 \\
1 & 1{,}840 & 3{,}385{,}600 \\
1 & 1{,}980 & 3{,}920{,}400 \\
1 & 2{,}230 & 4{,}972{,}900 \\
1 & 2{,}400 & 5{,}760{,}000 \\
1 & 2{,}930 & 8{,}584{,}900
\end{bmatrix}
\end{array}
$$

Then

$$
\mathbf{X'X} = \begin{bmatrix}
10 & 18{,}800 & 37{,}755{,}400 \\
18{,}800 & 37{,}755{,}400 & 8{,}093.9 \times 10^{7} \\
37{,}755{,}400 & 8{,}093.9 \times 10^{7} & 1.843 \times 10^{14}
\end{bmatrix}
$$

$$
\mathbf{X'Y} = \begin{bmatrix}
15{,}947 \\
31{,}283{,}250 \\
6.53069 \times 10^{10}
\end{bmatrix}
$$

and (obtained using a statistical software package):

$$
(\mathbf{X'X})^{-1} = \begin{bmatrix}
26.9156 & -.027027 & 6.3554 \times 10^{-6} \\
-.027027 & 2.75914 \times 10^{-5} & -6.5804 \times 10^{-9} \\
6.3554 \times 10^{-6} & -6.5804 \times 10^{-9} & 1.5934 \times 10^{-12}
\end{bmatrix}
$$

Finally, performing the multiplication, we obtain

$$
\hat{\boldsymbol{\beta}} = (\mathbf{X'X})^{-1}\mathbf{X'Y}
$$

$$
= \begin{bmatrix}
26.9156 & -.027027 & 6.3554 \times 10^{-6} \\
-.027027 & 2.75914 \times 10^{-5} & -6.5804 \times 10^{-9} \\
6.3554 \times 10^{-6} & -6.5804 \times 10^{-9} & 1.5934 \times 10^{-12}
\end{bmatrix}
\begin{bmatrix}
15{,}947 \\
31{,}283{,}250 \\
6.53069 \times 10^{10}
\end{bmatrix}
$$

$$
= \begin{bmatrix}
-1{,}216.14389 \\
2.39893 \\
-.00045
\end{bmatrix}
$$

Thus,

$$\hat{\beta}_0 = -1{,}216.14389$$

$$\hat{\beta}_1 = 2.39893$$

$$\hat{\beta}_2 = -.00045$$

and the prediction equation is

$$\hat{y} = -1{,}216.14389 + 2.39893x - .00045x^2$$

The SAS printout for the regression analysis is shown in Figure A.1. Note that the β estimates we obtained agree with the shaded values.

FIGURE A.1
SAS printout for the power usage data, Example A.6

ANALYSIS OF VARIANCE

SOURCE	DF	SUM OF SQUARES	MEAN SQUARE	F VALUE	PROB>F
MODEL	2	831069.55	415534.77	189.710	0.0001
ERROR	7	15332.55363	2190.36480		
C TOTAL	9	846402.10			

ROOT MSE	46.80133	R-SQUARE	0.9819
DEP MEAN	1594.7	ADJ R-SQ	0.9767
C.V.	2.934805		

PARAMETER ESTIMATES

VARIABLE	DF	PARAMETER ESTIMATE	STANDARD ERROR	T FOR H0: PARAMETER=0	PROB > |T|
INTERCEP	1	-1216.14389	242.80637	-5.009	0.0016
X	1	2.39893018	0.24583560	9.758	0.0001
XX	1	-0.000450040	0.000059077	-7.618	0.0001

EXERCISES

A.16 Use the method of least squares to fit a straight line to the five data points:

x	−2	−1	0	1	2
y	4	3	3	1	−1

a. Construct **Y** and **X** matrices for the data.
b. Find **X′X** and **X′Y**.
c. Find the least squares estimates $\hat{\boldsymbol{\beta}} = (\mathbf{X}'\mathbf{X})^{-1}\mathbf{X}'\mathbf{Y}$. [*Note*: See Theorem A.1 for information on finding $(\mathbf{X}'\mathbf{X})^{-1}$.]
d. Give the prediction equation.

Note that the matrix procedure gives the same solution as that obtained in Exercise 3.7.

A.17 Use the method of least squares to fit the model $E(y) = \beta_0 + \beta_1 x$ to the six data points:

x	1	2	3	4	5	6
y	1	2	2	3	5	5

a. Construct **Y** and **X** matrices for the data.
b. Find **X′X** and **X′Y**.
c. Verify that

$$(\mathbf{X'X})^{-1} = \begin{bmatrix} \frac{13}{15} & -\frac{7}{35} \\ -\frac{7}{35} & \frac{2}{35} \end{bmatrix}$$

d. Find the $\hat{\boldsymbol{\beta}}$ matrix.
e. Give the prediction equation.

Note that the matrix procedure gives the same solution as that obtained in Exercise 3.6.

A.18 An experiment was conducted in which two y observations were collected for each of five values of x:

x	−2		−1		0		1		2	
y	1.1	1.3	2.0	2.1	2.7	2.8	3.4	3.6	4.1	4.0

Use the method of least squares to fit the second-order model, $E(y) = \beta_0 + \beta_1 x + \beta_2 x^2$, to the 10 data points.

a. Give the dimensions of the **Y** and **X** matrices.
b. Verify that

$$(\mathbf{X'X})^{-1} = \begin{bmatrix} \frac{17}{70} & 0 & -\frac{1}{14} \\ 0 & \frac{1}{20} & 0 \\ -\frac{1}{14} & 0 & \frac{1}{28} \end{bmatrix}$$

c. Both $\mathbf{X'X}$ and $(\mathbf{X'X})^{-1}$ are symmetric matrices. What is a symmetric matrix?
d. Find the $\hat{\boldsymbol{\beta}}$ matrix and the least squares prediction equation.
e. Plot the data points and graph the prediction equation.

A.6 Calculating SSE and s^2

You will recall that the variances of the estimators of all the β parameters and of $\hat{y}$ depend on the value of σ^2, the variance of the random error ε that appears in the linear model. Since σ^2 will rarely be known in advance, we must use the sample data to estimate its value.

Formulas for SSE and s^2

$$\text{SSE} = \mathbf{Y'Y} - \hat{\boldsymbol{\beta}}'\mathbf{X'Y}$$

$$s^2 = \frac{\text{SSE}}{n - \text{Number of } \beta \text{ parameters in model}}$$

We demonstrate the use of these formulas with the advertising–sales data of Example A.5.

EXAMPLE A.7

Find the SSE for the advertising–sales data of Example A.5.

Solution

From Example A.5,

$$\hat{\boldsymbol{\beta}} = \begin{bmatrix} -.1 \\ .7 \end{bmatrix} \quad \text{and} \quad \mathbf{X'Y} = \begin{bmatrix} 10 \\ 37 \end{bmatrix}$$

Then,

$$\mathbf{Y'Y} = [1 \quad 1 \quad 2 \quad 2 \quad 4] \begin{bmatrix} 1 \\ 1 \\ 2 \\ 2 \\ 4 \end{bmatrix} = 26$$

and

$$\hat{\boldsymbol{\beta}}'\mathbf{X'Y} = [-.1 \quad .7] \begin{bmatrix} 10 \\ 37 \end{bmatrix} = 24.9$$

So

$$\text{SSE} = \mathbf{Y'Y} - \hat{\boldsymbol{\beta}}'\mathbf{X'Y} = 26 - 24.9 = 1.1$$

(Note that this is the same answer as that obtained in Section 3.3.)
Finally,

$$s^2 = \frac{\text{SSE}}{n - \text{Number of } \beta \text{ parameters in model}} = \frac{1.1}{5 - 2} = .367$$

This estimate is needed to construct a confidence interval for β_1, to test a hypothesis concerning its value, or to construct a confidence interval for the mean sales for a given advertising expenditure.

A.7 Standard Errors of Estimators, Test Statistics, and Confidence Intervals for $\boldsymbol{\beta}_0, \boldsymbol{\beta}_1, \ldots, \boldsymbol{\beta}_k$

This appendix is important because all the relevant information pertaining to the standard errors of the sampling distributions of $\hat{\beta}_0, \hat{\beta}_1, \ldots, \hat{\beta}_k$ (and hence of $\hat{Y}$) is contained in $(\mathbf{X'X})^{-1}$. Thus, if we denote the $(\mathbf{X'X})^{-1}$ matrix as

$$(\mathbf{X'X})^{-1} = \begin{bmatrix} c_{00} & c_{01} & \cdots & c_{0k} \\ c_{10} & c_{11} & \cdots & c_{1k} \\ c_{20} & c_{21} & \cdots & c_{2k} \\ \vdots & \vdots & \vdots & \vdots \\ c_{k0} & c_{k1} & \cdots & c_{kk} \end{bmatrix}$$

then it can be shown (proof omitted) that the standard errors of the sampling distributions of $\hat{\beta}_0, \hat{\beta}_1, \ldots, \hat{\beta}_k$ are

$$\sigma_{\hat{\beta}_0} = \sigma\sqrt{c_{00}}$$
$$\sigma_{\hat{\beta}_1} = \sigma\sqrt{c_{11}}$$
$$\sigma_{\hat{\beta}_2} = \sigma\sqrt{c_{22}}$$
$$\vdots$$
$$\sigma_{\hat{\beta}_k} = \sigma\sqrt{c_{kk}}$$

where σ is the standard deviation of the random error ε. In other words, the diagonal elements of $(\mathbf{X}'\mathbf{X})^{-1}$ give the values of $c_{00}, c_{11}, \ldots, c_{kk}$ that are required for finding the standard errors of the estimators $\hat{\beta}_0, \hat{\beta}_1, \ldots, \hat{\beta}_k$. The estimated values of the standard errors are obtained by replacing σ by s in the formulas for the standard errors. Thus, the estimated standard error of $\hat{\beta}_1$ is $s_{\hat{\beta}_1} = s\sqrt{c_{11}}$.

The confidence interval for a single β parameter, β_i, is given in the next box.

Confidence Interval for β_i

$$\hat{\beta}_i \pm t_{\alpha/2}(\text{Estimated standard error of } \hat{\beta}_i)$$

or

$$\hat{\beta}_i \pm t_{\alpha/2} s\sqrt{c_{ii}}$$

where $t_{\alpha/2}$ is based on the number of degrees of freedom associated with s.

Similarly, the test statistic for testing the null hypothesis H_0: $\beta_i = 0$ is as shown in the following box.

Test Statistic for H_0: $\beta_i = 0$

$$t = \frac{\hat{\beta}_i}{s\sqrt{c_{ii}}}$$

EXAMPLE A.8

Refer to Example A.5 and find the estimated standard error for the sampling distribution of $\hat{\beta}_1$, the estimator of the slope of the line β_1. Then give a 95% confidence interval for β_1.

Solution

The $(\mathbf{X}'\mathbf{X})^{-1}$ matrix for the least squares solution of Example A.5 was

$$(\mathbf{X}'\mathbf{X})^{-1} = \begin{bmatrix} 1.1 & -.3 \\ -.3 & .1 \end{bmatrix}$$

Therefore, $c_{00} = 1.1$, $c_{11} = .1$, and the estimated standard error for $\hat{\beta}_1$ is

$$s_{\hat{\beta}_1} = s\sqrt{c_{11}} = \sqrt{.367}(\sqrt{.1}) = .192$$

The value for s, $\sqrt{.367}$, was obtained from Example A.7.

A 95% confidence interval for β_1 is

$$\hat{\beta}_1 \pm t_{\alpha/2} s\sqrt{c_{11}}$$

$$.7 \pm (3.182)(.192) = (.09, 1.31)$$

The t value, $t_{.025}$, is based on $(n - 2) = 3$ df. Observe that this is the same confidence interval as the one obtained in Section 3.6.

EXAMPLE A.9

Refer to Example A.6 and the least squares solution for fitting power usage y to the size of a home x using the model

$$y = \beta_0 + \beta_1 x + \beta_2 x^2 + \varepsilon$$

The SAS printout for the analysis is reproduced in Figure A.2.

a. Compute the estimated standard error for $\hat{\beta}_1$, and compare this result with the value shaded in Figure A.2.
b. Compute the value of the test statistic for testing H_0: $\beta_2 = 0$. Compare this with the value shaded in Figure A.2.

FIGURE A.2 SAS printout for the power usage model

ANALYSIS OF VARIANCE

SOURCE	DF	SUM OF SQUARES	MEAN SQUARE	F VALUE	PROB>F
MODEL	2	831069.55	415534.77	189.710	0.0001
ERROR	7	15332.55363	2190.36480		
C TOTAL	9	846402.10			

ROOT MSE	46.80133	R-SQUARE	0.9819
DEP MEAN	1594.7	ADJ R-SQ	0.9767
C.V.	2.934805		

PARAMETER ESTIMATES

VARIABLE	DF	PARAMETER ESTIMATE	STANDARD ERROR	T FOR H0: PARAMETER=0	PROB > |T|
INTERCEP	1	-1216.14389	242.80637	-5.009	0.0016
X	1	2.39893018	0.24583560	9.758	0.0001
XX	1	-0.000450040	0.000059077	-7.618	0.0001

Solution

The fitted model is

$$\hat{y} = -1{,}216.14389 + 2.39893x - .00045x^2$$

The $(\mathbf{X}'\mathbf{X})^{-1}$ matrix, obtained in Example A.6, is

$$(\mathbf{X}'\mathbf{X})^{-1} = \begin{bmatrix} 26.9156 & -.027027 & 6.3554 \times 10^{-6} \\ -.027027 & 2.75914 \times 10^{-5} & -6.5804 \times 10^{-9} \\ 6.3554 \times 10^{-6} & -6.5804 \times 10^{-9} & 1.5934 \times 10^{-12} \end{bmatrix}$$

From $(\mathbf{X}'\mathbf{X})^{-1}$, we know that

$$c_{00} = 26.9156$$
$$c_{11} = 2.75914 \times 10^{-5}$$
$$c_{22} = 1.5934 \times 10^{-12}$$

and from the printout, $s = 46.80133$.

a. The estimated standard error of $\hat{\beta}_1$ is

$$s_{\hat{\beta}_1} = s\sqrt{c_{11}}$$
$$= (46.801)\sqrt{2.75914 \times 10^{-1}} = .24583$$

Notice that this agrees with the value of $s_{\hat{\beta}_1}$ shaded in the SAS printout (Figure A.2).

b. The value of the test statistic for testing H_0: $\beta_2 = 0$ is

$$t = \frac{\hat{\beta}_2}{s\sqrt{c_{22}}} = \frac{-.00045}{(46.801)\sqrt{1.5934 \times 10^{-12}}} = -7.62$$

Notice that this value of the t statistic agrees with the value -7.618 given in the column headed **T FOR H0: PARAMETER = 0** shaded in the printout (Figure A.2).

EXERCISES

A.19 Do the data given in Exercise A.16 provide sufficient evidence to indicate that x contributes information for the prediction of y? Test H_0: $\beta_1 = 0$ against H_a: $\beta_1 \neq 0$ using $\alpha = .05$.

A.20 Find a 90% confidence interval for the slope of the line in Exercise A.19.

A.21 The term in the second-order model $E(y) = \beta_0 + \beta_1 x + \beta_2 x^2$ that controls the curvature in its graph is $\beta_2 x^2$. If $\beta_2 = 0$, $E(y)$ graphs as a straight line. Do the data given in Exercise A.18 provide sufficient evidence to indicate curvature in the model for $E(y)$? Test H_0: $\beta_2 = 0$ against H_a: $\beta_2 \neq 0$ using $\alpha = .10$.

A.8 A Confidence Interval for a Linear Function of the β Parameters; a Confidence Interval for $E(y)$

Suppose we were to postulate that the mean value of the productivity, y, of a company is related to the size of the company, x, and that the relationship could be modeled by the expression

$$E(y) = \beta_0 + \beta_1 x + \beta_2 x^2$$

A graph of $E(y)$ might appear as shown in Figure A.3.

We might have several reasons for collecting data on the productivity and size of a set of n companies and for finding the least squares prediction equation,

$$\hat{y} = \hat{\beta}_0 + \hat{\beta}_1 x + \hat{\beta}_2 x^2$$

FIGURE A.3
Graph of mean productivity $E(y)$

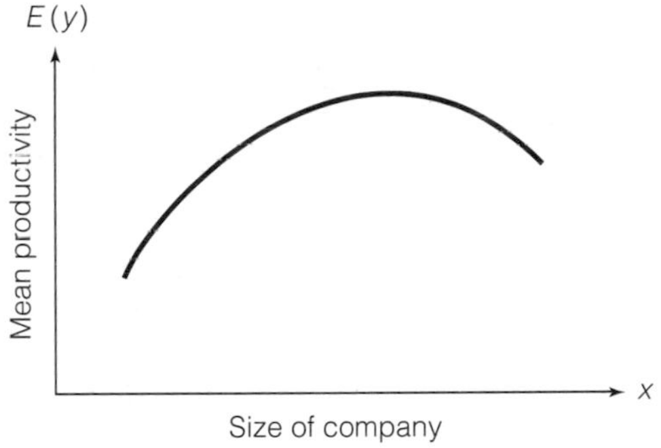

For example, we might wish to estimate the mean productivity for a company of a given size (say, $x = 2$). That is, we might wish to estimate

$$\begin{aligned} E(y) &= \beta_0 + \beta_1 x + \beta_2 x^2 \\ &= \beta_0 + 2\beta_1 + 4\beta_2 \qquad \text{where} \quad x = 2 \end{aligned}$$

Or we might wish to estimate the marginal increase in productivity, the slope of a tangent to the curve, when $x = 2$ (see Figure A.4). The marginal productivity for y when $x = 2$ is the rate of change of $E(y)$ with respect to x, evaluated at $x =$

FIGURE A.4
Marginal productivity

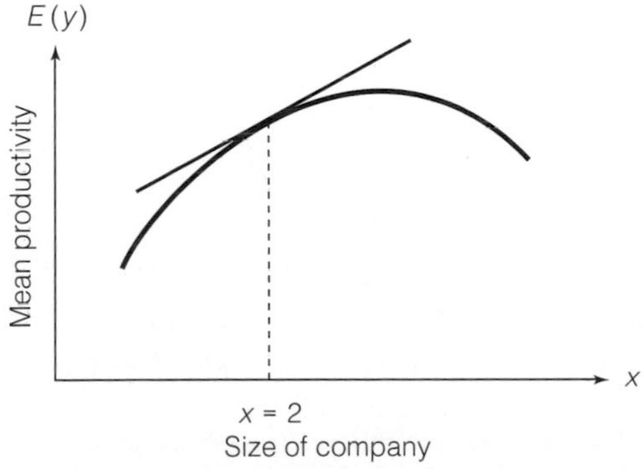

2.* The marginal productivity for a value of x, denoted by the symbol $dE(y)/dx$, can be shown (proof omitted) to be

$$\frac{dE(y)}{dx} = \beta_1 + 2\beta_2 x$$

Therefore, the marginal productivity at $x = 2$ is

$$\frac{dE(y)}{dx} = \beta_1 + 2\beta_2(2) = \beta_1 + 4\beta_2$$

For $x = 2$, both $E(y)$ and the marginal productivity are *linear* functions of the unknown parameters β_0, β_1, β_2 in the model. The problem we pose in this section is that of finding confidence intervals for linear functions of β parameters or testing hypotheses concerning their values. The information necessary to solve this problem is rarely given in a standard multiple regression analysis computer printout, but we can find these confidence intervals or values of the appropriate test statistics from knowledge of $(\mathbf{X}'\mathbf{X})^{-1}$.

For the model

$$y = \beta_0 + \beta_1 x_1 + \cdots + \beta_k x_k + \varepsilon$$

we can make an inference about a linear function of the β parameters, say,

$$a_0\beta_0 + a_1\beta_1 + \cdots + a_k\beta_k$$

where $a_0, a_1, \ldots, a_k$ are known constants. We will use the corresponding linear function of least squares estimates,

$$\ell = a_0\hat{\beta}_0 + a_1\hat{\beta}_1 + \cdots + a_k\hat{\beta}_k$$

as our best estimate of $a_0\beta_0 + a_1\beta_1 + \cdots + a_k\beta_k$.

Then, for the assumptions on the random error ε (stated in Section 4.2), the sampling distribution for the estimator ℓ will be normal, with mean and standard error as given in the first box on page 795. This indicates that ℓ is an unbiased estimator of

$$E(\ell) = a_0\beta_0 + a_1\beta_1 + \cdots + a_k\beta_k$$

and that its sampling distribution would appear as shown in Figure A.5.

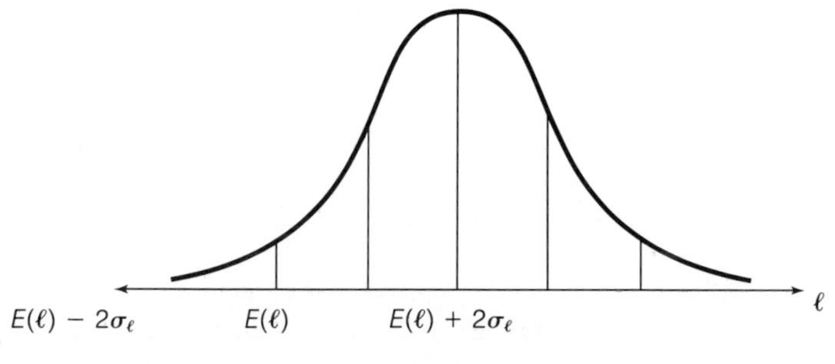

FIGURE A.5
Sampling distribution for ℓ

*If you have had calculus, you can see that the marginal productivity for y given x is the first derivative of $E(y) = \beta_0 + \beta_1 x + \beta_2 x^2$ with respect to x.

Mean and Standard Error of ℓ

$$E(\ell) = a_0\beta_0 + a_1\beta_1 + \cdots + a_k\beta_k$$
$$\sigma_\ell = \sqrt{\sigma^2 \mathbf{a}'(\mathbf{X}'\mathbf{X})^{-1}\mathbf{a}}$$

where σ^2 is the variance of ε, $(\mathbf{X}'\mathbf{X})^{-1}$ is the inverse matrix obtained in fitting the least squares model to the set of data, and

$$\mathbf{a} = \begin{bmatrix} a_0 \\ a_1 \\ a_2 \\ \vdots \\ a_k \end{bmatrix}$$

It can be demonstrated that a $100(1 - \alpha)\%$ confidence interval for $E(\ell)$ is as shown in the next box.

A $100(1 - \alpha)\%$ Confidence Interval for $E(\ell)$

$$\ell \pm t_{\alpha/2}\sqrt{s^2 \mathbf{a}'(\mathbf{X}'\mathbf{X})^{-1}\mathbf{a}}$$

where

$$E(\ell) = a_0\beta_0 + a_1\beta_1 + \cdots + a_k\beta_k$$

$$\ell = a_0\hat{\beta}_0 + a_1\hat{\beta}_1 + \cdots + a_k\hat{\beta}_k \qquad \mathbf{a} = \begin{bmatrix} a_0 \\ a_1 \\ a_2 \\ \vdots \\ a_k \end{bmatrix}$$

s^2 and $(\mathbf{X}'\mathbf{X})^{-1}$ are obtained from the least squares procedure, and $t_{\alpha/2}$ is based on the number of degrees of freedom associated with s^2.

The linear function of the β parameters that is most often the focus of our attention is

$$E(y) = \beta_0 + \beta_1 x_1 + \cdots + \beta_k x_k$$

That is, we want to find a confidence interval for $E(y)$ for specific values of x_1, $x_2, \ldots, x_k$. For this special case,

$$\ell = \hat{y}$$

and the **a** matrix is

$$\mathbf{a} = \begin{bmatrix} 1 \\ x_1 \\ x_2 \\ \cdot \\ \cdot \\ \cdot \\ x_k \end{bmatrix}$$

where the symbols $x_1, x_2, \ldots, x_k$ in the **a** matrix indicate the specific numerical values assumed by these variables. Thus, the procedure for forming a confidence interval for $E(y)$ is as shown in the box.

A 100(1 − α)% Confidence Interval for E(y)

$$\ell \pm t_{\alpha/2}\sqrt{s^2\mathbf{a}'(\mathbf{X}'\mathbf{X})^{-1}\mathbf{a}}$$

where

$$E(y) = \beta_0 + \beta_1 x_1 + \beta_2 x_2 + \cdots + \beta_k x_k$$

$$\ell = \hat{y} = \hat{\beta}_0 + \hat{\beta}_1 x_1 + \cdots + \hat{\beta}_k x_k \qquad \mathbf{a} = \begin{bmatrix} 1 \\ x_1 \\ x_2 \\ \cdot \\ \cdot \\ \cdot \\ x_k \end{bmatrix}$$

s^2 and $(\mathbf{X}'\mathbf{X})^{-1}$ are obtained from the least squares analysis, and $t_{\alpha/2}$ is based on the number of degrees of freedom associated with s^2, namely, $n - (k + 1)$.

EXAMPLE A.10

Refer to the data of Example A.5 for sales revenue y and advertising expenditure x. Find a 95% confidence interval for the mean sales revenue $E(y)$ when advertising expenditure is $x = 4$.

Solution

The confidence interval for $E(y)$ for a given value of x is

$$\hat{y} \pm t_{\alpha/2}\sqrt{s^2\mathbf{a}'(\mathbf{X}'\mathbf{X})^{-1}\mathbf{a}}$$

Consequently, we need to find and substitute the values of $\mathbf{a}'(\mathbf{X}'\mathbf{X})^{-1}\mathbf{a}$, $t_{\alpha/2}$, and $\hat{y}$ into this formula. Since we wish to estimate

$$\begin{aligned} E(y) &= \beta_0 + \beta_1 x \\ &= \beta_0 + \beta_1(4) \qquad \text{when} \quad x = 4 \\ &= \beta_0 + 4\beta_1 \end{aligned}$$

it follows that the coefficients of β_0 and β_1 are $a_0 = 1$ and $a_1 = 4$, and thus,

$$\mathbf{a} = \begin{bmatrix} 1 \\ 4 \end{bmatrix}$$

From Examples A.5 and A.7, $\hat{y} = -.1 + .7x$,

$$(\mathbf{X}'\mathbf{X})^{-1} = \begin{bmatrix} 1.1 & -.3 \\ -.3 & .1 \end{bmatrix}$$

and $s^2 = .367$. Then,

$$\mathbf{a}'(\mathbf{X}'\mathbf{X})^{-1}\mathbf{a} = [1 \quad 4]\begin{bmatrix} 1.1 & -.3 \\ -.3 & .1 \end{bmatrix}\begin{bmatrix} 1 \\ 4 \end{bmatrix}$$

We first calculate

$$\mathbf{a}'(\mathbf{X}'\mathbf{X})^{-1} = [1 \quad 4]\begin{bmatrix} 1.1 & -.3 \\ -.3 & .1 \end{bmatrix} = [-.1 \quad .1]$$

Then,

$$\mathbf{a}'(\mathbf{X}'\mathbf{X})^{-1}\mathbf{a} = [-.1 \quad .1]\begin{bmatrix} 1 \\ 4 \end{bmatrix} = .3$$

The t value, $t_{.025}$, based on 3 df is 3.182. So, a 95% confidence interval for the mean sales revenue with an advertising expenditure of 4 is

$$\hat{y} \pm t_{\alpha/2}\sqrt{s^2\mathbf{a}'(\mathbf{X}'\mathbf{X})^{-1}\mathbf{a}}$$

Since $\hat{y} = -.1 + .7x = -.1 + (.7)(4) = 2.7$, the 95% confidence interval for $E(y)$ when $x = 4$ is

$$2.7 \pm (3.182)\sqrt{(.367)(.3)}$$
$$2.7 \pm 1.1$$

Notice that this is exactly the same result as obtained in Example 3.4.

EXAMPLE A.11

An economist recorded a measure of productivity y and the size x for each of 100 companies producing cement. A regression model,

$$y = \beta_0 + \beta_1 x + \beta_2 x^2 + \varepsilon$$

fit to the $n = 100$ data points produced the following results:

$$\hat{y} = 2.6 + .7x - .2x^2$$

where x is coded to take values in the interval $-2 < x < 2$,* and

$$(\mathbf{X}'\mathbf{X})^{-1} = \begin{bmatrix} .0025 & .0005 & -.0070 \\ .0005 & .0055 & 0 \\ -.0070 & 0 & .0050 \end{bmatrix} \qquad s = .14$$

Find a 95% confidence interval for the marginal increase in productivity given that the coded size of a plant is $x = 1.5$.

Solution

The mean value of y for a given value of x is

$$E(y) = \beta_0 + \beta_1 x + \beta_2 x^2$$

Therefore, the marginal increase in y for $x = 1.5$ is

$$\frac{dE(y)}{dx} = \beta_1 + 2\beta_2 x$$
$$= \beta_1 + 2(1.5)\beta_2$$

Or,

$$E(\ell) = \beta_1 + 3\beta_2 \qquad \text{when} \quad x = 1.5$$

Note from the prediction equation, $\hat{y} = 2.6 + .7x - .2x^2$, that $\hat{\beta}_1 = .7$ and $\hat{\beta}_2 = -.2$. Therefore,

$$\ell = \hat{\beta}_1 + 3\hat{\beta}_2 = .7 + 3(-.2) = .1$$

and

$$\mathbf{a} = \begin{bmatrix} a_0 \\ a_1 \\ a_2 \end{bmatrix} = \begin{bmatrix} 0 \\ 1 \\ 3 \end{bmatrix}$$

We next calculate

$$\mathbf{a}'(\mathbf{X}'\mathbf{X})^{-1}\mathbf{a} = [0 \quad 1 \quad 3] \begin{bmatrix} .0025 & .0005 & -.0070 \\ .0005 & .0055 & 0 \\ -.0070 & 0 & .0050 \end{bmatrix} \begin{bmatrix} 0 \\ 1 \\ 3 \end{bmatrix} = .0505$$

Then, since s is based on $n - (k + 1) = 100 - 3 = 97$ df, $t_{.025} \approx 1.96$, and a 95% confidence interval for the marginal increase in productivity when $x = 1.5$ is

$$\ell \pm t_{.025}\sqrt{(s^2)\mathbf{a}'(\mathbf{X}'\mathbf{X})^{-1}\mathbf{a}}$$

*We give a formula for *coding* observational data in Section 5.6.

or

$$.1 \pm (1.96)\sqrt{(.14)^2(.0505)}$$
$$.1 \pm .062$$

Thus, the marginal increase in productivity, the slope of the tangent to the curve

$$E(y) = \beta_0 + \beta_1 x + \beta_2 x^2$$

is estimated to lie in the interval .1 ± .062 at $x = 1.5$. A graph of $\hat{y} = 2.6 + .7x - .2x^2$ is shown in Figure A.6.

FIGURE A.6
A graph of $\hat{y} = 2.6 + .7x - .2x^2$

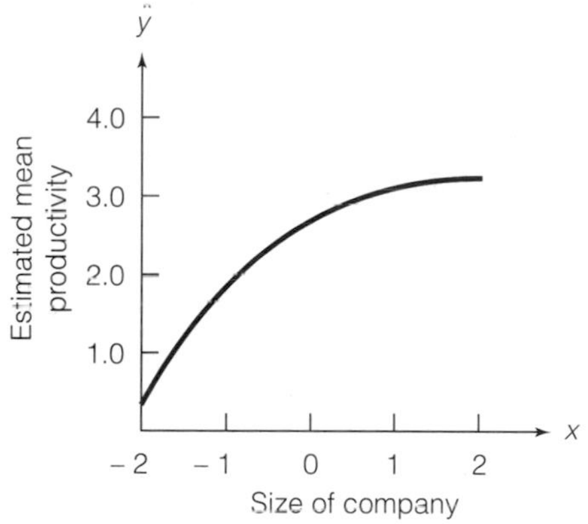

A.9 A Prediction Interval for Some Value of y to Be Observed in the Future

We have indicated in Sections 3.9 and 4.8 that two of the most important applications of the least squares predictor $\hat{y}$ are estimating the mean value of y (the topic of the preceding section) and predicting a new value of y, yet unobserved, for specific values of $x_1, x_2, \ldots, x_k$. The difference between these two inferential problems (when each would be pertinent) was explained in Chapters 3 and 4, but we will give another example to make certain that the distinction is clear.

Suppose you are the manager of a manufacturing plant and that y, the daily profit, is a function of various process variables $x_1, x_2, \ldots, x_k$. Suppose you want to know how much money you would make *in the long run* if the x's are set at specific values. For this case, you would be interested in finding a confidence interval for the mean profit per day, $E(y)$. In contrast, suppose you planned to operate the plant for just one more day! Then you would be interested in predicting the value of y, the profit associated with tomorrow's production.

We have indicated that the error of prediction is always larger than the error of estimating $E(y)$. You can see this by comparing the formula for the prediction interval (shown in the box on page 800) with the formula for the confidence interval for $E(y)$ that was given in Section A.8.

A $100(1-\alpha)\%$ Prediction Interval for y

$$\hat{y} \pm t_{\alpha/2}\sqrt{s^2 + s^2\mathbf{a}'(\mathbf{X}'\mathbf{X})^{-1}\mathbf{a}} = \hat{y} \pm t_{\alpha/2}\sqrt{s^2[1 + \mathbf{a}'(\mathbf{X}'\mathbf{X})^{-1}\mathbf{a}]}$$

where

$$\hat{y} = \hat{\beta}_0 + \hat{\beta}_1 x_1 + \cdots + \hat{\beta}_k x_k$$

s^2 and $(\mathbf{X}'\mathbf{X})^{-1}$ are obtained from the least squares analysis,

$$\mathbf{a} = \begin{bmatrix} 1 \\ x_1 \\ x_2 \\ \cdot \\ \cdot \\ \cdot \\ x_k \end{bmatrix}$$

contains the numerical values of $x_1, x_2, \ldots, x_k$, and $t_{\alpha/2}$ is based on the number of degrees of freedom associated with s^2, namely, $n - (k + 1)$.

EXAMPLE A.12

Refer to the sales–advertising expenditure example (Example A.10). Find a 95% prediction interval for the sales revenue next month, if it is known that next month's advertising expenditure will be $x = 4$.

Solution

The 95% prediction interval for sales revenue y is

$$\hat{y} \pm t_{\alpha/2}\sqrt{s^2[1 + \mathbf{a}'(\mathbf{X}'\mathbf{X})^{-1}\mathbf{a}]}$$

From Example A.10, when $x = 4$, $\hat{y} = -.1 + .7x = -.1 + (.7)(4) = 2.7$, $s^2 = .367$, $t_{.025} = 3.182$, and $\mathbf{a}'(\mathbf{X}'\mathbf{X})^{-1}\mathbf{a} = .3$. Then the 95% prediction interval for y is

$$2.7 \pm (3.182)\sqrt{(.367)(1 + .3)}$$

$$2.7 \pm 2.2$$

You will find that this is the same solution as obtained in Example 3.5.

EXERCISES

A.22 Refer to Exercise A.16. Find a 90% confidence interval for $E(y)$ when $x = 1$. Interpret the interval.

A.23 Refer to Exercise A.16. Suppose you plan to observe y for $x = 1$. Find a 90% prediction interval for that value of y. Interpret the interval.

A.24 Refer to Exercise A.17. Find a 90% confidence interval for $E(y)$ when $x = 2$. Interpret the interval.

A.25 Refer to Exercise A.17. Find a 90% prediction interval for a value of y to be observed in the future when $x = 2$. Interpret the interval.

A.26 Refer to Exercise A.18. Find a 90% confidence interval for the mean value of y when $x = 1$. Interpret the interval.

A.27 Refer to Exercise A.18. Find a 90% prediction interval for a value of y to be observed in the future when $x = 1$.

A.28 The productivity (items produced per hour) per worker on a manufacturing assembly line is expected to increase as piecework pay rate (in dollars) increases; it is expected to stabilize after a certain pay rate has been reached. The productivity of five different workers was recorded for each of five piecework pay rates, \$.80, \$.90, \$1.00, \$1.10, \$1.20, thus giving $n = 25$ data points. A multiple regression analysis using a second-order model,

$$E(y) = \beta_0 + \beta_1 x + \beta_2 x^2$$

gave

$$\hat{y} = 2.08 + 8.42x - 1.65x^2$$

$$\text{SSE} = 26.62,\ \text{SS}_{yy} = 784.11, \text{ and}$$

$$(\mathbf{X}'\mathbf{X})^{-1} = \begin{bmatrix} .020 & -.010 & .015 \\ -.010 & .040 & -.006 \\ .015 & -.006 & .028 \end{bmatrix}$$

a. Find s^2.
b. Find a 95% confidence interval for the mean productivity when the pay rate is \$1.10. Interpret this interval.
c. Find a 95% prediction interval for the production of an individual worker who is paid at a rate of \$1.10 per piece. Interpret the interval.
d. Find R^2 and interpret the value.

Summary

Except for the tedious process of inverting a matrix (discussed in Appendix B), we have covered the major steps performed by a computer in fitting a linear statistical model to a set of data using the method of least squares. We have also explained how to find the confidence intervals, prediction intervals, and values of test statistics that would be pertinent in a regression analysis.

In addition to providing a better understanding of a multiple regression analysis, the most important contributions of this appendix are contained in Sections A.8 and A.9. If you want to make a specific inference concerning the mean value of y or any linear function of the β parameters and if you are unable to obtain the results from the computer package you are using, you will find the contents of Sections A.8 and A.9 very useful. Since you will almost always be able to find a computer program package to find $(\mathbf{X}'\mathbf{X})^{-1}$, you will be able to calculate the desired confidence interval(s) and so forth on your own.

SUPPLEMENTARY EXERCISES

A.29 Use the method of least squares to fit a straight line to the six data points:

x	-5	-3	-1	1	3	5
y	1.1	1.9	3.0	3.8	5.1	6.0

a. Construct **Y** and **X** matrices for the data.
b. Find **X′X** and **X′Y**.
c. Find the least squares estimates,

$$\hat{\boldsymbol{\beta}} = (\mathbf{X'X})^{-1}\mathbf{X'Y}$$

[*Note*: See Theorem A.1 for information on finding $(\mathbf{X'X})^{-1}$.]
d. Give the prediction equation.
e. Find SSE and s^2.
f. Does the model contribute information for the prediction of y? Test H_0: $\beta_1 = 0$. Use $\alpha = .05$.
g. Find r^2 and interpret its value.
h. Find a 90% confidence interval for $E(y)$ when $x = .5$. Interpret the interval.

A.30 An experiment was conducted to investigate the effect of extrusion pressure P and temperature T on the strength y of a new type of plastic. Two plastic specimens were prepared for each of five combinations of pressure and temperature. The specimens were then tested in random order, and the breaking strength for each specimen was recorded. The independent variables were coded to simplify computations, i.e.,

$$x_1 = \frac{P - 200}{10} \qquad x_2 = \frac{T - 400}{25}$$

The $n = 10$ data points are listed in the table.

y	x_1	x_2
5.2; 5.0	-2	2
.3; $-.1$	-1	-1
-1.2; -1.1	0	-2
2.2; 2.0	1	-1
6.2; 6.1	2	2

a. Give the **Y** and **X** matrices needed to fit the model $y = \beta_0 + \beta_1x_1 + \beta_2x_2 + \varepsilon$.
b. Find the least squares prediction equation.
c. Find SSE and s^2.
d. Does the model contribute information for the prediction of y? Test using $\alpha = .05$.

e. Find R^2 and interpret its value.
f. Test the null hypothesis that $\beta_1 = 0$. Use $\alpha = .05$. What is the practical implication of the test?
g. Find a 90% confidence interval for the mean strength of the plastic for $x_1 = -2$ and $x_2 = 2$.
h. Suppose a single specimen of the plastic is to be installed in the engine mount of a Douglas DC-10 aircraft. Find a 90% prediction interval for the strength of this specimen if $x_1 = -2$ and $x_2 = 2$.

A.31 Suppose we obtained two replications of the experiment described in Exercise A.17; i.e., two values of y were observed for each of the six values of x. The data are shown here.

x	1		2		3		4		5		6	
y	1.1	.5	1.8	2.0	2.0	2.9	3.8	3.4	4.1	5.0	5.0	5.8

a. Suppose (as in Exercise A.17) you wish to fit the model $E(y) = \beta_0 + \beta_1 x$. Construct **Y** and **X** matrices for the data. [*Hint:* Remember, the **Y** matrix must be of dimension 12×1.]
b. Find **X′X** and **X′Y**.
c. Compare the **X′X** matrix for two replications of the experiment with the **X′X** matrix obtained for a single replication (part **b** of Exercise A.17). What is the relationship between the elements in the two matrices?
d. Observe the $(\mathbf{X}'\mathbf{X})^{-1}$ matrix for a single replication (see part **c** of Exercise A.17). Verify that the $(\mathbf{X}'\mathbf{X})^{-1}$ matrix for two replications contains elements that are equal to $\frac{1}{2}$ of the values of the corresponding elements in the $(\mathbf{X}'\mathbf{X})^{-1}$ matrix for a single replication of the experiment. [*Hint:* Show that the product of the $(\mathbf{X}'\mathbf{X})^{-1}$ matrix (for two replications) and the **X′X** matrix from part **c** equals the identity matrix **I**.]
e. Find the prediction equation.
f. Find SSE and s^2.
g. Do the data provide sufficient information to indicate that x contributes information for the prediction of y? Test using $\alpha = .05$.
h. Find r^2 and interpret its value.

A.32 Refer to Exercise A.31.
a. Find a 90% confidence interval for $E(y)$ when $x = 4.5$. Interpret the interval.
b. Suppose we wish to predict the value of y if, in the future, $x = 4.5$. Find a 90% prediction interval for y and interpret the interval.

A.33 Refer to Exercise A.31. Suppose you replicated the experiment described in Exercise A.17 three times; i.e., you collected three observations on y for each value of x. Then $n = 18$.
a. What would be the dimensions of the **Y** matrix?
b. Write the **X** matrix for three replications. Compare with the **X** matrices for one and for two replications. Note the pattern.
c. Examine the **X′X** matrices obtained for one and two replications of the experiment (obtained in Exercises A.17 and A.31, respectively). Deduce the values of the elements of the **X′X** matrix for three replications.

d. Look at your answer to Exercise A.31, part **d**. Deduce the values of the elements in the $(\mathbf{X}'\mathbf{X})^{-1}$ matrix for three replications.

e. Suppose you wanted to find a 90% confidence interval for $E(y)$ when $x = 4.5$ based on three replications of the experiment. Find the value of $\mathbf{a}'(\mathbf{X}'\mathbf{X})^{-1}\mathbf{a}$ that appears in the confidence interval and compare with the value of $\mathbf{a}'(\mathbf{X}'\mathbf{X})^{-1}\mathbf{a}$ that would be obtained for a single replication of the experiment.

f. Approximately how much of a reduction in the width of the confidence interval is obtained by using three versus two replications? [*Note*: The values of s computed from the two sets of data will almost certainly be different.]

References

Draper, N. and Smith, H. *Applied Regression Analysis*. New York: Wiley, 1966.

Graybill, F. A. *Theory and Application of the Linear Model*. North Scituate, Mass.: Duxbury, 1976.

Kleinbaum, D., and Kupper, L. *Applied Regression Analysis and Other Multivariable Methods*. North Scituate, Mass.: Duxbury, 1978.

Mendenhall, W. *Introduction to Linear Models and the Design and Analysis of Experiments*. Belmont, Calif.: Wadsworth, 1968.

Neter, J., Wasserman, W., and Kutner, M. H. *Applied Linear Statistical Models*, 3rd ed. Homewood, Ill.: Richard D. Irwin, 1989.

APPENDIX B A Procedure for Inverting a Matrix

There are several different methods for inverting matrices. All are tedious and time-consuming. Consequently, in practice, you will invert almost all matrices using a computer. The purpose of this section is to present one method for inverting small (2×2 or 3×3) matrices manually, thus giving you an appreciation of the enormous computing problem involved in inverting large matrices (and, consequently, in fitting linear models containing many terms to a set of data). In particular, you will be able to understand why rounding errors creep into the inversion process and, consequently, why two different computer programs might invert the same matrix and produce inverse matrices with slightly different corresponding elements.

The procedure we will demonstrate to invert a matrix **A** requires us to perform a series of operations on the rows of the **A** matrix. For example, suppose

$$\mathbf{A} = \begin{bmatrix} 1 & -2 \\ -2 & 6 \end{bmatrix}$$

We will identify two different ways to operate on a row of a matrix:*

1. We can multiply every element in one particular row by a constant, c. For example, we could operate on the first row of the **A** matrix by multiplying every element in the row by a constant, say, 2. Then the resulting row would be $[2 \quad -4]$.
2. We can operate on a row by multiplying another row of the matrix by a constant and then adding (or subtracting) the elements of that row to elements in corresponding positions in the row operated upon. For example, we could operate on the first row of the **A** matrix by multiplying the second row by a constant, say, 2:

$$2[-2 \quad 6] = [-4 \quad 12]$$

*We omit a third row operation, because it would add little and could be confusing.

Then we add this row to row 1:

$$[(1 - 4) \quad (-2 + 12)] = [-3 \quad 10]$$

Note one important point. We operated on the *first* row of the **A** matrix. Although we used the second row of the matrix to perform the operation, *the second row would remain unchanged*. Therefore, the row operation on the **A** matrix that we have just described would produce the new matrix,

$$\begin{bmatrix} -3 & 10 \\ -2 & 6 \end{bmatrix}$$

Matrix inversion using row operations is based on an elementary result from matrix algebra. It can be shown (proof omitted) that performing a series of row operations on a matrix **A** is equivalent to multiplying **A** by a matrix **B**; i.e., row operations produce a new matrix, **BA**. This result is used as follows: Place the **A** matrix and an identity matrix **I** of the same dimensions side by side. Then perform the same series of row operations on both **A** and **I** until the **A** matrix has been changed into the identity matrix **I**. This means that you have multiplied both **A** and **I** by some matrix **B** such that:

$$\mathbf{A} = \begin{bmatrix} \quad & & \quad \\ & & \\ & & \end{bmatrix} \qquad \mathbf{I} = \begin{bmatrix} 1 & 0 & 0 & \cdots & 0 \\ 0 & 1 & 0 & \cdots & 0 \\ 0 & 0 & 1 & \cdots & 0 \\ \vdots & \vdots & \vdots & & \vdots \\ 0 & 0 & 0 & \cdots & 1 \end{bmatrix}$$

$$\downarrow \qquad \leftarrow \text{Row operations change } \mathbf{A} \text{ to } \mathbf{I} \rightarrow \qquad \downarrow$$

$$\mathbf{I} = \begin{bmatrix} \quad & & \quad \\ & & \\ & & \end{bmatrix} \qquad \mathbf{B} = \begin{bmatrix} \quad & & \quad \\ & & \\ & & \end{bmatrix}$$

$$\mathbf{BA} = \mathbf{I} \quad \text{and} \quad \mathbf{BI} = \mathbf{B}$$

Since $\mathbf{BA} = \mathbf{I}$, it follows that $\mathbf{B} = \mathbf{A}^{-1}$. Therefore, as the **A** matrix is transformed by row operations into the identity matrix **I**, the identity matrix **I** is transformed into $\mathbf{A}^{-1}$, i.e.,

$$\mathbf{BI} = \mathbf{B} = \mathbf{A}^{-1}$$

We will show you how this procedure works with two examples.

EXAMPLE B.1

Find the inverse of the matrix

$$\mathbf{A} = \begin{bmatrix} 1 & -2 \\ -2 & 6 \end{bmatrix}$$

Solution

Place the **A** matrix and a 2 × 2 identity matrix side by side and then perform the following series of row operations (we will indicate by an arrow the row operated upon in each operation):

$$\mathbf{A} = \begin{bmatrix} 1 & -2 \\ -2 & 6 \end{bmatrix} \qquad \mathbf{I} = \begin{bmatrix} 1 & 0 \\ 0 & 1 \end{bmatrix}$$

OPERATION 1 Multiply the first row by 2 and add it to the second row:

$$\rightarrow \begin{bmatrix} 1 & -2 \\ 0 & 2 \end{bmatrix} \qquad \begin{bmatrix} 1 & 0 \\ 2 & 1 \end{bmatrix}$$

OPERATION 2 Multiply the second row by $\frac{1}{2}$:

$$\rightarrow \begin{bmatrix} 1 & -2 \\ 0 & 1 \end{bmatrix} \qquad \begin{bmatrix} 1 & 0 \\ 1 & \frac{1}{2} \end{bmatrix}$$

OPERATION 3 Multiply the second row by 2 and add it to the first row:

$$\rightarrow \begin{bmatrix} 1 & 0 \\ 0 & 1 \end{bmatrix} \qquad \begin{bmatrix} 3 & 1 \\ 1 & \frac{1}{2} \end{bmatrix}$$

Thus,

$$\mathbf{A}^{-1} = \begin{bmatrix} 3 & 1 \\ 1 & \frac{1}{2} \end{bmatrix}$$

(Note that our solution matches the one obtained using Theorem A.2.)

The final step in finding an inverse is to check your solution by finding the product $\mathbf{A}^{-1}\mathbf{A}$ to see whether it equals the identity matrix **I**. To check:

$$\mathbf{A}^{-1}\mathbf{A} = \begin{bmatrix} 3 & 1 \\ 1 & \frac{1}{2} \end{bmatrix} \begin{bmatrix} 1 & -2 \\ -2 & 6 \end{bmatrix} = \begin{bmatrix} 1 & 0 \\ 0 & 1 \end{bmatrix}$$

Since this product is equal to the identity matrix, it follows that our solution for $\mathbf{A}^{-1}$ is correct.

EXAMPLE B.2

Find the inverse of the matrix

$$\mathbf{A} = \begin{bmatrix} 2 & 0 & 3 \\ 0 & 4 & 1 \\ 3 & 1 & 2 \end{bmatrix}$$

Solution

Place an identity matrix alongside the **A** matrix and perform the row operations:

OPERATION 1 Multiply row 1 by $\frac{1}{2}$:

$$\rightarrow \begin{bmatrix} 1 & 0 & \frac{3}{2} \\ 0 & 4 & 1 \\ 3 & 1 & 2 \end{bmatrix} \qquad \begin{bmatrix} \frac{1}{2} & 0 & 0 \\ 0 & 1 & 0 \\ 0 & 0 & 1 \end{bmatrix}$$

OPERATION 2 Multiply row 1 by 3 and subtract from row 3:

$$\begin{bmatrix} 1 & 0 & \frac{3}{2} \\ 0 & 4 & 1 \\ 0 & 1 & -\frac{5}{2} \end{bmatrix} \leftarrow \qquad \begin{bmatrix} \frac{1}{2} & 0 & 0 \\ 0 & 1 & 0 \\ -\frac{3}{2} & 0 & 1 \end{bmatrix}$$

OPERATION 3 Multiply row 2 by $\frac{1}{4}$:

$$\begin{bmatrix} 1 & 0 & \frac{3}{2} \\ 0 & 1 & \frac{1}{4} \\ 0 & 1 & -\frac{5}{2} \end{bmatrix} \qquad \begin{bmatrix} \frac{1}{2} & 0 & 0 \\ 0 & \frac{1}{4} & 0 \\ -\frac{3}{2} & 0 & 1 \end{bmatrix}$$

OPERATION 4 Subtract row 2 from row 3:

$$\begin{bmatrix} 1 & 0 & \frac{3}{2} \\ 0 & 1 & \frac{1}{4} \\ 0 & 0 & -\frac{11}{4} \end{bmatrix} \qquad \begin{bmatrix} \frac{1}{2} & 0 & 0 \\ 0 & \frac{1}{4} & 0 \\ -\frac{3}{2} & -\frac{1}{4} & 1 \end{bmatrix}$$

OPERATION 5 Multiply row 3 by $-\frac{4}{11}$:

$$\begin{bmatrix} 1 & 0 & \frac{3}{2} \\ 0 & 1 & \frac{1}{4} \\ 0 & 0 & 1 \end{bmatrix} \qquad \begin{bmatrix} \frac{1}{2} & 0 & 0 \\ 0 & \frac{1}{4} & 0 \\ \frac{12}{22} & \frac{1}{11} & -\frac{4}{11} \end{bmatrix}$$

OPERATION 6 Operate on row 2 by subtracting $\frac{1}{4}$ of row 3:

$$\begin{bmatrix} 1 & 0 & \frac{3}{2} \\ 0 & 1 & 0 \\ 0 & 0 & 1 \end{bmatrix} \qquad \begin{bmatrix} \frac{1}{2} & 0 & 0 \\ -\frac{3}{22} & \frac{5}{22} & \frac{1}{11} \\ \frac{12}{22} & \frac{1}{11} & -\frac{4}{11} \end{bmatrix}$$

OPERATION 7 Operate on row 1 by subtracting $\frac{3}{2}$ of row 3:

$$\rightarrow \begin{bmatrix} 1 & 0 & 0 \\ 0 & 1 & 0 \\ 0 & 0 & 1 \end{bmatrix} \qquad \begin{bmatrix} -\frac{7}{22} & -\frac{3}{22} & \frac{6}{11} \\ -\frac{3}{22} & \frac{5}{22} & \frac{1}{11} \\ \frac{6}{11} & \frac{1}{11} & -\frac{4}{11} \end{bmatrix} = \mathbf{A}^{-1}$$

To check the solution, we find the product:

$$\mathbf{A}^{-1}\mathbf{A} = \begin{bmatrix} -\frac{7}{22} & -\frac{3}{22} & \frac{6}{11} \\ -\frac{3}{22} & \frac{5}{22} & \frac{1}{11} \\ \frac{6}{11} & \frac{1}{11} & -\frac{4}{11} \end{bmatrix} \begin{bmatrix} 2 & 0 & 3 \\ 0 & 4 & 1 \\ 3 & 1 & 2 \end{bmatrix} = \begin{bmatrix} 1 & 0 & 0 \\ 0 & 1 & 0 \\ 0 & 0 & 1 \end{bmatrix}$$

Since the product $\mathbf{A}^{-1}\mathbf{A}$ is equal to the identity matrix, it follows that our solution for $\mathbf{A}^{-1}$ is correct.

Examples B.1 and B.2 indicate the strategy employed when performing row operations on the **A** matrix to change it into an identity matrix. Multiply the first row by a constant to change the element in the top left row into a 1. Then perform operations to change all elements in the first column into 0's. Then operate on the second row and change the second diagonal element into a 1. Then operate to change all elements in the second column beneath row 2 into 0's. Then operate on the diagonal element in row 3, etc. When all elements on the main diagonal are 1's and all below the main diagonal are 0's, perform row operations to change the last column to 0; then the next-to-last, etc., until you get back to the first column. The procedure for changing the off-diagonal elements to 0's is indicated diagrammatically as shown:

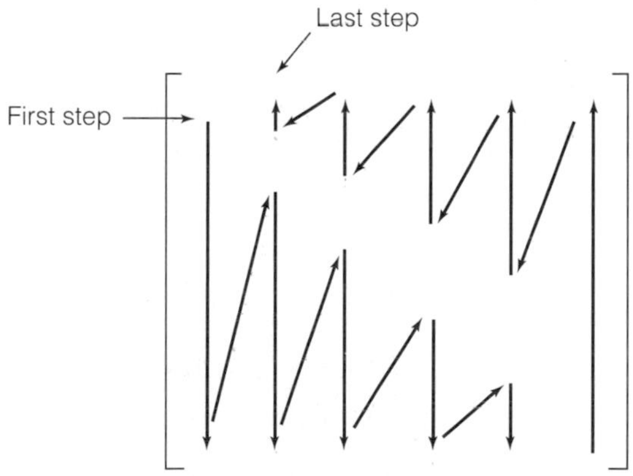

The preceding instructions on how to invert a matrix using row operations suggest that the inversion of a large matrix would involve many multiplications, subtractions, and additions and, consequently, could produce large rounding errors in the calculations unless you carry a large number of significant figures in the calculations. This explains why two different multiple regression analysis computer programs may produce different estimates of the same β parameters, and it emphasizes the importance of carrying a large number of significant figures in all computations when inverting a matrix.

You can find other methods for inverting matrices in any linear algebra textbook. All work—exactly—in theory. It is only in the actual process of performing the calculations that the rounding errors occur.

EXERCISE

B.1 Invert the following matrices and check your answers to make certain that $\mathbf{A}^{-1}\mathbf{A} = \mathbf{A}\mathbf{A}^{-1} = \mathbf{I}$:

a. $\mathbf{A} = \begin{bmatrix} 3 & 2 \\ 4 & 5 \end{bmatrix}$ b. $\mathbf{A} = \begin{bmatrix} 3 & 0 & -2 \\ 1 & 4 & 2 \\ 5 & 1 & 1 \end{bmatrix}$

c. $\mathbf{A} = \begin{bmatrix} 1 & 0 & 1 \\ 0 & 2 & 1 \\ 1 & 1 & 3 \end{bmatrix}$ d. $\mathbf{A} = \begin{bmatrix} 4 & 0 & 10 \\ 0 & 10 & 0 \\ 10 & 0 & 5 \end{bmatrix}$

[*Note*: No answers are given to these exercises. You will know whether your answer is correct if $\mathbf{A}^{-1}\mathbf{A} = \mathbf{I}$.]

APPENDIX C

Useful Statistical Tables

CONTENTS

TABLE 1 Normal Curve Areas

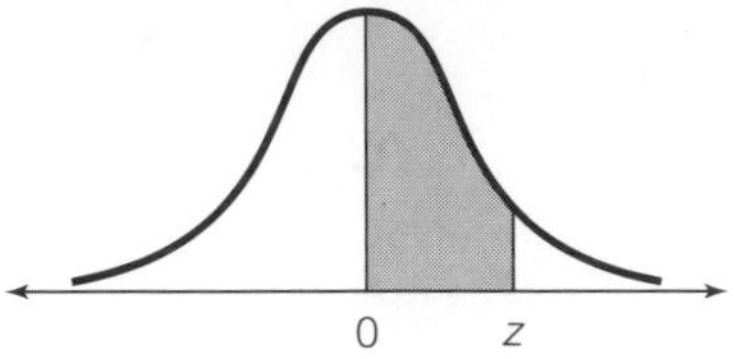

z	.00	.01	.02	.03	.04	.05	.06	.07	.08	.09
.0	.0000	.0040	.0080	.0120	.0160	.0199	.0239	.0279	.0319	.0359
.1	.0398	.0438	.0478	.0517	.0557	.0596	.0636	.0675	.0714	.0753
.2	.0793	.0832	.0871	.0910	.0948	.0987	.1026	.1064	.1103	.1141
.3	.1179	.1217	.1255	.1293	.1331	.1368	.1406	.1443	.1480	.1517
.4	.1554	.1591	.1628	.1664	.1700	.1736	.1772	.1808	.1844	.1879
.5	.1915	.1950	.1985	.2019	.2054	.2088	.2123	.2157	.2190	.2224
.6	.2257	.2291	.2324	.2357	.2389	.2422	.2454	.2486	.2517	.2549
.7	.2580	.2611	.2642	.2673	.2704	.2734	.2764	.2794	.2823	.2852
.8	.2881	.2910	.2939	.2967	.2995	.3023	.3051	.3078	.3106	.3133
.9	.3159	.3186	.3212	.3238	.3264	.3289	.3315	.3340	.3365	.3389
1.0	.3413	.3438	.3461	.3485	.3508	.3531	.3554	.3577	.3599	.3621
1.1	.3643	.3665	.3686	.3708	.3729	.3749	.3770	.3790	.3810	.3830
1.2	.3849	.3869	.3888	.3907	.3925	.3944	.3962	.3980	.3997	.4015
1.3	.4032	.4049	.4066	.4082	.4099	.4115	.4131	.4147	.4162	.4177
1.4	.4192	.4207	.4222	.4236	.4251	.4265	.4279	.4292	.4306	.4319
1.5	.4332	.4345	.4357	.4370	.4382	.4394	.4406	.4418	.4429	.4441
1.6	.4452	.4463	.4474	.4484	.4495	.4505	.4515	.4525	.4535	.4545
1.7	.4554	.4564	.4573	.4582	.4591	.4599	.4608	.4616	.4625	.4633
1.8	.4641	.4649	.4656	.4664	.4671	.4678	.4686	.4693	.4699	.4706
1.9	.4713	.4719	.4726	.4732	.4738	.4744	.4750	.4756	.4761	.4767
2.0	.4772	.4778	.4783	.4788	.4793	.4798	.4803	.4808	.4812	.4817
2.1	.4821	.4826	.4830	.4834	.4838	.4842	.4846	.4850	.4854	.4857
2.2	.4861	.4864	.4868	.4871	.4875	.4878	.4881	.4884	.4887	.4890
2.3	.4893	.4896	.4898	.4901	.4904	.4906	.4909	.4911	.4913	.4916
2.4	.4918	.4920	.4922	.4925	.4927	.4929	.4931	.4932	.4934	.4936
2.5	.4938	.4940	.4941	.4943	.4945	.4946	.4948	.4949	.4951	.4952
2.6	.4953	.4955	.4956	.4957	.4959	.4960	.4961	.4962	.4963	.4964
2.7	.4965	.4966	.4967	.4968	.4969	.4970	.4971	.4972	.4973	.4974
2.8	.4974	.4975	.4976	.4977	.4977	.4978	.4979	.4979	.4980	.4981
2.9	.4981	.4982	.4982	.4983	.4984	.4984	.4985	.4985	.4986	.4986
3.0	.4987	.4987	.4987	.4988	.4988	.4989	.4989	.4989	.4990	.4990

Source: Abridged from Table I of A. Hald, *Statistical Tables and Formulas* (New York: John Wiley & Sons, Inc.), 1952. Reproduced by permission of the publisher.

TABLE 2 Critical Values for Student's t

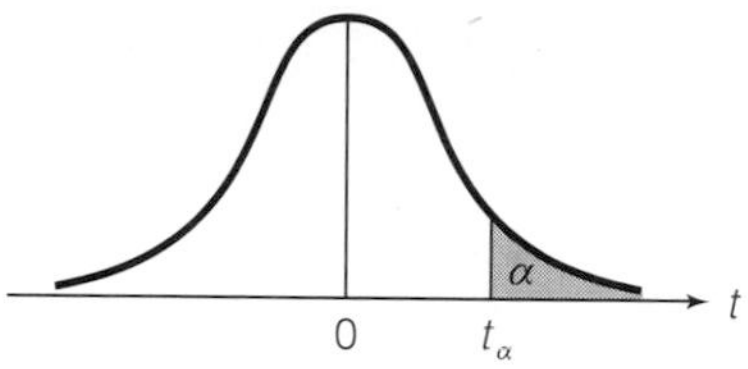

ν	$t_{.100}$	$t_{.050}$	$t_{.025}$	$t_{.010}$	$t_{.005}$	$t_{.001}$	$t_{.0005}$
1	3.078	6.314	12.706	31.821	63.657	318.31	636.62
2	1.886	2.920	4.303	6.965	9.925	22.326	31.598
3	1.638	2.353	3.182	4.541	5.841	10.213	12.924
4	1.533	2.132	2.776	3.747	4.604	7.173	8.610
5	1.476	2.015	2.571	3.365	4.032	5.893	6.869
6	1.440	1.943	2.447	3.143	3.707	5.208	5.959
7	1.415	1.895	2.365	2.998	3.499	4.785	5.408
8	1.397	1.860	2.306	2.896	3.355	4.501	5.041
9	1.383	1.833	2.262	2.821	3.250	4.297	4.781
10	1.372	1.812	2.228	2.764	3.169	4.144	4.587
11	1.363	1.796	2.201	2.718	3.106	4.025	4.437
12	1.356	1.782	2.179	2.681	3.055	3.930	4.318
13	1.350	1.771	2.160	2.650	3.012	3.852	4.221
14	1.345	1.761	2.145	2.624	2.977	3.787	4.140
15	1.341	1.753	2.131	2.602	2.947	3.733	4.073
16	1.337	1.746	2.120	2.583	2.921	3.686	4.015
17	1.333	1.740	2.110	2.567	2.898	3.646	3.965
18	1.330	1.734	2.101	2.552	2.878	3.610	3.922
19	1.328	1.729	2.093	2.539	2.861	3.579	3.883
20	1.325	1.725	2.086	2.528	2.845	3.552	3.850
21	1.323	1.721	2.080	2.518	2.831	3.527	3.819
22	1.321	1.717	2.074	2.508	2.819	3.505	3.792
23	1.319	1.714	2.069	2.500	2.807	3.485	3.767
24	1.318	1.711	2.064	2.492	2.797	3.467	3.745
25	1.316	1.708	2.060	2.485	2.787	3.450	3.725
26	1.315	1.706	2.056	2.479	2.779	3.435	3.707
27	1.314	1.703	2.052	2.473	2.771	3.421	3.690
28	1.313	1.701	2.048	2.467	2.763	3.408	3.674
29	1.311	1.699	2.045	2.462	2.756	3.396	3.659
30	1.310	1.697	2.042	2.457	2.750	3.385	3.646
40	1.303	1.684	2.021	2.423	2.704	3.307	3.551
60	1.296	1.671	2.000	2.390	2.660	3.232	3.460
120	1.289	1.658	1.980	2.358	2.617	3.160	3.373
∞	1.282	1.645	1.960	2.326	2.576	3.090	3.291

Source: This table is reproduced with the kind permission of the Trustees of Biometrika from E. S. Pearson and H. O. Hartley (eds.), *The Biometrika Tables for Statisticians*, Vol. 1, 3rd ed., *Biometrika*, 1966.

TABLE 3 **Critical Values for the *F* Statistic: $F_{.10}$**

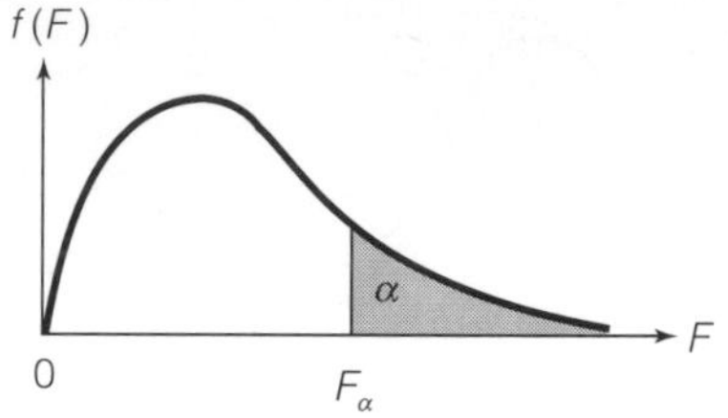

ν_2 \ ν_1 (Numerator Degrees of Freedom)	1	2	3	4	5	6	7	8	9
1	39.86	49.50	53.59	55.83	57.24	58.20	58.91	59.44	59.86
2	8.53	9.00	9.16	9.24	9.29	9.33	9.35	9.37	9.38
3	5.54	5.46	5.39	5.34	5.31	5.28	5.27	5.25	5.24
4	4.54	4.32	4.19	4.11	4.05	4.01	3.98	3.95	3.94
5	4.06	3.78	3.62	3.52	3.45	3.40	3.37	3.34	3.32
6	3.78	3.46	3.29	3.18	3.11	3.05	3.01	2.98	2.96
7	3.59	3.26	3.07	2.96	2.88	2.83	2.78	2.75	2.72
8	3.46	3.11	2.92	2.81	2.73	2.67	2.62	2.59	2.56
9	3.36	3.01	2.81	2.69	2.61	2.55	2.51	2.47	2.44
10	3.29	2.92	2.73	2.61	2.52	2.46	2.41	2.38	2.35
11	3.23	2.86	2.66	2.54	2.45	2.39	2.34	2.30	2.27
12	3.18	2.81	2.61	2.48	2.39	2.33	2.28	2.24	2.21
13	3.14	2.76	2.56	2.43	2.35	2.28	2.23	2.20	2.16
14	3.10	2.73	2.52	2.39	2.31	2.24	2.19	2.15	2.12
15	3.07	2.70	2.49	2.36	2.27	2.21	2.16	2.12	2.09
16	3.05	2.67	2.46	2.33	2.24	2.18	2.13	2.09	2.06
17	3.03	2.64	2.44	2.31	2.22	2.15	2.10	2.06	2.03
18	3.01	2.62	2.42	2.29	2.20	2.13	2.08	2.04	2.00
19	2.99	2.61	2.40	2.27	2.18	2.11	2.06	2.02	1.98
20	2.97	2.59	2.38	2.25	2.16	2.09	2.04	2.00	1.96
21	2.96	2.57	2.36	2.23	2.14	2.08	2.02	1.98	1.95
22	2.95	2.56	2.35	2.22	2.13	2.06	2.01	1.97	1.93
23	2.94	2.55	2.34	2.21	2.11	2.05	1.99	1.95	1.92
24	2.93	2.54	2.33	2.19	2.10	2.04	1.98	1.94	1.91
25	2.92	2.53	2.32	2.18	2.09	2.02	1.97	1.93	1.89
26	2.91	2.52	2.31	2.17	2.08	2.01	1.96	1.92	1.88
27	2.90	2.51	2.30	2.17	2.07	2.00	1.95	1.91	1.87
28	2.89	2.50	2.29	2.16	2.06	2.00	1.94	1.90	1.87
29	2.89	2.50	2.28	2.15	2.06	1.99	1.93	1.89	1.86
30	2.88	2.49	2.28	2.14	2.05	1.98	1.93	1.88	1.85
40	2.84	2.44	2.23	2.09	2.00	1.93	1.87	1.83	1.79
60	2.79	2.39	2.18	2.04	1.95	1.87	1.82	1.77	1.74
120	2.75	2.35	2.13	1.99	1.90	1.82	1.77	1.72	1.68
∞	2.71	2.30	2.08	1.94	1.85	1.77	1.72	1.67	1.63

(Rows: DENOMINATOR DEGREES OF FREEDOM)

ν_2 \ ν_1 (NUMERATOR DEGREES OF FREEDOM)	10	12	15	20	24	30	40	60	120	∞
1	60.19	60.71	61.22	61.74	62.00	62.26	62.53	62.79	63.06	63.33
2	9.39	9.41	9.42	9.44	9.45	9.46	9.47	9.47	9.48	9.49
3	5.23	5.22	5.20	5.18	5.18	5.17	5.16	5.15	5.14	5.13
4	3.92	3.90	3.87	3.84	3.83	3.82	3.80	3.79	3.78	3.76
5	3.30	3.27	3.24	3.21	3.19	3.17	3.16	3.14	3.12	3.10
6	2.94	2.90	2.87	2.84	2.82	2.80	2.78	2.76	2.74	2.72
7	2.70	2.67	2.63	2.59	2.58	2.56	2.54	2.51	2.49	2.47
8	2.54	2.50	2.46	2.42	2.40	2.38	2.36	2.34	2.32	2.29
9	2.42	2.38	2.34	2.30	2.28	2.25	2.23	2.21	2.18	2.16
10	2.32	2.28	2.24	2.20	2.18	2.16	2.13	2.11	2.08	2.06
11	2.25	2.21	2.17	2.12	2.10	2.08	2.05	2.03	2.00	1.97
12	2.19	2.15	2.10	2.06	2.04	2.01	1.99	1.96	1.93	1.90
13	2.14	2.10	2.05	2.01	1.98	1.96	1.93	1.90	1.88	1.85
14	2.10	2.05	2.01	1.96	1.94	1.91	1.89	1.86	1.83	1.00
15	2.06	2.02	1.97	1.92	1.90	1.87	1.85	1.82	1.79	1.76
16	2.03	1.99	1.94	1.89	1.87	1.84	1.81	1.78	1.75	1.72
17	2.00	1.96	1.91	1.86	1.84	1.81	1.78	1.75	1.72	1.69
18	1.98	1.93	1.89	1.84	1.81	1.78	1.75	1.72	1.69	1.66
19	1.96	1.91	1.86	1.81	1.79	1.76	1.73	1.70	1.67	1.63
20	1.94	1.89	1.84	1.79	1.77	1.74	1.71	1.68	1.64	1.61
21	1.92	1.87	1.83	1.78	1.75	1.72	1.69	1.66	1.62	1.59
22	1.90	1.86	1.81	1.76	1.73	1.70	1.67	1.64	1.60	1.57
23	1.89	1.84	1.80	1.74	1.72	1.69	1.66	1.62	1.59	1.55
24	1.88	1.83	1.78	1.73	1.70	1.67	1.64	1.61	1.57	1.53
25	1.87	1.82	1.77	1.72	1.69	1.66	1.63	1.59	1.56	1.52
26	1.86	1.81	1.76	1.71	1.68	1.65	1.61	1.58	1.54	1.50
27	1.85	1.80	1.75	1.70	1.67	1.64	1.60	1.57	1.53	1.49
28	1.84	1.79	1.74	1.69	1.66	1.63	1.59	1.56	1.52	1.48
29	1.83	1.78	1.73	1.68	1.65	1.62	1.58	1.55	1.51	1.47
30	1.82	1.77	1.72	1.67	1.64	1.61	1.57	1.54	1.50	1.46
40	1.76	1.71	1.66	1.61	1.57	1.54	1.51	1.47	1.42	1.38
60	1.71	1.66	1.60	1.54	1.51	1.48	1.44	1.40	1.35	1.29
120	1.65	1.60	1.55	1.48	1.45	1.41	1.37	1.32	1.26	1.19
∞	1.60	1.55	1.49	1.42	1.38	1.34	1.30	1.24	1.17	1.00

DENOMINATOR DEGREES OF FREEDOM (ν_2)

Source: From M. Merrington and C. M. Thompson, "Tables of percentage points of the inverted beta (*F*)-distribution," *Biometrika*, 1943, 33, 73–88. Reproduced by permission of the *Biometrika* Trustees.

TABLE 4 **Critical Values for the *F* Statistic: $F_{.05}$**

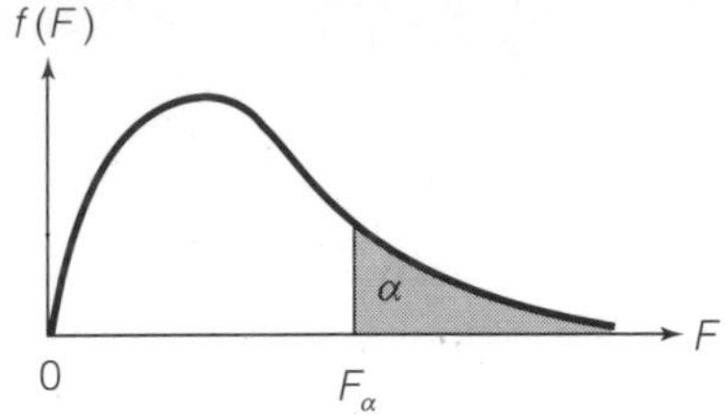

ν_2 \ ν_1 NUMERATOR DEGREES OF FREEDOM	1	2	3	4	5	6	7	8	9
1	161.4	199.5	215.7	224.6	230.2	234.0	236.8	238.9	240.5
2	18.51	19.00	19.16	19.25	19.30	19.33	19.35	19.37	19.38
3	10.13	9.55	9.28	9.12	9.01	8.94	8.89	8.85	8.81
4	7.71	6.94	6.59	6.39	6.26	6.16	6.09	6.04	6.00
5	6.61	5.79	5.41	5.19	5.05	4.95	4.88	4.82	4.77
6	5.99	5.14	4.76	4.53	4.39	4.28	4.21	4.15	4.10
7	5.59	4.74	4.35	4.12	3.97	3.87	3.79	3.73	3.68
8	5.32	4.46	4.07	3.84	3.69	3.58	3.50	3.44	3.39
9	5.12	4.26	3.86	3.63	3.48	3.37	3.29	3.23	3.18
10	4.96	4.10	3.71	3.48	3.33	3.22	3.14	3.07	3.02
11	4.84	3.98	3.59	3.36	3.20	3.09	3.01	2.95	2.90
12	4.75	3.89	3.49	3.26	3.11	3.00	2.91	2.85	2.80
13	4.67	3.81	3.41	3.18	3.03	2.92	2.83	2.77	2.71
14	4.60	3.74	3.34	3.11	2.96	2.85	2.76	2.70	2.65
15	4.54	3.68	3.29	3.06	2.90	2.79	2.71	2.64	2.59
16	4.49	3.63	3.24	3.01	2.85	2.74	2.66	2.59	2.54
17	4.45	3.59	3.20	2.96	2.81	2.70	2.61	2.55	2.49
18	4.41	3.55	3.16	2.93	2.77	2.66	2.58	2.51	2.46
19	4.38	3.52	3.13	2.90	2.74	2.63	2.54	2.48	2.42
20	4.35	3.49	3.10	2.87	2.71	2.60	2.51	2.45	2.39
21	4.32	3.47	3.07	2.84	2.68	2.57	2.49	2.42	2.37
22	4.30	3.44	3.05	2.82	2.66	2.55	2.46	2.40	2.34
23	4.28	3.42	3.03	2.80	2.64	2.53	2.44	2.37	2.32
24	4.26	3.40	3.01	2.78	2.62	2.51	2.42	2.36	2.30
25	4.24	3.39	2.99	2.76	2.60	2.49	2.40	2.34	2.28
26	4.23	3.37	2.98	2.74	2.59	2.47	2.39	2.32	2.27
27	4.21	3.35	2.96	2.73	2.57	2.46	2.37	2.31	2.25
28	4.20	3.34	2.95	2.71	2.56	2.45	2.36	2.29	2.24
29	4.18	3.33	2.93	2.70	2.55	2.43	2.35	2.28	2.22
30	4.17	3.32	2.92	2.69	2.53	2.42	2.33	2.27	2.21
40	4.08	3.23	2.84	2.61	2.45	2.34	2.25	2.18	2.12
60	4.00	3.15	2.76	2.53	2.37	2.25	2.17	2.10	2.04
120	3.92	3.07	2.68	2.45	2.29	2.17	2.09	2.02	1.96
∞	3.84	3.00	2.60	2.37	2.21	2.10	2.01	1.94	1.88

DENOMINATOR DEGREES OF FREEDOM

ν_2 (DENOMINATOR DEGREES OF FREEDOM) \ ν_1 (NUMERATOR DEGREES OF FREEDOM)	10	12	15	20	24	30	40	60	120	∞
1	241.9	243.9	245.9	248.0	249.1	250.1	251.1	252.2	253.3	254.3
2	19.40	19.41	19.43	19.45	19.45	19.46	19.47	19.48	19.49	19.50
3	8.79	8.74	8.70	8.66	8.64	8.62	8.59	8.57	8.55	8.53
4	5.96	5.91	5.86	5.80	5.77	5.75	5.72	5.69	5.66	5.63
5	4.74	4.68	4.62	4.56	4.53	4.50	4.46	4.43	4.40	4.36
6	4.06	4.00	3.94	3.87	3.84	3.81	3.77	3.74	3.70	3.67
7	3.64	3.57	3.51	3.44	3.41	3.38	3.34	3.30	3.27	3.23
8	3.35	3.28	3.22	3.15	3.12	3.08	3.04	3.01	2.97	2.93
9	3.14	3.07	3.01	2.94	2.90	2.86	2.83	2.79	2.75	2.71
10	2.98	2.91	2.85	2.77	2.74	2.70	2.66	2.62	2.58	2.54
11	2.85	2.79	2.72	2.65	2.61	2.57	2.53	2.49	2.45	2.40
12	2.75	2.69	2.62	2.54	2.51	2.47	2.43	2.38	2.34	2.30
13	2.67	2.60	2.53	2.46	2.42	2.38	2.34	2.30	2.25	2.21
14	2.60	2.53	2.46	2.39	2.35	2.31	2.27	2.22	2.18	2.13
15	2.54	2.48	2.40	2.33	2.29	2.25	2.20	2.16	2.11	2.07
16	2.49	2.42	2.35	2.28	2.24	2.19	2.15	2.11	2.06	2.01
17	2.45	2.38	2.31	2.23	2.19	2.15	2.10	2.06	2.01	1.96
18	2.41	2.34	2.27	2.19	2.15	2.11	2.06	2.02	1.97	1.92
19	2.38	2.31	2.23	2.16	2.11	2.07	2.03	1.98	1.93	1.88
20	2.35	2.28	2.20	2.12	2.08	2.04	1.99	1.95	1.90	1.84
21	2.32	2.25	2.18	2.10	2.05	2.01	1.96	1.92	1.87	1.81
22	2.30	2.23	2.15	2.07	2.03	1.98	1.94	1.89	1.84	1.78
23	2.27	2.20	2.13	2.05	2.01	1.96	1.91	1.86	1.81	1.76
24	2.25	2.18	2.11	2.03	1.98	1.94	1.89	1.84	1.79	1.73
25	2.24	2.16	2.09	2.01	1.96	1.92	1.87	1.82	1.77	1.71
26	2.22	2.15	2.07	1.99	1.95	1.90	1.85	1.80	1.75	1.69
27	2.20	2.13	2.06	1.97	1.93	1.88	1.84	1.79	1.73	1.67
28	2.19	2.12	2.04	1.96	1.91	1.87	1.82	1.77	1.71	1.65
29	2.18	2.10	2.03	1.94	1.90	1.85	1.81	1.75	1.70	1.64
30	2.16	2.09	2.01	1.93	1.89	1.84	1.79	1.74	1.68	1.62
40	2.08	2.00	1.92	1.84	1.79	1.74	1.69	1.64	1.58	1.51
60	1.99	1.92	1.84	1.75	1.70	1.65	1.59	1.53	1.47	1.39
120	1.91	1.83	1.75	1.66	1.61	1.55	1.50	1.43	1.35	1.25
∞	1.83	1.75	1.67	1.57	1.52	1.46	1.39	1.32	1.22	1.00

Source: From M. Merrington and C. M. Thompson, "Tables of percentage points of the inverted beta (*F*)-distribution," *Biometrika*, 1943, 33, 73–88. Reproduced by permission of the *Biometrika* Trustees.

TABLE 5 Critical Values for the *F* Statistic: $F_{.025}$

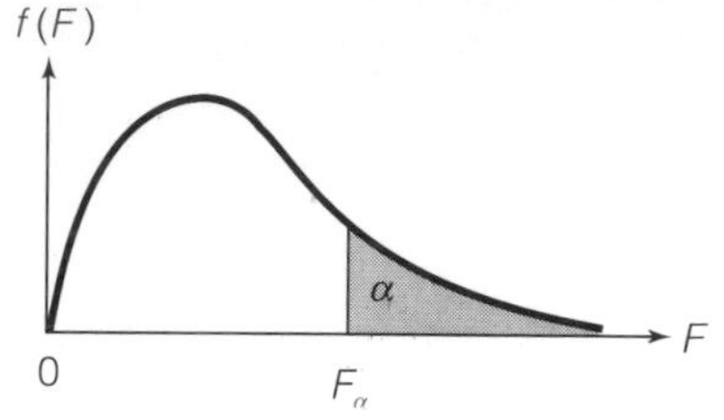

NUMERATOR DEGREES OF FREEDOM

DENOMINATOR DEGREES OF FREEDOM

ν_2 \ ν_1	1	2	3	4	5	6	7	8	9
1	647.8	799.5	864.2	899.6	921.8	937.1	948.2	956.7	963.3
2	38.51	39.00	39.17	39.25	39.30	39.33	39.36	39.37	39.39
3	17.44	16.04	15.44	15.10	14.88	14.73	14.62	14.54	14.47
4	12.22	10.65	9.98	9.60	9.36	9.20	9.07	8.98	8.90
5	10.01	8.43	7.76	7.39	7.15	6.98	6.85	6.76	6.68
6	8.81	7.26	6.60	6.23	5.99	5.82	5.70	5.60	5.52
7	8.07	6.54	5.89	5.52	5.29	5.12	4.99	4.90	4.82
8	7.57	6.06	5.42	5.05	4.82	4.65	4.53	4.43	4.36
9	7.21	5.71	5.08	4.72	4.48	4.32	4.20	4.10	4.03
10	6.94	5.46	4.83	4.47	4.24	4.07	3.95	3.85	3.78
11	6.72	5.26	4.63	4.28	4.04	3.88	3.76	3.66	3.59
12	6.55	5.10	4.47	4.12	3.89	3.73	3.61	3.51	3.44
13	6.41	4.97	4.35	4.00	3.77	3.60	3.48	3.39	3.31
14	6.30	4.86	4.24	3.89	3.66	3.50	3.38	3.29	3.21
15	6.20	4.77	4.15	3.80	3.58	3.41	3.29	3.20	3.12
16	6.12	4.69	4.08	3.73	3.50	3.34	3.22	3.12	3.05
17	6.04	4.62	4.01	3.66	3.44	3.28	3.16	3.06	2.98
18	5.98	4.56	3.95	3.61	3.38	3.22	3.10	3.01	2.93
19	5.92	4.51	3.90	3.56	3.33	3.17	3.05	2.96	2.88
20	5.87	4.46	3.86	3.51	3.29	3.13	3.01	2.91	2.84
21	5.83	4.42	3.82	3.48	3.25	3.09	2.97	2.87	2.80
22	5.79	4.38	3.78	3.44	3.22	3.05	2.93	2.84	2.76
23	5.75	4.35	3.75	3.41	3.18	3.02	2.90	2.81	2.73
24	5.72	4.32	3.72	3.38	3.15	2.99	2.87	2.78	2.70
25	5.69	4.29	3.69	3.35	3.13	2.97	2.85	2.75	2.68
26	5.66	4.27	3.67	3.33	3.10	2.94	2.82	2.73	2.65
27	5.63	4.24	3.65	3.31	3.08	2.92	2.80	2.71	2.63
28	5.61	4.22	3.63	3.29	3.06	2.90	2.78	2.69	2.61
29	5.59	4.20	3.61	3.27	3.04	2.88	2.76	2.67	2.59
30	5.57	4.18	3.59	3.25	3.03	2.87	2.75	2.65	2.57
40	5.42	4.05	3.46	3.13	2.90	2.74	2.62	2.53	2.45
60	5.29	3.93	3.34	3.01	2.79	2.63	2.51	2.41	2.33
120	5.15	3.80	3.23	2.89	2.67	2.52	2.39	2.30	2.22
∞	5.02	3.69	3.12	2.79	2.57	2.41	2.29	2.19	2.11

ν_2 (DENOMINATOR DEGREES OF FREEDOM) \ ν_1 (NUMERATOR DEGREES OF FREEDOM)	10	12	15	20	24	30	40	60	120	∞
1	968.6	976.7	984.9	993.1	997.2	1001	1006	1010	1014	1018
2	39.40	39.41	39.43	39.45	39.46	39.46	39.47	39.48	39.49	39.50
3	14.42	14.34	14.25	14.17	14.12	14.08	14.04	13.99	13.95	13.90
4	8.84	8.75	8.66	8.56	8.51	8.46	8.41	8.36	8.31	8.26
5	6.62	6.52	6.43	6.33	6.28	6.23	6.18	6.12	6.07	6.02
6	5.46	5.37	5.27	5.17	5.12	5.07	5.01	4.96	4.90	4.85
7	4.76	4.67	4.57	4.47	4.42	4.36	4.31	4.25	4.20	4.14
8	4.30	4.20	4.10	4.00	3.95	3.89	3.84	3.78	3.73	3.67
9	3.96	3.87	3.77	3.67	3.61	3.56	3.51	3.45	3.39	3.33
10	3.72	3.62	3.52	3.42	3.37	3.31	3.26	3.20	3.14	3.08
11	3.53	3.43	3.33	3.23	3.17	3.12	3.06	3.00	2.94	2.88
12	3.37	3.28	3.18	3.07	3.02	2.96	2.91	2.85	2.79	2.72
13	3.25	3.15	3.05	2.95	2.89	2.84	2.78	2.72	2.66	2.60
14	3.15	3.05	2.95	2.84	2.79	2.73	2.67	2.61	2.55	2.49
15	3.06	2.96	2.86	2.76	2.70	2.64	2.59	2.52	2.46	2.40
16	2.99	2.89	2.79	2.68	2.63	2.57	2.51	2.45	2.38	2.32
17	2.92	2.82	2.72	2.62	2.56	2.50	2.44	2.38	2.32	2.25
18	2.87	2.77	2.67	2.56	2.50	2.44	2.38	2.32	2.26	2.19
19	2.82	2.72	2.62	2.51	2.45	2.39	2.33	2.27	2.20	2.13
20	2.77	2.68	2.57	2.46	2.41	2.35	2.29	2.22	2.16	2.09
21	2.73	2.64	2.53	2.42	2.37	2.31	2.25	2.18	2.11	2.04
22	2.70	2.60	2.50	2.39	2.33	2.27	2.21	2.14	2.08	2.00
23	2.67	2.57	2.47	2.36	2.30	2.24	2.18	2.11	2.04	1.97
24	2.64	2.54	2.44	2.33	2.27	2.21	2.15	2.08	2.01	1.94
25	2.61	2.51	2.41	2.30	2.24	2.18	2.12	2.05	1.98	1.91
26	2.59	2.49	2.39	2.28	2.22	2.16	2.09	2.03	1.95	1.88
27	2.57	2.47	2.36	2.25	2.19	2.13	2.07	2.00	1.93	1.85
28	2.55	2.45	2.34	2.23	2.17	2.11	2.05	1.98	1.91	1.83
29	2.53	2.43	2.32	2.21	2.15	2.09	2.03	1.96	1.89	1.81
30	2.51	2.41	2.31	2.20	2.14	2.07	2.01	1.94	1.87	1.79
40	2.39	2.29	2.18	2.07	2.01	1.94	1.88	1.80	1.72	1.64
60	2.27	2.17	2.06	1.94	1.88	1.82	1.74	1.67	1.58	1.48
120	2.16	2.05	1.94	1.82	1.76	1.69	1.61	1.53	1.43	1.31
∞	2.05	1.94	1.83	1.71	1.64	1.57	1.48	1.39	1.27	1.00

Source: From M. Merrington and C. M. Thompson, "Tables of percentage points of the inverted beta (*F*)-distribution," *Biometrika*, 1943, *33*, 73–88. Reproduced by permission of the *Biometrika* Trustees.

TABLE 6 Critical Values for the F Statistic: $F_{.01}$

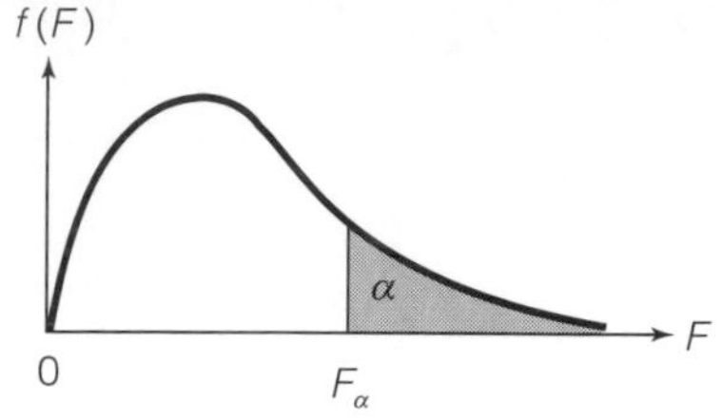

ν_2 \ ν_1 (NUMERATOR DEGREES OF FREEDOM)	1	2	3	4	5	6	7	8	9
1	4,052	4,999.5	5,403	5,625	5,764	5,859	5,928	5,982	6,022
2	98.50	99.00	99.17	99.25	99.30	99.33	99.36	99.37	99.39
3	34.12	30.82	29.46	28.71	28.24	27.91	27.67	27.49	27.35
4	21.20	18.00	16.69	15.98	15.52	15.21	14.98	14.80	14.66
5	16.26	13.27	12.06	11.39	10.97	10.67	10.46	10.29	10.16
6	13.75	10.92	9.78	9.15	8.75	8.47	8.26	8.10	7.98
7	12.25	9.55	8.45	7.85	7.46	7.19	6.99	6.84	6.72
8	11.26	8.65	7.59	7.01	6.63	6.37	6.18	6.03	5.91
9	10.56	8.02	6.99	6.42	6.06	5.80	5.61	5.47	5.35
10	10.04	7.56	6.55	5.99	5.64	5.39	5.20	5.06	4.94
11	9.65	7.21	6.22	5.67	5.32	5.07	4.89	4.74	4.63
12	9.33	6.93	5.95	5.41	5.06	4.82	4.64	4.50	4.39
13	9.07	6.70	5.74	5.21	4.86	4.62	4.44	4.30	4.19
14	8.86	6.51	5.56	5.04	4.69	4.46	4.28	4.14	4.03
15	8.68	6.36	5.42	4.89	4.56	4.32	4.14	4.00	3.89
16	8.53	6.23	5.29	4.77	4.44	4.20	4.03	3.89	3.78
17	8.40	6.11	5.18	4.67	4.34	4.10	3.93	3.79	3.68
18	8.29	6.01	5.09	4.58	4.25	4.01	3.84	3.71	3.60
19	8.18	5.93	5.01	4.50	4.17	3.94	3.77	3.63	3.52
20	8.10	5.85	4.94	4.43	4.10	3.87	3.70	3.56	3.46
21	8.02	5.78	4.87	4.37	4.04	3.81	3.64	3.51	3.40
22	7.95	5.72	4.82	4.31	3.99	3.76	3.59	3.45	3.35
23	7.88	5.66	4.76	4.26	3.94	3.71	3.54	3.41	3.30
24	7.82	5.61	4.72	4.22	3.90	3.67	3.50	3.36	3.26
25	7.77	5.57	4.68	4.18	3.85	3.63	3.46	3.32	3.22
26	7.72	5.53	4.64	4.14	3.82	3.59	3.42	3.29	3.18
27	7.68	5.49	4.60	4.11	3.78	3.56	3.39	3.26	3.15
28	7.64	5.45	4.57	4.07	3.75	3.53	3.36	3.23	3.12
29	7.60	5.42	4.54	4.04	3.73	3.50	3.33	3.20	3.09
30	7.56	5.39	4.51	4.02	3.70	3.47	3.30	3.17	3.07
40	7.31	5.18	4.31	3.83	3.51	3.29	3.12	2.99	2.89
60	7.08	4.98	4.13	3.65	3.34	3.12	2.95	2.82	2.72
120	6.85	4.79	3.95	3.48	3.17	2.96	2.79	2.66	2.56
∞	6.63	4.61	3.78	3.32	3.02	2.80	2.64	2.51	2.41

DENOMINATOR DEGREES OF FREEDOM (ν_2)

ν_2 \ ν_1	NUMERATOR DEGREES OF FREEDOM 10	12	15	20	24	30	40	60	120	∞
1	6,056	6,106	6,157	6,209	6,235	6,261	6,287	6,313	6,339	6,366
2	99.40	99.42	99.43	99.45	99.46	99.47	99.47	99.48	99.49	99.50
3	27.23	27.05	26.87	26.69	26.60	26.50	26.41	26.32	26.22	26.13
4	14.55	14.37	14.20	14.02	13.93	13.84	13.75	13.65	13.56	13.46
5	10.05	9.89	9.72	9.55	9.47	9.38	9.29	9.20	9.11	9.02
6	7.87	7.72	7.56	7.40	7.31	7.23	7.14	7.06	6.97	6.88
7	6.62	6.47	6.31	6.16	6.07	5.99	5.91	5.82	5.74	5.65
8	5.81	5.67	5.52	5.36	5.28	5.20	5.12	5.03	4.95	4.86
9	5.26	5.11	4.96	4.81	4.73	4.65	4.57	4.48	4.40	4.31
DENOMINATOR DEGREES OF FREEDOM 10	4.85	4.71	4.56	4.41	4.33	4.25	4.17	4.08	4.00	3.91
11	4.54	4.40	4.25	4.10	4.02	3.94	3.86	3.78	3.69	3.60
12	4.30	4.16	4.01	3.86	3.78	3.70	3.62	3.54	3.45	3.36
13	4.10	3.96	3.82	3.66	3.59	3.51	3.43	3.34	3.25	3.17
14	3.94	3.80	3.66	3.51	3.43	3.35	3.27	3.18	3.09	3.00
15	3.80	3.67	3.52	3.37	3.29	3.21	3.13	3.05	2.96	2.87
16	3.69	3.55	3.41	3.26	3.18	3.10	3.02	2.93	2.84	2.75
17	3.59	3.46	3.31	3.16	3.08	3.00	2.92	2.83	2.75	2.65
18	3.51	3.37	3.23	3.08	3.00	2.92	2.84	2.75	2.66	2.57
19	3.43	3.30	3.15	3.00	2.92	2.84	2.76	2.67	2.58	2.49
20	3.37	3.23	3.09	2.94	2.86	2.78	2.69	2.61	2.52	2.42
21	3.31	3.17	3.03	2.88	2.80	2.72	2.64	2.55	2.46	2.36
22	3.26	3.12	2.98	2.83	2.75	2.67	2.58	2.50	2.40	2.31
23	3.21	3.07	2.93	2.78	2.70	2.62	2.54	2.45	2.35	2.26
24	3.17	3.03	2.89	2.74	2.66	2.58	2.49	2.40	2.31	2.21
25	3.13	2.99	2.85	2.70	2.62	2.54	2.45	2.36	2.27	2.17
26	3.09	2.96	2.81	2.66	2.58	2.50	2.42	2.33	2.23	2.13
27	3.06	2.93	2.78	2.63	2.55	2.47	2.38	2.29	2.20	2.10
28	3.03	2.90	2.75	2.60	2.52	2.44	2.35	2.26	2.17	2.06
29	3.00	2.87	2.73	2.57	2.49	2.41	2.33	2.23	2.14	2.03
30	2.98	2.84	2.70	2.55	2.47	2.39	2.30	2.21	2.11	2.01
40	2.80	2.66	2.52	2.37	2.29	2.20	2.11	2.02	1.92	1.80
60	2.63	2.50	2.35	2.20	2.12	2.03	1.94	1.84	1.73	1.60
120	2.47	2.34	2.19	2.03	1.95	1.86	1.76	1.66	1.53	1.38
∞	2.32	2.18	2.04	1.88	1.79	1.70	1.59	1.47	1.32	1.00

Source: From M. Merrington and C. M. Thompson, "Tables of percentage points of the inverted beta (F)-distribution," *Biometrika*, 1943, *33*, 73–88. Reproduced by permission of the *Biometrika* Trustees.

TABLE 7 **Random Numbers**

ROW \ COLUMN	1	2	3	4	5	6	7	8	9	10	11	12	13	14
1	10480	15011	01536	02011	81647	91646	69179	14194	62590	36207	20969	99570	91291	90700
2	22368	46573	25595	85393	30995	89198	27982	53402	93965	34095	52666	19174	39615	99505
3	24130	48360	22527	97265	76393	64809	15179	24830	49340	32081	30680	19655	63348	58629
4	42167	93093	06243	61680	07856	16376	39440	53537	71341	57004	00849	74917	97758	16379
5	37570	39975	81837	16656	06121	91782	60468	81305	49684	60672	14110	06927	01263	54613
6	77921	06907	11008	42751	27756	53498	18602	70659	90655	15053	21916	81825	44394	42880
7	99562	72905	56420	69994	98872	31016	71194	18738	44013	48840	63213	21069	10634	12952
8	96301	91977	05463	07972	18876	20922	94595	56869	69014	60045	18425	84903	42508	32307
9	89579	14342	63661	10281	17453	18103	57740	84378	25331	12566	58678	44947	05585	56941
10	85475	36857	53342	53988	53060	59533	38867	62300	08158	17983	16439	11458	18593	64952
11	28918	69578	88231	33276	70997	79936	56865	05859	90106	31595	01547	85590	91610	78188
12	63553	40961	48235	03427	49626	69445	18663	72695	52180	20847	12234	90511	33703	90322
13	09429	93969	52636	92737	88974	33488	36320	17617	30015	08272	84115	27156	30613	74952
14	10365	61129	87529	85689	48237	52267	67689	93394	01511	26358	85104	20285	29975	89868
15	07119	97336	71048	08178	77233	13916	47564	81056	97735	85977	29372	74461	28551	90707
16	51085	12765	51821	51259	77452	16308	60756	92144	49442	53900	70960	63990	75601	40719
17	02368	21382	52404	60268	89368	19885	55322	44819	01188	65255	64835	44919	05944	55157
18	01011	54092	33362	94904	31273	04146	18594	29852	71585	85030	51132	01915	92747	64951
19	52162	53916	46369	58586	23216	14513	83149	98736	23495	64350	94738	17752	35156	35749
20	07056	97628	33787	09998	42698	06691	76988	13602	51851	46104	88916	19509	25625	58104
21	48663	91245	85828	14346	09172	30168	90229	04734	59193	22178	30421	61666	99904	32812
22	54164	58492	22421	74103	47070	25306	76468	26384	58151	06646	21524	15227	96909	44592
23	32639	32363	05597	24200	13363	38005	94342	28728	35806	06912	17012	64161	18296	22851
24	29334	27001	87637	87308	58731	00256	45834	15398	46557	41135	10367	07684	36188	18510
25	02488	33062	28834	07351	19731	92420	60952	61280	50001	67658	32586	86679	50720	94953
26	81525	72295	04839	96423	24878	82651	66566	14778	76797	14780	13300	87074	79666	95725
27	29676	20591	68086	26432	46901	20849	89768	81536	86645	12659	92259	57102	80428	25280
28	00742	57392	39064	66432	84673	40027	32832	61362	98947	96067	64760	64584	96096	98253
29	05366	04213	25669	26422	44407	44048	37937	63904	45766	66134	75470	66520	34693	90449
30	91921	26418	64117	94305	26766	25940	39972	22209	71500	64568	91402	42416	07844	69618
31	00582	04711	87917	77341	42206	35126	74087	99547	81817	42607	43808	76655	62028	76630
32	00725	69884	62797	56170	86324	88072	76222	36086	84637	93161	76038	65855	77919	88006
33	69011	65795	95876	55293	18988	27354	26575	08625	40801	59920	29841	80150	12777	48501
34	25976	57948	29888	88604	67917	48708	18912	82271	65424	69774	33611	54262	85963	03547
35	09763	83473	73577	12908	30883	18317	28290	35797	05998	41688	34952	37888	38917	88050

TABLE 7 *(Continued)*

ROW \ COLUMN	1	2	3	4	5	6	7	8	9	10	11	12	13	14
36	91576	42595	27958	30134	04024	86385	29880	99730	55536	84855	29080	09250	79656	73211
37	17955	56349	90999	49127	20044	59931	06115	20542	18059	02008	73708	83517	36103	42791
38	46503	18584	18845	49618	02304	51038	20655	58727	28168	15475	56942	53389	20562	87338
39	92157	89634	94824	78171	84610	82834	09922	25417	44137	48413	25555	21246	35509	20468
40	14577	62765	35605	81263	39667	47358	56873	56307	61607	49518	89656	20103	77490	18062
41	98427	07523	33362	64270	01638	92477	66969	98420	04880	45585	46565	04102	46880	45709
42	34914	63976	88720	82765	34476	17032	87589	40836	32427	70002	70663	88863	77775	69348
43	70060	28277	39475	46473	23219	53416	94970	25832	69975	94884	19661	72828	00102	66794
44	53976	54914	06990	67245	68350	82948	11398	42878	80287	88267	47363	46634	06541	97809
45	76072	29515	40980	07391	58745	25774	22987	80059	39911	96189	41151	14222	60697	59583
46	90725	52210	83974	29992	65831	38857	50490	83765	55657	14361	31720	57375	56228	41546
47	64364	67412	33339	31926	14883	24413	59744	92351	97473	89286	35931	04110	23726	51900
48	08962	00358	31662	25388	61642	34072	81249	35648	56891	69352	48373	45578	78547	81788
49	95012	68379	93526	70765	10592	04542	76463	54328	02349	17247	28865	14777	62730	92277
50	15664	10493	20492	38391	91132	21999	59516	81652	27195	48223	46751	22923	32261	85653
51	16408	81899	04153	53381	79401	21438	83035	92350	36693	31238	59649	91754	72772	02338
52	18629	81953	05520	91962	04739	13092	97662	24822	94730	06496	35090	04822	86774	98289
53	73115	35101	47498	87637	99016	71060	88824	71013	18735	20286	23153	72924	35165	43040
54	57491	16703	23167	49323	45021	33132	12544	41035	80780	45393	44812	12515	98931	91202
55	30405	83946	23792	14422	15059	45799	22716	19792	09983	74353	68668	30429	70735	25499
56	16631	35006	85900	98275	32388	52390	16815	69298	82732	38480	73817	32523	41961	44437
57	96773	20206	42559	78985	05300	22164	24369	54224	35083	19687	11052	91491	60383	19746
58	38935	64202	14349	82674	66523	44133	00697	35552	35970	19124	63318	29686	03387	59846
59	31624	76384	17403	53363	44167	64486	64758	75366	76554	31601	12614	33072	60332	92325
60	78919	19474	23632	27889	47914	02584	37680	20801	72152	39339	34806	08930	85001	87820
61	03931	33309	57047	74211	63445	17361	62825	39908	05607	91284	68833	25570	38818	46920
62	74426	33278	43972	10119	89917	15665	52872	73823	73144	88662	88970	74492	51805	99378
63	09066	00903	20795	95452	92648	45454	09552	88815	16553	51125	79375	97596	16296	66092
64	42238	12426	87025	14267	20979	04508	64535	31355	86064	29472	47689	05974	52468	16834
65	16153	08002	26504	41744	81959	65642	74240	56302	00033	67107	77510	70625	28725	34191
66	21457	40742	29820	96783	29400	21840	15035	34537	33310	06116	95240	15957	16572	06004
67	21581	57802	02050	89728	17937	37621	47075	42080	97403	48626	68995	43805	33386	21597
68	55612	78095	83197	33732	05810	24813	86902	60397	16489	03264	88525	42786	05269	92532
69	44657	66999	99324	51281	84463	60563	79312	93454	68876	25471	93911	25650	12682	73572

(continued)

TABLE 7 **Continued**

ROW \ COLUMN	1	2	3	4	5	6	7	8	9	10	11	12	13	14
70	91340	84979	46949	81973	37949	61023	43997	15263	80644	43942	89203	71795	99533	50501
71	91227	21199	31935	27022	84067	05462	35216	14486	29891	68607	41867	14951	91696	85065
72	50001	38140	66321	19924	72163	09538	12151	06878	91903	18749	34405	56087	82790	70925
73	65390	05224	72958	28609	81406	39147	25549	48542	42627	45233	57202	94617	23772	07896
74	27504	96131	83944	41575	10573	08619	64482	73923	36152	05184	94142	25299	84387	34925
75	37169	94851	39117	89632	00959	16487	65536	49071	39782	17095	02330	74301	00275	48280
76	11508	70225	51111	38351	19444	66499	71945	05422	13442	78675	84081	66938	93654	59894
77	37449	30362	06694	54690	04052	53115	62757	95348	78662	11163	81651	50245	34971	52924
78	46515	70331	85922	38329	57015	15765	97161	17869	45349	61796	66345	81073	49106	79860
79	30986	81223	42416	58353	21532	30502	32305	86482	05174	07901	54339	58861	74818	46942
80	63798	64995	46583	09785	44160	78128	83991	42865	92520	83531	80377	35909	81250	54238
81	82486	84846	99254	67632	43218	50076	21361	64816	51202	88124	41870	52689	51275	83556
82	21885	32906	92431	09060	64297	51674	64126	62570	26123	05155	59194	52799	28225	85762
83	60336	98782	07408	53458	13564	59089	26445	29789	85205	41001	12535	12133	14645	23541
84	43937	46891	24010	25560	86355	33941	25786	54990	71899	15475	95434	98227	21824	19585
85	97656	63175	89303	16275	07100	92063	21942	18611	47348	20203	18534	03862	78095	50136
86	03299	01221	05418	38982	55758	92237	26759	86367	21216	98442	08303	56613	91511	75928
87	79626	06486	03574	17668	07785	76020	79924	25651	83325	88428	85076	72811	22717	50585
88	85636	68335	47539	03129	65651	11977	02510	26113	99447	68645	34327	15152	55230	93448
89	18039	14367	61337	06177	12143	46609	32989	74014	64708	00533	35398	58408	13261	47908
90	08362	15656	60627	36478	65648	16764	53412	09013	07832	41574	17639	82163	60859	75567
91	79556	29068	04142	16268	15387	12856	66227	38358	22478	73373	88732	09443	82558	05250
92	92608	82674	27072	32534	17075	27698	98204	63863	11951	34648	88022	56148	34925	57031
93	23982	25835	40055	67006	12293	02753	14827	23235	35071	99704	37543	11601	35503	85171
94	09915	96306	05908	97901	28395	14186	00821	80703	70426	75647	76310	88717	37890	40129
95	59037	33300	26695	62247	69927	76123	50842	43834	86654	70959	79725	93872	28117	19233
96	42488	78077	69882	61657	34136	79180	97526	43092	04098	73571	80799	76536	71255	64239
97	46764	86273	63003	93017	31204	36692	40202	35275	57306	55543	53203	18098	47625	88684
98	03237	45430	55417	63282	90816	17349	88298	90183	36600	78406	06216	95787	42579	90730
99	86591	81482	52667	61582	14972	90053	89534	76036	49199	43716	97548	04379	46370	28672
100	38534	01715	94964	87288	65680	43772	39560	12918	86537	62738	19636	51132	25739	56947

Source: Abridged from W. H. Beyer (ed.). *CRC Standard Mathematical Tables*, 24th edition. Cleveland: The Chemical Rubber Company, 1976.

TABLE 8 **Critical Values for the Durbin–Watson *d* Statistic ($\alpha = .05$)**

n	$k = 1$		$k = 2$		$k = 3$		$k = 4$		$k = 5$	
	d_L	d_U	d_L	d_U	d_L	d_U	d_L	d_U	d_L	d_U
15	1.08	1.36	.95	1.54	.82	1.75	.69	1.97	.56	2.21
16	1.10	1.37	.98	1.54	.86	1.73	.74	1.93	.62	2.15
17	1.13	1.38	1.02	1.54	.90	1.71	.78	1.90	.67	2.10
18	1.16	1.39	1.05	1.53	.93	1.69	.82	1.87	.71	2.06
19	1.18	1.40	1.08	1.53	.97	1.68	.86	1.85	.75	2.02
20	1.20	1.41	1.10	1.54	1.00	1.68	.90	1.83	.79	1.99
21	1.22	1.42	1.13	1.54	1.03	1.67	.93	1.81	.83	1.96
22	1.24	1.43	1.15	1.54	1.05	1.66	.96	1.80	.86	1.94
23	1.26	1.44	1.17	1.54	1.08	1.66	.99	1.79	.90	1.92
24	1.27	1.45	1.19	1.55	1.10	1.66	1.01	1.78	.93	1.90
25	1.29	1.45	1.21	1.55	1.12	1.66	1.04	1.77	.95	1.89
26	1.30	1.46	1.22	1.55	1.14	1.65	1.06	1.76	.98	1.88
27	1.32	1.47	1.24	1.56	1.16	1.65	1.08	1.76	1.01	1.86
28	1.33	1.48	1.26	1.56	1.18	1.65	1.10	1.75	1.03	1.85
29	1.34	1.48	1.27	1.56	1.20	1.65	1.12	1.74	1.05	1.84
30	1.35	1.49	1.28	1.57	1.21	1.65	1.14	1.74	1.07	1.83
31	1.36	1.50	1.30	1.57	1.23	1.65	1.16	1.74	1.09	1.83
32	1.37	1.50	1.31	1.57	1.24	1.65	1.18	1.73	1.11	1.82
33	1.38	1.51	1.32	1.58	1.26	1.65	1.19	1.73	1.13	1.81
34	1.39	1.51	1.33	1.58	1.27	1.65	1.21	1.73	1.15	1.81
35	1.40	1.52	1.34	1.58	1.28	1.65	1.22	1.73	1.16	1.80
36	1.41	1.52	1.35	1.59	1.29	1.65	1.24	1.73	1.18	1.80
37	1.42	1.53	1.36	1.59	1.31	1.66	1.25	1.72	1.19	1.80
38	1.43	1.54	1.37	1.59	1.32	1.66	1.26	1.72	1.21	1.79
39	1.43	1.54	1.38	1.60	1.33	1.66	1.27	1.72	1.22	1.79
40	1.44	1.54	1.39	1.60	1.34	1.66	1.29	1.72	1.23	1.79
45	1.48	1.57	1.43	1.62	1.38	1.67	1.34	1.72	1.29	1.78
50	1.50	1.59	1.46	1.63	1.42	1.67	1.38	1.72	1.34	1.77
55	1.53	1.60	1.49	1.64	1.45	1.68	1.41	1.72	1.38	1.77
60	1.55	1.62	1.51	1.65	1.48	1.69	1.44	1.73	1.41	1.77
65	1.57	1.63	1.54	1.66	1.50	1.70	1.47	1.73	1.44	1.77
70	1.58	1.64	1.55	1.67	1.52	1.70	1.49	1.74	1.46	1.77
75	1.60	1.65	1.57	1.68	1.54	1.71	1.51	1.74	1.49	1.77
80	1.61	1.66	1.59	1.69	1.56	1.72	1.53	1.74	1.51	1.77
85	1.62	1.67	1.60	1.70	1.57	1.72	1.55	1.75	1.52	1.77
90	1.63	1.68	1.61	1.70	1.59	1.73	1.57	1.75	1.54	1.78
95	1.64	1.69	1.62	1.71	1.60	1.73	1.58	1.75	1.56	1.78
100	1.65	1.69	1.63	1.72	1.61	1.74	1.59	1.76	1.57	1.78

Source: From J. Durbin and G. S. Watson, "Testing for serial correlation in least squares regression, II," *Biometrika*, 1951, *30*, 159–178. Reproduced by permission of the *Biometrika* Trustees.

TABLE 9 Critical Values for the Durbin–Watson *d* Statistic (α = .01)

n	k = 1		k = 2		k = 3		k = 4		k = 5	
	d_L	d_U	d_L	d_U	d_L	d_U	d_L	d_U	d_L	d_U
15	.81	1.07	.70	1.25	.59	1.46	.49	1.70	.39	1.96
16	.84	1.09	.74	1.25	.63	1.44	.53	1.66	.44	1.90
17	.87	1.10	.77	1.25	.67	1.43	.57	1.63	.48	1.85
18	.90	1.12	.80	1.26	.71	1.42	.61	1.60	.52	1.80
19	.93	1.13	.83	1.26	.74	1.41	.65	1.58	.56	1.77
20	.95	1.15	.86	1.27	.77	1.41	.68	1.57	.60	1.74
21	.97	1.16	.89	1.27	.80	1.41	.72	1.55	.63	1.71
22	1.00	1.17	.91	1.28	.83	1.40	.75	1.54	.66	1.69
23	1.02	1.19	.94	1.29	.86	1.40	.77	1.53	.70	1.67
24	1.04	1.20	.96	1.30	.88	1.41	.80	1.53	.72	1.66
25	1.05	1.21	.98	1.30	.90	1.41	.83	1.52	.75	1.65
26	1.07	1.22	1.00	1.31	.93	1.41	.85	1.52	.78	1.64
27	1.09	1.23	1.02	1.32	.95	1.41	.88	1.51	.81	1.63
28	1.10	1.24	1.04	1.32	.97	1.41	.90	1.51	.83	1.62
29	1.12	1.25	1.05	1.33	.99	1.42	.92	1.51	.85	1.61
30	1.13	1.26	1.07	1.34	1.01	1.42	.94	1.51	.88	1.61
31	1.15	1.27	1.08	1.34	1.02	1.42	.96	1.51	.90	1.60
32	1.16	1.28	1.10	1.35	1.04	1.43	.98	1.51	.92	1.60
33	1.17	1.29	1.11	1.36	1.05	1.43	1.00	1.51	.94	1.59
34	1.18	1.30	1.13	1.36	1.07	1.43	1.01	1.51	.95	1.59
35	1.19	1.31	1.14	1.37	1.08	1.44	1.03	1.51	.97	1.59
36	1.21	1.32	1.15	1.38	1.10	1.44	1.04	1.51	.99	1.59
37	1.22	1.32	1.16	1.38	1.11	1.45	1.06	1.51	1.00	1.59
38	1.23	1.33	1.18	1.39	1.12	1.45	1.07	1.52	1.02	1.58
39	1.24	1.34	1.19	1.39	1.14	1.45	1.09	1.52	1.03	1.58
40	1.25	1.34	1.20	1.40	1.15	1.46	1.10	1.52	1.05	1.58
45	1.29	1.38	1.24	1.42	1.20	1.48	1.16	1.53	1.11	1.58
50	1.32	1.40	1.28	1.45	1.24	1.49	1.20	1.54	1.16	1.59
55	1.36	1.43	1.32	1.47	1.28	1.51	1.25	1.55	1.21	1.59
60	1.38	1.45	1.35	1.48	1.32	1.52	1.28	1.56	1.25	1.60
65	1.41	1.47	1.38	1.50	1.35	1.53	1.31	1.57	1.28	1.61
70	1.43	1.49	1.40	1.52	1.37	1.55	1.34	1.58	1.31	1.61
75	1.45	1.50	1.42	1.53	1.39	1.56	1.37	1.59	1.34	1.62
80	1.47	1.52	1.44	1.54	1.42	1.57	1.39	1.60	1.36	1.62
85	1.48	1.53	1.46	1.55	1.43	1.58	1.41	1.60	1.39	1.63
90	1.50	1.54	1.47	1.56	1.45	1.59	1.43	1.61	1.41	1.64
95	1.51	1.55	1.49	1.57	1.47	1.60	1.45	1.62	1.42	1.64
100	1.52	1.56	1.50	1.58	1.48	1.60	1.46	1.63	1.44	1.65

Source: From J. Durbin and G. S. Watson, "Testing for serial correlation in least squares regression, II," *Biometrika*, 1951, *30*, 159–178. Reproduced by permission of the *Biometrika* Trustees.

TABLE 10 Critical Values for the χ^2 Statistic

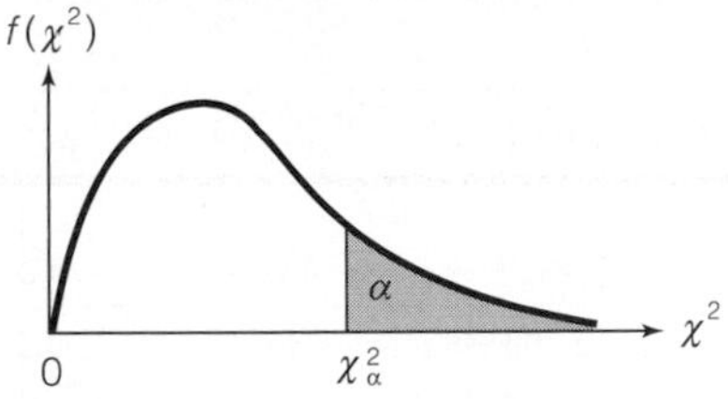

DEGREES OF FREEDOM	$\chi^2_{.995}$	$\chi^2_{.990}$	$\chi^2_{.975}$	$\chi^2_{.950}$	$\chi^2_{.900}$
1	.0000393	.0001571	.0009821	.0039321	.0157908
2	.0100251	.0201007	.0506356	.102587	.210720
3	.0717212	.114832	.215795	.351846	.584375
4	.206990	.297110	.484419	.710721	1.063623
5	.411740	.554300	.831211	1.145476	1.61031
6	.675727	.872085	1.237347	1.63539	2.20413
7	.989265	1.239043	1.68987	2.16735	2.83311
8	1.344419	1.646482	2.17973	2.73264	3.48954
9	1.734926	2.087912	2.70039	3.32511	4.16816
10	2.15585	2.55821	3.24697	3.94030	4.86518
11	2.60321	3.05347	3.81575	4.57481	5.57779
12	3.07382	3.57056	4.40379	5.22603	6.30380
13	3.56503	4.10691	5.00874	5.89186	7.04150
14	4.07468	4.66043	5.62872	6.57063	7.78953
15	4.60094	5.22935	6.26214	7.26094	8.54675
16	5.14224	5.81221	6.90766	7.96164	9.31223
17	5.69724	6.40776	7.56418	8.67176	10.0852
18	6.26481	7.01491	8.23075	9.39046	10.8649
19	6.84398	7.63273	8.90655	10.1170	11.6509
20	7.43386	8.26040	9.59083	10.8508	12.4426
21	8.03366	0.09720	10.28293	11.5913	13.2396
22	8.64272	9.54249	10.9823	12.3380	14.0415
23	9.26042	10.19567	11.6885	13.0905	14.8479
24	9.88623	10.8564	12.4011	13.8484	15.6587
25	10.5197	11.5240	13.1197	14.6114	16.4734
26	11.1603	12.1981	13.8439	15.3791	17.2919
27	11.8076	12.8786	14.5733	16.1513	18.1138
28	12.4613	13.5648	15.3079	16.9279	18.9392
29	13.1211	14.2565	16.0471	17.7083	19.7677
30	13.7867	14.9535	16.7908	18.4926	20.5992
40	20.7065	22.1643	24.4331	26.5093	29.0505
50	27.9907	29.7067	32.3574	34.7642	37.6886
60	35.5346	37.4848	40.4817	43.1879	46.4589
70	43.2752	45.4418	48.7576	51.7393	55.3290
80	51.1720	53.5400	57.1532	60.3915	64.2778
90	59.1963	61.7541	65.6466	69.1260	73.2912
100	67.3276	70.0648	74.2219	77.9295	82.3581
150	109.142	112.668	117.985	122.692	128.275
200	152.241	156.432	162.728	168.279	174.835
300	240.663	245.972	253.912	260.878	269.068
400	330.903	337.155	346.482	354.641	364.207
500	422.303	429.388	439.936	449.147	459.926

(continued)

TABLE 10 **Continued**

DEGREES OF FREEDOM	$\chi^2_{.100}$	$\chi^2_{.050}$	$\chi^2_{.025}$	$\chi^2_{.010}$	$\chi^2_{.005}$
1	2.70554	3.84146	5.02389	6.63490	7.87944
2	4.60517	5.99147	7.37776	9.21034	10.5966
3	6.25139	7.81473	9.34840	11.3449	12.8381
4	7.77944	9.48773	11.1433	13.2767	14.8602
5	9.23635	11.0705	12.8325	15.0863	16.7496
6	10.6446	12.5916	14.4494	16.8119	18.5476
7	12.0170	14.0671	16.0128	18.4753	20.2777
8	13.3616	15.5073	17.5346	20.0902	21.9550
9	14.6837	16.9190	19.0228	21.6660	23.5893
10	15.9871	18.3070	20.4831	23.2093	25.1882
11	17.2750	19.6751	21.9200	24.7250	26.7569
12	18.5494	21.0261	23.3367	26.2170	28.2995
13	19.8119	22.3621	24.7356	27.6883	29.8194
14	21.0642	23.6848	26.1190	29.1413	31.3193
15	22.3072	24.9958	27.4884	30.5779	32.8013
16	23.5418	26.2962	28.8454	31.9999	34.2672
17	24.7690	27.5871	30.1910	33.4087	35.7185
18	25.9894	28.8693	31.5264	34.8053	37.1564
19	27.2036	30.1435	32.8523	36.1908	38.5822
20	28.4120	31.4104	34.1696	37.5662	39.9968
21	29.6151	32.6705	35.4789	38.9321	41.4010
22	30.8133	33.9244	36.7807	40.2894	42.7956
23	32.0069	35.1725	38.0757	41.6384	44.1813
24	33.1963	36.4151	39.3641	42.9798	45.5585
25	34.3816	37.6525	40.6465	44.3141	46.9278
26	36.5631	38.8852	41.9232	45.6417	48.2899
27	36.7412	40.1133	43.1944	46.9630	49.6449
28	37.9159	41.3372	44.4607	48.2782	50.9933
29	39.0875	42.5569	45.7222	49.5879	52.3356
30	40.2560	43.7729	46.9792	50.8922	53.6720
40	51.8050	55.7585	59.3417	63.6907	66.7659
50	63.1671	67.5048	71.4202	76.1539	79.4900
60	74.3970	79.0819	83.2976	88.3794	91.9517
70	85.5271	90.5312	95.0231	100.425	104.215
80	96.5782	101.879	106.629	112.329	116.321
90	107.565	113.145	118.136	124.116	128.299
100	118.498	124.342	129.561	135.807	140.169
150	172.581	179.581	185.800	193.208	198.360
200	226.021	233.994	241.058	249.445	255.264
300	331.789	341.395	349.874	359.906	366.844
400	436.649	447.632	457.305	468.724	476.606
500	540.930	553.127	563.852	576.493	585.207

Source: From C. M. Thompson, "Tables of the Percentage Points of the χ^2-Distribution." *Biometrika*, 1941, Vol. 32, pp. 188–189. Reproduced by permission of the *Biometrika* trustees.

TABLE 11 **Percentage Points of the Studentized Range $q(p, \nu)$, Upper 5%**

ν \ p	2	3	4	5	6	7	8	9	10	11
1	17.97	26.98	32.82	37.08	40.41	43.12	45.40	47.36	49.07	50.59
2	6.08	8.33	9.80	10.88	11.74	12.44	13.03	13.54	13.99	14.39
3	4.50	5.91	6.82	7.50	8.04	8.48	8.85	9.18	9.46	9.72
4	3.93	5.04	5.76	6.29	6.71	7.05	7.35	7.60	7.83	8.03
5	3.64	4.60	5.22	5.67	6.03	6.33	6.58	6.80	6.99	7.17
6	3.46	4.34	4.90	5.30	5.63	5.90	6.12	6.32	6.49	6.65
7	3.34	4.16	4.68	5.06	5.36	5.61	5.82	6.00	6.16	6.30
8	3.26	4.04	4.53	4.89	5.17	5.40	5.60	5.77	5.92	6.05
9	3.20	3.95	4.41	4.76	5.02	5.24	5.43	5.59	5.74	5.87
10	3.15	3.88	4.33	4.65	4.91	5.12	5.30	5.46	5.60	5.72
11	3.11	3.82	4.26	4.57	4.82	5.03	5.20	5.35	5.49	5.61
12	3.08	3.77	4.20	4.51	4.75	4.95	5.12	5.27	5.39	5.51
13	3.06	3.73	4.15	4.45	4.69	4.88	5.05	5.19	5.32	5.43
14	3.03	3.70	4.11	4.41	4.64	4.83	4.99	5.13	5.25	5.36
15	3.01	3.67	4.08	4.37	4.60	4.78	4.94	5.08	5.20	5.31
16	3.00	3.65	4.05	4.33	4.56	4.74	4.90	5.03	5.15	5.26
17	2.98	3.63	4.02	4.30	4.52	4.70	4.86	4.99	5.11	5.21
18	2.97	3.61	4.00	4.28	4.49	4.67	4.82	4.96	5.07	5.17
19	2.96	3.59	3.98	4.25	4.47	4.65	4.79	4.92	5.04	5.14
20	2.95	3.58	3.96	4.23	4.45	4.62	4.77	4.90	5.01	5.11
24	2.92	3.53	3.90	4.17	4.37	4.54	4.68	4.81	4.92	5.01
30	2.89	3.49	3.85	4.10	4.30	4.46	4.60	4.72	4.82	4.92
40	2.86	3.44	3.79	4.04	4.23	4.39	4.52	4.63	4.73	4.82
60	2.83	3.40	3.74	3.98	4.16	4.31	4.44	4.55	4.65	4.73
120	2.80	3.36	3.68	3.92	4.10	4.24	4.36	4.47	4.56	4.64
∞	2.77	3.31	3.63	3.86	4.03	4.17	4.29	4.39	4.47	4.55

(continued)

TABLE 11 **Continued**

ν \ p	12	13	14	15	16	17	18	19	20
1	51.96	53.20	54.33	55.36	56.32	57.22	58.04	58.83	59.56
2	14.75	15.08	15.38	15.65	15.91	16.14	16.37	16.57	16.77
3	9.95	10.15	10.35	10.52	10.69	10.84	10.98	11.11	11.24
4	8.21	8.37	8.52	8.66	8.79	8.91	9.03	9.13	9.23
5	7.32	7.47	7.60	7.72	7.83	7.93	8.03	8.12	8.21
6	6.79	6.92	7.03	7.14	7.24	7.34	7.43	7.51	7.59
7	6.43	6.55	6.66	6.76	6.85	6.94	7.02	7.10	7.17
8	6.18	6.29	6.39	6.48	6.57	6.65	6.73	6.80	6.87
9	5.98	6.09	6.19	6.28	6.36	6.44	6.51	6.58	6.64
10	5.83	5.93	6.03	6.11	6.19	6.27	6.34	6.40	6.47
11	5.71	5.81	5.90	5.98	6.06	6.13	6.20	6.27	6.33
12	5.61	5.71	5.80	5.88	5.95	6.02	6.09	6.15	6.21
13	5.53	5.63	5.71	5.79	5.86	5.93	5.99	6.05	6.11
14	5.46	5.55	5.64	5.71	5.79	5.85	5.91	5.97	6.03
15	5.40	5.49	5.57	5.65	5.72	5.78	5.85	5.90	5.96
16	5.35	5.44	5.52	5.59	5.66	5.73	5.79	5.84	5.90
17	5.31	5.39	5.47	5.54	5.61	5.67	5.73	5.79	5.84
18	5.27	5.35	5.43	5.50	5.57	5.63	5.69	5.74	5.79
19	5.23	5.31	5.39	5.46	5.53	5.59	5.65	5.70	5.75
20	5.20	5.28	5.36	5.43	5.49	5.55	5.61	5.66	5.71
24	5.10	5.18	5.25	5.32	5.38	5.44	5.49	5.55	5.59
30	5.00	5.08	5.15	5.21	5.27	5.33	5.38	5.43	5.47
40	4.90	4.98	5.04	5.11	5.16	5.22	5.27	5.31	5.36
60	4.81	4.88	4.94	5.00	5.06	5.11	5.15	5.20	5.24
120	4.71	4.78	4.84	4.90	4.95	5.00	5.04	5.09	5.13
∞	4.62	4.68	4.74	4.80	4.85	4.89	4.93	4.97	5.01

Source: *Biometrika Tables for Statisticians*, Vol. I, 3rd ed., edited by E. S. Pearson and H. O. Hartley (Cambridge University Press, 1966). Reproduced by permission of Professor E. S. Pearson and the *Biometrika* Trustees.

TABLE 12 **Percentage Points of the Studentized Range $q(p, \nu)$, Upper 1%**

ν \ p	2	3	4	5	6	7	8	9	10	11
1	90.03	135.0	164.3	185.6	202.2	215.8	227.2	237.0	245.6	253.2
2	14.04	19.02	22.29	24.72	26.63	28.20	29.53	30.68	31.69	32.59
3	8.26	10.62	12.17	13.33	14.24	15.00	15.64	16.20	16.69	17.13
4	6.51	8.12	9.17	9.96	10.58	11.10	11.55	11.93	12.27	12.57
5	5.70	6.98	7.80	8.42	8.91	9.32	9.67	9.97	10.24	10.48
6	5.24	6.33	7.03	7.56	7.97	8.32	8.61	8.87	9.10	9.30
7	4.95	5.92	6.54	7.01	7.37	7.68	7.94	8.17	8.37	8.55
8	4.75	5.64	6.20	6.62	6.96	7.24	7.47	7.68	7.86	8.03
9	4.60	5.43	5.96	6.35	6.66	6.91	7.13	7.33	7.49	7.65
10	4.48	5.27	5.77	6.14	6.43	6.67	6.87	7.05	7.21	7.36
11	4.39	5.15	5.62	5.97	6.25	6.48	6.67	6.84	6.99	7.13
12	4.32	5.05	5.50	5.84	6.10	6.32	6.51	6.67	6.81	6.94
13	4.26	4.96	5.40	5.73	5.98	6.19	6.37	6.53	6.67	6.79
14	4.21	4.89	5.32	5.63	5.88	6.08	6.26	6.41	6.54	6.66
15	4.17	4.84	5.25	5.56	5.80	5.99	6.16	6.31	6.44	6.55
16	4.13	4.79	5.19	5.49	5.72	5.92	6.08	6.22	6.35	6.46
17	4.10	4.74	5.14	5.43	5.66	5.85	6.01	6.15	6.27	6.38
18	4.07	4.70	5.09	5.38	5.60	5.79	5.94	6.08	6.20	6.31
19	4.05	4.67	5.05	5.33	5.55	5.73	5.89	6.02	6.14	6.25
20	4.02	4.64	5.02	5.29	5.51	5.69	5.84	5.97	6.09	6.19
24	3.96	4.55	4.91	5.17	5.37	5.54	5.69	5.81	5.92	6.02
30	3.89	4.45	4.80	5.05	5.24	5.40	5.54	5.65	5.76	5.85
40	3.82	4.37	4.70	4.93	5.11	5.26	5.39	5.50	5.60	5.69
60	3.76	4.28	4.59	4.82	4.99	5.13	5.25	5.36	5.45	5.53
120	3.70	4.20	4.50	4.71	4.87	5.01	5.12	5.21	5.30	5.37
∞	3.64	4.12	4.40	4.60	4.76	4.88	4.99	5.08	5.16	5.23

(continued)

TABLE 12 **Continued**

ν \ p	12	13	14	15	16	17	18	19	20
1	260.0	266.2	271.8	277.0	281.8	286.3	290.0	294.3	298.0
2	33.40	34.13	34.81	35.43	36.00	36.53	37.03	37.50	37.95
3	17.53	17.89	18.22	18.52	18.81	19.07	19.32	19.55	19.77
4	12.84	13.09	13.32	13.53	13.73	13.91	14.08	14.24	14.40
5	10.70	10.89	11.08	11.24	11.40	11.55	11.68	11.81	11.93
6	9.48	9.65	9.81	9.95	10.08	10.21	10.32	10.43	10.54
7	8.71	8.86	9.00	9.12	9.24	9.35	9.46	9.55	9.65
8	8.18	8.31	8.44	8.55	8.66	8.76	8.85	8.94	9.03
9	7.78	7.91	8.03	8.13	8.23	8.33	8.41	8.49	8.57
10	7.49	7.60	7.71	7.81	7.91	7.99	8.08	8.15	8.23
11	7.25	7.36	7.46	7.56	7.65	7.73	7.81	7.88	7.95
12	7.06	7.17	7.26	7.36	7.44	7.52	7.59	7.66	7.73
13	6.90	7.01	7.10	7.19	7.27	7.35	7.42	7.48	7.55
14	6.77	6.87	6.96	7.05	7.13	7.20	7.27	7.33	7.39
15	6.66	6.76	6.84	6.93	7.00	7.07	7.14	7.20	7.26
16	6.56	6.66	6.74	6.82	6.90	6.97	7.03	7.09	7.15
17	6.48	6.57	6.66	6.73	6.81	6.87	6.94	7.00	7.05
18	6.41	6.50	6.58	6.65	6.72	6.79	6.85	6.91	6.97
19	6.34	6.43	6.51	6.58	6.65	6.72	6.78	6.84	6.89
20	6.28	6.37	6.45	6.52	6.59	6.65	6.71	6.77	6.82
24	6.11	6.19	6.26	6.33	6.39	6.45	6.51	6.56	6.61
30	5.93	6.01	6.08	6.14	6.20	6.26	6.31	6.36	6.41
40	5.76	5.83	5.90	5.96	6.02	6.07	6.12	6.16	6.21
60	5.60	5.67	5.73	5.78	5.84	5.89	5.93	5.97	6.01
120	5.44	5.50	5.56	5.61	5.66	5.71	5.75	5.79	5.83
∞	5.29	5.35	5.40	5.45	5.49	5.54	5.57	5.61	5.65

Source: *Biometrika Tables for Statisticians*, Vol. I, 3rd ed., edited by E. S. Pearson and H. O. Hartley (Cambridge University Press, 1966). Reproduced by permission of Professor E. S. Pearson and the *Biometrika* Trustees.

APPENDIX D SAS Tutorial

CONTENTS

D.1 Introduction

This appendix is a brief tutorial on how to analyze data using SAS statistical software. SAS requires the user to enter a list of commands, or instructions, in a specific form. Three basic types of instructions are utilized, as follows:

1. *Data entry commands:* Instructions on how the data will be entered
2. *Input data values:* Values of the variables in the data set
3. *Statistical analysis commands:* Instructions on what type of analysis is to be conducted on the data

Note: With few exceptions, the SAS commands provided in this tutorial are appropriate for the large mainframe and PC versions of the software. When a mainframe computer is being used, however, these statements must be preceded by the job control language (JCL) command required at your institution.

D.2 Creating a SAS Data Set

In this section, we list the steps necessary to create a data set ready for analysis by SAS. This involves specifying **data entry commands** and **input data values**. (The appropriate statistical analysis commands are provided in the sections that follow.)

The data set of interest is listed in Table D.1. These are the sale price data for five residential properties extracted from Appendix I.

TABLE D.1 **Data for Five Properties Extracted from Appendix I**

OBSERVATION	SALE PRICE	LAND VALUE	IMPROVEMENTS	NEIGHBORHOOD
1	775,000	113,998	535,227	E
2	224,900	57,024	112,601	A
3	71,400	17,672	48,153	F
4	156,900	30,000	80,655	B
5	35,000	8,246	19,368	D

The SAS commands for creating this data set are given in Program D.1.

PROGRAM D.1 Creating a SAS data set

Command Line

```
DATA SALES;
INPUT SALEPRIC LANDVAL IMPROVAL NBRHOOD $;     }
TOTVAL = LANDVAL + IMPROVAL;                   }
RATIO = SALEPRIC/TOTVAL;                       } Data entry instructions
LOGPRIC = LOG(SALEPRIC);                       }
SQRTPRIC = SQRT(SALEPRIC);                     }
CARDS;
775000  113998  535227  E  }
224900   57024  112601  A  }
 71400   17672   48153  F  } Input data values
156900   30000   80655  B  } (1 observation per line)
 35000    8246   19368  D  }
PROC PRINT;    } Print instruction
```

COMMAND 1 SALES is an arbitrarily chosen name used to identify the data set. (Data set names are restricted to a maximum of eight characters.)

COMMAND 2 SALEPRIC, LANDVAL, IMPROVAL, and NBRHOOD are arbitrarily chosen names for the variables on the data set. (Variable names are also restricted to a maximum of eight characters.) A dollar sign ($) must follow the name of any nonnumeric variable on the data set.

COMMANDS 3–6 TOTVAL (total appraised value) is calculated as the sum of LANDVAL and IMPROVAL. RATIO is calculated as the ratio of sale price to total appraised value. (The standard arithmetic operations symbols, +, −, *, and /, are used for addition, subtraction, multiplication, and division, respectively.) In regression, two other important transformations are the natural logarithm and the square root transformations. The SAS functions LOG (line 5) and SQRT (line 6) perform these transformations.

COMMAND 7 CARDS signals SAS that the input data values are to follow.

COMMANDS 8–12 Each data line gives the value of the variables on the data set for a single observation (property) in the order in which the variables are listed in the INPUT command. Input data values must be separated by at least one blank space; commas are not permitted in numeric values.

COMMAND 13 The PRINT procedure (PROC) will produce a listing of the entire data set. In addition to the INPUT variables, the data set will contain any variables created using the standard arithmetic operations (e.g., TOTVAL, RATIO, LOGPRIC, and SQRTPRIC).

GENERAL All SAS commands must end with a semicolon; the only exceptions to this rule are the input data values.

D.3 Accessing an External Data File

Data created by other software and saved in an external file as an ASCII data set can also be accessed and analyzed by SAS. For example, the sales data of Table D.1 are extracted from a much larger data set containing sales information for 707 residential properties (see Appendix I). This data set is saved in an ASCII file called APPI.DAT on a 3½″ diskette available from the publisher. Program D.2 gives the appropriate SAS commands for reading the data on this external file.

PROGRAM D.2 Accessing the sales file of Appendix I

Command Line

```
DATA SALES;                                        }
INFILE 'A:\APPI.DAT';                              } Data entry instructions
INPUT NBRHOOD $ LANDVAL IMPROVAL SALEPRIC;         }
```

COMMAND 2 The INFILE statement in SAS is used to read external ASCII data files. The location and name of the file are specified in single quotes. The command shown in Program D.2 indicates that the APPI.DAT file is stored on a 3½″ diskette in drive A of a personal computer.

D.4 Relative Frequency Distributions, Descriptive Statistics, Correlations, and Plots

A preliminary analysis of the regression data may include examining relative frequency distributions and descriptive statistics (e.g., mean, median, and standard deviation) for both the dependent and independent variables, correlations between pairs of variables, and exploratory plots of the dependent variable against each of the independent variables. Consider a preliminary analysis of the data in Appendix J, where the dependent variable (y) is the sale price of a condominium unit (PRICPAID), the quantitative independent variables are floor height (FLOORHGT) and distance (in units) from the elevator (DISTELEV), and the qualitative independent variables are ocean/bay view (VIEWOCEN), furnished/not furnished (FURN), and end-unit/not end-unit (ENDUNT).

The necessary SAS commands for conducting a preliminary analysis of the data are given in Program D.3. The program will produce the following: (1) a relative frequency distribution for the dependent variable (sale price); (2) descriptive statistics for the quantitative variables (sale price, floor height, and distance from elevator); (3) tables of frequencies for the different levels of the independent qualitative variables (view, furnished, and end-unit); (4) pairwise correlations between all quantitative variables; and (5) plots of sale price (y) versus both quantitative independent variables (floor height and distance from elevator).

PROGRAM D.3 Preliminary analysis of the condominium data in Appendix J

Command Line		
1	`DATA CONDO;`	Data entry instructions
2	`INFILE 'A:\APPJ.DAT';`	
3	`INPUT PRICPAID FLOORHGT DISTELEV`	
	`      VIEWOCEN FURN ENDUNT;`	
4	`PROC CHART;`	Relative frequency histogram
5	`   VBAR PRICPAID/TYPE=PERCENT;`	
6	`PROC FREQ;`	Frequency tables
7	`   TABLES VIEWOCEN FURN ENDUNT;`	
8	`PROC UNIVARIATE;`	Descriptive statistics
9	`   VAR PRICPAID FLOORHGT DISTELEV;`	
10	`PROC CORR;`	Matrix of pairwise correlations
11	`VAR PRICPAID FLOORHGT DISTELEV;`	
12	`PROC PLOT;`	Plots of dependent versus independent variables
13	`PLOT PRICPAID*(FLOORHGT DISTELEV)=VIEWOCEN;`	

COMMAND 2 The INFILE statement is used to access the data stored on disk.

COMMANDS 4–5 The CHART procedure is used to generate relative frequency and frequency distributions (histograms) for quantitative data. The key word VBAR followed by the variable name PRICPAID produces a frequency histogram for the sale prices. Relative frequency histograms are produced by adding the option TYPE=PERCENT. SAS will automatically select suitable class intervals for the histogram.*

COMMANDS 6–7 The FREQ procedure generates frequency tables for the qualitative variables specified in the TABLES statement.

COMMANDS 8–9 The UNIVARIATE procedure generates descriptive statistics for the quantitative variables specified in the VAR statement.

COMMANDS 10–11 The CORR procedure computes the Pearson product moment correlation between all pairs of quantitative variables specified in the VAR statement. The two-tailed p-value for testing H_0: $\rho = 0$ is also produced.

COMMANDS 12–13 The PLOT procedure produces a scatterplot. The variable specified to the left of the asterisk (*) is plotted on the vertical (y) axis, whereas the variable specified to the right is plotted on the horizontal (x) axis. One plot is produced for each x variable specified. The option =VIEWOCEN generates scatterplots with the values of the qualitative variable VIEWOCEN (0 or 1) as plotting symbols.

D.5 Simple Linear Regression

The SAS commands and instructions given in Program D.4 generate the simple linear regression printouts for the fire damage data of Section 3.10.

PROGRAM D.4 Simple linear regression of fire damage data

Command Line

```
 1   DATA FIRE;      } Data entry instructions
 2   INPUT X Y;      }
 3   CARDS;
 4   3.4  26.2  }
 5   1.8  17.8  }
 .    .     .   } Input data values
 .    .     .   }
18   3.8  26.1  }
19   PROC REG;             }
20      MODEL Y = X/P CLI;  } Regression analysis/prediction intervals
21      ID X;              }
```

COMMAND 19 The REG procedure performs a complete simple linear regression analysis on the data.

---

*The MIDPOINTS option allows the user to select the class intervals. Consult the SAS references given at the end of this tutorial for details on how to use the MIDPOINTS option in PROC CHART.

COMMAND 20 In the MODEL statement, the dependent variable is listed to the left of the equals sign and the independent variable to the right. The option P (following the slash) prints predicted values and residuals, and the option CLI prints corresponding lower and upper 95% prediction limits for all observations in the data set. Specify CLM to obtain 95% confidence intervals for $E(y)$. [*Note:* To predict y for a value of x that is not included in the data set (e.g., $x = 3.5$), you must include an "extra" observation in the data set. This observation has the specified value of x (e.g., 3.5), but a missing value for y (i.e., a single decimal point).]

COMMAND 21 The optional ID statement identifies the value of x for each 95% prediction (or confidence) interval.

D.6 Multiple Regression

Program D.5 fits the multiple regression model

$$E(y) = \beta_0 + \beta_1 x_1 + \beta_2 x_2 + \beta_3 x_1 x_2 + \beta_4 x_1^2 + \beta_5 x_1^2 x_2$$

to data collected for a sample of residential properties in two neighborhoods of Appendix I, where

$$y = \text{Sale price of a property}$$

$$x_1 = \text{Total appraised value of property}$$

$$x_2 = \begin{cases} 1 & \text{if property located in neighborhood B} \\ 0 & \text{if not} \end{cases}$$

PROGRAM D.5 Multiple regression analysis of sale price

Command Line

```
1   DATA SALES;
2   INFILE 'A:\APPI.DAT';
3   INPUT NBRHOOD $ LANDVAL IMPROVAL SALEPRIC;   ⎫
4   X1 = LANDVAL + IMPROVAL;                     ⎪
5   IF NBRHOOD='B' THEN X2=1;                    ⎬ Data entry instructions
6      ELSE X2=0;                                ⎪
7   X1X2=X1*X2;                                  ⎭
8   X1SQ=X1*X1;
9   X1SQX2=X1*X1*X2;
10  PROC REG;                                    } Regression analysis
11    MODEL SALEPRIC = X1 X2 X1X2 X1SQ X1SQX2/P CLI;  } 95% prediction limits
12    INT_TEST: TEST X1X2, X1SQX2;     } Nested model F test of interaction
```

COMMANDS 5–6 A two-level dummy variable for neighborhood is created using IF, THEN, ELSE statements.

COMMANDS 7–9 Interactions and squared terms are created using the multiplication operator *.

COMMAND 10 The REG procedure fits general linear models in addition to simple linear regression models.

COMMAND 11 In the MODEL statement, the dependent variable is listed to the left of the equals sign and the independent variables to the right. The option P (following the slash) prints predicted values and residuals, and the option CLI prints corresponding lower and upper 95% prediction limits. Specify CLM to obtain 95% confidence intervals for $E(y)$.

COMMAND 12 The TEST statement will conduct a nested model partial F test on the model terms specified (e.g., X1X2 and X1SQX2). These terms must be separated by commas. An optional label (INT_TEST), followed by a colon, may be specified in front of the TEST statement.

D.7 Stepwise Regression

Recall that Appendix H contains data on fixed and competitive road construction contracts. Program D.6 gives the SAS commands that produced the stepwise regression on contract cost in Section 4.13.

PROGRAM D.6 Stepwise regression of road contract cost data

Command Line

```
1    DATA ROAD;                                          } Data entry instructions
2    INFILE 'A:\APPH.DAT';
3    INPUT COST DOTEST B2B1RAT B3B1RAT BHB1RAT
4          STATUS DISTRICT BTPRATIO DAYSEST;
5    PROC REG;                                           } Stepwise regression
6       MODEL COST = DOTEST B2B1RAT B3B1RAT BHB1RAT
7       STATUS DISTRICT BTPRATIO DAYSEST
8       /METHOD=STEPWISE SLE=.05 SLS=.05;
```

COMMANDS 5–8 The REG procedure with the /METHOD=STEPWISE option (line 8) performs a stepwise regression on the data.

COMMANDS 6–7 In the MODEL statement, the dependent variable is listed to the left of the equals sign and the independent variables to be analyzed to the right.

COMMAND 8 Other optional stepwise selection methods include FORWARD (forward selection), BACKWARD (backward selection), and RSQUARE (all-possible-regressions selection). The SLE option specifies the significance level α required for a variable to enter into the model. (The default SLE is .15.) The SLS option specifies the significance level α required for a variable to stay in the model. (The default SLS is .15.)

D.8 Residual Analysis and Regression Diagnostics

Refer again to the data in Appendix H. Consider the following model for contract cost (y):

$$E(y) = \beta_0 + \beta_1 x_1 + \beta_2 x_2 + \beta_3 x_3$$

where x_1 = DOTEST, x_2 = STATUS, and x_3 = DAYSEST. Program D.7 produces regression diagnostics and a residual analysis of the model.

PROGRAM D.7 Residual analysis and diagnostics

Command Line

```
 1   DATA ROAD;                                      }
 2   INFILE 'A:\APPH.DAT';                           } Data entry instructions
 3   INPUT COST DOTEST B2B1RAT B3B1RAT BHB1RAT       }
 4         STATUS DISTRICT BTPRATIO DAYSEST;         }
 5   PROC REG;                                   }
 6      MODEL COST = DOTEST STATUS DAYSEST       } Residuals, influence diagnostics,
 7      / R INFLUENCE PARTIAL VIF;               } partial residual plots, variance
 8   OUTPUT OUT=RESIDS P=YHAT R=RESID;           } inflation factors
 9   PROC PLOT;                           }
10      PLOT RESID*(YHAT DOTEST);         } Residual plots
11   PROC CHART;                         }
12      VBAR RESID/TYPE=PERCENT;         } Histogram of residuals
13   PROC UNIVARIATE PLOT NORMAL;         } Stem-and-leaf plot of residuals,
14      VAR RESID;                        } normal probability plot
```

COMMAND 7 The R option produces a list of residuals, predicted values, Studentized residuals, and Cook's D statistic for all observations in the regression analysis. The INFLUENCE option requests a detailed analysis of the influence of each observation on the β estimates. This includes leverage values and Studentized deleted residuals. The PARTIAL option generates a partial residual plot for each independent variable in the model. The VIF option produces variance inflation factors for the independent variables.

COMMAND 8 The residuals and predicted values from the regression are saved in the data set specified after OUT=.

COMMANDS 9–10 Two plots are produced: residuals versus predicted ($\hat{y}$) and residuals versus the quantitative dependent variable, DOTEST.

COMMANDS 11–12 The CHART procedure is used to produce a histogram for the regression residuals.

COMMANDS 13–14 The PLOT option of the UNIVARIATE procedure produces a stem-and-leaf plot for the specified variable, RESID. The NORMAL option produces a normal probability plot for the variable.

D.9 Logistic Regression

Program D.8 gives the SAS commands for conducting the logistic regression of contract bid status in Section 8.6. The data, in Table 8.5, contain the following variables:

$$y = \begin{cases} 1 & \text{if fixed bid} \\ 0 & \text{if competitive bid} \end{cases} \quad \text{(STATUS)}$$

x_1 = Number of bidders (NUMBIDS)

x_2 = Percent difference between bid and DOT estimate (DOTEST)

PROGRAM D.8 Logistic regression of bid data in Table 8.5

Command Line

```
 1   DATA BIDS;                                   }
 2   INPUT STATUS $ NUMBIDS DOTEST;               } Data entry instructions
 3   CARDS;                                       }
 4   FIX   4 19.2     }
 5   FIX   2 24.1     }
 6   COM   4 -7.1     } Input data values
 .   .  .     .       }
 .   .  .     .       }
34   COM 10   -8.4    }
35   PROC LOGISTIC;                               } Logistic regression
36      MODEL STATUS=NUMBIDS DOTEST;              }
37   OUTPUT OUT=RESULTS P=PRED L=CLLOWER U=CLUPPER;             } Predicted values,
38   PROC PRINT;                                                } 95% prediction limits
39      VAR NUMBIDS DOTEST STATUS PRED CLLOWER CLUPPER;         }
```

COMMAND 35 The LOGISTIC procedure fits a logit model.

COMMAND 36 The MODEL statement specifies the dependent variable to the left of the equals sign and the independent variables to the right. [*Note:* The categories of the dependent variable (e.g., FIX and COM) are ordered alphabetically or numerically; SAS chooses the category probability to be predicted for the first category in the ordered list. Thus, in this program, the model predicts the probability of a competitive (COM) contract.]

COMMAND 37 The OUTPUT statement specifies an output data set that will contain the predicted values and lower and upper 95% confidence limits.

COMMAND 38 The PRINT procedure prints the predicted values and confidence limits saved in the OUTPUT data set.

D.10 Time Series Forecasting Models and Durbin–Watson Test

Several of the forecasting techniques outlined in Chapter 9 can be performed in SAS. The exponential smoothing model, a regression model, and a time series autoregressive error model are applied to the quarterly power load time series of Table 9.1. in Program D.9. Moving averages can be computed using SAS programming commands. (Consult the references at the end of this tutorial.)

PROGRAM D.9 Time series analysis of quarterly power loads in Table 9.1

```
Command
  Line

 1    DATA POWER;        }
 2    INPUT T LOAD;      } Data entry instructions
 3    CARDS;             }
 4     1 103.5      }
 5     2  94.7      }
 .     .    .       } Input data values
 .     .    .       } (1 observation per line)
19    16 169.0      }
20    PROC FORECAST OUT=PRED METHOD=EXPO TREND=1   }
                    WEIGHT=.7 LEAD=1 OUTDATA;      } Exponential smoothing
21       VAR LOAD;                                 }
22       PROC PRINT;         }
23    PROC REG;              } Durbin–Watson test
24       MODEL LOAD = T/DW;  }
25    PROC AUTOREG;              }
26       MODEL LOAD = T/NLAG = 1; } AR(1) error model
```

COMMANDS 20–22 The FORECAST procedure with the METHOD=EXPO TREND=1 options produces exponentially smoothed forecasts of the time series variable specified in command 21. The LEAD option specifies how many time periods ahead (e.g., 1) are to be forecast. OUTDATA requests that the actual time series data be output in addition to the forecasted value(s).

COMMANDS 23–24 The Durbin–Watson *d* test is produced by specifying the DW option after the slash in the MODEL statement of the REG procedure.

COMMAND 25 The AUTOREG procedure in SAS fits time series models with autoregressive errors.

COMMAND 26 In the MODEL statement, specify the dependent variable to the left of the equals (=) sign and the independent variables in the deterministic portion of the model to the right. The option NLAG=1 following the slash (/) specifies a first-order autoregressive model for the random (correlated) error component.

D.11 Analysis of Variance

ANOVAs for a wide variety of designed experiments can be performed in SAS. The key to performing an ANOVA using SAS is identifying the source(s) of variation for the experiment, that is, treatments for completely randomized designs, treatments and blocks for randomized block designs, and main effects and factor interaction for factorial designs. The SAS commands for conducting the ANOVA for the factorial experiment of Example 11.12 are given in Program D.10. Here, we need to specify three sources of variation: (1) ratio of raw material allocation (main effect #1); (2) supply of raw material (main effect #2); and (3) ratio–supply interaction.

PROGRAM D.10 Factorial experiment (data in Example 11.11)

Command Line

```
1    DATA FACT;                                  } Data entry instructions
2    INPUT RATIO SUPPLY PROFIT;
3    CARDS;
4    .5  15  23                                  } Input data values
5    .5  15  20                                    (1 observation per line)
.     .   .   .
.     .   .   .
30    2  21  24
31   PROC ANOVA;                                 } Analysis of variance
32      CLASSES RATIO SUPPLY;
33      MODEL PROFIT=RATIO SUPPLY RATIO*SUPPLY;
34   MEANS RATIO SUPPLY/TUKEY ALPHA=.01 LINES;   } Multiple comparison of means
```

COMMAND 31 The ANOVA procedure performs an analysis of variance.

COMMAND 32 The CLASSES statement identifies the independent variables (factors) for the experiment. In SAS, factors can be either quantitative or qualitative variables.

COMMAND 33 The sources of variation are specified to the right of the equals sign (=) in the MODEL statement, the dependent (response) variable to the left. Interactions are specified by placing an asterisk (*) between the factors (e.g., RATIO*SUPPLY).

COMMAND 34 The MEANS command produces a multiple comparisons analysis of the means of the specified source(s). The TUKEY option selects Tukey's multiple comparisons procedure. (Specify BON for Bonferroni's and SCHEFFE for Scheffé's method.) The LINES option connects the means that are not significantly different. (If LINES is omitted, confidence intervals on the differences between all pairs of means for each specified factor are displayed.) The ALPHA option specifies the experimentwise error rate to be used. (The default is $\alpha = .05$.)

References

SAS Language Guide for Personal Computers, Version 6. Cary, N.C.: SAS Institute, Inc.

SAS Language and Procedures, Version 6. Cary, N.C.: SAS Institute, Inc.

SAS Procedures Guide for Personal Computers, Version 6. Cary, N.C.: SAS Institute, Inc.

SAS/STAT User's Guide, Version 6. Cary, N.C.: SAS Institute, Inc.

APPENDIX E SPSS Tutorial

CONTENTS

E.1 Introduction

This appendix is a brief tutorial on how to analyze data using SPSS statistical software. SPSS requires the user to enter a list of commands, or instructions, in a specific form. Three basic types of instructions are utilized, as follows:

1. *Data entry commands:* Instructions on how the data will be entered
2. *Input data values:* Values of the variables in the data set
3. *Statistical analysis commands:* Instructions on what type of analysis is to be conducted on the data

Note: With few exceptions, the SPSS commands provided in this tutorial are appropriate for the large mainframe and PC versions of the software. When a mainframe computer is being used, however, these statements must be preceded by the job control language (JCL) command required at your institution.

E.2 Creating an SPSS Data File

In this section, we list the steps necessary to create a data file ready for analysis by SPSS. This involves specifying **data entry commands** and **input data values**. (The appropriate statistical analysis commands are provided in the sections that follow.)

The data set of interest is listed in Table E.1. These are the sale price data for five residential properties extracted from Appendix I.

TABLE E.1 **Data for Five Properties Extracted from Appendix I**

OBSERVATION	SALE PRICE	LAND VALUE	IMPROVEMENTS	NEIGHBORHOOD
1	775,000	113,998	535,227	E
2	224,900	57,024	112,601	A
3	71,400	17,672	48,153	F
4	156,900	30,000	80,655	B
5	35,000	8,246	19,368	D

The SPSS commands for creating this data file are given in Program E.1.

PROGRAM E.1 Creating an SPSS data file

Command Line

```
DATA LIST FREE/SALEPRIC LANDVAL IMPROVAL NBRHOOD (A1).  }
COMPUTE TOTVAL = LANDVAL + IMPROVAL.                     }  Data entry
COMPUTE RATIO = SALEPRIC/TOTVAL.                         }  instructions
COMPUTE LOGPRIC = LN(SALEPRIC).                          }
COMPUTE SQRTPRIC = SQRT(SALEPRIC).                       }
BEGIN DATA.
775000  113998  535227  E  }
224900   57024  112601  A  }  Input data values
 71400   17672   48153  F  }  (1 observation per line)
156900   30000   80655  B  }
 35000    8246   19368  D  }
END DATA.
LIST.    } Print instruction
```

COMMAND 1 SALEPRIC, LANDVAL, IMPROVAL, and NBRHOOD are arbitrarily chosen names for the variables on the data set. (Variable names are also restricted to a maximum of eight characters.) An alphanumeric format of the form (A*n*) must be specified, in parentheses, after the name of any nonnumeric variable. For example, A1 specifies that the nonnumeric variable NBRHOOD will occupy one column on the input data lines.

COMMANDS 2–5 TOTVAL (total appraised value) is calculated as the sum of LANDVAL and IMPROVAL. RATIO is calculated as the ratio of sale price to total appraised value. (The standard arithmetic operation symbols, +, −, *, and /, are used for addition, subtraction, multiplication, and division, respectively.) In regression, two other important transformations are the natural logarithm and the square root transformations. The SPSS functions LN (line 4) and SQRT (line 5) perform these transformations.

COMMAND 6 BEGIN DATA signals SPSS that the input data values are to follow.

COMMANDS 7–11 Each data line gives the values of the variables on the data set for a single observation (property) in the order in which the variables are listed in the DATA LIST command. Values in the data list must be separated by at least one blank space; commas are not permitted in numeric values.

COMMAND 12 END DATA signals SPSS that all input data values have been entered.

COMMAND 13 The LIST command generates a listing of the data for all the variables on the data file, including the variables created using COMPUTE commands.

GENERAL In the PC environment, all SPSS commands must end with a command terminator (usually a period); the only exceptions to this rule are the input data values. Omit the periods when using mainframe SPSS.

E.3 Accessing an External Data File

Data created by other software and saved in an external file as an ASCII data set can also be accessed and analyzed by SPSS. For example, the sales data of Table E.1 are extracted from a much larger data set containing sales information for 707 residential properties (see Appendix I). This data set is saved in an ASCII file called APPI.DAT on a 3½″ diskette available from the publisher. Program E.2 gives the appropriate SPSS commands for reading the data on this external file.

PROGRAM E.2 Accessing the sales file of Appendix I

Command Line

```
1   DATA LIST FILE='A:\APPI.DAT' FREE                    } Data entry instructions
2      /NBRHOOD (A1) LANDVAL IMPROVAL SALEPRIC.          }
```

COMMAND 1 The FILE command in SPSS is used to read external ASCII data files. The location and name of the file are specified in single quotes. The command shown in Program E.2 indicates that the APPI.DAT file is stored in drive A of a personal computer.

E.4 Relative Frequency Distributions, Descriptive Statistics, Correlations, and Plots

A preliminary analysis of the regression data may include examining relative frequency distributions and descriptive statistics (e.g., mean, median, and standard deviation) for both the dependent and independent variables, correlations between pairs of variables, and exploratory plots of the dependent variable against each of the independent variables. Consider a preliminary analysis of the data in Appendix J, where the dependent variable (y) is the sale price of a condominium unit (PRICPAID), the quantitative independent variables are floor height (FLOORHGT) and distance (in units) from the elevator (DISTELEV), and the qualitative independent variables are ocean/bay view (VIEWOCEN), furnished/not furnished (FURN), and end-unit/not end-unit (ENDUNT).

The necessary SPSS commands for conducting a preliminary analysis of the data are given in Program E.3. The program will produce the following: (1) a relative frequency distribution for the dependent variable (sale price), (2) descriptive statistics for the quantitative variables (sale price, floor height, and distance from elevator), (3) tables of frequencies for the different levels of the independent qualitative variables (view, furnished, and end-unit), (4) pairwise correlations between all quantitative variables, and (5) plots of sale price (y) versus both quantitative independent variables (floor height and distance from elevator).

PROGRAM E.3 Preliminary analysis of the condominium data in Appendix J

Command Line

```
1   DATA LIST 'A:\APPJ.DAT' FREE                          }
2     /PRICPAID FLOORHGT DISTELEV                         } Data entry instructions
3     VIEWOCEN FURN ENDUNT.                               }
4   FREQUENCIES VARIABLES=PRICPAID/                       } Relative frequency histogram
5      HISTOGRAM=PERCENT.                                 }
6   FREQUENCIES VARIABLES=VIEWOCEN FURN ENDUNT.           } Frequency tables
7   EXAMINE VARIABLES=PRICPAID FLOORHGT DISTELEV/         } Descriptive statistics
8      STATISTICS=DESCRIPTIVE.                            }
9   CORRELATION VARIABLES=                                } Matrix of pairwise correlations
10     PRICPAID FLOORHGT DISTELEV.                        }
11  PLOT PLOT=PRICPAID WITH FLOORHGT DISTELEV BY VIEWOCEN.  } Plots
```

COMMAND 1 The location of the data stored on disk is specified in the DATA LIST command.

COMMANDS 4–5 The FREQUENCIES command is used to generate relative frequency and frequency distributions (histograms) for quantitative data. The subcommand HISTOGRAM will produce a frequency histogram for the quantitative variables (e.g., PRICPAID) specified in the VARIABLES subcommand. Relative frequency histograms are generated by adding the =PERCENT option to the HISTOGRAM subcommand. SPSS will automatically select suitable class intervals for the histogram.

COMMAND 6 The FREQUENCIES command also produces frequency tables for the qualitative variables specified in the VARIABLES subcommand.

COMMANDS 7–8 The EXAMINE command with the STATISTICS=DESCRIPTIVE subcommand produces descriptive statistics for the quantitative variables specified.

COMMANDS 9–10 The CORRELATION command computes the Pearson product moment correlation between all pairs of quantitative variables specified in the VARIABLES subcommand and gives the one-tailed p-value for testing H_0: $\rho = 0$.

COMMAND 11 Scatterplots are generated with the PLOT command. The first variable listed after PLOT= is plotted on the vertical axis (e.g., PRICPAID). The variables following WITH (e.g., FLOORHGT and DISTELEV) are plotted on the horizontal axis. The option BY VIEWOCEN produces scatterplots with the values of the qualitative ocean-view variable (0 or 1) as plotting symbols.

E.5 Simple Linear Regression

The SPSS commands and instructions given in Program E.4 generate the simple linear regression printouts for the fire damage data of Section 3.10.

PROGRAM E.4 Simple linear regression of fire damage data

Command Line

```
 1  DATA LIST FREE/ X Y.        } Data entry instructions
 2  BEGIN DATA.
 3  3.4  26.2   }
 4  1.8  17.8   }
 .   .     .    } Input data values
 .   .     .    }
17  3.8  26.1   }
18  END DATA.
19  REGRESSION VARIABLES=Y, X/  }
20      DEPENDENT=Y/            } Regression analysis
21      METHOD=ENTER X/         }
22      CASEWISE=ALL.     } Predicted values
```

COMMANDS 19–21 The REGRESSION command performs a complete simple linear regression analysis on the data. The dependent and independent variables are specified in the DEPENDENT and METHOD=ENTER subcommands, respectively.

COMMAND 22 The CASEWISE=ALL subcommand prints predicted values and residuals for all observations (cases) in the analysis.

E.6 Multiple Regression

Program E.5 fits the multiple regression model

$$E(y) = \beta_0 + \beta_1 x_1 + \beta_2 x_2 + \beta_3 x_1 x_2 + \beta_4 x_1^2 + \beta_5 x_1^2 x_2$$

to data collected for residential properties in two neighborhoods of Appendix I, where

y = Sale price of property

x_1 = Total appraised value of the property

$$x_2 = \begin{cases} 1 & \text{if property located in neighborhood B} \\ 0 & \text{if not} \end{cases}$$

PROGRAM E.5 Multiple regression analysis of sale price

Command Line

```
1   DATA LIST 'A:\APPI.DAT' FREE/                                   } Data entry instructions (lines 1-8)
2      NBRHOOD (A1) LANDVAL IMPROVAL SALEPRIC.
3   COMPUTE X1 = LANDVAL + IMPROVAL.
4   IF (NBRHOOD='B') X2=1.
5   IF (NBRHOOD NE 'B') X2=0.
6   COMPUTE X1X2=X1*X2.
7   COMPUTE X1SQ=X1*X1.
8   COMPUTE X1SQX2=X1*X1*X2.
9   REGRESSION VARIABLES=SALEPRIC X1 X2 X1X2 X1SQ X1SQX2/           } Regression analysis (lines 9-12)
10     CRITERIA=TOLERANCE(.00001)/
11     DEPENDENT=SALEPRIC/
12     METHOD=ENTER X1 X2 X1X2 X1SQ X1SQX2/
13     METHOD=TEST (X1X2 X1SQX2)/     } Nested model F test of interaction
14     STATISTICS=ALL/     } Confidence intervals for β's
15     CASEWISE=ALL.     } Predicted values
```

COMMANDS 4–5 A two-level dummy variable for neighborhood is created using IF commands.

COMMANDS 6–8 Interactions and squared terms are created using COMPUTE commands with the multiplication operator *.

COMMAND 9 The REGRESSION command fits general linear models. All variables analyzed, both dependent and independent, are listed on the VARIABLES subcommand.

COMMAND 10 A low tolerance level (.00001) is specified to guarantee that all the independent variables will be entered into the regression equation. (SPSS will omit an independent variable from the model if its tolerance is less than the level specified. Consult the references for more information on tolerance levels in regression.)

COMMAND 13 METHOD=TEST will conduct a nested model partial F test on the model terms specified in parentheses (e.g., the interaction terms, X1X2 and X1SQX2).

COMMAND 14 In addition to other optional statistics, STATISTICS=ALL will compute 95% confidence intervals for all the β parameters in the model.

E.7 Stepwise Regression

Recall that Appendix H contains data on fixed and competitive road construction contracts. Program E.6 gives the SPSS commands that produced the stepwise regression on contract cost in Section 4.13.

PROGRAM E.6 Stepwise regression of road contract cost data

Command Line

```
1  DATA LIST 'A:\APPH.DAT' FREE/                      }
2     COST DOTEST B2B1RAT B3B1RAT BHB1RAT             } Data entry instructions
3     STATUS DISTRICT BTPRATIO DAYSEST.               }
4  REGRESSION VARIABLES=ALL/                 }
5     CRITERIA=PIN(.05) POUT(.10)/           } Stepwise regression
6     DEPENDENT=COST/                        }
7     METHOD=STEPWISE.                       }
```

COMMANDS 4–7 The REGRESSION command with the METHOD=STEPWISE option (line 7) performs a stepwise regression on the data. Other optional stepwise selection methods include FORWARD (forward selection) and BACKWARD (backward selection).

COMMAND 5 The PIN option of the CRITERIA subcommand specifies the significance level α required for a variable to enter into the model. (The default SLE is .05.) The POUT option specifies the significance level α required for a variable to stay in the model. (The default is .10.)

E.8 Residual Analysis and Regression Diagnostics

Refer again to the data in Appendix H. Consider the following model for contract cost (y):

$$E(y) = \beta_0 + \beta_1 x_1 + \beta_2 x_2 + \beta_3 x_3$$

where x_1 = DOTEST, x_2 = STATUS, and x_3 = DAYSEST. Program E.7 produces regression diagnostics and a residual analysis of the model.

PROGRAM E.7 Residual analysis and diagnostics

Command Line

```
1   DATA LIST 'A:\APPH.DAT' FREE/                          }
2      COST DOTEST B2B1RAT B3B1RAT BHB1RAT                 } Data entry instructions
3      STATUS DISTRICT BTPRATIO DAYSEST.                   }
4   REGRESSION VARIABLES=COST DOTEST STATUS DAYSEST/       }
5      CRITERIA=TOLERANCE(.00001)/                         }
6      DEPENDENT=COST/                                     } Regression diagostics
7      METHOD=ENTER DOTEST STATUS DAYSEST/                 }
8      STATISTICS=ALL/   } Variance inflation factors
9      RESIDUALS/   } Residuals, stem-and-leaf plots, normality test
10     CASEWISE=DEFAULT ALL SRESID SDRESID COOK LEVER/   } Influence diagnostics
11     SCATTERPLOT=(*RESID,*PRED) (*RESID,DOTEST)/   } Residual plots
12     PARTIALPLOT.   } Partial residual plots
```

COMMAND 9 The RESIDUALS subcommand generates residuals for the regression. In addition, a histogram and normal probability plot of the standardized residuals, as well as a list of the 10 "worst" outliers, is produced.

COMMAND 10 The CASEWISE subcommand produces a list of the residuals and predicted values (DEFAULT) for all observations used in the analysis. As options, Studentized residuals (SRESID), Studentized deleted residuals (SDRESID), Cook's distances (COOK), and leverage values (LEVER) for all observations (ALL) can also be produced.

COMMAND 11 Two residual plots are produced: residuals versus predicted values ($\hat{y}$) and residuals versus the quantitative variable, DOTEST.

COMMAND 12 The PARTIALPLOT option generates a partial residual plot for each independent variable in the model.

E.9 Logistic Regression

Program E.8 on page 852 gives the SPSS commands for conducting the logistic regression of contract bid status in Section 8.6. The data, in Table 8.5, contains the following variables:

$$y = \begin{cases} 1 & \text{if fixed bid} \\ 0 & \text{if competitive bid} \end{cases} \quad \text{(STATUS)}$$

x_1 = Number of bidders (NUMBIDS)

x_2 = Percent difference between bid and DOT estimate (DOTEST)

PROGRAM E.8 Logistic regression of bid data in Table 8.5

```
Command
Line
 1   DATA LIST FREE/                                   } Data entry instructions
 2        STATUS NUMBIDS DOTEST.
 3   BEGIN DATA.
 4    1   4   19.2                                     } Input data values
 5    1   2   24.1
 6    0   4   -7.1
 .    .   .    .
 .    .   .    .
34    0  10   -8.4
35   END DATA.
36   LOGISTIC REGRESSION STATUS WITH NUMBIDS, DOTEST.  } Logit regression
```

COMMAND 36 The LOGISTIC REGRESSION command fits a logit model. The 0–1 dependent variable (STATUS) is specified before the WITH subcommand, whereas the independent variables are specified after WITH.

E.10 Analysis of Variance

ANOVAs for a wide variety of designed experiments can be performed in SPSS. The key to performing an ANOVA using SPSS is identifying the source(s) of variation for the experiment, i.e., treatments for completely randomized designs, treatments and blocks for randomized block designs, and main effects and factor interaction for factorial designs. The SPSS commands for conducting the ANOVA for the factorial experiment of Example 11.12 are given in Program E.9. Here, we need to specify three sources of variation: (1) ratio of raw material allocation (main effect #1); (2) supply of raw material (main effect #2); and (3) ratio–supply interaction.

PROGRAM E.9 Factorial experiment (data in Example 11.11)

```
DATA LIST FREE/                              } Data entry instructions
     RATIO SUPPLY PROFIT.
BEGIN DATA.
 1  1   23                                   } Input data values
 1  1   20                                     (1 observation per line)
 .  .   .
 .  .   .
 3  3  24
END DATA.
ANOVA PROFIT BY RATIO(1,3) SUPPLY(1,3).      } Analysis of variance
```

INPUT DATA VALUES All values of the factors (e.g., RATIO and SUPPLY) must be coded as numerical whole numbers (e.g., 1, 2, and 3 for treatment 1, treatment 2, and treatment 3, respectively).

COMMAND 32 The dependent (response) variable is listed to the left of BY in the ANOVA command, whereas the sources of variation are listed to the right. The range of coded values of the sources must be specified in parentheses after each source. To exclude interaction between the factors (as in a randomized block design), use the subcommand OPTIONS=3.

GENERAL Multiple comparisons are not available in the SPSS ANOVA procedure. However, multiple comparisons for a completely randomized design can be obtained by using the ONEWAY command:

```
ONEWAY PROFIT BY RATIO(1,3)/RANGES=TUKEY.
```

The keyword TUKEY performs Tukey's procedure. To perform Scheffe's and Bonferroni's tests, use the keywords SCHEFFE and MODLSD, respectively.

References

Norusis, M. M. *SPSS/PC+ 4.0 Base Manual*, SPSS, Inc.

Norusis, M. J. *SPSS/PC+ Statistics 4.0, SPSS, Inc.*

APPENDIX F MINITAB Tutorial

CONTENTS

F.1 Introduction

This appendix is a brief tutorial on how to analyze data using MINITAB statistical software. MINITAB requires the user to enter a list of commands, or instructions, in a specific form. Three basic types of instructions are utilized, as follows:

1. *Data entry commands:* Instructions on how the data will be entered
2. *Input data values:* Values of the variables in the data set
3. *Statistical analysis commands:* Instruction on what type of analysis is to be conducted on the data

Note: With few exceptions, the MINITAB commands provided in this tutorial are appropriate for the large mainframe and PC versions of the software. When a mainframe computer is being used, however, these statements must be preceded by the job control language (JCL) command required at your institution.

F.2 Creating a MINITAB Data Worksheet

In this section, we list the steps necessary to create a data set—called a worksheet in MINITAB—ready for analysis. This involves specifying **data entry commands** and **input data values**. (The appropriate statistical analysis commands are provided in subsequent sections.)

The data set of interest is listed in Table F.1. These are the sale price data for five residential properties extracted from Appendix I.

TABLE F.1 **Data for Five Properties Extracted from Appendix I**

OBSERVATION	SALE PRICE	LAND VALUE	IMPROVEMENTS	NEIGHBORHOOD
1	775,000	113,998	535,227	E
2	224,900	57,024	112,601	A
3	71,400	17,672	48,153	F
4	156,900	30,000	80,655	B
5	35,000	8,246	19,368	D

The MINITAB commands for creating this data worksheet are given in Program F.1.

PROGRAM F.1 Creating a MINITAB worksheet

Command Line

```
READ C1 C2 C3 C4 } Data entry instruction
775000  113998  535227  5 }
224900   57024  112601  1 }
 71400   17672   48153  6 }  Input data values
156900   30000   80655  2 }  (1 observation per line)
 35000    8246   19368  4 }
ADD C2 C3 PUT INTO C5         }
DIVIDE C1 BY C5 PUT INTO C6   }  Data entry instructions
LOGE C1 PUT INTO C7           }
SQRT C1 PUT INTO C8           }
NAME C1='SALEPRIC' C2='LANDVAL' C3='IMPROVAL' }
NAME C4='NBRHOOD' C5='TOTVAL' C6='RATIO'      }  Naming variables
NAME C7='LOGPRIC' C8='SQRTPRIC'               }
PRINT C1-C8   } Print instruction
STOP
```

COMMAND 1 The four variables to be read onto the MINITAB worksheet are identified by the columns into which they are placed, C1, C2, C3, and C4. (MINITAB does not, in general, recognize variable names.) Thus, sale price will be read in column 1, land value in column 2, etc.

COMMANDS 2–6 Each data line gives the values of the variables read in the worksheet columns for a single observation (property). Input data values must be separated by at least one blank space; commas are not permitted. MINITAB also requires that all data used in statistical analysis be numerical. Thus, the values of the nonnumeric variable neighborhood are converted to numbers in C4. (Arbitrarily, let 1 represent A, 2 represent B, etc.)

COMMANDS 7–10 MINITAB uses the word commands ADD, SUBTRACT, MULTIPLY, and DIVIDE to perform the usual arithmetic operations on variables. The sum of land value (C2) and improvements value (C3), that is, total appraised value, is stored in C5; the ratio of sale price (C1) to total appraised value (C5) is stored in C6. In regression, two other important transformations are the natural logarithm and the square root transformations. The MINITAB functions LOGE (line 9) and SQRT (line 10) perform these transformations.

COMMANDS 11–13 The NAME command is used to name the columns of the MINITAB worksheet for labeling printouts. In future commands, you may refer to the columns by these names (e.g., SALEPRIC) or by the column numbers (e.g., C1).

COMMAND 14 The PRINT command will produce a listing of the data in the MINITAB worksheet for the specified variables (columns).

COMMAND 15 All MINITAB programs terminate with the STOP command.

F.3 Accessing an External Data File

Data created by other software and saved in an external file as an ASCII data set can also be accessed and analyzed by MINITAB. For example, the sales data of Table F.1 are extracted from a much larger data set containing sales information for 707 residential properties (see Appendix I). This data set is saved in an ASCII file called APPI.NUM on a 3½″ diskette available from the publisher. Program F.2 gives the appropriate MINITAB commands for reading the data on this external file.

PROGRAM F.2 Accessing the sales file of Appendix I

Command Line

```
READ 'A:\APPI.NUM' C1 C2 C3 C4
NAME C1='NBRHOOD' C2='LANDVAL'
     C3='IMPROVAL' C4='SALEPRIC'
```

} **Data entry instructions**

COMMAND 1 The READ statement in MINITAB is used to read external ASCII data files. The location and name of the file are specified in single quotes. The READ command shown in Program F.2 indicates that the APPI.NUM file is stored on a 3½″ diskette in drive A of a personal computer.

F.4 Relative Frequency Distributions, Descriptive Statistics, Correlations, and Plots

A preliminary analysis of the regression data may include examining relative frequency distributions and descriptive statistics (e.g., mean, median, and standard deviation) for both the dependent and independent variables, correlations between pairs of variables, and exploratory plots of the dependent variable against each of the independent variables. Consider a preliminary analysis of the data in Appendix J, where the dependent variable (y) is the sale price of a condominium unit (PRICPAID), the quantitative independent variables are floor height (FLOORHGT) and distance (in units) from the elevator (DISTELEV), and the qualitative independent variables are ocean/bay view (VIEWOCEN), furnished/not furnished (FURN), and end-unit/not end-unit (ENDUNT).

The necessary MINITAB commands for conducting a preliminary analysis of the data are given in Program F.3. The program will produce the following: (1) a relative frequency distribution for the dependent variable (sale price), (2) descriptive statistics for the quantitative variables (sale price, floor height, and distance from elevator), (3) tables of frequencies for the different levels of the independent qualitative variables (view, furnished, and end-unit), (4) pairwise correlations between all quantitative variables, and (5) plots of sale price (y) versus both quantitative independent variables (floor height and distance from elevator).

PROGRAM F.3 Preliminary analysis of the condominium data in Appendix J

Command Line

```
1  READ 'A:\APPJ.DAT' C1-C6                              }
2  NAME C1='PRICPAID' C2='FLOORHGT' C3='DISTELEV'        } Data entry instructions
3  NAME C4='VIEWOCEN' C5='FURN' C6'ENDUNT'               }
4  HISTOGRAM C1        } Relative frequency histogram
5  TALLY C4 C5 C6      } Frequency tables
6  DESCRIBE C1 C2 C3   } Descriptive statistics
7  CORRELATION C1-C3   } Matrix of pairwise correlations
8  PLOT C1 VS. C2      } Plots of dependent versus
9  PLOT C1 VS. C3      } independent variables
```

COMMAND 1 The READ command is used to access the data stored on disk.

COMMAND 4 The HISTOGRAM command will generate horizontal frequency distributions (histograms) for quantitative data. MINITAB will automatically select suitable class intervals for the frequency histogram of the prices located in column 1 (C1).* To generate a relative frequency histogram, use the command HISTOGRAM=PERCENT.

*The optional commands INCREMENT and START allow the user to select the class intervals. Consult the references given at the end of this tutorial for details on how to use these HISTOGRAM options.

COMMAND 5 The TALLY command produces frequency tables for the qualitative variables in the specified columns.

COMMAND 6 The DESCRIBE command prints descriptive statistics (mean median, standard deviation, lower quartile, and upper quartile) for the quantitative variables in the specified columns.

COMMAND 7 The CORRELATION command computes the Pearson product moment correlation between all pairs of quantitative variables in the specified columns.

COMMANDS 8–9 A scatterplot of the data is generated with the PLOT command. The variable in the first column listed (C1) is plotted on the vertical axis, and the variable in the second column listed is plotted along the horizontal axis.

F.5 Simple Linear Regression

The MINITAB commands and instructions given in Program F.4 conduct a simple linear regression for the fire damage data of Section 3.10.

PROGRAM F.4 Simple linear regression of fire damage data

Command Line

```
 1   READ C1 C2       } Data entry instructions
 2   3.4   26.2  )
 3   1.8   17.8  |
 .    .     .    } Input data values
 .    .     .    |
16   3.8   26.1  )
17   NAME C1='X' C2='Y'                      }
18   REGRESS C2 ON 1 PREDICTOR IN C1;        } Simple linear regression
19      PREDICT 3.5.    } Prediction interval
```

COMMAND 18 The REGRESS procedure performs a complete linear regression analysis on the data. The column in which the dependent variable appears must be specified first (e.g., C2), followed by the number of predictors (independent variables) in the model (e.g., 1), and the column(s) in which the predictor(s) appears (e.g., C1).

COMMAND 19 PREDICT is a subcommand of the main REGRESS command that produces a 95% confidence interval for $E(y)$ and a 95% prediction interval for y for the value of the independent variable specified (e.g., 3.5).

F.6 Multiple Regression

Program F.5 fits the multiple regression model

$$E(y) = \beta_0 + \beta_1 x_1 + \beta_2 x_2 + \beta_3 x_1 x_2 + \beta_4 x_1^2 + \beta_5 x_1^2 x_2$$

to data collected for residential properties in two neighborhoods of Appendix I, where

$$y = \text{Sale price of a property}$$

$$x_1 = \text{Total appraised value of property}$$

$$x_2 = \begin{cases} 1 & \text{if property located in neighborhood B} \\ 0 & \text{if not} \end{cases}$$

PROGRAM F.5 Multiple regression analysis of sale price

Command Line

```
1   READ 'A:\APPI.NUM' C1-C4                           } Data entry instructions
2   NAME C1='NBRHOOD' C2='LANDVAL'
3   NAME C3='IMPROVAL' C4='SALEPRIC'
4   ADD C2 C3 PUT IN C5                                } Data transformations
5   CODE (2) TO 1, (1 3 4 5 6) TO 0, IN C1 PUT IN C6
6   NAME C5='X1' C6='X2'
7   LET C7=C5*C6
8   LET C8=C5*C5
9   LET C9=C5*C5*C6
10  NAME C7='X1X2' C8='X1SQ' C9='X1SQX2'
11  REGRESS C4 5 C5-C9, FITS IN C10                    } Regression analysis
12  NAME C10='PREDICT'
13  PRINT C5 C6 C10
```

COMMAND 5 A two-level dummy variable for neighborhood is created using the CODE command. Since neighborhood B in C1 is coded on the data file as 2, all values of 2 (specified in parentheses) are changed to 1. The remaining values of neighborhood (1, 3, 4, 5, and 6) are coded as 0. These coded values are stored in C6.

COMMANDS 7–9 Interactions and squared terms are created using the LET command with the multiplication operator *.

COMMAND 11 The REGRESS command fits general linear models. The column number (C4) of the dependent variable is listed first, followed by the number of predictors in the model (5) and the columns where the independent variables are located (C5–C9). Predicted values are saved in the last column (C10) specified.

F.7 Stepwise Regression

Recall that Appendix H contains data on fixed and competitive road construction contracts. Program F.6 on page 860 gives the MINITAB commands for conducting the stepwise regression on contract cost in Section 4.13.

PROGRAM F.6 Stepwise regression of road contract cost data

Command Line

```
1   READ 'A:\APPH.DAT' C1-C9
2   NAME C1='COST' C2='DOTEST' C3='B2B1RAT'
3   NAME C4='B3B1RAT' C5='BHB1RAT' C6='STATUS'
4   NAME C7='DISTRICT' C8='BTPRATIO' C9='DAYSEST'
5   STEPWISE C1, PREDICTORS IN C2-C9;
6       FENTER=4  FREMOVE=4.
```

Data entry instructions (lines 1–4)

Stepwise regression (lines 5–6)

COMMAND 5 The STEPWISE command is used for stepwise regression. The column containing the dependent variable (e.g., C1) is listed first, followed by the columns containing the independent variables (e.g., C2–C9).

COMMAND 6 To enter into the model, an independent variable's F value must exceed the value specified on the FENTER subcommand. (The default FENTER is 4.) Once entered, a variable is removed from the model if its F value is less than the value specified on the FREMOVE subcommand. (The default FREMOVE is 4.) For forward stepwise selection, select FREMOVE=0; for backward stepwise selection, use the subcommand FORWARD=100000, ENTER C2–C9.

GENERAL To perform all-possible-regressions selection with the max-R^2 criterion, use the command BREG C1, ON PREDICTORS IN C2–C9.

F.8 Residual Analysis and Regression Diagnostics

Refer again to the data in Appendix H. Consider the following model for contract cost (y):

$$E(y) = \beta_0 + \beta_1 x_1 + \beta_2 x_2 + \beta_3 x_3$$

where x_1 = DOTEST, x_2 = STATUS, and x_3 = DAYSEST. Program F.7 produces regression diagnostics and a residual analysis of the model.

COMMAND 5 Predicted values are saved in the column (e.g., C10) that follows the independent variable columns on the REGRESS command.

COMMAND 6 The RESIDUALS subcommand stores residuals in the assigned column (C11) for purposes of plotting.

COMMAND 7 The HI subcommand stores leverage values in the assigned column (C12) for purposes of printing.

COMMAND 8 The TRESIDUALS subcommand stores Studentized residuals in the assigned column (C13) for purposes of printing.

COMMAND 9 The COOKD subcommand stores Cook's distances in the assigned column (C14) for purposes of printing.

PROGRAM F.7 Residual analysis and diagnostics cost data

Command Line

```
1   READ 'A:\APPH.DAT' C1-C9                                   ⎫
2   NAME C1='COST' C2='DOTEST' C3='B2B1RAT'                    ⎬ Data entry instructions
3   NAME C4='B3B1RAT' C5='BHB1RAT' C6='STATUS'                 ⎪
4   NAME C7='DISTRICT' C8='BTPRATIO' C9='DAYSEST'              ⎭
5   REGRESS C1 3 C2 C6 C9, FITS IN C10;
6      RESIDUALS C11;     } Residuals
7      HI C12;     } Leverage values
8      TRESIDUALS C13;     } Studentized residuals
9      COOKD C14;     } Cook's distances
10     VIF.     } Variable inflation factors
11  NAME C10='PREDICT' C11='RESID' C12='LEVERAGE'              ⎫ Naming variables
12  NAME C12='STUDRES' C13='COOKDIST'                          ⎭
13  PLOT C11 VS. C10  ⎫ Residual plots
14  PLOT C11 VS. C2   ⎭
15  STEM-AND-LEAF C11     } Stem-and-leaf display of residuals
16  NSCORES C11 C14
17  NAME C14='NORMRES'
18  PLOT C11 C14     } Normal probability plot
19  PRINT C12 C13 C14     } Print influence diagnostics
```

COMMAND 10 The VIF subcommand produces variance inflation factors on the regression printout.

COMMANDS 13–14 Two residual plots are produced: residuals versus predicted values ($\hat{y}$) and residuals versus DOTEST.

COMMAND 15 A stem-and-leaf display of the residuals is produced.

COMMANDS 16–18 "Normal scores" for the residuals in C11 are created by the NSCORES command (command 16). These normal scores (saved in C14) are the standard expected values of the data points, assuming the data are normally distributed. The PLOT command (command 18) produces the normal probability plot by plotting the actual residuals on the vertical axis and the normal scores on the horizontal axis.

F.9 Time Series Smoothing Methods and Durbin–Watson Test

Two methods for smoothing a time series, moving averages and exponential smoothing, are available in MINITAB. Also, MINITAB can perform the Durbin–Watson d test for correlated error. Program F.8 on page 862 provides the commands for performing these analyses on the quarterly power load data of Table 9.1.

COMMANDS 19–20 Moving averages are produced in the form of a control chart with the MACHART command. The variable in the column that is to be averaged is listed first (e.g., C2), followed by the column that represents the different time periods (e.g., C1). The SPAN option specifies the number of time series values to be averaged (i.e., the number of "points").

PROGRAM F.8

Command Line

```
1   READ C1 C2 } Data entry instruction
2    1  103.5 )
3    2   94.7 |
.    .     .  | Input data values
.    .     .  | (1 observation per line)
17  16  169.0 )
18  NAME C1='T' C2='LOAD'
19  MACHART C2 C1;  }
20     SPAN=4.      } 4-point moving average
21  EWMACHART C2 C1; }
22     WEIGHT=.7.    } Exponential smoothing
23  REGRESS C2 1 C1; }
24     DW.           } Durbin–Watson test
```

COMMANDS 21–22 Exponentially smoothed values of a time series are produced in the form of a control chart with the EWMACHART command. The variable in the column that is to be averaged is listed first (e.g., C2), followed by the column that represents the different time periods (e.g., C1). The smoothing constant *w* is specified on the WEIGHT command.

COMMANDS 23–24 The Durbin–Watson *d* test is performed by using the DW option of the REGRESS command.

F.10 Analysis of Variance

ANOVAs for a wide variety of designed experiments can be performed in MINITAB. The key to performing an ANOVA is identifying the source(s) of variation for the experiment, i.e., treatments for completely randomized designs, treatments and blocks for randomized block designs, and main effects and factor interaction for factorial designs. The MINITAB commands for conducting the ANOVA for the factorial experiment of Example 11.12 are given in Program F.9. Here, we need to specify three sources of variation: (1) ratio of raw material allocation (main effect #1), (2) supply of raw material (main effect #2), and (3) ratio–supply interaction.

PROGRAM F.9 Factorial experiment (data in Example 11.11)

Command Line

```
READ C1 C2 C3                                    }
NAME C1='RATIO' C2='SUPPLY' C3='PROFIT'          } Data entry instructions
 1  1   23 )
 1  1   20 |
 .  .   .  | Input data values
 .  .   .  | (1 observation per line)
 3  3   24 )
ANOVA C3 = C1 C2 C1*C2;    } Analysis of variance
   MEANS C1 C2.    } Factor means
```

INPUT DATA VALUES All values of the factors (e.g., RATIO and SUPPLY) must be coded as numerical whole numbers (e.g., 1, 2, and 3 for treatment 1, treatment 2, and treatment 3, respectively).

COMMAND 30 The ANOVA command performs an analysis of variance for balanced experimental designs. (For unbalanced data, replace ANOVA with GLM.) The column containing the response variable (C3) is given to the left of the equals sign and the sources of variation are listed to the right. For this factorial design, the columns containing the two factors (C1 and C2) are specified. Interactions are specified by including an asterisk between the factors that are interacted (e.g., C1*C2).

COMMAND 31 The MEANS command prints factor means and associated 95% confidence intervals for each factor column listed. (*Note:* Multiple comparisons analysis of the means is not available in MINITAB.)

References

MINITAB Primer: An Introduction to MINITAB Statistical Software, State College, Penn.: Minitab, Inc., 1986.

MINITAB Reference Manual, Release 8. State College, Penn.: Minitab, Inc., 1989.

MINITAB User Guide, DOS Microcomputer Version, Release 7. State College, Penn.: Minitab, Inc., 1989.

Ryan, B. F., Joiner, B. L., and Ryan, T. A. *Minitab Handbook*, 2nd ed. Boston: PWS-Kent, 1990 (revised printing).

APPENDIX G ASP Tutorial

CONTENTS

G.1 Introduction

This appendix provides an overview of the ASP program. It gives the minimal hardware requirements and start-up procedures necessary to begin an ASP session on a personal computer (PC). This tutorial is not intended to replace any of the ASP documentation manuals available from the publisher or DMC Software, Inc.

G.2 Hardware Requirements

ASP must be run on an IBM-compatible PC with at least 512K of memory, two disk drives (either one hard drive and one floppy drive, or two floppy drives), and DOS 2.0 or higher. A blank formatted floppy disk is also required for data storage, unless your PC has a hard drive (i.e., fixed disk) available for storing data.

G.3 Getting Started

To use the ASP program, first load it into the memory of the computer. Follow these steps to start ASP from a floppy disk:

1. Insert your copy of ASP into either of your two disk drives, drive A or drive B. (Assume drive A.)
2. Type A: and press ENTER to make drive A the current drive:

```
A: <ENTER>
```

3. Type ASP and press ENTER to load the ASP program into memory:

```
ASP <ENTER>
```

The ASP disk must remain in drive A for as long as you are using the program

To start ASP from a fixed disk or hard drive (e.g., drive C), first install ASP on the fixed disk. Place your copy of the ASP disk into drive A, and enter the following commands at the DOS prompt:

```
C:            <ENTER>
MD \ASP       <ENTER>
CD \ASP       <ENTER>
COPY A:*.*    <ENTER>
```

(In this sequence of DOS commands, we assume that the drive letter of the fixed disk is C and that the subdirectory in which the ASP program resides is \ASP.) Once ASP has been installed on the fixed disk, it need not be installed again. The ASP program can then be started at any point in the future by entering the following commands at the DOS prompt:

```
C:            <ENTER>
CD \ASP       <ENTER>
ASP           <ENTER>
```

G.4 The Main Menu

The initial screen displays copyright and licensing information. After reading this information, press any key to obtain the MAIN MENU shown in Figure G.1.

FIGURE G.1 The ASP MAIN MENU

```
                 **************** MAIN MENU ****************

  A Statistical Package for Business, Economics, and The Social Sciences
           Copyright 1994 by DMC Software, Inc.   (Version 2.60)
=============================================================================
  A. Analysis of Variance     B. Regression Analysis    C. Correlation Matrix
  D. Summary Statistics       E. Probability Dists.     F. File Management Menu
  G. Time Series Analysis     H. Hypothesis Tests       I. INSTRUCTIONS
  J. Factor Analysis          K. Miscellaneous Plots    L. Crosstab/Contingency
  M. Auxiliary Programs       N. Enter a DOS Command    O. Scr./Data Dir. Dflts
=============================================================================
 F1 = ALT COMMANDS MENU   F2 = CALCULATOR   F3 = TOGGLE PRINT (OFF)   X = EXIT
```

The MAIN MENU is a typical ASP "bounce bar" menu. The highlighted bar can be moved from option to option by pressing the SPACE BAR, the cursor control keys (→ ← ↑ ↓), or the TAB key. Once your selection is made, press ENTER to display submenus associated with the option. (You can also make a selection by pressing the letter of the desired option.)

Table G.1 gives a brief description of each of the MAIN MENU options together with the corresponding chapters in this text. Several of these options contain statistical procedures that are beyond the scope of this text. Only the statistical routines that we have covered are described in the table.

G.5 Alternate Commands Menu

All of the statistical routines in ASP are accessible through the MAIN MENU. However, additional commands can be executed through the ALT COMMANDS MENU. The ALT COMMANDS MENU is called by pressing the F1 function key anytime within the ASP program. When F1 is pressed from the MAIN MENU, the ALT COMMANDS MENU appears as shown in Figure G.2 on page 868.

TABLE G.1 **Options on the Main Menu**

OPTION	DESCRIPTION	CHAPTER(S)
A. Analysis of Variance	ANOVA for designed experiments	10, 11
B. Regression Analysis	Simple and multiple regression; residual analysis; stepwise regression	3–7
C. Correlation Matrix	Bivariate correlations	3
D. Summary Statistics	Mean, median, st. dev., etc.	1
E. Probability Dists.	Binomial, normal, etc.	1
F. File Management Menu	Creating, saving, editing data	—
G. Time Series Analysis	Moving averages, exponential smoothing, simple linear forecasts	9
H. Hypothesis Tests	Confidence intervals and hypothesis tests for means, proportions, and variances; one-way table χ^2 test; nonparametric tests	1
I. INSTRUCTIONS	A short tutorial on the use of ASP	—
J. Factor Analysis	(Beyond the scope of this text)	—
K. Miscellaneous Plots	Stem-and-leaf display, boxplot, normal probability plot, scatterplot	1, 3
L. Crosstab/Contingency	(Beyond the scope of this text)	—
M. Auxiliary Programs	(Beyond the scope of this text)	—
N. Enter a DOS Command	Enter and execute DOS commands within an ASP session	—
O. Scr./Data Dir. Dflts.	Set the color scheme on the monitor; set the default directory and printer port	—

You can execute the commands on the ALT COMMANDS MENU either by moving the cursor to the desired option and pressing ENTER or by pressing the letter associated with the option. You will find this menu most useful for

Editing or creating data sets (option E)

Listing data (option L)

Getting data from an existing ASP data set (option G)

Creating new variables for a data set (option T)

Adding or deleting variables and/or cases (option A)

Changing the names of variables (option I)

Getting or saving data in an external ASCII file (option B)

Saving an ASP data set (option S)

FIGURE G.2 The ALT COMMANDS MENU

```
       *  E = Edit Or Create Data Matrix                      **
   A Statistical  G = Get Data Matrix From ASP File          ocial Sciences
            Copy  S = Save Data Matrix In ASP File           2.60)
                  L = List Data Matrix
                  Q = Sort Or Transpose Data Matrix
 A. Analysis of V R = Recode Variable                        relation Matrix
 D. Summary Stati M = Change Missing Value Code              e Management Menu
 G. Time Series A J = Combine Or Break Down Variables        TRUCTIONS
 J. Factor Analys I = Change Names/Labels/Cases/Vars.        sstab/Contingency
 M. Auxiliary Pro A = Add Or Delete Variable Or Case         ./Data Dir. Dflts
                  B = Get Or Save ASCII File
F1 = ALT COMMANDS N = Enter A DOS Command                     T (OFF)    X = EXIT
                  T = Variable Transformation Menu
                  F = File Management Menu
                  V = View/Rename/Delete OUTPUT File
                  D = Summary Statistics
                  H = Hypothesis Tests Menu
                  P = Probability Distributions Menu
                  K = Miscellaneous Plots Menu
                  C = Change No. Of Digits In Display
                  O = Scr./Data Dir./Prt. Port Dflts.
```

G.6 Creating a Data Matrix

Typically, you will use ASP to analyze a data set. To do this, you must first create an ASP "data matrix." Select E = Edit Or Create Data Matrix on the ALT COMMANDS MENU and ASP responds with a series of questions and prompts. The first question is

```
EDIT or CREATE?   E
```

Note that the ASP default answer is E for EDIT. This is used when you want to edit an existing ASP data matrix. To create a data matrix, press the letter C (for CREATE). You are now prompted with the question:

```
Number of Variables?    1
```

Change the default to the correct number and press ENTER. ASP creates names for the variables using the convention Var1, Var2, Var3, etc., then asks

```
Are Names OK?   Y
```

To change the names, Press N (for No). ASP will then ask you to enter the new name of each variable. Once this is completed, ASP will prompt you, one case (i.e., one observation) and one variable at a time, to enter the data into the data matrix. **The ASP data editor will not accept letters or special characters (e.g.,**

dollar sign, comma) as data. Only whole numbers or numbers with decimals should be entered into the data matrix.

When data entry is complete, press X to exit the numerical data editor. Several questions will be asked, the most important being

```
Do You Wish to Save the Data Matrix?    Y
```

Answer "yes" by pressing ENTER. ASP will then ask for the drive letter (e.g., drive A) and directory of the disk where you want to save the data:

```
DATA DIRECTORY:     A:\
```

If the default is correct, press ENTER. Otherwise, enter the correct drive/path. You will be asked to name the ASP data file, to provide a file label (optional), and whether you want to save all variables and all cases.

Suppose you enter the following file name:

```
File Name:    MYDATA
```

ASP will save your data matrix in the ASP file named MYDATA.ASP in the directory specified previously. In future ASP sessions, you can access this data set by first selecting the option G = Get Data Matrix From ASP File from the ALT COMMANDS MENU, and then selecting MYDATA from the resulting list of ASP data files.

G.7 Accessing an External Data File

To access an external (ASCII) data file on hard or floppy disk, select B = Get Or Save ASCII File from the ALT COMMANDS MENU and specify G (for Get). ASP will initially ask for the location of the file (e.g., C:\DATA) and then for the data file name (e.g., APPJ.DAT). Next, specify the number of variables on the data set (e.g., 8). Finally, if you wish, change the ASP assigned names of the variables. Save the newly created data matrix (as outlined in Section G.6). Your data are now ready for analysis.

G.8 Analyzing a Data Matrix

To analyze an ASP data matrix that you have just created or accessed, return to the MAIN MENU by pressing X or ESC. From the MAIN MENU, select the desired statistical routine. Each choice will result in a series of submenus, prompts, and/or questions similar to those shown previously. After making your selections, ASP will perform the analysis and display the results immediately on the monitor screen. ASP menu selections at the bottom of the screen permit you to send the output directly to a printer or to save the output in a file for future use.

G.9 Available Documentation

ASP User's Manual (by DMC Software, Inc.) is available free to adopters of the text from the publisher of the text, Prentice-Hall Publishing Company.

ASP Tutorial and Student Guide (by George Blackford) can be purchased directly from DMC Software, Inc., or from your campus bookstore.

APPENDIX H

Data Set: Sealed Bid Data for Fixed and Competitive Highway Construction Contracts (See Section 4.13)

Note: The data set is available on a 3½″ diskette from the publisher.

OBS	COST	DOTEST	B2B1RAT	B3B1RAT	BHB1RAT	STATUS	DISTRICT	BTPRATIO	DAYSEST
1	1379.43	1386.29	1.01397	1.03303	1.06121	1	0	0.33333	250
2	134.03	85.71	1.00995	1.01092	1.01092	1	1	0.75000	45
3	202.33	248.89	1.12084	1.22498	1.30546	0	0	0.50000	120
4	397.12	467.49	1.00588	1.11035	1.26733	0	0	0.50000	180
5	158.54	117.72	1.01053	1.10247	1.10247	1	0	0.37500	80
6	1128.11	1008.91	1.06208	1.09137	1.09137	1	0	0.60000	200
7	400.33	472.98	1.10275	1.13560	1.13560	1	1	0.60000	70
8	581.64	785.39	1.09346	1.16794	1.33349	0	0	0.50000	200
9	353.96	370.02	1.05063	1.28312	1.47836	0	1	0.57143	75
10	138.71	174.25	1.07047	1.19279	1.27559	0	0	0.83333	70
11	383.66	410.95	1.07508	1.13970	1.13970	1	1	0.42857	60
12	3910.94	3405.94	1.02768	1.04733	1.07683	1	1	0.45455	350
13	362.92	385.96	1.01691	1.04658	1.04658	0	1	0.37500	100
14	196.50	235.41	1.16398	1.19491	1.62532	0	0	0.70000	120
15	637.99	627.41	1.07043	1.16355	1.58125	0	0	0.50000	140
16	152.06	175.40	1.07504	1.24451	1.24451	1	1	0.50000	75
17	375.00	432.33	1.05025	1.20642	1.30949	0	0	0.57143	120
18	2284.56	1499.04	1.01600	1.20033	1.20033	1	0	0.60000	270
19	551.45	497.74	1.06668	1.10932	1.10932	1	1	0.60000	100
20	239.67	194.65	1.02302	1.21276	1.21276	1	1	0.60000	65
21	207.87	167.99	1.05143	1.08977	1.15240	1	1	0.66667	60
22	640.48	767.80	1.06059	1.08447	1.27066	0	0	0.40000	90
23	230.54	260.30	1.11029	1.12570	1.12570	1	1	0.42857	125
24	299.87	247.04	1.08411	1.10180	1.10180	1	1	0.60000	80
25	2368.84	2456.77	1.17209	1.18020	1.48550	0	0	0.30769	320
26	496.49	879.40	1.00453	1.17145	1.38498	0	0	0.58333	140
27	1564.87	1303.40	1.00374	1.04983	1.04983	1	0	0.33333	200
28	7387.03	6107.93	1.01878	1.05413	1.05718	0	1	0.66667	340
29	195.68	199.09	1.04290	1.27466	1.27466	0	1	0.60000	50
30	830.47	715.46	1.01755	1.02450	1.08833	1	0	0.57143	135
31	179.06	208.72	1.02474	1.03067	1.60580	0	1	0.62500	90
32	150.35	199.09	1.00893	1.06483	1.55218	0	0	0.63636	100
33	240.06	429.24	1.10055	1.16394	1.72898	0	0	0.71429	120
34	586.81	709.85	1.01241	1.08838	1.38652	0	0	0.60000	120
35	537.17	676.41	1.03962	1.06037	1.25739	0	0	0.72727	225
36	392.69	490.55	1.07153	1.12770	1.64803	0	1	0.50000	180
37	216.47	406.47	1.05636	1.13153	1.57543	0	1	0.82353	130
38	1559.37	1925.31	1.07850	1.08130	1.60339	0	1	0.47619	250
39	88.31	143.07	1.09813	1.26329	1.50073	0	0	0.71429	55

OBS	COST	DOTEST	B2B1RAT	B3B1RAT	BHB1RAT	STATUS	DISTRICT	BTPRATIO	DAYSEST
40	268.45	308.09	1.14764	1.17190	1.32518	0	1	0.66667	75
41	189.02	269.55	1.00993	1.14649	1.95409	0	0	0.85714	115
42	192.81	227.70	1.04378	1.15395	1.45160	0	1	0.83333	60
43	256.22	436.79	1.00000	1.09973	1.89401	0	0	0.88235	125
44	113.61	132.39	1.01195	1.01307	1.60670	0	0	0.69231	70
45	124.99	121.61	1.00000	1.11019	1.26999	0	0	0.57143	40
46	116.57	114.21	1.00000	1.21566	1.91806	0	0	0.57143	35
47	143.13	172.71	1.08608	1.13900	1.38149	0	0	0.60000	50
48	36.19	64.44	1.25303	1.31504	1.49919	0	1	0.62500	60
49	2518.39	3124.39	1.02196	1.04278	1.31920	0	0	0.57143	255
50	1353.51	1617.53	1.12729	1.22658	1.40600	0	1	0.41176	200
51	332.82	376.37	1.00024	1.05449	1.53705	0	0	0.61538	140
52	202.50	300.32	1.18810	1.23180	1.92381	0	0	0.41667	100
53	6043.31	7074.99	1.02471	1.02528	1.22949	0	0	0.57895	350
54	2280.81	2823.87	1.08084	1.09406	1.39083	0	0	0.53333	330
55	99.92	118.99	1.16879	1.29648	1.58897	1	0	0.55556	70
56	1461.59	1774.72	1.01678	1.16689	1.54772	0	1	0.57143	220
57	1217.57	1341.08	1.01074	1.01149	1.39080	0	0	0.91667	350
58	258.44	306.44	1.00453	1.01727	1.25857	0	0	0.70000	75
59	115.42	117.94	1.06379	1.09767	1.44878	0	1	0.85714	65
60	463.93	540.01	1.07317	1.10858	1.35774	0	1	0.62500	120
61	728.86	763.02	1.02446	1.03732	1.44687	0	0	0.73333	200
62	3929.92	3941.57	1.00506	1.06041	1.23232	0	0	0.66667	400
63	181.69	194.82	1.08679	1.16042	1.37565	0	1	0.62500	60
64	479.47	487.17	1.00000	1.04831	1.35510	0	0	0.53333	140
65	93.48	92.36	1.00468	1.02595	1.19858	0	0	0.83333	60
66	2301.07	2505.60	1.06746	1.09047	1.38057	0	0	0.77778	400
67	136.06	181.09	1.13520	1.23219	1.23219	0	1	0.33333	100
68	144.06	252.92	1.30227	1.30894	1.71178	0	1	0.66667	90
69	65.17	84.75	1.20310	1.36565	1.96397	0	0	0.53846	60
70	161.33	164.03	1.07334	1.09596	1.47418	0	1	0.80000	100
71	1138.54	1254.62	1.00892	1.03438	1.37670	0	0	0.68421	200
72	84.79	97.63	1.05202	1.10115	1.36417	0	0	0.60000	50
73	749.13	859.34	1.00000	1.04832	1.49429	0	0	0.92857	180
74	43.67	41.09	1.00048	1.21624	1.33987	0	1	0.80000	30
75	2920.71	2812.50	1.05215	1.11637	1.22283	0	0	0.50000	315
76	32.63	40.05	1.06642	1.25626	2.08540	0	0	0.70000	35
77	1115.12	1148.53	1.00244	1.08541	1.45950	0	0	0.64286	250
78	50.66	59.86	1.29181	1.63089	2.39326	0	0	0.57143	50
79	2229.34	2434.60	1.00386	1.09355	1.21600	0	0	0.46154	450
80	2159.85	2698.59	1.00454	1.05874	1.32056	0	0	0.50000	360
81	45.91	61.89	1.14934	1.51780	2.10760	0	1	0.57143	60
82	127.31	137.52	1.07749	1.11993	1.38302	0	0	0.66667	30
83	147.81	143.34	1.00567	1.16406	1.16406	1	0	0.60000	30
84	470.71	447.75	1.00000	1.01164	1.37056	0	0	0.57143	150
85	188.67	202.46	1.00000	1.09388	1.69629	0	0	0.53846	120
86	4765.17	5035.94	1.00785	1.04760	1.27208	0	0	0.52381	300
87	168.53	163.67	1.05127	1.08435	1.30180	0	0	0.80000	30
88	95.86	95.63	1.06483	1.09471	1.40106	0	0	0.80000	30
89	106.92	107.89	1.03253	1.07409	1.28517	0	0	0.70000	30
90	698.48	646.43	1.01875	1.10615	1.64604	0	0	0.58333	180
91	796.00	969.69	1.14418	1.16051	1.28223	0	0	0.63636	175
92	689.73	801.61	1.06850	1.14537	1.27266	0	0	0.38462	210
93	831.84	906.84	1.00519	1.03516	1.22892	0	1	0.64286	190
94	2150.15	2161.37	1.04553	1.06808	1.29205	0	0	0.62500	400
95	169.75	187.32	1.11882	1.19117	1.19117	0	0	0.75000	100
96	923.58	887.37	1.00000	1.00012	1.29230	0	0	0.87500	130
97	2527.47	2616.81	1.01785	1.14500	1.40809	0	1	0.50000	350
98	726.58	778.27	1.04401	1.08922	1.21345	0	1	0.45455	220
99	1187.10	1573.45	1.05288	1.10879	1.35808	0	1	0.50000	230
100	138.02	149.28	1.04753	1.27350	1.30600	0	0	0.83333	40
101	147.56	162.23	1.02199	1.24037	1.26737	0	0	0.66667	40
102	94.24	116.09	1.13259	1.15708	1.54419	0	0	0.58333	75
103	580.52	675.41	1.00626	1.08359	1.37753	0	0	0.75000	225
104	445.52	435.03	1.13385	1.21180	1.41720	0	0	0.63636	150
105	110.46	120.07	1.08633	1.13347	1.96465	0	0	0.71429	70
106	45.17	68.28	1.12017	1.13175	1.13175	0	0	0.75000	65
107	800.60	1031.45	1.20374	1.23253	1.45298	0	0	0.72727	425
108	495.47	541.81	1.00323	1.13667	1.24085	0	0	0.83333	140
109	1370.06	1377.92	1.04485	1.10819	1.32836	0	0	0.58333	400
110	607.51	809.09	1.01111	1.05622	1.16072	0	0	0.66667	185
111	152.72	161.24	1.02685	1.10447	1.39143	0	0	0.75000	155
112	728.20	916.97	1.02795	1.09383	1.17993	0	0	0.66667	185
113	181.59	146.46	1.01158	1.43074	1.43074	0	0	0.75000	135
114	462.92	504.79	1.06679	1.07253	1.20283	0	0	0.50000	175
115	169.38	144.51	1.00382	1.02281	1.02281	0	1	0.50000	145
116	2473.26	2618.24	1.01709	1.04063	1.05926	0	1	0.33333	630
117	2346.77	2447.81	1.08238	1.08388	1.34398	0	0	0.80000	455
118	170.42	196.75	1.00000	1.03571	1.06790	0	0	0.75000	75
119	77.85	109.91	1.12864	1.16302	1.16302	0	0	0.60000	80
120	4770.88	7511.33	1.04645	1.11915	1.42217	0	1	0.52000	600
121	303.34	341.22	1.09503	1.20479	1.40115	0	0	0.77778	210

(continued)

OBS	COST	DOTEST	B2B1RAT	B3B1RAT	BHB1RAT	STATUS	DISTRICT	BTPRATIO	DAYSEST
122	395.98	419.00	1.21029	1.25946	1.25946	0	0	0.42857	185
123	150.55	174.48	1.05048	1.73452	1.73452	0	0	0.50000	110
124	1404.08	1573.83	1.02724	1.04925	1.24881	0	0	0.58333	550
125	1691.66	1627.08	1.03387	1.11274	1.11898	0	0	0.62500	600
126	5196.22	6365.13	1.02538	1.06196	1.30446	0	1	0.42857	805
127	3815.88	4960.82	1.01846	1.04353	1.07254	0	1	0.18182	450
128	122.62	95.38	1.04459	1.05195	1.07457	0	0	0.40000	120
129	1571.15	1759.21	1.01214	1.12645	1.27038	0	1	0.62500	385
130	4385.47	5556.82	1.12799	1.16978	1.72492	0	1	0.31818	600
131	4497.56	5186.30	1.00691	1.33380	1.51646	0	1	0.26316	750
132	23.67	32.54	1.05197	1.18120	2.22753	0	0	0.77778	60
133	1048.86	1040.53	1.05138	1.07009	1.27610	0	0	0.66667	300
134	239.51	315.11	1.05008	1.07829	1.17735	0	1	0.80000	100
135	260.64	351.80	1.02397	1.04081	1.17632	0	1	0.80000	120
136	138.89	123.31	1.00729	1.07116	1.07116	0	1	0.50000	150
137	128.38	151.89	1.00059	1.12683	1.12683	0	1	0.60000	75
138	284.98	315.97	1.04283	1.10622	1.10622	0	1	0.50000	110
139	77.32	101.04	1.00690	1.30480	1.30480	0	0	0.50000	90
140	5411.51	5086.25	1.02548	1.05641	1.29599	0	1	0.38889	815
141	3864.60	3991.03	1.02963	1.03230	1.48893	0	1	0.41176	800
142	2976.03	2832.43	1.06799	1.17414	1.56334	0	1	0.37500	440
143	257.51	205.86	1.01018	1.04526	1.05595	1	1	0.80000	130
144	36.44	42.04	1.02332	1.09791	1.09791	0	1	0.75000	45
145	182.52	223.13	1.00000	1.26493	1.26493	0	0	0.40000	90
146	1367.07	1433.62	1.07465	1.08446	1.35155	0	0	0.80000	475
147	76.81	75.25	1.01507	1.05527	1.05527	1	1	0.75000	90
148	1747.88	1493.45	1.01231	1.19420	1.31394	0	0	0.54545	445
149	5734.42	5427.31	1.02020	1.02571	1.32330	0	1	0.88889	700
150	5884.70	6097.41	1.03037	1.08206	1.26745	0	1	0.38889	900
151	346.52	331.10	1.12303	1.12316	1.47592	0	0	0.62500	190
152	646.40	818.54	1.29112	1.38469	1.59691	0	1	0.45455	400
153	760.84	718.24	1.02365	1.05158	1.05158	1	0	0.50000	185
154	169.77	175.95	1.02389	1.02754	1.05433	1	0	0.44444	125
155	138.79	151.62	1.00853	1.08094	1.08094	0	1	0.75000	60
156	346.76	394.21	1.10806	1.11556	1.11556	0	0	0.37500	150
157	1082.17	1085.87	1.07610	1.08797	1.34776	0	1	0.66667	400
158	253.68	270.93	1.07228	1.34120	1.34120	0	0	0.60000	200
159	433.15	545.26	1.00422	1.18435	1.24967	0	0	0.71429	230
160	10270.45	10467.40	1.03748	1.04612	1.28400	0	1	0.40000	720
161	1398.03	1414.73	1.09989	1.12889	1.22787	0	0	0.71429	460
162	2140.88	2152.01	1.00491	1.02566	1.02566	0	1	0.42857	400
163	6584.11	5949.35	1.02135	1.03414	1.37884	0	1	0.50000	675
164	666.77	641.52	1.14124	1.24950	1.31278	0	0	0.55556	240
165	108.09	99.56	1.08943	1.21201	1.21201	0	0	0.50000	65
166	106.10	95.29	1.00661	1.07263	1.33137	0	0	0.85714	125
167	549.64	413.08	1.02910	1.12878	1.12878	1	1	0.60000	120
168	1272.04	949.46	1.01918	1.02475	1.10157	1	0	0.55556	450
169	122.82	132.26	1.06736	1.30510	1.30510	0	0	0.30000	130
170	359.45	333.45	1.03525	1.04301	1.29319	0	1	0.50000	190
171	1731.47	1672.53	1.19267	1.21635	1.21635	0	1	0.33333	400
172	31.72	28.30	1.06263	1.22120	1.22120	0	0	0.50000	60
173	3299.96	2805.89	1.00757	1.05891	1.08968	1	1	0.44444	525
174	480.56	480.31	1.13607	1.34698	1.36586	0	0	0.66667	125
175	673.09	655.81	1.00000	1.08450	1.10744	0	0	0.83333	100
176	116.99	99.94	1.04192	1.07735	1.07735	1	0	0.75000	100
177	1157.39	891.21	1.01295	1.09076	1.09076	1	0	0.75000	450
178	166.80	131.99	1.07707	1.08335	1.08335	1	0	0.42857	120
179	668.53	596.89	1.03133	1.05542	1.05542	1	1	0.75000	120
180	7622.16	7871.19	1.06781	1.08947	1.18429	0	1	0.37500	700
181	201.32	182.94	1.04814	1.07143	1.07143	0	0	0.42857	90
182	1270.08	1306.33	1.02258	1.07352	1.07352	1	1	0.75000	195
183	1055.14	1148.65	1.03627	1.10087	1.33284	0	1	0.45455	400
184	5212.23	5090.86	1.01774	1.01786	1.25398	0	1	0.56250	500
185	5654.86	5447.59	1.04491	1.06438	1.06438	1	1	0.37500	500
186	856.46	938.14	1.06181	1.15976	1.23706	0	1	0.50000	375
187	88.98	66.06	1.15552	1.18257	1.19208	1	1	0.50000	90
188	200.00	168.99	1.10151	1.12477	1.12477	1	1	0.75000	90
189	234.04	179.74	1.03977	1.04869	1.07225	0	0	0.80000	170
190	116.56	125.85	1.05611	1.07894	1.07894	0	1	0.75000	80
191	82.11	93.04	1.00000	1.15889	1.39368	0	0	0.75000	100
192	207.81	214.25	1.07698	1.09489	1.09489	0	0	0.50000	155
193	463.28	474.89	1.00903	1.04904	1.18654	0	0	0.88889	215
194	7385.55	8460.87	1.04472	1.05852	1.05852	0	0	0.23077	505
195	91.66	100.31	1.02867	1.12586	1.18879	0	1	0.57143	90
196	546.16	622.92	1.00235	1.07635	1.07635	0	0	0.37500	165
197	740.30	810.26	1.00000	1.03483	1.14590	0	0	0.44444	175
198	888.44	883.30	1.01844	1.03710	1.18272	1	0	0.83333	250
199	656.75	750.82	1.03327	1.06556	1.11905	1	1	0.44444	180
200	1884.39	1550.49	1.01914	1.08680	1.08680	1	1	0.42857	350
201	4448.13	4197.79	1.01046	1.02215	1.02215	1	0	0.50000	660
202	258.20	181.95	1.00732	1.02541	1.04932	1	1	0.80000	130
203	1949.63	1880.83	1.05165	1.10803	1.17919	1	1	0.44444	330

OBS	COST	DOTEST	B2B1RAT	B3B1RAT	BHB1RAT	STATUS	DISTRICT	BTPRATIO	DAYSEST
204	235.28	230.75	1.01587	1.08762	1.12906	1	0	0.83333	90
205	35.18	39.21	1.03338	1.39979	1.39979	0	1	0.60000	45
206	244.76	221.88	1.00543	1.02878	1.17723	1	0	0.80000	90
207	648.92	563.88	1.02119	1.02659	1.02659	1	0	0.60000	140
208	391.47	358.53	1.02829	1.09437	1.09437	1	0	0.60000	100
209	267.78	249.91	1.03914	1.06844	1.11820	1	0	0.36364	255
210	2130.04	2019.87	1.10956	1.16759	1.19220	0	1	0.71429	450
211	301.23	303.19	1.07610	1.10834	1.10834	1	0	0.60000	110
212	1077.90	878.72	1.04175	1.06434	1.06768	1	0	0.80000	190
213	927.38	902.03	1.11036	1.16285	1.16285	0	1	0.25000	400
214	241.70	243.97	1.04946	1.16941	1.16941	1	1	0.75000	45
215	65.79	82.36	1.18645	1.20456	1.22890	0	1	0.44444	60
216	1208.44	1230.33	1.00000	1.30919	1.49820	0	0	0.30769	295
217	9453.35	9479.73	1.02255	1.03217	1.14419	0	1	0.31579	500
218	7098.11	8296.80	1.00855	1.03726	1.19543	0	1	0.50000	510
219	912.06	1137.65	1.00000	1.28672	1.28672	0	0	0.33333	220
220	259.99	319.59	1.00717	1.06833	1.06854	1	0	0.80000	90
221	8992.25	10743.60	1.03058	1.05344	1.36599	0	1	0.45455	650
222	339.88	428.82	1.20245	1.23939	1.23939	0	1	0.37500	165
223	833.66	859.74	1.05191	1.06098	6.04598	1	0	0.33333	450
224	4833.82	6225.04	1.00000	1.06601	1.37437	0	0	0.53333	520
225	271.94	223.89	1.01232	1.03402	1.10971	1	1	0.66667	110
226	2966.28	4433.47	1.07730	1.30852	1.51367	0	0	0.25000	720
227	577.37	701.07	1.00000	1.25713	1.25713	0	0	0.25000	150
228	10480.32	10276.29	1.02502	1.03832	1.30423	0	1	0.68750	570
229	462.39	444.19	1.04262	1.04489	1.05778	0	1	0.80000	120
230	2558.19	2741.05	1.14482	1.16483	1.19685	0	1	0.44444	365
231	2814.91	2816.73	1.02002	1.11954	1.26368	0	0	0.54545	540
232	119.81	122.16	1.00000	1.06686	1.29526	0	0	0.66667	90
233	3184.86	3373.04	1.00000	1.02879	1.35838	0	1	0.58333	240
234	473.20	548.01	1.11100	1.12516	1.12516	0	0	0.37500	130
235	400.48	496.68	1.06915	1.08216	1.18507	0	1	0.50000	90

APPENDIX I

Data Set: Real Estate Appraisals and Sales Data for Six Neighborhoods in Tampa, Florida (See Case Study 12)

Note: The data set is available on a 3½″ diskette from the publisher.

NBRHOOD=A

OBS	LANDVAL	IMPROVAL	SALEPRIC	OBS	LANDVAL	IMPROVAL	SALEPRIC
1	$14,000	$41,633	$77,500	2	$14,938	$55,186	$84,700
3	$11,741	$64,471	$93,900	4	$16,480	$52,449	$97,900
5	$13,860	$48,083	$92,300	6	$17,870	$59,700	$96,000
7	$18,400	$55,641	$70,000	8	$21,792	$53,950	$78,700
9	$22,880	$61,260	$95,000	10	$44,442	$117,257	$165,000
11	$25,751	$79,736	$123,000	12	$25,751	$73,551	$113,500
13	$25,751	$84,805	$118,000	14	$24,564	$67,909	$113,000
15	$28,492	$91,670	$127,000	16	$45,893	$126,773	$222,000
17	$46,589	$96,459	$145,000	18	$57,024	$112,601	$224,900
19	$47,170	$157,007	$279,000	20	$22,824	$95,426	$135,000
21	$22,824	$92,775	$157,500	22	$68,309	$141,199	$375,000
23	$12,804	$69,124	$98,000	24	$16,500	$47,956	$81,900
25	$16,053	$47,676	$85,000	26	$15,538	$47,676	$86,000
27	$16,374	$47,676	$83,300	28	$15,572	$73,936	$108,000
29	$15,510	$62,774	$97,500	30	$22,250	$68,961	$116,500
31	$38,648	$90,497	$140,500	32	$30,896	$65,412	$116,500
33	$22,250	$84,286	$119,900	34	$23,124	$79,072	$120,700
35	$22,028	$105,624	$147,500	36	$31,114	$70,776	$95,000
37	$22,250	$73,338	$128,500	38	$28,936	$108,072	$150,000
39	$32,000	$80,269	$110,000	40	$27,160	$93,519	$145,800
41	$22,116	$91,803	$139,900	42	$22,945	$94,500	$155,000
43	$32,628	$115,203	$194,000	44	$33,675	$98,731	$183,000
45	$62,160	$96,089	$150,000	46	$43,680	$99,001	$180,000
47	$44,100	$93,184	$181,000	48	$46,620	$107,219	$163,000
49	$50,544	$125,980	$187,500	50	$30,141	$124,451	$207,000
51	$31,310	$68,759	$107,500	52	$27,636	$105,454	$157,800
53	$33,055	$103,538	$167,500	54	$28,454	$75,720	$189,900
55	$31,299	$101,855	$160,000	56	$34,295	$99,271	$165,500
57	$34,457	$101,205	$165,000	58	$30,631	$89,922	$127,000
59	$30,030	$93,493	$158,400	60	$30,130	$81,669	$131,000
61	$31,900	$83,013	$132,900	62	$26,695	$87,046	$140,000
63	$26,695	$74,837	$121,300	64	$26,695	$75,240	$125,000
65	$30,139	$72,028	$124,500	66	$32,292	$70,710	$119,000
67	$16,256	$70,040	$116,000	68	$16,256	$72,991	$120,000
69	$16,256	$70,980	$118,000	70	$19,665	$70,980	$119,000
71	$28,634	$94,899	$132,500	72	$32,678	$88,745	$127,500
73	$33,992	$82,548	$124,000	74	$31,941	$83,165	$132,000

NBRHOOD=A

OBS	LANDVAL	IMPROVAL	SALEPRIC	OBS	LANDVAL	IMPROVAL	SALEPRIC
75	$38,036	$86,734	$121,500	76	$38,133	$79,699	$126,000
77	$34,489	$81,529	$123,500	78	$34,201	$87,889	$139,000
79	$19,782	$76,989	$118,000	80	$20,853	$64,346	$100,000
81	$17,358	$83,851	$129,900	82	$19,980	$78,314	$126,900
83	$18,663	$81,507	$123,500	84	$38,218	$120,337	$185,500
85	$43,097	$104,552	$178,000	86	$48,263	$106,646	$180,500
87	$46,652	$105,480	$174,500	88	$20,394	$51,342	$78,900
89	$20,181	$39,081	$68,000	90	$16,632	$44,499	$80,200
91	$17,808	$45,785	$77,000	92	$15,600	$44,378	$78,000
93	$16,128	$42,028	$74,500	94	$16,128	$64,179	$93,000
95	$16,800	$37,044	$69,900	96	$13,709	$40,406	$69,000
97	$17,234	$50,961	$69,000	98	$24,908	$41,606	$79,000
99	$13,709	$41,229	$68,900	100	$13,709	$43,273	$67,000
101	$16,255	$37,636	$61,500	102	$15,540	$38,642	$77,400
103	$16,000	$43,687	$68,900	104	$13,138	$40,085	$61,000
105	$17,948	$39,790	$72,000	106	$17,626	$43,553	$68,500
107	$13,138	$43,131	$77,900	108	$13,138	$48,305	$72,000
109	$13,709	$60,890	$91,900	110	$17,626	$43,207	$67,500
111	$14,541	$43,473	$69,500	112	$19,492	$39,416	$68,500
113	$15,060	$51,216	$78,000	114	$16,334	$38,161	$72,000
115	$13,202	$38,707	$67,000	116	$16,597	$30,948	$59,900
117	$14,350	$50,780	$82,500	118	$16,482	$50,966	$80,000
119	$14,841	$61,484	$92,000	120	$14,296	$52,664	$80,500
121	$14,423	$51,489	$82,000	122	$15,349	$52,664	$80,900
123	$14,451	$53,727	$78,000	124	$14,884	$51,462	$84,000
125	$14,494	$40,900	$64,500	126	$14,760	$35,344	$59,000
127	$46,641	$132,079	$230,000	128	$45,255	$103,920	$167,000
129	$25,320	$69,907	$110,000	130	$24,095	$68,218	$123,000
131	$30,818	$84,824	$128,500	132	$35,612	$69,381	$113,000
133	$58,992	$134,143	$295,000	134	$58,800	$164,668	$272,500
135	$74,645	$167,270	$250,000	136	$69,960	$155,962	$260,000
137	$54,075	$147,155	$277,000	138	$52,500	$136,279	$256,000
139	$51,720	$133,000	$216,500	140	$39,178	$135,631	$225,000
141	$48,855	$137,997	$205,000	142	$43,105	$97,882	$158,000
143	$48,719	$116,883	$179,000	144	$40,905	$98,002	$165,000
145	$36,360	$109,495	$191,000	146	$44,726	$147,405	$240,500
147	$24,543	$102,007	$145,000	148	$33,465	$82,588	$135,200
149	$59,386	$77,841	$132,000	150	$49,688	$84,477	$153,500
151	$63,400	$139,457	$262,100	152	$91,795	$113,171	$242,000
153	$44,888	$85,660	$172,000	154	$37,715	$90,189	$148,500
155	$36,720	$70,139	$125,000	156	$54,899	$132,266	$305,000
157	$90,629	$164,276	$300,000	158	$129,360	$167,838	$363,000
159	$37,526	$120,552	$227,500	160	$67,098	$95,451	$139,000
161	$84,084	$104,550	$205,000	162	$49,000	$99,167	$225,000
163	$54,324	$82,665	$135,000	164	$49,844	$92,361	$159,000
165	$41,923	$104,505	$210,000	166	$35,862	$118,494	$245,000
167	$24,675	$102,851	$72,200	168	$16,256	$55,312	$86,000
169	$30,192	$101,258	$134,900				

NBRHOOD=B

OBS	LANDVAL	IMPROVAL	SALEPRIC	OBS	LANDVAL	IMPROVAL	SALEPRIC
				170	$30,000	$49,760	$95,000
171	$30,000	$68,480	$116,500	172	$30,000	$80,655	$156,900
173	$30,000	$66,859	$111,000	174	$30,000	$70,861	$100,100
175	$30,000	$75,230	$100,000	176	$30,000	$64,798	$130,000
177	$49,394	$90,456	$170,400	178	$51,989	$118,352	$211,500
179	$44,520	$110,617	$185,000	180	$53,568	$117,094	$179,700
181	$46,651	$139,288	$208,000	182	$44,625	$142,832	$208,900
183	$47,775	$158,489	$210,000	184	$50,673	$173,180	$255,000
185	$46,997	$95,818	$150,000	186	$46,503	$82,789	$149,900
187	$98,704	$181,546	$360,000	188	$95,020	$273,883	$425,000
189	$32,211	$78,789	$130,000	190	$56,227	$98,341	$170,000
191	$43,294	$98,074	$152,500	192	$40,577	$84,059	$144,500
193	$90,000	$245,873	$310,000	194	$90,000	$209,460	$293,000
195	$101,856	$227,719	$300,000	196	$96,320	$227,932	$345,000
197	$90,410	$250,896	$475,000	198	$26,995	$79,778	$138,000
199	$24,538	$70,801	$110,000	200	$40,000	$102,258	$172,000
201	$57,760	$108,418	$196,000	202	$40,000	$111,310	$195,000
203	$40,422	$129,732	$190,000	204	$55,040	$124,191	$206,000
205	$33,658	$91,695	$170,000	206	$45,155	$108,501	$174,700
207	$32,077	$84,312	$137,000	208	$30,720	$93,718	$154,000
209	$31,270	$87,941	$147,500	210	$31,270	$97,401	$164,300
211	$31,270	$108,533	$180,000	212	$33,024	$87,149	$162,000

(continued)

213	$166,544	$502,585	$805,000	214	$48,000	$79,981	$155,900
215	$48,000	$73,030	$136,000	216	$60,000	$84,690	$175,000
217	$38,250	$157,105	$267,000	218	$41,400	$129,900	$203,000
219	$33,353	$90,273	$159,900	220	$27,000	$75,760	$121,000
221	$27,000	$77,425	$120,000	222	$26,652	$72,219	$124,900
223	$25,200	$69,285	$108,000				

NBRHOOD=C

OBS	LANDVAL	IMPROVAL	SALEPRIC	OBS	LANDVAL	IMPROVAL	SALEPRIC
				224	$14,350	$56,548	$85,000
225	$16,236	$51,206	$72,000	226	$14,207	$59,990	$87,000
227	$17,712	$51,513	$82,500	228	$14,350	$35,836	$64,800
229	$16,597	$44,937	$70,000	230	$18,762	$51,774	$86,500
231	$13,776	$49,704	$76,000	232	$20,118	$52,888	$80,000
233	$20,099	$48,307	$71,000	234	$12,386	$42,505	$57,900
235	$10,750	$43,723	$79,500	236	$11,568	$37,998	$66,000
237	$10,750	$38,673	$69,400	238	$12,259	$42,490	$67,800
239	$11,580	$33,996	$63,000	240	$10,750	$33,034	$68,000
241	$10,750	$39,145	$61,000	242	$10,750	$33,159	$52,200
243	$10,984	$43,122	$47,900	244	$10,984	$44,322	$64,000
245	$18,720	$70,229	$109,900	246	$18,720	$61,921	$88,500
247	$18,720	$54,010	$78,500	248	$31,943	$80,535	$169,000
249	$27,463	$90,370	$158,000	250	$28,313	$93,563	$155,000
251	$23,258	$88,268	$64,500	252	$14,000	$50,033	$70,000
253	$15,300	$55,111	$76,900	254	$13,580	$55,656	$71,800
255	$17,934	$58,116	$84,500	256	$15,840	$56,874	$84,000
257	$13,440	$58,517	$79,900	258	$14,400	$54,454	$82,000
259	$14,000	$53,083	$90,700	260	$23,925	$20,662	$59,000
261	$3,910	$33,018	$57,000	262	$7,821	$14,165	$40,000
263	$16,498	$44,342	$78,700	264	$11,767	$45,652	$77,700
265	$12,933	$36,110	$66,900	266	$10,143	$35,353	$66,600
267	$10,764	$40,999	$71,600	268	$17,581	$40,643	$67,900
269	$10,764	$40,940	$69,700	270	$10,764	$45,920	$72,400
271	$17,522	$40,940	$65,000	272	$17,424	$38,136	$83,000
273	$14,362	$45,296	$81,500	274	$16,051	$53,230	$85,000
275	$18,139	$39,858	$78,900	276	$16,896	$55,626	$84,000
277	$19,080	$22,635	$70,000	278	$13,241	$34,074	$65,000
279	$12,831	$42,994	$77,500	280	$12,558	$32,120	$60,000
281	$12,558	$28,166	$57,000	282	$13,138	$35,209	$63,900
283	$15,989	$26,129	$58,000	284	$14,213	$29,390	$61,000
285	$15,725	$38,348	$80,000	286	$12,831	$28,608	$60,000
287	$14,137	$36,402	$69,900	288	$13,423	$30,876	$59,000
289	$13,621	$30,496	$64,000	290	$15,989	$38,348	$75,000
291	$13,463	$40,431	$80,000	292	$15,278	$32,404	$65,900
293	$14,463	$32,201	$61,000	294	$14,805	$28,471	$63,000
295	$14,213	$36,219	$56,800	296	$15,120	$35,171	$58,000
297	$16,645	$30,355	$50,000	298	$16,432	$45,940	$69,000
299	$13,423	$24,767	$54,000	300	$15,792	$38,946	$69,000
301	$14,213	$68,466	$79,000	302	$13,818	$28,575	$70,000
303	$14,511	$30,183	$68,400	304	$15,365	$39,218	$58,300
305	$14,511	$52,586	$40,800	306	$17,072	$35,766	$74,900
307	$16,218	$32,480	$68,000	308	$17,618	$38,653	$70,000
309	$17,279	$38,653	$77,000	310	$16,051	$42,361	$80,000
311	$17,642	$44,644	$91,000	312	$16,553	$48,187	$69,900
313	$21,998	$62,076	$85,100	314	$17,222	$55,176	$100,000
315	$17,107	$45,455	$76,000	316	$19,008	$53,916	$62,700
317	$17,054	$46,539	$80,000	318	$15,924	$46,049	$65,000
319	$16,544	$44,822	$79,900	320	$13,844	$53,052	$82,000
321	$11,970	$57,936	$75,000	322	$11,455	$43,183	$69,000
323	$9,167	$26,843	$57,100	324	$10,476	$47,355	$75,000
325	$8,832	$22,019	$45,000	326	$9,347	$33,641	$65,500
327	$9,347	$29,166	$54,900	328	$9,084	$24,882	$51,600
329	$8,528	$18,497	$47,500	330	$8,280	$26,476	$48,900
331	$10,419	$21,653	$47,700	332	$8,280	$24,328	$36,100
333	$10,796	$21,477	$51,100	334	$10,800	$26,425	$52,100
335	$12,028	$28,133	$60,400	336	$10,850	$25,654	$62,300
337	$9,982	$26,792	$49,000	338	$9,982	$28,344	$62,000
339	$9,982	$36,224	$60,000	340	$12,350	$27,692	$56,000
341	$9,488	$37,702	$70,000	342	$14,227	$52,605	$78,900
343	$14,463	$57,417	$84,000	344	$14,015	$39,601	$66,500
345	$14,511	$40,512	$74,500	346	$13,658	$35,349	$68,000
347	$15,151	$31,442	$41,000	348	$15,840	$42,766	$44,900
349	$14,080	$34,426	$65,500	350	$15,629	$35,557	$62,200
351	$14,520	$53,091	$91,500	352	$14,593	$38,908	$69,900
353	$13,728	$58,102	$84,900	354	$14,593	$33,396	$53,000
355	$14,593	$40,079	$72,500	356	$14,157	$49,694	$89,900
357	$14,362	$47,518	$84,900	358	$13,965	$26,777	$58,500
359	$11,856	$25,182	$47,000	360	$12,768	$35,248	$68,500
361	$13,202	$31,574	$58,900				

NBRHOOD=D

OBS	LANDVAL	IMPROVAL	SALEPRIC	OBS	LANDVAL	IMPROVAL	SALEPRIC
				362	$8,488	$36,132	$23,400
363	$24,084	$16,237	$44,000	364	$7,906	$20,320	$21,500
365	$8,180	$20,689	$13,700	366	$8,165	$17,245	$27,200
367	$8,883	$18,069	$24,500	368	$7,614	$14,996	$39,500
369	$7,614	$19,158	$19,800	370	$7,700	$25,758	$26,900
371	$7,700	$16,466	$35,000	372	$9,173	$14,107	$38,500
373	$7,820	$44,462	$30,000	374	$11,615	$15,066	$34,900
375	$5,474	$7,707	$14,500	376	$7,178	$14,236	$30,000
377	$5,693	$21,279	$15,000	378	$5,693	$16,200	$16,000
379	$5,633	$14,696	$14,000	380	$6,162	$16,098	$37,500
381	$5,459	$11,253	$33,678	382	$5,633	$16,166	$36,900
383	$6,162	$11,146	$31,900	384	$5,290	$17,565	$19,800
385	$11,150	$24,808	$22,000	386	$6,204	$8,152	$8,500
387	$6,620	$6,604	$22,900	388	$7,293	$10,586	$28,000
389	$12,150	$10,755	$24,900	390	$7,875	$19,535	$30,000
391	$23,782	$36,153	$49,100	392	$4,275	$8,272	$10,500
393	$8,978	$12,828	$9,000	394	$4,703	$41,766	$52,500
395	$8,131	$7,118	$20,000	396	$11,040	$25,164	$21,900
397	$8,292	$17,970	$22,000	398	$5,625	$38,537	$31,500
399	$8,246	$19,368	$35,000	400	$4,699	$17,137	$33,000
401	$15,000	$3,319	$45,000	402	$5,175	$9,053	$34,900
403	$9,492	$39,506	$14,300	404	$12,150	$11,899	$12,000
405	$7,125	$15,653	$70,000	406	$3,960	$10,634	$9,600
407	$7,082	$10,631	$70,000	408	$4,050	$13,632	$25,000
409	$3,645	$30,211	$32,500	410	$8,100	$14,651	$12,500
411	$7,836	$16,018	$33,000	412	$5,262	$12,496	$12,000
413	$6,486	$13,404	$39,900	414	$5,865	$23,816	$49,500
415	$6,843	$11,437	$37,900	416	$5,175	$16,135	$30,000
417	$7,337	$22,195	$39,000	418	$6,960	$21,164	$32,000
419	$5,113	$10,271	$10,000	420	$13,650	$23,397	$45,000
421	$6,548	$15,050	$33,000	422	$4,486	$10,603	$18,000
423	$5,980	$10,563	$12,900	424	$5,980	$16,367	$15,000
425	$5,980	$11,679	$19,500	426	$3,760	$7,196	$20,000
427	$7,360	$7,902	$12,000	428	$6,355	$5,787	$17,000
429	$7,360	$18,005	$35,000	430	$4,261	$11,776	$16,100
431	$5,340	$10,669	$22,300	432	$6,108	$12,414	$35,000
433	$5,175	$11,781	$11,500	434	$6,624	$26,039	$10,000
435	$5,544	$11,176	$15,000	436	$5,837	$12,338	$25,000
437	$11,551	$1,000	$9,000	438	$9,338	$7,603	$11,000
439	$5,255	$6,508	$9,000	440	$8,280	$20,621	$14,000
441	$11,040	$26,084	$20,000	442	$5,175	$11,074	$38,700
443	$5,175	$13,178	$8,500	444	$7,163	$10,424	$25,000
445	$7,160	$21,109	$19,900	446	$4,032	$3,679	$17,000
447	$3,534	$4,882	$12,000	448	$6,106	$7,796	$36,000

NBRHOOD=E

OBS	LANDVAL	IMPROVAL	SALEPRIC	OBS	LANDVAL	IMPROVAL	SALEPRIC
449	$40,600	$129,632	$231,200	450	$43,384	$106,541	$210,600
451	$39,400	$93,495	$155,000	452	$34,000	$118,532	$166,000
453	$38,189	$99,429	$158,500	454	$39,180	$117,058	$180,000
455	$34,850	$79,745	$132,000	456	$34,000	$94,535	$155,800
457	$38,300	$102,962	$159,000	458	$34,000	$92,204	$148,000
459	$33,033	$118,744	$204,000	460	$36,125	$90,045	$165,500
461	$21,473	$96,439	$151,500	462	$121,665	$348,561	$300,000
463	$124,526	$280,947	$315,000	464	$89,529	$114,102	$245,000
465	$95,528	$362,992	$430,000	466	$196,459	$303,073	$605,000
467	$129,439	$355,958	$452,500	468	$113,998	$535,227	$775,000
469	$439,317	$1037067	$1,146,000	470	$45,806	$124,545	$317,500
471	$28,608	$119,518	$166,000	472	$26,392	$89,872	$159,000

NBRHOOD=F

OBS	LANDVAL	IMPROVAL	SALEPRIC	OBS	LANDVAL	IMPROVAL	SALEPRIC
473	$18,883	$56,216	$85,500	474	$20,232	$70,656	$105,000
475	$18,991	$61,485	$102,000	476	$18,883	$68,026	$99,000
477	$19,473	$65,138	$110,900	478	$17,672	$66,810	$109,000
479	$19,187	$59,433	$93,000	480	$17,748	$68,933	$109,000
481	$20,419	$46,093	$83,000	482	$17,672	$48,153	$71,400
483	$17,136	$65,173	$106,500	484	$18,360	$54,347	$94,700
485	$19,584	$54,375	$94,000	486	$22,473	$50,116	$77,000
487	$19,339	$66,213	$95,500	488	$19,829	$51,722	$85,300
489	$20,441	$44,811	$73,000	490	$22,721	$55,614	$90,000

(*continued*)

NBRHOOD=F

OBS	LANDVAL	IMPROVAL	SALEPRIC	OBS	LANDVAL	IMPROVAL	SALEPRIC
491	$18,482	$51,382	$78,000	492	$18,934	$59,943	$91,500
493	$27,859	$69,891	$121,600	494	$27,949	$63,660	$107,000
495	$21,770	$74,466	$120,500	496	$46,361	$79,205	$122,000
497	$28,416	$60,035	$98,500	498	$23,818	$64,613	$109,900
499	$31,066	$65,945	$105,000	500	$30,192	$71,871	$123,000
501	$29,600	$86,485	$150,500	502	$30,344	$61,770	$109,000
503	$23,739	$74,675	$111,900	504	$34,276	$83,468	$133,000
505	$32,660	$104,179	$169,000	506	$29,126	$81,789	$133,500
507	$19,625	$59,548	$85,000	508	$17,945	$71,844	$100,000
509	$14,550	$49,446	$97,000	510	$21,224	$59,451	$94,000
511	$27,965	$84,050	$130,000	512	$29,485	$74,573	$127,500
513	$24,864	$86,181	$134,000	514	$37,222	$88,080	$127,000
515	$30,488	$96,472	$129,000	516	$30,784	$90,466	$130,000
517	$24,276	$74,000	$93,200	518	$11,278	$42,941	$69,900
519	$11,936	$44,309	$73,500	520	$13,980	$33,786	$64,900
521	$12,009	$36,323	$67,500	522	$17,735	$33,786	$65,000
523	$16,100	$88,447	$118,000	524	$18,770	$71,357	$97,000
525	$16,405	$74,093	$93,000	526	$20,628	$76,887	$116,000
527	$16,100	$91,119	$120,000	528	$17,710	$67,880	$99,500
529	$17,710	$61,676	$100,000	530	$20,700	$89,625	$129,000
531	$23,870	$111,001	$162,500	532	$37,145	$105,493	$160,000
533	$32,200	$107,682	$175,000	534	$30,492	$88,046	$135,900
535	$32,000	$85,895	$138,000	536	$12,100	$30,618	$59,900
537	$12,100	$36,323	$61,200	538	$12,100	$35,426	$58,900
539	$21,197	$75,882	$105,000	540	$19,339	$83,744	$125,000
541	$19,811	$77,400	$106,000	542	$22,810	$88,534	$127,500
543	$41,164	$92,833	$137,500	544	$31,570	$85,563	$129,900
545	$30,492	$78,996	$122,900	546	$42,695	$24,672	$87,500
547	$11,270	$43,873	$63,300	548	$11,270	$45,311	$57,500
549	$11,270	$47,465	$61,600	550	$13,101	$43,892	$75,500
551	$11,270	$42,796	$63,500	552	$11,270	$26,761	$42,500
553	$15,746	$50,638	$83,000	554	$24,647	$51,587	$98,000
555	$23,957	$48,319	$77,000	556	$24,840	$27,722	$56,000
557	$15,306	$77,667	$109,500	558	$12,938	$54,952	$82,000
559	$16,000	$72,714	$103,900	560	$14,490	$63,267	$94,000
561	$14,490	$69,705	$105,000	562	$14,490	$62,004	$90,000
563	$14,490	$54,066	$76,000	564	$9,266	$39,189	$50,000
565	$35,910	$53,816	$107,000	566	$18,479	$41,224	$75,300
567	$13,920	$53,430	$87,400	568	$14,760	$65,044	$90,000
569	$15,055	$53,153	$84,800	570	$13,920	$50,576	$81,000
571	$14,145	$40,776	$74,900	572	$13,776	$50,195	$88,500
573	$17,712	$61,918	$81,900	574	$13,776	$49,487	$78,000
575	$14,814	$45,024	$84,900	576	$13,489	$40,830	$64,500
577	$14,706	$41,202	$75,500	578	$15,050	$50,269	$85,000
579	$14,147	$50,296	$84,000	580	$14,147	$50,073	$84,500
581	$17,131	$83,029	$126,000	582	$15,754	$44,295	$78,500
583	$14,448	$51,159	$85,500	584	$14,448	$49,293	$92,300
585	$15,466	$62,606	$91,000	586	$17,210	$44,160	$83,000
587	$14,448	$73,110	$93,000	588	$14,448	$51,401	$93,800
589	$16,158	$71,530	$89,800	590	$15,792	$51,832	$83,000
591	$17,000	$57,728	$90,000	592	$14,448	$52,115	$82,900
593	$14,448	$58,974	$88,200	594	$16,787	$52,756	$81,600
595	$14,448	$56,360	$81,900	596	$14,448	$45,413	$61,100
597	$19,814	$55,713	$77,500	598	$15,792	$52,674	$89,000
599	$19,402	$52,566	$83,900	600	$15,415	$55,283	$76,000
601	$16,000	$60,458	$84,000	602	$16,005	$36,565	$67,500
603	$14,938	$50,391	$79,500	604	$15,585	$63,079	$98,000
605	$14,168	$37,755	$68,000	606	$14,168	$52,912	$77,000
607	$17,061	$64,190	$91,500	608	$15,903	$55,010	$93,000
609	$17,268	$41,918	$71,500	610	$14,784	$51,009	$85,000
611	$13,248	$54,589	$85,000	612	$15,744	$43,513	$75,100
613	$14,592	$49,691	$84,000	614	$15,048	$50,776	$90,000
615	$14,784	$54,731	$83,000	616	$16,369	$65,399	$77,300
617	$16,369	$46,943	$70,000	618	$15,120	$44,620	$74,000
619	$15,120	$51,025	$78,000	620	$15,120	$65,518	$99,000
621	$19,440	$61,771	$102,500	622	$15,120	$49,860	$83,900
623	$15,120	$48,172	$82,000	624	$15,278	$64,179	$94,000
625	$15,120	$50,409	$76,000	626	$19,440	$63,033	$97,500
627	$15,120	$71,488	$86,200	628	$21,567	$75,896	$86,000
629	$20,251	$65,880	$97,500	630	$15,120	$40,749	$66,900
631	$16,200	$51,116	$81,500	632	$16,200	$55,931	$86,000
633	$15,379	$41,900	$72,500	634	$15,379	$69,767	$130,000
635	$17,916	$79,358	$102,900	636	$22,298	$57,467	$82,100
637	$15,120	$42,942	$76,500	638	$15,120	$71,187	$100,000
639	$19,125	$67,058	$100,300	640	$20,166	$67,526	$101,000

OBS	LANDVAL	IMPROVAL	SALEPRIC	OBS	LANDVAL	IMPROVAL	SALEPRIC
641	$17,775	$60,060	$94,000	642	$15,356	$57,099	$89,000
643	$16,200	$57,288	$85,000	644	$20,628	$66,969	$93,000
645	$16,200	$74,291	$99,900	646	$20,318	$68,327	$113,800
647	$19,600	$69,859	$104,500	648	$19,600	$56,274	$83,000
649	$15,120	$52,048	$78,000	650	$17,280	$72,442	$113,000
651	$15,120	$52,214	$79,000	652	$16,706	$55,177	$88,500
653	$22,871	$54,064	$87,000	654	$17,672	$60,217	$96,000
655	$16,200	$63,305	$97,400	656	$15,120	$50,342	$87,500
657	$22,633	$71,728	$131,800	658	$20,974	$60,442	$87,200
659	$20,844	$53,011	$65,300	660	$15,049	$66,113	$96,000
661	$19,491	$54,485	$89,800	662	$15,278	$43,089	$65,000
663	$16,595	$64,663	$105,000	664	$14,683	$50,767	$78,100
665	$14,683	$73,569	$101,000	666	$14,683	$49,897	$83,500
667	$16,702	$81,707	$115,000	668	$20,807	$51,761	$91,000
669	$21,278	$51,071	$83,500	670	$18,469	$73,095	$109,500
671	$18,096	$65,599	$103,000	672	$17,600	$53,380	$92,000
673	$17,424	$51,917	$99,900	674	$17,952	$72,436	$97,500
675	$17,072	$73,508	$113,500	676	$15,919	$75,347	$110,000
677	$17,280	$77,948	$100,000	678	$18,014	$70,391	$105,000
679	$15,898	$78,477	$118,000	680	$15,919	$58,897	$86,000
681	$16,848	$64,334	$95,000	682	$17,296	$61,900	$110,000
683	$17,375	$72,738	$108,000	684	$18,900	$86,439	$102,800
685	$17,929	$78,903	$92,000	686	$16,848	$75,023	$104,500
687	$17,246	$55,241	$86,800	688	$16,261	$59,514	$90,500
689	$20,270	$71,053	$100,700	690	$16,412	$61,715	$99,500
691	$18,209	$67,839	$102,500	692	$20,872	$64,489	$94,500
693	$16,589	$69,057	$108,000	694	$17,280	$51,304	$83,400
695	$16,848	$80,058	$129,000	696	$21,384	$65,938	$91,000
697	$18,934	$60,155	$90,000	698	$21,263	$63,581	$90,000
699	$16,200	$53,559	$69,000	700	$17,213	$53,559	$87,000
701	$19,586	$50,433	$83,400	702	$17,299	$60,504	$88,500
703	$18,180	$66,152	$112,400	704	$16,416	$67,285	$91,000
705	$15,898	$48,684	$75,700	706	$17,089	$60,922	$95,900
707	$17,375	$58,035	$86,000				

APPENDIX J

Data Set: Condominium Sales Data (See Case Study 15)

Note: The data set is available on a 3½″ diskette from the publisher.

OBS	PRICPAID	FLOORHGT	DISTELEV	VIEWOCEN	ENDUNIT	FURN
1	$19,900	1	2	0	0	0
2	$20,400	1	13	0	0	0
3	$27,500	1	15	1	0	0
4	$20,900	2	14	0	0	0
5	$25,900	1	2	1	0	0
6	$26,400	1	9	1	0	0
7	$26,400	1	12	1	0	0
8	$26,400	1	13	1	0	0
9	$25,400	3	9	1	0	0
10	$26,400	3	15	1	0	0
11	$27,900	8	15	1	0	0
12	$20,400	1	12	0	0	0
13	$19,900	2	13	0	0	0
14	$24,900	2	15	1	0	0
15	$26,400	3	11	1	0	0
16	$20,900	3	14	0	0	0
17	$25,900	4	15	1	0	0
18	$20,400	1	14	0	0	0
19	$27,400	7	15	1	0	0
20	$19,900	1	3	0	0	0
21	$19,900	1	11	0	0	0
22	$27,400	2	14	1	0	0
23	$18,000	3	11	0	0	0
24	$25,400	3	12	1	0	0
25	$28,400	4	14	1	0	0
26	$26,900	3	5	1	0	0
27	$15,900	2	3	0	0	0
28	$19,900	1	6	0	0	0
29	$20,400	1	9	0	0	0
30	$19,000	2	11	0	0	0
31	$26,100	2	12	1	0	0
32	$15,900	2	12	0	0	0
33	$26,100	2	13	1	0	0
34	$16,900	3	6	0	0	0
35	$19,900	4	14	0	0	0
36	$18,900	5	14	0	0	0
37	$29,400	6	15	1	0	0
38	$19,900	6	14	0	0	0

OBS	PRICPAID	FLOORHGT	DISTELEV	VIEWOCEN	ENDUNIT	FURN
39	$20,400	2	6	0	0	0
40	$27,900	3	14	1	0	0
41	$15,900	6	9	0	0	0
42	$15,100	2	4	0	0	0
43	$15,100	2	5	0	0	0
44	$15,900	2	10	0	0	0
45	$19,000	8	12	0	0	0
46	$19,000	8	13	0	0	0
47	$17,500	1	4	0	0	0
48	$17,500	1	5	0	0	0
49	$17,500	1	10	0	0	0
50	$15,900	2	2	0	0	0
51	$16,300	3	13	0	0	0
52	$21,900	8	14	0	0	0
53	$16,100	3	5	0	0	0
54	$16,900	3	3	0	0	0
55	$16,900	3	4	0	0	0
56	$16,500	3	10	0	0	0
57	$16,900	3	12	0	0	0
58	$26,900	3	13	1	0	0
59	$17,600	4	11	0	0	0
60	$18,600	5	11	0	0	0
61	$19,500	8	11	0	0	0
62	$25,900	1	3	1	0	0
63	$23,500	1	4	1	0	0
64	$24,000	1	11	1	0	0
65	$15,900	2	1	0	0	0
66	$16,900	3	1	0	0	0
67	$26,000	4	1	1	0	0
68	$20,900	4	1	0	0	0
69	$17,600	4	6	0	0	0
70	$17,900	4	9	0	0	0
71	$17,900	4	12	0	0	0
72	$27,400	4	13	1	0	0
73	$17,900	5	13	0	0	0
74	$18,000	6	2	0	0	0
75	$19,900	6	6	0	0	0
76	$19,000	6	12	0	0	0
77	$21,000	1	1	1	0	0
78	$22,500	1	5	1	0	1
79	$20,000	1	6	1	1	1
80	$22,000	1	10	1	0	0
81	$21,000	2	1	1	0	0
82	$22,500	2	3	1	0	1
83	$22,500	2	4	1	0	1
84	[illegible]	2	5	1	0	1
85	$19,500	2	6	1	1	0
86	$19,000	2	9	1	0	0
87	$19,500	2	10	1	0	0
88	$20,000	3	1	1	0	0
89	$21,000	3	2	1	0	1
90	$17,000	3	2	0	0	1
91	$20,000	3	3	1	0	0
92	$18,000	3	6	1	1	0
93	$20,500	3	10	1	0	1
94	$21,500	4	2	1	0	0
95	$17,500	4	2	0	0	1
96	$20,000	4	3	1	0	0
97	$17,500	4	3	0	0	1
98	$19,500	4	4	1	0	0
99	$16,500	4	4	0	0	1
100	$19,500	4	5	1	0	0
101	$17,500	4	6	1	1	0
102	$20,000	4	9	1	0	1
103	$19,000	4	10	1	0	0
104	$16,000	4	10	0	0	0
105	$20,500	4	11	1	0	1
106	$19,000	4	12	1	0	0
107	$20,500	5	1	1	0	0
108	$17,500	5	1	0	0	1
109	$21,500	5	2	1	0	1
110	$22,000	5	3	1	0	1
111	$26,500	5	4	1	0	1
112	$17,500	5	4	0	0	1
113	$20,000	5	5	1	0	1
114	$19,500	5	6	1	1	1
115	$18,500	5	6	0	0	1
116	$19,500	5	9	1	0	1
117	$16,000	5	9	0	0	1
118	$20,500	5	10	1	0	1
119	$17,500	5	10	0	0	1
120	$20,500	5	11	1	0	1

(continued)

OBS	PRICPAID	FLOORHGT	DISTELEV	VIEWOCEN	ENDUNIT	FURN
121	$20,500	5	12	1	0	1
122	$16,600	5	12	0	0	1
123	$19,500	5	13	1	0	0
124	$20,500	5	15	1	0	0
125	$21,000	6	1	0	0	1
126	$16,500	6	1	0	0	0
127	$22,000	6	2	1	0	0
128	$18,000	6	2	0	0	1
129	$21,500	6	3	1	0	0
130	$17,500	6	3	0	0	0
131	$20,000	6	4	1	0	1
132	$16,500	6	4	0	0	0
133	$17,500	6	5	0	0	1
134	$18,500	6	6	1	0	0
135	$20,000	6	9	1	0	1
136	$16,500	6	9	0	0	0
137	$17,500	6	10	1	0	0
138	$17,000	6	10	0	0	1
139	$19,000	6	11	1	0	0
140	$17,000	6	11	0	0	0
141	$20,000	6	12	1	0	1
142	$19,500	6	13	1	0	0
143	$19,500	6	14	1	0	0
144	$20,500	7	1	1	0	0
145	$18,000	7	1	0	0	1
146	$19,500	7	2	1	0	0
147	$17,000	7	2	0	0	0
148	$19,500	7	3	1	0	0
149	$18,600	7	3	0	0	1
150	$20,000	7	4	1	0	0
151	$17,500	7	4	0	0	1
152	$19,000	7	5	1	0	0
153	$19,000	7	6	1	1	1
154	$19,500	7	9	1	0	0
155	$17,000	7	9	0	0	0
156	$20,000	7	10	1	0	0
157	$18,000	7	10	0	0	1
158	$19,000	7	11	1	0	0
159	$18,000	7	11	0	0	1
160	$19,000	7	12	1	0	0
161	$17,500	7	12	0	0	0
162	$19,500	7	14	1	0	0
163	$19,000	8	1	1	0	0
164	$18,000	8	1	0	0	1
165	$20,500	8	2	1	0	0

OBS	PRICPAID	FLOORHGT	DISTELEV	VIEWOCEN	ENDUNIT	FURN
166	$17,500	8	2	0	0	0
167	$21,500	8	3	1	0	1
168	$17,500	8	3	0	0	0
169	$19,500	8	4	1	0	0
170	$17,000	8	4	0	0	0
171	$18,500	8	5	1	0	0
172	$17,500	8	5	0	0	0
173	$17,500	8	6	1	1	0
174	$17,500	8	6	0	0	0
175	$20,500	8	9	1	0	1
176	$16,500	8	9	0	0	0
177	$20,000	8	10	1	0	0
178	$17,500	8	10	0	0	0
179	$20,500	8	11	1	0	0
180	$19,000	8	12	1	0	0
181	$20,500	8	13	1	0	1
182	$19,500	8	14	1	0	0
183	$15,000	3	13	0	0	1
184	$14,000	5	1	1	0	1
185	$13,000	5	2	0	0	1
186	$18,200	6	5	1	0	1
187	$17,500	5	1	0	0	1
188	$16,400	5	14	1	0	1
189	$24,900	4	1	1	0	1
190	$21,500	7	13	1	0	1
191	$19,900	2	12	0	0	1
192	$19,000	8	5	0	0	1
193	$29,500	1	13	1	0	1
194	$21,700	2	13	0	0	1
195	$26,500	3	10	1	0	1
196	$20,200	4	1	0	0	1
197	$17,700	4	4	0	0	1
198	$18,900	8	11	0	0	1
199	$19,700	3	12	0	0	1
200	$20,500	3	1	0	0	1
201	$20,600	2	13	0	0	1
202	$23,100	7	4	1	0	1
203	$25,500	4	10	1	0	1
204	$25,000	7	14	1	0	1
205	$23,000	1	14	0	0	1
206	$27,900	4	12	1	0	1
207	$21,500	6	1	0	0	1
208	$30,600	3	15	1	0	1
209	$19,000	3	6	0	0	1

ANSWERS

Answers to Odd-Numbered Exercises

Chapter 1

1.1a. New automobiles **b.** Model: qualitative; manufacturer: qualitative; transmission: qualitative; engine size: quantitative; number of cylinders: quantitative; city mpg: quantitative; highway mpg: quantitative **1.3** (1) Quantitative (2) Qualitative (3) Quantitative (4) Qualitative (5) Quantitative (6) Qualitative (7) Qualitative (8) Quantitative (9) Quantitative (10) Quantitative **1.5a.** Quantitative **b.** Quantitative **c.** Quantitative **d.** Qualitative **e.** Qualitative **1.7a.** Qualitative **b.** Qualitative **c.** Qualitative **d.** Quantitative **e.** Quantitative **1.9a.** Thion levels of all possible daily ambient air specimens that can be collected at the orchard **b.** Thion levels for the 13 ambient air specimens actually measured **1.11a.** Smokers and former smokers **b.** 3; qualitative **c.** Samples **1.13a.** Job status (quit or not) of all state lottery winners **b.** Job status of 576 lottery winners who returned questionnaire **c.** 11% of all state lottery winners quit their job during first year after winning **1.15a.** Opinions of all American adults concerning support of euthanasia **b.** No **c.** Results of survey could possibly be used to develop legislation regarding euthanasia **1.17a.** Frequency histogram **b.** 250 **c.** Yes; skewed to the right **1.19a.** .02, .02, .06, .08, .20, .14, .10, .08, .06, .04, .06, .04, .06, .04 **b.** No **1.21a.** Sample **1.23a.** 3; 7; 2.646 **b.** 2; 4.4; 2.098 **c.** 8; 18.667; 4.32 **d.** 4.75; 12.917; 3.594 **e.** 10; 91.5; 9.566 **f.** 52.0; 3.336; 57.76 **g.** -2; 1.6; 1.265 **h.** .333; .0587; .242 **1.25a.** (3.95, 12.03) **b.** No **1.27** $R = 900 - 50 = 850$; $s \approx 850/4 = 212.5$ **1.29a** 9.333; 32.506; 5.701 **b.** (-2.069, 20.736) **1.31a.** 14.682 **b.** 199.974; 14.141 **c.** $\approx .95$ **d.** $60/66 = .909$ **e.** Decrease; decrease **f.** 13.74; 11.96 **g.** $59/65 = .908$ **1.33a.** .6826 **b.** .9500 **c.** .9000 **d.** .9974 **1.35a.** -3 **b.** 1.96 **c.** 1.645 **d.** 1.0 **e.** $-.15$ **1.37a.** .0694 **b.** .4402 **1.39a.** .9406 **b.** .0068 **1.41a.** .5199 **b.** 4.393 **1.43b.** 4.68 **c.** 7.931 **1.45a.** Approximately normal; $\mu_{\bar{y}} = 15$; $\sigma_{\bar{y}} = 1.118$ **b.** ≈ 0 **c.** True value of μ is highly likely to be less than 15 **1.47a.** 5.4 **b.** 5.4 ± 1.09 **1.49a.** 74.31 ± 15.57 **b.** Yes **1.51a.** $5.99 + 3.14$ **c.** Distribution of TCDD levels is approximately normal **1.53a.** .95 **b.** 95% of all similarly constructed intervals contain μ **c.** 95% confident that true mean sampling rate falls between 49.66 and 51.48 **d.** Distribution of sampling rates is approximately normal **1.55a.** $1.94 \pm .13$ **b.** Increase n or decrease $(1 - \alpha)$ **1.57a.** H_a and α **b.** No **1.59a.** H_0: $\mu = 88{,}000$, H_a: $\mu \neq 88{,}000$ **1.61** Reject H_0; $z = 8.82$; $p = 0$ **1.63** $t = -3.89$; reject H_0 **1.65** Do not reject H_0; $t = -1.39$ **1.67** $t = -12.60$, reject H_0 **1.69a.** Normal **b.** Independent **1.71a.** $.38 \pm .22$ **b.** No; infer that $\mu_{old} > \mu_{new}$ **1.73a.** Small-sample t-test **b.** Normal populations **c.** No **d.** Fail to reject H_0: $\mu_1 = \mu_2$ **e.** Reject H_0: $\mu_1 = \mu_2$ **1.75** Statement valid **1.77a.** $.99 \pm .50$ **b.** Yes **1.79** No, $p = .50$; both investment/quad populations are approximately normal with equal variances **1.81** $F = 3.41$; reject H_0 **1.83** Yes (at $\alpha = .05$), $F = 2.43$ **1.85** $F = 5.87$; reject H_0 **1.87a.** 5; 4.637; 21.5 **b.** 16.75; 6.021; 36.25 **c.** 4.857; 5.460; 29.81 **d.** 4; 0; 0 **1.89a.** 4 below the mean **b.** .5 above the mean **c.** 0 **d.** 6 above **1.91** Brand name **1.93a.** 0 **b.** .05 **c.** .44 **d.** -1.09 **1.95a.** .0548 **b.** 97 days **1.97a.** .2033 **b.** No **c.** ≈ 0 **d.** No **1.99a.** 41.135 ± 6.173 **c.** Relative frequency distribution of foreign revenues is approximately normal **1.101a.** Approximately normal with $\mu_{\bar{y}} = 8$ and $\sigma_{\bar{y}} = .822$ **b** .0075 **c.** 8 ± 1.64 **1.103** $F = 4.06$; reject H_0 **1.105a.** .1 **b.** $.1 \pm .27$ **d.** Increase n's

Chapter 3

3.3a. $\beta_0 = 2; \beta_1 = 2$ **b.** $\beta_0 = 4; \beta_1 = 1$ **c.** $\beta_0 = -2; \beta_1 = 4$ **d.** $\beta_0 = -4; \beta_1 = -1$ **3.5a.** $\beta_1 = 2; \beta_0 = 3$ **b.** $\beta_1 = 1; \beta_0 = 1$ **c.** $\beta_1 = 3; \beta_0 = -2$ **d.** $\beta_1 = 5; \beta_0 = 0$ **e.** $\beta_1 = -2; \beta_0 = 4$ **3.7a.** $\hat{\beta}_0 = 2; \hat{\beta}_1 = -1.2$ **3.9b.** $\hat{y} = -.00105 + .00321x$ **3.11b.** $\hat{y} = 4.79 + .014x$ **3.13a.** Yes **b.** $\hat{\beta}_0 = 1.192, \hat{\beta}_1 = .987$ **3.15a.** 1.60; .533; .730 **b.** .00068; .0000523; .00723 **c.** 30.768; 2.051; 1.432 **d.** .2509; .0502; .2240 **3.17b.** $\hat{y} = .3537 + .000004426x$ **d.** .3892 **e.** SSE = .10218, $s^2 = .01022$ **f.** .10108 **3.19a.** $\hat{y} = -405.25 + .218x$ **c.** SSE = 115.81; $s^2 = 38.60$ **d.** 6.213 **3.21** Yes, $t = 5.05$ **3.23** $t = .256$; no **3.25a.** .953 ± .05 **3.27a.** Yes, $t = 7.13$ **b.** Yes, $t = 5.98$ **c.** Yes, $t = 4.98$ **d.** 7.07 **e.** 35.86 **f.** 1,390.08 **3.29b.** $\hat{y} = 78.52 - .2389x$ **d.** $t = -2.31$, do not reject H_0 **e.** Observation #5 is an outlier **f.** $\hat{y} = 139.759 - .44969x$; $t = -15.35$, reject H_0 **3.31** Possibly; positive **3.35c.** $t = 38.66$, reject H_0 **3.37b.** −.766 **c.** $t = -4.92$; reject H_0 **3.39** Yes; $t = 3.88$ **3.41c.** $t = 7.79$, reject H_0 **3.43a.** .0311 ± .0133 **b.** .0311 ± .0036 **d.** Possibly for the prediction interval; yes for the confidence interval **3.45a.** 6.27 ± .26 **b.** 6.27 ± .96 **3.47** .3891 ± .2423; model not useful **3.49** −398.7 ± 10.52 **3.51** $\hat{y} = 28.894 + .905x$; SSE = 13,236.45; $s^2 = 315.15$; $s = 17.75$; $r^2 = .0661$; $t = 1.725$ (p-value = .0919) for testing H_0: $\beta_1 = 0$ (do not reject H_0) **3.53** $\hat{y} = -.535 + 15.526x$; SSE = 6.974; $s^2 = .8718$; $s = .9337$; $r^2 = .9760$; $t = 18.05$ (p-value = .0001) for testing H_0: $\beta_1 = 0$ (reject H_0); 95% prediction interval for y when $x = .4$ is (3.357, 7.994) **3.55** $\hat{y} = .213 + 2.426x$ **b.** $r^2 = .837$ **c.** $t = 10.63$ **d.** ≈ 0 **e.** $s = .454$ **3.57a.** $\hat{y} = -9.2667x$ **b.** SSE = 12.8667; $s^2 = 32167$; $s = 1.7935$; **c.** Yes; $t = -28.30$ **d.** −9.2667 ± .9090 **e.** −9.2667 ± .9090 **f.** −9.2667 ± 5.0611 **3.59a.** $\hat{y} = 5.364x$ **b.** Yes; $t = 25.28$ **c.** 18.774 ± 6.300 **3.61a.** $\hat{y} = 51.18x$ **b.** Yes; $t = 154.56$ **c.** $\hat{y} = 1{,}855.35 + 47.07x$; yes, $t = 93.36$ **d.** $y = \beta_0 + \beta_1 x + \varepsilon$ (reject H_0: $\beta_0 = 0$, $t = 8.37$) **3.63** Scheduling: $t = 2.47$, reject H_0; synchron: $t = .77$, do not reject H_0; alloc.: $t = -2.83$, reject H_0; autonomy: $t = -4.92$, reject H_0; future: $t = 5.37$, reject H_0 **3.65a.** $t = 24.0$; yes **b.** $t = 9.33$; yes **c.** .941, .774 **3.67a.** Yes; $t = -6.69$ **b.** .04 **3.69a.** $\hat{y} = 14{,}012 - 1{,}783x$; no (at $\alpha = .05$), $t = -.98$ **b.** $\hat{y} = 19{,}680 - 3{,}887x$; yes (at $\alpha = .05$), $t = -2.29$ **c.** Predicting outside range of x (1.52–4.11) **3.71b.** $\hat{y} = 5.977 + 74.068x$ **d.** 11.162 **e.** 11.162 ± 3.739 **f.** 11.162 ± 1.024 **3.73a.** Yes **b.** Yes **d.** 8.29 **e.** 21.15 **3.75** Probably; however, we cannot conduct a test since n is not given

Chapter 4

4.1 df = n − (number of independent variables + 1) **4.3a.** $E(y) = \beta_0 + \beta_1x_1 + \beta_2x_2 + \beta_3x_3$ **b.** Do not reject H_0: $\beta_2 = 0$ **4.5** Estimate of β_1 **4.7a.** Accountants: $F = 10.68$; reject H_0; truck drivers: $F = 22.07$, reject H_0 **b.** $\hat{\beta}_2$ **c.** Yes; $t = 3.23$ **d.** Yes; $t = 4.70$ **4.9a.** $E(y) = \beta_0 + \beta_1x_1 + \beta_2x_1^2$ **b.** Test H_0: $\beta_2 = 0$ vs. H_a: $\beta_2 < 0$ **4.11** $F = 1.056$; do not reject H_0 **b.** .05 **4.13b.** $t = -2.71$; reject H_0 **c.** Rental price, empl. growth, AFDC benefits, SSI benefits **d.** Inflated α error **4.15a.** $F = 9.6893$; reject H_0: $\beta_1 = \beta_2 = \beta_3 = 0$ **b.** $t = 1.444$; reject H_0: $\beta_1 = 0$ in favor of H_a: $\beta_1 > 0$ **4.17a.** $F = 72.11$, reject H_0 **b.** (47, 3,825) **4.19a.** Yes; $F = 120.651$ **b.** $t = 9.857$, reject H_0 **c.** (253.81, 821.39) **4.21a.** $E(y) = \beta_0 + \beta_1x_1 + \beta_2x_2$ **b.** $E(y) = \beta_0 + \beta_1x_1 + \beta_2x_2 + \beta_3x_3 + \beta_4x_4$

4.23a. $E(y) = \beta_0 + \beta_1x_1$, where $x = \begin{cases} 1 & \text{if A} \\ 0 & \text{if B} \end{cases}$

b. $E(y) = \beta_0 + \beta_1x_1 + \beta_2x_2 + \beta_3x_3$, where $x_1 = \begin{cases} 1 & \text{if A} \\ 0 & \text{if not} \end{cases}$ $x_2 = \begin{cases} 1 & \text{if B} \\ 0 & \text{if not} \end{cases}$ $x_3 = \begin{cases} 1 & \text{if C} \\ 0 & \text{if not} \end{cases}$

$\beta_0 = \mu_D$, $\beta_1 = \mu_A - \mu_D$, $\beta_2 = \mu_B - \mu_D$, $\beta_3 = \mu_C - \mu_D$ **4.25c.** Parallel lines **4.27b.** Second-order **c.** Different shapes **d.** Yes **e.** Shift curves along the x_1-axis **4.29a.** $\hat{y} = 64.82 + 1.05x_1 - 10.53x_2 + .27x_3 + 9.46x_4 - 92.97x_5$ **b.** β_1: Estimate y to increase \$1.05 for every 1-year increase in age holding all other x's fixed; β_4: estimate y to increase \$9.46 for each additional medication, holding all other x's fixed **c.** All x's significant except x_2 and x_3 **d.** Reject H_0: $\beta_1 = \beta_2 = \beta_3 = \beta_4 = \beta_5 = 0$ **e.** Model explains 44% of sample variation in y **f.** \$140.72 **4.31a.** Quantitative **b.** Quantitative **c.** Qualitative

d. $E(y) = \beta_0 + \beta_1x_1 + \beta_2x_2 + \beta_3x_3 + \beta_4x_4$, where $x_1 = \begin{cases} 1 & \text{if benzene} \\ 0 & \text{if not} \end{cases}$, $x_2 = \begin{cases} 1 & \text{if toluene} \\ 0 & \text{if not} \end{cases}$, $x_3 = \begin{cases} 1 & \text{if chloroform} \\ 0 & \text{if not} \end{cases}$, $x_4 = \begin{cases} 1 & \text{if methanol} \\ 0 & \text{if not} \end{cases}$

e. $\beta_0 = \mu_A$, $\beta_1 = \mu_B - \mu_A$, $\beta_2 = \mu_T - \mu_A$, $\beta_3 = \mu_C - \mu_A$, $\beta_4 = \mu_M - \mu_A$ **f.** Test H_0: $\beta_1 = \beta_2 = \beta_3 = \beta_4 = 0$ **4.33** $F = 70.46$; reject H_0: $\beta_1 = \beta_2 = \beta_3 = \beta_4 = 0$ **4.35a.** $F = 3{,}909.25$; reject H_0 **c.** H_0: $\beta_4 = 0$; H_a: $\beta_4 < 0$ **e.** No; since β_4 is positive **4.37** e(complete) and any other model; d(complete) and b; d(complete) and a; c(complete) and b; a(complete) and b **4.39a.** H_0: $\beta_5 = \beta_6 = \beta_7 = \beta_8 = 0$; $F > 2.37$ **b.** Yes **c.** Reject H_0 for both tests **4.41a.** H_0: $\beta_2 = 0$ **b.** Do not reject H_0 **4.43a.** $F = 2.94$; yes **b.** $F = 1.50$; no **c.** $F = 5.73$; reject H_0 **4.45a.** x_2; largest $|t|$ value ($t = -90$) **b.** Yes **c.** Fit all possible two-variable models, $E(y) = \beta_0 + \beta_1x_2 + \beta_2x_i$ **4.47a.** Use all but size (acres) and farm land (yes–no), testing at $\alpha = .01$

b.
$$E(y) = \beta_0 + \beta_1x_1 + \beta_2x_2 + \beta_3x_3 + \beta_4x_4 + \beta_5x_1x_2 + \beta_6x_1x_3 + \beta_7x_1x_4 + \underbrace{\beta_8x_2x_3 + \beta_9x_2x_4 + \beta_{10}x_3x_4 + \beta_{11}x_1^2 + \beta_{12}x_2^2 + \beta_{13}x_3^2 + \beta_{14}x_4^2}_{\text{quantitative terms}}$$
$$+ \beta_{15}x_5 + \beta_{16}x_6 + \beta_{17}x_5x_6 \; \} \text{ qualitative terms}$$
$$+ (\text{quantitative} \times \text{qualitative}) \; \} \text{ interaction terms}$$

where x_1 = seedlings and saplings x_2 = percent ponds
x_3 = distance to state park x_4 = site index
$x_5 = \begin{cases} 1 & \text{if residential land} \\ 0 & \text{if not} \end{cases}$ $x_6 = \begin{cases} 1 & \text{if branches or springs} \\ 0 & \text{if not} \end{cases}$

4.49a. (i) 4; (ii) 6; (iii) 4; (iv) 1 **b.** (i) max R^2= .2130, min MSE = 193.8, min C_p = 2.54, min PRESS = 10,507.4; (ii) max R^2 = .2473, min MSE = 189.1, min C_p = 2.34, min PRESS = 10,461.0; (iii) max R^2 = .2663, min MSE = 188.2, min C_p = 3.12, min PRESS = 10,489.3; (iv) max R^2 = .2682, min MSE = 191.7, min C_p = 5.00, min PRESS = 10,710.4 **4.51a.** Yes; positive **b.** Yes; positive **c.** t = 24.56; yes **d.** 1.278 + .505 **4.53a.** −75.51 ± 26.17 **b.** Do not reject H_0: t = 1.38 **d.** Yes; p-value < .01 **4.55a.** F = 17.8; yes **b.** t = −3.50; reject H_0: $\beta_1 = 0$ **c.** −6.38 ± 4.72 **4.57a.** $\hat{y} = 22.019 - .181x_1 - .25x_2 - 4.691x_3 + 3.674x_4 + 22.52x_5$ **b.** .599 **c.** 8.657 **d.** Yes; F = 87.45 **e.** Yes; t = −4.64 **f.** 3.674 ± .789 **g.** 22.52 ± 7.048 **4.59b.** t = 5; yes **c.** 825 **d.** Support **e.** The estimate of the difference in mean attendance between weekends and weekdays is $15x_3 - 700$
4.61a. $\hat{y} = 2.14 - .15x_1 + .03x_2 + 2.54x_3 - .34x_4 - .26x_5 - .72x_6$ **b.** Yes; F = 25.27 **c.** Yes; one-tailed p-value < .05/2 = .025 **d.** No; p-value > .05 **e.** H_0: $\beta_4 = \beta_5 = \beta_6 = 0$ **4.63b.** Test H_0: $\beta_2 = \beta_3 = 0$ **c.** t = −3.333; yes

Chapter 5

5.1a. Qualitative **b.** Quantitative **c.** Qualitative **d.** Quantitative **e.** Quantitative **f.** Qualitative
5.3a. Quantitative **b.** Quantitative **c.** Qualitative **d.** Qualitative **e.** Qualitative **f.** Quantitative **g.** Qualitative **h.** Qualitative **i.** Qualitative **j.** Quantitative **k.** Qualitative **5.5a.** (i) First-order (ii) Third-order (iii) First-order (iv) Second-order **b.** (i) $E(y) = \beta_0 + \beta_1 x$ (ii) $E(y) = \beta_0 + \beta_1 x + \beta_2 x^2 + \beta_3 x^3$ (iii) $E(y) = \beta_0 + \beta_1 x$ (iv) $E(y) = \beta_0 + \beta_1 x + \beta_2 x^2$ **c.** (i) $\beta_1 > 0$ (ii) $\beta_3 > 0$ (iii) $\beta_1 < 0$ (iv) $\beta_2 < 0$ **5.7** $E(y) = \beta_0 + \beta_1 x + \beta_2 x^2 + \beta_3 x^3$
5.9. $E(y) = \beta_0 + \beta_1 x + \beta_2 x^2$, where $\beta_2 > 0$ **5.13a.** $E(y) = \beta_0 + \beta_1 x_1 + \beta_2 x_2 + \beta_3 x_1 x_2 + \beta_4 x_1^2 + \beta_5 x_2^2$ **b.** $E(y) = \beta_0 + \beta_1 x_1 + \beta_2 x_2$ **c.** $E(y) = \beta_0 + \beta_1 x_1 + \beta_2 x_2 + \beta_3 x_1 x_2$ **d.** $\beta_1 + \beta_3 x_2$ **e.** $\beta_2 + \beta_3 x_1$
5.15a. $u = (x - 33)/2.16$ **b.** −1.389, −.926, −.463, 0, .463, .926, 1.389 **c.** .99966 **d.** 0 **e.** $\hat{y} = 37.5714 - .4629u - 5.3333u^2$
5.17a. $u = (x - 85.1)/14.81$ **b.** −.668, .446, 1.026, −1.411, −.223, 1.695, −.527, −.338 **c.** .9967 **d.** .3764 **e.** $\hat{y} = 110.953 + 14.373u + 7.421u^2$ **5.19a.** $\mu_{\text{(wife employed)}} < \mu_{\text{(wife unemployed)}}$
b. 2% of variation in job satisfaction is explained by the model
5.21a. $E(y) = \beta_0 + \beta_1 x_1 + \beta_2 x_2 + \beta_3 x_3 + \beta_4 x_4$ **b.** $\mu_{BA} - \mu_N$ **c.** $\mu_E - \mu_N$ **d.** $\mu_{LAS} - \mu_N$ **e.** $\mu_J - \mu_N$ **f.** $E(y) = (\beta_0 + \beta_5) + \beta_1 x_1 + \beta_2 x_2 + \beta_3 x_3 + \beta_4 x_4$ **g.** $\mu_{BA} - \mu_N$ **h.** $\mu_E - \mu_N$ **i.** $\mu_{LAS} - \mu_N$ **j.** $\mu_J - \mu_N$ **k.** $\mu_F - \mu_M$
l. Reject H_0: $\beta_5 = 0$; gender has an effect
5.23a. $E(y) = \beta_0 + \beta_1 x_1 + \beta_2 x_2 + \beta_3 x_3$, where $x_1 = \begin{cases} 1 & \text{if moderate concentration} \\ 0 & \text{if not} \end{cases}$, $x_2 = \begin{cases} 1 & \text{if high concentration} \\ 0 & \text{if not} \end{cases}$, $x_3 = \begin{cases} 1 & \text{if consumer type} \\ 0 & \text{if not} \end{cases}$ **c.** $E(y) = \beta_0 + \beta_1 x_1 + \beta_2 x_2 + \beta_3 x_3 + \beta_4 x_1 x_3 + \beta_5 x_2 x_3$ **e.** Test H_0: $\beta_4 = \beta_5 = 0$ using a partial F-test
5.25a. $E(y) = \beta_0 + \beta_1 x_2 + \beta_2 x_2^2$ **b.** Add $\beta_3 x_3 + \beta_4 x_4 + \beta_5 x_5 + \beta_6 x_6$ **c.** Add $\beta_7 x_2 x_3 + \beta_8 x_2 x_4 + \beta_9 x_2 x_5 + \beta_{10} x_2 x_6 + \beta_{11} x_2^2 x_3 + \beta_{12} x_2^2 x_4 + \beta_{13} x_2^2 x_5 + \beta_{14} x_2^2 x_6$ **d.** If $\beta_7 = \beta_8 = \cdots = \beta_{14} = 0$ **e.** If $\beta_2 = \beta_7 = \beta_8 = \cdots = \beta_{14} = 0$ **f.** If $\beta_3 = \beta_4 = \cdots = \beta_{14} = 0$ **5.27a.** F = 14.42, reject H_0: $\beta_1 = \beta_2 = \beta_3 = 0$; R^2 = .812; s = 8.057 **b.** F = 8.79; reject H_0: $\beta_4 = \beta_5 = 0$ **c.** DF-2: 2.14; blended: 4.865; adv. timing: 7.815
5.29a. $E(y) = \beta_0 + \beta_1 x_1 + \beta_2 x_2 + \beta_3 x_3$ **b.** Test H_0: $\beta_3 = 0$ versus H_a: $\beta_3 < 0$ using a t test **c.** $E(y) = \beta_0 + \beta_1 x_1 + \beta_2 x_2 + \beta_3 x_1 x_2 + \beta_4 x_1^2 + \beta_5 x_2^2 + \beta_6 x_3 + \beta_7 x_1 x_3 + \beta_8 x_2 x_3 + \beta_9 x_1 x_2 x_3 + \beta_{10} x_1^2 x_3 + \beta_{11} x_2^2 x_3$
d. Test H_0: $\beta_1 = \beta_3 = \beta_4 = \beta_7 = \beta_9 = \beta_{10} = 0$ using a partial F-test
5.31a. Quantitative **b.** Quantitative **c.** Qualitative **d.** Qualitative **e.** Qualitative **f.** Qualitative **g.** Quantitative **h.** Qualitative
5.33a. $E(y) = \beta_0 + \beta_1 x_1 + \beta_2 x_2 + \beta_3 x_3 + \beta_4 x_1 x_2 + \beta_5 x_1 x_3$, where $x_2 = \begin{cases} 1 & \text{if algorithm B} \\ 0 & \text{otherwise} \end{cases}$ and $x_3 = \begin{cases} 1 & \text{if algorithm C} \\ 0 & \text{if otherwise} \end{cases}$
b. F = 4.90, reject H_0 (p-value = .0394) **c.** $E(y) = \beta_0 + \beta_1 x_1 + \beta_2 x_2 + \beta_3 x_3$ **d.** F = 2.36; no
5.35a. $E(y) = \beta_0 + \beta_1 x_1 + \beta_2 x_2 + \beta_3 x_3 + \beta_4 x_4$; no interaction **b.** Include $\beta_5 x_1 x_2 + \beta_6 x_1 x_3 + \beta_7 x_1 x_4$ in model
5.37a. $E(y) = \beta_0 + \beta_1 x_1 + \beta_2 x_2$, where x_1 = years of education, $x_2 = \begin{cases} 1 & \text{if certified} \\ 0 & \text{if not} \end{cases}$ **b.** $E(y) = \beta_0 + \beta_1 x_1 + \beta_2 x_2 + \beta_3 x_1 x_2$
c. $E(y) = \beta_0 + \beta_1 x_1 + \beta_2 x_1^2 + \beta_3 x_2 + \beta_4 x_1 x_2 + \beta_5 x_1^2 x_2$ **5.39b.** H_0: $\beta_2 = \beta_5 = 0$ **c.** H_0: $\beta_3 = \beta_4 = \beta_5 = 0$
5.41a. 5 **b.** −1 **c.** −1 versus 1 **5.43a.** $E(y) = \beta_0 + \beta_1 x_1 + \beta_2 x_1^2 + \beta_3 x_2 + \beta_4 x_1 x_2 + \beta_5 x_1^2 x_2$
b. $E(y) = \beta_0 + \beta_1 x_3 + \beta_2 x_4 + \beta_3 x_3 x_4 + \beta_4 x_3^2 + \beta_5 x_4^2$ **c.** $E(y) = \beta_0 + \beta_1 x_1 + \beta_2 x_2 + \beta_3 x_3 + \beta_4 x_4$
d. $E(y) = \beta_0 + \beta_1 x_1 + \beta_2 x_2 + \beta_3 x_3 + \beta_4 x_4 + \beta_5 x_1 x_2 + \beta_6 x_2 x_3 + \beta_7 x_2 x_4$

Chapter 6

6.7 Drop Importance (since highly correlated with Support)
6.9 Unable to test model adequacy since there are no degrees of freedom available for estimating σ^2 (i.e., df $= n - 3 = 0$)
6.11a. $\hat{y} = 2.74 + .801x$; yes, $t = 15.918$ **b.** $\hat{y} = 1.66 + 12.395x_2$; yes, $t = 11.759$
c. $\hat{y} = -11.79 + 25.068x_3$; yes, $t = 2.512$
6.13 Possibly; 2 of 3 t-tests are nonsignificant in presence of significant F test **6.15** Two levels each; $n \geq 4$
6.17a. Yes, $F = 37.204$ (p-value $= .0007$) **b.** x_1 possibly correlated with other x's **c.** Possible multicollinearity
d. $r_{12} = .3275$; $r_{13} = .2307$; $r_{14} = .1658$; $r_{23} = .7898$; $r_{24} = .7909$; $r_{34} = .881$; yes **6.19a.** .0025; no **b.** .434; no **c.** No
d. $\hat{y} = -45.154 + 3.097x_1 + 1.032x_2$, $F = 39{,}222.34$, reject H_0: $\beta_1 = \beta_2 = 0$; $R^2 = .9998$ **e.** $-.8978$; high correlation **f.** No
6.21 df(Error) $= 0$, s^2 undefined, no test of model adequacy

Chapter 7

7.1a. $-.406, -.206, -.047, .053, .112, .212, .271, .471, .330, .230, -.411, -.611$ **b.** Yes; needs curvature **7.3a.** $\hat{y} = 40.35 - .207x$
b. $-4.64, -3.94, -1.83, .57, 2.58, 1.28, 4.69, 4.09, 4.39, 2.79, .50, 1.10, -6.09, -5.49$ **c.** Yes; model needs curvature
d. $\hat{y} = -1{,}051.108 + 66.186x - 1.006x^2$; yes, $t = -11.80$ **7.5a.** $.796, -.219, -1.004, .077, -1.071, 1.116, .868, .827, .223, -1.612$
d. 43.83, 20.36, 36.42, 31.88, 26.99, 40.41, 45.77, 25.15, 35.77, 45.16 **e.** 7.19, 2.34, 10.50, 3.91, 9.15, 6.23, 9.81, 8.49, 9.17, .94
7.7c. No; no curvature **7.9** Assumption of constant error variance appears satisfied; quadratic trend suggests need for curvature
7.11a. Yes; assumption of equal variances violated **b.** Use variance-stabilizing transformation $y^* = \sqrt{y}$
7.13a. $\hat{y} = .94 - .214x$ **b.** $0, .02, -.026, .034, .088, -.112, -.058, .002, .036, .016$ **c.** Football shape; unequal variances
d. Use the transformation $y^* = \sin^{-1}\sqrt{y}$ and fit the model $y^* = \beta_0 + \beta_1 x + \varepsilon$ **e.** $\hat{y}^* = 1.307 - .2496x$; possibly
7.15 Residuals are approximately normal **7.17** Residuals are approximately normal **7.19** No outliers **7.21a.** Yes; $F = 21.772$ ($p = .0001$)
b. Yes; s is reduced **c.** Model adequate ($F = 251.172$, $p = .0001$); residual for San Diego Harbor is relatively small **7.23** No outliers
7.25a. No **b.** Observation (child) #24 is influential **7.27b.** Model adequate at $\alpha = .05$ for all banks except bank 5
c. Reject H_0 (two-tailed at $\alpha = .05$) for banks 2 and 5; fail to reject H_0 for banks 4, 6 and 8; test inconclusive for banks 1, 3, 7, and 9
7.29a. Yes **b.** $d = .173$; reject H_0 ($d_L = 1.18$) **7.31a.** No, do not reject H_0; $d_U = 1.60$ **b.** Yes; reject H_0; $d_L = 1.39$
7.33a. Misspecified model; quadratic term missing **b.** Unequal variances **c.** Outlier **d.** Unequal variances **e.** Nonnormal errors
7.35a. Yes; $F_{.05} = 2.51$ **b.** No; $d_L = 1.03$, $d_U = 1.85$
7.37a. Residuals: $1.27, 12.63, -10.27, -.13, 20.72, 13.76, -34.47, -.05, 11.95, -11.91, -9.35, 3.88, 4.21, 4.32, -6.54$
b. $-72.18, -62.41, -77.41, -65.69, -54.32, -67.60, -113.46, -82.98, -70.98, -94.84, -100.18, -90.90, -86.62, -82.56, -93.42$
c. 350.2, 358.7, 335.8, 340.2, 358.2, 345.5, 300.1, 343.1, 355.1, 334.1, 339.5, 358.5, 364.5, 367.5, 359.5 **7.39a.** $\hat{y} = 1{,}604.81 - 64.1044t$
b. Residuals: $-773.7, -550.6, -241.5, 314.6, 773.7, 671.8, 709.9, 322.0, 39.1, -330.8, -359.7, -282.6, -292.5$; yes, runs of positive and negative residuals **c.** $d = .337$, reject H_0
7.41a. H_0: No residual correlation; H_a: Positive residual correlation; test statistic: d; rejection region: $d < 1.39$ **b.** Reject H_0

Chapter 8

8.1a. $E(y) = \beta_0 + \beta_1 x_1 + \beta_2(x_1 - 15)x_2$, where $x_1 = x$ and $x_2 = \begin{cases} 1 & \text{if } x_1 > 15 \\ 0 & \text{if not} \end{cases}$

b.

	y-INTERCEPT	SLOPE
$x \leq 15$	β_0	β_1
$x > 15$	$\beta_0 - 15\beta_2$	$\beta_1 + \beta_2$

c. Test H_0: $\beta_2 = 0$

8.3a. $E(y) = \beta_0 + \beta_1 x_1 + \beta_2(x_1 - 320)x_2 + \beta_3 x_2$, where $x_1 = x$, $x_2 = \begin{cases} 1 & \text{if } x_1 > 320 \\ 0 & \text{if not} \end{cases}$

b.

	y-INTERCEPT	SLOPE
$x \leq 320$	β_0	β_1
$x > 320$	$\beta_0 - 320\beta_2 + \beta_3$	$\beta_1 + \beta_2$

c. Test H_0: $\beta_2 = \beta_3 = 0$

8.5a. $E(y) = \beta_0 + \beta_1 x_1 + \beta_2(x_1 - 1{,}000)x_2$, where $x_1 = x$ and $x_2 = \begin{cases} 1 & \text{if } x_1 > 1{,}000 \\ 0 & \text{if not} \end{cases}$ **b.** $\hat{y} = 4.024 - .0021x_1 - .00139(x_1 - 1{,}000)x_2$
c. Yes; $F = 363.44$ (p-value $= .0001$) **d.** $-.0021 \pm .000366$ **8.7a.** 473.3 ± 540.2 **b.** Model is inadequate
8.9a. $\hat{y} = -2.03 + 6.06x$ **b.** Reject H_0: $t = 10.35$ **c.** $1.985 \pm .687$ **8.11a.** $\hat{y} = -1.2667 + .176x$; yes, $t = 4.09$ (p-value $= .0013$)
b. Residuals: $-1.33, 6.67, -5.33, -2.33, 1.67, -6.13, 3.87, -5.13, 9.87, -1.13, -7.93, 14.07, -6.93, 4.07, -3.93$; appears to be violated

c.

X	VARIANCE OF RESIDUALS; $w_i = 1/x_i^2$
100	20.7
150	44.3
200	85.2

d. $\hat{y} = -1.5143 + .1777x$ **8.15b.** $\hat{y} = -.5279 + .0750x_1 + .0747x_2 + .3912x_3$

c. Reject H_0; $F = 21.79$ d. Yes; $t = 4.01$ e. $(-.2122, .2047)$ **8.17a.** Reject H_0; $\chi^2 = 20.43$ b. Yes; $\chi^2 = 4.63$ c. (.00048, .40027)

Chapter 9

9.1b.

	I	II	III	IV
1989	—	—	332.8	335.4
1990	317.8	308.1	290.4	261.6
1991	256.6	251.0	230.7	249.9
1992	259.8	269.2	300.3	295.0
1993	301.6	310.0	321.3	—

c. Yes d. 86.88 e. 117.23
f. Quarter I: 286.7 (using $M_{21} \approx 330$); quarter II: 398 (using $M_{22} \approx 340$)

9.3a. Moving average: 15.17; exponential smoothing: 63.85; Holt–Winters: 8.27
b. Moving average: 17.12; exponential smoothing: 79.10; Holt–Winters: 9.47 c. Holt–Winters

9.5a. Yes b.

1980	—
1981	—
1982	283.56
1983	298.64
1984	309.84
1985	320.04
1986	331.20
1987	343.24
1988	357.06
1989	371.70
1990	386.32
1991	400.60
1992	—
1993	—
1995	forecast=456

c.

1980	—
1981	257.04
1982	269.86
1983	281.28
1984	293.21
1985	304.80
1986	314.24
1987	324.59
1988	336.46
1989	350.38
1990	366.75
1991	380.69
1992	393.69
1993	406.54
1995	forecast=414

d. 456

9.7a.

1971	1972	1973	1974	1975	1976	1977	1978	1979	1980
—	65.89	105.37	139.64	148.63	144.83	155.53	216.53	369.10	454.81

1981	1982	1983	1984	1985	1986	1987	1988	1989	1990
476.94	424.61	394.50	375.54	348.49	364.69	404.57	409.02	400.74	—

b. Approximately 400 for all three years

c.

1971	1972	1973	1974	1975	1976	1977	1978	1979	1980
41.25	55.14	89.28	145.62	158.24	131.49	144.94	183.79	283.00	541.41

1981	1982	1983	1984	1985	1986	1987	1988	1989	1990
468.79	393.10	437.84	375.80	329.00	360.10	399.15	429.37	390.84	385.43

d. 384.3 for all three years e. 1991: 381.4; 1992: 376.8; 1993: 372.1 f. Holt—Winters most accurate
9.9b. $\hat{y}_t = 39.4879 + 19.13032t - 1.31529t^2$ d. $(-31.25, 48.97)$
9.11b. Railroads: $\hat{y}_t = 74.527 - 8.239t$; buses: $\hat{y}_t = 35.260 - 2.442t$; air carriers: $\hat{y}_t = -13.173 + 10.915t$
d. Railroads: -24.35, $(-50.25, 1.56)$; buses: 5.96, $(-11.96, 23.88)$; air carriers: 117.81, (100.92, 134.70) **9.13a.** $\beta_1 = \mu_{\text{post}} - \mu_{\text{pre}}$ b. μ_{pre}
c. $-.55$ d. 2.53 e. 2.53 **9.15a.** No; $t = -1.39$ $(-t_{.05} = -1.645)$ b. 2,003.48 c. No; $t = -1.61$ $(-t_{.05} = -1.645)$ b. 1,901.81

9.17a. 0, 0, 0, .5, 0, 0, 0, .25, 0, 0, 0, .125, 0, 0, 0, .0625, 0, 0, 0, .03125
b. Autocorrelations for first-order model: .5, .25, .125, .0625, .03125, .0156, .0078, .0039, .0019, .0010, .0005, .0002, .0001, 0, 0, 0, 0, 0, 0, 0
9.19 $R_t = \phi_1 R_{t-1} + \phi_2 R_{t-2} + \phi_3 R_{t-3} + \phi_4 R_{t-4} + \varepsilon_t$ **9.21a.** $E(y_t) = \beta_0 + \beta_1 x_{1t} + \beta_2 x_{2t} + \beta_3 x_{3t} + \beta_4 t$
b. $E(y_t) = \beta_0 + \beta_1 x_{1t} + \beta_2 x_{2t} + \beta_3 x_{3t} + \beta_4 t + \beta_5 x_{1t} t + \beta_6 x_{2t} t + \beta_7 x_{3t} t$ **c.** $R_t = \phi R_{t-1} + \varepsilon_t$
9.23a. $E(y_t) = \beta_0 + \beta_1\left[\cos\left(\frac{2\pi}{365}\right)t\right] + \beta_2\left[\sin\left(\frac{2\pi}{365}\right)t\right]$
c. $E(y_t) = \beta_0 + \beta_1\left[\cos\left(\frac{2\pi}{365}\right)t\right] + \beta_2\left[\sin\left(\frac{2\pi}{365}\right)t\right] + \beta_3 t + \beta_4 t\left[\cos\left(\frac{2\pi}{365}\right)t\right] + \beta_5 t\left[\sin\left(\frac{2\pi}{365}\right)t\right]$ **d.** No; $R_t = \phi R_{t-1} + \varepsilon_t$
9.25a. $y_t = \beta_0 + \beta_1 t + \phi R_{t-1} + \varepsilon_t$ **b.** $\hat{y}_t = 4{,}787.82 + 22.34t + .736\hat{R}_{t-1}$ **d.** $R^2 = .8991$, $s = 43.61$
9.27a. $\hat{\beta}_0 = 434.93$; $\hat{\beta}_1 = 92.28$; $\hat{\phi} = .721$ **b.** .9057 **9.29a.** $F_{49} = 336.91$; $F_{50} = 323.41$; $F_{51} = 309.46$
b. y_{49}: 336.91 ± 6.48; y_{50}: 323.41 ± 8.34; y_{51}: 309.46 ± 9.36
9.31 Quarter 1: 5,221.1 ± 87.2; Quarter 2: 5,229.3 ± 108.3; Quarter 3: 5,241.2 ± 11.81; yes
9.33 1991: 2,660.1 ± 406.9; 1992: 2,672.2 ± 501.6; 1993: 2,706.7 ± 544.4; forecast interval for 1993 misses
9.35a. 2,136.2 **b.** (1,404.3, 3,249.7) **c.** 1,944.0; (1,301.8, 2,902.9)

9.37a.

YEAR	JAN.	FEB.	MAR.	APR.	MAY	JUNE
1991	—	—	—	—	—	—
1992	8.02	7.91	7.92	7.92	7.80	7.84
1993	7.42	7.37	7.47	7.49	7.62	7.79

YEAR	JULY	AUG.	SEPT.	OCT.	NOV.	DEC.
1991	8.17	8.10	8.17	8.33	8.33	8.11
1992	7.84	7.72	7.67	7.47	7.37	7.36
1993	7.84	—	—	—	—	—

b. 7.0 (using $M_{37} = 8.4$)

YEAR	JAN.	FEB.	MAR.	APR.	MAY	JUNE
1991	8.00	7.22	7.81	8.76	9.81	9.20
1992	7.04	7.32	8.99	9.23	8.43	7.99
1993	6.13	6.65	7.28	7.83	7.75	8.14

YEAR	JULY	AUG.	SEPT.	OCT.	NOV.	DEC.
1991	9.74	8.34	7.59	8.26	7.26	6.81
1992	8.48	7.89	7.42	7.35	7.20	6.78
1993	8.24	8.45	7.82	8.41	8.88	7.81

d. 7.38 **e.** 7.45
f. $y_t = \beta_0 + \beta_1 t + \beta_2 M_1 + \beta_3 M_2 + \cdots + \beta_{12} M_{11} + \phi R_{t-1} + \varepsilon_t$, where $M_1 = \begin{cases}1 & \text{if Jan.}\\ 0 & \text{if not}\end{cases}$, $M_2 = \begin{cases}1 & \text{if Feb.}\\ 0 & \text{if not}\end{cases}$, . . . , $M_{11} = \begin{cases}1 & \text{if Nov.}\\ 0 & \text{if not}\end{cases}$
g. $\hat{y}_t = 7.126 - .01445t + .077M_1 + .157M_2 + 1.761M_3 + 2.106M_4 + 1.820M_5 + 1.434M_6 + 2.215M_7 + .997M_8 + .379M_9 + 1.465M_{10} + .863M_{11} + .293\hat{R}_{t-1}$ **h.** 6.67 ± 1.83
9.39b. $y_t = \beta_0 + \beta_1 t + \beta_2 Q_1 + \beta_3 Q_2 + \beta_4 Q_3 + \phi R_{t-1} + \varepsilon_t$, where Q_1, Q_2, and Q_3 are dummy variables for quarters; $\hat{y}_t = -173.933 + 1{,}623.684t - 859.249Q_1 - 141.867Q_2 + 826.733Q_3 + .1702\hat{R}_{t-1}$ **c.** 20,429.19; 20,429.19 ± 2,915.69 **e.** No **9.41a.** $\hat{y}_t = 160.05 + 2.48t$
b. 215 **c.** Residuals: −13.53, −9.01, −6.49, −5.97, −1.45, 4.07, 6.59, 14.11, 11.63, 11.15, 8.67, 3.19, 1.71, 2.23, −2.26, −2.74, −3.22 −.70, −5.18, −7.66, −5.14; yes **d.** Durbin–Watson test; $d = .225$, reject H_0 **e.** $y_t = \beta_0 + \beta_1 t + \phi R_{t-1} + \varepsilon_t$; $\hat{y}_t = 154.83 + 2.73t + .792\hat{R}_{t-1}$
f. 210.8 ± 7.65 **9.43b.** $y_t = \beta_0 + \beta_1 t + \phi R_{t-1} + \varepsilon_t$
d. $\hat{y}_t = 1{,}101.83 + 4.918t + .792\hat{R}_{t-1}$ **e.** 1,315.05 ± 516.68

Chapter 10

10.1 Noise (variability) and volume (n) **10.3a.** Flextime, staggered, and fixed work schedules
b. Randomly assign 20 workers to each work schedule

c. $E(y) = \beta_0 + \beta_1 x_1 + \beta_2 x_2$, where $x_1 = \begin{cases} 1 \text{ if flextime} \\ 0 \text{ if not} \end{cases}$, $x_2 = \begin{cases} 1 \text{ if staggered} \\ 0 \text{ if not} \end{cases}$
10.5a. $y_{B1} = \beta_0 + \beta_2 + \beta_4 + \varepsilon_{B1}$; $y_{B2} = \beta_0 + \beta_2 + \beta_5 + \varepsilon_{B2}$; . . . ; $y_{B,10} = \beta_0 + \beta_2 + \varepsilon_{B,10}$; $\bar{y}_B = \beta_0 + \beta_2 + (\beta_4 + \beta_5 + \cdots + \beta_{12})/10 + \bar{\varepsilon}_B$ **b.** $y_{D1} = \beta_0 + \beta_4 + \varepsilon_{D1}$; $y_{D2} = \beta_0 + \beta_5 + \varepsilon_{D2}$; . . . ; $y_{D,10} = \beta_0 + \varepsilon_{D,10}$; $\bar{y}_D = \beta_0 + (\beta_4 + \beta_5 + \cdots + \beta_{12})/10 + \bar{\varepsilon}_D$ **10.7a.** 3 × 3 factorial **b.** Factors: pay rate (quantitative) and length of workday (quantitative) **c.** Treatments: P_1L_1, P_1L_2, P_1L_3, P_2L_1, P_2L_2, P_2L_3, P_3L_1, P_3L_2, P_3L_3 **10.9a.** No
10.11 $E(y) = \beta_0 + \beta_1 x_1 + \beta_2 x_2 + \beta_3 x_3 + \beta_4 x_4 + \beta_5 x_5 + \beta_6 x_1 x_2 + \beta_7 x_1 x_3 + \beta_8 x_1 x_4 + \beta_9 x_1 x_5 + \beta_{10} x_2 x_4 + \beta_{11} x_2 x_5 + \beta_{12} x_3 x_4 + \beta_{13} x_3 x_5 + \beta_{14} x_1 x_2 x_4 + \beta_{15} x_1 x_2 x_5 + \beta_{16} x_1 x_3 x_4 + \beta_{17} x_1 x_3 x_5$, where x_1 = quantitative factor A; x_2, x_3 are dummy variables for qualitative factor B; x_4, x_5 are dummy variables for qualitative factor C **10.13** Cannot investigate factor interaction **10.15** 7
10.21 8 treatments: A_1B_1, A_1B_2, A_1B_3, A_1B_4, A_2B_1, A_2B_2, A_2B_3, A_2B_4 **10.23** $E(y) = \beta_0 + \beta_1 x_1 + \beta_2 x_2 + \beta_3 x_3 + \beta_4 x_4 + \beta_5 x_5$; 10
10.25a. Sex and weight **b.** Both qualitative **c.** 4; (ML), (MH), (FL), and (FH)

Chapter 11

11.3a. $E(y) = \beta_0 + \beta_1 x$, where $x = \begin{cases} 1 \text{ if treatment 1} \\ 0 \text{ if treatment 2} \end{cases}$ **b.** $\hat{y} = 10.667 - 1.524x$; $t = -1.775$, do not reject H_0
11.5a. $t = -1.78$; do not reject H_0 **c.** Two-tailed **11.7a.** Patients with eating disorders; depressed patients; normal eaters **b.** H_0: $\mu_1 = \mu_2 = \mu_3$ **c.** df(Treatments) = 2; df(Error) = 80, df(Total) = 82 **d.** Reject H_0 **11.9a.** Completely randomized **b.** A/R, A/P, and control groups **c.** df(groups) = 2, df(error) = 42, SSE = 321.47, MS(groups) = 35.755, $F = 4.67$ **d.** Group means differ at $\alpha = .05$ **11.11** No; do not reject H_0, $F = .10$ ($p = .9566$) **11.13a.** Five filtering methods **b.** Relevance rating **c.** Reject H_0: $\mu_1 = \mu_2 = \mu_3 = \mu_4 = \mu_5$ **11.15a.** $E(y) = \beta_0 + \beta_1 x_1 + \beta_2 x_2$, where $x_1 = \begin{cases} 1 \text{ if entrepreneurs,} \\ 0 \text{ if not} \end{cases}$, $x_2 = \begin{cases} 1 \text{ if transferred} \\ 0 \text{ if not} \end{cases}$
b. $\hat{y} = 66.97 + 4.03x_1 + 5.55x_2$ **11.17a.** No; do not reject H_0 **b.** Reject H_0, p-value = .065 **11.19a.** Three positions **b.** Ten students **c.** Medial rotation **d.** Attempt to remove extraneous source of variation due to differences in medial rotation of college students
e. $E(y) = \beta_0 + \beta_1 x_1 + \beta_2 x_2 + \beta_3 x_3 + \cdots + \beta_{11} x_{11}$, where $x_1 = \begin{cases} 1 \text{ if beginning position} \\ 0 \text{ if not} \end{cases}$, $x_2 = \begin{cases} 1 \text{ if change directions} \\ 0 \text{ if not} \end{cases}$
x_3–x_{11} are dummy variables for students **11.21a.** Yes; $F = 52.81$
11.23. No evidence of a difference among the three plant session means; $F = .019$
11.25a. $E(y) = \beta_0 + \beta_1 x_1 + \beta_2 x_2 + \beta_3 x_3 + \cdots + \beta_8 x_8$, where
$x_1 = \begin{cases} 1 \text{ if rater 1} \\ 0 \text{ if not} \end{cases}$ $x_2 = \begin{cases} 1 \text{ if rater 2} \\ 0 \text{ if not} \end{cases}$ x_3–x_8 are dummy variables for candidates
b. $E(y) = \beta_0 + \beta_3 x_3 + \cdots + \beta_8 x_8$ **c.** $E(y) = \beta_0 + \beta_1 x_1 + \beta_2 x_2$ **11.27a.** Yes; $F = 5.06$ **b.** Do not reject H_0; $F = 2.28$

11.29a.

SOURCE	df
Period	1
Gender	1
P × G	1
Error	120
Total	123

b. Complete: $E(y) = \beta_0 + \beta_1 x_1 + \beta_2 x_2 + \beta_3 x_1 x_2$, where
$x_1 = \begin{cases} 1 \text{ if 16 hours or less} \\ 0 \text{ if more than 16 hours} \end{cases}$, $x_2 = \begin{cases} 1 \text{ if male} \\ 0 \text{ if female} \end{cases}$; Reduced: $E(y) = \beta_0 + \beta_1 x_1 + \beta_2 x_2$
c. Difference in mean body weight gains of males and females does not depend on photoperiod **d.** $\mu_{16 \text{ or less}} \neq \mu_{\text{more } 16}$; $\mu_M \neq \mu_F$
11.31a. Problem type and group independently affect proportion of ideas recalled
b. No evidence of a difference between the means of the two problem types **c.** Evidence of difference among the means of the four groups

11.33a.

SOURCE	df	SS	MS	F
Amount	3	104.19	34.73	20.12
Method	3	28.63	9.54	5.53
Amount × Method	9	25.13	2.79	1.62
Error	32	55.25	1.73	
Total	47	213.20		

b. Do not reject H_0; $F = 1.62$
c. Difference in mean shear strengths for any two levels of antimony amount does not depend on cooling method
d. Amount: reject H_0, $F = 20.12$; Method: reject H_0, $F = 5.53$
11.35a. Factors (levels): accounts receivable (completed, not completed); verification (completed, not completed); treatments: CC, CN, NC, NN
c. Yes **11.37a.** No evidence of interaction **b.** No evidence of window size main effect **c.** Evidence of jump length main effect
11.39 Evidence of interaction ($p = .0001$)

11.41a.

SOURCE	df
A	2
B	3
C	1
AB	6
AC	2
BC	3
ABC	6
Error	120
Total	143

b. $F = 5.21$; yes **c.** $F = 2.79$; yes
d. SS(Total) $= 34.99$, $R^2 = .52$

11.43a. $E(y) = \beta_0 + \beta_1x_1 + \beta_2x_1^2$ **b.** $E(y) = (\beta_0 + \beta_3) + (\beta_1 + \beta_6)x_1 + (\beta_2 + \beta_9)x_1^2$
c. $E(y) = (\beta_0 + \beta_3 + \beta_4 + \beta_5) + (\beta_1 + \beta_6 + \beta_7 + \beta_8)x_1 + (\beta_2 + \beta_9 + \beta_{10} + \beta_{11})x_1^2$
d. $\hat{y} = 31.15 + .153x_1 - .00396x_1^2 + 17.05x_2 + 19.1x_3 - 14.3x_2x_3 + .151x_1x_2 + .017x_1x_3 - .08x_1x_2x_3 - .00356x_1^2x_2 + .0006x_1^2x_3 + .0012x_1^2x_2x_3$
e. Rolled/inconel: $\hat{y} = 53 + .241x_1 - .00572x_1^2$; Rolled/incoloy: $\hat{y} = 50.25 + .17x_1 + .00336x_1^2$; Drawn/inconel: $\hat{y} = 48.2 + .304x_1 - .00752x_1^2$; Drawn/incoloy: $\hat{y} = 31.15 + .153x_1 - .00396x_1^2$ **11.45a.** $3 \times 4 \times 3 \times 3 = 108$
b. The complete model has 108 terms, including β_0, 9 main effect terms, 30 two-way interactions, 44 three-way interactions, and 24 four-way interactions **c.** H_0: $\beta_{10} = \beta_{11} = \cdots = \beta_{107} = 0$ **11.47a.** Reject H_0 **b.** $\mu_T < (\mu_V, \mu_R, \mu_L, \mu_S)$
11.49a. Reject H_0: $\mu_R = \mu_P = \mu_D = \mu_A = \mu_B$ **b.** $\mu_R < \mu_P < (\mu_D, \mu_A, \mu_B)$; $\mu_D < \mu_B$
11.51a. Evidence of accuracy × vocabulary interaction **b.** Yes
c. 75%: means for all three accuracy levels are significantly different; 87.5%: means for all three accuracy levels are significantly different; 100%: $\mu_{90\%} > (\mu_{99\%}, \mu_{95\%})$
11.53a. Policy 1 mean differs from each of policies 3–18; 2 and 3 differ from 4–18; 4 differs from 8–18; 5, 6, and 7 differ from 9–18; 8 differs from 12–18; 9, 10, and 11 differ from 16–18 **b.** Yes **11.55** $\omega = 1.82$; $(\mu_5, \mu_3, \mu_0) > (\mu_{10})$
11.57 The following treatment pairs are significantly different: (jail correctional, jail mental health), (jail correctional, county mental health), and (jail correctional, other mental health) **11.59a.** Yes; $F = 9.50$ ($p = .006$) **b.** $\omega = 8.67$; $\mu_{\text{PD-1}} > \mu_{\text{IADC 5-1-7}}$
11.67a. Winn-Dixie, Publix, and Kash N' Karry
b. $E(y) = \beta_0 + \beta_1x_1 + \beta_2x_2 + \beta_3x_3 + \cdots + \beta_{61}x_{61}$, where $x_1 = \begin{cases} 1 & \text{if Winn-Dixie} \\ 0 & \text{if not} \end{cases}$, $x_2 = \begin{cases} 1 & \text{if Publix} \\ 0 & \text{if not} \end{cases}$, and $x_3, \ldots, x_{61}$ are dummy variables for items (blocks) **c.** $E(y) = \beta_0 + \beta_3x_3 + \cdots + \beta_{61}x_{61}$

e.

SOURCE	df	SS	MS	F
Supermarkets	2	2.641	1.321	39.23
Items	59	215.595	3.654	108.54
Error	118	3.97	.034	
Total	179	222.206		

d. Reject H_0, $F = 39.23$
f. Reject H_0, $F = 108.54$ **g.** $\omega = .099$; $\mu_{WD} < (\mu_P, \mu_{KK})$

11.69 Reject H_0: $F = 17.66$ **11.71a.** Evidence of $N \times I$ interaction; ignore tests for main effects
b. Agree; interaction implies differences among N means depend on level of I **11.73** $(\mu_{\text{Rest}}, \mu_A) < \mu_B < (\mu_C, \mu_D, \mu_E)$ **11.75a.** Factorial
b. No replications **c.** $E(y) = \beta_0 + \beta_1x_1 + \beta_2x_2 + \beta_3x_1x_2 + \beta_4x_1^2 + \beta_5x_2^2$ **d.** Test H_0: $\beta_3 = 0$
e. $\hat{y} = -384.75 + 3.73x_1 + 12.72x_2 - .05x_1x_2 - .009x_1^2 - .322x_2^2$; $t = -2.05$, reject H_0 (p-value $= .07$)
11.77a. $E(y) = \beta_0 + \beta_1x_1 + \beta_2x_2$, where
$x_1 = \begin{cases} 1 & \text{if small company} \\ 0 & \text{if not} \end{cases}$, $x_2 = \begin{cases} 1 & \text{if medium company} \\ 0 & \text{if not} \end{cases}$ **b.** H_0: $\beta_1 = \beta_2 = 0$
c. df(size) $= 2$; df(error) $= 121$; SS(size) $= 15.5$; SS(Total) $= 205.5$; MS(size) $= 7.75$; MSE $= 1.57$ **d.** Yes; $F_{.05} = 3.07$

11.79a.

SOURCE	df	SS	MS	F
Methods	2	.19	.10	.08
Brands	5	605.70	121.14	93.18
Error	10	13.05	1.30	
Total	17	618.94		

c. No, do not reject H_0; $F = .08$ **d.** $-.233 \pm 1.469$

11.81

SOURCE	df	SS	MS	F
Groups	2	273.068	136.534	79.22
Error	342	589.418	1.723	
Total	344	862.486		

Reject H_0: $\mu_{NT} = \mu_{CAT} = \mu_{CTW}$ at $\alpha = .05$; Bonferroni comparisons ($\alpha = .06$): All three means are significantly different
11.83a. $E(y) = \beta_0 + \beta_1 x_1 + \beta_2 x_2 + \beta_3 x_1 x_2 + \beta_4 x_1^2 + \beta_5 x_2^2$ **b.** $\hat{y} = 29.86 + .56x_1 - .1625x_2 - .1135x_1x_2 - .275x_1^2 - .23125x_2^2$ c. The two models are different d. $R^2 = -.842$ e. Yes; $F = 5.67$

11.85a

SOURCE	df	SS	MS	F
Buyers (B)	1	227.8126	227.8126	.52
Sellers (S)	1	4,018.6126	4,018.6126	9.11
(BS)	1	1,757.8122	1,757.8122	3.99
Error	76	33,516.0000	441.0000	
Total	79	39,520.2374		

c. Reject H_0: $F = 3.99$

d. Complete model: $E(y) = \beta_0 + \beta_1 x_1 + \beta_2 x_2 + \beta_3 x_1 x_2$, where $x_1 = \begin{cases} 1 \text{ if BC} \\ 0 \text{ if BNC} \end{cases}$, $x_2 = \begin{cases} 1 \text{ if SC} \\ 0 \text{ if SNC} \end{cases}$;
Reduced model: $E(y) = \beta_0 + \beta_1 x_1 + \beta_2 x_2$ e. -12.75 ± 10.92 **11.87a.** Yes; $F = 33.86$ is significant at $\alpha = .01$
b. $R^2 = .9338$; 93.38% of total variability is explained by the model c. Yes d. Yes e. No; $t = .04$
f. $\hat{y} = -4{,}026.64 + 385.08x_1 - 24.67x_1^2 + 661.58x_2 - 37.17x_2^2 + .25x_1x_2$

Appendix A

A.1a. $\begin{bmatrix} 6 & 3 \\ -2 & -5 \end{bmatrix}$ **b.** $\begin{bmatrix} 3 & 0 & 9 \\ -9 & 4 & 5 \end{bmatrix}$ c. $\begin{bmatrix} 5 & 4 \\ 1 & -4 \end{bmatrix}$
A.3a. 3×4 **b.** No; the number of elements in a row of **B** does not match the number of elements in a column of **A**
A.5a. $\begin{bmatrix} 2 & 3 \\ -9 & 0 \\ 8 & 2 \end{bmatrix}$ b. $[3 \quad 0 \quad 4]$ c. $[14 \quad 7]$ **A.7a.** $\begin{bmatrix} 1 & 0 \\ 0 & 1 \end{bmatrix}$ c. $\begin{bmatrix} 1 & 0 & 0 \\ 0 & 1 & 0 \\ 0 & 0 & 1 \end{bmatrix}$ **A.13** $\begin{bmatrix} 3/8 & 1/8 \\ -1/4 & 1/4 \end{bmatrix}$
A.15a. $\mathbf{A} = \begin{bmatrix} 10 & 0 & 20 \\ 0 & 20 & 0 \\ 20 & 0 & 68 \end{bmatrix}$; $\mathbf{V} = \begin{bmatrix} v_1 \\ v_2 \\ v_3 \end{bmatrix}$; $\mathbf{G} = \begin{bmatrix} 60 \\ 60 \\ 176 \end{bmatrix}$ c. $\begin{bmatrix} 2 \\ 3 \\ 2 \end{bmatrix}$
A.17a. $\mathbf{Y} = \begin{bmatrix} 1 \\ 2 \\ 2 \\ 3 \\ 5 \\ 5 \end{bmatrix}$; $\mathbf{X} = \begin{bmatrix} 1 & 1 \\ 1 & 2 \\ 1 & 3 \\ 1 & 4 \\ 1 & 5 \\ 1 & 6 \end{bmatrix}$ b. $\mathbf{X'X} = \begin{bmatrix} 6 & 21 \\ 21 & 91 \end{bmatrix}$; $\mathbf{X'Y} = \begin{bmatrix} 18 \\ 78 \end{bmatrix}$ d. $\hat{\boldsymbol{\beta}} = \begin{bmatrix} 0 \\ .8571 \end{bmatrix}$ e. $\hat{y} = .8571x$
A.19 $t = -5.196$; reject H_0 **A.21** $t = -2.222$; reject H_0 **A.23** $(-1.1593, 2.7593)$ **A.25** $(.4153, 3.0131)$ **A.27** $(3.2719, 3.6581)$

A.29a. $\mathbf{X} = \begin{bmatrix} 1 & -5 \\ 1 & -3 \\ 1 & -1 \\ 1 & 1 \\ 1 & 3 \\ 1 & 5 \end{bmatrix}$; $\mathbf{Y} = \begin{bmatrix} 1.1 \\ 1.9 \\ 3.0 \\ 3.8 \\ 5.1 \\ 6.0 \end{bmatrix}$ b. $\mathbf{X'X} = \begin{bmatrix} 6 & 0 \\ 0 & 70 \end{bmatrix}$; $\mathbf{X'Y} = \begin{bmatrix} 20.9 \\ 34.9 \end{bmatrix}$ c. $\hat{\boldsymbol{\beta}} = \begin{bmatrix} 3.4833 \\ .4986 \end{bmatrix}$ d. $\hat{y} = 3.4833 + .4986x$

e. SSE = .0682; $s^2 = .0170$ f. $t = 31.95$; yes g. $r^2 = .9961$ h. (3.62, 3.85)

A.31a. $\mathbf{X} = \begin{bmatrix} 1 & 1 \\ 1 & 1 \\ 1 & 2 \\ 1 & 2 \\ 1 & 3 \\ 1 & 3 \\ 1 & 4 \\ 1 & 4 \\ 1 & 5 \\ 1 & 5 \\ 1 & 6 \\ 1 & 6 \end{bmatrix}$; $\mathbf{Y} = \begin{bmatrix} 1.1 \\ .5 \\ 1.8 \\ 2.0 \\ 2.0 \\ 2.9 \\ 3.8 \\ 3.4 \\ 4.1 \\ 5.0 \\ 5.0 \\ 5.8 \end{bmatrix}$ b. $\mathbf{X'X} = \begin{bmatrix} 12 & 42 \\ 42 & 182 \end{bmatrix}$; $\mathbf{X'Y} = \begin{bmatrix} 37.4 \\ 163.0 \end{bmatrix}$

c. The elements of $\mathbf{X'X}$ are increased by a factor of 2.

d. $(\mathbf{X'X})^{-1} = \begin{bmatrix} .4333 & -.1 \\ -.1 & .02857 \end{bmatrix}$ e. $\hat{\boldsymbol{\beta}} = \begin{bmatrix} -.09333 \\ .91714 \end{bmatrix}$; $\hat{y} = -.09333 + .91714x$ f. SSE = 1.5564; $s^2 = .15564$ g. $t = 13.75$; yes

h. $r^2 = .9498$

A.33a. 18 × 1 b. $\mathbf{X} = \begin{bmatrix} 1 & 1 \\ 1 & 1 \\ 1 & 1 \\ 1 & 2 \\ 1 & 2 \\ 1 & 2 \\ 1 & 3 \\ 1 & 3 \\ 1 & 3 \\ 1 & 4 \\ 1 & 4 \\ 1 & 4 \\ 1 & 5 \\ 1 & 5 \\ 1 & 5 \\ 1 & 6 \\ 1 & 6 \\ 1 & 6 \end{bmatrix}$ c. $\begin{bmatrix} 18 & 63 \\ 63 & 273 \end{bmatrix}$ d. $(\mathbf{X'X})^{-1} = \begin{bmatrix} .28889 & -.06667 \\ -.06667 & .019048 \end{bmatrix}$ e. $\mathbf{a}'(\mathbf{X'X})^{-1}\mathbf{a} = .0746$

f. Width is reduced by approximately 21%

Index

A

B

C